SANAMJIT
(Sonia)

PSYCHOLOGY

PSYCHOLOGY

Ronald E. Smith
University of Washington

West Publishing Company
Minneapolis/St. Paul   New York   San Francisco   Los Angeles

PRODUCTION CREDITS

COPYEDITING   Beverly Peavler
COMPOSITION   Parkwood Composition
ARTWORK   Mary Albury-Noyes Graphics
INDEX   Terry Casey
COVER IMAGE   Hologram provided courtesy of the
AORN Journal, 2170 South Parker
Rd., Denver, CO 80231. Copyright
1989. All rights reserved.
PRODUCTION, PREPRESS, PRINTING, AND
BINDING   West Publishing Company

WEST'S COMMITMENT TO THE ENVIRONMENT

In 1906, West Publishing Company began recycling
materials left over from the production of books. This
began a tradition of efficient and responsible use of
resources. Today, up to 95 percent of our legal books
and 70 percent of our college texts are printed on
recycled, acid-free stock. West also recycles nearly
22 million pounds of scrap paper annually—the
equivalent of 181,717 trees. Since the 1960s, West
has devised ways to capture and recycle waste inks,
solvents, oils, and vapors created in the printing process. We also recycle plastics of all kinds, wood,
glass, corrugated cardboard, and batteries, and have
eliminated the use of styrofoam book packaging. We
at West are proud of the longevity and the scope of
our commitment to our environment.

Production, Prepress, Printing and Binding by West
Publishing Company.

COPYRIGHT ©1993 By WEST PUBLISHING
COMPANY
610 Opperman Drive
P.O. Box 64526
St. Paul, MN 55164-0526

Printed in the United States of America

00 99 98 97 96 95 94 93   8 7 6 5 4 3 2 1

Library of Congress Cataloging-in-Publication
Data

Smith, Ronald Edward, 1940–
    Psychology / Ronald E. Smith.
       p.   cm.
    Includes index.
    ISBN 0-314-00768-7
    1. Psychology.   I. Title.
BF121.S58   1993
150--dc20   92-19803

  CIP

Contents-in-Brief

Contents

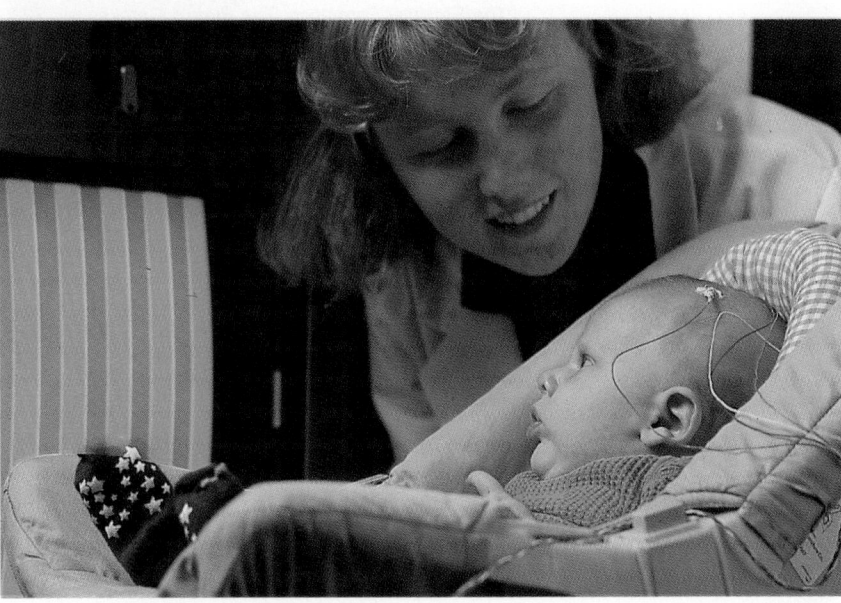

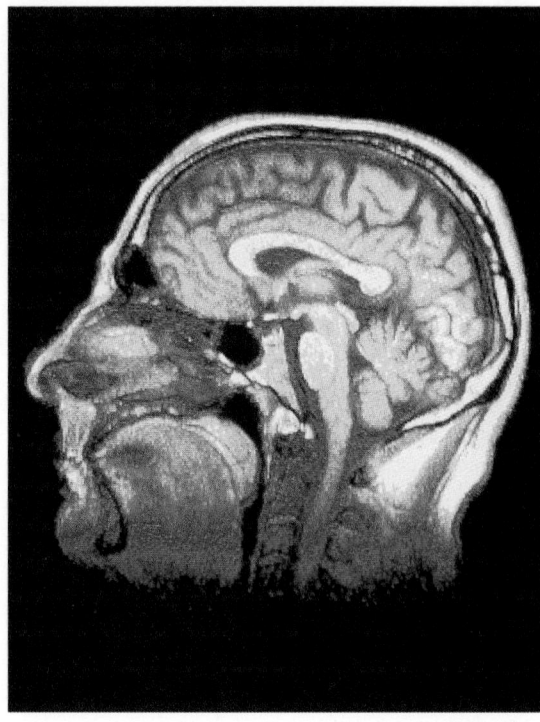

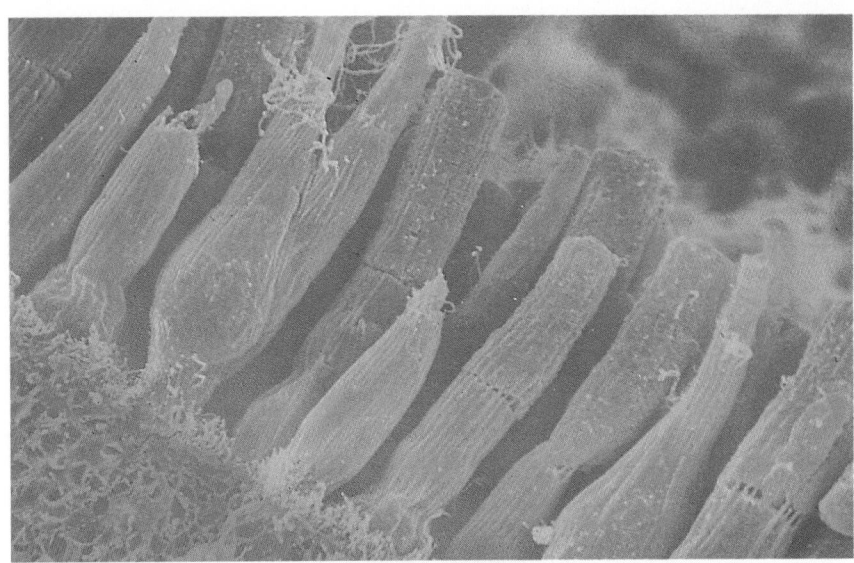

Chapter 8
States of Consciousness   229

Chapter 9
Learning   261

Physiological responses (e.g., brain waves)

Verbal self-report of experiences

Nonverbal behaviors from which inner experience or state of consciousness is inferred

Chapter 15
Stress, Coping and Well-Being 464

Chapter 16
Psychological Disorders 494

Chapter 17
Treatment of Psychological
Disorders   534

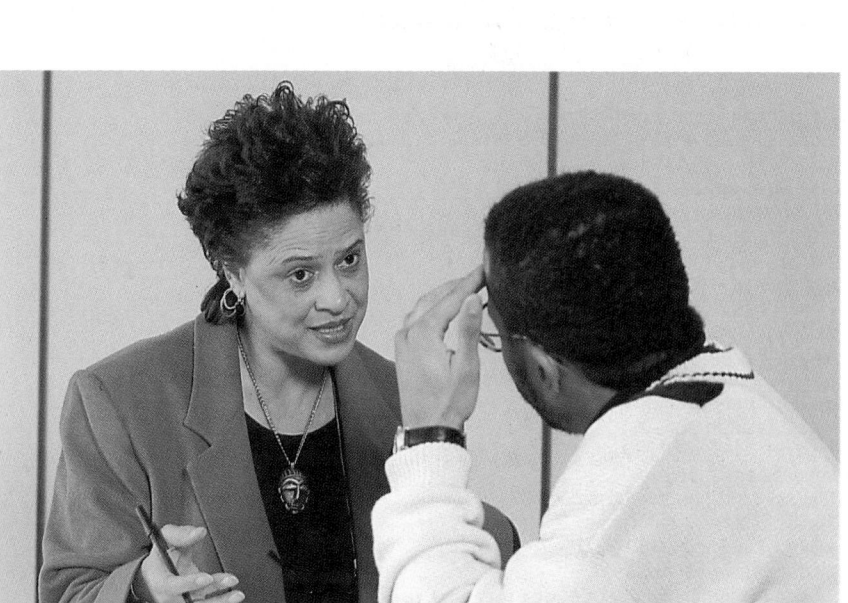

Chapter 18
Social Influences On Behavior   569

Preface

While the planning and preparation of *Psychology* has been in many ways the most challenging enterprise of my career as a psychologist, it is one that I have approached with great enthusiasm. Part of my enthusiasm stems from 18 years of experience in teaching introductory psychology. My enduring goal over this period has been to present psychology to students in a way that will create in them the excitement that psychological phenomena generate in me. This entails trying to make psychology (both the concepts and their applications) come alive in such a way that students will find themselves thinking about their experiences and the world of behavior in the same way a psychologist does. By presenting theory, research, and applications as intellectual detective work, I try to prompt students to approach behavioral phenomena with an inquiring, analytic mindset. Teaching students to examine behavior from the diverse perspectives that have dominated the intellectual and scientific traditions in psychology also helps them to develop the intellectual flexibility that critical thinking demands. My goal as a teacher is to promote a level of conceptual sophistication that students will carry with them long after they have forgotten the many facts that they are called upon to learn in an introductory psychology course. I have tried to carry these teaching goals into this textbook.

A second source of the enthusiasm I feel for this project stems from the very nature of present-day psychology. In the 1990s, psychology stands on the threshold of the most exciting phase in its history. Partly as the result of technical advances in the biological sciences, psychology is entering a revolutionary period in which new understandings of the links between psychological events and biological processes are emerging. For the first time in our scientific history, we are gaining more than fleeting glimpses of psychobiological interactions—that is, how the ''mind'' and the body interact and influence one another—and we are finding answers to questions that have perplexed and challenged researchers since serious inquiry began. Where is memory? What is thought? How can beliefs produce illness or protect us against disease? When and how does a genotype interact with environmental influences to produce the biopsychosocial product we call schizophrenia? Are basic aspects of temperament inborn? If so, can they be modified by experience? How do the activities of the brain create mental processes, and how do psychological processes alter the brain? Questions like these now guide a science of psychology that is probing new and uncharted frontiers of behavior and experience in this, the ''Decade of the Brain.'' These explorations are already producing new insights into who and what we are as humans and how we function as biopsychosocial beings.

A major goal of my book is to communicate to students what we presently know about the ways in which biological, psychological, and environmental factors interact to produce the experiences and behaviors that are the focus of psychology while at the same time achieving a balanced coverage of the traditional topics and theories. A second key goal is to introduce students to the methods being used to probe new frontiers and the questions that remain to be answered. I am convinced that this approach will serve to integrate current knowledge in psychology within a framework that students will find understandable, engaging, and thought-provoking and that introductory psychology instructors will find representative of the major themes in contemporary psychology.

A New Perspective on Perspectives: Interacting Causal Factors

A major challenge for both the student and the instructor lies in the great number of facts, concepts, and content areas that must be covered in an introductory psychology course. It is easy for students to feel lost in a dense forest of apparently disconnected facts, theories, and topics. A major objective of the approach I have taken in *Psychology* is not only to guide students through the forest but to bring the forest to life as an integrated ecosystem that represents the interactions between person, behavior, and the environment.

The way I have chosen to do this is to organize content around five perspectives on behavior—biological, psychodynamic, cognitive, behavioral, and humanistic—that guide the thinking and activities of contemporary psychologists and form a framework for understanding developments in the field. I emphasize not only how these perspectives differ in their conceptions of human nature and their approaches to understanding behavioral phenomena but also how they complement one another to provide a comprehensive understanding of human behavior and experience. I have found that the perspectives provide a very effective method of integrating the content of introductory psychology, because theories and causal factors can readily be accommodated within them. However, I do not believe that previous introductory psychology textbooks have succeeded in tapping the true potential of these perspectives. Indeed, most books treat them briefly in the first chapter and rarely if ever cite them again. What is needed, therefore, are pedagogical devices that will more effectively tap the conceptual and organizational potential of the perspectives.

Traditionally, the perspectives have been used to present alternative theoretical vantage points for viewing and trying to understand behavior. In this sense, the perspectives serve as lenses through which the world of behavior is seen, and they reflect differing conceptions of human nature (for example, views of a human as a biological being, a reactor to the environment, a thinker and information processor, an organism driven by internal psychodynamic forces, a free and choosing being, and so on).

Beyond this, however, the perspectives determine which class of *causal factors*—biological, cognitive, intrapsychic, or environmental—we focus on and what we learn about the complex determinants of behavior. These causal factors often interact with one another as determinants of behavior, and it is a focus on interacting causal factors that I have tried to carry to a new level throughout the book in textual and graphic form. This pedagogy is intended to help students (a) to organize what is known about the diverse causes of behavior; (b) to understand that many behaviors have not a single cause but rather an array of biological, cognitive, intrapsychic, and environmental causes which may interact with one another in various ways; and (c) to acquire a mental set for viewing behavior from differing perspectives. This approach goes to the very heart of the definition of *psychology,* which is "the scientific study of behavior and its *causes.*"

■ ▭ Major Themes and Features

Psychology was written with an eye to presenting conceptually rigorous material in a highly readable fashion. I have tried to write in a conversational tone, as if I were speaking directly to the student. I regard a good introductory psychology teacher as one who can do justice to the complexity of contemporary theories and research results, yet make the content comprehensible, interesting, and personally meaningful to students. I have sought to make this book a good teacher that engages the reader in the enterprise of psychology by focusing not only on the outcome of research but also on how the process of inquiry works (and sometimes doesn't work). I make a special effort to integrate principles, examples, and applications to make the material personally meaningful to the student and to illustrate the contributions that the science of psychology can make to understanding our world and promoting human betterment.

Several important themes are carried throughout the book. The first is the aforementioned focus on causal interactions among biological, psychological, and environmental factors. Of course, these interactions are discussed in the body of the text. Each chapter beyond Chapter 1 also contains a special *Psychobiological Interactions* feature, an in-depth discussion of a body–mind topic relevant to the content of the chapter. These features do not appear as isolated boxes, which can disrupt the flow of a book. Rather, they appear at the ends of relevant sections of the chapters. The Psychobiological Interactions feature is a product of enduring professional interests, reflecting in a sense my dual-track doctoral training in clinical–personality and physiological psychology. I believe that it also reflects a major thrust of contemporary psychology.

A second major feature that explicitly deals with causal interactions is entitled *Understanding the Causes of Behavior.* As noted earlier, I have divided causal factors into four classes: biological, cognitive, intrapsychic (including variables derived from psychodynamic and humanistic theories), and environmental. In special graphic features throughout the book, a major psychological phenomenon or process discussed in that chapter is analyzed and graphically presented in terms of the four classes of causal factors to summarize current knowledge. For instance, the Feature in Chapter 3 describes these four classes of causal factors in relation to immune system functioning, and the feature in Chapter 15 describes vulnerability factors that affect responses to stressors. These graphic features serve to summarize material discussed in the text and to continually reinforce the student's appreciation for the fact that many behaviors are multidetermined. The goal is to help students achieve a higher level of conceptual sophistication in understanding causal variables. Indeed, the logo associated with this feature presents Kurt Lewin's classic formula $B = f(P,E)$: "Behavior is a function of the person interacting with the environment."

The third pedagogical feature in *Psychology* is called **Enhancing Human Performance.** These special in-depth features highlight the practical implications of basic research in psychology for helping humans function more effectively. They provide research-based practical guidelines for developing psychological skills in such areas as critically evaluating research results, improving memory, solving problems, controlling pain, resisting social influence attempts, managing stress, and enhancing academic performance. Although these features have an applied focus, they continue to review relevant studies and summarize data in a manner that portrays research and application as complementary enterprises.

Most instructors (including myself) have the explicit goal of developing critical thinking skills in students. To facilitate such thinking, I have included more than 35 *Thinking Critically About...* features in the margins throughout the text. These features may present caveats about the topic being discussed in the adjacent text, may describe new discoveries that raise important new issues, or may challenge students to solve problems related to the issue at hand. A few even present mini-projects aimed at involving students personally and directly in the topic under discussion.

Finally, I have tried to accurately reflect the wide-ranging interest in multicultural and gender issues in contemporary psychology. At many points throughout the book, relevant research and theoretical contributions are described. Indeed, the book concludes with a section entitled ''Increasing Multicultural Tolerance and Understanding.''

These pedagogical features are intended to contribute to the cutting-edge character of the book and to help me achieve my goal of contributing an intellectually respectable and conceptually sophisticated book that presents theories, methodology, research results, and psychological applications in a way that engages and excites the student. There is no subject more fascinating and relevant to people's lives than psychology, and I have tried in every way to capitalize on its inherent interest value so as to showcase the discipline.

Supporting Materials

Psychology is part of a comprehensive resource package designed to assist instructors in teaching and enriching their courses. Some of the supporting materials are designed for the instructor, and others are intended to broaden the student's introductory psychology experience.

Resources for Students

Study Guide. A good study guide can be of great value, helping students to identify key concepts and research results, promoting critical thinking, and providing ways for students to assess their current knowledge and prepare for tests. Michael Passer of the University of Washington has prepared a study guide that is second to none in its comprehensiveness and quality. As the coordinator of introductory psychology offerings at Washington, as well as a gifted teacher in his own right, Dr. Passer has a keen understanding of how to help students master course content. Students will find the Study Guide to be a valuable resource that can significantly enhance their accomplishments in the course.

Three additional resources are offered free to students at the option of the instructor.

Enhancing Human Performance Handbook. Drawing on my own research and consulting experiences, I have prepared this handbook to help students acquire psychological skills that can enhance their performance not only in their academic work but also in other areas of their lives. Based on a cognitive–behavioral model of self-regulation, the handbook provides guidelines in such areas as time management, goal setting, behavioral self-control, and stress management. This handbook, offered free to students, will serve as an in-depth supplement to some of the material presented in the *Enhancing Human Performance* features in the text.

College Survival Guide Second Edition. This booklet, written by Bruce M. Rowe of Los Angeles Pierce College and available free to students, offers many tips for enhancing academic performance. Topics include tips on note taking, study skills, and exam-taking.

Cross-Cultural Perspectives in Introductory Psychology. Edited by William Price and Rich Crapo, this new book contains provocative articles and commentaries on cross-cultural topics. The material is organized to conform to the topics covered in the typical introductory psychology course. The book is also free and will expand upon and enhance the multicultural content in the text.

Software

The computer age has provided opportunities for students to enjoy a new kind of hands-on exposure to psychological phenomena. Three software programs accompany the textbook.

Microguide. A computerized version of the Study Guide is available to students. This interactive software is available in both IBM PC-compatible and Macintosh formats. The interactive nature of the program provides immediate feedback to students concerning their mastery of the material.

Mind Scope. This unique program for IBM PC-compatible computers consists of 20 modules on classic psychological phenomena. Students actually run the experiments on themselves, producing real data, which they are then called upon to interpret in a workbook that accompanies the program.

Psychware. Designed to enrich the introductory course, Psychware is a computer-assisted instructional package for Apple II computers that consists of simulations, tutorials, and experiments that feature engaging graphics. Students are able to experience classic experiments and demonstrations through interactive learning.

Resources for Instructors

Teaching an introductory psychology course can be a daunting assignment. We therefore provide a comprehensive package of resources that can make the task easier and also enhance the quality of the course.

Instructor's Planning Guide. This useful handbook integrates the entire instructional package by offering suggestions on how the printed, multimedia, and software supplements can be used with each chapter in the textbook.

Instructor's Manual. The cornerstone of the resource package is the comprehensive Instructor's Manual, prepared by Wendy Domjan of the University of Texas at Austin. I am confident that you will find this manual a real treasure in planning and improving your course. Rarely have I seen as much thought and wisdom go into an IM. The manual contains learning objectives for each chapter, demonstrations and lecture material, film suggestions, and other helpful materials. The manual alone contains enough material to support a highly successful course.

Test Bank. The test bank, also prepared by Wendy Domjan, consists of more than 100 carefully crafted test items for each chapter. Both printed and computerized versions of the test bank are available to instructors.

Software/Media

Computerized Testing. The computerized version of the test bank *(WesTest 3.0)* is available for both IBM PC-compatible and Macintosh computers. This program makes it easy for instructors to select items for tests, arrange the items in different orders to produce alternative forms, and even add their own items.

Color Transparencies. To augment lectures and integrate them with material in the text, a set of over 100 color acetate transparencies is offered to adopters.

Discovering Psychology Video Series. Strategically planned videotape presentations can greatly embellish lecture material. *Discovering Psychology* is a series of 26 half-hour videotapes covering all of the major topic areas of introductory psychology. In color, featuring beautiful computer animation, the series is designed to not only present concepts and demonstrations but also to challenge and motivate students while fostering critical thinking. A manual accompanies the video series.

Psychology Laser Disc. The Psychology Laser Disc, which contains a varied array of resources over 15 topical areas, can add a new dimension to classroom presentations.

Enhancing Human Performance Videos. Building on the performance enhancement theme, West has produced a series of three videotapes to accompany the text. The first, *Enhancing Academic Performance,* features a classroom lecture by this book's author on general principles of performance enhancement and shows how the principles can be applied to academic performance enhancement. *Enhancing Sport Performance* focuses on a psychological skills training program that I direct within the Houston Astros professional baseball organization. Filmed at the Astros' spring training complex, it features interviews with prominent baseball people as well as a sport psychology presentation to the athletes. The third tape, *Enhancing Tolerance and Understanding in a Multicultural Society,* features an informative roundtable discussion by a multicultural group of social scientists. The participants talk about measures that can be used to increase tolerance and understanding as well as the challenges that confront members of various ethnic groups on campus and the coping skills these individuals need to deal effectively with academic challenges and prejudice.

In addition to these resources, Psychware and Mind Scope software (described earlier) are available to adopters for use in their classes or quiz sections. We believe that this comprehensive package of resources can help the instructor plan and present an exceptionally fine introductory psychology course.

Acknowledgements

A great many people have contributed to the development of this book. These contributions began almost as the book was conceived and continued until the final day of production.

I have been blessed with an unusually generous group of consultants and reviewers. Because I wanted to emphasize psychobiological interactions, I invited a number of prominent psychologists—Robert Ader, Albert Bandura, John Cacioppo, Richard Davidson, and Earl Hunt—to form a "body–mind advisory committee." These valued colleagues contributed suggestions, reprints, and preprints of their own and others' work. Earl Hunt, my colleague at the University of Washington, also provided working drafts of the two cognitive chapters. Bryant Robinson of the University of North Carolina, Charlotte, furnished similar assistance in the preparation of the two developmental psychology chapters. Michael Passer not only produced a splendid study guide, but also provided many useful comments and suggestions that enhanced the final product. To these colleagues, I express my deepest appreciation.

I am greatly indebted to another group of colleagues who provided detailed reviews of each chapter. They supplied valuable feedback and suggestions, and many of their recommendations have helped enrich the text. To the following psychologists, I express my gratitude:

Vincent Adesso,
University of Wisconsin-Milwaukee

Leland Asa,
Westmont College

Barbara Basden,
California State University-Fresno

LTC Johnston Beach
West Point Military Academy

James Beaird,
Western Oregon State College

Darryl Beale,
Cerritos College

Linda Bosmajian,
Hood College

Paul Bronstein,
University of Michigan

Gary Brosvic,
Glassboro State College

Frederick Brown,
Pennsylvania State University

Gail A. Bruder,
SUNY-Buffalo

James Calhoun,
University of Georgia

John Caruso,
Southeastern Massachusetts University

Walter Charles,
Oregon State University

Eric Cooley,
Western Oregon State College

Jaime Diaz,
University of Washington

Janet Dizinno,
St. Mary's University

Wendy Domjan,
University of Texas at Austin

Roland Engelhart,
University of Windsor

John Flanagan,
Eastern Kentucky University

J. Fleishman,
Southwest Texas State University

William Gibson,
Northern Arizona University

Christopher Grace,
Biola University

Charles Gray,
Austin Peay State University

Larry Gregory,
New Mexico State University

Richard Griggs,
University of Florida

Carlos Grijalva,
University of California at Los Angeles

David Hogan,
Northern Kentucky University

Charles Honts,
University of North Dakota

Philip Hurst,
Georgia Southern University

Jeri Janowsky,
University of Oregon

Bruce King,
University of New Orleans

Stephen Klein,
Fort Hays State University

James Knight,
Humboldt State University

Michael Knight,
Central State University

R. Lakowski,
University of British Columbia

David Leonard,
University of Georgia

Ted Lewandowski,
Delaware County Community College

Richard Martin,
Gustavus Adolphus College

Angela McGlynn,
Mercer County Community College

T. Mark Morey,
SUNY-Oswego

Tom Nelson,
Adrian College

Michael Passer,
University of Washington

David Perkins,
Ball State University

Kent Pierce,
Purdue University-Calumet

Faye Pritchard,
LaSalle University

Laura Puckett,
North Hennepin Community
College

Robin Raygor,
Anoka Ramsey Community
College

Michael Ross,
St. Louis University

Peter Rowe,
College of Charleston

Bonnie Seegmiller,
Hunter College

David Shantz,
Oakland University

K. L. Shapiro,
University of Calgary

Mark Shatz,
Ohio University

Robert Smith,
George Mason University

Stuart Taylor,
Kent State University

Roger Thomas,
Texas Christian University

Michael Vitiello,
University of Washington

Brent Vulcano,
St. Mary's University

Walter Wagor,
Indiana University East

Benjamin Wallace,
Cleveland State University

Julia Wallace,
University of Northern Iowa

Paul A. Watson,
University of Tennessee
at Chattanooga

Paul Wellman,
Texas A & M University

Fred Whitford,
Montana State University

Once a manuscript is completed, the editorial and production staffs play critical roles in determining the quality of the final product. Again, I have been blessed with the assistance of a wonderfully talented group of people. Carolyn Smith and Chris Olson provided valuable input during the early stages of the project, as did Theresa O'Dell thereafter. John Orr, my production editor, coordinated the entire project during the design and production stages. His congenial and helpful manner made him a pleasure to work with, and the attractiveness of the book is due in no small part to his careful attention and abundant talents. The book's handsome illustration program is a product of the computer graphics skills of Lee Anne Storey and the artistic talents of Mary Albury-Noyes. Sheree Mattson did a wonderful job as photo researcher. Her persistence and good judgment are very much appreciated. Heartfelt thanks are also extended to Beverly Peavler, whose artful job of copy editing has contributed greatly to the readability of the book. She is a truly gifted professional, and I feel very fortunate to have had her assistance. Finally, I would like to thank Ann Swift for her many contributions to the marketing of the book and Beth Hoeppner for coordinating the production of the *Enhancing Human Performance* videotapes that accompany the book.

The most positive fate that can occur to any author is the opportunity to work with Clyde Perlee, Editor in Chief of West Educational Publishing. His creative genius, gentle guidance, and unwavering support contributed mightily to whatever success the book might enjoy. In the process of working with Clyde, I have not only seen a book born but have also formed an enduring friendship.

In many ways, the process of writing this book dominated my life for the better part of three years. However, it has never dominated my heart. To my wife Kay, whose love, devotion, and gentle support helped sustain my efforts, I dedicate this book.

Ronald E. Smith

Psychology: The Science of Behavior

1

■ ▢

C H A P T E R   O U T L I N E

n the predawn hours of August 24, 1992, the 160-mile-per-hour winds of Hurricane Andrew slammed into the coastal regions of southern Florida. The winds and torrential rains left in their wake the twisted wreckage of people's homes, businesses, and lives.

As dazed communities struggled to cope with the catastrophe, a broad panorama of human behavior unfolded. Some people were able to cope amazingly well with the stressful circumstances, while others collapsed psychologically under the strain. The best and worst sides of human nature were plainly exhibited as thousands of volunteers worked tirelessly to help the victims while, at the same time, a smaller number callously looted the survivors' few remaining possessions.

Among those who helped were groups of psychologists who ministered to the needs of emotionally exhausted victims and helpers. Psychological researchers were also at work, observing and interviewing people in an attempt to advance scientific knowledge about the personal and situational factors that affect people's reactions to catastrophic life events. The physical and emotional wreckage left behind by Hurricane Andrew thus provided a real-life laboratory for scientific research designed to answer important questions about human behavior, as well as a setting for the direct application of psychological principles to enhance human welfare.

On a hot summer evening in Austin, a University of Texas student wrote the following letter:

I don't really understand myself these days. I am supposed to be an average, reasonable, and intelligent young man. However, lately (I can't recall when it started) I have been the victim of many unusual and irrational thoughts. These thoughts constantly recur, and it requires a tremendous mental effort to concentrate on useful and progressive tasks. In March when my parents made a physical break I noticed a great deal of stress. I consulted a Dr. Cochrum at the University Health Center and asked him to recommend someone that I could consult with about some psychiatric disorders I felt I had. I talked with a doctor once for about two hours and tried to convey to him my fears that I felt overcome by overwhelming violent impulses. After one session I never saw the doctor again, and since then I have been fighting my mental turmoil alone, and seemingly to no avail. After my death I wish that an autopsy would be performed on me to see if there is any visible physical disorder. I have had some tremendous headaches in the past and have consumed two large bottles of Excedrin in the past three months.

▶ **Figure 1.1** *The aftermath of Hurricane Andrew not only provided an opportunity for psychologists to respond to human needs, but also to study a panorama of behavioral reactions to this catastrophic life event.*

Later that night Charles Whitman killed his wife and mother. The next morning he went to a tower on the University of Texas campus and began shooting the people below with a high-powered hunting rifle. In 90 horrifying minutes he killed 14 people, wounded another 24, and even managed to hit an airplane before police stormed the tower and shot him to death.

What caused a mild-mannered college student to go on a murderous rampage? (See Figure 1.2.) Perhaps the letter he wrote provides some clues. Following up his reference to intense headaches, a postmortem examination revealed a highly malignant tumor in an area of the brain known to be involved in aggressive behavior. Some experts therefore suggested that Whitman's damaged brain might have predisposed him to violent behavior. Others, however, maintained that additional causal factors may have combined to influence his violent outburst. For example, some focused on the "unusual and irrational thoughts" to which he referred. Still others sought the answer in Whitman's previous learning experiences. A study of his past revealed a long history of fascination and rewarding experiences with guns, as well as exposure to a brutally abusive father who often beat his mother and siblings. There was also speculation that Whitman's "overwhelming violent impulses" had been bottled up for many years and had finally exploded into action because of the recent life stresses that he described in his letter.

We cannot be certain how these potential causes might have combined to influence the final choices that led Whitman to the campus tower. Nonetheless, this tragic incident illustrates the many vantage points from which we can view a given act and seek an understanding of its causes.

The crowd at the U.S. Olympic Sports Festival hushed as the young weightlifter prepared for the second of his three attempts to perform a feat that defines a master in his sport. Derrick Crass, an American Olympic hopeful, was about to try to lift more than double his own 198 lb. body weight over his head. Cold and unyielding, the 411 lb. barbell lay at his feet. In one powerful motion, Crass reached down, "cleaned" the weight to his chest, then, with a triumphant yell, thrust it straight up over his head.

In the next instant, however, triumph turned to tragedy. Crass's rear foot slipped from the platform, he lost his balance, and the huge weight crashed down on him, driving his head and shoulders into the wooden platform. He lay unconscious and motionless as officials and other lifters rushed to his aid. The barbell was lifted off him and he was gingerly placed on a stretcher to be carried to a waiting ambulance.

As the weightlifter was borne from the arena, he suddenly regained consciousness. Crass rose from the stretcher and demanded his right to a third attempt to lift the weight. Dumbfounded, the trainers and physicians examined him and were amazed that they could find no sign of serious injury. It was as if Derrick Crass's bones, muscles, and connective tissue had refused to obey the laws of medicine and physics!

Derrick Crass returned to the platform as the crowd gasped in disbelief. He confidently strode to the weight and rolled it into position on the platform. He then reached down and, marshaling all of his physical and mental resources, cleaned and lifted the barbell over his head. Then, as the crowd roared and the officials signaled a successful lift, Derrick went a giant step further (see Figure 1.3). He broke into a big smile and, as cameras clicked, lifted one foot off the platform and balanced the weight on *one* leg!

There are rare and inspiring moments when the human spirit seems to rise above physical impossi-

▲ **Figure 1.3** *The dramatic manner in which Derrick Crass transformed tragedy into triumph illustrates the power that mind can exert over body.*

inspiring case of Derrick Crass represents another theme that is a centerpiece of psychology in the 1990s—the complex ways in which body, mind, and behavior relate to one another.

Psychology is defined as *the scientific study of behavior and its causes.* In this definition, the term *behavior* is used in its broadest sense to include anything that a human or animal can do. We are thus concerned with both **overt behaviors**—the actions that we can actually observe—and **covert behaviors,** such as thoughts, feelings, images, and biological processes that we cannot observe directly. Body, mind, and behavior are all part of psychology's broad focus.

The science of psychology relates to virtually every aspect of our lives. It explores the nature and causes of our behavior and feelings, our motives and thoughts. Psychology has also assumed an increasingly important role in solving human problems and promoting the welfare of the inhabitants of this complex and rapidly changing world. As you will discover, psychologists are concerned with an enormous range of questions about behavior. The following is just a sample of the issues we will be viewing through the window of psychology:

■ How do brain processes influence consciousness and behavior?
■ How does one's culture influence behavior, and what kinds of cultural differences seem to be most important?
■ What are the causes of aggression, and how can aggression be controlled?
■ How do the genes we inherit from our parents interact with the environment in which we develop to affect our abilities, traits, and behavior?
■ Which child-rearing methods produce psychologically healthy adults?
■ Why do we sleep, and what functions do our dreams have?
■ What are the causes of mental illness, and how can behavior disorders be treated and prevented?
■ How do drugs alter brain functioning and thereby affect consciousness and behavior?
■ Is extrasensory perception (ESP) really possible?
■ What are the most effective methods for preventing and treating addictions?
■ What causes individual differences in personality?
■ What is intelligence? Are current measures culturally fair and valid?
■ What effects do noise, crowding, and pollution have on our behavior and well-being?
■ Can stress kill? What are effective ways of coping with stress?

bilities. At such times, mind and body unite in a "supernormal" performance. What are the psychological principles that underlie such moments of peak performance?

■ ▣

The Nature and Scope of Psychology

The real-life cases of Charles Whitman and Derrick Crass introduce some of the themes and questions that will arise repeatedly as we explore the vast domain of behavior. First, the Charles Whitman case reflects a central theme of this book: that many causal factors may underlie a given behavior—some biological, some mental, and some environmental. The

These are only a few of the questions we will consider as we explore the domains of psychology. Because behavior is so complex and so personal, its scientific study poses special challenges. As you become familiar with the kinds of evidence necessary to validate scientific conclusions, you can become a better informed consumer of the many claims made in the name of psychology.

Psychology as a Basic and Applied Science

Working within a scientific discipline, psychologists employ a variety of research methods for building and testing theories about behavior and its causes. A distinction is sometimes made between **basic research,** the quest for knowledge purely for its own sake, and **applied research,** which is designed to solve specific practical problems. In psychology, the goal of basic research is to identify the factors that influence or cause a particular type of behavior. Such research may be carried out in the laboratory or in real-world settings. Applied research uses principles discovered through basic research to solve practical problems. Thus, as in the Hurricane Andrew disaster, one psychologist may be involved in basic research on the factors that influence how people cope effectively with catastrophic life events. Another psychologist may be interested in how this information can be applied in helping victims cope more effectively. As we survey the major areas of psychology, we will frequently notice the intimate link between basic and applied science. Not only can knowledge gained through basic research be applied to solving real-life problems, but the findings of applied science can also raise new questions that fuel basic research (Stricker, 1992). ▼

Psychological research and applications have four basic goals:

1. to *describe* behavior
2. to *understand* (explain) its causes
3. to *predict* how people will behave
4. to *influence* behavior

These four goals are not, of course, limited to the world of science; they reflect basic human endeavors. On a day-to-day basis, we all ask questions such as "What's happening? What am I (or they) doing?" (description); "Why did that happen?" (understanding or explanation); "What will happen if I do that?" (prediction); and "What can I do to make sure things turn out well?" (influence or control). Thus description, understanding, prediction, and influence are

goals shared by psychologists and lay people alike, although the specific methods used to attain these goals may differ somewhat.

Modern-day psychology is a sprawling intellectual domain that stretches from the borders of medicine and the biological sciences to those of the social sciences and on into the realm of philosophy. Within the American Psychological Association, more than 70,000 psychologists have organized themselves into nearly fifty specialty areas, or divisions, which range from General Psychology (Division 1) to Exercise and Sport Psychology (Division 47). The divisions illustrate the great diversity of interest areas that attract the attention of today's psychologists.

Because of the enormous breadth of psychology's subject matter, no psychologist can be an expert on all aspects of behavior, just as no physician can be an expert in all areas of medicine. As in other scholarly disciplines, areas of specialization have emerged within psychology. The major specialty areas are described in Table 1.1. You will be introduced to the ideas of leading theorists and researchers from each of these subfields throughout this book and in your introductory psychology course.

A career in most of the subfields described in Table 1.1 requires a doctoral degree based on four to six years of training beyond the bachelor's degree. Graduate training in psychology includes broad exposure to the theories and body of knowledge in the field, concentrated study in one or more of the subfields, and extensive training in research methods. In some areas, such as clinical, counseling, and school psychology, an additional year of supervised practical experience in a hospital, clinic, or school setting is generally required.

Besides the fascinating subject matter, the rich variety of career options and work settings available to the well-trained professional attracts many people to a career in psychology. Figure 1.4 shows some of the major settings in which psychologists work. Many psychologists teach, engage in research, or apply psychological principles and techniques to help solve personal or social problems.

Psychological Perspectives on Human Nature

We have noted that psychologists share our basic personal goals of description, understanding, prediction, and influence. Partly because psychology has its roots in such varied disciplines as philosophy, medicine, and the biological and physical sciences, a number of different ways of viewing people and their

Table 1.1 Major Specialty Areas Within Psychology

Specialty	Percentage	Major Focus
Clinical	45	Diagnosis and treatment of emotional disorders; research on personality and abnormal behavior.
Counseling	12	Consultation with clients concerning personal adjustment and vocational and career plans; interest and aptitude testing.
Educational	10	Psychological aspects of the educational process; curriculum and instructional research; teacher training.
Experimental	8	Research on basic psychological processes such as learning, memory, perception, and motivation, much of it conducted in laboratory settings.
Industrial	6	Examination of behavior in work settings; study of factors related to morale and productivity; design of training programs; preparation of machines and tasks to fit human capabilities.
Developmental	4	Study of physical, mental, emotional, and social development across the entire life span, from birth to old age.
Social	4	All aspects of social behavior and the conditions that affect it.
Personality	3	Individual differences in personality and their effects on behavior; factors involved in personality development and change.
Physiological	2	Biological foundations of behavior; brain/behavior relationships, genetic processes, and the functioning of sensory and motor systems.
Quantitative	2	Measurement and data analysis; development of mathematical models of behavior; computer science.
Others	4	
Total	100	

Source: American Psychological Association, 1992.

behavior make up its intellectual and scientific traditions. These diverse viewpoints, or, as we shall call them, *perspectives,* guide and enrich our attempts to understand behavior and its causes (see Figure 1.5).

Although opposing viewpoints may sometimes be uncomfortable for us in personal situations, they are the lifeblood of social, technical, and scientific advances. If everyone thought and viewed the world in exactly the same way, originality and creativity would be severely limited. In science, progress is often stimulated by disagreement. As one scientist noted, "Conciliatory smoothness is the lifeblood of diplomacy; it is the death of science. Diplomacy consists of producing agreement. . . . Science consists of organizing controversy or, if need be, generating it" (Murphy, 1982).

Each perspective focuses on a different aspect of our functioning and on different causes of human behavior. Psychologists often use such perspectives as tools for understanding and discovery, switching from one to another to view a behavior from different vantage points. Like our own personal viewpoints, psychological perspectives serve as lenses through which the world of behavior is viewed, and they reflect and shape our conception of human nature. They also determine which aspects of behavior we consider important and worthy of study, which questions we ask, and which study methods we employ. Perspectives on behavior influence the directions in which psychology develops, what it learns about behavior, and the kinds of contributions it makes to improving the human condition.

Taken together, the perspectives provide us with a unifying framework for understanding the many facets of who we are and why we behave as we do.

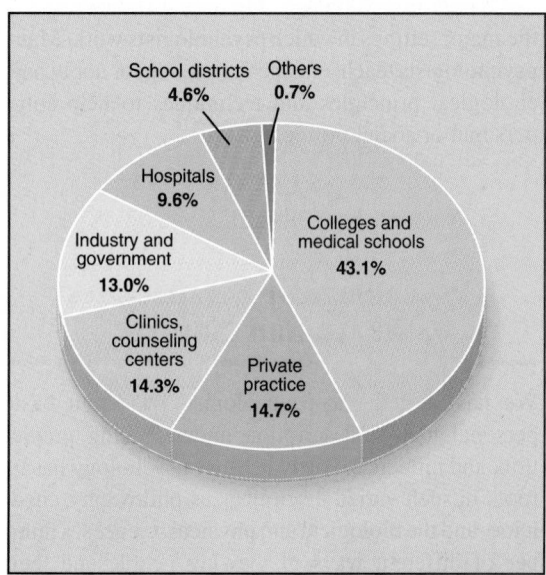

▶ **Figure 1.4** *Work Settings of Psychologists* Source: *American Psychological Association.*

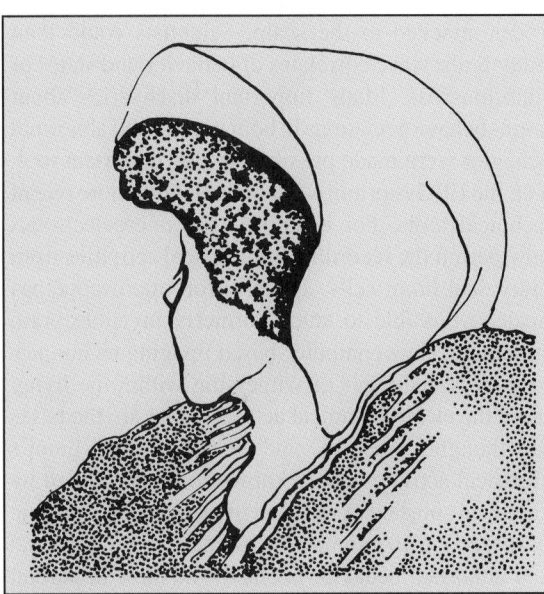

Figure 1.5 *Youth and beauty? . . . . or maturity and wisdom? If you examine this drawing, you will see both a young woman and an old one. Like many aspects of our experience, what we perceive depends on our perspective at the moment.*

They also provide us with a historical framework for tracing the intellectual and scientific traditions that fostered the development of modern-day psychology. The five major perspectives we will consider are the biological perspective, the psychodynamic perspective, the cognitive perspective, the behavioral perspective, and the humanistic perspective. (Figure 1.6).

The Biological Perspective: The Human Animal

The **biological perspective** focuses on the physical side of human nature, seeking to understand thought, emotion, and behavior in terms of physical processes taking place within the body. It emphasizes the role of our highly developed brain; the biochemical processes that underlie our every thought, emotion, and action; and a process of individual development that is partly programmed by genetic factors (Buss, 1991; Dewsbury, 1991; Loehlin, 1992).

Humans have long sought to understand the role of biological factors in their behavior. The ancient Greeks could not agree on the vital question of where mental processes originate in the body. Pythagoras, Plato, and Galen all believed that the brain is the seat of the mind and the intellect. Aristotle disagreed, believing that the mind is located in the heart. The Greek physician Hippocrates sought to account for differences in temperament in terms of proportions of four body fluids, or *humors*: black bile (which makes us moody or depressed); yellow bile (which produces excitability and impulsiveness); phlegm (which pro-

duces inactivity—hence the term *phlegmatic*); and blood (which presumably results in sociability and liveliness). Later advances in the biological sciences proved Pythagoras, Plato, and Galen to be correct, but the ideas of all these mind–body pioneers kept attention focused on the biological side of human nature.

Scientific Advances in Understanding the Nervous System

Because the biological perspective focuses on processes that are largely invisible to the naked eye, its development has depended on scientific and technological developments. In the sixteenth century, a number of scientific advances occurred in the fields of anatomy, physiology, and biology. Physicians began to dissect human cadavers to study anatomy. Experiments were conducted on the heart and circulatory system. The microscope was invented and cells were discovered. In 1664, Thomas Willis, an English physician, wrote the first accurate treatise on the brain and demonstrated that nerves emanated from it. Willis's book marked the beginning of Western medicine's focus on the brain as the organ of the mind.

Perhaps the most important discoveries for the future science of psychology concerned the electrical nature of nerve conduction. In a landmark experiment in the late 1700s, Luigi Galvani discovered that the severed leg of a frog would move if an electrical current was applied to it. Galvani's reports were ridiculed by philosophers who believed that all bodily movements were caused by spiritual forces from the soul, but further experiments confirmed Galvani's findings. Soon many experiments on electrical nerve conduction were underway, borne on a wave of excitement about the discovery of "nervous energy."

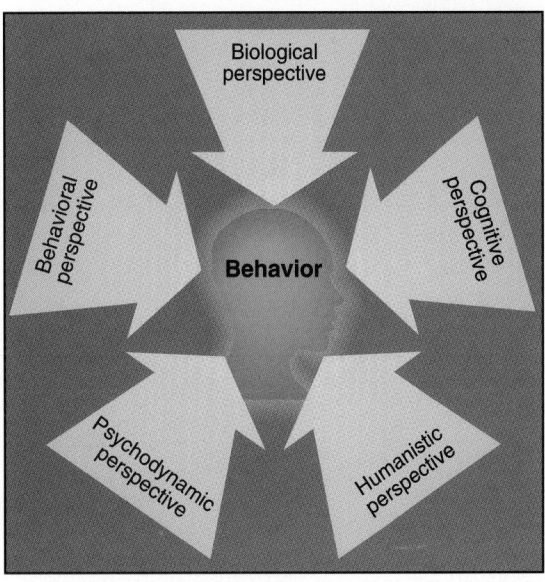

Figure 1.6 *Five major perspectives—biological, psychodynamic, cognitive, behavioral, and humanistic—guide modern psychology's attempts to understand human behavior.*

By 1870, researchers at the University of Berlin were applying electrical stimulation directly to the exposed brains of experimental animals. These researchers discovered that stimulation of a particular area on the surface of the brain now known as the *motor cortex* resulted in specific body movements. During this same period, many clinical reports appeared linking damage in specific areas of the brain with behavioral impairments of various kinds. For example, it was found that damage to a region on the left side of the brain resulted in the loss of the ability to understand or produce language.

As psychology entered the twentieth century, the study of brain–behavior relations was still in its infancy. Karl Lashley, perhaps the most important figure in the early development of biological psychology in America, was interested in brain mechanisms in learning. His approach was to create lesions (damage) in specific brain regions and to study their effects on the learning abilities and memories of experimental animals who had been trained to run mazes. Try as he might, however, Lashley was unable to find a specific area of the brain whose removal resulted in a complete loss of memory for the maze. He therefore concluded that memories must be stored throughout the brain. As we shall see in Chapter 10, the manner in which the brain stores memories is still being studied today. Lashley's research inspired many other attempts to study brain–behavior relations experimentally (see Figure 1.7).

In 1929, the invention of the electroencephalogram (EEG) allowed researchers to measure the electrical activity of large areas of the brain through electrodes attached to the scalp. Scientists could then study brain-wave correlates of behavior and states of consciousness. Many important discoveries about brain–behavior relations in both normal and abnormal behavior were made possible by this important tool. Yet, the EEG is primitive compared with more recent technical tools. For example, tiny microelectrodes now permit the recording of electrical activities from individual brain cells. The electron microscope has made it possible to study formerly invisible brain structures. New computer-based imaging techniques have provided ways of witnessing within the living brain the electrochemical activities that are the bases for thought, emotion, and behavior. The brain's electrical activity is now known to be controlled by chemical substances released by nerve cells. The role of these *neurotransmitter* substances in both normal and abnormal behavior is one of the most important areas of current research.

Although the brain is separated from the outer world by a bony skull, this organ's development and functioning cannot be insulated from the environment. We now know that an environment that provides plentiful stimulation and many learning opportunities can positively affect brain development and later capabilities, and that impoverished environments can have negative effects on brain development (Kolb, 1989; Renner, 1987). We have also learned that the two sides, or hemispheres, of the brain—the ''right brain'' and the ''left brain''—have different mental and emotional functions (Fox & Davidson, 1991; Sperry, 1970). Although the hemispheres ordinarily work together, under certain very specific conditions they are capable of functioning independently, as if there were two minds in one body. We are on the threshold of many other revolutionary discoveries of brain–behavior relations.

Evolution and Behavior: From Darwin to Evolutionary Psychology

We do not often stop to consider that as thinking and acting organisms, we go back a long way—long before our birth. Our species exists today because of our ancestors' ability to adapt, both biologically and behaviorally, to a changing and often hostile environment.

In 1859, the publication of Charles Darwin's book *On the Origin of Species* generated shock waves that are still felt today. In his theory of evolution, Darwin proposed that new species evolve over time in response to environmental conditions through a process called **natural selection,** or ''survival of the fittest.'' Natural selection means that any inheritable characteristic that increases the likelihood of survival will be maintained in the species because individuals hav-

Figure 1.7 *Relations between brain functions and behavior have long been a focus of the biological perspective. Here, a physiological psychologist has implanted a tiny electrode in a brain area thought to be involved in aggression. A mild electric current delivered through the electrode results in an immediate attack on another animal.*

ing the characteristic will be more likely to survive and reproduce. In addition, characteristics that reduce chances for survival will be eliminated from the species over time because creatures having such characteristics will not survive to pass on their genes (see Figure 1.8).

Darwin assumed that the principle of natural selection could be applied to all living things, including human beings. Contrary to a popular misconception, Darwin did *not* say that humans are the direct descendants of modern apes. Rather, he believed that both human beings and apes had a common ancestor in the distant past.

Evolution has relevance to more than just physical development. An organism's biology determines its behavioral capabilities, and its behavior determines whether or not it will survive. Psychologists with an evolutionary perspective stress that in the history of the human species, successful behavior evolved along with a changing body. One theory is that when dwindling vegetation in some parts of the world forced apelike animals from the trees and required that they hunt for food, chances for survival were greater for those who were capable of **bipedal locomotion** (walking on two legs) (Pilbeam, 1984). By freeing the hands, bipedalism in turn fostered the development and use of improved tools and weapons, and hunting in groups encouraged social organization.

Tool use and bipedal locomotion put new natural selection pressures on many parts of the body, including the teeth, the hands, and the pelvis. But the greatest pressure was placed on the brain structures involved in the abilities most critical to the emerging way of life: attention, memory, language, and thought. These mental abilities became important to survival in an environment that required the ability to learn and to solve problems. Between the early humanlike creature *Australopithecus* of 2 million years ago and the Neanderthal of 75,000 years ago, the brain tripled in size, and the most dramatic increase in brain tissue occurred in the cerebrum, the seat of the higher mental processes (see Figure 1.9). Thus, changes in behavior seem to have contributed to the development of the brain, just as the growth of the brain contributed to the development of human behavior.

The missing links that connect natural selection pressures of the distant past with behavioral tendencies of today's human species are sought within an emerging discipline known as **evolutionary psychology** (Buss, 1991; Tooby & Cosmides, 1989). Today's theorists have gone beyond the simple notion that specific behavior patterns have been programmed into human nature because they enhanced the survival of *Australopithecus* or the Neanderthal. Rather, they believe that evolutionary pressures resulted in the de-

Figure 1.8 *Natural selection pressures result in physical changes. The peppered moth's natural color is that of the lighter insect. However, over many generations, peppered moths who live in grimy polluted areas have become darker because the darker insects blended into their environment and were more likely to survive predators.*

velopment of innate learning and information-processing mechanisms that direct attention to specific kinds of stimuli that are relevant to individual and species survival (such as danger and sexual stimuli), that organize perception and memory, and that facilitate judgments and choices based on the current situation (Crawford & Anderson, 1989). These information-processing mechanisms are thought to apply to narrowly defined, or ''domain-specific,'' areas of human activity, such as aggressive threat, mate choice, sexual behavior, pair bonding, parenting, kinship, predator avoidance, and language acquisition (Cosmides & Tooby, 1987). The important point is that behavior is not ''stamped in'' by these brain-based evolutionary mechanisms; rather, these mechanisms allow us to respond more efficiently to the present environment in which we live, an environment that is far different from that of our ancestors and requires different behaviors. The goal of evolutionary psychology is to identify the psychological mechanisms that have been shaped by past and present selective pressures and to understand how the brain processes information to help us behave adaptively.

Behavior Genetics

Although scientists sometimes disagree about the role of evolution in the development of the human species, there is no question that many aspects of our development and behavior can be affected by the genetic blueprint with which we are born (Loehlin, 1992; Plomin & Rende, 1991). Psychologists have had a long-standing interest in **behavior genetics,** the study of how behavioral tendencies are influenced by genetic factors.

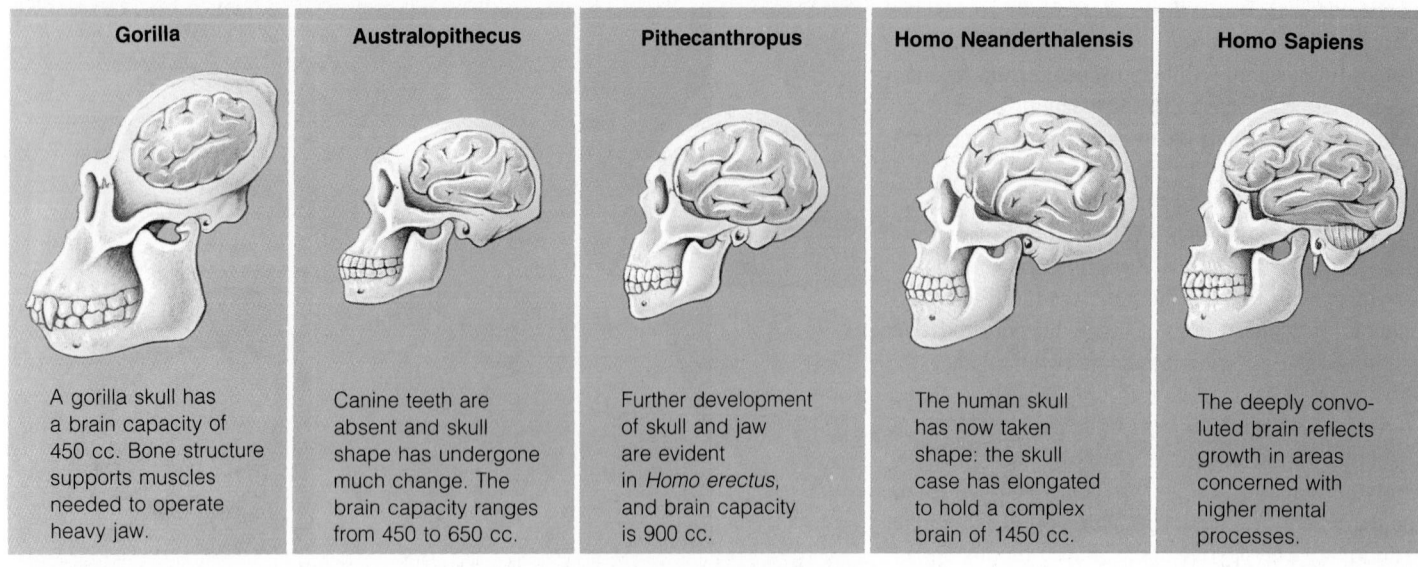

Gorilla	Australopithecus	Pithecanthropus	Homo Neanderthalensis	Homo Sapiens
A gorilla skull has a brain capacity of 450 cc. Bone structure supports muscles needed to operate heavy jaw.	Canine teeth are absent and skull shape has undergone much change. The brain capacity ranges from 450 to 650 cc.	Further development of skull and jaw are evident in *Homo erectus*, and brain capacity is 900 cc.	The human skull has now taken shape: the skull case has elongated to hold a complex brain of 1450 cc.	The deeply convoluted brain reflects growth in areas concerned with higher mental processes.

Figure 1.9 *The human brain evolved over a period of several million years. The greatest growth occurred in those areas concerned with the higher mental processes, particularly memory, thought, and language.*

Animals can be selectively bred for specific traits such as aggression or intelligence (see Figure 1.10). This is done by allowing highly aggressive or very bright males and females to mate with one another over a number of generations. In Thailand, where gambling on fish fights has long been a national pasttime, the selective breeding of winners has produced the Siamese fighting fish. The male of this species will instantly attack his own image in a mirror and can sometimes engage in fighting contests that last up to 6 hours.

There is little doubt that human behavior can also be influenced by genetic factors. Research with humans indicates that identical twins, who have exactly the same genetic makeup, are far more similar on many behavioral traits than are genetically different fraternal twins, even when the identical twins have been reared in different homes and very dissimilar environments (Bouchard & others, 1990; Pederson & others, 1988; Tellegen & others, 1988). Genetic factors are also implicated in certain brain dysfunctions that produce disturbed behavior (Gottesman, 1991; Martin, 1987).

Scientific advances in genetics now allow entire chromosomes to be created and manipulated (McClearn & others, 1991). Human chromosomes can be duplicated within host yeast cells, and it may not be long before artificial chromosomes are able to carry the large gene clusters that play important roles in animal and human functioning. This could lead to breakthroughs in the treatment of certain genetically based disorders.

The importance of biological factors in human behavior is underscored by many recent discoveries about brain processes and genetic determinants. In view of the technical advances that are occurring in the biosciences, there is good reason to anticipate revolutionary discoveries concerning the biological bases of experience and behavior.

The Psychodynamic Perspective: Impulse, Defense, and the Unconscious

Each of us is a unique person, with our own developmental history and an individual pattern of traits, motives, and inner conflicts that defines our personality. The concept of personality reflects an attempt to account for the important behavioral differences that define individual identities and that seem to originate within the person. Many psychologists refer to these personality factors as *psychodynamic* factors. The **psychodynamic perspective** searches for the causes of behavior within the personality structure of the person, emphasizing the role of unconscious processes and unresolved conflicts from the past. There are a number of different psychodynamic theories of behavior, but the first and most influential of them was Sigmund Freud's theory of psychoanalysis.

Psychoanalysis: Freud's Great Challenge

Although the shadowy underworld of hidden motives and meanings has enticed thinkers throughout history, modern humans have traditionally viewed themselves as creatures ruled by reason and conscious thought. But late in the nineteenth century, as the aftershocks produced by Darwin's evolutionary theory were still being felt throughout the intellectual world, Sigmund Freud (1856–1939) mounted a second and equally shocking assault on the prevailing conception of hu-

Figure 1.10 *Selective breeding can produce both physical and behavioral characteristics. This tiny horse (left) was produced by selectively breeding small horses, and the pedigree dogs competing at this dog show (above) are also the products of selective breeding.*

man beings as rational, civilized creatures. Freud was heavily influenced by Darwin, and he regarded humans as organisms whose inherently destructive nature is kept under control by the constraints of society. Unlike Darwin, however, Freud emphasized the role of complex psychological forces in controlling human behavior.

As a young Viennese medical student in the early 1880s, Freud was intensely interested in the workings of the brain (Miller, 1991). He began to focus his attention on the treatment of **hysteria,** a mysterious disorder in which physical symptoms such as blindness, pain, or paralysis develop without any apparent organic cause. Freud treated hysterical patients, first by using hypnosis and later by a technique he developed called **free association.** In free association, the patient was to say whatever came to mind and to let one association lead freely to another, even if the order did not seem logical or rational (see Figure 1.11). To Freud's surprise, his patients consistently reported and relived painful and long-''forgotten'' childhood sexual experiences and desires. After reliving these experiences, the patients' symptoms often showed considerable improvement. Even though Freud was the product of a Victorian culture that regarded sexuality as a taboo topic, he at first believed the reports of sexual abuse given by his clients. Later, he concluded that, in all likelihood, most of these childhood sexual experiences had never actually oc-

curred because too many of his hysterical patients reported them. (This conclusion is presently a topic of controversy in psychoanalytic circles, given recent

Figure 1.11 *According to Freud, psychodynamics often involve conflicting feelings toward important people in our lives. This portion of a homework assignment involving an exercise similar to free association ("Write the first words that come to your mind when you think of parents ") was completed by a young boy shortly after he was "grounded" as punishment for a misbehavior. Would you care to speculate on his emotional state at this time?*

> Brainstorming
> Parents
>
> mean   nerds   stupid
> uncool   nice   smart
> strict   cool   love
> lame   generous
> nerd   religious
> stupid   friends
> geeks

research reports of a notably higher incidence of childhood sexual abuse than was previously assumed.) Freud was now faced with the problem of explaining how the ''reliving'' of events that had never actually occurred could abolish the symptoms of hysteria. He became convinced that his patients were prompted to create these fantasies because of a compelling and unsatisfied sexual drive.

Freud also observed that sexual material often emerged in dreams and in slips of the tongue (so-called ''Freudian slips''). These observations, plus an intensive period of self-analysis, led Freud to propose that much of human behavior is influenced by forces of which we are unaware. He claimed that we have inborn sexual and aggressive drives, or instincts, and he believed that our adult personality is strongly influenced by the ways in which we cope with these forces as we grow up.

Freud speculated that because early sexual desires and needs are punished, we learn to fear them. Consequently, we learn to use a defense mechanism called **repression** to push them down into the unconscious depths of the mind. There they remain as sources of energy, continually striving for release. To keep the forbidden instincts under control, elaborate psychological defenses are constructed by the personality. All behavior, whether it is normal or abnormal, is a reflection of the never-ending and largely unconscious internal struggle between the *psychodynamics* created by the conflicting psychic forces of the instincts and the defenses (see Figure 1.12). Pathological acts such as Charles Whitman's shooting rampage appear when the defenses fail to control the instincts. Freud's daughter, Anna Freud, who also became a prominent psychoanalyst, identified many of the defense mechanisms and linked them to various per-

Figure 1.12. *In the psychodynamic perspective, some theorists believe that there is a never-ending internal struggle between impulses and defenses, with impulses sometimes being expressed indirectly.*

Figure 1.13 *For more than 50 years, Sigmund Freud probed the hidden recesses of the human mind. His daughter, Anna Freud, also made important contributions to psychoanalysis.*

sonality disorders (see Figure 1.13). (We will discuss these defense mechanisms in Chapter 14.)

One of the great thinkers of the 20th century, Freud wrote numerous works of both psychological and literary significance. The theory of psychoanalysis gave rise to many other psychodynamic theories, some of which differed from Freud's in attaching less importance to sexual instincts and fantasies and more to conscious and reality factors. (These theories will also be discussed in Chapter 14.) Regardless of their specifics, however, all psychodynamic theories emphasize the role of inner personality factors and unconscious processes in explaining behavior.

The Cognitive Perspective: Humans As Information Processors

If you were asked what sets humans apart from other organisms, chances are that you would emphasize our mental capabilities. The **cognitive perspective** (from the Latin *cogitare,* to think) emphasizes the ways in which people mentally process incoming information, evaluate it, and decide how to respond to it. Whereas psychodynamic theories focus primarily on the role of unconscious and nonrational mental forces, the cognitive perspective views humans as rational problem solvers whose actions are governed by conscious thought and planning (see Figure 1.14).

An important assumption of present-day cognitive psychology can be traced back to the philosopher J. F. Herbart (1776–1841), who stated that the way in which we receive information from the world is strongly influenced by the existing contents of the mind. Today's cognitive psychologists express this same conviction in their focus on concepts such as expectancies, belief systems, mental association networks, and information-processing systems. These psychologists are concerned with the manner in which information is internally organized, the content of the mental structures of the mind, and the ways in which information is processed and retrieved to create memories, problem-solving strategies, and creative thoughts (Estes, 1991; Hunt, 1989).

Psychology has been concerned with mental processes from its very beginning. In its early years, several important schools of psychology developed, each of which had its own way of studying mental processes and each of which contributed to the cognitive tradition. These schools included structuralism, functionalism, and Gestalt psychology.

Structuralism and Functionalism

Wilhelm Wundt (1832–1920) founded the first laboratory of experimental psychology at Leipzig, Germany, in 1879 (see Figure 1.15). There, he helped train the first generation of experimental psychologists. One of his students was Edward Tichener, who later established a psychological laboratory at Cornell University. Tichener was a kind of mental chemist. He believed that the mind could be studied by breaking it down into its basic components or structures, as a chemist might do in studying a complex chemical compound. This approach was therefore known as **structuralism.**

The structuralists believed that sensations are the basic elements of consciousness, and they set out to study sensations through the method of **introspection** (looking within). Subjects were exposed to all sorts of sensory stimuli—lights, sounds, tastes—and were asked to describe their inner experiences. Through such attempts to understand the conscious mind, the structuralists helped initiate a scientific tradition in the study of cognition.

In the United States, structuralism eventually gave way to an approach called **functionalism,** largely because of dissatisfaction with the scientific yield of introspection combined with a desire to study larger questions about the mind and how it directs behavior. Two of the chief architects of functionalism were William James and John Dewey. As their name suggests, functionalists were more interested in how the mind *functions* than in how it is structured. In part, functionalism was influenced by evolutionary theory, which stressed the importance of adaptive behavior

Figure 1.14 *The thinking human is the focus of the cognitive perspective.*

in survival, and much of the early research on the nature of learning and problem solving in humans and animals was done by functionalists. At one point, the eminent psychologist William James concurrently taught courses in physiology, psychology, and philosophy at Harvard University. James's broad functionalist approach helped widen the scope of psy-

Figure 1.15 *Wilhelm Wundt (center) established the first laboratory of experimental psychology to study the nature of consciousness.*

► **Figure 1.16** *This painting illustrates the Gestalt principle that the whole is often greater than the sum of its parts. Once you have perceived the organized image of a portrait, you are less likely to perceive the sea creatures as separate elements.* Source: Water *by Arcimboldo from Kunsthistorisches Museum, Vienna.*

◄ **Figure 1.17** *A modern-day counterpart of Sultan demonstrates insight learning by using a series of shorter sticks to pull in a stick that is long enough to reach the delicacy.*

chology to include body, mind, and behavior. Although it no longer exists as a formal approach within psychology, the tradition of functionalism endures in modern-day cognitive psychology as an emphasis on how the mind processes information and directs behavior.

Gestalt Psychology

In the 1920s, a German school of thought known as **Gestalt psychology** became influential in the United States. The word *gestalt* may be translated as "whole" or "organization." The Gestalt approach was the opposite of that taken by the structuralists; instead of trying to break consciousness down into its basic elements, the Gestalt psychologists argued that our perceptions and other mental processes are organized so that the whole is not only greater than, but also quite different from, the sum of its parts.

As an example, consider the painting in Figure 1.16. When you first look at it, you probably perceive it as a portrait of some kind. You are less likely to see it as a collection of individual sea creatures. The Gestalt psychologists believed that the tendency to perceive wholes, like other forms of perceptual organization, is built into our nervous system.

Wolfgang Köhler (1887–1967), one of the leaders of Gestalt psychology, conducted research with apes and other animals at a research station in the Canary Islands during World War I. Köhler concluded that the ability to perceive relationships is the essence of what we call intelligence, and he termed the sudden perception of a useful relationship **insight.**

Several examples of insight were demonstrated by Sultan, one of Köhler's apes. One day, Köhler hung a banana from the top of Sultan's cage, out of the ape's reach. Sultan seemed perplexed at first, but then he looked about his cage, noticed a box in one corner, and placed the box beneath the dangling banana so that he could reach it. Another time, Sultan joined two sticks together to reach a banana that had been placed on the ground outside his cage, a feat that has gone down in history as an act of simian genius (see Figure 1.17). Gestalt psychology's demonstrations of insight learning in both animals and humans stimulated new interest in human cognitive processes.

In addition to the schools of structuralism, functionalism, and Gestalt psychology, several prominent theorists exerted a strong influence on the development of the cognitive perspective. Three of these individuals were Jean Piaget, Albert Ellis, and Aaron Beck.

Piaget and the Development of Thought

A giant figure in the history of cognitive psychology is a man who reshaped our conceptions of how thought develops in children. A zoologist by training, Jean Piaget (1896–1980) spent more than 50 years studying how children think, reason, and solve problems. Like the functionalists, Piaget was concerned with how the mind and its development contributes to our ability to adapt to our environment.

Piaget's primary techniques included careful observation and **empathic inference,** in which he watched how children approached specific problems and then tried to imagine how they must have experienced the situation to respond as they did (see Figure 1.18). Piaget concluded that new and specific stages of cognitive development unfold naturally as children mature and that these abilities cannot be explained by the accumulation of past experiences. Rather, the stages represent fundamentally different ways of learning about and understanding the world. We shall consider these cognitive stages in detail in Chapter 4.

Cognitive Approaches to Psychological Disorders: Ellis and Beck

The cognitive perspective has strongly influenced our understanding of human unhappiness and problems in living. Two prominent psychotherapists, Albert Ellis (1962) and Aaron Beck (1976), have led the attempt to understand how dysfunctional and irrational thought patterns create emotional problems. By emphasizing the fact that distress and maladaptive behavior are caused not by external situations but by what we tell ourselves about those situations, and by developing psychotherapeutic approaches to helping people change self-defeating thought habits, Ellis and Beck have made notable contributions to the understanding and treatment of clinical disorders. We will consider their contributions in greater detail in later chapters.

Modern Cognitive Science

The cognitive perspective has evolved into today's *cognitive science.* As an area of psychology, cognitive science has links with computer science, linguistics, biology, and mathematics (Estes, 1991; Hunt, 1989). One area of cognitive science, **artificial intelligence,** tries to develop models of complex human thought, reasoning, and problem solving, often treating the mind as if it were a highly complex computer. Artificial intelligence researchers reason that by developing computer models that seem to duplicate natural cognitive processes, they will have a better understanding of how humans think. Cognitive scientists are also interested in how people produce and recognize speech, how memory operates, and how creative solutions to problems are produced. Like the evolutionary psychologists we encountered earlier, cognitive scientists are interested in understanding the internal ''hardware'' of the brain that underlies our cognitive abilities. This important area of contemporary psychology will be described in detail in Chapters 10 and 11.

The cognitive perspective assigns us an active role in shaping our own behavior. In the cognitive view, people are less what their experiences make them than what they make of their experiences. Far from being

▲ **Figure 1.18** *Jean Piaget was a master of observation. Many of his conclusions about stages of cognitive development came from watching children solve problems and inferring how they must have thought about them to respond as they did.*

passive reactors to our environment, cognitive psychologists believe, we mentally create the reality to which we respond. Indeed, my emphasis on the importance of psychology's differing perspectives is based in part on this assumption from the cognitive perspective. Our conceptions of human nature and the factors that affect behavior depend on our theoretical vantage point. For example, the image of the human animal inspired by the biological perspective is far different than the image of the human thinker that comes to us from the cognitive perspective, or the image of a being governed by intrapsychic forces as represented by the psychodynamic perspective. Moreover, all of these images differ from the conception of human nature furnished by the behavioral perspective.

The Behavioral Perspective: Environment, Learning, and Behavior

The biological, cognitive, and psychodynamic perspectives regard processes within the individual—biological factors, needs, conflicts, perceptions, and thought—as the important determinants of behavior. The **behavioral perspective** concentrates instead on the role of the external environment in shaping and governing our actions. Although behaviorists acknowledge the important role of biological factors, those who refer to themselves as **radical behaviorists** deny that people freely choose the ways in which they behave. The factors that control human behavior, they say, ultimately reside in the *external* environment rather than *within* the individual. People's behavior is jointly determined by their previous life experiences and by their immediate environment. Particular emphasis is placed on the effect of rewards and punishment in shaping behavior (Rachlin, 1991).

The behavioral perspective is rooted in a seventeenth-century school of philosophy known as **British empiricism.** The empiricists believed that all ideas and knowledge are gained *empirically*—that is, through sensory experiences. According to John Locke (1632–1704), one of the early empiricists, the human mind is initially a *tabula rasa,* a ''blank slate,'' on which our experiences make impressions. Human beings thus behave according to the dictates of their environment. Empiricism also maintained that observation was a more valid approach to knowledge than reason. To empiricists, seeing was believing, whereas reasoning was fraught with the potential for error. This idea has been enormously influential in the development of science, whose methods are rooted in empirical observation.

Radical Behaviorism: Watson and Skinner

Behaviorism emerged early in this century as an outspoken alternative to the cognitive and psychodynamic perspectives. One leader in the new movement was John B. Watson (1878–1958) (see Figure 1.19), who argued that the proper subject matter of psychology was observable, or overt, behavior, not unobservable inner consciousness. Human beings, he said, are products of their conditioning experiences, and their behavior can be controlled completely by manipulating their environment. So passionately did Watson hold this position that in 1924 he issued the following challenge:

> Give me a dozen healthy infants, well-formed, and my own specialized world to bring them up in and I'll guarantee you to take any one of them at random and train him to become any type of specialist I might select—doctor, lawyer, artist, merchant-chief and, yes, even beggar-man and thief, regardless of his talents, penchants, tendencies, abilities, vocations, and race of his ancestors. (p. 82)

Clearly, the behaviorists' approach of examining behavior strictly from the ''outside'' differs a great deal from our usual approach to understanding our inner selves. This approach is spoofed in the tongue-in-cheek story of the radical behaviorist who, after making love, turned to his partner and said, ''That was great for you. How was it for me?''

Because of the behaviorists' belief that we are what we are because of what we learn, they devoted their efforts to discovering the laws that govern learning and performance. Behaviorists believed that the same basic principles of learning apply to all organisms, and their research with both humans and animals led to many discoveries and applications of these principles. Many would argue that the discovery of the laws of learning was the greatest contribution made by American psychology. We will discuss these principles in detail in Chapter 9.

The leading modern figure in behaviorism was B. F. Skinner (1904–1990) of Harvard University (see Figure 1.20). Although Skinner did not deny that mental events, images, and feelings occur within us, he maintained that these are themselves behaviors and not causes. ''No account of what is happening inside the human body, no matter how complete, will explain the origins of human behavior,'' he insisted (Skinner, 1989, p. 18). For Skinner, there was no room for the ''mind'' or unobservable ''mental events'' in a scientific account of the causes of human behavior. The erroneous belief that human behavior is caused by inner factors, Skinner said, diverts attention from the real causes of behavior, which reside in the outer world: ''A person does not act upon the world, the world acts upon him'' (Skinner, 1971, p. 211). If human beings are to be changed, indeed saved, Skinner maintained, we must manipulate the environment that controls behavior through its pattern of rewards and punishments. Skinner believed that large-scale control over human behavior is possible today but that the chief barrier to creating a better world through ''social engineering'' is an outmoded conception of people as free agents. Needless to say, this was a highly controversial position, but Skinner's contributions prompted psychologists to appreciate the power of environmental forces.

▶ **Figure 1.19** *John B. Watson founded the school of behaviorism.*

Cultural Learning and Behavior

Every person has his or her individual learning history, but each of us is also part of a larger cultural context that provides us with common learning experiences and helps shape our behavior. **Culture** refers to the enduring values, beliefs, behaviors, and traditions that are shared by a large group of people and passed on from one generation to the next (Brislin, 1988). All cultural groups develop their own social norms. **Norms** are rules that specify what is acceptable and expected behavior for members of that group. The fact that norms can differ widely from culture to culture—and even at different times within the same culture—introduces another environmental factor that must be considered if we are to understand the causes of behavior. The effects of cultural learning factors on behavior are an important focus of a field known as **cross-cultural psychology** (Kagitcibasi & Berry, 1989).

Cultures differ from one another in many ways, but one of the most important differences from a psychological perspective is the extent to which they emphasize individualism versus collectivism (Markus & Kitayama, 1991; Triandis, 1989). Most industrialized cultures of northern Europe and North America promote **individualism,** an emphasis on personal goals and a self-identity based primarily on one's own attributes and achievements. In contrast, many cultures in Asia, Africa, and South America nurture **collectivism,** in which individual goals are subordinated to those of the group and personal identity is defined largely by the ties that bind one to family and other social groups.

Japan and the United States differ significantly on the individualism–collectivism dimension, with Japan being far more of a collectivist culture. These differences are created by social learning experiences that begin in childhood and continue thereafter in the form of social customs (Locke, 1992). For example, observational studies in Japanese and American schools have shown that Japanese children work more often as part of a group having a common assignment, whereas American children are more likely to work alone on individual projects and assignments (White, 1987). Moreover, even when American children are working in groups, American teachers are far more likely than Japanese teachers to direct their comments to individuals rather than to the group as a whole (Hamilton & others, 1991). Cultural learning experiences similar to these undoubtedly reflect and reinforce cultural norms (Lamal, 1991). At many points in this book, we shall note how the cultural environment can affect the entire spectrum of human behavior.

▲ **Figure 1.20** *B. F. Skinner was a major figure in modern behaviorism.*

Cognitive Behaviorism

An important recent development within the behavioral perspective is known as **cognitive behaviorism.** Cognitive behaviorism attempts to bridge the gap between the behavioral and cognitive perspectives and to combine them into a more comprehensive theory. The leading proponent of this approach is Albert Bandura of Stanford University (see Figure 1.21), whose theory emphasizes the role of thought, planning, and anticipated outcomes (Bandura, 1989).

Cognitive behaviorists such as Bandura believe that the environment exerts its effects on behavior not directly, as Watson or Skinner would maintain, but rather through the influence of thought. In other words, our behavior is affected not only by our im-

◀ **Figure 1.21** *Albert Bandura has played a key role in merging the cognitive and behavioral perspectives into cognitive behaviorism.*

mediate environment but also by our memories of the past and anticipations of the future. In this view, learning experiences give us the information we need to behave effectively (Bandura, 1986). Cognitive behaviorists also stress that we can learn through the experiences of others; that is, we can learn new behaviors by observing the actions of others and storing this information in memory. Finally, these theorists maintain that our cognitive abilities allow us to regulate our own behavior and thereby influence our environment (Cervone, 1992). By combining the cognitive and behavioral perspectives, cognitive behaviorists believe that a more useful conception of human behavior and its causes will emerge in which the individual is viewed as an active participant.

The Humanistic Perspective: Freedom and Self-Actualization

Not all psychologists were ready to accept the psychoanalytic notion that our behavior is determined by unconscious factors and early childhood experiences, nor were they ready to accept the behavioristic notion that we are shaped and controlled by our environment. Like psychodynamic theorists, psychologists holding the **humanistic perspective** emphasize the effect of **intrapsychic,** or inner personality factors on behavior. Of particular importance is the internal *self,* which organizes experience and directs behavior. However, humanistic theorists advance a far different conception of human nature than does psychoanalysis, be-

cause they stress the importance of conscious motives, freedom, and choice (Valle & Halling, 1989).

The historical roots of humanistic theories are found in philosophical and religious systems that have stressed the dignity, inherent goodness, and freedom of human nature. Among the most influential of the humanistic theorists were Carl Rogers (1902–1987) and Abraham Maslow (1908–1970). Both theorists assumed that in every human being there is an active force toward growth and **self-actualization,** the reaching of one's individual potential (see Figure 1.22). When the human personality unfolds in a benign and supportive environment that allows these creative forces free rein, the positive inner nature of a person emerges. Human misery and pathology, in contrast, are fostered by environments that frustrate the innate tendencies toward self-actualization. This idea was reflected by Steven J. Gould in *The Panda's Thumb* (1980): ''I am somehow less interested in the weight and convolutions of Einstein's brain than in the near certainty that people of equal talent have lived and died in cotton fields and sweatshops.''

Adding to the scope of the humanistic movement are theorists such as Rollo May (1961) and R. D. Laing (1967), who emphasize rising above environmental forces through self-determination, choice, and responsibility. ''We *are* our choices,'' these theorists maintain. To them, our existence and its meaning are squarely in our own hands, for we alone can decide what our attitudes and behaviors will be. These humanists also emphasize the importance of coming to terms with the meaning of life and death. As the German philosopher Friedrich Nietzsche once noted, ''He who has a why can bear almost any how.''

Humanistic theorists believe that scientific psychology misses the mark if it dwells only on observable behavior and neglects the individual's inner life. They believe that inner experience and the search for the meaning of our existence should be a primary focus of psychology.

In many respects, the humanistic viewpoint is more a philosophical position than a formal scientific theory. Nevertheless, this important perspective has addressed crucial aspects of human existence, and it has enriched our understanding of motivation and personality, as well as the understanding and treatment of psychological disorders.

As we have just seen, the five psychological perspectives provide us with differing conceptions of human nature, they focus on different causes of behavior, and they use different methods for discovering these causes. Table 1.2 summarizes these themes. We should keep in mind that most psychologists view these perspectives as *complementing* one another and as being useful for understanding particular aspects of human behavior and experience. To understand the whole person in his or her complexity, all of the causal

➤ **Figure 1.22** *The humanistic perspective recognizes the ability of the human spirit to rise above even the most formidable obstacles in striving for self-actualization.*

Table 1.2 Comparison of the Five Psychological Perspectives on Human Behavior

Dominant Theme	Perspective				
	Biological	**Psychodynamic**	**Cognitive**	**Behavioral**	**Humanistic**
Conception of human nature	The human animal	Humans in conflict	Humans as thinkers and information processors	Humans as reactors to the environment	Humans as free agents, seeking self-actualization and personal meaning
Causal factors in behavior	Genetic and evolutionary factors; brain and biochemical processes	Unconscious motives, conflicts, and defenses; role of early childhood experiences	Thought, planning, perception, memory processes	Past learning and present environment	Free will, choice, and drives to self-actualize and find meaning in life
Predominant focus and methods of discovery	Study of brain–behavior relations; role of hormones and biochemical processes; behavior genetics	Study of unconscious motives, conflicts, and defenses; clinical observations in psychotherapy	Study of conscious mental processes, often in laboratory settings	Study of learning and the effects of environmental stimuli	Study of meaning, values, and purpose in life

factors suggested by these five perspectives need to be considered. Nonetheless, we will find that some of the perspectives have a wider range of application than others. For example, the biological, cognitive, and behavioral perspectives apply to virtually all of the topics we will consider during our journey through the realm of psychology. The psychodynamic and humanistic perspectives have a narrower focus on personality and its development, motivation, and disordered behavior; they have much less to say about topics such as sensation and perception or cognitive science. Still, I will try to bring in all of the perspectives when they apply, because I believe that it is important for you to appreciate different viewpoints on behavior.

Integrating the Perspectives: Causal Interactions and Behavior

Psychology stands at a scientific junction formed by the five perspectives on behavior. Each perspective focuses on different pieces of the jigsaw puzzle of causality, and each has its own methods for studying its pieces of the puzzle. Yet, all of the perspectives are needed because the relative influence exerted by the various causes varies for different behaviors, for different individuals, and under differing circumstances. Sigmund Freud clearly recognized the importance of studying behavior from several vantage points when he wrote, "Let the biologists go as far as they can, and let us go as far as we can. One day the two will meet" (Freud, 1900, p. 276).

The five perspectives guide us to four different classes of causal factors—*biological, intrapsychic* (the internal personality factors that are the focus of the psychodynamic and humanistic perspectives), *cognitive,* and *environmental* (see Figure 1.23). The first three factors operate within the person, the fourth outside. To be sure, these causal factors do not usually operate in isolation, nor do they operate independently. This truism was captured many years ago by the social psychologist Kurt Lewin (1935) in the form of a simple but elegant formula:

$$B = f(P,E),$$

which reads,

"Behavior is a function of *interacting* personal and environmental factors."

For example, the effect of a particular environmental (*E*) event, such as not being invited to join acquaintances for dinner, may depend on a number of personal (*P*) factors, such as how hungry the person is (biological processes), how the person interprets

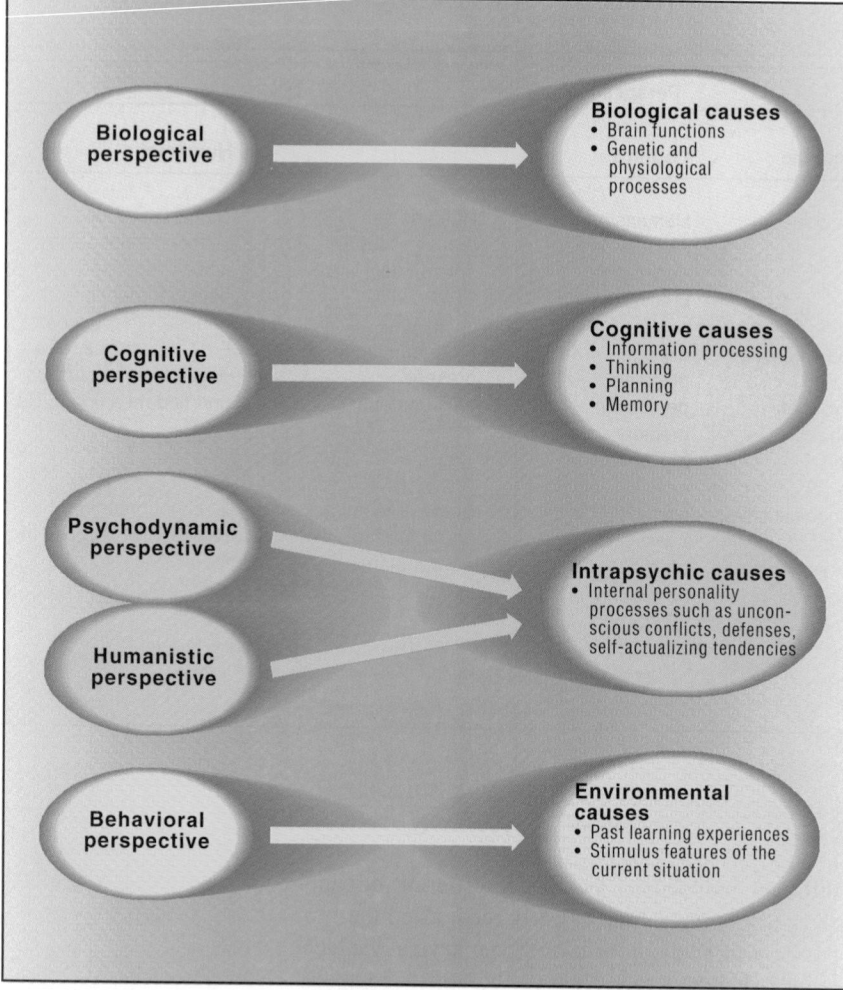

Figure 1.23 *The five perspectives on behavior provide us with four major classes of causal factors: biological, cognitive, intrapsychic (psychodynamic and humanistic perspectives), and environmental.*

the event (cognitive processes), and that individual's personality characteristics (intrapsychic influences). Thus, a person who is hungry, who interprets the lack of invitation as a sign that the group did not want his or her company, and who is very insecure and sensitive to being rejected is more likely to be upset than an individual who has just eaten, who interprets the situation as an unintentional oversight, and who is personally unconcerned about being liked or disliked. Keeping in mind that causal factors usually combine or interact with one another in many ways, it is nonetheless convenient to classify them into these four categories as a way of organizing the various causes of behavior. Therefore, throughout the book, I will attempt to bring some order to your understanding of the causes of behavior by means of special features called Understanding the Causes of Behavior. These features will summarize in graphic form what is currently known (or, in some instances, theorized) about the major biological, cognitive, intrapsychic, and en-

vironmental determinants of important behavioral phenomena.

To appreciate how the four classes of causal factors relate to a particular behavior, let us briefly summarize what is known about the most commonly experienced psychological problem, depression. A more extended treatment of these factors awaits you in Chapter 16.

An Example of Causal Interactions: Understanding Depression

Most of us have probably experienced feelings of sadness, grief, or "the blues" at some time in our lives. These feelings are usually normal responses to negative events or meaningful losses that we have experienced. However, when these emotional responses remain intense over a long time period and when they are accompanied by thoughts of hopelessness and an inability to experience pleasure, we have crossed the boundary between a normal reaction and clinical depression. Depression has sometimes been referred to as the "common cold" of emotional disturbances, because it is experienced by so many people. Even if we consider only severe depressive disorders, studies indicate that one fourth of the women and one eighth of the men in the United States can expect to experience a major depression during their lifetime (Comer, 1992).

Research on depression has shown that its causes span the entire range of causal factors. Causal links have been forged between depressive disorders and biological, intrapsychic, cognitive, and environmental factors, all of which will be considered in greater detail in Chapter 16. For now, I will simply summarize these factors to show you how differing perspectives on a psychological phenomenon can direct our attention to different causes of behavior.

Various biological factors have been implicated in depression. First, genetic factors appear to be involved in at least some cases of depression. In one study, relatives of people who had developed a major depression before age 20 were eight times more likely to eventually become depressed than were relatives of nondepressed people (Weissman & others, 1984). It thus seems likely that some people are genetically predisposed to develop depression, particularly if they experience severe losses in their lives (Plomin & Rende, 1991).

Evidence also exists that depression is related to certain biochemical factors in the brain (Depue, 1992). Special attention is being directed at the role of chemical neurotransmitters, which are involved in the transmission of nerve impulses within the brain. The most effective antidepressant drugs seem to operate by restoring a normal balance of these neurotransmitters. Also, evidence of disruptions in biological rhythms that underlie functions such as sleep have been found in the brain waves of depressed people (Campbell & Gillin, 1987).

Biological factors are not the whole story, however. Many psychodynamic and humanistic theorists believe that severe losses or rejections in childhood set the stage for later depression. In support of this notion, studies of depressed patients show that they are more likely than nondepressed subjects to have experienced the loss of a parent through death or separation during childhood (Barnes & Prosen, 1985; Brown & others, 1977). Depression is also related to childhood histories of abuse, parental rejection, and family discord (Hammen, 1991). People who have been subjected to severe loss and neglect may develop personalities that predispose them to slide into depression in the face of later life stresses. Finally, as humanistic theorists would predict, depression is frequently triggered by disillusionment and a perceived loss of meaning in one's life (Van Deurzen-Smith, 1989).

The third set of causal factors in depression is cognitive. Many studies have shown that depression is associated with a particular thinking style in which the person interprets events in a pessimistic way (Beck, 1976; Seligman, 1990). Depressed people can find the black cloud that surrounds every silver lining. They tend to blame themselves for negative things that occur while taking no personal credit for good things that happen, and they generally feel that the world, the self, and the future are bleak and hopeless (Beck, 1991).

Finally, the environment plays a major role in depression. According to the behavioral view, a vicious cycle begins when the environment provides few rewards for the person, triggering depression. As depression intensifies, such people tend to stop doing the things that ordinarily give them pleasure, a pattern that decreases environmental rewards still further. To make things worse, depressed people complain a good deal, seek excessive support from others, and generally become less likeable. These behaviors alienate others and cause them to begin avoiding the depressed person. The net result is a worsening environment with fewer rewards, a reduction in support from others, and the unhappiness and hopeless pessimism that characterize chronic depression (Lewinsohn & others, 1985).

The Understanding the Causes of Behavior feature on page 22 summarizes some potential causal factors in depression that are supported by theory and research conducted within the various perspectives. Some of these causal factors have more scientific support than others, but indirect evidence supports all of them. Although I have separated these causal factors

into four classes, keep two points in mind. First, these causal factors can differ from case to case, and they can combine or interact with one another in ways that vary according to the person and the situation. For example, a person who has a strong biological predisposition for depression may become depressed when faced with a relatively minor setback in life, whereas a person who does not have this biological predisposition may require a major life crisis to cause depression. Second, we are often dealing with what Albert Bandura (1986) refers to as **reciprocal (or two-way) causal relations** between behavior and the four classes of causal factors. That is, behaviors can have environmental, biological, cognitive, and psychodynamic consequences, just as these four sets of factors can have behavioral consequences. For example, depression can cause people to behave in ways that alienate other people, thereby creating an increasingly less supportive social *environment* for the depressed person. Likewise, a depressed person's behaviors, such as poor dietary and sleep habits and a lack of exercise, can affect *biological* functioning and cause chronic fatigue. Behavior also affects *cognitive* factors such as attitudes and beliefs about ourselves and the environment. Thus, the ineffective and socially alienating behaviors of depressed people tend to reinforce their beliefs that they are inadequate and their lives are hopeless. Finally, behavior can affect the extent to which we resolve *intrapsychic* conflicts and attain self-actualization. For many depressed people, the failure to maintain supportive relationships with others results in repeated frustration of their needs for human love and closeness (Beck, 1976). Thus, not only is behavior influenced by factors within the person and outside in the environment, but behavior can also influence these factors (Bandura, 1989). We could, therefore, reverse Lewin's classic formula to read:

$$P,E = f(B),$$

> "The person and the environment are influenced by the person's behavior."

Some of the most exciting discoveries in psychology involve interactions between biological and psychological factors, or what are popularly referred to as *mind–body interactions*. In depression, such interactions might involve relations between mental events and biological processes that accompany or produce depressed feelings and behavior. So important are the scientific discoveries linking biological and psychological processes that in 1989, President Bush signed into law congressional legislation declaring the 1990s "The Decade of the Brain." The legislation noted that "advances in neuroscience have brought us to a threshold as important and as prom-

Depression:
Factors Suggested by Theory and Research

$B=f(P,E)$

Causal Factors

Biological
- Genetic vulnerability to depression
- Biochemical imbalance in brain's transmitter systems

Cognitive
- Negative self, world views
- Self-blame for negative outcomes
- Ignoring positive aspects of life

Intrapsychic
- Unresolved grief over early loss
- Guilt and self-reproach for shortcomings
- Loss of meaning in life

Environmental
- Losses and setbacks in significant life areas
- Decreases in rewarding experiences
- Loss of or low social support from other people

Depression

Depression is a function of interacting personal and environmental causal factors. These factors may vary and may interact with one another in particular ways, depending on the person and the situation.

ising as the first launch into space—but this threshold involves a delicate step inside the human brain." Beginning in Chapter 2, each chapter will contain a special Psychobiological Interactions feature that highlights a current area of mind–body research.

As we will see throughout the book, psychological principles discovered through basic research can be applied to many areas of our lives and to the solution of important social problems. All specialties of psychology have contributed such principles. For example, educational psychology, which deals with the teaching and learning processes, has provided practical guidelines that may enhance your academic performance. Our first Enhancing Human Performance feature provides some pointers that should help you to be more successful in your coursework.

ACADEMIC PERFORMANCE ENHANCEMENT STRATEGIES

ENHANCING HUMAN PERFORMANCE

Psychologists have been researching educational and skill-enhancement processes for many years, and they have devised strategies for enhancing learning and performance in academic, occupational, and sport settings. Let us consider some principles derived from basic research that can help you improve your academic performance not only in this course but throughout your academic career. Four classes of strategies—time management, study skills, test-preparation strategies, and test-taking skills—are particularly useful for maximizing your learning and academic performance (see Figure 1.24).

Effective Time Management

Skills are needed in order to manage your time and allocate your efforts efficiently. College life provides many conflicting demands that can challenge even the most organized students. And, of course, many things that can soak up your time are more enjoyable than the hard work of studying. However, if you manage your time efficiently, you can allocate the time needed for study and have a clear conscience when it's time for recreational activities and relaxation.

Many businesses spend thousands of dollars annually on courses designed to teach their executives how to organize their time more efficiently and thereby increase their productivity while reducing stress (Haynes, 1987). These principles are as applicable to a student's life as they are in the business world.

First, it is essential to develop a written schedule. A written schedule forces you to decide how you are going to allocate your time to meet particular course demands and increases your commitment to the plan. Begin your master schedule by writing in all of your class meetings and other responsibilities, such as your job schedule. Then, block in definite study times, taking into account how long you can study efficiently at one time and avoiding times when you are likely to be tired. Try to distribute your study times throughout the week. If possible, schedule some of your study times immediately before enjoyable activities so that you can use the latter as rewards for studying.

Once your study times are set, you are ready to apply some of the other important time management principles. One is **prioritizing** (Lakein, 1973). We all tend to work on routine or simple tasks while putting off the most demanding ones until we "have more time." Unfortunately, this can result in never getting to the major tasks (such as a term paper or a major reading assignment) until it is too late to devote sufficient time to them. Prioritizing means asking yourself weekly or even daily, "What is the most important thing to get done?" Do that task first, then move to the second most important, and so on.

Often, the large or important task is too big to complete all at once. Time management experts tell us to break the large task down into smaller ones that can be completed at specific times (Haynes, 1987). Also, define each task in terms of a specific goal (for example, number of pages to be read or amount of material to be studied). Achieving these goals is rewarding, and such success strengthens your study skills and increases your feelings of mastery. It is important to make these goals meaningful, yet reachable.

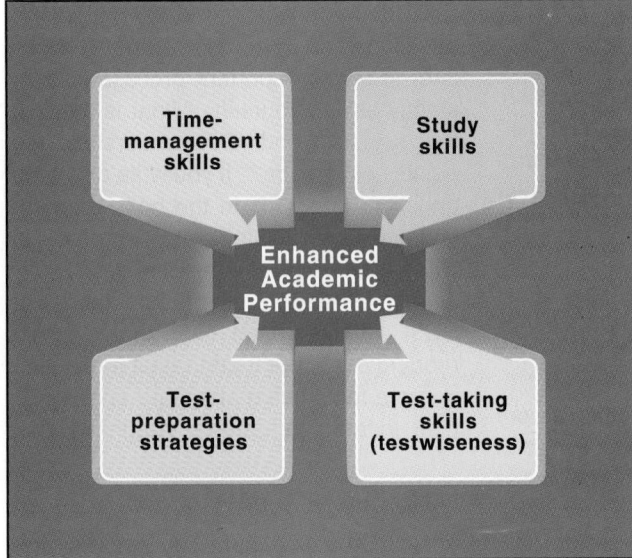

Figure 1.24 *Academic performance-enhancement methods for students include strategies for managing and allocating time more effectively, study skills, test-preparation strategies, and test-taking skills.*

Like any other skill, time management requires practice. With time, you'll get better at developing realistic schedules and setting priorities. The important tasks are (1) creating written schedules, (2) prioritizing, and (3) constantly monitoring your progress so you can modify your weekly schedule as necessary. The effort put into time management is more than repaid by the satisfaction of feeling on top of things—and by improved efficiency.

Studying More Effectively

Once you have planned your study time, you will want to use that time most effectively. *Where* you study can make a difference. Choose a place where you can concentrate and where there are no distracting influences. Most students can study better in a quiet library than in front of a TV or in the middle of a Student Union cafeteria. According to a principle of learning that we will study in Chapter 9, an excellent practice is to choose a quiet place where you do nothing but study. Over time, that place will become associated with study behaviors and it will be easier to study there (Watson & Tharp, 1989).

How you study is vital to your academic success. Rather than simply reading the material and passively letting it soak in, you must engage in an active process to study effectively. For example, as you read this book, you and I should form a relationship that entails more than my simply lecturing to you. Although I cannot physically be with you, our exchange should be more like a discussion.

Psychological research has confirmed the value of an active approach to learning (Glaser & Bassok, 1989). One popular active approach to reading is called the *SQ3R approach* (Robinson, 1970). The SQ3R acronym stands for *survey, question, read, recite,* and *review.* Here's how it works and how you can use it with this book.

Start by surveying the chapter to get an overall idea of its content. First, look over the chapter outline. Then go to the end of the chapter and read the Summary, which reviews the chapter's main points. You will then have a good idea of

the information you are going to be processing.

Ask questions about the material you are going to read and answer them after you've read the material. Most textbooks are organized into sections by means of headings. You can turn a heading such as "Psychology as a Basic and Applied Science" into one or more questions, such as "In what ways is psychology a basic and an applied science?" or "What is a basic science, and what is an applied science?" Then *read* the material with an eye toward answering the questions that you've posed. When you finish the section, actually *recite* an answer to the questions in your own words and check back to make sure that your answers are correct. Sometimes you may choose to read the material first, then formulate the questions and try to answer them. That's fine, too. The important process is constantly asking yourself, "What is this author saying?" and "Do I understand the points being made?" If you write down the questions (perhaps in the book margin), you will have a built-in *review* process in place after you finish the chapter.

Active reading using a method like SQ3R requires more effort than passive reading does, but it can result in the end in more facts being absorbed and principles understood (Estes & Vaughn, 1985).

Preparing for Tests

The time management and study strategies we've discussed can pay dividends

when preparing for tests. First, the written study schedule helps you to distribute your learning of the material over time and to avoid the last-minute cramming that characterizes the test-preparation habits of many students. Cramming is a less effective way to study because it is fatiguing and it strains your memory abilities. Moreover, it increases many students' test anxiety, a factor that can interfere both with the learning process and with actual test performance (Sarason & Sarason, 1990). The ideal situation as you near an exam is to have a solid familiarity with the material through previous study and to use the time before the test to reinforce and refine what you already know at a more general level.

As an undergraduate, I came upon a highly effective preparation procedure for taking tests that I have shared with many of my students over the years. This approach, the Directed Questions Study Method, can be highly compatible with the SQ3R approach described previously if the questions you formulate are very specific ones. Here's how it works.

As you read the material in the text, compose a question about every single point that is made. This forces you to actively identify what is being communicated. By the end of the chapter, you may have 50–70 questions that relate to concepts, facts, people, research studies, and so on. This sounds like a lot of work, and it is, but it pays rich dividends later on. If you have asked the right questions, you will have covered every point in the chapter that could be the basis for a test question. You can now study from your list of questions, referring back to the text to make sure that you are answering them correctly. As you go through your list of questions repeatedly, it takes less and less time, because you'll have developed a kind of mental shorthand to answer them. In the final stages of study, you may find, as my students do, that you can go through your list in perhaps 10–15 minutes. The question serves as a stimulus for the correct response, resulting in thorough learning.

To show you how specific the questions should be, here are some directed questions that I developed for the introductory paragraph to this feature and the section on time management. Can you answer them?

1. What are four classes of strategies that can improve academic performance?
2. Name two important principles of time management.
3. Give three reasons why a written schedule is important.
4. What self-defeating tendency does prioritizing combat?
5. What should be done if a high-priority task seems too big to deal with all at once?
6. How should subtasks be defined, and why?

Besides helping you to master the many facts and concepts that you have to learn in a survey course, the Directed Questions method has two additional benefits. First, at every stage of the study process, you have a good idea of exactly what you know and what you have not yet mastered. Research shows that there is almost no relation between what students *think* they know and how well they actually perform on tests, mainly because students have only a general idea of what they know and are relatively unaware of how well they have mastered the information required to answer test questions (Glenberg & others, 1987; Pressley & others, 1987). However, the specific questions that you prepare in the Directed Questions method allow you to realistically appraise your current level of mastery. Second, the method can reduce test anxiety. If you know that you can answer questions on every point in the text, you are likely to go into a test more confidently, and such confidence tends to enhance performance (Bandura, 1989).

Test-Taking Strategies

Once in the test, you are faced with a final challenge: translating what you have learned into test performance. Some students are more effective test takers than others. They know how to take advantage of the kind of test they are taking (e.g., multiple choice or essay format) to maximize their performance. Such skills are called *testwiseness* (Fagley, 1987). Here

are some of the strategies that testwise students use (Millman & others, 1965):

1. Because you have a time limit in which to complete the test, use the time wisely. Check your progress occasionally to make sure that you are on track. Answer the questions you know first (and, in the case of essay exams, the ones that count for the most points). Do not get bogged down on a question you find difficult to answer. Mark it and come back to it later.
2. On essay exams, organize your answer before you begin writing. Make a rough outline of the points you want to make. (You will often receive credit for points you didn't have time to make if the instructor sees them in the outline.) On essay exams, try to cover all of the critical points in enough detail to communicate what you know without needless verbiage.
3. On a test in an introductory psychology course, you are likely to have multiple-choice questions, and there are some key strategies for dealing with them. As you read the question, try to answer it without looking at the alternatives. (This process is facilitated if you have used the Directed Questions method of preparation.) If you find your answer among the alternatives, it is probably the correct alternative. Nonetheless, read all other alternatives to make sure that you chose the best one.

4. A widely held belief among both professors and students is that one should not change answers on multiple-choice tests because the first guess is most likely to be correct. Psychologists have checked out this belief and have found it to be untrue. Ludy Benjamin and his colleagues (1984) reviewed 20 different studies that investigated the consequences of changing answers. The results are summarized in Figure 1.25. As you can see, changing an answer is far more likely to result in a wrong answer becoming a correct one than vice versa. Therefore, don't be reluctant to change an answer if you are fairly sure that another alternative is better.
5. Most multiple-choice items have one or two alternatives that you can rule out

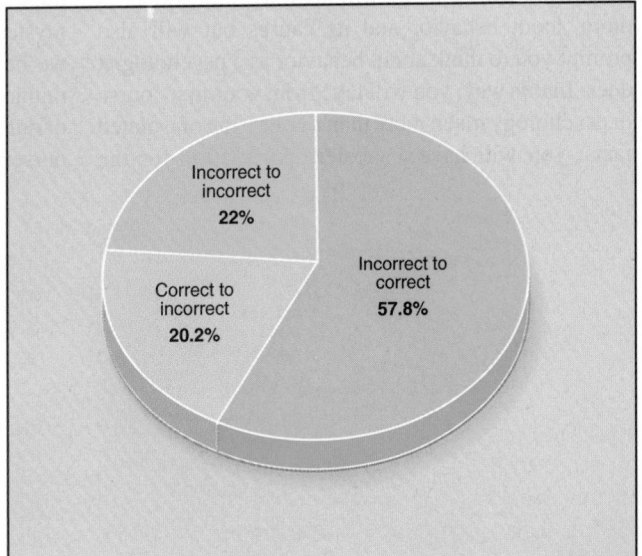

Incorrect to incorrect
22%

Correct to incorrect
20.2%

Incorrect to correct
57.8%

Figure 1.25 *Combined results of 20 studies on the effects of changing answers on multiple-choice examinations contradict the widespread belief that one's first-chosen answer is most likely to be correct and therefore should not be changed. (Data from Benjamin & others, 1984).*

immediately. Eliminate them first, then choose your answer from the remaining alternatives, which are likely to have at least a grain of truth in them.

6. Some questions have "all of the above" as an alternative. If one of the other three or four alternatives is clearly incorrect, eliminate this option; if you are sure at least two of the other alternatives are correct but are not sure about the third, choose "all of the above."

7. Because findings in science tend to be seen as tentative, alternatives containing terms such as *always, never, universally, totally,* and so on are probably incorrect. Conversely, qualified terms such as *tend, often, generally,* and *may* are often contained in correct alternatives.

The preceding strategies can help you improve your academic performance. Remember, however, that such skills are not acquired overnight; they require effort and practice. Yet, psychology is an ideal course in which to acquire or refine them, because the subject matter often directly pertains to performance enhancement. At various points in the book, other special features entitled Enhancing Human Performance will focus on performance enhancement strategies that relate to the material in those particular chapters. For example, in Chapter 9, we will discuss how principles derived from the behavioral perspective can be applied to gain greater self-control over behavior (including studying). In Chapter 10, we will dis-

cuss methods derived by cognitive psychologists for improving your memory. Finally, in Chapter 15, you can learn some specific coping skills that clinical psychologists have developed for dealing with stressful situations (including tests). You are invited to move ahead to these features and to incorporate the various performance-enhancement methods into your approach to this course. There is no better way of learning these principles than by applying them in your own life.

A Final Word and a Welcome

I hope that this book will serve as a warm and informative welcome to your study of psychology. The study of mind and behavior is one of the most fascinating and important activities in which you can engage. Although you may not choose a career in psychology, as I have, I am confident that what you learn in your introductory psychology course will contribute to your understanding of yourself and others and to the quality of your life. If some of my enthusiasm for psychology rubs off on you as you read this book, I will have succeeded in one of my goals in writing it.

I hope that this book will not only help you learn more about behavior and its causes but will also prompt you to think about behavior as a psychologist does. In this way, you will take from your first course in psychology much more than a collection of isolated facts; you will have a greater appreciation for the

complexities of behavior, a means of thinking about it critically, and an appreciation for the role of research in understanding behavior and in helping to separate truth from fiction.

Nearly a half century has passed since the English literary master and visionary Aldous Huxley looked into the future:

> We have had religious revolutions, we have had political, economic and nationalistic revolutions. All of them, as our descendants will discover, are but ripples in an ocean of conservatism—trivial by comparison with the psychological revolution toward which we are so rapidly moving.

We are now in the midst of the psychological revolution that Huxley predicted. On many fronts, important advances are being made in unraveling the mysteries of human behavior, in understanding how we behave, and why. In this book, I hope to communicate the excitement that exists on these frontiers of our attempts to know, to understand, and to change ourselves and the world of the 1990s.

The Nature and Scope of Psychology

● Psychology is the scientific study of behavior and its causes. Most psychologists use the term *behavior* in its broadest sense to include anything that a human or animal can do, including both overt and covert behaviors.

Psychology as a Basic and Applied Science

● The basic goals of psychological research and applications are to describe, understand (explain), predict, and influence behavior.

● Psychologists specialize in numerous subfields and work in many settings. Their professional activities include teaching, research, clinical work, and application of psychological principles in social settings.

Psychological Perspectives on Human Nature

● A number of important perspectives on human behavior have shaped the development of psychology. These perspectives serve as lenses through which the world of behavior is viewed, and they help to determine which aspects of behavior are studied and how. Each perspective provides a different conception of human nature.

The Biological Perspective: The Human Animal

● The biological perspective views humans as complex animals and focuses on genetic and physiological influences on behavior.

● Research in behavior genetics indicates that many complex human behaviors may be influenced by genetic factors.

The Psychodynamic Perspective: Impulse, Defense, and the Unconscious

● The psychodynamic perspective stresses the influence of internal conflicts and unconscious motivation on behavior. This perspective emphasizes the mind's conflicting psychic forces and counterforces striving for superiority and often sees behavior as a compromise between these forces. Freud's psychoanalytic theory has perhaps been the most influential of the psychodynamic theories.

The Cognitive Perspective: Humans as Information Processors

● The cognitive perspective views humans as rational information processors and problem solvers whose higher mental processes allow them to think, judge, imagine, and plan. The roots of the cognitive perspective lie in structuralism, functionalism, Gestalt psychology, and the work of Piaget, Ellis, and Beck.

The Behavioral Perspective: Environment, Learning, and Behavior

● The behavioral perspective had its roots in the philosophical tradition of empiricism. Behaviorists emphasize the role of the external environment and learning in behavior. They deny that humans freely choose how to behave.

● Behaviorists such as Watson and Skinner believed that psychology should restrict itself to the study of observable stimuli and responses; cognitive behaviorists such as Bandura have tried to combine the behavioral and cognitive perspectives into a more comprehensive theory of behavior.

The Humanistic Perspective: Freedom and Self-Actualization

● Humanistic theories present a concept of free and responsible humans with an innate drive toward self-actualization. Unless thwarted by the environment, this drive will help people fulfill themselves. This approach rejects the deterministic assumptions of psychoanalysis and behaviorism.

Integrating the Perspectives: Causal Interactions and Behavior

● The perspectives provide us with four classes of causal factors: biological; intrapsychic (psychodynamic and humanistic perspectives); cognitive; and environmental (behavioral perspective). In this chapter, the manner in which these causal factors may influence behavior was illustrated by relating them to depression. It was noted that behavior can, in turn, have biological, intrapsychic, and cognitive consequences for the person, and can exert an influence on the environment.

Academic Performance-Enhancement Strategies

● Psychological principles can be applied to enhance performance in many life settings, including college. Important skills are time management, study skills, test-preparation strategies, and test-taking skills.

K E Y   T E R M S   A N D   C O N C E P T S

applied research (p. 5)
artificial intelligence (p. 15)
basic research (p. 5)
behavioral perspective (p. 15)
behavior genetics (p. 9)
behaviorism (p. 16)
biological perspective (p. 7)
bipedal locomotion (p. 9)
British empiricism (p. 16)
cognitive behaviorism (p. 17)

cognitive perspective (p. 12)
collectivism (p. 17)
covert behavior (p. 4)
cross-cultural psychology (p. 17)
culture (p. 17)
empathic inference (p. 14)
evolutionary psychology (p. 9)
free association (p. 11)
functionalism (p. 13)
Gestalt psychology (p. 14)

humanistic perspective (p. 18)
hysteria (p. 11)
individualism (p. 17)
insight (Gestalt) (p. 14)
intrapsychic (p. 18)
introspection (p. 13)
natural selection (p. 8)
norms (p. 17)
overt behavior (p. 4)
prioritizing (p. 23)

psychodynamic perspective (p. 10)
psychology (p. 4)
radical behaviorism (p. 15)
reciprocal causal relations (p. 21)
repression (p. 12)
self-actualization (p. 18)
structuralism (p. 13)

S U G G E S T E D   R E A D I N G S

American Psychological Association (1986). *Careers in psychology.* Washington, D.C.: American Psychological Association. A booklet describing the many opportunities for careers in psychology. A free copy can be obtained by writing to the American Psychological Association, 750 First Street, N.E., Washington, D.C. 20002-4242.

Hothersall, D. (1984). *History of psychology.* New York: Random House. An engaging account of psychology's development as a science and profession that traces the intellectual and scientific traditions found in today's perspectives on behavior.

Journal of Cross-Cultural Psychology. Students interested in multicultural issues will find this quarterly scientific journal an excellent source of articles on many cross-cultural topics.

2 Research Methods In Psychology

As she returned to her New York City apartment late one night, Kitty Genovese was attacked by a knife-wielding stalker. "Oh, my God, he stabbed me," she screamed into the stillness of the night. "Please help me!" Her screams attracted the attention of 38 of her neighbors in nearby apartment buildings, some of whom leaned out their windows to see what was happening. One couple turned out their lights and pulled chairs up to their window so they could watch the grisly scene. On one occasion, a shout from one of the bystanders caused the attacker to flee, but he returned shortly thereafter to stab the screaming woman eight more times and sexually molest her. Despite her repeated pleas for help, not a single one of the 38 witnesses came to the aid of Kitty Genovese. Before the police were finally called, she died from her wounds.

In another incident, an 18-year-old switchboard operator was attacked, raped, and beaten as she worked alone in her office during the noon hour. Escaping from her assailant, she ran naked and bleeding into the street screaming for help. A crowd of 40 passersby gathered and watched as the rapist tried to drag her back into the building. No one came to her aid. Fortunately, two policemen happened by and arrested the assailant (Latané & Darley, 1970).

In the aftermath of these incidents, many commentators decried the shocking lack of concern for others that seemed so graphically displayed in these and other instances in which people refused to "get involved" when others clearly needed help. However, it seemed unlikely to two social psychologists, Bibb Latané and John Darley, that all of the 78 bystanders in the two incidents were cruel and indifferent. They wondered if the bystanders' failure to help could be due to psychological processes created when a number of bystanders are present in an emergency. Each bystander might assume that someone else surely will help, resulting in a decrease in feelings of personal responsibility. Latané and Darley referred to this phenomenon as **diffusion of responsibility** through the group of bystanders. Indeed, many of the witnesses to the Kitty Genovese incident insisted that they had been very concerned but that they had known that many other people were also aware of what was occurring and therefore had assumed that someone else was going to her rescue or had called the police. Latané and Darley hypothesized that a victim may be better off, then, if there is only one person present to help, because that person is totally responsible for helping.

To test this hypothesis, Darley and Latané (1968) created an emergency in their experimental laboratory at Columbia University. They told subjects that they would be participating in a discussion of "personal problems faced by normal college students." To en-

sure anonymity, subjects would be situated in separate rooms and would communicate through an intercom system. Each subject would have two minutes to speak, after which the speaker's microphone would automatically switch off. Subjects then heard, over the intercom, a speaker begin to describe his difficulties adjusting to college life. With some embarrassment, he disclosed that he occasionally suffered from severe epileptic seizures, especially when under stress. Somewhat later, this speaker began to gasp and stammer that he was having "a problem . . . because I—er—I—uh—I've got one of the sei—er—er things coming on." His voice became louder and more incoherent as he gasped, "If somebody would—er—give me a little h-help—uh—er—er c-ould somebody—er—er—help (choking sounds) . . . . I'm gonna die—er—er—I'm gonna die—er—help—seizure" (chokes, then silence) (Latané & Darley, 1970, pp. 95–96).

The subjects were actually listening to a carefully prepared tape recording to ensure that all of them were exposed to the identical "emergency." To test the effect of number of bystanders, Darley and Latané manipulated the number of other people that the subjects believed were present. In one condition, subjects thought they were alone with the victim; in another, they thought there was another subject besides themselves and the victim. In a third condition, they were told that there were five other subjects, including the victim. The researchers were interested in two measures of helping behavior: the percentages of subjects who tried to help by going to the victim or going to another room to get the experimenter, and the speed with which help was given.

Figure 2.1 shows the impact of the number of people present. When subjects thought they were alone with the victim, virtually everyone helped, usually within the first minute. With an increase in the number of others who were supposedly present, however, the proportion of people who helped and the speed with which they did so decreased noticeably.

Similar findings occurred in another laboratory experiment by Latané and Darley (1970). As subjects completed a series of questionnaires, the woman experimenter went into an adjoining room and switched on a tape recorder that broadcast the sounds of a filing cabinet crashing to the floor and a scream of pain from the woman: "Oh, my God, my foot . . . I can't move it . . . I can't get this thing off me." When only one subject was present, 70 percent of the subjects went to the woman's aid. But when other subjects (actually accomplices of the experimenters who were programmed not to help) were present, as few as 10 percent of the real subjects helped.

In many ways, the classic Latané and Darley experiments on helping behavior illustrate how psychological research can contradict commonsense ad-

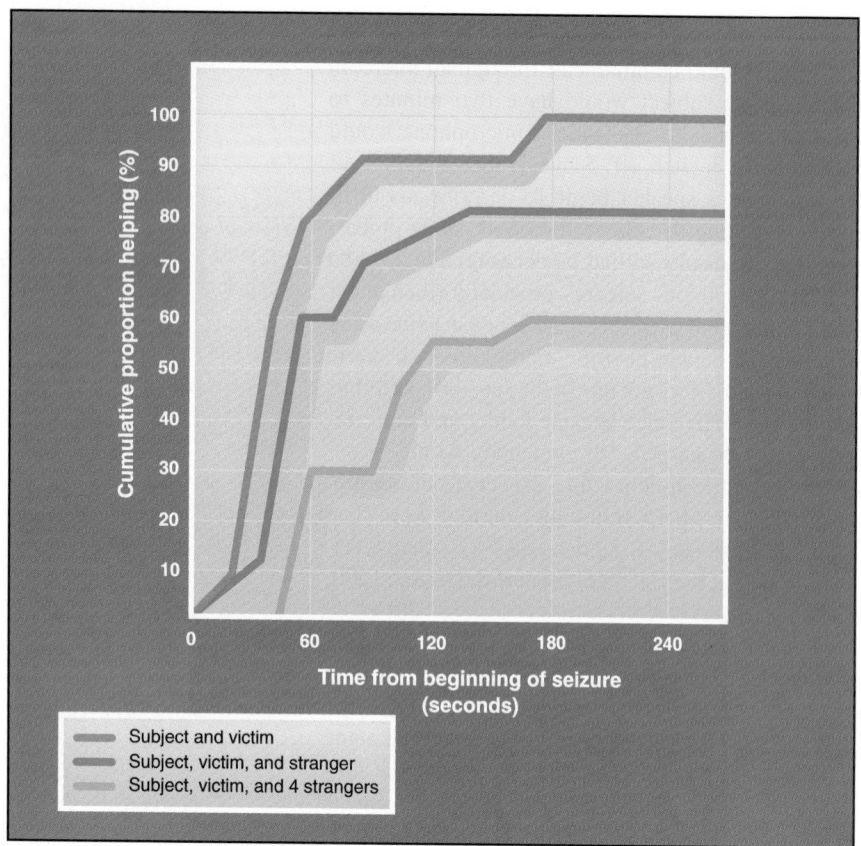

◀ **Figure 2.1** *This figure shows the cumulative (total) proportion of subjects who helped a student who was apparently having an epileptic seizure under three experimental conditions: when the subject believed he was alone with the victim; when he believed one additional subject was present; and when he believed four additional subjects were present. Each cumulative curve plots the percentage of subjects who intervened at any given time after the emergency began. Thus, both likelihood and speed of intervention were greatest when subjects believed themselves to be alone with the victim. (Latané & Darley, 1970).*

Like the master detective, the good scientist is an incurable skeptic. Even when it looks as if all the evidence is in and the mystery solved, he or she asks: How reliable is the evidence? Was the research designed and carried out carefully enough to control for other factors that might influence the behavior in question? Are there other possible explanations for the results? If so, what additional information is needed to rule them out?

Scientific study involves a continuous interplay between observation and attempts to explain and understand what was observed. Figure 2.2 shows the steps through which scientific inquiry typically proceeds. The scientific process always begins with some kind of noteworthy observation. Latané and Darley's work, for example, was inspired by a number of widely publicized incidents in which bystanders failed to help victims.

At the second stage of the scientific process, Latané and Darley tried to figure out what could have been responsible for the failure of bystanders to help the victims. Behaving just as nonscientists would, they used reason and logic to arrive at an initial, tentative explanation. They rejected the notion that people were simply uncaring and looked for other possible explanations. Noting that in each case, a large number of bystanders had witnessed the emergency, they reasoned that something in the group setting made people less likely to help. They reasoned that in such a situation, a diffusion of responsibility could reduce the likelihood that any one person would feel totally responsible for helping. (As we will see in Chapter 19, they identified several other psychological factors that could reduce helping as well.)

Casual observers might be satisfied at this point that they understood why the bystanders did not help, but the scientific method takes us a crucial step further. Recognizing that the explanation is still only tentative, the scientist goes on to *test* this understanding by means of additional observations. First, though, a hypothesis is formulated. A **hypothesis** is an "if, then" statement that can be tested with new observations. Latané and Darley's hypothesis could be stated: *"If* individuals confront an emergency in the company of other bystanders, *then* they will be

ages like "There's safety in numbers." As you will see at many points in this book, a number of commonsense beliefs have not survived the cutting edge of psychological research. More importantly, however, psychological research such as Latané and Darley's can help identify the psychological laws and processes that underlie a limitless variety of behavioral phenomena.

In this chapter, we explore the scientific principles that form the foundation of psychological research, as well as the methods that are used to describe, predict, influence, and understand behavior. Virtually all of what you will learn about human behavior in your introductory psychology course is a product of these methods.

■■ ■■

Scientific Principles in Psychology

As we will see on many occasions during our survey of psychology, science frequently has all the mystery and drama of a detective story. The mysteries that challenge the psychologist relate to behavior and its causes. But nature does not give up its secrets easily. False leads, blind alleys, and apparent contradictions are all part of the scientific enterprise.

less likely to intervene to help the victim than if they were alone when confronting the emergency.'' Latané and Darley created a number of situations to test their hypothesis. When their observations were consistent with their prediction, they considered the hypothesis supported.

The goal of the first four steps of the scientific process is the development of theories. A psychological **theory** is a set of formal statements that specify lawful relations between certain behaviors and their causes. A good theory has three important characteristics:

1. It incorporates many existing facts, observations, and known relations within a single broad framework.
2. It gives rise to additional hypotheses that can be tested by making new observations. In this way, a theory leads to new knowledge. Even if the new observations do not support the theory, the theory will still perform a valuable function by leading to a better and more inclusive theory. It is just as important to know what is *not* true as what is true. Thus, to be scientifically useful, a theory must be testable and capable of being refuted. It should be able to tell us what kind of relations are *not* possible as well as what kind are possible. Theories that seem capable of accounting for everything, even seemingly contradictory facts, are not good theories, because they can't be proven wrong.
3. It conforms to the law of **parsimony.** That is, it is not needlessly complex. If two theories can account for the same phenomena and generate the same number of testable hypotheses, the simpler of the theories is the preferred one.

Compared with those of the physical sciences, psychological theories are less explicit and well-developed, largely because of the bewildering complexity of behavior and its causes. The trend in psychology is away from the grand theory that tries to explain everything and toward small-scale theories that relate to a limited area of behavior and generate precise and testable hypotheses.

Two Ways of Understanding Behavior

As noted in Chapter 1, a basic human goal is to understand—that is, to be able to answer the questions ''Why?'' and ''How?'' For the psychologist, understanding means being able to specify the *causes* of behavior, the conditions responsible for its occurrence. There are two basic approaches to understanding, and they illustrate the difference between nonscientific and scientific understanding.

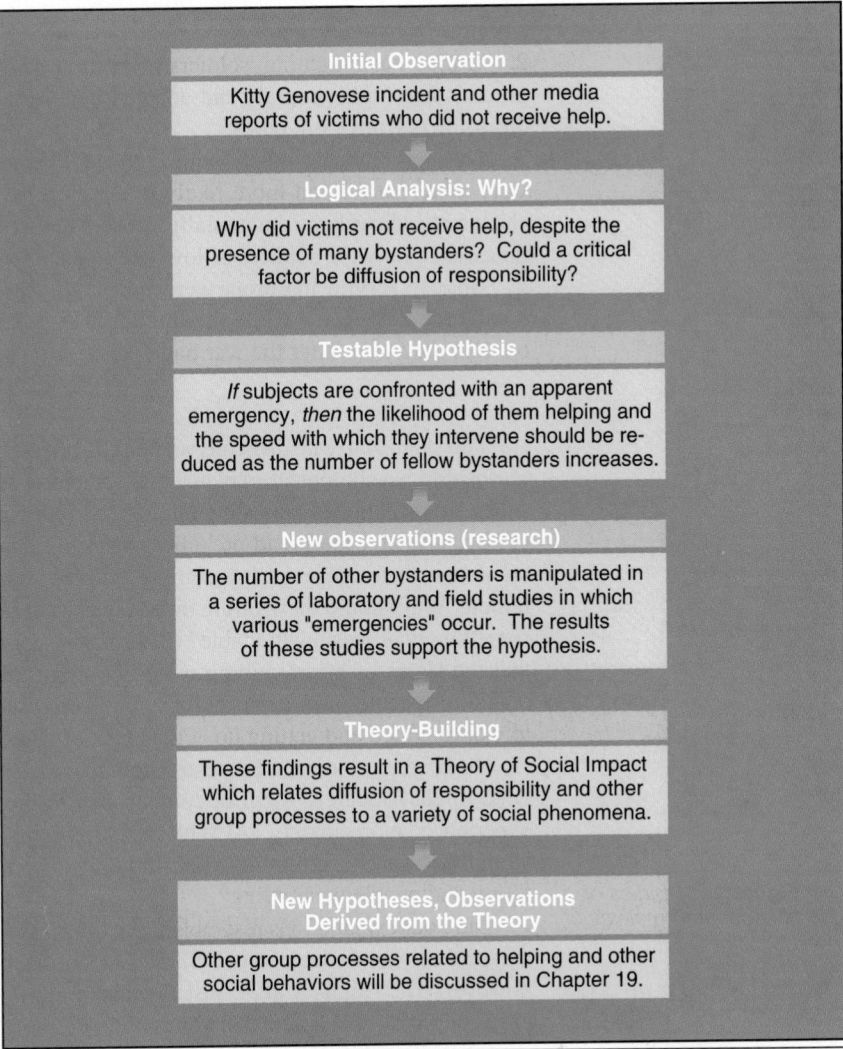

Initial Observation

Kitty Genovese incident and other media reports of victims who did not receive help.

Logical Analysis: Why?

Why did victims not receive help, despite the presence of many bystanders? Could a critical factor be diffusion of responsibility?

Testable Hypothesis

If subjects are confronted with an apparent emergency, *then* the likelihood of them helping and the speed with which they intervene should be reduced as the number of fellow bystanders increases.

New observations (research)

The number of other bystanders is manipulated in a series of laboratory and field studies in which various "emergencies" occur. The results of these studies support the hypothesis.

Theory-Building

These findings result in a Theory of Social Impact which relates diffusion of responsibility and other group processes to a variety of social phenomena.

New Hypotheses, Observations Derived from the Theory

Other group processes related to helping and other social behaviors will be discussed in Chapter 19.

Figure 2.2 *The path of scientific understanding often proceeds from informal observation through theory development to the use of the theory to generate new hypotheses and observations. We can see this progression in the research on bystanders' intervention in emergencies.*

After-the-Fact Understanding

One sometimes hears the statement that psychology is nothing more than common sense (Kelley, 1992). ''I knew that all along'' is a common response to findings from psychological research. In fact, exactly this criticism was leveled by a *New York Times* book reviewer some years ago. The report he was reviewing, *The American Soldier* (Stouffer & others, 1949a, 1949b), summarized the results of a large-scale study of the goals, attitudes, and behavior of U.S. soldiers during World War II (see Figure 2.3). The reviewer blasted the government for spending a considerable amount of money to ''tell us nothing we don't already know.''

Consider the following statements. How would you account for each of them?

1. The motivation to become officers was higher among white soldiers than among blacks.

2. During basic training, soldiers from rural backgrounds had higher morale and adapted better than did soldiers from large cities.

3. During combat, soldiers with high intelligence were more fearful and more likely to develop psychosomatic disorders (emotionally caused physical illnesses) than were soldiers of low intelligence.

4. Soldiers serving in Europe were more highly motivated to return home while the fighting was going on than they were after the war had ended.

You should have no difficulty arriving at perfectly reasonable psychological explanations for these results. A typical line of reasoning might be as follows: (1) Because of widespread prejudice, black soldiers knew that their chances of becoming officers were remote. Why should they torture themselves wanting something that was unattainable? (2) It makes sense that the rigors of basic training would be more tolerable for people from farm settings who were used to working hard and getting up at the crack of dawn. (3) The brighter soldiers were smart enough to realize what might happen to them in combat; hence, they experienced more anxiety. (4) Who in his right mind would *not* want to go home while the bullets were flying and people were dying?

Did your explanations resemble these? If so, they are perfectly reasonable ones. There *is* one catch, however. The results you've just explained are the exact opposite of the actual findings. The data presented in *The American Soldier* actually indicated that black soldiers were *more* highly motivated than

Figure 2.3 *Studies of the attitudes and motives of U.S. soldiers during World War II were criticized for "telling us nothing we don't already know." However, common sense may sometimes result in false conclusions.*

whites to become officers. Moreover, city boys had higher morale than farm boys during basic training, and soldiers of low intelligence were more anxious and more likely to develop psychosomatic problems in combat. Finally, soldiers were actually more eager to return home *after* the war had ended than they were during the fighting.

I often use this demonstration in my introductory psychology class to illustrate how easy it is to arrive at completely reasonable after-the-fact explanations for almost any result. Students quickly find equally plausible explanations for the real findings. (They also learn that they should not accept research findings uncritically but should instead think of conditions under which the results might *not* apply.)

Trying to explain a behavior by taking into account the conditions that existed at the time it occurred is probably our most common method of trying to understand our own and others' behavior. In the words of the Danish philosopher Søren Kierkegaard, "Life is lived forwards, but understood backwards." The major difficulty with after-the-fact understanding, however, is that past events can be explained in many ways, and there is no sure way to determine which, if any, of the alternative explanations is correct. Explanatory "truths" that seemingly contradict one another are found in such common sayings as "Absence makes the heart grow fonder" and "Out of sight, out of mind"; "Opposites attract" and "Birds of a feather flock together"; "You're never too old to learn" and "You can't teach an old dog new tricks."

We should not conclude that after-the-fact understanding is never useful or valid. Because we can't always reconstruct past events, there may be no alternative. This approach can give us valuable leads and insights, and it is usually the foundation on which further scientific inquiry is built.

Achieving Understanding through Prediction and Control

Scientists favor another approach to understanding, one that allows them to test their theories about causes directly. For scientists, the acid test of understanding is the ability to make accurate predictions. If we understand the causes of a given behavior, then we should be able to specify the conditions under which that behavior will occur in the future. Furthermore, if we can control or manipulate those conditions, then we should be able to control the occurrence of the behavior. We do this in our daily lives when we try to influence others by creating certain conditions or behaving in a particular way, and scientists do the same thing when they test a scientific hypothesis. Understanding through prediction and control is the scientific alternative to after-the-fact understanding.

Even when a hypothesis is supported by successful prediction and control, it is never regarded as an absolute truth, because it is always possible that some new observation will contradict it. If this happens, however, scientists don't necessarily wring their hands in despair, because the disproving of accepted and established hypotheses frequently opens up new frontiers for investigation. The displacement of old beliefs and "truths" by new ones is the essence of science.

Constructs and Operational Definitions

To conduct scientific research, we must clearly identify the phenomena that we are seeking to understand. The vocabulary of psychology is filled with terms like *aggression, personality, stress, learning,* and *motivation.* All of these are simply words or concepts—scientists prefer the term **constructs**—that refer to classes of behaviors and situations. Because these words represent nonmaterial ideas and not real things, they may have different meanings for different people. For example, the term *dependency* refers to a particular class of behaviors, but the specific types of behavior that are labeled "dependent" may differ from one person to another. Unless two people have a common definition of what *dependent* means, they can't be sure they're communicating effectively when

they talk about "dependent" people. "What do you mean by that?" is a question psychologists must answer very precisely if they are to study a psychological phenomenon.

Operational definitions help solve the communication problem by translating an abstract term into something observable and measurable. That observable event may be a stimulus, something that is *done to* a subject. For example, the construct *hunger* may be operationally defined as "the number of hours that a subject is deprived of food." Conversely, the event may be a response, something that the subject does. Thus, hunger may be operationally defined in terms of subjects' ratings of how hungry they feel or in terms of how much effort they will make to obtain food. To summarize, a construct may be operationally defined in terms of either stimuli or responses. Figure 2.4 shows some of the operational definitions of the construct *stress* that have been used in psychological research.

Unless a construct can be tied to something observable, it cannot be studied scientifically. For example, the construct *free will* has been an important concept in the history of Western thought, but it cannot be studied by scientists because no one can agree on how to operationally define or measure it. How could we ever know whether an act was truly free, as a humanistic theorist would maintain, or whether it was completely determined by the person's past and present environment, as a behaviorist would

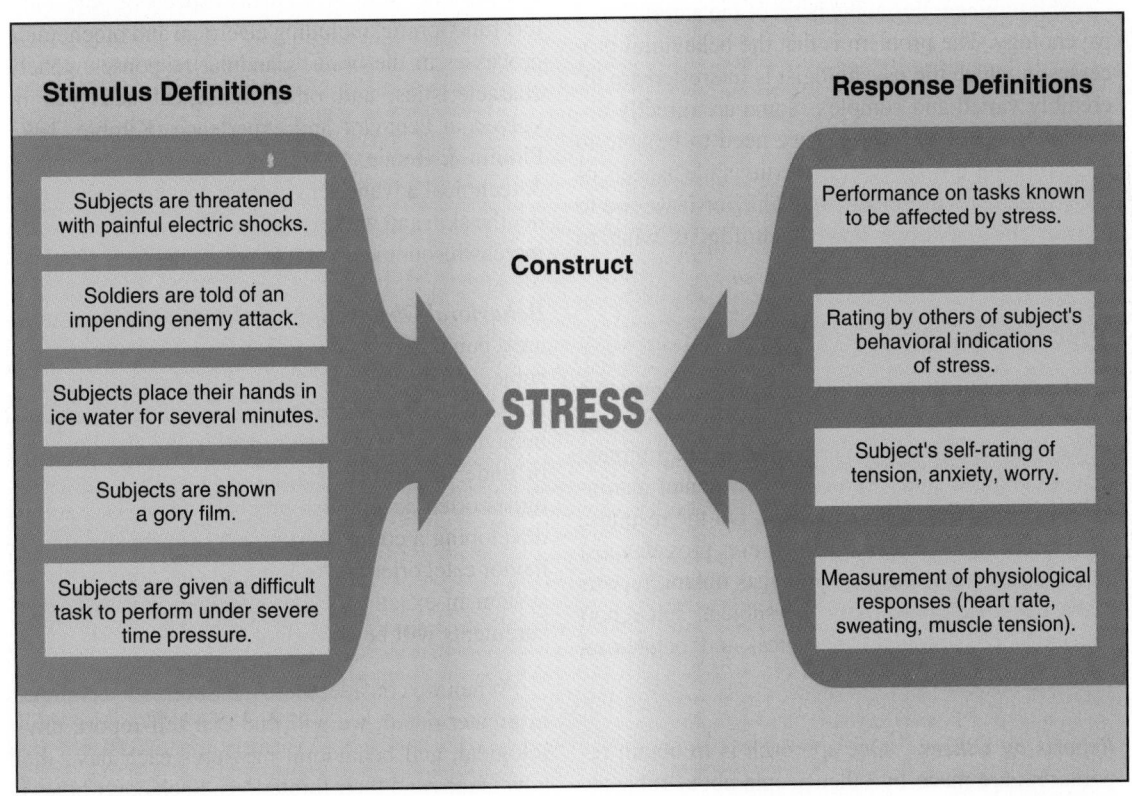

Stimulus Definitions

Subjects are threatened with painful electric shocks.

Soldiers are told of an impending enemy attack.

Subjects place their hands in ice water for several minutes.

Subjects are shown a gory film.

Subjects are given a difficult task to perform under severe time pressure.

Construct

STRESS

Response Definitions

Performance on tasks known to be affected by stress.

Rating by others of subject's behavioral indications of stress.

Subject's self-rating of tension, anxiety, worry.

Measurement of physiological responses (heart rate, sweating, muscle tension).

Figure 2.4 *The construct* stress *may be operationally defined in terms of either stimulus conditions to which subjects are exposed or responses made by subjects.*

claim? Although we cannot study free will itself, we can study the causes and effects of a *belief* in free will, because we can operationally define and measure people's beliefs by interviewing them or giving them questionnaires. If we assume that people are telling us the truth, we can obtain a direct measure of their belief.

Operational definitions don't solve every problem. Different scientists may not agree on a particular definition, just as you and a friend may not agree about whether an acquaintance is really dependent. Furthermore, results based on one operational definition may not agree with results based on another operational definition of the same concept. For example, subjects' ratings of their level of stress frequently do not relate highly to measures of their actual physiological responses (Andreassi, 1989; Riley & Furedy, 1985). Thus, researchers must state their operational definitions in very precise terms.

Measurement in Psychology

Good operational definitions tie directly into measurement of the phenomena in which we are interested. One of my psychology instructors introduced the topic of measurement by noting, "In science, everything ultimately boils down to measurement. Once we can figure out how to validly measure whatever we are interested in, we're in a position to go out and collect the information we need. Without good measurement, we have nothing."

Measurement lies at the heart of the enterprise of psychology. The problem is that the behavioral processes in which the psychologist is interested are incredibly varied and complex. Some are directly observable; others are not. Yet we need to be able to measure both the visible and the invisible aspects of body, mind, environment, and behavior if we are to answer the questions that psychologists wish to address.

Types of Measures

As the operational definitions of *stress* in Figure 2.4 suggest, we can classify environments in various ways, and we can sometimes create the environment that we want to study through experimental manipulations, as Latané and Darley did. On the response side, four kinds of behavioral measures provide most of the information that psychologists obtain: reports made by others concerning the subject, self-report measures, physiological measures, and behavioral observations (see Figure 2.5).

Reports by Others. One approach is to obtain reports that are made by other people about subjects.

Parents, spouses, roommates, job supervisors, and others who know the subject may provide useful information about him or her. Supervisors might be asked to provide ratings of the subject's task performance or the extent to which the subject exhibited certain behaviors on the job. College roommates are sometimes asked to rate subjects on certain personality traits. In studies of marital interactions, spouses can provide information about subjects that would be virtually impossible to obtain in any other way.

Verbal Self-Report Measures. Self-report measures require subjects to report on their knowledge, beliefs, feelings, internal experiences, or behavior. Various methods can be used to gather such information, including interviews, questionnaires, surveys, and psychological tests. Psychological tests are specially designed instruments that can be used to measure mental or behavioral characteristics, such as intelligence, vocational interests and aptitudes, scholastic abilities, or personality factors.

Physiological Measures. Psychologists frequently have to depend on self-report to measure some of the subjective experiences that interest them. This does not mean, however, that it is never possible to get "inside" the person to directly measure what is happening there. Physiological measures of body responses are becoming increasingly important in psychology, and such measures are favored by scientists operating from the biological perspective. Scientists are now able to measure many aspects of physiological functioning, including electrical and biochemical processes in the brain, glandular responses, genetic characteristics, and other biological activities involved in behavior and experience (Kimble, 1992; Plomin & Rende, 1991). As we will see in Chapter 3, technical advances in measuring what goes on under the skin and within the nervous system are greatly increasing our understanding of mind–body relations.

Behavioral Observations. Behavioral observations are a popular method for obtaining information about subjects, and they are favored by psychologists espousing the behavioral perspective. Subjects' actual behaviors can be observed either in real-life situations or under controlled laboratory conditions. Psychologists often accomplish precision of observation by developing a coding system made up of specific behavior categories and training all observers to use the system in exactly the same way so that their measurements will be consistent.

When we consider these measurement techniques in greater detail, we will find that self-report, physiological, and behavioral measures each have their advantages and their limitations. Each contributes in

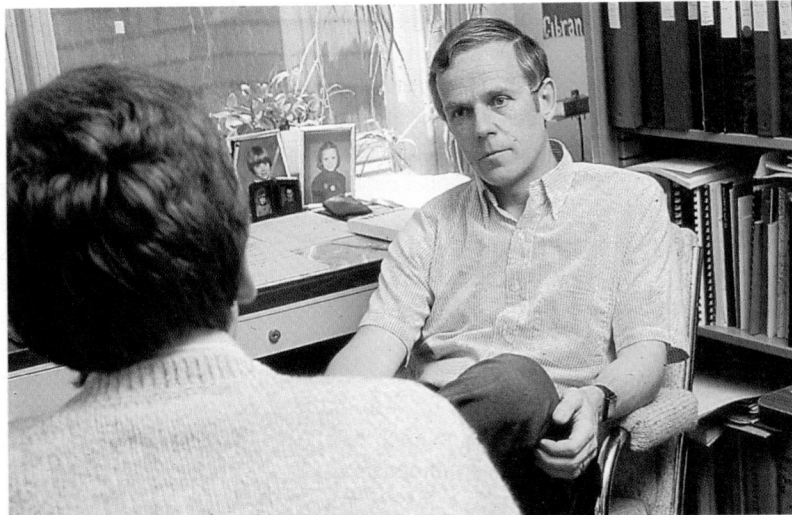

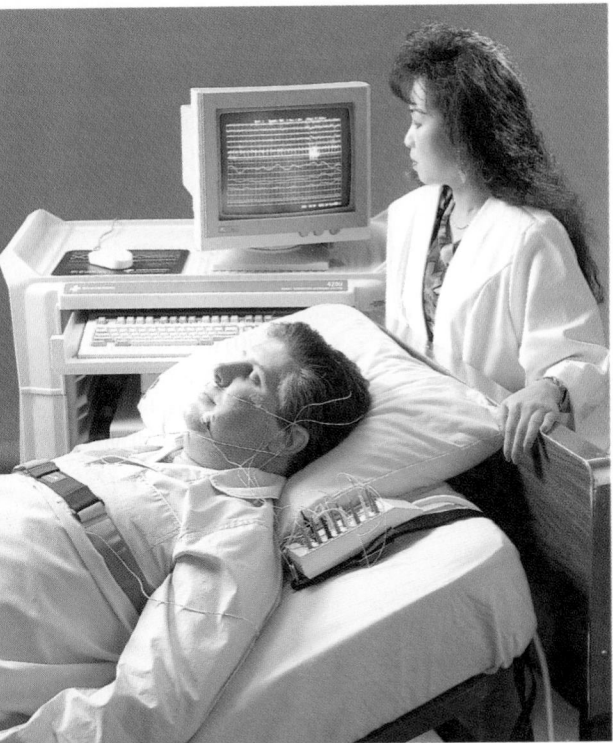

Figure 2.5 *Self-report, physiological, and behavioral measures are important scientific tools for psychologists.*

important ways to our understanding of person, environment, and behavior.

Data Collection Procedures

Having considered some of the principles underlying the scientific study of behavior, we now examine the specific ways in which observations, or **data,** are collected by psychologists. What methods a researcher chooses depends on the nature of the problem being studied, the objectives of the study, the researcher's perspective on behavior, and ethical principles relating to research methods.

Research Settings: Advantages and Trade-Offs

Some types of behavior can be studied only in their natural settings where little or no control is possible;

others can be studied under highly controlled laboratory conditions. The decision to study behavior in a natural setting as opposed to a laboratory involves some important trade-offs. On the one hand, identifying the true causes of behavior in a real-world setting poses problems because there is no way to rule out other possible causes by controlling them. On the other hand, when the subjects are observed in their native habitat, the researcher can have more confidence that the results can be applied to other similar real-life settings. The work of Jane Goodall and other researchers who have made painstaking observations of animals in their natural environments illustrates the scientific value that such research can have when it is carefully conducted.

The highly controlled conditions possible in the laboratory allow the researcher to be more confident that the causes of behavior *in that setting* have been identified—that is, that the study has high **internal validity.** Another important question remains, however: Can the results be generalized beyond the laboratory setting in which they occurred? In other words, to what extent do the results mirror what happens in the "real world"? The answer to this question, which defines a study's **external validity,** depends on how well the researcher has captured the important elements of the real-world situation to which the results are to be applied. Throughout the book, you will see many examples of the ingenuity that is required to achieve this goal.

We have seen how Bibb Latané and John Darley (1970) tried to move the Kitty Genovese incident into the laboratory to study under controlled conditions the effect of the presence of others on the likelihood that people will go to the aid of distressed victims. The researchers were able to create a highly standardized situation for all subjects to test and support their hypothesis that the presence of others reduces the likelihood that a person will help someone in distress. However, Latané and Darley could not be absolutely certain that the situations they had created in the laboratory had the essential features of the real-world situations that they were trying to understand. To establish that the hypothesis held across a range of situations, they and other researchers did nearly 50 additional experiments in natural settings ranging from subways and liquor stores to work and school settings (Batson, 1991; Clark, 1990). Consistently, the results indicated that when the situation was somewhat ambiguous and other bystanders were present, the likelihood that subjects would help was reduced. This research provides a good example of moving back and forth from the real world to the laboratory to study an important behavior, one that can have life-or-death implications.

Sampling

Before we consider research methods themselves, we should briefly examine sampling, because it relates in important ways to the interpretation of research results. There are few, if any, situations in which researchers can study every member of a **population** (all the relevant animals or people who might possibly be studied). Yet researchers want to arrive at conclusions that apply to the entire population. Unfortunately, research is almost always restricted to a segment, or **sample,** drawn from the larger population. If valid conclusions are to be drawn, the sample must reflect the important characteristics of the larger population.

A **representative sample** mirrors the population in every important respect (see Figure 2.6). Public opinion pollsters use samples that possess important characteristics (age, gender, political party, geographical location, and so on) in the same proportion as they exist in the population. Such a sample's responses are likely to mirror those of the larger population. For example, election forecasts derived from representative samples are often strikingly accurate, even if the sample constitutes less than 1 percent of the population.

Using unrepresentative, or biased, samples can produce distorted results. Other things being equal, large samples are better than small ones, because large samples are more likely to be representative of the population and conclusions are less likely to be biased by a few atypical subjects. Even a very large sample, however, can result in erroneous conclusions if it is not representative. For example, in 1936, a survey of more than 2 million *Literary Digest* readers indicated that Alf Landon would defeat Franklin Roosevelt by a landslide in the presidential election. Fortunately for Roosevelt, the views of the wealthy and highly educated *Literary Digest* readers were not representative of the general population. Since that time, poll-

Figure 2.6 *A representative sample possesses the important characteristics of the population in the same proportions. Data from a representative sample are more likely to apply to the larger population than data from an unrepresentative sample.*

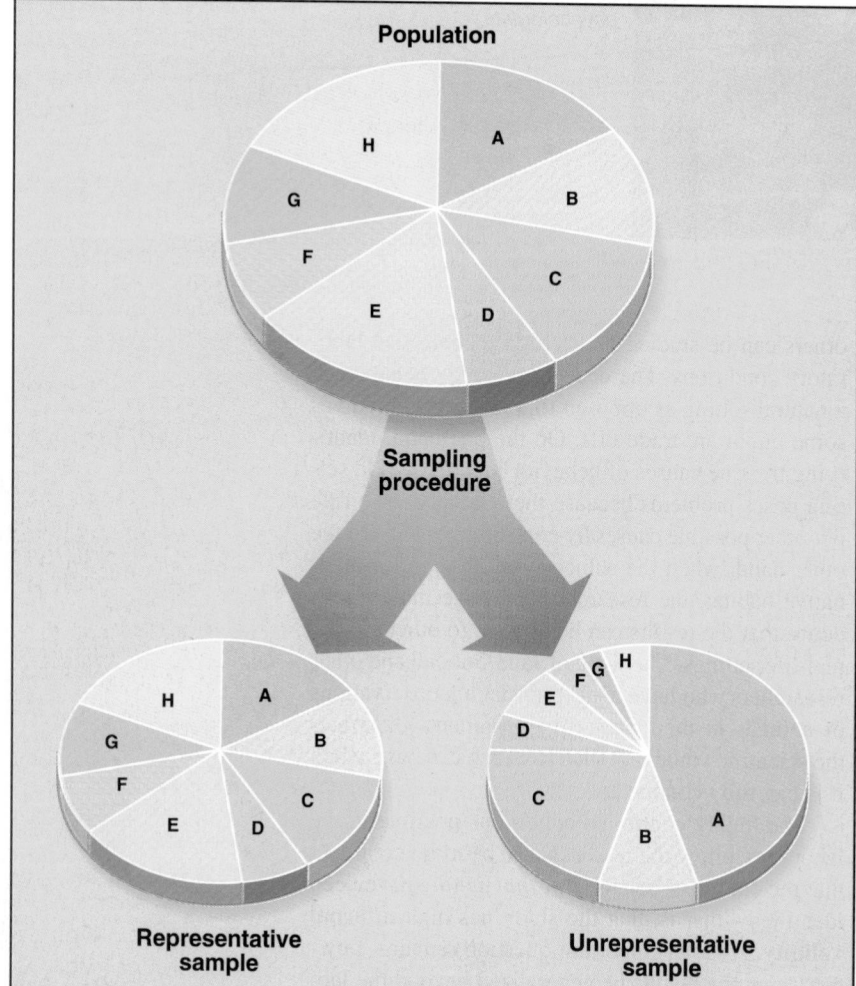

Population

Sampling procedure

Representative sample

Unrepresentative sample

sters have improved their techniques for obtaining representative samples of voters.

The nature of the sample should always be considered in the interpretation of research results. Just as the results of laboratory studies may not always generalize to real-life settings, research results derived from samples of college students or white rats (probably the two most-studied populations) may not apply to other populations, such as children or middle-aged males.

We turn now to a consideration of research methods. Four major methods are used by psychologists to study behavior and its causes. These include the case study, the observational approach, correlational research, and the controlled experiment. To show how these research methods are used, we will consider actual studies that illustrate each approach.

Case Studies

Case studies—detailed observations of an individual's or group's behavior—are often used by clinical and personality psychologists. The goal of most case studies is to identify or illustrate certain principles of individual behavior that are assumed to apply in a general sense. In many instances, case studies deal with phenomena that cannot be studied under controlled conditions because of practical or ethical constraints. Case studies can focus on individuals, on groups, or even on entire organizations. Many theories of personality, group behavior, and organizational functioning were originally derived from intensive case studies that raised important questions or suggested hypotheses that were later tested in more systematic and controlled research.

Rare or noteworthy examples of a particular phenomenon are often the subject of case studies. The following study suggests the profound effects that stress and cultural beliefs can have on physical well-being.

The Hmong Sudden Death Syndrome

Vang Xiong is a former Hmong (Laotian) soldier who was resettled in Chicago with his wife and child after escaping from Laos. Like many other victims of that war, Vang had vivid and traumatic memories of death and destruction as well as severe guilt about having had to leave his brothers and sisters behind when he fled with his family (see Figure 2.7). Moreover, the culture shock created by the move from his rural home to the busy urban environment of Chicago increased the stress he was experiencing. He began having problems almost immediately, according to a mental health team that reported on his case in a prominent psychiatric journal.

[He] could not sleep the first night in the apartment, nor the second, nor the third. After three days of sleeping very little, Vang came to see his resettlement worker, a young bilingual Hmong man named Moua Lee. Vang told Moua that the first night he woke suddenly, short of breath, from a dream in which a cat was sitting on his chest. The second night, the room suddenly grew darker, and a figure, like a large black dog, came to his bed and sat on his chest. He could not push the dog off and he grew quickly and dangerously short of breath. The third night, a tall, white-skinned female spirit came into his bedroom from the kitchen and lay on top of him. Her weight made it increasingly difficult for him to breathe, and as he grew frantic and tried to call out he could manage but a whisper. He attempted to turn onto his side, but found he was pinned down. After 15 minutes, the spirit left him and he awoke, screaming (Tobin & Friedman, 1983, p. 440).

Vang's report would not have attracted scientific interest had it not been for one fact: About 40 Laotian refugees in the United States had died of the "Hmong sudden death syndrome." The reports of the deaths are chillingly identical: A person in good health went to sleep and died in his or her sleep after exhibiting labored breathing, screams, and frantic movements similar to those reported by Vang. The Center for Disease Control investigated the mysterious deaths, but the medical investigators were unable to find a physical cause for them. The Center's investigators concluded that the deaths were psychologically induced and were a culture-specific response to the

Figure 2.7 *Many Hmong refugees who escaped the ravages of war in their homeland experienced great stress and guilt when they were resettled in the United States. This stress, combined with cultural beliefs about angry spirits, may have contributed to the Hmong sudden death syndrome, which claimed more than 40 lives.*

stress of resettlement and possibly to the guilt of abandoning family and relatives in Laos.

The authors of the case study concluded that Vang may have been a survivor of the sudden death syndrome. The role of cultural beliefs in the syndrome are suggested by what happened next. Vang went for treatment to a Hmong woman regarded as a shaman. She told him his problems were caused by unhappy spirits and performed the ceremonies needed to release the spirits. He encountered no further problems with nightmares or with his breathing during sleep.

As you will see throughout the book, interactions between mind and body are one of the most fascinating frontiers of psychological investigation. This case study certainly cannot prove that the Hmong sudden death syndrome is a fatal stress response produced by cultural beliefs (particularly since we cannot interview those who did not survive), but the case has stimulated additional scientific interest in the role of such beliefs in physical well-being (Sue & others, 1990). Multicultural research is an inviting area for such study because of the diversity of the cultural belief systems that can be studied.

In most case studies, explanations of the event occur after the fact, and there is little opportunity to rule out other possible explanations by controlling for them. Even the most intensive study of an individual case cannot assure us that the true causes of the behavior have been isolated. Nevertheless, such studies can provide important leads to be followed up by more controlled research. In addition, a single contradictory case study can cast doubt on an entire theory if the theory has been held to be true in all cases. Negative findings in case studies are sometimes the first indication that a theory is incomplete and must be expanded to take other factors into account.

The Observational Approach: Describing Behavior

The first steps in the scientific process are usually observation and description of some notable phenomenon. Some sciences are basically descriptive in nature. In astronomy and anatomy, for example, scientists carefully observe heavenly or earthly bodies and tell us what they see. Sometimes, psychologists also do research that is basically descriptive in nature. By describing certain behaviors and the specific settings in which they occur, researchers can obtain important information about possible cause-and-effect relations, although, like the case study, this method cannot definitely establish causality.

Observational research can be carried out in almost any setting. We will examine two very different examples. The first study was done in the natural environment; it is an example of **uncontrolled observation,** because the researchers could not regulate the conditions. The second example was carried out in a controlled laboratory setting under rigorously standardized conditions.

Uncontrolled Observation: When Prophecy Fails

People tend to strive for agreement, or consistency, among their beliefs, attitudes, and behavior. This basic idea is the foundation for the highly influential **theory of cognitive dissonance** developed by Leon Festinger (1957). People experience the uncomfortable state of dissonance when their cognitions are incompatible with one another. For example, the knowledge that one has just done something dishonest would be at odds with the belief that one is an honest person. It should therefore produce a state of dissonance. To bring the two cognitions into alignment, the person might justify the action as not being dishonest after all or might revise the belief that he or she is always honest. Dissonance theory, which will be discussed in greater detail in Chapter 18, has inspired many studies. The results suggest that people sometimes modify their beliefs and attitudes to make them consistent with their behavior.

There are times when psychologists have the opportunity to test predictions based on their theories in unique real-world situations. One such opportunity occurred for Festinger and his coworkers as they were developing cognitive dissonance theory in the 1950s (Festinger & others, 1956). They discovered a cult in Minneapolis organized around a clairvoyant, Mrs. Keech, who had prophesied the destruction of much of the United States by a cataclysmic flood, which was to occur on a specific date. Mrs. Keech claimed that the prophecy had come in a message sent from the planet Clarion by superior beings called Guardians and that she had received it through automatic writing. She had attracted a small but dedicated group of believers who, despite ridicule and criticism, had quit their jobs, given away their property, or dropped out of college. These believers, Mrs. Keech said, would be rescued by a spaceship from Clarion on the eve of the disaster.

When Festinger and his coworkers heard about the group, they joined it in order to observe the behavior of group members. They attended lengthy séances during which messages were received from the Guardians, and they dictated their observations onto tapes after each meeting. On the basis of dissonance theory, they predicted that when the prophesied disaster did not occur, a monumental clash would be created between the beliefs of the group members, their committed behaviors, and their knowledge that the flood had not occurred. Festinger therefore predicted that the group members would show an *increase* in their convictions and proselytizing activities. If they could convince others that their beliefs were correct, then the dissonance would not seem as great.

On the eve of the flood, the group waited to be picked up by the spaceship. When it did not appear, the group spent 5 hours in agonizing tension as the believers tried to maintain their faith. Then a message from the Guardians arrived through Mrs. Keech's automatic writing: Because this small group had such great faith, God had decided to spare the world.

The group received the glad tidings without question and experienced a great urge to share the news with others. By 6:00 A.M. they had contacted all newspapers and wire services to announce the message. For several days afterward, the group called press conferences to announce new messages received by Mrs. Keech from the Guardians, and the members showed a startling degree of commitment to their mission (see Figure 2.8). Most members of the group succeeded in convincing themselves that they had been correct all along in their beliefs and actions.

The uncontrolled observations of Festinger and his coworkers showed that although Mrs. Keech could not make very accurate predictions from her interplanetary messages, the researchers could make very accurate ones based on dissonance theory.

Controlled Observation: Blind Obedience to Authority

Our second example of the observational approach involves **controlled observation** of a most atypical variety. Indeed, because of the ethical issues it raised, this research evoked considerable controversy among psychologists. The study was carried out in a setting far different from the setting of Festinger's work, one in which it was possible to observe subjects under carefully contrived conditions. The behavior of interest—obedience—was operationally defined and measured very precisely.

After World War II, the famous Nuremberg trials were held to punish Nazi war criminals who had murdered millions of innocent people. In many instances, the defense offered by the defendants was that they had ''only followed orders.'' U.S. soldiers accused of similar acts in Vietnam gave the same explanation for their actions.

Just as the Nuremberg court did, many of us reject justifications based on obedience to authority as mere rationalizations, secure in our conviction that we would behave differently under such circumstances. However, the results of a series of ingenious laboratory studies performed by Stanley Milgram (1974) suggest that perhaps we should not be so sure of ourselves.

Figure 2.8 *As the observational study by Festinger and his coworkers suggested, the need for consistency among beliefs, attitudes, and actions can cause people to become extremely dedicated to justifying their beliefs by convincing others of their validity.*

To study the ability of an authority figure to command destructive obedience, Milgram devised a situation in which subjects thought they were assisting a Yale University researcher who was studying the effects of punishment on learning. The subject's task was to present the learning problems through a two-way intercom system to a learner who was strapped in a chair in an adjoining room. Each time the learner made an error, the subject was instructed to administer an electric shock through an apparatus having 30 numbered switches starting at 15 volts and going up to 450 volts. With each error, the shock was increased by 15 volts. Before beginning, each assistant was given a sample 45-volt shock, which was moderately painful (see Figure 2.9). *Obedience* was operationally defined as the maximum shock intensity the subject would administer when ordered to do so by the authority figure.

Forty men ranging in age from 20 to 50 years and representing a cross section of the male population in that age group served as subjects. They did not know that they were in a carefully contrived situation or that the learner was actually the experimenter's accomplice. No shocks were actually delivered, and the learner's responses, heard over an intercom, were tape-recorded so that they were the same for all subjects.

As the subjects increased the shock voltage after each error, the learner (who had earlier noted that he had a mild heart condition) showed increased distress. At 75 volts, he began to moan when the subject threw the shock switch. At 150 volts, he stated that he could not stand the pain any longer and began to complain that his heart was bothering him. He demanded to be

Stanley Milgram's obedience study generated shock waves among other psychologists. Many questioned the ethics of subjecting unknowing subjects to such a stressful situation. Some also suggested that participation in the study could have long-term negative effects on the self-concepts of subjects who had obeyed the experimenter's orders to harm another person. In response, Milgram maintained that the important social implications of what he was studying justified the methods he used. Do you agree? Can you think of any precautions that could have been taken to ensure that subjects were not psychologically harmed?

released. Beyond 200 volts, he emitted agonized screams every time a shock was delivered. He shrieked, ''Let me out! Let me out! I'm not in this experiment any more!'' Hysterical screams continued up to 345 volts, after which there was only silence. In response to the silence, the experimenter told the assistant to continue delivering the shocks because the learner was not giving correct responses.

The subject faced a terrible dilemma: Should he continue to hurt this innocent person, as the experimenter commanded, or should he refuse to go on? Whenever a subject became distressed and said that he was unwilling to continue with the experiment, the experimenter ordered him to continue. The only way that the subject could stop the proceedings was to openly defy the authority figure.

Place yourself in this situation. How far do you think you would go if you were one of Milgram's assistants? Before the experiment began, a panel of psychiatrists predicted that no more than 1 percent of the subjects would be ''pathologically sadistic'' enough to proceed to the 450-volt maximum. In fact, the average maximum shock administered was 368

volts, and 65 percent of the subjects gave the 450-volt maximum (see Figure 2.10).

Virtually all of the subjects who gave high levels of shock exhibited extreme discomfort, anxiety, and distress. Most of them balked at one time or another and said they would not go on. Yet they continued shocking the learner when ordered to do so by the experimenter, who assured them that he would take responsibility for whatever happened to the learner. As Milgram noted later, ''Even when the destructive effects of their work became patently clear, and they were asked to carry out actions incompatible with fundamental standards of morality, relatively few people have the resources needed to resist authority''(Milgram, 1974, p. 6). ▼

By contriving a situation with many real-life elements, Milgram was able to observe directly and under controlled conditions behaviors that in many ways resembled those of people in other settings who have claimed that ''I didn't want to do it, but I had to follow orders.'' Despite the carefully controlled conditions, however, this study is *not* an experiment, because all of the subjects were exposed to exactly the same sit-

Figure 2.9 *Stanley Milgram created a convincing setting for his controlled observations of obedience to authority. Shown here are the "shock generator," the "learner" being strapped into his chair, and a subject being directed to administer a severe shock and the subject refusing to go on. Despite their objections, most of the subjects obeyed the experimenter.*

(a)

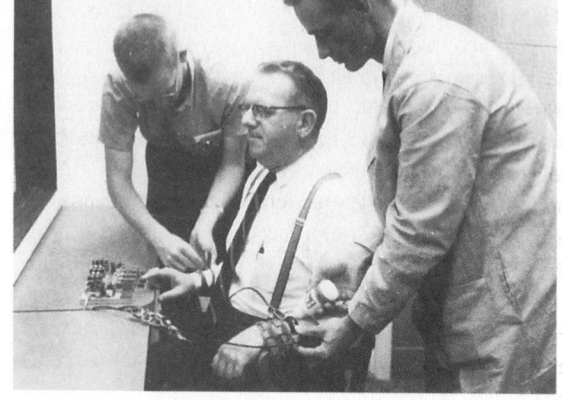

(b)

(d)

(c)

uation. A true experiment would include two or more distinct conditions that could be compared in terms of their effects on behavior.

The Correlational Approach: Studying Relations Between Observed Events

Psychologists often wish to study relations between naturally occurring events that they cannot directly control. For example, they may be interested in how scores on an intelligence test relate to college grades or how unemployment figures are related to crime rates. Such studies are called **correlational research,** because the objective is to find out how two things are co-*related*.

Correlational research is a valuable means of approaching many important societal issues, such as linkages between physical fitness and life expectancy or between television viewing habits and other behaviors. Although correlational research does not prove that one event causes the other, it often provides valuable leads to be followed up in other types of research that *can* demonstrate causality.

Early Parental Relationships and Midlife Adjustment

It has long been assumed that children's relationships with their parents play an important role in personality development and later adjustment. One of the most important parenting characteristics is the amount of warmth that the parent manifests in the parent–child relationship. Warm parents express affection and positive regard for the child, whereas cold parents tend to be disapproving, emotionless, or punitive toward their children.

In 1951, Robert Sears, Eleanor Maccoby, and Harry Levin (1957) began a landmark study of parenting styles and their effects on children. At the time, both child psychologists and the media held the view that parenting with strictness and discipline was the preferred approach to raising well-adjusted children. Based on interviews with 379 mothers, Sears and his coworkers were able to measure mothers and fathers along the warm–cold dimension and to relate this characteristic to a variety of child behaviors. The children were 5 years old at the time.

The researchers found that, contrary to popular wisdom of that era, maternal warmth was the best predictor of children's adjustment. Coldness was related to a variety of problems, including bed-wetting, feeding problems, greater aggression, and slower conscience development. By age 12, warmth of either parent was related to higher levels of self-esteem in the child (Sears, 1970).

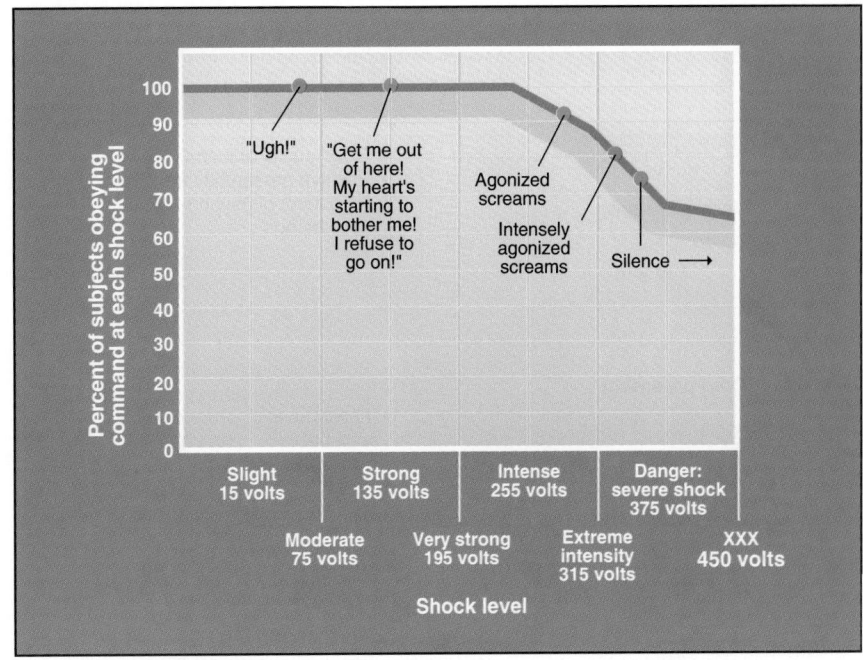

Until recently, little information was available on the relation between the well-being of adults and the parenting practices they had experienced as children. Most research was based on adults' retrospective accounts of what their parents were like, and their recall may have been biased by their level of adult adjustment. In 1991, however, Carol Franz, David McClelland, and Joel Weinberger published a 36-year follow-up of 76 subjects who had been studied as children by Sears and his coworkers. Of interest was the subjects' *conventional social accomplishment,* which the researchers defined as the ability to sustain long and relatively happy marriages, raise children, and sustain warm relationships with friends outside of the marriage. (The researchers did not assume that this lifestyle is the only adaptive one, but it was the one that had been chosen by most of the subjects. They therefore excluded subjects who had remained single.) To measure conventional adjustment, the researchers administered detailed questionnaires and interviews to the subjects, who were 41 years of age. The investigators then related the childhood measures that had been collected by Sears and his coworkers to the adult measures.

Franz and her coworkers found that parental warmth continued to be positively related to social adjustment in adulthood. The warmth of both the mother and the father toward children of 5 was related to good social adjustment at age 41. The subjects who were well adjusted socially were also better adjusted on measures of personality. This was especially true of the men, who were low in neuroticism and high in agreeableness, conscientiousness, and sociability. The men were also more satisfied with their mar-

Figure 2.10 *Results of the first Milgram study of obedience to authority. A startling 65 percent of the male subjects gave the learner the maximum shock level when ordered to do so by the experimenter. (Data from Milgram, 1974).*

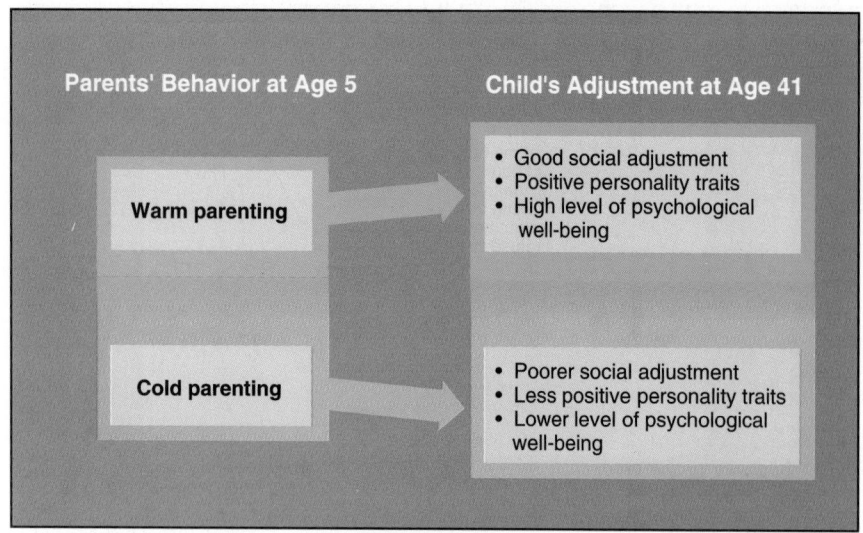

Parents' Behavior at Age 5

Warm parenting

Child's Adjustment at Age 41

- Good social adjustment
- Positive personality traits
- High level of psychological well-being

Cold parenting

- Poorer social adjustment
- Less positive personality traits
- Lower level of psychological well-being

▲ **Figure 2.11** *Correlational research by Franz and her colleagues (1991) has revealed the relations shown in the figure between parental warmth and later psychological well-being. Do these relations prove that warm parenting causes good midlife adjustment?*

riages, their jobs, and their own role as parents. The women had higher scores on measures of psychological well-being. In contrast, subjects who had experienced a cold parenting style as children were less well adjusted on these measures (see Figure 2.11). One interesting and unexpected finding was that the degree of harmony in their parents' relationship was unrelated to adults' social accomplishment. What mattered was the parents' relationships with the children.

This study established that there are indeed relations between childhood experiences with parents and later adult adjustment, and it might be tempting to conclude that the nature of the childhood experiences with parents caused or determined adult functioning. This conclusion *may* be valid, but it cannot be proven in a correlational study. As the researchers themselves point out, for example, the direction of causality could be just the opposite: Perhaps the warm parents were that way because they had children who were characteristically affectionate, sociable, and easy to raise. In other words, positive or negative characteristics of the child may have caused the warm or cold parenting, and these same childhood characteristics, if they persisted into adulthood, could have resulted in successful or unsuccessful social adjustment.

Perhaps the most important point to remember about correlational research is that *correlation does not necessarily mean that there is a causal relation between two events or measures.* The pages of history are filled with erroneous conclusions about causality drawn on the basis of correlational data. For example, medical authorities once concluded that general paresis (a fatal deterioration of the brain caused by the venereal disease syphilis) was caused by seawater, because the malady occurred so often among sailors. Many events that are correlated are

unlikely to be causally related. For example, did you know that: (1) a high correlation was found between the hourly salaries of Presbyterian ministers in Massachusetts and the price of rum in Havana; that (2) suicides and weddings both occur at their highest rates during June; or that (3) a high correlation was found between the number of storks seen nesting in French villages and the number of births that occurred in those locales? I'll leave it to you to speculate on what might be responsible for these relations.

The Correlation Coefficient

Psychological research is often designed to examine relations among variables. In the study just described, the researchers examined the relation between parental warmth scores and adjustment scores assigned to the children of these parents 36 years later. In other correlational studies, the relation between two sets of scores obtained from the same subjects is of interest. For example, suppose we want to know how scores on an intelligence test are related to students' grade-point averages. We can obtain a score on each of the two measures for each student in our sample and graph these data in a *scatter plot* like those shown in Figure 2.12. Each point in the scatter plot represents the intersection of an individual subject's scores on the two variables of interest, which we'll call variable X (intelligence) and variable Y (grade-point average).

The scatter plots in Figure 2.12 illustrate three kinds of correlational results: **positive,** in which high scores on intelligence are related to high grade-point averages; **negative,** in which high scores on intelligence are related to low grade-point averages; and a *zero correlation,* in which there is no relation between the two variables and the data points are scattered about in a random pattern.

The relation between two variables can be represented mathematically by the **correlation coefficient.** Correlation coefficients can range from -1.00 through $.00$ to $+1.00$. A coefficient of $+1.00$ means that there is a perfect positive relation between X and Y—that is, the person having the highest score on X also has the highest score on Y, the person having the second highest score on X has the second highest score on Y, and so on. A correlation of -1.00 signifies a perfect negative relation, and a correlation of $.00$ means that there is no relation at all between X and Y. The correlation coefficient thus indicates both the *direction* (positive or negative) and the *strength* of the statistical relation between the two measures. The closer to $+1.00$ or -1.00 the correlation, the more strongly the two variables are related. Thus, a correlation of $-.59$ indicates a stronger association between X and Y than does a correlation of $+.37$. (In case you're wondering about the previous examples, moderate positive correlations of about $+.35$ exist

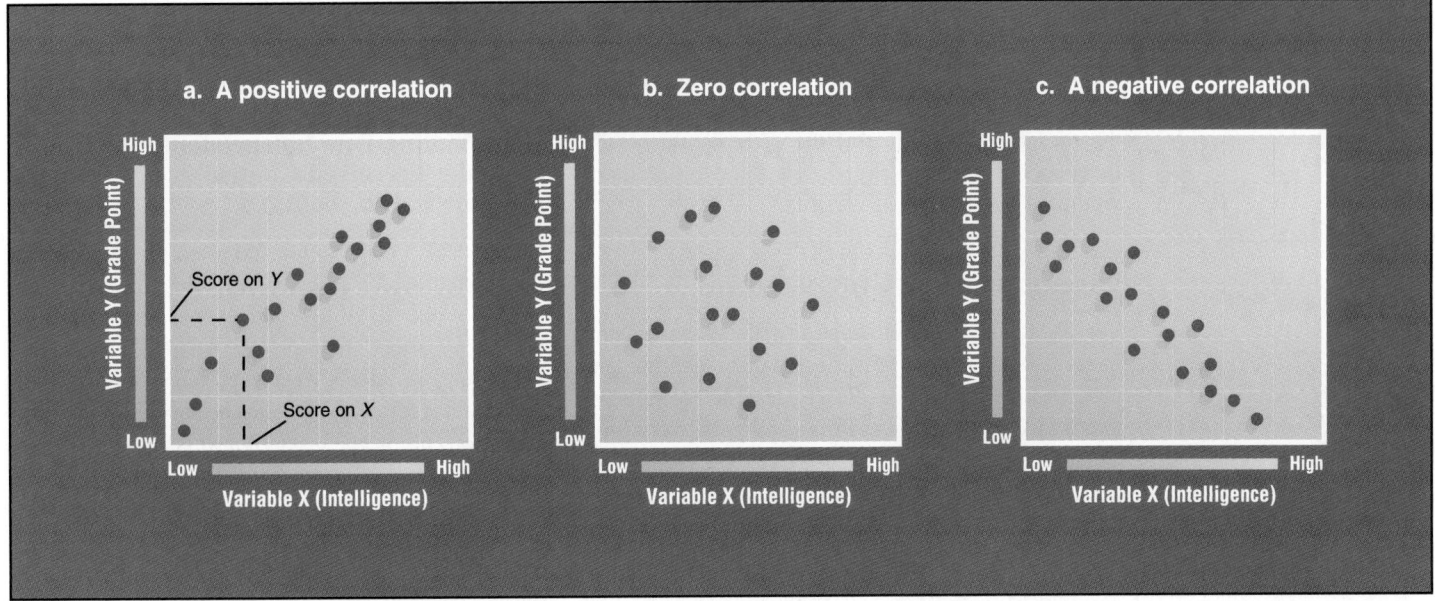

a. A positive correlation

High

Variable Y (Grade Point)

Score on Y

Score on X

Low

Low   High
Variable X (Intelligence)

b. Zero correlation

High

Variable Y (Grade Point)

Low

Low   High
Variable X (Intelligence)

c. A negative correlation

High

Variable Y (Grade Point)

Low

Low   High
Variable X (Intelligence)

between intelligence and college grade-point average and between parental warmth and midlife adjustment. As a basis for comparison, a correlation of about + .50 exists between height and weight in the general population.) If you wish to know more about how correlation coefficients are computed, you will find the formula and an example in Appendix A, which follows Chapter 20.

Correlation as a Basis for Prediction

Although correlational data do not allow us to establish causality, they do have a useful role in prediction. If two measures are highly related, either positively or negatively, knowledge of the score on one measure allows us to predict (within certain limits) the score on the other. Thus, college entrance examination scores are used by admissions officers to predict probable success in college because these measures are positively correlated. Insurance premiums are likewise established on the basis of correlations among certain factors. In a sense, your insurance company is betting you that you will not demolish your car, become seriously ill, or die before you are statistically ''supposed to.'' Because insurers' predictions are based on sound correlational data, the odds are solidly in their favor. If you doubt this, notice who owns some of the largest and newest buildings in your community.

The Experimental Approach: Demonstrating Cause and Effect

The psychologist's most powerful tool for establishing causal relations is the controlled experiment. The experimental method differs from the observational and correlational approaches because the experimenter can directly manipulate one or more factors and then measure how behavior has been affected. The logic behind this approach is that if two or more groups of equivalent subjects are treated identically in all respects but one, and if the behavior of the groups differs, then that difference in behavior is likely to have been caused by the factor that was varied.

Henceforth, we shall be using the term **variable.** A variable is, quite simply, anything that can vary. The term can refer to situations that differ, to behavioral measures that can take on different values (such as scores on a psychological test), or to characteristics on which subjects can differ, such as age, gender, personality factors, and so on. Correlational research looks for relations among variables, as does experimental research. The difference is that experimental research can demonstrate cause and effect.

Independent and Dependent Variables

In psychological experiments, the researcher is interested in relations between conditions that are manipulated and behaviors that are measured. The condition that is controlled or manipulated by the experimenter is called the **independent variable;** the resulting behavior that is measured is called the **dependent variable,** because it presumably depends on what the experimenter has done. To look at it another way, the independent variable is the *cause,* or the stimulus, and the dependent variable is the *effect,* or the response. In the studies on helping behavior, the number of other bystanders who were present was the independent variable. The percentage

Figure 2.12 *Scatter plots illustrating (a) a positive correlation, (b) absence of a statistical relationship (a correlation of .00), and (c) a negative correlation between two variables, X(intelligence) and Y (grade-point average). Each point represents the scores obtained by a particular subject on variable X and on variable Y.*

of subjects who intervened in each experimental condition, and the number of seconds it took them to do so, were the dependent variables. In an experiment testing the effects of a particular drug on memory, the presence or absence of the drug would be the independent variable and the measure of memory would be the dependent variable.

Experimental and Control Groups

For establishing causal relations, the experimental method is the most powerful of all scientific approaches because it is expressly designed to rule out alternative explanations of the results. If everything except the independent variable can be held constant, and if differences are found on the dependent variable, then the researcher can be fairly confident that a cause-and-effect relationship has been demonstrated.

Suppose we want to study the effects of noise on learning. We decide to expose a group of subjects to a tape recording of loud noises while the subjects are trying to learn a list of facts. This group is termed the **experimental group.** To be sure whether the noise is indeed having an effect on learning, however, we should measure the learning of a second group of subjects—a comparison or **control group**—that is not exposed to the noise. To make the two groups as similar as possible in all respects other than exposure to the noise, we assign subjects to the experimental and control groups on a random basis. To guarantee **random assignment,** we can assign each subject a number and then either draw numbers out of a hat or use a table of randomly ordered numbers devised by statisticians for this purpose (see Figure 2.13).

Having discussed the logic and some of the key concepts in the controlled experimental approach, let

us now consider two experimental designs that are frequently used in psychological research.

Manipulating One Independent Variable: Perceived Control and Survival in the Aged

A good deal of observation and research suggests that the extent to which animals and people have (or view themselves as having) control over their environments can affect their physical and psychological well-being. From his own experiences and his observations of fellow prisoners who survived Nazi concentration camps, the psychologist Bruno Bettelheim (1943) concluded that ''[survival] depended on one's ability to arrange, to preserve, some areas of independent action, to keep control of some important aspects of one's life despite an environment that seemed overwhelming and total'' (p. 287).

As elderly people have become an increasingly larger proportion of our population, concerns have arisen that declining health, decreased ability to care for themselves, and lessened control over their environment might contribute to psychological withdrawal, physical decline, and mortality (see Figure 2.14). An early suggestion that lack of perceived choice and control might hasten death came from a study in which elderly patients who were being admitted to a Cleveland nursing home were interviewed to determine whether they were coming to the nursing home by choice. Of the 55 patients interviewed, 17 indicated that the decision had been made by their families, not by themselves; the other 38 stated that they had decided to enter the nursing home on their own. Although the two groups of patients did not differ in age or in physical health on admission, striking differences were found in mortality rates. After 10 weeks, only one of the 38 patients who had chosen to enter the nursing home had died. But in the group whose families had decided, only one was still alive; the other 16 had died (Ferrari, 1962).

Although these results certainly are provocative, we cannot conclude that lack of personal control *caused* the difference in death rates. You may already realize that these are essentially correlational rather than experimental results. To demonstrate causality, we need an experiment in which we can directly manipulate as an independent variable a stimulus condition that affects subjects' sense of perceived control.

A number of experimental studies of this nature have been done (Rodin, 1986). One set of studies was carried out by Judith Rodin and Ellen Langer in a Connecticut nursing home. The investigators randomly selected two different floors of the nursing home. Patients had been assigned to these floors on a random basis. The investigators assured themselves

◆ **Figure 2.13** *In a conventional experimental design, subjects are randomly assigned to an experimental or control group. The experimental group is exposed to the independent variable. The behaviors that operationally define the dependent variable are then measured, and differences between the two groups are evaluated through statistical analysis to determine the effects of the independent variable. This experiment tests the effects of noise on learning.*

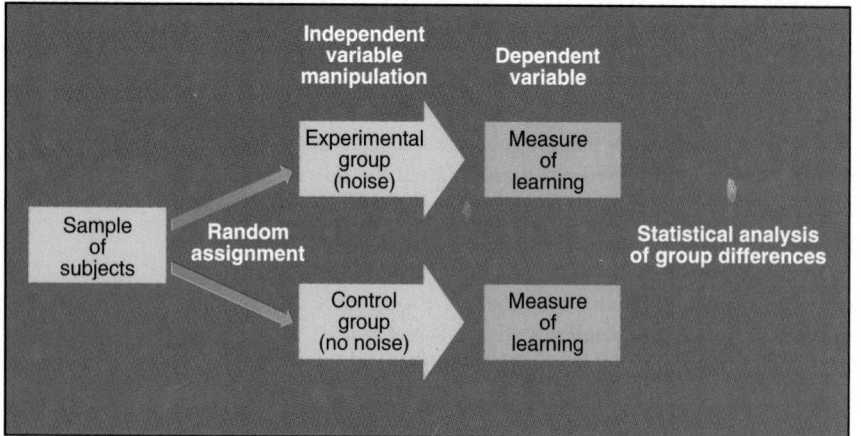

Figure 2.14 *Nursing home environments can vary widely in the extent to which patients are encouraged and empowered to exert control over their lives. Is it possible that a sense of personal control enhances physical and psychological well-being?*

that patients on the two floors rarely interacted and would therefore be unlikely to communicate with one another about the experimental manipulation.

The independent variable, perceived control, was manipulated in meetings called by the nursing home administrator. In the condition designed to enhance the patients' sense of personal control, the administrator stressed the many opportunities and the personal responsibility that patients had to exert control over their lives. They were reminded that they could and should decide how they wanted their rooms arranged, how they would spend their time, which activities they would participate in, which movies they would view, when the movies would be shown, and so on. The talk ended with the statement, ''It's *your* life here, and you can make of it whatever you want.'' To enhance further their sense of control, each patient was allowed to select a houseplant and to take responsibility for its care.

In the low-control condition, the administrator stressed the responsibility of the nursing home staff to care for the patients and to provide a range of activities (the type of message normally given to patients in custodial settings). The patients were told to ask the staff for help any time they needed it. The talk ended with the statement, ''We feel it's our responsibility to make this a home you can be proud of and happy in, and we want to do all we can to help you.'' Following the talk, each patient was given a plant selected by the staff and was told that the staff would water it.

Did the experimental manipulation affect mortality rates on the two floors of the nursing home? Although the two groups of patients did not differ in age or physical health at the beginning of the experiment, there was a difference in mortality rate after 18 months (see Figure 2.15). By this time, 30 percent of the low-control patients had died, compared with only 15 percent of the patients in the high-personal-control condition. The overall death rate at the nursing home in the 18 months preceding the beginning of the study was 25 percent. The results suggest that the experimental manipulation designed to increase the degree of perceived control may indeed have affected survival in the nursing home. Certainly, these results could have powerful implications for increasing well-being and survival in such settings, and the findings have already inspired attempts to give patients increased control in some progressive nursing homes.

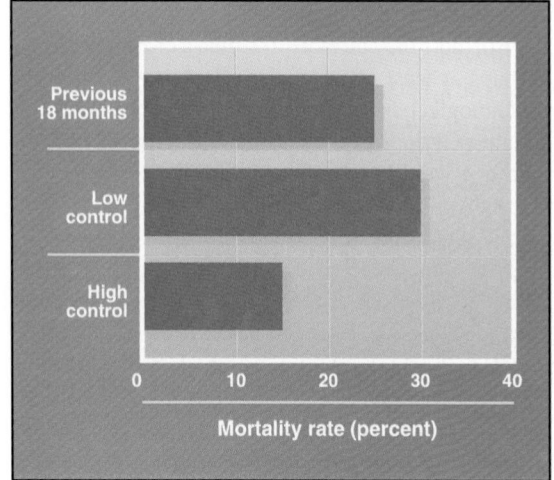

Figure 2.15 *Pictured are mortality rates after 18 months among nursing home patients who had been exposed to an experimental manipulation designed to induce a sense of either high or low personal control. The first bar shows the overall mortality rate at the nursing home during the 18 months preceding the experiment. (Data from Rodin & Langer, 1977).*

Although there is only one independent variable in this kind of experimental design, there can be more than one dependent variable, or measured outcome. (Indeed, having more than one dependent variable provides additional information about the effects of the independent variable.) In this study, Langer and Rodin studied several other dependent variables, including medical health based on physicians' ratings; nurses' ratings of how active, sociable, independent, and vigorous the patients were (neither the physicians nor the nurses were aware of the experimental manipulation); and patients' ratings of their life satisfaction. On all of these measures, the patients in the high-control condition showed better adjustment. These findings indicate not only that control is important in the lives of the elderly but also that psychological intervention programs that increase perceived control can enhance the well-being of the aged.

Manipulating Two Independent Variables: Psychological and Physiological Effects of Alcohol

Psychologists are often interested in measuring the effects of more than one independent variable at the same time. This allows them to determine how strongly each variable affects the behavior in question and whether certain combinations of independent variables have particular effects.

We've all encountered at one time or another, either directly or in stories, the mild-mannered person who is transformed after a few drinks into a loud, obnoxious, hostile fool, fully prepared to tear down the drapes or fight anyone in the house. Alcohol plays a major role in violent behavior. Well over half of all violent crimes are alcohol related, and there is general agreement that alcohol serves as a releaser of aggressive behavior (Marlatt and others, 1988). This increase in the potential for violence is typically attributed to the physiological effects of alcohol, which is known to depress areas of the brain that inhibit aggression (Siegel, 1990).

But there may be more to it than a chemical effect. Perhaps at least some of the effects of alcohol are psychological, based in part on our expectations that people will do things under the influence of alcohol that they would not ordinarily do. If people believe that they will lose their inhibitions when they drink, then perhaps they will actually do so.

How can a researcher separate the purely physiological effects of drinking from the psychological ones? The answer emerged in the form of an ingenious experimental design in which alcohol and belief were jointly controlled as independent variables. The researchers concocted a mixture of one part vodka and five parts tonic water (plus a squirt of lime juice).

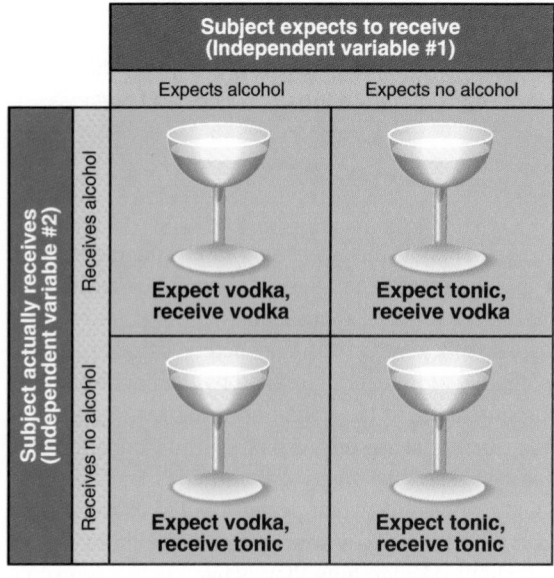

Figure 2.16 *In this experimental design, two independent variables—expectation of receiving alcohol and alcohol actually received—are manipulated at the same time to create four experimental conditions. This 2 × 2 design has been used to study the separate and combined effects of "thinking" and "drinking" on subsequent behavior.*

Pretesting established that subjects could not tell whether or not this mixture actually contained vodka. Under the guise of conducting taste tests of different brands of tonic water or vodka, the experimenters could manipulate subjects' expectations about whether or not they were drinking alcohol. Then the experimenters could give the subjects either tonic alone or vodka plus tonic.

As Figure 2.16 shows, this two-factor experimental design creates four possible combinations of factors. The *expect alcohol/receive alcohol* condition is the normal state of affairs when people drink. The *expect no alcohol/receive alcohol* condition assesses physiological effects alone, and the *expect alcohol/ receive no alcohol* condition isolates the effects of the belief that one is drinking. The *expect no alcohol/ receive no alcohol* condition creates a control group with which the other three conditions can be compared. Technically, this design is known as a 2 × 2 (two-by-two) design because it involves two levels of alcohol (*present* or *not present*) and two levels of belief (that one *is* or *is not* drinking alcohol).

Numerous experiments have been conducted using this design. In one study (Lang & others, 1975), males randomly assigned to the four experimental conditions performed the "taste test." Those actually given vodka were allowed to drink to a blood-alcohol level of 0.10 percent, the legal definition of intoxication in most states. Following the taste test, subjects were asked to assist the experimenter as a teacher in an experiment on "problem solving under stress." They had met the learner (actually the experimenter's accomplice) earlier and had had a friendly interaction with him. The teacher's job, as in the Milgram study described earlier, was to administer electric shocks to the learner when mistakes were made on a learning task. On each of 30 problem-solving trials, the teacher-subject saw either a green light (signaling a correct response by the learner) or a red one (indicating an incorrect response). When the red light appeared, which occurred on 20 of the 30 trials, the teacher was allowed to choose the shock level he wished to administer from among ten possibilities. The experimenters' operational definition of *aggression* was the average shock level chosen on the 20 incorrect trials. As in Milgram's study, no shock was actually delivered to the learner.

The results of the experiment are shown in Figure 2.17. As you can see, men who believed that they had received alcohol gave more intense shocks, regardless of whether or not they had actually been given vodka. An even more interesting finding occurred in the experimental conditions that directly pitted belief against drug: Men who thought they had consumed alcohol but actually had not were more aggressive than those who had been given vodka but thought they had been drinking only tonic.

In other studies using this research design, subjects who thought they had consumed alcohol (but had not) reported higher sexual arousal, more intense sexual fantasies, lower sexual inhibitions, and greater interest in viewing scenes of sexual violence than did subjects who thought they had consumed only tonic water (Crowe & George, 1989; George & others, 1989). Such results suggest that our beliefs about how drinking will affect us may be as important as the physiological effects of the alcohol, at least at the level legally defined as intoxication. These studies also illustrate the usefulness of experimental designs in which several independent variables are manipulated at the same time.

The causes of the "loss of control" that can occur when people drink thus involve more than the biological effects of alcohol (Steele & Joseph, 1990). As shown in the "think-drink" effect described above, cognitive factors may also be involved. So, too, may the two other classes of causal factors—environmental events and intrapsychic psychodynamic processes—that we discussed in Chapter 1. For example, past observation of others who lost control after drinking, as well as the presence of other uninhibited revelers in the current situation, are environmental factors that can increase the potential for aggression. Psychodynamic theorists believe that aggression can also result from intrapsychic factors, such as hostile impulses that are normally repressed

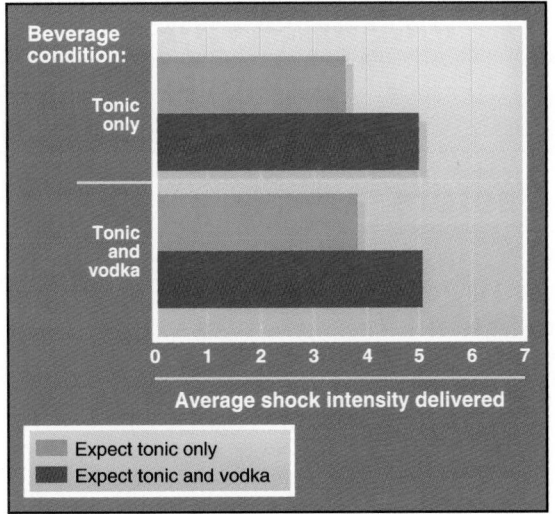

Figure 2.17 *This figure shows the results of the study by Lang and others (1975) on the think-drink effect and aggression. The experiment demonstrated that the belief that one has been drinking alcohol can increase aggression, whether or not one has actually consumed any alcohol. Notice that subjects who had actually drunk vodka but had believed they were drinking tonic water delivered lower levels of shock to the learner than subjects who had drunk no vodka but thought that they had.*

but that gain release as defenses are weakened after drinking. These four causal factors—biological, cognitive, environmental, and intrapsychic—can interact with one another in complex ways, depending on the person and the situation. The Understanding the Causes of Behavior feature on page 48 summarizes interacting biological, cognitive, intrapsychic, and environmental factors that can contribute to loss of control from alcohol use.

Threats to the Validity of Experimental Research

Because of the precision with which variables can be controlled and measured, the experiment is a powerful scientific tool for establishing cause-and-effect relations, but it is by no means infallible. Certain factors can seriously undermine the validity of experimental results. Four of the most serious are confounding of variables, reactivity, demand characteristics, and experimenter expectancy effects.

Confounding of Variables

The experimental method is based on the assumption that differences between experimental and control groups on the dependent variable are due to the manipulation of the independent variable. Sometimes, though, uncontrolled factors can have effects on the dependent variable that are indistinguishable from the possible effects of the independent variable. When this happens, **confounding** is said to occur. The independent variable and the uncontrolled variable are said to be confounded because the experimenter doesn't know which of them caused the observed differences in behavior.

Loss of Control from Alcohol:
Factors Suggested by Theory and Research

$B=f(P,E)$

Causal Factors

Biological
- Depressive effects of alcohol on brain regions that govern emotional control, judgment, and motor control

Cognitive
- Expectations about the effects of alcohol on mood and behavior
- Feelings of diminished personal responsibility

Intrapsychic
- Release of normally suppressed impulses
- Denial of personal choice over alcohol consumption and its consequences

Environmental
- Previous observations of other drinkers and their behavior
- Previous experiences of being absolved of personal responsibility when drunk
- Presence of other "loss of control" drinkers

Loss of Control from Alcohol

Loss of Control from Alcohol is a function of interacting personal and environmental causal factors. These factors may vary and may interact with one another in particular ways, depending on the person and the situation.

Experiments must be planned very carefully so that extraneous factors that could affect the results are controlled. For example, it would be unwise to assign only male subjects to an experimental group and only females to the control group; any difference between conditions might be due to gender differences rather than the independent variable manipulated by the experimenter, and there would be no way of disentangling the confounded variables and finding out which one was producing the results. Confounding of variables can threaten the validity of experimental results. "Confound it!" is probably the tamest thing that's likely to issue from the mouth of a researcher who has just discovered that confounding ruined his or her experiment.

Reactivity: The Effects of Knowing That One Is Being Studied

Even amateur photographers have discovered how difficult it is to get spontaneous poses when people know that they are being filmed. Experimenters have the same problem. How does one know that the behavior observed in an experimental setting is not the result of the subject's knowledge that he or she is being observed or studied? If subjects react to being observed by responding to the independent variable differently from the way they would respond in the real world, false conclusions can easily be drawn from experimental results.

Reactivity—behaviors caused by the knowledge that one is being studied—thus constitutes a threat to an experiment's validity. Researchers try to minimize reactivity in several ways. In most cases, they simply explain to the subject what the experiment is about and try to enlist the subject's collaboration. In some instances, however, the experimenter must hide the true purpose of the study in order to obtain a more valid sample of behavior. When deception is used, the subject is usually led to believe that the experiment involves some other topic. In Milgram's obedience study, for example, the subjects were told that the research dealt with the effects of punishment on learning.

Reactivity effects are usually less of a problem outside the laboratory, where behavior can often be observed in a less obvious fashion. This is one reason why psychologists emphasize the importance of comparing laboratory results with those observed in more natural settings. If the two types of results are consistent with one another, more confidence can be placed in both sets of results.

Nonreactive Measures. One approach to avoiding reactivity effects is to use **nonreactive,** or **unobtrusive, measures.** These are records that ac-

cumulate in the course of everyday living. Thus, subjects never have to know that they are being studied. For example, researchers assessed racial attitudes at different colleges by noting the degree to which black and white students mixed or clustered in lecture halls. Investigators gauged public interest in exhibits at a museum by measuring how worn the floor tiles were in front of each exhibit. To assess the effects of a "safe sex" program designed to encourage the use of condoms, researchers from the Centers for Disease Control counted the number of used condoms that turned up in a Baltimore sewage treatment plant before and after the program. These and many other ingenious unobtrusive measures have been used by psychologists to study psychological questions (Cook & Campbell, 1979; Webb & others, 1966).

Demand Characteristics

When we enter unfamiliar situations, it is quite natural for us to search for clues about how we are expected to behave. The clues that subjects pick up about the nature of an experiment and how they are supposed to behave are called **demand characteristics** (Orne, 1962). For example, having read about Milgram's obedience studies, what would you deduce if you took part in an experiment next week and were told by the experimenter that you were to shock another person in order to study the effects of punishment on learning? Sometimes subjects are able to guess the experimenter's hypothesis rather quickly (or, more properly, to *think* they've guessed it). Once this has occurred, subjects may respond in several different ways. People who are eager to be "good subjects" may try to give the experimenter the results they think he or she wants, while others may do just the opposite in an attempt to foil the experimenter (sometimes termed the "I'll fix you effect" as well as less printable terms). Some subjects may try to ignore the clues and behave "naturally."

Demand characteristics can threaten valid results by distorting subjects' true response tendencies. This is why researchers often feel a need to hide the true nature of an experiment. In many instances, experimenters also question subjects after the experiment to determine whether they were aware of the study's purpose and, if so, how their responses were affected. In this way, the data of "aware" subjects can be excluded if necessary.

Experimenter Expectancy Effects

Subjects aren't the only ones who develop expectations about how an experiment is supposed to come out. Experimenters may have a strong commitment

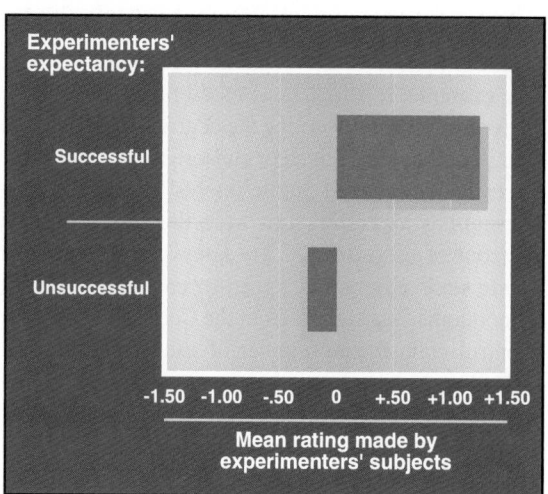

Figure 2.18 *The effects of experimenters' expectancies on their subjects' behavior were demonstrated in an experiment involving ratings of success based on photographs. Experimenters who had been led to believe that subjects would rate the people in the photos as successful obtained higher ratings of success from their subjects than a group of experimenters who had been told that their subjects would likely rate the people as unsuccessful. (Data from Rosenthal & Rubin, 1978).*

Experimenters' expectancy:

Successful

Unsuccessful

-1.50 -1.00 -.50 0 +.50 +1.00 +1.50

Mean rating made by experimenters' subjects

to the hypothesis they are testing, and they may subtly and unintentionally influence their subjects to respond in a way that is consistent with that hypothesis.

Many studies have shown that if experimenters expect to obtain certain results, they are more likely to do so (Rosenthal & Rubin, 1978). In some of these studies, undergraduate and graduate students were recruited to serve as experimenters. Their task was to show 20 subjects a standard set of facial photographs and to have the subjects rate how successful the persons in the photos had been. Some of the experimenters were told that the people in the photos had been very successful and that most past subjects had rated them as being successful. Other experimenters were told just the opposite. Actually, the people in the photos had been rated by earlier subjects as being neither successful nor unsuccessful; the purpose of giving the information to the experimenters was to see if their expectations would affect the data obtained from their subjects. The results indicated that the ex-

perimenters' expectancies did indeed have an effect (see Figure 2.18). Experimenters who expected ''successful'' ratings tended to get more of them, and those who expected low success ratings tended to receive such ratings, even though they apparently did nothing intentional to influence their subjects.

Because of potential problems involving **experimenter expectancy effects,** experiments are usually set up so that an experimenter collecting data from subjects is unaware of the experimental condition to which the subjects have been assigned. In research terms, the experimenter is *blind* to the independent variable as it applies to the subjects.

The Double-Blind Design. One way in which researchers try to eliminate both subject and experimenter expectancy effects is through the **double-blind procedure.** In this design, neither the subject nor the experimenter is aware of which experimental condition the subject is in. (If only the subject is unaware, the experiment uses a **single-blind procedure.**) The double-blind procedure is almost always used in drug studies, where some subjects receive a drug and others receive a **placebo** which has no physiological effects. If the person who is dispensing the drugs is also unaware of whether the subjects are getting the drug or the placebo, the possibility that the experimenter or the medical staff will react differently to the two groups of subjects is minimized.

We have discussed many of the factors that psychologists must take into account in order to do good research and to draw valid conclusions from research results. This chapter's Enhancing Human Performance feature gives you a chance to apply what you have learned by critically evaluating some research.

ENHANCING HUMAN PERFORMANCE

CRITICAL THINKING IN EVALUATING RESEARCH

The scientific knowledge explosion is upon us. On every side, it seems, the mass media bombard us with news about scientific discoveries. Many findings relate to various aspects of behavior, and they can have important personal and social implications.

Unfortunately, not all findings that bear the mark of science are equally valid. As we have learned, many pitfalls await the researcher, and doing good science is an incredibly challenging task.

The magnitude of this challenge is reflected in the fact that the better scientific journals reject up to 90 percent of the articles that are submitted to them for publication. The most frequent reason for rejection is that the research is judged by other scientists to contain methodological flaws that limit the conclusions that can be drawn.

To be an informed consumer of scientific findings, you must be able to critically evaluate research to identify features that

limit the validity of conclusions or that suggest alternative explanations for results. In fact, the development of critical thinking skills about behavior may be one of the most important benefits you'll derive from your psychology course. That is why these first two chapters have focused on how psychologists think about behavior and conduct their research.

Let us now critically evaluate some research results and see if we agree with the conclusions drawn by the researchers. Then we will focus on some guidelines for sharpening critical thinking skills.

Negative Life Change and Illness

As suggested by the Hmong sudden death syndrome, stress can have devastating effects on the body. Negative changes in our lives create stress. For many years it has been suggested that negative life events take a toll on the body's resources and thereby make a person vulnerable to disease and illness.

One researcher decided to test the hypothesis that negative life events predispose people to become ill. More than 300 men and women served as subjects. The subjects were first asked to complete a Seriousness of Illness scale that contained 126 different illnesses. They were instructed to check off any illness that they had experienced in the past three years. Next, the subjects were given a questionnaire containing a long list of negative life changes, such as changing jobs, getting divorced, experiencing a death in the family, and suffering a severe financial loss. Again, they were asked to check off any change that they had experienced during the past three years.

The researcher was interested in the relation between the number of negative life events that the subjects reported over the three-year period and the number of illnesses they had experienced during the same period. He found that high numbers of negative events were indeed associated with a high number of illnesses in both men and women, and he concluded that the results supported his hypothesis that negative life changes make people vulnerable to illness.

Do you agree with the researcher's conclusion? Please cover up the next paragraph and write down any criticisms you have. Let us assume that the obtained *result* is a valid one. How might you account for it?

Analysis Perhaps you have already recognized that this is a correlational study. Specifically, the researcher is examining the correlation between negative life events and illness. But, as noted earlier, even if a strong positive correlation is

found, we cannot conclude that one variable (life stress) *causes* the other (illness). It is possible, of course, that a causal relationship of that kind does exist (we will examine the evidence in Chapter 15), but there are other possibilities. For example, it is possible that just the opposite relation exists (that is, that illness causes high negative-event scores). Being ill frequently may cause people to look for reasons for their poor health and therefore to recall more negative life events or to conclude that more of the events they experienced were negative. Finally, it is possible that a third variable causes both high negative-event scores and high illness scores. One such variable might be neuroticism, the tendency to view the world negatively and to experience depression, anxiety, or anger frequently. Neurotic people perceive many things that happen to them in a negative light, and they tend to view themselves as unhealthy and to actually have more illnesses (McCrae & Costa, 1990). Indeed, when individual differences in neuroticism are eliminated in studies of this type, relations between life stress and illness tend to disappear (Schroeder & Costa, 1984). Thus, we see in this study the possibility of any of the causal relations discussed earlier: *A* (life stress) causes *B* (illness); *B* (illness) causes *A* (life stress reports); and some third variable, *C* (neuroticism), causes both *A* and *B*.

Having considered a correlational study, let us now critically evaluate an experiment.

Participative Management in the Classroom

Industrial studies in this country, as well as analyses of work settings in Japan and other nations, suggest that participative management—giving workers more freedom and responsibility to design their jobs—can increase morale (Aamodt, 1991). Might the same occur in colleges if students were allowed to decide on such crucial issues as how class time should be utilized, how many and what kind of tests should be administered, what out-of-class work should be assigned, and so on? One researcher (Kilmann, 1974) did an experiment to find out.

The subjects were 99 students enrolled in four sections of a graduate-level course. Two of the sections were taught in the daytime during the winter quarter and the other two were offered at night during the spring quarter. To control for instructor variables, the experimenter taught all four sections of the class himself. Because of concerns that the students in the two sections taught in a given quarter might communicate with one another and discover that the two sections were being taught in radically different ways, the two sections in the winter term were assigned to the experimental condition and the two sections in the spring quarter to a control condition.

In the experimental condition, students were given great responsibility for designing their own course, and in the control condition, the instructor took sole responsibility for all decisions regarding course content, exams, assignments, and so forth. The dependent variable was the students' ratings of the instructor's effectiveness in teaching the course and how much the students thought they had learned in the course. During the last week of the term, an assistant (not the instructor) had the students complete an anonymous evaluation form containing 22 items relating to these variables, with each item rated on a 5-point scale. The mean ratings of the students in the two experimental sections were compared with those of the students in the two control sections to test the hypothesis that the students in the experimental sections would evaluate the instructor and the course more favorably.

On 21 of the 22 items rated, the students who had been given the freedom to design their own course gave more favorable ratings. The experimenter concluded that "participative management" in the classroom causes students to evaluate their courses (or at least this particular course) more favorably, much as giving workers more decision-making control over their jobs increases morale in the work setting.

Do you agree with this conclusion, or are there other ways of accounting for the results? Cover up the next paragraph and write down any flaws that you can find in the design of this study. (Hint: There are at least three.)

Analysis Let us assume that we agree that the ratings favor the decision-making experimental condition. There are still some aspects of this study that could justify other interpretations of the results.

One serious problem is a confounding of day and night classes with the experimental conditions. Perhaps students who come to class at night are already fatigued after working all day and therefore do not enjoy the course as much. Or perhaps they are less used to the academic routine and find the course more demanding. It is also possible that there were differences between the students who registered for the course in the winter

and those who took it in the spring. Of course, we cannot be sure that student differences account for the results, but they cannot be ruled out as a possible explanation. That is what confounding does; it makes it impossible to rule out other explanations. Randomly assigning subjects to experimental conditions conducted at the same time would have helped the researcher to avoid problems such as these.

We might also wonder about instructor differences on at least two counts. One relates to the same confounding that applies to the students: It is possible that the instructor was a less effective teacher in the evening sections because of fatigue, which might account for the results. Second, there is the possibility of experimenter expectancy effects. If the instructor-experimenter believed that the hypothesis would be supported, he might have unintentionally behaved in a more friendly or favorable fashion in the day sections, and this factor could have influenced the students' ratings. The attempt to control for instructor effects by having the same instructor teach all sections was admirable, but it would have been better to have had an instructor who was unaware of the hypothesis. (However, there might still have been a problem if the "naive" instructor had developed his or her own hypothesis.)

Several other possible reasons for the results suggest themselves. Perhaps the students who designed their own course designed an easier one, which might account for their more favorable ratings. Or perhaps the course they designed was actually a better course that would have obtained more favorable ratings even if it had been totally designed by the instructor, as in the control condition. Ideally, one would want students to be exposed to exactly the same course in both conditions, with the only difference being that one group of students had been given decision-making power. As the experiment now stands, the decision-making variable was almost certainly confounded with course differences that might have produced the results. For all of the rea-

sons we have cited, therefore, we cannot conclude that the differences in students' decision-making power caused the differences in instructor and course evaluation, although it is *possible* that they did.

Some Critical-Thinking Principles Applied to Research

You were probably able to pick out some of the flaws of design and logic in the two research examples. Critical thinking requires practice, and you will get better at it if you continue to ask yourself, "Is that the only way to explain these findings?" Consider other interpretations of the data and look for flaws in the methods that were used. Also, keep in mind that common sense allows us to explain almost anything after the fact (Kelley, 1992). The question "Under what circumstances could exactly the *opposite* results occur?" often prompts an awareness of other factors that may be important in understanding the behavior at hand.

We may be especially ready to accept evidence that is consistent with our own beliefs. Do you believe that life stress causes illness or that giving people greater control over their lives increases their morale? Personal beliefs, attitudes, and emotions can act as psychological blinders that allow us to accept inadequate evidence as fact or to reject inconsistent evidence out of hand because we "know" that it can't be true. As critical thinkers, we must be open-minded and able to tolerate uncertainty. It may be comforting to have the conviction that we possess "truth," but a stubborn refusal to consider other viewpoints or evidence will not serve us well as critical thinkers. This does not mean that we should be so skeptical of everything that we believe nothing; rather, we should be willing to consider new evidence that might cause us to revise our conclusions. In psychology, you will frequently come upon research findings and viewpoints that challenge common wisdom and folklore. Openness to new ideas and a willingness to wonder about behavior and its causes will serve you well and make this course more meaningful for you.

Ethics in Human and Animal Research

Some of the studies we have reviewed in this chapter have involved exposing subjects to stressful conditions or using deception. Actually, most psychological research does not involve stress or deception, and most subjects (93 percent in a survey I conducted among several thousand introductory psychology students at my university) find their experiences as subjects pleasant and informative. Sometimes, however, in order to study important problems, researchers walk an ethical tightrope, balancing the importance of the knowledge to be gained and the benefits that may result from its application against the use of deception or the exposure of subjects to stressful conditions.

Many psychologists were gravely concerned and even outraged when Stanley Milgram published his first studies on obedience to authority in 1963 (e.g., Baumrind, 1964). Perhaps you had similar reactions while reading about this research. Milgram's critics questioned the ethics of exposing unsuspecting subjects to a situation that was likely to cause them considerable stress and that might even have lasting negative effects on them.

In reply, Milgram argued that the great social importance of the problem he was studying justified the methods he had used and that adequate precautions had been taken to protect the welfare of the subjects. He pointed out that in a debriefing immediately after the session, the subjects were informed that they had not actually shocked the learner. Then they had a friendly meeting with the learner. The purpose of the study was explained to them, and they were assured that their behavior in the situation was perfectly normal. Milgram also cited questionnaire responses collected from the subjects after they had received a complete report of the study's purposes and results. Eighty-four percent of the subjects stated that they were glad to have been in the study, and several noted that their experience had made them more tolerant of others or had changed them in other desirable ways. Only 1.3 percent of the subjects said that they were sorry they had participated (Milgram, 1964).

Many psychologists remain unconvinced that research such as Milgram's can be justified on ethical grounds. The controversy over Milgram's research has raged for nearly 30 years. In combination with other controversial issues, such as the use of deception in research and the potential for invasion of privacy, the discussion has prompted deep concern for protecting subjects' welfare (see Figure 2.19). It is unlikely that research like Milgram's could be con-

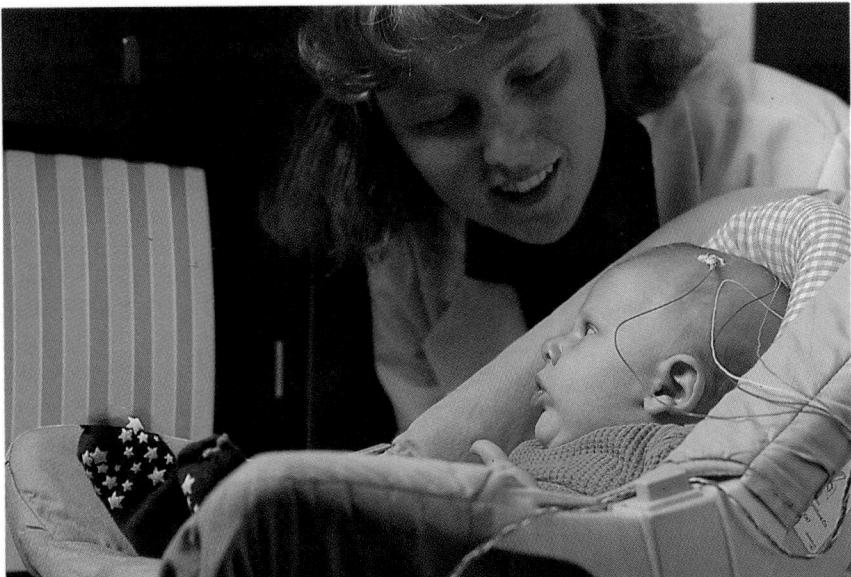

Figure 2.19 *Ethical standards are designed to protect the welfare of both human and animal subjects in psychological research.*

ducted in the United States or Canada today because of strict guidelines developed by government agencies and professional organizations. For example, according to the research guidelines of the American Psychological Association (APA), subjects cannot be placed in either physical or psychological jeopardy without their **informed consent.** This means that they must be told about the procedures to be followed and warned about any risks that might be involved. If deception is necessary in studies that do not involve such risk, then subjects must be completely debriefed after the experiment and the entire procedure must be explained to them. Special measures must be taken to protect the confidentiality of data, and subjects must be told that they are free to withdraw from a study at any time without penalty.

When children, seriously disturbed mental patients, or others who are not able to give true consent are involved, consent must be obtained from their parents or guardians. Strict guidelines also apply to research in prisons. Inmates cannot be forced to participate in research, nor can they be penalized for refusing to do so. In research dealing with rehabilitation programs, inmates must be permitted to share in decisions concerning program goals. Researchers who violate the code of research ethics face serious legal and professional consequences.

The ethical and moral issues in psychology are not simple ones. They are quite similar to those that confront medical researchers. In some instances, the only way to discover important knowledge about behavior or to develop new techniques to enhance human welfare is to deceive subjects or to expose them to potentially stressful situations. To help researchers balance the potential benefits against the risks involved and to ensure that the welfare of subjects is protected, academic and research institutions have created scientific panels that review every research proposal. If a proposed study is considered ethically questionable, or if the rights, welfare, and personal privacy of subjects are not sufficiently protected, the methods must be modified or the research cannot be conducted.

Concern about the rights of subjects extends to animals as well as humans. As in medical research, animals are frequently subjects in psychological studies considered too hazardous for humans. The APA's guidelines require that animals be treated humanely and that the risks to which they are exposed be justified by the potential importance of the research. This determination, however, is not always easy to make. For example, should researchers carry out studies in which animals undergo severe stress that causes ulcers—with the knowledge that some of them will die of ulcers—in the hope of discovering what types of stress cause ulcers and what can be done to prevent ulcers from developing? People of good will can disagree on questions such as these, and the judgment calls are not easy ones.

Despite increased attention to the humane treatment of animal subjects, many animal-rights advocates believe that current regulations are not strong enough. Indeed, the treatment of animal research subjects has become an important social issue, an issue that is also debated by psychologists. Psychological organizations such as the APA supported and provided input into the regulations and laboratory inspection procedures found in Congress's Animal

▶ **Figure 2.20** *The debate on animal research highlights the challenging task researchers face in their attempts to protect the welfare of animals while ensuring that society continues to receive the benefits that animal research provides.*

Welfare Act of 1985. Virtually all psychologists would agree that it is morally and ethically wrong to subject animals to needless suffering. Many scientists, however, do not agree with the head of the American Anti-Vivisection Society, who maintained that animals should never be used in research "which is not for the benefit of the animals involved" (Goodman, 1982, p. 61). These scientists point to the many important medical advances made possible by animal research (see Figure 2.20). For example, had Pasteur not subjected some dogs to suffering, he could not have developed the rabies vaccine, which has saved the lives of countless animals as well as humans. They ask, "Does the prospect of finding a cure for cancer justify creating tumors in a limited number of laboratory animals?" Many scientists and philosophers also dispute the assertion made by some animal-rights activists that human welfare should never be placed above that of animals. They point out that those of us who eat meat, go fishing, or kill mosquitoes and termites have made the behavioral decision that it is sometimes permissible to place human needs above the welfare of animals.

There are no easy answers to the ethical questions posed by animal research. It is encouraging that the welfare of animals in research is receiving the careful attention it deserves (see Phillips & Sechzer, 1989). Recent evidence from England indicates that the use of animals in psychological research has dropped by two thirds since 1977, and the use of electric shock and other stressors has declined considerably (Thomas & Blackman, 1991). As a science and a profession dedicated to promoting human and animal welfare, psychology cannot avoid coming to grips with the issues involved in animal research, as well as other areas of research ethics.

As we have seen in these first two chapters, the range of psychological phenomena that are the focus of research is almost limitless. Scientific breakthroughs are occurring so quickly that what was science fiction yesterday may be fact tomorrow. For this reason, some psychologists continue to research one of the most elusive topics of all: special classes of alleged mind–body phenomena that are termed *paranormal*.

PSYCHOBIOLOGICAL INTERACTIONS

Science and the Paranormal

Throughout, this chapter has stressed the advantages of the scientific method for understanding behavioral phenomena. Certainly, the realm of natural phenomena offers scientists a seemingly endless supply of fascinating questions. Yet for many of us, some of the most fascinating questions are those that seem to defy explanation in terms of normal causes. According to a recent survey, half of all adults in the United States believe in the existence of psychic or paranormal phenomena, and another 25 percent believe that such phenomena may exist (Gallup & Newport, 1991). These phenomena include *mental telepathy* (transmission of thoughts between individuals), *precognition* (foretelling of the future), *clairvoyance* (perception of remote objects or events, such as a plane crash in Asia), and *psychokinesis* ("mind over matter" demonstrations, such as bending metal keys through mental means or lifting file cabinets off the floor without touching them). Surely, no science concerned with the nature of physical and mental events can ignore the possibility that parapsychological phenomena occur, for if these phenomena really exist, they call for a reexamination of current scientific conceptions of human nature, particularly conceptions of

how the mental and physical realms interact. What kinds of sensory receptors in the body could respond to thoughts transmitted by others? What kinds of signals could the body emit that would bend a metal key? These are the kinds of scientific mind–body questions that would confront us if psychic phenomena were proved to exist.

Most scientists demand that we approach these phenomena with skepticism. This does not mean that we reject them out of hand because they seem "impossible" in terms of our present conceptions of reality but rather that we apply the same rigorous standards of proof that we do to any other phenomenon—no more, no less.

In 1976, the Committee for the Scientific Investigation of Claims of the Paranormal was formed to begin this task. Consisting of leading scientists, philosophers, and several magicians who are experts in the art of fakery, the committee has evaluated the validity of a wide range of paranormal phenomena. Its standard of proof requires that any presently known "natural" physical or psychological explanation for a psychic phenomenon be ruled out as an alternative explanation. Many of the committee's studies and conclusions are described in volumes edited by Kendrick

◀ **Figure 2.21** *The fact that, for some people, belief in paranormal phenomena such as mental telepathy satisfies psychological needs is an interesting and appropriate topic for psychological research.*

Frazier (1981, 1986). The committee also publishes a periodical called *The Skeptical Inquirer,* which can be found in many college libraries.

After more than a century of scientific research, it appears that, however much we might like to believe otherwise, there is no firm evidence to support the existence of paranormal phenomena (Alcock, 1990). To the contrary, the scientific journey through the realm of the paranormal has revealed a landscape of nonexistent effects, poor experimental designs, selective treatment of data (contrary data are frequently discarded on the grounds that the psychic was having an "off day"), and outright cheating and fraud (for example, an Israeli psychic, Uri Geller, has been shown to perform his feats, such as "mentally" bending metal spoons, through deception). Tallies of accurate predictions by psychics who claim to foretell the future have been unimpressive. For example, a daily check of 550 predictions made by 36 leading psychics in the nation's newspapers yielded only 24 correct predictions (Blodgett, 1986); another tally of 425 predictions made by the *National Enquirer's* leading psychics revealed a total of 2 correct ones (Strentz, 1984).

Several phenomena that were once attributed to psychic causes have proved to have natural causes after all. One example is the ability of bats to navigate in total darkness. At one time, scientists thought that they had ruled out all possibilities for explaining this phenomenon. They had covered the bats' eyes, sealed their noses, and coated their wings with varnish, yet the bats could still avoid wires strung in total darkness. What

could account for this paranormal ability except some form of extrasensory perception (ESP)? The answer came when scientists discovered the bat's natural "sonar" (Gibson, 1989). Today, many scientists who continue to study psychic phenomena hold out hope that their work will result in the discovery of new mind–body relations. Some psychic researchers maintain that science has not yet developed the methods needed to verify the existence of psychic phenomena.

As studies of psychic phenomena have become more tightly controlled, results have become more discouraging. This is unusual in scientific research; typically, tighter controls make for stronger and clearer results. More importantly, not a single psychic has ever been found who could demonstrate any paranormal power to the satisfaction of impartial scientists, nor has there been any psychic phenomenon that can be reproduced by independent investigators (Alcock, 1986). Indeed, James Randi, a magician and an expert in the art of psychic fraud who helped unmask Uri Geller, has for more than 20 years had a standing offer of $10,000 to anyone who can demonstrate *any* paranormal act under his scrutiny and in the presence of a panel of scientists. No one has yet collected.

Perhaps the most interesting psychological question of all is why beliefs in the paranormal continue to persist in a scientific and technological society like our own. The persistence of such beliefs in the face of contrary evidence has perplexed some of the scientists who have proved that the claims of well-known "psychics" are unsupportable: "Jeane Dixon and Uri Geller, for example, seem as unsinkable as rubber ducks—though some of us have attempted to make duck soup out of them" (Kurtz, 1986, p. 7).

One answer is that many people *want* to believe in the paranormal. Although we live in a technological society, many of our religious traditions promote belief in the supernatural. Moreover, many people welcome the notion that the course and meaning of their lives are shaped in part by cosmic forces and that there are people who can help them discover their destinies. The paranormal also appeals to our sense of wonder, our curiosity, our desire to know the unknown. And, ironically, the very institution—science—that is so skeptical of the paranormal helps promote our belief in it. The dizzying pace of scientific discovery reinforces the belief that almost *anything* is possible; in so many ways, what was science fiction a few years ago is fact today. Who knows what tomorrow's new facts will be?

Should a scientific psychology simply close the book on the paranormal? I think not. Let us have critical skepticism that demands solid scientific proof, but not a blind skepticism that rejects the unknown as the impossible. We should not be like the Italian philosophers who refused to look through Galileo's telescope because they already "knew" that the moons of Jupiter did not exist. Certainly, the burden of proof lies with those who believe in the paranormal, but rejections of their claims should be based on scientific evidence and not on blind prejudice.

S U M M A R Y

Scientific Principles in Psychology

● Scientific understanding usually proceeds through a number of steps: (1) informal observation and formulation of a question; (2) intuitive attempts to answer the question; (3) formulation of scientific hypotheses; (4) hypothesis testing; (5) theory construction; and (6) use of the theory to generate new observations and hypotheses.

● Good theories are able to incorporate already known facts, give rise to additional hypotheses that can be tested to generate new knowledge, and are testable and capable of being refuted. A theory should be parsimonious, incorporating as much as possible without being needlessly complex.

● In psychology, understanding means being able to specify the causes of behavior. There are two basic approaches to understanding. After-the-fact understanding is limited, because there may be countless possible explanations and no way to ascertain which is correct. Scientists prefer to test their understanding through prediction and control.

● In order for a psychological construct to be scientifically useful, it must be operationally defined either in terms of conditions imposed on the subject (in stimulus terms) or in terms of observable behaviors of the subject (in response terms). Thus, constructs are defined in terms of the operations used to measure them.

● Methods for measuring behavior include reports by others about subject behaviors, verbal self-report techniques, physiological measures, and behavioral observations.

Data Collection Procedures

● Behavioral research is carried out in both natural settings and under controlled laboratory conditions. Both kinds of settings have advantages and disadvantages. Ideally, research on a given phenomenon is done in both settings.

● Research is almost always done with samples drawn from the larger population about which conclusions will be drawn. Ideally, samples are representative of the population—that is, they mirror the population with regard to important characteristics that influence the behavior being studied. Large sample sizes and random assignment to experimental conditions are used to avoid sampling errors.

● Case studies involve the detailed study of a person, group, or organization. Although conclusions about causality are difficult to establish, case studies often lead to more systematic research, and they can show if a theory is invalid.

● Uncontrolled observation can be used in many real-life settings to gather useful information about behavior and about possible causal relationships. The study conducted by Festinger and his colleagues of the cult leader who prophesied the cataclysmic flood is an example of uncontrolled observation.

● Observation under controlled conditions allows psychologists to control and standardize the conditions to which subjects respond. Milgram's study of destructive obedience to authority used this approach. Because there was only one condition, this study does not qualify as an experiment.

● Correlational research explores relations among naturally occurring events that are not controlled by the researcher. The study by Franz and coworkers relating parental warmth to adult social adjustment illustrates this approach. One limitation is that causality cannot be established through correlation alone. Correlation can, however, serve as the basis for predictions.

The Experimental Approach: Demonstrating Cause and Effect

● Experiments involve the manipulation of one or more independent variables and an assessment of their effects on dependent variable behaviors. An attempt is made to hold everything constant except the independent variable so that cause-and-effect conclusions can be drawn.

● Comparisons between experimental and control conditions are the basis for drawing conclusions in experiments. Experimental manipulation may involve only one independent variable, as in the nursing home study in which an attempt was made to manipulate perceived personal control. In other experiments, more than one independent variable is manipulated, as in the research on the think-drink effect. In any experiment, more than one dependent variable can be (and often is) measured.

● Several factors can undermine the validity of conclusions drawn from experiments. These include confounding of independent and extraneous variables, reactivity (changes in behavior resulting from subjects' awareness that they are being studied), demand characteristics (stimuli that suggest to subjects how they are expected to behave), and experimenter expectancy effects (subtle influencing of subjects to provide data consistent with the experimenter's hypothesis).

Ethics in Human and Animal Research

● Psychologists are placing increasing emphasis on the protection of human and animal subjects used in research. Research panels must be assured that subjects' rights and welfare are protected before research is approved. Protections include provision for informed consent from subjects, debriefing after deception has been used, and freedom of subjects to decline to participate in or to withdraw from a study at any time. Serious issues about animal research are currently being debated.

Science and the Paranormal

● To date, no solid scientific evidence supports the existence of any paranormal phenomenon. Despite the evidence, many people continue to believe in the validity of paranormal events, which is in itself an interesting psychological phenomenon. Possible reasons for the popularity of such beliefs include religious traditions, an intrinsic fascination with the unknown, people's desire to understand and predict their destinies, and an era of rapid scientific discovery suggesting that almost anything is possible.

KEY TERMS AND CONCEPTS

case study (p. 37)
confounding (p. 47)
construct (p. 33)
control group (p. 44)
controlled observation (p. 39)
correlational research (p. 41)
correlation coefficient (p. 42)
data (p. 35)
demand characteristics (p. 49)
dependent variable (p. 43)
diffusion of responsibility (p. 29)
double-blind procedure (p. 50)

experimental group (p. 44)
experimenter expectancy effects (p. 50)
external validity (p. 36)
hypothesis (p. 30)
independent variable (p. 43)
informed consent (p. 53)
internal validity (p. 35)
negative correlation (p. 42)
nonreactive or unobtrusive
   measures (p. 49)
operational definition (p. 33)
parsimony (p. 31)

placebo (p. 50)
population (p. 36)
positive correlation (p. 42)
random assignment (p. 44)
reactivity (p. 49)
representative sample (p. 36)
sample (p. 36)
single-blind procedure (p. 50)
theory (p. 31)
theory of cognitive dissonance (p. 38)
uncontrolled observation (p. 38)
variable (p. 43)

SUGGESTED READINGS

Frazier, K. (Ed.) (1986). *Science confronts the paranormal.* Buffalo, N.Y.: Prometheus Books. A fascinating series of reports on paranormal phenomena written by scientists, philosophers, and experts in magic from a skeptical scientific viewpoint. These articles illuminate many psychological processes that underlie the appearance and acceptance of the paranormal.

Huck, S. W., and Sandler, H. M. (1979). *Rival hypotheses: Alternative interpretations of data based conclusions.* New York: Harper & Row. A delightful book that analyzes flaws in 100 interesting scientific reports and provides alternative explanations for their results.

Mitchell, M. & Jolley, J. (1992). *Research design explained.* Ft. Worth: Harcourt Brace Jovanovich. An interesting and readable introduction to research methods in psychology, sociology, and related fields.

Phillips, M. T., & Sechzer, J. A. (1989). *Animal research and ethical conflict.* New York: Springer-Verlag. A volume that brings together the major research, social issues, and scientific viewpoints concerning the ethical and moral treatment of animal research subjects. The full text of the Animal Welfare Act of 1985 is reproduced in an appendix.

Biological Bases of Behavior

3

 distraught woman appeared in the emergency room of Baltimore City Hospital three days before her 23rd birthday, pleading for help. The story she told was a strange one indeed.

She and two other girls had been delivered by the same midwife in Georgia's Okefenokee Swamp on a Friday the 13th. The obviously deranged midwife had, for reasons known only to herself, placed a curse on all three babies, proclaiming that one would die before her 16th birthday, another before her 21st birthday, and the third before her 23rd birthday.

True to the midwife's prediction, one of the girls had been killed in an auto accident during her 15th year; the second was accidentally shot to death in a night club as she celebrated her 21st birthday. Now, the third young woman waited in terror for her own death.

The emergency room psychiatrist reassured the terrified woman that no harm would come to her in the hospital and reluctantly admitted her for observation. Despite the doctor's reassurance, the woman remained convinced that she was doomed. The next morning, two days before her 23rd birthday, she was found dead in her hospital bed. Doctors were unable to determine a physical cause for her death (Rosenhan & Seligman, 1989).

The year was 1848. As the Vermont winter approached, a railroad construction crew hurried to complete its work on an important section of new track. They could not know that they were to witness one of the most celebrated incidents in the annals of neurology.

As a blasting crew prepared its charges, the dynamite accidentally exploded, propelling a spike more than 3 feet long and weighing 13 pounds through the face and head of Phineas Gage, a 25-year-old foreman. The spike entered through the left cheek, passed through the brain, and emerged through the top of the skull (see Figure 3.1). Dr. J. M. Harlow, who treated the case, described the incident:

> The patient was thrown upon his back by the explosion, and gave a few convulsive motions of the extremities, but spoke in a few minutes. He . . . seemed perfectly conscious, but was becoming exhausted from the hemorrhage, which by this time was quite profuse, the blood pouring from the lacerated sinus in the top of his head. . . . He bore his sufferings with firmness, and directed my attention to the hole in his cheek, saying, ''the iron entered there and passed through my head'' (Harlow, 1868, pp. 330–332).

Miraculously, Gage survived. Or did he?

His physical health is good, and I am inclined to say that he has recovered. Has no pain in his head, but says it has a queer feeling that he is not able to describe. Applied for his situation as foreman, but is undecided whether to work or travel. His contractors, who regarded him as the most efficient and capable foreman in their employ previous to his injury considered the change in his mind so marked that they could not give him his place again. The equilibrium or balance, so to speak, between his intellectual faculties and animal propensities, seems to have been destroyed. He is fitful, irreverent, indulging at times in the grossest profanity (which was not previously his custom), manifesting but little deference for his fellows, impatient of restraint or advice when it conflicts with his desires, at times pertinaciously obstinate, yet capricious and vacillating, devising many plans of future operations, which are no sooner arranged than they are abandoned in turn for others. . . . His mind is radically changed, so decidedly that his friends and acquaintances say that he is ''no longer Gage'' (Harlow, 1868, pp. 339–340).

Mind and body; body and mind. As the cases of the young woman's sudden death and the tragic accident to Phineas Gage illustrate, biological and psychological processes are intimately related. In one case, something in the ''mind'' apparently killed the body; in the other, damage to the body changed the mind so radically that a totally different person emerged in the recovered Phineas Gage.

After Albert Einstein died in 1955, his brain was preserved in a formaldehyde solution and placed in the care of a Missouri physician. Did any part of the genius who gave the world the theory of relativity still reside in that preserved brain? Most of us would

Figure 3.1 *The brain damage suffered by Phineas Gage seemed to change him into a new person.*

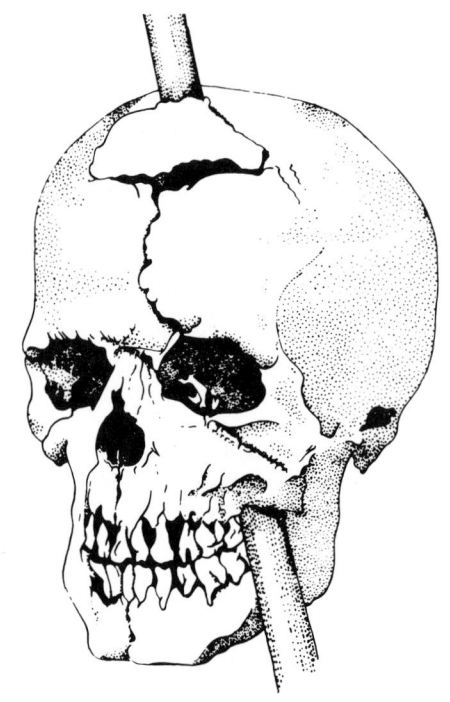

probably reply, ''No.'' But a much more profound question then follows: What was the essence of ''Einstein'' that made that brain tissue the residence of genius one instant and a lifeless lump of tissue the next?

Some would maintain that what left that brain was a spiritual entity, such as the soul. Such thinking is firmly rooted in many religious and philosophical traditions. Whether or not spiritual entities exist is not a question that science can currently address, however. Its province is the material world; the spiritual remains the domain of philosophy and theology. Therefore, a modern neuroscientist would most likely respond that the brain ceased to be Einstein when the electrical and chemical activities that defined his thoughts, feelings, and behaviors were stilled forever. The discoveries being made by neuroscientists about the specifics of those molecular, chemical, and electrical activities have profound implications both for self-understanding and for changing the biological processes that underlie human ills, both physical and psychological.

In order to understand behavior, we must know something about its biological foundations. After all, the processes that are the focus of psychology's psychodynamic, cognitive, humanistic, and behavioral perspectives result from the functioning of biological systems. Every psychological function—attending, sensing, perceiving, thinking, feeling, acting—involves the activities of complex biological systems that operate within our bodies. Indeed, powerful determinants of our physical and behavioral traits are inscribed on a genetic blueprint that existed long before we were born. These genetic factors will be addressed when we discuss human development. For now, we will concern ourselves with three systems whose activities are of special importance in understanding body–mind interactions. The first is the nervous system, the master control network whose activities underly our every thought, feeling, and behavior. Two other systems interact with the nervous system. The endocrine system influences many behaviors through the activities of hormones. The immune system, our body's biological defense network, is the site of some of the most profound recent discoveries of mind–body interactions.

The Neural Bases of Behavior

We live in a universe whose limits are so vast that we can scarcely comprehend them. Yet that vastness exists for us only within the confines of our grapefruit-sized brain, represented for us in the interplay of molecules across the surfaces of brain cells, or neurons.

We will now focus on the marvels of what has been termed ''our three-pound universe'' (Hooper & Teresi, 1986).

The Neuron

Specialized cells called **neurons** are the basic building blocks of the nervous system. They are linked together in circuits, not unlike the electrical circuits in a computer. At birth your brain contained about 100 billion neurons. You will never again have that many, for unlike other body cells, neurons are not replaced when they die. It is estimated that through normal cell death, about 10,000 of them are lost each day (Kolb & Whishaw, 1989).

Like all cells in the body, each neuron is a separate unit within which the vital processes of growth and metabolism occur. The neuron has three main parts: a soma (or cell body), dendrites, and an axon (see Figure 3.2). The **soma** contains a nucleus, which regulates the cell's life processes. Branch-like fibers called **dendrites** (from the Greek word meaning ''tree'') extend like leafless branches from the soma. The dendrites receive messages from neighboring neurons and conduct them to the soma. Extending from one side of the soma is a single **axon,** which branches at its end to form a number of axon terminals. The axon conducts electrical impulses away from the soma to as many as 50,000 of its neighbors, as well as to muscles and glands.

Nerve impulses normally move in only one direction—from dendrite or soma (which can also receive impulses from other neurons) to axon. Although a given neuron has only one axon, it may have 1,000 or more dendrites that receive nerve impulses from the axons of many other neurons. Thus, the number of potential connections among neurons is

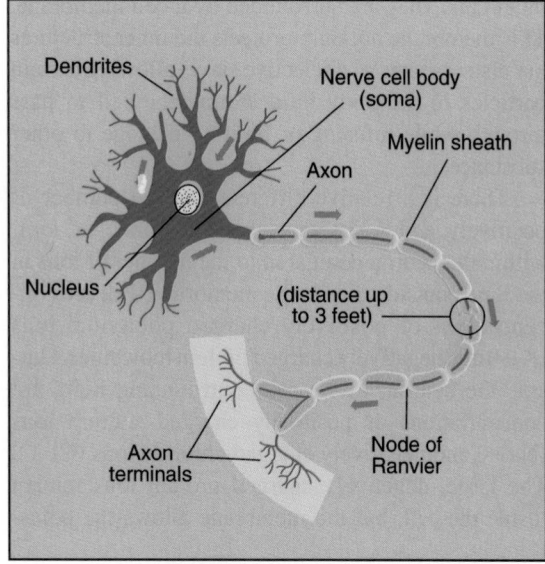

Figure 3.2 *Structural elements of a typical neuron. Stimulation received by the dendrites or soma (cell body) may trigger a nerve impulse, which travels down the axon to stimulate other neurons, muscles, or glands. Some axons have a fatty myelin sheath interrupted at intervals by the nodes of Ranvier. The myelin sheath helps increase the speed of nerve conduction.*

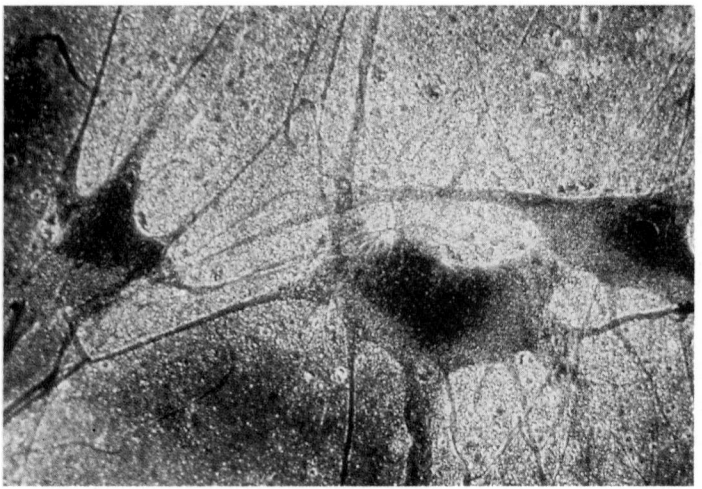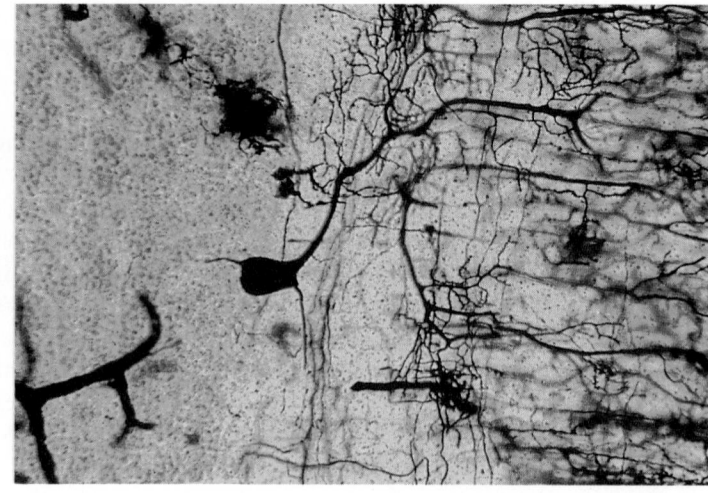

Figure 3.3 *As shown in these photographs taken through the electron microscope, neurons' structural characteristics can vary widely. Despite these differences, all neurons have only one cell body and one axon.*

very great, dwarfing even the largest, most complex computers.

Neurons can vary greatly in size and shape (see Figure 3.3). A neuron in your spinal cord may have an axon that extends several feet to one of your fingertips; another neuron up in your brain may be no more than a thousandth of an inch long. What you think of as nerves running through your body are actually bundles of axons extending from hundreds or even thousands of neurons.

Nerve Conduction

Neurons do two things: They generate electricity, and they release chemicals. Nerve conduction is thus an electrochemical process. The electrical properties of neurons have been known for more than a century, but we have only recently begun to learn about the chemical processes involved in neural activity. An understanding of how neurons generate electricity requires a brief excursion into chemistry.

Neurons function a bit like batteries in that their own chemical substances are a source of energy. Like other cells, they are surrounded by a cell membrane. This membrane not only protects the inner structures but also operates as a selective sieve, allowing certain particles in the body fluid around the cell to pass through while refusing or limiting passage to other substances.

There is a relative difference in the number of positively and negatively charged atoms, or *ions,* within the neuron compared to the number of ions in the fluids outside. Inside the membrane wall are concentrations of positively charged potassium ions (K+) and negatively charged protein molecules. Outside the neuron, in the salty surrounding fluid, are concentrations of positively charged sodium ions (Na+) and negatively charged chloride ions (Cl−). The large, negatively charged protein ions remain inside the cell, but the membrane allows the potas-

sium and chloride ions to flow in and out of the cell. As a result of this uneven distribution of ions, the inside of the cell is electrically negative compared to the outside by about 70 millivolts, or 70/1,000 of a volt. This is called the **resting potential.**

All cells in the body have a similar resting voltage. In some animals, specialized organs can combine this tiny voltage to generate very high voltages. For example, electric eels can generate 600 to 700 volts because their muscle tissue cell membranes are arranged so that the individual cell voltages add together to equal one big jolt.

Neurons and muscle cells have a unique property among body cells: sudden and extreme changes can occur in their resting potential voltage. A **nerve impulse** is a sudden reversal in the neuron's membrane voltage, during which the membrane voltage momentarily moves from −70 millivolts (inside) to +40 millivolts (see Figure 3.4).

What causes this sudden reversal? Through a series of sophisticated experiments that won them the Nobel Prize, British scientists A. L. Hodgkin and A. F. Huxley provided the answer. Recall that when the cell is resting, positively charged sodium ions are kept outside the cell. During an impulse, however, *sodium channels* in the axon membrane open for an instant, and sodium ions flood into the interior of the cell, pulled by the negative electrical force within the neuron. Because the sodium ions are positively charged, they cause the interior of the cell to become more positively charged than the outside. This change in polarity, called the **action potential,** starts a chain reaction and causes the *sodium gate* to open at adjacent membrane sites. In a reflex action to restore the resting polarity, the cell quickly closes the sodium channels, and tiny sodium pumps in the cell membrane pump out the excess sodium ions, restoring the cell's negatively charged resting potential. In less than 1/1,000 of a second, the process is over. Figure 3.4 shows this sequence of events.

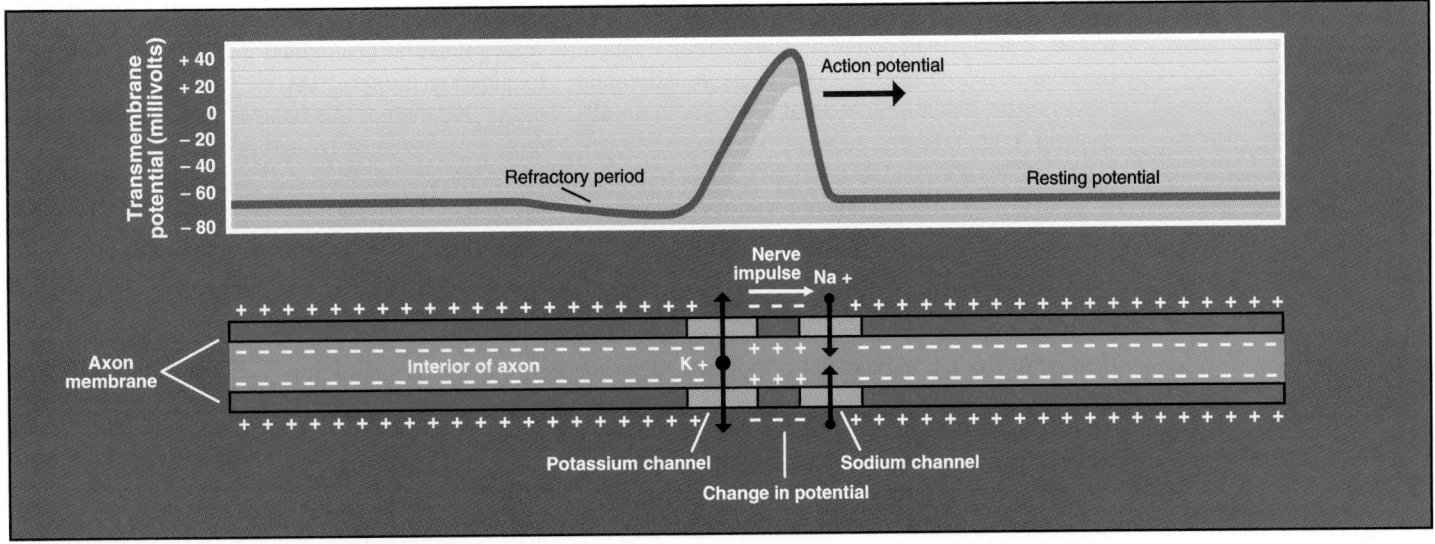

Figure 3.4 *The nerve impulse is a change in electrical potential. The axon membrane separates fluids that differ greatly in their concentration of sodium (Na+) and potassium (K+) ions. Because of this, the inside of the fiber is normally about 70 millivolts negative compared to the exterior (the resting potential). The movement of a nerve impulse along an axon involves the opening of a sodium gate, which allows positively charged sodium ions to flow into the cell, reversing the polarity to about +40 millivolts and creating the action potential. An instant later the sodium channels close, and the sodium ions are pumped back out of the cell, restoring the negative resting potential. After a brief refractory period, another impulse can follow.*

Once the electrical impulse is started at any point on the membrane, it travels down the full length of the axon in bucket-brigade fashion. Immediately after an impulse passes a point along the axon, there is a recovery period, lasting a few thousandths of a second, during which the membrane is not excitable and cannot discharge another impulse. This is called a **refractory period,** and it places an upper limit on the rate at which impulses can be triggered in a neuron. In humans the limit seems to be about 300 impulses per second (Kimble, 1992).

Some axons are covered by a fatty insulation layer called the **myelin sheath.** The myelin sheath is interrupted at regular intervals by the **nodes of Ranvier,** sites at which the myelin is either extremely thin or absent (see Figure 3.2). In myelinated fibers, electrical conduction can skip from node to node rather than having to travel along the entire axon, and these great leaps from one gap to another account for high conduction speeds of more than 200 miles per hour. But these high-speed fibers are 3 million times slower than the speed at which electricity courses through an electric wire, which is why your brain, though vastly more complex than any computer, cannot begin to match it in speed of reaction.

The myelin sheath, which developed late in the evolutionary process, is characteristic of the nervous systems of higher animals. In many nerve fibers, the sheath is not completely formed until some time after birth. This may be why some of our sensory and motor abilities do not mature until after we are born. For example, myelinization is partly responsible for the gains that infants exhibit in motor skills as they grow older (Kolb, 1989).

The tragic effects of damage to the myelin coating can be seen in people who suffer from multiple sclerosis. This progressive disease of the myelin sheath disrupts the delicate timing of nerve impulses, resulting in jerky, uncoordinated movements and, in the final stages, paralysis.

Synaptic Transmission

The nervous system operates as a giant communications network, and its action requires the transmission of nerve impulses from one neuron to another. Early in the history of brain research, scientists thought that the tip of the axon made physical contact with the dendrites or cell bodies of other neurons, so that electricity passed directly from one neuron to the next. With the advent of the electron microscope, however, researchers found that there is actually a tiny gap between the axon terminal and the next neuron. This space is known as the **synapse.**

Events that occur at the synapse determine whether or not neurons will fire. When the dendrites or the soma are stimulated by other nerve cells, small shifts occur in the cell membrane's electrical potential. These shifts, called **graded potentials,** are proportional to the amount and kind of incoming activity. If the graded potential is large enough to reach the required level of intensity, called the **action potential**

threshold, the neuron discharges with an action potential. If the graded potential is not strong enough, the neuron simply does not fire. Once an individual neuron fires, its action potential proceeds in an all-or-none fashion. In this sense, activating a nerve cell is like firing a gun: Unless a certain amount of energy is applied to the trigger, the gun will not fire; once it does fire, however, the velocity of the bullet bears no relation to how hard the trigger was pulled. Where nerve impulses are concerned, this is known as the **all-or-none principle** of nerve conduction. Although the size of the action potential is the same, a strong stimulus may increase the *rate* of firing of the neuron.

The synaptic activity of some neurons inhibits rather than excites the firing of other neurons. This process of **inhibition** prevents a runaway discharge of the nervous system, as occurs in an epileptic seizure. Certain drugs, such as strychnine, block inhibition and produce this very effect—massive discharges of neurons and electrochemical disruption of life-serving functions.

Every neuron is constantly bombarded with excitatory and inhibitory influences from other neurons, and the interplay of these influences determines whether or not the cell fires (see Figure 3.5). An ex-

quisite balance between excitatory and inhibitory processes must be maintained if the nervous system is to function properly. As we will see in Chapter 8, drugs that disrupt this balance can have striking effects on consciousness and behavior.

Neurotransmitters

If neurons do not physically touch the other neurons to which they send signals, how does transmission occur? If the action potential does not cross the synapse, what does? What carries the message?

We now know that in addition to generating electricity, neurons produce chemical molecules and pump them down their axons to be stored in chambers called **synaptic vesicles** within the axon terminals. A nerve impulse triggers from the vesicles the release of the chemical molecules known as **neurotransmitters,** which are "sprayed" across the fluid-filled space between the axon of the sending (presynaptic) neuron and the membrane of the receiving (postsynaptic) neuron's dendrite or soma. There the neurotransmitters *bind* or attach themselves to specific **receptor sites,** which are large protein molecules embedded in the receiving neuron's semi-liquid cell membrane. The receptor site, which looks somewhat like a lily pad, has a specially shaped surface that fits a specific transmitter molecule much like a lock accommodates a single key. When the transmitter molecule binds with the receptor site, the portion of the receptor inside the cell membrane changes shape, and a body known as a **G protein** binds with the receptor and is activated by it (see Figure 3.6). Once activated, the G protein can alter the polarity of the cell membrane and produce the graded potential that, alone or in combination with other excitatory synapses, causes the receiving neuron to fire. If, however, the neuron is an inhibitory one, the chemical reaction produced by its neurotransmitter will inhibit the firing of the postsynaptic neuron. The G protein can also change its shape and bind with and trigger *second messengers* that initiate actions within the cell, making possible an array of cellular events that molecular biologists are only beginning to understand (Hyman & Nestler, 1992).

Once a transmitter molecule binds to its receptor, it will keep activating or inhibiting the neuron unless it is shut off or deactivated. The transmitter molecule can be deactivated in several ways. Some transmitter substances are destroyed almost immediately by other chemicals located in the synaptic space. In other cases, the transmitter molecules are rapidly sucked back into the presynaptic axon terminal, a process known as **reuptake.** When the receptor is again vacant, the G protein ceases its activities inside the neuron and returns to its former shape and inactive state.

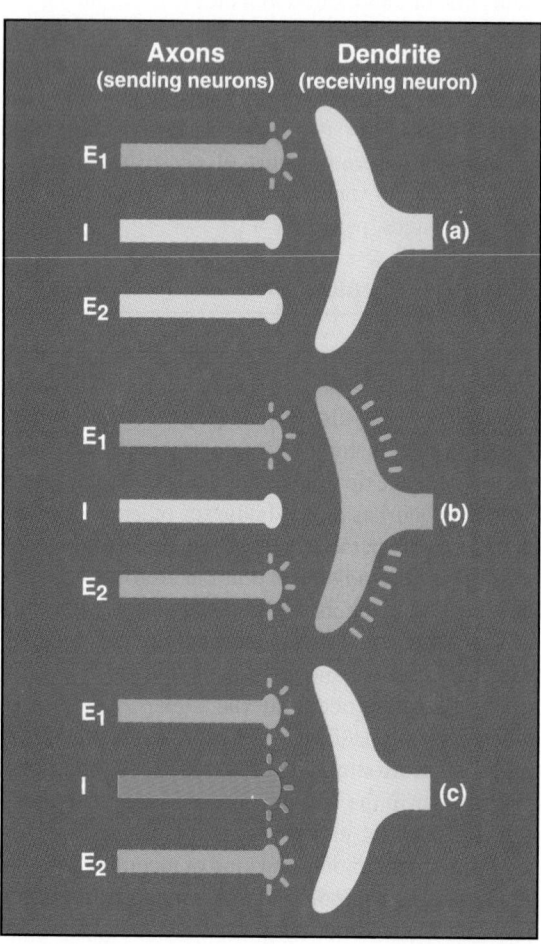

▶ **Figure 3.5** *Excitatory and inhibitory influences interact to affect neural transmission. In this example, three neurons— two excitatory (E_1 and E_2) and one inhibitory (I)—can stimulate the dendrite with their neurotransmitters. Stimulation by E_1 alone (a) is not enough to fire the postsynaptic neuron; simultaneous stimulation by E_1 and E_2 is required (b). However, if the inhibitory neuron stimulates the neuron at the same time as E_1 and E_2, postsynaptic firing will be inhibited (c). The interaction of inhibitory and excitatory influences makes possible an exquisite fine-tuning of neural activity.*

Axons
(sending neurons)

Dendrite
(receiving neuron)

E_1
I
(a)
E_2

E_1
I
(b)
E_2

E_1
I
(c)
E_2

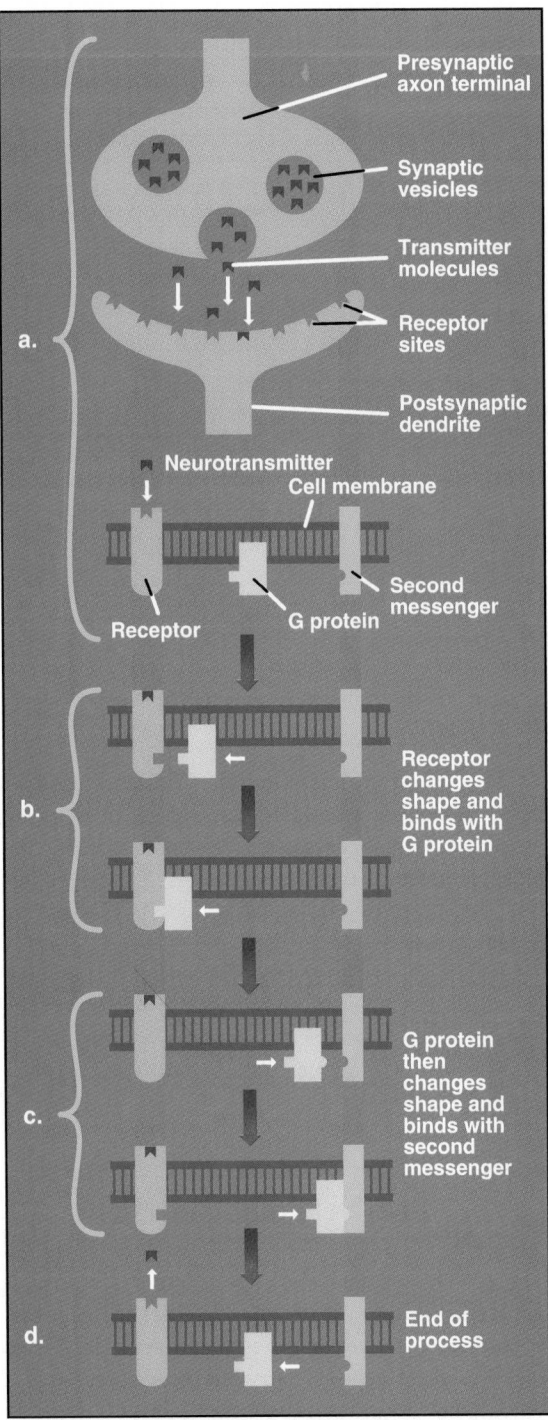

a.

- Presynaptic axon terminal
- Synaptic vesicles
- Transmitter molecules
- Receptor sites
- Postsynaptic dendrite

- Neurotransmitter
- Cell membrane
- Second messenger
- Receptor
- G protein

b.

Receptor changes shape and binds with G protein

c.

G protein then changes shape and binds with second messenger

d.

End of process

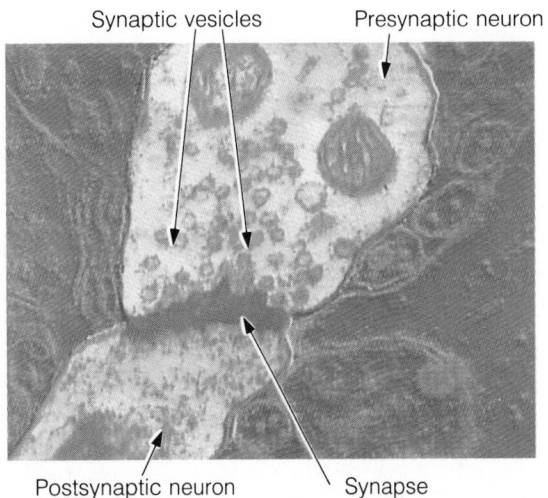

Synaptic vesicles   Presynaptic neuron

Postsynaptic neuron   Synapse

Figure 3.6 *A synapse between two neurons. The action potential travels to the axon terminals, where it stimulates the secretion of transmitter molecules from the synaptic vesicles. These molecules travel across the synapse and bind to specially keyed receptor sites on the dendrite of the postsynaptic neuron (a). Binding causes the portion of the receptor inside the neuron to change shape, enabling it to bind with the G protein (b). Once the G protein has been activated, it also changes shape, allowing it to bind to a second messenger that can trigger depolarization or other processes within the neuron (c). When the receptor is vacant, the G protein returns to its original position and shape (d).*

Through the use of chemical transmitters, Nature has found an ingenious way of dividing up the brain into systems that are uniquely sensitive to certain messages. There is only one kind of electricity, but there are myriad shapes that can be assumed by transmitter molecules. Because the various systems in the brain recognize only certain chemical messengers, they are immune to "cross talk" from other systems. At present, around 40 different substances are known or suspected transmitters in the brain, but there may be hundreds more (Kimble, 1992). Each substance has a specific excitatory or inhibitory effect on certain neurons. Table 3.1 lists several of the more important transmitters that have been linked to psychological phenomena.

Perhaps the best understood neurotransmitter is **acetylcholine (ACh),** which is found in various brain regions that are believed to be involved in memory. Underproduction of acetylcholine is thought to be an important factor in the profound memory impairments experienced by patients who suffer from **Alzheimer's disease,** a degenerative brain disorder that afflicts between 5 and 10 percent of all people over 65 years of age (Selkoe, 1991). Acetylcholine is also known to be the excitatory transmitter through which neurons activate muscle cells (Sherwood, 1991). Drugs that block the action of ACh can result in fatal muscular paralysis. For example, curare, a plant extract used by native people of South America to poison their arrows, prevents ACh from acting because its molecules cover up the transmitter receptor sites on the muscle cell. The muscles, unable to respond to nerve impulses, become paralyzed, including those involved in breathing. A different but equally deadly kind of blocking action is performed at ACh synapses in botulism, a serious type of food poisoning. The toxin formed by the *Clostridium botulinum* bacteria appears to block the release of ACh from the axon terminal, again resulting in a paralysis

Table 3.1 Major Neurotransmitter Substances

Neurotransmitter	Function	Disorder Associated with Malfunctioning
Acetylcholine	Excitatory at synapses involved in movement and memory	Paralysis; Alzheimer's disease (undersupply)
Norepinephrine	Found in circuits controlling learning, memory, arousal, wakefulness, eating; also a hormone	Depression (undersupply)
Serotonin	Involved in neural networks governing sleep, appetite, and mood	Depression (undersupply)
Dopamine	Found in circuits involving movement, learning, emotional arousal, and reward centers	Schizophrenia (oversupply); Parkinson's disease (undersupply)
GABA	Major inhibitory transmitter; involved in movement	Huntington's disease, seizures (undersupply)
Endorphins	Mostly inhibitory; inhibit pain	None established

Source: Julian, 1991.

of the muscles, including those of the respiratory system.

The medical treatment of emotionally disturbed people has been revolutionized by the development of *psychoactive* drugs, which affect experience and behavior. These drugs operate by either enhancing or inhibiting the actions of certain transmitters at the synapse. For example, the antipsychotic drugs chlorpromazine and haloperidol (known commercially as Thorazine and Haldol) fit into the receptor "locks" meant for an excitatory transmitter called **dopamine,** thus preventing dopamine from stimulating neurons (Cohen & Servan-Schreber, 1992). Abnormally high concentrations of dopamine and dopamine receptors have been found in the brains of patients suffering from schizophrenia, a severe disorder of thought, emotion, and behavior. Researchers speculate that one factor in schizophrenia may be overactivity in the brain's dopamine transmitter system and that certain antipsychotic drugs help to restore a more normal transmitter balance, thereby reducing symptoms (Depue, 1991; Fowles, 1992). One scientist who is trying to find possible chemical bases for psychiatric disorders echoes the theme that stirs the hopes of many workers in this field:

There are thousands and thousands of different types of molecules involved—not just transmitters and receptors, but also the enzymes that manufacture and degrade them. . . . And—think about this—every time we discover a molecule we have discovered the potential for at least two diseases. Some people will surely have too much of that molecule; others will have too little. . . . it doesn't take a genius to understand that the next century is going to see a dramatic process of discovery in which molecular defects are connected, one after an-

other, to mental illnesses (quoted in Franklin, 1987, pp. 91–92).

In addition to improving the treatment of disordered behavior, solving the mysteries of synaptic transmission may be the key to understanding the physical bases of thinking, learning, memory, emotion, and other psychological processes (Thompson & Gluck, 1992).

Having described some of the basic structures and processes that underlie the functioning of the nervous system, let us consider the nervous system's organization and its complex role in our consciousness and behavior.

■ ▢

The Nervous System

The nervous system is the body's master control center. It consists of increasingly complex structures that appear as one moves up the evolutionary scale. Three major types of neurons carry out the system's input, output, and integration functions. **Sensory neurons** carry input messages from the sense organs to the spinal cord and brain. **Motor neurons** transmit output impulses from the brain and spinal cord to the body's muscles and organs. **Interneurons** perform a connective or associative function between regions within the nervous system.

The nervous system may be broken down into several subsystems, although the parts of the system are interrelated (see Figure 3.7). The two major divisions are the **central nervous system** (all the neurons in the brain and spinal cord) and the **peripheral nervous system** (all the neurons that connect the cen-

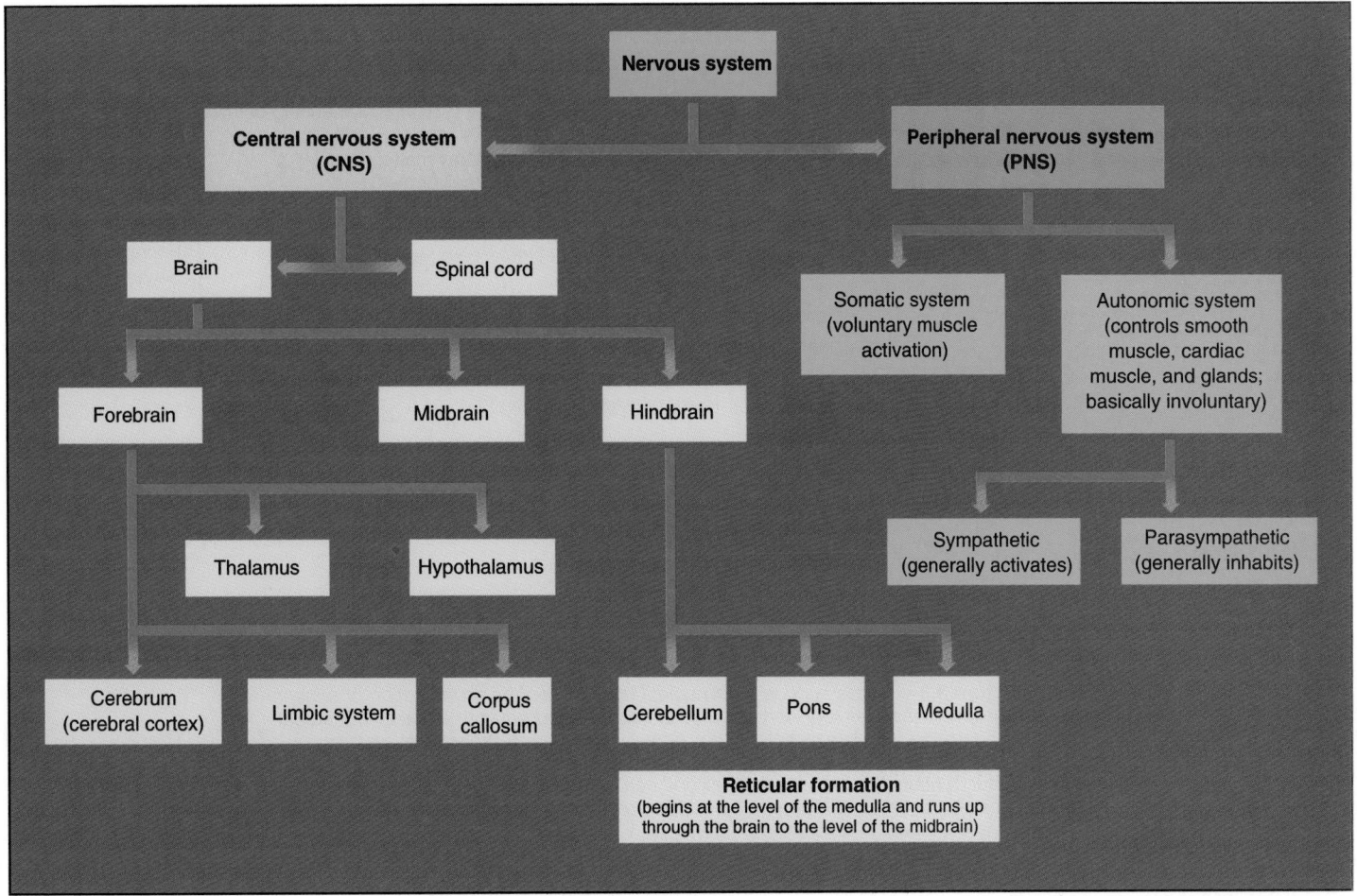

Figure 3.7 at top showing the structural organization of the nervous system:

Nervous system
→ Central nervous system (CNS)
  → Brain
    → Forebrain
      → Thalamus
      → Hypothalamus
      → Cerebrum (cerebral cortex)
      → Limbic system
      → Corpus callosum
    → Midbrain
    → Hindbrain
      → Cerebellum
      → Pons
      → Medulla
      → Reticular formation (begins at the level of the medulla and runs up through the brain to the level of the midbrain)
  → Spinal cord
→ Peripheral nervous system (PNS)
  → Somatic system (voluntary muscle activation)
  → Autonomic system (controls smooth muscle, cardiac muscle, and glands; basically involuntary)
    → Sympathetic (generally activates)
    → Parasympathetic (generally inhibits)

tral nervous system with the muscles, glands, and sensory receptors). The peripheral nervous system may be subdivided further into the **somatic system,** which provides input from the sensory system and output to the skeletal muscles responsible for voluntary movement, and the **autonomic nervous system,** which directs the activities of the body's glands and internal organs.

The Spinal Cord

Most nerves enter and leave the central nervous system by way of the spinal cord, where they are protected by the vertebrae (bones of the spine). When the spinal cord is viewed in cross section (Figure 3.8), its central portion resembles an H. The H-shaped portion is the **gray matter,** which consists largely of gray-colored neuron cell bodies and their interconnections. Surrounding the gray matter is the **white matter,** composed almost entirely of white-colored myelinated axons that connect various levels of the spinal cord with each other and with the higher centers of the brain.

Emerging from both sides of the spinal cord all along its length are the **dorsal** (backside) and **ventral roots.** The dorsal root consists of sensory nerves, and the ventral root contains motor nerves.

Some simple stimulus/response sequences, known as **spinal reflexes,** can be generated at the level of the spinal cord without any involvement of the brain. For example, a tap on the kneecap produces the familiar knee-jerk response. As another example, if you touch something hot, sensory receptors in your skin trigger nerve impulses that enter your spinal cord through the dorsal root and synapse with the interneurons in the cord's gray matter. These, in turn, excite motor neurons in the ventral root so that your hand jerks away. The sensory neurons have also synapsed with other neurons that carry the message about these events to your brain, but it is a good thing that you don't have to wait for the brain to tell you what to do in such emergencies. Getting messages to and from the brain takes slightly longer, so the spinal cord reflex system significantly reduces reaction time.

The Brain

The three pounds of protein, fat, and water that you carry around inside your skull is the most complex structure in the known universe and the only one that

▲ **Figure 3.7** *Structural Organization of the Nervous System*

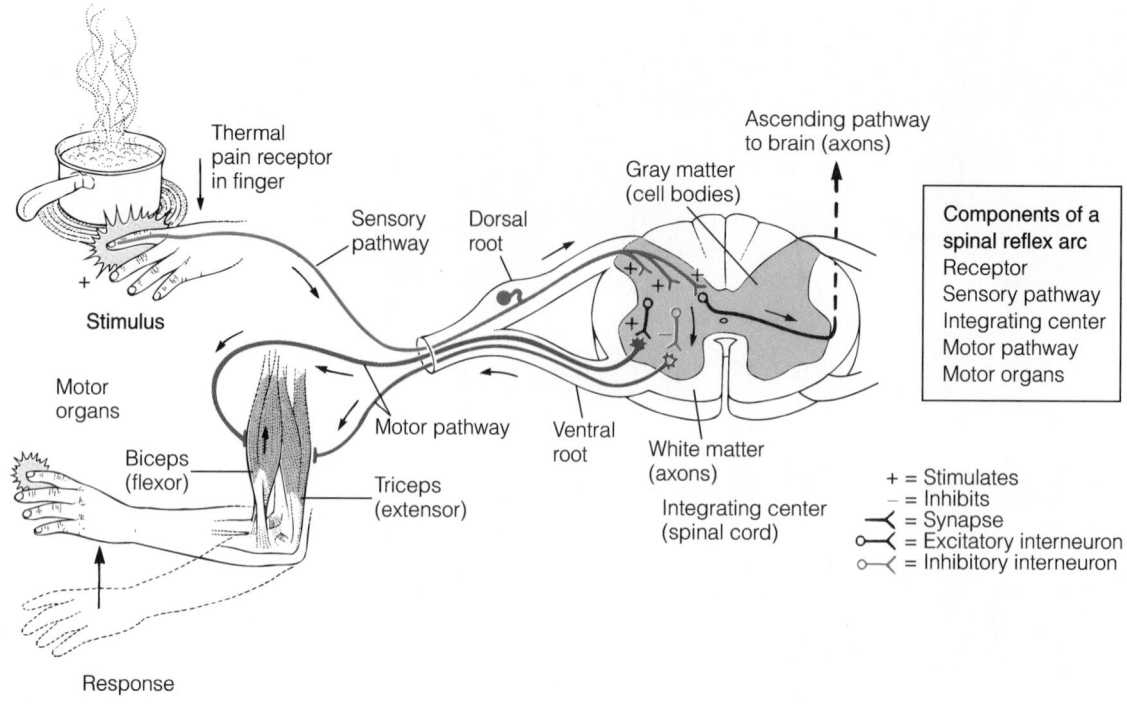

Thermal
pain receptor
in finger

Sensory
pathway

Dorsal
root

Gray matter
(cell bodies)

Ascending pathway
to brain (axons)

Stimulus

Motor
organs

Biceps
(flexor)

Triceps
(extensor)

Motor pathway

Ventral
root

White matter
(axons)

Integrating center
(spinal cord)

Response

**Components of a
spinal reflex arc**
Receptor
Sensory pathway
Integrating center
Motor pathway
Motor organs

+ = Stimulates
− = Inhibits
⊰ = Synapse
o⊰ = Excitatory interneuron
o⊰ = Inhibitory interneuron

Figure 3.8 *A cross section of the spinal cord shows the organization of sensory and motor nerves. Sensory nerves enter the spinal cord on both sides of the spinal column through the dorsal roots; motor nerves exit through the ventral roots. Interneurons within the spinal gray matter can serve a connective function, as shown here, but in many cases, sensory neurons can also synapse directly with motor neurons. At this level of the nervous system, reflex activity is possible without involving the brain.*

can wonder about itself. As befits this biological marvel, your brain is the most active energy consumer of all your body organs. Although it accounts for only about 2 percent of your total body weight, your brain consumes about 20 percent of the oxygen you use in a resting state (Iversen, 1979). Moreover, the brain never rests; its rate of energy metabolism is relatively constant day and night. In fact, when you dream, the brain's metabolic rate actually increases slightly.

One of psychology's greatest challenges is to understand how the brain functions. Recent years have witnessed a burgeoning of knowledge about brain processes that are tied to thought, emotion, and behavior. Before describing these linkages, let us consider the tools and techniques of discovery that are used in this quest for understanding.

Unlocking the Secrets of the Brain

More has been learned about the brain in the past three decades than was known in all the preceding ages. Various methods are used by brain investigators to study the brain's structures and activities. Some of the new technical breakthroughs permit detailed study of the living brain.

Destruction and Stimulation Techniques. We can often learn a great deal about a particular structure in the brain by studying the behavioral effects of brain damage. In **lesioning,** tissue is destroyed with electricity, with cold or heat, or with chemicals. In surgical **ablation,** a part of the brain is surgically removed. Most experiments of this kind are performed on animals, but sometimes humans can also be studied when accident or disease produces a lesion or when abnormal brain tissue must be surgically removed.

In a sense, the opposite of destroying neurons is stimulating them. A specific region of the brain can be stimulated by a mild electric current or by chemicals that excite neurons. Electrodes can be permanently implanted so that the region of interest can be stimulated repeatedly. In chemical stimulation studies, a tiny tube is inserted into the brain so that a small amount of the chemical can be delivered directly to the area to be studied. Again, most of these techniques are used with animals.

Electrical Recording Techniques. It is also possible to eavesdrop on the electrical conversations occurring within the brain. Electrodes can record brain activity as well as stimulate it. Neurons' electrical

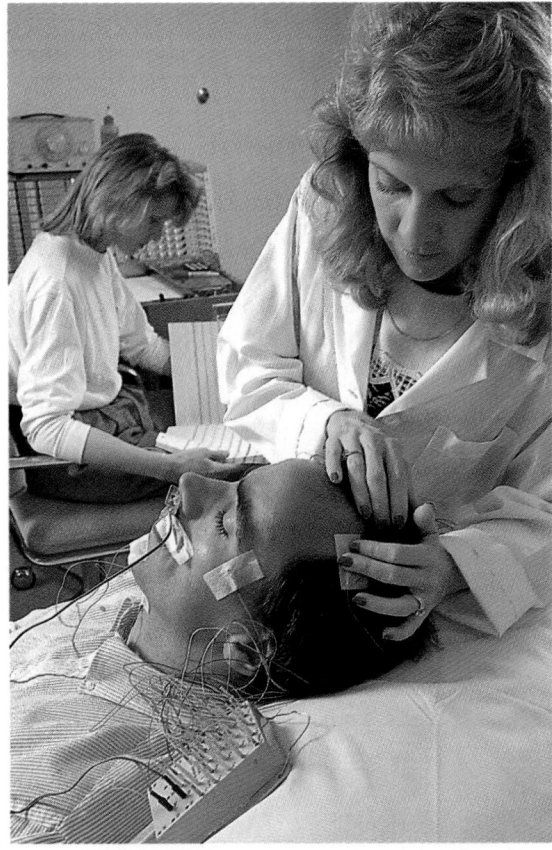

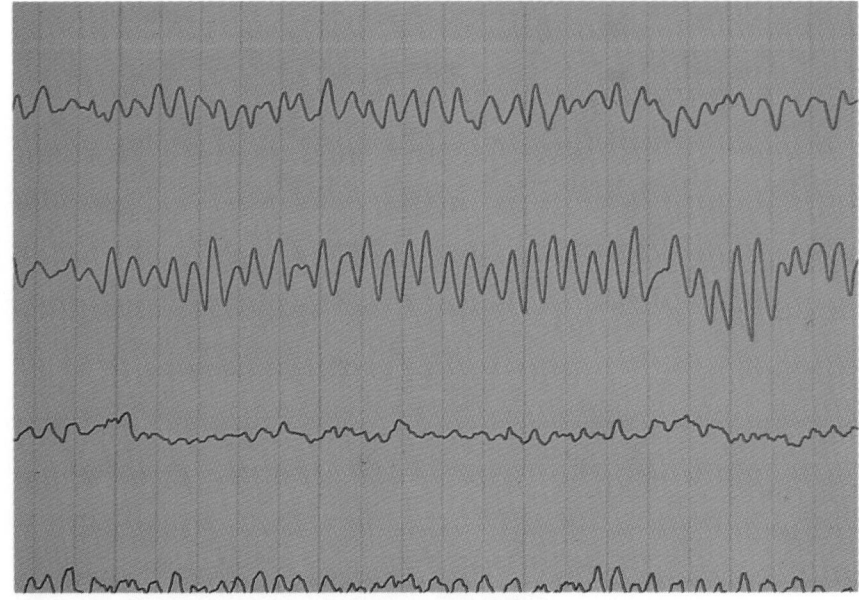

activity can be measured by inserting small electrodes in particular areas of the brain or even in individual neurons.

In addition to measuring individual voices, scientists can tune in to "crowd noise" by placing larger electrodes on the scalp to measure the activity of large groups of neurons with the **electroencephalograph (EEG)** (see Figure 3.9). Although the EEG is a rather gross measure that taps the electrical activity of thousands of neurons, specific EEG patterns relate to various states of consciousness, such as wakefulness and sleep. The EEG can also be used clinically to help determine whether a brain abnormality is present.

Brain Imaging Techniques. The newest tools are imaging techniques that permit neuroscientists to peer into the living brain. The most important of these technological "windows" are CAT scans, PET scans, and magnetic resonance imagery (MRI).

Developed in the 1970s, the technique of **computerized axial tomography (CAT scan)** is 100 times more sensitive than standard X-ray procedures. A narrow beam of X-rays scans the patient's brain 160 times to take pictures of narrow slices of the brain. A computer analyzes the X-rays and creates pictures of the brain's interior from many different angles (Figure 3.10). Pinpointing where injuries or deterioration have occurred helps clarify relations be-

tween brain damage and psychological functioning. The technological advance represented by the CAT-scan technique was so dramatic that its developers, Allan Cormack and Godfrey Hounsfield, were awarded the 1979 Nobel Prize for medicine.

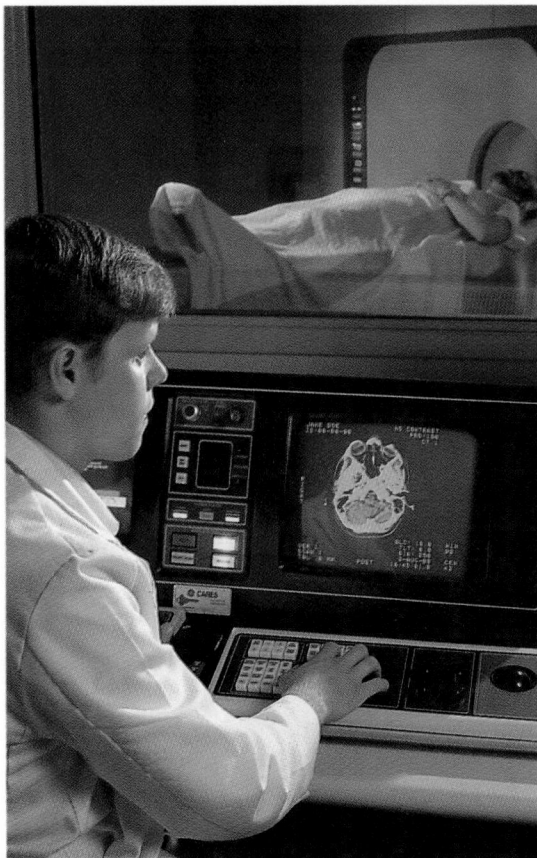

Figure 3.10 *The CAT scan uses narrow beams of X-rays to construct a composite picture of brain structures.*

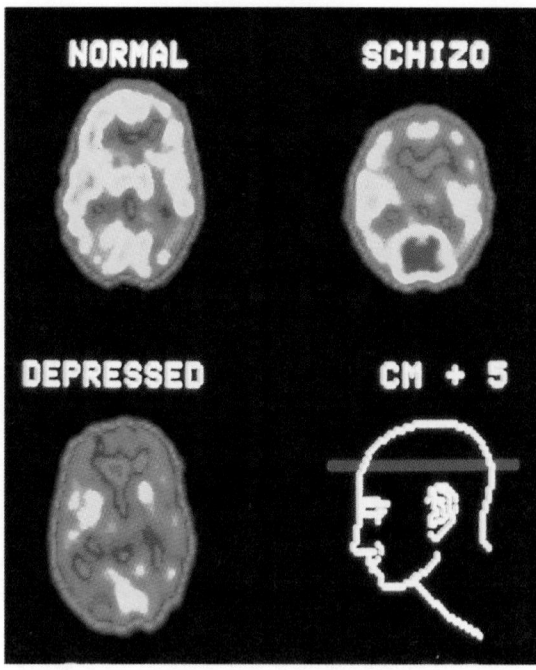

NORMAL   SCHIZO

DEPRESSED   CM + 5

Another type of scanner has revolutionized brain research. Unlike the CAT scan, which is used to study brain structures, **positron emission tomography (PET scan)** is used to investigate brain metabolism, blood flow, and neurotransmitter activity. One use of PET is to scan the absorption of a safe form of radioactive **deoxyglucose,** which is injected into the bloodstream and travels to the brain. Deoxyglucose is chemically similar to glucose, the main fuel of neurons, except that it is not ''digested'' when the neuron consumes it for food. Researchers can therefore tell how active particular neurons are by the amount of deoxyglucose that accumulates in them. If a subject is performing a mental reasoning task, for example, a researcher can tell by the deoxyglucose concentration pattern which parts of the brain were activated by the task (Raichle, 1992). The energy emitted by the radioactive substance is measured by the PET scan, and the data are fed into a computer that uses the readings to produce a color picture of the brain on a display screen (Figure 3.11). Scientists can now map the activity of brain structures in a living animal or human in a way never before possible, and brain activity can be studied in relation to cognitive processes, behavior, and even forms of mental illness (Crisp & others, 1991; Depue, 1992).

In addition to the deoxyglucose tracer used to study glucose metabolism, radioactive tracers have been developed to measure such diverse functions as local blood flow, blood volume, oxygen consumption, tissue pH, and tissue drug distribution in living brains (Raichle, 1992). An especially promising development uses the PET scan to discover neurotransmitter

binding sites in living brains. Radioactive transmitter substances are injected and the radioactively lit trails of receptors are traced throughout the brain. This method allows researchers to study the neurochemistry of brain functions. They can, for example, find out where certain neurotransmitters operate in the brain (Duncan & Stumpf, 1991).

The newest tool for viewing the living brain is **magnetic resonance imaging (MRI).** MRI, which combines features of CAT and PET, can be used to study both brain structures and brain activity. It focuses on the nuclei of atoms in living tissue and creates images based on how the atoms respond to a magnetic pulse delivered to an organ. The part of the body to be studied is placed in the hollow core of a long magnetic cylinder, and the atoms in the subject's body are exposed to a uniform magnetic field. The field is then altered, and when the magnetic field is shut off, the energy absorbed by the nuclei becomes a small electrical voltage. The voltage is picked up by detectors and relayed to a computer for analysis and reconstruction of a two- or three-dimensional image that serves as a biochemical blueprint of chemical activity. In addition to providing color images of the tissue, MRI also tells which chemicals are active in the tissue (see Figure 3.12).

A particularly promising new development is **fast magnetic resonance imaging,** which can produce pictures less than a second apart (compared with 5 to 10 minutes apart for other techniques). Fast MRI dis-

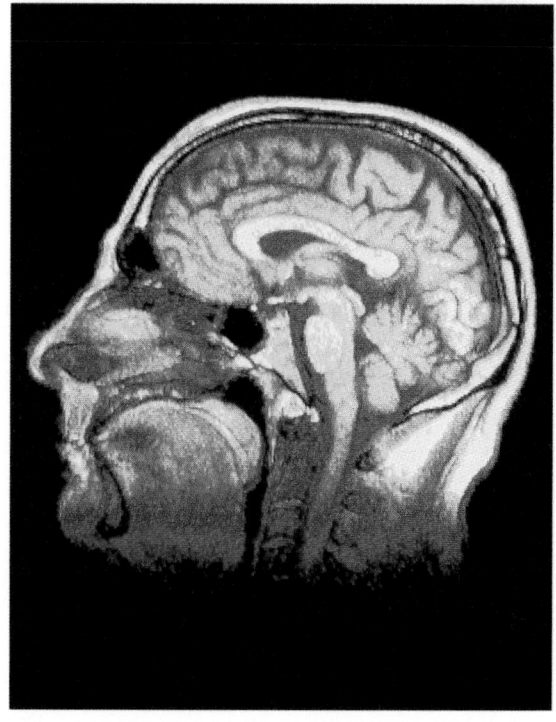

plays the pattern of blood flow throughout the brain (Kwong & others, 1992; see Figure 3.12b). Researchers can now, quite literally, watch thoughts being produced within the brain as different regions of the brain light up when subjects are given problems to solve.

Advances in every area of brain research are making this one of the most exciting frontiers of psychology. The brain is beginning to yield its many secrets to scientists, yet we have still only begun to learn about this wondrous organ. As one observer noted, ''If the brain were so simple that we could understand it, we would be so simple that we couldn't'' (Pugh, 1977).

██ ▭

Brain Structure and Functions

The human brain (shown in Figure 3.13) consists of three major divisions: the **hindbrain,** which is the lowest and most primitive level of the brain; the **midbrain,** which lies above the hindbrain; and the **forebrain.** The forebrain contains the cerebrum, the biological seat of Einstein's creativity, Hitler's mad vision of world conquest, Mother Teresa's compassion, and that which makes you a unique human being.

In an evolutionary sense, your brain is far older than you are. The brain's structure represents perhaps 500 million years of development and fine tuning. This many-layered organ has been likened to an onion. Level upon level has been added to the simple nerve nets that constitute the nervous systems of primitive animals. At the brain's core, the hindbrain structures govern the basic physiological functions, such as breathing and heart rate, that keep us alive. These we share with all other vertebrates (animals having backbones). Built upon these basic structures are other systems that involve progressively more complex functions—sensing, emoting, wanting, thinking, reasoning. Evolutionary theorists believe that these structures developed because they were needed for survival as animals faced more complex environmental demands. Let us, therefore, travel up the brain from the spinal cord to the two sides, or hemispheres, of the cerebral cortex. As we do, we move from basic biological survival functions toward those that define the human mode of being.

The Hindbrain

As the spinal cord enters the brain, it enlarges to form the medulla and the pons, the structures that compose the stalklike **brain stem.** Attached to the brain stem is the other major portion of the hindbrain, the cerebellum. Buried within the brain stem is the reticular formation, which extends from the hindbrain into the midbrain.

► Figure 3.12b *The newly developed fast MRI allows researchers to study ongoing brain activity without invading the brain in any manner. In this series of photos, the fast MRI is used to study the response of the visual cortex (whose location is shown in part a) to the intermittent presentation of a light stimulus. The scan detects small differences in cerebral blood flow, providing a measure of the activity of the neurons. The top right photo (b) shows the actual cortical response, with red indicating the neurons that are most active. In the lower series, (c) scans taken 3.5 seconds apart show the brain's response to the on-off pattern of stimulation. (Photos courtesy of John W. Belliveau, Harvard Medical School)*

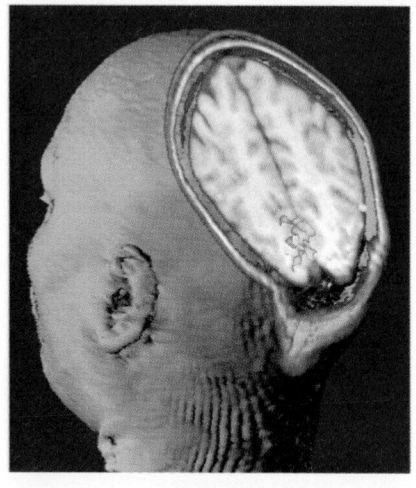
(a)

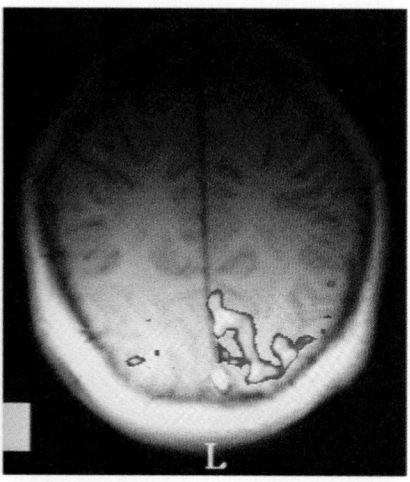
(b)

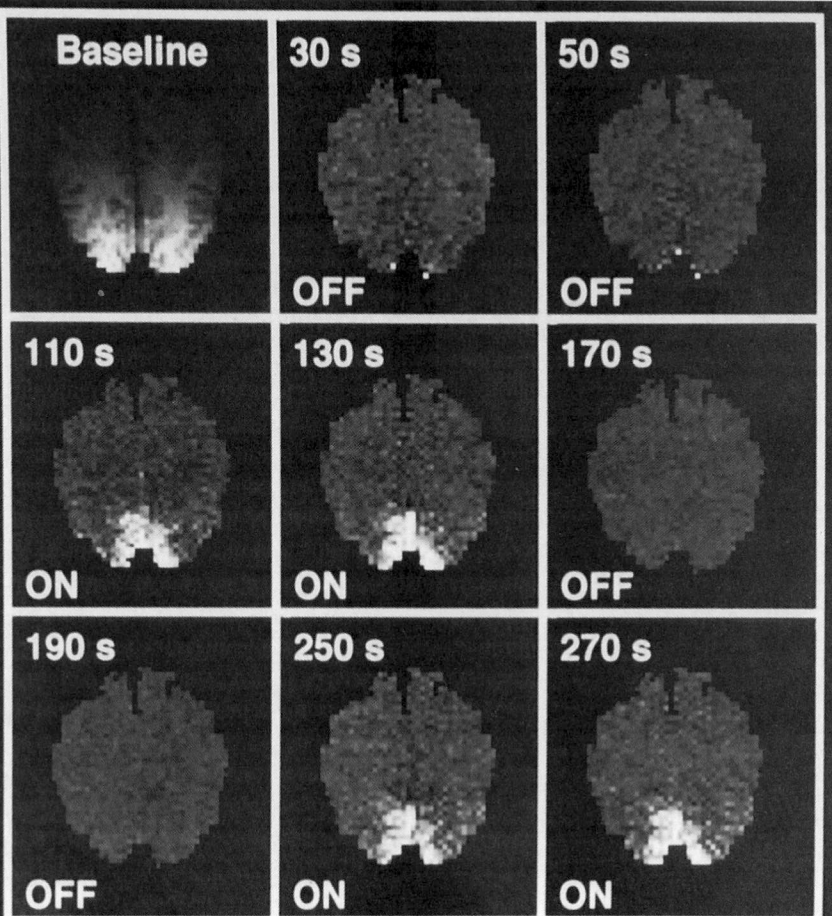
(c)

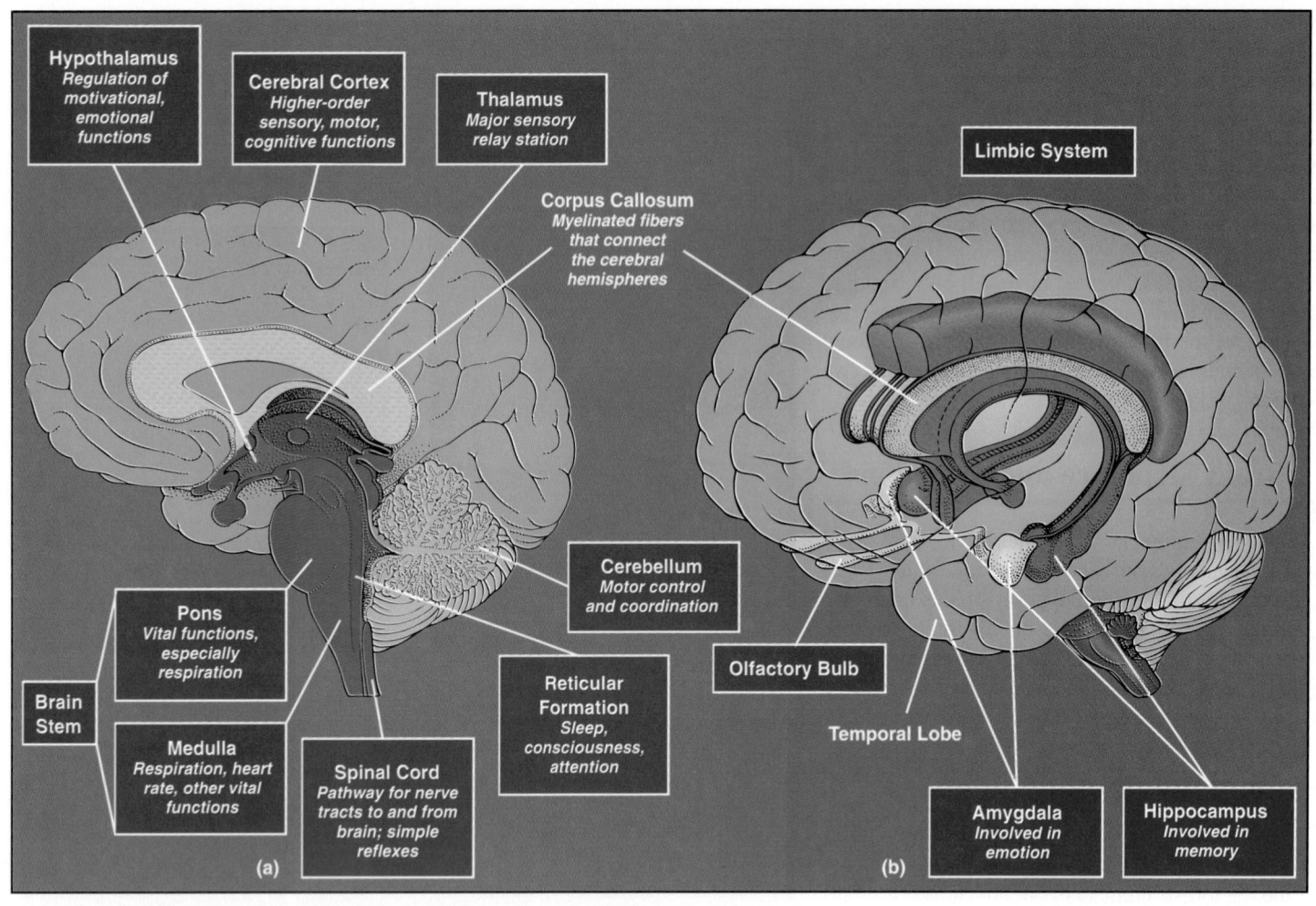

Figure 3.13 (a) The structures of the brain and their major functions:

Hypothalamus
Regulation of motivational, emotional functions

Cerebral Cortex
Higher-order sensory, motor, cognitive functions

Thalamus
Major sensory relay station

Corpus Callosum
Myelinated fibers that connect the cerebral hemispheres

Limbic System

Cerebellum
Motor control and coordination

Pons
Vital functions, especially respiration

Brain Stem

Medulla
Respiration, heart rate, other vital functions

Spinal Cord
Pathway for nerve tracts to and from brain; simple reflexes

Reticular Formation
Sleep, consciousness, attention

Olfactory Bulb

Temporal Lobe

Amygdala
Involved in emotion

Hippocampus
Involved in memory

(a)　　　(b)

Figure 3.13 (a) The structures of the brain and their major functions are shown as they would appear if the brain was sectioned at its midline. (b) This partially transparent view of the brain reveals the structures of the limbic system. Of special interest to psychologists are the amygdala and the hippocampus.

The Medulla and Pons: Life Support Systems

The **medulla** is the first structure encountered after leaving the spinal cord. This inch-and-a-half-long structure, which is well-developed at birth, plays an important role in vital body functions such as heart rate and respiration. The medulla is also a two-way thoroughfare for all the sensory and motor nerve tracts coming up from the spinal cord and descending from the brain. Most of these tracts cross over within the medulla, so the left side of the brain receives sensory input from and exerts motor control over the right side of the body, and the right side of the brain serves the left side of the body. Why this crossover occurs is one of the unsolved mysteries of brain function.

The **pons** (meaning "bridge" in Latin) lies just above the medulla. As its name suggests, it serves as a bridge carrying nerve impulses between higher and lower levels of the nervous system. It also contains motor neurons that control the muscles and glands of the face and neck. Like the medulla, the pons helps to control vital functions, especially respiration. Because the medulla and pons play such a vital role in

our basic bodily functions, damage to them can be fatal. So-called "brain death" occurs when these structures cease to function.

The Reticular Formation: The Brain's Gatekeeper

Buried within the brain stem is the lower portion of the **reticular formation,** a complex mixture of nerve fibers and cell bodies that extends up into the midbrain. This structure receives its name from its resemblance to a reticulum, or net. The reticular formation acts as a kind of sentry, having both alerting and admitting functions. These are represented in an *ascending* part, which sends input to higher regions of the brain, and a *descending* portion, through which higher brain centers can either admit or block out sensory input.

The reticular formation has attracted a great deal of interest from psychologists because of its central role in consciousness, attention, and sleep. The ascending reticular formation rouses higher centers in the brain and prepares them to receive input from our sense organs. Without reticular excitation, messages from our sense organs do not register in consciousness, even though the nerve impulses may reach the appropriate higher areas of the brain. In fact, some general anesthetics work by deactivating neurons of the ascending reticular formation so that the sensory impulses that ordinarily would be experienced as pain never make it through to the sensory areas of the brain (Derogatis, 1986).

Sleep and wakefulness are also affected by the reticular formation. Electrical stimulation of certain portions of the reticular formation can produce sleep in a wakeful animal and wakefulness in a sleeping animal. As you might expect, severe damage to the reticular formation can produce a permanent coma.

The reticular formation is also known to play an important role in attention. Attention is an active process in which only important or meaningful sensory inputs get through to our consciousness; other inputs are toned down or completely blocked out. The descending reticular formation appears to play an important part in this process, serving as a gate through which some inputs are admitted while others are blocked due to signals coming down from higher brain centers.

The Cerebellum: Motor Coordination Center

The **cerebellum** looks like a miniature brain attached to the rear of the brain stem directly above the pons. It is covered by a convoluted or wrinkled cortex having a large number of lobes (hills) separated by fissures (canyons). This covering consists mainly of gray cell bodies (gray matter). The cerebellum is concerned primarily with motor coordination. Specific motor movements are initiated in higher brain centers, but their timing and coordination depend on the cerebellum (Thatch & others, 1992). The cerebellum regulates complex, rapidly changing movements that require exquisite timing, such as those of a ballet dancer or a competitive diver.

Damage to the cerebellum results in severe motor disturbances characterized by jerky, uncoordinated movements, as well as an inability to perform habitual movements such as walking. The behavioral effects of damage to the cerebellum are apparent in the following case:

By the third day, Ed could no longer walk a straight line. His gait involved wide separation of his legs. The timing of his steps was jerky and irregular, causing him to lurch from side to side. He could no longer manage changes in position smoothly, and turning or rising from a chair caused him to nearly fall. By the fifth day he could no longer stand without assistance, and he began to display rapid and jerky eye movements. Ed was ad-

mitted to a hospital, where imaging techniques revealed a cerebellar tumor. Surgical removal of the tumor resulted in a marked improvement in his motor coordination (Gazzaniga & others, 1979).

The Midbrain

The midbrain, which lies just above the hindbrain, contains important clusters of sensory and motor neurons, as well as many sensory and motor fiber tracts that connect higher and lower portions of the nervous system. The sensory portion of the midbrain contains important relay centers for the visual and auditory systems. Here, nerve impulses from the eyes and ears are organized and sent to forebrain structures involved in visual and auditory perception (Kimble, 1992). The midbrain also contains motor neurons that control eye movements. For example, if you see movement out of the corner of your eye, midbrain activity causes your eyes to swing toward the source of the movement in order to identify it. Extending well into the core of the midbrain is the upper portion of the reticular formation.

The Forebrain

The most profound biological difference between your brain and that of a lower animal is the size and complexity of your forebrain, particularly your cerebral cortex. The forebrain consists of two large cerebral hemispheres that wrap around the brain stem, as well as a number of important structures buried in the central regions of the hemispheres. We will consider these inner structures first.

The Thalamus: The Brain's Switchboard

The **thalamus** is located above the midbrain. It resembles two small footballs, one within each cerebral hemisphere. The thalamus is an important sensory relay station and has sometimes been compared to a switchboard that organizes sensory inputs and routes them to the appropriate areas of the brain. The visual, auditory, and body senses all have major relay stations in the thalamus.

The Hypothalamus: Motivation and Emotion

The **hypothalamus** (literally, "under the thalamus") consists of tiny groups of neuron cell bodies that lie at the base of the brain, above the roof of the mouth. This small structure plays a major role in many aspects of motivational and emotional behavior, including sexual behavior, temperature regulation, sleeping, eating, drinking, aggression, and the expression of emotion. Damage to the hypothalamus can disrupt all of these behaviors. For example, destruction of one area of a male's hypothalamus results in a complete loss of sex drive; damage to another portion produces an overwhelming urge to eat and marked obesity. Through its connection with the pituitary gland (the master gland of the endocrine system), the hypothalamus also directly controls many hormonal secretions that regulate sexual development and sexual behavior, metabolism, and reactions to stress.

The Limbic System: Learning and Organization of Behavior

As we journey up through the brain, we come to the **limbic system,** which consists of a number of structures lying deep within the cerebral hemispheres. These structures, which are shaped like a wishbone, encircle the brain stem. The limbic system has many neural interconnections and forms an important partnership with the hypothalamus (so much so that some brain scientists consider the hypothalamus part of the limbic system). It seems to be involved in organizing the behaviors needed to satisfy the basic motivational and emotional urges that arise in the hypothalamus, and one of its structures, the **hippocampus,** appears to be a site where learning occurs in both simple and complex animals (Squire, 1992). If certain parts of your limbic system were injured, you would be unable to carry out organized sequences of actions to satisfy your needs. A small distraction would make you forget what you had set out to do. Many instinctive activities in lower animals, such as fleeing from danger, mating, attacking, and feeding, appear to be organized by the limbic system (Davis, 1992).

The limbic system also affects emotional behavior, particularly aggression. A key structure is the **amygdala,** which organizes emotional response patterns (Le Doux, 1992). Lesions in certain areas of this structure produce extreme rage reactions to the slightest provocation, whereas damage to other areas results in an inability to respond aggressively, even in self-defense.

Finally, the limbic system contains "reward" and "punishment" areas that have important motivational functions. When a reward area is stimulated with a mild electric current, animals will learn and perform behaviors in order to keep receiving their electrical reward; likewise, they will learn to stop performing behaviors that are followed by stimulation of one of the punishment regions (White & Milner, 1992; Wise & Rompre, 1989). Certain drugs, such as cocaine and marijuana, seem to induce pleasure by stimulating limbic reward areas (Grilly, 1989; Holloway, 1991). Depressed patients seem to have abnormally low levels of some of the neurotransmitters that activate the reward areas, suggesting the limbic system's possible role in human depression as well (Depue & Iacono, 1989).

The Cerebral Hemispheres: Crown of the Brain

The cerebral cortex, which forms the outermost layer of the human brain, is the crowning achievement of brain evolution. Fish and amphibians have no cerebral cortex, and the progression from more primitive to more advanced mammals is marked by a dramatic increase in the proportion of cortex compared to the total amount of brain tissue. This quarter-inch-thick sheet of gray matter is not essential for survival in the way that the brain stem structures are, but it is essential for life as a human being. How much so is evident in this description of patients who, as a result of an accident during prenatal development, were born without a cerebral cortex:

> Some of these individuals may survive for years, in one case of mine for twenty years. From these cases, it appears that the human brain-stem and thalamic "preparation" sleeps and wakes; it reacts to hunger, loud sounds, and crude visual stimuli by movement of eyes, eyelids, and facial muscles; it may see and hear, it may be able to taste and smell, to reject the unpalatable and accept such food as it likes; it can itself utter crude sounds, can cry and smile, showing displeasure when hungry and pleasure, in a babyish way, when being sung to; it may be able to perform spontaneously crude movements of its limbs (Cairns, 1952, p. 109).

The two **cerebral hemispheres** constitute the largest part of the human brain. They consist of an outer gray cortex composed primarily of neuron cell bodies and unmyelinated fibers and an internal white core of myelinated fibers that connect the hemispheres with each other and with other parts of the brain.

Most sensory systems send information to specific regions of the cerebral cortex. Motor systems that control the activity of muscles and glands are situated in other cortical regions. The basic organization of the cortex's sensory and motor areas is quite similar from rat to human. However, the relative proportion of **association cortex,** made up of interneurons that are neither sensory nor motor but are instead involved in more complex behavioral functions, increases dramatically from lower animals to humans.

Because the cortex is wrinkled and convoluted, like a wadded-up piece of paper, a tremendous amount of cortical tissue is compressed into a relatively small space inside the skull. Perhaps three quarters of the cerebral cortex's total surface area lies within its folds, or *fissures.* Two of these fissures serve as major landmarks within each hemisphere. The **central fissure** divides the cerebrum into anterior (front) and posterior (rear) halves, and the **lateral fissure** runs from front to rear along the side of the brain. On the basis of these landmarks, neurologists have divided each hemisphere into four lobes: **frontal, parietal, occipital,** and **temporal.** The frontal lobe is separated from the parietal lobe by the central fissure, the temporal lobe lies beneath the lateral fissure, and the occipital lobe is at the rear of the brain (see Figure 3.14).

Fortunately, the cerebrum is not a random collection of neurons. Each of the four cerebral lobes is associated with particular sensory and motor functions (also shown in Figure 3.14). Speech and skeletal motor functions are localized in the frontal lobe. The area governing body sensations is located in the parietal lobe immediately behind the central fissure. Messages from the auditory system are sent to a region in the top of the temporal lobe, and the brain's visual area is located in the occipital lobe (Kaas, 1987). The areas in Figure 3.14 that are not correlated with either sensory or motor functions are the association areas.

Two areas that govern the understanding and production of speech are localized in the cortex. **Wernicke's area,** located in the left temporal lobe (see Figure 3.14) is involved in speech comprehension. The area is named for Carl Wernicke, who in 1874 discovered that damage to this cortical region left patients unable to understand written or spoken speech. These patients often spoke in meaningless gibberish. **Broca's area,** located in the left frontal lobe, is involved in the production of speech through its connections with the motor cortex region that controls the muscles used in speech. Its discoverer, Paul Broca, found that damage to this frontal area left patients with the ability to comprehend speech but not to express themselves in words or sentences. These two speech areas normally work in concert when we are conversing with another person. They allow us to comprehend what the other person is saying and to express our thoughts (Werker & Tees, 1992). In this example, input from the ears to the auditory cortex is routed to Wernicke's area for comprehension, and nerve impulses from Wernicke's area to Broca's area result in the forming of a verbal response.

The Motor Cortex

The cortical area that controls body movements lies in the frontal lobe just in front of the central fissure.

Figure 3.14 *Division of the brain into frontal, parietal, occipital, and temporal lobes, and localization of sensory and motor functions in the cortex. The remainder is primarily association cortex, consisting of interneurons.*

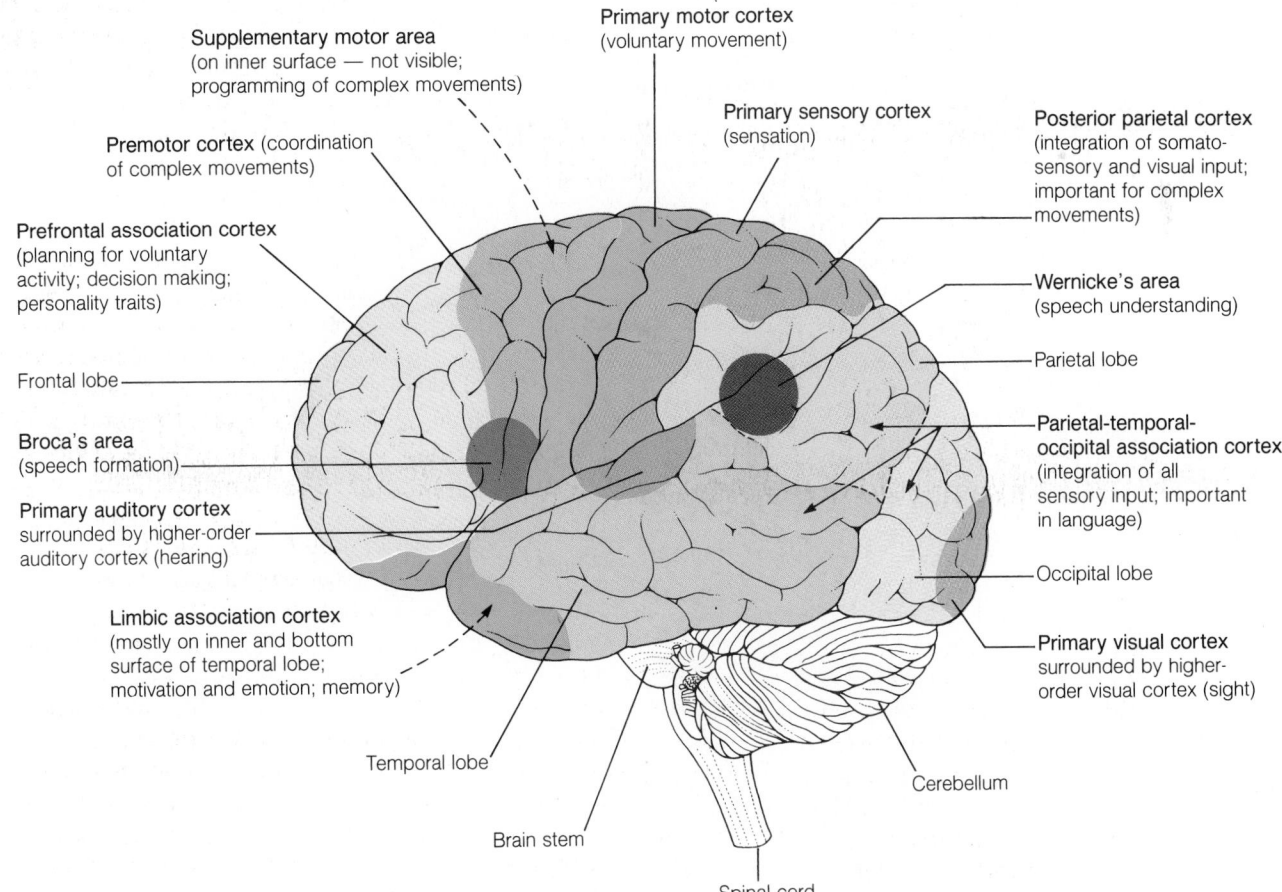

Supplementary motor area (on inner surface — not visible; programming of complex movements)

Primary motor cortex (voluntary movement)

Primary sensory cortex (sensation)

Posterior parietal cortex (integration of somato-sensory and visual input; important for complex movements)

Premotor cortex (coordination of complex movements)

Prefrontal association cortex (planning for voluntary activity; decision making; personality traits)

Frontal lobe

Broca's area (speech formation)

Primary auditory cortex surrounded by higher-order auditory cortex (hearing)

Limbic association cortex (mostly on inner and bottom surface of temporal lobe; motivation and emotion; memory)

Wernicke's area (speech understanding)

Parietal lobe

Parietal-temporal-occipital association cortex (integration of all sensory input; important in language)

Occipital lobe

Primary visual cortex surrounded by higher-order visual cortex (sight)

Cerebellum

Temporal lobe

Brain stem

Spinal cord

As noted earlier, each hemisphere governs movement on the opposite side of the body. Specific body areas are represented in different parts of the motor cortex, and the amount of cortex devoted to each area depends on the complexity of the movements that are involved. The left side of Figure 3.15 shows the relative organization of function within the motor cortex. Electrical stimulation of a particular point results in movements of the muscles governed by that part of the motor cortex.

The Sensory Cortex

Input from each of the sensory systems is directed to particular areas of the cortex known as **cortical projection areas.** With the exception of taste and smell, at least one projection area in the cortex has been identified for each of the senses.

The projection areas for heat, touch, cold, and our senses of balance and body movement (kinesthesis) lie behind the motor cortex, separated from it by the central fissure. Each side of the body projects to the opposite hemisphere. Like the motor area, this somatic sensory area is basically organized in an upside-down fashion, and the amount of cortex devoted to each body area is directly proportional to that region's sensitivity. The organization of the sensory cortex is shown on the right side of Figure 3.15. As far as our sensory cortex is concerned, we are mainly fingers, lips, and tongue.

The auditory area lies on the surface of the temporal lobe at the side of each hemisphere. Each ear sends messages to the auditory areas of both hemispheres, so the loss of one temporal lobe has little effect on hearing. The sensory projection area for vision lies at the rear of the occipital lobe. Here messages from the visual receptors are analyzed, integrated, and translated into sight. As in the auditory system, both eyes send input to both hemispheres.

Within each sensory area, neurons respond to particular aspects of the sensory stimulus; they are tuned in to specific aspects of the environment. Thus, certain cells in the visual cortex fire only when a subject looks at a particular kind of stimulus, such as

Figure 3.15 *Both the somatic sensory and the motor cortex are highly specialized so that every site is associated with a particular part of the body. The amount of cortex devoted to each body part is proportional to the sensitivity of that area's motor or sensory functions. Both the sensory and motor cortex are arranged in an upside-down fashion and serve the opposite side of the body.*

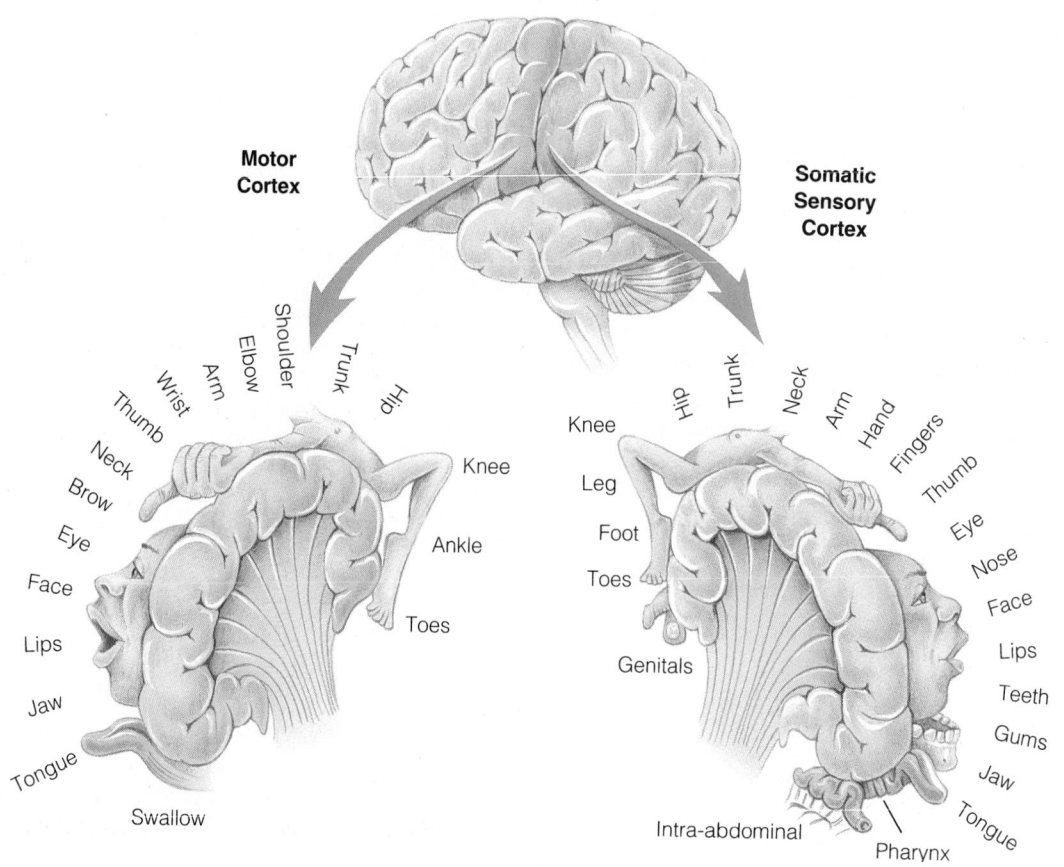

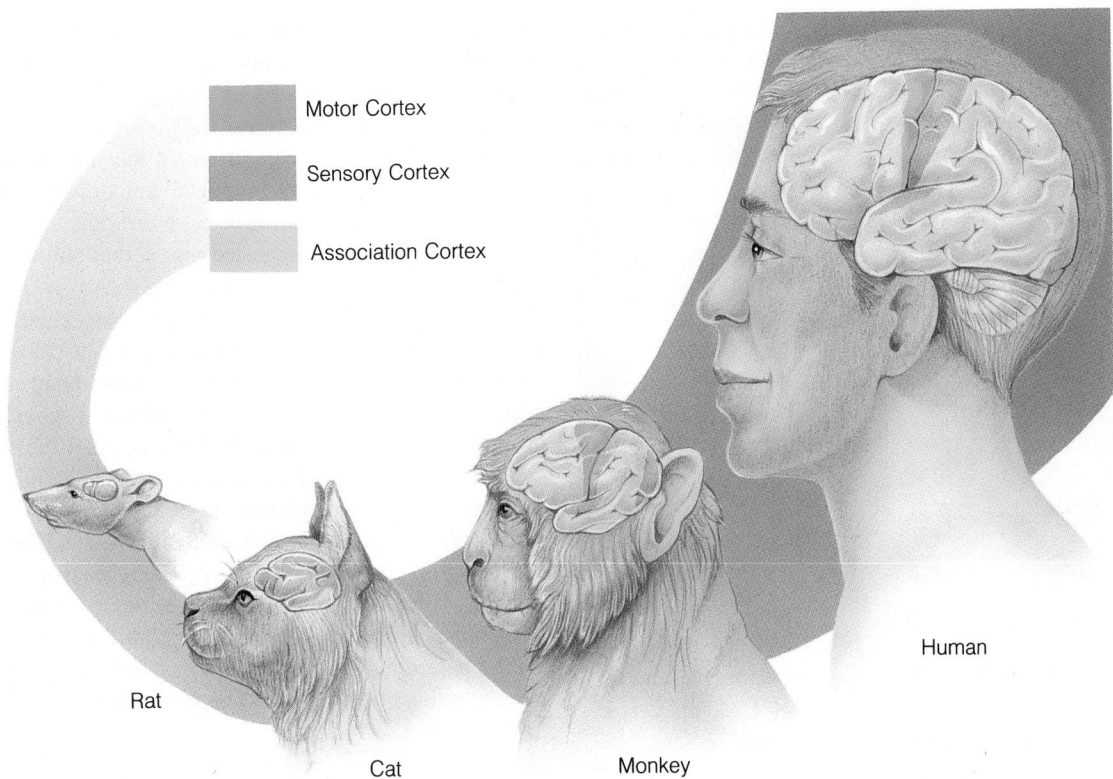

Motor Cortex

Sensory Cortex

Association Cortex

Rat

Cat

Monkey

Human

Figure 3.16 *The amount of association cortex increases greatly as one moves up the phylogenetic scale, underlying species' differences in "higher" mental functions.*

a vertical line or a corner (Hubel & Wiesel, 1979). In the auditory cortex, some neurons fire only in response to high tones, whereas others respond only to tones having some other specific frequency. Many of these single-cell responses are present at birth, suggesting that we are "prewired" to perceive many aspects of our sensory environment (Shair & others, 1991).

The Association Cortex

The association cortex covers the largest area of the cerebral hemisphere. Association areas are known to be critically involved in perception, language, and thought. Damage to specific parts of the association cortex causes disruption or loss of functions such as speech, understanding, thinking, and problem solving. As seen in Figure 3.16, the amount of association cortex increases dramatically as we move from animals to humans.

Together with underlying structures such as the hippocampus, the association cortex plays a crucial role in complex cognitive behaviors, as is seen in the case of a young man who developed a severe memory impairment after a temporal lobe operation for epilepsy:

He could no longer recognize the hospital staff, apart from Dr. Scoville himself, whom he had known for many years; he did not remember and could not relearn the way to the bathroom, and he seemed to retain nothing of the day-to-day happenings in the hospital. . . .

Although he mows the lawn regularly, and quite expertly, his mother has to tell him where to find the lawnmower, even when he had been using it the day before. The same forgetfulness applies to people he has met since the operation, even to those neighbors who have been visiting the house regularly for the past six years. He does not recognize any of them if he meets them in the street (Milner, 1966, p. 113).

The Frontal Lobes:
The Human Difference

One prominent neurologist has suggested that the entire period of human evolutionary existence can be considered the "age of the frontal lobe." This mass of cortex residing behind our eyes and forehead hardly exists in mammals such as mice and rats. The frontal lobes comprise about 3.5 percent of the cerebral cortex in the cat, 7 percent in the dog, and 17 percent in the chimpanzee. In a human, the frontal lobes constitute 29 percent of the cortex (see Figure 3.17). The site of such human qualities as self-awareness, planning, initiative, and responsibility, the frontal lobes are in some respects the most mysterious and least understood part of the brain.

Much of what we know about the frontal lobes comes from detailed studies of patients having brain damage there. Such people often cannot carry out tasks, even when they can verbalize what they should do. It is as if will gets separated from action. Frontal lobe damage results not so much in a loss of intellectual abilities as in an inability to plan and carry

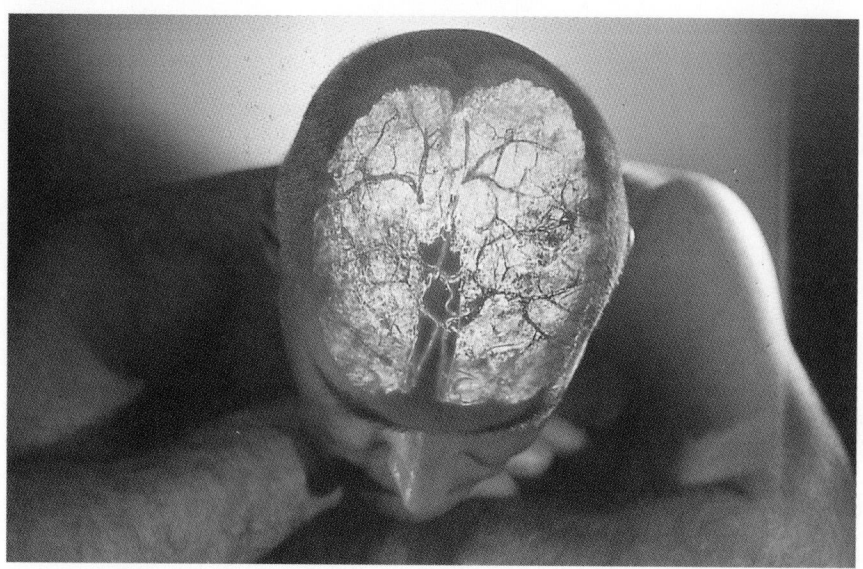

Figure 3.17 *The frontal lobes (behind and above the eyes) are the seat of many functions that define human nature.*

out a sequence of actions, as well as difficulty in correcting actions that are clearly erroneous and self-defeating (Shallice & Burgess, 1991). This was evident in the case of Phineas Gage, whose frontal lobe was severely damaged by the spike that tore through his brain; he became "capricious and vacillating" (Harlow, 1868).

Attitudes of apathy and lack of concern are common in patients with frontal lobe damage, as typified in this conversation between a neurologist and a patient:

> Testing left-right discrimination was oddly difficult, because she said left or right indifferently (though there was not, in reaction, any confusion of the two. . .). When I drew her attention to this, she said: "Left/right. Right/left. Why the fuss? What's the difference?"
>
> "Is there a difference?" I asked.
>
> "Of course," she said with a chemist's precision. . . . "But they mean nothing to *me*. They're no different *for me*. Hands. . . Doctors. . . Sisters," she added, seeing my puzzlement. "Don't you understand? They mean nothing—nothing to me. *Nothing means anything*. . . at least to me."
>
> I found this somewhat shocking—her friends and family did too—but she herself, though not without insight, was uncaring, indifferent, even with a sort of funny-dreadful nonchalance or levity. . . . Mrs. B., though acute and intelligent, was somehow not present—"desouled"—as a person (Sacks, 1986, p. 174).

Hemispheric Localization: The Left and Right Brains

The cerebral hemispheres are connected by a broad white band of nerve fibers called the **corpus callosum**. This neural bridge acts as a communication link between the two hemispheres and allows them to function as a single unit. However, clinical obser-

vations and research studies indicate differences between the psychological functions of the two cerebral hemispheres.

Medical studies of patients who had suffered various types of brain damage provided the first clues that certain complex psychological functions were localized within one hemisphere or the other. The patients' impairments suggested that verbal abilities and speech are localized in the left hemisphere, as are mathematical and symbolic abilities. Most left-handed people seem, like right-handers, to have speech localized in the left hemisphere, but about a third of them process speech in the right hemisphere or in both hemispheres (Bloom & Lazerson, 1988).

When Broca's or Wernicke's speech areas are damaged, the result is **aphasia**, the partial or total loss of the ability to communicate. C. Scott Moss, a clinical psychologist who temporarily became aphasic and was paralyzed on his right side as the result of a left-hemisphere stroke that affected both the speech comprehension and production areas, has provided some insights into what it is like to be aphasic:

> I recollect trying to read the headlines of the Chicago Tribune but they didn't make any sense to me at all. I didn't have any difficulty focusing; it was simply that the words, individually or in combination, didn't have meaning, and even more amazing, I was only a trifle bothered by that fact. . . .
>
> The second week I ran into a colleague who happened to mention that it must be very frustrating for me to be aphasic since prior to that I had been so verbally facile. (I) later found myself wondering why it was not. I think part of the explanation was relatively simple. If I had lost the ability to converse with others, I had also lost the ability to engage in self-talk. In other words, I did not have the ability to think about the future—to worry, or anticipate or perceive it—at least not with words. Thus, for the first five or six weeks after hospitalization I simply existed. So the fact that I could not use words even internally was, in fact, a safeguard (Moss, 1972, pp. 4–5).

When the right hemisphere is damaged, the clinical picture is quite different. Language functions are not ordinarily affected, but the person has great difficulty in performing certain spatial tasks. She or he may have a hard time understanding complex pictures or recognizing faces and may even forget a well-traveled route (Springer & Deutsch, 1989). It appears that mental imagery, musical and artistic abilities, and the ability to perceive and understand spatial relationships are primarily right-hemisphere functions.

The two hemispheres differ not only in the cognitive functions that reside there but also in the emotions that do. EEG studies have shown that the right hemisphere is relatively more active when negative emotions such as sadness and anger are being experienced. Positive emotions such as joy and happiness are accompanied by relatively greater left-hemisphere activation (Fox & Davidson, 1991; Tomarken & others, 1992).

The Split Brain: Two Minds in One Body?

Despite the localization of specific functions in the two cerebral hemispheres, the brain normally functions as a unified whole because the two hemispheres communicate with one another through the corpus callosum. But what would happen if this communication link between the two hemispheres were cut? Would we, in effect, produce two different and largely independent minds in the same person? A series of Nobel Prize–winning studies by Roger Sperry (1970) and his associates at the California Institute of Technology suggest that something akin to this can happen when we ''split'' the brain.

Like many scientific advances, this one resulted from human misfortune. Some patients suffer from a form of epilepsy characterized by a seizure—an uncontrolled electrical discharge of neurons—that begins on one side of the brain and spreads to the other hemisphere. Years ago, neurosurgeons found that some patients could be helped by cutting the nerve fibers of the corpus callosum. The operations successfully prevented the seizures from spreading to the other hemisphere through the corpus callosum, and they seemed to have no negative side effects on other psychological functions. Sperry's studies of patients who had had such operations involved some ingenious ways to test the functions of the two hemispheres after the corpus callosum was cut.

Split-brain research was made possible by the way in which our visual input to the brain is ''wired.'' Some of the fibers of the optic nerve from each eye split and cross over at the **optic chiasma** and travel to the opposite brain hemisphere (see Figure 3.18). Fibers that transmit messages from the right side of each eye's visual field project to the left hemisphere; fibers from the visual field's left half project to the right hemisphere. Despite this arrangement, we experience a unified visual world rather than two half-worlds because the hemispheres' visual projection areas are normally connected by the corpus callosum. When the corpus callosum is cut, however, visual input to one hemisphere can be restricted by projecting the stimulus to either the right side of the visual field (in which case it goes to the left hemisphere) or to the left side of the visual field (which sends it to the right hemisphere).

In Sperry's experiments, **split-brain patients** looked at a fixation point, a dot on the center of a screen, while slides containing visual stimuli (words, pictures, and so on) were flashed briefly to the right

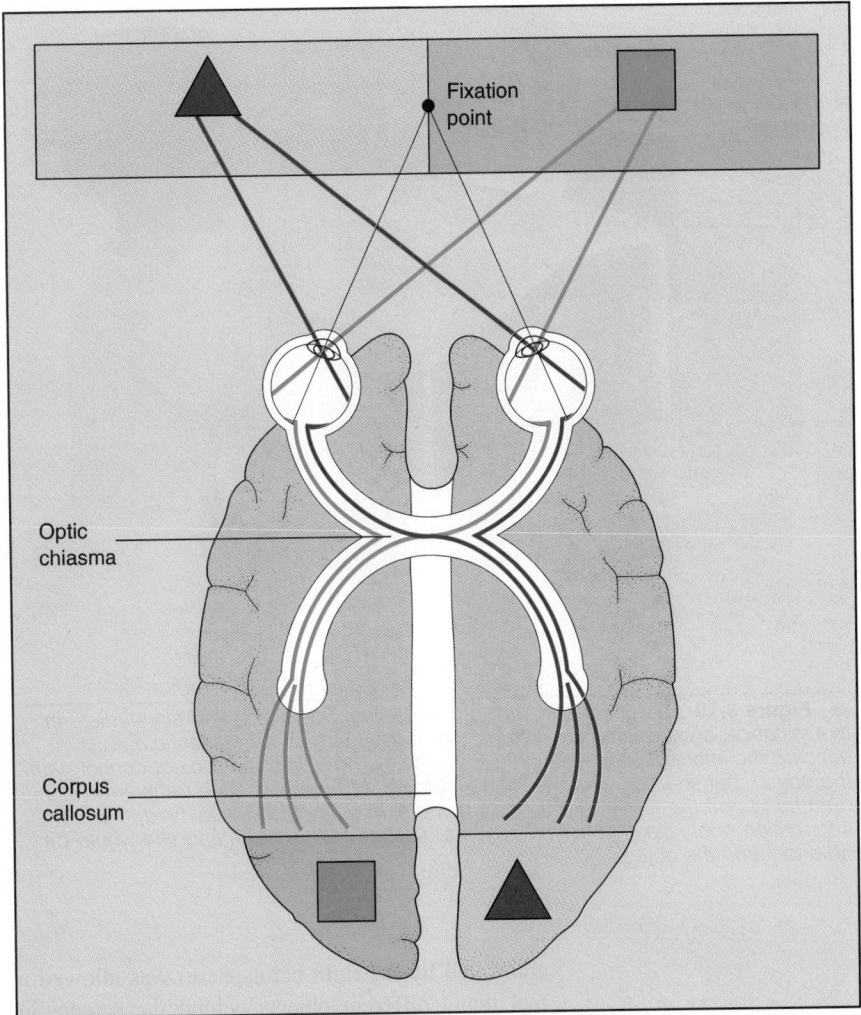

Figure 3.18 *The visual system's anatomy made studies of split-brain subjects possible. Images entering the eye are reversed by the lens. The right side of each eye's field projects to the visual cortex of the left hemisphere, whereas the left visual field projects to the right hemisphere. When the corpus callosum is cut, the two hemispheres no longer communicate with each other. By presenting stimuli to either side of the visual fixation point, researchers can control which hemisphere receives the information.*

or left side of their visual field (see Figure 3.19). The subject could respond verbally or with movements of either hand. The hands were concealed behind a screen so that they could not be seen by the subject.

Sperry found that when words were flashed to the language-rich left hemisphere, subjects could immediately say them and could write them with their right hand (which is controlled by the left hemisphere). However, if words were flashed to the right hemisphere, the subjects could neither say nor write them, because the right hemisphere does not have well-developed language abilities.

This did not mean, however, that the right hemisphere was incapable of recognizing objects. If a picture of an object (for example, a spoon) was flashed to the right hemisphere and the left hand (which is

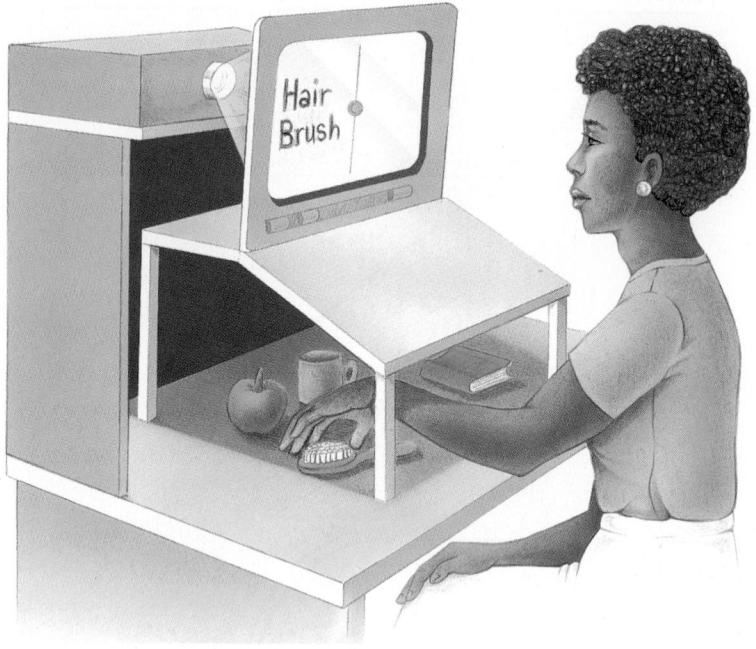

← **Figure 3.19** *The apparatus shown was used in Sperry's split-brain studies. In this instance, a word is briefly projected to the left side of the visual field, thus sending the information to the right hemisphere. The split-brain subject cannot name the object, but she can find it with her left hand. If the object were transferred to her right hand or if the word were flashed to the right side of the visual field, the information would be sent to the language-rich left hemisphere, and she would be able to name the object.*

controlled by the right hemisphere) was allowed to feel many different objects behind the screen, including the object shown in the picture, the person's hand would immediately select the spoon and hold it up. As long as the person continued to hold the spoon in the left hand, sending sensory input about the object to the "nonverbal" right hemisphere, the subject was unable to name it. However, if the spoon was transferred to the right hand, the person could immediately name it. In other words, until the object was transferred to the right hand, the left hemisphere had no knowledge of what the right hemisphere was experiencing.

Later research showed the right hemisphere's definite superiority over the left in the recognition of patterns. In one study, three split-brain subjects were presented with photographs of similar-looking faces projected in either the left or right visual fields. On each trial, the subjects were asked to select the photo they had just seen from a set of 10 cards. As Figure 3.20 shows, the right hemisphere was far more accurate than the left hemisphere, probably because the similar faces could not be differentiated by means of a verbal description (Gazzaniga & Smylie, 1983).

Some psychologists have suggested that what we call the conscious self resides in the left hemisphere,

because consciousness is based on our ability to verbalize about the past and present. Is the right hemisphere, then, an unconscious (nonverbal) mind? Yes, these psychologists answer, except when it communicates with the left hemisphere across the corpus callosum. When the connections between the two hemispheres are cut, the experiences of the right hemisphere are not part of conscious awareness. A person may have emotions or other experiences without being able to verbalize them, as in the following case:

> In one of our experiments we would present a series of ordinary objects and then suddenly flash a picture of a nude woman. This evoked an amused reaction regardless of whether the picture was presented to the left hemisphere or to the right. When the picture was flashed to the left hemisphere of a female patient, she laughed and verbally identified the picture as a nude. When it was later presented to the right hemisphere, she said in reply to a question that she saw nothing, but almost immediately a sly smile spread over her face and she began to chuckle. Asked what she was laughing at, she said, "I don't know. . . nothing. . . Oh—that funny machine." Although the right hemisphere could not describe what it had seen, the sight nevertheless elicited an emotional response like the one evoked from the left hemisphere (Gazzaniga, 1967, p. 29).

Is the right hemisphere totally lacking in language ability? The initial conclusion of split-brain researchers that the right hemisphere has no language capabilities has softened somewhat in recent years. At least 5 of the first 44 split-brain subjects studied in the United States gave clear evidence of language skills in the right hemisphere. These skills ranged from simply being able to name objects to complex language skills that were essentially identical to left-hemisphere abilities. In other patients, the right hemisphere demonstrated reading abilities as well as the ability to recognize isolated words (Levy, 1983). It now appears that there may be more hemispheric interaction in language than was originally assumed. Recent PET scan studies measuring cerebral blood flow in the brains of normal people indicate that both hemispheres are involved in speaking, reading, and listening. The same is undoubtedly true of other brain functions (Springer & Deutsch, 1989).

Brain Damage and Recovery of Function

Because brain injuries can have such devastating effects on psychological and behavioral functioning, the study of various types of brain damage and the factors that influence recovery from them has interested psychologists for many years. Several common types of brain injury differ in their effects on a person's physical and psychological welfare.

Varieties of Brain Damage

Concussions and contusions result from severe blows to the head. A **concussion** is a jarring of the brain which can cause minor damage to neurons and blood vessels. **Contusions** are more serious, because the brain may be severely bruised or even torn when it strikes the hard inner surface of the skull. Both injuries commonly result in a loss of consciousness followed by confusion, headaches, and loss of memory for the events leading up to the blow, but the symptoms are typically more severe and long lasting in contusions because of the more serious tissue damage. People usually show complete recovery from concussions, but contusions may have more permanent effects, especially if repeated (as is seen in punchdrunk boxers who didn't duck often enough).

Strokes, or **cerebrovascular accidents** (CVAs), result either from a blood clot that blocks circulation or from the bursting of a blood vessel in the brain. In either case, blood supply is disrupted, causing neurons to die from lack of oxygen or glucose (see Figure 3.21). Depending on which area of the brain is affected, speech and memory may be temporarily or permanently impaired, and varying degrees of paralysis are common. Strokes are the third-ranking cause of death in the United States and Canada, after heart attacks and cancer (Comer, 1992). Approximately 500,000 new strokes and 200,000 deaths from strokes occur in the United States each year. More than 80 percent of stroke victims are over the age of 65, but people of any age can be affected. The risk of stroke is increased by smoking, high blood pressure, and elevated serum cholesterol levels (Taylor, 1991).

The term **epilepsy** comes from a Greek word meaning "to seize" or "to attack." About 3 out of every 1,000 Americans suffer from some form of epilepsy. Epileptic seizures result from uncontrolled electrical discharges, most often produced by scar tissue in the brain (Levinthal, 1990). The scar tissue may result from disease or injury, or it may have been present at birth. Whether or not seizures occur as well as the extent to which they spread depend in part on the location of the scar tissue in the brain. The temporal lobe is especially prone to seizures.

Finally, **tumors** (uncontrolled cell growth) can appear in any part of the brain. Tumors' effects depend on their size and the role that neurons damaged or affected by them play in physical or psychological functions. Tumors can be treated successfully with surgery, radiation therapy, or chemotherapy.

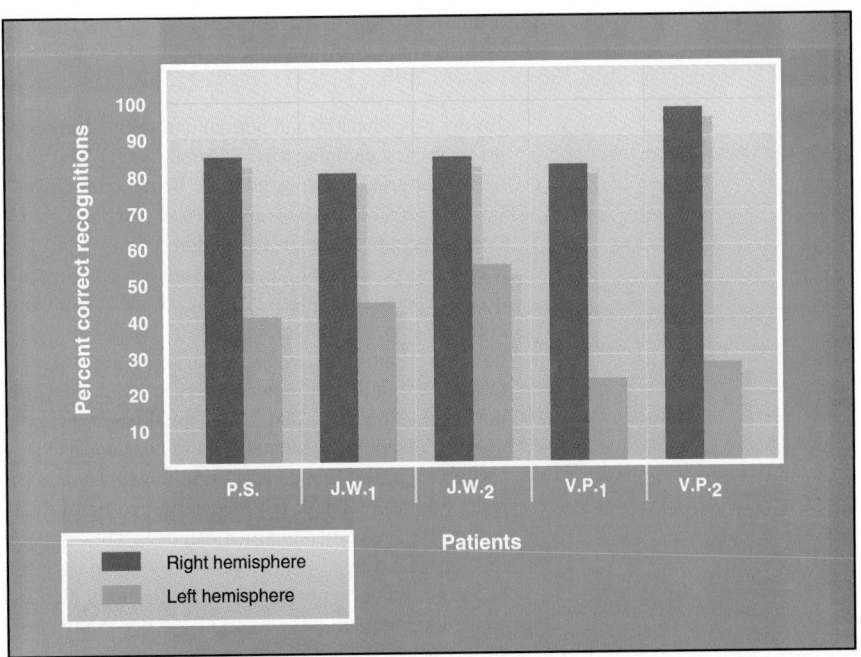

Figure 3.20 *Facial recognition accuracy by the right and left hemispheres of three split-brain patients. Patients J. W. and V. P. were tested twice. Because the faces were quite similar, the left hemispheres' verbal abilities were not very useful; the pattern-recognition abilities of the right hemisphere contributed to more accurate recognition of faces. (Gazzaniga & Smylie, 1983).*

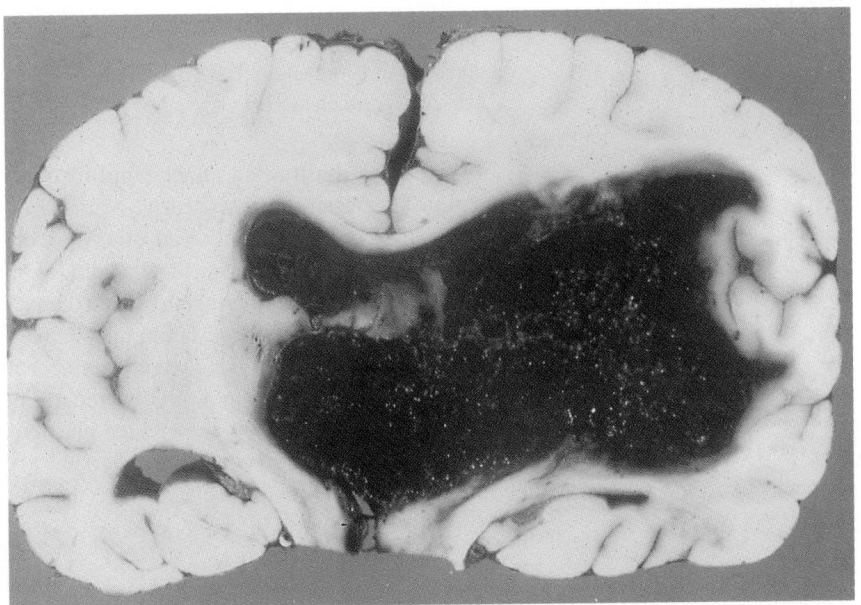

Neural Plasticity

As noted earlier, neurons are not replaced when they die. This means that when an injury results in the destruction of brain tissue, other neurons must take over the lost functions if recovery is to occur. The brain's ability to transfer functions in this manner is known as **neural plasticity.** At times the brain shows

Figure 3.21 *The devastating damage that can be caused by a stroke is shown in the brain of a deceased patient. Note the enlargement of the right hemisphere as a result of a massive hemorrhage.*

an amazing flexibility and recovery of function, as the following case illustrates:

Jimmy was a healthy and normal five year old about to go on his first camping trip in the mountains. The night before the trip, he appeared more irritable than usual, but in the rush of packing no one took much notice. He later woke up crying in the middle of the night and seemed to be in pain, but he had no temperature and dropped back off to sleep in a few minutes after being comforted by his mother's presence. By the next day, however, Jimmy's parents were sure that something was terribly wrong. Jimmy appeared very drowsy and would not speak. He was rushed to a hospital where his condition was quickly evaluated. Jimmy was aphasic—he could not speak—and he was slightly paralyzed on the right side of his body. It was determined that he had suffered a stroke of unknown origin in the temporal lobe of his left hemisphere. A blood vessel in his brain had ruptured or had been blocked by a blood clot and an area of the brain "downstream" from the site of the stroke had died when its blood supply was interrupted.

For Jimmy's father, it was like reliving a nightmare. His own grandfather had also suffered a stroke. The old man never recovered his speech and he remained paralyzed until his eventual death. But for Jimmy, the chances of recovery were much greater because of his young age. Nature took its course, and within three months, Jimmy was again speaking normally, and his paralysis had disappeared completely. He was ready to resume the life of a normal five year old. All that remained of his ordeal was a frightening memory (Gazzaniga & others, 1979).

Jimmy's case illustrates a rather rapid recovery of function after brain injury. Clearly, neural reorganization in Jimmy's brain allowed other neurons to take over the functions of those that had died. This case also illustrates a general principle: Brain damage suffered early in life is less devastating than damage suffered as an adult. Jimmy recovered his speech quickly; his great-grandfather never recovered it. The brain seems to be capable of far greater plasticity early in life. For example, when researchers cut the neural pathways in a young monkey's arm, the area of the sensory cortex that formerly had received this input soon began to respond with evoked potentials when the animal's face was touched (Barnes, 1990). In another study using rats, a motor tract connecting the motor cortex to a limb was cut. Within a few hours, stimulation of the point in the motor cortex that formerly had stimulated the paralyzed area resulted in movements in a different part of the body as the motor cortex reorganized itself (Jacobs & Donoghue, 1991).

Studies using the electron microscope may explain why such plasticity is possible early in life. Peter Huttenlocher of the University of Chicago found that a 1- to 2-year-old child has about 50 percent more brain synapses than mature adults do (Huttenlocher, 1979). This overproduction of synapses may help to explain why children can recover from brain damage more quickly and completely than adults. But, sadly, the days of synaptic riches don't last forever. Unused or weaker synapses deteriorate with age so that the brain loses some of its potential flexibility (Kolb, 1989). Apparently, this is another instance of the adage, "Use it or lose it."

Yet even adults can recover some functions after brain injury. When nerve tissue is destroyed, surviving neurons can restore functioning by modifying themselves in two major ways (Kolb & Whishaw, 1989; Sokolov, 1992). First, they can alter their structure by sprouting enlarged networks of dendrites and extending axons from surviving neurons to form new synapses. The second mechanism is neurochemical in nature. Surviving neurons may make up for the loss of other cells by increasing the amount of neurotransmitters they release, or postsynaptic neurons may increase their sensitivity to transmitter substances by forming more receptors so that they can fire in response to lower concentrations of their transmitter.

Are natural healing processes the only hope for victims of neurological damage? There is hope that new treatments will help victims recover lost functions. The following feature focuses on some recent advances in neuroscience.

 **ENHANCING HUMAN PERFORMANCE**

NEW HOPE FOR VICTIMS OF NEUROLOGICAL DAMAGE

The sterile laboratory of the brain researcher may seem far removed from the not-so-tidy world of people with neurologically based performance problems. Yet, discoveries in the laboratory are offering hope to millions of people who have lost abilities ranging from basic movement to the most complex memory and thought processes. Physiological psychologists and other neuroscientists are developing and testing revolutionary treatment approaches to neurological problems that, until recently, physicians could only diagnose and helplessly observe. Given the incidence of strokes, spinal injuries, Parkinson's disease, muscular dystrophy, Alzheimer's disease, and other neurologically based disorders, there is good reason to expect that you or someone close to you will one day benefit from one of these new treatments.

A challenging yet promising area of research focuses on the restoration of functions that are lost when neurons are destroyed by physical trauma or disease. Ten years ago, dead neurons were thought impossible to replace or repair. Although severed fingers and toes can be reattached and regain their functions, the same has not been true in the damaged spinal cord and brain. Thus, paralyzed individuals with spinal injuries have had little hope for recovery of motor and sensory functions. Patients having Parkinson's disease—a disorder involving uncontrollable tremors, progressive difficulties in movement, and body rigidity caused by the destruction of dopamine-producing cells in the brain—have also had little hope for a cure. They could obtain some relief with L-dopa, a drug that restores missing dopamine and helps alleviate movement problems. Unfortunately, after 5 to 10 years on the drug, many patients must stop taking it because of serious side effects, whereupon their symptoms return and become progressively worse (National Institutes of Health, 1989).

Hope for victims of neurological disorders has been rekindled by the discovery that damaged central nervous system neurons can be replaced—that the impossible is possible. In one experiment, axons in rat spinal cords were severed, and the neurons from which the axons originated were placed under a weak electrical current. This current stimulated regrowth of axons out of the cell bodies. The axons grew over the injury to seek their predamage positions on the other side of the cut (National Institutes of Health, 1989). In another study, nerve tissue was taken from the legs of eight hamsters that had been blinded by severing the optic nerve, which carries sensory information from the eye to the brain. The transplanted nerve tissue was laid along the trail that the experimenters wanted optic nerve regrowth to follow. The researchers knew that transplanted tissue could not conduct signals, but they hoped that it might guide regenerating nerves along the desired path. After about four

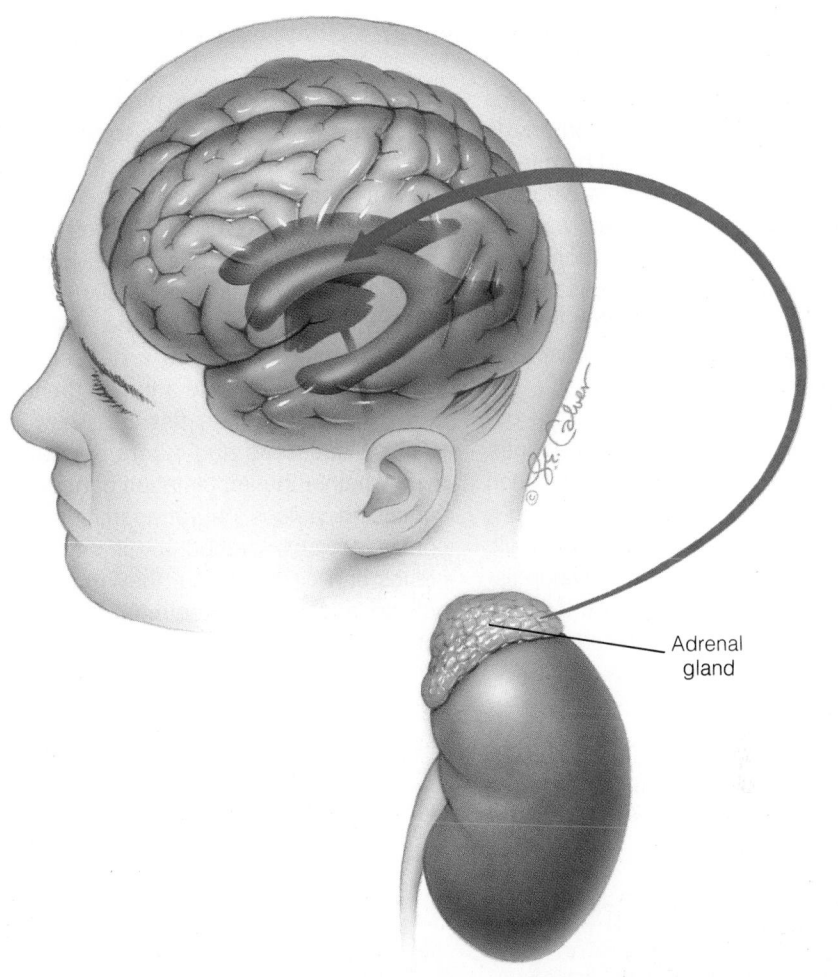

Figure 3.22 *In a new experimental treatment for Parkinson's disease, dopamine-producing cells from a patient's adrenal gland are implanted in a motor control area of the brain to increase dopamine production and reduce motor symptoms.*

Adrenal gland

months, electrical responses occurred in the visual cortex in six of the hamsters when a light was flashed in front of their eyes (Keirstead & others, 1989). Establishing what the animals were "seeing" through their regenerated optic nerves awaits further research, but this study shows that neural regeneration can occur over a fairly long distance. More importantly, such research, although very preliminary, gives scientists hope that neural regeneration may one day fix what has long been irreparable—the severed spinal cord.

Attempts have also been made to transplant healthy neural tissue into diseased areas of the brain in order to restore neurological function. These techniques are still highly experimental and their effectiveness is uncertain, but some intriguing results have been reported in both animals and humans. In several an-

imal studies, dopamine-producing cells in the brains of mice were destroyed, producing Parkinson-like motor symptoms. The researcher then implanted healthy, dopamine-producing neurons taken from the brains of mouse embryos into the region of destruction, an area deep in the brain that regulates body movement. The grafted cells were not rejected and soon began to produce dopamine, resulting in the animals' recovery from their motor disorder (Fine, 1986).

Successes with animal implants have stimulated experiments with human patients. Scientists have taken dopamine-producing cells from patients' own adrenal glands and implanted them into the brain region affected by Parkinson's disease in the hope that they would produce the dopamine needed to reverse the patients' symptoms (see Figure 3.22). So far, the results have been variable, with dramatic improvement occurring in some cases and no improvement in others. In one of the successes reported by a team of Mexican scientists, a patient who had been confined to a wheelchair was out playing soccer with his son 10 months after the surgery (Madrazo & others, 1987).

Recent studies suggest that human fetal tissue is even better for transplants than a patient's own adrenal tissue, because fetal tissue seems to secrete dopamine more readily and to last longer. However, serious concerns have been raised by antiabortionists who fear that a market for aborted fetuses may result, and researchers are trying to develop tissue cultures of human fetal cells that can be used in transplants (National Institutes

of Health, 1989). In the meantime, scientists are trying to answer some important questions about the transplant procedure: What factors have accounted for the successes and for the failures experienced so far? How long will an implant last? Will the disease eventually kill the implanted cells as it did the formerly healthy neurons? Is there a danger that the implant will grow like a tumor, thereby damaging surrounding tissue? Answers to these questions and others will determine whether the implantation of neurons containing various neurotransmitters becomes a viable procedure. If the techniques can be perfected, they may spur new advances in the treatment of Parkinson's disease as well as disorders such

as Alzheimer's disease (which is linked to the destruction of neurons that produce acetylcholine) and epilepsy (which often results from a deficiency of the inhibitory transmitter GABA).

While waiting for answers to the mysteries of nerve regeneration, scientists have been using microcomputer technology to develop *functional neuromuscular stimulation* devices for patients who are paralyzed as a result of spinal cord injuries. Implanted electrodes pass a current into paralyzed muscles to stimulate a movement. "Smart" probes can be implanted in the spinal cord to intercept electrical impulses coming down from the brain, route them around the damaged area of the spinal cord, and deliver them

Figure 3.23 *A functional neuromuscular stimulation device that forms a sensorimotor closed loop from limb to brain enables this patient, normally paralyzed from the neck down, to use his left arm and hand for various activities.*

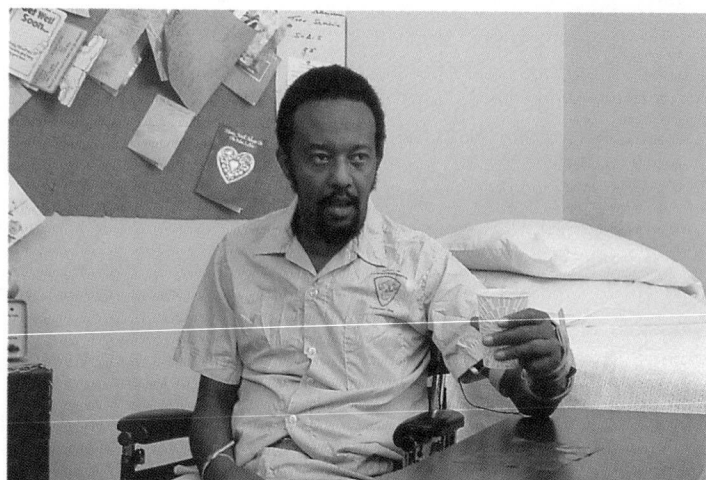
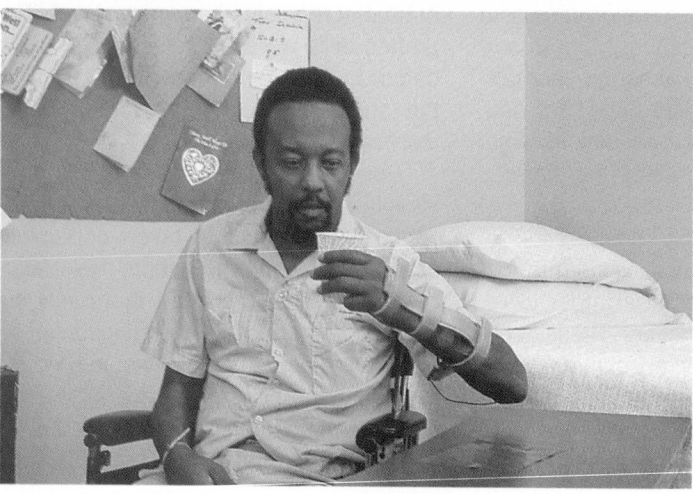

to the appropriate muscles. Similar probes can pick up nerve impulses from the muscles of paralyzed limbs and relay them back to the brain, creating a sensorimotor closed loop that allows a person to "will" a limb movement and then feel its response so that corrective movements can be made. Figure 3.23 shows a paralyzed patient using a prosthetic sensorimotor device that allows him to use his arm and hand to drink from a paper cup without spilling a drop or crushing the cup. The patient can also comb his hair, write with a pen, and perform other movements. The development and refinement of such devices could change the lives of people whose paralyzed bodies are now incapable of sensation or movement.

The current "Decade of the Brain" promises dramatic advances in our knowledge of how the nervous system operates, and this knowledge is certain to revolutionize the treatment of many performance-disrupting disorders, bringing new hope to millions of afflicted people.

■ ▭
The Autonomic Nervous System

Our ability to behave and, indeed, to survive depends on the coordinated functioning of our internal organs and glands. These structures are also involved in many aspects of motivation, emotional behavior, and response to stress. The body's internal environment is regulated largely through the activities of the autonomic nervous system and the endocrine system.

The peripheral nervous system, which connects the body's organs and muscles with the brain and spinal cord, consists of two divisions (refer back to Figure 3.7). The somatic system, which we have already discussed, includes the major sensory systems and the motor nerves that activate skeletal muscles. The other major division, the **autonomic nervous system,** controls the glands and the smooth (involuntary) muscles that form the heart, blood vessels, and the lining of the stomach and intestines. The autonomic system controls such body functions as respiration, circulation, and digestion, and it is especially important in emotional behavior.

The autonomic nervous system consists of two subdivisions, the **sympathetic nervous system** and the **parasympathetic nervous system** (see Figure 3.24). Often these two divisions affect the same organ or gland in opposing ways. By working together, the two divisions can maintain a delicately balanced internal state known as **homeostasis.**

We will consider the autonomic nervous system in greater depth when we discuss emotion (Chapter 13). For now, we will briefly outline its two major divisions and their functions.

Sympathetic Nervous System

The sympathetic neurons have their cell bodies in the spinal cord. They run out through the ventral root to a chain of cell bodies called **sympathetic ganglia,** which run parallel to the spinal cord. In the sympathetic ganglia these fibers synapse with nerves that fan out to activate the internal organs of the body.

The sympathetic system has an arousal function and tends to act as a unit. For example, when you encounter a stressful situation, your sympathetic nervous system simultaneously speeds your heart rate, dilates your pupils, slows down your digestive system, increases your rate of respiration, and, in general, mobilizes your body to confront the stressor. This is sometimes called the *fight or flight response.* The sympathetic system also stimulates the adrenal glands of the endocrine system to secrete stress hormones, such as adrenaline, into the bloodstream in order to maintain or increase the level of arousal.

Parasympathetic Nervous System

Whereas the sympathetic system tends to act as a unit, the parasympathetic system is more specific in its actions, affecting one or a few organs at a time. The parasympathetic nervous system slows down body processes and maintains a state of tranquility. Thus, your sympathetic system speeds up your heart rate; your parasympathetic system slows it down. The two divisions of the autonomic nervous system work together to maintain a state of equilibrium in the internal organs. Some acts require a sequence of sympathetic and parasympathetic activities. For example, sexual activity in the male involves erection of the penis (a primarily parasympathetic function) followed by ejaculation (a primarily sympathetic function) (Masters & others, 1988).

The autonomic nervous system thus produces its effects in two ways: by direct neural stimulation of body organs and by stimulating the release of hormones from the glands of the endocrine system.

■ ▭
The Endocrine System

Although the endocrine system is not a part of the nervous system, it has important interactions with it. The **endocrine system** consists of numerous glands distributed throughout the body. Like the nervous system, the endocrine system's function is to convey

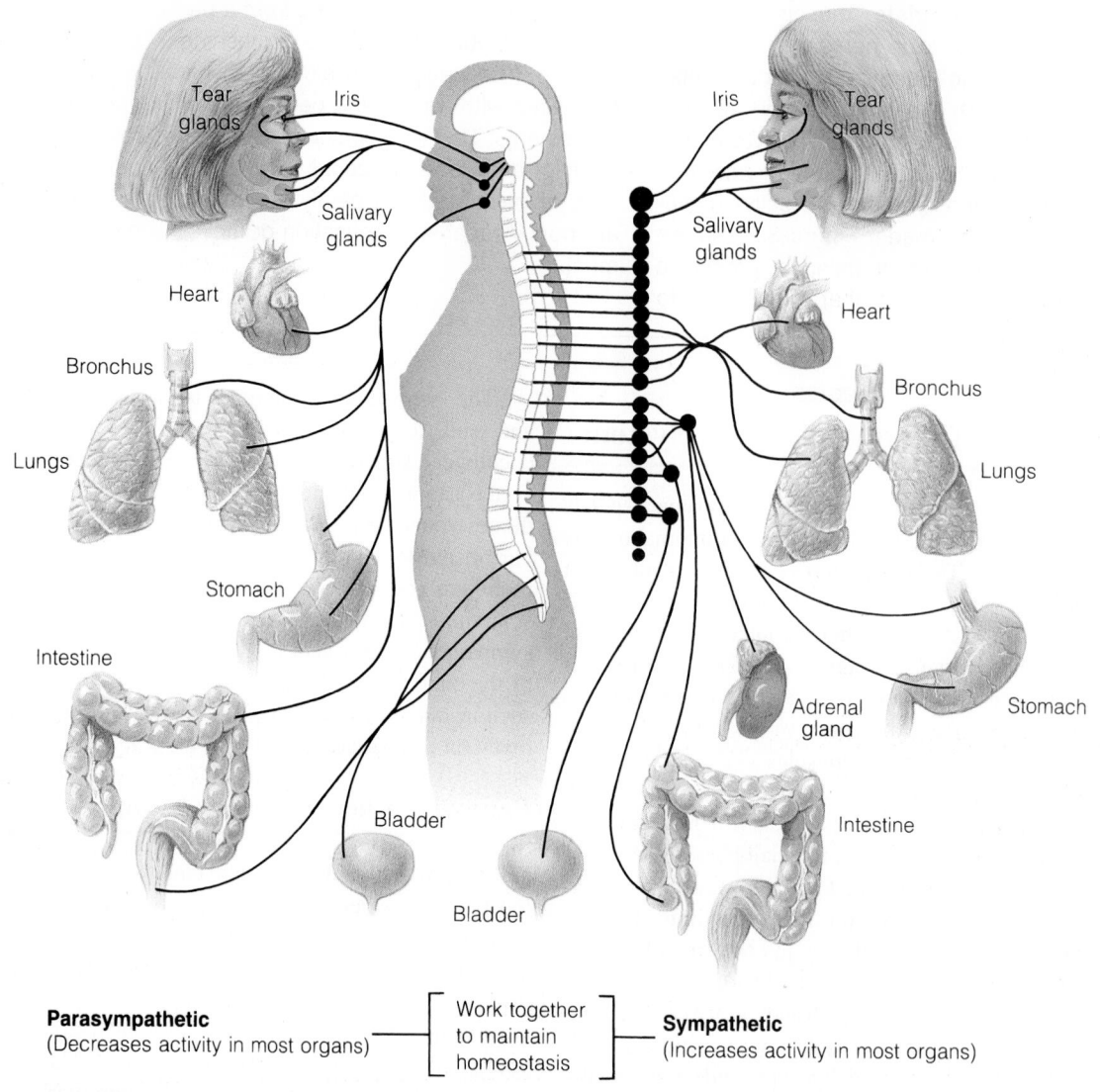

Parasympathetic
(Decreases activity in most organs)

Work together
to maintain
homeostasis

Sympathetic
(Increases activity in most organs)

Figure 3.24 *The sympathetic branch of the autonomic nervous system arouses the body and speeds up its vital processes, whereas the parasympathetic division slows down body processes. The two divisions work together to maintain an equilibrium within the body.*

information from one area of the body to another. Rather than using nerve impulses, however, the endocrine system conveys information in the form of chemical messengers called **hormones,** which are secreted into the bloodstream.

The nervous system transmits information rapidly, with the speed of nerve impulses. The endocrine system is much slower because delivery of its messages depends on the rate of blood flow. Also, whereas a particular neuron in the nervous system usually synapses directly with a relatively small number of other neurons, hormones travel throughout the body in the bloodstream and can reach millions of individual cells. Thus, when the brain has important information to transmit, it has the choice of sending it in the form of nerve impulses to a relatively small number of neurons or by means of hormones to a large number

of cells. Often, both communication networks are used.

Just as neurons have receptors for certain neurotransmitters, cells in the body (including neurons) have receptor molecules that respond to specific hormones from the endocrine glands. The approximate locations of the endocrine glands within the human body and a list of their functions are presented in Figure 3.25. Many of the hormones secreted by these glands affect psychological development and functioning (Becker & others, 1992). As noted earlier, the hypothalamus has many connections with the pituitary gland, the master gland that stimulates other glands to action.

Of special interest to psychologists are the **adrenal glands,** because their actions relate to the functions of both the central and the autonomic ner-

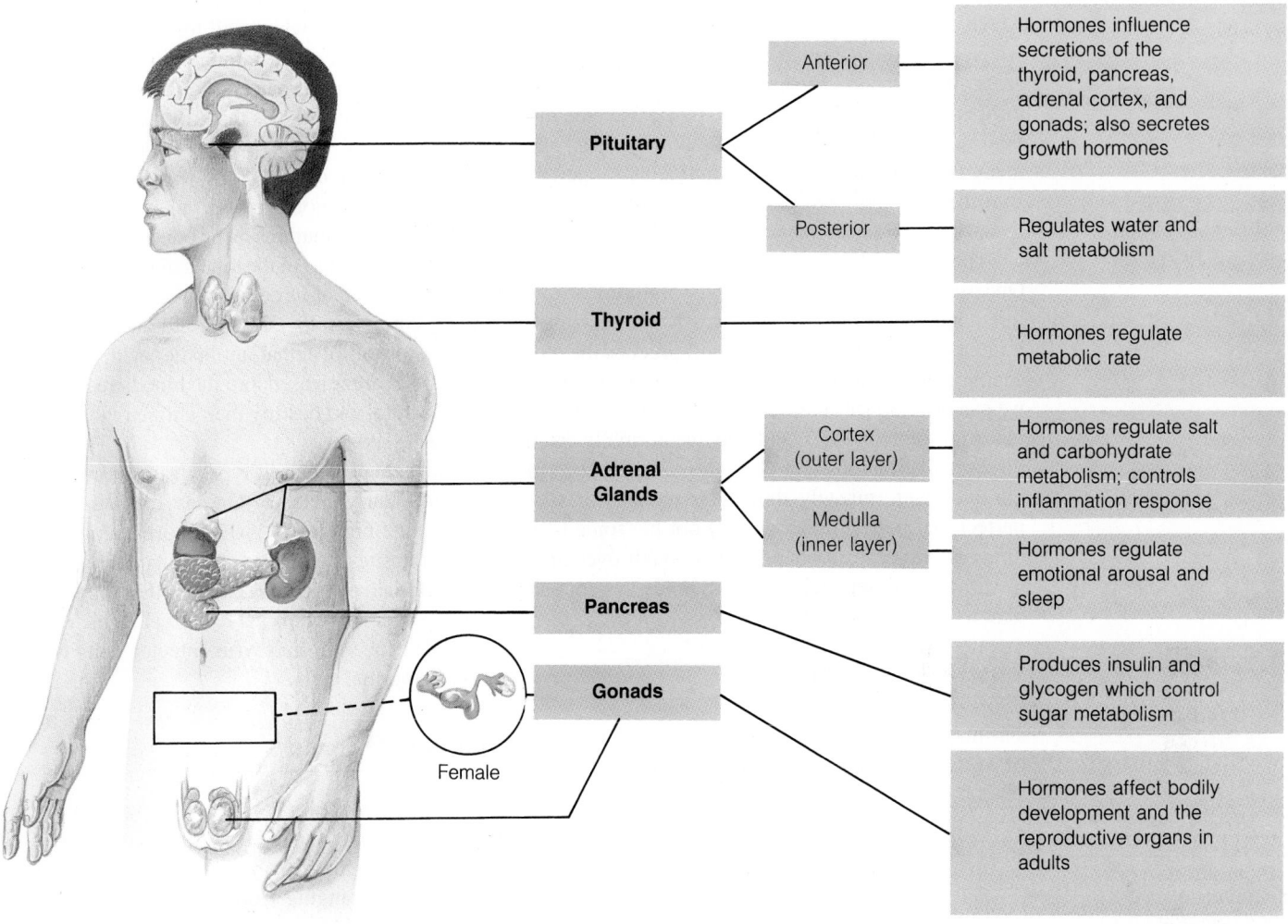

Pituitary	Anterior	Hormones influence secretions of the thyroid, pancreas, adrenal cortex, and gonads; also secretes growth hormones
	Posterior	Regulates water and salt metabolism
Thyroid		Hormones regulate metabolic rate
Adrenal Glands	Cortex (outer layer)	Hormones regulate salt and carbohydrate metabolism; controls inflammation response
	Medulla (inner layer)	Hormones regulate emotional arousal and sleep
Pancreas		Produces insulin and glycogen which control sugar metabolism
Gonads		Hormones affect bodily development and the reproductive organs in adults

Female

Figure 3.25 *The glands that comprise the endocrine system and the effects of their hormones on bodily functions.*

vous systems. The adrenal glands have two distinct anatomical divisions. The **adrenal cortex,** the outer portion of the gland, is quite literally a drug factory. It secretes about 50 different hormones that regulate many metabolic processes within the body, including metabolism of carbohydrates, functioning of the reproductive organs, and balancing of sodium- and potassium-containing body fluids that surround the neurons and other body cells.

Lying beneath the adrenal cortex is the **adrenal medulla**. It secretes epinephrine (also known as adrenaline) and norepinephrine (noradrenaline). Epinephrine and norepinephrine can elicit many of the same effects as those produced by the sympathetic nervous system. In an emergency, the adrenal medulla is activated by the sympathetic branch of the autonomic nervous system, and epinephrine or norepinephrine is secreted into the bloodstream. Because hormones remain in the bloodstream for some time, the action of the adrenal medulla and its hormones is especially important in circumstances of prolonged stress.

Brain, Behavior, and the Immune System

At this moment, microscopic sentinels patrol every part of your body, searching for biological invaders that could disable or kill you. They are part of your immune system, a wondrous biological defense network that scientists are only now beginning to understand. The immune system has extensive two-way communication links with both the nervous and endocrine systems, a fact that is revolutionizing the ways in which we think about the interaction of mind and body (Ader & others, 1990; Gorman & Kertzner, 1991). Recently, two young sciences, immunology and psychology, have joined forces to study how the mind can operate as either healer or slayer, creating a new discipline known as **psychoneuroimmunology.**

A normal, healthy immune system is a wonder of nature. Programmed into each member of this legion of tiny defenders is an innate ability to recognize which cells and molecules belong to the body and which are foreigners that must be destroyed. Such recognition occurs because substances known as **antigens** trigger a biochemical response from the immune system. Bacteria, viruses, abnormal cells, and many chemical molecules with antigenic properties start the wars that rage inside our bodies every moment of every day.

The immune system has a remarkable memory. Once it has encountered one of the millions of different antigens that enter the body, it will recognize it immediately in the future and will produce the biochemical weapons needed to destroy it. This is why we can develop vaccines to protect animals and people from some diseases, and why we normally catch diseases like mumps and chicken pox only once in our lives. Unfortunately, though the memory may be perfect, our body's defenses may not be; some bacteria and viruses can change just enough over time to slip past the sentinels in our immune system and give us this year's cold or flu.

The Defense Team

The major actors in the immune system are two kinds of white blood cells, or **lymphocytes.** Together with several other kinds of cells, lymphocytes detect and sound the alarm on invaders, produce antibodies, destroy the target, call off the attack, and clean up the debris.

Immune system cells originate in the bone marrow and then follow different developmental paths. Some are carried by the bloodstream to the endocrine system's thymus gland, where hormones cause them to develop into **T-cells** (T as in thymus). There are several types of T-cells, the most important of which are **helper T-cells,** which call for or increase the aggressive action of other immune cells; **killer T-cells,** which destroy cancerous and virus-infected cells by secreting toxic chemicals that kill the foreign tissue; and **suppressor T-cells,** which suppress the activity of other immune cells.

The other major lymphocyte is the **B-cell**, so named because it matures in the bone marrow. B-cells are an important part of the total defense system. They have receptors that fit certain antigens like a key fits a lock. Once B-cells ''lock'' onto an antigen, they create a torrent of lethal antibodies with similar receptors that are released into the bloodstream to seek out, attach to, and destroy their antigen victims (Ada & Nossal, 1987).

Two other major cell types in the immune army are particularly notable. One is the **macrophage** (Greek for ''big eater''), which oozes, amoeba-like, around the site of an infection, eating debris, viruses, and bacteria (see Figure 3.26). Another immune system defender is the **natural killer cell,** which attacks and kills cancerous and virus-infected cells without harming normal cells.

Immune Disorders

The immune system is a natural marvel that is easy to take for granted when it is functioning normally. Unfortunately, things can sometimes go awry, with consequences ranging from discomfort to devastation.

The antigens to which the immune system responds can originate externally (a flu virus or a pollen) or internally (a cancerous tumor). Problems arise when the immune system has either an underactive or an overactive response. Figure 3.27 shows the consequences of under- and overreaction.

An underactive immune-system response to external antigens is dramatically illustrated in acquired immune deficiency syndrome (AIDS). The human immunodeficiency virus (HIV) attacks the helper T-cells, which are so important in strengthening the response of other immune cells (see Figure 3.28). A healthy person has twice as many helper T-cells as suppressor T-cells (which reduce the action of other immune cells); in an AIDS victim, the reverse is true (Taylor, 1991). As a result, the individual's immune system holds itself back from attacking invaders, leaving the body defenseless against virtually anything that can infect humans: bacteria, viruses of all kinds, fungi, and protozoa.

An overactive response to an external antigen presents problems in the form of an **allergy.** The immune system produces the symptoms experienced during an allergic reaction. For example, in its violent re-

➡ **Figure 3.26** A macrophage extends several pseudopods to seize bacteria. The bacteria that have already been pulled to the surface of the macrophage will be engulfed and devoured.

action to an allergen, an asthmatic's immune system releases a torrent of histamine, a chemical that causes critical breathing muscles around the bronchial tubes to contract, leaving the asthmatic person wheezing and gasping for air.

Underreaction because of failure to recognize or inability to cope with an internal antigen occurs in cancer. Abnormal body cells are allowed to proliferate, resulting in the formation of tumors.

Finally, certain **autoimmune reactions** result when the immune system attacks the body's own healthy tissue. Somehow, the system mistakenly identifies part of the body as an enemy and attacks it. For example, in rheumatoid arthritis, the immune system attacks the collagen, part of the connective tissue in the joints, causing inflammation, pain, and loss of flexibility.

Immune—Nervous System Interactions

So far, we have learned that the immune system, like the nervous system, has an exquisite capacity to receive, interpret, and respond to specific forms of stimulation. Despite these similarities, research on the two systems proceeded along independent paths for many years, with only a few visionaries suggesting that the two systems might be able to communicate and influence each others' activities. Recent technical advances in biochemistry and the neurosciences have shown, however, that the nervous, endocrine, and immune systems are integrated parts of a communication network so completely underlying our every mental, emotional, and physical action that one expert has dubbed it "bodymind" (Pert, 1986).

Pieces of this communication puzzle began to fall into place with several key discoveries. The first was that selective electrical stimulation or destruction of certain areas of the hypothalamus and cerebral cortex resulted in almost instantaneous increases or decreases in immune-system activity. Conversely, activation of the immune system by injecting antigens into the body resulted in increased electrical activity in several brain regions (Felten & others, 1990).

Research with the electron microscope yielded another important discovery: the thymus, bone marrow, and lymph nodes—all key sites of immune-cell development and activation—are laced with nerve connections to and from the brain. These nerve connections even extend to the lymphocytes themselves. Considering all the "talking" the brain does with the immune system, the two must be communicating something important to one another.

Recent findings have highlighted the chemical connections among the systems and have discredited the notion that the immune system operates in iso-

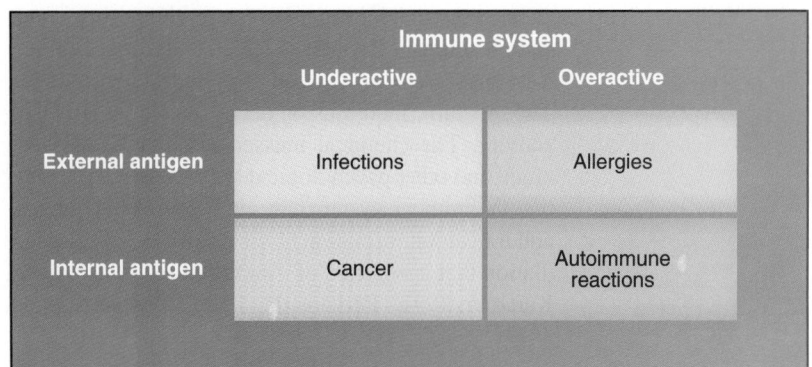

	Immune system	
	Underactive	**Overactive**
External antigen	Infections	Allergies
Internal antigen	Cancer	Autoimmune reactions

Figure 3.27 *Disorders of the immune system created by under- or overreaction to either internal or external antigens.*

lation as a kind of "headless horseman." Much of this research has centered on **neuropeptides,** the 50 to 60 amino acid compounds manufactured by brain cells. Like the neurotransmitters discussed earlier, these chemicals bind to matched receptors on cells and change the cells' functioning in some way. The neuropeptides and their receptors form a highly specific communication network that underlies much of the nervous system's functioning.

Imagine, then, the stir in the scientific community caused by reports from Candace Pert's laboratory at the National Institute of Health that the immune-system cells contain receptors keyed to specific neuropeptides (Pert & others, 1985). This means that the action of immune cells can be directly influenced by chemical messengers from the brain. An equally startling discovery was that immune cells can actually produce hormones, neurotransmitters, and neuropeptides, allowing them to directly influence brain and endocrine system functioning (Goetzl & others, 1990; Roszman & Carlson, 1990). The communication loop is thus a complete one. For example, when immune cells circulating through the blood encounter viruses

Figure 3.28 *Acquired immune deficiency syndrome (AIDS) is caused by the HIV virus. Here, the virus (blue) attacks a helper T-cell (pink), whose function is to increase immune-system activity.*

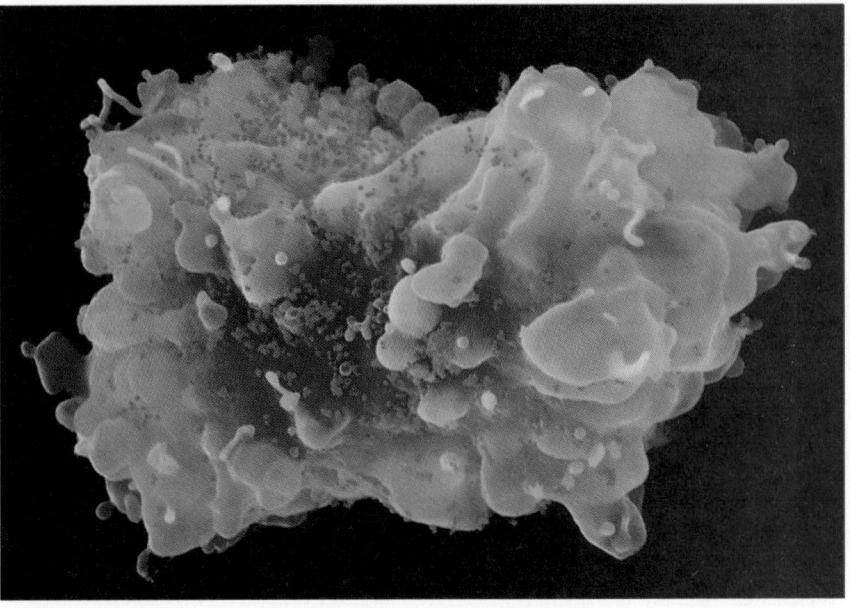

or bacteria, in addition to attacking them, they send chemical signals through the blood to the brain, telling it to turn on the production of endocrine hormones. This, in turn, increases or decreases immune cells' activity. The chemical messengers can also affect mood and other psychological states. Indeed, the fact that the immune system can sense chemical changes and transmit information to the brain has led to speculation that it is a kind of "sixth sense" (Gorman & Kertzner, 1991). Perhaps this helps to explain some people's reports that they somehow "know" that they are going to become ill even before they experience actual symptoms.

Discoveries about relationships among the immune, endocrine, and nervous systems provide clues to how mind and body can affect one another and how psychological factors are related to health and illness. Some of the recent findings in the new field of psychoneuroimmunology are described in this chapter's Psychobiological Interactions feature.

PSYCHOBIOLOGICAL INTERACTIONS

Psychoneuroimmunology: How Psychological Factors Affect Health

It has been known for a long time that psychological factors affect health and illness—and, as in the case of the woman cursed by the midwife, even life and death. It's also been known that the immune system is critically important in maintaining health. What was missing was an understanding of how mental events "get into" the immune system and affect its functioning. During the past decade, researchers have pieced together some parts of the puzzle, and psychologists have teamed with immunologists to form a new discipline called psychoneuroimmunology. Workers in this field study how psychosocial factors affect immune-system functioning and, ultimately, health and illness (Ader & others, 1990).

Stress is known to increase the risk of illness (Cohen & Williamson, 1991). Research by Ronald Glaser, Janet Kiecolt-Glaser, and their coworkers at Ohio State University has shown that one possible reason for the stress–illness relationship is reduced immune-system effectiveness. Medical students were studied over a one-year period. Blood samples collected during three stressful academic examination periods were compared with samples collected a month before each examination to measure T-cell activity. The researchers found that immune-system effectiveness was reduced during the stressful exam periods and that this reduction was linked to the likelihood of becoming ill (Glaser & others, 1987, 1990). Other studies showed that hormones and neuropeptides released into the bloodstream as part of the brain's response to stress suppress the number of natural killer cells and other immune-system cells, possibly increasing the likelihood of illness (Kiecolt-Glaser & Glaser, 1990).

School examinations are stressful, but they pale in comparison with some other life stressors. The death of a loved one is a profoundly stressful life event that can have telling effects on survivors' health. Within one year of the death of a spouse, about 67 percent of widows decline in health. An increased rate of mortality is also found, particularly in widowers. To study the impact of bereavement on immune-system functioning, Michael Irwin and his associates monitored the natural killer cell activity of women before and after the death of their husbands. They found a decrease in immune-cell activity, but only in women who reacted to the loss with depressive symptoms (Irwin & others, 1987). Depression thus appears to weaken the immune system, which can increase the body's vulnerability to viral diseases and, possibly, to cancer cells (Stein & others, 1990).

Psychodynamic and environmental factors have been implicated in other ways as well. David McClelland and his coworkers reported that people who have a strong need for power show decreased immune-system functioning when they are exposed to high levels of stress or frustration of their power needs (Jemmott & others, 1988; McClelland, 1989). In a long-term European study, people who were experiencing high levels of stress but were too emotionally restrained to express negative feelings had a significantly higher rate of cancer in the future than did highly stressed people who were not so emotionally restrained (Eysenck & Grossarth-Marticek, 1991). Thus, persons with certain personality patterns appear to be at increased risk for illness when they are subjected to stress.

If negative emotions such as anxiety and depression can suppress immune activity, can positive feelings and attitudes and a will to live boost immune-system functioning? Many cancer specialists are convinced that an aggressive and determined attitude and a will to live characterize cancer survivors, whereas patients who resign

Immune System Functioning:
Factors Suggested by Theory and Research

$B = f(P, E)$

Causal Factors

Biological
- Presence of antigens
- CNS-immune system interactions

Cognitive
- Stress-producing cognitions
- Resignation vs. determination
- Beliefs that others are supportive

Intrapsychic
- Unconscious conflicts that increase negative reactions to threat, loss
- Avoidance defenses
- Sense of meaning, purpose

Environmental
- Stressful life events
- Availability of social support

Immune System Functioning

Immune System Functioning is a function of interacting personal and environmental causal factors. These factors may vary and may interact with one another in particular ways, depending on the person and the situation.

themselves to their fate have a less favorable prognosis (Greer & others, 1979; Taylor & Brown, 1988). High levels of social support from the environment are also believed to increase immune-system functioning (Hall & O'Grady, 1990). In one study involving the spouses of cancer patients, individuals who reported high levels of social support from others exhibited a stronger immune response when they were injected with antigens than did those who reported low levels of social support (Baron & others, 1990).

The immune system thus appears to be affected by biological, environmental, cognitive, and intrapsychic factors. These factors, shown in the accompanying Understanding the Causes of Behavior feature, may interact with one another in currently unknown ways.

Can anything be done to actively enhance immune-system functioning? This question is one of the most fascinating ones in psychoneuroimmunology. Although there is a great need for more controlled studies, research suggests that techniques involving imagery, relaxation, and stress management may affect immune functioning. In one investigation, Janice Kiecolt-Glaser and her colleagues (1985) found that relaxation training to reduce stress and strengthen one's sense of personal control improved natural killer cell activity in geriatric patients who were compared with a control group of similar patients who received only social visits from a college student. The relaxation group also reported less illness during the course of the experiment. In Europe, a treatment program was designed to help emotionally constrained people who had not yet developed cancer. You will recall that such people constitute an at-risk population. The program focused on building stress-coping skills and on helping the people learn how to express their emotions. A follow-up 13 years later revealed that 90 percent of the treated subjects were still alive, compared with only 38 percent of an untreated control group of similar at-risk people (Eysenck & Grossarth-Marticek, 1991). Finally, in a study of 86 women undergoing breast cancer treatment at Stanford Medical School, women were randomly assigned to either a weekly therapy group designed to strengthen their coping skills and social support or to a no-treatment control group. Those in the therapy groups survived an average of 37 months compared with an average of 19 months in the controls (Spiegel & others, 1989).

Obviously, the immune system does not "know" that a feared examination is at hand, that a spouse has died, or that social support is available. But the brain knows, and there is increasing evidence that what the brain knows and does can affect how well the immune system protects us. The implications are attracting an increasing number of psychologists to the new field of psychoneuroimmunology.

S U M M A R Y

The Neural Bases of Behavior

● Neurons are the basic building blocks of the nervous system. Each neuron has dendrites, which receive nerve impulses from other neurons; a cell body, or soma, which controls the vital processes of the cell; and an axon, which conducts nerve impulses to adjacent neurons, muscles, and glands.

● Neural transmission is an electrochemical process. The nerve impulse is a brief reversal in the electrical potential of the cell membrane as sodium ions from the surrounding fluid flow into the cell through a sodium gate. Passage of the impulse across the synapse—the microscopic space between neurons—is mediated by chemical transmitter substances released from the axon terminals.

● Some neurotransmitters excite neurons, whereas others inhibit firing of the postsynaptic neuron. Acetylcholine is an important excitatory transmitter. Psychoactive drugs affect behavior by modifying neurotransmitter activity at the synapse, and there is evidence that some mood and behavior disorders may involve defects in neurotransmitter systems.

The Nervous System

● The nervous system is made up of sensory neurons, motor neurons, and interneurons (associative neurons). Its two major divisions are the central nervous system, consisting of the brain and spinal cord, and the peripheral nervous system. The latter is divided into the somatic system, which has sensory and motor functions, and the autonomic nervous system, which directs the activity of the body's internal organs and glands.

● The dorsal roots of the spinal cord contain sensory neurons and the ventral roots contain motor neurons. Interneurons inside the spinal cord serve a connective function. Simple stimulus-response connections can occur as spinal reflexes.

● Discoveries about brain–behavior relations are made using techniques such as lesioning and surgical ablation, electrical and chemical stimulation of the brain, electrical recording techniques, and scanning procedures. Recently developed methods for producing computer-generated pictures of structures and processes within the living brain include CAT and PET scans and magnetic resonance imaging (MRI). Deoxyglucose and other radioactive tracers are used in conjunction with the PET scan to study activities in the living brain such as glucose metabolism, blood volume, and neurotransmitter binding.

Brain Structure and Functions

• The human brain consists of the hindbrain, the midbrain, and the forebrain. Major structures within the hindbrain include the medulla, which monitors and controls vital body functions; the pons, which contains important groups of sensory and motor neurons; and the cerebellum, which is concerned with motor coordination.

• The midbrain contains important sensory and motor neurons, as well as many sensory and motor tracts connecting higher and lower parts of the nervous system.

• The reticular formation extends from the hindbrain up into the midbrain. It plays a vital role in consciousness, attention, and sleep. Activity of the ascending reticular formation excites higher areas of the brain and prepares them to respond to stimulation. The descending reticular formation acts as a gate, determining which stimuli get through to enter into consciousness.

• The forebrain is highly developed in humans. It consists of two cerebral hemispheres and a number of subcortical structures. The cerebral hemispheres are connected by a band of fibers known as the corpus callosum.

• The thalamus acts as a switchboard through which impulses originating in sense organs are routed to the appropriate sensory projection areas. The hypothalamus plays a major role in many aspects of motivational and emotional behavior. The limbic system seems to be involved in organizing the behaviors involved in motivation and emotion.

• The convoluted outer portion of the cerebral hemispheres, the cerebral cortex, is highly developed in humans. It is divided into frontal, parietal, occipital, and temporal lobes. Some areas of the cerebral cortex receive sensory input, some control motor functions, and others (the association cortex) are believed to be involved in the higher mental processes in humans. The frontal lobes are particularly important in planning, voluntary behavior, and self-awareness.

• Although the two cerebral hemispheres ordinarily work in coordination with one another, they appear to have different functions and abilities. Studies of split-brain patients who have had the corpus callosum cut indicate that the left hemisphere commands language and mathematical abilities, whereas the right hemisphere has well-developed spatial abilities but a generally limited ability to communicate through speech. Positive emotions are believed to be linked to relatively greater left-hemisphere activation and negative ones to relatively greater right-hemisphere involvement.

Brain Damage and Recovery of Function

• Common types of brain damage include concussions, contusions, strokes, and epilepsy.

• A person's ability to recover from brain damage depends on several factors, including the nature, location, and extent of the injury and the age of the victim. Other things being equal, recovery is greatest early in life and declines with age.

• Neural plasticity refers to the brain's ability to reorganize itself and recover functions following injury. Neurons are not replaced when they die, but surviving neurons can sprout enlarged dendritic networks and extend axons to form new synapses. Neurons can also increase the amount of neurotransmitter substance they release and the number of receptors on postsynaptic neurons so that they are more sensitive to stimulation.

• Recent experiments in treating neurological disorders include neuron regeneration, the grafting of nerve tissue that produces dopamine into the brains of Parkinson's disease patients, and the development of prosthetic devices to restore sensorimotor functions to patients who are paralyzed as a result of spinal injuries. Although these methods are experimental at this point, they offer hope for major treatment advances.

The Autonomic Nervous System

• The autonomic nervous system consists of sympathetic and parasympathetic divisions. The sympathetic system has an arousal function and tends to act as a unit. The parasympathetic system slows down body processes and is more specific in its actions. Together, the two divisions maintain a state of homeostasis.

The Endocrine System

• The endocrine system secretes hormones into the bloodstream. These chemical messengers affect many body processes. Because of the adrenal glands' relation to functions of the nervous system, they are of particular interest to psychologists.

Brain, Behavior, and the Immune System

• The lymphocytes (white blood cells), macrophages, and natural killer cells are the main members of the immune system defense team. These cells detect and attack antigens.

• Disorders can occur because of either an underactive or an overactive immune system. Allergic reactions and autoimmune conditions are caused by overactivity; cancer and AIDS result from underactivity.

• The immune system has direct neural and biochemical connections with the nervous and endocrine systems, and all three systems can affect one another's functioning.

• The new field of psychoneuroimmunology studies relations between psychological factors and immune-system functioning.

KEY TERMS AND CONCEPTS

ablation (p. 68)
acetylcholine (ACh) (p. 65)
action potential (p. 62)
action potential threshold (p. 63)
adrenal cortex (p. 87)
adrenal glands (p. 86)
adrenal medulla (p. 87)
allergy (p. 88)
all-or-none principle (p. 64)
Alzheimer's disease (p. 65)
amygdala (p. 74)
antigen (p. 88)
aphasia (p. 78)
association cortex (p. 74)

autoimmune reactions (p. 89)
autonomic nervous system (p. 85)
axon (p. 61)
B-cell (p. 88)
brain stem (p. 71)
Broca's area (p. 75)
CAT scan (p. 69)
central fissure (p. 75)
central nervous system (p. 66)
cerebellum (p. 73)
cerebral hemispheres (p. 74)
computerized axial tomography (see CAT scan)
concussion (p. 81)

contusion (p. 81)
corpus callosum (p. 78)
cortical projection areas (p. 76)
dendrite (p. 61)
deoxyglucose (p. 70)
dopamine (p. 66)
dorsal root (p. 67)
electroencephalograph (EEG) (p. 69)
endocrine system (p. 85)
epilepsy (p. 81)
fast MRI (p. 70)
forebrain (p. 71)
frontal lobe (p. 75)

G protein (p. 64)
graded potentials (p. 63)
gray matter (p. 67)
helper T-cells (p. 88)
hindbrain (p. 71)
hippocampus (p. 74)
homeostasis (p. 85)
hormones (p. 86)
hypothalamus (p. 73)
inhibition (p. 64)
interneuron (p. 66)
killer T-cells (p. 88)
lateral fissure (p. 75)
lesioning (p. 68)
limbic system (p. 74)
lymphocytes (p. 88)
macrophages (p. 88)
magnetic resonance imaging (*see* MRI)
medulla (p. 72)
midbrain (p. 71)
motor neurons (p. 66)
MRI (p. 70)

myelin sheath (p. 63)
natural killer cells (p. 88)
nerve impulse (p. 62)
neural plasticity (p. 81)
neuron (p. 61)
neuropeptides (p. 89)
neurotransmitters (p. 64)
nodes of Ranvier (p. 63)
occipital lobe (p. 75)
optic chiasma (p. 79)
parasympathetic nervous system (p. 85)
parietal lobe (p. 75)
peripheral nervous system (p. 66)
PET scan (p. 70)
pons (p. 72)
positron emission tomography (*see* PET scan)
psychoneuroimmunology (p. 87)
receptor sites (p. 64)
refractory period (p. 63)
resting potential (p. 62)
reticular formation (p. 72)
reuptake (p. 64)

sensory neurons (p. 66)
soma (p. 61)
somatic system (p. 67)
spinal reflexes (p. 67)
split-brain patients (p. 79)
stroke or cerebrovascular accident (p. 81)
suppressor T-cells (p. 88)
sympathetic ganglia (p. 85)
sympathetic nervous system (p. 85)
synapse (p. 63)
synaptic vesicles (p. 64)
T-cells (p. 88)
temporal lobe (p. 75)
thalamus (p. 73)
tumors (p. 81)
ventral root (p. 67)
Wernicke's area (p. 75)
white matter (p. 67)

SUGGESTED READINGS

Ader, R., Cohen, N., & Felten, D. L. (Eds.). (1990). *Psychoneuroimmunology II.* New York: Academic Press. Although this book is somewhat advanced, it is by far the most up-to-date reference on the many fascinating directions in which research on the immune system and psychological factors is proceeding.

Bloom, F. E., & Lazerson, A. (1988). *Brain, mind, and behavior.* New York: Freeman. This introductory-level text provides an excellent overview of many of the topics discussed in this chapter. The book is comprehensive, illustrated with many color photographs and drawings, and focuses on recent discoveries in brain science.

Gazzaniga, M. S., Steen, D., & Volpe, B. T. (1979). *Functional neuroscience.* New York: Harper & Row. If you enjoyed the case studies presented in this chapter, you will find many more in this overview of brain–behavior relations.

Hooper, J., & Teresi, D. (1986). *The three-pound universe.* New York: Macmillan. Visits to the laboratories of the world's leading neuroscientists provide fascinating glimpses of the current frontiers of brain–behavior research.

Infant and Child Development 4

■ ■

C H A P T E R   O U T L I N E

ragic stories of child abuse are all too common. However, few children experience an environment as deprived and pathological as Genie's. Genie was the unwanted child of a brutal father who terrorized his family. One of his children died of pneumonia after the father banished her to their unheated garage so that he would not have to put up with her crying. When Genie was born, she was a normal-weight full-term baby. Her father became increasingly jealous of the attention Genie received from her mother and expressed growing hatred for the child. When Genie was 20 months old, his rage exploded into action, and he locked Genie in a barren room by herself. For more than 11 years she lived there, chained by day to a potty and tied up at night in a sleeping bag. She was beaten with a large piece of wood whenever she cried. When her father came to bring her food or to tie her in for the night, he growled like a dog, bared his teeth, and raked her with fingernails that he let grow long for this purpose. During her 11-year period of abuse, no one ever spoke human language to her.

Genie's mother was too terrified of the father to intervene. Finally, when Genie was 13 years old, her mother took Genie with her and escaped from the house to seek assistance at a family aid facility. Upon hearing what had taken place, the caseworker immediately notified the police, and charges were filed against the parents. On the day of the hearing, Genie's father killed himself. A suicide note read, ''The world will never understand.''

When Genie was liberated from her prison, she was 4 feet 6 inches tall and weighed only 59 pounds. She could not walk normally; instead, she shuffled and swayed from side to side. She rarely made a sound, showed no emotions, and was not toilet trained. Eventually, Genie learned to control her bowels and walk normally, but she never acquired normal language. Sophisticated tests of language functions indicated that Genie's language abilities were localized in the right hemisphere of her brain rather than in the left hemisphere, the normal site for a right-handed person like Genie. Seven years after her rescue, Genie's language was still less sophisticated than that of a normal 5-year-old despite extensive language training (Curtiss, 1977).

Not surprisingly, Genie had no social skills when she was found. Although she became attached to some of the people who lived in the hospital rehabilitation unit where she resided and to Susan Curtiss, the UCLA scientist who befriended her and studied her development, she never developed mature social behaviors. In remarkable contrast to her linguistic and social deficits, however, Genie's performance on psychological tests revealed an amazing ability to perceive and think about spatial relationships. For ex-

ample, one test required Genie to inspect a small part of a larger object and identify which of several objects the part belonged to. She responded with a degree of speed and accuracy that astonished the testers, and she scored higher on this test than 98 percent of adults do.

Thankfully, cases such as Genie's are very rare. However, this tragedy does raise important questions about the conditions that are required in order for normal human development to occur. Take, for example, Genie's failure to acquire normal language. Some psycholinguists, who study the development and nature of language, believe that there may be a **critical period** in development—probably between the age of 2 and puberty—when a child *must* be exposed to language in order for normal language development to proceed. Normal lateralization of language in the left hemisphere may depend on linguistic input to the brain during this critical period or, at the very least, during a **sensitive period**—a period in which development occurs most easily (Lenneberg, 1967). Susan Curtiss (1977), who studied Genie's language abilities intensively, fears that after such a developmental period, the left-hemisphere language areas may atrophy from disuse, resulting in localization of language within the less linguistic right hemisphere.

Considering Genie's social and emotional deficits, we might also ask whether critical periods (when some experience must occur for normal development to proceed) or sensitive periods (when the organism profits most from the experience) also exist for social development and whether it is possible for a developing child to be damaged beyond repair in the absence of normal human interactions. Given the degree of deprivation that Genie experienced, we might likewise wonder if any remnants of normal human desires for closeness remain. In partial answer to this question, the drawing in Figure 4.1 and Susan Curtiss's poignant description of the circumstances under which it was drawn suggest an enduring attachment and yearning for the mother from whom she was isolated early in life.

Finally, how might we account for Genie's remarkable spatial abilities? Are they the result of some special innate capacity conferred upon her by her genetic heritage, or did they develop as a result of her immobility and her socially isolated environment? Genie's case leaves many of our queries unanswered, but we shall encounter in this chapter many attempts to address, through theory and research, these and other important questions about the developing child.

Developmental psychology is the scientific study of the biological, cognitive, and behavioral changes that occur from the moment of conception until death and of the factors that cause these changes (see Figure 4.2). The journey across the human life span will occupy this chapter and the next one. This chapter considers the early years of life, from conception through the end of childhood. Chapter 5 will explore the rapidly expanding study of development through adolescence, adulthood, and old age.

■ ■ Two Important Developmental Issues

Two issues have surfaced repeatedly in the study of human development. One issue concerns the very nature of change. Does it proceed gradually and continuously, or do people pass through a series of distinct and separate stages in which totally new behaviors and abilities suddenly appear? The second issue, the **nature–nurture controversy,** concerns the relative importance of biological and experiential factors in causing the observed changes. Let us examine these issues.

Everyone agrees that adults differ from children, and even from adolescents. But how did those differences come about? Are they *quantitative* in nature, the product of gradual, cumulative growth, as we might see in the physical growth of a tree from a seedling? Or are they *qualitative,* reflecting a progression through specific stages that differ not in degree but in kind, as when a creeping caterpillar suddenly becomes a soaring butterfly?

When specific patterns of skills or behaviors seem to emerge suddenly and occur in a specific order in virtually all members of a species, we are tempted to think in terms of distinct **stages.** Presumably, each of these stages represents a distinct phase within a larger sequence of development. For example, some theorists believe that adults solve problems more effectively than children do because they think in a way that is different in *kind* (that is, qualitatively different) from the thought processes of children. In contrast, developmentalists who emphasize the importance of learning emphasize continuity in development rather than distinct stages. They view development as a gradual and continuous process in which one experience builds upon another in the same way cell growth and division build a bigger tree. They would say that adult thinking is simply a more advanced form of children's thinking.

The stage-versus-continuity issue relates to the nature of development. The nature–nurture debate relates to its causes. Here, two sets of causal factors are involved: heredity and environment. Those who emphasize the importance of hereditary factors view development as an unfolding of fairly fixed innate ca-

Figure 4.1 *According to Susan Curtiss (1977), who studied Genie for more than 7 years after her liberation, "this drawing is testimony to the importance of the mother–child relationship for all human beings, and to Genie's need for a sense of her own history. Early in 1977, filled with loneliness and longing, Genie drew this picture. At first she drew only the picture of her mother and then labeled it 'I miss Mama.' She then suddenly began to draw more. The moment she finished she took my hand, placed it next to what she had just drawn, motioning me to write, and said 'Baby Genie.' Then she pointed under her drawing and said, 'Mama hand.' I dictated all the letters. Satisfied, she sat back and stared at the picture. There she was, a baby in her mother's arms. She had created her own reality" (p. 1).*

pacities. Strict hereditarians believe that intelligence is determined by an individual's genetic endowment and that it is changeable only within rather narrow limits. In contrast, those on the nurture side of the dispute view the environment in which people are raised as the key factor in their intellectual development.

It has long been recognized that an "either–or" approach to heredity and environment is an exercise in futility because most behavior is a product of *interactions* between genetic factors and the environment. The prevailing view today is that genetic factors create a range of possibilities within which environmental factors operate to positively or negatively affect characteristics and behaviors.

Figure 4.2 *Developmental psychology studies development and the factors that influence it across the entire life span.*

It is difficult to imagine the square root of a shoulder or the factoring of an equation involving a series of body parts.

Psychological characteristics and behaviors vary in the relative importance of genetic and environmental causal factors as well as in the precise ways in which these factors interact (McClearn & others, 1991). Therefore, many of today's most important research questions concern how nature and nurture interact to affect the countless varieties of behavior that are the focus of developmental research.

The Study of Development

Developmental psychologists are interested in describing the process of change and explaining its causes. Suppose, for example, we were researchers interested in how memory abilities change with age. We might pose questions like the following: Is childhood memory as good as adult memory? Does memory improve with age? When does it reach its peak efficiency? Does memory show a decline in old age? To answer these questions, we might decide to study the developmental course of memory from the early school years to old age. Our measure of memory might be the ability to recall lists containing nonsense syllables, such as *bxj* and *frp*. How could we determine how performance on this memory task is affected by age?

Among the critical environmental factors is the culture in which one is reared. Consider, for example, the ability to solve algebraic problems. The Oksapmin people of New Guinea do their arithmetic with a basic set of 29 numbers that correspond to specific body parts (see Figure 4.3). Although Oksapmin children appear to have the same ability to grasp number concepts as children growing up in Montreal or Denver, they find it next to impossible to solve algebra problems because their number system does not support the development of algebraic thinking (Saxe, 1981).

Figure 4.3 *Culture influences the development of cognitive abilities. The Oksapmin of New Guinea do their arithmetic using a basic set of 29 numbers corresponding to a sequence of specific body parts. This number system does not support the development of algebraic reasoning, although other number skills in the Oksapmin are as advanced as those of Europeans and North Americans (Based on Saxe, 1981).*

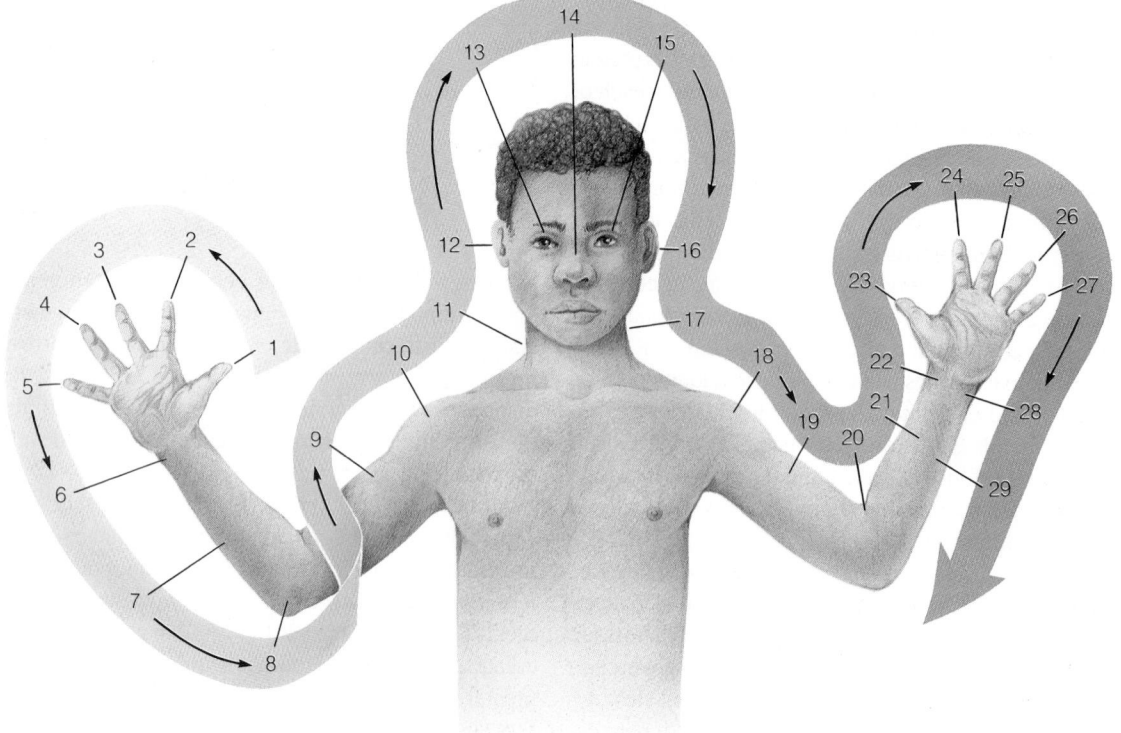

Two basic research designs have been used in studies designed to assess the course of development: the cross-sectional design and the longitudinal design. These designs are shown graphically in Figure 4.4.

The **cross-sectional design** compares groups that represent a cross section of ages at a particular point in time. Thus, in 1995, we might compare groups of 7-, 10-, 20-, 30-, 50-, and 70-year-olds on our memory task. The cross-sectional design is the most widely used design in developmental research. Because many age groups can be measured at a given point in time, the data can be collected quickly and comparisons can be made among the age groups. We can also obtain large and representative samples at each age.

Despite these advantages, the cross-sectional design has a major drawback that may already have occurred to you. However careful we might be in selecting our age groups, these groups may differ in ways *other* than age. For example, suppose we find that the 70-year-old group scores significantly lower on our memory measure than the 20-year-old group. These results might reflect a universal tendency for memory to decline in old age. But they might also reflect factors related to the generations, or **cohorts,** in which the different groups grew up. Thus, the 70-year-olds, who grew up during the Great Depression, may have had poorer nutrition as children or less schooling. To the extent that these factors affect the development of memory, they are confounded with the age differences and could lead us to an erroneous conclusion.

A more expensive and time-consuming alternative to the cross-sectional design is the longitudinal design. With a **longitudinal design,** the same subjects are studied over the entire time interval in question. In this case, we would begin assessing memory in 1995 when the subjects were 7 years of age and then retest the subjects when they were 10, 20, 30, 50, and 70 years of age. Consistent with the concept of development, this design traces changes that occur in the same people over time. The longitudinal design also eliminates systematic differences between people of different age cohorts because, of course, there is only one group of subjects. However, it does *not* control for factors specific to a particular cohort that might affect the behaviors of interest. If, for example, an environmental pollutant that negatively affects memory existed in this cohort's environment for a period of 10 years, the subjects could show a decrease in memory that is not caused by the aging process. This could pose difficulties in generalizing findings to other cohorts.

Longitudinal studies have other drawbacks as well. They are more time-consuming than cross-sectional studies, and because humans mature so slowly, a long-term longitudinal study might well out-

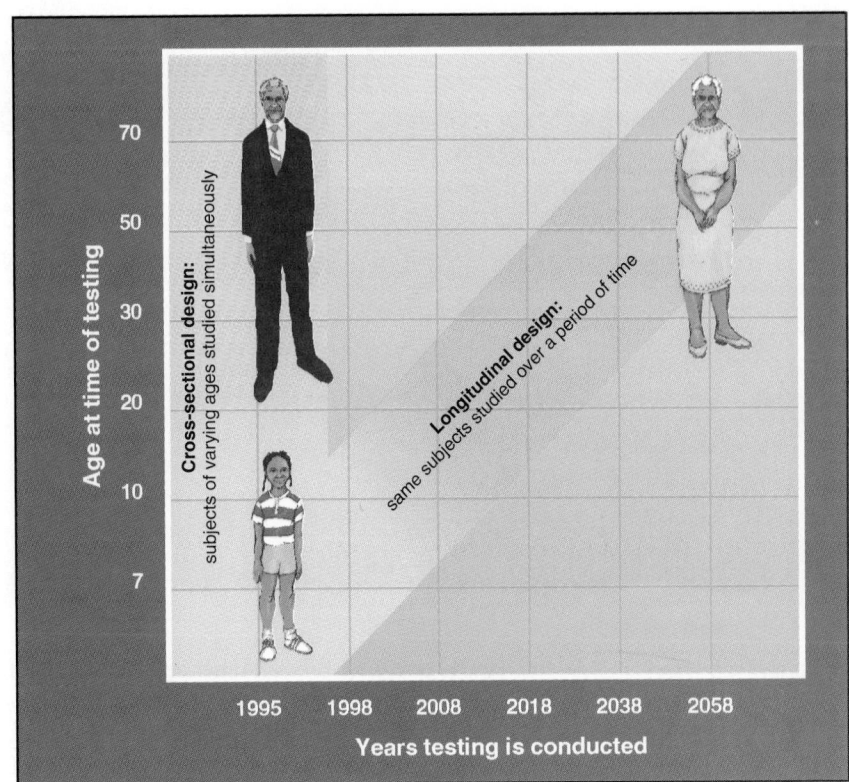

last the researcher. For example, our longitudinal study would not end until the year 2058. Moreover, the findings may be biased in unknown ways as certain subjects move away, withdraw from the study, or die. Finally, retesting the same subjects a number of times may affect the results. In this case, subjects might develop more effective memory strategies that improve their recall simply because they are tested repeatedly.

There are ways to use the longitudinal method to capitalize on its best features while minimizing its limitations (Menard, 1991). For example, a short-term longitudinal study lasting perhaps 5 years may trace a particular behavior during a period when great change in that behavior is expected. Thus, we might study the development of the child's self-concept during the critical elementary school years.

The course of development actually begins before birth, for critical determinants of what each person will become are encoded in the genes of that person's parents. Let us therefore begin our study of child development by examining its genetic bases.

Figure 4.4 *A graphic representation of the difference between cross-sectional and longitudinal research designs, based on the hypothetical study of memory development described in the text.*

■ ▭

Genetic Foundations of Development

The union of two cells, the egg from the mother and the sperm from the father, is the beginning of a new

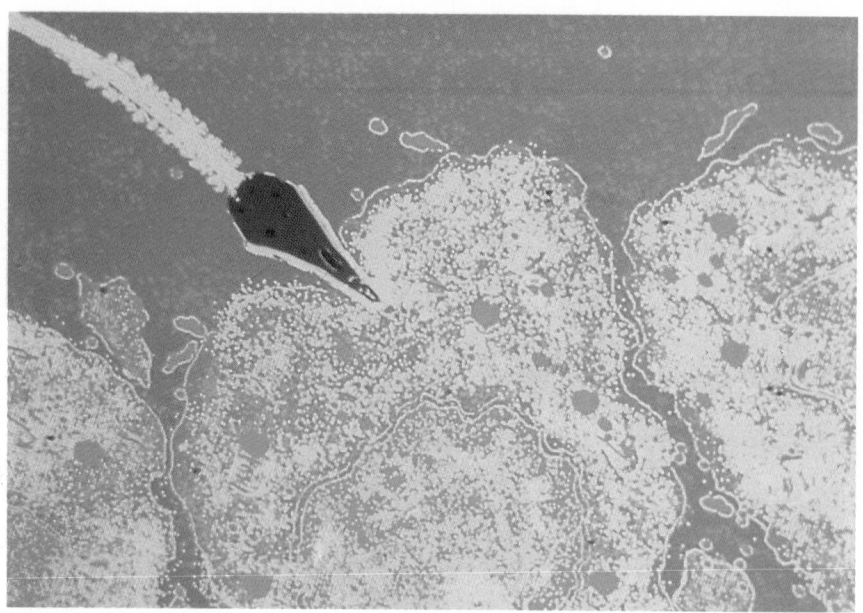

(Sherwood, 1991). Genes can be likened to a giant computer file of information about a person's characteristics, potentials, and limitations. Every moment of every day, the strands of DNA silently transmit their detailed instructions for cellular functioning. Genetic instructions give some of us blue eyes and curly hair and, as we shall see, even contribute to how shy or how outgoing we will be (Kagan & Snidman, 1991).

With one exception, every kind of cell in a normal person contains 46 chromosomes arranged in 23 pairs. The exception is the sex cell, the egg or the sperm, which has only 23 chromosomes. At conception, the egg and sperm unite to form a new cell, which contains the full 46 chromosomes, half furnished by each parent. Because of the large number of genes in each chromosome, a human parent could produce several trillion genetically different egg or sperm cells, making for enormous potential genetic variation even among children in the same family. The only exception to this uniqueness occurs in *monozygotic* (identical) twins, whose heredity is identical because they develop from the same fertilized egg. Fraternal, or *dizygotic*, twins result from the fertilization of two different eggs, and they are no more genetically similar than any other pair of siblings.

life (see Figure 4.5). Like all other cells, the egg and the sperm carry within them the material of heredity in the form of rodlike units called **chromosomes.** A chromosome is a tightly coiled molecule of **deoxyribonucleic acid (DNA)** partly covered by protein (see Figure 4.6). All the information of heredity is encoded in the combinations of molecules that make up the approximately 3 feet of DNA chains that exist in each of our cells.

The DNA portion of the chromosome carries the hereditary blueprint in units called **genes.** Each human chromosome consists of about 20,000 genes

Sex Determination

The sex of a baby is determined by a single gene on the 23rd pair of chromosomes formed by the union of sperm and egg. A normal female's 23rd pair contains two X chromosomes (XX), so called because of their shape. A normal male's 23rd pair contains an X and a Y chromosome (XY). Women carry only X chromosomes, so the 23rd chromosome in the egg is always an X. The 23rd chromosome in the sperm is an X in about half of the cases and a Y in the other half. The Y chromosome normally contains the specific gene (known as the **TDF gene**) that triggers male sexual development (see Figure 4.7). The union of an egg with a sperm cell having a Y chromosome results in an XY combination and therefore a boy. A sperm containing an X chromosome produces an XX chromosome combination and so a baby girl. Thus, it is the father's chromosomal contribution that determines the sex of the baby. Unfortunately, many women throughout history have been belittled, divorced, or even beheaded for failing to bear a male heir. Clearly, they were victims of mistaken causality.

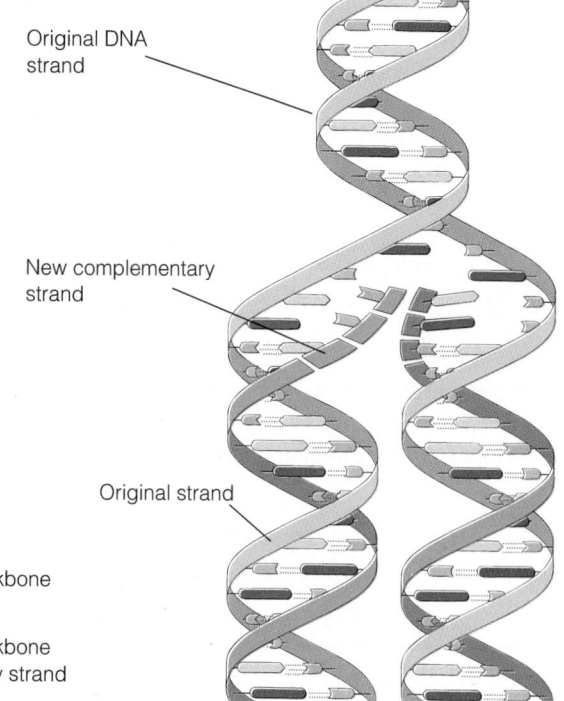

Original DNA strand

New complementary strand

Original strand

Molecular Elements
▬◖ = Adenine
◖▬ = Thymine
▭ = Guanine
◖ = Cytosine

▨ = Sugar-phosphate backbone of original strand

▬ = Sugar-phosphate backbone of new complementary strand

◀ **Figure 4.6** *Chromosomes consist of two long, twisted strands of DNA, the chemical that carries genetic information. The inverted ladder of the DNA molecule can "unzip" up the center and reproduce the missing halves, so that each DNA molecule contains the complete code of the original.*

Dominant and Recessive Genes

The genes contributed by each parent may be either dominant or recessive in their control of a particular characteristic. If a gene is **dominant,** then the characteristic it controls will be displayed in the offspring. If a gene is **recessive,** its effect will be masked unless it is paired with another recessive gene. For example, the gene for brown eyes is dominant (D), and the one for blue eyes is recessive (d). Therefore, children have brown eyes when they have two dominant genes (DD) or when they have a dominant and a recessive gene (Dd). They have blue eyes only when they have two recessive genes (dd). When both genes of a given pair are the same (for example, DD or dd), the person is said to be **homozygous** for that gene. When the two genes are different (for example, Dd), the person is **heterozygous** for that gene.

Because of the interactions between dominant and recessive genes, geneticists make an important distinction between genotype and phenotype. **Genotype** refers to the inherited genetic pattern itself, such as DD, Dd, or dd. The actual expression of the genetic pattern in physical traits or behavior is known as the **phenotype.** It is important to note that even though the traits controlled by a recessive gene may remain hidden, recessive genes can be passed on to an offspring. If that offspring mates with a person who also has the recessive gene, the characteristic controlled by that gene may appear in the next generation.

About 5 percent of newborns have chromosomal or genetic defects that produce a physical or mental handicap (Plomin & others, 1990). As Table 4.1 shows, some of the more common genetic defects are produced by a dominant gene, others by the combination of two recessive genes. To minimize the chances of giving birth to a baby with a genetic defect, many couples are seeking genetic counseling before deciding to have a child. The likelihood that parents will have a child with a chromosomal or genetic disorder can be estimated on the basis of a detailed study of family records or by means of laboratory tests that may detect a chromosomal or genetic abnormality in either parent.

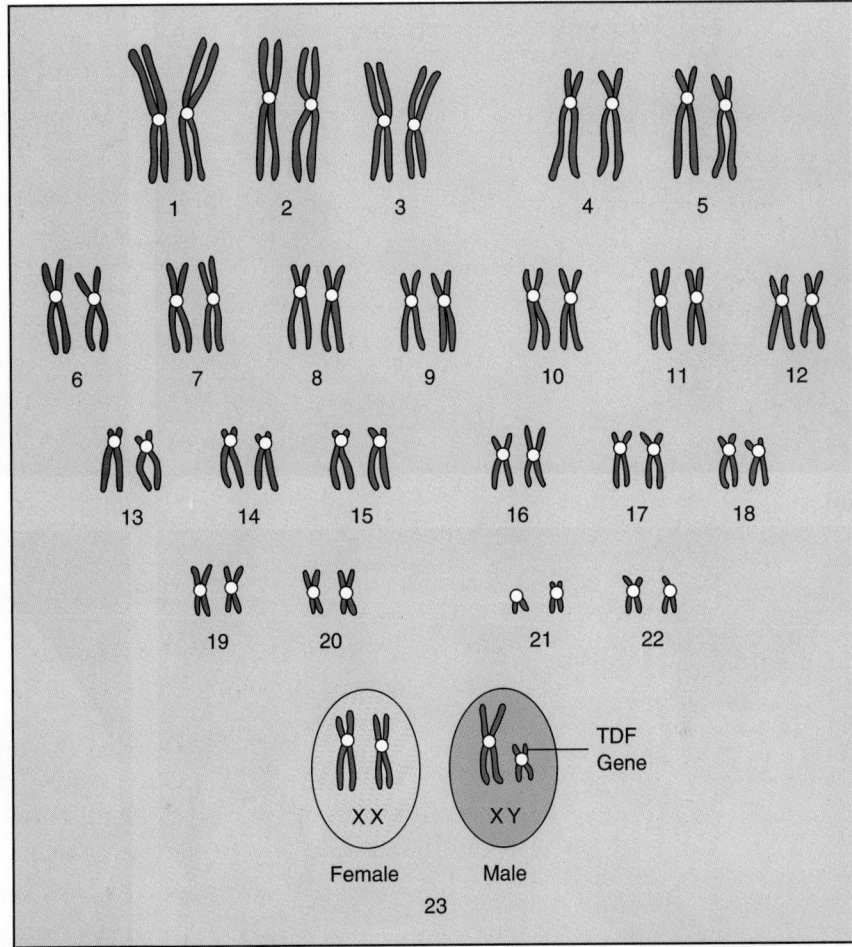

Figure 4.7 *Human beings have 23 pairs of chromosomes, one set from each parent. Sex is determined by the 23rd pair. In females, the pair contains two X chromosomes (XX genotype). In males, it contains an X chromosome and a Y chromosome (XY genotype). The TGF gene on the Y chromosome throws the switch that triggers male development.*

Prenatal Development

Prenatal development occurs from the moment of conception until birth. During this period of about 266 days, the unborn child develops from a single-

Table 4.1 Physical Defects Produced by Dominant or Recessive Genes		
Dominant or Recessive	**Trait or Characteristic**	**Description**
Dominant	Cataract	Opaqueness of lens of eye
Dominant	Huntington's disease	Degeneration of particular brain centers
Dominant	Amyloidosis	Congestive heart failure
Recessive	Albinism	Lack of pigment in hair, eyes, and skin
Recessive	Congenital deafness	Deafness from birth
Recessive	Microcephaly	Abnormally small head

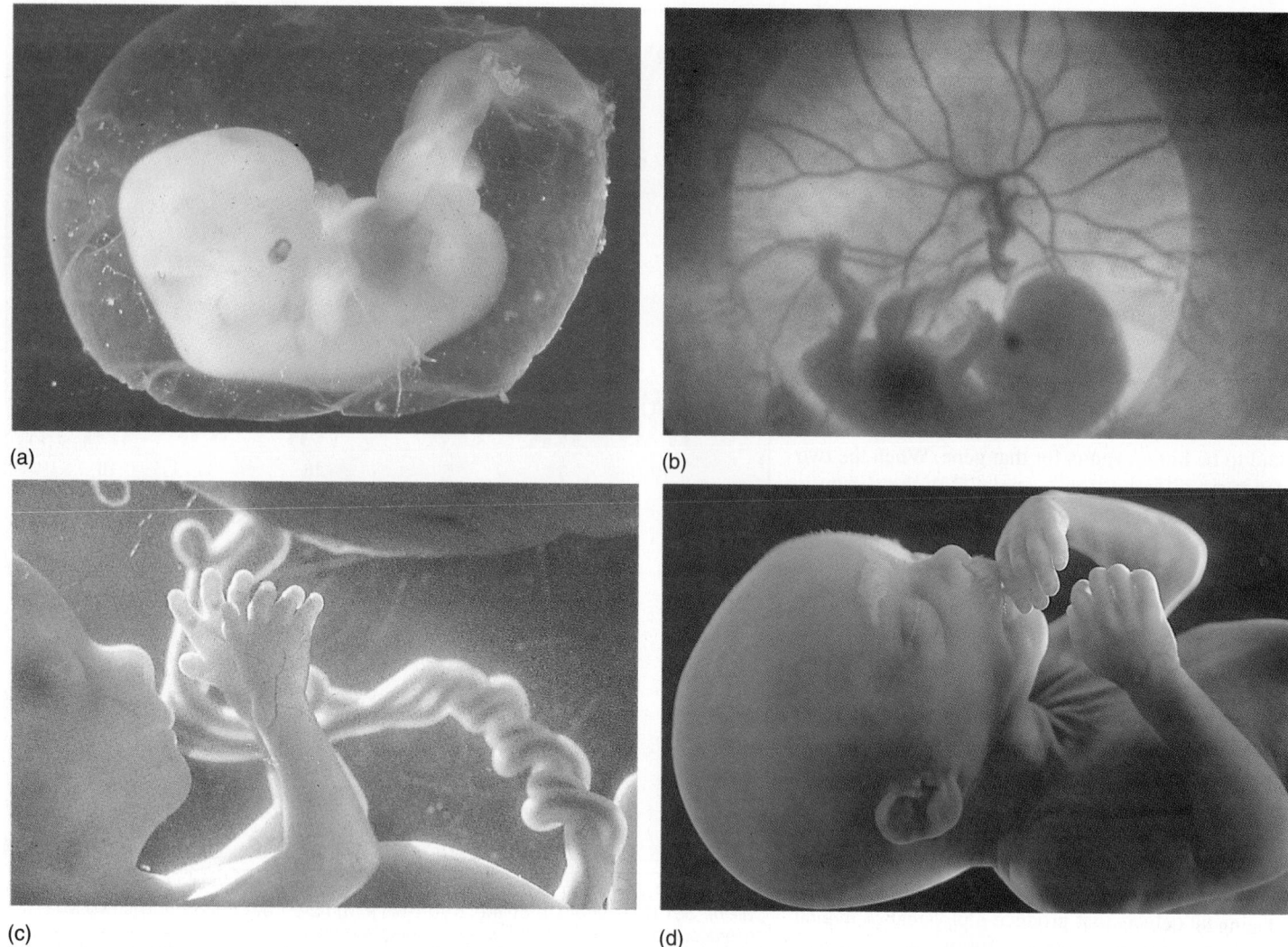

(a)

(b)

(c)

(d)

◆ **Figure 4.8** *The course of prenatal development is shown in these remarkable photos, taken at (a) 6–7 weeks; (b) 11–12 weeks; (c) 4 months, and (d) 5 months. By 5 months of age, the fetus is capable of sucking its thumb.*

cell organism into a fully formed person (see Figure 4.8). The **zygote** phase comprises the first 2 weeks following conception, and the **embryo** phase extends from the end of the 2nd week through the 8th week. At the end of this period, the embryo is no larger than a pea, but it has a beating heart and a growing brain.

The next phase, the period of the **fetus,** extends from 9 weeks after fertilization until birth. This period of rapid growth is supported by oxygen and nutrients from the mother's blood. These substances pass through the **placenta,** an organ that filters the mother's blood and provides nutrients to the fetus through the umbilical cord.

Diseases, injuries, drugs, chemicals, and radiation can all affect the fetus. For example, rubella (German measles) in a mother can cause deafness, heart disorders, and mental retardation in the offspring, particularly if the mother is infected early in pregnancy. Drugs can cross the placenta and enter the fetus, sometimes causing grave damage. For example, babies born of mothers who use heroin, cocaine, or morphine are often addicted when they are born, and they may die from withdrawal symptoms when they are deprived of the mother's blood supply. Substances such

as these, which can disrupt fetal development, are known as **teratogens.**

Nicotine and alcohol also are teratogens. Smoking reduces the amount of oxygen in the mother's blood and increases the risk of spontaneous abortion. Furthermore, infants of mothers who smoke tend to weigh less and to be in poorer physical condition (Spady, 1987).

A very serious disorder known as **fetal alcohol syndrome (FAS)** can increase the risk of fetal death, as well as produce congenital heart defects, brain damage, and other birth defects (see Figure 4.9). Most FAS babies are later found to have below-normal IQs (Streissguth & others, 1990). FAS occurs in 33 to 44 percent of the babies of alcoholic women, but even small amounts of alcohol that have no apparent effects on the mother can damage the fetus. "Social drinking" (alcohol intake of 1 to 3 ounces per day) can thus increase the risk of fetal damage (Schardein, 1985).

This is clearly an instance in which it is better to be safe than sorry. Pregnant women are advised to quit smoking and drinking completely and to take no drugs at all unless they are prescribed and have been tested and shown to be safe (Apgar & Beck, 1974). The fetus is extremely vulnerable to a wide range of teratogens, and the consequences of exposure to them can be tragic.

■ ■
Neonatal Behavior

What must the world be like for a newborn baby? Does the **neonate,** as the child is called during the first 4 weeks after birth, have anything resembling consciousness as we know it? How prepared are these newborns to perceive the sights, sounds, and smells in their new environment? These questions have fired the imaginations of many developmentalists, and their research has begun to provide answers.

Sensory Capabilities and Preferences

To study the sensory capabilities of very young infants, developmental psychologists have developed a number of testing techniques. Some involve the measurement of physiological responses, such as *visual evoked potentials (VEPs)* recorded through electrodes placed on the scalp above the infant's visual cortex (Slater, 1989). VEPs are present at birth, indicating that sensory input from the visual system is being routed to the appropriate areas of the brain. By placing grids of lines that differ in spacing and thickness in the neonate's visual field and then measuring the cortical responses to the stimulus, researchers can tell if the stimuli are "registering" in the visual cortex. This method has established that visual acuity—the ability to see detail—is present at birth. However, the neonate is very nearsighted, with visual acuity estimated by various researchers at about 20/800 (Cornell & McDonnell, 1986). That is, they can see at 20 feet what an adult with normal vision would see at 800 feet. Visual acuity improves steadily during the first 6 months of life as the visual cortex matures and rapidly develops more synapses (Atkinson & Braddick, 1989).

We now know that infants come into the world equipped with preferences for various kinds of stimuli. In the early 1960s, Robert Fantz introduced the *preferential looking procedure* to measure visual preferences in infants. Infants were laid on their backs and two visual stimuli were presented, one on each side of the visual field (see Figure 4.10). Fantz filmed the infants' eye movements to measure how long they looked at each of the stimuli. This technique showed that infants prefer striped and checkerboard patterns over solid colors, and they prefer new patterns to familiar ones (Fantz & Nevis, 1967). Infants also pre-

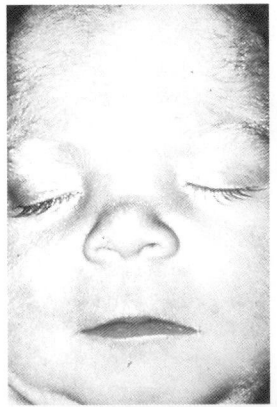
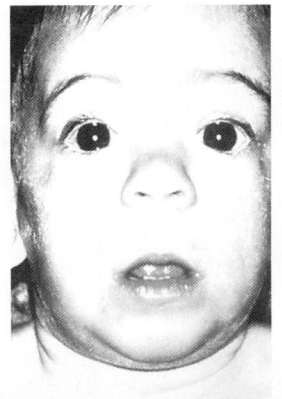
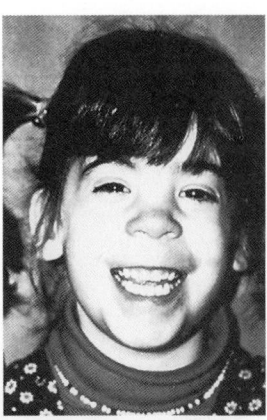
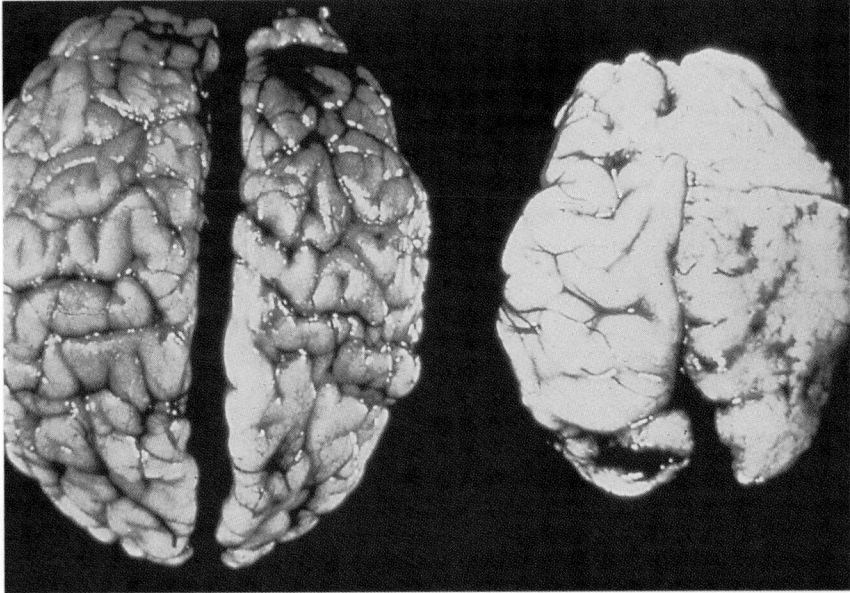

Figure 4.9 *Children who suffer from fetal alcohol syndrome (FAS) not only look different but have brains that are underdeveloped, resulting in severe retardation. The FAS child's brain (right) fails to exhibit the normal pattern of cortical convolutions.*

fer to look at the human face (Dannemiller & Stephens, 1988), and visual preference responses show that they can discriminate their mother's face from those of other familiar caregivers in the first months of life (Kurzweil, 1988).

Researchers can also measure infants' interest in various stimuli by measuring the vigor with which neonates suck on a special nipple equipped with sensors (see Figure 4.11). Hearing abilities and preferences can be studied by observing how infants orient, or turn their heads and eyes toward the source of sounds. Such observations indicate that infants prefer the sound of the human voice to other sounds, and they orient more to high-pitched tones, typical of their mother's voice, than to low-pitched sounds like those of the father's voice (Aslin, 1987). It is possible that the newborn's preference for the mother's voice results from having become familiar with her voice during the later stages of pregnancy, when sound

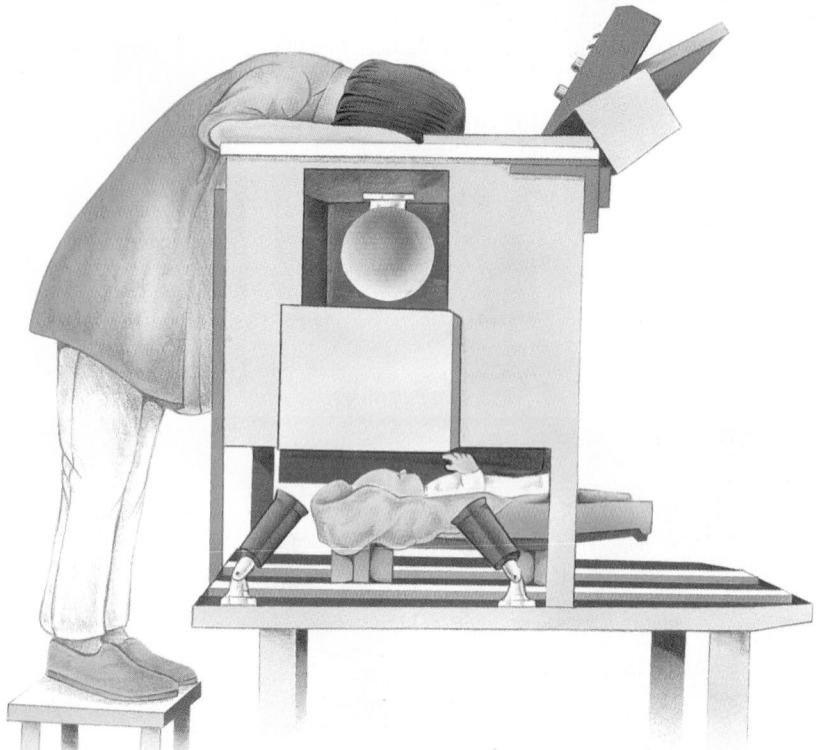

Figure 4.10 *In the early 1960s, Robert Fantz developed this "looking chamber" to study the infant's preferences for various kinds of visual stimuli. The researcher can present stimuli to the left or right side of the chamber and determine where the infant's gaze is directed, or a camera can record eye movements.*

vival (Bowlby, 1958). The reflexive smile will develop into social smiles toward human faces and voices at 2 to 8 weeks of age.

When we consider the newborn's limited visual abilities and uncoordinated movements, the notion that they can discriminate adults' facial expressions and imitate them may seem farfetched. It therefore came as a considerable surprise to developmentalists when Andrew Meltzoff and Keith Moore (1977, 1983) produced photos and videotapes of neonates reproducing the facial expressions of an adult (see Figure 4.12). Tiffany Field and her coworkers (1983) took this demonstration one step further and found support for Meltzoff and Moore's conclusion that neonates are capable of at least a primitive form of imitation. In Field's study, an adult modeled three facial expressions—happy, sad, and surprised—for neonates who were only 36 hours old. The babies demonstrated, first of all, that they could distinguish among the model's expressions by paying close attention to her when she modeled a new one. Most important, the babies appeared to imitate these

waves from her voice were transmitted through her body to the womb (DeCasper & Spence, 1986).

Neonates are attracted to the chemical odors of breast-feeding mothers. If exposed to pads from inside the bras of several nursing mothers, including their own, infants as young as a week old will orient toward their mother's pad (Cernoch & Porter, 1985; Makin & Porter, 1989). Early recognition through chemical signals may contribute to the infant–mother relationship.

Response Capabilities

Neonates enter the world equipped with a variety of **reflexes**—automatic, inborn behaviors that occur in response to specific stimuli. The major neonatal reflexes are presented in Table 4.2. Although many of these primitive reflexes disappear within the first year of life, they are good indicators of neurological maturity at birth. Moreover, some of the reflexes, such as grasping, sucking, crying, and smiling, serve as building blocks for later development. Thus, the newborn's reflexive grasp of her mother's finger lays the foundation for later voluntary motor acts, such as picking up blocks and balls. Some theorists suggest that the early reflexive smile serves as a stimulus to attract parents and increase their interactions with their babies, thereby helping to ensure care and sur-

Figure 4.11 *By measuring how vigorously an infant sucks on the nipple when visual stimuli are flashed on the screen, this developmental psychologist can measure the infant's degree of interest in the stimulus.*

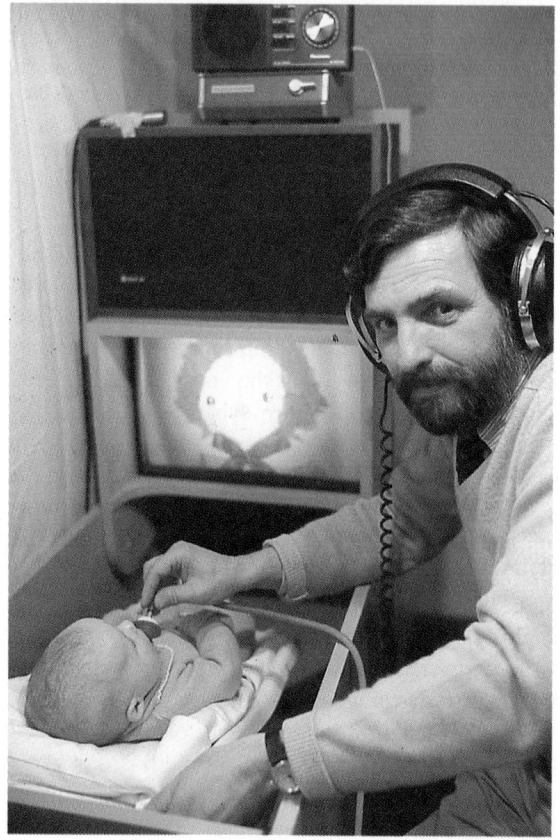

Table 4.2 Reflexes Present at Birth

Reflex Name	Description	Developmental Course	Significance
Babinski	When the bottom of the baby's foot is stroked, the toes fan out and then curl	Disappears in 8 to 12 months	Presence at birth and normal course of decline are a basic index of normal neurological condition
Breathing	Repetitive, rhythmic inhalation and exhalation	Permanent	Provides oxygen and removes carbon dioxide
Crawling	When baby is placed on stomach and pressure is applied to the soles of the feet, rhythmic movements of the arms and legs are elicited	Disappears after 3 to 4 months; possible reappearance at 6 to 7 months as component of voluntary crawling	Uncertain
Eyeblink	Rapid closing of eyes	Permanent	Protection against aversive stimuli such as bright lights or foreign objects
Grasping	When a finger or some other object is pressed against the baby's palm, the baby's fingers close around it	Disappears in 3 to 4 months; replaced by voluntary grasping	Presence at birth and later disappearance is a basic sign of normal neurological development
Moro	If the baby is allowed to drop unexpectedly while being held, or if there is a loud noise, the baby will throw his or her arms outward while arching the back, and then bring the arms together as if grasping something	Disappears in 6 to 7 months (although startle to loud noises is permanent)	Disputed; its presence at birth and later disappearance are a basic sign of normal neurological development; possibly functions as facilitator of mother–infant bonding
Rooting	Turning the head and opening the mouth when touched on the cheek	Disappears between 3 and 6 months	Component of nursing
Stepping	When the baby is held upright over a flat surface, he or she will make rhythmic leg movements	Disappears in first 2 months	Disputed; it may be only a kicking motion, or it may be a component of later voluntary walking
Sucking	Sucking elicited by putting something into the baby's mouth	Permanent	Fundamental component of nursing

Source: Cole & Cole, 1989, p. 128.

expressions. An adult who watched the neonates but could not see the model was able to guess which expression the model was exhibiting with accuracy that far exceeded chance.

The past 20 years have radically altered psychologists' conception of the neonate. They have come to see the neonate for what it is: a surprisingly sophisticated perceiver and information processor with an impressive ability to respond to the emotional, physical, and social features of its environment. In a sense, the helpless neonate of the 1960s has become the newborn ''prodigy'' of the 1990s. The biologically programmed sensory and response capacities that neonates bring into the world lay the foundations for later physical, cognitive, and social development. We now examine the course of these three areas of interrelated development during childhood, beginning with physical and motor development.

Physical and Motor Development

Rapid development occurs in physical structures and in motor (movement) capabilities during infancy and early childhood. This biological unfolding of the individual according to the plan contained in the genes

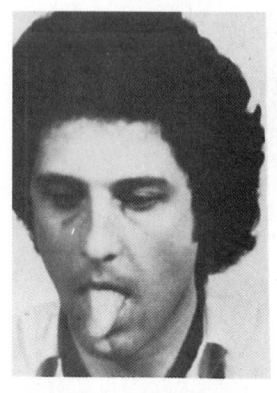
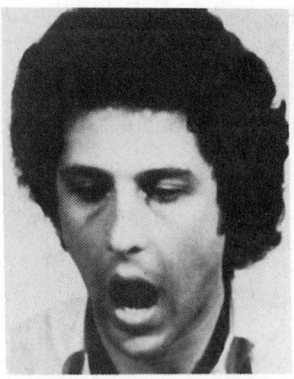
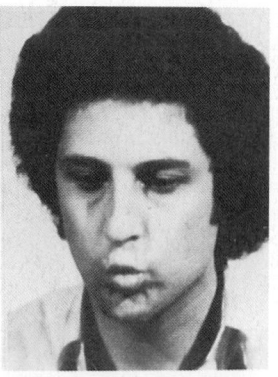
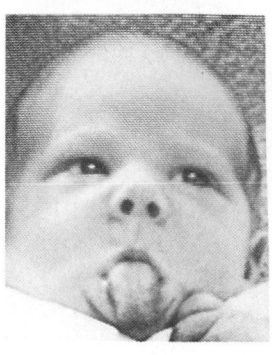
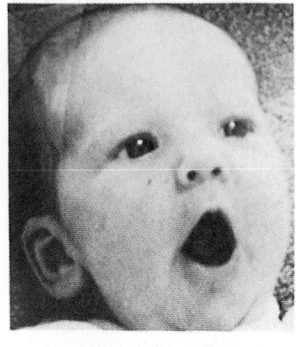
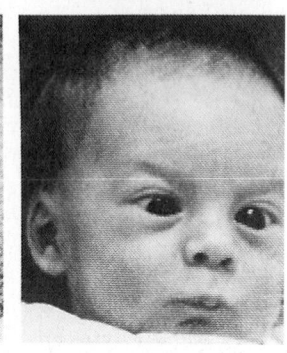

Figure 4.12 *Andrew Meltzoff demonstrates facial imitation in an 18-day-old infant. Infants can discriminate and imitate facial responses almost from birth.*

is known as **maturation.** General norms for motor development are shown in Figure 4.13. It is important to emphasize that these norms reflect the *average* timetable for motor skills and that children vary around these averages. What does not normally vary is the sequence in which the skills appear.

The **cephalocaudal principle** reflects the tendency for development to proceed in a head-to-foot direction. Thus, a baby's head may seem disproportionately large because physical growth begins with the head and proceeds toward the lower part of the body (see Figure 4.14). The same pattern is evident in the development of motor control. Infants lift their heads first, then they lift their shoulders, and later they gain control over their legs. Physical and motor development also follow the **proximodistal principle,** which states that development begins along the innermost parts of the body and continues toward the outermost parts. Thus, the arms develop before the hands and fingers. At birth, infants have control of their shoulders but randomly wave their arms because they lack control over arm and hand muscles. Later in the first year, they will develop the ability to grasp objects placed in their palms, to reach out and brush at objects, and eventually to reach out and grab objects in the palm with consistent skill. Typically, they cannot pick up an object with thumb and forefinger until they are about 9 months old.

A third growth pattern is the principle of **differentiation,** which states that growth proceeds from generalized behaviors to more specific ones. The observation that infants will swipe at an object before

they can pick it up between thumb and forefinger represents this principle. Differentiation is eventually followed by **integration,** through which the developing body systems become better coordinated and integrated with one another. According to the principle of integration, as children develop, the physical–motor, cognitive, and social–emotional subsystems become more integrated into a "whole person" whose behavior often reflects the coordinated actions of all of these subsystems.

No organ in the human body undergoes faster and more dramatic development than the brain. At birth, the brain has all of the 100 billion neurons it will ever have, but it is far from mature. The complex neural networks that form the basis for cognitive and motor skills are just beginning to form, and the brain has attained only about 25 percent of its eventual adult weight. As Figure 4.15 shows, neural networks develop rapidly. The brain of a child 6 months of age already has reached 50 percent of its adult weight, and by the time the child is 2, it will have attained 75 percent of its eventual weight. The increase in brain weight occurs through cell growth, the development of interconnections among neurons, and the development of the insulating myelin sheath over many axons (see Chapter 3, p. 63).

The brain develops in an orderly fashion that underlies the maturational patterns we have already discussed. Subcortical and brain-stem areas governing basic biological survival processes like heartbeat and respiration develop first. In the first few months after birth, the primary motor area of the cerebral cortex develops rapidly, increasing voluntary control of movements. The sensory areas of the brain develop as well, and the integration of sensory and motor abilities allows infants to reach out and touch objects they see by the fourth month. Biological maturation of the cerebellum at the rear of the brain creates the degree of motor control needed to master walking near the end of the first year. The association areas of the cortex, which are involved in memory, thought, and language, are the last brain areas to develop.

Genetically controlled maturation of the nervous system sets limits on behavioral capabilities. For example, no infant can be toilet-trained before the nerve fibers that permit bladder control have developed the insulating myelin sheath that permits them to function efficiently. To expect such control before it exists is to court disaster. This does not mean, however, that maturation cannot be affected by environmental factors. Brain maturation *can* be influenced by the environment in which the organism matures (Wachs, 1992).

In a series of landmark studies by Mark Rosenzweig and his University of California coworkers, rat pups from the same litters were randomly assigned

(a)

⬥ **Figure 4.13** (a) *Children are capable of complex motor behaviors at an early age once their nervous systems and muscles have matured sufficiently. Part (b) of the figure shows that motor development in babies occurs in an orderly sequence, but there is variation in the ages at which certain abilities emerge. The bottom end of the bar represents the age by which 25 percent of children exhibit the skill; the top end represents the age by which 90 percent have mastered it.*

to be raised in either enriched environments, replete with lots of toys and playmates, or in standard laboratory cages (see Figure 4.16). At the end of the experimental periods, which lasted from a few weeks to several months, behavioral tests and examinations of the animals' brains revealed many differences that favored the rats raised in the enriched environment. These animals had greater overall brain weight, larger neurons, more synaptic connections, and greater amounts of *acetylcholine,* a brain neurotransmitter

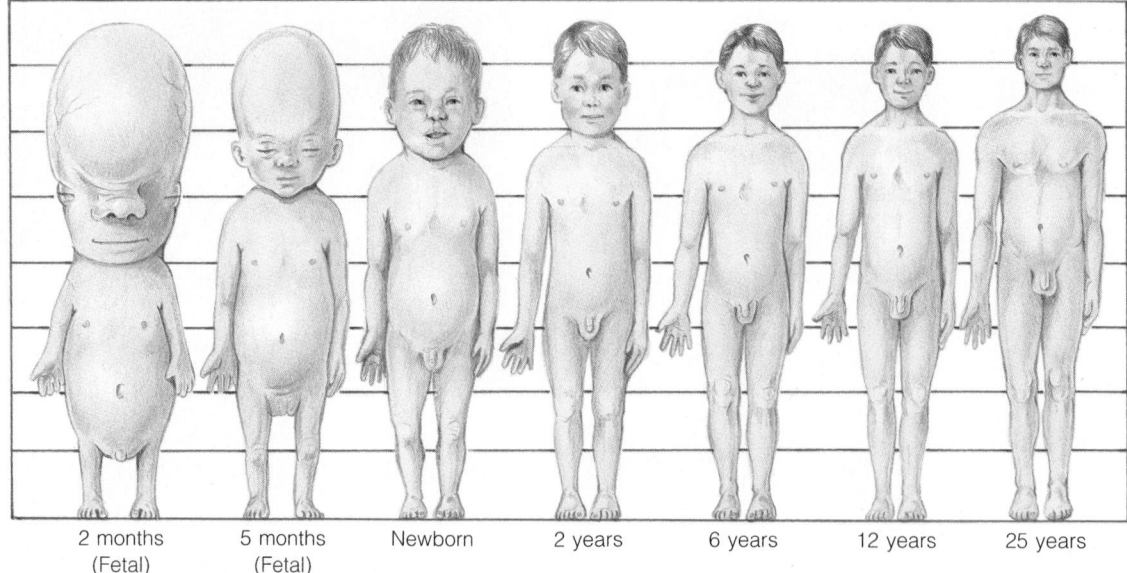

Figure 4.14 *The cephalocaudal principle of physical development is clearly shown in the changes that occur in body proportions as the human ages. The head develops earlier than the lower portions of the body. (Adapted from Robbins, 1929).*

| 2 months (Fetal) | 5 months (Fetal) | Newborn | 2 years | 6 years | 12 years | 25 years |

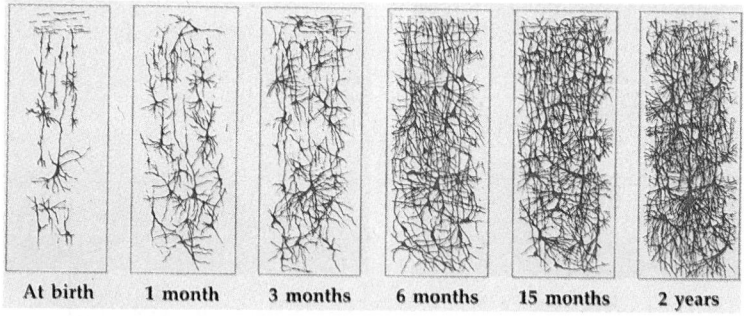

| At birth | 1 month | 3 months | 6 months | 15 months | 2 years |

Figure 4.15 *Increases in the density of neural networks during early development are apparent in these drawings of tissue from the human cerebral cortex.*

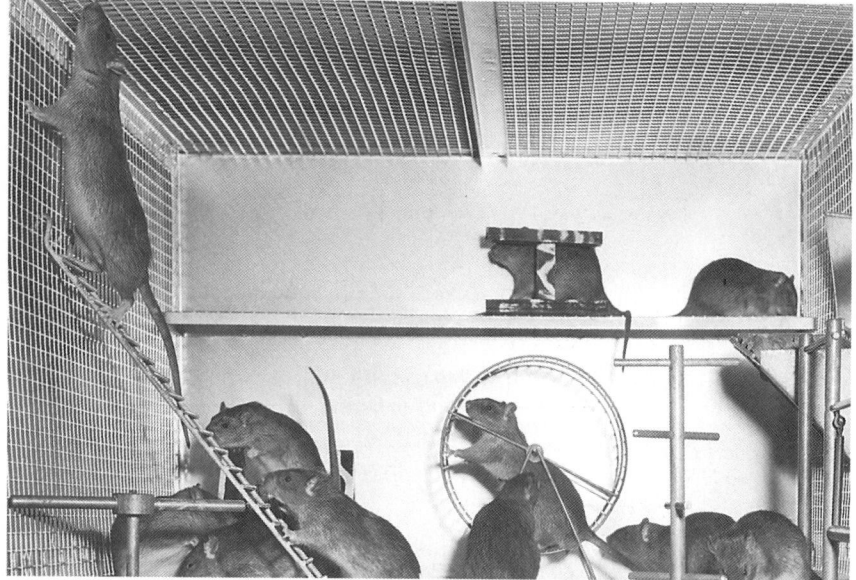

Figure 4.16 *The manner in which environment can affect both biological development and behavioral capabilities was demonstrated in studies in which rats were reared alone in laboratory cages or in "enriched" environments replete with playmates and toys.*

that enhances learning. These neural differences were reflected in faster learning of laboratory mazes (Rosenzweig, 1984). Similar results have been obtained with human babies. For example, premature infants who are caressed and massaged on a regular basis gain weight more rapidly and show faster neurological development (Field & others, 1986). As is often the case, reciprocal (two-way) interactions between biological and environmental factors are at work in these situations. In Rosenzweig's rat studies, for example, an enriched environment made it possible for certain play and social behaviors to occur. These behaviors apparently stimulated brain development, which in turn supported more complex forms of behavior, such as the ability to learn mazes (Rosenzweig, 1984).

The rapid rate of growth that characterized the first three years of life slows down during the remaining preschool years as the refinement and coordination of physical–motor abilities takes priority. As motor development proceeds through experience and the continuing maturation of the nervous system, clumsy, inaccurate efforts are replaced by smoother and more coordinated movements, allowing children to move about with greater confidence and ease. As predicted by the principles of differentiation and integration, gross motor behaviors such as running, kicking, and jumping improve before fine motor behaviors such as holding a crayon or using scissors.

The brain of the 5-year-old child has reached almost 90 percent of its adult size—closer to adult weight than any other part of the body (Tanner, 1978). Within the nervous system, the soft white myelin sheath coats perhaps half of all axons, insulating them and allowing nerve impulses to be transmitted more rapidly. This process of myelinization continues throughout childhood and adolescence, contributing to the child's growth in physical coordination and cognitive abilities.

Although there is little actual increase in the size of the brain between the ages of 5 and 10 years, the maturation process continues inside the brain. New synapses are formed, the association areas of the cerebral cortex mature, and the cerebral hemispheres become more highly specialized. Neural connections between the left and right hemispheres are fairly complete by age 7 or 8, allowing greater communication and coordination between them. Maturation of the brain and nervous system, together with a history of experiences in the physical and social worlds, usher in a process of cognitive development that permits children to think in increasingly logical ways and to master a language. Let us turn to the details of that development.

Figure 4.17 *Jean Piaget's careful observations of children as they solved problems were the foundation of his influential theory of cognitive development.*

■ ▫
Cognitive and Linguistic Development

What are the thought processes and cognitive abilities of children like? How do they change as the child matures? These questions captivated Jean Piaget, a Swiss developmental psychologist who spent more than 50 years charting the course of cognitive development in children. Piaget is truly the father, or perhaps the grandfather, of cognitive development research, and his ideas have influenced several generations of developmental psychologists.

Early in his career, Piaget worked for Alfred Binet, one of the originators of intelligence testing, helping to develop test questions. As he administered the questions to children of various ages, Piaget became intrigued by the nature of their *incorrect* answers. It seemed to him that there were important patterns in the errors children made, with children of the same age often making similar mistakes. Piaget came to believe that the critical issue in understanding how children think was not whether children got the right answers but *how* they arrived at their answers. This principle guided his work for the rest of his career.

Piaget's research approach was to closely observe how children tried to solve problems and to infer how they must be thinking about the problems to approach them as they did (see Figure 4.17). Such observations convinced Piaget that the mind of a child is not a miniature version of an adult's. The way in which children think about the world is qualitatively different from the way adults think. Indeed, children of different ages even differ from one another.

For Piaget, cognitive development occurs as a result of physical maturation combined with the child's interactions with the physical and social worlds. He viewed children as miniature scientists whose cognitive development represents an active, voluntary exploration of themselves and their world in a never-ending attempt to find meaning and understanding. To achieve these goals, the child's brain builds **schemas,** organized patterns of thought and action that the child uses to understand and respond to experience. Schemas are constructed and modified by two important processes, which Piaget termed assimilation and accommodation. **Assimilation** is the process by which children incorporate new experiences into existing schemas, interpreting and reacting to their experiences in terms of their current understanding. **Accommodation** is the process whereby children change schemas so that they can incorporate new experiences that do not "fit" existing schemas. For example, a child who sees a camel for the first time will try to assimilate this experience into one of her existing schemas for four-legged animals and may think of this creature as a "doggie." However, she may quickly notice that this is indeed a strange doggie and seek a better understanding of her observation. The process of accommodation may be aided by the parent who points to the animal and says, "That's a camel." The child can now modify, or accommodate,

Table 4.3 Piaget's Stages of Cognitive Development

Name	Age Period	Basic Concepts
Sensorimotor Stage	birth–2 yrs.	*Object permanence.* The stage develops gradually and is not fully complete until the child is about 18 months of age. At 6 months, babies will look for an object that has been hidden under a cloth while they are watching. But they do not keep looking for long, and if the object is hidden under a series of cloths, they will look under only the first one. By about 18 months of age, infants will search for objects they have not actually seen being hidden. Until then, children have no mental image or word to represent the existence of an object when it is not in sight. *Object constancy.* The child comes to understand that even if things appear different because of distance, light, viewing angle, and so on, they actually are the same.
Preoperational Stage	2–7 yrs.	*Object representation.* Children acquire the ability to represent objects and events to themselves through images or with a few words. *Object classification.* Children understand that objects can be classified and grouped. At first, children group things on the basis of what they can do with them—things you can throw, things you can put in your mouth, things that mothers use, things people ride in, and so forth. By the end of the period, children group things more systematically, often by color or shape. *Lessening of egocentrism.* Younger children are not able to imagine that an object looks different from another person's viewpoint. At the end of the period, they can describe things as they look to someone else—for example, someone sitting across from and facing them.
Concrete Operational Stage	7–12 yrs.	*Operations.* Children grasp the idea that certain processes are reversible. *Conservation concepts.* Children learn the idea that objects have fundamental qualities that do not change even when their outward appearance changes. Conservation concepts apply to length, number, quantity, and volume (see Figure 4.20). Some, such as volume, may not be understood even by a 12- to 14-year-old. *Class inclusion.* Children grasp the idea that one class is included in a larger class—for example, that in a bunch of flowers containing mostly daffodils there are more flowers (the larger class) than daffodils. *Mental representation.* Children acquire the ability to draw and use maps.
Formal Operational Stage	12 yrs. and beyond	*Deductive logic.* Children are able to use a general statement or theory to predict specific outcomes.

her schema of four-legged animals to include the new category ''camels.''

The accommodative process of seeking a fit and resolving imbalances between existing schemas and new experiences forces the child to new levels of cognitive development. Piaget charted the course of cognitive growth as a series of four major developmental stages that begin at birth and stretch into adulthood. These stages—sensorimotor, preoperational, concrete operational, and formal operational—are described in Table 4.3. The stages provide a useful framework for considering the course of cognitive development.

The Sensorimotor Stage

The first stage, which begins at birth, is the **sensorimotor stage.** As noted earlier, humans are born with a set of innate reflexive behaviors. For Piaget, these innate stimulus–response patterns are the earliest schemas that guide thought and action. Newborns use their sucking and grasping reflexes to assimiliate the properties of objects. They suck on any object placed near their mouths, be it a rattle, a pacifier, a blanket, or a nipple, and they grasp any object placed in their palms. In the first months of life, accommodation begins to occur as these schemas

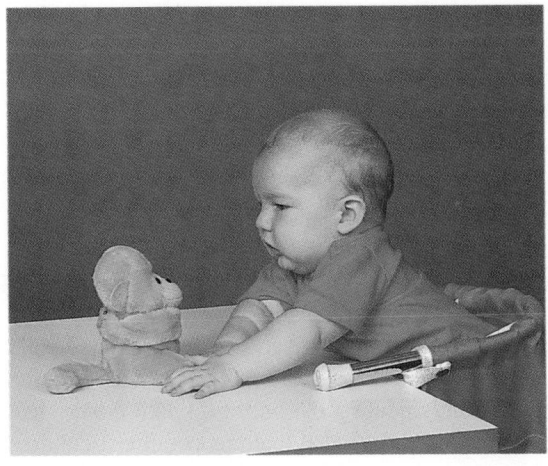

(a)

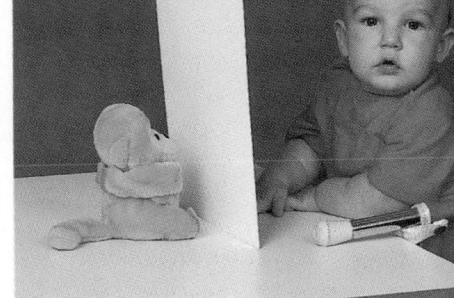

(b)

Figure 4.18 *During the sensorimotor period, a baby will reach for a visible toy* (a), *but not for one that is hidden from view* (b). *According to Piaget, the child lacks the concept of object permanence; when something is out of sight, it ceases to exist.*

are modified and elaborated by new experiences and by the maturation of sensory and motor capabilities. For example, accommodation has occurred when hungry infants prefer their mother's breasts to their pacifiers. They have developed different schemas for milk-producing objects and objects that do not produce milk so that they can tell the difference between the two and respond differently to them.

The major developmental milestone of the sensorimotor period is the emergence of **object permanence** at about 8 months. Infants come to realize for the first time that objects and people exist even when they are out of sight. If you cover 6-month-old Cindy's favorite crib toy with a blanket, she will not search for it (see Figure 4.18). Apparently, because it is no longer within her range of vision, it no longer exists as far as she is concerned. But with the development of object permanence, Cindy will pull back the blanket and retrieve the favorite toy. Object permanence is a major cognitive accomplishment, for it frees the child from the here and now and makes things that are unseen and unheard a part of the child's conscious experience.

As their sensory and motor capacities increase, babies begin to experiment actively with their environment. They do so by taking objects apart and by finding many other ways to test their surroundings. I will not soon forget the time my 18-month-old son used a shoe horn to remove all of the wood screws from his crib, sending his mattress (with him and his twin brother on it) crashing to the floor like a runaway elevator, nor the time the twins peeled large sheets of latex paint from the wall of their nursery. When their horrified parents entered the room, one of them proudly proclaimed the operative schema: "Band-aid!"

Increasing motor abilities allow toddlers to move about and explore their world like the curious "scientists" that Piaget was convinced they are. These experiences give toddlers a better understanding of their world and usher in the beginning of **symbolic thought**—the use of mental images to represent objects that are not present. Thus, a child may go to his toy box to get the truck that he needs for an imaginary car game. Children also become attentive to the behavior of others and learn from their observations. Piaget attributed great importance to imitation as a means of learning and adapting.

Andrew Meltzoff (1988) found that as early as 14 months of age, infants can clearly imitate actions that they have observed on television. In his experiment, children were seated in front of a video monitor (see Figure 4.19). After watching a televised adult model pull apart an unfamiliar toy, 65 percent of the infants did exactly the same thing when the toy was put on the table in front of them. Children in a control group that had not seen the model perform the behavior were far less likely to pull the toy apart—only 20 percent did so. Meltzoff also found that infants' memory processes are sufficiently advanced by 14 months that imitation is possible even if the infant is not given the toy until 24 hours after observing the televised model. Under this "delayed" experimental condition, 40 percent of the children performed the behavior. Meltzoff's findings indicate that television content can affect children's behavior quite early in life.

The child's cognitive achievements during the sensorimotor period are quite remarkable. In the space of 2 years, infants have evolved from largely reflexive creatures into planful thinkers who can form simple concepts, solve some problems mentally, and even communicate some of their thoughts to others. As the child enters Piaget's second stage of cognitive development, mental symbols become the most important instruments of thought.

The Preoperational Stage

At about 2 years of age, children enter the **preoperational stage** of cognitive development. Piaget called this stage preoperational because the

(a)

(b)

(c)

Figure 4.19 *Recent studies indicate that the power of television to teach extends downward into infancy: (a) In the first photograph, a 14-month-old boy watches an adult pull apart a novel toy. (b) The infant is given the same toy, which (c) he immediately pulls apart as the model did. (Courtesy of Andrew Meltzoff).*

year-old will insist that a volume of juice becomes smaller when poured from a tall, narrow glass into a short, wide glass or larger when poured from a short, wide glass into a tall, narrow one (see Figure 4.20). This is because the child focuses only on the height dimension and is incapable of reversing the operation by mentally pouring the juice back into the original glass. Piaget concluded that preoperational children have not yet acquired concepts of **conservation** that would allow them to understand that basic properties of objects (such as mass, number, quantity, and area) stay the same, or are conserved, even though their outward appearance may change.

Despite the absence of operations, important cognitive advances occur during the preoperational years. Around the age of 2, children begin to represent objects and actions with some kind of internal symbols. These symbols may be visual representations, such as a mental image of an object, or they may be more abstract representations, such as words or sentences. The rapid development of language during this period helps the child in the process of classification and grouping. Understanding that objects can be classified and grouped is the basis for concept formation and one of the major accomplishments of the preoperational period.

Seen through Piaget's eyes, preoperational children are **egocentric** in their thinking. That is, they are unable to view the world from someone else's perspective, and they think that everyone sees things in the same way they do. You can demonstrate this quality of preoperational thought yourself. Ask a 4-year-old to stand on the opposite side of a table from you and to put a knife or fork next to your plate so you can pick them up and eat. Most preschoolers will arrange the utensils from their perspective, with the handles facing themselves. You will likely find yourself facing the sharp "business ends" of the utensils. In a more formal demonstration of egocentrism, Piaget and Barbel Inhelder (1956) showed preschool children a scene with three different-sized mountains, each having distinctive landmarks (see Figure 4.21). Then they asked the children what a person observing the scene from behind the large mountain would see. The children said that the person would see exactly what they saw from their vantage point (for example, the house and the road), indicating an inability to adopt another's perceptual perspective and realize that the mountain would block the other person's view of these features.

child is not yet capable of comprehending certain rules, or *operations.* One such rule is *reversibility,* the notion that actions can be reversed or undone to get back to the original state of affairs. Thus, a clay ball can be rolled into a cylinder, then rolled back into a ball. You can add two pennies to three to get five, then return to the original number of coins by subtracting two pennies. Lacking such concepts, a 4-

Parents need to be aware of the egocentric qualities of children's thought during this period. Acts that may appear selfish and inconsiderate to an adult are often a result of the child's limited cognitive abilities rather than a product of malevolent intentions. Refusing to share a toy with a peer probably reflects the child's lack of appreciation for how he or she would feel if the situation were reversed. During the later years of the preoperational period, children gradually become less egocentric and more able to adopt another's perspective.

The Concrete Operational Stage

Piaget's third stage, lasting from about age 7 to about age 12, is the **concrete operational stage.** During this period, children acquire many of the mental operations that they lacked earlier. Because they grasp the concept of reversibility, they can solve the conservation problems that baffled them as preschoolers. They realize that changing the shape of a ball of clay from a sausage to a pancake doesn't change the amount of clay. Such changes always fool preoperational children. In contrast, older children may say, "It's still the same amount because you haven't added anything or taken anything away." Conservation abilities emerge gradually and at different times between the ages of 6 and 12, depending on the difficulty of the specific problem and the cognitive maturity of the child.

At about age 7, children can grasp the concept of serial ordering. If you give a very young child a set of blocks that differ in height and ask her to put them in order, she will be unable to do it. A child in the concrete operational period can perform the task because she understands the concept of relative size.

Children in this stage can also form a mental representation of a series of actions. For example, a concrete operational child could draw you a map of how to get to school. A younger child might be able to lead the way to school, but could not represent the route symbolically.

Children who are in the concrete operational stage use an increasing number of mental principles, but they are not yet able to reason abstractly. Piaget named this period the *concrete* operational stage because children in it are largely limited to performing mental operations on problems involving concrete, or existing, objects. It is not until adolescence that one becomes capable of deductive logic, or "if, then" reasoning. Children in the concrete operational stage can reason inductively. That is, they can use specific observations to arrive at a more general theory or principle. But until they are about 12 or 13, they cannot reverse the process—that is, begin with the theory or principle and hypothesize about what ought

Figure 4.20 *Preoperational children cannot perform the mental operations needed to understand conservation of liquids. They are convinced that the tall glass contains more. This will occur even when the contents of the short glass are poured into the tall glass before their very eyes.*

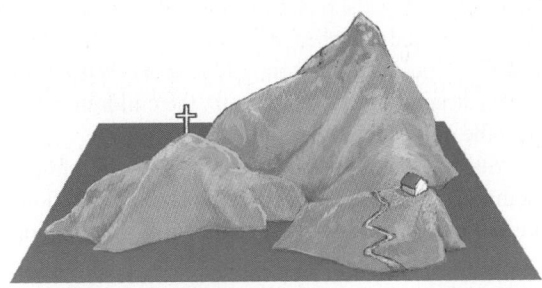

Figure 4.21 *Piaget used the three-mountain problem to illustrate the egocentrism of young children. Children viewing this scene often say that a person looking at the mountains from a different vantage point (for example, the other side of the large mountain) sees exactly what they see from their vantage point.*

to be observed if the theory is correct. We will examine the advance to formal operations in the next chapter.

Evaluating Piaget's Theory

As noted at the beginning of the chapter, one of the basic issues in developmental psychology revolves around the nature of development. Does development proceed through a series of discrete stages, or is development a continuous, incremental process?

Piaget's is a strict stage theory, for he maintained that each cognitive stage represents new modes of thinking that are impossible at earlier stages. What has the enormous amount of research inspired by Piaget's theory to say about this assumption? The answer may provide valuable insights into the nature of cognitive development.

As is typical in science, research has shed new light on some of Piaget's ideas (Gelman & Baillargeon, 1983; Shaffer, 1989). For one thing, it now appears that many cognitive skills begin to appear, at least in rudimentary form, much earlier than Piaget thought. For example, if test conditions are carefully arranged so that children's success does not depend on their language abilities (in this case, their understanding of what the experimenter means by "more" or "longer"), children presumed to be preoperational can succeed on number conservation problems that involve distinguishing between the number of objects in a set and the objects' spatial arrangement (Gelman & Gallistel, 1978). In one such study with 4- to 6-year-old children, the experimenter laid out two identical rows of objects and then pushed one row together and asked the children which row had fewer objects. As Piaget would have predicted, most children said that the shorter row had fewer objects, indicating that they had not yet mastered the principle of conservation. However, when the examiner told the children that she had a mischievous teddy bear who was always messing up the toys and then made the bear move one row of objects closer together, most of the children said the number of objects was the same (McGarrigle & Donaldson, 1974/1975). With a different structuring of the problem, the children exhibited the ability to conserve.

Second, there does not seem to be a strict line of demarcation between preoperational and operational thought; virtually all of the elements of concrete operational abilities appear to be present in some form in the preschool years. Undoubtedly, real changes in the way children think appear at age 6 or 7, but the changes seem to reflect not a new kind of thinking but rather a more mature form of what was already present at age 3 or 4 (Flavell, 1982). Critics of a pure stage scheme also point out that children often show marked inconsistencies in their thinking abilities.

Thus, a child may appear to be stuck at the preoperational stage on one task yet clearly demonstrate concrete operational abilities on another. This should not be possible if the child is at a single stage of development; we should see almost complete consistency in thinking abilities across tasks. In summary, while Piaget was correct about the sequence in which cognitive abilities develop, it appears that children can show different levels of cognitive ability on different tasks and that some cognitive abilities may emerge earlier than Piaget originally assumed.

Information-Processing Approaches to Cognitive Development

An alternative to Piaget's theory is the **information-processing approach.** Theorists who favor this approach argue that cognitive development represents not a series of distinct stages but rather a gradual increase in the abilities to attend to the environment and to learn, remember, and apply information. They regard development as a process whereby children *reduce limitations* on their ability to process information (Cole & Cole, 1989). These limitations are caused by uneven or deficient attention, limited memory, and poorly developed strategies for retaining information or approaching problems (Siegler, 1986). Thus, a younger child may be unable to solve a water conservation problem because he did not attend well enough to the task or because he cannot simultaneously hold enough pieces of information in memory to realize that the amount of water is the same even when the shape of the container changes.

Consider the two houses in Figure 4.22. Are they identical or different? How, precisely, did you decide? This is an easy task for you or me, but it is a difficult one for 3- and 4-year-olds because they approach the comparison less systematically than we do. Eliane Vurpillot (1968) showed these and other sets of houses to children aged 3 to 10 and recorded their eye movements while they examined the houses. The eye movements showed that the older children scanned the houses in a systematic manner, comparing each of the windows. In contrast, the preschoolers tended to look haphazardly at only a few of the windows, and they had a great deal of trouble detecting differences, particularly if the houses differed in only one or two ways. Clearly, the preschoolers showed only limited ability to select relevant details and search systematically for differences.

Young children, even 2- and 3-year-olds, can often surprise us with their ability to remember events or names. But when it comes to organizing information and using strategies to improve memory, they fall far short of school-aged children. For example, rehearsal of information is a very effective way to improve retention. In a cross-sectional study, John

Flavell (1970) gave children of various ages lists of words or numbers to remember. He observed that preschool children almost never used rehearsal spontaneously, whereas 8- to 10-year-olds could often be heard rehearsing the words or numbers under their breath. If the preschool children were taught to use rehearsal on a particular task, their recall improved, but if they were then given another problem in which rehearsal could be used, they failed to apply the strategy. Similar findings occur with regard to "chunking," an organizational strategy for grouping related objects or words together (Brown & others, 1983).

Young children not only fail to attend to and process information effectively, but they show almost no awareness of their own mental processes. With middle childhood comes the emergence of **metacognition,** the child's awareness and knowledge of his or her own cognitive activities (Flavell, 1985). For example, older children have a better idea of whether they have learned the material for a test than young children do, and they can judge how well they understand instructions, such as directions to a new friend's house. Such judgments can help them to decide more realistically if additional study is needed or if they need to ask their friend to draw a map. They can also describe how they go about memorizing material in school or how they solve particular types of problems. From the information-processing perspective, these metacognitive abilities are critical aids to thinking, learning, and remembering, and they help children to increase their problem-solving abilities (Flavell, 1985).

One conclusion shared by stage theorists and information-processing theorists is that cognitive abilities are linked to the maturation of the brain. During the preschool years, as we have seen, the brain increases in size, and myelinization of neural networks results in more effective communication between many areas of the brain. Thus, over time, the neural structures needed to support cognitive maturation develop, and the child becomes capable of increasingly complex and efficient cognitive operations. Nowhere is this more obvious than in the development of language. Cognitive maturation permits linguistic abilities to develop. These, in turn, contribute greatly to other cognitive and social competencies.

Language and Its Development

Language is one of the defining marks of humanity. It is a method of communication qualitatively different from that used by any other species. Most of the grunts, howls, barks, and whistles we hear from other animals are signals about the sender's motivational or emotional state—whether the animal is frightened, hungry, or amorous. By contrast, human language is

Figure 4.22 *Stimuli used by Vurpillot to assess visual inspection through filmed eye movements. Preschoolers fail to scan the pictures systematically, which often leads them to claim that the two houses are identical. (From Vurpillot, 1968).*

referential; we use language messages to talk about things other than our own desires. A seal can indicate that it is hungry, but only a human can discuss the relative merits of salmon and crab.

Language consists of a system of symbols and rules for combining these symbols in ways that can produce an infinite number of possible messages or meanings. This definition implies three critical properties that are essential to any language.

First, language is *symbolic.* It uses sounds, written signs, or gestures to refer to objects, events, ideas, and feelings. This means that objects that are not physically present and events that are not currently occurring can be represented and that meanings can be communicated through the symbols. As a communication vehicle, we can view language as a means by which a communicator attempts to develop a mental representation of an object, event, or idea in the mind of the person to whom the message is being directed. When this mental representation approximates that held by the communicator, we say that meaning has been successfully communicated.

Second, language is *structured.* That is, rules govern how symbols are combined to create meaningful communication units. Thus, if I ask you if *zpflrovc* is an English word, you will almost certainly say that it is not. Why? Because it violates rules of the English language that /z/ is not to be followed by /pf/ and that five consonants are not to be combined. Likewise, you would not consider the string of words "Bananas have sale for I no" an appropriate English sentence. We may not be able to verbalize all the rules of English, but we know them implicitly because they are part of the language we speak.

Third, language is *generative.* This means that the symbols can be combined to generate an infinite number of messages which can have novel meaning. Thus, if you are a speaker of English you can understand sentences like "Who put the nightingale under my strudel?" even though you are unlikely to have heard anything like them. You can even imagine circumstances in which they might be said.

Humans apparently are born linguists, and language acquisition seems to be a special case of the unfolding of an innate ability within a learning context. Many language experts believe that humans inherit a biological readiness to interpret the sounds people make in a certain way, so that each child eventually recognizes and produces the structure of the language of his or her society (Chomsky, 1965; Lieberman, 1984). However, this unfolding requires a linguistic environment that provides the necessary learning experiences (Bruner, 1983).

The Structure of Language

Psycholinguists describe language as having both a surface structure and a deep structure. The **surface structure** consists of the way symbols are combined within a given language. The rules for such combination are called the **syntax** of a language. **Deep structure** refers to the underlying meaning of the combined symbols. The rules for connecting the symbols to their referents, or meanings, are known as **semantics.** To see the difference between surface structure and deep structure, consider the following sentences:

1. Eloise ran over the pit bull with her Big Wheel.
2. The Big Wheel driven by Eloise ran over the pit bull.
3. The police must stop drinking after midnight.

The first two sentences have different surface structures but the same deep structure. In other words, they have different syntax but are similar at a semantic level. The third sentence is an ambiguous one that can have two different deep structures (Miller, 1981). The rules for both surface structure and deep structure are stored in memory. However, when we recall something, we are likely to retrieve deep structure (meaning) rather than the specific words.

In considering the formal structure of language, we can retreat to an even more elemental level and consider the basic building blocks that are combined into the symbols that convey meaning.

Human languages have a hierarchical structure. The lowest rung on the ladder is the phoneme. **Phonemes** are the smallest units of sound that are recognized as separate in a given language. Humans are capable of producing about 100 phonemes, but no language uses all of these sounds. For example, European and Asian languages do not use the clicking sounds heard in several African languages. The world's languages vary considerably in their phonemes, employing as few as 15 in some cases and more than 80 in others. English uses about 40 phonemes, consisting of the various vowel and consonant sounds, as well as certain letter combinations such as *th* and *sh.*

Phonemes are combined into **morphemes,** the smallest units of meaning in a language. Morphemes, which consist of a single syllable, include some words (*tree, ball, it*), as well as prefixes and suffixes such as *-ed, un-, -ous,* and *pre-.* The suffix *-ous* is formed from two phonemes, *uh* and *s.* In all languages, syntactic rules restrict how phonemes can be combined into morphemes. As noted earlier, for example, we cannot combine five consonants in English. Even with such restrictions, our 40 English phonemes can be combined into more than 100,000 morphemes. Morphemes, in turn, can be combined into nearly half a million words, words into countless phrases, and phrases into an almost infinite number of sentences. Thus, from the humble phoneme to the elegant sentence, we have a five-step language hierarchy (see Figure 4.23).

Language Development

The acquisition of language is one of the most striking events in the cognitive development of children. In a few short years, a totally nonverbal creature comes to understand and produce a complex language.

It was earlier noted that children seem to be born linguists. Analyses of young children's utterances have revealed that in the beginning, they vocalize the entire range of phonemes that are found in the world's languages. In the transition from babbling to talking, however, their range of utterances narrows until it includes only the phonemes that are part of their native tongue (Lieberman, 1984). It is as if human infants generate a sequence of "guesses" about the units of language and extend these guesses until they hit upon the correct rules for the language of their society. This is not a conscious process. It does appear

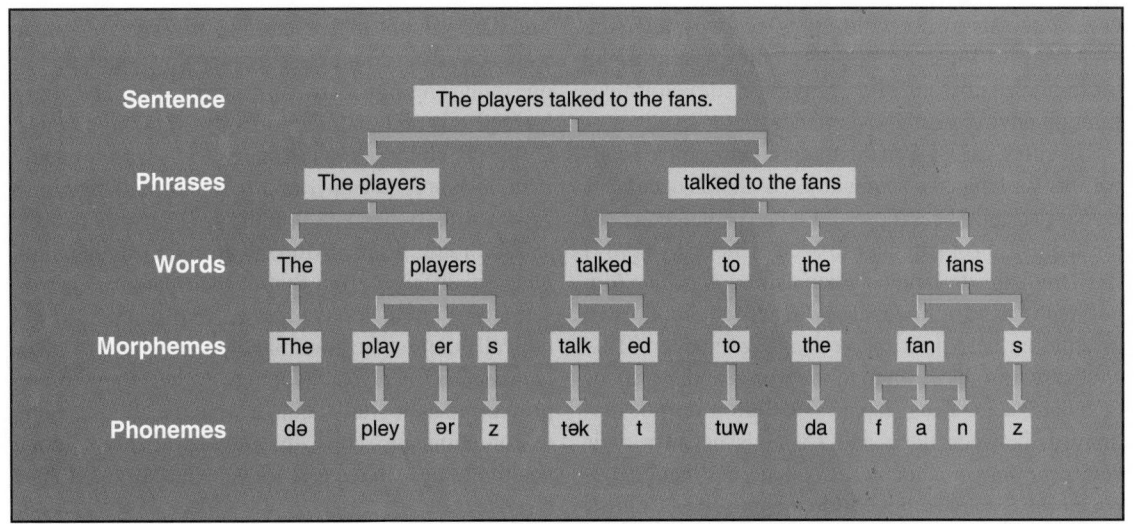

Figure 4.23 *Human language is structured in a hierarchical arrangement, with phonemes the most basic unit. The line of phonemes contains symbols used by linguists to denote particular sounds.*

to be a biologically based mechanism that will, in combination with input from the child's linguistic environment, eventually uncover the appropriate language—that is, any language spoken by humans. If this analysis is correct, children should learn language in a regular fashion as their guesses become progressively more refined and as their speech-production systems mature. This they do, regardless of their culture, in the age-related progression shown in Table 4.4.

The first stage of language development begins with reflexive crying. The four different sound patterns associated with this early crying seem to communicate anger, pain, hunger, and frustration (Wolf, 1969). The biological underpinnings of language development are evidenced by the fact that infants throughout the world utter exactly the same sounds in three distinct stages: (1) crying at birth; (2) cooing as the beginning of vowel sounds, which usually begins at 2 to 3 months of age; and (3) babbling, in which consonants are added to vowel sounds, which begins at 3 to 6 months of age (Oller, 1978). At about 6 months, however, the influence of the environment is observed as infants begin to make the sounds of their native tongue and discard those of other languages.

The analysis has another implication: All adult languages should have structural regularities that fit with the child's guesses. Again, regardless of the culture and the language studied, they seem to. In fact, the psycholinguist Noam Chomsky (1965, 1987) has been so impressed by the similarities among languages that he has suggested that the understanding of deep structure is a biological characteristic that is built into the human brain. He posits a **language acquisition device (LAD)** consisting of at least some inborn knowledge about the structural properties of language as well as a set of cognitive and perceptual abilities that are specialized for language learning.

Table 4.4 Language Development in Children

Age	Speech Characteristics
1–3 months	Infants can distinguish speech from nonspeech sounds, and they prefer speech sounds (phonemes); undifferentiated crying gives way to cooing when happy.
4–6 months	Babbling sounds begin to occur. These contain sounds from virtually every language. Child vocalizes in response to verbalizations of others.
7–11 months	Babbling sounds narrow to include only the phonemes heard in the languages spoken by others in the environment. Child moves tongue with vocalizations (lalling). Child discriminates between some words without understanding their meaning and begins to imitate word sounds heard from others.
12 months	First recognizable words typically spoken as one-word utterances to name familiar people and objects (e.g., *da-da* or *block*).
12–18 months	Child increases knowledge of word meanings and begins to use single words to express whole phrases or requests (e.g., *out* to express a desire to get out of the crib); uses primarily nouns.
18–24 months	Vocabulary expands to 50–100 words, and first rudimentary sentences appear, usually consisting of two words (e.g., *more milk*) with little or no use of articles *(the,a)*, conjunctions *(and)*, and auxiliary verbs *(can, will)*. This condensed, or telegraphic speech, is characteristic of first sentences throughout the world.
2–4 years	Vocabulary expands rapidly at the rate of several hundred words every 6 months. Two-word sentences give way to longer sentences that, though often grammatically incorrect, exhibit basic language syntax. Child begins to express concepts with words and to use language to describe imaginary objects and ideas, and sentences become more correct syntactically.
4–5 years	Most children have learned the basic grammatical rules for combining nouns, adjectives, articles, conjunctions, and verbs into meaningful sentences.

Other linguists are not willing to go so far as the LAD, preferring to focus on the developing brain as the biological substrate for language development through environmental experiences.

In either case, given the required biological foundations for language acquisition, all that is necessary is that the child be exposed to a native language for the acquisition of language to occur. Chomsky (1987) likens our innate language acquisition capacity to a box with banks of linguistic switches that are thrown as children hear their native language spoken. This exposure introduces them to the words and syntax of their language. Thus, Japanese children do not distinguish between the *r* and *l* sounds because their language does not make a phonetic distinction between the 2 sounds, but children exposed to English can discriminate the sounds at an early age. Likewise, Japanese-speaking children learn to put the object before the verb ("Sadahara the ball threw"), whereas English-speaking children learn the syntactic rule that the verb comes before the object ("John threw the ball").

As noted earlier, some linguists are also convinced that there is a critical period for language acquisition that extends from infancy to puberty (Lenneberg, 1967). One line of evidence for this assertion comes from studies of children who lived by themselves in the wild or who were isolated from human contact by disturbed parents. As we saw in the case of Genie, even with intensive language training, such children never acquire normal speech (Clarke & Clarke, 1976; Curtiss, 1977). However, Genie's case also suggests that Lenneberg's assertion that puberty is the end of the critical period for language acquisition needs to be softened, for Genie clearly showed some progress in language development in her teens. Perhaps it would be more accurate to say that the years prior to puberty seem to be a *sensitive period* for the *normal* learning of a first language (Shaffer, 1989). This sensitive period exists not only for spoken language but also for the acquisition of sign language by deaf children. Such children show a distinct language-learning deficit if they are not exposed to sign language before puberty (Meier, 1991).

Learning processes are also clearly involved in acquiring a language. Parents and others serve as models for verbal behavior, they teach their children words and syntax, and they reinforce children in a variety of ways for successful language. B. F. Skinner (1957, 1985) developed an elaborate learning explanation for language acquisition using basic principles of conditioning. The basic premise is that children's language development is governed by adults' rewarding of appropriate language and nonrewarding of inappropriate verbalizations. However, most modern psycholinguists reject Skinner's explanation and

find it very doubtful that learning principles alone can satisfactorily account for language development. For one thing, children learn too much too fast. They have learned several hundred words by 30 months of age. By age 6, children are estimated to be learning more than 15 words per day, and their vocabularies have grown to between 8,000 and 14,000 words (Carey, 1977; Smith, 1926). Moreover, much of their language is different from that of their parents, and observational studies have shown that parents do not typically correct the grammar of their children as their language skills are developing. Rather, they correct primarily on the truth value of what the child is trying to communicate. Thus, they will probably respond positively to "I have two foots," but not to "I have three feet."

The prevailing view is that language acquisition represents the unfolding of a biologically primed process within a learning environment and that it is part of the more general growth of cognitive capacities in the developing human. ▼

Piaget (1926) believed that as children develop intellectually, they produce increasingly sophisticated utterances, which cause adults to increase the complexity of their own speech (see Figure 4.24). This input results in accommodation of schemas to include increasingly more complex language. Jerome Bruner (1983), who studied how parents and children communicate with one another, suggested that the way adults structure their language input to children should be considered a **language acquisition support system (LASS),** the necessary complement to Chomsky's biologically based LAD.

Adults constitute an important part of the language-learning environment. Early on, they maintain their children's interest and attract their attention by conversing with them in a high-pitched intonation called *motherese*. In addition, they use falling intonations to comfort their infants and staccato bursts for prohibitions. Parents in all cultures use these intonations, and babies universally understand and respond to them (Fernald & others, 1989). Parents also teach their children words by pointing out objects and naming them, by reading aloud, and by responding to "What's that?" inquiries, which begin at about 18 months of age. Thereafter, children begin to combine their one-word utterances into two-word sentences. These sentences are examples of **telegraphic speech,** which typically includes nouns and verbs (for example, "Want cookie") but leaves out unessential words, as a telegram does. Parents often respond to such speech by taking into account the situational context in which the speech occurs.

Telegraphic speech signals the beginning of multiword grammar. Once the two-word stage ends, sometime after the 24th month, children begin uttering increasingly long and complex sentences that follow basic grammatical rules of their language. As children hear the speech of their culture, Chomsky believes, grammar switches are thrown in the LAD. Thereafter, the grammar of the language is easily learned, often with assistance from adults. Thus, English-speaking children learn to put the object in a sentence last (''I saw the dog''), whereas children who learn Japanese put the object before the verb (''I the dog saw''). A study of Korean and Chinese immigrants to the United States showed that if the children learned a second language early in life, they could master that grammar about as well as the grammar of their first language. After ages 3 to 7, however, the mastery of English grammar was progressively more difficult (Johnson & Newport, 1989).

Linguistic Influences on Thinking

Much of our thinking involves the use of language. In his **linguistic relativity hypothesis,** the linguist Benjamin Lee Whorf (1956) contended that language not only influences but *determines* how and what we think. He pointed out, for example, that Eskimos have many words for snow and concluded that as a result, they actually perceive this aspect of the world differently from English speakers who have only one word (see Figure 4.25). In this view, children's thinking should depend to some extent on the vocabulary they happen to have at a given time.

The opposing view is that thought shapes language, reflecting the ways in which our minds work. Eskimos have many words for snow because their well-being depends on this discrimination. Similarly, skiers develop concepts like *powder, sun crust,* and *corn snow* to make important discriminations.

If the linguistic relativity hypothesis is correct, then people whose cultures have only a few words for colors should have greater difficulty in perceiving the spectrum of colors than do people whose languages have many different color words. In one test of this proposition, Eleanor Rosch (1973) studied the Dani of New Guinea, who have only two color words in their language, one for bright warm colors, the other for cool dark ones. She found that, contrary to what strict linguistic determinism would suggest, the Dani *could* discriminate among and remember a wide assortment of hues in much the same manner as speakers of the English language, which contains many color names. Similar results occurred for shapes that were not represented in the Dani language.

Today, most linguists do not agree that language determines how we think. They would say instead that language reflects basic aspects of human perception and thought. They would agree, however, that language influences how efficiently we can categorize our experiences and perhaps how much detail we attend to in our daily experience (Hunt & Agnoli,

Figure 4.24 *Piaget and other developmentalists stress the importance of the language-learning environment that parents and others provide by introducing children to increasingly sophisticated language in response to the child's increasing language competencies.*

1991). This is of no minor importance, for the encoding of information affects perception and memory in important ways. The power of language to influence thinking makes vocabulary development a critical part of the educational process in any field. The vocabulary you are learning in this course will provide new concepts that will influence how you think about behavior in the future. Likewise, as their vocabularies expand, children become capable of thinking in more sophisticated ways.

Figure 4.25 *Eskimos have many different words for various kinds of snow. Does their language shape their thought processes, or does it reflect the way their minds work?*

Personality and Social Development

Personality refers to the distinctive and relatively consistent ways of thinking, feeling, and behaving that characterize our responses to the life situations that we encounter. Like other aspects of the developing child, the roots of personality and social behavior lie in the interaction of biological and environmental factors. As we shall see, our genetic makeup gives us certain emotional and behavioral predispositions which are reinforced or modified in our early social environment.

Stage Theories of Personality Development: Freud and Erikson

If Piaget is the father of cognitive developmental theory, then Sigmund Freud and Erik Erikson must be considered the progenitors of personality development theories. Paralleling Piaget's conception of fixed and invariant stages of cognitive development, Freud and Erikson both believed that personality development proceeds through a series of specific stages. Sigmund Freud (1933) maintained that adult personality is in large part established during the first 5 years of life as the child confronts conflicts between biological urges and the demands of society. In contrast, Erik Erikson (1980) viewed personality development

as occurring across the entire life span in response to a sequence of developmental tasks, or identity crises, that arise at specific stages of our lives.

The developmental stages proposed by the two theorists are shown in Table 4.5. Freud's theory will be considered in greater detail in Chapter 14. For now, we will focus on his viewpoints on personality development. Erikson's theory, which stretches across the entire life span, will be discussed in both this chapter and the next.

Freud's Psychosexual Theory

At each of Freud's psychosexual stages, the concerns of the child and society are focused on a specific pleasure-giving area of the body. On the basis of clinical observations of his adult patients, Freud became convinced that the circumstances of children's lives at each stage determine the course of personality development.

The first of these stages is the **oral stage,** which occurs during infancy. Infants gain primary satisfaction from taking in food and from sucking or chewing on a thumb, a breast, or some other object. Freud proposed that either excessive gratification or frustration of oral needs can result in a state of arrested development, or **fixation,** on oral themes of self-indulgence or dependency. When babies pass through this stage successfully, they become basically trusting of others but not overly dependent on them.

During the second and third years of life, children enter the **anal stage.** During this developmental pe-

Approximate Age (years)	Freud's Psychosexual Stages	Erikson's Psychosocial Stages and Developing Ego Qualities
0–1	Oral Stage	Oral–sensory Basic trust vs. basic mistrust
2–3	Anal stage	Muscular–anal Autonomy vs. shame, doubt
4–5	Phallic stage	Locomotor–genital Initiative vs. guilt
6–12	Latency stage	Latency Industry vs. inferiority
Adolescence 13–20	Genital stage	Adolescence Identity vs. role confusion
Early adulthood 20–40		Early adulthood Intimacy vs. isolation
Middle adulthood 40–65		Middle adulthood Generativity vs. stagnation
Late adulthood		Late Adulthood Ego-integrity vs. despair

Table 4.5 Freud's and Erikson's Stages of Personality Development

riod, pleasure becomes focused on the process of elimination, and the child is faced with society's first attempt to control a biological urge in the form of toilet training. Children who pass successfully through this stage become flexible, generous, and tidy adults. According to Freud, harsh toilet training can produce compulsions, overemphasis on cleanliness, obsessive concerns with orderliness, and insistence on excessive rules and rituals. In contrast, Freud speculated that a messy, negative, and dominant adult emerges when parents are too lax in toilet training.

The most controversial of Freud's stages is the **phallic stage,** which begins at 4 or 5 years of age. This is the time when children begin to derive pleasure from their sexual organs. Freud believed that during this stage of early sexual awakenings, the male child experiences erotic feelings toward his mother and desires to possess her sexually and eliminate his father. At the same time, however, these feelings arouse strong guilt and a fear of reprisal from the father in the form of **castration anxiety.** This conflictual situation is the **Oedipus complex,** named for the Greek character Oedipus, who unknowingly killed his father and married his mother. Girls, meanwhile, discover that they lack a penis, blame the mother for their lack of what Freud considered the more desirable sex organ, and wish to bear their father's child as a substitute for the penis they lack. The female version of the Oedipus complex was termed the **Electra complex.** Freud believed that children normally resolve these conflicts of the phallic stage by moving from a sexual attachment to the opposite-sex parent to identification with the same-sex parent, boys taking on the traits of fathers and girls identifying with their mothers. Freud speculated that this process of **identification** allows the child to possess the opposite-sex parent indirectly, or vicariously, while reducing the anxiety created by the complex. Freud considered identification the most important process in sex-role development.

As the phallic stage draws to a close at about 6 years of age, the child enters a **latency stage.** During this period of about 6 years, considerable social development occurs with same-sex peers, but these interactions are not erotic in nature. With the onset of puberty, sexual feelings toward the opposite sex return during the **genital stage,** but in a new form. In well-socialized adolescents and adults, the selfish sexuality of the earlier stages is transformed into a mature genital love, and the individual is capable of genuine caring and adult sexual satisfaction.

Freud's ideas about psychosexual development are undoubtedly the most controversial aspect of his theory. Although most theorists agree that childhood experiences are very important in the development of personality, many of them reject Freud's assertions about childhood sexuality as well as the notion of specific psychosexual stages.

Erikson's Psychosocial Theory

Inspired by Freud, Erik Erikson also developed a stage theory of personality development. He referred to these stages as *psychosocial* rather than *psychosexual* to emphasize his belief that socially influenced **identity crises** encountered at various periods of life are more important than crises caused by biological drives. In all, Erikson identified eight psychosocial stages (see Table 4.5). Four of them occur prior to adolescence and will be described here. The rest will be described in Chapter 5.

Stage 1: Oral–sensory.   During the first year of life, we are totally dependent on our parents. How adequately our needs are met and how much love and attention we receive determine whether we develop **basic trust** or **basic mistrust** of the world. Healthy personality development is built on a foundation of basic trust.

Stage 2: Muscular–anal.   During the second year of life, children who have developed basic trust become ready to separate themselves from their parents and exercise their individuality. Erikson viewed many of the rebellious ''terrible twos'' behaviors as attempts to achieve some measure of **autonomy.** If parents unduly restrict children or make harsh, unreasonable demands on them during toilet training, children tend to develop **shame and doubt** about their abilities and later lack the courage to be independent individuals.

Stage 3: Locomotor–genital.   During the third through fifth years, the autonomy and control issues of Stage 2 are supplanted by an exploratory curiosity about the world. Children at this stage want to know the ''whys'' and ''hows'' of things around them. If they are allowed freedom, receive answers to their questions, and are left free to explore their bodies and the environment, they develop a sense of **initiative.** If they are held back or punished, they develop **guilt** about their desires and suppress their basic curiosity.

Stage 4: Latency.   From the sixth year until puberty, the child's life expands into school experiences and a widening range of peer relationships. Children who experience a sense of pride in being able to master tasks and reach their goals develop what Erikson called **industry** (see Figure 4.26). If they fail repeatedly or do not receive encouragement and praise for trying, they develop a sense of **inferiority.**

Erikson captured in his stages many of the developmental issues that confront children as they interact with their environments and develop a sense of self. His outlook is more optimistic than Freud's because negative resolution of a developmental crisis

Figure 4.26 *According to Erikson, during the elementary-school years, mastery experiences engender a sense of industry, whereas important failures contribute to the development of a sense of inferiority.*

need not result in permanent damage or fixation at that stage. A need left unsatisfied at an earlier stage can be satisfied later. By expanding on Freud's developmental stages, Erikson stimulated interest in development across the entire life span.

Both Freud and Erikson viewed personality development as involving interactions of a biological organism with a social environment. Neither could know the extent to which today's researchers are finding this interaction to be important. Freud and Erikson were more concerned with biological universals than with individual differences in biological predispositions. However, research on temperament has emphasized how our predispositions differ. Let us examine some of these differences.

PSYCHOBIOLOGICAL INTERACTIONS

Temperament

Any parent with more than one child can attest to the fact that infants seem to differ from one another in important ways from the moment of birth. For example, some infants are placid and happy, whereas others are irritable and cry more. Some are outgoing, while others are inhibited. Considerable scientific evidence supports the view that children are, in fact, born with different **temperaments**—distinct styles of emotional reactivity and ways of interacting with the environment (Kagan & Snidman, 1991; Wachs, 1992).

In a landmark study of infant temperament, Alexander Thomas and Stella Chess (1977, 1986) studied the characteristics that 141 babies displayed in their observed interactions with their parents. They found that the behavioral patterns of these babies could be placed in three fairly distinct categories. The *easy* infants, who comprised 40 percent of the sample, were described as quick to develop regular feeding and sleep patterns. They related positively to new people and situations, they accepted frustrations with little fuss, and they were characterized by mild, mostly positive moods. In sharp contrast were *difficult* infants, described as irregular in eating and sleeping patterns, negative in their emotional reactions to new people and situations, subject to violent tantrums when frustrated, and characterized by intense, mostly negative moods. They constituted about 10

percent of the babies. The third group, comprising about 15 percent of the babies, was termed *slow to warm up*. Babies in this group had mildly negative responses to new people and situations, but they showed slow adaptability after repeated contact. The remaining 35 percent of the infants had a mixture of traits from the three major categories.

The temperamental patterns observed by Thomas and Chess have been confirmed in later research, so these differences appear to be real ones (Green & others, 1989). But how do they relate to what the child is like later in life? To answer this important question, Thomas and Chess did a longitudinal study in which they followed their infants over the next 10 years. They found that many of the behaviors were indeed stable over time. For example, newborns rated as "difficult" were more likely to have behavior problems during the preschool and elementary-school years. It seems likely that these problems were a product of both their negative behaviors, which were influenced by innate temperament, and the negative reactions that such behaviors would be expected to evoke from their social environments. If so, we have an example of how biological dispositions and environmental factors can support one another.

At Harvard University, Jerome Kagan and his coworkers have been studying the biological roots of shyness (Kagan & others, 1988; Kagan & Snidman, 1991). Like Thomas and Chess, the Harvard researchers have found that the early signs of shyness appear in infants. Such infants cry and withdraw in response to unfamiliar visual stimuli or the sound of a strange female voice saying nonsense syllables. Twenty-three percent of the infants these researchers observed showed the crying and withdrawal pattern. When retested with novel stimuli at 9, 14, and 21 months of age, these children continued to be more distressed and avoidant than the other infants. Physiological measures suggested that the shy children had lower thresholds of excitability in their limbic systems, resulting in higher levels of emotional arousal in response to novel stimuli. Kagan suggests that this tendency to experience high levels of fear or anxiety motivates withdrawal behavior.

In other studies, Kagan and his associates found that by the second year of life, about 15 percent of children are consistently shy and emotionally subdued in unfamiliar situations, whereas another 15 percent are consistently sociable and spontaneous. Beginning at 2 years of age, children who had previously been classified as either shy, quiet, and timid or as sociable, talkative, and spontaneous were observed in a laboratory room as they encountered unfamiliar people and objects. Each group of children was also observed on three other occasions, the last when the children were 7½ years of age. The later observations included laboratory play situations with 7 to 10 unfamiliar children of the same age and gender.

The findings were quite clear: The shy 2-year-olds developed into 7-year-olds who were quiet, cautious, and socially avoidant of peers and adults. In contrast, the outgoing 2-year-olds became 7-year-olds who were sociable and talkative. Moreover, these behavioral differences were mirrored by different patterns of physiological responses in unfamiliar situations, as with the inhibited infants described earlier. Shy children at every age had faster heart rates and higher levels of early morning salivary cortisol, a hormone that reflects stress-related activity in the hypothalamus and pituitary gland. In contrast, the uninhibited children did not have the biological readiness to experience stress in novel or unexpected situations. Instead, Kagan suggests, they found novelty to be stimulating in a positive fashion, and they developed a behavioral pattern of approach rather than avoidance. The behavioral and physiological findings of the Harvard studies thus support the notion that the two types of children have different genotypes, which interact with environmental events to produce a set of accompanying physiological and behavioral traits.

Another line of research indicates that childhood shyness may continue as a long-term personality pattern. Avshalom Caspi and his coworkers (1988) followed shy boys and girls from the time they were 10 to 12 years of age into their 40s. They found that men who had been shy boys tended to postpone marriage, fatherhood, and establishing a career. Caspi attributed these differences to a reluctance on the part of shy people to enter new and unfamiliar social situations, a reluctance apparently carried from childhood into adult life. Women who had been shy as children tended to follow a conventional pattern of marriage, childbearing, and homemaking. Caspi speculated that in U.S. culture, shyness may be more compatible with the traditional female gender role than it is with the gender demands that confronted the shy men (see Figure 4.27).

Temperament researchers believe that shyness and other temperamental predispositions are stable because inherited temperamental differences are reinforced over time by the environmental consequences they produce (Caspi & others, 1988; Kagan & Snidman, 1991; Scarr, 1992). In other words, our own behaviors tend to create circumstances that influence both how we see ourselves and how others respond to us. Thus, if we perceive ourselves as shy, we may avoid the kinds of social situations that could help us become more outgoing, or we may quite literally enter social situations and "stand in a corner." This passive behavior increases the likelihood that we will be overlooked, which, in turn, reinforces our belief that we are, in fact, shy and reserved. Thus, person–environment interaction patterns promote personality continuity through biological, behavioral, environmental, and cognitive mechanisms.

Figure 4.27 *The shyness exhibited by this child may have a biological basis that is reinforced by her withdrawn behaviors. In turn, shy behaviors reduce the likelihood that she will engage in the kinds of social interactions that might counteract her tendencies toward shyness.*

Attachment

The baby monkey had not been fed and was obviously hungry when it was returned to its cage in Harry Harlow's primate research laboratory at the University of Wisconsin. Inside the cage were the two artificial mothers with whom the monkey had lived since it was separated from its biological mother shortly after birth. One "mother" was a bare wire cylinder with a feeding bottle attached to its chest region. The other was also a cylinder, but it had no feeding bottle. Instead, it was covered with foam rubber and a soft terrycloth exterior.

The baby immediately ran to the terrycloth figure and clung tightly to it. Then, continuing to anchor itself to the terrycloth object with its rear feet, the baby gingerly stretched its body across to the wire mother and sucked on the bottle (see Figure 4.28). Later, the researchers placed in the monkey's cage a teddy bear that marched forward while beating a drum, knowing that baby monkeys, like humans, run to their mothers when they are frightened. The terrified baby fled, but not to the wire mother who fed it. Instead, it sought refuge with the terrycloth mother (Harlow, 1958).

Harry Harlow's classic monkey studies in the 1950s challenged the long-held belief that the primary basis for infants' attachment to their mothers is the mother's role in satisfying the infant's needs for physical nourishment. Harlow showed that perhaps even more basic is the need for body contact with a soft and comforting object. His experiments revealed that baby monkeys consistently preferred the cloth mother and clung to her for security, even though the wire mother provided their food. Subsequent studies with human babies have also shown the importance of being held and cuddled for the well-being of babies and for the process of emotional bonding with caregivers (Bee, 1989; Hunziker & Barr, 1986). Today, the study of **attachment**—the strong emotional bond that develops between children and their caregivers—is one of the most vigorously pursued areas in developmental psychology. Most developmentalists believe that the nature of the relationship that evolves between the developing child and his or her caregivers is a critical feature of personality and social development, and one that has a lifelong influence on the child's adjustment (Ainsworth & Bowlby, 1991; Franz & others, 1991).

Through behavioral observation studies, the course of attachment has been studied in a number of cultures, including the United States and Uganda. In all of the cultures, attachment seems to develop through four distinct phases (Ainsworth, 1989; Bowlby, 1982; see Figure 4.29). The first stage, *indiscriminate attachment,* occurs over the first 3 months of life. As we saw earlier, newborns have reflexive abilities to cry, vocalize, and smile. These behaviors evoke caregiving from and contact with adults. During this phase, neonates do not direct their signaling toward any specific person—hence the term *indiscriminate* attachment.

By 3 months of age, most infants can distinguish their caregivers' faces from those of other people, and they begin to direct more attachment behaviors toward them than toward strangers. The period from 3 to 6 months of age is therefore termed the stage of *discriminate attachment.*

By 7 or 8 months of age, infants have developed their first meaningful attachment to specific caregivers and enter the phase of *specific attachment.* They smile more at these caregivers, hold out their arms to be picked up by them, and want to be in their presence. They may experience distress when the caregivers leave and may reject overtures from strangers. Typically, the infant forms the first specific attachment with the primary caregiver. This single attachment later broadens to a series of separate attachments in the second year of life. The attachment behaviors are healthy signs that a bond has formed, and they are supported by other important changes going on at the same time. For example, the development of object

◆ **Figure 4.28** *Harlow's studies of baby monkeys separated from their biological mothers and placed with inanimate surrogates demonstrated the importance of touch and physical contact in the development of attachment. The babies reared with a cloth-covered surrogate clung to it as they would a real mother, and they preferred to remain in contact with the terrycloth mother even though the wire mother satisfied nutritional needs.*

sonality, providing a stable sense of personal identity and exerting strong influences on thoughts, feelings, and behavior. As the accompanying Understanding Causes feature indicates, its foundations in childhood reflect the interaction of many of the causal factors we have discussed in this chapter.

Our journey across the life span has now reached the end of childhood. At one time, developmental psychology was often termed *child psychology,* as if development stopped at the end of childhood. However, there is now increased awareness that important developmental processes occur throughout our lives, and the adult years are receiving more scientific attention. In the next chapter, we explore development in adolescence, adulthood, and old age.

SUMMARY

The Study of Development
● Developmental psychology is the scientific study of the biological, cognitive, and behavioral changes that occur from the moment of conception until death and of the factors that cause these changes.
● Two important issues concerning development are: (1) whether psychological development occurs continuously or through a series of discrete stages, and (2) how heredity and environment interact to affect the course and products of development.
● Cross-sectional research designs involve the simultaneous study of people who differ in age. Longitudinal designs involve the study of the same subjects over time.

Genetic Foundations of Development
● Hereditary potential is carried in the DNA of the chromosomes in units called genes. The biological sex of a human is determined by a single gene on the 23rd pair of chromosomes.
● Some genes are dominant, while others are recessive. The characteristic associated with a parent's recessive gene will not appear in an offspring unless it is paired with a recessive gene for the same trait from the other parent. The result is a difference between genotype and phenotype.

Prenatal Development
● The gestation period extends from conception to birth. It includes three stages: the zygote stage, the embryonic stage, and the fetal stage.
● During the fetal stage, development can be adversely affected by teratogens, harmful substances which can pass through the placental barrier into the fetus. Teratogens include nicotine, alcohol, and a wide variety of drugs.

Neonatal Behavior
● Neonatal development in many behavioral areas is built on innate reflexes, including grasping, crying, smiling, and sucking reflexes.
● Neonates have well-developed sensory capabilities. They show sensory discriminations and preferences, and they are able to imitate various facial expressions.

Physical and Motor Development
● Maturation refers to the biologically based unfolding of development in accordance with genetic programming.
● Physical and motor development proceeds in accordance with four principles. Development proceeds from the head to the lower part of the body (the cephalocaudal principle) and from the innermost parts of the body toward the extremities (the proximodistal principle). Development also entails differentiation of structures and functions followed by integration of the components into complex structures and behaviors.
● The brain shows rapid development after birth as a result of cell growth, the forming of neural interconnections, and the process of myelinization. By the age of 2 years, it has attained 75 percent of its adult weight. Research with both animals and humans indicates that environmental events can affect neural development and subsequent behavioral capabilities.
● There is little increase in the size of the brain during the elementary-school years (ages 6 through 12), but considerable development occurs within the brain. This development is reflected in impressive increases in cognitive abilities.

Cognitive and Linguistic Development
● According to Piaget, children pass through four stages of cognitive development. Infants are in the sensorimotor stage, in which assimilation and accommodation occur first through reflexes, then through the infants' growing awareness that they can affect the environment. The major developmental milestone is object permanence.

● During the preschool years, children refine their physical–motor and cognitive skills. Their thinking becomes more symbolic as they enter Piaget's preoperational period. Preoperational children are egocentric, and they have not yet acquired concepts of conservation.
● According to Piaget, children enter the stage of concrete operations during the elementary school years. In this stage they can mentally manipulate information, acquire conservation abilities, and think with limited logic.
● Research on cognitive development indicates that Piaget was correct concerning the sequence in which cognitive development occurs but that he underestimated the cognitive abilities of children of various ages.
● Some developmentalists who dispute Piaget's concept of stages have adopted an information-processing perspective. They view cognitive development not as a passage through discrete stages but as a gradual increase in abilities to attend to the environment and to learn, remember, and apply information. These abilities are enhanced with the emergence of metacognition, the awareness of one's own cognitive activities.
● Human language is symbolic, structured, and generative. The surface structure of a language refers to how symbols are combined; the deep structure refers to the underlying meaning of the symbols. Language elements are hierarchically arranged from phonemes to morphemes and on to words, phrases, and sentences.
● Language development seems to depend heavily on innate mechanisms that permit the learning and production of language, provided the child is exposed to an appropriate linguistic environment. There may be a sensitive period for exposure to language that extends from early childhood to puberty. Thereafter, normal linguistic development does not occur. Neither strictly biological nor strict environmental explanations appear capable of accounting for language development. Language does not appear to determine thought, but it does influence how effectively the child can think.

Personality and Social Development

- Both Freud and Erikson formulated stage theories of personality development. Freud's childhood theory has three major psychosexual stages—oral, anal, and phallic—followed by a latency stage during which sexual drives become dormant and finally a genital stage. Erikson's theory includes eight psychosocial stages extending from infancy through old age. Each stage provides psychosocial tasks to be mastered, and the success with which mastery occurs has important psychological consequences at each stage.

- Temperamental differences are evident in infants, and there is mounting evidence that temperament is in part biologically based and interacts with environmental events to help produce stable patterns of behavior.

- Attachment patterns begin to develop in infancy, and there is evidence that early attachment patterns are related to later behavior. The major attachment patterns demonstrated in the strange situation are secure and insecure attachment.

- Day-care studies indicate that more important than whether children are placed in day care is the quality of the program. Poor-quality programs appear to have a negative impact on both preschool and school-age children.

- At the time it occurs, divorce appears to affect younger children more adversely than older ones, but the long-term effects are greater for school-age children. The nature of the child's subsequent relationships with biological parents and stepparents is the most important factor in his or her adaptation to divorce.

- Parenting styles may be described as falling along the dimensions of warmth versus hostility and restrictiveness versus permissiveness to form four patterns: authoritative, authoritarian, permissive, and neglecting. The authoritative pattern seems related to the most positive outcomes.

- Gender identity develops during early childhood. Freud believed that sex-role development resulted from psychosexual conflict in the phallic stage. Other theorists point to the pervasive role of sex typing, in which boys are consistently treated differently from girls. Most children have developed gender identity by the time they are 3, but gender constancy is not attained until the age of 6 or 7.

- The self-concept evolves out of self-awareness and provides a sense of personal identity. It is influenced by the reactions of others and by comparison of oneself with others. Once formed, it helps to direct behavior, often in ways that help the child attain the qualities of his or her ideal self.

KEY TERMS AND CONCEPTS

accommodation (p. 109)
anal stage (p. 120)
assimilation (p. 109)
attachment (p. 124)
authoritarian parent (p. 130)
authoritative parent (p. 129)
autonomy (p. 121)
basic mistrust (p. 121)
basic trust (p. 121)
castration anxiety (p. 121)
cephalocaudal principle (p. 106)
chromosomes (p. 100)
cohort (p. 99)
concrete operational stage (p. 113)
conservation (p. 112)
critical period (p. 96)
cross-sectional design (p. 99)
deep structure (p. 116)
deoxyribonucleic acid (DNA) (p. 100)
developmental psychology (p. 96)
differentiation (p. 106)
dominant gene (p. 101)
egocentrism (p. 112)
Electra complex (p. 121)
embryo (p. 102)
fetal alcohol syndrome (FAS) (p. 102)
fetus (p. 102)
fixation (p. 120)
gender constancy (p. 130)

gender identity (p. 130)
genes (p. 100)
genital stage (p. 121)
genotype (p. 101)
guilt (p. 121)
heterozygous (p. 101)
homozygous (p. 101)
ideal self (p. 131)
identification (p. 121)
identity crises (p. 121)
indulgent parent (p. 130)
industry (p. 121)
inferiority (p. 121)
information-processing approach (p. 114)
initiative (p. 121)
integration (p. 106)
language (p. 115)
language-acquisition device (LAD) (p. 117)
language-acquisition support system (LASS) (p. 118)
latency stage (p. 121)
linguistic relativity hypothesis (p. 119)
longitudinal design (p. 99)
maturation (p. 106)
metacognition (p. 115)
morpheme (p. 116)
nature–nurture controversy (p. 97)
neglecting parents (p. 130)
neonate (p. 103)

object permanence (p. 111)
Oedipus complex (p. 121)
oral stage (p. 120)
phallic stage (p. 121)
phenotype (p. 101)
phoneme (p. 116)
placenta (p. 102)
preoperational stage (p. 111)
proximodistal principle (p. 106)
recessive gene (p. 101)
reflex (p. 104)
schema (p. 109)
semantics (p. 116)
sensitive period (p. 96)
sensorimotor stage (p. 110)
sex-role stereotyping (p. 130)
sex typing (p. 130)
shame and doubt (p. 121)
stage (p. 97)
strange situation (p. 125)
stranger anxiety (p. 125)
surface structure (p. 116)
symbolic thought (p. 111)
syntax (p. 116)
TDF gene (p. 100)
telegraphic speech (p. 118)
temperament (p. 122)
teratogens (p. 102)
zygote (p. 102)

SUGGESTED READINGS

Berndt, T. J. (1992). *Child development.* Ft. Worth: Harcourt Brace Jovanovich. A good overview of current knowledge concerning many aspects of child development, including in-depth discussions about virtually all of the topics covered in this chapter.

Chess, S., & Thomas, A. (1987). *Know your child.* New York: Basic Books. A discussion of how effective child rearing adjusts to the temperamental traits of the individual child, written by leading researchers on child temperament.

Maurer, D., & Maurer, C. (1988). *The world of the newborn.* New York: Basic Books. A highly readable and award-winning treatment of what is currently known about how the world appears to the neonate.

Adolescent and Adult Development 5

■□

C H A P T E R   O U T L I N E

We call it Sunrise Dance. It's the biggest ceremony of the White Mountain Apache—when a girl passes from childhood to womanhood. When my time came at fourteen, I didn't want to have one. I felt embarrassed. All my friends would be watching me. But my parents encouraged me, ''Then you will live to an old age.''

On Friday evening Godmother dressed me and pinned an eagle feather on my head and an abalone shell pendant on my forehead. The feather will help me live until my hair turns gray. The pendant is the sign of Changing Woman, mother of all Apache people. . . .

The most important thing Godmother does is to massage my body. She is giving me all her knowledge. For hours around the fire I follow a dancer who impersonates a protective spirit.

Saturday is like an endurance test. Men begin prayer chants at dawn. Godmother tells me to dance while kneeling on a buckskin pad facing the sun—the creator. In that position, Apache women grind corn. When the time comes for running, I go fast around a sacred cane, so nobody evil will ever catch up with me. Aunt Dolly runs behind me, followed by Godmother. Rain begins, and my ten pound costume gets heavier and heavier. But I don't fall. I don't even get tired. . . .

Dolly's daughter wants me to blow in her baby's mouth. That's because during the dance I have power to keep evil spirits away. Next, my father pours candies and corn kernels over me to protect me from famine. My family passes out crates of candy and pop—this means the people will always have food. . . .

My Godfather directs my dancing on Sunday with an eagle feather in each hand. My father holds my sacred cane. When I'm old, I'll use the cane for walking. It's decorated with feathers of the even-tempered oriole to give me a good disposition.

Godfather paints me from the top of my head to the bottom of my buckskin boots. I am blessed and protected from all four sides. Four is the most important number to the Apache.

On Monday there is more visiting and blessing. I was really strong all the way; I didn't cry like some girls do. I'm really glad I had a Sunrise Dance. It made me realize how much my parents care for me and want me to grow up right. They know my small age is past and treat me like a woman. If I have a daughter, I want her to have a Sunrise Dance too (Quintero, 1980, pp. 262–271).

I n some cultures, initiation ceremonies like the Sunrise Dance clearly mark the transition from childhood into adulthood (see Figure 5.1). These rites of passage formally declare the new adult status with all its obligations and rights. As in the Sunrise Dance, the rites are often filled with symbolism concerning the life tasks that are to occur in the adult years and the traits that are deemed desirable in the culture.

For most teenagers in our culture, there is no such event to confer formal adult status. In preindustrial times, biological maturity was the major criterion for adult status. But the Industrial Revolution of the early 19th century brought advanced technology and with it a need for more years of schooling. The time between biological maturity and recognition of adult status thus lengthened and the transition period we call *adolescence* emerged. In important ways, adolescents in our culture are neither children nor adults. Their physical and cognitive development are adultlike in many respects, but they are still childlike in their economic dependence on parents. From a social perspective, one becomes an adult by accomplishing certain developmental tasks, such as being financially independent, having a steady job, being married and raising a family, or gaining some degree of recognition within the community (Havighurst, 1972).

Like the childhood years, adolescence brings important developmental demands. So, however, do early adulthood (ages 21 to 40), middle adulthood (ages 41 to 65), and late adulthood (age 65 and beyond). These demands ensure that development never stops. Although important foundations of personal identity are laid down in childhood, people continue to change in significant ways as their lives unfold. No account of human development would be complete without considering development after childhood.

▶ **Figure 5.1** *Nita Quintero participates in the Sunrise Dance, which initiates her into adult status in the White Mountain Apache tribe. These initiation rites formalize the transition into adulthood. In most Western cultures, the transition is far lengthier and not so well defined.*

Adolescence

Adolescence extends from the beginnings of sexual maturity to the attainment of independent adult status. For G. Stanley Hall (1916), the first psychologist to formally examine this period, adolescence was a time of ''storm and stress'' caused by the sometimes conflicting forces of biological maturation, economic and emotional dependence, and striving for personal identity. As Hall would have predicted, many individuals beyond the age of 30 do indeed recall adolescence as a period of conflict and alienation that they would not wish to relive (Macfarlane, 1964). On the other hand, not everyone agrees with the ''storm and stress'' characterization of adolescence. Survey studies reveal that many young people find adolescence to be an enjoyable and relatively carefree period of their lives, and they report positive feelings about themselves and their parents during this period (Hunter & Youniss, 1982; Rosenberg, 1985). But whether the path of adolescence is rocky or smooth in the individual case, there is no debate about the importance of physical maturation during this developmental period.

Physical Development

Adolescence begins at **puberty,** a period of sexual maturation and rapid physical growth that is triggered by hormonal influences. Hormones from the pituitary gland stimulate the production of other growth-producing glands, including the thyroid, the adrenals, and the ovaries and testes. These hormones not only produce physical changes, but also affect moods and behavior (Buchanan & others, 1992). Beginning at about age 11 in girls and age 13 in boys, a 2-year period of rapid growth occurs. Boys may grow 10 inches during this period, and girls about 3 inches a year. At approximately age 14, boys overtake girls in both height and weight (see Figure 5.2).

During the adolescent growth spurt, hormones direct the development of the reproductive organs, or **primary sex characteristics,** as well as the appearance of **secondary sex characteristics,** such as the appearance of pubic and underarm hair in males and females, facial hair and a deepening of the voice in males, and breast development and widening of the hips in females. The pubertal landmark in girls is **menarche,** the first menstrual flow. For boys, it is the production of sperm and the first ejaculation. These landmarks occur at about age 12 or 13 for girls and at about age 14 for boys. Once puberty occurs, reproduction is possible.

Recent findings indicate that psychological reactions to life events may hasten the onset of menarche in girls. Terrie Moffit and her coworkers (1992) found that girls who grow up in families with high levels of stress and conflict experience an earlier menarche. One suggestion is that the physiological stress response to family dysfunction may lower metabolism and bring about an earlier menarche, but the precise mechanism by which stress may hasten maturation is at present unknown.

As in the earlier stages of development, the sequence of physical changes is far more predictable than their timing. Thus, some girls and boys mature earlier or later than the norm (see Figure 5.3). Both early and late maturation can have important psychological consequences. Research on timing of maturation indicates that the most positive behavioral and psychological outcomes occur for boys who mature early and for girls who reach puberty at about the

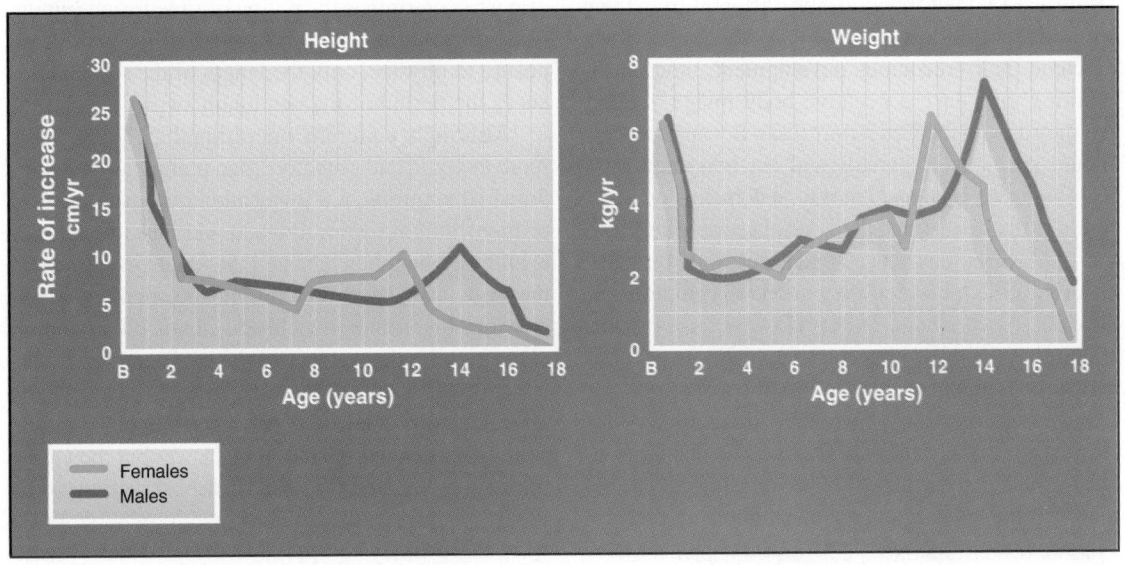

Figure 5.2 *Growth curves reflect adolescent spurts in height and weight. Girls experience their maximum increases around age 12, boys at about age 14. (Smith & others, 1983).*

Figure 5.3 *Biological development during adolescence occurs in fixed stages, but there is wide variation in the timing of the changes.*

expected age of 12 to 13. Conversely, the most negative outcomes occur for early maturing girls and late-maturing boys.

Early maturing boys generally have greater physical strength and size, which makes them superior in athletics and other physical activities that contribute to leadership status in early adolescence. They have a more positive body image and tend to be more popular with their peers than do late maturers who lack these prized physical characteristics (Duke & others, 1982; Sigelman & Shaffer, 1991).

In contrast, early maturing girls may be handicapped by their precocious development. Having reached their adult height and full breast development before age 13, they are noticeably different from their peers. Recent studies indicate that while some girls welcome their precocious development, other early maturing girls have a negative body image, feeling that they are too fat (Peterson, 1987). Because of their mature appearance, parents and teachers may mistakenly place social and emotional demands on early maturers that are beyond their current coping abilities, and older boys may place sexual demands on early maturing girls for which they are totally unprepared (Magnusson & others, 1986). However, it is worth noting that the most important factor in the psychological consequences of maturation seems to be the teenager's *perception* of whether maturation is occurring too early or too late (Lerner, 1987; Peterson, 1987). Such perceptions are based on culturally transmitted standards accompanied by the adolescents' comparisons of themselves with peers.

Cognitive Development

Changes in cognitive development during adolescence can be nearly as dramatic as the physical changes that occur. Teenagers acquire a new level of cognitive maturity that enables them to reason abstractly and hypothetically and to reflect on their own and others' thoughts.

Development of Formal Operations

The final stage of cognitive development proposed by Piaget is typically attained during adolescence. During the period between ages 11 and 15, many adolescents achieve an adultlike way of thinking that Piaget termed **formal operations.** A more powerful set of cognitive skills expands their reasoning abilities beyond the limitations of concrete thinking and allows them to consider the abstract and the hypothetical. As we saw in Chapter 4 (p. 113), children in the preceding period, the concrete operational stage, can use *inductive* reasoning to derive general principles from a series of specific observations. Formal operational thinkers can, in addition, do the opposite: They can solve complex problems in a systematic way through the use of *deductive* reasoning. That is, they can begin with a general principle and derive specific "if, then" hypotheses or conclusions. This is the basis for advanced scientific thinking (see Figure 5.4). Formal operations also permit the adolescent to think about possibilities and abstractions.

Piaget and his colleague Barbel Inhelder illustrated differences between formal operational thinking and earlier stages of cognitive development by giving youngsters ranging in age from 5 to 15 the pendulum problem shown in Figure 5.5 (Inhelder & Piaget, 1958). The problem requires the subject to figure out which combination of four variables (length of string, weight of object, force of push, and height of push) determines the period of time for one swing of the pendulum. (As you may recall from your exposure to physics, only the length of the string influences the period of the pendulum swing.)

Although concrete operational children were more analytic and objective than preoperational children in their problem-solving attempts, many features of their thinking were illogical and unscientific. For example, when they adjusted the length of the string, they often adjusted the weight, too, making it impossible to draw a conclusion about either factor. (This is a classic example of the confounding of variables, which, as we saw in Chapter 2, can plague researchers as well.) Concrete operational children sometimes discovered the right answer but then drew the wrong conclusions from their observations.

In contrast to the younger children, adolescents were more likely to approach the problem systematically, trying out all possible combinations of the variables and carefully observing the results. For example, even though many of them initially thought that the heavier weights would swing faster, they still tried out all possible combinations. Based on their observations, they then drew the correct logical conclusion: The shorter the string, the more frequently the pendulum swings back and forth, regardless of the weight of the object.

Inhelder and Piaget's research on formal operations is among their most original and interesting work. It stimulated a great deal of research by other investigators, some of which has challenged Piaget's assumptions about formal operational development (Richards & Commons, 1990). For example, Piaget assumed that virtually all people of average intelligence attain formal operations. However, it now appears that formal operational thinking is by no means a universal phenomenon. Some studies suggest that perhaps only 50 to 60 percent of 18- to 20-year-olds use formal operations at all, let alone consistently (Keating, 1980). Some people do seem to use formal operations a good deal of the time, but others rarely or never do. In between are people who apply formal operational logic to familiar problem areas but not to novel problems (Neimark, 1982). Nonetheless, most experts agree with Piaget's conclusion that a remarkable development of cognitive capabilities occurs during adolescence. These changes are manifested in many areas of cognitive activity, one of which is moral reasoning.

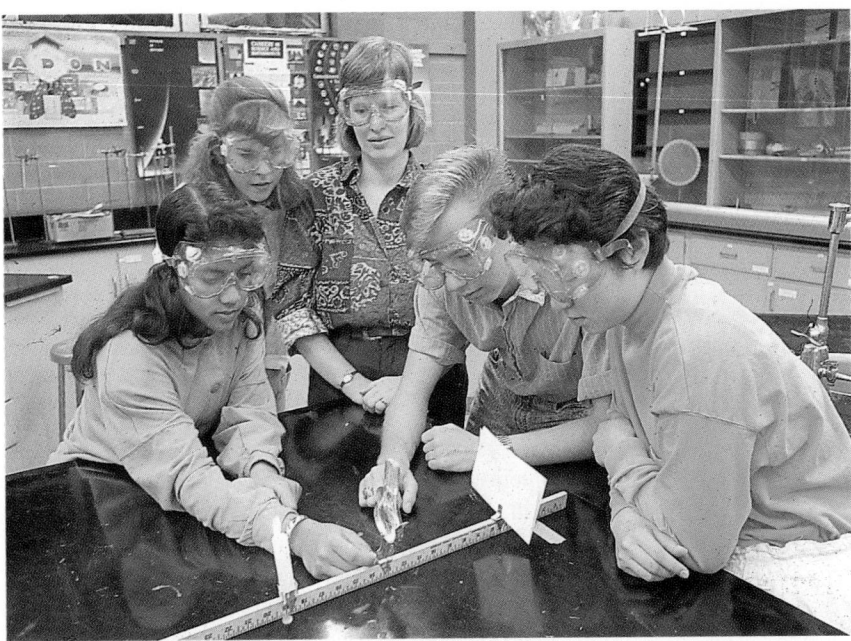

▲ **Figure 5.4** *The development of formal operations during adolescence permits the use of deductive reasoning and the systematic solution of science problems.*

Moral Reasoning

Adolescents restructure their thinking about moral questions as they develop abstract reasoning abilities. This aspect of cognitive development has been charted by Lawrence Kohlberg (1963, 1984), who expanded Piaget's earlier work to develop an influential stage theory of moral reasoning. In doing so, Kohlberg drew upon Piaget's conception that cognitive development involves a movement from concrete to abstract thinking.

In a series of investigations to examine moral reasoning, Kohlberg presented children, adolescents,

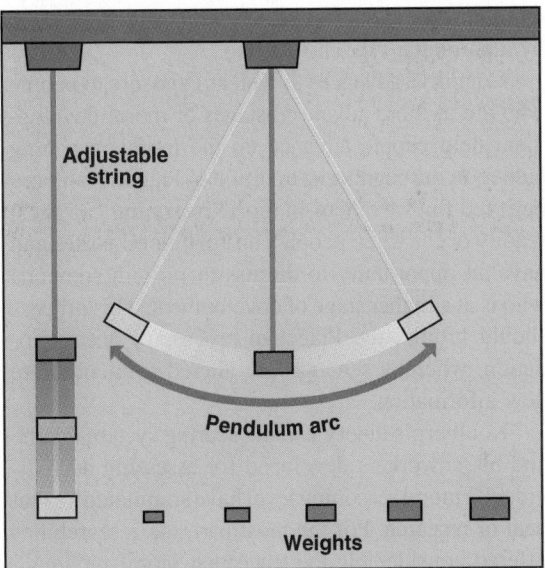

◀ **Figure 5.5** *The materials for the pendulum problem used by Inhelder and Piaget include an adjustable string and a set of weights. The problem is to determine what factors influence the speed of the pendulum through its arc. (Adapted from Inhelder & Piaget, 1958).*

Adjustable string

Pendulum arc

Weights

and adults with hypothetical moral dilemmas like the following:

> Heinz's wife was dying from cancer. A rare drug might save her, but the druggist—who made the drug for 200 dollars—would not sell it for a penny less than $2,000. Heinz tried hard, but he could only raise $1,000. The druggist refused to give Heinz the drug for that price even though Heinz promised to pay the balance later. So Heinz broke into the store to steal the drug.
>
> What do you think? Should Heinz have stolen the drug? Why or why not?

In his analysis of moral reasoning, Kohlberg was interested not in whether subjects agreed or disagreed with Heinz's behavior but in the *reasons* for their judgment. He believed that the analysis of such reasoning would enable him to construct a developmental model of the human being as a moral philosopher. Based on analyses of responses to this and other moral dilemmas, Kohlberg concluded that there are three main levels of moral reasoning—preconventional, conventional, and postconventional—with two substages within each level (see Table 5.1).

At the **preconventional** level, people make their judgments based on the punishments or rewards that will result from particular courses of action. What is good for *them* is good. At the **conventional** level, morality moves beyond this limited self-interest and is based on conformity to the standards of the social group and a desire to obey rules set down by the social order. **Postconventional** morality, the highest level, goes beyond the social group and is based on abstract moral principles, such as universal principles of justice. The person examines, thinks through, and internalizes such principles as part of his or her system of values. Each of Kohlberg's stages builds on, reorganizes, and includes the one before it, and each is thought to be a distinct structural unit characterized by a particular type of thinking.

Cognitive advances as well as exposure to people who are at more advanced stages of moral development help people advance up the moral reasoning ladder. In the cognitivist tradition of Piaget, Kohlberg believed that advances in moral reasoning can most readily occur when people confront moral issues and have an opportunity to discuss them with someone who is at a higher stage of development. This process should prompt the Piagetian process of accommodation, whereby schemas are altered to incorporate new information.

Kohlberg's theory and the scoring system that he and his coworkers developed for assessing an individual's moral reasoning level have stimulated a great deal of research. For the most part, the research has offered considerable evidence that moral judgment changes over time in the sequence that Kohlberg described (Colby & others, 1983; Rest, 1983; Snarey, 1987). Studies carried out in a number of cultures, including the United States, Taiwan, Turkey, Mexico, Kenya, India, and Israel, indicate that preconventional thinking is characteristic of middle childhood and is also found among many early adolescents. Conventional moral reasoning (Stages 3 and 4) emerges in middle adolescence and remains the most characteristic form in adulthood. As Kohlberg defined it, postconventional reasoning is uncommon even in adulthood, and it may be largely limited to Western societies that value individuality. These patterns are evident in Figure 5.6, which shows the findings from a longitudinal study of 58 American boys who were tested repeatedly over a 20-year period (Colby & others, 1983). The results indicate a decrease in preconventional reasoning over time and a corresponding increase in conventional reasoning beginning in adolescence. Stage 5 reasoning emerges late in adolescence and is shown by only a few of the subjects at any age. Kohlberg (1978) had earlier concluded that Stage 6, reasoning based on universal ethical principles, is extremely rare and may be found only in a few unusual people, such as Martin Luther King, Gandhi, and Mother Teresa. Consequently, it was not even assessed in this longitudinal study.

Despite the research support it has received, Kohlberg's theory is not without its critics. The model has been criticized as having a Western cultural bias and as being too limited in its emphasis on justice and fairness as the highest moral ideal. For example, Kohlberg's stages do not seem to take account of moral principles that are based on the common good or on the ideal of caring and responsibility to others. In some communal societies, an ethic based on a commitment to the common good may be more adaptive than one based on abstract moral principles of justice (Gilligan & others, 1990). Moreover, Carol Gilligan (1982) has argued that Kohlberg's emphasis on abstract principles of justice may have a gender bias even as it applies to Western culture. Gilligan maintained that by studying moral development from a male's perspective and by using primarily male subjects, Kohlberg has devalued an emphasis on caring and responsibility for others' welfare that is characteristic of highly moral women.

Gilligan's assertion of gender differences in justice versus caring as a basis for moral reasoning has not been supported by subsequent research. Females can and do use justice reasoning when the situation calls for it, and males use reasoning based on caring and relationships as often as females do (Friedman & others, 1987; Walker, 1987). Nevertheless, Gilligan's criticisms have focused attention on the implicit value judgments that underlie the study of moral principles. In some respects, moral maturity is in the eye of the beholder. ▼

▼
Thinking Critically About "Moral Maturity"

One of the controversies in the study of moral maturity concerns how it should be defined. Theorists who take a behavioral approach take issue with Kohlberg and other cognitive theorists who define moral maturity in terms of the reasoning bases for moral judgments. They point out that moral reasoning is not the same thing as moral behavior and that there is a very imperfect relation (and at times, no relation whatever) between moral reasoning and moral behavior (Bandura, 1991; Mussen & Eisenberg-Berg, 1977). Moral reasoning, they argue, truly reflects moral maturity only to the extent that it contributes to moral behavior. It is the latter that reflects the level of moral maturity. Moral reasoning theorists reply that the "same" moral behavior may reflect very different levels of moral reasoning. What do you think? When the two conflict, does moral maturity reside in the sophistication of a person's moral reasoning or in the behavioral choices he or she makes?

Table 5.1 Kohlberg's Stages of Moral Reasoning

Levels and Stages	Definition	Typical Response to Heinz Dilemma
Level I **Preconventional Level**	People obey external rules in order to avoid external punishment or to obtain rewards.	
Stage 1 Punishment and obedience orientation	The physical consequences of an act determine its moral goodness or badness, regardless of the human meaning or value of these consequences.	"Heinz should steal the drug because if he lets his wife die, he will get in trouble" or "Heinz should not steal the drug because he might get put in jail."
Stage 2 Instrumental relativist orientation	Moral judgments are based on rewards and exchanges. Satisfaction of personal needs is the most important consideration for answers. But trade-offs and deals are accepted when people see something in it for themselves.	"He wouldn't get much time even if he stole the drug; a little time is okay if he can save his wife" or "If he steals everyone will think he's a thief, he will go to jail, and his wife will be dead before he gets out."
Level II **Conventional Level**	Moral reasoning is based on conformity to the expectations of the social group. People want to please peers and authority figures by following their standards and conforming to the social order.	
Stage 3 Good boy—good girl orientation.	Moral decisions are based on the individual's ability to gain approval and maintain good relations with others.	"People would think that Heinz is bad if he doesn't steal the drug to save his wife" or "Heinz should not steal the drug because it's not nice to steal and people won't like you if you take things that don't belong to you."
Stage 4 Law and order orientation	Reasoning at this stage is based on rigid rules and maintenance of the social order. Moral behavior consists of doing one's duty, showing respect for authority, and maintaining the social order for its own sake.	"Heinz should steal the drug, because it's his responsibility if his wife dies; it would be the same as murder" or "It's against the law to steal. Heinz should not take the drug without permission, but he can find another way to get it."
Level III **Postconventional Level**	Individuals make moral decisions from general moral principles that have been examined, thought out, and internalized as part of their value systems. Right and wrong are based on internal belief systems rather than external standards, punishments, or rewards.	
Stage 5 Social-contract legalistic orientation	Morality is thought of in terms of general rights agreed on by society and the welfare of the community. Moral judgments are based on the will of the majority, but there is an emphasis on changing laws if they lose their social utility. There is an increasing orientation toward internal decisions based on conscience.	"Heinz should have stole the drug. Human life is above financial gain. It doesn't matter who is dying, even a total stranger, we have a duty to save that person from dying" or "If everybody went out and stole like Heinz, there would be no laws for us to live in harmony."
Stage 6 Universal ethical principle orientation	Moral reasoning reaches its highest—and least often achieved—state. Behaviors are guided by abstract ethical principles such as the Golden Rule.	"By the law of society Heinz would be wrong to steal the drug, but by the law of nature the druggist was wrong and Heinz was justified" or "If he steals the drug he will never be able to live with himself for not living up to his good conscience."

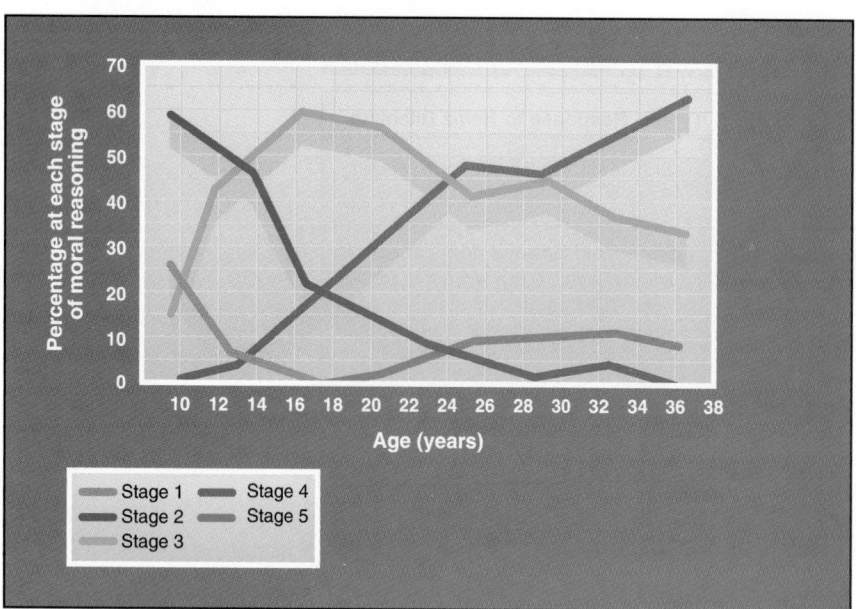

Figure 5.6 *Changes in Kohlberg's stages of moral reasoning over time. Fifty-eight American boys responded to moral dilemmas over more than 20 years. As they grew older, shifts occurred, with conventional morality taking precedence during the high-school years. Stage 5 moral reasoning was not common at any age, and Stage 6 was not measured. (Colby & others, 1983).*

Personality and Social Development

During adolescence, the search for a personal identity assumes great importance. Relationships with parents and peers change in important ways, and social development accelerates toward an adult role. We now consider these important personal and social transitions.

Self-Identity

No developmental task is of greater importance to the adolescent than the search for a stable sense of personal identity. ''Who am I?'' ''What do I believe in?'' ''How do I want to live my life?'' These are the questions that confront adolescents (Adams & others, 1992). Finding answers to them can be a confusing and sometimes painful process for both adolescents and the significant others in their lives.

Erik Erikson, the developmental theorist whose stage theory we encountered in Chapter 4, viewed adolescence as one of the most critical life periods because of the central role that the self-concept plays in how we think, feel, and behave. Erikson termed the developmental crisis of the adolescent years *identity versus role confusion.* As the bridge between childhood and adulthood is crossed, teenagers typically experiment with different roles in their quest for an identity they can call their own. In the process, their attitudes and self-concepts may show sudden changes, and they may adopt dress patterns, view-

points, and behavior patterns that are at odds with those of their parents (see Figure 5.7). This process is less likely to disrupt family relationships when parents encourage self-exploration while remaining a willing source of support and guidance for the adolescent. Needless to say, this role is not an easy one for parents to assume, especially if the adolescent begins to reexamine or challenge some of their central attitudes and values.

The struggle for self-identity can have a number of different outcomes. The best outcome is, of course, the attainment of a stable and comfortable identity as adolescents integrate the various experimental ''selves'' into a comfortable sense of knowing who they are, what they value and believe in, and where they want to go in life.

According to James Marcia (1980), who carried out detailed interviews with adolescents, this process of adolescent *identity achievement* normally develops in two stages: a *crisis,* during which differing roles and values are tried out and evaluated, and a *commitment* to some specific role or ideology. Marcia concluded that as they enter adolescence, most children are in a state of **identity diffusion,** a condition in which they have not yet begun to examine their goals or values. Many adolescents later enter a **moratorium** period during which they experience the crisis phase—trying out various roles, evaluating different viewpoints and values, and considering what they want to do in life—before making a commitment. During the moratorium phase, adolescents may read about or discuss different religious or social views, critically evaluate the strong and weak points of other people (especially adults), and fantasize about different life paths. Commitments usually occur at different times for different areas of self-identity, such as values, sexual standards, social behaviors, and vocational choices. For those who go to college, the moratorium phase may continue into the 20s. Indeed, one longitudinal study of college students indicated that some of them actually moved from an initial identity achievement to a new moratorium as their college experiences caused them to question their prior commitments (Adams & Fitch, 1982).

Some adolescents make a premature commitment without having experienced the crisis, either adopting or rejecting out of hand the identity offered by parents or society. This pattern of **foreclosure** can spare the teenager the sometimes painful process of self-exploration, but it can also pave the way for an identity upheaval later in life if he or she begins to question the premature commitments made in adolescence.

Still other adolescents, unable to reconcile conflicts and uncertainties in personal identity, experience the *role confusion* identified by Erikson. They have no clear idea of who they really are or where they are going in life. This adolescent expresses the sense of uncertainty that attends role confusion: "What I like least about myself are my vacillating ideas. I never seem to get a clear viewpoint of what I am doing, or what I want to do, or what I have done. . . . It's a feeling of being lost—no sense of direction" (Martin, 1971, p. 410).

The importance that Erikson and other theorists attach to identity attainment is supported by research. Compared with teenagers in the role confusion and foreclosure statuses, those in the identity achievement or moratorium statuses are more independent and autonomous, achieve more highly in school, reason at the level of formal operations more frequently, are more successful in establishing intimate relationships, and have higher self-esteem (LaVoie, 1976; Marcia, 1980). However, a stable personal identity is not readily achieved during the adolescent years. Cross-sectional studies of both males and females have shown that most people do not attain a stable identity until they are in their 20s. Identity attainment is, in fact, an ongoing process (see Figure 5.8).

Parental and Peer Relationships

An important part of establishing a personal identity is gaining some degree of independence from parents. Although this process begins in middle childhood, it accelerates during the teen years. As parental influence wanes, peer influence increases (Brown & others, 1986). This does not necessarily mean that relationships between adolescents and parents are fraught with conflict. On the contrary, research has shown that the popular image of the teenage years as a time of intergenerational warfare is more myth than reality (Steinberg, 1987). In one survey study in which teenagers were asked how well they got along with their parents, 56 percent answered "very well," and 41 percent, "fairly well." Only 2 percent answered "not at all well" (Gallup, 1977). The conflicts that do develop tend to peak in the early years of pubertal change (grades 7 through 10) and then decline (Furman & Buhrmeister, 1992). Nonetheless, some degree of conflict is a normal part of the separation process. Parents who understand this and respectfully discuss the issues with their adolescents are more likely to discourage destructive rebellion and to maintain a positive relationship with their sons or daughters. The most successful parents are able to grant their teenager some room to make independent judgments while continuing to maintain reasonable limits on behavior (National Institute of Mental Health, 1981).

Peer relationships become more important during the adolescent years than at any time previously. As Erikson (1968) has pointed out, relationships with peers (unlike those with parents) are interactions between equals, so they allow the young person to prac-

Figure 5.7 In their search for personal identity, teenagers may adopt clothing and hairstyles that contrast markedly with conventional norms.

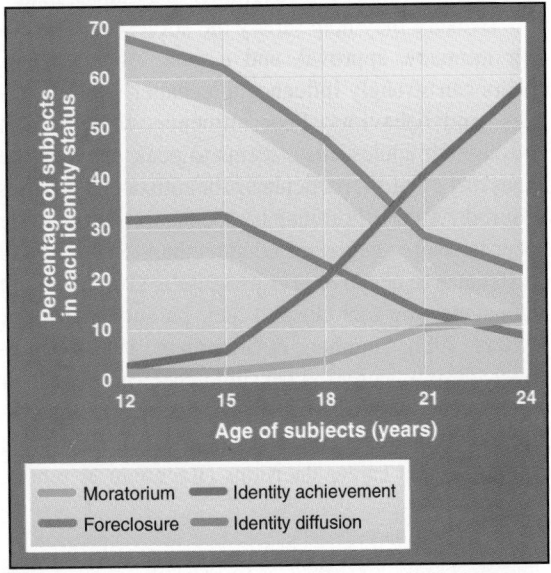

Figure 5.8 Percentage of subjects in each of Marcia's four identity statuses at various ages, based on interviews. These data suggest that most young people attain identity much later than Erikson suggested. (Data from Meilman, 1979).

tice many of the skills that will be needed in later adult relationships. Peer relationships are also a critical part of the process of separating from parents and establishing one's own identity.

Adolescents report that they spend more time talking with peers than in any other activity, and they tend to identify more with peers than with adults (Csikszentmihalyi & Larson, 1984). Adolescent friendships are typically more intimate than those at previous ages. Figure 5.9 shows the results of a study in which children and teenagers rated the intimacy of

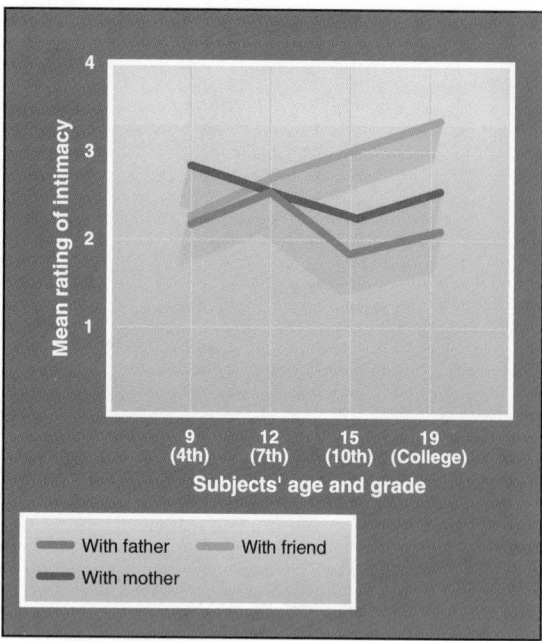

Figure 5.9 *Ratings of intimacy in relationships with parents and best friends. (Hunter & Youniss, 1982).*

Mean rating of intimacy

4

3

2

1

9 (4th)   12 (7th)   15 (10th)   19 (College)

Subjects' age and grade

— With father   — With friend
— With mother

1987). In these important areas, the so-called "generation gap" is far narrower than we might expect.

Patterns of peer interaction show a notable shift during the teenage years. Two trends are apparent in the data shown in Figure 5.10. First, the amount of time spent in groups decreases across the high-school years. Second, progressively more time is spent with members of the opposite sex. This occurs first in mixed-sex groups, where teenagers have the opportunity to learn heterosexual social skills within a protected setting, and then in relationships with a single person of the opposite sex (Csikszentmihalyi & Larson, 1984). These heterosexual interaction patterns, together with part-time jobs and scholastic preparation for college or work, help prepare adolescents for the major developmental tasks of young adulthood.

Adolescent Sexuality

The past 30 years have witnessed a revolutionary change in sexual attitudes and behaviors. As attitudes toward sexuality have become more liberal, adolescents have been engaging in sexual behavior at an earlier age and at an increasing rate. In the 1930s and 1940s, Alfred Kinsey and his coworkers (1948, 1953) reported that fewer than 20 percent of the females and 40 percent of the males they interviewed had engaged in sexual intercourse before age 20. Today, surveys of adolescents indicate that at least half of all adolescent boys and girls have experienced intercourse, many before the age of 16 (Brooks-Gunn & Furstenberg, 1989).

One of the most troubling consequences of adolescent sexuality is the risk of infection by the AIDS virus (DiClemente, 1992). Another is a rapidly increasing rate of teenage pregnancy. Close to a million girls become pregnant each year, and many of them are under 15 years of age (Dryfoos, 1990). Indeed, the United States has by far the highest rate of teenage pregnancy among industrialized countries (see Figure 5.11). If present trends continue, it is estimated that

their relationships with their parents and their best friends. Intimacy, defined as the ability to discuss problems and to be understood by the other person, increased with best friends and declined with parents over the age range studied (Hunter & Youniss, 1982).

Because they help satisfy the adolescent's needs for intimacy, approval, and a sense of belonging, peers can strongly influence a teenager's ideas, values, and behaviors. Peer influence, though high throughout adolescence, seems to peak between the ages of 12 and 14, particularly for antisocial activities (Berndt, 1982). Fortunately, teenagers report more peer pressure *against* misconduct than toward it, and resistance to negative peer pressure is greater among teenagers who feel close to their parents (Brown & others, 1986; Steinberg & Silverberg, 1986). Moreover, despite increased peer influence on dress, hair styles, and attitudes toward other people, parental influence remains high on issues of politics and religion, morality, and career decisions (Bachman & others,

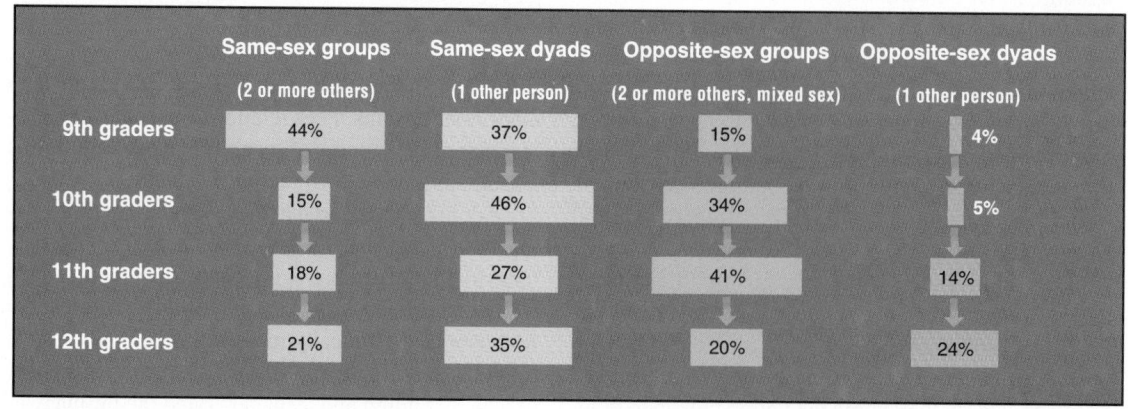

Figure 5.10 *Changes in interaction patterns during the high-school years. A progressive increase in time spent with one individual of the opposite sex is apparent. (Csikszentmihalyi & Larson, 1984).*

	Same-sex groups (2 or more others)	Same-sex dyads (1 other person)	Opposite-sex groups (2 or more others, mixed sex)	Opposite-sex dyads (1 other person)
9th graders	44%	37%	15%	4%
10th graders	15%	46%	34%	5%
11th graders	18%	27%	41%	14%
12th graders	21%	35%	20%	24%

nearly half of today's 14-year-old girls will be pregnant at least once before the age of 20 (Dryfoos, 1990). In many cases, these mothers will be ill equipped to provide secure homes for their babies (see Figure 5.12). Children of teenage mothers have high rates of illness and mortality, and they are at risk for child abuse from a parent who lacks the maturity and emotional control to tolerate the difficulties of child rearing (Jorgensen, 1992). The children themselves are likely to have adjustment problems as they grow up. A 17-year follow-up study of nearly 300 children born to teenage mothers revealed that they had a significantly higher incidence of school failure, behavior problems, and delinquency than children of older mothers. They were also more likely to repeat the cycle by engaging in sexual activity at a young age and becoming pregnant or fathering a child (Furstenberg & others, 1987).

Many experts attribute the problem of teenage pregnancy to a culture that glorifies sex in movies and television and encourages early experimentation, yet fails to provide the educational resources needed to inform teenagers about sex and to encourage either abstinence from sexual intercourse or appropriate precautions to prevent pregnancy. Sex education is a controversial topic in the United States, and the provision of contraceptives to teenagers is even more controversial. It is noteworthy that the differences in the incidence of teenage pregnancy shown in Figure 5.11 are *not* attributable to a higher rate of sexual activity in U.S. teenagers (Brozan, 1985). Instead, they are due to a higher incidence of contraceptive use among teenagers in the other countries. Surveys indicate that fewer than one third of sexually active U.S. teenagers regularly use a contraceptive, and about one fourth never do (Dryfoos, 1990). Even among educated students, the findings are alarming. A recent study of college students revealed that only about 40 percent of them used contraception the first time they had sexual intercourse (Darling & others, 1992). It would appear that a key to decreasing unwanted teenage pregnancy is educating young people in ways that will increase either abstinence or contraceptive use (Miller & others, 1992).

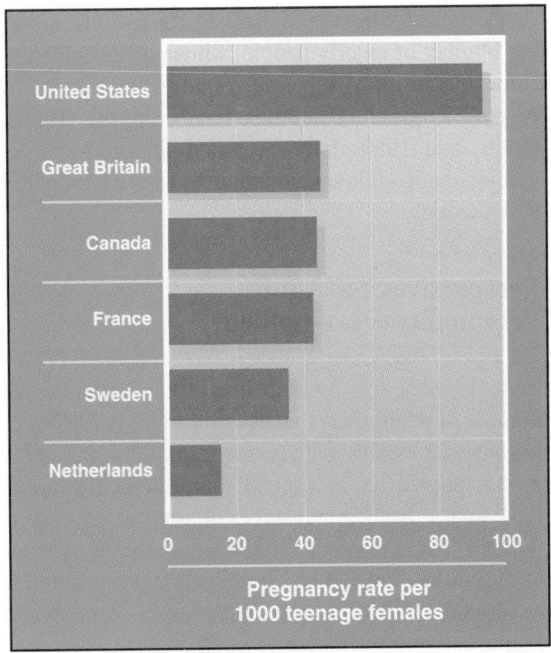

Figure 5.11 *Teenage pregnancy rates for various industrialized countries. The rate in the United States (9.5 percent) is more than double that of any of the other countries. (Data from Alan Guttmacher Institute, 1985).*

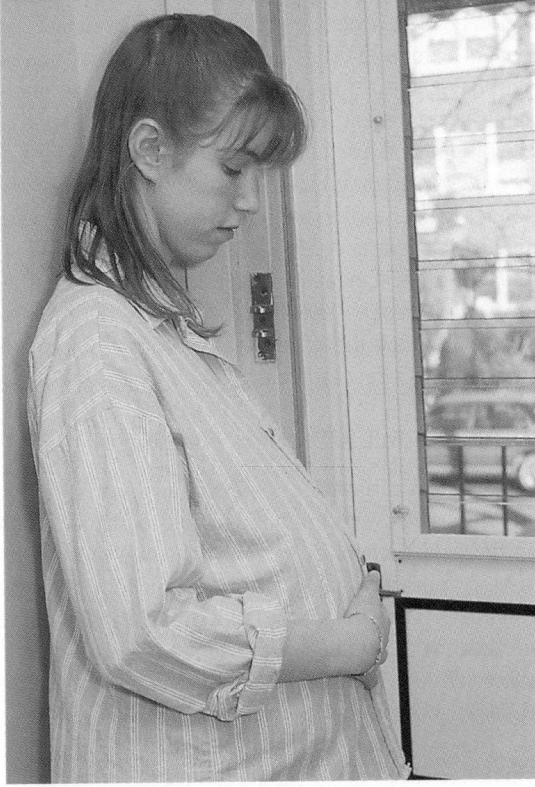

Figure 5.12 *The fact that many teenage mothers are themselves children who lack the maturity and resilience for child rearing raises grave concerns about the consequences of many teenage pregnancies.*

Adult Development and Aging

The past three decades have seen a notable increase in research and theorizing on adult development. One reason why activity in this area was slow in getting started is that early theorists of great influence, such as Freud and Piaget, focused almost entirely on childhood and adolescence. Freud believed that personality is basically formed in childhood, and Piaget's stages of cognitive development ended with the development of formal operations in adolescence and early adulthood (Piaget, 1972).

Erik Erikson's (1950) theory was the first to extend personality development through the remainder of the life cycle, and it made psychologists aware of the need for more research on adult development. Interest in adult development in the United States and

Canada has also been stimulated by the nations' growing number of elderly people, whose needs have become increasingly apparent. Finally, the results of several longitudinal studies begun in the 1930s, 1940s, and 1950s have provided important information about adult development and have stimulated new theories.

Perspectives on Adult Personality Development

In some ways, it is more difficult to chart the development of adults than that of children or adolescents because personality development in adulthood is far less regulated by biological maturation. Theorists have focused on general stages of adult development that are linked to age-related life transitions such as entry into the work force, establishment of a family, experiencing the ''empty nest'' as children leave home, and retirement. However, these transitions occur at different times for different people. Adult development is strongly influenced by individual experiences, and the fact that these experiences can occur at different ages makes chronological age an unreliable basis for drawing generalizations about adult development. As Bernice Neugarten, a leading developmental researcher, has noted, ''If you look at people's lives, they're like the spreading of a fan. The longer they live, the greater the differences between them'' (Neugarten & Hall, 1980, p. 78). Thus, 4-year-olds are likely to be much more similar to one another than 40-year-olds. We should keep this fact in mind as we examine the efforts of theorists to chart the course of life development through the adult years.

Erikson's Adult Psychosocial Stages

As noted in earlier discussions of Erikson's theory, the experiences of childhood and adolescence result in the development of basic trust, autonomy, initiative, competence, and identity on the one hand or mistrust, shame and doubt, guilt, inferiority, and role confusion on the other. In the remaining years of life, three additional tasks remain: the development of intimacy, generativity, and integrity.

According to Erikson, the major developmental challenge faced in young adulthood (ages 20 to 40) is the conflict of *intimacy versus isolation.* This is the period during which many people fall in love, marry, raise children, and form close adult friendships. **Intimacy,** the ability to open oneself to another and to form close, loving relationships, is influenced by how successfully one has resolved the earlier conflicts. For example, achieving intimacy obviously requires the ability to trust other people. Adults who developed a sense of basic mistrust earlier in life may therefore have great difficulty in experiencing inti-

macy. Likewise, young adults who have a sense of inferiority often fear that if they let others close to them, friends and lovers will discover their shortcomings and ultimately reject them. They are therefore locked in conflict, craving intimacy yet fearing emotional vulnerability and possible rejection. When intimacy begins to develop, they may become frightened and feel a need to distance themselves from others. Though surrounded by other people, they may feel isolated and cut off from them.

According to Erikson, middle adulthood—the ages of 40 to 60—brings with it the issue of *generativity versus stagnation.* Once adults have established intimacy, their interests move beyond current adult relationships to a focus on the next generation (Crain, 1985). **Generativity** is experienced by doing things for others, raising children, exercising leadership in society, and generally making the world a better place to live. Having children is by no means the only way of achieving generativity; many single people and childless couples achieve generativity through community work, close friendships, church and synagogue activities, or within their careers.

At this stage, we see once again the importance of having mastered the developmental tasks of earlier periods. Adults who are still struggling with identity and intimacy issues are so preoccupied with their own needs and problems that they are often incapable of expressing care for others. Failure to exercise generativity leads to a childish self-indulgence that is accompanied by a pervading sense of personal impoverishment (Erikson, 1963).

The end of the life cycle brings the final conflict, *integrity versus despair.* According to Erikson, older adults review the course of life and evaluate its meaning and value. If the central conflicts of the earlier phases of life have been favorably resolved, the basic trust, autonomy, industry, identity, intimacy, and generativity that have been achieved all contribute to a sense of integrity. By **integrity** Erikson means a sense of completeness, wholeness, and fulfillment that is strong enough to offset the downward psychological pull of one's inevitable physical decline.

As Erikson reached his mid 80s, he and his wife, Joan, reflected on their own experiences and expanded his theory to focus on the *wisdom of the aged* (Erikson & others, 1986; Goleman, 1988). They concluded that in old age, the lessons learned in each of the earlier stages can ripen into a wisdom that is the culmination of life and a peaceful preparation for death. Table 5.2 shows how successful resolution of the developmental tasks at each phase of life contribute to the wisdom of old age.

Unfortunately, not everyone achieves the final triumph of integrity and wisdom. Instead, older adults who have failed to achieve positive outcomes at the earlier stages may live the final years of their lives in a state of *despair.* According to Erikson, such people have an intense fear of death and a bitter regret that they cannot relive their lives in a more fulfilling fashion. They cannot respond affirmatively to the most important question of their lives: ''As I face death, can I consider my life to have been a worthwhile and meaningful one?''

The Grant Study of Adult Development

Erikson's ideas were based primarily on his own astute observations rather than empirical research. Fortunately, there is now a growing body of research results that bear on his seminal ideas. In 1937, Harvard University received funding from a philanthropist, William T. Grant, to conduct a longitudinal study of adult development. A sample of 95 well-adjusted Harvard graduates has been followed through the adult years by means of detailed questionnaires and interviews.

George Vaillant (1977) analyzed the longitudinal data from the Grant Study and found considerable support for Erikson's basic adult stages of intimacy, generativity, and integrity. Moreover, he concurred with Erikson on the importance of mastering each stage before moving on to the next; those who did not do so were generally unsuccessful in dealing with the next developmental issue.

On the other hand, Vaillant also concluded that Erikson's stages are incomplete. He found evidence for two additional transitional periods in the 30s and 40s. Between the development of intimacy in the 20s and the generativity of middle age, Vaillant inserted a new stage, *career consolidation.* During this period following marriage and the establishment of strong friendships, the Harvard men tended to become preoccupied with advancing their careers. They became conforming, status oriented, and materialistic. This period was followed by a reexamination of basic values, which occurred when the men reached their 40s. Nearly 80 percent of the men went through a period of inner turmoil during which they questioned their goals, their life priorities, and the quality of their marriages and relationships. Some of the men made external changes in their lives, such as divorce or occupational shifts, whereas others made internal changes in their values and commitments. Men who successfully resolved this *midlife transition* became more content with their lives and more compassionate and loving in their relationships (Vaillant, 1977). They were more ready to move into the stage of generativity.

Vaillant's observations are sometimes cited as evidence for the so-called midlife crisis that has become part of our everyday vocabulary. However, Vaillant emphasizes that although some dissatisfac-

Table 5.2 How Successful Resolution of Life-Span Crises Contributes to the Wisdom of the Aged

Successful Resolution	Contribution to Wisdom
Old age: Integrity	Understanding of personal completion and wholeness
Middle adulthood: Generativity	Caring and empathy for others
Early adulthood: Intimacy	Appreciation for the complexity of relationships; valuing of the ability to love freely
Adolescence: Identity	Capacity for commitment and fidelity; appreciation for the complexity of living; merging of sensory, logical, and aesthetic perception
Middle childhood: Industry	Humility; a realistic appreciation of limits and abilities
Early childhood: Initiative	Resilience in the face of adversity; humor concerning shortcomings in self and others
Toddlerhood: Autonomy	Acceptance of physical deterioration
Infancy: Basic trust	Appreciation of interdependence with others

Source: Based on Erikson & others, 1986 and on Goleman, 1988.

tion and emotional turmoil may occur during this period of reevaluation and growth, it is best regarded as a transition period rather than a full-blown crisis. Many men pass through this transition phase with little or no upheaval in their lives. In considering this and other conclusions drawn from the Grant Study, it should be noted that a sample of Harvard men is hardly a representative sample of the U.S. or Canadian population. The results are certainly provocative, but generalization of Vaillant's findings awaits additional research with more representative samples, including women.

Levinson's Study of Life Structures

One of the most intensive studies of adult development was carried out by Daniel Levinson and his coworkers at Yale University (Levinson & others, 1978; Levinson, 1990). In 1969, Levinson began a longitudinal study of 40 men (10 executives, 10 biologists, 10 novelists, and 10 factory workers), who at the time were 35 to 45 years of age. The researchers have now conducted 5 to 10 detailed interviews of about 2 hours' duration with each man. The subjects were asked to describe their life stories and their present hopes, dreams, frustrations, occupational experiences, and relationships.

Based on findings from his admittedly small and unrepresentative sample, Levinson concluded that at any given point in time, a person has a **life structure** that provides an underlying pattern for the person's life. Life structures evolve through a series of stable periods, each lasting 5 to 10 years. These stable pe-

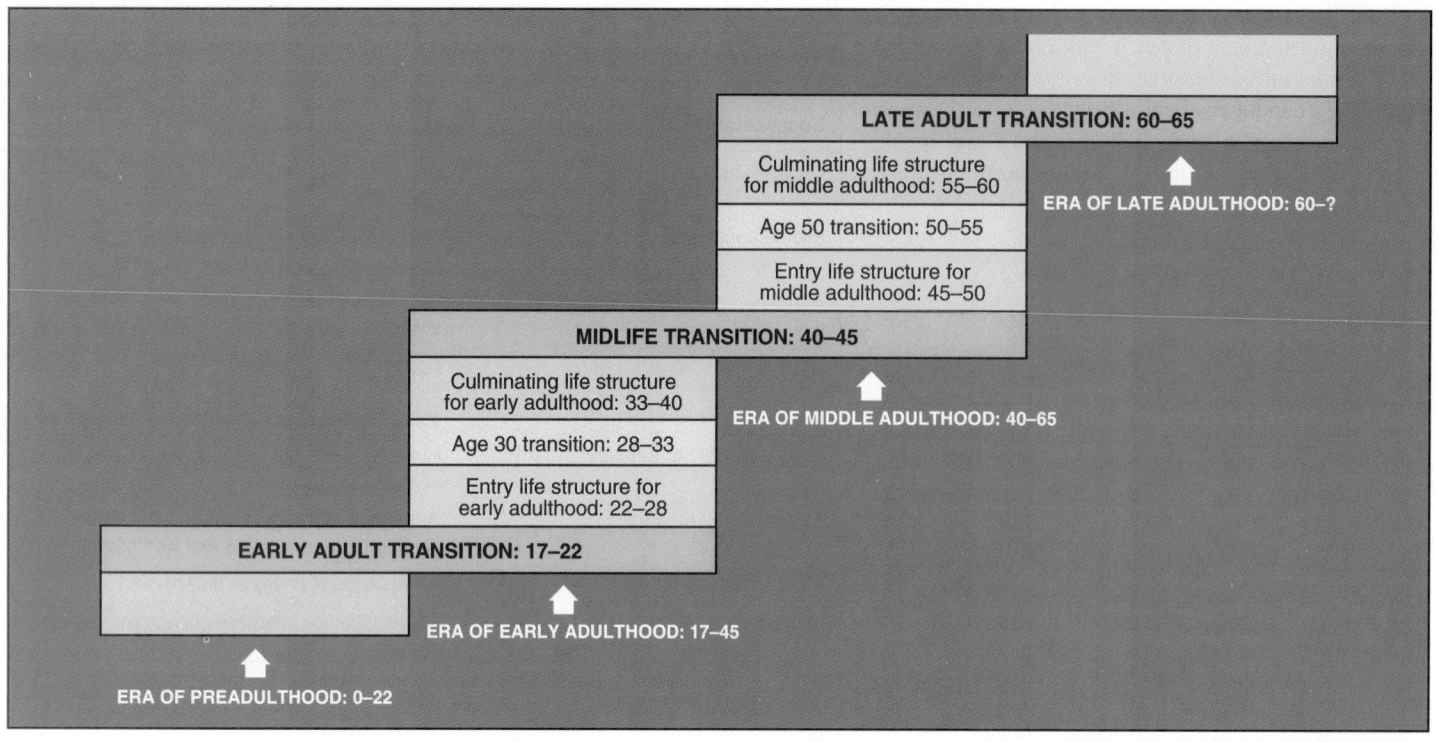

LATE ADULT TRANSITION: 60–65

Culminating life structure
for middle adulthood: 55–60

ERA OF LATE ADULTHOOD: 60–?

Age 50 transition: 50–55

Entry life structure for
middle adulthood: 45–50

MIDLIFE TRANSITION: 40–45

Culminating life structure
for early adulthood: 33–40

ERA OF MIDDLE ADULTHOOD: 40–65

Age 30 transition: 28–33

Entry life structure for
early adulthood: 22–28

EARLY ADULT TRANSITION: 17–22

ERA OF EARLY ADULTHOOD: 17–45

ERA OF PREADULTHOOD: 0–22

◆ **Figure 5.13** *Levinson's proposed stages of adult development. Each of the age-related life structures is framed by important transition periods. (Levinson, 1986).*

riods are bounded by transition periods that change the life structure in fundamental ways and are often crucial periods of reappraisal (see Figure 5.13).

In Levinson's sample, the first of these transition periods occurred as the men broke away from their preadult environments and entered the adult world of work and relationships. During their 20s, they were often guided in their work and relationships by highly idealized "dreams." At the end of their 20s, another transitional period occurred in which the men took stock of their lives and sometimes questioned their vocational and marriage choices. Men who had made no vocational or relationship commitments during their 20s often became disenchanted with their lack of roots and felt a need to "settle in." Levinson views this period of introspection as an opportunity to work out flaws in the life structure and create a basis for a more satisfying one. During this period, many of the men found an older person who served as a *mentor,* giving them guidance and serving as a confidant.

The 30s served as a period of career advancement and a time of tending to family life. During this period, family and occupational demands were especially high. In the late 30s, a distinct phase occurred that Levinson called *becoming one's own man.* At this time, ambition peaked, and the men became more independent, authoritative, and confident.

The midlife transition occurred between the ages of 40 and 45. The men again looked back and appraised their life structures. For the first time, they began to focus on their own mortality and to realize that time was now limited and had to be used wisely.

For many of them, the dream of fame and fortune had to be abandoned, and those who had achieved this dream often realized that doing so had not brought them the happiness they expected. Many of Levinson's subjects experienced psychological turmoil during this period, and some of them made major changes in their lives in an attempt to attain greater satisfaction and meaningfulness. Once the crises were over, the men tended to deepen their attachments, became more compassionate and reflective, and set about completing their careers. Most of them found the years from 50 to 60 to be fulfilling ones because of the issues they had confronted and worked out for themselves during the midlife transition. However, those men who did not negotiate the midlife transition satisfactorily found their lives to be "increasingly trivial or stagnant" (Levinson, 1986, p. 5).

Levinson's study has not yet provided data on the later stages of adult development, and the applicability of his conclusions to non-Caucasian ethnic populations and to women are not yet clear. Levinson (1986) reported that a new study in which 45 women were interviewed indicates the same basic developmental sequence for women. Priscilla Roberts and Peter Newton (1987) reviewed similar studies done with women and concluded that the nature and timing of the women's developmental tasks were quite similar to those for men. Like men, women developed a dream of what they wanted to achieve in their lives during the early adult transition. However, in contrast to men's dreams, which were mainly focused on career, women's involved both career and a deep commitment to intimacy in their relationships. In general, women found it more difficult than men to balance their career and relationship aspirations, and a strong source of dissatisfaction to many of them was the cultural expectation that they sacrifice their career when the two conflicted.

Levinson's model provides the most detailed description of adult development, but critics of the theory question not only its generalizability to other populations but also the notion of rigid, time-bound stages. They point out that in today's U.S. and Canadian cultures, there are no longer rigid expectations or time constraints for finishing one's education, entering the work force, marrying, starting a family, and retiring. Individual life paths may differ sharply, and so may individual developmental timetables during the adult years.

Research results tend to support Vaillant's more benign midlife transition as opposed to Levinson's more crisis-oriented one (Newman & Newman, 1991). Although some midlifers undoubtedly experience turmoil, studies done with far larger samples than Levinson's find little if any evidence that life-crisis indicators, such as job dissatisfaction, divorce, suicide, feelings of meaningless, and life dissatisfaction, peak during the presumably critical period of 40 to 45 years (McCrae & Costa, 1990; Schaie & Willis, 1986). Instead, these indicators tend to remain relatively stable across the adult years.

Possible Selves in Adulthood

According to Hazel Markus and Paula Nurius (1986), people have not only current self-concepts but also hopes and fears about what they might become in the future. These make up people's **possible selves.** The hoped-for self is similar to the ideal self discussed in Chapter 4, and it motivates the person's attempts to attain the desired state. In contrast, the feared self motivates the person to avoid the feared conditions.

Several recent studies have examined possible selves at various stages of adulthood, under the assumption that they reflect the dominant motivations and concerns of each age group. In a cross-sectional study, Susan Cross and Hazel Markus (1991) used questionnaires to measure the hoped-for and feared selves of men and women at four age levels: 18–24, 25–39, 40–59, and 60 and older. Figure 5.14 shows the frequency with which hoped-for selves were related to family, occupation, physical status, and lifestyle for each group.

Analysis of the hoped-for selves revealed that the youngest group tended to have extremely positive ideal selves, such as being rich, famous, and perfectly happy. These were reminiscent of Levinson's notion of the young adult's dreams. By the 30s, however, the goals were more modest and seemed to reflect the

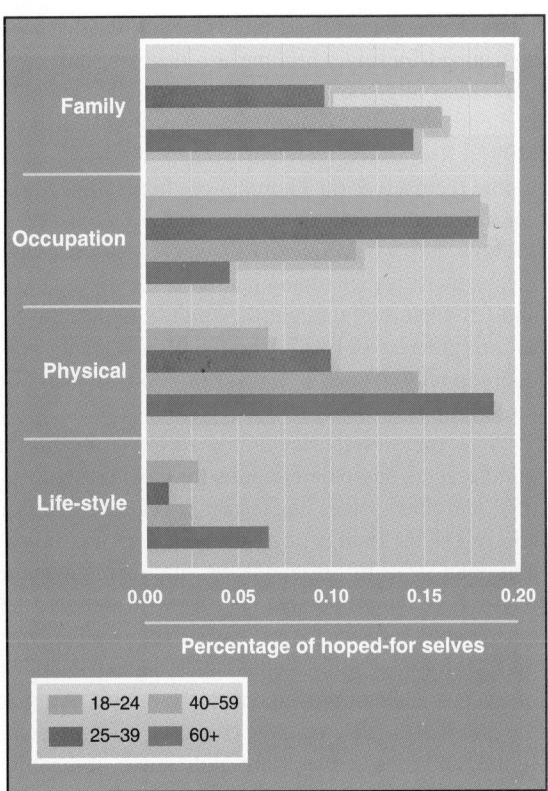

Figure 5.14 *Percentages of hoped-for selves falling into four general life categories at various ages. (Cross & Markus, 1991).*

settling down that Levinson described in the men he studied. The men and women wanted to be good mates and parents and to have success in their work, and they often expressed desires for travel and leisure.

The hoped-for selves of the members of the 40-to-59 age group seemed still more anchored in their current life situations, and they expressed desires for comfort, security, and a deepening of relationships. Finally, the possible selves of those over 60 indicated that personal growth and development were still important. They expressed wishes to maintain current selves (for example, to stay active and involved) as well as hopes of doing new tasks (such as writing a publishable novel).

The patterns of feared selves differed among the age groups as well. Although physical fears (for example, developing cancer) were most often mentioned by all of the groups, the young adults differed most from the other groups in expressing many concerns about possible occupational failure. Some of their statements reflected desperation about the possibility that they would not be able to marry or attain occupational success. The middle-aged adults had more concerns than other groups about material well-being. The oldest group had by far the greatest number of concerns about future physical well-being and life-style.

In general, both the positive and negative possible selves are quite consistent with the age-related themes emphasized by Erikson, Vaillant, and Levinson. One interesting aspect of the results is the finding that with age, hoped-for selves become less idealistic and move into closer alignment with the current self. This phenomenon is also revealed in a study by Carol Ryff (1991). Ryff asked men and women of various ages to rate themselves on a number of characteristics according to (a) their present perceptions of themselves; (b) how they would like to be—in other words, their ideal selves; (c) what they had been like in the past; and (d) what they thought they would be like in the future (the next 10 to 15 years). Self-acceptance was operationally defined in terms of the positiveness of these ratings.

The mean self-acceptance ratings of young, middle-aged, and elderly adults for past, present, future, and ideal selves are shown in Figure 5.15. For all groups, the ratings of past selves were less favorable than those of present selves, indicating a sense of perceived improvement over time. Moreover, the discrepancy between the present and future selves was greatest for the young adults, indicating expectations of even greater improvement in the future. Among the elderly, the discrepancies between past, present, future, and ideal selves were quite small, indicating that with age, people achieve a closer fit between their ideal and their actual self-perceptions and expect little change in the future. Ryff concluded that as they age, people come to have more realistic goals for themselves, expect less positive change, and seem more at peace with who they are.

Genetic Influences on Life Events

Most adult developmental theorists emphasize how much adult development is influenced by the life events that people encounter at various points in their lives. However, as we have seen in earlier chapters, characteristics of the individual may, in turn, influence the environment. Recently, behavior geneticists have begun to explore how genetically influenced characteristics such as cognitive skills, physical appearance, and temperament might influence the kinds of life events people encounter.

Robert Plomin and his coworkers (1990) studied the life events reported by adult twins. They examined 25 specific life events that involved relationships, changes in occupational and financial status, illnesses, difficulties with the law, and changes in lifestyle. Of particular interest was a comparison of identical and fraternal twins who had been separated early in life and reared in different environments. Plomin and his coworkers reasoned that if the genetically identical twin pairs raised in different environments were more similar in the events they reported than were the fraternal twins, a genetic influence on life events would be indicated. The results supported this hypothesis. As shown in Figure 5.16, life-event correlations were substantially higher for identical twin

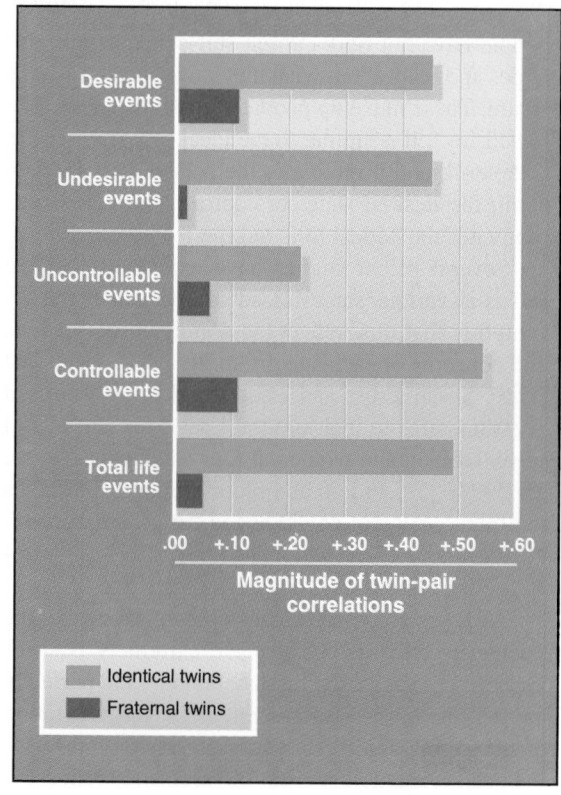

Figure 5.16 *Correlations between the life-event scores of identical and fraternal twins who were separated early in life and reared in different environments. The higher correlations (greater similarities) for identical twins suggest that genetic factors influence life events. (Data from Plomin & others, 1990).*

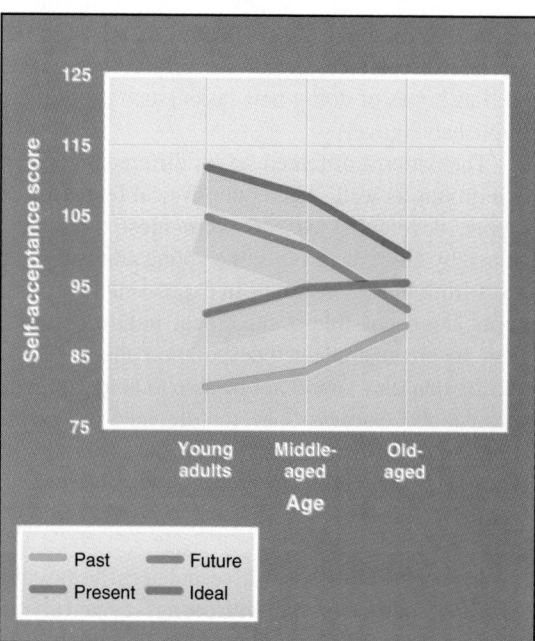

Figure 5.15 *Self-acceptance ratings of past, present, ideal, and future (possible) selves at various developmental periods of adulthood. Note the convergence of these various aspects of the self among the elderly. (Ryff, 1991).*

pairs than for fraternal twins. Moreover, the largest difference in the magnitude of the correlations involved a subset of *controllable* events, such as conflicts with spouses and occupational success, which could presumably be influenced by a person's behavior. By comparing the correlations for identical and fraternal twins, Plomin and his coworkers estimated that approximately 40 percent of the variance in life-event scores could be attributed to genetic differences among individuals.

Development involves a constant interplay between the individual and the environment. As we have seen, this is a reciprocal interaction in which the characteristics of the environment influence the individual and, in turn, the characteristics of the person influence the environment (Bandura, 1986; Plomin & Rende, 1991). Within this complex pattern of person–environment interactions, a wide range of individual developmental outcomes are possible.

Physical Development and Health

Young Adulthood

Young adults in their 20s and 30s are at the peak of their physical, sexual, and perceptual functioning. Maximum muscle strength in the legs, arms, and other parts of the body is reached at age 25 to 30. Women reach the peak of their reproductive capacities in their 20s, when the uterus is still growing and the lining is most amenable to implantation (Sherwood, 1991). Most of the physical changes that begin to occur during young adulthood involve the internal organs and are not readily observable. For example, heart and lung capacities gradually decline, but this decreased functioning is not noticeable until about age 40 (Belsky, 1990). Figure 5.17 shows the rate of decline in several physiological functions from young adulthood into old age.

Visual and auditory acuity reach their peak in the teens and early 20s and undergo a gradual loss in efficiency that is typically not noticeable until 45 to 60 years of age (Verrillo & Verrillo, 1985; Hayslip & Panek, 1989). Reaction time and coordination improve from childhood until about 19 years, remain constant until about age 26, and then begin a gradual decline (Hayslip & Panek, 1989). The strength, speed, and quick reactions of young adults give them an edge in competitive sports and other activities requiring physical coordination and endurance. During the middle to late 20s, athletes in many sports are considered to be in their prime (see Figure 5.18).

In contrast to the more chronic conditions that appear in middle and late adulthood, most illnesses suffered by young adults are acute, or temporary. Younger adults, especially men under the age of 40,

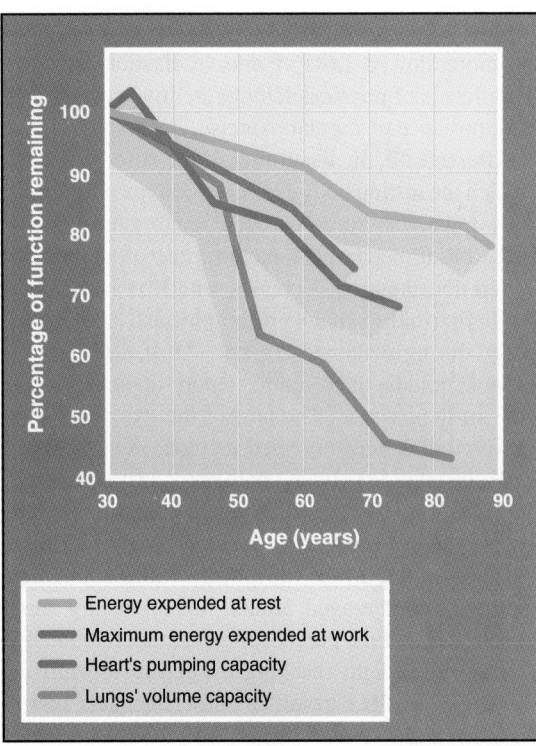

Figure 5.17 *Rates of decline in various physical functions from early to late adulthood. (Data from Insel & Roth, 1976).*

are more likely to die from violent causes such as automobile accidents or homicides than from chronic illnesses (Bayer & others, 1982).

Middle Adulthood

Physical status begins to decline at midlife. Some of the earliest changes occur in motor abilities. After age 33, hand and finger movements become progressively more clumsy (Troll, 1985). A 10-percent loss in muscle strength occurs between 30 and 60 years of age.

Figure 5.18 *Because of physical maturation factors, many athletes reach the peaks of their careers between the ages of 25 and 30. At 25, Jose Canseco became the first baseball player in history to hit more than 40 home runs and steal more than 40 bases in the same season in an unequaled display of power and speed.*

Muscles become stiffer and tend to tense, relax, and heal more slowly. Loss of muscle elasticity occurs where levels of physical activity are low, suggesting the importance of regular exercise.

After age 40, the **basal metabolic rate**—the rate at which the resting body converts food into energy—slows down, resulting in a tendency to gain weight. As the basal metabolism declines, the efficiency of oxygen consumption decreases, and it is harder for the 40-year-old to maintain the physical endurance needed during sustained exercise (Troll, 1985).

Most middle-aged adults report noticeable declines in their vision. The lens of the eye continues to grow, but it does not shed its older cells (Corso, 1977). Instead, it yellows, hardens, and loses some of its elasticity. By age 40, the lens is too large and stiff for the eye muscles to focus properly on close objects, resulting in the farsighted condition characteristic of middle-aged adults. Visual acuity also worsens because the pupil becomes smaller, reducing the amount of light reaching the retina (Fozard & others, 1977). As a result of these changes, many adults need glasses and bright light for reading and doing other close-range work. Accompanying these visual changes is a decrease in the ability to hear high-frequency tones, which is caused by degenerative changes in the auditory system (Corso, 1977). High-frequency hearing losses are greater for men than for women. Loss of auditory sensitivity impairs speech perception.

Although physical declines are noticeable in middle adulthood, it is not necessarily a period of poor health and bodily deterioration (see Figure 5.19). Many adults live through the middle years without becoming sick or incapacitated. However, infections and disease sometimes surface because of wear and tear on the body and poor health habits, including smoking and excessive use of alcohol. The greatest health risks to Americans in middle adulthood are posed by the two leading killers in the United States, heart disease and cancer. The incidence of heart attacks increases among middle-aged men; and those who smoke, have high-fat diets, or lead inactive or highly stressful lives are at special risk (Taylor, 1991). The incidence of breast cancer increases among middle-aged women; this form of cancer is the principal killer of women between 35 and 50 (National Center for Health Statistics, 1990).

Late Adulthood

The graying of America is an indisputable reality. The fastest-growing segment of the U.S. population is made up of people over 65 years of age. Greater control of malnutrition and infectious diseases, combined with improved medical treatment, diet, and exercise, is allowing more people to reach old age than ever before. White females born in 1970 can expect to live 78.2 years, African-American females 72.7 years, white males 70.6 years, and African-American males 64 years (National Center for Health Statistics, 1990). As the baby boom generation reaches old age in the early 2000s, the older population is expected to more than double in size from its current level of 36 million to 82 million persons and there will be more 80- and 90-year-olds than ever before.

As Figure 5.20 shows, the number of adults 60 years of age or older increased from 4.9 million in 1900 to 35.6 million in 1980. Meanwhile, the population under age 60 increased at only one fourth this rate. Demographers expect this rapid growth rate to continue through the first third of the 21st century (Fowles, 1983). By 2030, one in five Americans will be over 65 years of age if present trends continue (Bureau of the Census, 1991).

The physical and structural changes of middle adulthood become more pronounced in late adulthood. About 80 percent of a young adult's body consists of so-called lean body mass (muscles, organs, and bone), and the remaining 20 percent consists of fatty, or adipose, tissue. But after age 30, the muscles begin to atrophy, the skin thins out, and lean body mass is replaced by adipose tissue at an average rate of 5 percent a decade. By age 70, the balance between lean and fat body mass may be 50–50. Deterioration of the skeletal frame and spinal discs results in a height decrease of about an inch between the ages of 40 and 70 (Troll, 1982). Bones lose calcium and become more brittle and slower to heal, and hardened ligaments hamper movement and make movements stiffer and slower (Weg, 1983).

▶ **Figure 5.19** *Physical declines in midlife can be slowed by regular exercise.*

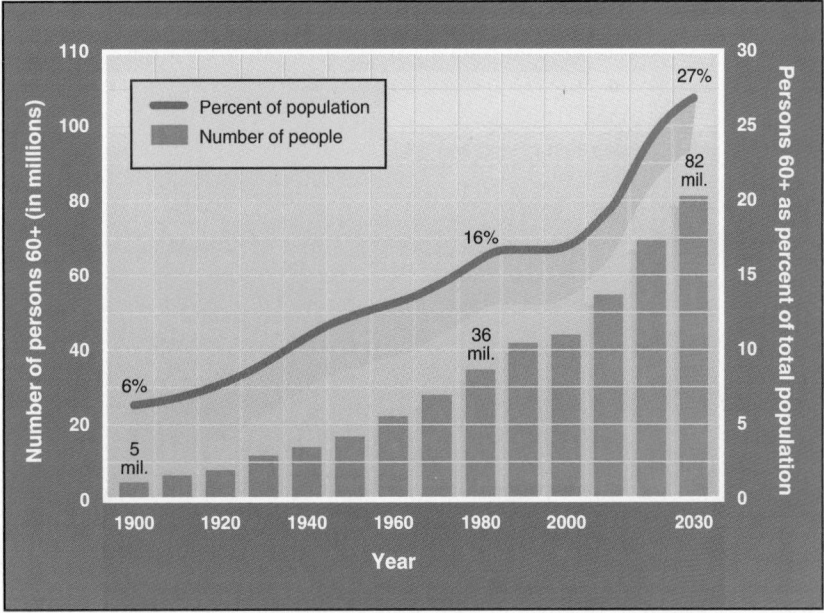

◀ **Figure 5.20** *Increase in the late adult population (60 years and older) from 1900 to 2030. (U.S. Bureau of the Census, 1992).*

Can any of these bodily changes be delayed or reversed? Recent attempts to do so have involved injections of human growth hormone (HGH), a pituitary substance that stimulates the growth of lean tissue and bone in children and whose decline in late adulthood has long been thought to play a role in the aging process. In one recent study, injections of synthetic HGH 3 times a week for 6 months resulted in significant gains in 12 elderly men. They showed an 8.8 percent increase in muscle and other lean tissue, a 14.4 percent decrease in adipose tissue, and increases in skin thickness and in density of the vertebrae of the lower back (Rudman & others, 1990). More research is needed to assess possible negative side effects of the treatment and to establish whether gains can be maintained over time, but medical researchers are hopeful that HGH therapy can allow some of the elderly to be more active and productive in their final years. It may also combine with other medical advances to extend life for the aged.

The brains of people over 30 begin to shrink as neurons are lost each year (Troll, 1982). At 90, the brain has lost 5 to 10 percent of its early adult weight (Whitbourne, 1985). Among the consequences of brain alterations are disruptions of sleep. The elderly find it more difficult to sleep soundly, and they have a higher incidence of sleep disturbances than any other age group (Monk, 1989). A more serious dysfunction is Alzheimer's disease, a progressive and degenerative neurological disorder that severely affects memory and other cognitive functions (Larson & others, 1992). The disease strikes 10 percent of Americans by age 75 and nearly half by age 85. In the United States, approximately 2.5 million persons over 65 are afflicted each year (Jarvik & Winograd, 1988).

Recent studies of autonomic nervous system (ANS) activity in the elderly indicate that the physiological component of emotion decreases with age, although the emotional experience does not. In one of the first studies comparing elderly people (aged 77 to 81) with younger ones (aged 18 to 30), Robert Levenson, Laura Carstensen, Wallace Friesen, and Paul Ekman (1991) asked subjects to imagine and relive past experiences in which they had experienced anger, fear, sadness, and disgust. Measures of heart rate, finger temperature, and facial activity were obtained, and the subjects also rated the subjective intensity of each of their emotional responses as they reexperienced them.

The investigators found no differences in the rated intensity of the relived experiences or in the strength of facial expressions accompanying the emotional responses. However, as shown in Figure 5.21, the physiological responses of the elderly subjects were less intense than those of the younger subjects. The researchers suggested that "emotion-specific ANS activity has been selected by evolution for its adaptive functions that are critical to survival. These functions might become less important once the primary reproductive period has ended, thus diminishing, albeit not eliminating, the ANS component of emotion" (Levenson & others, 1991, p. 33).

The physical declines that occur during the aging process are undeniable. But we have seen on numerous occasions the many ways in which biological and psychological processes are linked. Thus, we should not be surprised to find that there is considerable scientific evidence for the adage "You're only as old as you feel."

Figure 5.21 *Changes in mean heart rate (in beats per minute, or BPM) and finger temperature in young and old adults as they relived negative emotional experiences. Despite their generally lower physiological reactivity, the older subjects rated their subjective emotional reactions as equally intense, and their facial expressions were equally strong. (Levenson & others, 1991).*

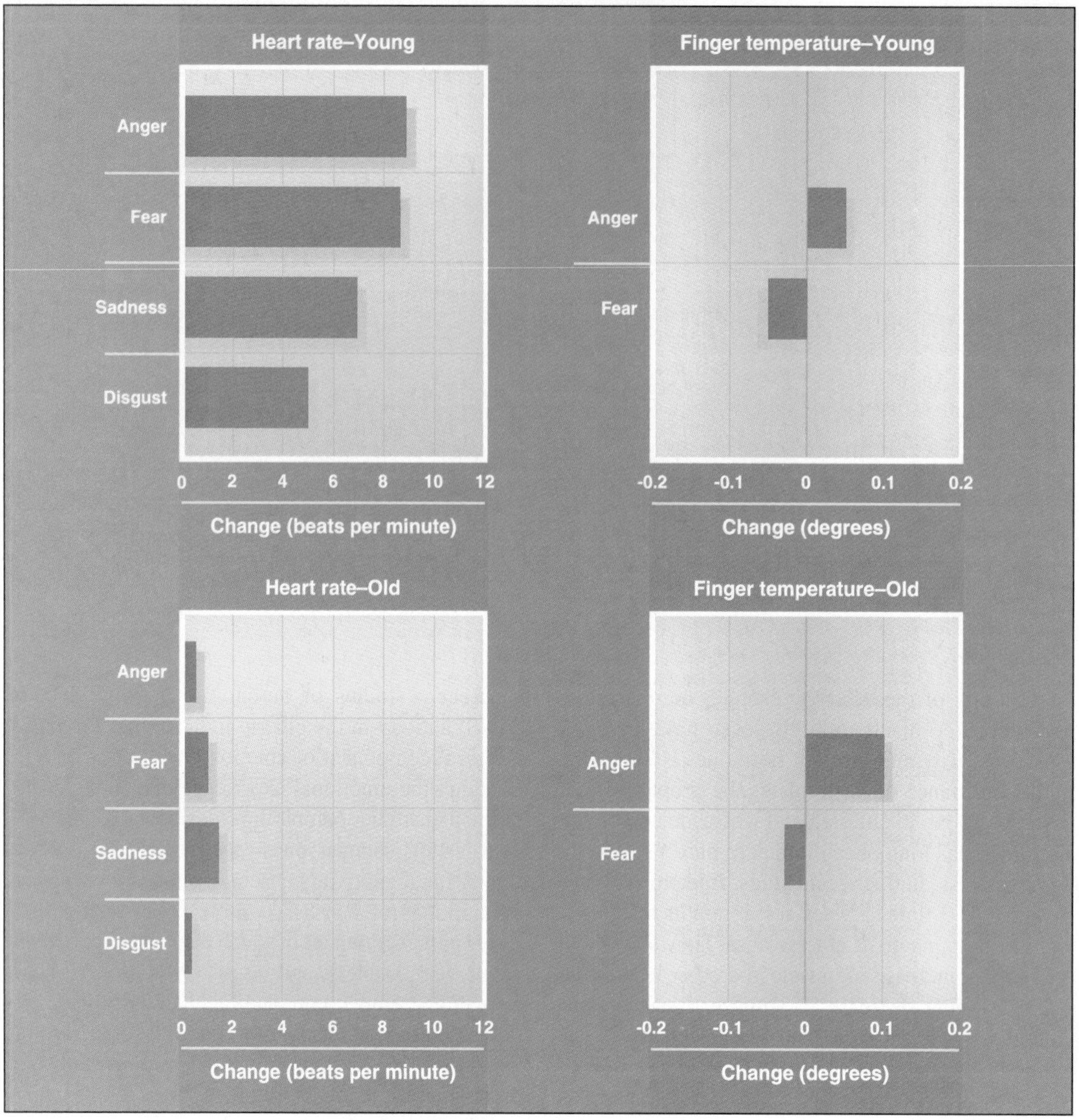

Heart rate–Young

Anger
Fear
Sadness
Disgust

0 2 4 6 8 10 12
Change (beats per minute)

Finger temperature–Young

Anger
Fear

-0.2 -0.1 0 0.1 0.2
Change (degrees)

Heart rate–Old

Anger
Fear
Sadness
Disgust

0 2 4 6 8 10 12
Change (beats per minute)

Finger temperature–Old

Anger
Fear

-0.2 -0.1 0 0.1 0.2
Change (degrees)

PSYCHOBIOLOGICAL INTERACTIONS

Aging as a State of Body *And* Mind

As people move into their 40s and 50s, the obvious physical signs of aging—wrinkles, middle-age flab, failing vision, and the loss and graying of hair—bring the sudden realization that the twilight of life is approaching. Psychological reactions to this realization are as diverse as the different physical patterns of aging. Some view midlife as a time of crisis and become anxious and depressed. They see themselves as "over the hill" and feel their days are numbered. But others view midlife as a time of gaining new insights, self-understanding, and personal fulfillment.

At midlife, many adults respond to signs of physical aging by focusing more attention on their bodies (Gould, 1972). Bernice Neugarten (1968) found an increase in *body monitoring* among middle-aged men and women. Confronted with an aging body, many middle-aged adults become concerned with its upkeep. They may spend an increasing amount of time before a mirror, begin an exercise program to tone up their muscles, or resort to hair color, wigs, creams, and other cosmetic devices.

Middle-aged adults who are very body conscious have more psychological difficulties with becoming older. Adults who value themselves for their beauty, strength, or other physical traits tend to experience negative psychological reactions as soon as their bodies begin to show wear and tear. In contrast, people who place importance on non-physical attributes such as intelligence or interpersonal skills usually continue to function well and feel young for many years after their hair turns gray and their muscles weaken (Troll, 1985).

Middle-aged adults not only think more about their bodies but also become more concerned about their health. A national survey of 25,000 middle-aged Americans revealed that 42 percent of the respondents thought about their health more than about almost anything else, including love, work, and money. Those who were highly body conscious (that is, more often combed their hair, looked in mirrors, flexed muscles, or checked for body odors) felt less healthy than those who were less body conscious, even though the two groups were equally healthy (Rubenstein, 1982). The results also revealed that how people feel about their health is as important as how healthy they actually are. A person's actual physical health status did not always correspond with how healthy that person felt. "Health optimists" often felt healthy despite physical ailments, whereas "health pessimists" frequently felt ill despite apparent good health.

People respond quite differently to their concerns about deterioration in health and other physical attributes. Three notable response patterns were found. *Health vigilants* pursued health with a vengeance and believed that diet and exercise could conquer any health threat. *True believers* thought illness could best be combated through positive thinking, faith, prayer, optimism, and friendship. *Fatalists* believed that their health was determined by fate and luck or by genetic endowment and that they could do little to influence it. Not surprisingly, the fatalists were the most unhappy of the three groups. In contrast, the health vigilants, who took maximum responsibility for their own health, were physically and psychologically the healthiest (Rubenstein, 1982).

Robert Peck (1968) analyzed the specific developmental tasks of old age and concluded that one of the most important is acceptance of one's inevitable physical decline, accompanied by a shift from valuing physical powers to valuing wisdom and relationships. Levinson (1978) also found that as they entered middle age, many of his subjects redefined the self, placing less emphasis on physical appearance and performance and more emphasis on knowledge and experience. In this way, they focused on remaining productive in activities

Figure 5.22 *An active lifestyle can contribute to physical vigor in the elderly. Many older people illustrate the truism that aging is a state of mind as well as body.*

where their functioning was less affected by the physical aging process. The success with which many aging adults accomplish this task is suggested by cross-sectional studies of subjective well-being. In one analysis of the results of 119 such studies, age groups ranging from adolescence through old age were virtually indistinguishable in their ratings of personal happiness (Stock & others, 1983). In another study of subjective well-being carried out in eight Western European countries, an identical 78 percent of adolescents, middle-aged adults, and adults over 65 reported themselves to be "satisfied" or "very satisfied" with their lives (Ingelhart & Rabier, 1986).

Physical deterioration and feelings of growing old can begin in young adulthood, especially for those who practice poor nutrition and health habits and lead an inactive life. In contrast, many adults claim they didn't hit their peak until they reached their 40s or 50s, and some elderly persons begin running marathons at age 70 (see Figure 5.22). In a very real sense, all of these groups *are* as old as they feel. Ironically, regardless of one's age, the conviction that one is "getting old" may result in behaviors, such as withdrawal from physical activity and poor dietary habits, that speed up the biological process of aging.

Cognitive Development

As noted earlier, Piaget believed that cognitive development ends in adolescence with the attainment of formal operations. According to Piaget (1972), the period from 15 to 20 years marks the beginning of what he termed **professional specialization** in abstract reasoning. Piaget proposed that young adults attain and apply formal operations at different times and in different areas according to their aptitudes and their professional specializations. Thus, they often apply abstract thought in their fields of interest but not in other fields. For example, Carl, a physicist who reasons at a highly abstract level in his profession, may have great difficulty applying abstract reasoning to a problem involving contract law. Mary is an attorney whose logic in verbal discourse and judicial concepts is superior to Carl's. Asked to reason on the theory of relativity, however, she will probably have the same difficulty Carl has with contract law, because concepts are involved that she is unfamiliar with or has forgotten.

Piaget never suggested another *kind* of thinking beyond formal operations. However, he acknowledged that adults continue to advance in their cognitive skills. According to Piaget, this occurs because their accumulated experiences give adults more schemas than adolescents have, and the broader world view produced by experiences in educational settings and the workplace gives them greater skill in applying these schemas.

Other theorists dispute Piaget's contention that cognitive development ends with formal operations, suggesting a possible fifth stage (Richards & Commons, 1990). For example, Patricia Arlin (1984) proposed that adults progress to a new level of cognitive maturity that she called **problem finding.** Problem finding involves posing new questions about the world and trying to discover novel solutions to old problems. Arlin viewed this mode of thinking as the foundation for creativity, and she maintained that the ways in which people think about the world continue to develop in the adult years. Another theorist, Klaus Riegel (1973), suggested that adults attain a fifth stage of reasoning, **postformal thought,** in which they can reason about opposing points of view and accept contradictions and irreconcilable differences. This form of reasoning has shown up in studies in which subjects of varying ages were asked to reason about social dilemmas, such as a disagreement between a man and a woman about whether to abort an unplanned pregnancy. Adolescents almost always tried to find reasons to justify only one side of the argument. In contrast, adults were more likely to accept both sides of the disagreement as legitimate, as the notion of postformal thought would predict (Blanchard-Fields, 1986).

Given the declines in physical and perceptual abilities that become noticeable in middle age, many people naturally assume that cognitive functions also decline during this period. However, psychologists have discovered that this is not necessarily so. Although there are some declines in reaction time and in speed of performance on certain tasks, other abilities, such as verbal skills, actually peak during midlife (Willis, 1989). Short-term memory shows no notable decline through middle adulthood (Wingfield & Byrnes, 1981), and long-term memory shows only a slight decrease on measures of *recall* (for example, retrieving factual information on an essay exam). In contrast, *recognition* measures of long-term memory (such as recalling facts on a multiple-choice test) show no decline in middle age. Moreover, middle-aged adults can profit greatly from training in how to organize material for learning and recall (Zivian & Darges, 1983). Finally, the learning and problem-solving skills of middle-aged people differ little, if at all, from those of adolescents and young adults, particularly among those midlifers who regularly exercise their cognitive skills in academic or occupational settings (Wagner & others, 1992).

Intellectual Changes

Age-related changes in the cognitive skills measured by intelligence tests have been the subject of a great deal of research and controversy. Do intellectual skills decline like physical skills, or do they remain largely intact through middle and late adulthood? The answer to this question depends in large part on how the research is conducted. As noted in Chapter 4, research designs in developmental psychology are of two major types, cross sectional and longitudinal. When early cross-sectional studies of intelligence were carried out, they yielded results like those shown in Figure 5.23. The conclusion seemed fairly clear: Intellectual abilities decline sharply and progressively after age 50. Until the 1950s, this conclusion went virtually unchallenged because the age-related differences between subjects tested at the same time were attributed to the aging process.

There is, however, an important alternative explanation that cannot be ruled out in cross-sectional studies of this kind. As discussed in Chapter 4, how can we be sure that the differences are not due at least in part to the generation, or *cohort,* in which the different age groups were reared? For example, we know that successive generations have received more formal education. More recent generations are also more likely to have jobs that require the constant use of cognitive skills. Finally, dietary practices and health care have improved greatly over the past half century. Any or all of these factors could contribute to higher intellectual functioning in younger groups and account for the results in Figure 5.23. The weaknesses of the cross-sectional design caused some critics of the early work to question whether intellectual abilities decline as these studies suggested (Schaie & Strother, 1968).

One means of controlling for cohort effects is the longitudinal study, in which the same subjects are tested repeatedly over time. One of the best longitudinal studies of intellectual functioning is the Seattle Longitudinal Study, conducted by K. Warner Schaie and his coworkers (Schaie, 1983, 1987). The subjects ranged in age from 18 to 67 years of age when the study began, and they have been tested repeatedly over a 21-year period. The results therefore provide a reasonably good picture of age-related changes in intellectual abilities that are not confounded with cohort effects.

Schaie's data look quite different from the cross-sectional results, and they suggest a far different conclusion about the course of intellectual deterioration (see Figure 5.24). Schaie found that although there is some decline in intellectual abilities in the late 60s and 70s, it is not until age 81 that the average person falls below the midrange of performance for young adults. Moreover, individuals' relative rankings

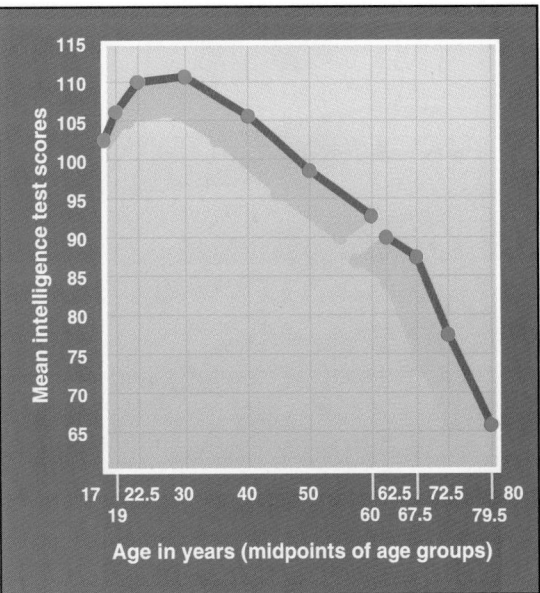

Figure 5.23 *Cross-sectional data suggest a notable decline in scores on the Wechsler Adult Intelligence Scale after age 40. These data, collected in the 1950s, supported the conclusion that intelligence declines sharply with age. (Doppelt & Wallace, 1955).*

within their cohort group are highly stable over time (Hertzog & Schaie, 1986); the brightest at age 60 are also likely to be the brightest at age 80.

It thus appears that intellectual functions remain largely intact through much of the late adult period.

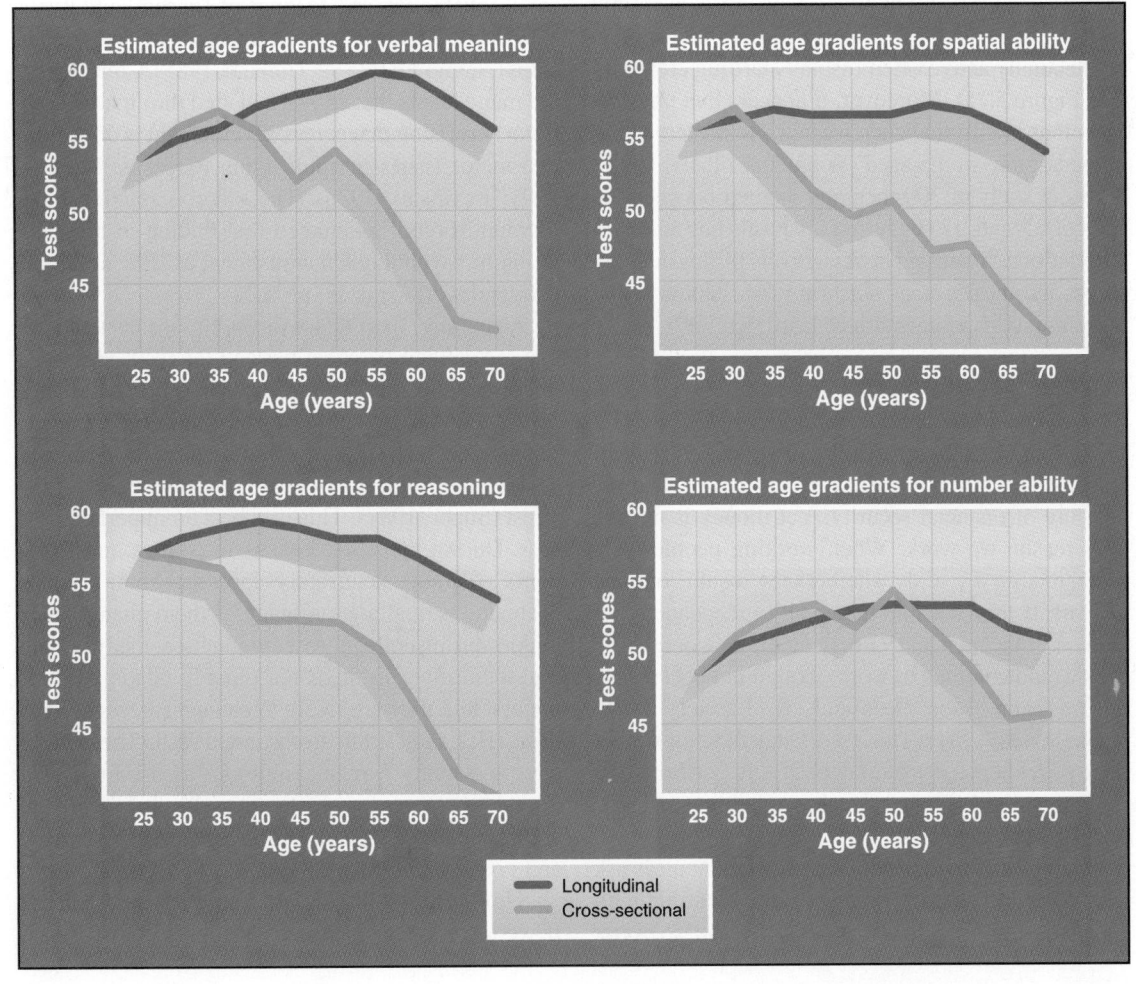

Figure 5.24 *Longitudinal data indicate that mental abilities decline with aging far less than cross-sectional methods suggested. Here, longitudinal data remain fairly stable to age 70. The cross-sectional declines are likely attributable to cohort effects. (Schaie & Strother, 1968).*

→ **Figure 5.25** *Continuous mental activity can preserve cognitive abilities far into late adulthood. The Guggenheim Museum in New York was designed by the architect Frank Lloyd Wright when he was 89 years old.*

This is especially true for people who exercise these skills through regular involvement in cognitive activities. As in the case of physical exercise, the moral is, "Use it or lose it." Elderly people who remain intellectually active often display startling creativity (see Figure 5.25). Moreover, it appears that physical as well as intellectual exercise helps to preserve cognitive abilities in the aged (Wagner & others, 1992). A recent study of 300 men and women between the ages of 55 and 91 suggested a causal (not merely a correlational) relation between levels of physical exercise and measures of reaction time, memory, and reasoning (Clarkson-Smith & Hartley, 1990).

Career Development

Work is a central part of our lives for a variety of reasons. The most obvious is the need to achieve some measure of financial security. Yet money is not the only reason we work. When working people were asked in a survey study whether they would continue to work if they became financially independent, 84 percent of the men and 77 percent of the women said they would continue to work, though not necessarily at the same jobs (Renwick & Lawler, 1978; Yankelovich, 1981). Thus, work has functions other than providing for material needs. It performs the important psychological function of helping to define our personal identities.

One of the first questions new acquaintances ask is, "What do you do?" Adults tend to identify themselves as teachers, lawyers, bankers, and so forth.

Work also helps us structure and organize our lives; it counteracts boredom; it provides an outlet for personal satisfaction and feelings of success; and it is a significant source of social interactions and friendships (Havighurst, 1982; Holland, 1985). Considering the many needs that can be satisfied through work, it is not surprising that career development is one of the two major issues in adult living (Cross & Markus, 1991; Levinson, 1978). The other is relationships. Sigmund Freud anticipated this finding in his definition of psychological adjustment as "the ability to love and work" (1935, p. 112).

Generally, men and women choose occupations that match their personalities and interests, and these interests are usually established by age 17 (Holland, 1985; Shinkman, 1981). When choosing a career, young adults frequently match their self-images against their images of people in certain fields of interest (Super, 1981). This is at best an imperfect process. During their first 2 years in college, most students cannot accurately predict their future occupations, and a great many of them change their majors during college. After graduation, many people find themselves in fields not directly related to their majors, and they are likely to change careers at least once (Holland, 1985; Rothstein, 1980). These facts have led many career counselors to recommend a liberal education that fosters breadth of knowledge and varied learning skills as opposed to a more narrow and vocationally focused one.

How successful are adults in their career choices? If we use job satisfaction as an index of success, it appears at first that the majority of adults make appropriate choices. In one major survey, about 90 percent of respondents replied affirmatively to the question "Are you satisfied with your job?" However, the picture changed considerably when the same respondents were asked, "If you could start over, would you seek the same job you have now?" To this question, fewer than half of white-collar workers and only about a fourth of blue-collar workers responded yes, suggesting that job satisfaction is generally less than optimal (Weaver, 1980). Job satisfaction is lower among younger workers than among older ones, and younger workers change jobs far more frequently. There are also developmental changes in what people see as most important in work. Younger workers are most interested in salary and advancement, but in middle adulthood, job security becomes more important to workers (Krausz, 1982).

Women and Work

Perhaps the most notable trend in the work force is the increasing number of women who hold jobs outside the home. In the early 1950s, only one in five women between the ages of 25 and 44 worked outside the home. That figure has now risen to nearly 70 percent (U.S. Department of Labor, 1992). The most dramatic increase has occurred among married women—from 24 percent to 57 percent. Among couples in the 25–34 age range, about one wife in five earns more than her husband (U.S. Department of Labor, 1992).

The range of occupations accessible to women has broadened considerably as gender stereotypes and sex discrimination have been challenged. An increasing number of women work in what were formerly male-dominated professions, such as law, medicine, and the sciences. Labor statistics show, however, that at every level of educational attainment, women's pay is lower than men's. Overall, for every dollar that men earn, women earn about 68 cents (Barrett, 1987). One reason is that many women enter low-paying occupations offering only limited opportunities for advancement, such as secretarial work, elementary-school teaching, and social work. But even at the higher occupational levels, including positions in science and engineering, women are paid less (Rother, 1987).

The increasing tendency for married women to work outside the home has resulted in studies of **interrole conflict.** The term refers to the difficulties people can experience in trying to meet the demands of spouse, children, and employer (Sigelman & Shaffer, 1991). Such problems can be especially acute for working women who have children (see Figure 5.26). Women who have full-time positions not only work the same number of hours as their husbands but

frequently are also responsible for most of the household and child-rearing duties (Gustafson & Magnusson, 1991). A mother with a full-time job spends about 80 hours a week meeting work and home responsibilities, compared with about 62 hours for the father (Vanek, 1980). Not surprisingly, interrole conflict in dual-work families generally is a greater problem for women than for men. However, for women in careers that provide opportunities for advancement and greater responsibilities (as opposed to jobs that do not), the costs may be offset by financial, status, and personal fulfillment rewards (Gilbert & others, 1981).

Work at Midlife

Potential interrole conflict is likely to decrease markedly as children grow older and leave home. With the children gone, many middle-aged women who have worked primarily in the home begin to find rewarding activities outside the home. Some enter the work force for the first time in years. Research suggests that work acts as a stabilizing force in midlife role transitions, especially for women. During the middle-adult years, women who work outside the home have higher self-esteem, report being in better physical health, and experience less psychological distress than homemakers do (Adelmann & others, 1990; Frankenheuser & others, 1991). Love and work may well serve different needs in women. In one study of a large sample of women between the ages of 35 and 55, paid work was the best predictor of a woman's sense of *mastery,* whereas her relationship with her husband and children was the best predictor of *pleasure* (Baruch & others, 1983).

Figure 5.26 *Balancing career and family demands can result in interrole conflict, especially for women.*

Many adults find satisfaction and material rewards in their careers at midlife. They frequently have moved into positions of leadership as department heads, chiefs of staff, supervisors, and directors. They are the power brokers and decision makers. They also enjoy more of the material comforts of life than they did in early adulthood, and major financial commitments such as buying and furnishing a home have been completed. There is more time and money for leisure and travel.

Unfortunately, this description of the ''good life'' doesn't fit all midlifers. Some experience gnawing worries and regrets about jobs that have turned sour. Middle-aged adults who cannot compete or advance may have a hard time holding onto their jobs and making ends meet on their poor salaries. Major problems can occur when workers fail to keep up with technological changes in their fields or hit career plateaus and become bored or feel unchallenged (Campbell & Cellini, 1981). Some workers are forced out of work by technological changes or economic problems that eliminate their jobs. Prolonged unemployment and job-related problems can pose serious threats to mental and physical well-being (Belsky, 1990; Liem & Rayman, 1982).

Job dissatisfaction may lead to midcareer changes as adults begin to reassess their work and life values (Holland & Gottfredson, 1981). Fortunately, midcareer change is more possible in the 1990s than ever before because of increased life expectancy, an emphasis on lifelong learning for all ages, and a cultural focus on the quality and meaning of life.

Retirement

Retirement is an important milestone of late adulthood. An increasing number of people are retiring early. Between 1947 and 1987, the percentage of men between the ages of 55 and 64 who were participating in the work force dropped from 89.6 percent to 67 percent. For those over 65 years, the percentage declined from 47.8 percent to 16.6 percent (Ruhm, 1989). Although the changes were less dramatic for older women, their involvement in the labor force also decreased significantly (Ruhm, 1989).

Attitudes toward retirement are as varied as individual personalities and life circumstances. Some older adults view retirement as a reminder that they are growing older, nearing death, and losing their place in society. Older adults who are in poor health, who have low incomes, or who were forced out of the labor market because of mandatory retirement rules tend to be more poorly adjusted and more dissatisfied with retirement (Beck, 1982; Herzog & others, 1991). Retirees with strong traditional work values are more apt to miss their jobs and become dissatisfied with retirement than those whose lives

did not revolve around their work (Hooker & Ventis, 1984).

Fortunately, for the majority of retirees, the picture is considerably brighter. Retirement is viewed as a blessing by many older adults, who look forward to leisure time and an opportunity to do things that they were unable to do while working or to the prospect of continuing their current work activities at a more leisurely pace. And even for people who are apprehensive about retirement, research indicates that once it has occurred, retirement does not cause major dissatisfaction with life, a decline in physical or mental health, or a lower life expectancy. Findings also indicate that most retired people do not miss their jobs and do not suffer an increase in loneliness, anxiety, or depression upon retirement (Atchley, 1976; George, 1980). Instead, they remain as optimistic as before they retired, continue to feel useful, and express more positive than negative feelings about retirement (McConnell, 1983). Over 40 percent of people between the ages of 50 and 74 perform some form of volunteer work, and many of these people find positions in which they can share the expertise they've gained over the years.

Several recent studies indicate that whether a person continues to work is unrelated to measures of physical and psychological well-being (Herzog & others, 1991; Swan & others, 1991). What is important is whether the person is satisfied with his or her current work or retirement status. In a study of 1,339 people over age 55, A. Regula Herzog and coworkers (1991) found that those whose work or retirement status reflected their personal preferences reported higher levels of physical and psychological well-being than did those who were either forced to continue working by external factors or those who had involuntarily retired. In another large-scale study of retirees, who averaged 72 years of age, Gary Swan, Alison Dame, and Dorit Carmelli (1991) found that compared with voluntary retirees, those who reported involuntary retirement had a more difficult time adjusting, more illnesses, poorer physical status, and more depressive symptoms.

Relationships

Young adulthood is the time when most people marry and establish families. Today's young adult expects a great deal from marriage, including satisfaction of social, emotional, and sexual needs. While many couples realize these goals, a rising divorce rate indicates that happiness is by no means an automatic outcome. Successful marriages are characterized by positive communication and the ability to negotiate the solution of problems. Partners in such marriages experience mutual caring and emotional closeness, high levels of physical intimacy, agreement on basic values, shared activities, and a willingness to accept and even support changes in the partner and in the nature of the relationship (Gottman & Levenson, 1992).

The birth of the first baby represents a major change in the way couples spend their time, and it may affect the marriage in important ways. Most research shows that marital satisfaction is lowest during the childbearing years (Glenn & McLanahan, 1982; Rollins, 1989). Graphs of marital satisfaction over time are typically U-shaped, reflecting high levels of marital comfort before children are born, a drop in satisfaction during the child-rearing years, and a positive rebound after the children leave home (Robinson & Barret, 1986). In one study of adults' adjustment to parenthood, the largest decline in marital satisfaction occurred in the first 18 months after the baby's birth (Cowan & others, 1985). For the new parents, dissatisfaction tended to center around changes in role demands, a decreased level of sexual contact, and the experiencing of higher life stress and lower social support from their spouses. Women's roles were affected the most. They tended to quit work or work shorter hours, and they were more involved physically and psychologically in parenting activities. Women sometimes felt that their husbands were pulling away from the family and were not dependable sources of help and support. The men tended to see themselves as good providers who contributed to their families' welfare through their work role rather than by taking on more responsibilities at home. The arrival of children often places such severe demands on a couple that little time or energy is left to fuel the marriage relationship, and it therefore suffers, at least temporarily (Rollins, 1989).

Despite the stresses and strains of marriage and parenthood, research shows that married people are happier and healthier; have lower rates of chronic illness, depression, stress, and disabilities; and live longer than nonmarried adults (Shumaker & Hill, 1991; Verbrugge, 1979). Divorced and separated adults have the worst health status, including high rates of acute and chronic conditions that limit social activity. When marriages are dissolved, some adults attempt to relieve stress through drinking, smoking, and other behaviors associated with health risks (Verbrugge, 1979).

One of the major decisions a married couple faces is when to begin having children. In terms of health, the 20s are an optimal time for women to bear children. Their reproductive organs are in peak condition, they are more likely to have healthy babies, and they have the high level of stamina needed to care for their young ones. However, an increasing number of married couples are delaying parenthood until their 30s and 40s because of personal, educational, and career commitments. Younger readers may make a similar decision in the coming years. The implications of this decision are discussed in our next feature.

| ISSUES IN DELAYING PARENTHOOD UNTIL MIDLIFE | ENHANCING HUMAN PERFORMANCE |

Forty-year-old Caroline and her 42-year-old husband Mark are expecting their first child. Their parents and even some friends say they have waited too long to begin having children. But the couple felt that only by delaying could they achieve the level in their careers and marriage at which they would feel comfortable taking on the responsibility of a child. They are among the increasing number of career couples who are postponing having their first child until midlife (see Figure 5.27). Statistics show that the percentage of couples having their first child after age 30 increased fourfold between 1970 and 1987 (Roosa, 1988).

Delaying childbearing results from many factors, including a growing trend to postpone marriage until the late 20s and early 30s, an increase in the use of contraception, a decline in unwanted births as a result of legalized abortion, increased educational and economic opportunities for women, and the changing roles of women who are completing college educations and establishing professional careers (Giordano, 1988; Wilkie, 1981). Like Caroline and Mark, couples who delay parenthood feel that they are more financially and emotionally prepared to have children once their careers are in place, and that they will, therefore, perform better as parents.

Research shows that delayed parenthood can involve advantages for the mother–infant relationship. In one study, researchers questioned mothers between the ages of 16 and 38 about their parenting role and observed them interacting with their babies one month after hospital

◆ **Figure 5.27** *An increasing number of married couples are delaying parenthood until their 30s and even their 40s. Such delays can result in both risks and benefits for the parents and children.*

discharge. The mothers in their mid 30s were more satisfied with and committed to their parenting role, were more sensitive to their infants' needs, and were more likely to behave in ways that fostered the infants' social–emotional and cognitive growth (Ragozin & others, 1982).

Despite these positive outcomes, delayed childbearing is associated with certain medical risks. As noted earlier, the bodies of women in their 20s are optimally prepared to carry a child. Delayed childbearing increases risks for both mother and baby. Deterioration of the lining of the uterus, diabetes, high blood pressure, and other physical problems are more common in women after age 35.

Stillbirths, miscarriages, cleft palate, Down syndrome, and other physical problems also increase, along with the incidence of delivery by caesarean section (Scott, 1986). Moreover, fertility drops sharply after age 30, meaning that women who wait have an increased risk of being unable to conceive (Federation CECOS et al., 1982).

The good news, however, is that risks for all pregnancies have decreased over the years because of advances in medical science and improvements in health practices. Some developmental experts argue that when couples postpone parenthood until they are emotionally and financially ready, medical risks are offset by increases in psychological stability that can positively affect the outcomes of pregnancy (Westoff, 1980).

Effectively performing the role of parents so as to raise a healthy, well-adjusted child is of great concern to most couples. Scientific findings concerning the effects of delaying child-bearing offer couples important information that can inform their decision about when to begin parenthood.

Midlife Relationships

During the years of middle adulthood, many adults experience the so-called *empty nest* when their last grown child leaves home. In the past, this stage was characterized as a time of extreme depression and loneliness for parents, especially mothers. That image

▶ **Figure 5.28** *Research contradicts the stereotype of the "empty-nest syndrome." In fact, many couples find the years after their children leave home a time of marital renewal.*

has been tempered by research showing that most middle-aged couples do not become significantly depressed or suffer midlife crises when their children leave home (Chiriboga, 1989; Newman & Newman, 1991). As children grow up and leave home, feelings of loss are natural for parents. Their task at this point is to accept the grown children as adults who have lives separate from their own. Findings from interview and questionnaire studies indicate that most parents accomplish this with little difficulty and continue to maintain meaningful and positive relationships with their children (Chiriboga, 1989).

Many middle-aged adults feel that the empty nest gives them new freedom to travel and pursue other activities (Hooyman & Kiyak, 1988). As noted earlier, marital satisfaction frequently increases when children leave home and couples have more time to do things together (see Figure 5.28). Many studies, in fact, report that the postparental years are a time of marital renewal, a ''second honeymoon'' (Lewis & Roberts, 1982; Rollins, 1989).

The 40s and 50s bring with them a decline in estrogen and progesterone levels in women, leading to the final menstrual period, the **menopause.** Men show a decline in testosterone levels during the same period. Despite these physical changes, the capacity of both men and women to enjoy sexual relations continues throughout life. In some cases, an actual increase in sexual desire and activity occurs in post-menopausal couples (Masters & others, 1989; Wade & Cirese, 1992). In one study, many middle-aged women reported a stronger sex drive and greater sexual enjoyment once the risk of pregnancy was no longer a worry (Neugarten & others, 1968). However, both men and women are slower to respond physically to sexual stimulation in middle age, and the frequency of sexual intercourse decreases from an average of three times a week in young adulthood to once a week among 45- to 65-year-olds (Wade & Cirese, 1992).

Selectivity in Social Interactions

People maintain social connections with others throughout life. However, both cross-sectional and longitudinal studies indicate that a narrowing of social interactions begins to occur in the later part of adulthood (Carstensen, 1987; Cumming & Henry, 1961). One interpretation of this finding comes from **disengagement theory** (Cumming & Henry, 1961), which views withdrawal from relationships as a central feature of the process of preparing for death. An alternative explanation is offered by **selectivity theory** (Carstensen, 1987), which states that as part of the aging process, people become more selective in choosing social partners as a way of reducing energy expenditure and reducing the negative emotional costs of later separation and ending of relationships when the new acquaintances die (see Figure 5.29).

To test the central hypothesis of selectivity theory, Barbara Fredrickson and Laura Carstensen (1990) asked subjects ranging from adolescence to old age to indicate preferences for interacting with familiar people or meeting new acquaintances in hypothetical situations. Sixty-five percent of the subjects under age 30 preferred to interact with a social partner they had not met before, whereas only 35 percent of those over age 65 preferred the novel partner. The researchers attributed this to concerns in the elderly about investing in new relationships that might soon end. In a follow-up study with only young people, they found that when they structured a hypothetical situation in a way that made it clear that there would be a quick social ending of the relationship with the novel person, young people, like the elderly people in the first study, showed a marked preference for interacting with someone they already knew. Thus, the narrowing of social relationships in old age may be a means of reducing emotional costs associated with establishing relationships that have a social ending in sight, rather than the symbolic preparation for death proposed by disengagement theory. Nonetheless, the maintenance of close relationships and a social support network remains very important for the well-being of the elderly (Russell & Cutrona, 1991).

Loss and Bereavement

The death of a spouse is one of the most stressful events in life and one of the most difficult to adjust to (McCubbin & Patterson, 1982). Sixty percent of

Figure 5.29 As people age, they show an increasing tendency to restrict their social lives to interactions with familiar people. Disengagement theory and selectivity theory offer differing explanations for this phenomenon.

widowed adults in the United States are over 65 years of age (Blackwell, 1981). Because women have a longer life span than men and because they typically marry men who are older than they are, there are six times more widows than widowers in the United States (DiGiulio, 1989). Three out of four American wives can expect to become widows (Blackwell, 1981).

Loss of a mate can bring with it trauma, grief, loneliness, economic hardship, and the need to restructure one's life (see Figure 5.30). These stresses can lead to a decline in physical and mental health among widows and widowers. Compared with other adults of the same age, widows and widowers report greater depression, more illnesses, and greater use of medications (Gallagher & others, 1983; Shumaker & Hill, 1991). The suicide rate is also higher among the widowed population than among their married counterparts, especially among males (Stroebe & Stroebe, 1983).

Based largely on clinical lore and on theories of loss and coping, certain assumptions about the grieving process have been widely accepted, both by medical and mental health professionals and by the general public. These include the assumptions that intense depression is inevitable following loss, that a failure to experience and express grief is maladaptive, and that eventual recovery and resolution are to be expected following an irrevocable loss. Camille Wortman and Roxane Silver (1989) reviewed the research literature on bereavement and concluded that all of these assumptions are probably myths.

▶ **Figure 5.30** *The loss of a spouse is one of the most stressful of life events.*

Although the majority of widows and widowers do experience depressed moods, these reactions are typically not as strong as those occurring in clinical depression. Somewhat surprisingly, in view of the widespread belief that grieving is adaptive, those who react initially with strong distress are *more* likely to experience physical and emotional difficulties later on. Finally, the assumption that after a period of mourning, the bereaved person will accept the loss and achieve a state of normal functioning has also been called into question. Years after the death of a spouse, as many as 40 percent of widows and widowers are still grieving and have failed to accept the loss emotionally. Unexpected deaths tend to have a stronger and more lasting negative impact than deaths for which there is forewarning (Parkes & Weiss, 1983).

The practical implications of these findings are clear: First, we need to recognize that a failure to respond to the loss of a loved one with intense grieving is not unusual and does not indicate a lack of caring or a pathological emotional reaction. Second, we need to be attentive to the long-range needs of the person who has suffered the loss and not assume that "time heals all." The family network is the major support system on which widowed persons depend for their recovery from bereavement and their ultimate well-being (O'Bryant, 1988; Shumaker & Hill, 1991). A recent study of people who had lost a spouse indicated that depression was more intense 9 months after the loss if social support from family, friends, and acquaintances was not forthcoming (Norris & Murrell, 1990).

Death and Dying

All of us will eventually face the specter of death: the deaths of our parents, family members and friends, and finally ourselves. Death is for all seasons. Says Herman Feifel, "It is not the restricted domain of the combat soldier, dying person, elderly individual, or suicidal person. Children as young as two years of age are already wrestling with the idea of death" (1977, p. 7).

Nevertheless, death has different meanings for a 2-year-old child, a 20-year-old college student, a 40-year-old career woman and mother who is dying of cancer, and an 80-year-old ailing grandfather. Older adults have had more experience with death than anyone else in the life cycle. Elderly adults have usually lost more friends and loved ones, attended more funerals, and thought more about their own deaths than have young or middle-aged adults. With age, understanding of death becomes clearer and acceptance of this inevitable part of life seems easier (Atwood, 1984). Understandably, then, the elderly are more accepting of their own deaths than any other age group (Kalish & Reynolds, 1977).

Preparing to Die

In her pioneering work on death and dying, Elisabeth Kübler-Ross (1969), a physician, conducted interviews with over 200 terminally ill patients (see Figure 5.31). She concluded that the typical dying person goes through five stages in the process of coping with impending death: denial, anger, bargaining, depression, and acceptance. Moreover, family and friends of the dying person frequently experience these same reactions. Kübler-Ross stressed that these stages do not always occur in the same order and that several may occur simultaneously.

The first stage is generally *denial,* the "No, not me!" reaction. The person may experience shock and disbelief, seek other medical opinions, or pursue some kind of miracle cure. Even when death has been partially accepted, fleeting periods of denial may still occur. Denial gives way to *anger:* "Why me?" (and, by implication, "Why not you?"). Next, as the inevitability of death becomes more real, the person may turn to *bargaining:* "God, it's okay for me to die if I can just live long enough to see my grandchild" or "If you let me off this time, I promise to straighten up." *Depression* ushers in the fourth stage, as dying patients begin to grieve for themselves and to acknowledge the impending loss of everything they love in life. *Acceptance* of the inevitability of death constitutes the final stage. At this stage, many dying people experience a resigned sense of peacefulness.

Critics of Kübler-Ross's proposed stages question the generalizability of the five stages, as well as the notion that they comprise the "normal" or "correct" way to face death. They cite research showing that not all dying persons experience all five stages and that some move back and forth between stages (Schulz & Aderman, 1980). As we have also seen, the elderly are generally more accepting of their own deaths than any other age group, and they may be less likely to experience the first four stages of Kübler-Ross's sequence.

Although some of its features have been called into question, Kübler-Ross's theory has contributed to an increased emphasis on understanding and helping people to cope with impending death, and this may be the theory's most lasting contribution. The past decade has seen an increased willingness to deal more openly and humanely with the processes of death and grieving. Important ethical issues, such as the propriety of removing life supports and even giving terminally ill individuals the right to end their own lives, are being openly debated.

An especially welcome development is the work of hospice organizations, which provide special facilities and services to support the terminally ill and their families (see Figure 5.32). In many instances, hospice workers care for patients in their own homes and help involve family members in the process of caring for and supporting the patients in the final days of life. Facing death with dignity and the support of loved ones helps a person to complete the life cycle with a sense of meaningfulness and completion. Life can be celebrated even as death approaches, and we can wish no more for those we love, or for ourselves.

Figure 5.31 Elisabeth Kübler-Ross contributed greatly to our understanding of and concern with the process of coping with impending death.

to the issues of stages versus continuity and stability versus change that have been so long debated in developmental psychology. Nevertheless, these debates have fueled thinking about the entire range of human development, and they have inspired a great deal of research that has given us a better understanding of development, a greater appreciation for its complexities, and some of the knowledge needed to influence its course in ways that enhance human existence.

Final Reflections on Life-Span Development

We have now completed our far-ranging study of life-span development. We have seen that during every period of life, development is affected by our biological endowment, by environmental events, and by our own thoughts, feelings, and behaviors. This chapter's Understanding Causes feature (page 166) shows how the aging process is affected by the interplay among all of these factors.

Human development is fairly orderly in some areas, as stage theorists would predict, yet highly individual in others, as the continuity viewpoint would suggest. There is also evidence for both stability in characteristics across the life span and the capacity for dramatic change. Thus, there are no easy answers

Figure 5.32 Hospice, an approach to ensuring death with dignity and support, is enriching the last days of many people. This dying woman is comforted by her great-grandchildren.

Aging:
Factors Suggested by Theory and Research

$B=f(P,E)$

Causal Factors

Biological
- Genetically programmed cellular decline over time
- Exercise and nutrition, which affect condition of the body at all ages
- Biological conditions created by stress and lifestyle factors

Cognitive
- Attitudes and expectations concerning aging, including possible selves
- Self-views upon witnessing skill and physical deterioration
- Degree to which cognitive skills are regularly exercised

Intrapsychic
- Personality trait of optimism vs. pessimism
- Outcomes of previous psychosocial stages and success in attaining generativity and integrity in middle and late adulthood
- Value attached to forming new close relationships

Environmental
- Exposure to harsh environmental agents that promote physical aging
- Stressful life events that take their toll on the body
- Quality of social support available from the social environment

Aging

Aging is a function of interacting personal and environmental causal factors. These factors may vary and may interact with one another in particular ways, depending on the person and the situation.

Adolescence

- Unlike cultures in which initiation rites formally confer adult status, ours has a rather lengthy transition period of adolescence. Adolescents attain adulthood by reaching physical maturity and meeting certain social criteria, such as becoming financially independent, having a steady job, being married and raising a family, or gaining recognition in the community.

- The onset of adolescence is marked by puberty, a period of rapid physical growth and sexual maturation. Some adolescents mature earlier and others later than the norm. Generally, early maturation is more advantageous for boys than for girls.

- According to Piaget, adolescents reach a stage of thinking called formal operations, in which they can reason abstractly and deductively.

- Humans restructure their thinking about social and moral questions as they mature. Lawrence Kohlberg constructed a six-stage theory of moral reasoning that parallels Piaget's stages of cognitive development. During adolescence, the bases for moral decision making shift from the reward-and-punishment orientation of preconventional morality to conventional morality based on conforming to the expectations of the social group.

- Erikson viewed the central conflict of adolescence as identity versus role confusion. An important part of establishing a personal identity involves gaining some degree of independence from parents. As parental influence wanes, peer influence increases, and relationships with peers tend to become more intimate than relationships with parents. However, in the important areas of values, morality, and career decisions, parents and adolescents experience less of a "generation gap" than is often assumed.

- Teenage pregnancies have become a major issue in the United States. Factors affecting this phenomenon include liberal cultural standards for sexual activity and failure of many adolescents to use contraceptives.

Adult Personality Development

- According to Erikson, the major adult developmental tasks are the achievement of intimacy in young adulthood, generativity during middle age, and integrity in old age. Erikson has also discussed the wisdom of the aged, the culmination of successful coping with previous life challenges.

- Several longitudinal studies have provided important information about adult develop-

ment. The Grant Study led Vaillant to posit several additional stages of adult development, and Levinson's concept of life structures resulted in a stage model more detailed than Erikson's.

- Recent research on possible selves in adulthood tends to support the stages suggested by Erikson, Vaillant, and Levinson. It appears that discrepancies between the ideal self, the current self, and future selves decrease in old age.

- Recent findings indicate that genetic factors play a role in the life events experienced by adults. This work illustrates the reciprocal relations between personal and environmental characteristics.

Physical Development and Health

- Young adults in their 20s and 30s are at the peak of their physical capabilities. By the 30s, however, declines have begun to occur in physical systems, although signs of these declines generally do not begin to show up until sometime later.

- Middle adulthood, the period between ages 40 and 64, is a turning point in life. The physical and perceptual signs of aging that began in young adulthood are more pronounced. Rates of aging vary depending on lifestyle, life circumstances, genetic factors, and psychological responses to the aging process.

- The physical and structural changes of middle adulthood become more pronounced in late adulthood. Recent research suggests the possibility that treatment with human growth hormone may slow or even, to some extent, reverse the physical aging process. Recent studies of autonomic nervous system activity in the elderly indicate that the physiological component of emotion decreases with age, although the experienced intensity of emotional states does not.

Cognitive Development

- According to Piaget, as a result of their diverse aptitudes and interests, young adults become professional specialists and tend to apply formal operations in their fields of interest more than in other fields. Theorists such as Patricia Arlin and Klaus Riegel have proposed modes of thinking beyond formal operations, such as problem finding, which are the basis for creative thought.

- Although there are some declines in reaction time and speed of performance, cognitive development continues in middle adulthood, and verbal skills tend to peak during middle age. The significant intellectual declines with age found in cross-sectional studies

do not appear in longitudinal analyses of intellectual changes. Significant declines in most abilities do not appear until the 80s.

Career Development

- Work serves several important functions, such as providing material resources, helping establish personal identity, structuring time, and providing social interactions.

- Choosing and preparing for a career is an important task of young adulthood. Research suggests that most adults are at least moderately successful in finding careers that match their talents and interests, although the process often involves several changes of educational objectives and exposure to more than one career path.

- The number of women working outside the home has increased markedly over the past four decades. Despite entry into traditionally male professions, women are paid less than men overall. Moreover, many married and unmarried women with children experience interrole conflict as they are called on to respond to the demands of work and family life.

- For many people, retirement is occurring earlier in the life span. Research indicates that voluntary retirement results in positive adaptation to the new lifestyle. Those who retire involuntarily tend to experience more physical and psychological problems.

Relationships

- Marriage and parenthood place strong demands on both men and women. Marital satisfaction is generally lowest during the child-rearing years, and satisfaction increases for most middle-aged couples after the children leave home. There is little evidence for an empty-nest syndrome.

- An increasing number of couples are electing to delay parenthood until their late 30s and 40s. Doing so increases the medical risks for mother and child, but the parents' greater psychological stability may compensate for the risks.

- As people age, they tend to become more selective in their relationships and to increasingly withdraw from new social interactions. Disengagement theory views this as part of the process of preparing for death, whereas selectivity theory attributes it to an attempt to reduce the emotional costs of establishing relationships that may have an imminent social ending.

- Older adults have had more experience with death than anyone else in the life cycle, and they are more accepting of death than any other age group. Nonetheless, the experience of losing a mate, an event experienced by many women over 65, is one of the most stressful of life events. Recent research has challenged many assumptions about the bereavement process, including the notions that it is important to express strong distress and that feelings of loss pass with time.

Death and Dying

● Kübler-Ross has proposed a five-stage model of people's psychological responses to their impending deaths. The stages are denial, anger, bargaining, depression, and acceptance. Research indicates that many people either do not pass through all of these stages or do not do so in the order suggested by Kübler-Ross.

KEY TERMS AND CONCEPTS

adolescence (p. 137)
basal metabolic rate (p. 152)
conventional morality (p. 140)
disengagement theory (p. 163)
foreclosure (p. 142)
formal operations (p. 138)
generativity (p. 146)
identity diffusion (p. 142)
integrity (p. 146)

interrole conflict (p. 159)
intimacy (p. 146)
life structure (p. 147)
menarche (p. 137)
menopause (p. 162)
moratorium (p. 142)
possible selves (p. 149)
postconventional morality (p. 140)
postformal thought (p. 156)

preconventional morality (p. 140)
primary sex characteristics (p. 137)
problem finding (p. 156)
professional specialization (p. 156)
puberty (p. 137)
secondary sex characteristics (p. 137)
selectivity theory (p. 163)

SUGGESTED READINGS

Alexander, C. N., & Langer, E. J. (Eds.) (1990). *Higher stages of human development: Perspectives on adult growth.* New York: Oxford University Press. An excellent anthology that contains chapters written by leading researchers in the field of adult development. These experts summarize theory and research relating to physical, cognitive, personality, and social development during the adult years.

Belsky, J. K. (1990). *The psychology of aging: Theory, research, and intervention.* Pacific Grove, Calif.: Brooks-Cole. Written by a leading developmental researcher, this book brings together a wealth of information on theories of aging, research results, and the role of both theory and research in the design of interventions intended to enhance quality of life in the aged.

Gustafson, S. B., & Magnusson, D. (1991). *Female life careers: A pattern approach.* Hillsdale, N.J.: Erlbaum. A comprehensive study of women's career paths and factors that influence their course.

Sensation 6

When I turn my gaze skyward I see the flattened dome of sky and the sun's brilliant disk and a hundred other visible things underneath it. What are the steps which bring this about? A pencil of light from the sun enters the eye and is focused there on the retina. It gives rise to a change, which in turn travels to the nerve layer at the top of the brain. The whole chain of these events, from the sun to the top of my brain, is physical. Each step is an electrical reaction. But now there succeeds a change wholly unlike any which led up to it, and wholly inexplicable by us. A visual scene presents itself to the mind; I see the dome of the sky and the sun in it, and a hundred other visual things besides. In fact, I perceive a picture of the world around me. When this visual scene appears, I ought, I suppose, to feel startled; but I am too accustomed to feel even surprised (Sherrington, 1950, p. 3).

L ike Sir Charles Sherrington, the eminent brain researcher who made these observations, you probably take your sensory windows to the world for granted most of the time. If our sense organs are not defective, we experience light waves as brightnesses and colors, air vibrations as sounds, and so on. However, such is not the case for people who experience a condition called **synesthesia,**—literally, "mixing of the senses." For synesthetes, sensory impressions get mixed up; they may experience sounds as colors or tastes as tactile sensations that have different shapes.

One synesthete was studied by the Russian psychologist A. R. Luria (1968). The man was a highly successful writer and musician whose life was a perpetual stream of mixed-up sensations. For example, when Luria asked him to report what he experienced while listening to electronically generated musical tones of various pitches, a pitch of 30 cycles per second evoked a visual image of a strip the color of tarnished silver. A slightly higher tone conjured up a brown strip with red edges and a sweet and sour flavor. A very high-pitched tone evoked the following sensation: "It looks something like a fireworks tinged with a pink-red hue. The strip of color feels rough and unpleasant, and it has an ugly taste—rather like that of a briny pickle. . . . You could hurt your hand on this."

These mixed sensations also occurred in the man's daily life, and they were sometimes disconcerting. On one occasion, he asked an ice cream vendor what flavors she sold. "But she answered in such a tone that a whole pile of coals, of black cinders, came bursting out of her mouth, and I couldn't bring myself to buy any ice cream after she answered that way."

Synesthesia is a rare condition, occurring once in perhaps every 500,000 people, and its cause remains a mystery. Nevertheless, synesthesia has recently attracted new scientific interest because it raises some basic questions about the biological and psychological factors that frame our sensory experiences. In a sense, our neurons are storytellers; they shape and select what they pass along on the way from sensory organ to brain. We know, for example, that synesthetes' mixed sensations are unique. The same tone may be experienced as green and sharp by one synesthete and as brown and sweet by another, which may cause you to wonder, is your green the same as my green?

Basic questions about how we come to know and experience ourselves and our world have intrigued thinkers since before Plato and Aristotle. Psychologists have been concerned with the same questions for more than a century. Recall that Wilhelm Wundt established the first psychology laboratory at Leipzig to study sensations, which he regarded as the basic units of the mind. Today, psychologists continue to search for the answers.

This chapter and the next will explore the mysteries of sensation and perception. In some ways, sensation and perception are so intimately related that they are difficult to separate, for the stimulation we receive through our sense organs is instantaneously organized and integrated into the experiences that we refer to as perceptions. Nevertheless, we will adopt the common distinction used among psychologists and regard **sensation** as the stimulus-detection process by which our sense organs transform environmental stimuli into nerve impulses that are sent to the brain. **Perception**—making "sense" of what our senses tell us—is the active process of organizing this stimulus input and giving it meaning (Banks & Krajicek, 1991). Because our thoughts, feelings, and behaviors are responses to what we experience as "reality," sensation and perception are related to virtually every topic in psychology.

As we will see in these two chapters, what we experience as reality is not a mirror of the outside world—far from it. In ways not yet completely understood, our nervous system acts on, organizes, and gives meaning to the sound and light waves, chemical molecules, and other physical stimuli that impinge on us and are detected by our sense organs. From the electrochemical responses of our sensors and the neurons they stimulate, our brain creates the "product" that we call perceptions. Because perception is an active and creative process, the same sensory input may be perceived in different ways at different times. For example, read the two sets of symbols in Figure 6.1. The middle symbols in both lines are exactly the same, but you probably perceived them differently. Your interpretation, or perception, of the characters was influenced by their context—that is, by the characters that preceded and followed them. This is a simple illustration of how perception takes us a step beyond sensation.

In this chapter we explore the sensory systems that provide our brain with the basic data from which our experiences are constructed. Then, in Chapter 7, we will consider the ways in which those sensory data are acted on and organized in the process of perception. As we shall see, biological, cognitive, intrapsychic, and environmental factors combine to influence both sensation and perception.

■ ▭

Basic Principles of Sensation: Simplicity and Selectivity

Like other parts of our body, our sensory system is adapted to the world we live in and to our survival needs. At any given instant, we are being bombarded with millions of stimuli. Look around you right now and consider the countless visual elements on which you could choose to focus. Such complexity would be impossible to handle if all stimuli came in at once. Besides, we don't need to be aware of everything. For this reason, our sensory system is governed by one overriding principle: Simplify! Sense what is important at this instant!

Sensory input is simplified in two major ways. First, sensory systems are *selective*. Each sensory system is designed to extract specific bits of information from the chaos of stimuli coming from the outside world, letting some in and keeping the rest out. In part, our senses provide information related to survival needs, which helps account for the striking differences among species' sensory capabilities. For example, you and I experience infrared waves as heat, but insects need to be able to *see* this form of energy in order to survive. An eagle needs to have eyes like—well, like an eagle—in order to hunt. As nocturnal hunters, cats need their reflective eyes to see in the dark.

In addition to their selectivity, sensory systems are specifically designed to respond to *changes* in stimulation. Sensory neurons respond to a constant stimulus by decreasing their activity. This decreased activity is responsible for the phenomenon of **sensory adaptation.** If, for example, you dive into a swimming pool, the water may feel cold at first because your body's temperature sensors respond to the change in temperature. With time, however, you become used to the water temperature. If you then leave the pool and take a room-temperature shower, it will feel much warmer than it would have if you had showered before entering the pool.

Adaptation occurs in all sensory modalities, including vision. Why, then, you might wonder, don't objects simply fade from sight when we stare at them without moving our eyes? The reason is that tiny,

Figure 6.1 *Quickly read these two lines of symbols out loud. Did your perception of the middle symbol in each line depend on the symbols that surrounded it?*

Figure 6.2 *Sensory systems simplify the world by selecting the most important stimuli from among the millions of sensations bombarding our sense organs every instant. Otherwise, we would be overwhelmed with stimulation.*

involuntary eye movements keep images moving about the retina. Were it not for these eye movements, images would vanish in time, just as the sensation of coldness does in a swimming pool. In an ingenious demonstration, R. M. Pritchard (1961) invented a method of guaranteeing that visual images would maintain a constant position on the retina. He attached a tiny projector to a contact lens worn by the subjects (see Figure 6.3[a]). When an image was projected through the lens onto the retina, subjects reported that the image appeared in its entirety for a time, then

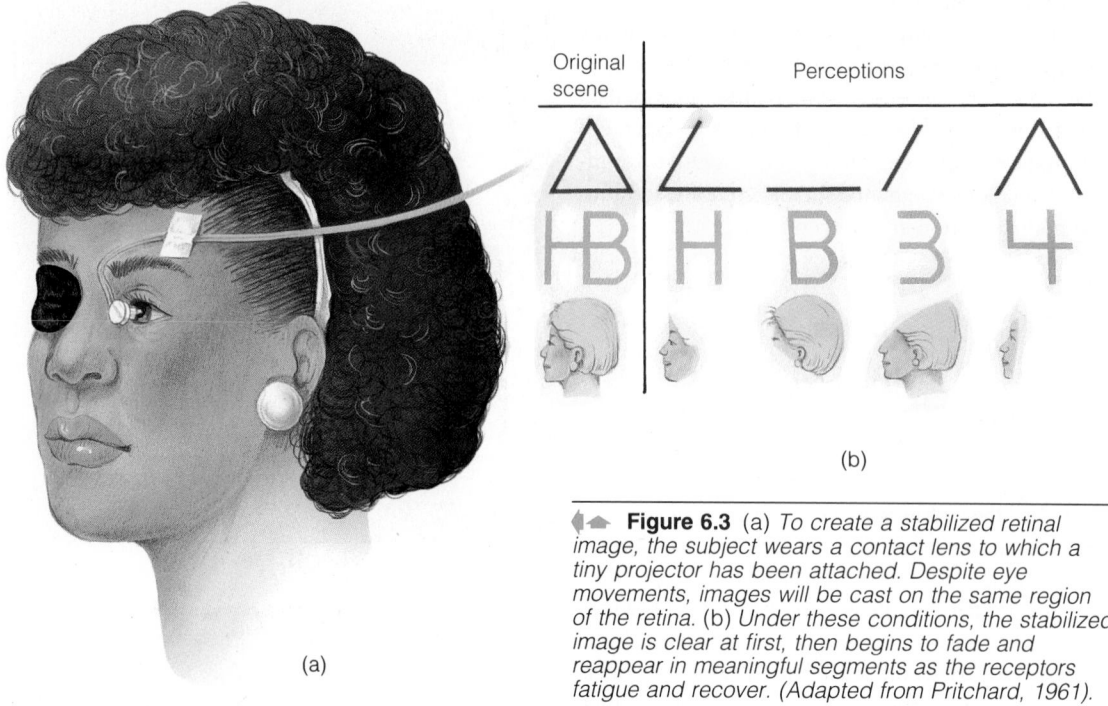

Original scene | Perceptions

(b)

Figure 6.3 (a) *To create a stabilized retinal image, the subject wears a contact lens to which a tiny projector has been attached. Despite eye movements, images will be cast on the same region of the retina. (b) Under these conditions, the stabilized image is clear at first, then begins to fade and reappear in meaningful segments as the receptors fatigue and recover. (Adapted from Pritchard, 1961).*

(a)

began to vanish and reappear as parts of the original stimulus (Figure 6.3[b]). When the stimuli were words, the images that reappeared and then vanished tended to be meaningful new words that were part of the old word, indicating that the meanings extracted from the original stimulus influenced what the subjects perceived. This result illustrates a point that will be made repeatedly in the next chapter: The perceptual system actively constructs and organizes our perceptions from the raw stimulus input.

Although ignoring constant stimuli may reduce our overall sensitivity, it frees our senses to pick up informative changes in the environment. Such changes are likely to be important to our survival, so the phenomenon of adaptation again demonstrates that sensory principles are tied in with survival needs.

Having considered some of the basic principles of sensory processes, let us now consider how psychologists study our sensory capabilities and functions.

■ ▢

The Study of Sensory Capabilities

Interest in sensory processes among psychologists goes back to the first laboratory of experimental psychology, founded by Wundt in 1879. The work of Wundt and his colleagues constituted the first sci-

entific attempt to link the physical world of objectively measured energies with the psychological realm of experience. Like the early structuralists, many modern psychologists are interested in testing the limits of sensory abilities in both animals and humans. Some of the methods they use derive from the early days of psychological research, whereas others reflect the new technologies for studying the nervous system described in Chapter 3.

Measuring Sensory Capabilities

Researchers in the field known as **psychophysics** study how sensitive our sensory systems are. In this investigation, psychologists have been concerned with two kinds of sensitivity. The first kind concerns the absolute limits of sensitivity. For example, what is the dimmest light or the softest sound that can be detected? The second kind of sensitivity has to do with differences between stimuli. By how much must two tones differ before we can tell that they are not identical? Both kinds of sensitivity involve relations between physical energy and sensory experience, so the term *psycho-physics* is applicable to the study of such relations.

Stimulus Detection: The Absolute Threshold

How strong must a point of light, a whisper, or a brush on the skin be before we can detect its presence?

The minimum amount of stimulus energy that can be sensed is called the **absolute threshold.** The lower the absolute threshold, the greater the sensitivity. Recognizing that barely perceptible stimuli occur within a range of some uncertainty for subjects, researchers operationally define the absolute threshold as the intensity at which a stimulus can be detected 50 percent of the time.

The absolute threshold can be established in a number of ways. The most common technique is known as the **method of constant stimuli.** To study your absolute threshold for sound, for example, a sound that was loud enough for you to detect almost every time would be chosen. Then, one that you could almost never detect would be selected. Finally, the middle range would be filled in with about six sounds that varied in volume in equally spaced increments. The eight stimuli would be presented in a random order accompanied by a light. Your task would be to tell if you were able to hear a tone when the light appeared. The random presentations would continue until each of the stimuli had been presented perhaps 50 times. The number of times you had reported hearing each of the tones could be plotted, and the intensity at which the tone could be heard 50 percent of the time could be estimated quite closely.

Absolute thresholds vary, depending on the conditions under which the stimulus occurs, such as the number of possibly distracting stimuli, and on the characteristics of the perceiver, such as the degree of sensory adaptation that has occurred from exposure to previous stimuli. The general limits of human sensitivity for the five major senses can be estimated, however. Some examples are presented in Table 6.1. As you can see, many of our senses are surprisingly sensitive. A human's ability to see a candle from 30 miles, for example, required entire cities to be completely blacked out during the threat of air attacks during World War II.

Signal Detection Theory

I can remember lying in bed as a child after I had seen a horror movie, straining my ears to detect any unusual sound that might signal the presence of a monster in the house. I recall hearing faint sounds that would have probably gone unnoticed had I seen a comedy or a western earlier in the evening. Perhaps you have had a similar experience.

At one time it was assumed that each person had a more or less fixed level of sensitivity for each sense. But psychologists and engineers who study stimulus detection have found that people's apparent sensitivity can fluctuate quite a bit. They have concluded that the concept of a fixed absolute threshold has to be modified, because there is no single point on the intensity scale that separates nondetection from detec-

Table 6.1 Sensitivity of Various Senses: Some Approximate Absolute Thresholds

Sense Modality	Absolute Threshold
Vision	Candle flame seen at 30 miles on a clear, dark night
Hearing	Tick of a watch under quiet conditions at 20 feet
Taste	1 teaspoon of sugar in 2 gallons of water
Smell	1 drop of perfume diffused into the entire volume of a large apartment
Touch	Wing of a fly or bee falling on your cheek from a distance of 1 centimeter

Source: Based on Galanter, 1962.

tion of a stimulus. There is instead a range of uncertainty, and people set their own **decision criterion,** a standard of how certain they must be that a stimulus is present before they will say they detect it. The decision criterion can also change from time to time. **Signal detection theory** is concerned with the factors that influence such decisions.

In a typical signal detection experiment, subjects are told that after a warning light appears, a tone may or may not be presented. Their task is to tell the experimenter whether or not they heard the tone. Under these conditions, there are four possible outcomes, as shown in Figure 6.4. When the tone is in fact presented, the subject may say "yes" (a *hit*) or "no" (a *miss*). When no tone is presented, the subject may also say "yes" (a *false alarm*) or "no" (a *correct rejection*).

At low stimulus intensities, both the subject's and the situation's characteristics influence the decision criterion (Pitz & Sachs, 1984). Bold subjects who frequently say "yes" have more hits but also have more false alarms than do conservative subjects. Subjects can also be influenced to become bolder or more

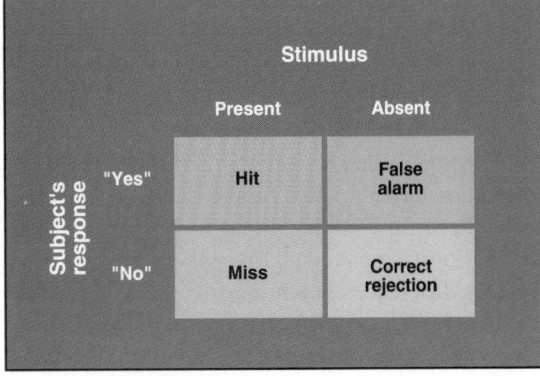

Figure 6.4 *This matrix shows the four possible outcomes in a signal detection experiment. The percentages of responses that fall within each category can be affected by both subject characteristics and the nature of the situation.*

conservative by manipulating the rewards and costs for giving correct or incorrect responses. Increasing rewards for hits relative to the costs for false alarms results in lower thresholds (more "yes" responses at low intensities). Conversely, subjects become more conservative in their "yes" responses as costs for false alarms are increased relative to rewards, resulting in higher thresholds.

The decision processes involved in signal detection experiments are similar to those faced by a physician who must decide whether or not a given disease is present. The consequences of the diagnostic decision will affect the doctor's decision criterion (Grossberg & Grant, 1978; Swets, 1992). On the one hand, most physicians will not require much evidence of a bacterial infection to give a patient antibiotics, since they and the patient have little to lose in the case of a false alarm and much to gain if an infection actually is present and can be cured. On the other hand, physicians will not make certain diagnoses (especially those that will result in radical interventions, such as open-heart surgery) unless they have compelling evidence to support the diagnosis, because the consequences of a false alarm would be too costly to them, to the patient, and, perhaps, to the company that provides them with malpractice insurance.

The Difference Threshold

Sometimes, subtle differences between stimuli are important. The smallest difference between two stimuli that people can perceive is called the **difference threshold** or the *just noticeable difference (jnd)*.

German physiologist Ernst Weber made an important discovery about the difference threshold about 150 years ago. He found that the difference threshold, or jnd, is proportional to the intensity of the stimulus with which the comparison is being made and that the specific proportions differ for the various senses. For example, the jnd value for weights is approximately 0.02, or 1/50. This means that if you lift a weight of 100 grams, a second weight must weigh at least 102 grams (i.e., 2/100 = 1/50) for you to discriminate between them. If the first weight is 200 grams, the second must be at least 4 grams heavier, and if the first weight is 400 grams, the second one must be at least 408 grams. **Weber's law** holds up well within the most frequently encountered middle ranges of stimulation, but it breaks down at extremely high or low intensities of stimulation.

Weber and other researchers also found that specific ratios differ for the various senses, indicating that some sensory modalities are more sensitive than others. For example, sound receptors are very sensitive to differences in stimulation; the Weber constant for differences in pitch is approximately 1/333. Taste is the least sensitive of our senses, with a ratio

of 1/5 for detecting differences in salt concentrations. The jnd for discriminations among lights of differing intensities is about 1/60.

Recording and Scanning Methods

Some of the same techniques used to study the brain's functions can be used to study sensation. For example, electrical recording and brain imaging techniques can detect whether certain stimuli are registering in the sensory systems.

Electrical recording techniques have proved to be useful in studies of infants' visual capabilities. Through electrodes attached to the infant's scalp above the visual cortex, researchers can measure *evoked potentials*, the electrical responses that occur in the cortex as visual stimuli are presented. This method can be used over time to measure the maturation of sensory capabilities (see Figure 6.5). For example, evoked potentials have shown that infants can perceive shapes even at birth and that their visual sensitivity to detail grows rapidly during the first 6 months of life (Slater, 1989).

PET scans used to measure the activities of neurons in the sensory system have provided valuable information on how the system responds to various types of stimulation (Duncan & Stumpf, 1991). Ra-

◆ **Figure 6.5** *Evoked cortical potentials can be used to test when certain kinds of stimuli begin to register in the baby's nervous system and provide information about the development of visual capabilities.*

dioactive deoxyglucose is injected into a human or animal, and the subject is then exposed to various stimuli. The amount of deoxyglucose absorbed by various neurons in the sensory pathways and the cortex shows where the stimuli are being processed (see Figure 6.6). This approach, as well as the fast MRI technique described in Chapter 3, promises to receive more widespread use in the years ahead, and imaging techniques will undoubtedly shed light on many aspects of sensory functioning.

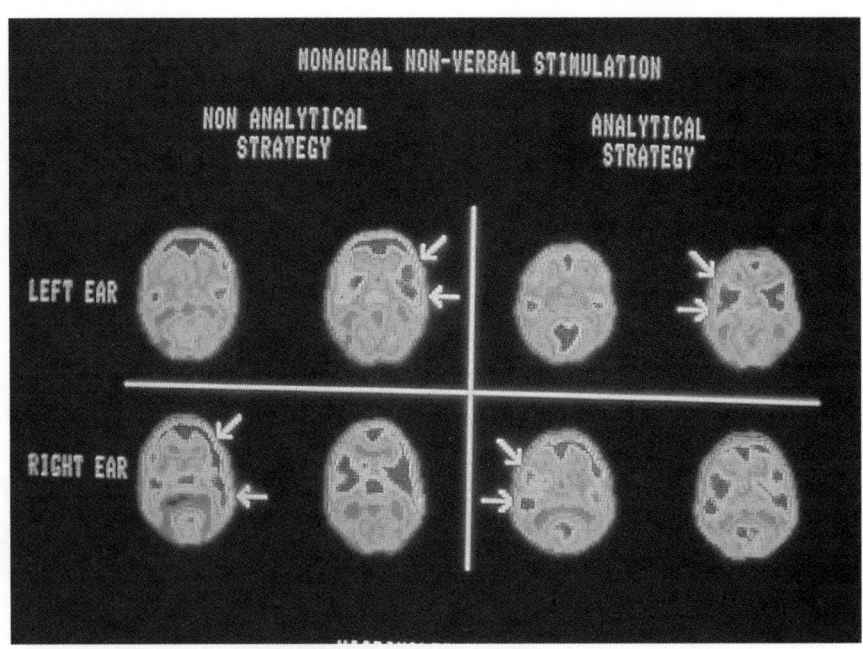

Figure 6.6 *PET scans can be used to pinpoint the areas of the brain that are activated by various types of sensory stimulation.*

The Sensory Systems

The only language that your brain understands is the electrochemical language of your nervous system. Locked within the silent, dark recesses of your skull, the brain cannot "understand" light waves, sound waves, or the other forms of energy that make up the language of the environment. Contact with the outer world is possible only because certain neurons have developed into specialized sensory receptors that can transform, or *transduce,* different types of energy, such as sound, light, and temperature, into the code language of nerve impulses.

How many senses are there? It really depends on how you classify them. Certainly there appear to be more than the five classical senses with which we are familiar—vision, audition (hearing), touch, taste, and smell. For example, there are senses that provide information about balance and body position. Also, because of the many different receptors in the skin, touch may be broken down into the separate senses of pressure, pain, and temperature. Receptors deep within the brain monitor the chemical makeup and temperature of the bloodstream, and we now know that the immune system has sensory functions that allow it to communicate with the brain.

One popular way of classifying sensory systems is in terms of the types of stimuli to which they respond (Coren & Ward, 1989; Levine & Shefner, 1992). For each of the senses presented in Table 6.2, we will discuss the sensory receptors as well as the **transduction** process by which the physical stimulus is translated into the language of nerve impulses that are sent to the brain.

Vision

The normal stimulus for the visual sense is electromagnetic energy, or light waves. In addition to that small portion of the electromagnetic spectrum that humans can perceive, there are X-rays, television and radio signals, and infrared and ultraviolet rays (see Figure 6.7). Such energies may be described in terms of their *wavelengths,* which are measured in **nanometers.** (A nanometer [nm] is one billionth of a meter.) The human visual system is sensitive to wavelengths extending from about 400 nanometers (blue-violet) to about 700 nanometers (red), only a tiny fraction of the electromagnetic spectrum.

The Human Eye

The eye is a complex and highly specialized sensory receptor organ; its main structures are shown in

Table 6.2 Classification of Sensory Systems in Terms of Stimuli to Which They Respond

Stimulus	Sense	Receptors
Electromagnetic energy	Vision	Rods and cones in retina
Mechanical energy		
Sound waves	Audition	Hair cells in the basilar membrane, inner ear
Displacement of skin; pressure	Skin senses	Various types in skin and tissues
Movement of joints	Kinesthetic body sense	Nerve endings in tendons, muscles, and joints
Gravity, acceleration	Vestibular body sense	Hair cells in semicircular canals of ear
Thermal	Skin senses	Various types in skin and tissues
Chemical substances		
Dissolved in saliva	Taste	Taste buds on the tongue
Molecules in air	Olfaction (smell)	Cells in upper nasal cavity

Source: Based on Levine & Shefner, 1992; Uttal, 1973.

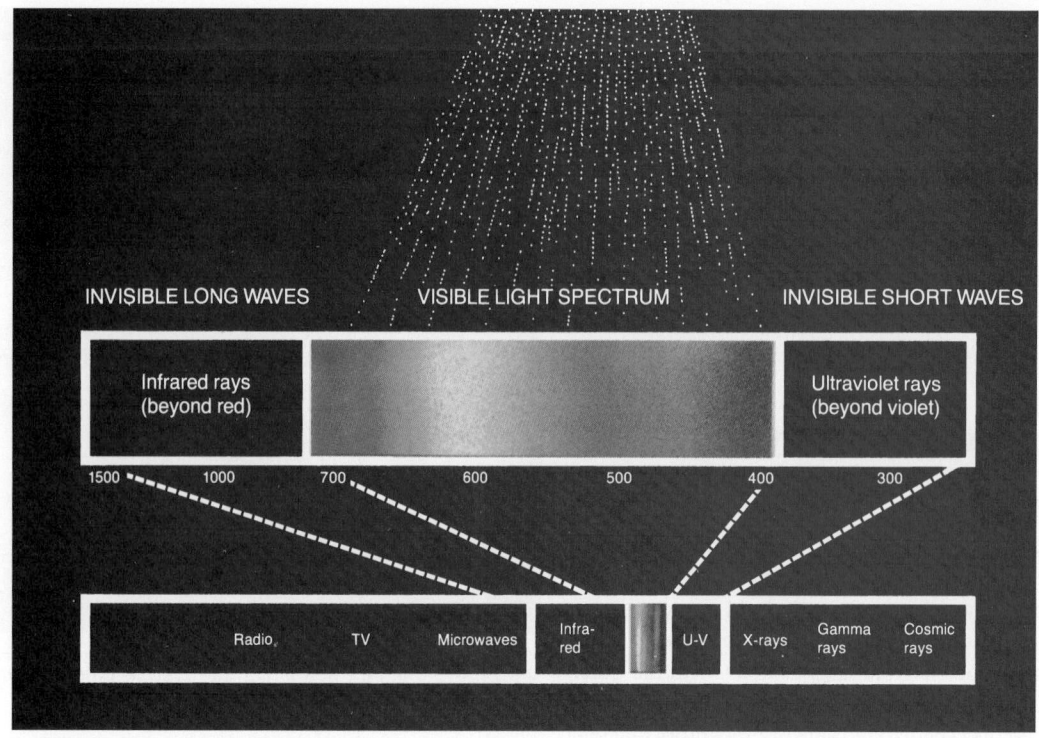

INVISIBLE LONG WAVES   VISIBLE LIGHT SPECTRUM   INVISIBLE SHORT WAVES

| Infrared rays (beyond red) | | Ultraviolet rays (beyond violet) |

1500   1000   700   600   500   400   300

| Radio | TV | Microwaves | Infra-red | | U-V | X-rays | Gamma rays | Cosmic rays |

Figure 6.7 *The full spectrum of electromagnetic radiation. Only the narrow band between 400 and 700 nanometers (nm) is visible to the human eye. One nanometer = 1,000,000,000th of a meter.*

Figure 6.8 *This cross section shows the major parts of the human eye. The iris regulates the size of the pupil. The ciliary muscles (or ciliary body) regulate the shape of the lens. The image entering the eye is reversed by the lens and cast on the retina, which contains the photoreceptor cells. The optic disk, where the optic nerve exits the eye, has no receptors and produces a "blind spot" as demonstrated in Figure 6.12.*

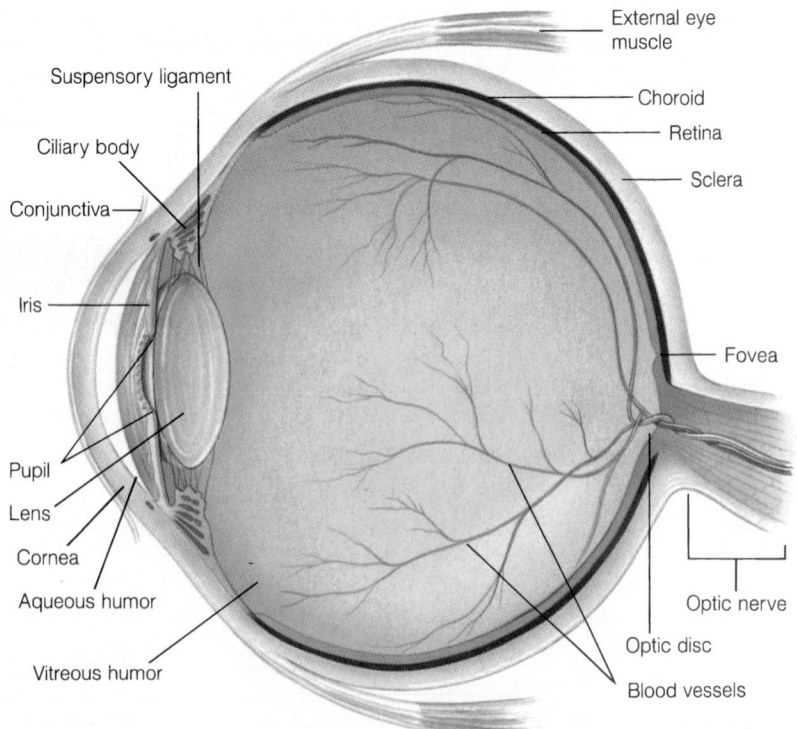

Suspensory ligament
Ciliary body
Conjunctiva
Iris
Pupil
Lens
Cornea
Aqueous humor
Vitreous humor

External eye muscle
Choroid
Retina
Sclera
Fovea
Optic nerve
Optic disc
Blood vessels

Figure 6.8. Light rays enter the eye through the transparent **cornea.** The amount of light allowed to enter is regulated by the colored **iris,** which regulates the size of the **pupil,** the hole in the center of the iris. Tiny muscles in the iris cause the pupil to dilate or constrict, depending on the brightness of the light and other factors, such as one's emotional state. Low levels of illumination and emotional arousal cause the pupil to dilate, letting more light into the eye to improve optical clarity.

The interior of the eyeball is filled with clear liquids called **aqueous humor** (in front of the lens) and **vitreous humor** (behind the lens). The aqueous humor nourishes the cornea, and the vitreous humor helps the eyeball maintain its shape.

The **lens** is an elastic structure whose shape varies with the distance of the object at which you're looking. Through the action of the **ciliary muscles,** the lens becomes thinner to focus on distant objects and thicker to focus on nearby objects. Just as a camera lens focuses an image on a photosensitive material (film), so the lens of the eye focuses the image on the **retina,** which contains the visual receptors.

Several common visual defects involve dysfunction of the lens. In nearsightedness, or **myopia,** the lens is too thick. When a nearsighted person looks at a distant object, the lens forms an image that falls in front of the retina instead of directly on it, resulting in a blurred image. Visual perception of nearby objects is not affected. This condition can be corrected by eyeglasses or contact lenses with negative, or concave, lenses, which are thicker on the edges than in the center. Such lenses correct for the natural lens' inability to become thin enough to focus the distant object's image directly onto the retina (see Figure 6.9).

Farsightedness, or **hyperopia,** occurs when the lens does not thicken enough to focus the image of nearby objects directly onto the retina. Perception of distant objects is not affected by hyperopia. A positive, or convex, lens—thicker in the center than on the edges—is used to correct this problem.

The Rods and Cones

Embedded in the retina at the back of each eye are more than 125 million photoreceptor cells, called **rods** and **cones** because of their shapes (see Figure 6.10). The rods outnumber the cones by more than 10 to 1 and are found throughout the retina except in a small central region called the **fovea,** which contains only cones. The cones decrease in number as one moves away from the center of the retina.

Interestingly, the rods and cones form the *rear* layer of the retina; there are other layers of cells between the retina and the lens. One of these layers includes the **bipolar cells,** which make direct synaptic connections with the rods and cones. The bipolar cells, in turn, synapse with the **ganglion cells** in the frontmost layer, whose axons are collected into a bundle to form the **optic nerve.**

Surprisingly, the light-sensitive ends of the rods and cones face *away from* the direction of the entering light. Because of this, and because of the structures and the liquid substances that lie in front of the receptors, only a small portion of the total light energy entering the eyeball actually reaches the rods and cones.

The rods and the cones play different roles in vision. The more numerous rods are about 500 times more sensitive to light than the cones, but they do not give rise to color sensations. The cones, which function only when the light is relatively bright, are the retina's color receptors. Thus, the rods are a bit like black-and-white film; the cones are like color film.

Figure 6.11 shows the photoreceptor connections in the retina. Each rod and cone is connected to one or more bipolar cells. Typically, many rods are connected to the same bipolar cell and can combine or "funnel" their individual electrical messages to fire it. This arrangement is especially good for vision under dim light conditions, because the sensitivities of individual rods are summed and can fire the bipolar cell.

The cones in the periphery of the retina also share bipolar cells, but in the fovea each cone has its own.

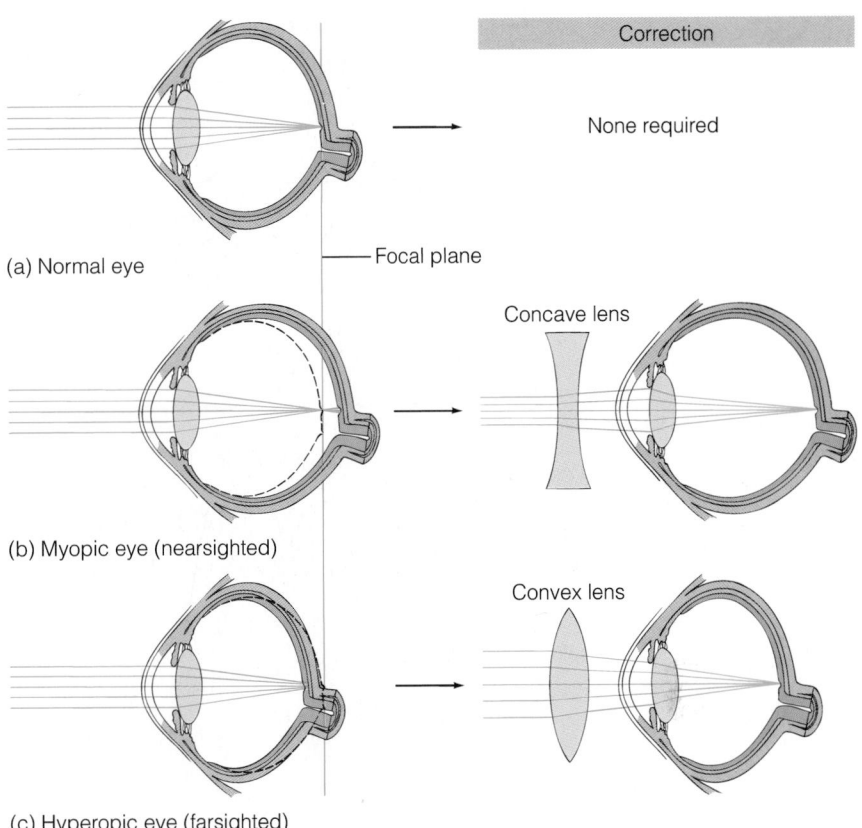

(a) Normal eye

(b) Myopic eye (nearsighted)

(c) Hyperopic eye (farsighted)

Figure 6.9 *Nearsightedness (myopia) and farsightedness (hyperopia) are caused by incorrect focusing of distant or nearby objects onto the retina by the lens of the eye. Negative (concave) lenses are used to correct nearsightedness, whereas positive (convex) lenses are used to correct farsightedness.*

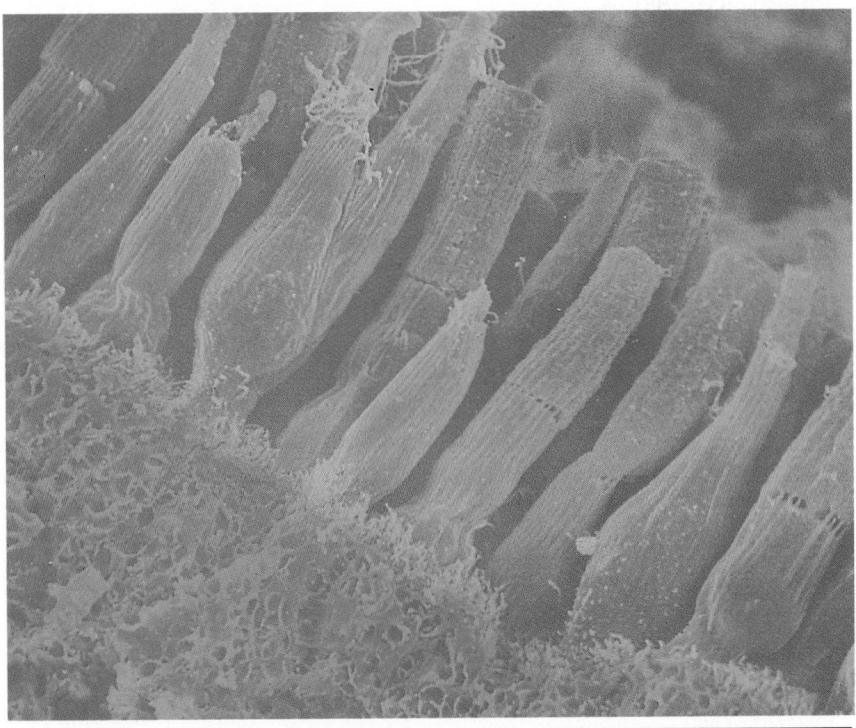

Figure 6.10 *Rods and cones as seen through an electron microscope. In this photo, the rods are pictured in blue and the cones in green.*

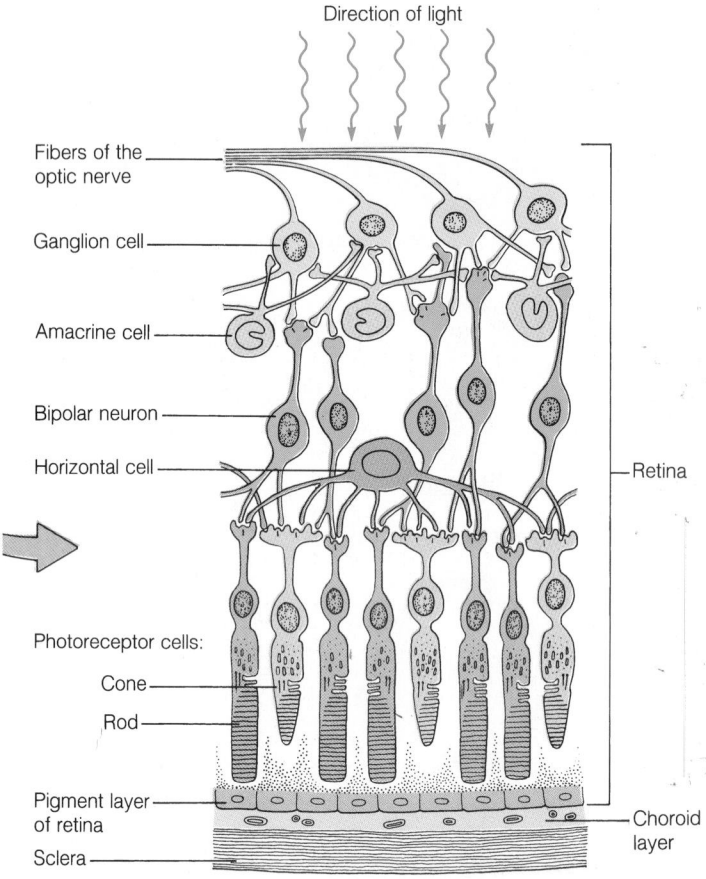

Direction of light

Fibers of the optic nerve

Ganglion cell

Amacrine cell

Bipolar neuron

Horizontal cell

Retina

Photoreceptor cells:

Cone

Rod

Pigment layer of retina

Sclera

Choroid layer

▲ **Figure 6.11** *There are two types of photoreceptor connections in the retina. The rods and cones synapse with bipolar cells, which in turn synapse with ganglion cells, whose axons form the optic nerve. The horizontal and amacrine cells help to integrate these connections within the retina.*

This "private line," plus the fact that the cones in the fovea are very tightly packed together, means that our **visual acuity,** the ability to see fine detail, is greatest when the image projects directly onto the fovea and results in the firing of a large number of cones and bipolar cells.

The rods and the cones thus contribute to different aspects of visual sensitivity. Color and fine detail are best seen when objects are looked at directly, because this focuses the image on the densely packed cones in the fovea. Because cones do not function under dim illumination, however, we can more easily detect a faint stimulus, such as a dim star, if we look slightly to one side so that its image falls not on the fovea but on that portion of the retina where the rods are packed most densely. This is why soldiers are trained to fixate slightly to one side of an object during night combat.

The Transduction Process: From Light Waves to Nerve Impulses

How do the rods and cones translate light waves into nerve impulses? Not all the details of the process are

fully understood, but it is known that each rod and cone contains several million chemical molecules called **photopigments** (Stryer, 1987). The absorption of light by these molecules produces a chemical reaction in the receptor cell. If the chemical reaction is strong enough, a change occurs in the electrical potential in the receptor's cell membrane. This *graded potential,* which is directly proportional to the intensity of the stimulus, changes the rate of neurotransmitter release at the receptor's synapse with the bipolar cells. The greater the change in transmitter release, the stronger the signal passed on to the bipolar cell and the more likely it is that an all-or-none *action potential* will be triggered in the next layer of ganglion cells (the first place at which action potentials can occur). If nerve responses are triggered at each of the three levels (rod or cone, bipolar cell, and ganglion cell), the message is instantaneously on its way to its final destination, the visual cortex of the brain.

The optic nerve exits through the back of the eye not far from the fovea. Because there are no receptors at this point, there is a **blind spot** there whose existence can be shown through the demonstration in Figure 6.12. Ordinarily, we are unaware of the blind spot because our perceptual system "fills in" the missing part of the visual field. Notice, for example, how you continue to see the entire checkerboard pattern surrounding the figures in Figure 6.12 even when they fall on the blind spot and are no longer visible.

Brightness Vision

Brightness is probably the most elementary visual sensation. Some organisms have sense organs that are responsive only to differences in illumination. In the human eye, brightness vision is a more complex pro-

▲ **Figure 6.12** *Close your left eye and from a distance of about 12 inches, focus steadily on the X with your right eye as you slowly move the book toward your face. At some point the image of the dot will cross your optic disk (blind spot) and disappear. It will reappear after it crosses the blind spot. Note how the checkerboard remains wholly visible even though part of it falls on the blind spot. Your perceptual system fills in the missing information.*

cess, because humans have more than one type of photoreceptor.

As noted earlier, rods are far more sensitive to low illumination than are cones. Nonetheless, the brightness sensitivity of both the rods and the cones depends in part on the wavelength of the light. Psychologists have studied the absolute thresholds of rods and cones for light energy at various wavelengths. This research has shown that rods have a much greater brightness sensitivity than cones throughout the color spectrum except at the red end, where rods are relatively insensitive. Cones, in contrast, are most sensitive to low illumination in the greenish-yellow range of the spectrum. These findings have prompted many cities to change the color of their fire engines from the traditional red to yellow-green in order to increase the vehicles' visibility to both rods and cones in dim lighting (see Figure 6.13). Similarly, airport landing lights are blue because this color is picked up well by the rods during night vision.

Dark Adaptation

Perhaps you have had the embarrassing experience of entering a movie theater from bright sunlight, groping around in the darkness, and finally sitting down in someone's lap. Although one can meet interesting people this way, most of us prefer to stand in the rear of the theater until our eyes become accustomed to the dimly lit interior. This improvement in sensitivity is called **dark adaptation.**

Dark adaptation occurs as the result of changes in the receptors' photopigment molecules. After absorbing light, the receptor molecule undergoes a chemical change and is depleted of pigment for a period of time. Until the photopigment is regenerated, visual sensitivity is lost in that receptor. If the eye has been exposed to conditions of high illumination, such as bright sunlight, a substantial amount of photopigment will be exhausted. During dark adaptation, the photopigment molecules are regenerated, and the receptor's sensitivity increases greatly. It is estimated that after complete adaptation, rods are able to detect light intensities only 1/10,000 as great as those that could be detected before dark adaptation began (Stryer, 1987).

Studies of the process of dark adaptation have provided further evidence for sensitivity differences between rods and cones. Figure 6.14 shows a typical dark adaptation curve. Such curves are calculated by having people look at a bright light until their retinas become adapted to it. The people are then placed in darkness, and their absolute thresholds to light flashes of different intensities and wavelengths are measured as the visual system gradually recovers its sensitivity.

Note that the curve has two distinct parts. By changing the wavelength (color) of the light and the area of the retina being tested (so that either rods or cones are being stimulated), it can be shown that the first part of the curve is due to dark adaptation of the cones and the second part to dark adaptation of the rods. The cones gradually become sensitive to fainter lights as time passes, but after about 5 minutes in the dark, their sensitivity has reached its maximum. The rods, however, do not reach their maximum sensitivity for about half an hour. The reason is differences in regeneration rates of the pigments in rods and cones.

Principles of dark adaptation had an important wartime application for fighter pilots who needed to be able to take off on a moment's notice and see their

Figure 6.13 *Knowledge about the sensitivity of rods and cones under low illumination has resulted in a new phenomenon—the yellow-green fire engine.*

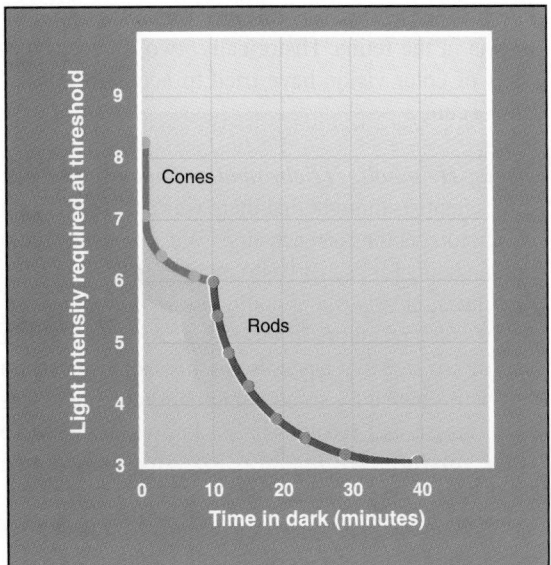

Figure 6.14 *The course of dark adaptation is graphed over time. The curve has two parts, one for cones and one for rods. The cones adapt completely in about 5 minutes, whereas the rods continue to increase their sensitivity.*

Figure 6.15 *Working in red light keeps the rods in a state of dark adaptation.*

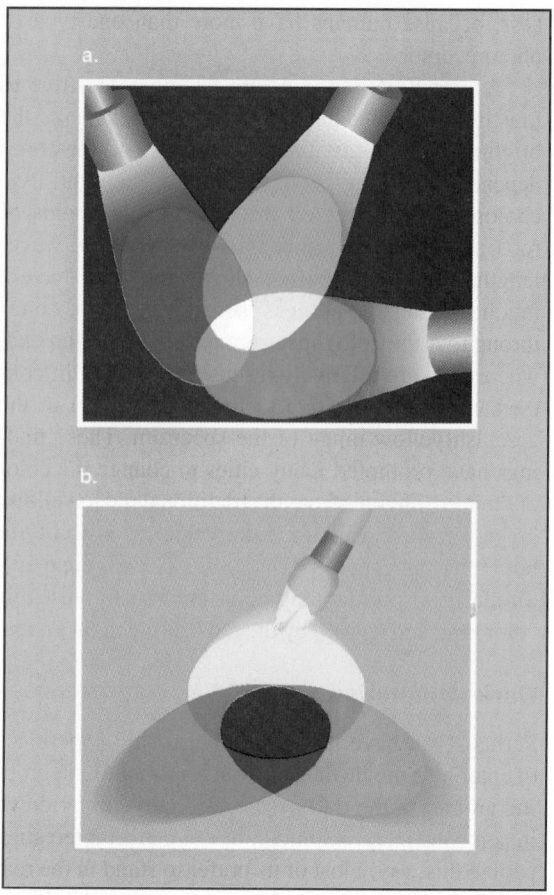

Figure 6.16 (a) *Additive color mixture. A beam of light of a specific wavelength directed onto a white surface is perceived as the color that corresponds to that wavelength on the visible spectrum. If beams of light that fall at certain points within the red, green, or blue color range are directed together onto the surface in the correct proportions, an additive mixture of wavelengths will result and any color in the visible spectrum can be produced (including white at the point where all three colors intersect). The Young-Helmholtz theory of color vision assumes that color perception results from the additive mixture of impulses from cones that are sensitive to red, blue, and green (see text). (b) Subtractive color mixture. Mixing pigments or paints produces new colors by subtraction—that is, by removing (i.e., absorbing) other wavelengths. Paints absorb (subtract) colors different from themselves while reflecting their own color. For example, blue paint mainly absorbs wavelengths that correspond to nonblue hues. Mixing blue paint with yellow paint (which absorbs wavelengths other than yellow) will produce a subtractive mixture that emits wavelengths between yellow and blue (i.e., green). Theoretically, certain wavelengths of the three primary colors of red, yellow (not green, as in additive mixture), and blue can produce the whole spectrum of colors by subtractive mixture.*

targets at night under conditions of very low illumination. An experimental psychologist familiar with the facts about dark adaptation provided a solution. Knowing that the rods are important in night vision and that they are relatively insensitive to red wavelengths, the psychologist suggested that fighter pilots either wear goggles with red lenses or work in rooms lit only by red lights while waiting to be called for a mission. Because red light stimulates only the cones, the rods remained in a state of dark adaptation, ready for service in the dark (see Figure 6.15).

Color Vision

The wavelength of light determines the color, or, more technically, the *hue* that we experience. The translation of wavelength signals into sensations of color begins in the retina. Historically, two different theories of color vision have tried to account for how this occurs.

Young-Helmholtz Trichromatic Theory. At one time scientists thought that there was a different kind of photoreceptor for each hue. We know now that human beings are sensitive to more than 200,000 distinct hues; clearly, there could not be that many different color receptors in the retina. Around 1800, it was discovered that any color in the visible spectrum can be produced by some combination of the colors blue, green, and red in what is known as **additive color mixture** (see Figure 6.16). This fact formed the basis of an important theory of color vision developed in 1867 by Thomas Young, an English physicist, and Hermann von Helmholtz, a German phys-

iologist. The **Young-Helmholtz trichromatic theory** assumes that there are three types of color receptors in the retina. Although all cones can be stimulated by most wavelengths to varying degrees, each cone is most sensitive to wavelengths that cor-

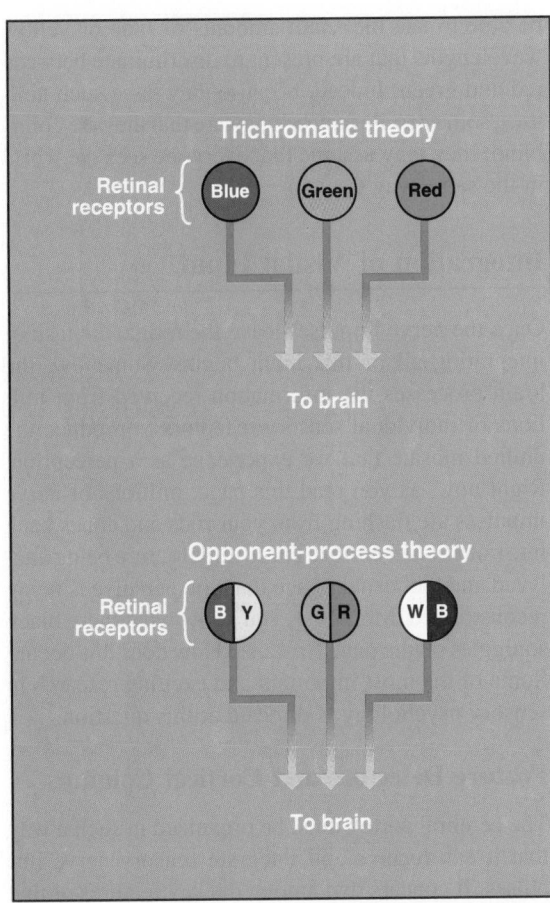

Figure 6.17 *Two classic theories of color vision. The Young-Helmholtz trichromatic theory proposes three different receptors, one for blue, one for red, and one for green. The ratio of activity in the three types of cones in response to a stimulus yields our experience of color. Hering's opponent-process theory also assumes that there are three different receptors, one for yellow-blue, one for red-green, and one for black-white. Each of the receptors can function in two possible ways, depending on the wavelength of the stimulus. Again, the pattern of activity in the receptors yields our perception of the hue.*

Hering's Opponent-Process Theory. A second influential color theory, formulated by Ewald Hering in 1870, also assumed that there are three types of cones. In this theory, however, each type of cone responds to *two* different wavelengths—one receptor to red or green, another to blue or yellow, and a third to black or white. Each receptor is assumed to be capable of two different chemical reactions, depending on the type of stimulation. For example, a red-green cone responds with one chemical reaction to a green stimulus and with its other chemical reaction to a red stimulus. Because the receptor cannot react both ways at the same time, Hering's theory has become known as the **opponent-process theory** (see Figure 6.17). You can experience one of the phenomena that supports the existence of opponent processes by staring at the flag in Figure 6.18. The color afterimage that you will later see in the blank space contains the colors specified by opponent-process theory.

Which theory is correct? It appears that both may be, but at different points in the visual system. According to recent findings, the photopigments of each cone contain one of three different visual proteins that are most sensitive to wavelengths roughly corresponding to the colors blue, red, and green (Baylor, 1987). These visual proteins bind together with retinal, a light-absorbing molecule that comes from vitamin A. When light waves of a particular wavelength are absorbed by the protein-retinal units in the cones sensitive to that wavelength, the units snap apart and the cones produce graded potentials. Different ratios of activity in the red-, blue-, and green-sensitive cones

respond to either blue, green, or red (see Figure 6.17). Presumably, each of these receptors sends messages to the brain, based on the extent to which they are activated by the wavelength of the stimulus. The visual system then combines the signals to recreate the original color.

Although the Young-Helmholtz theory is consistent with the laws of additive color mixture, there are some facts that do not fit the theory. For example, according to the theory, yellow is produced by activity in red and green receptors, yet certain people with red-green color blindness are able to experience yellow. This finding suggested to other scientists that there must be a different receptor for yellow, an observation that gave impetus to the next prominent theory to emerge.

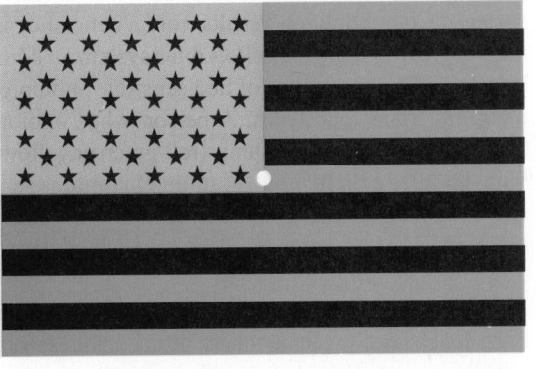

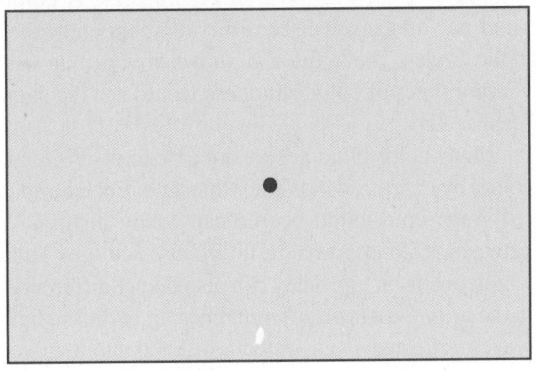

Figure 6.18 *Negative color afterimages have been thought to demonstrate opponent processes in the visual system. Stare steadily at the white dot in the center of the flag for about a minute, then shift your gaze to the black dot in the blank space. An American flag should appear. Theoretically, adaptation has occurred in the yellow, green, and black processes. When you shift your gaze to a blank surface, a rebound effect occurs, yielding activity in the blue, red, and white processes.*

can produce any hue in the spectrum. These photochemical processes in the cones seem consistent with the Young-Helmholtz trichromatic theory.

However, opponent processes also appear to be involved in color vision. Microelectrode studies done with monkeys (whose visual system is similar to ours) have shown that some bipolar cells in the retina (as well as some neurons in visual relay stations further up in the brain) respond to short wavelengths with a burst of impulses above their base rate of spontaneous firing, but they decrease their activity when the eye is stimulated by long wavelengths. This finding suggests that an opponent process operates not in the cones themselves, as the original Hering theory suggested, but further along the pathway from the eye to the brain (Jameson & Hurvich, 1989). It thus appears that there are yellow-blue and red-green opponent processes occurring as early as the first synapses of the rods and cones. The blue-sensitive cones stimulate the blue opponent process, and the red- and green-sensitive cones trigger their respective opponent processes. The yellow opponent process is triggered by certain levels of simultaneous input from the red- and green-sensitive cones.

Color Blindness. About 7 percent of the male population and 1 percent of the female population are unable to distinguish all the wavelengths (colors) from one another. As we've seen, the normal eye is capable of discriminating three fundamental systems of color: red-green, yellow-blue, and black-white. People with normal color vision are called **trichromats** because they are sensitive to all three systems. Color blindness results from a deficiency in the red-green system, the yellow-blue system, or both. It is caused by an absence of hue-sensitive photopigment in certain cone types. A person who is color-blind in only one of the systems (red-green or yellow-blue) is called a **dichromat.** A **monochromat** is sensitive only to the black-white system and is totally color-blind. Most color-blind people have a deficiency in the red-green system.

Several different tests of color blindness have been developed. Typically, these tests contain sets of colored dots such as those in Figure 6.19. A color-blind person cannot discern the numbers embedded in the circles. The figure also shows how people with varying types of color blindness would see the same scene.

Many color-blind people are able to discriminate colors by characteristics other than hue. For example, red-green color-blind people can easily distinguish between red and green traffic lights once they learn which one is on top. They can also detect differences in the brightnesses of different hues. In addition, light waves reflected from objects often contain mixed wavelengths, so a red-green color-blind person may

be able to use the small amounts of blue or yellow wavelengths that are present to discriminate between red and green. Indeed, because they have such abilities, some people may be unaware that they are color-blind; they may assume that everyone sees the world in the same way they do.

Integration of Visual Input

Once the nerve impulses leave the retina, the task of integrating all of this input begins. Somehow, the brain processes the information received from millions of individual sensory receptors to produce the unified mosaic that we experience as a perception. Right now, as you read this page, millions of nerve impulses are flashing from your rods and cones back into your visual cortex. These impulses are being analyzed and the visual image that you perceive is being reconstructed. Moreover, you know what these black squiggles on the page ''mean.'' How does this occur? Some of the most important and exciting research in sensory psychology is directed at this question.

Feature Detectors and Cortical Columns

The cerebral cortex must be organized in such a way that it can receive and integrate sensory nerve impulses. It appears that among the key features of that organization are the **cortical columns** (Hubel, 1982). These are vertically arranged groups of neurons that extend downward from the surface into other layers of the cortex.

Much of our knowledge about the role of cortical columns comes from research that won David Hubel and Torsten Wiesel of Harvard University the 1981 Nobel Prize. Using microelectrodes to record the activity of individual cells of the visual cortex of animals (see Figure 6.20), Hubel and Wiesel found that certain columns fired most frequently when lines of certain orientations were presented. For example, the cells of a particular column might fire most frequently when a horizontal line was presented; the cells of the next column would fire most frequently to a line of a slightly different orientation, and so on ''around the clock.'' Figure 6.21 shows how these cortical units, known as **orientation columns,** are arranged. Hubel and Wiesel also found that a column of cells dominated by the left eye is usually next to a column that receives input from the right eye. They called these alternating columns **ocular dominance columns.**

As shown in Figure 6.21, the individual columns are grouped into larger units called **hypercolumns.** Each hypercolumn is composed of about 400 to 1600 individual columns (Frisby, 1980). The hypercolumn's job is to inspect a particular region of the retina and to act as an information-processing subunit within the cortex. The total pattern of neural activity in each

(a)

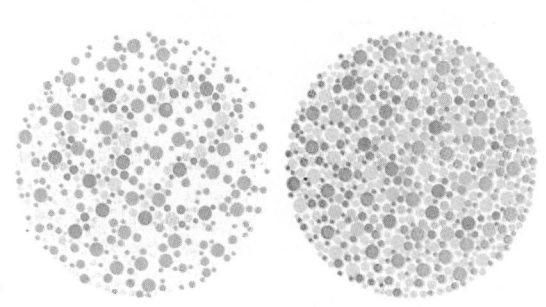

Figure 6.19 *The dotted figures below are used to test for color blindness. The one on the left is used to test for yellow-blue color blindness, the one on the right to assess red-green color blindness. Because the dots in the picture are of equal brightness, color is the only cue for perceiving the numbers in the chips. The pictures show how a scene might appear to a person with (a) normal color vision, (b) red-green blindness, (c) yellow-blue blindness, and (d) total color blindness, a monochromat.*

(b)

(c)

(d)

hypercolumn is believed to be the basis for the analysis and integration of inputs by the visual cortex, although how this occurs is still a mystery. Another Nobel Prize surely awaits the discoverer of how the hypercolumns work.

Hubel and Wiesel's discovery of cortical columns that respond selectively to specific stimuli revolutionized the field of vision research. Since then, scientists have studied the stimulus features to which specific cells in the visual system respond. So-called **feature detectors** have been identified by recording the electrical activity of individual cells in the retina and higher visual centers when various kinds of visual stimuli are presented. Cells have been found that respond most strongly to bars, slits, and edges in certain positions. The feature detectors send information about edges, contours, and angles to the cortex, where the information is integrated and analyzed by successively more complex feature-detector systems to produce our perception of objects. Based on record-

Figure 6.20 *A partially anesthetized monkey views an image projected on the screen while an electrode embedded in its visual cortex records the activity of a single neuron. This research by Hubel and Wiesel led to the discovery of feature detectors and cortical columns.*

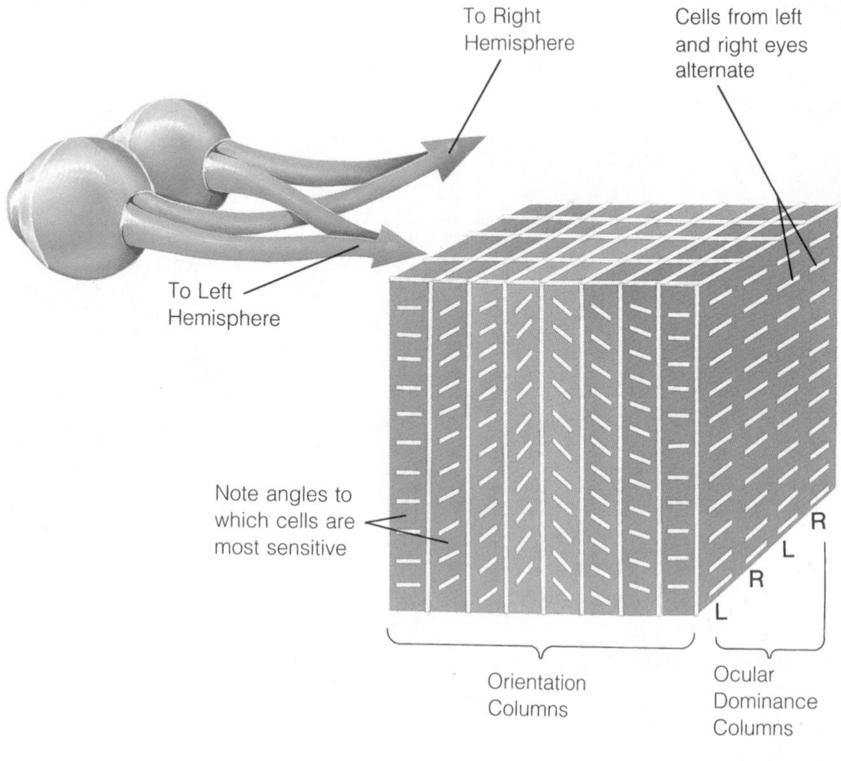

To Right Hemisphere

Cells from left and right eyes alternate

To Left Hemisphere

Note angles to which cells are most sensitive

Orientation Columns

Ocular Dominance Columns

Figure 6.21 *This representation of a portion of a hypercolumn in the left visual cortex shows the general arrangement of cortical columns. Stimuli having a particular orientation elicit maximum firing in cells within each orientation column. Input from the two eyes is alternated in ocular dominance columns lying side by side in the cortex. The patterns of neural activity in the 400 to 1,600 individual columns comprising a hypercolumn are analyzed to detect features of the visual stimulus.*

ings of neural responses to specific stimuli, color-coded computer models of how the cortical columns might be arranged have been generated.

Recently, patches of cells colloquially named *blobs* have been found interspersed among the form detectors. These blobs are sensitive to color and operate in an opponent-process fashion (Hubel & Livingstone, 1983). Still other feature detectors respond only to movement. Thus, the visual cortex seems to have feature receptors for form, movement, and color.

Spatial Frequency Filters

An important recent development, the **spatial frequency model,** has added to our understanding of how the brain receives and processes visual information. Any visual pattern can be represented as variations in brightness, darkness, and contrast, as in a black-and-white photograph. For example, the series of bars in Figure 6.22 can be represented as spatial frequency waves that reflect variations in brightness in terms of their position in the visual field. Evidence now suggests that specialized cells in the retina and in higher levels of the visual system respond to specific spatial frequencies (DeValois & DeValois, 1988). Some of these cells respond to low frequencies, such as general patterns of light and darkness that define shapes; others detect high frequencies, picking out fine details. Such cells are called **spatial frequency filters.** The theory states that the specific pattern of firing by the spatial frequency cells reflects the object's visual characteristics, such as its pattern of brightness, darkness, and shading. You've probably noticed, for example, that a black-and-white newspaper photo is composed of millions of small dots whose concentration determines the variations in lightness and darkness that produce contours and shading. The idea is that our perception of form arises from the visual system's analysis of these elements. Within the brain, these many bits of spatial frequency information from small areas of the retina are integrated to form a perception of the object (Graham, 1989).

Organization of the Visual Cortex

Microelectrode studies of the visual cortex have shown that, as in the case of other sensory systems, there is a point-to-point correspondence between receptor cells in the retina and cortical columns in the brain. In other words, stimulation of a particular point on the retina will activate a particular point on the cortex. Thus, the cortex "maps" the retina. As you might expect, the densely populated fovea is represented by a large area of the visual cortex, just as the somatic sensory area of the cortex devotes much space to the fingers, lips, and tongue. Somewhat surprising is the fact that there is more than one complete map of the retina; in fact, there are at least 10 of them, each a duplicate of the others. Other sensory systems also have duplicate maps, but not so many of them. At this point, we can only speculate that the many duplicate maps may reflect the special importance of vision in humans. Is it possible that the duplicate maps are nature's insurance against damage to any one of them? Or, perhaps, the duplicate maps somehow are involved in the integration of visual input. For now, the mystery remains unsolved.

Audition

The energy that stimulates our sense of hearing is fundamentally different from light. Light waves are electromagnetic energy, but sound waves are a form of mechanical energy. What we call sound is actually pressure waves in air, water, or some other conducting medium. Thus, when the stereo volume is high enough, you can actually see the cloth speaker covers moving in and out. The resulting vibrations cause successive waves of compression and expansion among the air molecules surrounding the source of the sound. These sound waves have two characteristics: *frequency* and *amplitude* (see Figure 6.23).

Frequency is the number of sound waves, or cycles, per second. The technical measure of cycles per second is the **Hertz (Hz);** 1 Hz equals one cycle per second. The sound waves' frequency is related to the *pitch* that we perceive; the higher the frequency in cycles per second, the higher the perceived pitch. Humans are capable of detecting sound frequencies from 20 Hz up to 20,000 Hz (about 12,000 Hz in

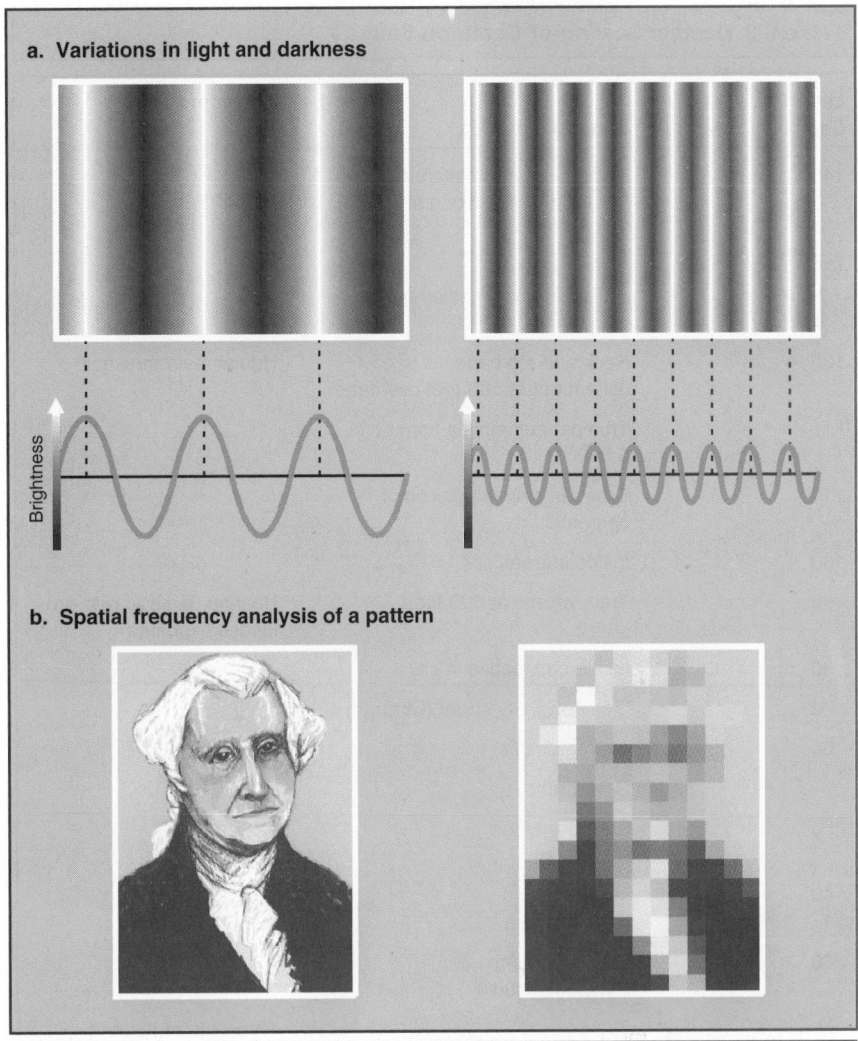

a. Variations in light and darkness

Brightness

b. Spatial frequency analysis of a pattern

⬆ **Figure 6.22** *A spatial frequency wave measures the location and extent of variations in brightness. This wave shows the amount of contrast between bands and the location and number of contrasts. Certain cells in the visual system are maximally sensitive to particular spatial frequencies. One theory is that the brain "sees" or reconstructs a visual pattern by analyzing which spatial frequency cells are firing.*

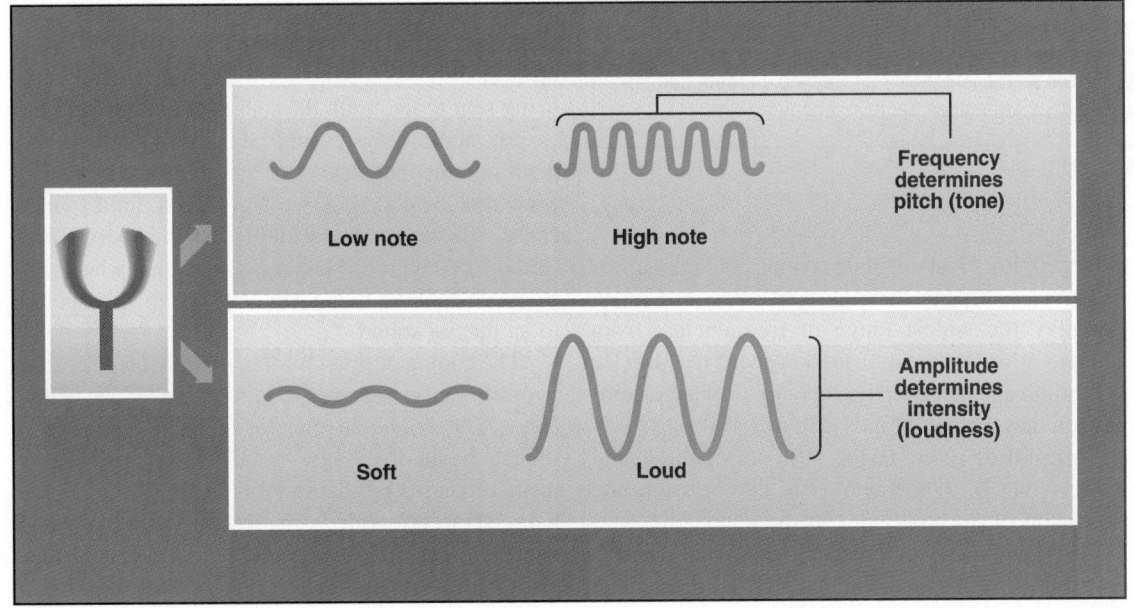

⬇ **Figure 6.23** *Sound waves are a form of mechanical energy. As the tuning fork vibrates, it produces successive waves of compression and expansion of air molecules. The number of maximum compressions per second (cycles per second) is its frequency (measured in Hz). The height of the wave above zero air pressure represents the sound's amplitude. Frequency determines pitch; amplitude determines loudness.*

Low note   High note   **Frequency determines pitch (tone)**

Soft   Loud   **Amplitude determines intensity (loudness)**

Table 6.3 Decibel Scaling of Common Sounds

Level in Decibels (db)	Common Sounds	Threshold Levels
140	50 hp siren at a distance of 100 feet; Jet fighter taking off at 80 feet from plane	
130	Boiler shop Air hammer at position of operator	
120	Rock and roll band Jet aircraft at 500 feet overhead	Human pain threshold
	Trumpet automobile horn at 3 feet	
110	Crosscut saw at position of operator	
100	Inside subway car	
90	Train whistle at 500 feet	Hearing damage with prolonged exposure
80	Inside automobile in city	
70	Downtown city street (Chicago)	
60	Average traffic	
	Restaurant	
50	Business office Classroom	
40	Inside church Hospital room	
30	Quiet bedroom Recording studio	
20		Threshold of hearing (young men)
10		Minimum threshold of hearing
0		

The decibel scale relates a physical quantity—sound intensity—to the human perception of that quantity—sound loudness. It is a logarithmic scale; that is, each increment of 10 decibels represents a tenfold increase in loudness. The table indicates the decibel ranges of some common sounds as well as the thresholds for hearing, hearing damage, and pain. Prolonged exposure at 150 decibels causes death in laboratory rats.

Source: Adapted from Christman, 1979, p. 236.

amplitude are expressed as **decibels,** a unit developed by scientists at the Bell Telephone Laboratories to measure the physical pressures that occur at the eardrum. Table 6.3 shows various common sounds scaled in decibels.

The Human Ear

The transduction system of the ear is made up of tiny bones, membranes, and liquid-filled tubes designed to translate pressure waves into nerve impulses (see Figure 6.24). Sound waves travel into an auditory canal leading to the **eardrum,** a movable membrane that vibrates in response to the sound waves. Beyond the eardrum is the middle ear, a cavity housing three small bones called (because of their shapes) the **hammer** (*malleus*), **anvil** (*incus*), and **stirrup** (*stapes*). The hammer is attached firmly to the eardrum, whereas the stirrup is attached to another membrane, the **oval window.** When the eardrum is activated by sound waves, its vibrations are passed along from the hammer through the other small bones of the middle ear to the oval window, which forms the boundary between the middle ear and the inner ear. The inner ear contains the **cochlea** (from the Latin for "snail"), a coiled tube filled with fluid. The cochlea contains two membranes, the **basilar membrane** and the **tectorial membrane.** Resting on the basilar membrane is the **organ of Corti,** which contains thousands of tiny hair cells whose ends are in contact with the tectorial membrane. These hair cells are the actual sound receptors.

Auditory Transduction

When sound waves strike the eardrum, pressure created at the oval window by the bony transmitters of the middle ear sets the fluid inside the cochlea into motion. These fluid waves shift the basilar and tectorial membranes in relation to one another so that the hair cells in the organ of Corti are bent, setting up an electrical potential that results in nerve impulses being sent to the brain through the auditory nerve.

The auditory system must transform loudness and pitch into the language of nerve impulses. Loudness appears to be coded in two ways. First, loud sounds cause a greater number of auditory nerve fibers to fire. Second, certain receptor neurons fire only when considerable bending of the hair cells occurs in response to an intense sound.

The coding of pitch is more complicated because two different processes—one for frequencies below about 400 Hz and another for higher frequencies—seem to be involved. Low-frequency sounds, such as those produced by the bass fiddle, cause individual hair cells to fire at the same frequency as the sound wave. Groups of individual hair cells in the cochlea also can coordinate their firing so that they fire at

older people). Most common sounds are in the lower frequencies. Among musical instruments, the piano can play the widest range of frequencies, from 27.5 Hz at the low end of the keyboard to 4,186 Hz at the high end. An operatic soprano's voice, in comparison, has a range of only 250 to 1,100 Hz.

Amplitude refers to the intensity of the sound waves—that is, to the amount of compression and expansion of the molecules in the conducting medium. The sound wave's amplitude is the primary determinant of the sound's loudness. Differences in

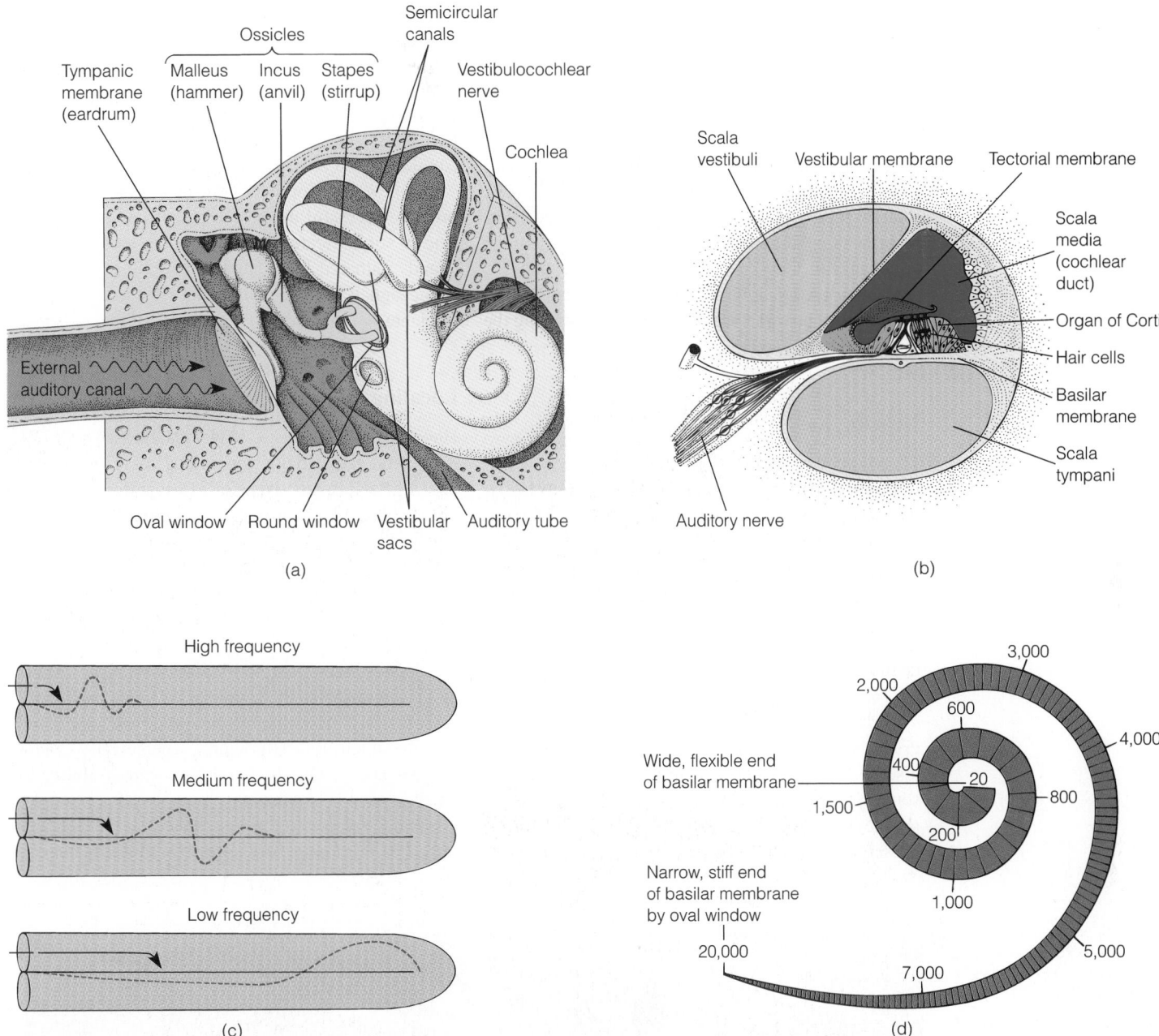

Labels in figure (a):
Ossicles
Tympanic membrane (eardrum)
Malleus (hammer)
Incus (anvil)
Stapes (stirrup)
Semicircular canals
Vestibulocochlear nerve
Cochlea
External auditory canal
Oval window
Round window
Vestibular sacs
Auditory tube

(a)

Labels in figure (b):
Scala vestibuli
Vestibular membrane
Tectorial membrane
Scala media (cochlear duct)
Organ of Corti
Hair cells
Basilar membrane
Scala tympani
Auditory nerve

(b)

Labels in figure (c):
High frequency
Medium frequency
Low frequency

(c)

Labels in figure (d):
3,000
2,000
600
4,000
400
800
Wide, flexible end of basilar membrane
20
1,500
200
Narrow, stiff end of basilar membrane by oval window
1,000
20,000
7,000
5,000

(d)

▲ **Figure 6.24** *A cross section of the ear (a) shows the structures that transmit sound waves from the auditory canal to the cochlea. There, sound waves are translated into fluid waves that stimulate hair cells in the organ of Corti (b). The resulting nerve impulses reach the brain via the auditory nerve. The semicircular and vestibular sacs of the inner ear contain sense organs for equilibrium. In (c), the fluid waves created by different sound frequencies are shown, and (d) shows the frequencies that maximally stimulate different areas of the basilar membrane. High-frequency waves peak quickly and stimulate the membrane close to the oval window.*

slightly different times, resulting in "volleys" of nerve impulses being sent through the auditory nerve at about the same frequency as the sound wave. This is known as the **frequency theory of pitch coding.**

Because refractory periods following nerve impulses limit the frequency of firing, individual impulses or volleys of impulses cannot produce high enough frequencies of firing to match sound wave frequencies above 400 Hz. Thus, frequencies above this range are coded in terms of the area of the basilar membrane that is displaced the most by the wave action in the cochlea. The point of maximum wave action on the basilar membrane serves as a frequency coding cue. The discoveries that led to this **place theory of pitch coding** won Georg von Bekesy the 1961 Nobel Prize. By cutting small holes in the cochleas of guinea pigs and human cadavers and observing cochlear events through a microscope, Bekesy (1957) found that high-frequency sounds produce a wave that peaks close to the oval window, whereas lower frequency vibrations produce a slower wave that peaks further down the cochlear canal.

As in the case of trichromatic and opponent-process theories of color vision, which were once thought to oppose one another, frequency and place theories of pitch transduction have both proved to be applicable in their own ways. At low frequencies, frequency theory holds true; at higher frequencies, place theory provides the mechanism for sensing the pitch of a sound.

Hearing Loss

There are two major types of hearing loss. **Conduction deafness** is caused by problems involving the mechanical system that transmits sound waves to the cochlea. For example, a punctured eardrum or a loss of function in the tiny bones of the middle ear may reduce the ear's capacity to transmit vibrations. Use of a hearing aid, which amplifies the sounds entering the ear, may correct many cases of conduction deafness.

Nerve deafness is an entirely different matter. This damage is to the receptors within the inner ear or to the auditory nerve itself. Although aging and disease can produce nerve deafness, exposure to loud sounds is a leading cause of nerve deafness in young people. Exposure to loud, damaging sounds of a particular frequency (as might be produced by a machine in a factory) causes people to eventually lose hair cells at one point on the basilar membrane, and also causes hearing loss for that frequency. Figure 6.25 shows the devastating results of a guinea pig's exposure to a sound level approximating that of loud rock music heard through earphones. Hearing aids can do little to remedy such problems.

A new development, cochlear implants, have proved successful in some cases of nerve deafness. These sophisticated electronic devices translate sounds gathered by a small microphone into electronic signals that reach the brain via a tiny electrode implanted in the cochlea.

Locating Sound Sources

Have you ever wondered why you have two ears, one located on each side of your head? As is usually the case, there is a good reason. Our ability to locate objects that emit sounds has important survival implications, and the two ears play a crucial role. The nervous system uses information concerning the time and intensity differences of sounds arriving at the two ears to locate the source of sounds in space (Middlebrooks & Green, 1991).

Sounds arrive first and loudest at the ear closest to the sound. When the source of the sound is directly in front of us, the sound reaches both ears at the same time and intensity, so the source is perceived as being straight ahead. Our binaural (two-eared) ability to localize sounds is amazingly sensitive; for example, a sound 3 degrees to the right arrives at the right ear only 300 millionths of a second before it arrives at

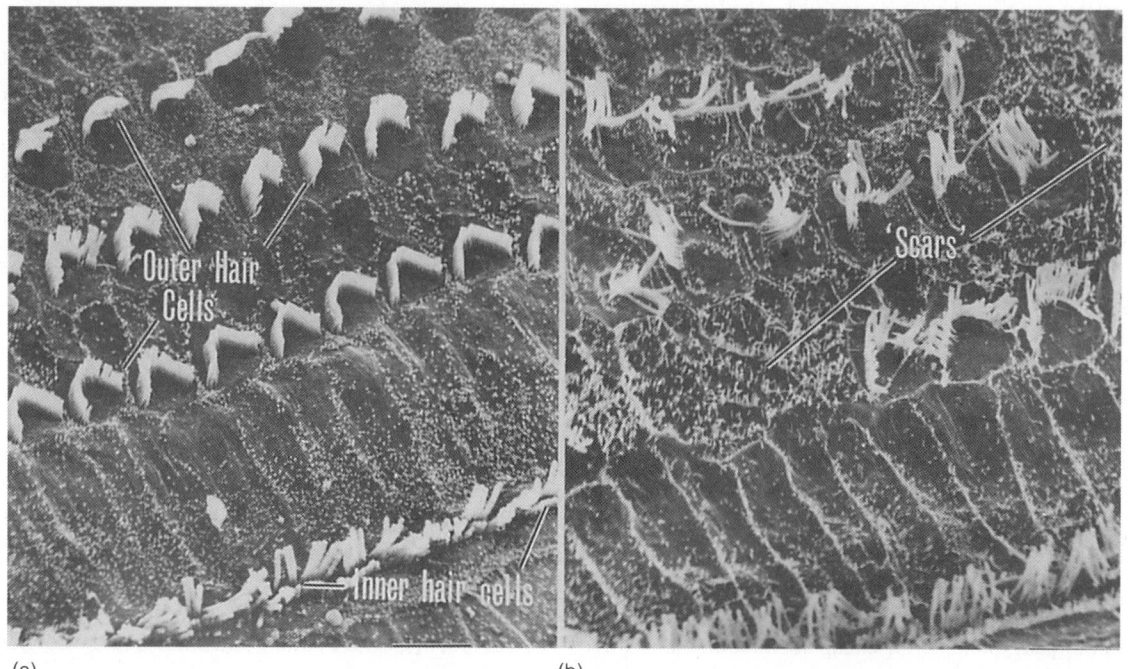

Figure 6.25 *Exposure to loud sounds can destroy auditory receptors in the inner ear. These pictures, taken through an electron microscope, show the hair cells of a guinea pig before (a) and after (b) exposure to 24 hours of noise comparable to that of a loud rock concert. (Micrographs by Robert E. Preston, courtesy of Professor J. E. Hawkins, Kresge Hearing Research Institute, University of Michigan.)*

(a)

(b)

the left ear, and yet we can tell that the source of the sound is not straight ahead (Yin & Kuwada, 1984).

Suppose that you were steering a ship through treacherous waters in a dense fog. Your vision would do you little good, and you would depend heavily on your auditory abilities to localize sounds. You might profit from a device like that shown in Figure 6.26. This device was actually used by sailors in the late 1800s to increase their ability to localize sounds. It assisted in two ways. First, because the two ear receptors were much larger than human ears, they could capture more sound waves. Even more importantly, the wider spacing between the receptors increased the time difference between the sound's arrival at the two human ears, thus increasing directional sensitivity.

Sound wave technology has resulted in several important applications in recent years. The Enhancing Human Performance feature highlights two of them. One device provides new "eyes" for blind people, and the other reduces the physically and psychologically damaging effects of certain kinds of noise.

PROFESSOR MAYER'S TOPOPHONE.

Figure 6.26 *This device, used by sailors to increase their ability to locate sounds in thick fog, worked primarily by increasing the time differences between sounds arriving at the two ears.*

NEW APPLICATIONS OF SOUND WAVE TECHNOLOGY: SONIC "EYES" AND ANTINOISE

ENHANCING HUMAN PERFORMANCE

Blindness not only deprives its victims of the visual delights that most of us take for granted, but it also limits their activities and performance in many ways. However, recent technological advances in *sensory substitution* provide hope that other senses can be tapped to partially compensate for the loss of vision. One promising development, a device known as a Sonicguide, provides new "eyes" by applying principles of auditory perception (Kay, 1982).

The Sonicguide (shown in Figure 6.27) works on the same principle as echolocation, which is used by bats to navigate in total darkness. The transmitter within the headset emits high-frequency sound waves beyond the range of human hearing. These waves bounce back from objects in the environment and are transformed by the Sonicguide into sounds that can be heard through the earphones. Different sound qualities match different features of external objects, and the wearer must learn to interpret the sonic messages. The sound's pitch tells the person how far

away the object is; a low pitch signals a nearby object and the pitch becomes higher with increasing distance. The loudness of the sound tells how large the object is, and the clarity of the sound (ranging from a static-like sound to a clear tone) signals the texture of the object, from very rough to very smooth. Finally, the auditory localization principle described previously tells the person where the object is located in the environment by means of differences in the time at which sounds arrive at the two ears.

In a heartening and scientifically illuminating test of the Sonicguide, psychologist T. G. R. Bower (1977) used the apparatus with six blind babies ranging in age from 5 to 16 months. He found that the babies quickly were able to use the device. In his first Sonicguide session with the youngest baby, Bower swung an object on a string until it lightly tapped the baby's nose. After only two presentations, the baby moved both eyes toward his nose as the object approached and moved both eyes away from his nose as the object swung away. On the seventh

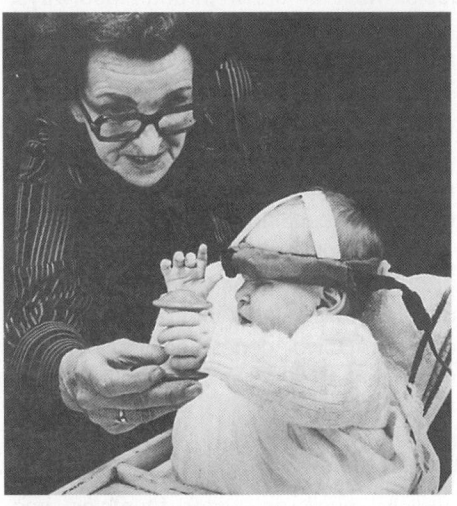

Figure 6.27 *This sonic device allows a blind baby to perceive the size, movement, shape, and texture of objects.*

trial, the baby reached out and blocked the object before it reached his face. The blind infant also began to follow the object with his eyes and head when it was moved on a right–left plane in front of him.

Within hours or days, all of the babies using the Sonicguide could reach for ob-

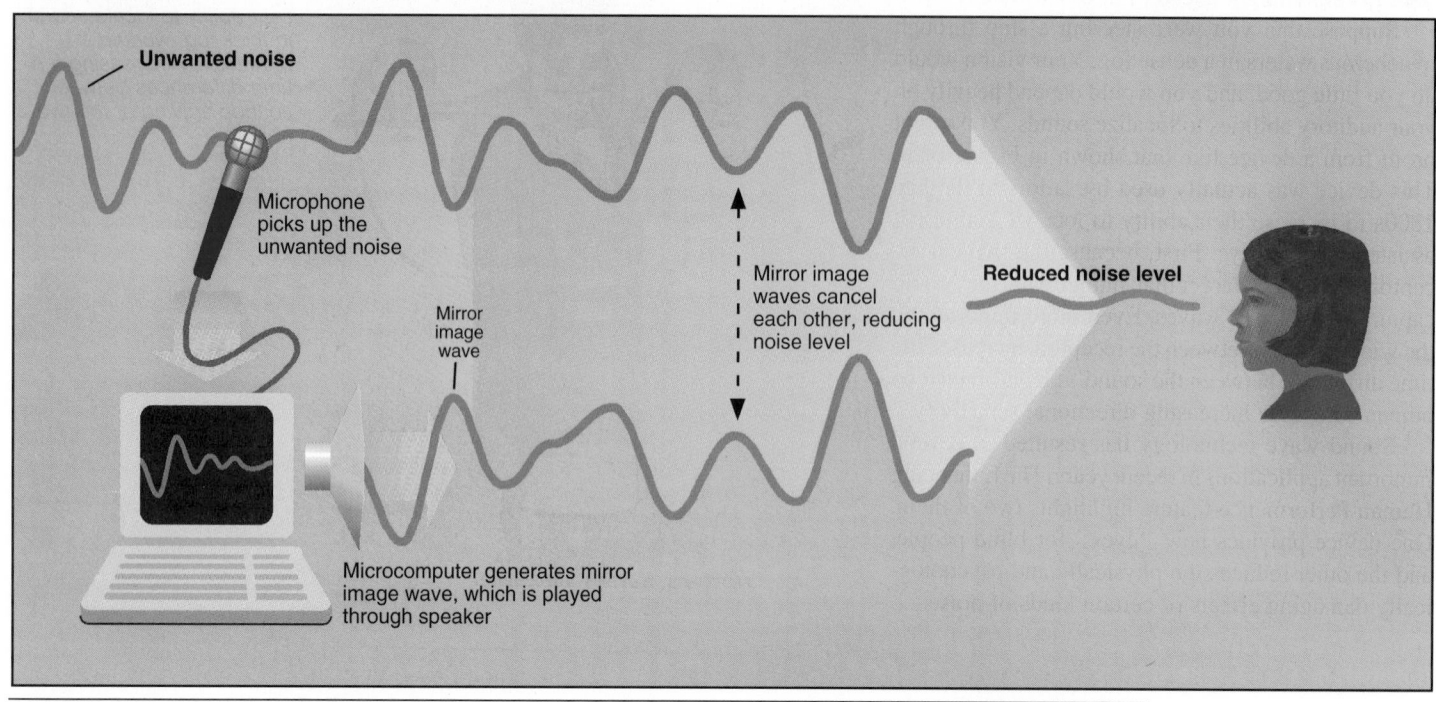

▲ **Figure 6.28** *Recently developed antinoise devices work by creating a mirror-image sound wave that cancels out the noise stimulus. A microphone detects the unwanted sound waves, and a microcomputer analyzes the offending wave's frequency and amplitude and generates an identical wave form 180 degrees out of phase.*

jects, walk or crawl through doorways, and listen to the movement of their hands and arms as they moved them about. They could even play peek-a-boo games with their parents. Moreover, their development of sensorimotor abilities, such as reaching for objects, recognizing favorite toys, and reaching out to be picked up when mother (but not someone else) approached, seemed to occur on the same developmental timetable as in sighted children. Bower concluded that blind infants can extract basically the same information from sonic cues as sighted babies do from visual cues. Older children trained with the device can easily find objects, such as water fountains and specific toys with which they want to play. They can thread their way through crowded school corridors and can even play hide-and-seek.

Some of the observations made during the Sonicguide trials also have implications for understanding sensory development. Older children and adults can learn to use the device, but not as easily as babies can. One reason seems to be that very young children do not treat the

auditory cues as "sound" but rather as basic information about the world. For them, auditory and visual information seems to be essentially interchangeable. In contrast, it appears that by the time children are a year old, they have already learned to differentiate between their senses. These toddlers seem to treat the sound as a property of the object itself rather than as raw information about the object's location and characteristics. For example, older children and adults sometimes hold the objects up to their ears to "listen" to them.

Sensory substitution systems promise important practical benefits for people with sensory deficits, and there could also be applications for improving sensory capabilities among other users, such as military personnel. Research in this area may also provide insights into factors affecting the development of auditory localization skills.

Antinoise Devices

It is estimated that more than 9 million American workers are exposed to haz-

ardous noise levels on the job. As we have already learned, exposure to loud noise can have damaging physical effects, including hearing loss. Noise is also a psychological stressor that negatively affects mood and task performance (Cohen & others, 1986; Stokols, 1992). Industrial psychologists and engineers have recently collaborated to develop an **antinoise** device that could have enormous practical value.

Noise is produced by sound waves that have specific wave frequencies and amplitudes. New antinoise devices are based on a simple principle: sound waves can be canceled out by other waves that are their mirror image, that are 180 degrees out of phase (see Figure 6.28). The antinoise devices have a microphone that picks up the offending sound wave, a minicomputer that analyzes the sound's frequency and amplitude, and a speaker system that instantaneously generates the sound's mirror image, thereby canceling it out. The result is a deadening of the sound. Sounds that the system wants to preserve, such as alarm bells or human voices, can be subtracted at the beginning of the process and added at the end (Elmer-DeWitt, 1989).

Antinoise devices counteract the destructive effects that noise has on physical and psychological well-being. In antinoise technology, as well as in the development of sensory substitution systems like the Sonicguide, we see how knowledge of basic sensory processes can be applied to promote human welfare and enhance performance.

The Chemical Senses

Taste and smell are termed chemical senses because their receptors are sensitive to chemical substances rather than to some form of energy or pressure. Humans are visually oriented creatures, but the chemical sense of smell (olfaction) is of great importance for many species. Bloodhounds, for example, have rather poor eyesight but an exquisitely developed olfactory sense that is thought to be about 2 million times more sensitive than ours (Thomas, 1974). A bloodhound can detect a person's scent in a footprint that is 4 days old. For humans, vision and audition are more important; our chemical senses are far less developed than are those of animals who depend heavily on them for survival.

People who fancy themselves to be gourmets are frequently surprised to learn that their sense of taste responds to only four qualities: sweet, sour, salty, and bitter. Every other taste experience is composed of a combination of these qualities and those of other senses, such as smell, temperature, and touch. Part of the experience of eating popcorn, for example, includes sensations of its texture, its crunchiness, and its odor.

Taste

The stimuli for taste are a variety of chemical substances that come into contact with sensory receptors in the mouth. These receptors, known as **taste buds,** are concentrated along the edges and back surface of the tongue. Humans have about 9,000 taste buds, each one consisting of several receptor cells arranged like the segments of an orange (see Figure 6.29). Hairlike structures project from the top of each cell into the taste pore, an opening to the outside surface of the tongue. When a substance is taken into the mouth, it interacts with saliva to form a chemical solution that flows into the taste pore and stimulates the receptor cells.

Olfaction

The stimuli for olfaction are also chemical molecules. This is why it is sometimes difficult to determine whether we are tasting or smelling something. Both chemical senses are undoubtedly involved in our enjoyment of a good meal or our dissatisfaction with a bad one. Remember how tasteless your meals seemed the last time you had a bad cold?

The receptors for smell are long cells that project through the lining of the upper part of the nasal cavity and into the mucous membrane. Our ability to discriminate among different odors is not well understood. One theory suggests that specifically shaped odor molecules fit into receptor slots like keys into locks (Levine & Shefner, 1991). Each odor then results in a particular pattern of firing among the neurons in the olfactory system, much as colors are mixed in an artist's palette. A competing theory is that olfactory receptors recognize odors individually rather than by mixing the activity of a smaller number of basic receptors. This is possible because a huge family of genes produce individual receptor proteins that can recognize any of the thousands of potential odor molecules (Buck & Axel, 1991). Further research is needed to determine which of these theories is more accurate.

Compared with vision and audition, olfaction's relation to human behavior has received much less attention. Some interesting discoveries are being made about our sense of smell, however, and findings suggest that perhaps we are led by the nose more than we realize. For example, recent research suggests the possible importance of olfaction in regulating sexual behavior.

Pheromones and Sexuality. There is considerable evidence that the sexual behavior of animals is heavily regulated by olfaction (Duvall & Silverstein, 1986),

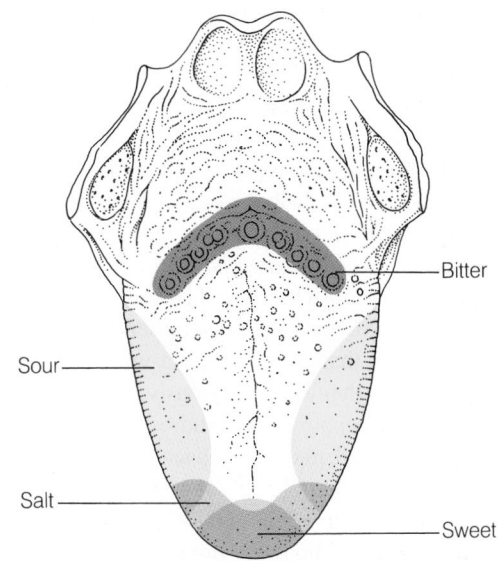

◀ **Figure 6.29** *The receptors for taste are specialized cells located in the tongue's taste buds. The taste buds are grouped in different areas according to the taste sensation they produce. The center of the tongue is relatively insensitive to taste qualities.*

as anyone who has owned a female dog or cat in heat could tell you. A huge cosmetics industry tries to convince us that we will increase our sexual attractiveness by smelling like limes, roses, and pine trees, and we do our best to camouflage natural body odors with deodorants and perfumes. The potential role of natural body odors in governing human sexual behavior has been largely ignored, but recent findings suggest that natural body scents produced by secreted substances known as **pheromones** may affect our sexual functioning at both a physiological and a behavioral level.

One interesting but puzzling observation was that women who live together or are close friends tend to have similar menstrual cycles. Psychologist Martha McClintock (1971) confirmed this informal observation in an early study. She tested 135 college women and found that during the course of an academic year, roommates moved from a mean of 8.5 days apart in their periods to 4.9 days apart. But why? Is it possible, McClintock asked, that the synchronizing factor is body odors?

Experiments carried out at the Monell Chemical Senses Center in Philadelphia have provided evidence that pheromones do indeed mediate menstrual synchrony. Ten women with regular cycles were daubed under the nose every few days with underarm secretions collected from other women. After 3 months, the subjects' cycles began to coincide with the sweat donors' cycles. A control group of women who were daubed with an alcohol solution rather than sweat showed no menstrual synchrony with a partner (Preti & others, 1986).

The Monell researchers have also linked pheromones to another menstrual phenomenon. Prompted by findings that females who regularly engage in sexual activity with males are more likely to have regular menstrual cycles, a study was conducted with college women who had abnormal cycles. In a double-blind experiment in which neither the subjects nor the experimenters were aware of the substance received, women in the experimental condition were daubed under the nose with male underarm secretions mixed with alcohol, whereas women in the control condition were daubed with alcohol alone. Over a 14-week period, the cycles in women exposed to the male pheromones sped up or slowed down to approach an average 28-day one. The control subjects continued to have irregular cycles (Cutler & others, 1986).

It appears that some men and women are emotionally and behaviorally responsive to pheromones secreted by the opposite sex. Androstenol, a substance secreted by adult males, has been the subject of research conducted by Victor Johnson (1985). Johnson measured the brain waves of male and female subjects as they viewed slides of same- and opposite-sex models. Of particular interest to Johnson was a brain-wave pattern known as P3, which appears to be related to positive emotional responses. The subjects were told that their respiration was being measured through a small tube under their noses. Actually, the tube contained a cotton swab saturated either with an alcohol solution containing androstenol or with alcohol alone. Johnson found that the P3 responses of female subjects were higher when they viewed slides of males when breathing androstenol than when breathing alcohol alone. Male P3 responses to slides of females were also highest in the presence of androstenol. Johnson suggests that body odors produced by certain pheromones may affect emotional responses to potential sexual stimuli. He also suggests that body hair and beards in males may help retain the odors produced by such secretions.

Pheromones known as **copulins** are secreted in the vagina, with peak secretions believed to occur during ovulation (Keverne, 1977). In an experiment involving 62 married couples, the wives were asked to apply one of four perfumes to their chests each night at bedtime according to a predetermined random schedule. The couples were unaware that one of the perfumes contained copulins. Each morning the couples completed questionnaires about their sexual behavior during the previous evening. The investigators found that the sexual responsiveness of 12 of the 62 couples was apparently affected by the copulins. These couples showed increases in sexual activity on the nights that the women wore copulins, and peak sexual activity occurred during the ovulation phase of the women's cycles (Morris & Udry, 1978). The fact that some couples, but not others, showed changes in their sexual behavior suggests that there are individual differences in sensitivity and/or responsiveness to copulins. If so, the reasons for these differences could be an interesting topic for future research.

The Skin and Body Senses

The skin and body senses include the senses of touch, kinesthesis, and equilibrium. The last two are called body senses because they inform us of the body's position and movement. They tell us, for example, if we are running or standing still, lying down or sitting up.

The Skin Senses

Touch is important to us in many ways. Sensitivity to extreme temperatures and to pain not only enables us to avoid external danger but also alerts us to disorders within our bodies. In addition, tactile sensations are a source of many of life's pleasures.

Humans are sensitive to at least four tactile sensations: pressure or touch, pain, warmth, and cold.

These sensations are conveyed by receptors in the skin and in our internal organs. Mixtures of these four sensations form the basis for all other common skin sensations, such as itch.

Considering the importance of our skin senses, surprisingly little is known about how they work. Although it is known that the skin contains a number of receptor structures, it has not been possible to find consistent relationships between all of the structures and specific sensations. It has been established that the primary receptors for pain are *free nerve endings* that terminate in the skin, and that nerve fibers situated at the base of hair follicles are receptors for touch and light pressure (Heller & Schiff, 1991). It is also known that there are "warm" and "cold" spots on the skin and that their simultaneous activation results in the sensation of warmth if they are stimulated for a sufficient length of time (See Figure 6.30).

The brain can locate sensations because, as noted in Chapter 3, skin receptors send their messages to the point in the sensory cortex that corresponds to the area of the body where the receptor is located. People who have had arms or legs amputated sometimes experience a *phantom limb* phenomenon, in which they feel vivid sensations coming from the missing limb (Warga, 1987). Apparently, an irritation of the nerves that used to originate in the limb fools the brain into interpreting the impulses as real sensations. The experience can be quite maddening. Imagine having an intense itch that you never can scratch! Even more disturbing, Joel Katz and Ronald Melzack (1990) studied 68 amputees who insisted that they experienced pain from the amputated limb that was vivid and immediate and not merely a recollection of what pain used to feel like in the phantom limb.

The Body Senses

We would be totally unable to coordinate our body movements if we did not receive constant feedback about our muscles' and joints' positions and movements. The sense of **kinesthesis,** or body movement, functions by means of nerve endings in the muscles, tendons, and joints. The information this sense gives us is the basis for making corrective movements (see Figure 6.31).

Cooperating with kinesthesis is the **vestibular sense**—the sense of body orientation or equilibrium. Those of us who have experienced seasickness, vertigo, or dizziness from an amusement park ride have encountered the vestibular sense's effort to tell us which end is up when neither end will stay still.

The sense organs for equilibrium are located in the **vestibular apparatus** of the inner ear (refer back to Figure 6.24). One part of the equilibrium system consists of three **semicircular canals,** each in a dif-

Figure 6.30 *This man has learned that due to the poor heat conductivity of wood coals, a quick walk across the embers will not result in the sensory and physical consequences of burning because the skin is in contact with the coals for only a fraction of a second.*

Figure 6.31 *A well-developed kinesthetic sense provides the feedback needed to execute a complex motor skill.*

ferent plane: left/right, backward/forward, or up/down. These canals are filled with fluid and lined with hairlike cells that function as receptors. When the head moves, the fluid in the appropriate canal shifts, stimulating the hair cells and firing associated neural fibers. The semicircular canals respond only to acceleration and deceleration. When a constant speed is reached (no matter how high), the fluid and the hair cells return to their normal resting state. That's why takeoffs and landings give a sense of movement, whereas flying at 500 mph on a cruising airliner doesn't.

The *vestibular sacs,* located at the base of the semicircular canals, compose the second part of the body-sense system. These structures, which are also lined with hair cells, respond to the position of the resting body and tell us whether we are upright or tilted at an angle.

Sensory Processing Without Awareness

Research in sensory psychology is concerned with the complex processes that occur when physical stimuli reach our sensory receptors, are translated into the language of nerve impulses, and are routed to the brain. Whether or not a particular stimulus results in a sensory experience depends on what occurs at numerous points in the nervous system. Many sensory messages may "register" at some level of the nervous system without crossing the threshold of awareness. Can such stimuli influence our thoughts, feelings, and behavior? The Psychobiological Interactions feature highlights this question's scientific and practical implications.

PSYCHOBIOLOGICAL INTERACTIONS

Can Subliminal Stimuli Influence Behavior?

United Nations (UPI). Satellites orbiting the earth can beam messages directly to television sets in viewers' homes to brainwash people without their even knowing it, according to a United Nations report.

By sending out so-called subliminal messages that are recorded only in viewers' subconscious, the technique can be used to mass-hypnotize and influence politics of other countries, the report said (November 4, 1974).

Certain stimuli are so weak or brief that, although they are received by the senses, they cannot be perceived consciously because they are below the perceptual threshold, or *limen.* The effect of these subliminal stimuli has been a matter of great controversy in psychology. Research has shown that the nervous system can indeed process incoming information "preconsciously"—that is, without our conscious awareness of it (Kihlstrom, 1990; Greenwald, 1992; Mandler & Nakamura, 1987). But can such stimuli affect behavior without our knowing it? The answer appears to be yes—to some extent. Let us consider some scientific evidence for subconscious perception.

A series of studies performed by Robert Zajonc and his University of Michigan coworkers showed that the more frequently subjects were exposed to stimuli—be they geometric shapes, faces, or other stimuli—the more subjects grew to like them (Zajonc, 1980). In the initial studies, the stimuli were presented for several seconds and subjects could see them clearly. What would happen if the stimuli were presented so briefly that subjects could see only flashes of light? The re-

sult, as reported in several recent studies, was pretty much the same. Whether the stimuli were geometric shapes or pictures of faces, those images presented subliminally a greater number of times were rated as being more likeable later on (Bornstein & others, 1987; Zajonc, 1984). In a more recent study, Jon Krosnick (1992) showed subjects nine slides of a particular person and then measured their attitudes toward the target person. For half of the subjects, each photograph was immediately preceded by an unpleasant picture (for example, a face on fire) that was presented subliminally. The remaining subjects saw pleasant subliminal stimuli, such as smiling babies. Subjects who were shown the unpleasant subliminal stimuli expressed more negative attitudes toward the target person than did those who saw the positive subliminal stimuli.

We might have anticipated such results by looking at findings from an earlier study. Sheldon Bach & George Klein (1957) showed subjects slides of people's faces and, at the same time, subliminally flashed the word "sad" or "happy." Later, when subjects were asked to rate the faces they had seen, those faces associated with "happy" were rated as being happier than those linked with "sad."

Perhaps inspired by these findings, James Vicary, a public-relations executive, arranged to have subliminal messages flashed on a theater screen during a movie shown in the late 1950s. These "secret" messages urged the audience to "drink Coca-Cola" and "eat popcorn." Vicary claimed that the subliminal messages increased popcorn sales by 50 percent and soft drink sales by 18 percent. Naturally, his claims aroused a public furor. Consumers and scientists worried about the possible abuse of subliminal messages for mind control and brainwashing. Advertising agencies and manufacturers gleefully foresaw an opportunity to have a more direct influence on the buying habits of millions of Americans. The National Association of Broadcasters reacted by outlawing subliminal messages on American television. Ironically, Vicary admitted years later that his study was a hoax designed to revive his foundering advertising agency. Nonetheless, his report stimulated a great deal of interest in subliminal stimuli and their possible ability to influence behavior.

The important issue, of course, is whether or not subliminal stimuli can affect people's subsequent actions to an extent that would be a cause for alarm. Numerous studies conducted in laboratories, on television and radio, and in movie theaters indicate that behavior is not profoundly influenced by subliminal stimuli. Attempts to reproduce Vicary's results under controlled conditions have ended in failure. After research had been conducted over many years, psychologist Norman Dixon (1981) reviewed the evidence concerning subliminal stimulation. He concluded that although some behaviors can be influenced in subtle ways, there is little reason to be seriously concerned about significant or widespread control of behavior through subliminal stimulation. Persuasive stimuli *above* the perceptual threshold appear to be far more influential, perhaps because we are more certain to get the total message.

Subliminal Self-Help Materials

Thus far, we have discussed the use of subliminal messages to influence behavior involuntarily. More frequently, however, individuals use subliminal materials in an effort to change their behavior or increase their abilities in various ways. In 1987 alone, American consumers spent an estimated $50 million on subliminal tapes intended to help them lose weight, gain self-confidence, stop smoking, make friends, conquer fears, and reach other personal-improvement goals (Natale, 1988). More than 200 companies in the United States and Canada currently market subliminal self-help materials (Oldenburg, 1990).

Most subliminal tapes are represented as providing below-threshold suggestions or affirmations (for example, "Stop smoking" or "You are no longer afraid of public speaking") that program the "powerful unconscious mind" in desirable ways.

However, when one investigator subjected subliminal tapes produced by four leading vendors to spectograms (or voice prints), none showed any signs of hidden speech (Merickle, 1988). Yet, many people who had used these tapes claimed that they had benefited from them. Why?

One possibility is that if people expect a desirable change to occur as a result of using subliminal tapes, their expectation alone might mobilize behavior change. To test this possibility, Anthony Greenwald and his coworkers (1991) conducted an experimental test of commercially produced subliminal tapes purporting either to increase self-esteem or improve memory. Through newspaper advertisements, the researchers recruited subjects who wanted to improve in these areas and pretested them for their level of self-esteem and their memory abilities. They then gave the subjects a subliminal tape to use daily for a month. At the end of the month, the subjects were retested for self-esteem and memory.

The experimental manipulation was the label on the tape. Half of the subjects who were given the tape labeled "self-esteem improvement" actually received the memory-improvement tape, and half of those who were given the tape labeled "memory improvement" actually got the self-esteem tape. The researchers reasoned that if the subliminal tapes were effective, the subjects should show improvement in the area that was targeted by the tape they actually received. If expectancy effects were at work, the subjects should show greater change in the area they thought they were improving with the tape.

Overall, the subjects improved significantly in *both* self-esteem and memory. As Figure 6.32 shows, the subjects who thought they were listening to a self-esteem-improvement tape but were actually given the memory-improvement tape showed a larger increase in self-esteem than did subjects who actually listened to the self-esteem tape. In the case of memory improvement, those who listened to the self-esteem tape did slightly better than those actually given the memory tape. Overall, the positive changes in self-esteem and memory that did occur seem attributable to a general expectancy or placebo effect that had nothing to do with the actual content of the subliminal tape.

At the request of the U.S. Army Research Institute, a panel of distinguished psychologists reviewed the scientific evidence concerning subliminal self-help materials. On the basis of their review, the committee concluded the following:

> But one cannot and should not assume that long-term changes in complex actions, cognitions, or emotions—such as smoking, self-confidence, or depression—can be affected by exposure to sublim-

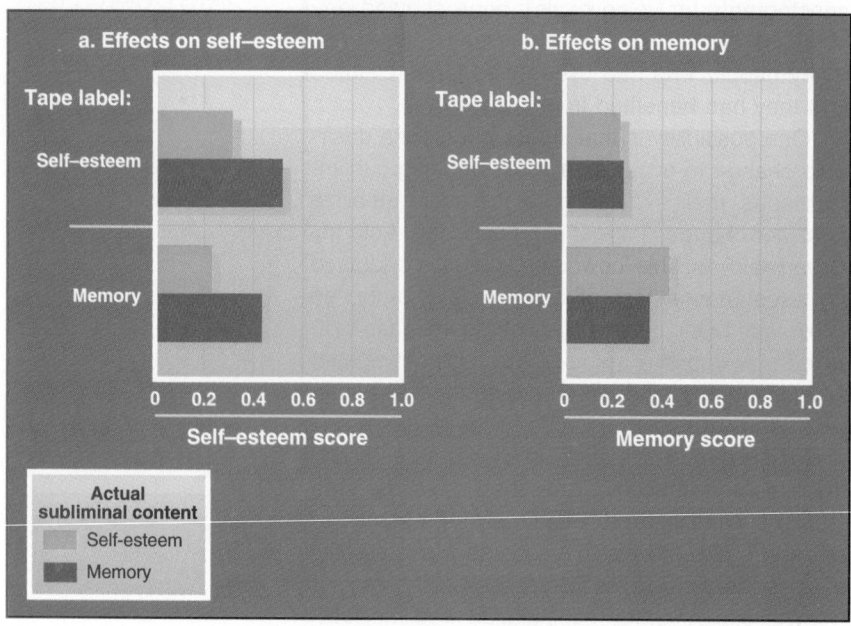

inal suggestions under such varied real-life circumstances as reading, relaxing, or even sleeping. Such effects, if any, remain to be conclusively established or rigorously explored (Eich & Hyman, 1991, p. 116).

Today, some people are concerned about the possibility that young people might be influenced by subliminal messages embedded in rock music. Although current evidence does not indicate persuasive effects from subliminal auditory messages, not much is known about the effects of long-term repeated exposure, as might occur if a person listened to the same message over and over for months or even years. Although subliminal stimulation has been the focus of research for more than 3 decades, some questions still need to be explored.

◆ **Figure 6.32** *The effects of subliminal self-help tapes on self-esteem and memory are shown. Subjects who were given a tape labeled as either self-esteem or memory improvement, but who actually received the opposite tape, improved as much or more than subjects whose subliminal tape actually corresponded to the label. (Greenwald & others, 1991).*

Cognitive and Psychodynamic Factors Affecting Sensation

Although we might be tempted to view sensation as a purely biological process in which specialized receptors respond to specific types of environmental energy, psychological factors also play a role. Our previous discussion of signal detection theory has shown us that cognitive factors, such as knowledge of the consequences that will follow a correct or incorrect judgment, can strongly affect sensory thresholds. Other cognitive factors, such as the importance attached to a particular stimulus and the expectation that the stimulus will occur, can also affect sensory capabilities.

Psychodynamic factors can produce some startling alterations of sensory capabilities. For example, in certain *somatoform disorders* (to be discussed in Chapter 16), sensory problems without any underlying organic cause may appear as a means of coping with unconscious conflicts or fears. For example, during World War II, some bomber pilots suddenly developed blindness. Physical examination revealed that their eyes were healthy; the blindness was being

produced further up in the visual system. Psychological factors were suspected because pilots who flew night bombing missions developed night blindness, whereas those who flew during the day developed day blindness (Ironside & Batchelor, 1945).

Another classic sensory disorder produced by psychodynamic factors is the so-called *glove anesthesia* observed by Sigmund Freud and other psychoanalysts. In this disorder, the patient reports a complete loss of feeling in the hand up to the wrist. As shown in Figure 6.33, this pattern of insensitivity is anatomically impossible, given what is known about the nerve pathways in the hand and arm. Psychodynamic psychotherapists have found glove anesthesia and other psychologically induced sensory disorders to be the products of psychological conflicts (for example, unconscious guilt feelings about masturbation). Such a disorder may disappear as quickly as it appeared once the patient consciously confronts and resolves the conflict or when changes in the environment (such as being relieved of combat flight duty) no longer makes it necessary (Holmes, 1990).

At any given time, we are aware of only a tiny portion of the millions of messages that are being sent out by our sensory receptors. Our sense organs do not select

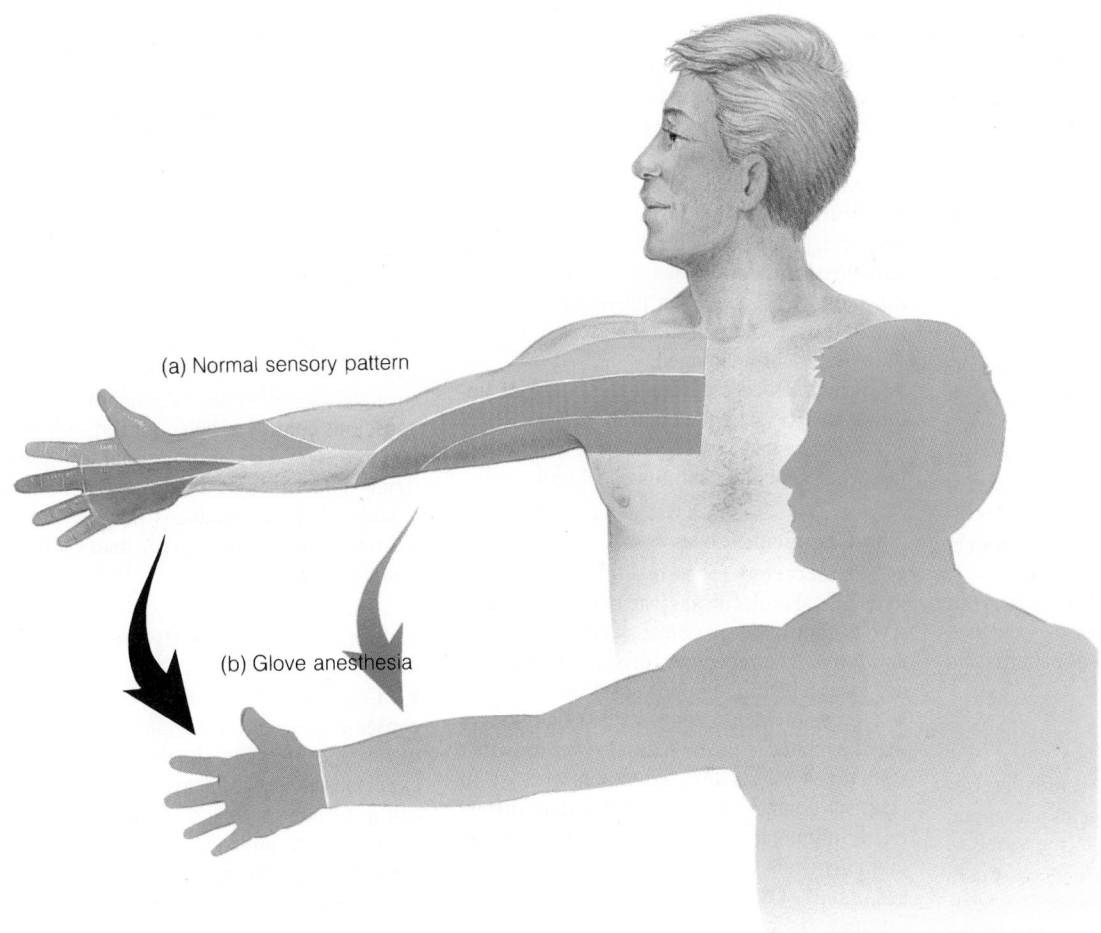

(a) Normal sensory pattern

(b) Glove anesthesia

Figure 6.33 *The skin areas served by nerves in the arm and shown in* (a) *make it anatomically impossible for the loss of sensation that characterizes a glove anesthesia, as seen in* (b). *Such a pattern of sensory loss indicates the influence of psychological factors.*

what we will be aware of or how we will experience it; they merely transmit as much information as they can through our nervous system. But sensory input is only the beginning of the story. Once in the nervous system, the stimuli are acted upon, processed, and transformed into perceptions. The fascinating process of perception, still barely understood, is affected by the biological features of the system, by the effects of learning, and by cognitive and intrapsychic factors. We explore these factors in the next chapter.

SUMMARY

Basic Principles of Sensation

● The principles of selectivity, adaptation, and comparison simplify sensory input, make it manageable, and permit us to respond to important changes in the environment.

The Study of Sensory Capabilities

● Psychophysics is the scientific study of how the physical properties of stimuli are related to sensory experiences. Sensory sensitivity is concerned with both the absolute threshold and the difference threshold. The absolute threshold is the intensity at which a stimulus is detected 50 percent of the time. Signal detection theory studies factors that influence decisions about whether or not a stimulus is present.

● The difference threshold (just noticeable difference, or jnd) is the amount by which two stimuli must differ in order for them to be perceived as different. Studies of the jnd led to Weber's law, which states that the jnd is proportional to the intensity of the original stimulus and is constant within a given sense modality.

● Electrical recording and scanning techniques provide important information about the development and functioning of the sensory systems.

The Sensory Systems

● The senses may be classified in terms of the energy to which they respond. These energy forms—electromagnetic, mechanical,

thermal, or chemical—are transformed into the common language of nerve impulses, a process called transduction.

Vision

● Light-sensitive visual receptor cells are located in the retina. The rods are brightness receptors and the less numerous cones are color receptors. Light energy striking the retina is converted into nerve impulses by chemical reactions in the photopigments of the rods and cones. Dark adaptation involves the gradual regeneration of photopigments that have been depleted by brighter illumination.

● The two classical color vision theories are the Young-Helmholtz trichromatic theory and Hering's opponent-process theory.

- Color vision appears to be a two-stage process involving both trichromatic and opponent-process components. The first stage involves the reactions of cones that are maximally sensitive to red, green, and blue wavelengths. In the second stage, color information from the cones is coded through an opponent-process mechanism further along in the visual system.

Integration of Visual Input

- The discovery of feature detectors in the nervous system has deepened our understanding about how sensory input may be processed and integrated. In the visual cortex, there are orientation columns (which respond to lines of particular orientations), ocular dominance columns, and hypercolumns (which are thought to be processing subunits).
- Recent research suggests that the nervous system responds to spatial frequencies and uses such input to create perception of patterns and objects.

Audition

- Sound waves have two characteristics: frequency, measured in terms of cycles per second or Hertzes (Hz), and amplitude, measured in terms of decibels. Frequency is related to pitch, amplitude to loudness. The receptors for hearing are hair cells in the organ of Corti of the inner ear.
- Loudness is coded in terms of the number and types of auditory nerve fibers that fire. Pitch is coded in two ways. Low-frequency tones are coded in terms of corresponding numbers of nerve impulses in individual receptors or of volleys of impulses from a number of receptors. Frequencies above 4,000 Hz are coded according to the region of the basilar membrane that is displaced most by the fluid wave in the cochlear canal.
- Hearing loss may result from conduction deafness, produced by problems involving the structures of the inner ear that transmit vibrations to the cochlea, or nerve deafness, in which the receptors of the inner ear or the auditory nerve are damaged.
- Principles derived from the study of audition have been applied in important practical advances such as sonic eyes for the blind and the development of antinoise techniques.

The Chemical Senses

- The receptors for taste and smell respond to chemical molecules. Taste buds are responsive to four basic qualities: sweet, sour, salty, and bitter. The receptors for smell (olfaction) are long cells in the upper nasal cavity.
- Recent evidence suggests that body odors may be related to the menstrual synchrony that sometimes occurs among women who are in frequent contact. There are individual differences in human sexual responsiveness to certain chemicals released in the urine or by the sex organs of the opposite sex. Human behavior may be influenced by olfactory stimuli more than was previously assumed.

The Skin and Body Senses

- The skin and body senses include touch, kinesthesis, and equilibrium. Receptors in the skin and body tissues are sensitive to touch, pain, warmth, and cold. These receptors send their messages to particular areas of the sensory cortex. Kinesthesis functions by means of nerve endings in the muscles, tendons, and joints. The sense organs for equilibrium are in the vestibular apparatus of the inner ear.

Sensory Processing without Awareness

- Research indicates that subliminal stimuli, which are not consciously perceived, can influence behavior in subtle ways, but not strongly enough to justify concerns about subconscious control of behavior through subliminal messages. Use of subliminal self-help materials sometimes results in positive behavior changes, but such changes may be produced by expectancy factors rather than by the subliminal messages.

Cognitive and Psychodynamic Factors Affecting Sensation

- Cognitive factors such as knowledge of the consequences of correct and incorrect judgments, the meaning attached to stimuli, and expectations about the appearance of stimuli, can influence sensory processes.
- Psychodynamic processes are evident in certain sensory-based somatoform disorders in which no organic damage to the sensory system is evident. In the case of glove anesthesia, the disorder is anatomically impossible.

KEY TERMS AND CONCEPTS

absolute threshold (p. 173)
additive color mixture (p. 180)
amplitude (p. 186)
antinoise (p. 190)
anvil (p. 186)
aqueous humor (p. 176)
basilar membrane (p. 186)
bipolar cells (p. 177)
blind spot (p. 178)
ciliary muscles (p. 176)
cochlea (p. 186)
conduction deafness (p. 188)
cones (p. 177)
copulins (p. 192)
cornea (p. 176)
cortical columns (p. 182)
dark adaptation (p. 179)
decibel (p. 186)
decision criterion (p. 173)

dichromat (p. 182)
difference threshold (jnd) (p. 174)
eardrum (p. 186)
feature detectors (p. 183)
fovea (p. 177)
frequency (p. 185)
frequency theory of pitch coding (p. 187)
ganglion cells (p. 177)
hammer (p. 186)
Hering's opponent-process theory (p. 181)
Hertz (Hz) (p. 185)
hypercolumns (p. 182)
hyperopia (p. 177)
iris (p. 176)
kinesthesis (p. 193)
lens (p. 176)
method of constant stimuli (p. 173)
monochromat (p. 182)
myopia (p. 176)

nanometer (p. 175)
nerve deafness (p. 188)
ocular dominance columns (p. 182)
opponent-process theory (*see* Hering's opponent-process theory)
optic nerve (p. 177)
organ of Corti (p. 186)
orientation columns (p. 182)
oval window (p. 186)
perception (p. 170)
pheromones (p. 192)
photopigments (p. 178)
place theory of pitch coding (p. 187)
psychophysics (p. 172)
pupil (p. 176)
retina (p. 176)
rods (p. 177)
semicircular canals (p. 193)
sensation (p. 170)

sensory adaptation (p. 171)
signal detection theory (p. 173)
spatial frequency filters (p. 184)
spatial frequency model (p. 184)
stirrup (p. 186)
synesthesia (p. 170)

taste bud (p. 191)
tectorial membrane (p. 186)
transduction (p. 175)
trichromat (p. 182)
vestibular apparatus (p. 193)
vestibular sense (p. 193)

visual acuity (p. 178)
vitreous humor (p. 176)
Weber's law (p. 174)
Young-Helmholtz trichromatic
  theory (p. 180)

SUGGESTED READINGS

Frisby, J. P. (1980). *Seeing: Illusion, brain, and mind.* Oxford, England: Oxford University Press. A fascinating and beautifully illustrated introduction to the visual system.

Gregory, R. L. (1978). *Eye and brain: The psychology of seeing* (3rd ed.). New York: McGraw-Hill. A classic popular introduction to vision and its psychological determinants.

Levine, M W. & Shefner, J. M. (1992). *Fundamentals of sensation and perception* (2nd ed.). Pacific Grove, CA: Brooks/Cole. A readable and comprehensive overview of all the senses.

7 Perception

The date: July 3, 1988. The place: The Persian Gulf off the coast of Iran. A Navy warship, the USS *Vincennes,* is engaged in a pitched battle with several speedy Iranian gunboats. In the midst of the battle, the *Vincennes'* highly advanced radar system detects an aircraft taking off from a military/civilian airfield in Iran and heading straight toward the American vessel. The plane is identified as an Iranian F-14 fighter, known to carry lethal air-to-surface missiles similar to those used in an earlier attack on the USS *Stark* which killed 37 crewmen. Repeated requests to the plane to identify itself yield no response. Soon, the ship's Combat Information Center warns that the plane is descending toward the *Vincennes,* a pattern consistent with an impending attack. The plane is now only 10 miles from the ship and, according to the crewman watching its progress on radar, still descending toward the *Vincennes.* A final warning receives no response, and Captain Will Rogers gives the command to fire on the plane. Two of the *Vincennes'* missiles streak into the sky. Moments later, all that remains of the plane is a shower of flaming debris.

The jubilation and relief of the *Vincennes'* crew was short-lived. Soon the awful truth was known: The plane they had shot down was not an attacking F-14 warplane. Instead, it was an Iranian commercial airliner carrying 290 passengers, all of whom died when the aircraft was blown from the sky. Moreover, videotape recordings of the electronic information that the crew of the Combat Information Center had used to identify the plane and its flight pattern showed conclusively that the aircraft was not an F-14 and that it had actually been *climbing* rather than descending toward the ship.

What had gone wrong? How could such a tragic error have been made by a well-trained and experienced crew with access to the world's most sophisticated radar information? That such an event could occur illustrates a key difference between sensation and perception. In this case, the sensory information provided by the radar system clearly showed that the plane was climbing. Yet the radar operator "saw" the plane diving toward the ship, and this perception resulted in the fateful decision to launch the missiles. At a Congressional hearing on the *Vincennes* incident, several prominent psychologists who study perception reconstructed the psychological environment that could have caused the radar operator's eyes to "lie."

Clearly, the situation was a stressful and dangerous one. The *Vincennes* was already under attack by Iranian gunboats, and other attacks could reasonably be expected. It was easy for the radar operator, observing a plane taking off from a military field and heading in the direction of the ship, to interpret this as the possible prelude to an air attack. The determination of the *Vincennes'* crew to avoid what had happened in the air attack on the USS *Stark* had produced a high level of vigilance to any stimuli that

suggested an impending attack. Fear and expectation thus created a certain psychological context within which the sensory input from the computer system was interpreted. The perception that the aircraft was a warplane and that it was descending toward the ship was consistent with the crew's expectations and fears, and it became the "reality" that they experienced. They had a **perceptual set**—a readiness to perceive stimuli in a particular way (see Figure 7.1).

The psychologists also presented scientific findings showing that under stress, people often place great confidence in their immediate judgments and those of others, and that these judgments resist change even in the face of conflicting sensory information. This factor could account for the crewman's continued perception that the plane was descending in the face of contradictory radar data, as well as the failure of other members of the Combat Information Center to check the computer records that would have shown them that the plane was actually climbing.

The *Vincennes* incident, as well as our own experiences, tell us that perception is not the same thing as reality. The brains of two different people may experience the same sensory information in radically different ways. Our experiences are not simply a one-to-one reflection of what is "out there." Rather, **perception** is an active, creative process in which raw sensory data are coded into the electrical language of the nervous system, organized, and given meanings derived from our unique personal experiences.

We know quite a bit more about how our sensory systems function than about how the real world and our perceptions of it are linked. As we shall see, a variety of factors influence the personal reality that

◆ **Figure 7.1** *The* Vincennes *incident in the Persian Gulf indicated how easily false perceptions can be created by psychological factors.*

we construct through our perceptions. The physical characteristics of stimuli are only one of those factors. Others are biological; they are built into our nervous systems. Still others result from our learning experiences. And, as the *Vincennes* affair demonstrates, what we perceive is also influenced by our expectations, our emotions, and our needs.

Attention as a Selective Process

As you read these words, 100 million sensory messages may be clamoring for your attention. Only a few of these messages register in awareness; the rest you perceive either dimly or not at all. But you can shift your attention to one of those "unregistered" stimuli at any time. (For example, how does the big toe of your right foot feel right now?) Attention, then, involves two processes of selection: (1) focusing on certain stimuli and (2) filtering out other incoming information (van der Heijden, 1991).

Attentional Shifts

The selective nature of attention is evident in many situations. Imagine that you are at a party having an interesting conversation with a group of your friends. Other people are talking nearby, but you are almost unaware of them until you hear someone in a group across the room mention your name. This meaningful

stimulus filters through, despite your inattention to the rest of the partygoers. You quickly shift part of your attention to the group across the room while trying at the same time to listen to what the person you have been talking to is saying.

This "cocktail party phenomenon" has been studied experimentally through a technique called **shadowing.** People wearing earphones listen simultaneously to two messages, one through each earphone. They are asked to repeat (or "shadow") one of the messages word for word as they listen. Most subjects can do this quite successfully, but only at the cost of not remembering what the other message was about. People can also shift their attention rapidly back and forth between the two messages, trying to attend to bits of each and drawing on their general knowledge of the English language and the subject matter in the messages to fill in the gaps. The results of these shadowing experiments have demonstrated conclusively that we cannot attend completely to more than one thing at a time but that we can shift our attention back and forth rapidly enough to get the sense of two different messages (Sperling, 1984).

Attention is strongly affected by both the nature of the stimulus and personal factors. Stimulus characteristics that attract our attention are intensity, novelty, movement, contrast, and repetition. Advertisers use these properties in their commercials and packaging, and they also appeal to our personal interests and motives (see Figure 7.2).

Personal Factors in Perception

Internal motivational and personality factors act as filters to help determine which stimuli in our environment we will notice. Motives and interests are very powerful filters. For example, when we are hungry, we are especially sensitive to food-related cues, such as those familiar golden arches. Our interests function in the same way. A botanist walking through a park is especially attentive to the plants; a landscape architect attends primarily to the layout of the park; a hungry person may take special note of the aroma coming from a nearby restaurant.

Perceptual Vigilance

As we saw earlier, the crew of the *Vincennes* had a perceptual set that made them highly attentive to signs of danger, and they quickly interpreted sensory input from their radar as an impending attack. Similarly, a person who has narrowly escaped from a fire may become very sensitive to the smell of smoke. People (as well as other organisms) appear to be especially attentive to stimuli that might represent a threat to their well-being. Some theorists believe that the perceptual system scans incoming stimuli and quickly

Figure 7.2 *Advertisers are adept at using attention-attracting stimulus characteristics. In this advertisement, we see the use of an unusual perspective that suggests the car is actually moving.*

locks in on those that could signal danger. Such a mechanism would clearly have biological survival value (Bargh, 1984; Izard, 1989).

Consider, for example, a study by Christine and Ranald Hansen (1988). They presented subjects with pictures showing groups of nine people. In half of the pictures, all of the people looked either angry or happy. In the other half, there was one discrepant face—either an angry face in a happy crowd or a happy face in an angry crowd. The subjects' task was to judge as quickly as possible whether there was a discrepant face in the crowd. The dependent variable was the length of time required to make this judgment, measured in milliseconds (thousandths of a second). The results, summarized in Figure 7.3, showed that subjects were much faster at detecting a single angry face in an otherwise happy crowd than at finding a happy face in an angry crowd. It was as if the angry face, which the experimenters assumed to have threat value, "jumped out" of the crowd when the stimuli were scanned.

Perceptual Defense

In some cases, the filtering process seems to serve a defensive function—to protect us from the anxiety that would be aroused if we allowed ourselves to perceive threatening stimuli. This phenomenon is known as **perceptual defense.**

Perceptual defense studies have been conducted since the late 1940s. In these studies, experimenters present slides of visual stimuli to subjects very briefly (for fractions of a second) by means of a projector-like instrument called a *tachistoscope* or present auditory stimuli very faintly through earphones. The subject's task is to report what, if anything, he or she saw or heard. The studies have shown that some people have higher thresholds (that is, require longer or louder exposures) for stimuli that are threatening or anxiety arousing than for emotionally neutral stimuli. Such stimuli may be words of a sexual or violent nature, or they may simply be meaningless stimuli (such as the syllable *bhx*) that have been paired with electric shock to condition fear responses to them. The use of these nonsense syllables would seem to rule out the possibility that the phenomenon is simply due to subjects' reluctance to report a word like *penis* to the experimenter unless they are *absolutely* sure they have seen or heard it (Erdelyi, 1988). Perhaps the most striking finding in these studies is that physiological indicators of anxiety, such as sweating palms and increases in heart rate, occur in response to these stimuli even when the subjects appear unable to consciously recognize them. This suggests that the anxiety-arousing stimuli are registering at an unconscious level (Greenwald, 1992; Kihlstrom, 1990; Kihlstrom & others, 1992). Perceptual defense studies

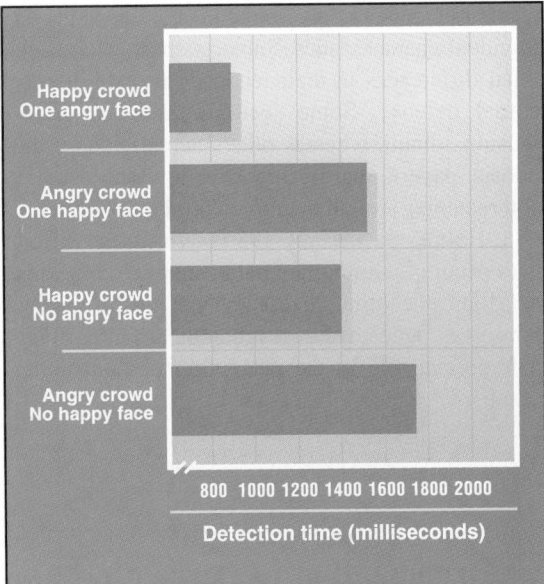

Figure 7.3 *Perceptual vigilance to threatening stimuli is exemplified in the finding that subjects required less time to detect an angry face in a happy crowd than to detect a happy face in an angry crowd or to determine if there was a discrepant face in a crowd that did not contain such faces. (Data from Hansen & Hansen, 1988).*

Happy crowd
One angry face

Angry crowd
One happy face

Happy crowd
No angry face

Angry crowd
No happy face

800 1000 1200 1400 1600 1800 2000

Detection time (milliseconds)

Figure 7.4 *Failing to see eye-to-eye, basketball coach Bobby Knight and two officials go jaw-to-jaw. Our personal needs can play a prominent role in perception.*

provide evidence that unconscious processing of sensory information may at times serve a defensive function (Kihlstrom, 1991).

Perceptual defense and perceptual vigilance might appear at first glance to be contradictory phenomena, but they actually can be part of the same process. Obviously, vigilance must occur first if the threatening stimuli are to be detected preconsciously.

Whether perceptual defense then occurs depends on individual characteristics. Subjects show wide individual differences in their tendency to exhibit perceptual defense. Some seem to avoid anxiety-arousing stimuli, whereas others actually show the opposite pattern; that is, they have lower thresholds for threatening stimuli than for neutral ones (Erdelyi, 1988; Holmes & McCaul, 1989). Why these differences occur is an important but unanswered question and a topic of continuing research, but the differences themselves indicate that psychological factors play an important role in the perception of threatening stimuli.

Patterning and Organization in Perception

The world we perceive is anything but random and meaningless to us. The bits of sensory information are somehow combined into a mosaic that we "know" or "understand." For example, have you ever stopped to wonder why we perceive the world as comprising distinct objects? After all, the retinal image is nothing but an array of varying intensities and frequencies of light. The rays coming from different parts of a single object have no more natural affinity for one another than those coming from two different objects. Yet we perceive scenes as involving separate objects, such as trees, mountains, and people. These perceptions, as noted, are not inherent in the picture focused on the retina; they are, instead, a product of an organization imposed by our nervous system. The process of perceptual organization occurs so automatically that we take it for granted. But Dr. Richard, a prominent psychologist who suffered brain damage in an accident, no longer does.

> The brain damage affected the ability of his brain to organize sensory input properly. There was nothing wrong with his eyes, yet the input he received from them was not put together correctly. Dr. Richard reported that if he saw a person, he sometimes would perceive the separate parts of the person as not belonging together in a single body. But if all the parts moved in the same direction, Dr. Richard then saw them as one complete person. At other times, he would perceive people in crowds wearing the same color clothes as "going together" rather than as separate people. The same thing might happen when several inanimate objects of the same color, such as an orange and a robin, appeared in his visual field at the same time, even if they were spatially separated from one another. He also had difficulty putting sights and sounds together. Sometimes, the movement of the lips did not correspond to the sounds he heard, as if he were watching a badly dubbed foreign movie. Dr. Richard's experience of his environment was thus disjointed and fragmented, quite unlike his experience before his accident affected the ability of his perceptual system to synthesize and organize his sensory input (Sacks, 1986, p. 76).

Although we may take perceptual organization for granted, psychologists interested in perception do not. Much theory and research have been directed at understanding the mysterious process by which sensory nonsense becomes perceptual sense. We now turn to the principles that govern the construction of perceptions.

Gestalt Principles of Perceptual Organization

Long before the discovery of feature detectors and cortical hypercolumns, the German school of Gestalt psychology addressed the basic question of how we organize the separate parts of our perceptual field into a unified and meaningful whole. As noted in Chapter 1, *gestalt* is the German term for pattern, shape, or configuration. The Gestalt psychologists argued that the whole is greater than (and frequently different from) the sum of its parts and attempted to discover the principles of perceptual organization that make it so.

The Gestalt theorists emphasized the importance of **figure-ground relations.** We tend to organize stimuli into a central, or foreground, figure and a background. In vision, the central figure is usually in front of or on top of what we perceive as background. It has a distinct shape and is more striking in our perceptions and memory than the background. The background flows around the shape of the figure; it has no edges of its own. We see contours wherever there is a distinct change in the color or brightness of the background, but we interpret these contours as part of the figure rather than part of the background. At times, separating figure from ground can be a challenging task, as in Bev Doolittle's *Pinto,* shown in Figure 7.5, yet our perceptual systems are usually equal to the task.

Consider the drawing in Figure 7.6. It is known as a reversible figure, because it can be seen in two equally plausible ways. If you examine it for awhile, two different perceptions will emerge. But whichever way you see the stimulus, the contour is always part of the figure, not the background. This same principle of figure and ground operates in relation to auditory stimuli: Most music is heard as a melody (figure) surrounded by other chords or harmonies (ground).

In addition to figure–ground relations, the Gestalt psychologists were also interested in how separate stimuli come to be perceived as parts of larger wholes.

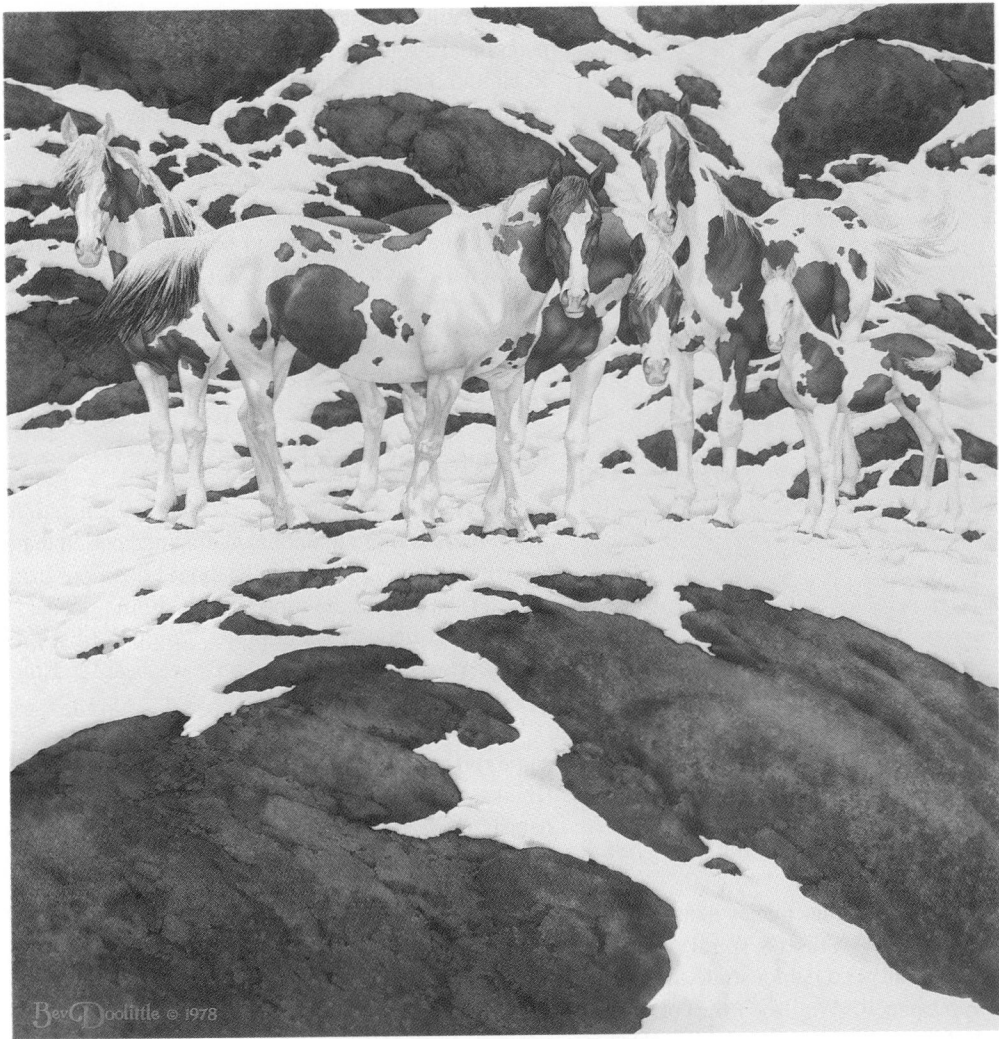

Figure 7.5 *The artist has created great similarity between figure and ground in this representation of natural camouflage, yet enough figural cues remain to permit most people to detect the ponies. (Source:* Pintos, *Bev Doolittle, 1979. The Greenwich Workshop, Trumbull, Conn.).*

They suggested that people group and interpret stimuli in accordance with four laws of perceptual organization: similarity, proximity, closure, and continuity. These organizing principles are illustrated in Figure 7.7.

The law of **similarity** states that when parts of a configuration are perceived as similar, they will be perceived as belonging together. For example, most people immediately perceive the dots in Figure 7.7*a* as two triangles formed by different-sized circles. The law of **proximity** says that elements that are near each other are likely to be perceived as part of the same configuration. Thus, most people perceive Figure 7.7*a* as three sets of lines rather than as six separate lines. The law of **closure,** also illustrated in Figure 7.7*a*, states that people tend to close the open edges of a figure or fill in gaps in an incomplete figure, so that what they see is more complete than what is actually there. Finally, the law of **continuity** holds that people link individual elements so they form a

Figure 7.6 *Figure–ground relations are demonstrated by this reversible figure, which can be seen in two different ways. Whichever percept exists at the moment is seen as figure against background.*

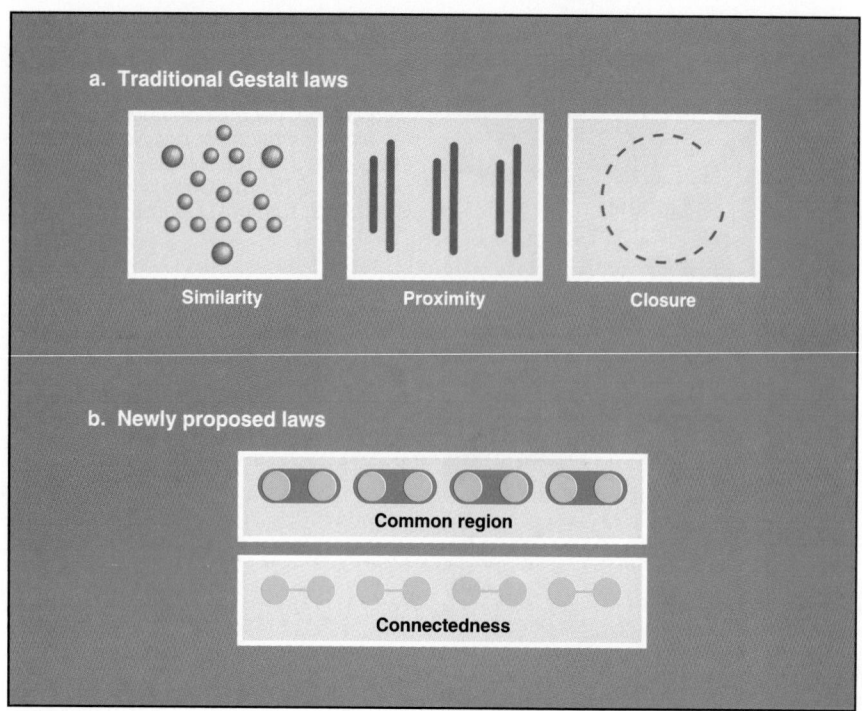

a. Traditional Gestalt laws

Similarity

Proximity

Closure

b. Newly proposed laws

Common region

Connectedness

⬆ **Figure 7.7** *Among the Gestalt principles for perceptual organization are the laws of similarity, proximity, and closure, illustrated in (a). In (b), the newly proposed laws of common region and connectedness are shown. Each principle allows us to organize stimuli into "wholes" that are greater than the sums of their parts.*

Recently, two additions to the Gestalt laws of perceptual grouping have been suggested by Irvin Rock and Stephen Palmer (1990). **Common region** refers to the tendency to group elements that are located in the same perceived region (see Figure 7.7*b*). **Connectedness,** which may be the most elementary grouping principle of all, refers to the powerful tendency of the visual system to perceive any uniform, connected region, such as a dot, a line, or a more extended area, as a single unit. This law may explain why each element in all the other configurations shown in Figure 7.7 is seen as a single entity to begin with.

Perception as Hypothesis Testing

As the Gestalt principles of perceptual organization show, there is more to understanding perception than knowing the biological details about how input gets into the system and how pattern recognition occurs. We need to understand how we "know" what the scenes we see, the spoken words we hear, and the objects we feel really are.

Recognition of a stimulus implies that we have some sort of internal representation to compare it with (Banks & Krajicek, 1991). Classification of sensory data is made possible by the existence of complex information structures known as **perceptual schemas,** which contain the critical features of objects, events, and other perceptual phenomena (Wade & Swanston, 1991). For example, our schema for "woman" has many similarities with the schema for "man," yet the schemas also have critical differences that enable us to make an instantaneous perceptual judgment of a person's gender.

Some of these internal schemas must be inborn—"hard-wired" in the brain over the eons during which mammals have sensed certain features of the world—for some of our perceptual interpretations seem to be present at birth (Gibson, 1988). For example, newborns will turn their heads in the direction of a human voice but will not respond in this manner to an artificial sound. They will gaze longer at a drawing of a human face than at other patterns (Fantz, 1963). Such stimuli seem to have innate meaning for the infant. But many other schemas are products of experience and memory. They contain the critical elements necessary for identification of your Uncle Harry (and from all different angles, at that), the sound of a fire engine, and the feel of a softball. The features of incoming stimuli are matched with various internal representations until the best fit is established. The closer the fit between stimulus features and internal concept, the more confident we are in our perception (Rock, 1983).

Perception is, in this sense, a search for the best interpretation of sensory information we can arrive

continuous line or pattern that makes sense. To illustrate, Figure 7.8 shows Fraser's spiral, which is not really a spiral at all! (To demonstrate, trace one of the circles with a pencil.) We "see" the concentric circles as a spiral because, to our nervous systems, a spiral gives better continuity between individual elements than does a set of circles. The spiral is created by us, not by the stimulus.

▶ **Figure 7.8** *Fraser's spiral illustrates the Gestalt law of continuity. If you follow any part of the "spiral" with your finger, you will find that it is not a spiral at all but a series of concentric circles. The "spiral" is created by your nervous system because that perception is more consistent with continuity of the individual elements.*

at based on our knowledge and experience. According to Irvin Rock (1983), perception is an exercise in problem solving that requires intelligent activity on the part of the perceptual system. The problem is to make sense of stimulus input. Likening the process to the scientific enterprise, Richard L. Gregory (1966) suggested that each perception is essentially a hypothesis about the nature of the object or, more generally, the meaning of the sensory information. The perceptual system actively searches its gigantic library of internal schemas for the interpretation that best fits the sensory data. If we have only partial data, we are often able to fill in the missing information. For example, can you decode the following sentence to extract its meaning?: Wi_h y_ur gre_t sc_em_s, yo_ a_e bou_d to _e a suc_e_s in l_fe, s_art_ng w_th an A _n t_is c_urse. When you read, you can skim the page and, because you have learned a lot about the style of written language, you can make good predictions the words you expect to see. In fact, your perceptual expectancies may have caused you to automatically fill in the missing ''about'' in the previous sentence or to not even notice that it was missing.

An example of how effortlessly our perceptual systems build up descriptions or hypotheses that best fit the available evidence is found in the upside-down comic strips created by Gustave Verbeek in the early 1900s. The *Sunday New York Herald* told Verbeek that his comic strip had to be restricted to 6 panels.

Verbeek wanted 12 panels; so he ingeniously created 12-panel cartoons in only 6 panels by drawing pictures like that shown in Figure 7.9*a*. When you turn your book upside down, a bird story becomes a fish story! The point is that you do not simply see an upside-down version of the same picture, even though the physical stimuli remain exactly the same. You see a radically different picture.

Another example of how the same stimulus can give rise to different perceptions is the Necker cube, shown in Figure 7.9*b*. As you stare at the cube, you will find that it changes before your eyes. The front of the cube suddenly becomes the back, and it appears that the cube is being viewed from a different angle as your nervous system tries out a new perceptual hypothesis. This occurs because the sensory information provided by this stimulus fits two different internal representations, and there is not enough information to permanently rule out one of them in favor of the other.

Bottom-Up and Top-Down Processing

There are two basic approaches to processing sensory information. One way is to use what is called *bottom-up processing*. In this kind of processing, the individual elements of the stimulus are inspected and then combined to somehow reproduce what is sensed. The sensory system operates in a bottom-up fashion when its feature detectors and spatial frequency filters take

Figure 7.9 *Two examples of how the same stimulus can give rise to different perceptions are found in the comic strips of Gustave Verbeek* (a) *and the Necker cube* (b). *To produce the reversals, turn the comic strip panel upside down and stare at the cube.*

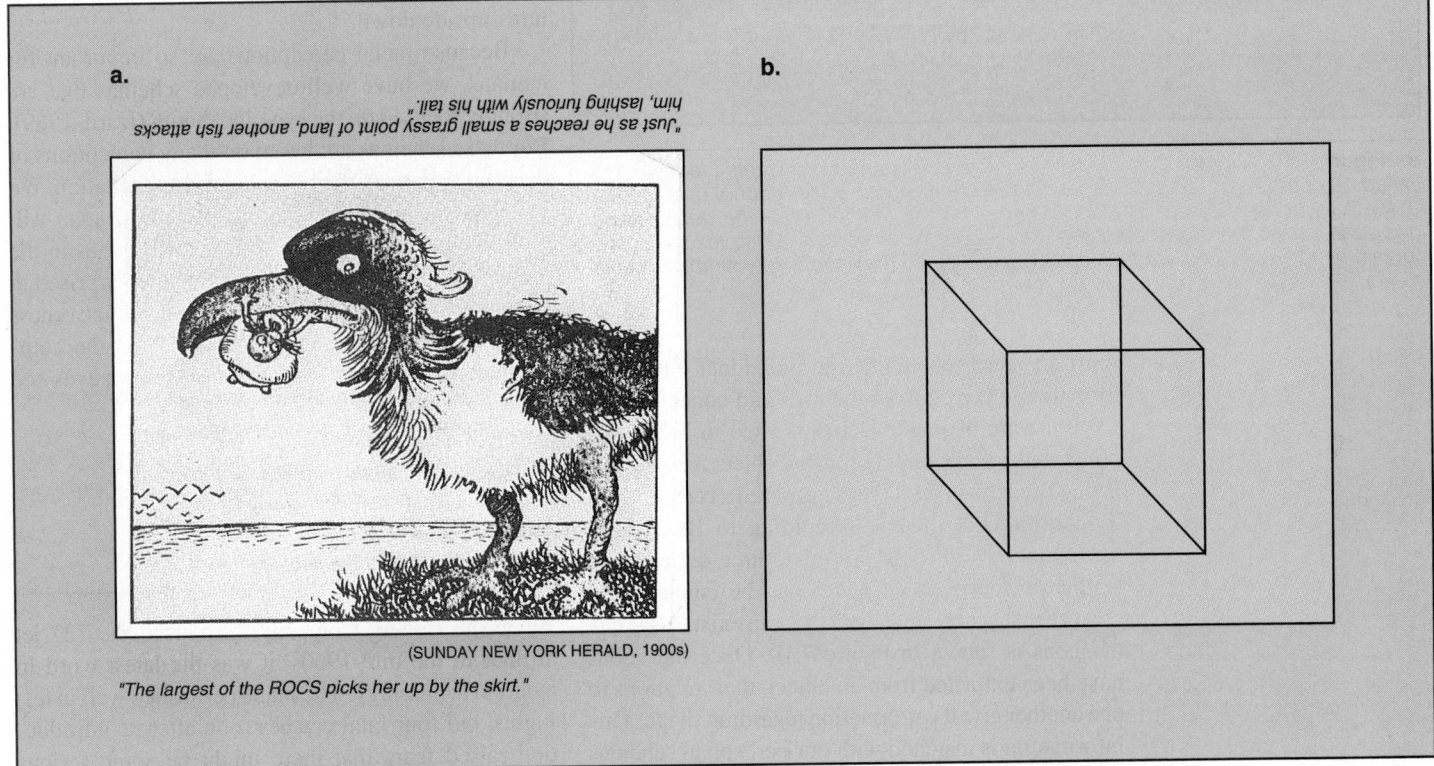

a.

"Just as he reaches a small grassy point of land, another fish attacks him, lashing furiously with his tail."

(SUNDAY NEW YORK HERALD, 1900s)

"The largest of the ROCS picks her up by the skirt."

b.

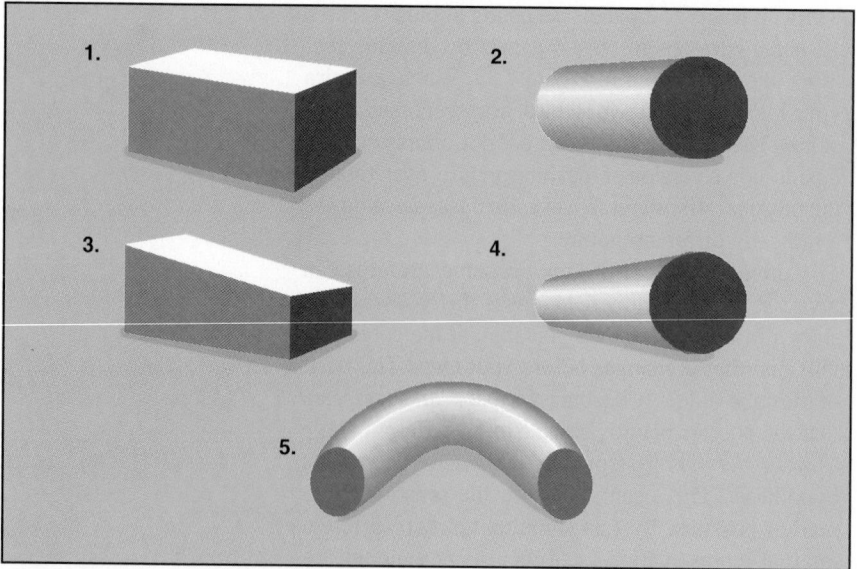

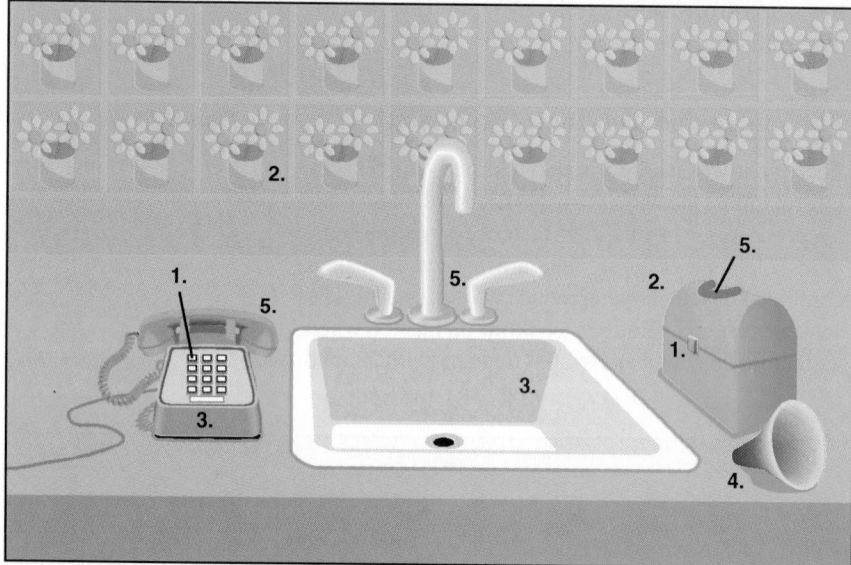

Figure 7.10 *According to Biederman's recognition-by-components theory, a limited number (25 to 35) of lower level three-dimensional forms (geons) underlie the ability to recognize objects. The upper part of the figure shows 5 of the geons; the lower part shows the presence of the geons in common objects. Complex shapes contain more geons and are thus easier to recognize than some very simple objects.*

apart and then recombine the individual bits of information received from the rods and cones.

What are the basic elements used in bottom-up processing? In the realm of visual object recognition, Irving Biederman (1987) has proposed a **recognition-by-components theory**. According to Biederman, approximately 25 to 35 primitive three-dimensional geometric forms called **geons** can be combined to create the shape of any object that can exist. A sample of geons is shown in Figure 7.10. Once the geons have been extracted from an object, their relations to one another give us information regarding shape. This information is matched with our perceptual schemas in memory. For example, if a cylinder has an arc on

the side, it corresponds to the schema for ''cup''; if the arc is over the top of the cylinder, it fits that for ''pail.'' The more geons we can extract from an object, the more easily we will recognize it. Support for this proposition comes from experiments in which pictures of objects are presented very briefly to subjects. As the recognition-by-components theory would predict, complex objects like airplanes (which are composed of many geons) are recognized more easily than simple objects like the faucet handles in Figure 7.10 (Banks & Krajicek, 1991).

Our perceptual systems seem to operate not only in a bottom-up fashion but also through *top-down processing,* a hypothesis-driven approach. The Gestalt emphasis on principles of perceptual organization is an example of a top-down approach to perception. For those like Rock and Gregory, who take a cognitive approach to perception, perceptual schemas and hypotheses comprise meaning, and the incoming stimuli are interpreted in light of this meaning. Thus, we start with the meaning structures and compare and fit the stimuli to them. In a top-down approach, ''sensory information is termed the 'support' for perception, much as evidence is taken as support for an argument or theoretical position'' (Banks & Krajicek, 1991, p. 324).

Top-down processing can mask an unusual perception. As an example, look at the pictures in Figure 7.11. You may notice that the picture on the right has been altered a bit around the eyes and mouth, but the woman probably still looks like an attractive person. Now, see what she looks like when you turn the pictures upside down.

Because facial perceptions are so important for humans, we have well-developed schemas that are strongly focused on the eyes and mouth (Izard, 1989). But these schemas are based on many perceptions of these body parts in their usual upright orientation. We thus have difficulty imagining what the woman will look like when that orientation is reversed, as in the picture on the right. You were probably surprised at how much your hypothesis of facial attractiveness was disconfirmed when you encountered the combination of an upright face and upside-down eyes and mouth.

Illusions: False Perceptual Hypotheses

When the Boeing Company introduced the 727 jet airliner in the mid-1960s, it was the latest word in aviation technology. The plane performed well in test flights, but four fatal crashes soon after its introduction raised fears that there might be some serious problems in its design.

The first accident occurred as a 727 made its approach to Chicago over Lake Michigan on a clear night. The plane plunged into the lake 19 miles offshore. About a month later, another airliner glided in over the Ohio River to land in Cincinnati. Unaccountably, it struck the ground about 12 feet below the runway elevation and burst into flames. The third accident occurred as an aircraft approached Salt Lake City over dark land. The lights of the city twinkled in the distance, but the plane made too rapid a descent and landed short of the runway. In the fourth accident, a Japanese airliner approached Tokyo at night. The flight ended unexpectedly and tragically as the plane, its landing gear not yet lowered, struck the waters of Tokyo Bay 6 miles from the runway and spun to destruction.

Analysis of these four accidents, as well as others, suggested a common pattern. Because all occurred at night under clear weather conditions, the pilots were operating under visual flight rules rather than performing instrument landings. In each instance, the plane was approaching city lights over dark areas of water or land. In all cases, the cities in the background sloped upward. Finally, all of the planes crashed short of the runway.

These observations led a Boeing psychologist, Conrad L. Kraft, to suspect that the cause of the crashes might be pilot error based on some sort of visual illusion. To test this possibility, Boeing constructed an apparatus to simulate night landings (see Figure 7.12). It consisted of a cockpit and a miniature lighted "city" named Nightertown. The city moved toward the cockpit on computer-controlled rollers and could be tilted to simulate various terrain slopes. The pilot could control simulated air speed and rate of climb and descent, and the Nightertown scene was controlled by the pilot's responses just as a true visual scene would be.

Kraft (1978) tested 12 experienced Boeing flight instructors, who made "landings" at Nightertown under various conditions. The results of the experiments confirmed Kraft's suspicion. When he duplicated the conditions of the fatal crashes by having the pilots approach an upward-sloping distant city over a dark area, the pilots were unable to detect the upward slope and consistently overestimated their altitude. They assumed that the background city was flat and adjusted their altitude accordingly. On a normal landing, the preferred altitude at 4.5 miles from the runway is about 1240 feet. As Figure 7.13 shows, the pilots approached at about this altitude when the simulated city was in a flat position. But when it was sloped upward, 11 of the 12 experienced pilot instructors reached zero altitude at about 4.5 miles out! The perceptual hypotheses of the flight instructors, like those of the pilots involved in the real crashes, were tragically incorrect. On the basis of Kraft's findings,

(a) (b)

Figure 7.11 *Try to imagine what the retouched photo on the right will look like when you turn your book upside down.*

Boeing urgently recommended that pilots attend carefully to their instruments when landing at night, even under perfect weather conditions. In this case, seeing should *not* be believing.

Illusions, then, are incorrect perceptions. Put another way, they are erroneous perceptual hypotheses about the nature of the stimulus. Illusions are frequently intriguing and sometimes delightful visual

Figure 7.12 *Conrad Kraft, a Boeing psychologist, created an apparatus to study how visual cues can affect the simulated landings of airline pilots. Pilots approached Nightertown in a simulated cockpit. The computer-controlled city could be tilted to reproduce the illusion (shown below) thought to be responsible for fatal air crashes.*

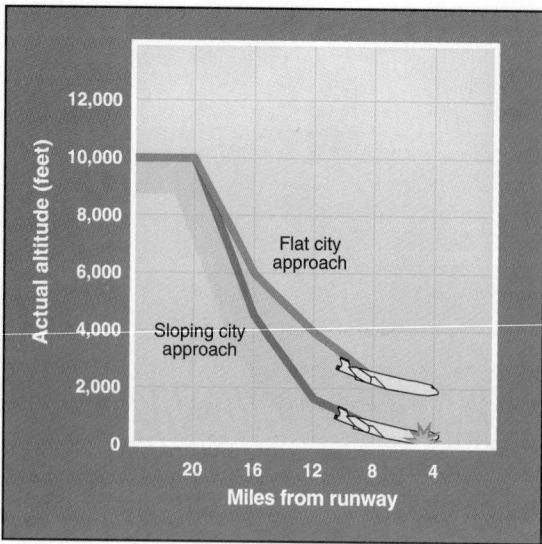

Figure 7.14 *Shape constancy makes it possible to recognize objects from many different perspectives.*

experiences. Perception researchers have long been interested in them because they give us important information about how our perceptual processes work under normal conditions. In particular, the analysis of illusions has served to indicate the central role played in our perceptions by perceptual constancies.

Perceptual Constancies as a Basis for Illusions

To understand the nature of illusions, we have to consider **perceptual constancies,** those compromises with sensory reality that allow us to recognize familiar stimuli under varying conditions. For example, *shape constancy* allows us to recognize objects from many different angles (see Figure 7.14). Perhaps you have had to sit off to one side of the screen in a crowded movie theater. At first, the picture probably looked distorted, but after awhile your visual system corrected for the distortion, and objects on the screen looked normal again.

Because of *brightness constancy,* the relative brightness of objects remains the same under different conditions of illumination. Brightness constancy occurs because the ratio of light intensity between an object and its surroundings is usually constant. The actual brightness of the light that illuminates the objects does not matter, as long as the same light intensity illuminates both an object and its surroundings.

Size constancy is an extremely important basis for perceptual hypotheses. Even though objects on our retina change in size with changes in distance, our perception of their sizes remains constant. When we fly in an airplane, for example, we know that the cars down there on the highway aren't the size of toys. We learn to use distance cues to judge the size

of objects. But distance cues can sometimes fool us. In Figure 7.15, the railroad tracks provide distance cues that make one bar appear farther away than the other. The bar that appears to be in the background looks larger than the one in the foreground. Actually, as you can prove to yourself by measuring them, the bars are equal in length. However, although the bars cast retinal images of the same size, our brains interpret the one that appears farther away as being larger. This is called the *Ponzo illusion.*

Distance cues can be manipulated to create striking size illusions. One occurs in the Ames Room, which is named after its designer, Adelbert Ames. Viewed through a peephole with one eye, the scene presents a startling size reversal (see Figure 7.16*a*). This occurs because we assume that the room has a normal rectangular shape. In reality, however, the left corner of the room is twice as far away as the right corner (see Figure 7.16*b*). Because we cannot detect this fact, size constancy breaks down, and we base our judgment of size on the sizes of the retinal images cast by the two people.

The study of perceptual constancies provides ample evidence that our perceptual hypotheses are strongly influenced by the *context,* or surroundings, in which a stimulus occurs. Consider, for example, the *moon illusion.* You have probably marveled at how much larger that beautiful harvest moon looks when it is just rising than it does when it is overhead in the sky. Obviously, the moon doesn't shrink during the night, as researchers have demonstrated by taking photos of the moon at the horizon and later when it is directly overhead. The moon looks larger at the horizon because we use objects in our field of vision, such as the ground, trees, and buildings, to estimate its distance. Laboratory studies have shown that objects look farther away when viewed through filled space than when viewed through empty space (Coren & Ward, 1989). Research has also shown that such cues cause us to estimate the distance of the moon on the horizon as two and one-half to four times farther away than when it is above us in the sky (Frisby, 1980). Because our size perceptions are based in part on distance cues, we perceive the ''more distant'' moon on the horizon as being larger. Figure 7.17 shows some other examples of how context can produce illusory perceptions.

Depth and Movement Perception

One of the more complicated aspects of perception is our ability to perceive depth. The retina receives information in two dimensions (length and width), but the brain translates these cues into three-dimensional perceptions. It does this by using both **monocular cues** (which require only one eye) and **binocular cues** (which require both eyes).

Monocular Cues

Judging the relative distances of objects is one important key to perceiving depth. Many distance cues require only one eye, and they are therefore classified as monocular depth cues. For example, look again at the railroad tracks in Figure 7.15. Parallel lines, such as real railroad tracks, seem to angle closer together as they recede in the distance. This phenomenon is called *linear perspective,* and we have already seen that the distance cues it provides can produce a size illusion. In his painting *Uncomposed Objects in Space,* Paul Klee used linear perspective to create a depth effect in which objects seem to be moving into

Figure 7.15 *The Ponzo illusion. Which bar is longer? Measure them and see. The distance cues provided by the converging railroad tracks affect size perception and disrupt size constancy.*

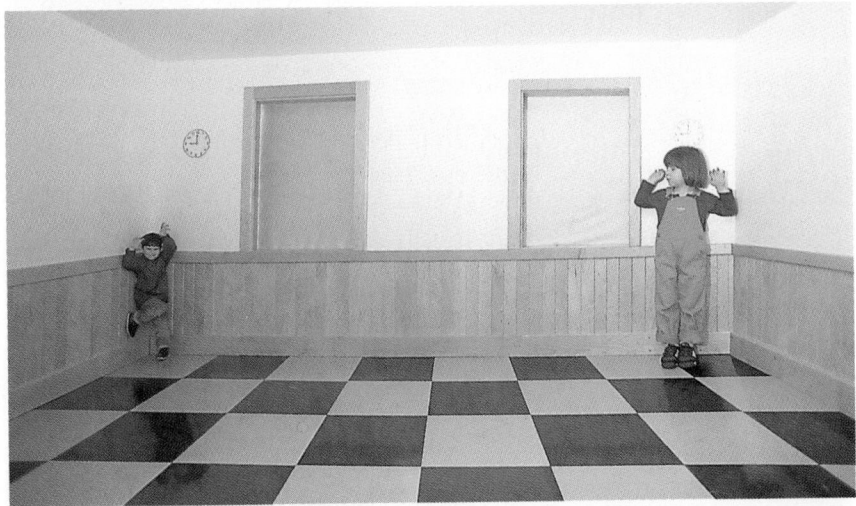

(a)

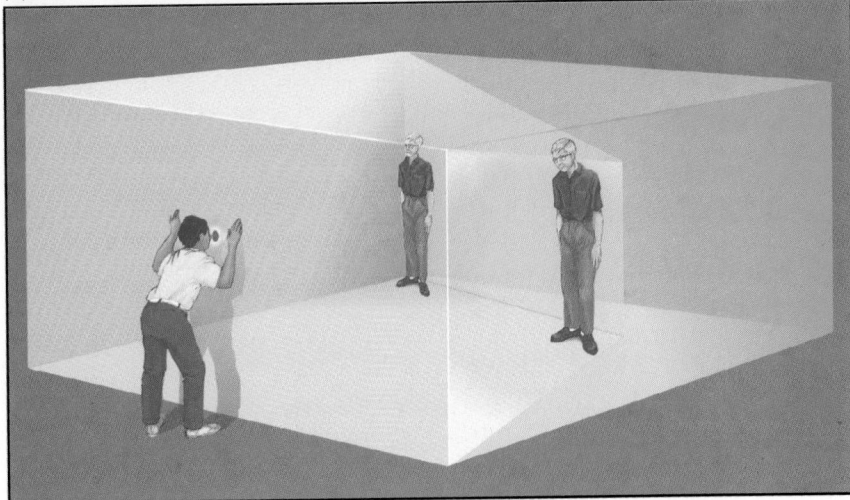

(b)

Figure 7.16 *The Ames Room produces a striking size perception because it is designed to appear rectangular* (a). *However, as* (b) *shows, the room is actually trapezoidal in shape, and the figure on the left is actually much farther away from the viewer than the one on the right.*

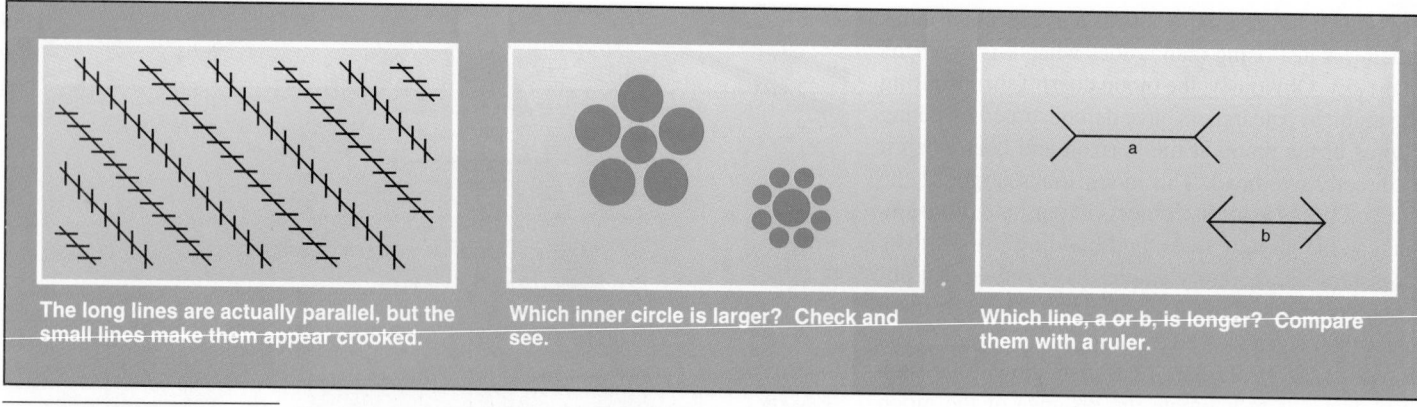

The long lines are actually parallel, but the small lines make them appear crooked.

Which inner circle is larger? Check and see.

Which line, a or b, is longer? Compare them with a ruler.

Figure 7.17 *Context-produced geometric illusions.*

and out of the dark space formed by the tallest rectangle (Figure 7.18).

Decreasing size is another distance cue; as objects move away from us, they produce smaller retinal images. An object's *height in the horizontal plane* also provides information (see Figure 7.19). For example, a ship five miles offshore appears in a higher plane and closer to the horizon than does one which is only one mile from shore. *Texture* is a fourth cue, because the texture or grain of an object appears finer as distance increases (see Figure 7.20). Finally, *clarity* can be an important cue for judging distance; we can see nearby hills more clearly than ones that are far away, especially on hazy days. These five perspective cues provide us with information that we can use to make judgments about distance and therefore about depth.

In addition to the five distance cues, there are two other important monocular depth cues. The first is patterns of *light and shadow*. The Dutch artist M. C. Escher skillfully used light and shadow to create the three-dimensional effect shown in Figure 7.21. The depth effect is as powerful if you close one eye as it is when you use both. Finally, since objects closer to us may cut off part of our view of more distant objects, the *interposition* of objects is an indication of distance and depth.

Because artists can draw in only two dimensions, they need to be skillful in using monocular depth cues. Like Escher, the artist Raphael Sanzio was a master at using such cues. *The School of Athens,* shown in Figure 7.22, illustrates all seven of the monocular depth cues just discussed.

Some of the most intriguing perceptual distortions are produced when monocular depth cues are manipulated to produce a figure or scene whose individual parts make sense but whose overall organization is "impossible" in terms of our existing perceptual schemas. Figure 7.23 shows two impossible figures. In each case, our brains extract information about depth from the individual features of the objects, but when this information is put together and matched with our existing schemas, the percept that results simply doesn't make sense. The "devil's tuning fork," for example, could not exist in our universe. It is a two-dimensional image containing paradoxical depth cues. Your brain, however, automatically interprets it as a three-dimensional object and matches it with its internal schema of a fork, a bad fit indeed.

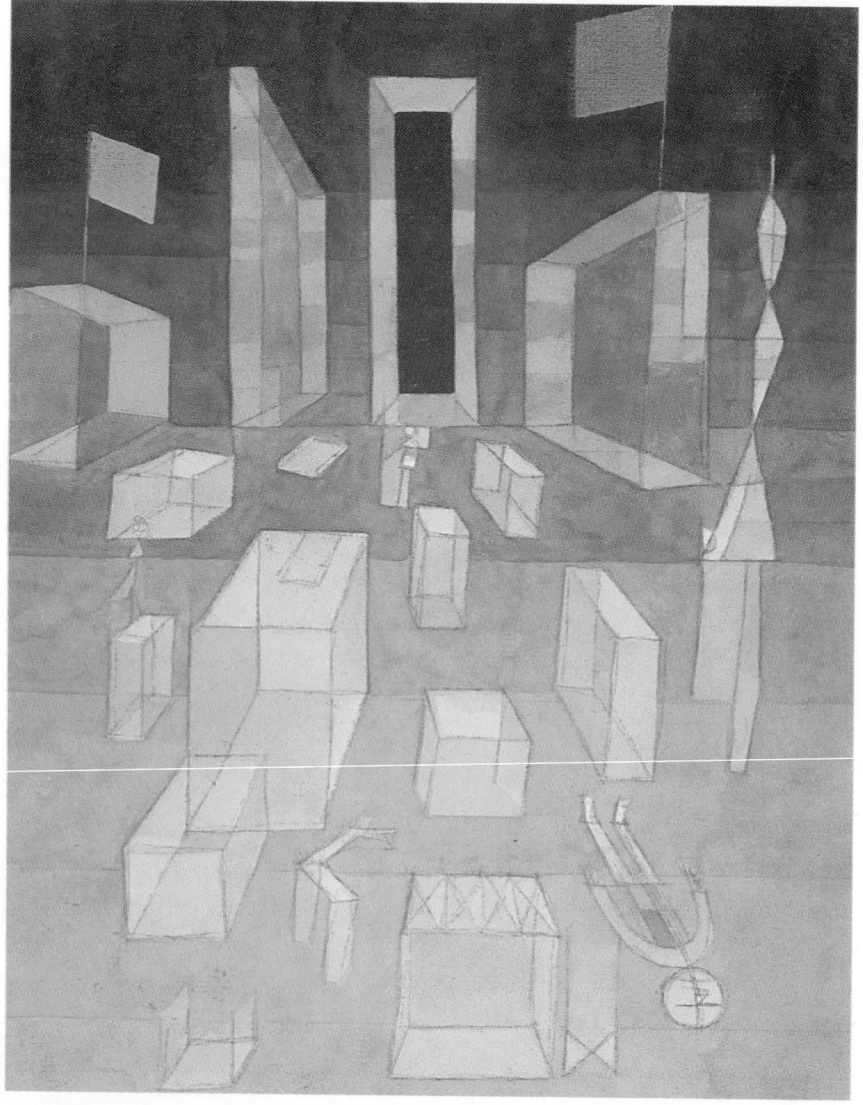

Figure 7.18 *The use of linear perspective to create depth is illustrated in* Uncomposed Objects in Space, *by Paul Klee.*

(© 1978 BY SIDNEY HARRIS/AMERICAN SCIENTIST MAGAZINE.)

Figure 7.19 *If he had taken this psychology course, he would have known that height in the horizontal plane is a monocular cue for depth and distance.*

Figure 7.20 *Texture is one of the monocular cues that influences perception of depth.*

A remarkable demonstration will acquaint you with one last monocular depth cue. This demonstration will also show how your brain tries to organize ambiguous depth cues. All you need in order to experience this phenomenon is a piece of fairly heavy paper and a little patience.

First, fold the paper down the middle and set it on a table with one of the open ends facing you. Close one eye and view the paper from a point above and directly along the line of the fold. Stare at a point midway along its length (see Figure 7.24).

At first, the object looks like a tent, but if you continue to stare at it intently, the paper will suddenly "stand up" and look like a corner viewed from the inside. When this happens, gently move your head back and forth. (Remember to use only one eye!) The effect produced by the movement is a striking one.

To analyze your experience, it is important to understand that both the "tent" and the "corner" cast identical images on your retina. After perceiving a tent for awhile, your brain shifted to the second perceptual hypothesis, as it did in response to the reversible figure shown in Figure 7.6. When the object was a "tent," all the depth information was consistent with that perception. But when you began to see it as a "corner" and then moved your head slowly back and forth, the object seemed to twist and turn as if it were made of rubber. This occurred because when you moved, the image of the near point of the fold moved across your retina faster than the image of the far point. This is the normal pattern of stimulation for points at different depths and is known as **motion parallax.** Thus, when you were seeing a tent, the monocular cue of motion parallax was consistent with

the shape of the object. When you later saw the object as standing upright, all the points along the fold appeared to be the same distance away, yet they were moving across the retina at different rates of speed! The only way your brain could maintain its "corner" perception in the face of the motion parallax cues was to see the object as twisting and turning. Again, as in other illusions, forcing all of the sensory data to fit the perceptual hypothesis produced an unusual experience.

Figure 7.21 *Patterns of light and shadow can serve as monocular depth cues, as shown in* Drawing Hands *by M. C. Escher.*

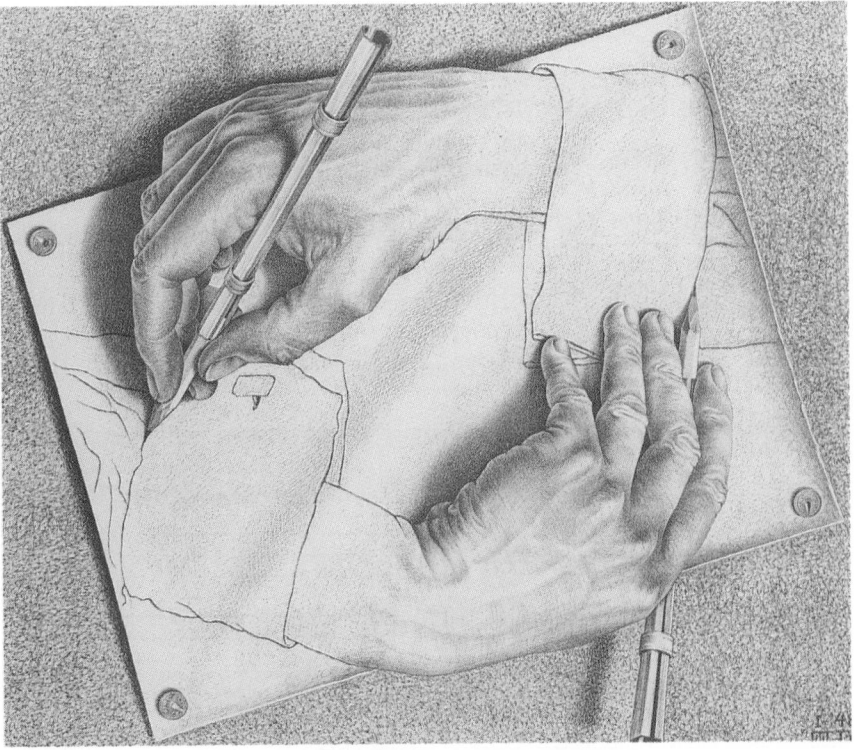

Figure 7.22 The School of Athens, *by Raphael Sanzio, illustrates seven monocular depth cues. (1) The converging lines of the corridor represent linear perspective. (2) The arches and the people in the background are smaller than those in front. (3) The back of the building is in a higher horizontal plane than the foreground. (4, 5) The objects in the background are less detailed than the closer ones (texture and clarity). (6) Light and shadow are used to create depth. (7) The arches and people in the front of the painting cut off parts of the corridor behind them (interposition).*

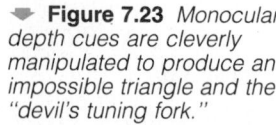

Figure 7.23 *Monocular depth cues are cleverly manipulated to produce an impossible triangle and the "devil's tuning fork."*

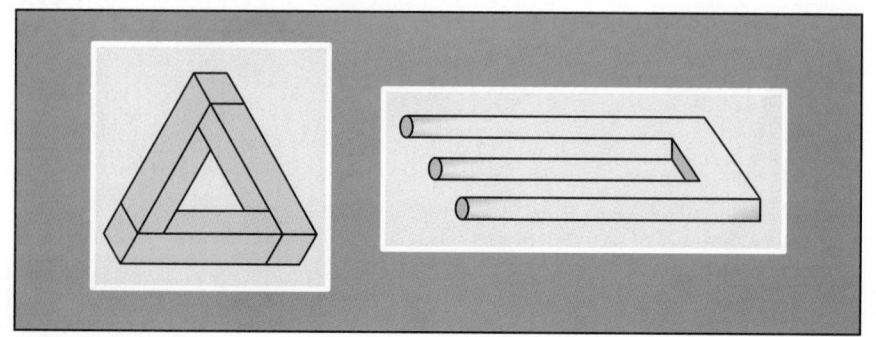

Binocular Cues: Stereopsis

Monocular cues can provide valuable information concerning depth and distance, but the most dramatic perceptions of depth arise when both eyes are used. If you extend your pencil or pen out in front of you and view it against the background with one eye shut and your head perfectly still, you will perceive little depth. But open the other eye and a much richer perception of depth will occur. The appearance of depth that results from the use of both eyes is called **stereopsis.**

Most of us are familiar with the delightful depth experiences provided by View Master slides, stereoscopes, and 3-D movies watched through special glasses. All of these devices make use of the principle of **binocular disparity.** In normal binocular vision, each eye sees a slightly different image, and the two images are fused by the brain into a single image that has depth.

Stereopsis does not occur in the eyes themselves but at higher levels of the visual system. Microelectrode studies of the visual cortex during binocular vision have found feature detector cells that respond only to stimuli that are either in front of or behind the fixation point (Poggio & Fischer, 1977; von der Heydt & others, 1978). Receptor channels near the fixation plane may be narrowly tuned for detailed vision of the fixated object, while other broader channels cover nearer and farther objects. The responses of these depth-sensitive neurons are probably integrated within the brain to produce the perception of depth (Wade & Swanston, 1991).

Although much remains to be learned, it now appears that information concerning shape, color, and spatial relations (including movement and depth) are processed by three independent pathways in the brain. This conclusion is based on painstaking research in which the electrical signals generated by forms, colors, and movement are traced from the retina through the brain. At higher levels of the brain, particularly in the visual centers of the thalamus and the cortex, these three sets of information are integrated to produce visual experiences like depth, recognition of forms, and perception of colors (Livingstone, 1988; Shapley, 1990).

Perception of Movement

The perception of movement is a complex process that requires the brain to integrate information from several different senses. For example, try this demonstration. Hold your pen in front of your face. Now, while holding your head still, move the pen back and forth. You will perceive the pen moving. Now hold the pen still and move your head back and forth at the same rate of speed. In both cases, the image of the pen moved across your retina in about the same way. When you moved your head, however, your brain took into account input from your kinesthetic and vestibular systems and "concluded" that you were moving but the pen was not.

If you sit in a dark room and stare at a stationary beam of light for awhile, the light will suddenly appear to move about. This perceived movement, known as the **autokinetic effect,** occurs because of random eye movements of which you are not aware. Movement of the light's image on your retina causes you to mistakenly conclude that the stationary light is moving.

The typical stimulus for perception of movement is the actual movement of the stimulus across the retina. Under optimal conditions, a retinal image need move only about one-fifth the diameter of a single cone in order for us to detect movement (Nakayama & Tyler, 1981). However, relative motion of an object against a structured background is an even stronger cue for movement because it provides more visual information (Gibson, 1979). For example, if you fixate on a moving object, such as a football in flight, the relative motion of the object against its background is a strong cue for perceived speed of movement. You may recognize this as another instance of motion parallax, which is a cue for movement as well as depth.

The illusory perception of smooth motion can be produced by the patterning of stimulus presentation. The Gestalt psychologists demonstrated this in their studies of **stroboscopic movement,** also known as the **phi phenomenon.** For example, they showed that if a light was briefly flashed in darkness and then, a few milliseconds later, another light was flashed nearby, the first light seemed to move from one place to the other in a manner indistinguishable from real movement. The timing of the two lights is critical, however. If the time interval is too short, the lights appear to be simultaneous; if it is too long, the lights appear as two lights without motion.

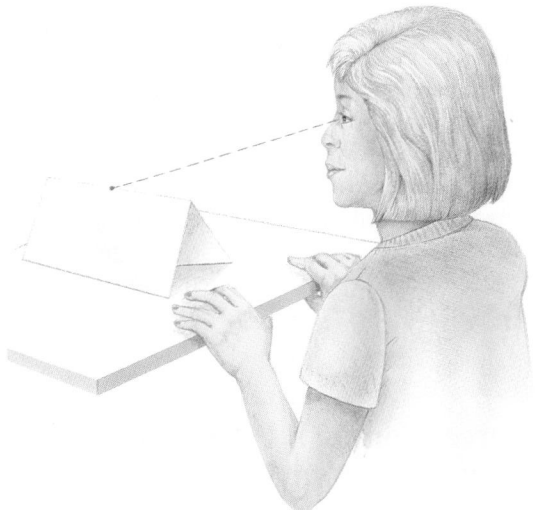

Figure 7.24 *To demonstrate how the visual system tries to deal with ambiguous monocular depth cues, fold a heavy piece of paper and place it on a table like a tent. Stare with one eye at a point midway along the fold (x). After awhile, the paper will suddenly appear to be a raised corner. When this occurs, gently move your head back and forth for some unusual visual effects.*

Stroboscopic movement has been used commercially in a number of ways. For example, we have all seen the strings of successively illuminated lights on theater marquees that seem to move endlessly around the border or that spell out messages in a "moving" cursive script. Stroboscopic movement is also the principle behind moving pictures (see Figure 7.25). The film is simply a series of still photographs, or frames, that are projected on a screen in rapid succession with dark intervals in between. The rate at which the frames are projected is critical to our perception of smooth movement. In the early movies, the frames were projected at only 16 frames per second, and the movement appeared fast and jerky. Today, the usual speed is 24 frames per second, which more perfectly

Figure 7.25 *Stroboscopic movement is produced in moving pictures as a series of still photographs projected at a rate of 24 per second.*

produces an illusion of smooth movement. Television presents up to 30 images per second.

The perception of depth and movement is critically important to our ability to interact with our physical environment. Again we see, however, that perceptual experiences that appear perfectly ''natural'' to us actually reflect a highly complex and finely calibrated series of neural processes that stretch from the individual receptors of the retina to the highest centers of the cerebral cortex.

■ ▢

Perception as a Psychobiological Phenomenon: Understanding Pain

Physical pain is surely one of the most unpleasant realities of life, and most of us do our best to avoid it. But despite its negative aspects, pain also has important survival functions. First, it serves as a warning signal when the body is being threatened or damaged. Second, it is part of a defensive system that triggers behavioral reactions ranging from simple reflexes to complex behavior patterns designed to help us cope with the threat. Pain is thus an important part of the natural ''biofeedback'' system that helps us adjust to our environment.

Because of its crucial survival function, as well as its role in physical illnesses and certain psychological problems, many psychologists are conducting research to discover the physiological and psychological causes of our perception of pain as well as ways in which we can control pain. We now know that pain is more than simply a sensory phenomenon. It is possible for people to experience excruciating pain in the absence of tissue damage, as occurs in certain *somatoform* disorders having psychological causes (Sarason & Sarason, 1993). Conversely, people may experience physical damage and yet experience no pain, as has occurred in soldiers who were unaware for several hours that they had been wounded in combat (Fordyce, 1988). Pain clearly has important motivational, emotional, and cognitive facets that determine our experience of it (Sternbach, 1987). From a psychological perspective, pain is one of the most fascinating of perceptual phenomena, and because it reflects the operation of psychological processes more than many other perceptual experiences do, we shall explore it in some detail.

Biological Mechanisms of Pain

Receptors for pain are found in the skin, joints, muscles, and all body tissues, with the exception of the brain, bones, hair, nails, and nonliving parts of the

teeth. The major receptors for pain are thought to be free nerve endings that respond to intense mechanical, thermal, or chemical stimulation. The receptors send their impulses into the dorsal horns of the spinal cord, where sensory tracts carrying pain information ascend to the brain (see Figure 3.8, p. 68). Recent studies using the PET scan to observe brain activity in response to painful stimulation indicate that precise information about pain intensity and location reaches small areas of both the somatosensory and frontal areas of the cerebral cortex (Talbot & others, 1991). Other tracts direct pain impulses to subcortical regions, especially the limbic system, which are known to be involved in motivation and emotion. These tracts seem to control the emotional component of pain (Melzack, 1990).

The role of the spinal cord in the transmission of pain impulses has been known for a long time. Beyond that, however, pain was one of the most mysterious aspects of perception. In recent years, however, a series of discoveries has revolutionized pain research and given us major new insights into the mechanisms of pain perception.

Gate-Control Theory

One major advance was the **gate-control theory** of pain, developed by a psychologist, Ronald Melzack, and a physiologist, Patrick Wall (1983). This theory deals with neural transmissions that can open or close a system of spinal ''gates'' between the pain receptors in the body tissues and the brain regions responsible for the perception of pain. Briefly, the theory holds that free nerve endings can activate both small-diameter and larger diameter sensory nerve fibers. The thin fibers carry pain impulses; the thick fibers convey information about touch. Whether or not we experience pain depends partly on the ratio of thin-fiber-to-thick-fiber transmissions. A high ratio of thin-fiber activity opens the gates, whereas thick-fiber activity closes them. It follows, then, that anything that can increase thick-fiber impulses can decrease our perception of pain. This is why rubbing a bruise or scratching an itch can make us feel better. Gate-control theorists also suggest that acupuncture achieves its pain-relieving effects because the acupuncture needles stimulate the thick fibers, closing the pain gates. Evidence supporting this explanation comes from research findings that acupuncture performed with needles reduces pain, whereas a newer form of acupuncture performed with laser beams does not (Brockhaus & Elger, 1990).

From a psychological perspective, the most intriguing aspect of gate-control theory is the notion that the gates can also be opened or closed by nerve impulses coming down from the brain (see Figure 7.26). This would help to explain how psychological

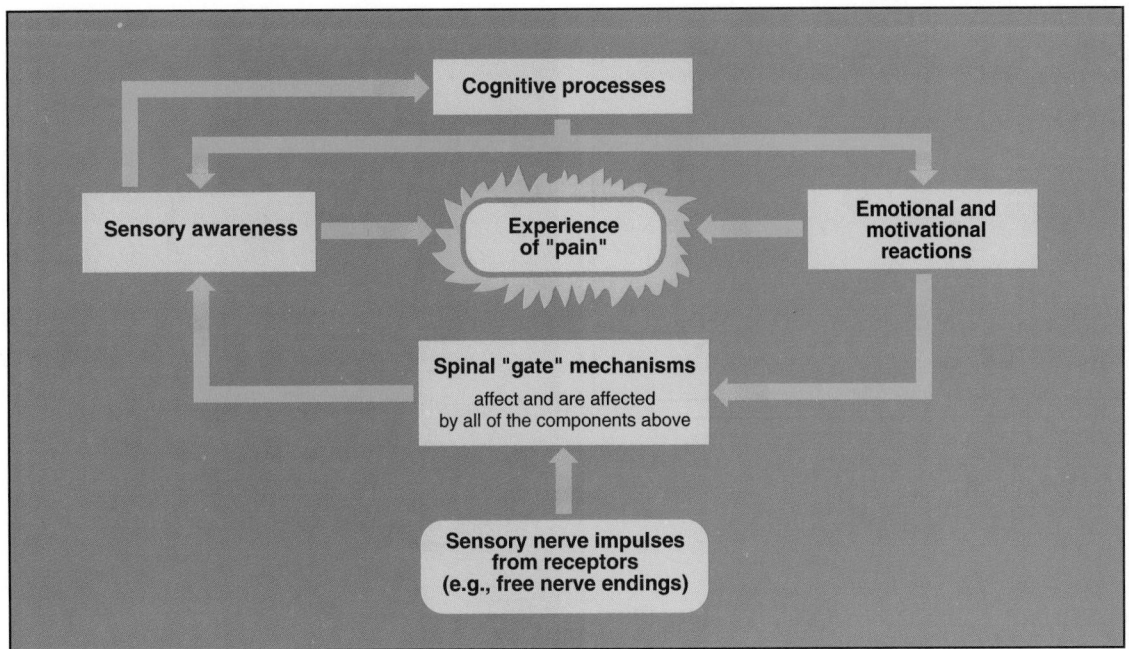

Figure 7.26 The gate-control theory holds that the perception of pain is affected by a series of "gates" in the nervous system that can be opened or closed either by tactile stimuli or by nerve impulses coming down from the brain. In this manner, psychological processes going on in the brain may be capable of increasing or decreasing our pain "sensations."

factors might increase or decrease our experience of pain.

Opiates of the Brain

A second major breakthrough in our understanding of pain was the discovery of the *endorphins.* Their discovery is one of the great success stories of modern scientific history.

Opiates (such as opium, morphine, and heroin) have been used to relieve pain for centuries. One of the striking features of the opiates is their profound and highly specific effects on the brain's pain and pleasure systems. This specificity and the minuscule amounts of the drugs needed to produce an effect led a neurochemist, Solomon Snyder, and his coworker, Candace Pert, to suspect that morphine produced its effects by locking into specific receptor sites in the brain. To demonstrate the presence of receptors, they tried injecting radioactive morphine into rat brains to see if it bound to any receptors. Attempt after attempt failed to show any indication of binding. There was something wrong with either their theory or the experiment.

One possibility was that morphine works so fast, snapping in and then out of receptors, that it was not active long enough to show up in their films of radioactive concentration. Snyder and Pert then produced a radioactive form of *naloxone,* a drug used to help people recover from heroin-induced comas. They reasoned that naloxone might counteract the action of the opiate drugs by taking over the suspected receptor sites and that naloxone, unlike morphine, might occupy the receptor sites long enough so that

the binding could be captured on radiation-sensitive film. When they injected the radioactive naloxone into brain tissue, sure enough, the naloxone bound tightly to the brain cells. There were opiate receptors, after all!

Later experiments showed that the "hot" binding sites for naloxone include brain stem structures known to be suppressed by opium and morphine, such as the respiration centers whose suppression results in many drug-induced deaths. Also filled with receptors are brain regions to which pain receptors send their nerve impulses and brain regions that, when stimulated electrically, produce reports of happiness and bliss in humans (the so-called reward centers described in Chapter 3). These binding regions correspond with the two major effects of the opiates on consciousness: pain suppression and pleasure.

But why would the brain have receptors for opiates unless there were some natural chemical in the brain for the receptor to receive? Later research disclosed what had to be true: The nervous system has its own built-in analgesics (painkillers) with opiate-like properties. These natural opiates were named **endorphins** (literally meaning "the morphines within"). Their discovery has helped unlock many mysteries of how the brain operates, including how pain is regulated.

Endorphins are thought to exert some of their pain-killing effects by inhibiting the release of **substance P,** one of the major neurotransmitters involved in the synaptic transmission of pain impulses from the spinal cord to the brain (Fessler, 1989). Some of the endorphins are enormously potent: One brain endorphin isolated by scientists is more than 200

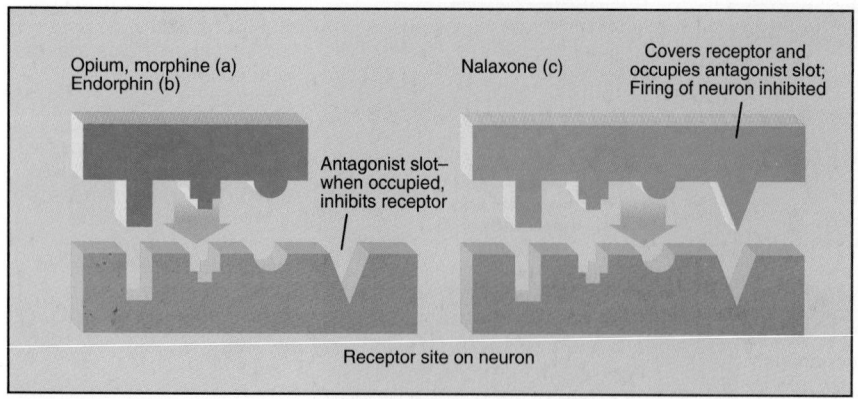

Figure 7.27 *Opiate receptors in the brain are tailored to receive molecules having very specific shapes, including drugs made from the opium poppy* (a), *the body's own endorphins* (b), *and the opiate antagonist naloxone* (c). *Antagonists are substances that counter the effects of a drug.*

times more powerful than morphine (Franklin, 1987). The discovery of the endorphins is helping us to account for the success of many analgesic procedures.

While the endorphins have been isolated and studied directly by biochemists, behavioral researchers have studied their action either by injecting endorphins into subjects and observing analgesic effects or by injecting naloxone and observing the consequences. If a procedure produces analgesia when naloxone is not used, but does not work when naloxone is present, we have indirect evidence that endorphins are responsible for the pain-reducing effects of the procedure (see Figure 7.27).

Endorphins, Acupuncture, and Gate Control

Acupuncture is one mysterious pain-reduction technique that may ultimately be understood in terms of endorphin mechanisms (see Figure 7.28). Research done in China has shown that injections of naloxone greatly reduce the analgesic effects of acupuncture. This finding and gate-control theory suggest that there may be two mechanisms for pain relief through acupuncture: thick-fiber stimulation and endorphin release. Endorphins may, in fact, be part of the gate-control mechanisms. Perhaps endorphins released by neurons in the spinal cord as a result of stimulation from the brain inhibit the release of substance P, the transmitter that excites neurons to send pain information to the brain. Such a mechanism would effectively close the gate and decrease the perception of pain (Bloom & Lazerson, 1988; Wall & Melzack, 1989).

Stress-Induced Analgesia

Under severe stress, people sometimes become oblivious to pain. About 65 percent of soldiers wounded

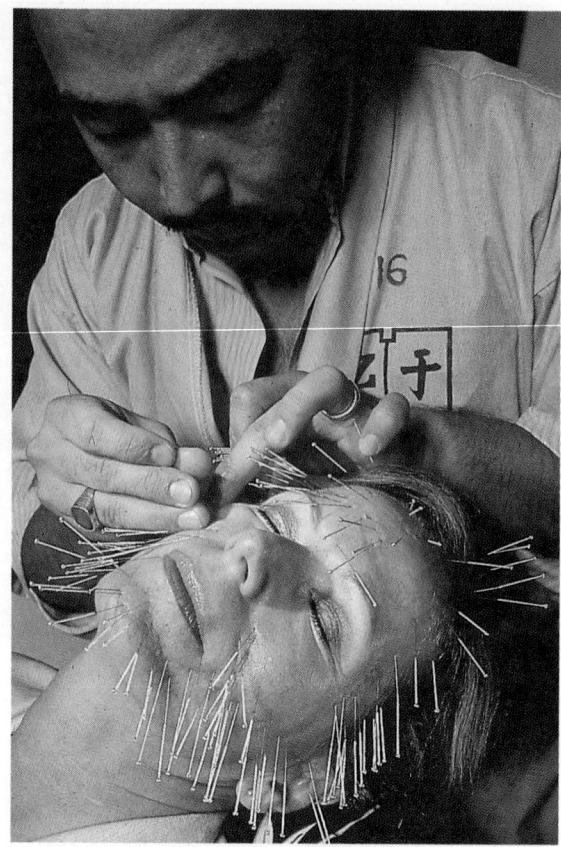

Figure 7.28 *Acupuncture treatments can reduce pain. The needles may produce an analgesic effect through thick-fiber stimulation or by stimulating the release of endorphins.*

during combat report having felt no pain at the time (Warga, 1987). Likewise, people involved in accidents are sometimes unaware of serious injuries until the crisis is over. Research using naloxone suggests that this phenomenon, known as **stress-induced analgesia,** is produced by the release of endorphins. Animals injected with naloxone and then exposed to stress fail to demonstrate the analgesic response and seem to experience a normal level of pain if subjected to painful stimuli (Fanselow, 1991).

What is the survival value of stress-induced analgesia? Michael Fanselow (1991) suggests that in a life-threatening situation, defensive behavior must be given immediate priority over normal responses to pain. By reducing or preventing pain sensations, stress-induced analgesia helps suppress these pain-related behaviors so that the person or animal can get on with the actions that are needed for immediate survival, such as fleeing, fighting, or getting help (see Figure 7.29).

Newborns are relatively insensitive to painful stimuli, and some scientists believe this may be a defense against the stresses of birth. It has been found that both the placenta and the amniotic fluid in which the fetus lives are richly endowed with endorphinlike substances when birth occurs (Franklin, 1987; Houck & others, 1980). The ''birth trauma'' proposed by several theories of personality may thus be less severe than was once thought, at least in terms of physical pain.

The release of endorphins seems to be part of the body's natural response to stress, but we may pay a price for this temporary relief from pain. It now appears that chronically high levels of endorphin release help block the activity of *natural killer cells,* lymph cells that recognize and selectively kill tumor cells as part of the body's immune system defenses. This may be one way in which stress makes us more susceptible to serious illnesses, such as cancer (Shavit, 1990).

The Psychology of Pain

Sensory input from pain receptors is only the first step in our ultimate experiencing of pain. Like all perceptions, pain is a subjective experience. Its quality and intensity are influenced not only by the physical stimulus but also by psychological factors, such as personal and cultural beliefs, customary methods of coping with difficulties, and the meanings attached to painful situations.

Cultural Factors in Pain: The Importance of Meaning

Childbirth can be a very painful event for some mothers. Yet in certain cultures, women work in the fields almost until the moment the baby arrives and show virtually no distress during childbirth. Indeed, in one culture, the woman's husband gets into bed and groans as if he were in great pain, while the woman calmly gives birth to the child. The husband stays in bed with the baby to recover from his terrible ordeal, and the mother returns to work in the fields almost immediately (Kroeber, 1948).

Although cross-cultural laboratory studies of pain reveal no consistent differences in the ability of various racial and ethnic groups to discriminate pain stimuli, members of different cultural groups may differ greatly in their interpretation of the meaning of pain (Zatzick & Dimsdale, 1990). In certain parts of India, for example, people practice an unusual hook-hanging ritual. A celebrant is chosen to bless the children and crops in a number of neighboring villages. Large steel hooks attached by ropes to the top of a special ceremonial cart are shoved under the skin and muscles on each side of his back, and he travels on the cart from village to village. At the climax of a ceremony in each village, the celebrant swings free, hanging only by the hooks embedded in his back, to bless the children and crops (see Figure

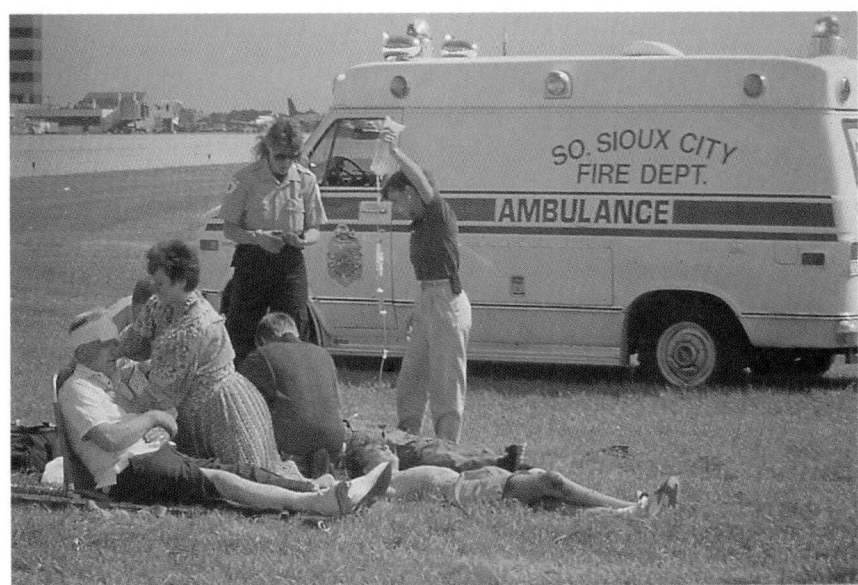

⬆ **Figure 7.29** *Stress-induced analgesia often occurs in disasters, and victims are sometimes unaware of their injuries until later.*

7.30). Incredibly, though impaled on the hooks, the celebrant shows no evidence of experiencing pain during the ritual; on the contrary, he appears to be in a state of ecstasy. When the hooks are removed, the wounds heal rapidly and are scarcely visible within two weeks (Kosambi, 1967).

Differences exist not only between cultural groups but also within them, as the physician Henry Beecher (1959) observed while working at Anzio Beachhead in World War II and later at Massachusetts General Hospital. Beecher found that only about 25 percent of the severely wounded soldiers he observed required pain medication, compared with 80 percent of civilian men who had received similarly serious ''wounds'' from surgeons at Massachusetts General. Why the difference? Beecher concluded that for the soldiers, the wounds had a fundamentally positive meaning: They spelled evacuation from the war zone and a ''ticket'' back home to their loved ones. For the civilian surgical patients, on the other hand, the operations meant a major disruption in their normal lives. The different meanings attributed to the pain stimuli resulted in very different levels of suffering and, consequently, different needs for pain relief.

Intrapsychic Factors in Pain

Sigmund Freud and other psychodynamic theorists have suggested that psychodynamic processes can play a role both in the experiencing of pain and in responses to painful stimuli. Freud treated a number of patients whose physical pain symptoms were found to be without physical cause. Today, such problems are called *somatoform disorders* (Task Force on DSM

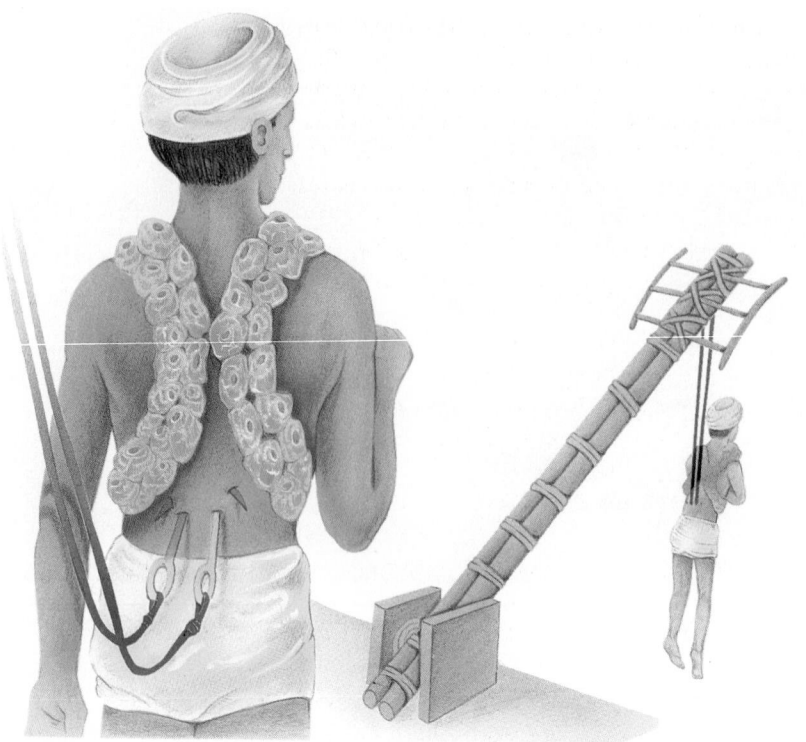

Figure 7.30 *A hook-swinging ceremony practiced in remote villages in India illustrates the importance of the meaning attributed to pain stimuli. Steel hooks are jammed into the back of the celebrant, who is decked with garlands, and he travels from village to village on a cart. The hooks are attached with ropes to a large crossbeam on the cart. After blessing all the children and farm fields in a village, he leaps from the cart and hangs suspended by the hooks. The crowds cheer at each swing; and during the ceremony the celebrant, in a state of ecstasy, shows no sign of pain. (Adapted from Kosambi, 1967).*

In some cases, pain disorders, such as tension and migraine headaches, can result from personal intrapsychic vulnerabilities (Sarason & Sarason, 1993). Former Supreme Court Justice William O. Douglas related how his treatment by a psychoanalyst affected his experience of pain:

> My problem was migraine headaches, which threatened to ruin my career. I had gone to several New York specialists. . . . Draper eventually psychoanalyzed me and helped me discover and understand the stresses and strains that produced the headaches. Once I faced up to them, the migraines disappeared. . . . He was a seminal influence because having discovered that I had been launched in life as a package of fears, he tried to convince me that all fears are illusory (Douglas, 1974, pp. 177, 181, 182).

Many researchers have sought to uncover personality traits that predict an exaggerated response to painful stimuli or the development of somatoform disorders in the absence of actual tissue damage. Although no specific pattern of traits has been consistently found, commonly reported characteristics include a pessimistic and bitter approach to life based on unfulfilled dependency and love needs and a repressive personality style that causes people to be out of touch with personally unacceptable feelings, which are expressed in the form of physical symptoms (Colbach, 1987; Van Houndenhove, 1986).

Individual Coping Styles and Recovery from Pain

Individuals may respond to pain and injuries in a variety of ways. Some regard pain as an unpleasant inconvenience and go about their business as best they can. Others have an exaggerated response to the pain, become preoccupied with it, go to great lengths to protect themselves from it, and eventually become chronic pain patients.

In England, researchers studying factors that influence recovery from injury have advanced a **fear-avoidance theory** to account for exaggerated pain perception (Lethem & others, 1983). They note that fear is the normal response to the threat of pain. People respond to fear of pain in two basically different ways, which they term *confrontation* and *avoidance*.

People who adopt the response of confrontation regard the pain as a temporary nuisance, are strongly motivated to return to normal work, social, and leisure activities, and do so as soon as the injury allows. They test the reality of the pain experience at every stage and maintain an accurate perception of their true physical state. Their fear of further pain realistically dissipates over time as their physical condition improves. They see themselves as healed.

IV, 1991). For some of these patients, the nature or location of the pain bore a symbolic relation to an unconscious conflict or an anxiety-related impulse. For example, one woman experienced stabbing pain in her hands when deeply defended hostile impulses to choke her tyrannical father threatened to erupt into consciousness and action. Freud interpreted this as a turning inward of the forbidden hostile impulses, as well as a form of self-punishment for having them.

Pain can also be a way of attaining certain goals. For some bitter and deprived people, pain can be a way of dramatizing their unhappiness, eliciting caring, sympathy, or guilt from others, or gaining favors from them. Pain may also be a way of escaping from or avoiding threatening situations. For example, an athlete who dreads the possibility of failing may avoid the feared competitive situation by experiencing severe pain that prevents a return to action (May & Sieb, 1987). This process can occur at a subconscious level that is different from simply "faking" being hurt. The pain experienced by the athlete can thus provide a socially and personally justifiable reason for staying away from the psychologically dangerous competitive arena.

Avoiders, on the other hand, do their best to prevent any recurrence of the pain. They take no chances of reinjuring themselves or of worsening their pain. They avoid physical and social activities, and many retreat into a self-protective shell. With fewer opportunities to test reality, many avoiders develop an exaggerated sense of their physical damage and their vulnerability to further injury. Instead of dissipating, their fear increases, and they become chronic pain cases long after the physical injury has apparently healed, particularly if people in their environment encourage or reward their avoidance responses (Slade & others, 1983; Fordyce, 1988).

Self-Efficacy: The Conviction That One Can Cope

The statement ''I can take it'' may be more than an idle boast or a reassuring phrase. Research is demonstrating that **self-efficacy,** the conviction that one can cope, is a major factor in pain tolerance (Bandura & others, 1987; Litt, 1988). In laboratory studies, subjects' self-efficacy expectations that they can tolerate pain result in higher pain thresholds (lower ratings of pain intensity) and greater ability to tolerate painful stimulation from electric shocks, increasing pressure placed on a fingertip, or icy water. The same finding occurs outside of the laboratory. One study examined the perception of women who had completed childbirth classes that they could exercise con-

trol over pain while giving birth. It was found that the higher a woman's perceived self-efficacy, the longer she tolerated the pain of labor before requesting medication and the less medication she required (Manning & Wright, 1983). Likewise, a study of chronic arthritis patients who were equated for degree of physical disability revealed that those who believed that they could exercise some control over their pain led more active lives and reported experiencing less pain (Shoor & Holman, 1984).

Why does self-efficacy improve pain tolerance? The answer is suggested by the results of a study by Albert Bandura and his coworkers (1987). They suggested that high self-efficacy expectations are likely to make people willing to expose themselves to the more intense pain stimuli that activate the endorphin release found in stress-induced analgesia. Endorphin release, in turn, reduces the noxiousness of the stimuli, resulting in a lesser experiencing of pain. In support of their hypothesis, they found that injecting subjects having high self-efficacy for pain tolerance with naloxone (which interferes with endorphins) greatly reduced their ability to endure intensely painful stimuli.

The finding that cognitive factors like interpretation of meaning and self-efficacy expectations can affect the ability to tolerate pain suggests that it might be possible to train people to cope more effectively with pain. The Enhancing Human Performance feature provides some research-derived guidelines that you can use to increase your own pain tolerance.

COPING WITH PAIN: COGNITIVE AND BEHAVIORAL STRATEGIES

ENHANCING HUMAN PERFORMANCE

We all experience pain occasionally, but for some people, pain is a never-ending nightmare. It is estimated that as many as 40 million Americans suffer from long-term and chronic pain of arthritis, cancer, headaches, and physical injury. To assist people who suffer from pain, researchers have increasingly turned their attention to psychological pain control strategies (Davison & Darke, 1991; Keefe & others, 1990). The effectiveness of these techniques can be tested in patients who suffer from body damage, or they can be tested under controlled experimental conditions. In laboratory experiments, subjects are taught specific cognitive or behavioral strategies that they can use during exposure to a painful stimulus, which may be immersion of the hand in

ice water of 2°C (the *cold-pressor test*), painful pressure applied to a finger, or electric shock. The length of time that subjects can tolerate the pain, their physiological stress responses, and their ratings of pain intensity are compared with those of control subjects who have received no pain-control instructions.

Cognitive Strategies

Recent attention has focused on two classes of cognitive techniques known as **dissociative** and **associative strategies.** As the name implies, the first strategy involves dissociating, or distracting, yourself from the painful sensory input. You can do this in a variety of ways: by directing your attention to some other feature of the external situation, by vividly

imagining a pleasurable experience, or by repeating a word or thought to yourself. Research has shown that dissociative strategies are most effective when they require a great deal of concentration or cognitive activity. Thus, if you concentrate on some aspect of the environment, it is best to involve it in a cognitive activity, such as counting the indentations in the ceiling tiles above the dentist's chair. If you use imagery to dissociate from the pain, make the image as vivid as possible and focus on fine details. If you are imagining an experience (preferably a pleasant one), make the internal "movie" as engrossing and personally involving as possible. It is helpful to have several pleasurable fantasies prepared beforehand so that you can switch from one to the other if necessary. Finally, try to experience the fantasies in all sensory modalities and direct your attention to specific details of the scenes.

If you are a recreational jogger or a long-distance runner, you are familiar with the discomfort that can result from extending yourself. Endurance running seems an ideal real-life task to use in the study of cognitive strategies. In a study done at the University of Wisconsin by William Morgan and his coworkers, the effects of a dissociative strategy were studied under laboratory conditions. Male subjects ran to exhaustion on a treadmill at 80 percent of their maximum aerobic capacity to test their pain endurance. They were then randomly assigned to either a control group, which received no strategy instructions, or to an experimental group in which subjects were given a simple dissociative strategy. They were instructed to focus their attention on a spot in front of them and say "down" each time their right foot came down on the treadmill. Then all the men were retested on the treadmill.

Physiological measures taken during the second treadmill run showed that the two groups were similar in their bodily reactions. Yet the dissociation group was able to run the treadmill 32 percent longer, indicating that their strategy enabled them to tolerate the discomfort (Morgan & others, 1983).

Associative strategies are just the opposite of dissociative ones. Here, you focus your attention on the physical sensations but do so in a detached and unemotional fashion, taking care not to label them as painful or difficult to tolerate. It appears that when pain is intense, associative strategies that focus unemotionally on the basic sensory aspects of the pain become more effective than dissociative ones (Ahles & others, 1983; McCaul & Malott, 1984). Perhaps there is a point at which pain stimuli become too intense to ignore, and dissociative strategies break down at this point. One possibly effective strategy is to use dissociation as long as possible and then to shift to an associative mode when the pain becomes too intense to permit distraction. This strategy may be successfully combined with pos-

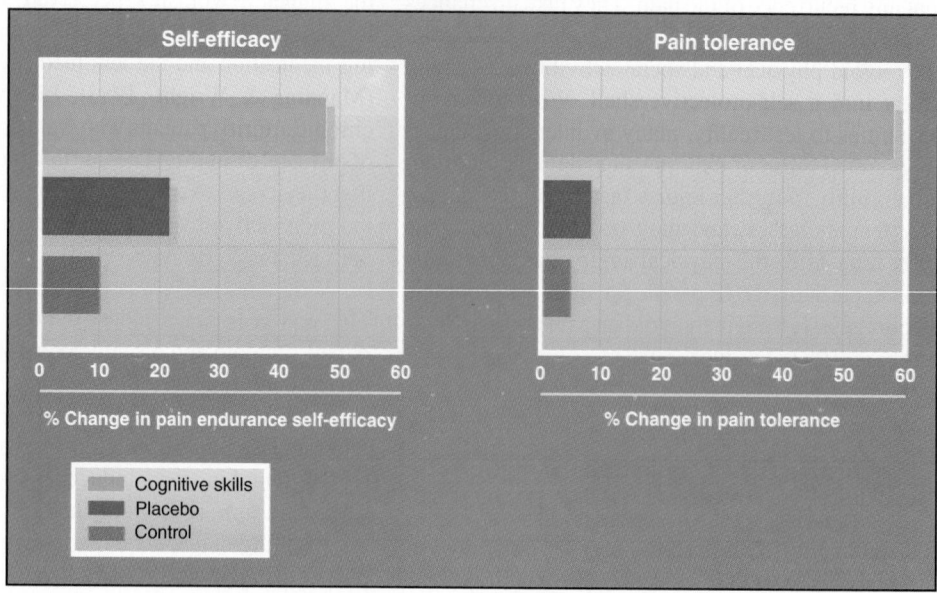

▲ **Figure 7.31** *Effects of training in cognitive pain-control skills on self-efficacy for controlling pain and actual pain tolerance on the cold-pressor task. Subjects trained in the cognitive techniques showed much greater increases in both self-efficacy and pain tolerance than subjects given a placebo and untreated subjects. (Bandura & others, 1987).*

itive self-statements emphasizing that although you do not like the pain, you can stand it and you have control over your tolerance of it (Meichenbaum, 1985).

We have already seen how important self-efficacy is in pain tolerance. Several studies have shown that learning cognitive pain-control strategies increases self-efficacy and the ability to withstand pain. In one study conducted by Albert Bandura and his coworkers (1987), subjects were given the cold-pressor (ice-water) test after estimating how long they could tolerate it. One group of subjects was then trained in and practiced a number of cognitive coping strategies, such as attention diversion, use of distracting imagery, imagining that the hand soaking in the ice water was detached from the body, and nonemotional focusing on the pain sensations. Then they made a new estimate of how long they thought they could tolerate the cold water and were given a second cold-pressor test. The self-efficacy and pain tolerance of the trained subjects were compared with those of two control groups. One control group was given a placebo represented to them as an analgesic agent, while the other received neither training nor placebo. As shown in Figure 7.31, the

cognitive-skills training resulted in large increases in both self-efficacy and pain tolerance. The subjects who learned the skills increased nearly 50 percent in self-efficacy and nearly 60 percent in pain tolerance. In another study, people who suffered from arthritic knee pain were trained in coping skills. Both at the end of treatment and 6 months later, these patients exhibited significantly lower psychological and physical disability than patients who had not received coping-skills training (Keefe & others, 1990).

An Important Behavioral Strategy: Keeping Active

As we saw earlier, patients who avoid activity and become overly protective of an injured body part are at risk for developing a chronic pain condition. It is important to return to activity after an injury as soon as the healing process will allow (but not so soon or so vigorously as to risk reinjury). Wilbert Fordyce, a leader in the behavioral treatment of pain, emphasizes the negative effects that unnecessary rest and disuse of a body part can have on recovery.

[T]he lavish prescription of rest virtually ensures adverse disuse effects. With disuse in the musculoskeletal system, movement then becomes painful. But pain from disuse risks being interpreted by patient and professional as an indication of lack of healing. The result may become more prescribed rest or practical disuse and yet more pain with movement. . . . Pain problems originating in tissue injury but in which healing has occurred are made better by use. Patients must be helped to understand the dictum "To make it better, use it." . . . People who have something better to do don't suffer as much (Fordyce, 1988, p. 282).

Other behavioral skills are useful in coping with pain. One of the most useful is the ability to relax deeply, a coping skill that is taught in the *Enhancing Human Performance* feature of Chapter 15. Voluntary relaxation has been shown in many studies to decrease pain, and relaxation combined with the cognitive strategies just described appears to make these strategies even more effective (Turk & others, 1983).

As we have seen, pain is far more than a sensory experience. It is a psychological phenomenon influenced by interacting biological, environmental, cognitive, and intrapsychic factors. The accompanying Understanding Causes schematic (page 224) summarizes some of the major factors that influence the experience of pain.

Plasticity, Critical Periods, and Perceptual Development

The Ba Mbuti pygmies live in the rain forests of central Africa. Their environment is a closed-in green world of densely packed trees without open spaces. The anthropologist C. M. Turnbull once brought one of the pygmies, a man named Kenge, out of the forest to the edge of a vast plain. A herd of buffalo grazed in the distance. To Turnbull's surprise, Kenge remarked that he had never seen insects of that kind. When told that they were buffalo, not insects, the man was deeply offended and felt that Turnbull was insulting his intelligence. To prove his point, Turnbull drove his jeep toward the animals. Kenge's eyes widened in amazement as the "insects" grew into buffalo before his eyes. To explain his perceptual experience to himself, he concluded that witchcraft was being used to fool him.

We can explain Kenge's misperception as a failure in size constancy. Having lived in an environment without open spaces, he had no experience in judging the size of objects at great distances. But this story also raises a larger issue: What roles do learning and experience have in perceptual development? Are our perceptual abilities determined by a preengineered set of sensory receptors and brain mechanisms that unfold naturally as we mature? Or can perceptual abilities and their underlying physiological structures be altered by sensory experience?

As we might anticipate in light of this chapter's discussion of learned perceptual schemas, experience helps shape our perceptual abilities. The degree to which perceptual systems can be modified, referred to as **plasticity,** parallels the degree of recovery described in Chapter 3 in relation to brain injury. There is considerable evidence that certain experiential and learning factors are critical to the development of perceptual abilities as well as the underlying sensory and neural apparatus. For some aspects of perception, there are also **critical periods** during which certain kinds of experiences must occur if perceptual abilities are to develop normally.

As is often the case, we can learn a good deal about normal development by studying abnormal development. We will focus on the latter here, because it provides us with important facts about plasticity and critical periods.

An Example of Plasticity: Seeing with the Auditory Cortex

Plasticity in perception must involve changes in the underlying sensory and integrative systems that give rise to perceptions, and scientists have been exploring the possibility of such changes. For example, recent studies carried out at the Massachusetts Institute of Technology illustrate the extent to which sensory systems can exhibit plasticity if normal development is disrupted very early in life. The animal chosen for these experiments was the ferret, whose visual system is very immature at birth.

In a number of experimental animals, the visual cortex and the major visual relay station in the thalamus (the sensory "switchboard") were surgically removed from one hemisphere. At the same time, auditory tracts from the ears to that hemisphere's auditory relay station in the thalamus were also removed, but the auditory relay system was left intact. The question was this: Could the auditory system "take over" visual functions in that hemisphere?

The animals were studied into adulthood. Electrical recording techniques indicated that, indeed, axons from the eyes rerouted themselves into the auditory thalamus and that the latter was now sending visual input to the auditory cortex. As various types of visual stimuli were presented to the eyes of the ferrets, recordings from the auditory cortex indicated that neurons there were functioning as visual feature detectors that responded to certain shapes, directions

Causal Factors

Biological
- Stimulation of pain receptors in body
- Release of substance P, endorphins, and other neurotransmitters that affect brain regions involved in pain perception
- Opening and closing of spinal "gates"

Cognitive
- Perceived "meaning" of pain stimuli
- Placebo expectancy effects
- Use of cognitive pain-control strategies
- Coping self-efficacy beliefs

Intrapsychic
- Unresolved conflicts in somatoform pain disorders
- Pain as a means of controlling others
- Confrontation vs. avoidance coping styles
- Personality conflicts that increase vulnerability to stress

Environmental
- Cultural factors that influence perceived meaning of pain stimuli
- Previous learning about how to deal with pain
- Environmental support or discouragement for confrontation/avoidance coping styles

Pain

Pain is a function of interacting personal and environmental causal factors. These factors may vary and may interact with one another in particular ways, depending on the person and the situation.

of movement, and so forth (Sur & others, 1988). The animals were now, in a sense, seeing with their auditory cortex. It thus appears that the development of the sensory and perceptual apparatus may be determined by the kinds of inputs it receives during critical periods early in development (Kimble, 1992; Kolb, 1989).

Manipulating the Visual Environment

Another approach to studying the impact of experience on perceptual development is to control and manipulate the specific sensory inputs received by subjects and then to observe the effects on perceptual abilities. Earlier, we saw that the visual cortex has orientation columns composed of neurons that respond only to lines at particular angles. What would happen if newborn animals grew up in a world in which they saw only certain angles?

In a classic study, British researchers Colin Blakemore and Grahame Cooper (1970) created such a world for newborn kittens. The animals were raised in the dark except for a 5-hour period each day during which they were placed in round chambers that had either vertical or horizonal stripes on the walls. Figure 7.32 shows one of the kittens in a vertically striped chamber. A special collar prevented the kittens from seeing their own bodies while they were in the chambers.

When the kittens were 5 months of age, Blakemore and Cooper presented bars of light at differing angles to them and tested the electrical responses of individual cells in their visual cortexes with microelectrodes. The results for animals raised in the vertically striped environment are shown in Figure 7.32b). As you can see, the kittens had no cells that fired in response to horizontal stimuli. They also had visual impairments. For example, they acted as if they could not see a pencil when it was held in a horizontal position and waved in front of them. However, as soon as the pencil was rotated to a vertical position, the animals began to follow it with their eyes as it was moved back and forth.

As you might expect, the animals raised in the horizontally striped environment showed the opposite effects. They had no feature detectors for vertical stimuli and did not seem to see them. Thus, the cortical neurons of both groups of kittens developed in accordance with the stimulus features of their environments.

When the Blind See

Suppose people who had been blind from birth suddenly had their vision restored during adulthood.

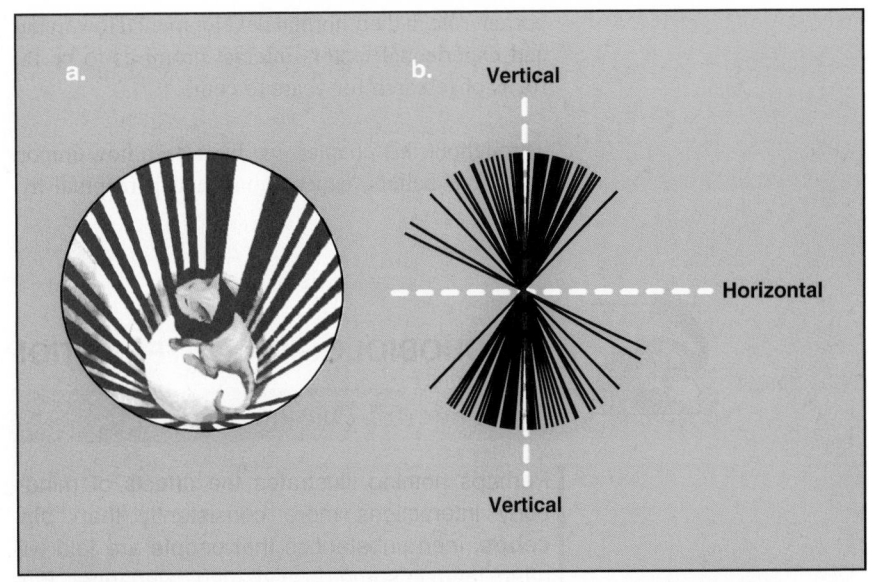

🔹 **Figure 7.32** *Kittens raised in a vertically striped chamber such as the one shown in* (a) *lacked cortical cells that fired in response to horizontal stimuli. The orientation column "holes" are easily seen in* (b), *which shows the orientation angles that resulted in evoked potentials from feature detectors. (Adapted from Blakemore & Cooper, 1970).*

What would they see? Could they perceive visually the things that they had learned to identify through their other senses?

People who are born with congenital cataracts grow up in a visual world without form. The clouded lenses of their eyes permit them to perceive light, but not patterns or shapes. A German physician, von Senden (1960), compiled data on adult patients with congenital cataracts who were tested soon after their cataracts were surgically removed. These people were immediately able to perceive figure–ground relations, to scan objects visually, and to follow moving targets with their eyes, indicating that such abilities are innate. However, they could not visually identify objects that they were familiar with through touch, such as eating utensils, nor were they able to distinguish simple geometric figures without counting the corners or tracing the figures with their fingers.

After several weeks of training, the patients were able to identify simple objects by sight, but their perceptual constancy was very poor. Often, they were unable to recognize the same shape in another color, even though they could discriminate between colors. Years after their vision had been restored, some of the patients could identify only a few of the faces of people they knew well. Many also had great difficulty judging distances. Apparently, no amount of subsequent experience could make up for their lack of visual experience during childhood.

All of these lines of evidence suggest that biological and experiential factors interact in complex ways. Some of our perceptual abilities are at least partially present at birth, but experience plays an important role in their normal development. How innate and experiential factors interact promises to be the focus of research for years to come.

Throughout this chapter, we have seen how importantly our beliefs, expectations, and perceptual hypotheses influence our experiences. The feature that follows draws together much of what we have discussed and illustrates how beliefs and perceptions can interact with actual bodily states.

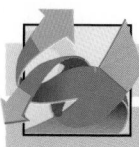

PSYCHOBIOLOGICAL INTERACTIONS

The Powerful Placebo

Perhaps nothing illustrates the effects of mind–body interactions more consistently than **placebos,** inert substances that people are told will affect them in some positive medical manner. Placebos seem capable of affecting every system of the body. The range of medical problems that have responded to them includes seasickness, headaches, high blood pressure, angina, anxiety, depression, warts, colds, insomnia, acne, ulcers, allergies, and many other disorders (Friedman & DiMatteo, 1989; Taylor, 1991).

In his book *Persuasion and Healing* (1973), the psychiatrist Jerome Frank described an experiment done by a German physician, Hans Rheder, on three bedridden patients. One of the patients had an inflamed gall bladder and chronic gallstones. The second was having difficulty recovering from pancreas surgery and had experienced such severe weight loss that Rheder described her as "skeletal." The third patient was dying from cancer that had spread throughout her body. Since conventional medicine had done all that was possible for the women, Rheder decided to try the unconventional: He told each of the women that he had discovered a very powerful faith healer who could cure with remarkable success by simply directing his healing power to a particular place. Rheder told each woman that he had arranged for the miraculous healing power to be projected to her room on a specific day and hour. (Actually, he had already tried the healer without telling the women and without success. The healer was no longer involved in the cases.)

Within a few days of the appointed healing date, the woman who had been wasting away began to eat and subsequently gained 30 pounds. The patient with gallstones lost all of her symptoms, returned home, and remained symptom-free for a year. The patient with cancer was already a terminal case, but her body soon excreted excess fluids that had made her bloated, she gained strength, and her blood count improved. She was able to return home and lived for three months in relative comfort.

Can placebos also affect our perception of pain? Clearly, they can. In one study, either a placebo or a morphine injection was given to 122 surgical patients suffering postoperative pain from their wounds. Sixty-seven percent of those who received morphine reported relief, but 42 percent of those given placebos reported equal relief (Beecher, 1959).

The power of belief and expectation not only can cause placebos to relieve pain but also can completely reverse the usual pharmacological effects of a drug. In one extraordinary experiment, pregnant women suffering from nausea caused by morning sickness were given what was described to them as a new wonder drug to relieve their nausea. In reality, however, they were given syrup of ipecac, a medication used to induce vomiting in people who have swallowed certain poisons. The ipecac should have made the women even sicker, but instead, some of the women reported immediate relief from their morning sickness (Haas & others, 1959).

Placebos work only if people believe they are going to work. Without faith and expectation of relief, the inert interventions are exactly that. But given the expectation of relief, how do placebos work at a physiological level? Where perception of pain is concerned, it appears that placebos bring about their analgesic effects by stimulating the release of endorphins. One piece of evidence supporting this mechanism comes from a study in which subjects who had just had their wisdom teeth removed were given a placebo. About 40 percent of the patients responded to the placebo with reports of reduced pain after one hour. Those reporting relief were then given a second "pain relief" injection, which was either a second placebo or naloxone, the drug that blocks endorphin effects. Under naloxone, the pain-reducing placebo effects of the second injection were completely eliminated, and these subjects reported sharply increased levels of pain. Patients who had not responded to the original placebo and who had been given naloxone on the second injection reported no change in their experience of pain. This pattern of results suggests that when placebos produce analgesic effects, they do so by stimulating the release of endorphins (Levine & others, 1978).

Over the course of medical history, patients have been successfully treated with potions ranging from frog sperm, lizard tongues, and animal dung to modern wonder drugs. The fact that many patients over the ages have responded to medicines and procedures now known to lack medical value suggests that the effects we now label "placebo effects" have always been operative, stimulated by faith in the shaman, the medicine man, or the physician. It seems likely that it was the *belief* in the remedy that helped mobilize innate self-healing mechanisms within the body. Understanding the mechanisms by which placebos work may not only provide us with ways to strengthen these innate healing systems but also help us to gain fresh insights into how mind and body interact.

S U M M A R Y

Sensation and Perception

● Although sensation and perception are interrelated, sensation refers to the activities by which our sense organs receive and transmit information, while perception involves the brain's processing and interpretation of the information.

Attention as a Selective Process

● Attention is an active process in which we focus on certain stimuli while blocking out other stimuli. We cannot attend completely to more than one thing at a time, but we are capable of rapid attentional shifts.

● Attentional processes are affected by the nature of the stimulus as well as by personal factors such as motives and interests. The perceptual system appears to be especially vigilant to stimuli that denote threat or danger. However, sometimes threatening or anxiety-arousing stimuli are not consciously perceived, a phenomenon known as perceptual defense.

Patterning and Organization in Perception

● The Gestalt psychologists identified a number of principles of perceptual organization, including figure–ground relations and the laws of similarity, proximity, closure, and continuity. R. L. Gregory suggested that perception is essentially a hypothesis about what a stimulus is, based on previous experience and the nature of the stimulus. According to this view, illusions are incorrect hypotheses.

● Perceptual constancies allow us to recognize familiar stimuli under changing conditions. In the visual realm, there are three constancies: shape, brightness, and size. Constancies are the basis of many illusions.

Depth and Movement Perception

● Several monocular cues help us to judge distance. These include linear perspective, decreasing size, height in the horizontal plane, texture, and clarity.

● The five distance cues also help us to judge depth. Depth perception also occurs through the monocular cues of light and shadow patterns and interposition and through binocular cues.

● Stereopsis is the perception of depth that results from the use of both eyes. Binocular disparity is the basis for stereopsis.

● The stimulus for perception of movement is absolute movement of a stimulus across the retina or relative movement of an object in relation to its background. Autokinetic and stroboscopic movement are illusory.

Pain as a Perceptual Phenomenon

● The major pain receptors appear to be free nerve endings. Gate-control theory proposes that once pain impulses have been sent toward the brain, a series of neural gates may be opened or closed to influence pain perception. The nervous system also contains opiates called endorphins, which appear to play a major role in pain perception. Endorphins released in response to stress produce analgesia and thus increase pain tolerance. Recent evidence indicates, however, that the endorphins block the activity of natural killer cells that are part of the body's defenses against tumors.

● Psychological factors strongly influence responses to painful stimuli. Coping styles involving inappropriate avoidance of additional pain appear to be related to chronic pain problems. Cultural factors also influence the manner in which painful stimuli are appraised and responded to, as do expectations and self-efficacy beliefs.

● Cognitive control of pain is possible through a number of strategies. Dissociative strategies appear useful with milder forms of pain, while associative strategies seem to produce better results when pain is intense.

Plasticity, Critical Periods, and Perceptual Development

● Perceptual development involves both physical maturation and learning. Certain perceptual abilities are innate or develop shortly after birth, whereas others require particular experiences in order to develop.

● There appear to be critical periods for the development of certain perceptual abilities. Visual deprivation studies, manipulation of visual input, and studies of restored vision have shown that the normal biological development of the perceptual system depends on certain sensory experiences.

associative strategies (p. 221)
autokinetic effect (p. 215)
binocular cues (p. 211)
binocular disparity (p. 214)
common region (p. 206)
connectedness (p. 206)
critical period (p. 223)
dissociative strategies (p. 221)
endorphins (p. 217)
fear-avoidance theory of pain (p. 220)
figure-ground relations (p. 204)
gate-control theory (p. 216)

geons (p. 208)
illusion (p. 209)
law of closure (p. 205)
law of continuity (p. 205)
law of proximity (p. 205)
law of similarity (p. 205)
monocular cues (p. 211)
motion parallax (p. 213)
perception (p. 201)
perceptual constancies (p. 210)
perceptual defense (p. 203)
perceptual schemas (p. 206)

perceptual set (p. 201)
placebo (p. 226)
plasticity (p. 223)
recognition-by-components theory (p. 208)
self-efficacy (p. 221)
shadowing (p. 202)
stereopsis (p. 214)
stress-induced analgesia (p. 218)
stroboscopic movement (phi phenomenon) (p. 215)
substance P (p. 217)

SUGGESTED READINGS

Coren, S., & Ward, L. (1989). *Sensation and perception.* New York: Harcourt, Brace. A comprehensive and readable introduction to basic principles of sensation and perception.

Melzack, R. (1973). *The puzzle of pain.* A somewhat dated but classic description of the development of the gate-control theory of pain, well worth reading for its vivid description of the process of discovery.

Rock, I. (1984). *Perception.* New York: Scientific American Books. Many basic topics in perception are dealt with in this beautifully illustrated book.

White, L., Tursky, B., & Schwartz, G. E. (Eds.) (1985). *Placebo: Theory, research, and mechanism.* Leading investigators of placebo effects and their underlying mechanisms report on their work.

States of Consciousness

8

One autumn afternoon in 1943, Albert Hofmann, a Swiss chemist, was beset by giddiness and an inability to concentrate. More alarmingly, he noticed that the shapes of his assistants kept changing. He went home to bed, but instead of normal sleep, he experienced fantastic dreams with intense and fluid colors.

Returning to his laboratory the next day, Hofmann examined a chemical substance he had been synthesizing and concluded that he must have absorbed a small amount of it through his skin. Overcome by curiosity, he put a tiny bit on his tongue. Soon he began to experience a strong sense of uneasiness and felt he was splitting into two people. His alarmed assistants took him home, where his strange experiences continued:

> The dizziness and sensation of fainting became so strong at times that I could no longer hold myself erect and had to lie down on a sofa. My surroundings had transformed themselves in more terrifying ways. Everything in the room spun around and the familiar objects and pieces of furniture assumed grotesque, mostly threatening forms. . . . The neighbor woman who brought me milk . . . I scarcely recognized any longer. She was no longer Mrs. R., but rather a malevolent insidious witch with a colored mask. Even worse than these demonic transformations of the outer world were the alterations that I perceived in myself, in my inner being. Every exertion of my will, to put an end to the disintegration of the outer world and the dissolution of my ego, seemed a wasted effort. A demon had invaded me and had taken possession of my body, mind and soul. I jumped up and screamed in order to free myself from him, but then sank down again powerless on the sofa. The substance, with which I had wanted to experiment, had vanquished me (Hofmann, 1980, p. 58).

So it was that Albert Hofmann accidentally discovered the striking alterations in conscious experience that can be produced by a dose of lysergic acid diethylamide (LSD) no larger than the tip of a pin.

Billy Milligan is a most unusual person. In fact, he may be as many as ten unusual people. Billy's multiple personalities became known shortly after he was arrested for raping several women in Columbus, Ohio. A psychologist began a jailhouse interview by asking him if he was William Milligan. "Billy's asleep," came the reply. "I'm David."

An intensive psychological study of Milligan revealed a dramatic division of consciousness that psychologists call **dissociation.** Over time, there emerged at least nine distinct personalities in addition to the core personality, Billy. Most of them were unaware of the others. The other personalities included Christene, a loving 3-year-old girl who liked to draw flowers and butterflies; Adelena, a young female homosexual; David, a withdrawn youngster who banged his head against the wall when he was upset; an escape artist named Tommy, who slithered out of a straitjacket in less than 10 seconds; Arthur, an intellectual who spoke with a British accent; Ragan, an aggressive male with a Slavic accent who considered himself the others' protector and once threatened to fire the defense lawyers; and Allen, an 18-year-old who played the drums and was the only one who smoked. When given intelligence tests, the various personalities obtained IQs ranging from 68 to over 130 (Keyes, 1982).

Albert Hofmann's LSD experience and the multiple personalities of Billy Milligan may seem to illustrate extreme departures from the states of consciousness to which we are accustomed. And yet they are not as far removed from our normal functioning as we might think. We all drift into and out of various states of consciousness and awareness, though in far less extreme and dramatic ways than Albert Hofmann and Billy Milligan did. Our conscious self-awareness provides us with a stable personal identity that has a past, a present, and a future. But a moment's reflection tells us that even when we are fully awake, our consciousness is not a unitary state. At any instant, for example, we may be looking, listening, feeling, planning, or anticipating. The many processes and experiences that occur in our normal stream of consciousness are so familiar to us that we often take them for granted and forget how wonderfully varied they are.

We are far more aware of the fluctuations in consciousness that occur as we pass from wakefulness into sleep, where we may at times experience vivid dreams that rival Hofmann's hallucinations and where there occurs a kind of dissociation that we rarely think about. Have you ever wondered why you don't fall out of bed while you are asleep, as young children sometimes do? Despite the fact that "you" are sound asleep, a part of you somehow knows where the edge of the bed is, and you remain on it despite the 8 to 12 major posture shifts that you are likely to make during the night.

In this chapter, we explore the spectrum of consciousness, which stretches from the many varieties of normal waking activity and fantasy, to sleep and the world of dreams, and on into the more exotic realms of meditative and hypnotic experiences and drug-induced states of consciousness. As we shall see, the phenomena of consciousness lie squarely at the crossroads of biological–psychological interactions. Their study is not only revealing a great deal about how brain and experience are related but also is forcing us to rethink some long-standing conceptions about the nature of the mind.

The Scientific Study of Consciousness

Consciousness refers to our moment-to-moment awareness of ourselves and our environment. It involves subjective awareness of thoughts, percepts, and feelings. Because of its subjective nature, the scientific study of consciousness is a challenging enterprise. Charles Dickens recognized the problem when he observed that "Every human creature is constituted to be that profound secret and mystery to every other." I cannot directly know what reality is for you, nor can you enter directly into my experience. Even if we were observing the same sunset, we couldn't be sure that our conscious experience was the same, because at any instant, our consciousness is affected by two general classes of stimulation: (1) stimuli from the external environment being processed by our sensory and perceptual systems, and (2) internal stimuli generated by the brain in the form of thoughts, images, memories, and so on (Singer, 1988). Scientists, then, are limited to the study of externally observable behaviors that may indicate what the subject is experiencing subjectively. Figure 8.1 shows the types of observable behavior used to study consciousness.

The most common of these behaviors is verbal self-report, in which subjects describe their inner experiences. But although self-reports are frequently our only tool for studying certain aspects of consciousness, such reports are not always reliable and are often impossible to verify. This is why behaviorists have always opposed the use of introspection for scientific purposes. Moreover, subjects sometimes do not have words to describe certain types of experiences that occur in unusual states of consciousness.

A second class of behaviors is physiological responses. Because all experience involves the functioning of the nervous system, physiological measures that are consistently associated with verbal reports of particular mental processes or inner experiences can provide valuable indirect measures of mental events. As we shall see, such measures have been extremely useful in the study of sleep and dreaming. Thanks to increasingly sophisticated ways of measuring and analyzing the electrical activity of the brain, scientists can now measure a variety of mental activities and perhaps even subjective experiences (Lydic & Biebuyck, 1989).

Nonverbal behaviors are a third class of indicators scientists use to infer mental events. Suppose, for example, that you want to know if chimpanzees are self-aware. You might do what one scientist did (Gallup, 1979). He anesthetized a chimp and put a red spot on its face. When the chimp awoke, it was

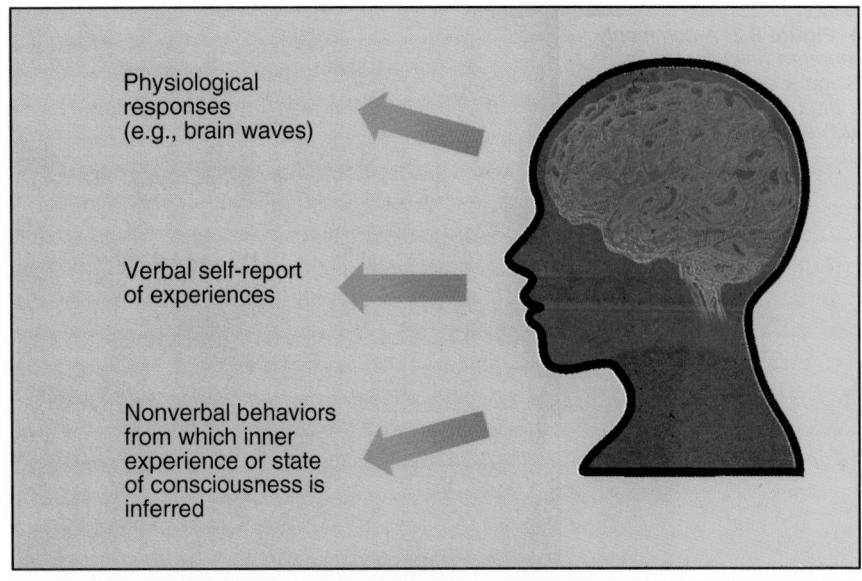

Figure 8.1 *Because it is a private event, consciousness cannot be observed directly. However, conscious experience can be studied scientifically through three major classes of externally observable and measurable responses: physiological responses, verbal self-reports, and nonverbal behavior.*

handed a mirror. Seeing its reflection in the mirror, the chimp immediately raised a hand to its face and tried to rub off the spot, indicating that (a) it knew that the mirror image was a reflection of itself and (b) it was aware that the red spot was something new. These nonverbal behaviors imply some degree of conscious self-awareness on the part of the chimp. As we saw in Chapter 4, this same procedure has been used to establish that most human infants achieve a sense of self-awareness during the second year of life (Gallup & Suarez, 1986).

In another example, Ronald Siegel (1977) of UCLA trained human volunteers to use a complex keyboard whose keys represented various forms, colors, and movements. The keyboard was then used by volunteers to report on the hallucinations they experienced after taking LSD and other drugs. Experts in the use of the keyboard could bang out detailed information concerning up to 20 images per minute. Using this technique in conjunction with verbal report, Siegel identified a common four-stage pattern of drug hallucinations, which proceeds from vague black-and-white floating forms in the first stage to the appearance of complex geometric forms like the spiral tunnel shown in Figure 8.2 in the second stage. Blue is the most common color at first, but red begins to predominate later. The third stage contains meaningful images and scenes from memory, which become more like surreal movie "special effects" in the fourth stage.

In the study of human consciousness, all three of these response systems can be used at the same time. For example, if we wish to study a person's waking

fantasies, we can observe her behavior (for example, whether she is reading or staring into space), take EEG measures to assess her brain-wave patterns, and ask her what she is thinking about. Each of these measures can provide valuable information that the others would not capture.

Emerging Conceptions of Mind and Consciousness

The study of consciousness demands not only imaginative methods of study but also some conception of what consciousness is and how the mind operates. Research has shown that a great deal of cognitive activity goes on outside of our awareness, and the study of these events by cognitive scientists has resulted in an important distinction between automatic processing and controlled processing. This distinction is also captured in the contrast made by Ellen Langer (1989) between mindlessness and mindfulness.

Automatic and Controlled Processing

Many mental activities, such as figuring out how to solve a problem or paying careful attention to what your professor is saying as you take notes, involve attention and conscious effort. Such activities are said to involve **controlled processing.** Other activities which seem not to require conscious attention, are said to represent **automatic processing.** A wide range of mental activities proceed in a completely automatic fashion. These include the perceptual schemas used to interpret stimuli, as well as knowledge structures that are used to understand and produce language and to commit information to memory. That stimuli can be automatically processed is illustrated by the fact that so-called subliminal stimuli can evoke physiological reactions even though a person does not consciously perceive them (Erdelyi, 1988; Kihlstrom, 1990). Automatic processing commonly occurs when we carry out a well-learned activity, such as driving a car, while daydreaming about something completely different. Through years of practice, athletes program themselves to execute complex skills with a minimum of conscious thought (see Figure 8.3). Yogi Berra, the former Yankee catcher, captured the importance of automatic processing in his classic pronouncement, ''You can't think and hit at the same time.''

Because of automatic processing, a great deal of complex cognitive activity can go on outside of conscious awareness. We carry out mental activities and make judgments that we are completely unaware of, and we may not even know exactly why we have made them. Ellen Langer (1989) points out that automatic processing, which she calls *mindlessness,* also has its disadvantages. Despite the speed and economy of effort that it provides, mindlessness can keep us from challenging old ways of viewing the world and can rob us of chances to be aware of problems and to find new ways of approaching problems.

Levels of Consciousness

Controlled and automatic processing are, of course, related to our degree of awareness of mental processes. How consciously aware we are of a stimulus, a memory, a feeling, or our own thought processes may vary. Sigmund Freud was one of the first theorists to focus on varying levels of awareness and to emphasize the importance of psychic processes other than conscious ones. Today, many psychologists favor a classification scheme that specifies four levels of conscious awarenessness.

The term **conscious** describes contents of mind that are in our immediate awareness. For example, you are conscious of what you are reading at this moment.

Subconscious awareness occurs when we are not attending directly to a stimulus, but the stimulus is being processed automatically. For example, when you walk, you are not aware of the position of your limbs unless something goes awry. Similarly, you may not be aware of a background stimulus, such as a strange sound, until someone tells you it is important.

Preconscious events are outside of conscious awareness but can be recalled under certain conditions. For instance, you may not have thought about a childhood friend for years; but when another person mentions your friend's name, a flood of memories may return.

Finally, as Freud noted, **unconscious** material cannot be brought into conscious awareness under ordinary circumstances. Some unconscious content, such as the automatic processing mechanisms themselves, are never conscious. According to psychodynamic theorists, other mental events are actively kept out of awareness because they would arouse anxiety, guilt, or some other negative emotion.

The Mind as Multiple Modules

Traditionally, the human mind has been portrayed as a single, unified entity. To be sure, the mind was viewed as having different functions, like memory, perception, thought, and language, but all were under the control of an "executive" that oversaw and coordinated their functions.

This traditional view of mind has been challenged in recent years by a new conception that views the mind not as a unified entity but as a collection of largely independent modules, or "little minds" (Estes, 1991; Fodor, 1983; Gazzaniga, 1985). These modules are information-processing units devoted to performing simple and specific tasks in particular situations. They operate automatically at an unconscious level, but their contents can ascend into consciousness in a process controlled by higher level integrative modules. Some modules process sensory information; others swing into action when we select a restaurant, walk into a classroom on the first day of classes, or are confronted by an angry person. The modules interact with one another to produce the bottom-up and top-down processing of information discussed in Chapter 7 (Estes, 1991; Rummelhart & McClelland, 1986). At any given moment, the ongoing activity of the modules accounts for the ever-changing "stream of consciousness" that the early psychologist William James described.

The most important aspect of the modular model of mind is the notion that a number of modules can all be processing the same information at the same time. From a modular perspective, conflicting thoughts or feelings and even multiple personalities may reflect the successive emergence into consciousness of the contents of different modules when the integrative modules fail to consistently control what appears in consciousness.

The multiple-module notion of mind and consciousness is viewed by many scientists as being more consistent with the facts of subliminal perception, observations of split-brain patients and other forms of brain damage, and the sometimes divided nature of consciousness than the traditional model of the unitary mind (Kihlstrom, 1990). Only time will tell

Figure 8.3 *Automatic processing permits elite athletes like Michael Jordan to execute complex skills "mindlessly."*

how useful this model will be in advancing our understanding of body–mind relations.

We now turn to the phemonena of consciousness that are in the forefront of current psychological research: sleep and dreaming, fantasy, meditation, hypnosis, and drug-induced alterations of consciousness.

Sleeping and Dreaming

We probably spend from 30 to 40 percent of our lives asleep. No wonder we sometimes feel that there are not enough hours in the day! Yet despite many recent advances in sleep research, scientists do not agree on why we sleep so much or, for that matter, why we sleep at all (Ellman & Antrobus, 1991; Hobson, 1989).

One theory of sleep has an evolutionary focus. It holds that the sleep cycle keeps organisms inactive (and usually hidden) during the period of day or night when they would be especially vulnerable to predators (Webb, 1974). Thus, the tendency of humans to sleep during the night hours is viewed as a product of natural selection that favored those prehistoric humans who avoided in this way the jaws of the predators who prowled in their nocturnal world.

Another long-standing idea is that sleep restores us. When we are fatigued, sleep gives our bodies a chance to recuperate. Consistent with this hypothesis are recent findings of a complex interaction of more than 30 chemicals in the brain, the endocrine system, and the immune system (Inouye, 1989). One of the results of this process is the release of a growth hormone, *somatotropin,* which aids in protein synthesis and tissue regeneration. Most of the body's supply of this hormone is produced during deep sleep (Krueger, 1989).

But other findings do not fit the hypothesis that we sleep because the body needs to recuperate. For example, our bodies use about the same amount of oxygen and glucose during sleep as during relaxed wakefulness, and we do not seem to rid ourselves of any body toxins during sleep (Horne, 1988). Moreover, scientists have studied unusual people who customarily sleep as little as 15 to 30 minutes a night with no ill effects (Moore-Ede & others, 1982).

Despite a range of speculations, then, the question of exactly why we sleep remains unanswered. Nonetheless, it is clear that sleep is a part of a natural biological activity cycle that regulates many aspects of our behavior.

The Circadian Rhythm

Most of us regulate periods of sleep and wakefulness in accordance with external events, such as changes in light and darkness, mealtimes, and the unwelcome buzzing of alarm clocks. But underlying these artificial regulators of the sleep cycle is a biologically based 24-hour activity cycle that becomes evident when sleep and waking are not regulated by external stimuli. Over the billions of years during which life has been evolving, the biological activities of humans, as well as those of other species, including plants, have become linked to the 24-hour cycle resulting from the earth's rotation on its axis. In humans, the 24-hour **circadian rhythm** (from the Latin *circa,* "around," and *dia,* "day") involves daily cyclical changes in body temperature, blood pressure, blood-plasma volume, hormonal secretions, and other bodily processes. We normally sleep during the low point of the daily temperature cycle.

Disruption of the circadian rhythm by an extreme change in sleeping patterns may result in a kind of fatigue and disorientation similar to the jet lag that people experience when they cross several time zones in one day (see Figure 8.4). Our bodies may require a week or more to adapt completely to a major disruption of the circadian rhythm. With jet lag, speed of readjustment depends in part on whether one has lost time flying east, or gained time flying west. It takes less time for people flying west to resynchronize their biological rhythms with the new time frame, presumably because the lengthening of the day by the "gaining" of hours is more compatible with the natural circadian rhythm than is the effective shortening of the day that results from going west to east (Kimble, 1992).

Whether you are traveling east or west across time zones, adjusting your sleep cycle to the new locale (perhaps by changing your bedtime even before you leave) speeds the resynchronization process. A more exotic means of doing so has been developed by Charles Czeisler, a sleep researcher at Harvard Medical School (Czeisler & others, 1986). Evidence that bright light can affect the release of hormones thought to be involved in the sleep cycle led Czeisler to wonder if biological clocks could be reset by exposure of subjects to bright fluorescent lights on a schedule corresponding with a new day–night cycle (see Figure 8.5). An experiment with a woman whose biological clock, for unknown reasons, was chronically 6 hours out of phase with her Boston environment was successful. More recently, Czeisler demonstrated that 5 hours of bright light on each of 3 successive days can reset internal clocks by as much as 12 hours. Normally, such a change would take about 12 days (Kimble, 1992).

It appears that the light treatment works by altering the temperature cycle that seems to be an important factor in the circadian rhythm (Hobson, 1989). In any case, this form of treatment may offer new hope for people who suffer from sleep disorders related to circadian rhythm. Exposure to the bright fluorescent lights also helps people who suffer from **seasonal affective disorder,** a cyclic tendency to become extremely depressed during the winter months because of the decreased amount of daylight (Lewy & others, 1987).

Figure 8.4 *Crossing many time zones, as in traveling from North America to New Zealand, can disrupt the circadian rhythm.*

Given the intimate links that exist between the circadian cycle and physiological functions, it is perhaps not surprising that both medical catastrophes and human error are related to brain and sleep clocks (Mitler and others, 1988). We now know that the neural processes controlling alertness and sleep produce sleepiness and diminished capacity to function during the early morning hours (2:00–7:00 A.M.) and, to a lesser degree, during the midafternoon (2:00–5:00 P.M.). Death—particularly sudden death—strikes most often in the early morning hours, with a major peak occurring between 2:00 and 6:00 A.M. Job performance errors, fatal auto accidents, and engineering and industrial disasters show the same pattern, with the major peak occurring between 2:00 and 4:00 A.M. (see Figure 8.6). Alarmingly, major nuclear accidents at Chernobyl, Russia; at Three Mile Island; and at two other plants in the United States all occurred between 1:30 and 5:00 A.M. (Akerstedt, 1988; Mitler & others, 1988). Night workers consistently report sleepiness at this period of the early morning, when the circadian temperature cycle is at its lowest point (Akerstedt, 1988). Clearly, both laboratory and field research are needed to develop countermeasures to this dangerous pattern.

Stages of Sleep

Much of the research on sleep and dreaming has been carried out in specially equipped sleep laboratories where the physiological responses of sleeping subjects are monitored and analyzed on computers (see Figure 8.7). A more recent technique permits subjects to sleep at home in their own beds while their physiological data are transmitted through computer telephone hookups to laboratories miles away (Rosekind & others, 1978).

The most important technological advance in sleep research was the development of the electroencephalogram (EEG) for measuring the brain's electrical activity. EEG recordings during the sleep cycle resemble those shown in Figure 8.8. These records show that there are five fairly distinct stages of sleep. A relaxed waking state is represented by a brain-wave pattern of 8 to 12 cycles per second (cps), known as an **alpha rhythm.** At the onset of sleep, the alpha rhythm is replaced by the fast, irregular rhythm of stage 1, a form of light sleep from which we can easily be awakened. At stage 2, **sleep spindles**—periodic bursts of brain-wave activity—appear in the EEG as sleep becomes deeper. As sleep progresses into stage 3, brain waves become progressively slower and larger. The deepest sleep, which occurs in stage 4, is characterized by a slow (0.5–2 cps), synchronized pattern of the brain waves, known as **delta waves.** The changes in wave patterns from stage 1 to stage

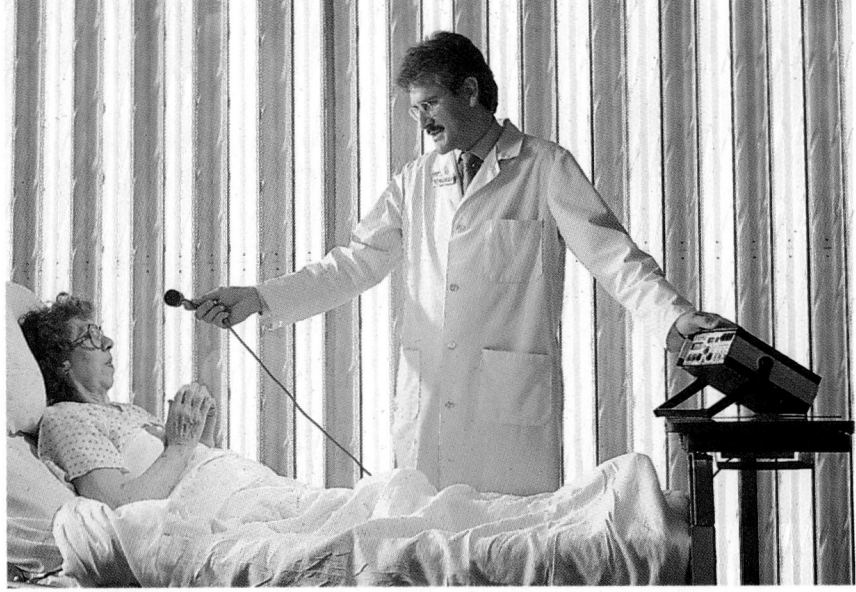

Figure 8.5 *By exposing subjects to bright fluorescent lights corresponding to a particular day–night cycle, sleep researcher Charles Czeisler can "reset" the circadian rhythm.*

4 reflect increasing synchronization in the electrical firing of millions of brain cells.

In 1953, two sleep researchers, Eugene Aserinsky and Nathaniel Kleitman, identified a fifth sleep stage that begins about an hour after we fall asleep and occurs approximately every 90 minutes thereafter. Returning through stages 3 and 2, we enter a new stage quite unlike the rest. The EEG pattern for this stage resembles wakefulness—which caused it to be labeled *paradoxical sleep*—but the stage also involves increases in heart rate, more rapid and irregular

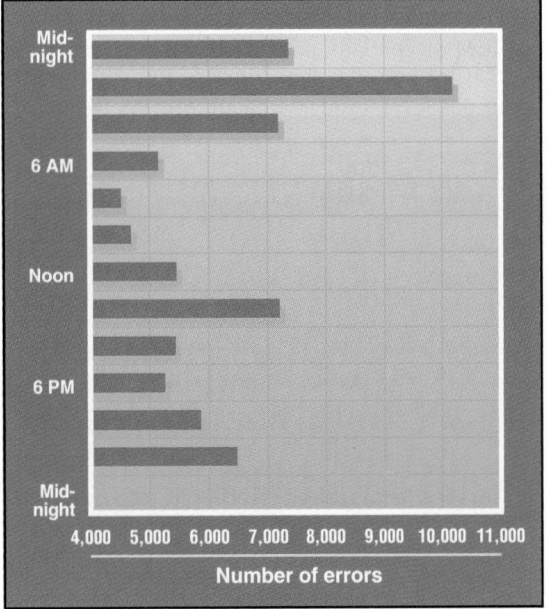

Figure 8.6 *The temporal distribution of 74,927 industrial meter-reading errors shows the typical peak in the early morning hours, when workers complain about sleepiness. (Data from Bjerner & others, 1955; Mitler & others, 1988).*

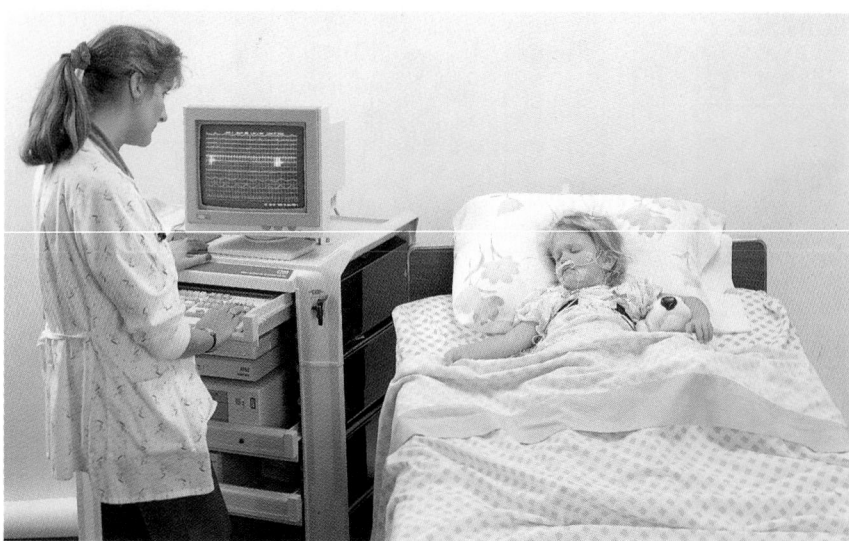

Figure 8.7 *In a modern sleep laboratory, subjects sleep while their physiological responses are monitored and recorded in an adjoining room. The electrodes attached to the scalp area record the subjects' EEG brain-wave patterns. Electrodes attached beside the eyes can record eye movements during sleep. The combined EEG and eye movement records can be used to study dreaming.*

breathing, genital responses (erections in men, vaginal congestion and lubrication in women), and bursts of muscular activity that produce rapid eye movements (REMs) every half-minute or so. Because of the characteristic eye movements, paradoxical sleep is often called **REM sleep**. Aserinsky and Kleitman found that people who were awakened during REM periods almost always reported that they had been dreaming. Research stimulated by this discovery has yielded great insights into the nature of sleep and dreaming.

The Nature of Dreams

Infants spend about 50 percent of their sleeping hours in REM sleep. This proportion drops to about 25 percent between the ages 5 and 9 and continues at about this level throughout adult life. As Figure 8.9

Figure 8.8 *Brain-wave changes define the various stages of sleep. Typical brain-wave patterns of each stage appear on this EEG record. Note that the brain waves become slower and larger as sleep deepens. Note also that the pattern of REM sleep is similar to that of stage 1.*

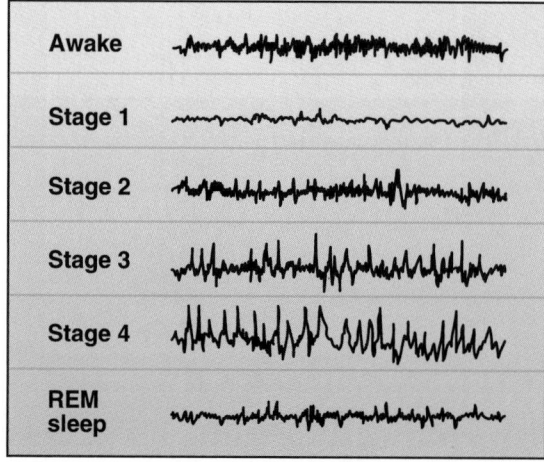

shows, adults have about five REM periods each night. These REM periods become progressively longer as the night wears on and may last as long as 60 minutes (Hobson, 1989). Because subjects awakened during REM sleep reported having been dreaming on about 80 percent of the occasions, it was formerly believed that dreams occur only during REM sleep. But it now appears that some degree of mental activity also occurs during non-REM sleep. Clearly, the brain is mentally active throughout the sleep cycle, although the dreams during the REM phase are likely to be most vivid, detailed, and easily recalled (Antrobus, 1991).

Many dreams involve vigorous physical activity, such as running, jumping, or struggling. Recordings of brain activity show that the motor cortex of the brain is quite active during such dreams. The body, however, remains almost motionless, because neurons in the brain stem block nerve impulses from the brain to the skeletal muscles (but not to the muscles controlling eye movement and respiration). Cats with damage to this brain-stem mechanism lose the motor inhibition and physically act out their dreams. Though sound asleep, they typically groom themselves, then get up and chase something around their cages. While chasing the mouse of their dreams, they ignore real mice placed in their cages, showing that they are definitely asleep and that they are apparently responding to internally produced images (Morrison, 1983).

The brain processes that create dreams are not completely understood, but recent theoretical advances have been made. John Antrobus (1991) has summarized the results of many years of research findings and, using the concept of brain modules described earlier, has developed a promising theory of dreaming as a neurocognitive process. His major thesis is that the images and thoughts that occur during dreaming are modified forms of waking perceptual and cognitive activities and that they therefore must be produced by activation of the same processing modules in the brain. Citing the similarities between EEG wave forms in the waking state and in the state of paradoxical (REM) sleep in which dreams are most vivid, Antrobus suggests that the interacting outputs of perceptual, motor, cognitive, motivational, and emotional modules in the brain are the stuff of which dreams are made.

Antrobus believes that the modules are stimulated into action by a high level of general cortical arousal, which occurs in REM sleep but not in the non-REM stages. This arousal is evident in the fast-wave EEG activity in waking and REM stages (see Figure 8.9). It also shows up in PET scans using radioactive deoxyglucose to measure cerebral energy expenditure (Gottschalk & others, 1991). The activation is thought to be produced by stimulation of the cerebral cortex by the reticular formation, which, as you may recall from Chapter 3, alerts the cortex to incoming stimuli under waking conditions (see Figure 8.10). In REM sleep, however, thresholds for external sensory stimulation are extremely high, effectively blocking external stimulation; so all the brain has to work with is its own internal stimulation produced by the processing modules. Thus, perceptual modules in the cerebral cortex may spontaneously produce images, which are then interpreted in a "bottom-up" manner by cognitive modules that specialize in thought and meaning. Motor modules may also react to the images, but, as noted earlier, the inputs of these modules to the skeletal muscles are blocked. (Antrobus suggests that this blocking of motor inputs may be responsible for the frequent report of dreamers that they find themselves unable to move.) Once a "theme" has been selected by the cognitive modules that interpret the internal images, these modules may stimulate the perceptual modules to produce additional images that go along with the theme, and motivational and emotional modules may also be called into play, producing the emotional content of the dream. In this manner, the "top-down" processing and stimulation of perceptual input by the cognitive modules may create the conceptual theme of the dream.

Dream content sometimes has a bizarre quality, involving events or images that "couldn't really happen." Antrobus attributes this to the fact that in waking consciousness, the activity of the perceptual modules is controlled in part by sensory and perceptual input from the external world. In sleep, however, this input is absent; the cognitive modules are processing only internally produced signals from the other modules. Under the weight of such input, the logical abilities of the cognitive modules, which are trying to achieve the "best fit" interpretations of the images, may be overwhelmed, resulting in unusual or bizarre dreams.

Antrobus's theory is an attempt to understand complicated mental and physiological phenomena by using a modular approach to mind and brain. The processes that are assumed to produce dreams under high levels of cortical arousal are consistent with much existing evidence related to the brain processes that occur during sleep and wakefulness, as well as with the subjective experiences that people report when they describe their dreams.

Scientific research has begun to part the veil of mystery that has long shrouded the world of dreams. Some of the other facts discovered in recent research are summarized in Table 8.1.

The Functions of Dreams

Through the ages, people have sought to understand the shadowy world of dreams. Because dreams often

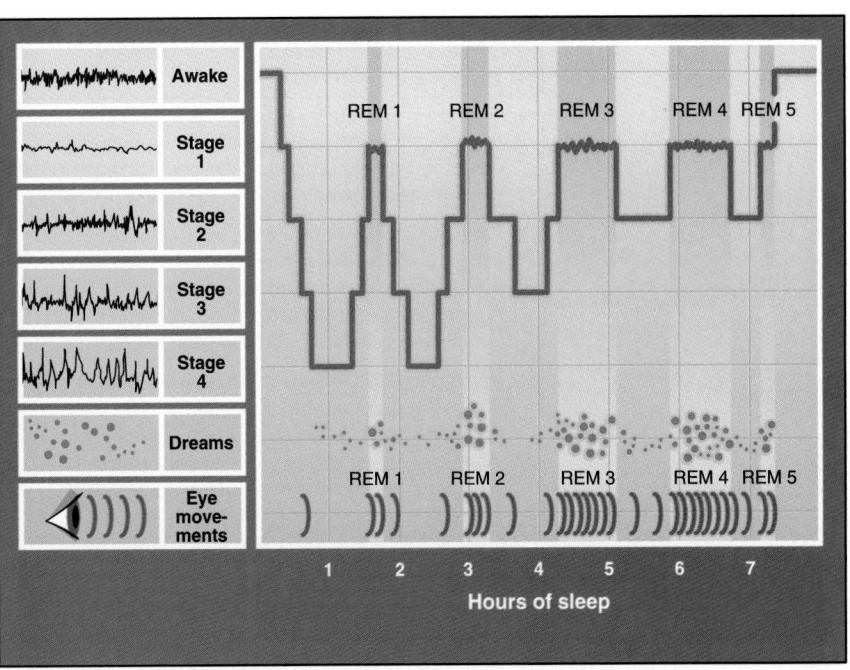

Figure 8.9 *A record of a typical night's sleep. The REM stages are shown in bars. Subjects typically average four to five REM periods during the night. These tend to become longer as the night wears on.*

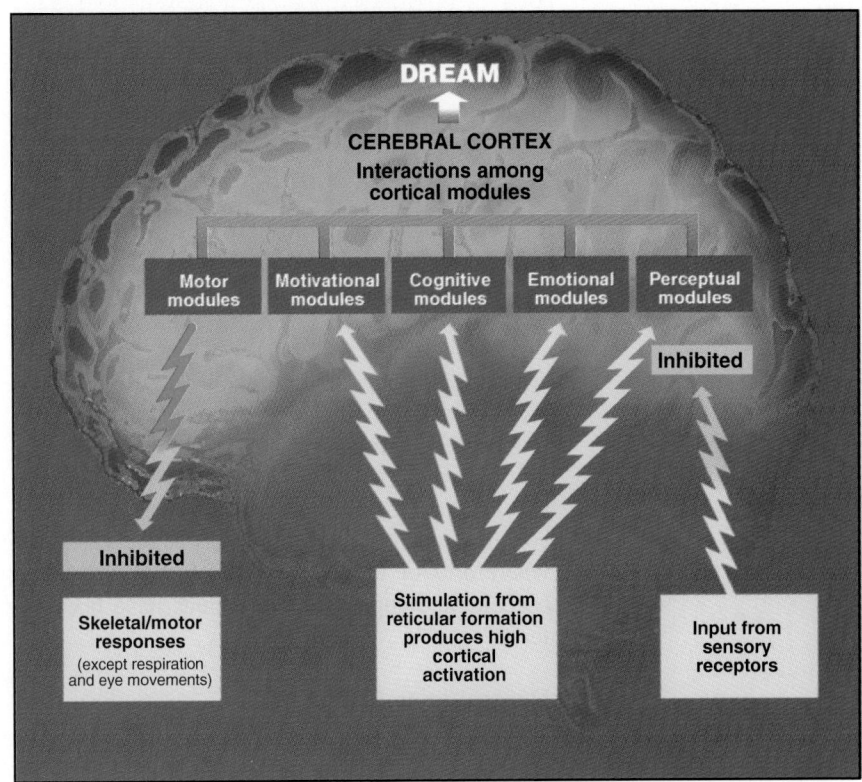

Figure 8.10 *According to Antrobus's (1991) theory, dreams are variations of normal perceptual, cognitive, and motor activities. Under a high level of cortical arousal, produced by stimulation of the cortex by the reticular formation, together with a blocking of sensory input and motor output, various modules in the cortex interact with one another to produce the images and themes present in dreams, together with emotional responses to the dream content.*

Table 8.1 Some Facts About Dreams, Dreaming, and Dreamers

- It appears that everyone dreams, and people who do not recall their dreams have about as much REM sleep as people who do.

- When subjects are awakened from REM sleep and asked to act out their dreams, the length of time it takes them to do so is about as long as the REM episode, suggesting that incidents in dreams last about as long as they would in "real life."

- Some people have lucid dreams, meaning that they are aware that they are dreaming. They voluntarily initiate actions in their dreams (like suspending themselves in midair) to prove to themselves that they are indeed dreaming. From their sleep state, they can signal an experimenter that they are dreaming by activating a mechanical switch.

- People can control their dream content to varying degrees by means of presleep suggestions that they will have a particular dream.

- Sleepwalking and sleeptalking generally take place in the non-REM stages of deep sleep, as do the night terrors that cause some children to cry out in their sleep.

- Dreams occurring during the night's first REM periods tend to be related to events of the preceding day, while those in later REM periods tend to be more vivid, unusual, and sometimes anxiety provoking.

- Men's dreams tend to be more active and aggressive than women's. Men use more action terms to describe their dreams, while women use more emotional terms.

- Dreams are frequently reported to be in color. Colorblind people dream in the colors they see when awake, and people blind from birth dream in the senses they know, mainly hearing and touch.

seem to have some sort of symbolic significance, people have tended to think of them as informative, even prophetic. In psychology, the possible symbolic significance of dreams has been of special interest to psychodynamic theorists, but brain researchers and cognitive scientists have also sought the whys and wherefores of dreaming. Thus, biological, intrapsychic, and cognitive explanations have been offered.

Dreaming as Homeostasis

Research that followed the discovery of REM sleep showed that people seem to have a definite need for REM sleep. When subjects were prevented from dreaming for several nights by being awakened each time they entered an REM phase, they spent more time in REM sleep on subsequent nights, as if they needed to catch up on their dreaming. They also

tended to slip into REM phases much sooner after they had gone to sleep (Dement, 1974). This **REM rebound effect** suggested that REM sleep might maintain some kind of an internal equilibrium, or homeostasis, in the brain.

One speculation is that dreams may give the right hemisphere of the brain a chance to be more active than it is during waking activity, which typically involves the left hemisphere more than the right. Consistent with this view is the finding that people whose waking time is dominated by left-hemisphere verbal–logical activity seem to show a greater REM rebound effect the night after they have been repeatedly awakened from REM sleep, as if they had more catching up to do (Cartwright, 1977).

Psychodynamics and Dreaming

Sigmund Freud has had a great impact on how people think about dreams. Freud believed that dreams are stimulated by unconscious impulses and that the aim of any dream is **wish fulfillment,** the gratification of some need. Because of Freud's conviction that dreams allow the unconscious mind to disguise forbidden thoughts and desires and slip them past our defenses, he regarded dreams as "the royal road to the unconscious."

Freud distinguished between a dream's **manifest content** (the story or symbols that the dreamer reports) and its **latent content** (its true psychological meaning). Manifest content involving long and upstanding objects, such as umbrellas and trees, for example, might symbolically represent the penis (Freud, 1938). The process by which the dream's latent content is transformed for defensive purposes into the manifest content is called **dream work.** Freud believed that if the latent content of the dream were to appear in undisguised form, it might frighten or awaken the sleeper. Indeed, Freud regarded nightmares as dreams in which the latent content was insufficiently disguised.

Because they believe that dreams are a means of releasing mental tension, resolving conflicts, and compensating for things that are lacking in people's waking lives, psychodynamic therapists often use dream interpretation as a central part of treatment. Applied to Antrobus's (1991) theory, psychoanalysts might suggest that dream content reflects important personal themes that affect how perceptual and cognitive modules create and process information. In using dream analysis, therapists hope to help patients achieve insight into the psychodynamics that underlie their problems (Whitmont & Perera, 1990).

Dreaming and Memory Consolidation

Dreaming clearly involves some kind of brain activity, and perhaps this activity in some way improves the brain's mental functioning. One suggestion is that dreaming may help us to *consolidate,* or strengthen, the synapses that constitute memories of things we learned while awake (Winson, 1990). Perhaps dreams replay important experiences and reinforce the crucial synaptic connections, or perhaps they aid in memory consolidation in some less direct fashion.

In one study that is frequently cited by supporters of the consolidation theory, subjects who had been asleep in the laboratory for 5 hours were awakened and told that they were going to learn something before going back to sleep. They were shown a series of slides depicting common objects and were asked to write down the names of all the objects they could remember. Then they went back to sleep for another 2 hours, and their EEG patterns and eye movements were monitored. When they woke up, those subjects who had experienced REM sleep during the interval either showed no memory loss or remembered even more of the objects than before. But those who had not had any REM sleep showed significantly poorer recall (Barker, 1972). Although these correlational results cannot tell us whether REM sleep actually caused the better memory, findings like these have fueled speculation that REM sleep is linked to cognitive processes in the brain.

A more recent notion is that dreaming enhances our mental functioning not by helping us remember but by helping us *forget.* Francis Crick and Graeme Mitchison (1983, 1986) view REM sleep as fundamentally an *erasing* process rather than a consolidating one. Crick and Mitchison maintain that if all of the information processed during a day were permanently stored in the brain's synaptic connections, even the gargantuan neocortex would soon run out of storage space. They suggest that dreaming is the brain's way of purging itself of unwanted or unimportant mental content that might compete or interfere with significant material stored in the brain's neural circuits. They also suggest that we are operating at cross-purposes with nature when we try to remember information that our brains are trying to prune from memory.

Although we do not yet have definitive answers to why we sleep and dream, both are clearly important to our physical, mental, and emotional well-being. For this reason, scientific interest in sleep disorders has surged in recent years.

Sleep Disorders

Most of us take our relatively stable sleep cycles for granted, but the physiological mechanisms involved in sleep are complex, and they can go wrong in a variety of ways. Many millions of people suffer from sleep problems, whose effects range from relatively mild to life threatening. These disorders fall into two main classes: **insomnia,** or abnormal wakefulness, and **hypersomnia,** or uncontrollable sleepiness (Thorpy, 1990).

Insomnia, the inability to fall asleep or remain asleep, is the most common chronic sleep complaint, afflicting between 10 and 25 percent of the U.S. population. Insomnia is not a single disorder; it may be associated with a variety of physiological disorders, with alcohol and drug abuse, and with emotional problems such as anxiety and depression (Lydic & Biebuyck, 1989).

Insomniacs who suffer from a **delayed sleep phase syndrome** are unable to go to sleep until 2:00 to 6:00 A.M. They awaken for work or school the next morning feeling exhausted. On weekends, however, they sleep late (waking somewhere from 11:00 A.M. to 2:00 P.M.) and awaken refreshed. Victims of delayed sleep phase have been treated successfully by resetting their biological clocks. The person being treated goes to bed 3 hours later each day over the course of a week, moving all the way around the clock until the biological clock has been reset to an acceptable time for sleeping and waking. The patient maintains this bedtime to set the clock permanently (Weitzman & others, 1983).

Some people suffer not from an inability to sleep but from an inability to stay awake. A serious form of hypersomnia is **narcolepsy,** a condition in which people suffer sudden and uncontrollable sleep attacks. Perhaps 100,000 Americans suffer from this disorder (Reite & others, 1990). In its milder forms, the disorder may cause a person to simply "go blank" for a brief period; then the person continues his or her activities as if nothing had happened. Children with this disorder may be mistakenly labeled as inattentive or thought to be daydreaming when, in fact, they are briefly asleep. In more severe cases, narcoleptics suddenly fall asleep during the day and may even collapse in the middle of a vigorous activity. Physiological recordings show the sudden appearance of REM sleep during narcoleptic attacks. The safety hazards created by narcoleptics who drive automobiles are self-evident.

The causes of narcolepsy are unknown, and so is its cure. However, animals can also have the disorder, and there appears to be a genetic basis for it. Through selective breeding, William Dement (1983) and his coworkers at Stanford University have produced a colony of narcoleptic dogs (see Figure 8.11). Research on these animals may advance our understanding of this baffling disorder.

Sleep apnea is a serious and life-threatening disorder in which breathing stops during sleep, as often as 500 times per night. After a minute or so without oxygen, the person—generally an overweight male—takes in air with a loud snore. Air is cut off by a

collapse of the pharynx, which results in an obstruction of the upper airway (Remmers, 1983). Although the respiration rate continues, no air gets through until reflexes result in the loud "snore." Cardiac failure is one possible consequence of the obstruction and is probably a leading cause of death in apnea sufferers.

Links have been suggested between sleep apnea and Sudden Infant Death Syndrome (SIDS), or "crib death," which claims the lives of infants in their sleep. One speculation is that middle-aged apnea victims may be survivors of SIDS; perhaps they remain alive because their reflex response to oxygen depletion occurs in time to prevent death (Harper, 1983).

Three other sleep disorders—sleepwalking, sleeptalking, and night terrors—are specific to stage 4 sleep, and they are more common in children than in adults. In sleepwalking and sleeptalking, the person seems vaguely conscious of the environment. Sleeptalkers sometimes respond to questions and commands, and sleepwalkers can sometimes navigate through furniture-filled rooms. Contrary to common belief, awakening sleepwalkers is not harmful, although they will usually appear very confused when wakened.

Night terrors occur in children, who awaken in response to these events with terrified screams. Night terrors should not be confused with nightmares, which occur during REM sleep. Children who experience night terrors typically do not report that they were dreaming, and the experiences do not appear to be harmful. Usually, the children do not recall the experiences in the morning.

Sleep disorders occur over the entire life span, from infancy to old age. Some conditions, such as narcolepsy, appear in childhood or adolescence and never disappear, whereas others, like sleepwalking and night terrors, seem to be outgrown. Still others, like sleep apnea and insomnia, may appear later in life. Most of us can look forward to a decrease in sleep efficiency as we get older. It doesn't appear that the *need* for sleep decreases. Rather, the ability to sleep soundly seems to deteriorate as we age (Hobson, 1989). The establishment of sleep disorder centers in major hospitals and universities promises to speed progress in understanding the nature and functions of sleep and the conditions that give rise to sleep problems.

Waking Fantasies and Daydreams

Our fantasy lives are hardly restricted to the nocturnal realm of dreams. When we are awake, we experience a continuous stream of consciousness that includes thoughts, memories, images, and other mental events. Fantasies appear to be an important part of our waking consciousness (Singer, 1988).

In *The Secret Life of Walter Mitty,* James Thurber vividly portrayed a person who transformed his humdrum existence into an exhilarating fantasy world of adventure and personal fulfillment. Freud, too, speculated that fantasy and daydreams (the more fanciful of our waking fantasies) are a means of fulfilling our needs and discharging impulses.

Waking fantasy has other adaptive functions as well (see Figure 8.12). It can provide stimulation during periods of boredom, and it can help us experience positive emotions. Fantasy can also help us find solutions to problems and rehearse different ways of approaching situations. Fantasy can allow us to make plans and anticipate possible consequences of our behavior, thereby contributing to self-regulation of behavior (Bandura, 1986).

Patterns of Daydreaming

How do daydreams compare with the nocturnal variety? Researchers have been comparing ratings of the vividness and content of dreams made by subjects awakened during REM sleep with similar ratings of daydreams made by the same subjects. Subjects tend to rate their daydreams as less vivid and realistic than their night dreams, probably because during the day they can distinguish between fantasy and reality. There is, however, a surprising degree of similarity in the themes of the night dreams and the waking fantasies, suggesting that the nocturnal dreams may be an extension of daytime fantasy (Antrobus & others, 1984; Singer, 1988).

Jerome Singer (1975, 1988) and his coworkers have for more than 2 decades been exploring the realm of waking fantasy. They have devised a number of questionnaires and interview methods to gain information about the nature of people's daydreams. In some of their studies, subjects have worn beepers that were programmed to go off at random times during the day. Subjects then described what they were thinking about at the time.

These studies have shown that people vary in the frequency and content of their daydreams. Singer has identified three different patterns of daydreaming. The first is associated with a tendency toward distractibility, mind wandering, and fleeting daydreams that are largely negative and sometimes fearful in nature. People displaying this pattern report that they have trouble concentrating and focusing their attention, and they do not tend to report long-lasting daydreams.

The second pattern is characterized by a wide range of daydreams centered around unpleasant emotions such as fear of failure, guilt, hostility, and aggressive impulses. People who show this pattern also report daydreams of achieving, but they are generally preoccupied with self-doubt and guilt.

Singer characterizes people displaying the third pattern as "happy daydreamers." Their daydreams tend to be built around positive emotions, their imagery during daydreaming is vivid, and they frequently use their daydreams for planning. These people tend to be well adjusted. They value and enjoy their private fantasies and can use them for self-amusement during periods of boredom.

In another research laboratory, Theodore Barber has been studying people who live in a vivid fantasy world much of the time (Wilson & Barber, 1984). *Fantasy-prone personalities* comprise about 4 percent of the population. The majority of them are females, and they are no better or more poorly adjusted than the general population. They differ, however, in the frequency and richness of their daydreams. For example, three quarters of those studied were able to achieve sexual orgasm by merely fantasizing sexual activity. All of them could experience fantasies "as real as real" in all five senses. Typically, they were avid readers who had grown up without television sets. As children, they had had many imaginary playmates. They had regarded their stuffed animals as real beings and had engaged in intense make-believe play with them. This rich fantasy life continued in adulthood, and most of the subjects spent at least half of their waking time in a fantasy world. They were extremely hypnotizable, had vivid nocturnal dreams, and were so easily overwhelmed by drugs that they

Figure 8.12 *Daydreams and fantasy can serve a number of important psychological functions.*

avoided them. Indeed, Barber suggested that their normal fantasy experiences, though under their control, were precisely the kind of altered experiences that many people seek through drugs.

Although most people cannot direct their consciousness into the vivid realm that is home to the fantasy-prone personality, most of us have an active fantasy life that is an important part of our mental activity. Research on this normal stream of consciousness promises to advance our understanding of how we interact with the world.▼

■■■

Meditation

Meditation has a long and varied history. It has been performed throughout the world for ages in connection with religious, military, therapeutic, and recreational activities. In the Western world, however, much of the current scientific interest in meditation was stimulated by the Transcendental Meditation (TM) movement, founded by the Maharishi Mahesh Yogi. TM may have as many as half a million disciples in the United States. The attractiveness of meditation may in part reflect a search for peace and tranquility in a world that has become increasingly chaotic and stressful.

A distinction is sometimes made between active and passive meditation techniques. *Active meditation* techniques require practitioners to make strenuous efforts to focus their attention. In certain yoga techniques, for example, practitioners maintain specific

▼

Thinking Critically About Racial Differences in Daydreams

In a study designed to assess racial differences in waking fantasies, Giambra (1982) compared questionnaire reports of daydreams made by Caucasian and African-American subjects matched on important variables like age, income, and education. The two groups did not differ in their reports of how vivid, how sexual, or how frightening their fantasies were. However, African Americans' daydreams had significantly more achievement themes as well as more hostile content. How might you account for these differences using concepts from (1) psychodynamic theories such as Freud's and (2) the cognitive–behavioral perspective, which emphasizes the role of social learning experiences?

postures and control their breathing. Other meditative techniques, such as TM, are *passive* approaches. Passive meditators remain in a quiet atmosphere and make a relaxed attempt to achieve a state of inner peace by concentrating on a particular thought or on their breathing. Most passive techniques are practiced for one or two 20-minute periods each day.

Popular as well as scientific interest in meditation was sparked by reports that meditation, like drugs, can produce dramatically altered states of consciousness. However, research suggests that few people have bizarre or mystical experiences while meditating (Goleman, 1977).

Proponents of passive meditation do report positive personality changes, improved interpersonal functioning, increased energy and mental efficiency, reduced use of drugs, and reduction in tension and stress (Delmonte, 1985; Dillbeck & Orme-Johnson, 1987). Not all scientific evidence supports these claims (Pagano & Warrenburg, 1983; Shapiro & Walsh, 1984), but there is little doubt that many people find meditative techniques helpful. People report feeling deeply relaxed, free from stress, and refreshed by meditation. However, there is no compelling evidence that these stress-reduction effects are greater than those that occur when people simply take time out to quietly relax (Davison & Pirozzolo, 1991).

EEG recordings made during passive meditation show brain-wave patterns that are typically associated with relaxation and drowsiness. Most notable are increases in alpha rhythm, the brain-wave pattern of 8 to 12 cycles per second that is associated with the relaxed waking state, a pleasant state of relaxation and low physiological arousal. EEG studies also suggest that meditators may spend as much as 40 percent of their meditation time actually asleep (Pagano & Warrenburg, 1983). There are also decreases in respiration rate, heart rate, and concentrations of blood lactate, a chemical associated with fatigue and anxiety. In addition, meditators show improved reflex responses during or after meditating, suggesting that the practice of meditation produces a state of restful alertness rather than simply arousal reduction (Dillbeck & Orme-Johnson, 1987).

Like other forms of quiet relaxation, meditation is believed to affect the autonomic nervous system, whose sympathetic branch arouses the body for action and whose parasympathetic branch calms it down. The physiological responses of meditators suggest that the procedure causes an increase in parasympathetic activity, a decrease in sympathetic activity, or both. The net result is a state of general relaxation that is quite the opposite of the body's fight-or-flight response to danger and stress. Herbert Benson (1975) of Harvard University has referred to the restful physiological response produced by meditation as the **relaxation response.**

Benson maintains that the relaxation response is a generalized physical and mental reaction. But other researchers believe that a distinction should be made between **somatic** (bodily) and **cognitive** (mental) relaxation (Davidson, 1978). If you have had the experience of trying to go to sleep while your body was deeply relaxed but your mind was racing, you have first-hand knowledge of the difference between somatic and cognitive relaxation.

Meditation has been found to be effective for producing somatic relaxation, but often no more effective than other techniques, such as voluntary relaxation of the muscles, exercise, and restful reading (Holmes, 1984; Shoicket & Bertelson, 1988). On the other hand, meditation seems ideally suited for producing cognitive relaxation, since attention is diverted from intrusive and anxiety-arousing thoughts and concentrated instead on a neutral word, an idea, or one's breathing. The mental technique practiced in TM is said to lead to a state of "pure consciousness" without the activity of thought, in which "consciousness is awake to itself alone" (Dillbeck & Orme-Johnson, 1987, p. 880). Indeed, where stress-management effects are concerned, the important element in any relaxation technique, including meditation, may be the temporary withdrawal it provides from the stresses and strains of daily living.

Hypnosis

During the 18th century, a Viennese physician named Anton Mesmer achieved fame as a result of a series of dramatic cures of physical and psychological afflictions. He claimed that these cures were brought about by magnetic forces that radiated from the planets. Mesmer treated his patients by exposing them to magnetic objects and fluids in order to restore their "bodily harmony," and he called his technique *animal magnetism* (see Figure 8.13). Later, it was termed *mesmerism* in his honor.

Despite the impressive cures that Mesmer and his patients reported, the medical and religious communities became fearful that mesmerism might be a dangerous spiritual force. Concerned that young women could be seduced easily while under its influence, a French scientific commission recommended that mesmerism be outlawed in France, and for a time it was.

James Braid, a Scottish surgeon, was impressed by the fact that patients undergoing mesmerism often went into a "trance" in which they appeared to be oblivious to their surroundings. He decided that mesmerism was a state of "nervous sleep" resulting from concentrated attention rather than magnetic forces. Braid renamed the phenomenon **hypnosis,** after Hypnos, the Greek god of sleep.

The Scientific Study of Hypnosis

Much of what we know about hypnosis has been learned only in the last 30 years. Controlled research has been made possible by the development of **hypnotic susceptibility scales.** These scales contain a series of items that investigators can read to subjects following a general hypnotic induction. Each item involves a different suggested behavior (for example, ''You cannot move your arm''). Subjects are given a ''pass'' or ''fail'' on each item, depending on whether or not they meet specific criteria for compliance with the suggestion. The total hypnotic susceptibility score is based on the number of ''passes.'' Some items from one of the most widely used research scales, the Stanford Hypnotic Susceptibility Scale, are presented in Table 8.2. Other measures have been developed to explore the subjective experiences that people have while hypnotized. Such scales ask subjects to rate the intensity of various experiences they may have had during hypnosis (Hilgard, 1987).

People differ considerably in how responsive they are to hypnotic suggestions, and hypnotic susceptibility appears to be a stable trait. In one study, Stanford alumni who had been tested as students were again tested over periods of 10, 15, and 25 years. Their responses on the retests were very similar to their original scores; the average subject differed by no more than one point on the 12-item scale even after a quarter-century (Piccione & others, 1989).

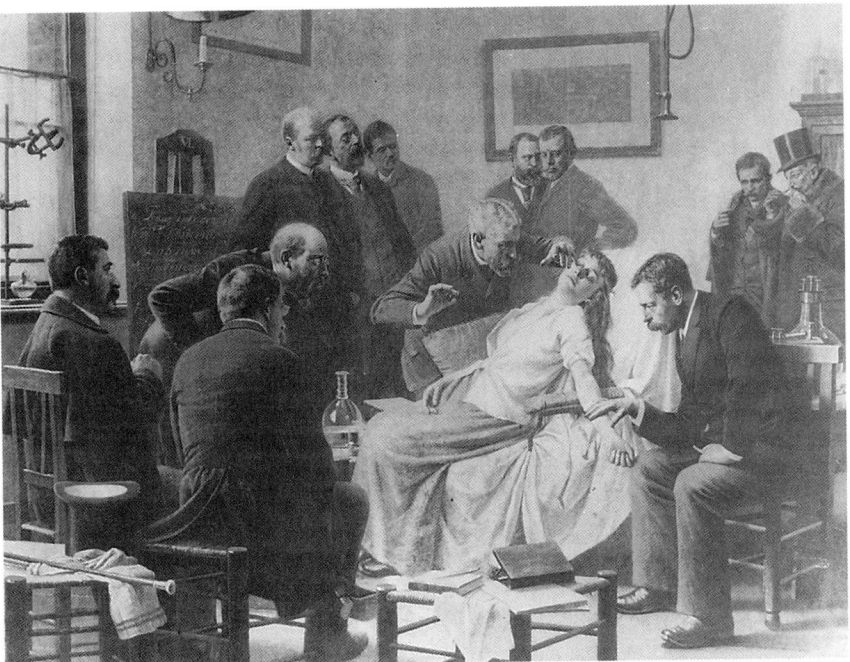

⬤ **Figure 8.13** *This 19th-century painting shows an ''animal magnetizer'' putting his patient into a trance.*

Hypnosis and Memory

Instances of posthypnotic amnesia are also commonly observed. If told to forget what occurred under hypnosis, some suggestible subjects show an absence of recall until they are later told by the hypnotist that they can remember (Kihlstrom & Shor, 1978).

The use of hypnosis to try to improve memory has a long history, but the topic is now being studied with new vigor. One reason is the increasing use of

Hypnotic Behaviors and Experiences

Hypnosis can produce striking changes in consciousness and behavior. The most notable characteristic of hypnotized subjects is an increase in their suggestibility. In one study, Martin Orne and Frederick Evans (1965) found that many hypnotized subjects could be induced to dip their hands briefly in a foaming solution they were told was acid and then to throw the ''acid'' in another person's face. This might appear at first to be a striking example of the power of hypnosis to induce people to act ''against their will.'' However, members of a control group of subjects who were asked to simply *pretend* they were hypnotized were just as likely to perform the behaviors. As demonstrated by Milgram's obedience experiments, discussed in Chapter 2, an authority figure in a legitimate context can induce people to commit some unlikely acts, whether they are hypnotized or not.

Table 8.2 Sample Test Items and Criteria for Passing from the Stanford Hypnotic Susceptibility Scale, Form C

Item	Suggested Behavior	Criterion for Passing
Arm lowering	Right arm is held out; subject is told arm will become heavy and drop.	Arm is lowered at least 6 inches in 10 seconds.
Moving hands apart	With hands extended and close together, subject is asked to imagine a force acting to push them apart.	Hands are 6 or more inches apart in 10 seconds.
Mosquito hallucination	It is suggested that a mosquito buzzing nearby lights on the subject.	Any grimacing movement or acknowledgment of mosquito that occurs.
Posthypnotic amnesia	Subject is awakened and asked to recall suggestions after being told they cannot be remembered.	Three or fewer items are recalled before subject is told, "Now you can remember everything."

Source: Adapted from Weitzenhoffer and Hilgard, 1962.

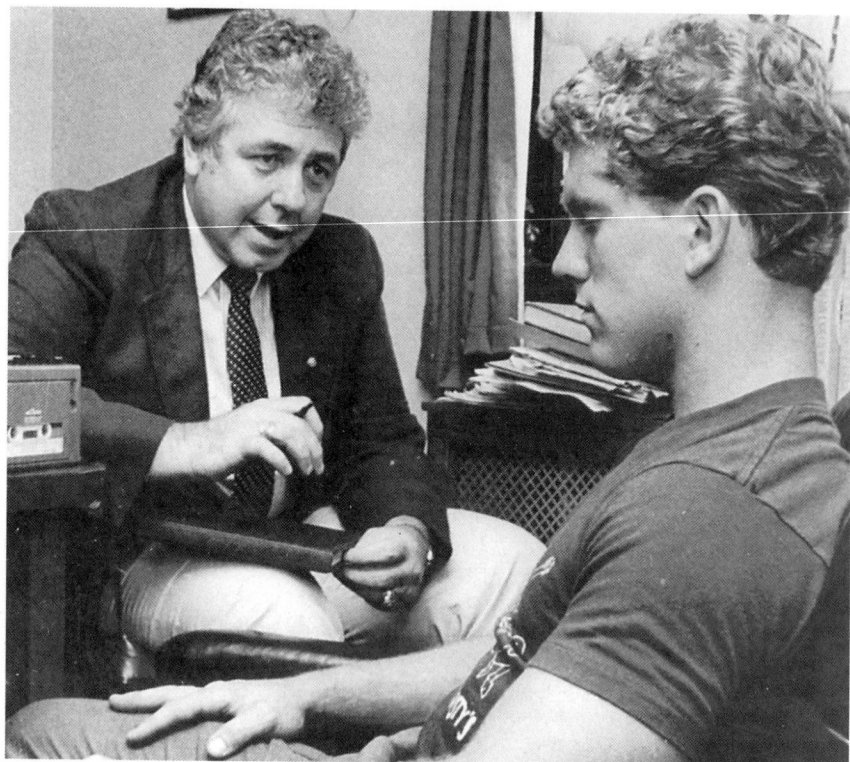

Figure 8.14 *Hypnosis is sometimes used in criminal investigations in attempts to enhance the recall of witnesses to crimes. The sessions can be either audiotaped or videotaped for later presentation in court. Recent research suggests that witnesses' "memories" in such situations may be inaccurate, however.*

hypnosis by police (see Figure 8.14) to aid the recall of eyewitnesses to crimes (Hibler, 1984). Unfortunately, scientific evidence casts serious doubt on the assumption that hypnosis can aid recall. Many carefully controlled studies indicate that when proper control groups are used, hypnosis does not significantly improve memory (Pettinati, 1988; Register & Kihlstrom, 1987). Even more disturbing from a criminal justice perspective is the fact that some of the "memories" recalled under hypnosis are actually created during the hypnotic period, when subjects are more suggestible, on the basis of inadvertent suggestions or "facts" implied by the questions (Sheehan & Statham, 1989). Afterwards, during court testimony, an eyewitness may report "facts" that never occurred (but were implied by the questions) as actual memories of the event (McCann & Sheehan, 1988). These findings have alarming implications, and many courts are becoming appropriately cautious in their view of evidence produced through investigative hypnosis.

Physiological Effects

Hypnosis can have striking physiological effects. Nearsighted people see more clearly; allergic responses are inhibited; warts are cured; stomach acidity can be increased. However, well-controlled studies have shown that nonhypnotized control subjects who are given the same suggestions can exhibit these same responses (Spanos & Chaves, 1988). The power

of suggestion alone can apparently produce some rather remarkable physiological effects.

An investigation that illustrates the powerful effects that suggestions can have, with or without hypnosis, involved 13 subjects who were strongly allergic to two poisonous types of trees. Five were hypnotized and the other 8 served as controls. Each subject was blindfolded and told that one arm was being touched by leaves from a harmless tree when in fact it was being touched by leaves from a poisonous tree. Four out of the 5 hypnotized subjects and 7 out of the 8 nonhypnotized controls had no allergic reaction. Next, the subject's other arm was rubbed with leaves from a harmless tree, and he or she was told that the leaves were poisonous. All subjects, both hypnotized and control, responded to this suggestion with mild to severe allergic reactions (Ikemi & Nakagawa, 1962). As we have seen in our previous discussion of placebos, beliefs and expectations can produce real physiological effects.

Most hypnotism shows contain several "amazing physical feats" performed by "entranced" subjects. One is the so-called human plank routine. A male subject is placed between two chairs, one chair beneath the calves of his legs, the other beneath his shoulders. He is told that his body is absolutely rigid, and an attractive woman is asked to stand on his chest. The audience attributes the man's ability to support the woman to his "profound hypnotic trance." What they don't know is that an average man suspended in this manner can support at least 300 pounds on his chest with little discomfort and no need of a hypnotic trance (see Figure 8.15). However, stage hypnotists are not known for their insistence on nonhypnotized control subjects.

Increased Pain Tolerance

Virtually every surgical procedure known to medicine has been accomplished under hypnosis (Ewin, 1984). Hypnosis has been used successfully to control pain during surgery since the 19th century (see Figure 8.16). The Scottish surgeon James Esdaile performed more than 300 major operations in the mid-1800s using hypnosis as the sole anesthetic. Joseph Barber (1977), a noted hypnotherapist, needed an average of only 11 minutes to hypnotically produce analgesia in 99 out of 100 dental patients. Controlled clinical and laboratory studies have also shown dramatic increases in pain tolerance associated with hypnosis (Brown & Fromm, 1987). What we don't know at this point is exactly how the effects are produced. At a physiological level, hypnosis may be involved in the release of endorphins, as appears to occur in the case of placebos. Other mechanisms are also possible. By reducing anxiety and fear; by establishing positive attitudes, motivations, and expectations; by distracting

↟ **Figure 8.15** *The "human plank" demonstration, a favorite of stage hypnotists, seems to demonstrate the power of the hypnotic trance. Most of the audience is unaware that the average man suspended in this manner can support a person on his chest without hypnosis. In the photo, The Amazing Kreskin, a professional magician, demonstrates this fact with a group of unhypnotized men.*

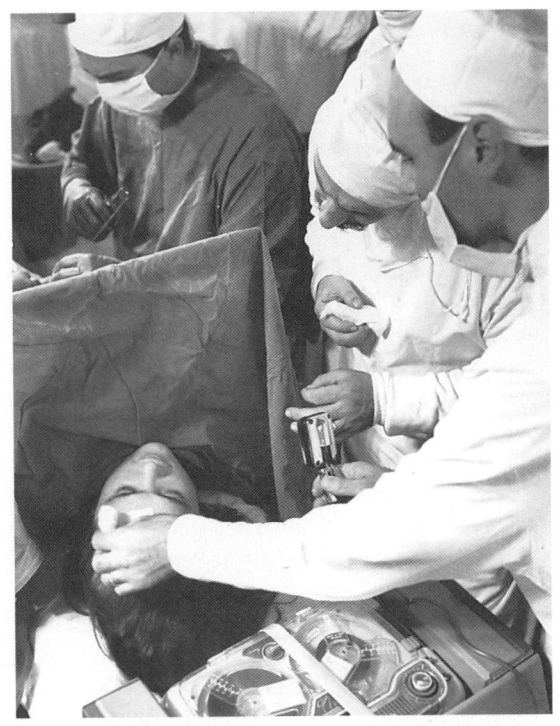

↟ **Figure 8.16** *This patient is undergoing an appendectomy with hypnosis as the sole anesthetic. Hypnotic suggestions that the patient can feel no pain are being delivered through the tape recorder.*

patients from their pain; by exposing them to believable suggestions that they will not experience pain; or by somehow helping them to separate the pain from conscious experience, hypnosis may be unusually effective in increasing tolerance to pain (Miller & Bowers, 1986; Spanos & Katsanis, 1989).

Theories of Hypnosis

Although hypnosis produces a range of sometimes striking effects, scientists do not agree on what hypnosis is and how it exerts its influence. Moreover, we have seen that nonhypnotized controls often exhibit the same dramatic changes in experience and behavior that hypnotized people report. Several prominent theories offer differing conceptions of hypnosis and the psychological processes that govern its effects.

Hypnosis: A Unique Physiological State?

What is hypnosis, and how does it produce its effects? The best way to begin to answer this question is to state what hypnosis is *not*. It is not sleep, nor is it any other state of consciousness with unique physiological properties. The EEGs of subjects under hypnosis are not like those of people in any of the recognized stages of sleep. Instead, they resemble those of people in a waking state, and they change continuously, depending on what activities the person is engaging in. No physiological measure shows a unique pattern for hypnosis that would enable us to tell who is hypnotized and who isn't (Bauer & McCanne, 1980).

This fact has important implications. If we wish to say that a specific physiological state, the "hypnotic trance," is the scientific explanation for hypnotic behavior, then we must be able to define and measure that state in some way other than in terms of the behaviors it is assumed to produce. If we can't do that, we find ourselves on the scientifically uncomfortable merry-go-round of circular reasoning: "Why do hypnotized people behave as they do? Because they are in a trance. How do we know that they are in a trance? Because they behave as they do." Clearly, we've explained nothing.

Because hypnosis does not seem to be a distinct physiological state and because hypnotized and nonhypnotized subjects often behave in identical ways, psychologists have sought to understand hypnosis in terms of other psychological processes, including role playing, imagination, and dissociation.

Hypnosis as Role Playing

A number of theorists have advanced a **role theory of hypnosis.** They suggest that being hypnotized involves taking on the role of a hypnotized person (Sarbin & Coe, 1972). In our culture, most people have a general idea of how hypnotized individuals are supposed to behave: They are supposed to have a trance-like appearance, be responsive to suggestions, and lose their self-consciousness. People who are motivated to conform to this role, who are free from fears or inhibitions, and who expect to be able to experience hypnosis are likely to adopt the role of hypnotized subject and to experience the suggested effects.

The importance of beliefs and expectations about the hypnotic role was shown in a study conducted by Martin Orne of the University of Pennsylvania. During a classroom demonstration, college students were told that hypnotized people frequently exhibit "catalepsy (stiffening of the muscles) of the dominant hand." Actually, catalepsy of the hand rarely, if ever, occurs spontaneously in hypnosis. An accomplice of the lecturer was then hypnotized, and, sure enough, he "spontaneously" exhibited the cataleptic response. When students who had seen the demonstration were later hypnotized, 55 percent of them exhibited the catalepsy spontaneously without any suggestion from the hypnotist. A group of control subjects saw a demonstration without a mention or exhibition of catalepsy. Not one of them exhibited catalepsy when hypnotized later (Orne, 1959).

Does the role-playing explanation of hypnosis mean that people are simply faking or playacting when they are hypnotized? Not at all. Role theorists stress that we are constantly taking on roles in our daily lives. Being a hypnotic subject is simply another specific role having cognitive and behavioral components (Spanos & Chaves, 1988). When people become truly immersed in this role, the experiences and behaviors that result are as completely real to them as the role of "college student reading a book" is to you right now. They are not merely playacting.

Hypnosis and Imagination

Hypnotic experiences and behaviors can also be seen as the result of imagination. To an individual who can become actively involved in imagining, it may seem as if the imagined events actually do occur. Research has shown that imagining an event often produces the same bodily changes as the event itself. For example, individuals who imagine themselves moving body parts actually do have small but measurable movements in those muscles (Feltz & others, 1988). During hypnosis, this "as if" process is supported by the hypnotist's suggestions. When a hyp-notist suggests to a subject that his or her arm feels heavy, the subject may imagine previous experiences in which the arm did feel heavy and may reexperience the sensations. Researchers have found that people who are especially responsive to hypnotic suggestions have rich imaginative lives and tend to become absorbed in the themes of their imagery (Lynn & Rhue, 1986).

Hypnosis and Dissociation

The case of Billy Milligan's multiple personalities illustrates how mental events can become so split off from each other that distinct personalities, some totally unaware of the others, can coexist within the same person. Less extreme forms of dissociation occur in our daily lives.

Ernest Hilgard (1977, 1987) has studied the possible role of dissociation in several hypnotic phenomena. Hilgard's basic approach is to try to communicate with what he calls the **hidden observer,** a subconscious mind that remains in contact with reality while the person is hypnotized. For example, procedures that are normally quite painful, such as placing the hand and forearm in ice water (see Figure 8.17a), can be experienced as painless by hypnotized subjects who have received the suggestion that they will feel no pain. But suppose it is suggested to the subject that all awareness of the arm that is not immersed in the ice water will be lost but that this "dissociated" arm will write down how the person really feels. In this case, the nonstressed arm may report a rise in pain even while the hypnotized person verbally reports feeling very little pain (see Figure 8.17b). The "hidden observer" can also report sounds presented while the subject is hypnotically deaf and remember facts that the hypnotized subject cannot recall because of amnesia instructions.

Individual differences in hypnotic susceptibility may be linked to differences in the ability to dissociate. Perhaps people who are highly susceptible to hypnosis can dissociate better than people whose susceptibility is low because they can register and respond to information that they do not consciously perceive. Future research on hypnosis may help us to understand the process of dissociation not only in hypnosis but also in multiple personalities and in other states of consciousness. Certainly, the dissociation theory is consistent with the emerging notion that the mind consists of separate modules that can sometimes function independently of one another.

Modularity of mind may involve not only consciousness but also related biological processes. As the following feature indicates, recent studies of multiple personality disorder dramatically illustrate the intimate connections that can exist between psychological and biological phenomena.

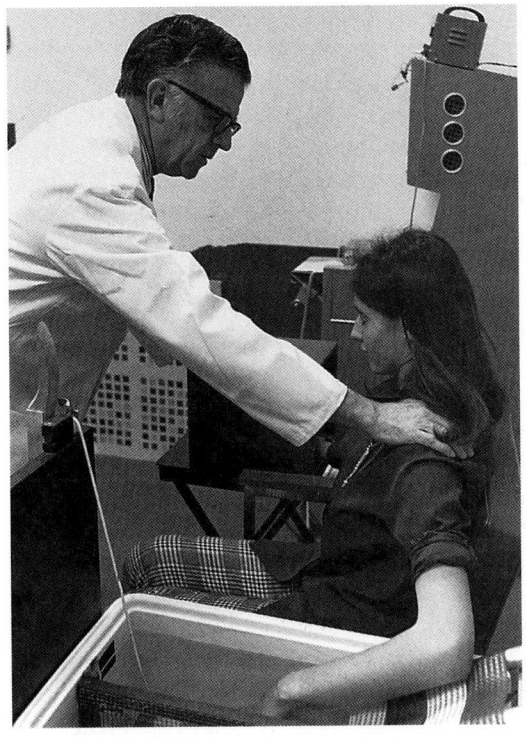

(a)

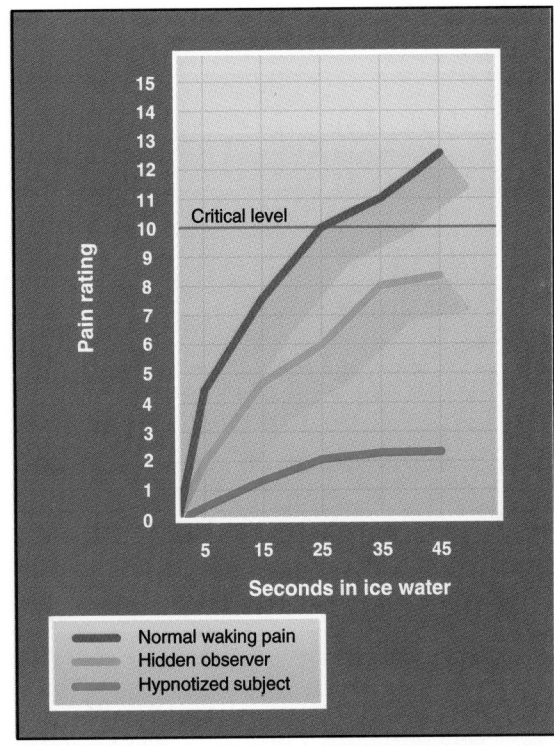

(b)

Figure 8.17 (a) *This hypnotic subject's hand is immersed in painfully cold ice water. By placing his hand on her shoulder, Ernest Hilgard, the researcher, contacts her dissociated "hidden observer."* (b) *This figure shows the pain intensity ratings given by the subject when she is not hypnotized, by the subject under hypnosis, and by the hidden observer in the same hypnotic state. The hidden observer reports more pain than the hypnotized subject but less than the subject when she is not hypnotized. (Data from Hilgard, 1977).*

PSYCHOBIOLOGICAL INTERACTIONS

Multiple Personality: Dissociated Minds *and* Bodies?

The case of Billy Milligan, described at the beginning of the chapter, exemplifies perhaps the most extreme form of dissociation that we know of, the multiple personality disorder (MPD). In this disorder, two or more distinct personalities coexist within a person. Each personality maintains its own pattern of behavior, thinking, and social relationships over an extended period of time. Several celebrated cases of multiple personality have been described in books and movies, such as *The Three Faces of Eve* and *Sybil*. Once thought to be a rare disorder, MPD has received greater attention in recent years, and the disorder may be far more common than psychologists previously believed. During the early 1980s, scientists at the National Institute of Mental Health (NIMH) in Washington, D.C., surveyed more than 150 cases of MPD (Putnam, 1984, 1989). In many cases, they were able to study the physiological responses of the patients when different personalities were active. The results of these studies suggest that the alternate selves within a multiple personality may be different in both mind and body. If Eve had three faces, she may also have had three voices, three memory systems, and, in a limited sense, three biological response systems.

Prior to the NIMH studies, physicians and mental health workers had frequently reported dramatic physical differences among the alternate personalities of MPD patients. The differences include such phenomena as physical health differences, voice changes, and even changes in right- and left-handedness. The alternate personalities in MPD patients often respond in different ways to medications. Some patients have severe allergies when one personality is present but no allergies when the others are active. One patient nearly died of a violent allergic reaction to a bee sting; a week later, when an alternate personality was active, another sting produced no reaction. Female patients frequently have different menstrual cycles for each female personality; one patient had three periods per month. Other patients need eyeglasses with different prescriptions for different personalities; one may be farsighted, another nearsighted (Miller & others, 1991).

Physiological studies of MPD patients under controlled laboratory conditions have also shown differences between the various personalities. In-

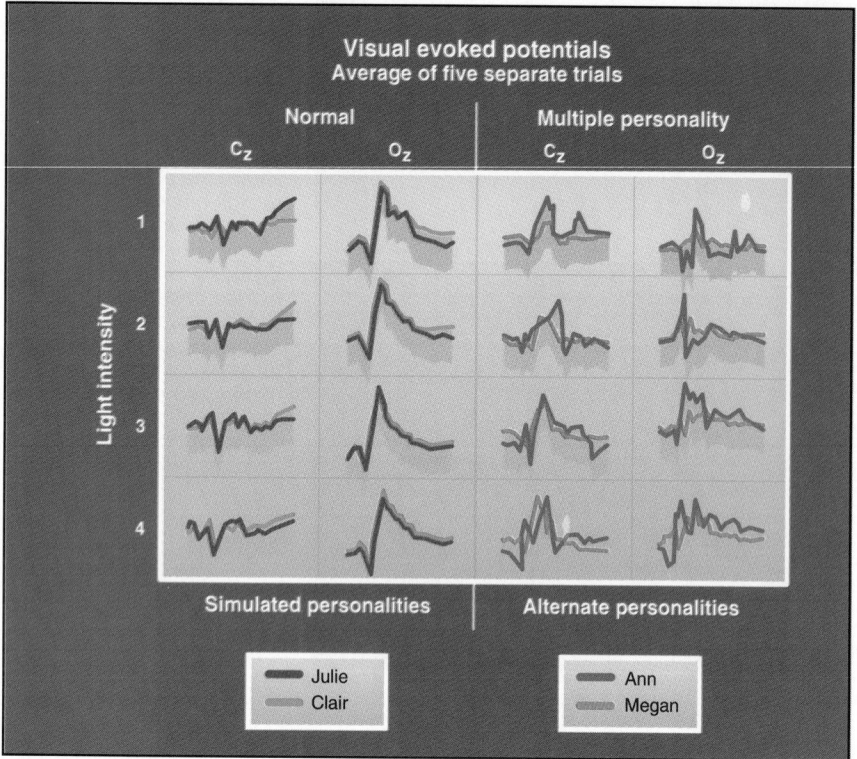

Visual evoked potentials
Average of five separate trials

♣ **Figure 8.18** *Comparison of averaged evoked potentials from two cortical regions (C_2 and O_2) of a control subject simulating a second personality (Julie and Clair) and a multiple personality patient (Ann and Megan) in response to four levels of brightness of light. (Putnam, 1984).*

deed, the responses of the different personalities frequently appear as different as if they had come from different people. For example, Christine Ludlow of the National Institute of Neurological and Communicative Disorders and Stroke did computerized spectral analyses ("voice prints") of audio recordings made by alternate personalities. She found that the voices were very distinct from one another (Putnam, 1984). Frank Putnam, an NIMH researcher, used electrical recording and brain-scanning techniques to study brain differences associated with alternate personalities. He found that cerebral blood-flow patterns differed among the personalities. Moreover, Putnam found shifts in EEG measures of hemispheric dominance when the individual had separate right-handed and left-handed personalities. When a left-handed personality appeared, the right hemisphere became more active.

Multiple personalities appear to differ even in their neural responses to simple visual stimuli. In one study, researchers tested 11 MPD patients who had three or more alternate personalities,

measuring the electrical response of the visual cortex to four intensities of light flashes. Each personality was tested on 5 different days, and the results were compared with those obtained from normal control subjects of the same age and gender who were asked to simulate different personalities.

The results of one such comparison are shown in Figure 8.18. The averaged potentials of Ann and Megan (the MPD patient) appear to differ more from one another than do those of Julie (the control) and her simulated Clair. Statistical analyses of the cortical responses of all the subjects confirmed this pattern; the evoked potentials of the MPD patients differed more than those of the controls (Putnam, 1984).

The emergence of new personalities in MPD is thought to occur in response to severe stress; a literal "imaginary playmate" who can somehow handle the stress more effectively comes into existence. For a vast majority of MPD patients, this begins to occur in early childhood, frequently in response to severe physical and sexual abuse. The children appear to engage in something akin to self-hypnosis as a means of protecting themselves, and they often create another self to handle the stressor (O'Regan, 1984). Over time, it is theorized, the protective functions served by the new personality remain separate in the form of an alternate personality, rather than being integrated into the core personality. Psychological treatment of MPD is intended to achieve that integration (Meyer & Osborne, 1987; Putnam, 1989).

Although more research is needed, the picture that has emerged so far suggests that the divided consciousness seen in the MPD patient is associated with physiological differences. This fact raises intriguing questions about the unity of the self. Perhaps all of us, to some extent, harbor other potential selves linked to our development. For most of us, however, the self has a continuity that extends across time. What holds the self together? Some theorists, speaking from the biological perspective, suggest that what we call *self* is in part a production of frontal-lobe and left-hemisphere language abilities that allow us to interpret and theorize about the world and our place in it and to fuse our multiple selves into a coherent unitary self (Gazzaniga, 1985; Ornstein, 1986). Perhaps, they suggest, these processes are the glue with which the many facets of conscious experience are fused into the stable "I" that we call the self.

Drug-Induced Alterations of Consciousness

A **drug** is any substance, other than food, whose chemical action alters the structure or functioning of the body. There are many different kinds of drugs, but our present concern is with drugs that affect the functioning of the nervous system and thereby produce alterations in consciousness.

Like any cell, a neuron is essentially a fragile bag of chemicals floating in a liquid medium that has specific chemical properties. The neuron's life and activities are governed by chemical interactions with other neurons, with the surrounding fluid, and within the neuron itself. It should not be surprising that this delicate chemical balancing act makes neurons highly vulnerable to invading chemicals. To protect neurons, certain cells in the nervous system form a **blood–brain barrier** that screens out foreign chemicals while letting in substances that the neurons need. Generally, the blood–brain barrier does a very effective job, but some chemical substances can pass through the barrier and affect the workings of neurons. Alcohol is one of them. Others come from the opium poppy, the peyote cactus, and the coca and hemp plants. Additional substances are produced artificially in pharmaceutical laboratories. Because these substances affect consciousness, mood, and behavior, they are known as **psychoactive drugs,** and they are the fastest, the most effective, and, in some instances, the most dangerous way of artificially altering states of consciousness.

Mechanisms of Drug Action

Psychoactive drugs produce their effects by altering the normal functioning of neurons. By stimulating or inhibiting the neuron's naturally occurring processes, a psychoactive drug can speed up, slow down, or stop synaptic transmission.

Drugs can affect synaptic transmission in at least five ways (Julien, 1991). First, some drugs mimic, or imitate, certain natural neurotransmitters. Their molecules are shaped like the natural neurotransmitters, so they can occupy receptor sites on the neuron and fire it, just as the natural neurotransmitter would. Drugs known as stimulants often act in this way. Second, drugs can prevent neural firing by occupying the receptor site and keeping the natural neurotransmitter from reaching the neuron. Tranquilizing drugs sometimes operate in this fashion.

Drugs can influence neural functioning in other ways as well. A third mode of influence is to invade the neuron's membrane and prevent it from manufacturing transmitter substances. Fourth, a drug can

prevent the release of the neurotransmitters into the synaptic space. As a result, the neuron's ability to transmit information is lost. Finally, a drug that prevents the reuptake of a neurotransmitter from the synaptic space allows the transmitter to keep stimulating other neurons and greatly increases neural firing.

A particular drug may affect different people in different, and unpredictable, ways. The effects of any drug can be heightened or diminished by several factors: dosage, frequency of use, the person's size and physical condition, his or her psychological state, whether other drugs have been taken or food eaten, expectations concerning the drug's effects (recall the think-drink phenomenon described in Chapter 2, in which alcohol expectancies influenced behavior more than alcohol itself), and the setting in which the drug is taken. Thus, in describing how psychoactive drugs affect consciousness and behavior, we have to speak in generalities while keeping the important role of these other factors in mind.

Tolerance, Dependence, and Addiction

As we consider the effects of specific drugs, we need to have in mind the definitions of three terms: tolerance, dependence, and addiction. When a person repeatedly uses a drug, the body adapts to it, and larger and larger doses are needed to produce the original effects. This need for increasingly larger doses is called **tolerance.** In an attempt to restore homeostasis, the nervous tissue has begun to counter the effect of the drug with **compensatory responses,** which produce effects opposite to the drug's effects. More drug is needed to overcome the body's ''protest'' (Poulos & Cappell, 1991).

When tolerance develops, it is frequently accompanied by **dependence** on the drug. *Physical dependence* means that when the drug is not taken, the person experiences unpleasant withdrawal symptoms as the body's protest response against the drug continues. *Psychological dependence* means that the person simply wants the drug because of its pleasurable effects, not because he or she wants to avoid withdrawal symptoms. Psychological dependence can occur without physical dependence.

Drug **addiction** is defined as a strong physiological and psychological dependence on a habit-forming drug. Addicts lose their ability to control their drug intake. They take drugs compulsively and experience a craving when they are unavailable. Both tolerance and dependence undoubtedly underlie addiction.

Depressants

Depressants decrease the level of activity in the nervous system. In moderate dosages, they reduce feelings of tension and anxiety and produce a state of relaxed euphoria. In extremely high dosages, however, depressants can slow down vital life processes to the point at which death occurs.

Alcohol

When ingested, alcohol passes directly through the walls of the stomach and small intestine and is absorbed immediately into the bloodstream and carried to the brain. The **blood alcohol level** is a measure of alcohol concentration in the body. In most of the United States and Canada, a person whose blood alcohol level is 0.10 percent is considered legally intoxicated and unfit to operate a motor vehicle. One rough rule of thumb used to approximate how much a person can drink and metabolize in an hour without raising the blood alcohol level is to divide body weight (in pounds) by five times the percentage of alcohol in the beverage (Ray, 1978). Thus, a 150-pound person could drink about 6 ounces of 5-percent beer per hour (150 lb./[5 × 5 percent] = 6 oz.).

If you get a "high" from drinking, you may be surprised to find alcohol classified as a depressant, but it is so classified because it acts directly on neural cell membranes to reduce electrical impulses, and it also increases the activity of GABA, a neurotransmitter that inhibits synaptic activity (Goldstein, 1992).

Once inside the brain, alcohol affects the ascending reticular formation first. As noted earlier, in relation to dreaming, the ascending reticular system normally alerts and stimulates the cerebral cortex, but this process slows down under the influence of alcohol. The decreased input from the reticular formation results in a depression of inhibitory control mechanisms in the cortex. This release of inhibitions is seen in the euphoric "high" experienced at low blood alcohol levels by many people. But the release of inhibitions also makes it impossible to predict specific behavioral effects. Which behaviors are suppressed and which are released from inhibition depends on the individual, and here intrapsychic factors enter the picture. Thus, a usually shy person may become a live wire equipped with a lamp shade, while a typically friendly one may become a modern version of Attila the Hun. An important contributor to such behaviors is a reduction in self-consciousness and self-awareness, which causes people to monitor and evaluate their behaviors less than they normally would (Steele & Josephs, 1990). ▼

As the concentration of alcohol in the blood increases, other parts of the brain, including the cerebral cortex, are directly affected. The behavioral and cognitive effects of progressively higher blood alcohol levels are shown in Table 8.3. As you can see, after

Table 8.3 Effects of Blood Alcohol Levels on Consciousness and Behavior

Blood Alcohol Level (Percent)	Behavioral Effects
0.00	Sober
0.05	Lowered alertness, usually good feeling, release of inhibitions, impaired judgment
0.10	Slowed reaction time, impaired motor function, less caution; legal intoxication in many states
0.15	Large, consistent increases in reaction time
0.20	Marked depression in sensory and motor capability; decidedly intoxicated
0.25	Severe motor disturbance, such as staggering; sensory perceptions greatly impaired; "wiped out," "plastered"
0.30	Stuporous but conscious; no comprehension of the immediate environment
0.35	Surgical anesthesia; possible death at this point and beyond

Source: Adapted from Ray, 1983; and Bogen, 1932.

the initial excitement phase, the body begins to react in quite the opposite way. Feelings of fatigue, nausea, unhappiness, and depression may ocur, exactly as we would expect from a depressant drug. Thought processes and physical coordination become progressively more disorganized as cortical control is depressed. Reaction time, eye–hand coordination, and decision making are all impaired, making the drunk driver a true menace to self and others (see Figure 8.19).

Thus, the effect on conscious experience of an increase in blood alcohol level seems to have two phases: an initial "upper" from the release of inhibitions, followed by a "downer" as higher brain centers are depressed (Marlatt & others, 1988). Unfortunately, some people respond to the second phase by drinking even more in the hope that it will make them feel "high" again, a self-defeating strategy if ever there was one.

Barbiturates and Tranquilizers

Physicians frequently prescribe barbiturates and tranquilizers as sedatives, relaxants, and sleeping pills.

▼

Thinking Critically About Alcohol and Aggression

A normally mild-mannered man who has been drinking alcohol begins to slur his speech and lose his train of thought. Presently, he approaches another man, becomes increasingly abusive and physiologically aroused, and then challenges the other person to a fight. How might you explain the physiological arousal and the aggressive behavior in terms of (1) the physiological effects of alcohol, (2) psychodynamic factors, and (3) cognitive factors, such as the "think–drink" effect described in Chapter 2?

Barbiturates—such as Nembutal ("yellow jackets"), Seconal ("redbirds"), and phenobarbital and amobarbital ("the purple hearts")—and tranquilizers—such as Valium and Xanax—are grouped together because both groups depress the nervous system by interfering with synaptic transmission. They either prevent the release of excitatory neurotransmitters or cause the release of inhibitory ones, particularly GABA (Grilly, 1989; Julien, 1991).

Mild doses of barbiturates are effective as sleeping pills. Higher doses, such as those used by addicts, trigger an initial period of excitation, followed by slurred speech, loss of coordination, extreme depression, and severe impairment of memory and thinking. Overdoses, particularly when they are taken with alcohol, may cause unconsciousness, coma, and death.

Users can build up a tolerance for barbiturates. Addicts may take as many as 50 sleeping pills a day to regain the initial high. Barbiturates are highly addictive, and heavy users may die if the drugs are withdrawn suddenly. Several months of gradual, supervised withdrawal may be needed before addicts lose their physical dependence.

The overuse of tranquilizers is extensive in U.S. society. Americans spend almost half a billion dollars a year on Valium alone. Nearly 90 million tranquilizer prescriptions are filled each year, and perhaps half a million Americans use tranquilizers for nonmedical purposes (Julien, 1991). Many people mistakenly regard Valium as harmless, but it is not. The body develops a tolerance to Valium, and physical and psychological dependence can occur. Many people do not know they have become addicted until they try to stop taking the drug and experience serious withdrawal symptoms. Tranquilizers are involved in perhaps a quarter of all drug-related deaths (Vischi & others, 1980).

Stimulants (C)

Stimulants are drugs that increase neural firing and activate the nervous system. Two of the most widely used stimulants are amphetamines and cocaine.

Amphetamines

Amphetamines—popularly known as speed, uppers, and bennies—are powerful stimulants of the brain and the autonomic nervous system. They increase the release of the neurotransmitters norepinephrine and dopamine, triggering synapses and spreading excitation throughout the nervous system. They also cause leakage of norepinephrine and dopamine from axon terminals, which increases firing even more. Amphetamines are prescribed to reduce appetite, fatigue, and the need for sleep and to alleviate depression.

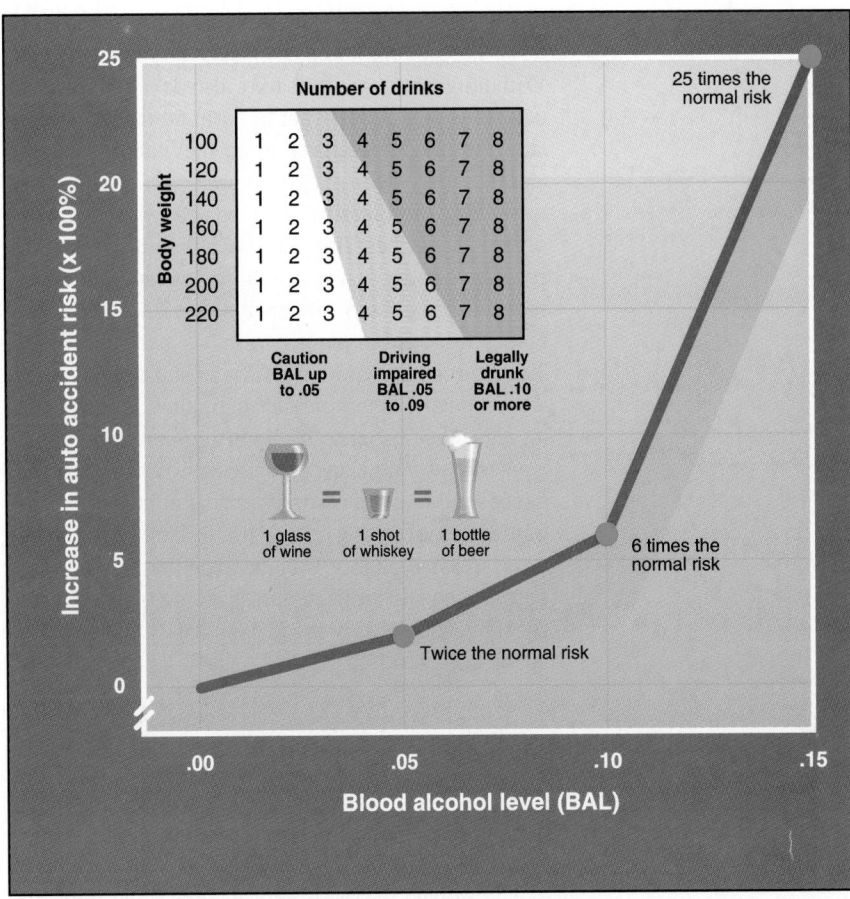

Figure 8.19 *Relation between blood alcohol level and risk of having an auto accident. At 0.10, the legal definition of intoxication in most states, the risk is 6 times greater than at 0.00, and the risk climbs to 25 times higher at a BAL of 0.15. (Based on National Safety Council, 1992).*

Amphetamines appear to have no harmful effects if they are used in moderation. However, people who use higher dosages quickly develop tolerance, and they often acquire a strong psychological dependence. Eventually, many heavy users start injecting, or mainlining, large quantities of the drug. When speed is mainlined, a sudden flash, or rush, of intense pleasure envelops the body within seconds and a great surge of energy is experienced. This energy surge is one reason why amphetamines are sometimes used by athletes to gain a competitive edge (Tricker & Cook, 1990). As one professional football player said during the 1970s, "You look at your opponent and he's staring at you wild-eyed with big dilated pupils and drooling all over himself. I'm not about to go out there unless I'm in the same condition" (Mandell, 1978). Fortunately, amphetamine use by athletes during competition has been reduced by stringent anti-drug legislation and drug testing.

Amphetamine addicts may mainline the drug repeatedly and remain awake continuously for as long as a week. During this period, their body systems are racing at breakneck speed. They become increasingly tense and anxious and may suffer a large weight loss. With long-term use, users may also develop paranoid delusions that others want to harm them. When they stop the injections, there is an inevitable "crash," and they may sleep deeply for one or two days, only to wake up profoundly depressed and exhausted, with severe headaches and intense irritability. The depressive crash is brought about by the amphetamine-induced depletion of the excitatory transmitters norepinephrine and dopamine from the axon terminals. The neurons are, quite literally, exhausted.

When amphetamines are mainlined, there occurs an enormous increase in blood pressure, which can lead to heart failure and cerebral hemorrhage (stroke). Considerable evidence shows that repeated use of high doses of speed causes brain damage. Thought processes and memory can become permanently impaired. Because amphetamines tax the body so heavily, addicts have a short life expectancy. This type of speed kills, too.

Cocaine

Cocaine is a stimulant derived from the coca plant, which grows mainly in western South America. Cocaine was once used widely as a local anesthetic in eye, nose, and throat surgery. Unlike other local anesthetics, however, cocaine also acts as a powerful central nervous system stimulant, apparently by stimulating the release and preventing the reuptake of the excitatory transmitters norepinephrine and dopamine (Gawin, 1991).

Cocaine is a white or colorless crystalline powder that is usually either inhaled (snorted) or injected (mainlined). More recently *crack,* a chemically converted cocaine "freebase" which can be smoked, has appeared. Its effects are faster, more intense, and more dangerous (Grilly, 1989; Ray, 1983). Overdoses of freebase can cause sudden death from cardiorespiratory arrest.

Hailed at various times in its history as a wonder drug and as a menace, cocaine has a wide range of possible effects. It can induce euphoria, excitation, anxiety, a sense of increased muscular strength, talkativeness, and liveliness. The stimulant effect occurs within minutes and lasts about 30 minutes. Cocaine causes pupils to dilate and heart rate and blood pressure to increase. In larger doses, it can produce fever, vomiting, convulsions, hallucinations, and paranoid delusions similar in many respects to the effects of amphetamines. Crack works even faster and produces a more intense reaction that dissipates more quickly. A severe crash and depressive mood swing may occur after the cocaine high, particularly with repeated doses. Although there is no evidence that they become

physically dependent, cocaine users often develop a strong psychological dependence on the drug.

Narcotics

The term **narcotic** applies to opium and opium derivatives, such as morphine, heroin, and codeine. Products of the opium poppy, an annual plant that grows in hot dry climates, have been used to reduce pain and produce pleasure for at least 6,000 years. Narcotics are indispensable in the practice of medicine—they are the most effective agents known for the relief of intense pain. Unfortunately, they have also caused untold misery and destroyed many lives.

The 1970s witnessed our first real glimpses into how narcotics affect the nervous system. Opiate receptors were found in the brain, and it was discovered that the body produces its own opiates, the endorphins. Portions of the brain stem and thalamus that seem important in pain perception and parts of the limbic system that are involved in emotional reactions were both found to be packed with opiate receptors. These sites of receptor concentration may help to account for two different and important effects of narcotics: (1) pain relief and (2) mood changes that sometimes produce euphoria.

Heroin, a widely abused narcotic, mainly causes emotional changes. Experienced users feel a "thrill" within several minutes of an injection. It resembles, some say, a sexual orgasm, except that the sensation is in the abdomen rather than the genitals. For a time, users feel as if they are "on top of the world," with no worries, no concerns. They feel peaceful and non-aggressive. Their psychological functions are not impaired, as they are with alcohol and barbiturates, and heroin users can perform well on certain kinds of skilled tasks.

But tolerance and both physical and psychological dependence on narcotics develop quickly. Some people think that if narcotics are not taken intravenously, one cannot become addicted. That is simply not so.

Traumatic withdrawal symptoms occur when heavy narcotics users stop taking the drugs, and many addicts continue to "shoot up" in order to avoid them, even if the injections no longer make them feel high (see Figure 8.20). The following description of withdrawal comes from a young woman who succeeded in "kicking" her heroin habit.

> It's like a terrible case of flu. Your joints move involuntarily. That's where the phrase "kick the habit" comes from. You jerk and twitch and you just can't control it. You throw up. You can't control your bowels either and this goes on for four or five days afterwards. You can't sleep and you cough up blood, because if you're on drugs, you can't eat and that's all there is to cough up.

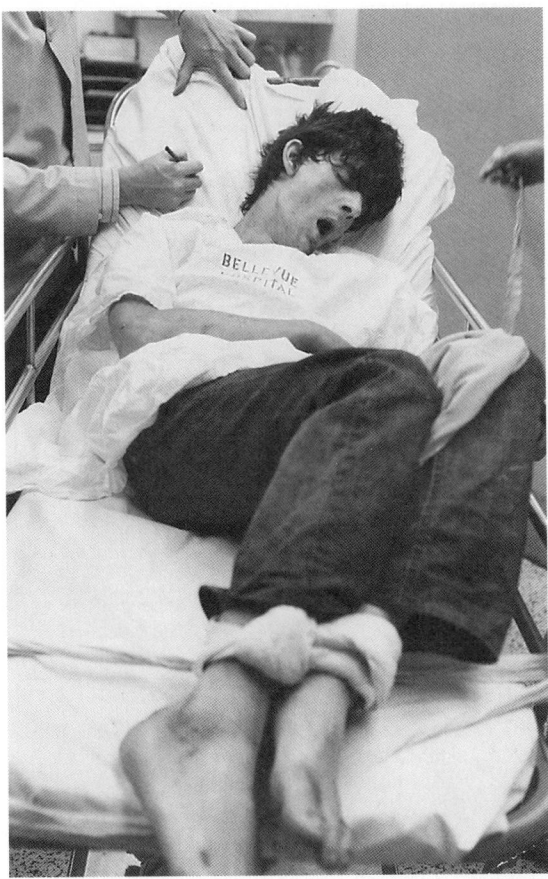

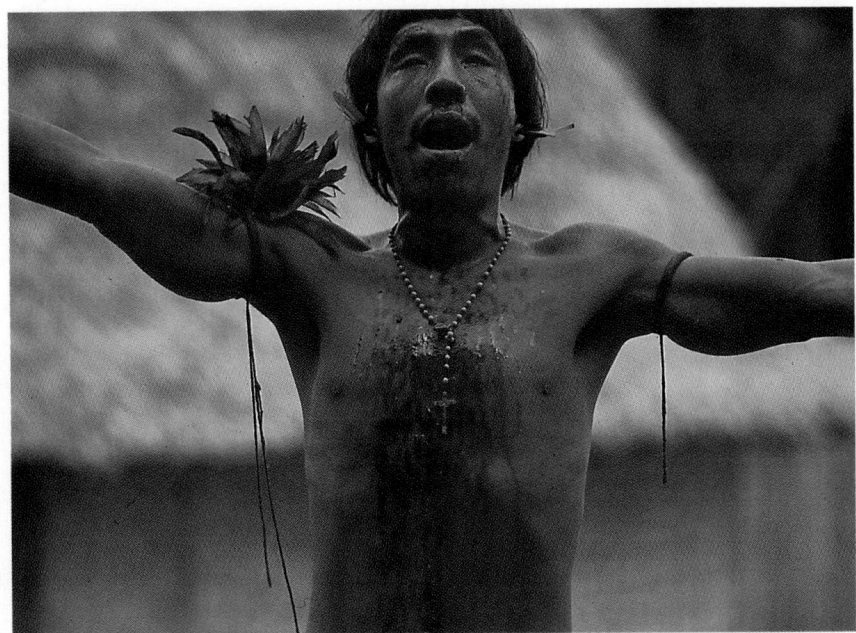

Figure 8.21 *In some cultures, hallucinogenic drugs are thought to have spiritual powers. Under the influence of peyote, this modern Indian shaman prepares to conduct a religious ceremony.*

 Figure 8.20 *The agonies of narcotic withdrawal can be so severe that addicts who would like to kick the habit continue to shoot up in order to avoid withdrawal.*

Hallucinogens (E)

The **hallucinogens,** or psychotomimetic drugs, are the most powerful of the mind-altering drugs. *Psychotomimetic* literally means "imitation of psychosis." The term is used because some of the effects of these drugs are very close to symptoms of severe mental disorders. The plants from which some of the hallucinogens are derived are considered sacred in many primitive cultures. Because of their ability to produce "unearthly" states of consciousness, they are thought in some societies to contain spiritual forces (see Figure 8.21).

The effects of a hallucinogen are not determined solely by the drug; they are heavily influenced by the user's mood, mental attitude, and environment. Hallucinogens usually distort or intensify sensory experience, and they can blur the boundaries between fact and fantasy. Users may speak of seeing sounds and hearing colors. They may lose their sense of direction and distance and their ability to make objective judgments.

The mental effects of hallucinogens are always unpredictable, even if the drugs are taken repeatedly, and their effects may recur as *flashbacks* days or even months after the drugs have been taken. Hallucinogens may cause mystical experiences, illusions, exhilaration, withdrawal from reality, violent outbursts, self-destruction, or sheer panic. This unpredictability constitutes the greatest danger to users. Unlike depressants and narcotics, hallucinogens are apparently not physically addictive, but psychological dependence may develop.

LSD

Lysergic acid diethylamide (LSD-25) is many times more potent than other hallucinogens, such as the cactus-derived peyote. In its natural form, LSD is synthesized from ergot fungus, a disease that affects rye and wheat grain. It can also be produced synthetically.

By inhibiting the release of certain neurotransmitters (particularly serotonin) and thereby affecting control mechanisms in the reticular formation and other brain regions, LSD causes a runaway flooding of excitation in the nervous system. A dose no larger than the tip of a pin can take a user on a "trip" for 8 to 16 hours. During and after such trips, users may suffer acute panic or depression. Some even suffer short- or long-term psychoses. We do not yet know whether the drug actually causes the psychotic disorder or merely precipitates it in people who were marginally adjusted to begin with.

Table 8.4 Effects of the Major Pychoactive Drugs

Class	Typical Effects	Effects of Overdose	Tolerance/Dependence
DEPRESSANTS Alcohol	Biphasic reaction: initial "high," followed by depressed physical and psychological functioning	Disorientation, loss of consciousness, possible death at extremely high blood alcohol levels	Tolerance; physical and psychological dependence; withdrawal symptoms
Barbiturates Tranquilizers	Depressed reflexes and impaired motor functioning, tension reduction	Shallow respiration, clammy skin, dilated pupils, weak and rapid pulse, coma, possible death	Tolerance; high psychological and physical dependence on barbiturates, low to moderate on such tranquilizers as Valium; withdrawal symptoms
STIMULANTS Amphetamines Cocaine	Increased alertness, excitation, euphoria, increased pulse rate and blood pressure, sleeplessness	Agitation, hallucinations (e.g., "cocaine bugs"), paranoid delusions, convulsions, death	Tolerance; psychological but probably not physical dependence
NARCOTICS Opium Morphine	Euphoria, drowsiness, "rush" of pleasure, little impairment of psychological functions	Slow, shallow breathing, clammy skin, convulsions, coma, possible death	High tolerance; physical and psychological dependence; severe withdrawal symptoms
HALLUCINOGENS LSD PCP	Illusions, hallucinations, distortions in time perception, loss of reality contact; with PCP, possible violent behavior	Psychotic reactions, particularly with PCP; possible death	Tolerance; no physical dependence for LSD, degree unknown for PCP; high psychological dependence for PCP, degree unknown for LSD
MARIJUANA	Euphoria, relaxed inhibitions, increased appetite, possible disorientation	Fatigue, disoriented behavior, possible psychosis	Tolerance and psychological dependence

Source: The National Board of Narcotics, 1992.

Although pure LSD is manufactured, its use is generally restricted to government-sponsored research projects. Most "acid" sold on the street has been made in a "basement lab" and may contain other chemicals, such as speed and strychnine. The addition of these other drugs may make the effects of the drug even more unpredictable and increase the likelihood of a "bad trip."

PCP

Phencyclidine (PCP) was introduced in the 1950s as a synthetic anesthetic. In 1967 it was made commercially available as an anesthetic in veterinary medicine. That same year it began to appear in the drug culture in San Francisco. After a number of PCP users experienced bad trips, its popularity declined rapidly.

Later, however, it reappeared as "angel dust." It is often mixed with other drugs or represented as other drugs and sold to naive buyers.

We don't know exactly how PCP affects the nervous system, but its effects on consciousness and behavior are alarmingly apparent. The drug is highly variable in its effects. Rapid and involuntary eye movements, a blank stare, and an exaggerated gait are among those most commonly observed. Image distortion (as in a fun-house mirror), auditory hallucinations, and severe mood disorders may also occur. Some people experience acute anxiety and feelings of impending doom, while others become paranoid and hostile. Users may commit violent assaults on others, and a number of bizarre murders have been directly attributed to PCP use (Siegel, 1989).

Perhaps PCP's most notable characteristic is its ability to produce psychotic reactions that are indistinguishable from schizophrenia. As many as 15 to 20 percent of those taking the drug become temporarily psychotic (Lerner & Burns, 1978; Schatzberg & Cole, 1991). Normal behavior and thought patterns return, usually in about a week, but in severe cases recovery may take 12 to 18 months (Young & others, 1987).

Marijuana

Marijuana, the product of **cannabis,** the hemp plant, has become an important recreational drug. The major active ingredient of marijuana is the chemical substance *tetrahydrocannabinol,* or THC. As with most drugs, the effects that any individual experiences and the intensity of those effects depend on the dosage, the individual's sensitivity to the drug, his or her psychological state, and the setting in which the drug is taken.

Usually inhaled, but sometimes eaten, the drug starts to take effect within about 15 minutes. Depending on drug potency and dosage, its effects can last up to 4 hours. Low doses may cause people to feel an increased sense of relaxation and well-being. Their sense of space and time may be expanded. Sensations can become more intense, and a craving for food (''the munchies'') often occurs, even though blood sugar level has not changed.

With higher doses, marijuana users may experience rapid changes in emotions and sensory imagery, a dulling of the ability to attend, and more pronounced alterations in thought formation and expression. These distortions can produce temporary feelings of panic and anxiety in some individuals. Very high doses may cause distortions in body image and sense of personal identity, as well as hallucinations.

Individuals under the influence of marijuana may have a hard time making decisions that require clear thinking and may be highly susceptible to the suggestions of other people. Their ability to perform tasks that require quick reflexes and thinking is impaired, and so is memory and learning ability (Siegel, 1989). Moreover, experimental evidence derived from performance on driver test courses and under actual traffic conditions clearly shows that driving under the influence of marijuana (even ''social doses'') can be hazardous (Grilly, 1989).

Table 8.4 summarizes the major properties and effects of marijuana and the other drugs that we have considered.

Perhaps the most serious consequence of drug use is the potential for addiction. Drug addiction ruins lives, increases crime rates, and produces tremendous costs in health care and job productivity. Since addiction is a behavioral phenomenon that has both biological and psychological facets, psychology has the potential to contribute strongly to the understanding and modification of addictions. Our next feature surveys what is known about the process of overcoming addictions.

UNDERSTANDING AND OVERCOMING ADDICTIONS

ENHANCING HUMAN PERFORMANCE

A variety of behaviors can be labeled *addictive*. These include drinking, smoking, and other forms of substance abuse. Addictive behaviors have in common a repetitive habit pattern that increases the risk of disease or personal problems. These habit patterns are often experienced as involving loss of control, and attempts to stop or reduce the behaviors are marked by great discomfort (withdrawal symptoms) and high potential for relapse. Addictive behaviors typically involve a pattern of immediate gratification (short-term reward) and long-term costs.

In recent years, many psychologists have come to view addictions as a family of problem behaviors that have certain important commonalities in terms of how they develop and how they can be changed. An emerging *biopsychosocial model* suggests that the processes associated with becoming addicted and (for those fortunate enough to do so) overcoming the addiction fall into a sequence of developmental stages (Marlatt & others, 1988). These stages are shown in Figure 8.22. Recent research has begun to uncover the key biological, psychological, and social factors that influence the processes in each of these phases. Most of this research has focused on alcohol and substance abuse.

The *initiation phase* encompasses those factors that place a person at risk for later addictive behaviors. Although no specific gene has been conclusively identified, there is good reason to believe that genetic factors may be relevant (Holden, 1991). For example, it appears that children of alcoholics are up to four times as likely to develop alcoholism as children of nonalcoholics, even if they leave their biological parents early in life and grow up in another household (Schuckit, 1987). The link is strongest for males whose fathers are alcoholic.

Studies of adolescent drug use have identified a number of psychosocial risk factors. These include exposure to peers who use drugs, parental drug use, poor self-esteem, high needs for novelty and excitement, lack of social conformity, and a combination of stressful life changes and poorly developed coping skills (Newcomb & McGee, 1991). Recent studies of adolescent drug involvement indicate that it develops in stages, beginning with increasing use of beer and wine and moving on to liquor and cigarettes, then to marijuana, and finally to stimulant and depressant drugs. For both males and females, the link from marijuana to stimulant drugs is stronger than the link to later use of depressants (Windle & others, 1989).

Next in the process is the *transition phase* from social and recreational use into addiction. Here, again, both biological and psychological factors have been identified. There is increasing evidence that the rewarding effects of drugs are mediated by their effects on neurotransmitters, including dopamine, norepinephrine, and the endorphins (Grilly, 1989). One theory is that dopamine release in the reward centers of the limbic system is triggered by addictive drugs, producing intense pleasure (Holloway, 1991). The initial pleasurable feelings associated with the drug motivate the user to continue using it. In fact, the drug does not even need to make the person feel good—merely *better* than before (Barrett, 1985). Tolerance and dependence strengthen the tendency to repeat the addictive behavior, and withdrawal reactions punish the failure to do so (Babor & others, 1987).

Emerging as key factors in the transition phase are expectations concerning the addictive behavior. As we saw in the research on the think-drink effect described in Chapter 2, expectancies may be as important as pharmacological effects. Studies of addicts and those on their way to addiction consistently show that these people have higher expectations than others that the drug will enhance their pleasure or the effectiveness of their behavior (Christiansen & others, 1989; Marlatt & others, 1988). Another important expectancy is their belief that they are incompetent to deal with stressful events or negative moods on their own and that the object of addiction will be helpful in this regard (Litman, 1986).

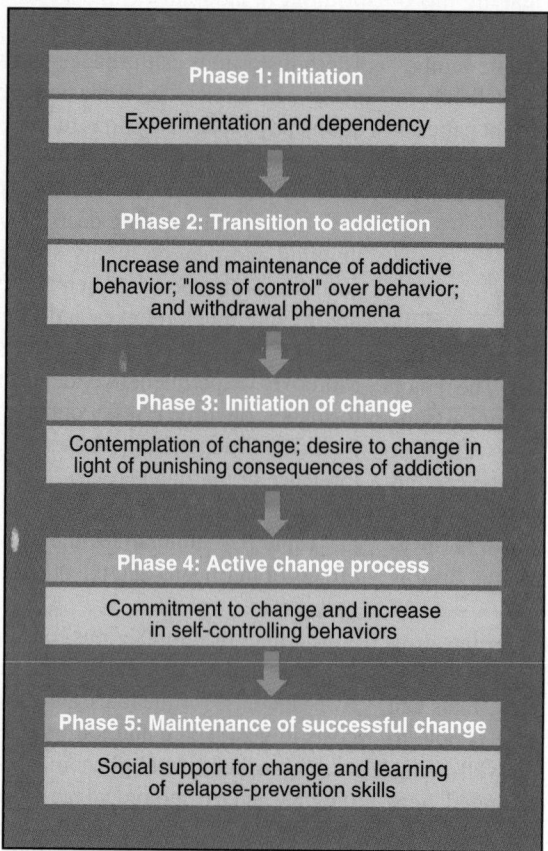

Figure 8.22 *A biopsychosocial model of how addictions develop and are overcome. (Marlatt & others, 1988).*

Eventually, as addicts experience increasingly serious difficulties in their lives, many of them begin to contemplate and desire change in their addictive behaviors. This desire triggers the *initiation of change phase,* and it forms the bridge to the next phase, that of *active change.* During this fourth phase, the person must actively engage in behaviors that can overcome the biopsychosocial factors that have maintained the addiction. These behaviors include maintaining the motivation and determination to change, reducing or stopping the addictive behaviors, and maintaining the change.

Studies of people who have overcome addictions on their own show that success in self-change is enhanced by public announcements of the intention to change, social support for efforts to change, changes in activities (especially avoidance of the people and situations linked to the addictive behaviors), and development of other strategies for coping with stress, such as meditation or exercise. Successful quitters also change

their belief that the addictive behavior will produce positive results for them (Stall & Biernacki, 1986).

In their desire to change, some addicts enter formal treatment programs. Where alcohol is concerned, it appears that many different treatment programs have moderate (30- to 50-percent) success rates, but no one treatment has emerged as clearly the most effective (Marlatt & others, 1988; Miller & Hester, 1986). Especially promising, however, are treatments that teach addicts more effective coping skills for dealing with their addictive urges and with situations that invite relapse, such as stressful circumstances and social situations in which temptations arise (Marlatt & Gordon, 1985).

Successful change in addictive behaviors begins the final phase, *maintenance of change.* Many studies indicate that it is far easier to change than to maintain the change. For example, formal smoking cessation programs are even less successful than alcohol treatment programs, with only 20 to 30 percent remaining abstinent 6 to 12 months after the program has ended. People who have quit on their own have even lower 12-month abstinence rates of 4 to 7 percent, although light smokers, who smoke fewer than 21 cigarettes per day, have nearly double the success rate of heavy smokers (Cohen & others, 1989).

High rates of relapse are found across the entire range of addictive behaviors. In one recent study of more than 14,000 people who had received treatment for alcoholism, fewer than half maintained abstinence or controlled drinking (Riley & others, 1988). Other studies have found relapse rates as high as 85 percent (Tims & Leukefeld, 1986). A study of 5,389 people who tried to quit smoking on their own found that of the fewer than 10 percent who successfully abstained for 6 months, up to 35 percent returned to regular smoking in the next 6-month period (Cohen & others, 1989).

Faced with these rather grim statistics, psychologists are working on programs that will not only change addictive behaviors but also reduce relapse. For example, Alan Marlatt and Judith Gordon (1985) have designed a **relapse prevention** program that trains clients to recognize and deal with situations that threaten to result in relapse, such as stressful events and peer pressure. Addicts also learn that a relapse does not mean that "it's no use." Rather, lapses are viewed as temporary setbacks and learning situations that invite the development of new skills so that the person can cope more successfully the next time. An addiction is seldom overcome on the first try; quitting often requires many attempts, each of which provides new information about the barriers to quitting and the strategies that work best. Thus, the best advice is to keep trying until one succeeds. Success does not result from "willpower"; rather, it depends on the development of self-control *behaviors* that counter the addiction. Some ways of increasing behavioral self-control will be described in the *Enhancing Human Performance* features of Chapters 9 and 15.

Multiple Determinants of Drug Effects

As we have seen, the effects of drugs on consciousness and behavior are produced by a combination of interacting factors. The drug itself produces pharmacological effects on brain processes, but environmental, cognitive, and intrapsychic factors can also influence the drug experience.

At the environmental level, the physical and social setting in which the drug is taken can have a marked influence. For example, the behavior of other people who are sharing the drug experience provides important cues for how to respond. It appears that a hostile environment may increase the chances of a bad trip with drugs such as LSD (Palfai & Jankiewicz, 1991). Cultural learning experiences may also affect our beliefs about a drug's effects and thereby influence our experiences.

As we saw in Chapter 2 with regard to the think-drink effect and in Chapter 7 with regard to placebo effects, beliefs and expectancies are powerful cognitive influences. These factors are able not only to affect our psychological responses to drugs but even to override their pharmacological effects. Many of the environmental factors just described probably work their influences through these cognitive factors. Thus, if a person's fellow drinkers are acting happy and gregarious, he or she may expect to respond to drinking in the same way.

Finally, intrapsychic factors also exert an effect. Psychodynamic theorists have long suggested that many of the atypical behaviors and experiences that may occur under the influence of drugs result from the weakening of defenses and the emergence of repressed or inhibited impulses. Moreover, people who are maladjusted or whose contact with reality is marginal may be particularly at risk of experiencing severe psychiatric reactions to drugs when their already strained controls are further diminished by drug reactions (Ray & Ksir, 1987; Young & others, 1987). Finally, humanistic theorists would not be surprised by the finding that an intrapsychic factor highly related to drug use among young people is a sense of meaninglessness and lack of direction in life (Newcomb & Harlow, 1986).

Some of the major biological, environmental, cognitive, and intrapsychic factors that may interact to determine drug experiences are summarized in this chapter's Understanding Causes feature (page 258).

Frontiers of Consciousness

Many people seek altered states in the hope that their experiences will reveal alternate views of reality not shaped by previous learning and cultural influences. But learning from altered states may not be easy. Some of the experiences appear to be **state dependent;** that is, they are so different from normal mental functioning that it is difficult to translate what has been experienced within an altered state into the thinking, feeling, and remembering of normal experience. A person may feel that he or she has had a great insight or new mode of understanding yet be unable to recall what it was or express it in the language that we use to describe "normal" reality.

Drug-Induced States of Consciousness:
Factors Suggested by Theory and Research

$B=f(P,E)$

Causal Factors

Biological
- Effects of drug on neuro-transmitters
- Genetic factors that influence biological response to specific drugs
- Body weight in the case of alcohol

Cognitive
- Attitudes toward the drug
- Expectancies concerning drug effects

Intrapsychic
- Possible release of inhibited impulses
- Individual's level of personal adjustment, which can influence the likelihood of a negative experience

Environmental
- Cultural background and context
- Social setting in which drug is taken

Drug-Induced States of Consciousness

Drug-Induced States of Conciousness are a function of interacting personal and environmental causal factors. These factors may vary and may interact with one another in particular ways, depending on the person and the situation.

Throughout history, people have felt themselves influenced by mystical and spiritual experiences. Now, for the first time in history, science is making a concerted attempt to understand such experiences, and these efforts may expand our understanding of both consciousness and reality. The words of William James, one of the founding fathers of psychology, are as pertinent today as they were nearly a century ago:

Our normal waking consciousness is but one special type of consciousness, whilst all about it, parted from it by the filmiest of screens, there lie potential forms of consciousness entirely different. We may go through life without suspecting their existence, but apply the requisite stimulus, and at a touch they are there in all their completeness, definite types of mentality which probably nowhere have their field of application and adoption. No account of the universe in its totality can be final which leaves these other forms of consciousness quite disregarded. How to regard them is the question. . . . At any rate, they forbid our premature closing of accounts with reality. (1902, p. 298)

SUMMARY

The Scientific Study of Consciousness

● Because consciousness is a private and subjective experience, it cannot be studied directly. Three classes of observable behavior—verbal self-report, physiological responses, and nonverbal behaviors—are the major sources of information about states of consciousness.

Emerging Conceptions of Mind and Consciousness

● The distinction between automatic and controlled processing is an important one in understanding consciousness. Psychologists also distinguish between conscious, subconscious, preconscious, and unconscious phenomena.

● A newly emerging conception of the mind represents it as multiple and largely independent modules devoted to specific types of information processing, emotions, and behavior.

Sleeping and Dreaming

● Scientists do not fully understand why people sleep. Periods of sleep and wakefulness are in part regulated by a 24-hour circadian rhythm, which involves cyclical changes in various bodily processes. The physiological and psychological problems of jet lag and work-shift changes result from a disruption of the circadian rhythm, and circadian factors have been related to death and to human errors.

● EEG recordings during the sleep cycle indicate that it contains five distinct stages. The REM stage, characterized by rapid eye movements and reports of dreams, occurs about every 90 minutes during the night. The proportion of REM sleep decreases from about 50 percent in infancy to about 25 percent between the ages of 5 to 9. Although dreams are very likely to be reported during REM sleep, they also occur in non-REM sleep.

● Various theories about the nature and functions of dreams have been proposed. Antrobus has advanced a theory of dreaming based on a modular model of brain processes. The REM rebound effect has led to suggestions that dreams are part of a homeostatic mechanism in the nervous system. According to Freud, dreams reflect psychodynamic processes. They allow some degree of wish fulfillment, and their manifest content is thought to be a symbolic manifestation of the latent content, or true psychological meaning. Another theory is that dreams help to consolidate memories formed in the waking state. But other theorists suggest that dreams reflect the erasure of unneeded memories.

● Insomnia is the most common sleep disorder. More serious are narcolepsy, a condition in which people suffer sudden and uncontrollable sleep attacks, and sleep apnea, in which air intake is blocked by an occlusion of the upper airway.

Waking Fantasies and Daydreams

● Waking fantasies can serve a number of adaptive functions, including wish fulfillment, the production of positive mood states, self-stimulation to relieve boredom, problem solving, and self-regulation of behavior.

● Studies have identified several types of daydreamers, whose fantasies vary in frequency and content. Other research has studied fantasy-prone personalities, who spend a great portion of their time in vivid fantasy.

Meditation

● Meditation appears to result in a state of relaxed alertness that involves reduced physiological arousal and, at times, a ''pure consciousness'' that is relatively free of thought processes. Meditation seems particularly useful for producing cognitive relaxation.

Hypnosis

● There is no physiological state that is unique to hypnosis. Research has shown that many of the phenomena produced by hypnosis can also be exhibited by unhypnotized control groups. This has given rise to attempts to identify the psychological principles that underlie hypnosis.

● Some theorists have suggested that hypnosis involves taking on the role of a hypnotized person and behaving in accordance with role expectations. Others have stressed the role of imagination and its possible effects on behavior and experience in hypnosis. A third point of view suggests that dissociation accounts for many hypnotic phenomena, and Hilgard has developed a technique for communicating with a presumably dissociated ''hidden observer'' during hypnosis.

● Recent studies of multiple personality disorder indicate the presence of striking physiological differences between alternate personalities in the same person, suggesting physiological as well as mental dissociation.

Drug-Induced Alterations of Consciousness

● A drug is any substance other than food whose chemical action alters the structure and functioning of the body. Certain psychoactive drugs are able to pass through the blood–brain barrier and affect the nervous system, producing changes in consciousness and behavior.

● Drugs work by duplicating, stimulating, or inhibiting neuronal processes. Some drugs mimic neurotransmitters; others affect their manufacture, release, or reuptake. A drug's effects depend on dosage, frequency of use, individual differences, and the setting in which the drug is taken.

● Tolerance is the need for increasingly larger doses of a drug to reproduce its original effects. Physical dependence results in withdrawal symptoms when the drug is not taken. People can also become psychologically dependent on a drug. Physical and/or strong psychological dependence on a drug results in addiction.

• Depressants decrease the level of activity in the nervous system, resulting in relaxation and feelings of well-being. Moderate doses reduce tension and anxiety; extremely high doses can slow down vital life processes to the point of death. Alcohol, barbiturates, and tranquilizers are depressants.

• Stimulants increase neural firing and activate the nervous system. Amphetamines mimic the transmitters norepinephrine and dopamine and also cause them to leak out of the axon terminals, increasing neural activity still further. Cocaine works by stimulating norepinephrine and dopamine release and preventing reuptake.

• Opiate receptors in certain regions of the brain account for two different effects of narcotics: pain relief and mood changes that may produce euphoria. Morphine primarily produces pain relief, while heroin mainly causes mood changes. Tolerance, dependence, and addiction occur readily, and withdrawal effects are especially traumatic.

• Hallucinogens are the most powerful of the mind-altering drugs. Hallucinogens usually distort or intensify sensory experience, and they frequently cause hallucinations and delusions. Their effects are very unpredictable and are influenced by the user's mood, expectations, and environment.

• Emerging developmental models of addiction are helping to identify the biological, psychological, and social variables that influence addictive behaviors and their modification.

Frontiers of Consciousness

• Experiences involving altered states of consciousness are sometimes state dependent and difficult to translate into the language of everyday life. Although traditional scientific methods are not well suited to the study of such states, the willingness of psychological researchers to study them may expand our understanding of important psychological processes.

KEY TERMS AND CONCEPTS

addiction (p. 249)
alpha rhythm (p. 235)
automatic processing (p. 232)
blood alcohol level (p. 250)
blood–brain barrier (p. 249)
cannabis (p. 255)
circadian rhythm (p. 234)
cognitive relaxation (p. 242)
compensatory response (p. 249)
conscious (p. 232)
consciousness (p. 231)
controlled processing (p. 232)
delayed sleep phase syndrome (p. 239)
delta wave (p. 235)
dependence (p. 249)
depressant (p. 249)

dissociation (p. 230)
dream work (p. 238)
drug (p. 249)
hallucinogen (p. 253)
hidden observer (p. 246)
hypersomnia (p. 239)
hypnosis (p. 243)
hypnotic susceptibility scales (p. 243)
insomnia (p. 239)
latent content (p. 238)
lysergic acid diethylamide (LSD-25) (p. 253)
manifest content (p. 238)
narcolepsy (p. 239)
narcotic (p. 252)
phencyclidine (PCP) (p. 254)
preconscious (p. 232)

psychoactive drug (p. 249)
relaxation response (p. 242)
REM rebound effect (p. 238)
REM sleep (p. 236)
relapse prevention (p. 257)
role theory of hypnosis (p. 246)
seasonal affective disorder (p. 234)
sleep apnea (p. 239)
sleep spindles (p. 235)
somatic relaxation (p. 242)
state-dependent experience (p. 257)
stimulant (p. 251)
subconscious (p. 232)
tolerance (p. 249)
unconscious (p. 233)
wish fulfillment (p. 238)

SUGGESTED READINGS

Hobson, J. A. (1989). *Sleep.* New York: Freeman. An authoritative summary of the latest findings on sleep and dreaming, including a discussion of the various theories of dreaming.

Long, M. E. (1987). What is this thing called sleep? *National Geographic, 172* (6), 787–821. An unusually comprehensive and beautifully illustrated article on sleep research.

Siegel, R. K. (1989). *Intoxication.* New York: Dutton. A fascinating description of drug effects and research on drugs.

Spanos, N. P., & Chaves, J. F. (Eds.) (1988). *Hypnosis: The cognitive–behavioral perspective.* Buffalo, N.Y.: Prometheus Books. An outstanding collection of articles that discuss hypnosis primarily from the perspective of role theory.

Learning 9

CHAPTER OUTLINE

261

Hilda, an attractive 33-year-old married woman, sought help for an unusual phobia: She was terrified of snow. Her phobia had appeared suddenly and for no apparent reason 2 years earlier when she and her husband moved to a suburb of a city in the eastern United States, and it seemed to be getting progressively worse. As the following report by her psychotherapist indicates, the phobia had a significant impact on her life.

> It is hard to picture adequately the extent of fear; this woman's fear of snow petrified her. She could not stand to go out in it; she could not stand to see it; in winter she could not listen to weather reports because someone might make some reference to snow! Any reference to snow, or even subjective thoughts about it, would make her uncomfortable, frightened, and tense. The many, many ways in which this phobia could affect her day-to-day living were almost incredible. The effects were . . . profound (Laughlin, 1967).

A middle-aged man has been playing roulette in a Las Vegas casino for nearly 36 hours. His clothes are disheveled and his hair hangs limply over his forehead. Hope and desperation are alternately mirrored on his face as he peers through the smoke-filled air at the whirling roulette wheel.

Nearby, a casino guard nudges a blackjack dealer and mutters, "That poor guy's really got the fever. He's been in here since yesterday. A real loser, too—I'll bet he's blown thousands. He's in hock up to his ears. I'll never understand what keeps these guys going. It's a sickness."

A judge in Staten Island, New York, prohibited two teen-age brothers from watching professional wrestling on television because he said they were becoming too violent. According to records filed in Family Court, the boys practiced body slams, choke holds, and figure-four locks with such zest that they were inflicting injuries on one another and frightening their mother. The mother reported that on one occasion, her 13-year-old son tried to apply the dreaded sleeper hold on her as she was in the kitchen stir-frying vegetables. Fortunately, she was able to break the hold before losing consciousness and before the vegetables burned. According to the judge, she also reported that the boy frequently addressed her "in a bizarre manner, shaking violently, calling himself Rowdy Roddy Piper and graphically describing the terrible things he was going to do to her." The judge told the mother that if the boys were allowed to watch wrestling in the future, he would have the family's TV set removed from the house and might even place the boys in foster homes (*The Sporting News*, August 19, 1985).

We begin with three instances of human behavior, each different, each distinctive. Yet they share one important thing: They are products of learning, a process that has been termed "the window of the mind." More specifically, they exemplify the three major types of learning with which we will be concerned: classical conditioning (learning through association); operant conditioning (learning through consequences); and modeling (learning through observation).

The study of learning is fundamental to an understanding of most aspects of human behavior. Unlike lower animals, people do not come equipped with the built-in blueprints for behavior called instincts. Instincts require that complex innate patterns of behavior occur invariably when certain stimuli are present. Human behavior is far more flexible than this. What humans have, instead of instincts, is a matchless capacity to adapt to the ever-changing circumstances of their lives by learning new ways of responding. The products of learning include knowledge and intellectual skills, attitudes and emotional responses, social behaviors and movement skills. Through our interactions with our unique personal environments, we learn to think, act, and feel in the ways that contribute most richly to our individual human identities.

Unfortunately, as demonstrated in the examples above, we can also learn to respond in ways that are harmful and self-defeating. For example, how did the young woman learn her intense and irrational fear of snow, and why has the fear become so pervasive? How did the compulsive gambler get that way, and why is he so strongly compelled to go on playing even in the face of terrible financial loss? How much is our behavior, like that of the teen-age wrestling enthusiasts, affected by observing the actions of others? This chapter focuses on these and many other questions. It describes some of the ways in which principles of learning established within the behavioral perspective have been applied to the understanding and solution of personal and social problems. It also shows how the cognitive, biological, and intrapsychic perspectives have added to our understanding of the processes that govern and limit learning. The humanistic perspective has not been explicitly concerned with the learning process—that is, *how* people learn—and so the chapter will have little to say from that perspective.

The Nature and Scope of Learning

We can define **learning** as *a change in behavior or in potential behavior that occurs as a result of ex-*

perience. This definition has several important elements. First, it excludes changes in behavior that occur as a result of purely physical factors such as maturation, injury, fatigue, or drugs. Second, by including the term *potential behavior,* the definition includes two different aspects of learning: ''knowing how'' and ''doing.'' This reminds us that learning is actually a construct referring to some hypothesized change within the organism that results from experience. Thus, when we see ourselves improve our abilities through practice, we infer that learning has occurred, and we know that we have the potential to perform better than before.

Although great strides have been made in understanding what happens in people's nervous systems when they learn, we can't see this internal process called learning. All we can see is some change in *performance.* For scientific purposes, then, performance changes are our operational definition of learning. Yet we know that learning is not always reflected in performance. For example, you probably know how to go about robbing a bank. Even though you haven't done so, the *potential* behaviors have been learned. Likewise, all of us have seen top athletes perform poorly—the superstar basketball player who suddenly loses his shooting touch or the champion gymnast who suddenly seems unable to walk a straight line when the pressure mounts during competition. There is no question that the *potential* for better performance is there, but it is being masked by other factors. Thus, in order to capture all that learning involves, the definition of learning must take into account potential as well as actual changes in behavior (Houston, 1992).

The products of learning are many and diverse, but they appear to be based on three major ways of learning: (1) learning through association, (2) learning through the positive or negative consequences our behaviors produce for us, and (3) learning by observing the behaviors of others. The formal terms for these three kinds of learning are *classical conditioning, operant conditioning,* and *observational learning,* or *modeling.*

Classical Conditioning: Learning Through Association

Our lives are full of reminders of things past. For example, you may feel good when you hear a particular song because it was associated with a pleasurable event or person in your life. Or perhaps you have had an instant and involuntary negative reaction to an individual who reminded you of some unpleasant person you once knew. For many of us, the mere aroma of popcorn or freshly baked bread is enough to induce mouth-watering hunger.

Back around the turn of the century, Ivan Pavlov, a Russian physiologist, was studying salivation in dogs as part of the research on digestion that won him the Nobel Prize in 1904. To study digestive processes, Pavlov built an apparatus that allowed him to collect and measure samples of dogs' saliva (see Figure 9.1). Pavlov's procedure was to place various kinds of food in front of the dogs and measure the natural salivary response of the animals in measuring tubes surgically attached to their salivary glands. But, as often occurs in science, Pavlov was about to make an important accidental discovery through astute observation. He noticed that with repeated testing, the dogs began to salivate *before* the food was actually presented. For example, Pavlov observed that the footsteps of the approaching experimenter could induce salivation, almost as if the footsteps were a substitute for the food itself.

Pavlov began to study this ''stimulus substitution.'' It soon became clear that if some stimulus that would not ordinarily cause salivation, such as a tone or a touch to the leg, was presented to the dogs slightly before a small amount of dried meat powder was squirted directly into their mouths, the sound of the tone or the touch alone would soon make the dogs salivate. Since these responses were not caused by the appropriate biological stimulus (food), Pavlov began to refer to them as ''psychic secretions.'' Figure 9.1*b* shows the apparatus Pavlov built to study classical conditioning in his laboratory (Goodwin, 1991).

In formal terms, the principle underlying **classical conditioning** is this: If a neutral stimulus (that is, one that at first elicits no response) is paired with a stimulus that already evokes a reflex response, then eventually the new stimulus will by itself evoke a similar response. The original stimulus (in Pavlov's experiments, the meat) is called the **unconditioned stimulus (UCS),** and the response it naturally evokes (salivation) is called the **unconditioned response (UCR).** The neutral stimulus that is then introduced (for example, a tone) is called the **conditioned stimulus (CS),** and the new response that it eventually evokes (salivation) is called the **conditioned response (CR)** (see Figure 9.2). Incidentally, it is widely believed that Pavlov used a bell for the CS. In reality, however, Pavlov found the bell to be a poor CS because it startled the dogs (Pavlov, 1906).

You may be wondering why we have different terms (UCR and CR) for what seems to be exactly the same response (salivation). There are two reasons. First, in Pavlov's studies, one of the responses (the UCR) was an unlearned reflex; the other was a conditioned, or learned, one. Second, even though the CR is a very close match, it usually is not identical

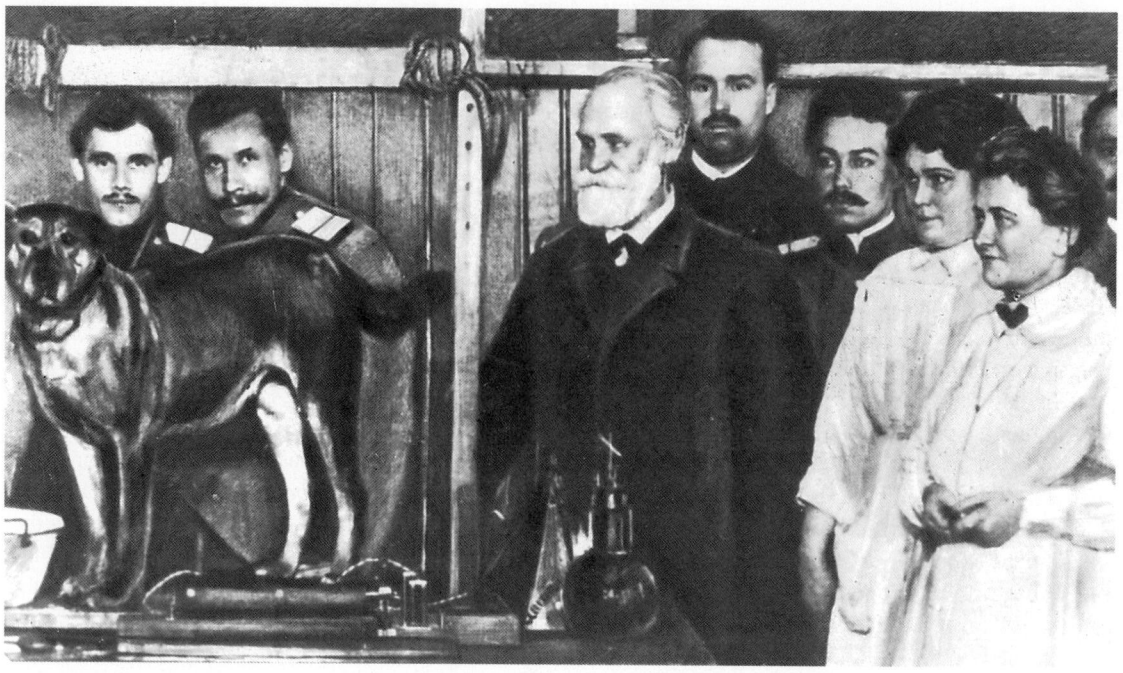

(a)

Figure 9.1 (a) *Ivan Pavlov (the man with the white beard) is shown here with colleagues and one of his canine subjects.* (b) *The apparatus with which Pavlov studied classical conditioning. The harness restrained the dog. A tube inserted in the dog's salivary gland permitted the precise measurement of salivation (far right). During training, the experimenter pulled one of the cords to deliver tactile stimulation (the conditioned stimulus, or CS) to the dog's front or hind leg shortly before food (the unconditioned stimulus, or UCS) was placed before the dog. After a number of CS–UCS pairings, the tactile stimulus alone elicited the salivary response.*

to the UCR in every respect. In Pavlov's experiments, for example, the touch to the leg usually did not make the dogs salivate quite as much as the meat did.

Acquisition, Extinction, and Spontaneous Recovery

During the acquisition, or learning, phase of classical conditioning, each **learning trial,** or pairing of the CS with the UCS, strengthens the connection between the CS and the CR. The time interval between the occurrence of the CS and that of the UCS makes a difference; typically, the strongest and fastest conditioning occurs when the CS is presented about one-half to one second before the UCS (Klein, 1987). The critical feature of the CS–UCS pairing is that the CS signals that an important event is about to occur (Rescorla, 1988).

The strength of the CS–CR bond and the speed with which it forms may vary considerably. Typically, a number of pairings are required to establish a CR; but in some cases, particularly those involving a traumatic UCS and a distinctive CS, conditioning may require only one CS–UCS pairing. Once a CR has been established, it may last for an extremely long time without the presentation of the UCS. In one

study, hospitalized Navy veterans who had seen combat in World War II showed strong physiological responses to the sound of a "call-to-battle-stations" gong, even though 15 years had passed since this stimulus was associated with danger. Hospitalized Army veterans, who had not served on ships, were much less emotionally responsive to this stimulus (Edwards, 1962).

If behaviors acquired through classical conditioning are to be responsive to changes in the environment, there must be a way of eliminating the CR when it is no longer appropriate. Fortunately, there is. If the CS is presented repeatedly in the absence of the UCS, the CS–CR bond will become weaker, and the conditioned response will eventually disappear. This process is called **extinction.** In his experiments, Pavlov found that if he kept applying the tactile stimuli without giving the dogs meat, they salivated less and less and eventually stopped salivating altogether. Occasional re-pairings of the CS and the UCS are required to maintain a classically conditioned response.

Even when a CR has been extinguished, however, it may suddenly reappear (usually in weakened form) if the CS is presented after a period of time. This phenomenon is called **spontaneous recovery.** Such a response will extinguish again very rapidly in the absence of the UCS (see Figure 9.3).

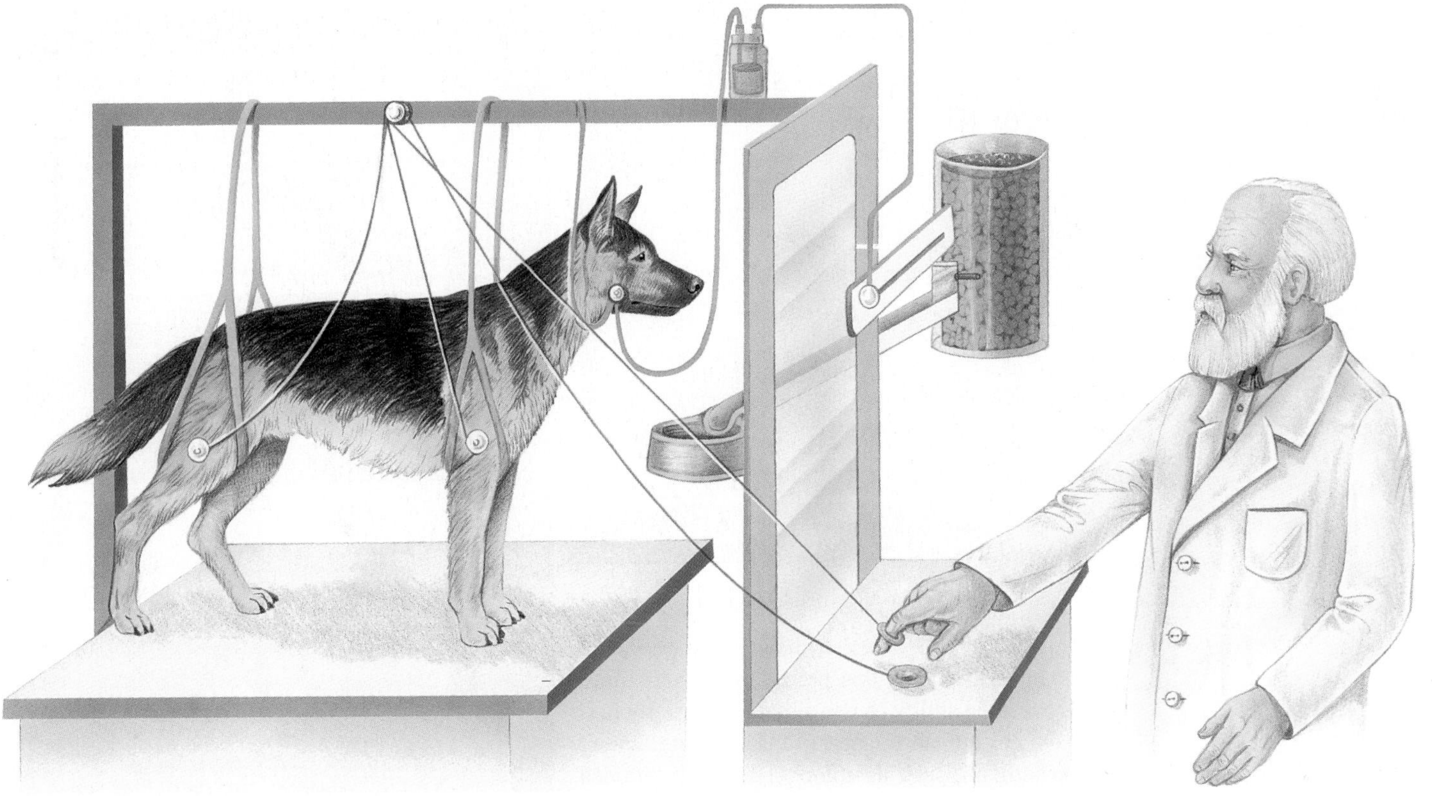

(b)

Generalization and Discrimination

Once conditioning has occurred, the subject may respond not only to the CS but also to stimuli that are similar to it. The more similar a stimulus is to the original CS, the more likely the subject is to respond with the CR. For example, the emotional responses of the Navy veterans could probably have been evoked by sounds similar to the battle-stations gong. Learning theorists refer to this phenomenon as **stimulus generalization** (see Figure 9.4*a*). Many of our likes and dislikes of new people and situations come from generalization based on similarities to past experiences.

Discrimination is in a sense the opposite of generalization. It is the ability to detect differences among stimuli. In classical conditioning, discrimination is demonstrated when a conditioned response occurs to one stimulus but not others that differ from it. Researchers can establish discrimination during classical conditioning by presenting a series of similar stimuli

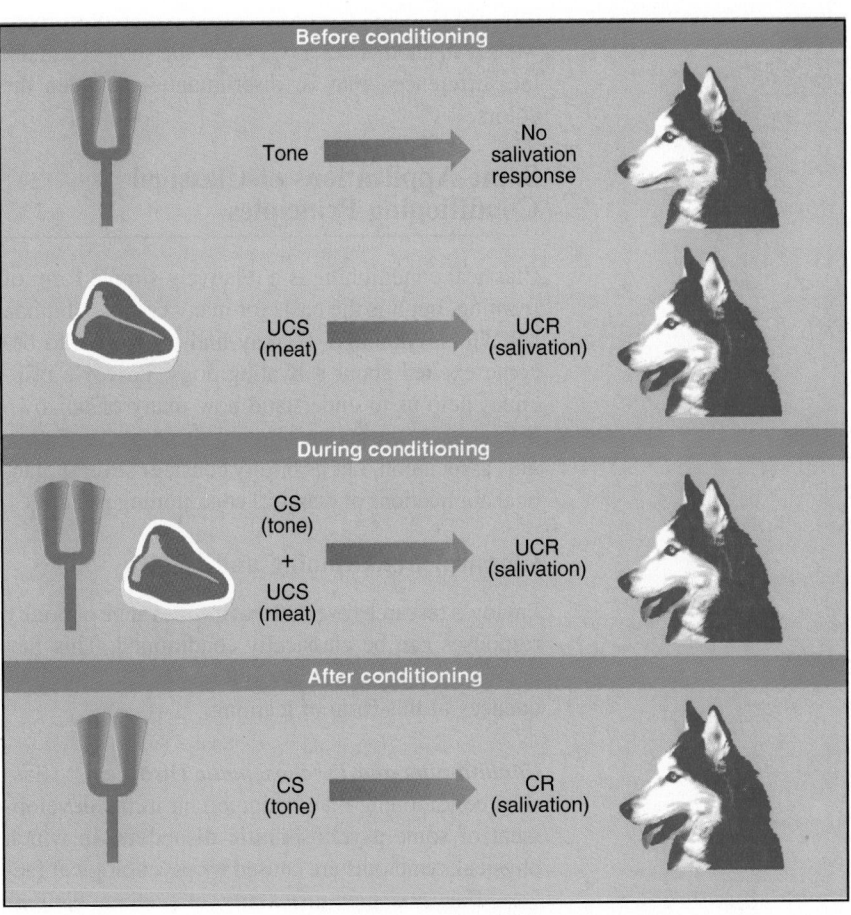

Before conditioning

Tone → No salivation response

UCS (meat) → UCR (salivation)

During conditioning

CS (tone) + UCS (meat) → UCR (salivation)

After conditioning

CS (tone) → CR (salivation)

▶ **Figure 9.2** *In classical conditioning, after a stimulus such as a tone (conditioned stimulus) is associated with the meat (unconditioned stimulus) on a number of occasions, the tone becomes capable of eliciting the salivation response (conditioned response).*

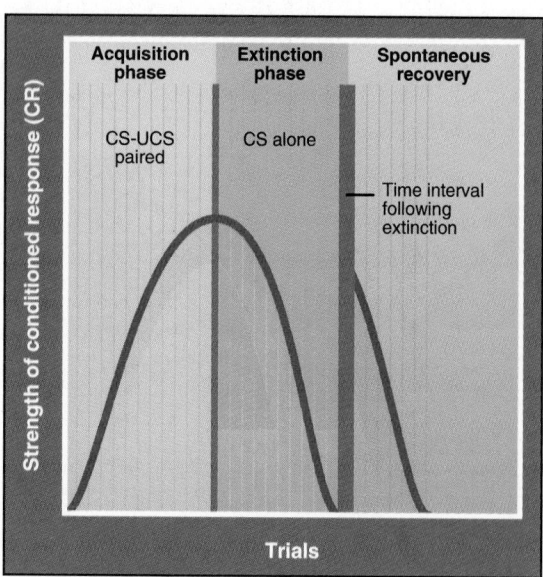

Figure 9.3 *Acquisition, extinction, and spontaneous recovery of a classically conditioned response. The strength of the CR increases during the acquisition phase as the CS and the UCS are paired on each trial. During the extinction phase, only the CS is presented, and the strength of the CR decreases until it finally disappears. After a period of time following extinction, presentation of the CS elicits a weak response (spontaneous recovery), which quickly extinguishes again.*

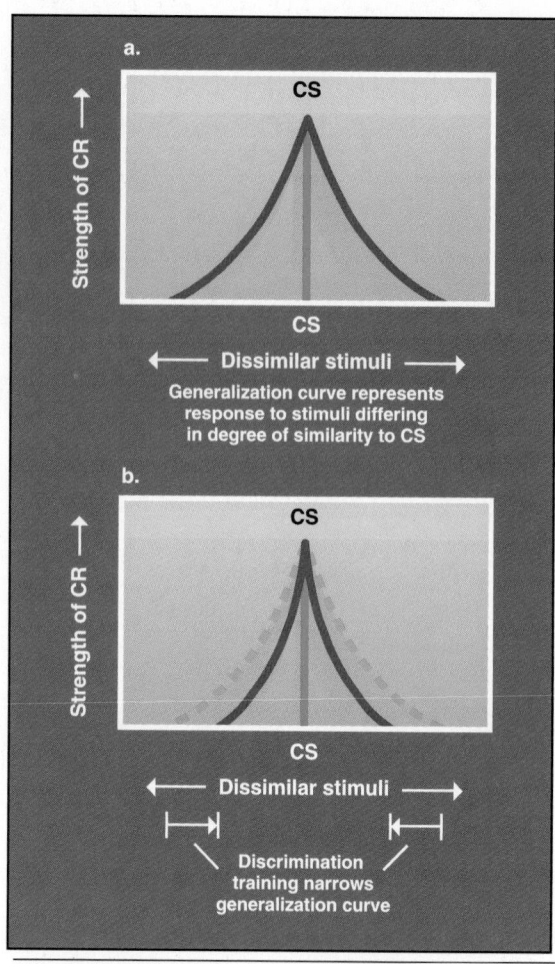

Figure 9.4 (a) *A stimulus generalization curve shows that the strongest CR is evoked by the exact stimulus that was originally paired with the UCS. Progressively weaker responses are evoked by stimuli less similar to that CS.* (b) *The generalization gradient narrows after a series of discrimination learning trials in which the original CS is paired with the UCS while the other stimuli are not paired, so that the CRs to the other stimuli begin to extinguish.*

but only pairing one of them with the UCS (see Figure 9.4b). In fact, exactly this procedure is sometimes used to test the ability of nonverbal subjects, such as animals and human infants, to discriminate among various stimuli, such as colors. The unconditioned stimulus in such studies is often a gentle puff of air directed at the eye, a stimulus that evokes an unconditioned eyeblink. If a subject responds with a conditioned eyeblink to one color and not at all or more weakly to another color, we know the subject can tell the difference—that is, discriminate—between the colors.

Some Applications of Classical Conditioning Principles

Classical conditioning is a relatively simple form of learning, but it is the basis for many complex human behaviors. Although we may find it difficult to become excited about salivating dogs, Pavlov's principles help us to understand how many of our own behaviors can be learned through this process of stimulus association. Let us briefly consider several practical applications of classical conditioning principles.

Classical Conditioning and Health

Pavlov's research revealed that a wide range of bodily responses can be classically conditioned. This fact has led psychologists to explore the health consequences of this form of learning.

Conditioning and Psychosomatic Disorders Classical conditioning may be important in the development of some **psychosomatic disorders,** in which physical symptoms are caused by psychological factors. For example, one study of asthma patients revealed that their attacks of wheezing often occurred in the presence of specific conditioned stimuli such as goldfish, the national anthem, radio speeches by influential politicians, and waterfalls. Although the original CS-UCS pairings could not always be uncovered, once the critical stimuli had been identified, the investigators were able to induce asthma attacks by presenting the critical stimuli or fascimiles of them. In many cases, the attacks generalized from living objects to inanimate ones. The researchers described one such case.

Patient L had told us that she got an asthmatic attack from looking at a goldfish. After a baseline (measure of normal respiratory function) had been obtained, a goldfish in a bowl was brought into the room. . . . Under our eyes she developed a severe asthmatic attack with loud wheezing, followed by a gradual remission after the goldfish had been taken from the room. During the next experiment the goldfish was replaced by a plastic toy fish which was easily recognized as such . . . but a fierce attack resulted (Dekker & Groen, 1956, p. 62).

In another case, a man began to have violent attacks of wheezing and difficulty in breathing while having sex with his wife in their bedroom. The removal from the room of the critical CS—a large, scowling portrait of his mother-in-law—ended the man's respiratory problems (and greatly enhanced the couple's sexual relationship).

Can the Immune System Be Trained? One of the most significant discoveries of recent years is that the immune system can also learn through classical conditioning. We now know that the immune system, far from being an automatic system, can learn and, indeed, can be trained.

The discovery, like many other important discoveries in science, was a fortuitous one. At the University of Rochester, a psychologist, Robert Ader, was studying the classical conditioning of food aversions in rats. If you've ever became sick to your stomach after eating a certain food and found later that you had developed an aversion to that food, you've had first-hand experience with the subject of Ader's research. Ader's procedure was to pair saccharin-flavored water (the CS) with the injection of a drug that made the animals violently ill (the UCS). It usually took no more than one pairing to produce a conditioned aversion to the saccharin flavor. The experiments were going well except for one complication: Many of the rats were getting sick and dying long after the drug was out of their systems. Mystified by these unexpected illnesses, Ader analyzed every facet of his procedure. When he examined the nausea-producing drug he was using as a UCS, he found that it had an important side effect: It also suppressed the immune system. This was the breakthrough discovery. Ader concluded that he had conditioned not only an aversion to the flavored water but also a suppression of the immune system that made the animals more susceptible to disease and death.

Ader repeated the experiment many times with similar results, and so did other experimenters (Ader & Cohen, 1990). Figure 9.5 shows data from one such study (McCoy & others, 1986). As in Ader's studies, saccharine-flavored water served as the CS. Rats assigned to the conditioning group received an injection of an immune-suppressant drug 30 minutes after drinking the water, while those in the placebo control group got an injection of saline instead. Three days later, the animals were injected with an antigen, and then the thirsty animals were allowed to drink saccharine-flavored water again. The researchers then measured the number of antibodies produced by the

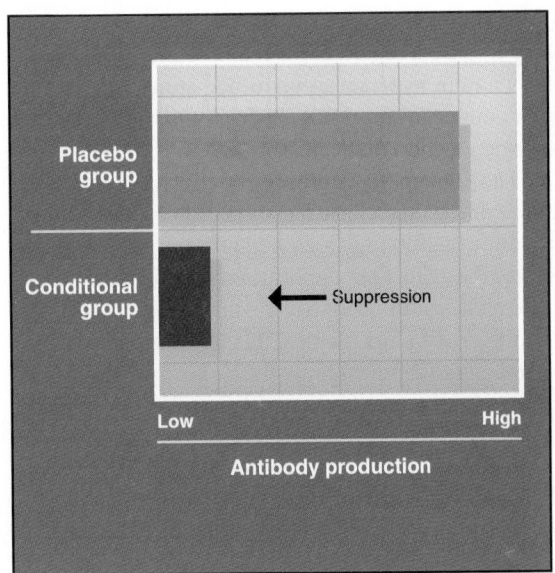

Figure 9.5 *Classically conditioned suppression of the immune system. Rats in the conditioned group received a saccharine solution to drink and then were injected with a drug that suppresses the immune system. The animals in the control group received a placebo injection that does not affect the immune system. Seven days later, the rats were injected with an allergen that ordinarily triggers a strong immune-system response. The thirsty rats were given saccharine water to drink (the CS) and then antibody production was measured. The conditioned animals showed far less antibody production. (Data from McCoy & others, 1986).*

animals during the next 6 days. As Figure 9.5 shows, the conditioned animals produced fewer antibodies than those who had received the placebo injection.

If classical conditioning can cause suppression of immune functioning, can it also be used to increase immunity? Recent evidence indicates that the answer is yes (Ader & Cohen, 1990). Reginald Gorczynski and his colleagues at the University of Toronto (1982, 1987) used skin grafts from unrelated mice to produce an immune response (the so-called rejection response sometimes exhibited after organ transplants). To achieve classical conditioning, they paired the skin grafts from the unrelated animals (the UCS) with another set of skin grafts, these from the animals' own tissue (which would not produce a rejection response). Later, however, when the researchers again grafted the animals' own skin onto them, the animals mounted an enhanced immune response. They had developed a conditioned immune response to their own tissue.

Classical conditioning of the immune system was a landmark discovery because it demonstrated that the supposedly independent and isolated immune system could be influenced by life experiences in a manner that indicated communication between this system and the brain, where experiences are stored. Conditioning of immune system functioning could have significant health implications if—and this is a big *if* at this point—the conditioning effects are strong enough and controllable enough to be clinically meaningful. For example, it might be possible to condition certain cues to increase immune system functioning in people who have been exposed to an antigen, who are fighting a cancerous tumor, or whose immune system has been disabled by AIDS. On the other hand, it might be possible to decrease immune functioning in other people, such as those who suffer from severe allergic reactions. We presently do this with drugs; epinephrine, for example, is given to people who are hypersensitive to bee stings to prevent their going into *anaphylactic shock,* an overwhelming allergic reaction that can be fatal.

The coming years promise to give us answers to important health-related questions related to immune-system conditioning and perhaps to provide psychologists with new opportunities to respond to an important health need. Meanwhile, research is continuing on the physiological mechanisms involved in such conditioning and how these mechanisms might be exploited to increase conditioning effects to clinically significant levels (Ader & Cohen, 1990).

Classical Conditioning, Tolerance, and Drug Overdoses

Chapter 8 discussed the fact that repeated use of a drug creates tolerance (the need for increasingly larger doses of the drug to achieve the initial effects) because the body begins to counter the drug's effects in an attempt to restore homeostasis. The bodily responses that counteract the drug's effects are called **compensatory responses.** For example, if amphetamines increase blood pressure, the compensatory response is a lowering of blood pressure.

Recent findings indicate that classical conditioning is partly responsible for this process. With repeated use of a drug, environmental stimuli associated with drug use, such as the sight of the drug, the needle, the presence of others with whom one customarily uses drugs, and the physical setting, may all become conditioned stimuli that begin to elicit the compensatory responses. As the conditioned compensatory responses become stronger, more and more of the drug is needed to counter them, and tolerance occurs (Poulos & Cappell, 1991). The compensatory responses also contribute to the strong, unpleasant craving that addicts experience when they are exposed to an environment in which they have frequently taken drugs.

There is a hidden and possibly fatal danger in this process, particularly for experienced drug users. The compensatory responses serve a protective function by countering part of the drug's effects in an attempt to restore homeostasis (Poulos & Cappell, 1991). However, if a user takes his or her usual high dose in an unfamiliar environment that lacks the CSs that ordinarily evoke the compensatory responses, the result may well be an overdose. Shepard Siegel, who introduced the theory of conditioned compensatory responses, interviewed heroin addicts who had experienced near-fatal overdoses. He found that in most cases, they had not taken a dose larger than their customary one. However, in more than 70 percent of the cases, they had injected themselves in unfamiliar

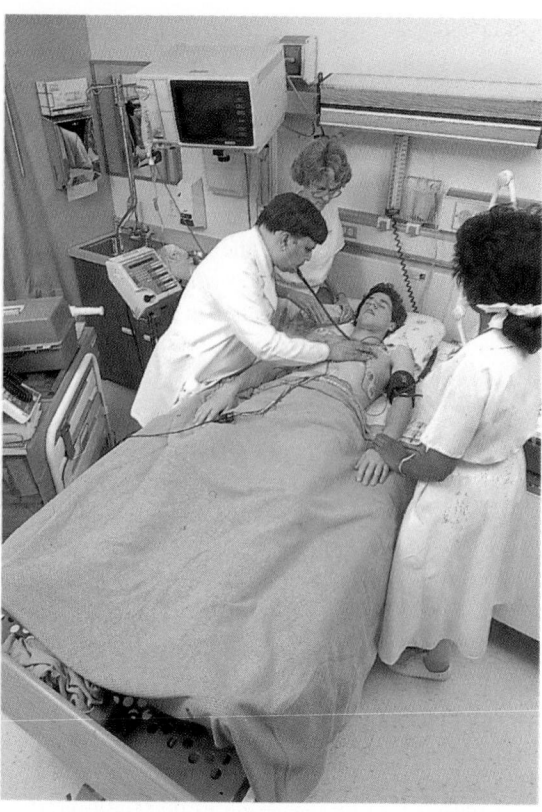

Figure 9.6 *Many people die each year from drug-overdose reactions. Recent evidence suggests that some of these reactions occur in unfamiliar environments, which fail to elicit the conditioned compensatory responses that underlie tolerance. As a result, the body is not "ready" for the user's typical dose level.*

environments (Siegel, 1984). As a result, Siegel concluded, they were not protected by the usual compensatory responses, and the drug had a much stronger physiological effect than usual, resulting in an overdose reaction (see Figure 9.6). Thus, it appears that classical conditioning processes pose yet another danger to the many already faced by drug users and that such processes may well contribute to drug-related fatalities.

Classical Conditioning of Attitudes

Emotional reactions are an important component of attitudes. When we say we have a positive or a negative attitude toward a person or situation, we are referring in part to the way the person or situation makes us feel. Some theorists believe that classical conditioning is critically important in establishing attitudes (Olson & Zanna, 1991; Staats, 1975). In classical conditioning terms, the attitude object or situation is the CS. If this CS is associated with another stimulus (the UCS) that already elicits a positive or negative emotional response (the UCR), we may develop a conditioned emotional response toward the CS without being fully aware of the process (van den

Hout & Merckelbach, 1991). For example, a song may have become a favorite because it was paired with a pleasurable situation or event, or it may arouse negative feelings because it was associated with a negative event.

But how can attitudes be classically conditioned to people or objects we've had no personal contact with? The concept of **higher order conditioning** provides a possible answer. Once a response has been conditioned to a CS, that CS can be used like a UCS to establish another CS. For example, the word *bad* has no meaning when it is presented initially to an infant; it is a neutral stimulus. But after *bad* has been paired with slaps or a spanking (pretty potent UCSs), the word alone becomes capable of triggering a variety of emotional responses. *Bad* has become a CS. If we now pair *bad* with the name of a person or group of people with whom the child has had no contact, it is possible that the child's negative emotional reactions to the word could be transferred to the new stimulus. The result: instant dislike. This process can occur with words that have either positive or negative learned connotations (Kuykendall & Keating, 1990).

Advertisers seem to have a great deal of faith in higher order conditioning (Allen & Janiszewski, 1989). They carefully link their products to attractive people and settings, to personal wealth, and most of all, to pleasurable interactions with the opposite sex (see Figure 9.7). When was the last time you saw an advertisement showing an unattractive, dirty person contentedly puffing on a cigarette in a cancer ward? ▼

Figure 9.7 *Attempts to classically condition favorable attitudes to products by associating them with other positive stimuli are readily apparent in many advertisements.*

Classical Conditioning, Psychodynamics, and Fear

Having discussed some of the basics of classical conditioning, let us return to one of the cases at the beginning of this chapter—the young woman with the snow phobia. Suppose that you were her therapist. Do you think that classical conditioning could help you explain any part of her problem?

One difficulty in fitting this case into a classical conditioning framework is the sudden appearance of the phobia in the absence of any clear conditioning event. However, in the course of psychodynamic treatment of Hilda, the traumatic event finally emerged.

> In this instance, we were most fortunate eventually to uncover what proved to have been the major precipitating event in the onset of the phobia. This was a traumatic experience dating from when the patient was eleven years old. This experience had lain completely out of sight, hidden in her unconscious, for twenty-one years—repressed but hardly dormant.
>
> In the winter of her eleventh year, she had accompanied an aunt and uncle to a ski lodge in Vermont.

One afternoon, she wandered off by herself, into a small ravine. . . . Suddenly she found herself in the path of a miniature avalanche. She was helpless to move out of the way in time and was engulfed. She was literally buried alive and unable to move or to extricate herself. Somehow, however, she [had] a channel so she could continue breathing. . . . The little girl remained there, absolutely petrified with fear, for an indeterminate period of time, until discovered through most fortuitous circumstances, by her worried uncle. It had seemed an eternity.

Her complete repression of this episode was believed to be caused by its unbearable horror, plus her certainty of death (Adapted from Laughlin, 1967).

It seems clear from this description that classical conditioning played a role in establishing Hilda's fear of snow. During her accident, conditioned stimuli relating to snow were associated with unconditioned stimuli that evoked the unconditioned responses of pain and terror. Hilda was left with a strong conditioned fear response. It is also clear that considerable stimulus generalization had occurred, so that stimuli such as weather reports and even thoughts about snow could evoke strong fear responses. These stimuli produced less anxiety than a walk through deep snow, however, as would be predicted on the basis of stimulus generalization.

As far removed as Pavlov's laboratory may seem from Freud's couch, Hilda's case illustrates the potential value of applying behavioral concepts to an understanding of psychodynamic phenomena. We see in this instance not only the classical conditioning of

▼
Thinking Critically About Classical Conditioning, Advertising, and Sexual Stereotypes

Consider the advertisement in Figure 9.7. Based on principles of higher order classical conditioning, analyze the ad, identifying the UCS, the CS, the UCR, and the CR. Then identify what value statements are implicit in the choice of stimuli. Do these values, reinforced through repeated classical conditioning experiences, help shape and support the sexual attitudes and stereotypes that are so prevalent in our culture, or do they merely reflect what's already there? How could such conditioning account for changes in values over time, and who should have the power to dictate what those changes might be?

a strong fear response but also an example of how psychodynamic factors might influence the products of learning. Hilda's "repression" of the original traumatic event (which could be viewed as a learned response of "not thinking") protected her from the conditioned fear response for many years. It is quite possible that personality dynamics can increase a person's susceptibility to certain learning experiences, thereby creating a psychological readiness to acquire certain conditioned responses (Erdelyi, 1985, 1988). For example, a person with a history of early parental rejection might find it very easy to learn to fear interpersonal closeness in later relationships. Memory for the aversive conditioning experiences may also be affected, as in Hilda's case (Riccio & Spear, 1991).

Although classical conditioning principles explain how Hilda's snow phobia was established, a number of important questions remain: Why doesn't the fear decrease? After all, the stimuli that relate to the snow are no longer being associated with the terror of being buried alive. Shouldn't the fear responses simply extinguish? Most puzzling of all, why does the client seem to be getting worse? She clearly realizes that her fear is irrational and seems highly motivated to get rid of it. In order to answer these questions, we must consider a second major type of learning: operant conditioning.

Operant Conditioning: Learning Through Consequences

At about the same time Pavlov was making his landmark discoveries of classical conditioning in Russia, an American psychologist, Edward L. Thorndike, was studying a somewhat different kind of learning. While Pavlov was exploring relations between involuntary responses and the stimuli that precede them, Thorndike was studying the trial-and-error learning that animals use to solve problems. The behaviors that Thorndike was studying were not involuntary reflexive responses to particular stimuli, as were Pavlov's conditioned responses. Instead, they were voluntary behaviors that were instrumental in helping the organism attain some goal, such as operating a latch to get out of a box and get food.

The terms **operant** and *instrumental,* which are often used interchangeably, refer to the fact that the behaviors in question produce some kind of an effect for the organism. The organism *operates* on its environment in some way; the behaviors in which it engages are *instrumental* to achieving some outcome (Houston, 1992).

Thorndike developed an elaborate theory of behavior. Its cornerstone was his **law of effect,** which can be summarized as follows: If a response is followed by a pleasant or "satisfying" consequence, that response will be strengthened. If a response is followed by an unpleasant or negative state of affairs, it will be weakened. This law of effect is the foundation of operant conditioning.

The Study of Operant Conditioning

Much of our current knowledge about operant conditioning stems from the research of Thorndike, B. F. Skinner, and other behaviorists who performed many laboratory studies with animals. A typical laboratory demonstration of operant conditioning might proceed as follows.

A rat that has been deprived of food for a number of hours is placed in an experimental chamber called a **Skinner box** (named for its inventor over his objections). There is a lever on one wall of the chamber. Beneath the lever is a small cup into which a pellet of food is dropped by an automatic dispenser whenever the rat presses the lever (see Figure 9.8). When put into the chamber, the rat first explores its surroundings. In the course of its explorations, it happens to press the lever. A pellet of food clinks into the cup, and the surprised rat eats it quickly. Sometime later, the rat again randomly presses the bar and receives another pellet. If we record the rat's behavior on a **cumulative recorder** (see Figure 9.9), we will find that the animal soon begins to press the bar more and more frequently. In the language of the learning psychologist, we would say that an operant bar-press response has now been established. Receiving the food pellet is a *reinforcement*—an outcome that increases the likelihood that the rat will press the bar again.

Suppose we now place a light on the panel above the bar. When the light is on, pressing the bar dispenses food, but when the light is off, no food is dispensed. The rat will soon learn to press the bar only when the light is on. That is, it will respond to the *discriminative stimulus* that signals the availability of reinforcement.

This general procedure has been used to study operant conditioning in many different species, including human beings. One need only modify the response to be made (for example, pigeons peck a disc instead of pressing a bar) and the type of reinforcer employed (children respond more enthusiastically to candy than to rat pellets).

We now consider the major principles of operant conditioning in greater detail and indicate ways in which these principles have enabled psychologists to understand and sometimes change behavior.

Antecedents, Consequences, and Behavior

The operant analysis of behavior involves the study of relations between three kinds of events: **antecedents** (A), or environmental stimuli; **behaviors** (B) in which the organism engages; and **consequences** (C) that follow the behaviors and either strengthen or weaken them. The relations that exist among these "if, then" elements are called **contingencies.** The ABCs of contingencies can be expressed in the following way:

IF antecedent stimuli (A) are present
AND behavior (B) is emitted,
THEN consequence (C) will occur.

Two aspects of these relations are of interest. The first is the relation between antecedents and behaviors (A and B); the second is the contingency between behavior and its consequences (B and C).

Antecedents: Stimulus Control of Behavior

Through experience, we learn which behaviors have which consequences under which conditions. Antecedents that signal the likely consequences of particular behaviors in given situations are known as **discriminative stimuli.** As we have seen, in the Skinner box, the light that signals the availability of food if the bar is pressed serves as a discriminative stimulus. Such signals help to guide behavior so that it is "appropriate" and most likely to lead to positive consequences. When antecedents are influential in governing a behavior (not in the reflex-like classical conditioning sense but rather in signaling the behavior's likely consequences), that behavior is said to be under **stimulus control** (Rilling, 1992). For example, the sight of a squad car occupied by a police officer

Figure 9.8 *A rat explores an operant experimental chamber (Skinner box). The animal has just pressed the bar, and a food reinforcer is being automatically delivered by the apparatus to the left of the box. The light above the bar can be used as a discriminative stimulus signaling the availability of the reinforcer.*

can exert powerful stimulus control over most people's driving behavior. Because we constantly respond to stimuli in our environment, many of our behaviors eventually come under stimulus control. As you will see later in the Enhancing Human Performance feature, we can use this principle to gain increased control over our own behavior.

Differences between Operant and Classical Conditioning

There are two main differences between classical and operant conditioning:

1. In classical conditioning, the conditioned behavior (CR) is triggered by a particular stimulus (CS)

Figure 9.9 *A cumulative recorder. The paper moves at a constant speed in the direction indicated. Each bar press operates an electromagnet that moves the pen one step upward. When the pen reaches the top of the paper, it activates a switch, which causes the pen to move back down to the bottom of the paper. In this way, the animal "draws" its own performance curve. Responses are also counted by an electric counter.*

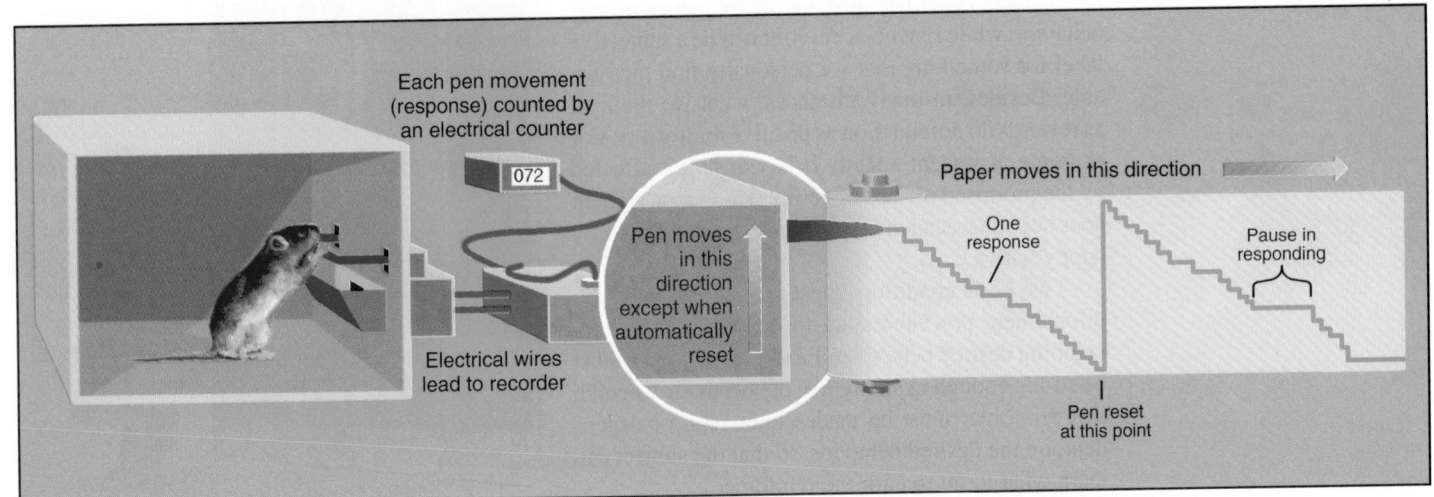

Each pen movement (response) counted by an electrical counter

072

Pen moves in this direction except when automatically reset

Electrical wires lead to recorder

Paper moves in this direction

One response

Pause in responding

Pen reset at this point

and is therefore called an **elicited behavior**. Operant behavior is **emitted behavior** in the sense that it occurs in a situation containing many stimuli and seems to be initiated by the organism. In a sense, the subject "chooses" when and how to respond.

2. In both classical and operant conditioning, a behavior is strengthened. The difference is that the classically conditioned behavior (CR) is affected by something that occurs *before* the behavior (the CS–UCS pairing). In contrast, the operant response is affected by what happens *after* the behavior—that is, by its consequences.

Although the procedures for classical and operant conditioning are quite different, many learning situations involve both processes. For example, if a young child is bitten by a large dog she has tried to pet, the bite is a punishing response consequence, so the child becomes operantly conditioned to avoid petting that dog again. In addition, the pain from the bite is paired with the stimuli coming from the dog, so the child may also develop a classically conditioned fear of the dog, which may generalize to other large dogs. However, discrimination is indicated if the child does not fear small dogs.

Positive Reinforcement and Extinction

We have emphasized that the key feature in operant conditioning is what happens after a response is made. Psychologists have done a great deal of research on how different types of consequences affect behavior.

Positive Reinforcement

A **positive reinforcer** is any stimulus or event that increases the likelihood of occurrence of a behavior that it follows. The term *reward* is often used as if it were synonymous with positive reinforcement. However, psychologists prefer the latter term, because *reinforcement* describes how the consequence affects behavior, while *reward* seems often to be a subjective label for something that we personally find pleasurable. Besides, in many instances, what we think of as rewards do not function as positive reinforcers. For example, a student's study behavior is not affected by the promised reward of getting an A if the student does not value academic achievement and is perfectly happy with a C.

Two basic conditions must be met if positive reinforcement procedures are to be successful in developing desired behaviors: First, the reinforcer must be strong enough to strengthen the behavior. Second, that reinforcer must be made contingent, or dependent, on the desired behavior, so that the subject can learn what to do to earn the reinforcer.

Primary and Secondary Reinforcers. Learning psychologists distinguish between **primary reinforcers** and **secondary, or conditioned, reinforcers.** Primary reinforcers satisfy biological needs. Food and water are examples. Because these reinforcers relate to innate physiological needs, they are unlearned reinforcers. However, we can also learn to want reinforcers that are not directly related to satisfaction of biological needs through a process of conditioning—hence the term *conditioned reinforcer.* Theoretically, any stimulus associated with the attainment of a primary reinforcer can become a conditioned reinforcer. Attention, verbal praise, trading stamps, and money are examples of secondary reinforcers. In an animal version of the secondary reinforcement properties of money, a chimpanzee will learn to value and work for (and even hoard) tokens it can place into a vending machine to obtain raisins (see Figure 9.10).

Shaping

Stiff trade winds buffeted the coconut palms and tropical plants at Sea Life Park in Hawaii. The blue-green

◀ **Figure 9.10** *A chimpanzee drops a token into the Chimp-O-Mat vending machine to obtain raisins. Through their association with a primary reinforcer (food), the tokens become valued secondary reinforcers for the animals, much as money acquires value for humans.*

waters of the Pacific shimmered in the distance beneath the warm afternoon sun. A sizable crowd had gathered in the stands around Whaler's Cove to watch the trained dolphins and killer whales. "Oohs" and "ahs" greeted the complex acrobatic tricks that the animals performed with great precision. As the buzzing crowd left the show, a young woman trainer in colorful Hawaiian garb was explaining to a group of interested spectators how the animals are trained to perform their remarkable feats (see Figure 9.11).

"The animals you're seeing are not geniuses, although they may look like it at times. Actually, what you're seeing is the end product of very systematic training. We use a method known as **shaping,** or the **method of successive approximations,** to gradually build the complex behaviors you see. This means that we reinforce, with a fish, behaviors that get closer and closer to the desired trick. For example, no dolphin or killer whale, regardless of how brilliant, is going to jump spontaneously through a hoop 10 feet above the water. We have to gradually shape her, first by immediately and consistently rewarding her when she swims into the area near the hoop, then when she breaks water, and so on. In other words, in order to

get her fish, she has to come closer and closer to what we want her to do eventually. This is basically how all animal acts are developed, whether here at Sea Life Park or in a circus. We can eventually put together long **behavior chains** in which a number of responses are run off in sequence, with reinforcement at the end of the chain."

The products of operant conditioning go far beyond rats pressing bars and pigeons pecking discs in Skinner boxes, and even beyond the feats performed by trained animals. Humans also learn many complex behaviors through shaping. Shaping is involved in learning a language and in developing educational skills. If we want to train children to be mathematicians, we do not expect them to solve complex calculus problems spontaneously. We start by teaching them basic arithmetic operations, and we successively build on what they have already learned. On a broader level, our acquisition of the behaviors, values, and attitudes of our society involves a great deal of shaping on the part of parents, teachers, and peers. ▼

◆ **Figure 9.11** *Shaping procedures have been used to train this dolphin at Sea Life Park in Hawaii. Trainers build up progressively more complex behaviors using fish as positive reinforcers.*

Operant Extinction

In operant conditioning, as in classical conditioning, **extinction** refers to the gradual disappearance of a learned response. Extinction of operant behaviors occurs when reinforcement stops. When previously reinforced behaviors no longer "pay off," we are likely to abandon them and replace them with more successful ones. It follows, therefore, that an effective way to change someone's negative behaviors is to make sure that he or she gets no reinforcement for the undesirable behaviors while at the same time reinforcing alternative behaviors that are more desirable. This principle has been employed to help many parents change the behavior of disruptive children (O'Leary & Wilson, 1987; Schroeder & Gordon, 1991). We might title the following case: "The Taming of Pascal the Rascal."

Mrs. Adams sought help at a child guidance clinic because of severe problems with her 4-year-old son Pascal. Pascal seemed to delight in misbehaving. "He'll go to any lengths just to make my life miserable," she complained. His behavior was especially disruptive, she added, when she was concentrating on her housework. Under the circumstances she found Pascal very difficult to love and felt guilty about her hostile feelings toward him.

Mrs. Adams was at her wit's end because nothing seemed to work. First she had tried to reason with him. Then she had resorted to yelling and screaming at him when he misbehaved. When that produced no effect, Mrs. Adams began using physical punishment. Even that did not work. "In fact," she reported, "he got worse."

Thinking Critically About Cultural Conditioning of Individualism and Collectivism

Chapter 1 pointed out that the United States and Canada have individualist cultures (focusing on individual achievement and rights), whereas cultures like Japan's exhibit collectivism (emphasizing the achievement and well-being of the larger group). Behaviorists would look for the roots of this cultural difference in social learning experiences. They might view social institutions as analogous to Skinner boxes in which behaviors are conditioned. What, for example, might teachers in the two cultures do to shape individualism and collectivism? To find out, researchers carried out detailed behavioral observations in 5th-grade classrooms in the United States and Japan (Hamilton & others, 1991). They found that Japanese teachers used many more group activities than U.S. teachers did. Teacher communications also differed markedly: U.S. teachers directed 72 percent of their comments to individual students, whereas the majority of the Japanese teachers' comments were directed to the group as a whole, often focusing on group solutions to problems.

How could we translate such findings into operant conditioning terms to understand the nature of the environment and the behaviors that are being conditioned? Would you agree with the "cultural Skinner box" analogy?

Like many parents, Mrs. Adams could not understand why measures like scolding and spanking not only failed to reduce her son's negative behaviors but even seemed to increase them. She did not realize that any sort of attention is such a powerful positive reinforcer for many children that it can overshadow the effects of the punishment it accompanies. Behavior patterns like Pascal's usually develop when parents do not reinforce desirable behaviors with attention; then the only way for a child to get their attention is to misbehave. This again illustrates the difference between reward and reinforcement. Parents are not likely to view punishment as a reward for negative behavior, but it certainly can function as a reinforcer by increasing the behavior.

Mrs. Adams was instructed to ignore Pascal's obnoxious behaviors whenever possible. She was warned that Pascal was likely to increase his negative behaviors for a period of time. When a reinforcer is removed, most people (as well as animals) try harder for awhile before they begin to decrease the behavior. This is the main reason why many people stop extinction procedures before they have a chance to work. They are afraid they are making matters even worse.

Because Pascal's behavior was so disruptive, it could not simply be ignored. The psychologist suggested a procedure called **time out**, which is short for ''time out from positive reinforcement'' and involves removing the child from the situation in which he can receive reinforcement. When Pascal's behavior was too disruptive to be ignored, Mrs. Adams was instructed to lock him in another room for a specified period of time. If Pascal threw a tantrum, as he did on the first two occasions, she told him that the time-out interval would begin when the tantrum ended. Because it was impossible for Pascal to receive attention during these periods, he soon began to reduce the behaviors that resulted in time out.

Mrs. Adams was also instructed to reinforce Pascal for desirable behaviors by paying attention to him. Because Pascal had strong needs for attention, simply extinguishing his negative behavior without establishing a way to reinforce him for positive behavior would not have been very effective. Use of the combination of extinction of misbehaviors and reinforcement of desired behaviors resulted in a radical positive change in Pascal's behavior. The family atmosphere at the Adams house improved immensely, and Mrs. Adams began to enjoy once again her relationship with Pascal, the ex-Rascal.

Schedules of Reinforcement

The environment that responds to behavior can be varied and unpredictable, and reinforcers can occur in different patterns and frequencies. Sometimes we receive reinforcement after every response of a given type, but more typically only a proportion of our responses are reinforced. These patterns, or **schedules of reinforcement,** have strong and predictable effects on learning, extinction, and performance. The discovery of their effects on behavior is one of the most important contributions made by Skinner and his coworkers (Ferster & Skinner, 1957).

The first important distinction is between continuous and partial reinforcement. On a **continuous reinforcement schedule,** every response of a particular type is reinforced. In contrast, on a **partial,** or **intermittent, reinforcement schedule,** only some of the responses are reinforced.

Partial reinforcement schedules can be categorized as ratio schedules or interval schedules. On **ratio schedules,** a certain percentage of the subject's responses are reinforced. On **interval schedules,** a certain amount of time must elapse between reinforcements, regardless of how many responses might occur during that interval.

Both types of partial schedules can be further subdivided into fixed and variable schedules. On **fixed schedules,** the reinforcement always occurs after a fixed number of responses or after a fixed time interval; on a **variable schedule,** the required number of responses or the time interval varies at random around an average. Figure 9.12 shows how all these partial reinforcement categories can be combined to produce four different reinforcement schedules: fixed-ratio (FR), variable-ratio (VR), fixed-interval (FI), and variable-interval (VI). As you can see by looking at the cumulative response curves, the different schedules have quite different effects on behavior. Let us see why.

Fixed-Ratio Schedule

On a **fixed-ratio (FR) schedule,** reinforcement is given after a fixed number of responses. For example, FR 10 means that reinforcement occurs after every 10th response, regardless of how long it takes for the subject to respond 10 times.

An FR schedule produces a high rate of responding with little hesitation between responses. That's one reason why some businesses prefer to pay piece-work wages based on a set number of items produced (Aamodt, 1991). For example, garment workers are often paid for every 5–10 pieces of clothing they sew.

It is possible to achieve a very high response rate by gradually increasing the ratio over time. Pigeons in a Skinner box have been known to literally wear down their beaks pecking a disc on an FR 20,000 schedule, for example. But if the ratio is increased too rapidly, the response may extinguish between reinforcements.

FR schedules have another characteristic effect. As shown in Figure 9.12, the subject pauses for awhile after each reinforcement, perhaps because the responses that immediately follow are never reinforced. The larger the number of subsequent responses needed to earn reinforcement, the longer the pause before the animal resumes responding.

Variable-Ratio Schedule

On a **variable-ratio (VR) schedule,** reinforcement varies around an average number of responses. A VR 10 schedule means that, *on average,* 10 responses are required for reinforcement. Because the schedule is variable, however, reinforcement can occur when fewer or more than 10 responses have been made.

A VR schedule, like an FR schedule, produces a high rate of responding. But because the occurrence of reinforcement is variable and unpredictable, there is no pause after reinforcement. Instead, there is a relatively steady rate of responding, as shown in Figure 9.12. Because each response is equally likely to result in reinforcement, the VR schedule can be physically taxing. Both animals and human beings may continue to respond to the point of exhaustion.

Let us return to the gambler described at the beginning of the chapter. As the casino guard remarked, the gambler has been responding without reinforcement for a long time. Is he indeed ''sick,'' as the guard suggests, or can we now understand his behavior in terms of the reinforcement conditions in that situation?

Gambling is a good example of behavior that is maintained on a variable-ratio schedule (see Figure 9.13). Because any spin of the roulette wheel or any pull of the lever on a slot machine is as likely as any other to be reinforced with a jackpot, it is easy to establish a high rate of responding that is very resistant to extinction. This is especially true when a person wins a jackpot early on.

Suppose, for example, that a slot machine is programmed on a VR 20 schedule. You drop a coin in, pull the lever, and receive a 10-coin jackpot. After two more attempts, you hit a 15-coin jackpot. But then, after 67 consecutive, unsuccessful attempts—nothing. You walk away muttering angrily about your lot in life, probably unaware that you've been ''hooked'' by the VR schedule. If you were to stay and play the machine indefinitely, you would receive a payoff for every 20 attempts, *on the average.* These ''one-armed bandits'' make a handsome profit for the casino because the average number of coins in a jackpot is smaller (perhaps 10 to 15 coins) than the average of 20 needed to trigger the jackpot.

Our gambler, then, may be seen as the unhappy victim of a difficult and compelling reinforcement

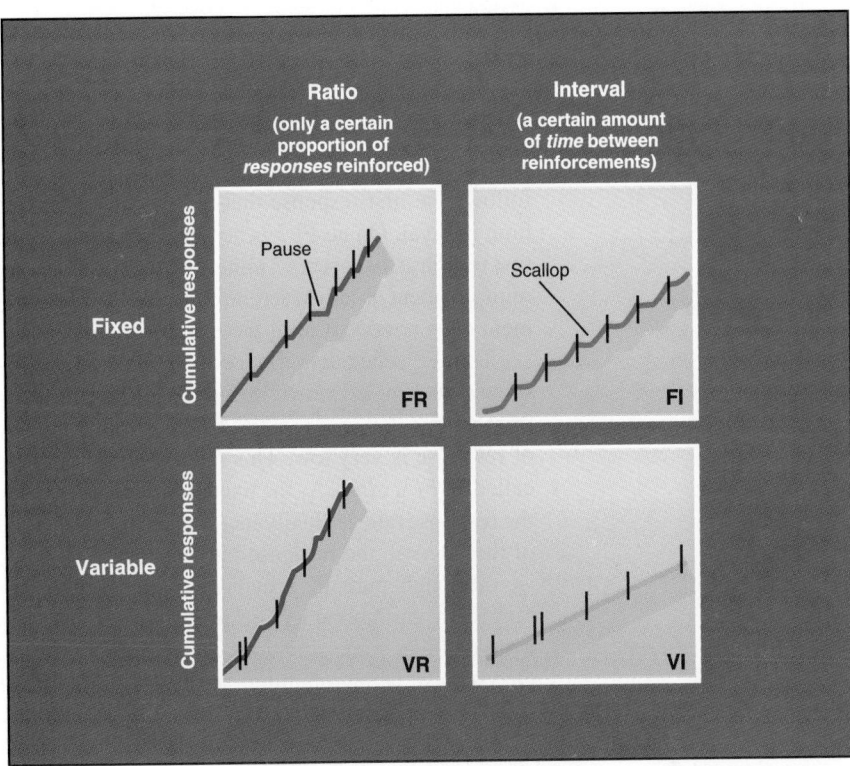

Figure 9.12 *Each type of positive reinforcement schedule produces a typical cumulative response curve. Ratio schedules produce a high rate of responding, as shown in the steep slopes of the curves. The variable-interval schedule produces a steady rate of responding. The fixed-interval schedule produces a scalloped curve because the subject learns to stop responding until the time for the next reinforcement approaches.*

Figure 9.13 *Slot machines, which operate on variable-ratio schedules, can elicit a high rate of response. The behavior is highly resistant to extinction because of the unpredictable schedule of jackpots.*

schedule rather than the victim of some mysterious sickness.

Fixed-Interval Schedule

On a **fixed-interval (FI) schedule,** reinforcement follows the first response that occurs after a certain time interval. On an FI 3 schedule, for example, the first response that occurs 3 minutes after the preceding reinforcement is always reinforced. The reinforcement does not occur until there is a response.

The FI schedule produces a characteristic response pattern, as shown in Figure 9.12. After each reinforcement, there is a period during which the rate of response is very low. This feature of the curve is called an *FI scallop.* As the fixed time interval passes, the response rate gradually increases until, by the end of the interval, the response rate is very rapid.

Although pure FI schedules such as those arranged in the laboratory are probably quite rare in everyday life, some situations do approximate them. One such situation—familiar, unfortunately, to all of us—is the schedule of tests in most college courses. Many instructors give three exams, one every 4 weeks. Let us assume that each exam offers you the opportunity for potent positive reinforcers in the form of a good grade, increased self-esteem, satisfaction of your insatiable thirst for knowledge, and approval from an attractive classmate. This situation is very similar to an FI schedule. What kind of pattern will your study behavior exhibit?

If you are like many students, the cumulative recording of the number of hours you spend studying may resemble the one shown in Figure 9.14. It shows very little study during the first 2 weeks of the Test 1 interval, somewhat more during the next week, and a great deal of studying during the days preceding the test. This "cramming" pattern demonstrates the potency of the FI reinforcement schedule. Study behavior is usually radically different in the face of a variable and hence unpredictable schedule of "pop

quizzes," as you are well aware if you have had a professor who used that system of testing. Because the quiz is unpredictable, you are more likely to study continuously.

Variable-Interval Schedule

On a **variable-interval (VI) schedule,** reinforcement occurs after a variable interval of time. Reinforcement is given for the first response that occurs after that interval. A VI 5 schedule means that, *on the average,* there is a 5-minute interval between opportunities for the subject to obtain reinforcement. Because the availability of reinforcement is apparently random, the VI schedule produces a rather steady response rate that is much different from the scallop pattern that occurs on an FI schedule. The rate of response on a VI schedule, although fairly steady, is affected by the size of the average interval between reinforcements. The longer the average interval, the lower the rate of response.

Fishing often approximates a VI schedule. You know that the fish are present, but it is difficult to predict the time when they will start biting. The very next cast may hook a lunker if "the bite is on." This fact that the reinforcement is available but unpredictable may keep you going even if you have not had a bite all day.

I myself am hooked on the VI fishing schedule. For years I have been flailing the waters of Pacific Northwest rivers with my fly line in the hope of landing a prize steelhead trout. My efforts have met with such a notable lack of success that my fishing partners have nicknamed me "Empty River." Yet I continue, with visions of a reinforcer like the one shown in Figure 9.15 keeping me going. One might surmise that the English critic Samuel Johnson had first-hand experience with an unfavorable VI fishing schedule when he wrote, "Angling: I can only compare it to a stick and a string, with a worm at one end and a fool at the other."

Effects of Reinforcement Schedules on Learning and Extinction

So far, we have seen that reinforcement schedules have profound effects on response patterns and rates. Reinforcement schedules also affect the course of learning and extinction.

As you might expect, learning occurs most rapidly on a schedule of continuous reinforcement. If each response is reinforced, then there is no opportunity for extinction to occur, and the relation between the behavior and its consequence is easily perceived.

Although learning occurs faster under continuous reinforcement, partial schedules produce behavior that is harder to extinguish, especially if the behavior was reinforced on a variable schedule. If reinforce-

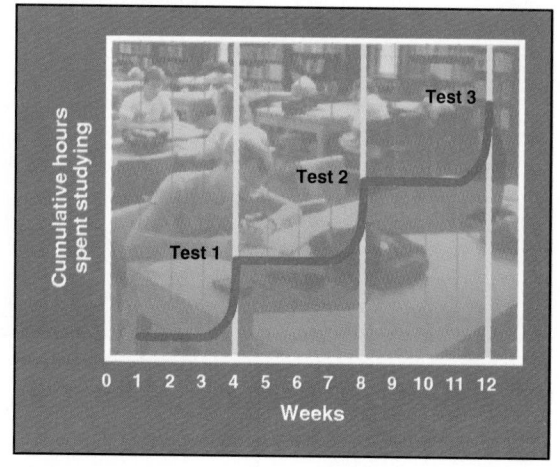

▶ **Figure 9.14** *Course examinations in college often follow a kind of fixed-interval schedule. The cumulative response curve of study behavior for many students shows a predictable scalloped pattern representing a gradually increasing amount of studying that reaches its maximum rate in "cramming" immediately before the test.*

Figure 9.15 *Fishing exemplifies a variable-interval schedule. This highly experienced fly fisherman put in over 50 hours of fishing time, often in freezing rain, before hooking this trophy steelhead trout (which he then released). Even a rarely obtained reinforcer like this makes it all worthwhile for many fishermen.*

ment has been unpredictable in the past, it takes subjects longer to realize that it is gone forever. If, on the other hand, the behavior has been reinforced on a continuous schedule, a change in the reinforcement pattern is quickly perceived, so extinction is likely to occur quite rapidly. Most people do not continue to drop coins into a candy machine that doesn't deliver, since vending machines are supposed to operate on a continuous schedule. As we have seen, their behavior toward a slot machine that doesn't deliver may be quite different.

To sum up, then, the best way to promote both fast learning and high resistance to extinction is to begin reinforcing the desired behavior on a continuous schedule until the behavior is fairly strong and then to shift to a partial (preferably variable) schedule that is gradually made more demanding. With a gradually increasing ratio on a VR schedule, for example, a pigeon may learn to peck a disk 12,000 times per hour to obtain a reinforcer given, on the average, once every 110 responses (Ferster & Skinner, 1957).

Negative Reinforcement: Escape and Avoidance Conditioning

As suggested earlier, we can understand many behaviors as attempts to maximize positive outcomes

and minimize negative ones. The discussion of positive reinforcement focused on positive outcomes. But that's only half the story. We now turn to those behaviors that we learn in order to escape from or avoid negative consequences. These behaviors are maintained through the process of negative reinforcement. They include such common responses as buckling one's seat belt before driving, applying sunscreen before going to the beach, and studying to avoid getting a low grade (as opposed to studying with the positive goal of getting an A, which would involve positive reinforcement).

A **negative reinforcer** is anything that increases a behavior that results in the reinforcer's *removal*. Don't confuse negative reinforcement with punishment. Although the same kinds of stimuli (for example, electric shock) may be involved, negative reinforcement (shock *removal) increases* a response that results in the reinforcement, whereas punishment (*being* shocked) *decreases* a response that produces the punishment. Both positive and negative reinforcement, then, involve a consequence that *increases* a response (see Figure 9.16).

Escape conditioning is one form of learning that results from negative reinforcement. In the laboratory, escape conditioning is carried out in the following manner: A rat is placed in one compartment of a shuttlebox, a rectangular chamber divided into two compartments by a partition with a doorway (see Figure 9.17). The floor of the shuttlebox is a grid through which electric shock can be delivered to either compartment. When shock is delivered in the rat's compartment, it evokes pain and fear, and the rat attempts to escape from the compartment. Sooner or later, the animal runs through the door into the other compartment, where the current is not on. When a shock is then delivered in that compartment, the rat can again escape by running back to the other side. Because the escape behavior of running through the door removes the shock, this consequence is a negative reinforcer for the behavior. As the conditioning proceeds, the

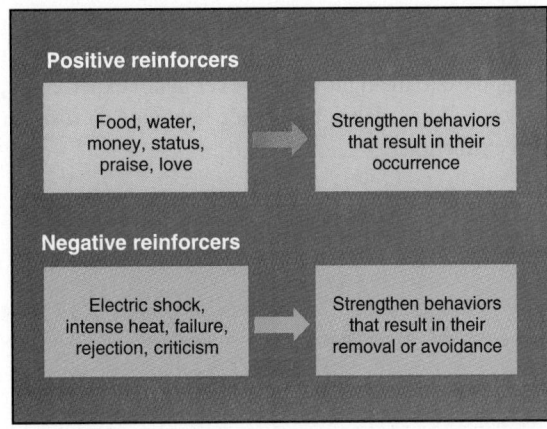

Figure 9.16 *Both positive and negative reinforcers increase and strengthen the responses that produce them.*

Positive reinforcers

Food, water, money, status, praise, love → Strengthen behaviors that result in their occurrence

Negative reinforcers

Electric shock, intense heat, failure, rejection, criticism → Strengthen behaviors that result in their removal or avoidance

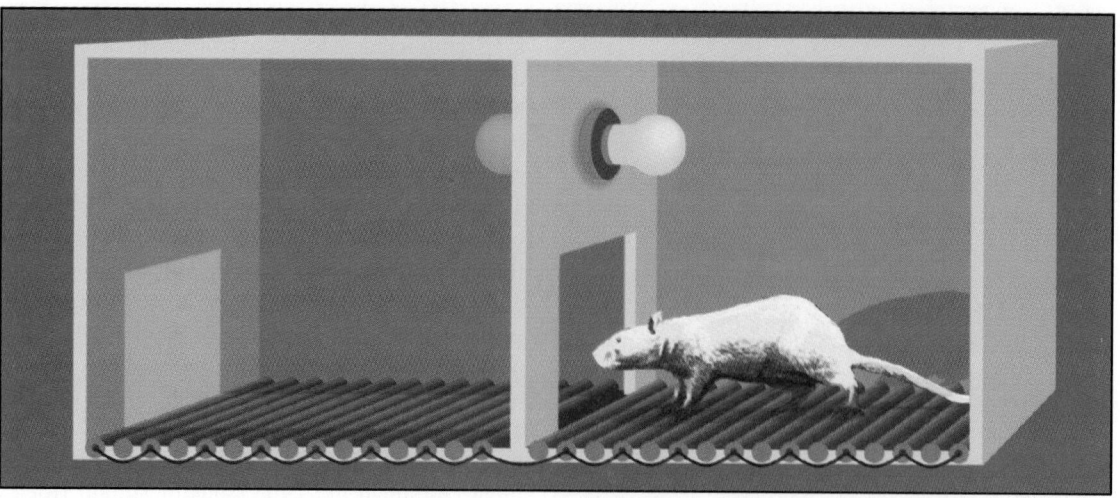

Figure 9.17 *The shuttlebox is used to study escape and avoidance learning. One side of the chamber is electrified, but the animal can learn to escape by going into the other compartment. If a light precedes the shock, the animal will learn to avoid the shock by running into the other compartment when the light comes on. In both cases, the shock is a negative reinforcer, because escaping or avoiding it strengthens the response of switching compartments.*

rat will require less and less time to escape the shock, until finally it will escape as soon as the shock is administered.

To study **avoidance conditioning,** all we need to do is introduce a warning light (as in Figure 9.17) or some other discriminative stimulus that precedes the shock. The animal will learn after the first several trials that the light signals impending shock, and it will begin to run to the other compartment after it sees the light and before the shock is administered, thereby avoiding it.

It is easy to identify examples of both escape and avoidance conditioning in daily life. For example, a student may drop a course because the professor is a terrible teacher and the course content is so totally uninteresting that going to class is an aversive experience. This would qualify as escape conditioning. If the student elects never to take another course in that subject because of his or her initial negative experience, we have an example of avoidance conditioning.

One aspect of avoidance conditioning that has intrigued psychologists is the remarkable strength of the avoidance behavior that may develop in only a few trials. Some dogs, for example, need only a few shocks before they learn to run into the other compartment of a shuttlebox at the sight of the warning light. After that, they may run hundreds of times in response to the light without ever again experiencing shock. What makes avoidance behavior so resistant to extinction?

The Two-Factor Theory of Avoidance Learning

One attempt to answer this question is the **two-factor theory of avoidance learning** (Rescorla & Solomon, 1967). The theory is so named because it explains avoidance conditioning in terms of two kinds of learning—classical conditioning and operant conditioning.

Because the warning stimulus (in our example, the light) is paired with shock (a UCS) in the beginning, the light becomes a CS that triggers a classically conditioned fear response. Since fear is an unpleasant state of affairs, responses that reduce it are strengthened through negative reinforcement. This is where the second process, operant conditioning, enters the picture. Fear reduction is a powerful negative reinforcer, and as long as the fear remains, the avoidance behavior that reduces it will continue.

Why doesn't the classically conditioned fear response extinguish? After all, the light is paired with the shock only a few times at the beginning of the training. Note that this is exactly the same question we asked earlier about Hilda's fear of snow. In her case, the snow stimuli had been associated with trauma on only one occasion more than 20 years earlier, yet the conditioned fear response did not weaken.

The answer to this puzzle is that successful avoidance responses can actually *prevent* the unlearning of fear (Denny, 1991). Recall that in order for a classically conditioned response to be extinguished, the CS (warning light, snow-related stimuli) must be presented without the UCS (shock, pain) long enough for extinction to occur. But once an avoidance response is learned, the subject may leave the fear-producing situation before finding out that the UCS will not occur. The dog in the shuttlebox has no opportunity to learn that the light (CS) is no longer followed by a shock because the animal is long gone by the time the shock would occur. Similarly, the young woman never allows herself to be in contact with snow long enough for her fear to extinguish (see Figure 9.18). The avoidance behaviors prevent the conditioned fear response from extinguishing, and the avoidance responses are in turn strengthened time after time through negative reinforcement (Houston,

1992). This helps to account for the fact that phobic avoidance often seems to become stronger over time, as appears to have been the case with the young woman's snow phobia.

The two-factor theory suggests not only a cause for phobic behavior but also a cure. To extinguish the conditioned fear response that motivates and maintains the phobic behavior, the avoidance response must be prevented from occurring so that the subject can be exposed to the feared CS in the absence of the UCS. This *stimulus exposure* approach has proved successful in eliminating learned fears in both animals and humans (Marks, 1987; Stampfl, 1991). Returning once more to the case of the snow phobia, an effective treatment approach might involve exposing Hilda to the feared snow stimuli (either in her imagination or in real life) long enough for the fear to extinguish. This form of treatment, known technically as **flooding,** evokes high levels of anxiety initially, but the anxiety diminishes as extinction occurs over time.

Exposure to a feared CS has been used by many people to conquer fears on their own. For example, G. Gordon Liddy, one of the main perpetrators of the Watergate break-in which led to the resignation of President Richard M. Nixon, described how he used his own version of this technique to conquer his fears:

> For example, to conquer my fear of thunder, I waited for a big storm and then sneaked out of the house and climbed up a seventy-five foot oak tree and lashed myself to the trunk with my belt. As the storm hit and chaos roared around me and the sky was rent with thunder and lightning, I shook my fist at the rolling black clouds and screamed, "Kill me! go ahead and try! I don't care! I don't care! . . .
>
> I repeated this kind of confrontation over a period of years, mastering one fear after another. . . . I feared heights so I scaled buildings with one of my friends (quoted in Meyer & Salmon, 1989, p. 120).

So far, we have discussed response consequences that are rewarding enough to increase the performance of certain behaviors. We now turn to the other side of the coin and consider what is probably the most frequently used method for controlling undesirable behavior—punishment.

Punishment

Punishment is any consequence that decreases the future occurrence of a behavior that produces it. We have already seen the difference between punishment and negative reinforcement. It is also important to distinguish punishment from extinction, a procedure that, like punishment, decreases a behavior. Punishment involves negative consequences that are con-

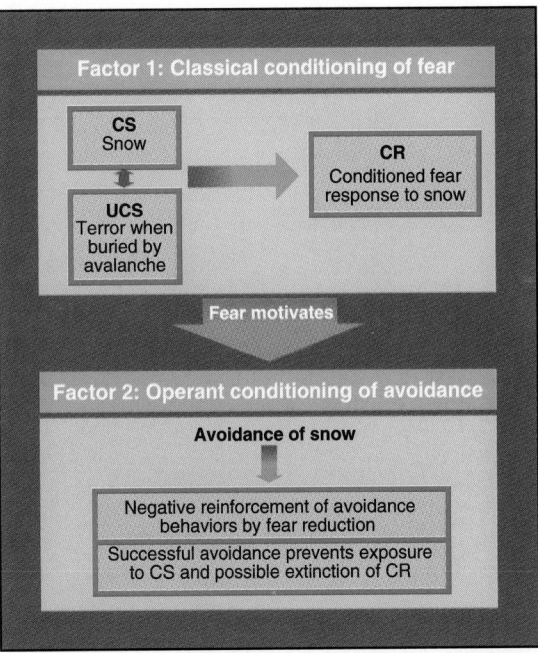

Figure 9.18 *The two-factor theory of avoidance learning would account for Hilda's snow phobia in terms of two sets of learning processes: classical conditioning of a fear response and the negative reinforcement of avoidance behavior by fear reduction.*

tingent on a given behavior, whereas extinction simply involves a failure to reinforce the behavior.

Punishment can be administered in two forms. The first, **aversive punishment,** involves the application of aversive stimuli, such as painful slaps or verbal reprimands. The second form of punishment, known as **response cost,** involves taking away positive reinforcers, such as privileges, social interactions, or possessions (see Figure 9.19). Notice that response cost is different from extinction because the reinforcer that is being taken away is not one that is reinforcing the undesired behavior. For example, a fine for speeding is punishment through response cost rather than extinction, because presumably money is not the reinforcer for speeding (unless, of course, the motorist is driving a getaway car from the scene of a robbery).

Applying Aversive Stimuli

When aversive or painful stimuli occur in response to a particular behavior, an inhibition, or *suppression,* of that behavior typically follows. This suppression usually results from fear of additional punishment (Axelrod & Apsche, 1983). In a sense, this form of punishment pits the suppressive effects of fear against the power of whatever is reinforcing the undesired behavior.

Aversive punishment has several advantages. First, it often produces rapid results. This can be an important consideration when it is necessary to stop a particularly dangerous behavior, such as a child's playing with a loaded gun or running out onto a busy street. Sometimes, punishment in the form of contingent electric shocks is used to stop the self-destructive

▶ **Figure 9.19** *Being deprived of the chance to practice with her soccer team is a potent response-cost punishment for this girl.*

out of or avoiding punishing school situations. Finally, the suppressive effects of strong punishment may generalize to other behaviors that are actually appropriate. A child who is severely punished for aggressive behavior may become generally unassertive, even in situations in which assertive behavior is called for, and one punished for sexual behaviors in childhood may suffer from sexual inhibitions as an adult (Wade & Cirese, 1992).

One of the greatest difficulties with punishment is the example that it sets. Aversive punishment amounts to control through aggression, and the message conveyed to the victim of punishment is that such behaviors are appropriate and effective. There is evidence that this lesson is quickly learned. One study found that by 13 to 35 months of age, children whose parents used severe physical punishment already displayed more aggression in day-care centers than a matched sample of children who were not physically punished (George & Main, 1979).

Punishment, then, is a two-edged sword. It is probably the quickest way to control unwanted behaviors, but it clearly has shortcomings and possible negative side effects. This is why most psychologists recommend that this form of behavior control not be used unless there are no other alternatives. If punishment must be used, it is very important to also focus on alternative positive behaviors, for punishment only teaches the recipient what *not* to do; it doesn't guarantee that desirable behavior will appear in its place. When punishment is used in conjunction with reinforcement of desirable alternative behaviors, and when language is used to help the recipient discriminate between appropriate and inappropriate behavior in particular situations, complete and relatively permanent suppression of problem behaviors can occur. Moreover, the reinforced desirable behaviors can appear in place of the punished ones, and problems stemming from fear and dislike can be minimized (Routh, 1982). Nonetheless, because of the aggressive component in aversive punishment, most learning psychologists recommend that extinction rather than aversive punishment be used whenever possible.

behaviors of profoundly disturbed or mentally retarded children who injure themselves by banging their heads on sharp objects or biting off chunks of their flesh (Matson & Gardner, 1991). In one case, a severely disturbed girl with a 6-year history of banging her head against sharp objects stopped after she had received only 15 contingent shocks (Lovaas, 1977).

We have already seen that extinction can be a very effective way to get rid of negative behaviors. However, in order to extinguish a behavior, we need to be able to control and eliminate the reinforcers of the behavior. Unfortunately, some positive reinforcers, such as those that maintain thrill-seeking behaviors, are beyond our control. In such cases, punishment may be the only way to bring a behavior under control.

Punishment often works, but it can also have undesirable side effects. One problem is that the suppression of the behavior may be temporary and may last only as long as the punisher is present ("When the cat's away . . ."). Another problem is that punishment arouses negative emotions, such as fear and anger, that can result in dislike for the person delivering the punishment or avoidance of the situation in which punishment occurs. Most parents do not want their children to dislike or fear them; similarly, teachers and administrators do not want students dropping

Response Cost: Punishment Through Removal of Reinforcers

The legendary baseball umpire Bill Klem once called a batter out on a close third strike. The enraged batter flung his bat high into the air and whirled around to argue the call. Klem whipped off his mask, fixed the batter with a steely gaze, and said, "If that bat comes down, it'll cost you 100 bucks."

Fines, loss of privileges, and "groundings" are all examples of a second form of punishment that involves the removal of *noncontingent reinforcers*—

that is, reinforcers other than those that maintain the behavior. This form of punishment, as mentioned earlier, is called *response cost* (as in "That'll cost you").

Punishment through deprivation has two distinct advantages over aversive punishment. First, even though response cost may arouse temporary frustration or anger, it does not create the kind of fear that aversive punishment does (Pazulinec & others, 1983). It is therefore less likely to cause avoidance of the punisher or the punishing situation, and it may actually increase the attractiveness of the withdrawn reinforcer (which can then be used to reinforce desired alternative behaviors). Second, the punisher is not setting the example of using physical aggression, so there is less opportunity for learning of aggression through imitation.

It is important to emphasize to parents that when response cost is used to punish behavior, the withheld reinforcer should be some prized object or activity, rather than love. When parents withhold love and reject a misbehaving child, the effects on the child's self-concept can be damaging (Sroufe & others, 1992). It is far better to deprive a child of some other prized reinforcer while continuing to communicate love and concern. The same principle applies to the use of aversive punishment: Communicate dislike for the *behavior,* not the child.

Figure 9.20 summarizes the types of response consequences we have discussed. As you can see, these involve the presentation or the removal of either positive or aversive stimuli.

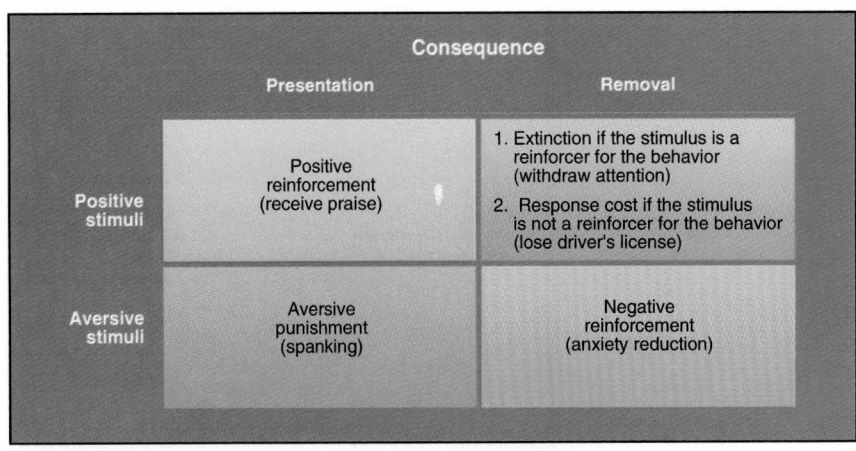

Figure 9.20 *The five kinds of response consequences that result from the presentation or removal of positive or aversive stimuli.*

example, some people destroy their love relationships again and again because they consciously or unconsciously fear being close to others and therefore vulnerable to being hurt or rejected. Their need to reduce their anxiety right now can be more potent than their need to be loved today or to avoid being lonely tomorrow. Social rejection, loss of important goals, loneliness, and even psychiatric hospitalization are the prices some people pay for immediate fear reduction.

Timing of Behavioral Consequences

The timing as well as the schedule of consequences can have important effects on behavior. Other things being equal, consequences that immediately follow a behavior have stronger effects than delayed consequences (Commons & others, 1984).

Some behaviors have both immediate and delayed consequences. Smoking, drinking, drug use, and criminal acts are all examples of behaviors that have immediate positive consequences and later negative ones: short-term "goods" and long-term "bads" (see Figure 9.21). Behaviors like these are difficult for many people to overcome because the immediate positive reinforcement for the behavior overrides the negative consequences that occur later on.

In his discussion of what he termed the **neurotic paradox,** the psychologist O. H. Mowrer (1950) tried to explain why many people seem to be trapped in a web of maladaptive and self-defeating behaviors. Mowrer suggested that the deviant behaviors are often maintained because they produce immediate negative reinforcement in the form of anxiety reduction. For

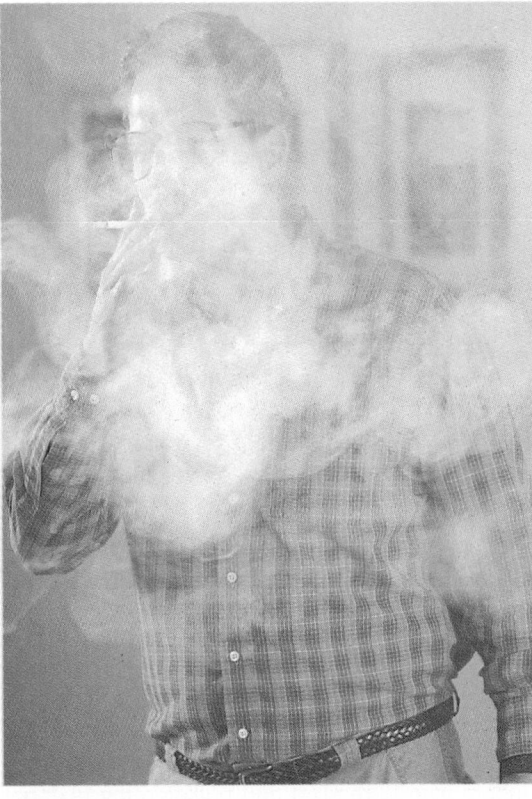

Figure 9.21 *Smoking is a behavior that is maintained despite long-term negative consequences because it has immediate positive consequences for smokers.*

Figure 9.22 *Many athletes show great dedication to their sport because they can imagine future long-term rewards for the sacrifices they make in the present.*

Despite their greater potency, immediate consequences do not always govern our behavior. Many people strive for long-term goals in the face of short-term difficulties (see Figure 9.22). To cite an example

close to home, think of the many day-to-day frustrations that you experience as you work toward your college degree.

Human behavior seems to be less influenced than animal behavior by the timing of behavioral consequences. One factor that makes a difference is our ability to imagine future events and thereby bring the distant consequences into the present. Many people can tolerate current unpleasantness associated with a behavior by imagining pleasures that will result from the behavior in the future. Likewise, imagining the long-term aversive outcomes of a behavior like taking illicit drugs may override the immediate positive reinforcement that could be obtained from taking the drug. Our cognitive abilities thus help to free us from the shackles of the reinforcement contingencies in our external environment.

Traditionally, the behavioral perspective has focused on how the external environment influences behavior, and there can be no doubt that the A–B–C (antecedent–behavior–consequences) contingencies exert considerable control over human as well as animal behavior. However, this does not mean that we are at the mercy of the external environment. As the following feature shows, we can use our knowledge of operant conditioning principles to gain greater control over our own behavior and to change ourselves in desired ways.

ENHANCING HUMAN PERFORMANCE

BEHAVIORAL SELF-CONTROL: OPERANT PRINCIPLES IN THE SERVICE OF SELF

A highly significant development within the behavioral perspective has been an increased emphasis on how people can use principles of learning to modify their own behavior (Kanfer, 1991; Marks, 1991). Concepts like "will power" and "self-control" have been translated into the concept of **self-regulation** (Cervone, 1992). The basic notion is that people can learn to operate as their own scientists and change themselves by using the principles of learning in their own behalf.

The flow chart in Figure 9.23 shows the basic steps for designing and carrying out a systematic self-control program. Throughout the program, the person collects data on antecedents, consequences, and the target behavior that he or she wants to change. To illustrate these procedures, we will consider how they might be used by a college student who

wants to increase the amount and effectiveness of studying.

Specifying the Problem

The first step in a self-control program is to pinpoint the behaviors you want to change. This may be more challenging than it sounds. We tend to use abstract words like *lazy, unmotivated, hostile,* and *dependent* to describe our problems. These fairly vague "trait" words do not tell us much about the actual behaviors and the situations in which they occur. One student described her study problem by saying, "I'm just not motivated to study hard." With a little help, she redefined her problem in behavioral terms as follows: "I don't spend enough time at my desk between the hours of 7 P.M. and 10 P.M. reading and outlining my textbook." This

redefinition specified both the target behaviors and the situation (time and place) in which she wanted the changes to occur.

Many problems can be defined in terms of competing behaviors, one desirable and the other undesirable (for example, studying versus not studying, not smoking versus smoking, being assertive versus being too submissive). A general rule is that whenever possible, self-change programs should be designed to increase the desirable alternative through positive reinforcement rather than to decrease the undesirable alternative through the use of punishment. As we learned earlier, punishment makes situations aversive, and simply decreasing some undesirable behavior does not guarantee that a desirable one will appear in its place. Thus, it is far better to reinforce yourself for studying than to punish yourself for not studying.

Collecting Baseline Data

The next step in the program is to collect preintervention, or **baseline,** data on your behavior. Accurate baseline data provide valuable information about how frequently and in which specific situations the target behavior presently occurs. Unless you have good baseline data, you will have no way of measuring change once you begin your program. Moreover, during the baseline period, people often discover some key information about the antecedents and consequences of the target behavior that are useful in planning the self-modification program (Watson & Tharp, 1993).

The most effective way to examine and detect behavioral changes is by plotting data on a graph, as is done in laboratory and clinical studies (Martin & Pear, 1992). The behavioral data collected by one student over a 2-week period are shown in Figure 9.24. As you can see, he graphed both the amount of time spent in the study situation and the amount of time spent in actual study (defined by him as reading and taking notes). To do this, he used a stopwatch that he ran only when he was actually studying. He found that a week of baseline data was enough to give him a good idea of how much time he was actually studying (and how much time he was wasting). In the second week, he began his change program. In cases where behavior varies greatly, it is necessary to collect baseline data over a longer period.

Identifying Antecedents and Consequences

Careful observation of your behavior and the situations in which it occurs should help you to identify conditions that are affecting the behavior. You should take careful note of situational factors that seem to trigger an undesirable target behavior or interfere with a desirable one. You also need to focus on the consequences of the behavior. These include both external consequences, such as compliments from others, and internal consequences, such as anxiety reduction or feelings of satisfaction. Once you have

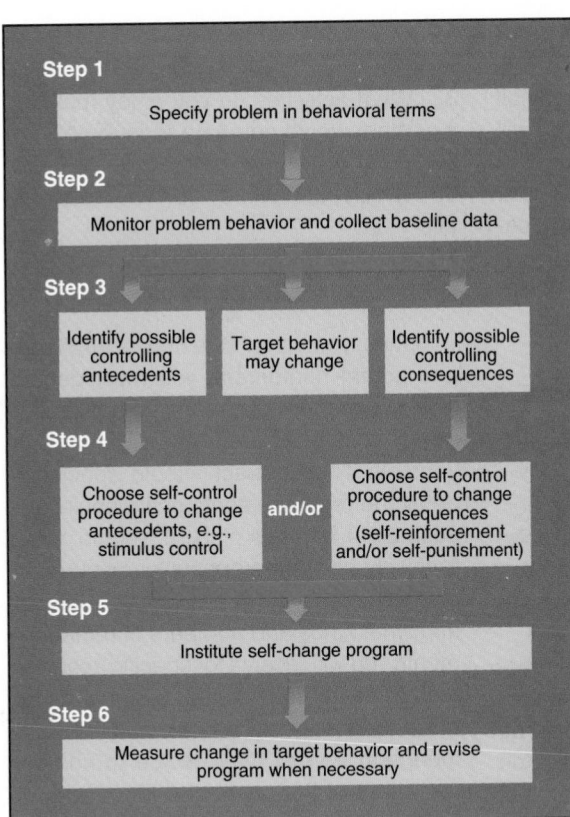

Step 1
Specify problem in behavioral terms

Step 2
Monitor problem behavior and collect baseline data

Step 3
Identify possible controlling antecedents | Target behavior may change | Identify possible controlling consequences

Step 4
Choose self-control procedure to change antecedents, e.g., stimulus control | and/or | Choose self-control procedure to change consequences (self-reinforcement and/or self-punishment)

Step 5
Institute self-change program

Step 6
Measure change in target behavior and revise program when necessary

Figure 9.23 *The basic steps and options in designing a self-control program that involves modifying the antecedents and consequences of behavior.*

identified the controlling antecedents and consequences, you are ready to apply your self-controlling behaviors. These behaviors may be attempts to alter antecedents, to rearrange consequences, or both.

Controlling Antecedents

We constantly respond to stimuli in our environment, and many of our behaviors

eventually come under stimulus control. Undesirable behaviors tend to occur within a specific range of situations. Students who have difficulty studying often find that certain stimuli, such as a television set or the presence of friends, trigger behaviors that are incompatible with studying. If a student's behavior is under this kind of stimulus control, then it should be possible for the student to change target behaviors by changing the stimulus environment.

Stimulus control techniques can be used very effectively to help increase studying. Select a place in which you do *nothing* but study. If you find your attention wandering or need to do something else, get up immediately and leave the study area. Your objective is to condition

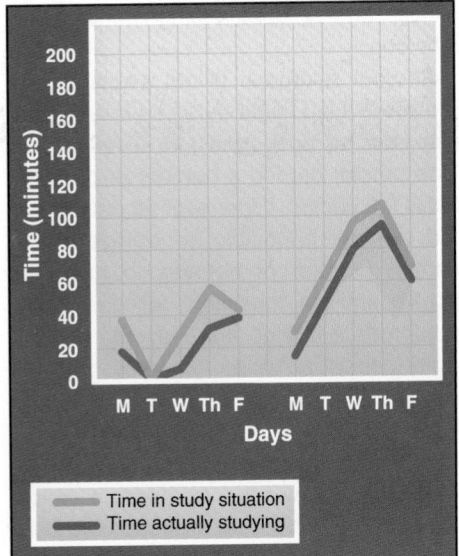

Figure 9.24 *Data collected over time by a student in a self-control program designed to increase study behavior. The student graphed both the amount of time he spent in the study situation and the amount of time he spent actually studying (that is, reading, outlining, and memorizing). He measured actual study time with a stopwatch. Note how study time increased when he began to self-reinforce study behavior in the 2nd week.*

yourself to study in response to the stimuli present in the study area. In time you will find that the study area is a powerful stimulus for studying. B. F. Skinner himself used this technique throughout his career. He did all of his writing at a particular desk and did nothing else there (Skinner, 1983).

Altering Response Consequences

Although antecedent conditions stimulate and guide our behavior, consequences determine whether we will repeat it. Fortunately, we have the power to arrange many of our own consequences, and this provides us with a powerful means of controlling our own behavior.

Self-administered positive reinforcement is one of the most effective self-modification procedures, and it should be the cornerstone of most programs. You need to find an effective reinforcer that you can control and then arrange to make it available to yourself only if you engage in the desired behavior. Virtually any object or activity can serve as a reinforcer if it is something that you enjoy having or doing and if you have complete control over it. Complete control is essential so that you can make the reinforcer contingent upon your behavior. It is best to avoid reinforcers that require the cooperation of other people unless you are sure they will cooperate. If you decide to reinforce yourself for good grades with a trip to Acapulco with money borrowed from your parents, make sure they are willing to lend it to you.

The reinforcer you select must also be potent enough to maintain the desired behavior. Awarding yourself a penny for each 40 hours of study time is unlikely to affect your study behavior. Moreover, the reinforcer must be potent enough to override the effects of the natural reinforcers that maintain the problem behaviors.

In choosing a reinforcer, you may find it helpful to ask yourself questions such as the following:

1. What kinds of things do you enjoy having?
2. What would be a nice present to receive?
3. What activities do you enjoy most?
4. What would you hate to give up?
5. What do you do to relax?
6. Which behaviors do you perform every day?
7. Are there other behaviors you perform instead of the target behaviors?

Once you have selected controllable and potent reinforcers, you must decide how to use them to change the target behavior. It helps to draw up a contract with yourself. The contract should specify in detail the reinforcement contingencies for each step of your plan. It should state precisely how often or how long you must or must not perform the target behavior and what kinds and numbers of reinforcements you will receive for specific achievements. Make your contract as clear, detailed, and loophole free as possible, and then sign it. You may decide to change the terms of the contract during the program, but you should always be operating under a specific contract.

Using Reinforcers Effectively

We have already seen that immediate reinforcement is more effective than delayed reinforcement. Thus, you should try to provide immediate reinforcement for your target behavior whenever possible. This is especially true when the alternative behavior is a strong habit you are trying to break or when the undesired behavior provides immediate reinforcement of its own, as does eating, drinking, or smoking.

If your reinforcer is not available immediately, you might try using *tokens* that can later be converted into a reinforcer. One person carried a number of pennies in his left pocket. Whenever he performed the desired behavior, he transferred a certain number of pennies to his right pocket until he "qualified" for his weekly reinforcer, a dinner at his favorite restaurant. Indeed, a "token economy" can be constructed, with a certain number of tokens redeemable for certain reinforcers. One student who wanted to increase her study time drew up a contract in which each 15-minute period of study time was worth one point. The points could be re-

deemed for a number of consequences that varied in their reinforcement value. For example, one point was worth 15 minutes of TV viewing, but 15 points earned the right to "do anything I want to, all day." As we will see in Chapter 17, token economies have been used very effectively to strengthen adaptive behaviors in hospitalized schizophrenics, who are very difficult to change with other treatments. If it works for them, it surely can work for you. Many studies have shown the effectiveness of token economies for people who want an effective means for modifying their own behavior (Watson & Tharp, 1993).

The Use of Shaping

A most effective way to build new behaviors is by shaping, or rewarding successive approximations. Shaping starts with the behaviors the person is already able to perform and proceeds from there by reinforcing behaviors that approximate the desired final product more and more closely.

If you collect good baseline data, you will know the level at which you currently perform your target behavior. Shaping requires that you begin at this level or *slightly* beyond it and begin to move *slowly* toward your goal, reinforcing yourself at each step. Start with a small change and make the steps small. If you have trouble, reduce the size of your steps. Through experimentation, you will discover the correct pace. It is far better to move forward slowly than to rush yourself and become discouraged by the failures that result. Impatience is probably the greatest threat to completion of self-modification projects.

Shaping should almost always be used to increase studying. Don't let your initial steps be influenced by how much you think you *should* be studying. In your project, start slightly (10 to 15 minutes) above your current daily level and reinforce yourself when you succeed. Successive increases should not exceed 10 or 15 minutes unless you find that you can succeed easily with larger ones. Remember, your self-modification program should not be a test of your pain tolerance. The goal is to bring about gradual change while enjoying plenty of honest reinforcers and the satisfaction of increasing your degree of self-mastery. The way in which you arrange the reinforcement contingencies is the most critical determinant of whether your goal will be achieved.

Few things of value come easily. Most people experience occasional setbacks or reach plateaus where progress seems to stop. When this happens, it is not a sign of personal weakness, but a sign that changes need to be made in the arrangement of antecedents, the contingencies, the shaping procedure, or perhaps all of these. Patience and resourcefulness are called for rather than discouragement and despair.

Behavioral self-control procedures have proved to be effective ways of helping people gain greater control of their lives. The development and testing of methods designed to increase behavioral self-control are attracting the attention of a growing number of psychologists, promising to give a new dimension of meaning to the phrase "Power to the people."

Cognition and Learning

Early behaviorists believed that learning involves the relatively automatic and mindless formation of bonds between stimuli and responses. Pavlov, for example, was convinced that the nervous system is built in such a way that the close pairing of a CS and a UCS automatically creates a neural bond between them (Pavlov, 1906). Radical behaviorists like Watson and Skinner always opposed any attempt to explain learning that went beyond observable stimuli and responses.

Even in the early days of psychology, other theorists disagreed with the radical behaviorists and emphasized the role of cognition. The Gestalt psychologists argued that learning involves the perception of relations among events. They cited experiments on insight learning in both animals (see Chapter 1, page 14) and humans to support their view (Kohler, 1925). Today, the cognitive perspective is an important force in learning theory (Healy & others, 1992).

Expectancies, Latent Learning, and Cognitive Maps

The most influential of the early cognitive learning theorists was Edward Tolman of the University of California, Berkeley. The basis of learning, argued Tolman, is the development of an **expectancy**, a cognitive representation of "what leads to what." In other words, stimuli serve as *signs* that certain events will follow. From this point of view, reinforcement does not "stamp in" behavior automatically. Instead, it provides *information* that a particular consequence will follow from a particular response.

In a famous series of experiments on what he called **latent learning**, Tolman and his associates demonstrated that learning can occur in the absence of reinforcement. In one experiment, three groups of rats were run in a complex maze. One group was run under normal conditions, with food always available at the end of the maze. A second group never received any food. For the critical third group, no food was available at the end of the maze for the first 10 days, but on the 11th day, food was introduced. According to traditional reinforcement theory, this last group should perform no better than animals who had never been in the maze, for they had not been reinforced. Therefore, no learning should have occurred.

The results of the experiment, shown in Figure 9.25, were very different from what reinforcement theory predicted. As soon as food was introduced, the performance of the third group became as good as that of the group that had been reinforced all along (Tolman & Honzik, 1930). Tolman concluded that these animals must have learned a *cognitive map* of the maze during the first 10 days. This learning remained latent, or hidden, until the rats had a good reason to get to the end of the maze, at which time it was manifested in performance. Tolman's research on latent learning gave impetus to a cognitive perspective on learning in animals as well as in humans. Today, it is widely accepted that cognitive factors are involved in both classical and operant conditioning (Houston, 1992; Rachman, 1991).

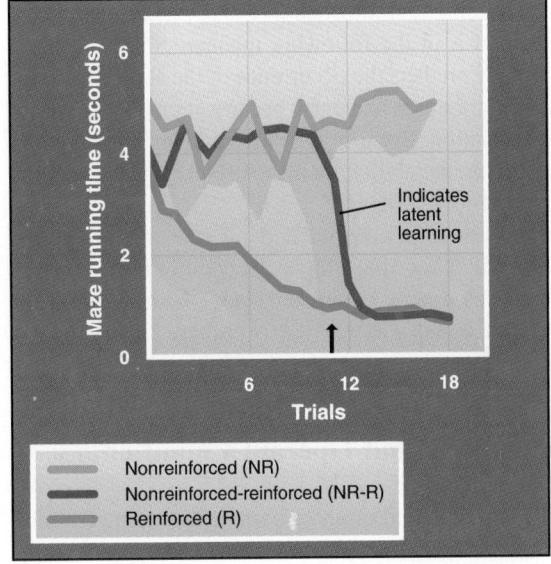

Figure 9.25 *Maze-running performance in one of Tolman's latent learning experiments. The rats had one trial in the maze on 18 consecutive days. Rats in Group NR received no reinforcement in the maze at any time. Rats in Group R were reinforced with food every time they reached the end of the maze. Rats in the critical group, NR-R, had no food reward until the 11th day. Their immediate and dramatic performance improvement indicated that they had already learned the maze. (Data from Tolman & Honzik, 1930).*

Cognition in Classical Conditioning

Tolman's concept of expectancy remains the cornerstone of cognitive theories about what is actually being learned in the various kinds of learning situations described so far in this chapter. Cognitive learning theorists believe that the basis of classical conditioning is the learning of an expectancy that the CS will be followed by the UCS (Bolles, 1979; Holland, 1992). The expectancy model predicts that the most important factor in classical conditioning is not *how often* the CS and the UCS are paired but *how predictably* the UCS follows the CS, since the animal is learning to predict one event (the UCS) from another earlier event (the CS) (Rescorla, 1988).

Here is the kind of experimental result that strengthens the cognitive position: If two groups of animals experience exactly the same number of CS–UCS pairings, but the second group receives additional presentations of the UCS in the absence of the CS, the first group shows much stronger classical conditioning (Rescorla & Holland, 1982). Apparently, the extra UCS presentations decrease CS predictability and thus weaken the conditioning.

Support for the cognitive interpretation of classical conditioning also comes from a phenomenon known as **blocking.** In a typical blocking experiment, subjects are exposed to repeated pairings of a light and an electric shock (UCS) until the light alone elicits a fear response. Then a second stimulus, such as a tone, is added so that both the light (the CS) and the tone occur together before the shock. We would expect that the tone will also become a CS, since it too is being regularly paired with the shock.

But that's not what happens. If the tone is later presented alone, it does not evoke the fear response. It has somehow been "blocked" from becoming a CS because of the previous conditioning involving the light. Pavlovian theory has a hard time explaining this finding, but the cognitive expectancy theory can explain it in the following manner: Since the light already predicts the occurrence of the shock, the new tone stimulus is irrelevant because it provides no new information. Because the new stimulus does not enhance predictability, it fails to become a CS (Rescorla & others, 1985).

These experiments challenge the traditional behavioral view that classical conditioning is a mechanistic process dependent solely on the association of the CS with the UCS. It may be that even in animals, cognitive processes play a key role.

Cognition and Operant Conditioning

The story is told of an operant conditioning demonstration that occurred in an introductory psychology class. The instructor sent one of the students out of the room for a few minutes and instructed another student in how to shape a response—flicking the light switch on and off—using M&Ms as the reinforcer. When the first student returned, he was reinforced first for looking at the wall that held the light switch, then for approaching the wall, and so on, until, 25 minutes later, he was flicking the switch and chomping one M&M after another.

At this point, another student asked if she could serve as experimenter. A new subject left the room for a moment while the class decided that he should be shaped to erase the blackboard. When the student reentered the classroom, the new experimenter quickly said, "John, if you'll erase the blackboard immediately, I'll give you this whole bag of M&Ms." This time, it took all of 5 seconds to get the desired behavior.

As this anecdote shows, there's more than one way to establish an operant response. The cognitive perspective stresses that *awareness*—knowing the relations between responses and their probable consequences—is important, if not essential, in operant conditioning. Awareness, however, is not as easy to establish scientifically as we might think. For one thing, animals cannot tell us what they know. Studies with humans are not foolproof, either. Even if subjects are able to verbalize the reinforcement contingency, it is impossible to determine exactly when they became aware and whether or not any learning had occurred prior to awareness. Despite these difficulties, however, the weight of evidence indicates that, at least in humans, awareness is very important.

Consider, for example, a *verbal conditioning* experiment by Charles Spielberger and L. D. DeNike (1966). The subjects' task was to make up a series of sentences. In one condition, they were reinforced by the experimenter with positive comments such as "mmm-hmm" and "good" whenever they used a certain kind of word in sentences they made up. In this case, the desired response was the use of nouns that could refer to humans, such as *boy*. A control group did not receive this reinforcement. Subjects in both conditions made up 10 sets of sentences. The change in the number of times subjects included human nouns in their sentences was measured. In addition, subjects were frequently asked questions to determine whether they were aware of the reinforcement contingency.

The results of the experiment are shown in Figure 9.26. Part *a* shows that the subjects who were aware of the reinforcement contingency showed a large increase in their use of human nouns, while unaware and control subjects displayed virtually no change. Part *b* shows the impact of awareness. There was a rapid increase in human noun responses at precisely the point at which subjects said they had become aware of the connection between what they were saying and the experimenter's positive comments.

It is important to note that, from the cognitive perspective, the best predictor of a person's behavior is the *perceived* contingency, not the actual one (see Figure 9.27). In many instances, the two are identical, but that's not always the case. Sometimes people perceive contingencies that do not actually exist. A good example of this involves the superstitious behavior in which a person thinks that good luck or bad luck will follow from performing or not performing a certain act. We have also described the potent effects that placebos can have on people who believe that they will be helped by them. A final example of a misperceived contingency is this anecdote:

> A psychologist reported that a frustrated mother once contacted him for assistance in the reduction of swearing behavior on the part of her two young sons. A behavior therapist, the psychologist recommended that she use punishment techniques. He told her that it was important to use immediate and severe punishment each and every time the swearing occurred. To maximize the impact of that punishment, he also recommended that she try to use each child as an example for the other—that is, punish him in front of his brother.
>
> Enthusiastic over this advice, the mother returned home. At breakfast the next morning, she sat down ready and raring to modify behavior. The older son opened the conversation by requesting that she ''pass the goddam Cheerios.'' With lightning fury, the mother lunged across the table and hit her son—sent both him and his chair sprawling to the floor. Pleased with her skillful execution of behavioral principles, the mother turned to her somewhat bewildered younger son. ''Well, what will you have?'' He paused a moment, glanced at his supine brother, and answered, ''You can bet your sweet ass it isn't Cheerios!'' (Mahoney, 1980, pp. 136–137).

Internal Self-Evaluations as Reinforcers and Punishers

For more than a decade, a middle-aged man referred to by students as Holy Hubert was a regular visitor to the campus where I teach. His fire-and-brimstone exhortations to repent and avoid damnation, delivered on the steps of the Student Union, often evoked reactions ranging from amused smiles to loud insults and ridicule. One could hardly imagine less positive consequences for an evangelist.

One day, I approached Hubert and asked him why he continued to preach when the response of students was so negative. He answered, ''I don't care what they say. When I know I'm doing the Lord's work, I feel so good that they could hang me for all I care.''

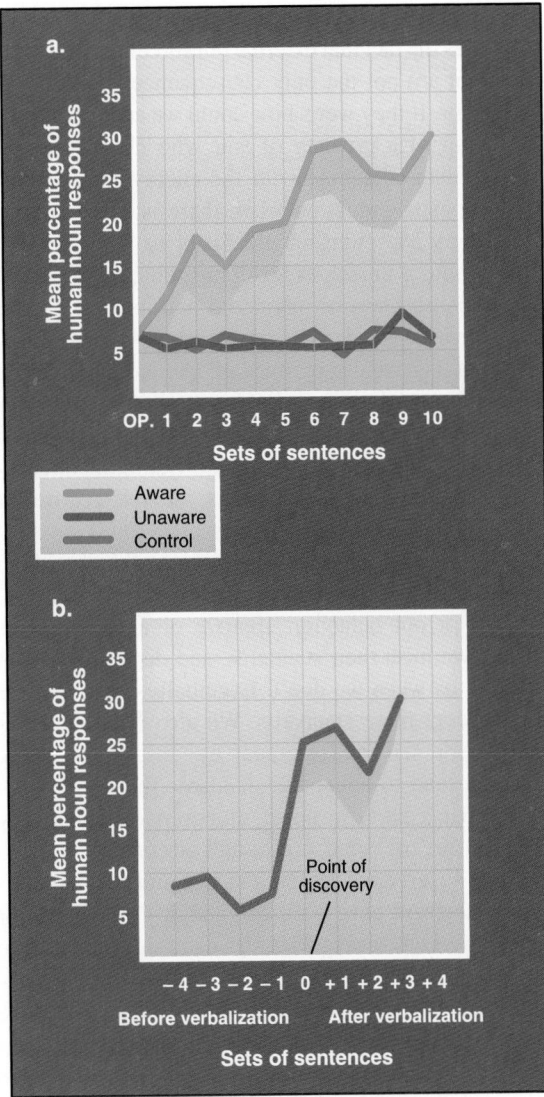

a.

b.

Point of discovery

−4 −3 −2 −1 0 +1 +2 +3 +4

Before verbalization   After verbalization

Sets of sentences

Figure 9.26 *Awareness has a dramatic effect on verbal conditioning. Part a shows that only subjects who were aware of what caused the experimenter to say "good" or "mmm-hmm" showed an increase in the desired responses. Part b shows levels of performance before and after the subjects were able to verbalize the contingency. (Data from Spielberger & DeNike, 1966).*

''Boy, have I got this guy conditioned! Every time I press the bar down, he drops in a piece of food.''

(Columbia Jester (1951); H. Mazzeo '52/P. Gardner '52.

Figure 9.27 *The cognitive perspective on operant conditioning holds that the behavior is governed by perceived relations between behaviors and their consequences, whether or not the perceptions are accurate.*

Hubert's persistence in the face of adversity illustrates the fact that external reinforcement and punishment are not the only consequences that control behavior. If they were, how could we account for the behavior of a prisoner of war who chooses to die rather than cooperate with the enemy, or a person who resists temptation when there is no chance of discovery and punishment? All of us have at times felt proud of ourselves for doing something, even if no one else knew or others did not approve. In this sense, virtue is indeed its own reward. At other times, most of us have disapproved of, berated, or devalued ourselves for failing to live up to our own internal standards. Behavioral psychologists have begun to pay increasing attention to internally administered reinforcements and punishments, or **self-evaluative processes** (Bandura, 1986; Cervone, 1992).

These internal processes are learned in a number of ways. Significant adults, such as parents, set standards for our behavior, approve of and reward us when we meet their standards, and disapprove of or punish us when we don't. Eventually, we ourselves may adopt these standards. We also establish standards for self-reinforcement by observing others. People tend to adopt the standards that others display, particularly in novel situations in which they are unsure of what constitutes acceptable performance (Cervone, 1992). Once standards of self-reinforcement have been adopted, a given behavior can have two consequences: an external consequence and a self-evaluative response. In some instances, when the two conflict with one another, the self-reinforcement system may override the external consequences. This is one way in which people achieve some degree of freedom from the constraints of the external environment.

Sometimes, unrealistic self-reinforcement standards result in maladjustment and unhappiness. Some people experience a great deal of distress because they have lofty standards that they can rarely meet. As a result, they suffer from depression, feelings of worthlessness, and self-devaluation. Helping such people relax their unrealistic standards can result in feelings of increased self-worth and a reduction in depression (Ellis & Dryden, 1990).

Modeling: Learning Through Observation of Others

We learn not only through our own experiences but also by observing others, a process called observational learning, or **modeling.** Children learn fears, prejudices, likes and dislikes, religious attitudes, social values, and social behaviors from their parents by imitating their behavior. They also can learn either positive or undesirable behaviors from other figures, such as friends, an older brother or sister, a rock star, a sports hero, or a teacher. The apprenticeship system, in which a novice watches and learns from an expert, in time creates a skilled craftsman.

Modeling is a very efficient way of learning that can save us time and effort. By imitating those behaviors that produce positive outcomes for others and avoiding those that do not, we can bypass the potentially dangerous process of learning through trial and error. For example, we obviously would not want members of our armed forces to learn how to use explosives and fly airplanes through trial and error.

When we observe models, we receive information not only on how to behave but also on what consequences the behavior is likely to have. Many studies have shown that while we can learn a behavior through observation alone, our future performance of the behavior depends on the consequences that we have observed or have come to expect (Bandura, 1989). Presumably, the teen-age wrestling fans described earlier not only learned the techniques that Rowdy Roddy and the other professional wrestlers exhibited on television, but also saw the wrestlers reinforced with success and crowd approval. Thus, much to their mother's chagrin, they were very ready, willing, and able to copy the behaviors.

The difference between observational learning and performance was demonstrated in a classic experiment performed by Albert Bandura (1965). Children watched a film in which a model engaged in a series of aggressive acts. One group of children saw the model rewarded with praise and candy, a second group saw the model reprimanded for aggression, and a third group saw no consequences for the model. After the film, the children were carefully observed to see how many of the aggressive responses they reproduced.

Those children who saw the model punished performed fewer imitative responses than those who had seen the model rewarded and those who had seen no consequences (see Figure 9.28). But did this lower level of performance mean that they had not learned the aggressive responses? To find out, the experimenter offered the children attractive prizes if they could do what the model had done. Many of the children quickly reproduced the model's aggressive acts.

Research on modeling is directly relevant to concerns that exposure to violent models in the mass media might increase aggressive behavior in viewers. We saw a vivid example of the potentially negative influence of televised violence in the case of the teen-age wrestling enthusiasts. As we shall see in Chapter 19, which considers aggression in greater detail, there is strong research evidence linking the amount of television violence watched by young boys with their

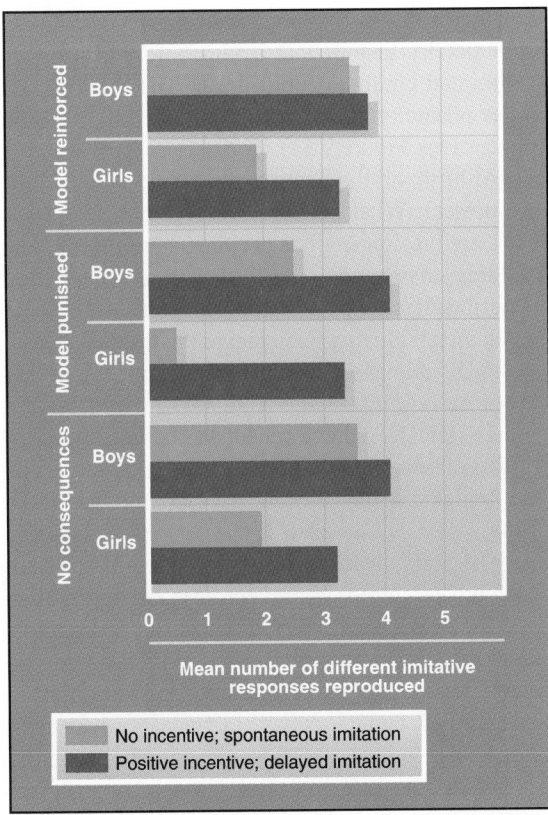

Figure 9.28 *The learning and performance of modeled aggressive responses. Children who saw an aggressive model punished spontaneously reproduced fewer of the aggressive behaviors than children who saw the model rewarded or saw no consequences. However, when the children were later offered incentives for reproducing the behaviors, both the boys and the girls showed that they had clearly learned the behaviors. (Bandura, 1965).*

Figure 9.29 *Children who watch violent television programs are exposed to many models for aggressive behavior, raising concerns about the impact of such viewing on their developing personalities.*

aggressiveness as teenagers and young adults (Bandura, 1986; Eron, 1987). While some researchers (e.g., Freedman, 1988) point out that we cannot conclude on the basis of correlational data that viewing violence causes aggression, the majority of researchers working in the area believe that by arousing aggressive impulses and violent ideas, reducing concerns about the suffering of victims, reducing the shock value of violence, and providing aggressive models, media violence increases the likelihood of aggression (Donnerstein & others, 1987; Geen & Thomas, 1986). Given the fact that during the impressionable elementary and junior-high-school years, the average U.S. child witnesses the violent destruction of some 13,000 human beings on television alone, it is difficult to dismiss the media's potential as a ''school for violence'' (see Figure 9.29).

Emotional responses can also be learned through modeling (Rachman, 1991). Children often acquire fears by observing fear responses of parents or other

adults. So do young rhesus monkeys, who become fearful of snakes after they observe an adult monkey exhibit fear of a snake (Cook & others, 1985). Indeed, it may be that more of our fears arise in this vicarious fashion than through direct classical conditioning based on our own direct experiencing of CS–UCS pairings.

Biological Factors and Learning

The changes in behavior that occur as the result of experience surely reflect underlying changes in the nervous system. What is the nature of these changes? Where and how do they occur? Does the structure of the nervous system, forged in part by evolutionary factors, limit what can be learned? Can the biological processes involved in learning be influenced in ways that will enhance learning capacity? For more than a hundred years, psychologists have searched for answers to these questions.

Three basic approaches have been taken in the search for linkages between biological and learning processes. These approaches are shown in Figure 9.30. In the first approach, scientists perform some biological intervention, such as injecting a drug or destroying a part of the brain, and observe the effects on learning. In the second, they do just the opposite: They perform some intervention that affects learning and measure the effects of the intervention on the biological system. For example, they might expose

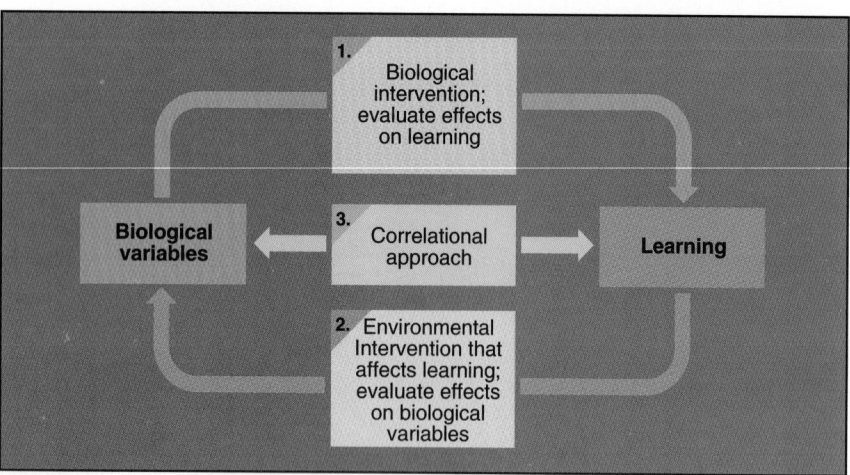

Figure 9.30 *In research on the biological bases of learning, biological interventions can be performed and their effects on learning studied (1). Conversely, the effects of learning on the brain can be studied (2). Finally, correlational research can be done on relations between biological and learning variables (3).*

one group of infants to a highly enriched early environment with many learning opportunities and study the effects of this manipulation on various biological measures of brain development. Finally, they can use the correlational approach to study natural relations between biological and learning variables. For example, relations have been discovered between the concentration of certain neurotransmitters in the brain and learning ability (White & Milner, 1992). All three of these approaches have resulted in important discoveries about the links between the organism and the environment.

Environment, Learning, and Brain Development

As we saw in Chapter 1, the human brain is the product of a long evolutionary history. Yet according to anthropologists, the brain probably achieved its present form some 50,000 years ago in the cranium of Cro-Magnon (Pilbeam, 1984). We might then wonder why it was not until perhaps 15,000 years ago that lifelike paintings began to appear on cave walls. Cities did not appear until 5000 B.C., and not until about 400 B.C. did humans find a way to store knowledge outside the brain in the form of writing (Rose, 1973). These time lags indicate that human thought and behavior depend on more than the physical structure of the brain. Clearly, the evolution of human behavior did not end 50,000 years ago.

The other important part of the human equation is experience and its product, learning. Our cranial capacity and the number of neurons in our brains may not have changed much since Cro-Magnon, but our environment has evolved by leaps and bounds. We

now know that each human brain has its own unique evolutionary history that begins before birth in the womb and continues until death. The brain's enormous plasticity allows it to be molded by its experiences (see Figure 9.31).

At birth, all the neurons the brain will ever have are present. What does increase dramatically, however, are the connections between them. By the time children enter grade school, their brains have more dendrites than those of adults and consume twice as much metabolic fuel (Chugani & Phelps, 1986; Kolb, 1989). By adolescence, however, the number of dendrites has shrunk to the adult level, a process that some scientists believe reflects a Darwinian process of natural selection that occurs as experience sculpts the brain and unused synapses are pruned (Ogg, 1988).

The brain clearly determines our ability to learn, but our learning environment also influences brain development (Wachs, 1992). We know, for example, that exposing young animals to enriched environments with many interesting toys and opportunities to learn new behaviors has biological consequences. Compared with normally reared animals, rats raised in enriched environments have more and longer dendrites, more synapses, greater brain weight, and greater concentrations of neurotransmitter substances (Kolb, 1989; Turner & Greenough, 1985). At the other end of the age spectrum, it appears that a lack of stimulation leads to neural decline in the aged. In some nursing home studies, notable drops in intelligence test scores were found in patients within 6 months of their entering the setting, whereas no such change was found in people of the same age who remained in their normal environments (Belsky, 1990). Environments that starve the brain of experience appear to exact a grim toll on brain functioning, particularly in the young and in the aged.

Thus, every day you are alive, your brain continues to evolve, its neural networks, transmitter substances, and electrochemical patterns affected by your experiences. Your accumulated sensory inputs, thoughts, motives, emotions, and actions weave your neurons into the unique tapestry of your mind, and your interactions with your environment help shape you biologically as well as behaviorally.

Is the plasticity of the brain so great that there are no limits to what we are capable of learning? Is experience the supreme shaper? As you might expect, there is another side to the interaction between biology and learning.

Biological Constraints on Learning

It has always been obvious that biological factors limit the complexity of the behaviors that various species can learn. Not even the most radical behaviorist of the 1920s ever suggested that the white rat could be conditioned to solve complex mathematical problems. But it was always assumed that the basic principles of classical and operant conditioning could be used to condition any behavior that the organism was physically capable of performing. Recent years have witnessed one challenge after another to that basic assumption. Let us examine some of these challenges and their implications.

The Misbehavior of Animals

Keller and Marian Breland had a farm in Florida where they trained animals for circuses, advertising agencies, and the movies. They used well-established operant techniques like shaping and the chaining of behaviors into complex sequences. These operant techniques were usually successful, but not always. Sometimes, the animals simply refused to behave according to the "laws" of learning.

On one occasion, the Brelands tried to train a chicken to play baseball. The game was arranged so that a small ball would roll toward home plate and the chicken would pull a chain to swing a small metal bat. If the ball was hit, a bell would ring and the chicken would run to first base to get its food. To the Brelands, this was no real challenge. The chicken was soon pulling the chain to swing the bat and running to first base when it heard the bell.

But then the ball was introduced into the game, and with it utter chaos. Whenever the chicken hit the ball, instead of running to first base to collect its food reinforcement, it would attempt to field the ball, pecking furiously at the ball, flapping its wings, and chasing the ball all around the diamond. Try as they might, the Brelands could not stop these behaviors. End of training and end of the chicken's baseball career. In this and other instances, animals simply refused to "shape up." But why?

Species Effects on Conditioned Aversions

Some years ago, a psychologist, John Garcia, discovered that rats quickly learned to avoid eating food that had been contaminated with a tasteless substance (lithium chloride) that made them violently ill (Garcia & others, 1970). These conditioned food aversions occurred after only one experience, even though the sickness (the UCS) did not occur until several hours after the rats had eaten the food (the CS). Before Garcia's studies, a CS–UCS interval of this length was virtually unknown in animal research. Moreover, the conditioning was very specific. That is, the rats' aversion was restricted to the taste of the specific food that had made them sick; it did not generalize to similar foods with different tastes.

Figure 9.31 *The environments in which we live our lives help to shape our brains, and our brains, in turn, govern our responses to our environments.*

Differences among species in conditioned aversions proved to be striking. It seems that there are definite biological limitations on the kinds of food aversions that can be learned. Rats quickly develop aversions to new tastes but not to new odors. For some other species, however, taste aversions are very hard to establish even if the animals are made very ill. Quail, for example, develop aversions on the basis of the visual characteristics of the food rather than its taste, even though they have an acute sense of taste (Wilcoxon & others, 1971). What do these findings mean in terms of the biological bases for learning?

Instinctive Drift and Preparedness

All of these findings—the misbehavior of the Brelands' animals and the species differences in conditioned aversions—indicate that there are biological limits on learning that go beyond the animals' physical capabilities. In every instance, it appears that the artificial learning conditions established by the experimenters were overridden by innate factors that are species specific.

For example, the Brelands found to their dismay that once a particular stimulus came to represent food, the animals began to act as if it *were* food. The chicken, for example, pecked at the seed-like ball as if it were something to eat. Raccoons insisted on "washing" tokens that were intended to act as secondary reinforcers. These instinctive responses are so deeply rooted in the animals' evolutionary history that

Figure 9.32 *As the Brelands found, innate behavior patterns may come to the fore once a particular stimulus has come to represent a primary reinforcer. When the Brelands tried to train a raccoon to place a token into a vending machine to obtain food, they could not break the raccoon of dipping the token in water, just as this raccoon is doing with real food.*

they simply take over under relevant conditions and override the conditioning procedure, a phenomenon known as **instinctive drift** (see Figure 9.32). Likewise, the species differences found in learned food aversions indicate that the evolutionary history of the animal must be important. The rat is a forager that eats many different kinds of food. If it is to survive, it must have a learning mechanism that protects it from foods that are poisonous. The rat thus has an innate readiness to learn which tastes are dangerous. Visual and odor cues are far less important than taste to its survival.

We must, then, consider the evolutionary history of the organism as well as its learning history (Crawford & Anderson, 1989). Martin Seligman (1970) has captured this general idea in his concept of **preparedness.** Seligman believes that animals are biologically prepared to form associations between stimuli, responses, and consequences that are related to their survival as a species. These *prepared* associations are learned with very little training. On the other hand, animals are *contraprepared* to learn associations that are contrary to their natural tendencies. These associatons are learned very slowly, if at all. Seligman argues that most of the behaviors that have been studied in the learning psychologist's laboratory, such as bar pressing and disc pecking, fall somewhere between these two classes of behaviors. That is why learning in the laboratory has always looked like a gradual process of establishing stimulus–response connections and why the findings that we have just discussed surprised many learning researchers.

Is the concept of preparedness relevant only to lower animals like rats, chickens, and pigeons? Are humans, because of our greater flexibility, immune to the influence of prepared associations? Perhaps not, as we see in our next feature.

PSYCHOBIOLOGICAL INTERACTIONS

Are We Biologically Prepared to Fear Certain Things?

Seligman's concept of preparedness suggests that both classical and operant conditioning are affected by biologically based predispositions to learn some associations more readily than others. Observations made by clinicians support the possibility that not all stimuli are equally conditionable. For example, a British psychotherapist, Isaac Marks (1977), tells of a 4-year-old girl who saw a snake while walking through a park. She found the snake interesting and showed no fear of it. A short time later, she returned to the family car, and her hand was smashed in the car door when it was closed. She developed a lifelong phobia not of car doors or automobiles, but of snakes.

The clinical literature indicates that human phobias tend to fall into certain narrow classes, most of which pertain to animals and dangerous places. Fear of snakes is the most common phobia, and fear of spiders, of the dark, of high places, and of closed-in places are also fairly common. Interestingly, in many phobics, no evidence can be found for previous classical conditioning of fear (see Figure 9.33).

Even more striking evidence for selective conditioning of fear in humans comes from a long series of experimental studies performed by Arne Öhman and his research team at the University of Uppsala in Sweden. In these experiments, the researchers paired various kinds of stimuli with electric shock and later presented these stimuli to subjects and measured the subjects' physiological responses (Öhman & others, 1985; Hygge & Öhman, 1978). People who received shocks each time pictures of snakes or spiders were projected on a screen quickly acquired conditioned emotional responses to these stimuli, often after a single pairing. But subjects who received shocks while looking at slides of flowers, houses, or berries usually required many more pairings before they showed fear conditioning. Moreover, once conditioning was established, the emotional response to the spider or snake took far longer to extinguish than the response to the flowers or houses. Other studies in Öhman's laboratory show that pictures of angry faces can trigger physiological responses even when they are presented too briefly to be consciously recognized, providing evidence of automatic cognitive processing of threat cues having evolutionary significance (Öhman, 1986).

Seligman (1971) proposed that, like other animals, humans are biologically prepared to acquire fears of some stimuli but not others. The stimuli that we are prepared to fear are those that have had evolutionary significance for our species. He points out that biological significance seems to be more important than cultural significance. For example, consider guns as a potential phobic object. According to Seligman, guns are too recent in our history as a species to have been prepared for fear conditioning, even though we have ample cultural preparation to view them as instruments of death. And in fact, when slides showing guns are used as stimuli in studies of selective emotional conditioning, they turn out to have the conditioning power of houses and flowers, not that of snakes and spiders (Hodes, 1981). (It is possible, of course, that at least some subjects view guns as signals for safety and sport rather than as dangerous objects.)

Recent research on prepared phobias, while generally supporting the conclusion that fears of evolutionary significance are most common, has called other preparedness assumptions into question (McNally, 1987). For example, preparedness theory views such phobias as reflecting primitive, noncognitive forms of associative learning. This notion is called into question by findings that in laboratory studies like those conducted by Öhman, emotional learning did not occur unless or until subjects became aware of exactly which slides were associated with shock (Dawson & others, 1986). This finding strongly suggests that cog-

Figure 9.33 *Are some common human fears the results of evolutionary factors rather than personal experience?*

nition rather than automatic associative learning is involved. Another finding is that, contrary to what Seligman's theory would predict, phobias involving objects with evolutionary significance, such as spiders, respond as quickly to treatment as those involving objects or situations that have no such significance (Foa & Kozak, 1986). Finally, it appears that vulnerability to particular phobias is not constant over the life span, but varies with age. Fears of animals tend to be acquired in childhood, social fears in adolescence, and agoraphobia (fear of open spaces and public places) in adulthood (Thyer & others, 1985).

Phobias thus appear to reflect the interaction of biological, cognitive, and developmental factors. Preparedness theorists are now focusing on the possibility that phobias arise out of innate responses to specific stimuli that we are biologically prepared to fear at various stages of our lives. This view, while more complex than Seligman's original suggestion, is also more likely to capture the complexities of human learning.

Advances in the understanding of learning principles are considered by many to be the greatest single contribution of North American psychology. At one time early in the history of behaviorism, research was driven by a stimulus–response model and emphasized control of behavior by the external environment. Over time, this view has broadened a great deal. As we have seen in this chapter, the biological, cognitive, and intrapsychic perspectives have all contributed to

our current understanding of learning as a process involving complex interactions between the environment and an organism that is being changed by its experiences. Partly by way of summary, and partly to emphasize once again how causal factors can interact, this chapter's Understanding Causes feature (page 294) provides an overview of biological, environmental, cognitive, and intrapsychic factors that influence what is learned.

Learning:
Factors Suggested by Theory and Research

$B=f(P,E)$

Causal Factors

Biological
- Evolution-based preparedness factors
- Activation of reward, punishment areas in brain
- Formation of synaptic circuits underlying learning

Cognitive
- Awareness of reinforcement contingencies
- CS-UCS and antecedent-response-outcome expectancies
- Cognitive self-evaluation standards

Intrapsychic
- Personality processes that affect awareness and memory for learning experiences
- Internalized standards that affect self-evaluative processes
- Anxiety that can affect learning, performance, memory

Environmental
- Classical conditioning experiences
- Operant conditioning experiences
- Exposure to modeled behaviors and their consequences

Learning

Learning is a function of interacting personal and environmental causal factors. These factors may vary and may interact with one another in particular ways, depending on the person and the situation.

SUMMARY

The Nature and Scope of Learning

● Learning is a change in behavior or in potential behavior that occurs as a result of experience. Learning is inferred from a change in performance. The three major types of learning are classical conditioning, operant (or instrumental) conditioning, and observational learning, or modeling.

Classical Conditioning: Learning Through Association

● Classical conditioning involves the pairing of an unconditioned stimulus (UCS) with a previously neutral stimulus (CS). The CS alone eventually evokes a conditioned response (CR), which is similar to the unconditioned response (UCR) previously evoked by the UCS.

● The acquisition phase of classical conditioning involves the pairing of the CS with the UCS. Extinction of the CR occurs when the CS is presented repeatedly in the absence of the UCS. Sometimes, however, spontaneous recovery occurs and the CS temporarily evokes a response even after extinction has occurred.

● Stimulus generalization occurs when a CR is evoked by stimuli other than the CS. Generalization depends on how similar the new stimulus is to the original CS. Discrimination is the ability to detect differences among stimuli.

● A wide range of bodily responses can be classically conditioned, and this process is believed to underlie the development of some psychosomatic disorders. The recent discovery that the immune system can be classically conditioned raises the possibility that individuals can be trained to increase or decrease immune reactions and thus enhance their physical health. Conditioned compensatory responses can contribute to drug tolerance and may result in overdose in unfamiliar settings.

● Once a response has been conditioned to a CS, that CS can sometimes be used like a UCS for subsequent classical conditioning of new stimuli. This process, known as higher order conditioning, may be important in attitude formation.

Operant Conditioning: Learning Through Consequences

● Thorndike's law of effect states that responses followed by pleasant or rewarding consequences will be strengthened, while those followed by unpleasant consequences will be weakened. This law is the cornerstone of operant conditioning, so called because the organism operates on its environment to achieve some outcome.

● Many laboratory studies of operant conditioning have been done with rats, pigeons, and other animals. The Skinner box and the cumulative response recorder are important tools for the operant researcher.

● The operant analysis of behavior involves relations between antecedents, behaviors, and consequences. Relations among these elements are called contingencies. Antecedents that signal the likely consequences of particular behaviors in a given situation are known as discriminative stimuli, and behaviors that are heavily influenced by such stimuli are said to be under stimulus control.

● Operant behaviors are emitted behaviors, whereas classically conditioned responses are elicited behaviors. Classically conditioned responses are influenced by what happens before the behavior (that is, by the CS–UCS pairing), whereas operant behaviors are influenced by consequences that occur after the behavior.

Positive Reinforcement

● A positive reinforcer is any stimulus or event that increases the occurrence of a behavior that it follows. Secondary or conditioned reinforcers acquire their value through their association with primary reinforcers which satisfy biological needs.

● Shaping, or the method of successive approximations, involves the reinforcement of behaviors that increasingly resemble the desired behavior.

● In operant conditioning, extinction refers to the weakening and eventual disappearance of a response when it is no longer reinforced.

Schedules of Reinforcement

● Schedules of reinforcement have important effects on learning, performance, and extinction. On a continuous schedule, every response is reinforced. Partial reinforcement schedules involve reinforcement of only some responses. Partial reinforcement may occur on a ratio schedule, in which a certain percentage of responses are reinforced, or on an interval schedule, in which a certain amount of time must pass before a response is reinforced.

● Ratio and interval schedules may be fixed, so that reinforcement always occurs after a fixed number of responses or a fixed time interval, or variable, so that the required number of responses or interval of time varies around some average. Each type of schedule results in a particular pattern of responding.

● Learning occurs most rapidly under continuous reinforcement, but partial schedules produce behaviors that are harder to extinguish.

Negative Reinforcement: Escape and Avoidance Conditioning

● A negative reinforcer is any stimulus that increases a behavior that results in the reinforcer's removal. Escape and avoidance conditioning are two types of learning that result from negative reinforcement. According to the two-factor theory of avoidance conditioning, fear is created through a process of classical conditioning. This fear motivates avoidance behavior, and avoidance behaviors are negatively reinforced and thereby strengthened through fear reduction.

Punishment

● Punishment is a consequence that decreases the occurrence of a behavior that it follows. Punishment can be administered through application of aversive stimuli or removal of reinforcers unrelated to the punished behavior (response cost).

● Aversive punishment can result in a quick suppression of an undesired behavior but can have undesirable side effects. These include generalization of its suppressive effects to other behaviors, development of fear and avoidance, and the modeling of aggressive behaviors. Punishment through response cost avoids some of these side effects.

● Punishment is most effective when desirable alternative behaviors are simultaneously strengthened through positive reinforcement.

Timing of Behavioral Consequences

● In general, immediate consequences have a stronger effect on behavior than delayed ones. Many maladaptive behaviors are maintained because they produce positive immediate consequences, even though the long-term consequences are negative.

Cognition and Learning

● Tolman's experiments on latent learning suggested that learning could occur in the absence of reinforcement and that cognitive factors were involved in the form of expectancies and cognitive maps.

● Cognitive interpretations of classical conditioning suggest that what is learned is an expectancy that the UCS will follow the CS. Studies of the blocking of a new CS by previous conditioning support the cognitive view of classical conditioning.

● Cognitive theorists attribute operant conditioning to the development of expectancies that certain behaviors will produce certain consequences under certain conditions. Research with humans suggests that awareness of re-

SUMMARY—*Continued*

inforcement contingencies greatly facilitates learning.

● Internal self-evaluations can function as rewards and punishers and, in some instances, may override external consequences. Standards for self-reinforcement are acquired through direct learning and through observation of others' standards.

Modeling: Learning Through Observation of Others

● Many behaviors are learned through modeling. Observation of others' behavior is suf-

ficient for learning to occur, but performance is affected by the consequences that the behaviors produce for the model. Emotional responses can also be learned through observation.

Biological Factors and Learning

● The brain determines the organism's ability to learn, but the learning environment also influences brain development.

● Research suggests that there are biological limitations on learning. An animal's evolutionary history may make it prepared to learn

certain associations but contraprepared to learn others.

● Evidence that humans show faster fear conditioning to CSs that have evolutionary significance has led to the suggestion that we are biologically prepared to acquire specific kinds of phobias.

KEY TERMS AND CONCEPTS

antecedent (p. 271)
aversive punishment (p. 279)
avoidance conditioning (p. 278)
baseline (p. 283)
behavior chain (p. 273)
blocking (p. 286)
classical conditioning (p. 263)
compensatory responses (p. 268)
conditioned response (CR) (p. 263)
conditioned stimulus (CS) (p. 263)
consequence (p. 271)
contingency (p. 271)
continuous reinforcement schedule (p. 274)
cumulative recorder (p. 270)
discrimination (p. 265)
discriminative stimuli (p. 271)
elicited behavior (p. 272)
emitted behavior (p. 272)
escape conditioning (p. 277)
expectancy (p. 285)
extinction (p. 264, 273)
fixed schedule (p. 274)

fixed-interval (FI) schedule (p. 276)
fixed-ratio (FR) schedule (p. 274)
flooding (p. 279)
higher order conditioning (p. 269)
instinctive drift (p. 292)
interval schedule (p. 274)
latent learning (p. 285)
law of effect (p. 270)
learning (p. 262)
learning trial (p. 264)
modeling (p. 288)
negative reinforcement (p. 277)
neurotic paradox (p. 281)
operant conditioning (p. 270)
partial (intermittent) reinforcement schedule (p. 274)
positive reinforcer (p. 272)
preparedness (p. 292)
primary reinforcer (p. 272)
psychosomatic disorder (p. 266)
punishment (p. 279)
ratio schedule (p. 274)

response cost (p. 279)
schedule of reinforcement (p. 274)
secondary, or conditioned, reinforcer (p. 272)
self-evaluative processes (p. 288)
self-regulation (p. 282)
shaping (method of successive approximations) (p. 273)
Skinner box (p. 270)
spontaneous recovery (p. 264)
stimulus control (p. 271)
stimulus generalization (p. 265)
time out (p. 274)
two-factor theory of avoidance learning (p. 278)
unconditioned response (UCR) (p. 263)
unconditioned stimulus (UCS) (p. 263)
variable schedule (p. 274)
variable-interval (VI) schedule (p. 276)
variable-ratio (VR) schedule (p. 275)

SUGGESTED READINGS

Bolles, R. C. (1979). *Learning theory* (2nd ed.). New York: Holt, Rinehart & Winston. A good introduction to current theories of learning and their historical development.

Houston, J. P. (1992). *Fundamentals of learning and memory*. Ft. Worth: Harcourt Brace Jovanovich. A readable introduction to learning principles and recent developments in the field.

Watson, D. D., and Tharp, R. G. (1993). *Self-directed behavior: Self-modification for personal adjustment* (6th ed.). Monterey, Calif.: Brooks/Cole. A detailed guide to the personal application of behavioral self-control principles. Contains many concrete examples and suggestions.

Skinner, B. F. (1977). *Upon further reflection.* Englewood Cliffs, N.J.: Prentice-Hall. A fascinating autobiographical glimpse into the career of this eminent scientist.

Memory

CHAPTER OUTLINE

**W**hen he was 7 years old, H. M. suffered a head injury in a bicycle accident. At first, it appeared that there were no ill effects, but 3 years later he had his first mild seizure. The seizures became progressively worse over the next 6 years, and medication had little effect on the major seizures that began when H. M. was 16 years old. By the time he was 27, the seizures were out of control, and so his doctors decided on a drastic treatment involving surgical removal of the area in the limbic system where the seizures began. In 1953 the doctors removed a portion of the brain that included most of the hippocampus and nearby cortical tissue.

The surgery had the hoped-for effect of reducing H. M.'s seizures, but an unexpected problem soon became apparent: H. M. could no longer learn new facts or remember recent experiences. He still cannot to this day. In effect, H. M.'s memory for events contains nothing after 1953. He lives in an eternal present, a prisoner of the moment.

If you met H. M., he would probably appear quite normal, since he has lost none of his language or social skills, but he would not remember you if you came to see him again the next day. He forgets the names of his doctors within minutes, no matter how often he is introduced to them. H. M. cannot remember that one of his favorite uncles has died, and so he experiences shock and grief each time he hears of his uncle's death. Within a few minutes, he forgets that he has mowed the lawn or eaten, and he cannot enjoy television stories because he quickly loses track of the plot. Here, he describes what his existence is like:

> Every day is alone in itself, whatever enjoyment I've had and whatever sorrow I've had. . . . Right now, I'm wondering, have I done anything amiss? You see, at this moment, everything looks clear to me, but what happened just before? It's like waking from a dream. I just don't remember (Milner, 1970, p. 37).

H. M. has been followed closely by several memory researchers for nearly 40 years (Corkin, 1984; Scoville & Milner, 1957). His case illustrates some of the complexities of human memory, and it raises some intriguing questions: What prevents H. M. from remembering experiences, while at the same time leaving all of the skills he has learned intact? Why is it that he can learn new skills and not remember having learned them? For example, H. M. has learned through repeated attempts how to solve a very complicated mechanical puzzle, but he will swear each time that he has never seen it before, and he will need to have the instructions for the task repeated. Are there different memory systems located at various places in the brain, each dealing with different kinds of in-

formation? In this chapter, we will explore these and other questions.

As we have seen in earlier chapters, many human responses are learned. We often respond to the present in the light of past experience, and our ability to record our experiences and make use of that record in the course of our daily activities is one of the most important of our mental capabilities. Every day, you use memory to deal with immediate problems—to understand what another person is saying to you, to learn information contained in textbooks, to find your way from one place to another, to recognize people you've met before—the list is endless.

Memory refers to the processes that allow us to record experiences and information and to retrieve that information later. The information may be maintained for any length of time, ranging from a split second to an entire lifetime. In this chapter, we will explore what has been learned in over a century of psychological and biological research on how we remember, why we forget, and how we can improve memory. First, let us consider how memory is studied.

Research Approaches to Memory

As a psychobiological phenomenon, memory can be approached from either a psychological or a biological perspective. Psychological approaches seek to describe and understand how memory operates and what variables affect it. This approach has spawned many theories of memory, as well as an enormous amount of research on memory and forgetting. Much of this research has been carried out in the experimental psychologist's laboratory, but memory is increasingly being studied outside the laboratory in real-world settings (Loftus, 1991; Tulving, 1991).

Physiological approaches to memory search for the neural processes that underlie the formation and retrieval of memories, as well as the brain structures involved in memory (Gormezano & Wasserman, 1992). A bit later in the chapter, we will consider some recent breakthroughs in knowledge about the neural bases of memory.

The psychological approach to memory has a long research tradition. A pioneer in this work was Hermann Ebbinghaus, who published a series of insightful studies in 1885 (see Figure 10.1). Ebbinghaus studied only one subject—himself. To provide material to memorize that would be uncontaminated by previous learning, Ebbinghaus created 2,300 **nonsense syllables,** meaningless letter combinations that consisted of a vowel sandwiched between two consonants (for example *biv, zaj, xew*). He made up lists of syllables and studied the memory process by reading the items aloud, then covering up the list, trying to recite the syllables from memory, and counting the number that he recalled correctly. Ebbinghaus's dedication to his scientific quest was quite remarkable; in one study, he went through over 14,000 practice repetitions as he tried to memorize 420 lists of nonsense syllables (Slamecka, 1985).

One of Ebbinghaus's major interests was the course of forgetting. In one series of studies, he retested his memory at various time intervals after mastering a list of nonsense syllables. His findings are presented in Figure 10.2. As you can see, forgetting occurred rapidly at first, as he was able to recall less than half of the syllables on a list after an hour's time interval. The steep drop-off in retention probably occurred because the nonsense syllables were quite meaningless. As we shall see later, the forgetting of meaningful material is far less pronounced (Houston, 1992).

The Measurement of Memory

Some of the methods for measuring memory that were introduced by Ebbinghaus are still used today. In his list-learning studies, he used the method of **recall,** which required that he reproduce material from memory without any cues. In an academic setting, recall is required on an essay examination or an oral quiz. In the **cued recall** method, "hints" are given that may stimulate recall of memories that are not accessible. For example, Ebbinghaus tried to stimulate recall of a list by uncovering the first word. The ability of subjects to recall information in response to cues has demonstrated that memories that cannot be spontaneously recalled may nevertheless persist and may be activated by appropriate cues (Humphreys & Tehan, 1992).

Another method of assessing memory is through **recognition,** as when eyewitnesses are asked to identify a person from a series of mug shots. The academic analogue of this procedure is the multiple-choice test. Recognition seems to involve a kind of matching process. We consider a given stimulus and decide whether it matches something already stored in memory.

A third measure of memory that has been used in research is the method of **relearning.** Here, the dif-

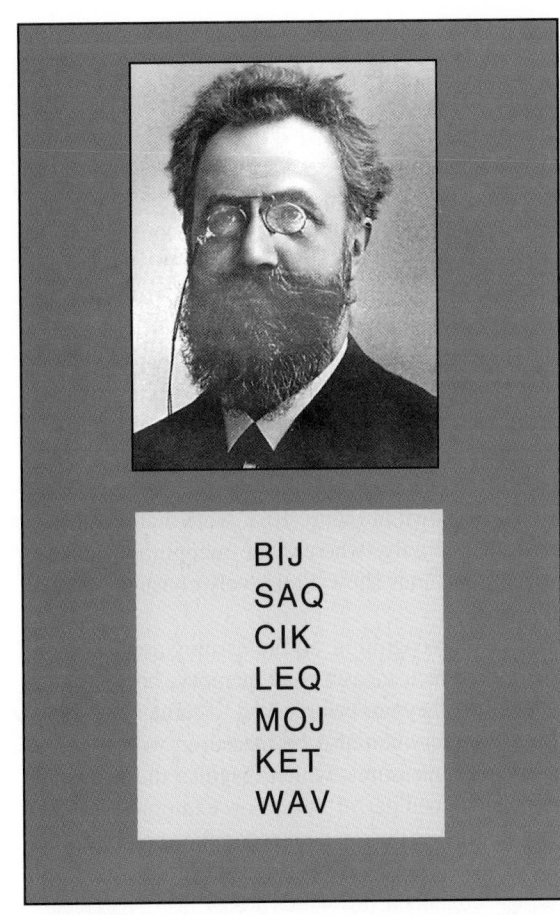

Figure 10.1 *Hermann Ebbinghaus was a pioneer in the experimental study of memory. He invented the nonsense syllable to provide himself with meaningless material to learn and remember.*

BIJ
SAQ
CIK
LEQ
MOJ
KET
WAV

ference between the amount of time (or number of trials) needed to recall material originally and the time (or trials) needed to learn it again (the *savings score*) measures how much of the material was retained. Ebbinghaus found that he could go back to a list of nonsense syllables he could no longer recall and relearn it much faster (that is, in fewer trials) than he had originally. Subjects may believe they "can't re-

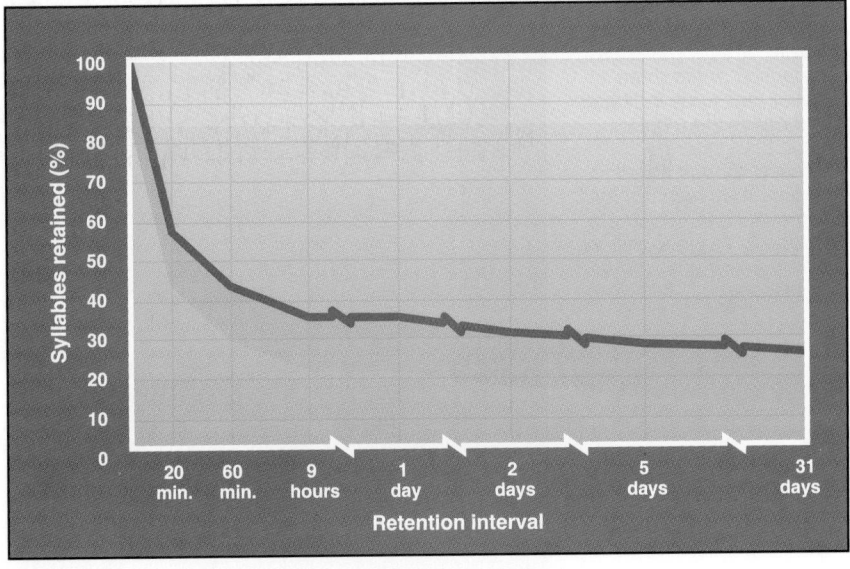

Figure 10.2 *Hermann Ebbinghaus's forgetting curve shows a rapid loss of memory for nonsense syllables at first, then a much more gradual decline. The rapid decline is probably due to the meaningless nature of the nonsense syllables. (Data from Ebbinghaus, 1885).*

member anything'' and recall none of the material, yet may be able to relearn it faster the second time around. Thus, reviewing for an exam will take less time and be more effective if the material was studied on previous occasions. Savings may be found even when the material was originally learned years before. Ebbinghaus did find, however, that the longer the time interval between learning and relearning, the less the savings. The greatest loss of savings occurred in the first day or so (Ebbinghaus, 1885).

Do you prefer essay exams or multiple-choice tests? Many students find multiple-choice tests easier. Consistent with these students' beliefs, recognition is an easier memory task than recall (Greene, 1992). The difference between the three memory measures is clearly shown in Figure 10.3. Note that recall falls off rather rapidly, whereas the recognition and relearning methods show a relatively constant residual after a day.

Recall, recognition, and relearning are called *explicit,* or direct, measures of memory, because subjects know they are being asked to remember something. Memory can also be measured with *implicit,* or indirect, measures, which disguise the testing of memory (Roediger, 1990). For example, subjects may insist that they cannot remember any item in a list of words they have learned. Let us assume that the list contained the words KITCHEN, MONTANA, and DEFEND. In a later task, the subjects are given word stems like KIT_____, MO_____, and DE_____ and asked to complete each stem to form a word. Subjects often come up with the words on the original list, even though they say they cannot remember them. This has occurred in studies of both brain-damaged and normal subjects, indicating that the memory for the word was indeed present, even though it could not be retrieved (and in the case of some brain-damaged subjects, even though they did not recall having seen the original list). The presence of the stem has cued the memory (Schacter, 1992).

Having considered some of the ways in which memory is studied, let us consider the nature of memory itself.

Perspectives on the Nature of Memory

The study of memory can be approached from a number of perspectives. First, we might explore the different *contents of memory* and consider the possibility that there are distinct kinds of memory. We see, for example, that H. M. can acquire new skills but that he cannot remember new experiences. Is memory for skills different from memory for events?

Second, we might view memory from an *information processing* perspective and ask what goes on between exposure to new information and later recall of that information. Here, we would be concerned not with memory contents but with the *processes* that govern how memory takes in and stores information.

Finally, we might explore the structure, or *architecture,* of memory and ask what the components of the memory system are and how they relate to one another. For example, our observations of H. M. might suggest that there is a part of the memory system that transfers new information to a relatively permanent storage system and that this mechanism was destroyed by the surgery in 1953. Let us further explore the three different perspectives.

Types of Memory: Episodic, Semantic, and Procedural Memory

What are we to infer about the nature of memory from our encounter with Patient H. M.? We find that he is capable of learning new skills, such as solving the complex mechanical puzzle, but has no recall of the previous occasions on which he worked on the puzzle. Although he is capable of learning new skills, his memory for personal experiences seems absent. Observations like these, as well as experimental research with animals indicating that selective brain damage can eliminate certain learned responses while preserving others, have led cognitive scientists to conclude that there are indeed distinct, though interacting, memory systems that process and store different kinds

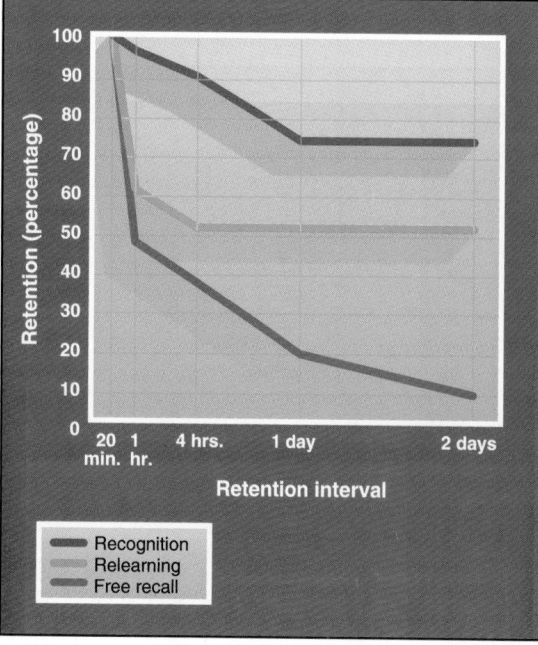

▶ **Figure 10.3** *Memory can be measured by recall, recognition, or time required to relearn (a measure of savings). This comparison of the three retrieval measures indicates that recall is the most difficult task, and the continued drop in recall over time may reflect a loss in retrieval cues, which are provided in the recognition and relearning procedures. (Luh, 1922).*

of memories (Squire & Zola-Morgan, 1991; Tulving & Schacter, 1990).

Three major types of memory have been identified by various theorists: episodic, semantic, and procedural (Tulving, 1972; Squire, 1987, 1992; see Figure 10.4). **Episodic memory** is personal, factual, and autobiographical. It is a store of information about past experiences—when, where, and what happened. It deals with episodes—the fact that I had chicken and white wine for dinner last Friday, the fact that one of my student research assistants came to see me a few minutes ago, the fact that I have to go to the dentist tomorrow afternoon, and so on. Episodic memory is constantly changing; information is rapidly lost as new information comes in (although it may be retrieved if we have the proper cues).

Semantic memory, in contrast, is organized, relatively stable knowledge about the world and language. It includes memory for words, concepts, rules, and abstract ideas. We make use of semantic memory when we read, converse, or solve problems. When we use the word *memory,* for instance, we're referring to a general concept that we have learned and stored in semantic memory.

A third type of memory, **procedural memory,** is our repository of skills. It consists of certain responses that are appropriate in particular situations, such as how to type, ride a bicycle, or shoot a basketball. Whereas the contents of episodic and semantic memory may be verbalized, causing some theorists to refer to them as **declarative memory,** procedural memories are those we use for doing rather than describing. These skill-related memories can replay without the need for conscious recollection. For this reason, procedural memory is sometimes referred to as **nondeclarative,** or **implicit, memory.**

Applying the concept of multiple memory systems to the case of H. M. sheds some light on his puzzling memory pattern. It appears that his procedural memory has not been lost, whereas his declarative memory system (particularly episodic memory), has been devastated by his brain damage. According to a number of contemporary theorists, the best way to account for the complexity and flexibility of human memory is to think of procedural, semantic, and episodic memory as distinct, though interrelated, systems (Tulving & Schacter, 1990). As we shall see, there is mounting evidence from neuropsychological studies that the operation of these memory systems may involve different operating modules in the brain (Squire & Zola-Morgan, 1991; Squire, 1992).

Information Processing Concepts: Encoding, Storage, and Retrieval

Another way to approach memory is in terms of its operating principles. Many of today's cognitive sci-

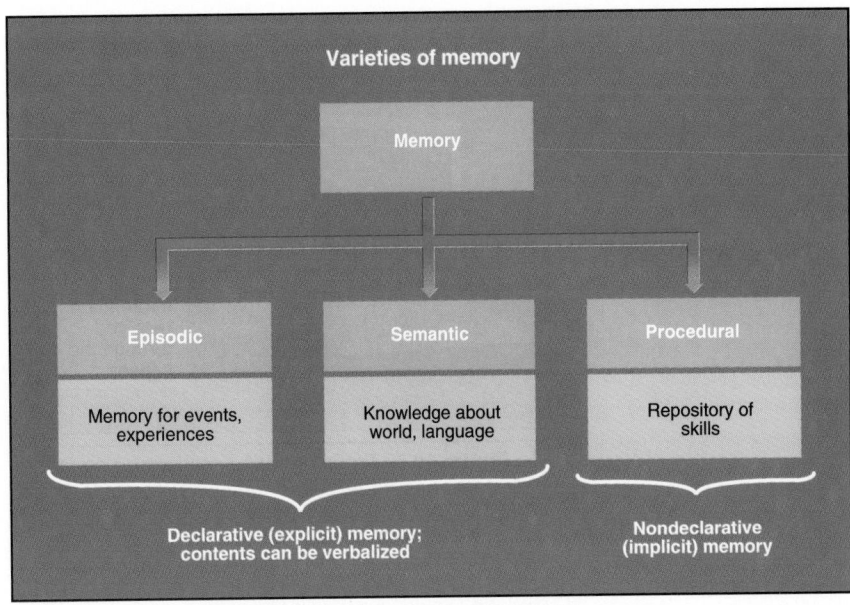

▲ **Figure 10.4** *Some theories have divided memory into three types: episodic, semantic, and procedural. Episodic and semantic memory are declarative, or explicit; their contents can be verbalized. Procedural memory is nondeclarative, or implicit; its contents cannot readily be verbalized.*

entists view memory as an information processing system and draw parallels between how we think and how other information processing systems, particularly computers, operate (Hunt, 1989). Where memory is concerned, there are some obvious parallels, and cognitive psychologists suggest that units of information are stored in the brain in much the same way that bits of information are stored in a computer's data bank. From this perspective, memory involves three important processes: **encoding** of information so that it can be incorporated into memory; **storage** of the information in the "memory bank"; and later **retrieval** of the information from memory (see Figure 10.5).

Encoding is the translation of incoming sensory information into the neural code that your brain can process. This is a little like what happens when a computer keyboard translates keystrokes into an electrical code that the internal processing system of the computer can understand. Once into the system, this input must be processed and then saved in memory so that the information can be stored indefinitely. Finally, there must be a way of retrieving the stored information from memory by giving the system certain cues for retrieval. In some respects, retrieving a fact or a memory of an experience is a bit like giving your computer the software commands that transfer, or retrieve, information from the computer's memory back to the screen where you can view it.

As we shall see, the concepts of encoding, storage, and retrieval help us to understand many important aspects of remembering (and forgetting), and they do

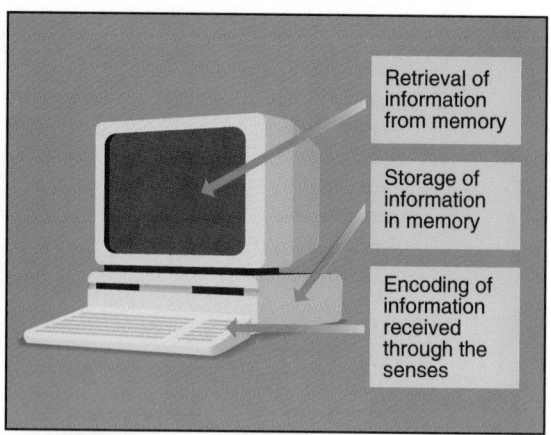

Figure 10.5 *The information processing concepts of encoding, storage, and retrieval are useful in understanding memory processes. Using the computer analogy, encoding is similar to entering data into a computer through the keyboard; storage is analogous to saving the information on a computer disk; and retrieval is similar to calling up the information from the computer's memory onto the screen with the appropriate commands, or retrieval cues.*

seem to describe some of the cognitive and underlying neural processes that occur between initial exposure to new information and later retrieval of it. Nonetheless, cognitive scientists rightfully point out that human memory processes are infinitely more complex than what goes on in a computer. When the human organism receives new information, the information is recoded and related to other contents of memory to create a changed pattern of total information within the storage system. Thus, memory is a highly dynamic

and ever-changing system whose complexity cannot be fully captured by any existing information processing model.

Architectural Concepts: The Structure of Memory

The concepts of encoding, storage, and retrieval relate to the processes of the memory system—that is, to what it does. We can also approach memory from the perspective of what the system is like and how it carries out these processes. We do this by considering what are called **architectural concepts,** which pertain to the structure of memory (Estes, 1991).

The architectural description of memory that most cognitive psychologists use today is a modification of ideas developed in the late 1960s by Richard Atkinson and Richard Shiffrin (1968). The current model is shown in graphic form in Figure 10.6. It consists of three major components: the sensory registers; the short-term or working memory system; and the long-term memory system.

The **sensory registers** are the initial information processors. They hold incoming information from the senses long enough for it to be evaluated and recognized. The **short-term memory** holds the information that people are conscious of at any given time. It is sometimes called **working memory** because conscious mental processing of information occurs in the short-term store. Finally, **long-term memory** is essentially a limitless store of all the declarative and procedural information that we know. Atkinson and

Figure 10.6 *Current architectural concepts of memory have three major components: (1) sensory registers, which receive incoming sensory information and hold it briefly so that it can be interpreted and given meaning; (2) a short-term (working) memory to which information is transferred from the sensory registers through a process of selected attention; and (3) a long-term memory, which can store information for lengthy periods, and perhaps permanently. When we remember, information is retrieved from long-term memory into short-term memory. (Based on Atkinson & Shiffrin, 1977).*

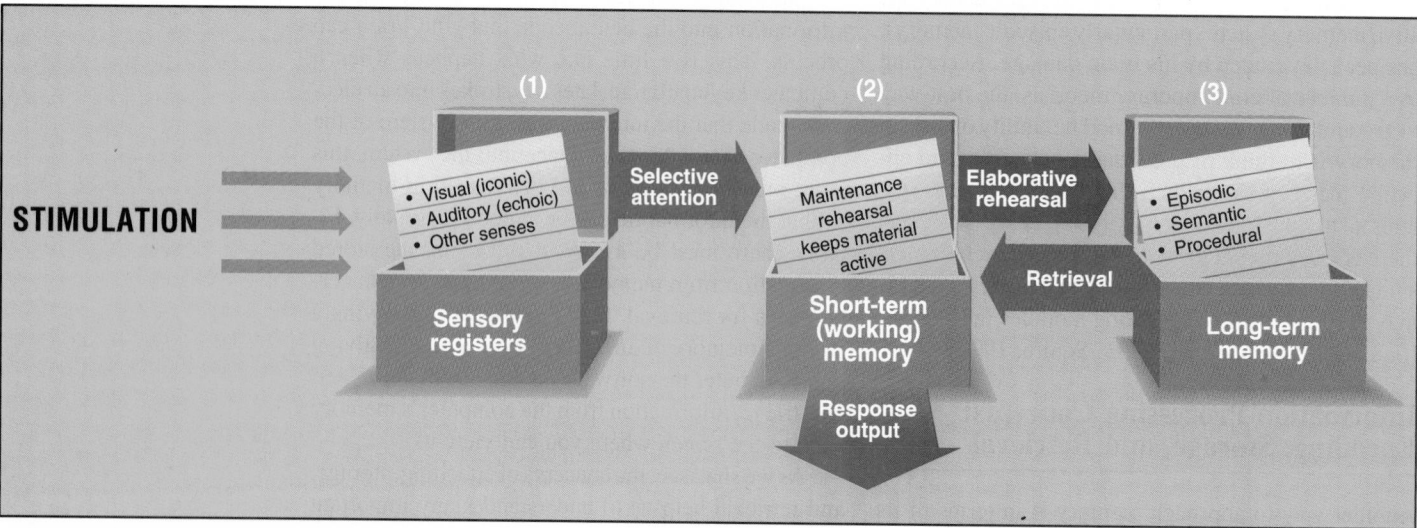

Shiffrin assume that people don't forget because they run out of space to store new information in long-term memory. Instead, they either (a) fail to put information into the long-term store at all or (b) put it in in such a way that it can't be retrieved when it is needed, rather as if they had misfiled a book in a library and then couldn't find it.

Let us examine the properties of these processing systems in more detail. Keep in mind that we should not assume that these units correspond with specific parts of the brain; they may involve the interrelated activities of many neural sites. The terms are being used by these theorists in a more abstract sense.

The Sensory Registers

When information first enters the sensory system (for example, the eyes or ears), it is stored very briefly and in its entirety in a sensory register connected to that sense (see Figure 10.7). The sensory registers hold incoming sensory information just long enough for recognition to occur. To examine the visual register, try glancing about you and then close your eyes and attempt to visualize what you just saw. You will see a fading image, rather like a picture that is being washed away. The visual register is called the **iconic store,** and the representation of visual input is called an *icon,* meaning copy or image (Neisser, 1967).

In 1960, George Sperling, a psychologist working at Bell Telephone Laboratories, conducted a classic experiment that illustrated some of the properties of the iconic store. Sperling showed subjects visual displays consisting of arrays of letters like the one shown in Figure 10.8. The arrays were presented through a tachistoscope for a very short time, about 1/20 of a second. The subjects were then asked to report as many letters as they could. They typically reported three to five letters, usually starting at the upper left-hand side of the array.

Sperling wondered if the subjects had processed the whole array, only to have their memories fade in the few seconds it took them to report the few letters they did. To test this possibility, Sperling repeated the experiment in a slightly different way. He told the subjects that they would be asked to report only one row of letters, but he didn't tell them which one. As soon as the stimulus disappeared, Sperling presented either a high, a medium, or a low tone, which signaled the observer to report either the first, the second, or the third row of the array. If the tone occurred within a few tenths of a second, subjects could report an entire row correctly. However, if the tone was delayed by more than a second, recall performance declined drastically. Sperling concluded that the subjects were "reading" a highly detailed, but rapidly fading, visual image. They had time to read any one of the lines, even if they did not know which

Figure 10.7 *The sensory registers take in enormous amounts of information, but most of it fades away almost immediately. What we choose to attend to, or what attracts our attention, is processed further by short-term memory.*

one it would be until the tone sounded, but the image was gone before they could read the entire array. As shown in Figure 10.8, by the time one second had elapsed, subjects' ability to report one line of letters (that is, their partial report) was no better than their ability to report the entire array (their whole report), suggesting that the image had faded. Sperling's study, as well as many others, indicates that it is very dif-

Figure 10.8 *In Sperling's study, subjects viewed arrays of letters like that in the insert, then were asked to report either the top, middle, or bottom row after varying intervals. The results indicate that the image of the array had faded from the iconic register within a second, whereupon partial report was no better than recall for the entire array. (Adapted from Sperling, 1960).*

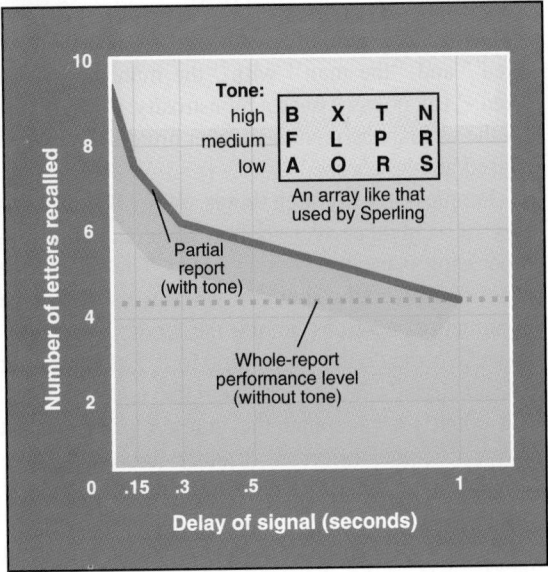

ficult, perhaps impossible, to retain information in purely visual form for more than a fraction of a second (Barsalou, 1992).

Other researchers have studied the auditory sensory register, which is called the **echoic store** (as in echo). This can be done by presenting sets of numbers or letters simultaneously through speakers situated to the left, middle, or right of the subject, then using a flashing light to indicate which of the sets should be reported (Darwin & others, 1972). Such studies yield results similar to Sperling's, but they suggest that the auditory memory lasts longer, perhaps for several seconds (Baddeley & Logie, 1992).

Without further processing, icons, echoes, and other sensory memories simply fade away. Processes of selective attention to specific stimuli control what is processed further by the next component of the model, the short-term store.

Short-Term (Working) Memory

Roughly speaking, short-term, or working, memory is memory for the things that are the focus of attention at the moment (Goldman-Rakic, 1992). Short-term memory is also quite limited, but not in the same way as the sensory registers. The short-term memory can hold material for perhaps 30 seconds—much longer than the sensory registers—but the amount it can hold is more limited.

Consider the following example. It's easy to understand the sentence "The rat ate the cheese." It's not hard to understand the sentence "The rat the cat chased ate the cheese." But the sentence "The rat the cat the woman owned chased ate the cheese" sounds a bit odd. It is a defensible English sentence, however; "the rat" can be replaced with "the rat the cat chased," and the sentence is still grammatically correct. Similarly, "the cat" can be replaced with "the cat the woman owned." We could go further, replacing "the woman" with "the woman the man liked" and "the man" with "the man the banker hired." But now we have a monstrosity: "The rat the cat the woman the man the banker hired liked owned chased ate the cheese."

People don't say such things. Why? Because this sort of sentence overwhelms their information-processing capacity. We can hold "The rat ate the cheese" in working memory while we sort out the grammatical relations among the words in the sentence. We can do the same thing for "The rat the cat chased ate the cheese," although this is a bit harder. But when we encounter the monster sentence just given, comprehension is virtually impossible. We simply cannot store the whole thing in working memory.

Short-term memory has a limited capacity, but just how limited is it? A great many studies using many different kinds of memory tasks indicate that people can hold no more than five to nine meaningful items in short-term memory, leading George Miller (1956) to set the capacity limit at "the magical number seven, plus or minus two."

To illustrate this point, read the line of letters below to yourself (about one per second). Then cover the line of letters and try to recall as many as you can, writing the letters on a sheet of paper in the order presented.

S R I M I B G B K I B F X T A

How did you do? You did quite well if you remembered four to eight of the 15 letters in order. Now suppose the letters just given are rearranged as follows:

IRS IBM KGB FBI TAX

Try reading and reproducing this sequence. You will find that the memory task is much easier. The limit on verbal short-term memory is a limit on the number of meaningful *units* that can be recalled, and in the new list the original 15 individual letters have been combined into five units that are meaningful. The combining of individual items into a larger unit of meaning is called **chunking.** As you can see, chunking can be a great aid to recall (see also Figure 10.9).

⬥ **Figure 10.9** *The impressive abilities of professional interpreters would not be possible if they translated from one language to another on a word-by-word basis. Instead, they chunk units of meaning consisting of phrases and sentences and then translate them.*

Maintenance Rehearsal. If retention of information in working memory is limited to 30 seconds or so, it is clear that, if we are to retain the information for a longer period of time, we have to either process it rather quickly or find a way to keep it active in working memory. How do we do this?

Perhaps the most common method for keeping material active in short-term memory is through **maintenance rehearsal.** An example of such rehearsal occurs when you look up a telephone number and keep repeating it to yourself so that you will not forget it while you wait to use a phone. It appears that maintenance rehearsal involves a kind of internal speech and that the information is reentered into short-term memory as it is ''heard'' again and again (Baddeley, 1982). If so, then it should be possible to demonstrate almost instantaneous forgetting when processing in working memory is interrupted before transfer of the information to long-term memory can take place.

Everyone has experienced this kind of instantaneous forgetting. Have you ever been introduced to someone, begun a conversation with that person, and then suddenly realized that you didn't have the foggiest idea what his or her name was? This occurred because the words in the conversation took over working memory before you had a chance to store the name.

Exactly the same phenomenon has been demonstrated experimentally. For example, Lloyd and Margaret Peterson (1959) presented subjects with syllables consisting of three consonants, such as BSX, followed by a three-digit number, such as 140. The subjects were then asked to count backward by threes from the number. If they counted backwards for as long as 18 seconds and were then asked to recall the letters, they could no longer do so (see Figure 10.10). The counting-backward task prevented rehearsal of the letters in working memory and disrupted the transfer of information to long-term memory.

Elaborative Rehearsal. Maintenance rehearsal alone does not guarantee that the information will be transferred into long-term memory. More permanent storage occurs when we go beyond simply repeating a piece of information to ourselves and engage in **elaborative rehearsal** by focusing on the meaning of the information, relating it to other things we know, or forming an image of it. In reading, for example, the general meaning of the information is what is typically coded, rather than the individual words. When you finish this paragraph, you will not be able to reproduce the exact words it contained, but you will remember its gist, or meaning. If you tried to remember all the words, your working memory would be quickly overwhelmed.

Rehearsal helps keep material alive in short-term memory, but it also aids in the transfer of material to long-term memory. Indeed, the two stores interact constantly (see Figure 10.11). Information from long-term memory allows us to interpret material in short-term memory. For example, without input from long-term semantic memory, you could not interpret the funny black squiggles you are visually processing at this moment. Moreover, once you do ''understand'' what you now have in the short-term memory store, you must relate that information to other information in episodic or semantic long-term memory. Long-

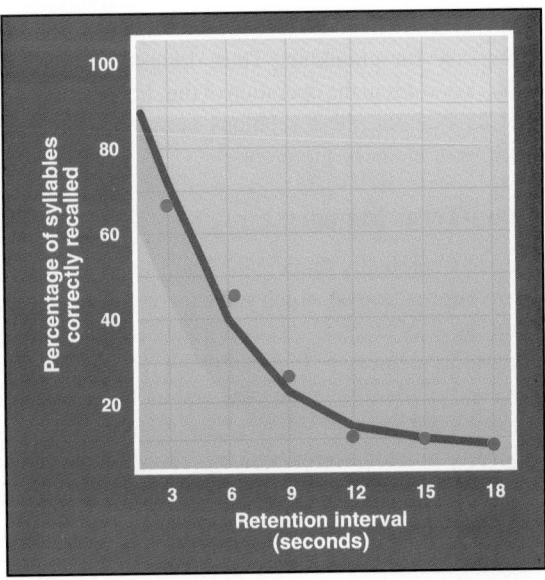

Figure 10.10 *Results of the Peterson and Peterson experiment. Subjects who were prevented from rehearsing three-letter syllables in working memory showed almost no recall of the letters within 18 seconds, illustrating the rapid decay of short-term memory. (Peterson & Peterson, 1959).*

Figure 10.11 *The distinction between short-term and long-term memory can have practical as well as theoretical significance.*

''The matters about which I'm being questioned, Your Honor, are all things I should have included in my long-term memory but which I mistakenly inserted in my short-term memory.''
(Drawing by Fisher, © 1983 The New Yorker Magazine, Inc.)

term semantic memory also provides the information necessary for chunking. Thus, long-term memory plays key roles in the operation of the short-term store. Let us examine these relations between short- and long-term memory more closely.

Long-Term Memory

You have probably spent many hours trying to memorize information on which you expected to be tested. Your goal, of course, was to store the information in long-term memory so that you could retrieve it when necessary. Memorization appears to be a process whereby information in working memory is ''implanted'' into long-term memory. Therefore, the content of long-term memory is determined by how we encode the material while it is in working memory.

List-learning experiments using a free recall procedure have taught researchers a great deal about the transfer from short-term to long-term memory. In a typical experiment, subjects are asked to recall a list of unrelated words immediately after the list has been presented. They can recall the words in any order they wish (hence the designation ''free recall''). The results typically reveal that (1) the easiest words to recall are the two or three at the end of the list; (2) the next-easiest words to recall are those at the beginning of the list; and (3) the words in the middle of the list are hardest to recall. This is illustrated more formally in Figure 10.12*a*, which shows the **serial position curve** that results when recall of a word is plotted as

a function of the word's position in a list. The same results have occurred in numerous studies, giving rise to the terms **primacy effect** and **recency effect** to describe the superior recall of the earliest-presented and the most recently presented words, respectively. Note that the primacy and recency effects occur whether 10-, 20-, or 30-word lists are used.

What is responsible for the primacy and recency effects? The answer to this question provides one reason why we distinguish between long-term and short-term memory. Consider what happens at the very beginning of a list-remembering task. As the first two or three words enter a subject's short-term memory, she can concentrate on and rehearse them, thereby ensuring that they are somehow ''written into'' long-term memory. However, as the list gets longer, her short-term memory fills up, so she cannot attend to any single item for long. Hence, it is hard to store information about the items in the middle of the list and, therefore, harder to learn those items.

As for why the recency effect occurs, one explanation is that these items are still in short-term memory when the list is recalled. That is, if the subject is allowed to begin reciting immediately after the experimenter stops reading the list, she will still have the last few words in working memory. She can simply read them out of the short-term store before she tries to recall any information from long-term memory.

If this explanation is correct, then we should be able to wipe out the recency effect by eliminating the recall from short-term memory. There are in fact at least two ways to do this. First, if the recall test is delayed for a minute or so, the last words will have faded from short-term memory, and they will be recalled no better than the words in the middle of the list (see Figure 10.12*b*). We can also eliminate the recency effect by asking the subject to do an arithmetic task, such as counting backwards from a number by threes, immediately after hearing the list (Glanzer & Cunitz, 1966). This time, the last words will be poorly recalled because the arithmetic task will occupy working memory and ''bump out'' the words at the end of the list.

These simple list-learning demonstrations illustrate two important facts about long-term memory. First, long-term memory depends on information transferred from working memory. Second, the information transferred will be determined by how attention is focused when the information is presented. A great many facts about human memory can be viewed as amplifications of these two principles, as we will see in the following sections.

To summarize, we have discussed three architectural components of memory: sensory registers, short-term (working) memory, and long-term memory. As we have seen, each has different characteristics and

➤ **Figure 10.12** *Immediate recall of word lists produces serial position curves like those in* (a), *where primacy and recency effects are both evident. However, as shown in* (b), *even a short delay of 30 seconds in recall eliminates the recency effect, indicating that the later items in the word list have disappeared from short-term memory. (Adapted from Postman & Phillips, 1965).*

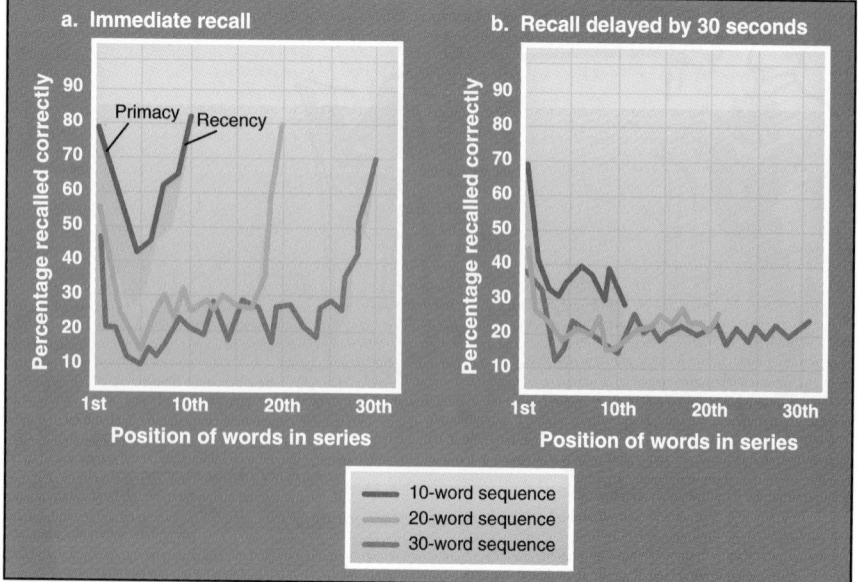

Table 10.1 The Three Architectural Components of Memory

Feature	Sensory Registers	Short-Term (Working) Memory	Long-Term Memory
Means of Entry	From sense organs	Selective attention	Elaborative rehearsal
Maintenance	Not possible	Maintenance rehearsal	Organization
Format	Literal copy of input	Largely acoustic (some imagery and semantic)	Largely semantic (some auditory and visual)
Capacity	Large	Small (7 ± 2 items)	Apparently unlimited
Loss	Decay, in seconds	Displacement (possibly decay)	Loss of retrieval cues or interference (possibly no loss)
Duration	¼–2 seconds	Up to 30 seconds	Minutes to years

capacities. Table 10.1 summarizes their major features.

Today's memory researchers are proceeding along two converging tracks. Cognitive scientists are studying the nature and types of memory to understand its information-processing principles and capabilities. Meanwhile, psychobiologists are gaining new insights into the "hardware" of memory—the physiological structures and processes that underlie the forms of memory we have discussed. The following feature focuses on some of this work.

PSYCHOBIOLOGICAL INTERACTIONS

The Physiology of Memory

The study of the biological bases of memory is one of the most active areas of psychobiological research. Technological advances, such as the new scanning devices, have provided tools of discovery that are making it possible to pursue the answers to a number of critical questions. Let us review some of the answers that are emerging.

Are There Distinct Kinds of Memory?

This chapter has made a number of distinctions among various types of memory—episodic, semantic, and procedural; short and long term; declarative and implicit. Do these distinctions have any basis in physical reality?

There is considerable research evidence to support the idea that these different types of memory do indeed have different biological underpinnings. One line of evidence comes from studies by neuropsychologists who have investigated how physical injuries to the brain influence memory. As we have seen, in some cases brain-damaged patients can retain short-term memories (that is, memories for events extending over a few seconds) but cannot retain memories for events once their "stream of consciousness" has been interrupted. The most famous of these cases involve people like H. M. who have suffered damage to the hippocampus, a banana-shaped structure in the limbic system, and adjacent cortical areas (see Figure 10.13). This area has been termed the **medial temporal lobe memory system** (Squire & Zola-Morgan, 1991). People whose hippocampus has been damaged can remember things that are in working memory; for instance, they can repeat a phone number, provided that they are asked to do so immediately. However, these patients do not display any long-term memory for events that occurred after their injury. Thus, a hippocampal patient may meet the same person day after day and have to be introduced again each time. They also display normal semantic memory for knowledge acquired prior to their injury. However, they do not acquire new semantic knowledge based on events that occurred after their injury. For example, one amnesic patient could recall the names of presidents who had been elected before the injury occurred, but not the names of presidents elected after the injury (Squire, 1987).

On the basis of studies of brain-damaged humans as well as experimental studies with monkeys, Larry Squire and Stuart Zola-Morgan (1991) have concluded that working memory is carried

There is also physiological evidence for the distinction between declarative (episodic and semantic) memory and procedural memory. Again, the medial temporal lobe memory system plays a prominent role in the distinction. Although, as we have seen, evidence demonstrates that this system is important in both declarative forms of memory, it appears *not* to be involved in the formation of procedural memories. Thus, individuals with hippocampal damage can learn procedural tasks similar to learning to type the same sequence of letters over and over again. What is striking, however, is that even though their performance improves, they don't remember learning the task. In other words, they display procedural knowledge based on training but have no declarative knowledge of having been trained.

Where in the Brain Are Memories Formed?

For more than 60 years, neuroscientists have been trying to map the neural circuitry of memory. Their findings suggest that there is not a single "memory center" somewhere in the brain. Instead, many areas of the brain interact with one another, with both cortical and subcortical areas involved in the encoding, storage, and retrieval of memories.

Recent discoveries do suggest, however, that different brain areas play particularly important roles in certain types of memory. Using a PET scan to record glucose activity in the brain as subjects learned and recalled a verbal task, researchers found that most of the brain activity occurred in the hippocampus while the subjects were learning the words. When they tried to recall the words, however, activity was concentrated not only in the hippocampus but also in the frontal lobes of the cerebral cortex, an area known to be involved in complex thinking (Squire, 1992).

Research by Richard Thompson and his co-workers indicates that the cerebellum, an ancient brain structure involved in control of movement, (see Figure 10.13), may be an important site for procedural memories (Thompson, 1985; Thompson & Steinmetz, 1992). The researchers established a conditioned eyeblink response in rabbits by pairing a tone (the CS) with a puff of air in the eye (the UCS). As the animal learned the conditioned response, electrical recordings revealed increased electrical activity in the cerebellum. Later, Thompson found that removing a tiny portion of the cerebellum completely abolished the memory for blinking—a very basic procedural memory—when the tone occurred.

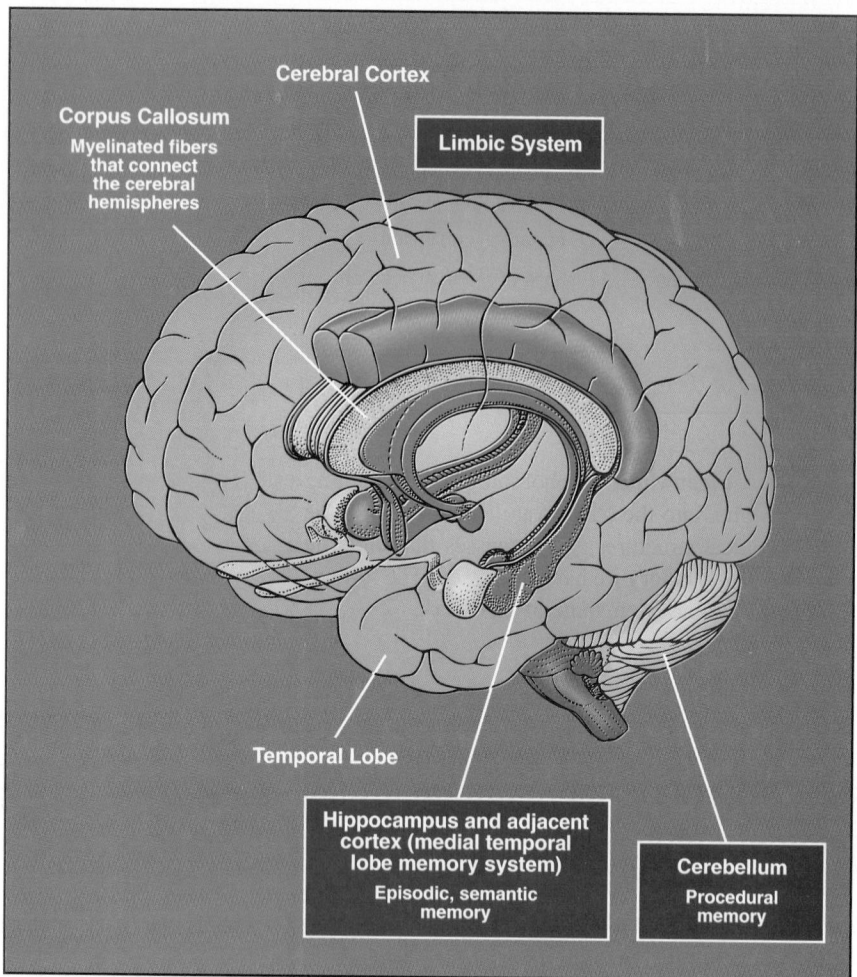

Corpus Callosum
Myelinated fibers that connect the cerebral hemispheres

Cerebral Cortex

Limbic System

Temporal Lobe

Hippocampus and adjacent cortex (medial temporal lobe memory system)
Episodic, semantic memory

Cerebellum
Procedural memory

◆ **Figure 10.13** *Numerous areas of the brain interact in memory, but several areas are particularly involved in certain types of memory. The medial temporal lobe memory system, which includes the hippocampus and adjacent cortex, is involved in episodic and semantic memory. The cerebellum seems to be an important site for procedural memories. The cerebral cortex plays a role in all types of memory.*

out in the cerebral cortex, where perceptual input from the sensory registers is processed and interpreted. However, they believe that the activity of the medial temporal lobe memory system is needed to temporarily bind together the storage sites in the cortex where the long-term memory will eventually be formed, at least until the cortical memory is firmly established. In the absence of this binding, permanent memories will not be formed in the cortex (Squire, 1992).

Experimental studies support this analysis. Monkeys whose medial temporal lobe structures were damaged showed a marked inability to perform on a task in which they were first presented with an object and then required to remember which object they had seen when two different objects were presented at time intervals ranging from 8 seconds to 10 minutes. As Figure 10.14 shows, by the time 10 minutes had passed, the brain-damaged monkeys were performing at only a 50 percent, or chance, level.

Taken together, these lines of research indicate that the hippocampus is part of the declarative memory system and the cerebellum is part of a separate procedural memory system. However, it is also clear that many other areas of the brain are involved in memory. For example, the cerebral cortex plays a key role in both working memory and long-term memory (Gormezano & Wasserman, 1992). Although giant strides have been made in unraveling the neural circuitry of memory, much remains to be learned.

How Are Memories Formed?

One of the enduring mysteries of memory research is perhaps also the most basic one: How are memories formed within the nervous system? The physical basis of memory is almost certain to involve changes in the mosaics of neurons linked with one another in the neural circuit that constitutes a memory.

One of the stars of current neuroscience research on memory is a marine snail, *Aplysia californica*. Clearly, *Aplysia* is no mental giant, and its remembrances of things past are probably quite limited. Yet this creature has attracted the attention of researchers like Eric Kandel of Columbia University for a number of important reasons. First, *Aplysia* is capable of learning and forming memories. For example, a gentle squirt of water onto its siphon—a breathing organ lying atop its gill—ordinarily results in the creature's retracting its gill slightly in an act of self-defense. However, if a squirt is paired a number of times with an electric shock to the tail, *Aplysia* acquires a conditioned defensive response in which the CS (the water squirt) causes it to cover its siphon and gill with a protective flap of skin (see Figure 10.15).

Why study conditioned responses in a sea slug? The answer is that *Aplysia* has some very important anatomical features. First of all, it has only about 20,000 neurons (compared with our 100 billion), and these neurons are larger and easier to study than ours. Moreover, these neurons seem otherwise to be very much like those of humans and are thought to operate in the same way. Finally, a single synapse links each sensory neuron in the siphon with a neuron controlling movement of the gill-protecting mechanism. Thus, researchers know that learning must occur at those synapses, and now they can study what happens physically to the neurons involved as learning occurs.

For more than 20 years, Kandel and other researchers have been studying *Aplysia* (Carew & others, 1990; Kandel & Hawkins, 1992). What they have found may be the beginnings of a true un-

derstanding of how memories are formed. Their research has shown that shocking the slug's tail triggers a complicated series of biochemical and genetic events that result in the formation of neural circuits involving the sensory neurons stimulated by the UCS, those stimulated by the CS, and the motor neurons that control the defensive gill-protection response.

A key step in the process is the activation of an enzyme, *protein kinase,* which results in a large increase in the amount of transmitter substance released by the sensory neurons into the synaptic space. This increase creates stronger activation of the motor neurons, as well as a biochemical bonding of the neural firings produced by the CS and the UCS. The amount of time the protein kinase is active seems to determine whether short-term memories become long-term memories. If only

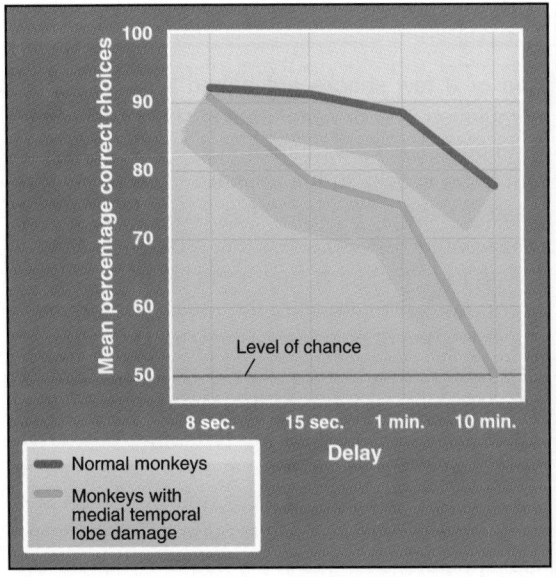

Figure 10.14 Performance on an episodic memory task by normal monkeys and monkeys whose medial temporal lobe memory systems had been damaged. (Data from Squire & Zola-Morgan, 1991).

Figure 10.15 Classical conditioning of Aplysia has helped unlock some of the physiological mechanisms of memory formation. Normally, the snail pulls in its gill slowly if its siphon is squirted. This is shown in the top part of the figure, together with the synaptic activity of the siphon sensory neuron and the gill motor neuron. The squirt to the gill cover can be used as a CS for a totally different response—a complete covering of the gill cover—by pairing the squirt with a shock to the tail (lower figure). After a CS (squirts from a WaterPik to the animal's siphon) is paired a number of times with a shock to the tail (a UCS), a conditioned defensive response to the squirt alone is established. This is accompanied by neurotransmitter increases in the sensory neurons that convey the CS and UCS information and an eventual neurotransmitter link between the sensory and motor neurons involved.

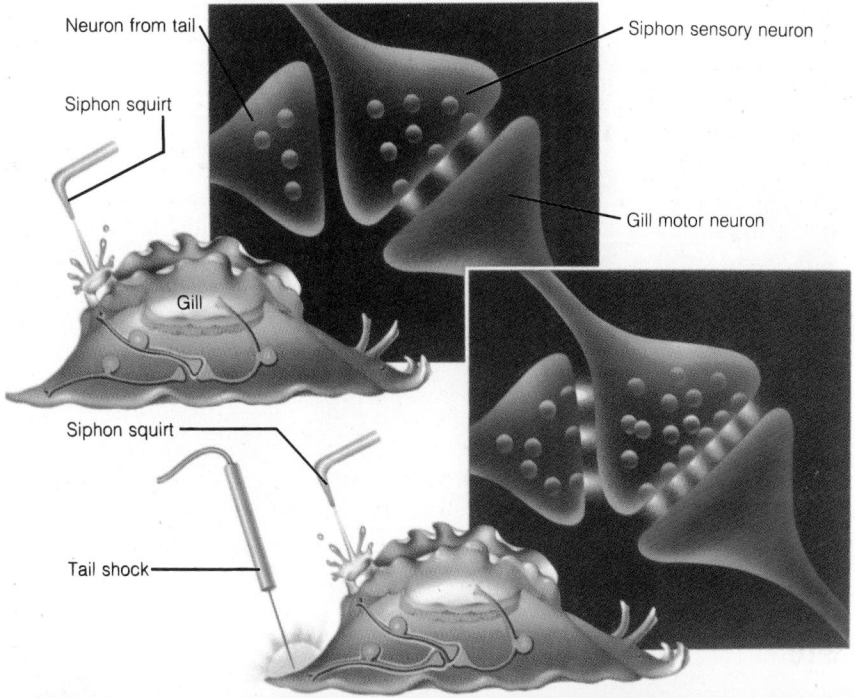

one or a few shocks are paired with the siphon stimulation, the protein kinase "shuts off" after a brief period, and no permanent memory is formed. But if the shocks to the animal's tail are given repeatedly (in a sense, if the situation becomes "meaningful" to *Aplysia*), the protein kinase remains in a long-term state of activation, resulting in repeated stimulation of the motor neuron and a consolidation of the new memory trace into a more permanent one. In *Aplysia,* this process must begin within 90 minutes or the memory will decay. Thus, the first stages in the formation of a short-term and then a long-term memory seem to involve a series of complex biochemical processes.

These events inside the neurons result in actual structural changes in the neurons themselves. Studies with the electron microscope have shown that long-term memory doubles the number of synaptic branches sent out by a siphon sensory neuron, which carries the CS message, toward the gill motor neuron. Further, the axon terminal of the siphon neuron becomes densely packed with neurotransmitter release points, resulting in a dramatic increase in transmitter activity (Bailey & Chen, 1992). Other researchers have found structural changes in postsynaptic neurons as well, including an increase in the number of receptor sites on the surface of the receiving neuron (Baudry & Davis, 1991). Together, these changes seem to result in greater ease of synaptic transmission and the development of a neural circuit that may be the basis for memory.

The complexities of human memory are only beginning to be understood at a physiological level, and researchers are looking for processes like those found in *Aplysia* within the brains of more complex creatures. The next decade could well produce, at last, an understanding of how our experiences leave their traces within the cells of our brains.

Encoding and Organization in Memory

Your long-term memory has infinitely more storage space than the largest of libraries. Yet its holdings, like those of a library, must be organized in terms of specific codes if the information is to be available when you wish to retrieve it (see Figure 10.16). In a library, information is organized according to a system of call numbers. As we shall see, our "call numbers" are known as retrieval cues. They allow us to address information stored in long-term memory and transfer it back into working memory. Some of the retrieval cues are generated by us; others reside in the environment. To understand how the retrieval cues operate, however, we need to consider first how the information in memory is encoded and organized. Three codes that represent information in long-term memory are verbal (linguistic) codes, imagery codes, and motor codes.

Verbal Coding

One of the most important memory codes is the verbal, or linguistic, code. Semantic memory is populated with these codes. Once we begin to acquire language, we can code concrete objects and events in terms of words and concepts. A **concept** is a linguistic category that includes objects having some important feature in common (for example, "vegetables," "professors," "coins," "loving people," "bad experiences"). For memory-encoding purposes, concepts are like storage bins in which individual bits of information may be deposited. The advantage of organizing information in this way is shown in clustering experiments, where it is found that people who cluster lists of unrelated words into categories like "animals" and "professions" can use the categories as retrieval cues and remember more of the words later on (Tulving & Pearlstone, 1966). People tended

Figure 10.16 *Memories are stored and filed like the holdings of a great library. Retrieving them requires the correct retrieval cues. Searching without the cues is rather like searching for a book without knowing its location or call number.*

to do this spontaneously, using whatever organizational scheme they could come up with on their own. This phenomenon, known as **subjective organization,** illustrates the need we have to organize material in memory.

The importance of imposing organization during the encoding process was also shown in an experiment by Gordon Bower and his coworkers (1969). They presented subjects with lists of words. For one group of subjects, the words were presented within a logically organized hierarchical tree like that shown in Figure 10.17a. Another group of subjects received the words placed randomly within the tree. As shown in Figure 10.17b, the difference in the percentage of words recalled in the two experimental conditions was quite dramatic. The subjects presented with a meaningful hierarchy remembered more than three times as many words.

Information can also be *re*coded in ways that make it easier to remember. You have already seen one example of this in the earlier discussion of chunking. Once you formed the 15 letters into acronyms like FBI and IRS, they became much easier to retain in memory because they now comprised five units instead of 15 units.

We are not often asked to recall lists of words, but we are frequently asked to explain the meaning of something that has been said to us or that we have read. In such situations, meaning becomes even more important. Our understanding of the information will control our encoding of it and hence our later memory of it. To illustrate, let us consider the following experiment.

In a study of verbally presented information, Bransford and Franks (1971) showed people sentences that formed a theme, such as:

1. The jelly was on the table.
2. The ants climbed the table.
3. The ants ate the jelly.
4. The picnic was ruined.

The subjects were then shown more sentences, some of which were ''old,'' in that they had been shown before, and some of which were ''new.'' The new sentences either presented the same information in a new way, as in ''The ants climbed the table and ate the jelly,'' or presented new information, as in ''The table had peanut butter and jelly on it.''

Figure 10.18 shows how often people called each type of sentence a ''new'' one. It is clear from the figure that people had trouble discriminating between the old sentences and the new sentences that presented the same information in a different way. What people had encoded was the *meaning* of the sentences, not the sentences themselves.

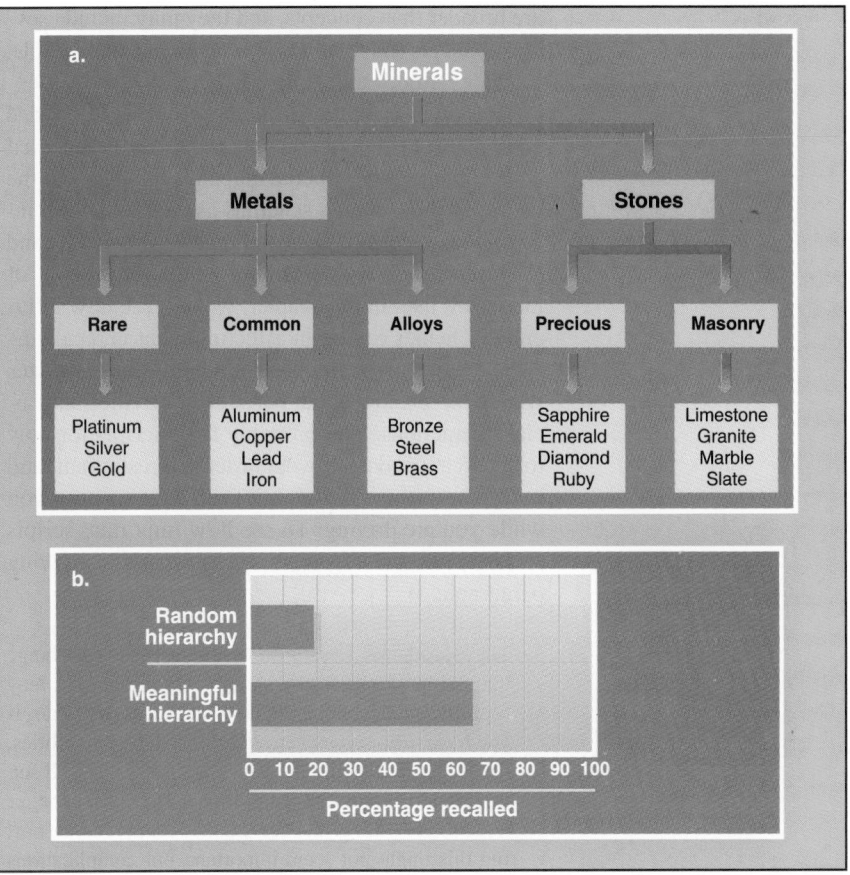

Schemas and Scripts

It is sometimes said that what we construct in memory is a broad-based theme that describes the meaning of an episode, rather than a precise record of what happened during the episode. The theme itself is called a *schema*. A **schema** is a mental representation of a class of people, events, situations, or objects (Fiske & Taylor, 1991; Greene, 1992). Thus, in describing the picnic example, a psychologist might say that what was stored in the subjects' memories was a schema describing how ants ruined a picnic. Schemas

Figure 10.17 *Effects of hierarchical organization on later recall. Words presented in a logically organized hierarchical structure like the one in (a) are remembered better than the same words placed randomly in a similar-looking structure. (Bower & others, 1969).*

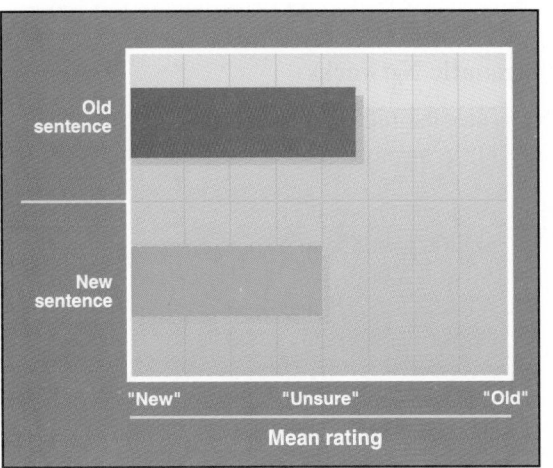

Figure 10.18 *Subjects' difficulty in discriminating between sentences they were originally shown (old sentences) and new sentences that communicated the same meaning in different words indicates that the subjects encoded a schema relating to the meaning of the sentences, rather than the sentences themselves. (Data from Bransford & Franks, 1982).*

are broader than concepts, and they may include several concepts and relations among them (for example, "ants," "ruin," and "picnics").

Information stored in memory is often encoded and organized around schemas. This means that what is eventually remembered depends in part on the nature of the person's schemas as well as on the information received from the sensory registers and short-term memory. When we examine retrieval of memories later in the chapter, we will see how influential schemas can be in affecting what is recalled.

A **script** is a specific type of schema that organizes what people know about particular activities and social interactions. You probably have scripts for how to act on a first date, how to order in a restaurant, and how to best respond to a police officer who stops you while you are driving. To see how important scripts can be in organizing memories, read the following paragraph:

> The procedure is actually quite simple. First you arrange things into different groups. Of course, one pile may be sufficient depending on how much there is to do. If you have to go somewhere else due to lack of facilities, that is the next step; otherwise you are pretty well set. It is important not to overdo things. That is, it is better to do too few things at once than too many. In the short run this might not seem important, but complications can easily arise. A mistake can be expensive as well. . . . After the procedure is completed, one arranges the materials into different groups again. Then they can be put into their appropriate places. Eventually they will be used once more, and the whole cycle will have to be repeated. However, that is part of life (Based on Bransford & Johnson, 1973).

Asked to recall as much as you can of the preceding paragraph, you would probably have difficulty remembering much of it. Certainly, the subjects in the original experiment did. However, suppose I tell you that the paragraph is about a common activity: washing clothes. Now, if you read the material again, you will find that the abstract ideas suddenly make sense, and you can use your script for washing clothes to organize the ideas and recall a great deal more.

Semantic Networks

Consider the following statements, and indicate as quickly as possible whether each one is true or false:

1. A raccoon has wings.
2. Madrid is in Spain.
3. A bat is a bird.
4. A script is a schema.
5. Coca-Cola is green.

Chances are, you were able to respond to these statements almost instantaneously. Considering their diversity, it is remarkable that you could access the facts so quickly. The fact that people perform such tasks routinely has caused cognitive psychologists to speculate on how information might be stored in semantic memory. One popular theory is that memory can be represented as a massive network of associated ideas and concepts (Best, 1992; Collins & Loftus, 1975). Figure 10.19 shows what a small portion of such a network might be like. The lines in this **semantic network** represent associations between concepts, with shorter lines indicating stronger associations.

Alan Collins and Elizabeth Loftus (1975) theorize that when people think about a concept, such as "fire engine," there is a *spreading activation* of related concepts throughout the network. Thus, in this case, related concepts like "truck," "fire," and "red" should be partially activated as well. This activation of related concepts, known as **priming,** makes it more likely that these concepts will also be accessed.

Priming is a highly adaptive phenomenon because it directs our thinking along lines that are relevant to the current situation. To illustrate, let us consider the role of priming in our ability to understand discourse. Read the following sentences:

> I can see those islands in the sun.
> Their palms are stretched up to the sky.

The sentences probably conjure up visions of a tree-laden tropical island. Now, read the next sentences:

> I can see those pilgrims praying.
> Their palms are stretched up to the sky.

This sentence pair presents quite a different meaning. Although the second sentence is the same in each instance, we have no trouble encoding the intended meaning, because the context of the preceding sentence has primed the appropriate semantic classes. Priming is obviously important in reading, because we must constantly encode and interpret the written element within the meaning context established by previous words, concepts, and ideas.

Imagery Coding

As noted earlier, long-term memory content is coded not only verbally, or linguistically, but also by means of images. Sometimes, both are used to code material, and Alan Paivio (1969) has proposed that such **dual coding** can improve later memory. He reasons that if we store two different kinds of information about an experience, the chances improve that at least one of the two codes will be available to support recall later on. Many popular memory improvement books (such as Lorayne & Lucas, 1974) recommend using imagery to dual-code information for later recall (for example, by forming unusual images of items on your grocery list), and there is a good deal of evidence that this procedure does indeed improve memory (Tye, 1991). A later section, on improving memory, will discuss the specifics of dual coding.

Use of Schemas

We have already considered the role of schemas in encoding and organizing verbal information. Schemas are also used to code images. In one demonstration of the role of schemas, the encoding and memory capabilities of expert and novice chess players were compared (Chase & Simon, 1973). The players glanced at pieces on a chess board. Then they looked away and attempted to reconstruct the board from memory. If their memory of the original board was incomplete, they looked at it again. This procedure continued until they had correctly placed all the pieces on a second board.

The contrast between the performance of the expert players and that of the novices was noteworthy. The expert players were much better able to reconstruct the original board, but only if the positions to be memorized were ones that might actually occur in a game of chess. If the pieces were randomly positioned on the board, there was no difference in recall capability between experts and novices.

These results were explained in terms of how the experts reconstructed the board. If the positions of the pieces were legitimate, experts would group together pieces that served the same function. For example, they would treat as a unit all pieces that were positioned to attack the king. The researchers referred to these units as encoded *chunks* of meaningful information. (Recall the chunking effect demonstrated earlier in the ''IBM FBI KGB IRS'' example.) Novices, who did not have the well-developed chess strategy schemas that the experts possessed, could not construct the chunks, so they had to try to memorize the position of each piece. However, if the pieces were not in positions that would occur in a real game, they were no more meaningful to the experts than to the novices. As a result, the experts lost their schematic advantage and had to approach the task on a piece-by-piece basis just as the novices did.

A more recent experiment by Daniel Garland and John Barry (1991) replicated these results in a study of memory for diagrams of football plays. Experienced football coaches and novices who had played football but had not coached were shown diagrams of football plays for 5 seconds and then were asked to reproduce the patterns of X's and O's. Some of the diagrams showed logical plays, whereas others were unstructured and illogical in nature. As you can see

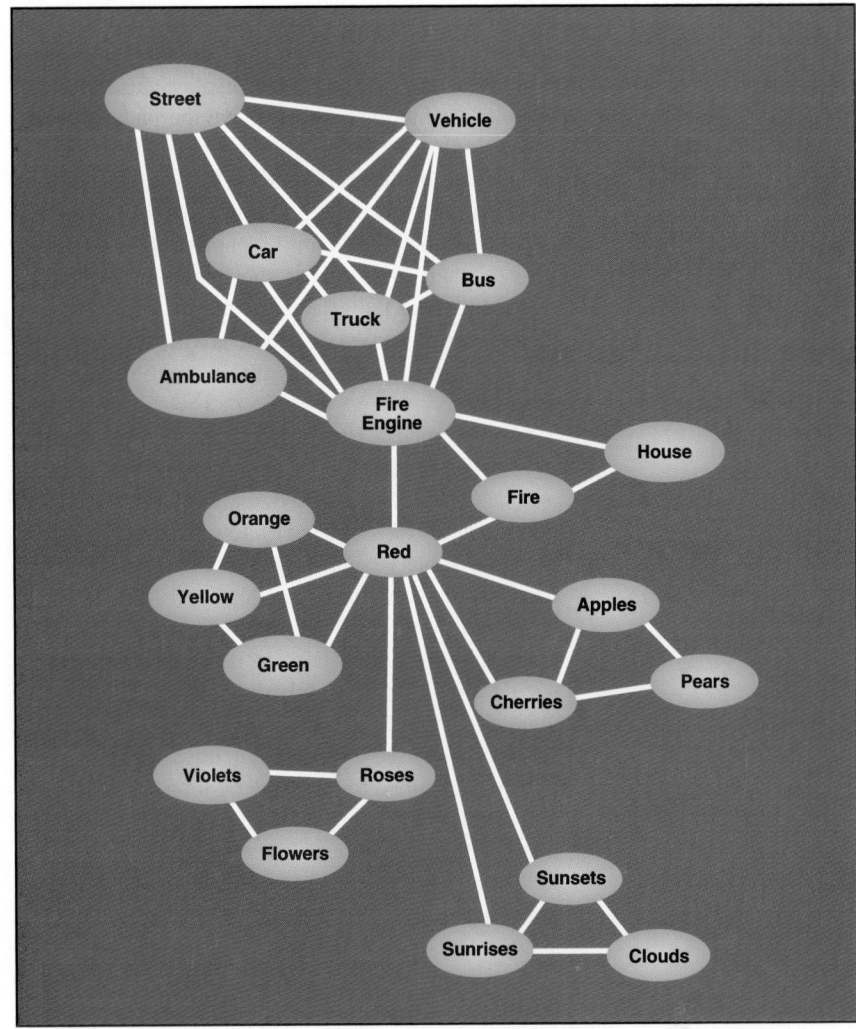

Figure 10.19 *A network of concepts in semantic memory. The lines in the semantic network represent associations between concepts, with shorter lines indicating stronger associations. (Collins & Loftus, 1975).*

in Figure 10.20, the experienced coaches were far superior to the novices in encoding and recalling the real plays. However, like the chess masters, their superiority largely disappeared when they could no longer use their football play schemas to organize the illogical plays.

Eidetic Imagery

Most of us can easily create images of objects or events when asked to do so. However, there are great individual differences in how vivid people report their images to be (Paivio, 1986). Some people claim to have a ''photographic memory'' that retains images as clearly and completely as a photograph. The technical name for this phenomenon is **eidetic imagery.**

A number of ingenious tests of eidetic imagery have been devised (Merritt, 1979). One of them is shown in Figure 10.21. Perception studies have shown that if the two patterns of meaningless dots are presented simultaneously, one to each eye, through a stereo display, the displays fuse and the person sees figures floating above the pattern. What has this to do with eidetic imagery? Charles Stromeyer and Joseph Psotka (1970) suggested that a person who has eidetic imagery should be able to look at the top pattern until a photographic image is formed, then superimpose the image on the lower figure to create the effect that occurs when the dot patterns are presented simultaneously to the two eyes. Try it yourself, following the instructions in Figure 10.21.

One woman, a Harvard teacher and artist studied by Stromeyer and Psotka, was able to pass the dot test, and she also reported impressive abilities on other imagery tasks. So have a few highly suggestible hypnotic subjects, but they could do so only when hypnotized (Crawford & Wallace, 1986). For the most part, however, tests like this one suggest that eidetic imagery, if it does exist, is extraordinarily rare, so you should not be unduly disappointed if you were unable to produce the stereo effect. In fact, one researcher who used the dot fusion test with many subjects who claimed to have eidetic imagery described eidetic imagery as a ''none in a million phenomenon.'' Other researchers, however, continue to look for subjects who truly have eidetic imagery in the hope that studying such people will provide new insights into the nature of imaginal coding and memory.

Motor Coding

Stop for a moment and answer the following question: What can you remember about the case of H. M., which opened this chapter? What you are now doing

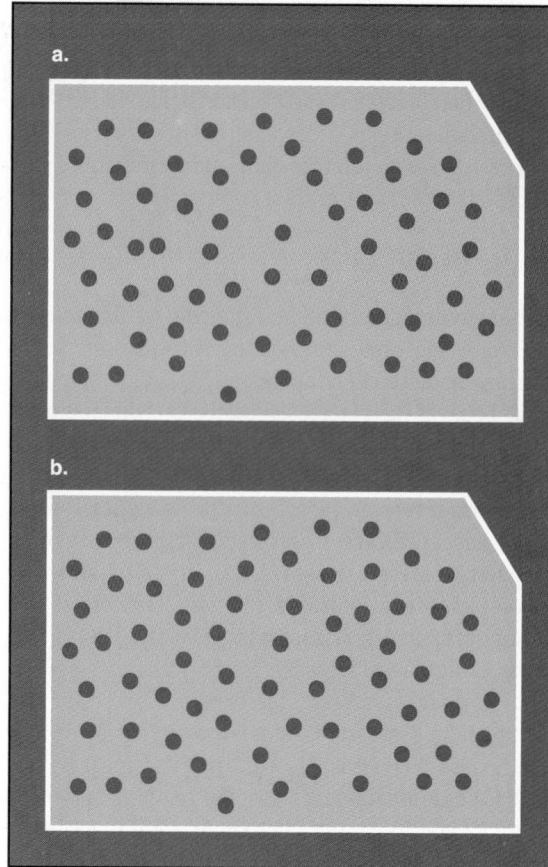

▲ **Figure 10.21** *Eidetic imagery test. Carefully examine the dot pattern in* (a) *for several minutes, moving your gaze about to inspect all details. Then shut your eyes and build up the most vivid image you can of the dot array. Open your eyes and superimpose the image you have formed of* (a) *onto* (b)*, making sure the borders of the figures coincide perfectly. If your image of* (a) *is sufficiently vivid and detailed, you will see numbers or letters when you fuse the two dot arrays. What a person with eidetic imagery should see is shown on the next page. (Merritt, 1979).*

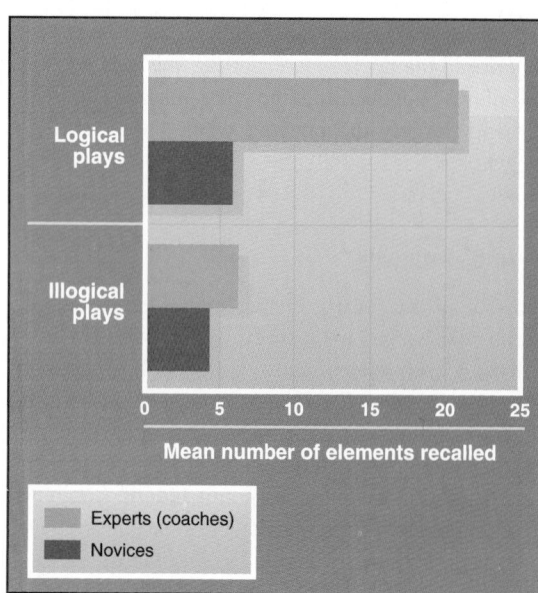

▶ **Figure 10.20** *Effects of schema sophistication on recall of football plays. The graph shows the mean number of elements of complex football plays recalled by experienced football coaches and novices after a 5-second exposure to diagrams of logical and illogical play diagrams. (Data from Garland & Barry, 1991).*

Mean number of elements recalled

Logical plays

Illogical plays

0   5   10   15   20   25

☐ Experts (coaches)
■ Novices

is an example of declarative memory: You have retrieved information about something you know and translated it into words. The memory was available for conscious inspection; that is, it could be declared.

Now try to describe how you balance on one foot. It is quite likely that although you can balance on one foot, you cannot describe just how you do it. This is an example of procedural memory: You know how to do something even though you may not be able to translate your knowledge into words very easily.

We have many procedural memories. Such memories are not limited to motor sequences, but memories for motor actions, such as riding a bicycle or swinging a bat, are among the best examples of procedural memory. Such memories are thought to be encoded in brain regions different from those in which verbal or imaginal memories are coded (Squire & Zola-Morgan, 1991), and less is known about motor codes. According to one view, motor schemas are built up through execution of tasks and the feedback that is received from the actions (Newell, 1991; Schmidt, 1975). Thus, repeated experience with a particular sequence of environmental events and reactions to them will produce an automated stimulus–response sequence so that whenever the stimulus occurs we can react to it without pausing to retrieve declarative information (see Figure 10.22).

Automated response sequences are often established by practicing exactly the same response to a stimulus over and over again. This is what concert pianists do when they practice a Chopin étude for 3 or 4 hours a day, often repeating a single measure 100 times. As a result of such training, responding becomes both automatic and extremely rapid. Likewise, experienced typists and pianists respond much more rapidly than they ever could if they had to consciously recall where particular keys were located on their respective keyboards.

As we have seen, the encoding of information into long-term memory is a complex process. However, encoding principles are very important in understanding the factors that influence how successful we are in retrieving memories from the long-term store. We now examine the processes involved in retrieval and in the retrieval failures that we refer to as forgetting.

■ ■

Retrieval of Memories

Memory would not be very useful to us if it were only a store. We have to be able to retrieve information as well as store it. As we shall see, our ability to remember depends in part on how (and how well) the information was encoded and partly on how effectively we are able to search and access the memory store.

Retrieval Cues

Memory, as noted earlier, is something like a vast library. Trying to find a particular book by starting in one room and looking at each book in turn would be a fruitless approach. However, if we have the call number and the book is shelved correctly, we can easily gain access to the book.

Remembering depends not only on having information coded and stored in long-term memory but also on having an appropriate **retrieval cue** that brings the memory into consciousness. If the cue is not present, even information that is well stored may be inaccessible. All of us have experienced the so-called *tip-of-the-tongue phenomenon*, in which we

◀ **Figure 10.22** *It takes many hours of practice to establish the procedural memories needed to perform the activities of a concert pianist.*

temporarily cannot recall a fact, a name, or some other piece of information that we "know as well as our own names." Sometimes it seems as if our retrieval cue has triggered another memory that blocks out the memory we want, as when we keep retrieving a name that is similar in some respects but clearly incorrect. At other times, we just can't seem to jog our memory strongly enough to retrieve the information when we need it. Thus, our recall of some fact might be blocked while we are taking a test, only to reappear a moment after we hand in the exam.

Priming is a good example of how one cue can trigger associated elements in memory. Thus, a particular external stimulus, a thought, or an idea can

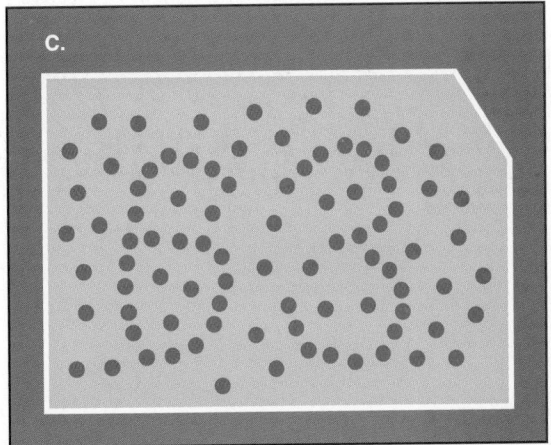

Fusion of dots in Figure 10.21a, b.

serve as a retrieval cue for memories that have long lain dormant in long-term memory.

Levels of Processing

The earlier discussion of how information is transferred from short-term to long-term memory pointed out that rehearsal of information plays a central role in this process. But not all rehearsal is created equal. We saw, for example, that maintenance rehearsal involves simply repeating the information to keep it in working memory, whereas elaborative rehearsal involves attempting to form associations between the new information and material already stored in memory.

Fergus Craik and Robert Lockhart (1972) believe that the more actively we process incoming information and form associations with other memories, the better our long-term recall will be. Indeed, Craik and Lockhart have challenged the distinction between short-term and long-term stores, suggesting that they may simply involve different levels, or depths, of information processing. The so-called **duplex theory of memory,** which posits separate short- and long-term stores, seems to have survived this challenge and remains highly influential. Nevertheless, the approach focusing on **levels of processing** has inspired many experiments that have demonstrated the importance of deeper forms of processing. For example, in one study people answered three types of word-related questions, each type requiring a different depth of processing. Structural questions required that they process only superficial features of the word (for example, "Does it begin with a capital letter?"). Phonemic questions required somewhat deeper processing ("Does the word rhyme with legal?"). Semantic questions demanded still deeper processing ("Does it fly?"). The subjects were then asked to recall the words to which the questions related. Figure 10.23 shows the results. Semantic processing clearly resulted in the strongest memories.

The fact that deeply processed material is generally recalled better than superficially processed information makes sense in terms of our previous discussion of retrieval cues. Associating new information with existing memories helps build up an associative network in which there are many possible retrieval cues. Dual coding in terms of verbal and imaginal cues could also provide more points of access to the new memory. As we shall see later, in this chapter's Enhancing Human Performance feature, levels-of-processing concepts provide us with several useful hints for improving memory.

Distinctiveness

Do you remember the moment in 1986 when you first heard about the explosion of the space shuttle Challenger (see Figure 10.24)? Many people can recall in vivid detail exactly where they were, what they were doing, how they learned of the event, and so on (Bohannon, 1988). Likewise, most people of my generation have clear recollections of when and where they received the news of President John F. Kennedy's assassination. Such memories have been termed **flashbulb memories** because of their vivid detail (Brown & Kulik, 1977). They are most likely to be maintained over long periods if the event in question evoked strong emotional reactions and was repeatedly recalled in conversations with friends or acquaintances (Bohannon, 1988).

The distinctiveness of information and experiences affects how well they are remembered. Again, we can understand this phenomenon in terms of the adequacy of retrieval cues. As the experience of having one memory interfere with another would suggest, a factor limiting the effectiveness of retrieval cues is how overloaded they become with associated memories. The greater the number of memories associated with a given cue, the less effectively the cue will trigger any one of those memories. Accordingly, distinctive information or experiences may be remembered so well because they are tied to only one or a few cues (Ross, 1992). Thus, the cue Challenger is associated far more strongly with the tragic event in 1986 and with your emotional reaction to that event than it is with any other memory. It therefore becomes a dependable retrieval cue for the vivid memory.

Figure 10.23 *Depth of processing facilitates recall. Subjects in this study saw words and were asked questions that required superficial structural processing of the word ("Does it begin with B?"), somewhat deeper phonemic processing ("Does it rhyme with "great?"), or deeper semantic processing ("Is it a four-legged animal?"). Depth of processing was related to later recognition of the words in a larger list. (Data from Craik & Tulving, 1975).*

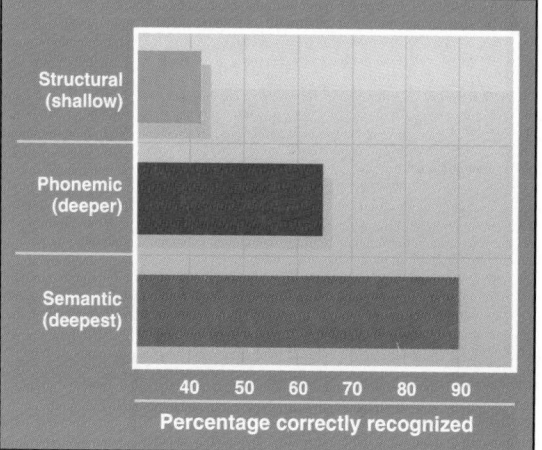

Percentage correctly recognized

Structural (shallow)

Phonemic (deeper)

Semantic (deepest)

40 50 60 70 80 90

Figure 10.24 *Incidents like the 1986 tragedy involving the Challenger space shuttle are so distinctive and emotionally involving that they often produce flashbulb memories.*

Encoding Specificity and Transfer-Appropriate Processing

The crucial role of retrieval cues in evoking memories has yet another important implication: We should expect that stimuli that are present at the time we experience something will become encoded as part of the memory and will therefore serve as retrieval cues. According to the **encoding specificity principle,** ease of recall will be influenced by the extent to which stimuli that are present when we are trying to remember something match those that were present when the memory was originally encoded (Tulving & Thompson, 1973). For example, returning to the elementary school you attended may awaken many memories because the sights and sounds of the school's physical environment were present when you originally encoded your earlier experiences. The encoding specificity hypothesis is in some ways similar to the concept of stimulus generalization discussed in Chapter 9: The more similar a stimulus is to the original conditioned stimulus, the more likely it is to evoke the conditioned response. In this case, the more similar the retrieval cues are to those that were present when the memory was encoded, the more likely they are to evoke the memory.

Thus, the kind of processing involved in the encoding of an event in memory can make a big difference later on. **Transfer-appropriate processing** is processing that is similar to the type that will be required when we are later called upon to recall the information (Morris & others, 1977). For example, if you know what kinds of questions you are likely to be asked on a test, memorizing material with those questions in mind will help you encode additional retrieval cues that can assist your later recall of the material.

Context, State, and Mood Effects on Memory

Almost any external or internal stimulus that is present when we have an experience can potentially serve as a retrieval cue. Therefore, it may be easier to remember information in the environment in which it was acquired, because the context can serve as an associative link to the memory store. This phenomenon, known as **context-dependent memory,** is one reason why police often take witnesses back to the scene of the crime and interrogate them there. This practice is well founded in terms of what we know about the effect of context on memory. For example, in an experiment by Duncan Godden and Allen Baddeley (1975), divers learned some lists of words underwater and some on dry land. When they were retested in the two environments, they had better recall of a list in the environment in which they had originally learned it (see Figure 10.25). Other studies

Figure 10.25 *Because of context-dependent memory, this diver may recall information learned underwater more readily when he is in this environment than when he is on land.*

have shown that simply asking subjects to imagine the original learning environment can serve as an aid to recall (Smith, 1979).

A person's internal physiological state at the time of learning is also part of the context, and recreating that state may also prime recall. Memory recalled with the aid of these internal retrieval cues is known as **state-dependent memory.** For example, Sirhan Sirhan, the man who assassinated Senator Robert F. Kennedy, was in a highly agitated emotional state when he did so. Later, he claimed that he had no recollection of committing the crime. According to Gordon Bower (1981), when Sirhan returned to the agitated emotional state under hypnosis, the memories of the event reportedly came flooding back to him in vivid detail (Bower, 1981; Kaiser, 1970). Although some experimental studies have demonstrated state-dependent memory by using drugs to induce particular states during learning and recall, many other studies have not been able to replicate such results, suggesting that state-dependent memory is an unreliable phenomenon (Blaney, 1986).

There is more consistent evidence for **mood-congruent recall.** Laboratory experiments using hypnosis to induce moods during learning and recall of information have shown that recall is significantly improved when people are in the same mood (for example, sad or happy) when they recall material as when they learned it (Blaney, 1986). People also show a pronounced tendency to selectively remember negative events when they are sad and positive events when they are happy (Teasdale & Fogarty, 1979). This seems to be one of the processes that maintains depression once people have entered a depressed state.

Memory as a Reconstructive Process

Retrieving information from long-term memory is not at all like viewing a taped replay on a video cassette recorder. Usually, our memories of things past are incomplete and sketchy. In such situations we may *reconstruct* a "reasonable" memory by embellishing directly retrieved memory with sensible elaborations. This is the process of **reconstructive memory.** Reconstruction sometimes works, in the sense that it may provide cues that trigger direct retrieval of accurate memories. However, reconstruction is clearly a dangerous business. We can easily fool ourselves into thinking that the "reasonable" reconstruction is what we actually experienced.

A classic experiment by Frederick Bartlett (1932) provides an excellent illustration of what can occur in the reconstructive process. Bartlett asked residents of Cambridge, England, to read stories. Months (in some cases years) later, he asked them to retell the stories. One of the stories, "The War of the Ghosts," is presented in Table 10.2. It is a Pacific Northwest Indian tale about a man who meets a group of warriors and goes on a raid with them. During the raid, he discovers that his companions are ghosts; subsequently, he dies a supernatural death.

Bartlett's memorizers, however, were 20th-century residents of England, not 18th-century Native Americans. When the English subjects retold the story, they reconstructed it in a way that made sense to them. Table 10.2 also contains one subject's memory of the story, retold after only 20 hours. The story is much shorter, and the plot has changed in significant ways. Now, the hero was fishing, not hunting seals. Also, the word *boat* is introduced, and the enemy, not the war party, is described as ghosts. Bartlett found that the longer the time interval between the reading and retelling of the story, the more the story changed to fit English culture.

Bartlett, who originally coined the term *schema,* believed that people have generalized ideas about how certain events happen and that they use these ideas to organize and, in some cases, to reconstruct their memories. Studies have shown that memory reconstruction using schemas is very common. In general, the use of appropriate schemas improves memory performance. People can often develop cues for recall by thinking systematically about what "had to have happened," given their knowledge of the situation. Thus, if you needed to remember whether you had turned off the headlights when you got out of your car, you might use your schema for "getting out of a car"—that is, your understanding of what happens when a driver leaves a car—to reconstruct what you did and to search that reconstruction for the act of turning off the headlights.

Sometimes, of course, schemas can be distracting. This is the case when the wrong schema is used to control recall or when the memorizer is unable to discriminate between what actually happened and his or her reconstruction of what "makes sense," given the schema used.

Advertisers often make use of people's tendency to elaborate and change their memories, thereby skirting laws against false advertising. Consider, for example, the following Listerine commercial:

"Wouldn't it be great," asks the mother, "if you could make him coldproof? Well, you can't. Nothing can do that. [Boy sneezes.] But there is something you can do that may help. Have him gargle with Listerine antiseptic. Listerine can't promise to keep him cold-free, but it may help him fight off colds. During the cold-catching season, have him gargle twice a day with full-strength Listerine. Watch his diet, see he gets plenty of sleep, and there's a good chance he'll have fewer colds, milder colds, this year" (Anderson, 1980, p. 203).

Original	Reconstruction
The War of the Ghosts	Bartlett then asked his subjects to try to retell the story. About 20 hours later, one subject recalled the story this way.
One night two young men from Egulac went down to the river to hunt seals, and while they were there it became foggy and calm. Then they heard war-cries, and they thought: "Maybe this is a war-party." They escaped to the shore and hid behind a log. Now canoes came up, and they heard the noise of paddles and saw one canoe coming up to them. There were five men in the canoe, and they said:	**The War of the Ghosts**
"What do you think? We wish to take you along. We are going up the river to make war on the people."	Two men from Edulac went fishing. While thus occupied by the river they heard a noise in the distance.
One of the young men said: "I have no arrows."	"It sounds like a cry," said one, and presently there appeared some men in canoes who invited them to join the party on their adventure. One of the young men refused to go, on the ground of family ties, but the other offered to go.
"Arrows are in the canoe," they said.	"But there are no arrows," he said.
"I will not go along. I might be killed. My relatives do not know where I have gone. But you," he said, turning to the other, "may go with them."	"The arrows are in the boat," was the reply.
So one of the young men went, but the other returned home.	He thereupon took his place, while his friend returned home. The party paddled up the river to Kaloma, and began to land on the banks of the river. The enemy came rushing upon them, and some sharp fighting ensued. Presently some one was injured, and the cry was raised that the enemy were ghosts.
And the warriors went up the river to a town on the other side of Kalama. The people came down to the water, and they began to fight, and many were killed. But presently the young man heard one of the warriors say: "Quick, let us go home: that Indian has been hit." Now he thought: "Oh, they are ghosts." He did not feel sick, but they said he had been shot.	The party returned down the stream, and the young man arrived home feeling none the worse for his experience. The next morning at dawn he endeavoured to recount his adventures. While he was talking something black issued from his mouth. Suddenly he uttered a cry and fell down. His friends gathered round him.
So the canoes went back to Egulac, and the young man went ashore to his house, and made a fire. And he told everybody and said: "Behold I accompanied the ghosts, and we went to fight. Many of our fellows were killed and many of those who attacked us were killed. They said I was hit, and I did not feel sick."	But he was dead.
He told it all, and then he became quiet. When the sun rose he fell down. Something black came out of his mouth. His face became contorted. The people jumped up and cried.	
He was dead.	

Source: Bartlett, 1932.

This commercial, with the name of the product changed to Gargoil, was used in a memory experiment (Harris, 1977). After subjects had heard the commercial and were later asked to recall it, they all agreed with the statement "Gargoil antiseptic helps prevent colds," even though the commercial did not say that. The subjects clearly elaborated on what the ad said when they reconstructed it in their memories. Undoubtedly, this is what the advertisers hoped would happen.

The use of schemas in reconstructive memory gives rise to an issue that is of great concern to the legal profession—namely, the possibility that eyewitness testimony might be affected by additional information received after the event. Such information might be incorporated into the witness' memory of the event and change the actual memory. In one celebrated case of mistaken eyewitness identification, Father Bernard Pagano, a Roman Catholic priest, was positively identified by seven eyewitnesses as the perpetrator of a series of armed robberies in the Wilmington, Delaware, area. The priest was saved from almost certain conviction when the true robber, dubbed the "gentleman bandit" because of his politeness and the concern he expressed for his victims, confessed to the crimes. I think you will agree that there was little physical resemblance between the priest and the robber (see Figure 10.26). What could account for the false eyewitness identifications?

Two pieces of information may have affected the witnesses' "memories." One is the fact that the gentlemanly and concerned manner of the robber is consistent with the schema many people have of priests. A second factor, which came to light later,

Figure 10.26 *Seven eyewitnesses to armed robberies committed by Ronald Clouser (left) mistakenly identified Father Bernard Pagano (right) as the robber, probably as a result of information from police that influenced their memory reconstructions. (United Press International).*

▼

Thinking Critically About Children's Testimony in Sexual Abuse Cases

In most cases involving sexual abuse of children by adults, the only witnesses to the event are the perpetrator and the victim. If an adult is accused of such a crime, the most important testimony is likely to be that offered by the child. The recent research evidence that children may be especially susceptible to distortions in reconstructive memory has raised important legal issues about the validity of children's testimony in such cases (Doris, 1991).

Suppose you were called as an expert witness in a hearing concerning whether children's testimony should be accepted in such trials. What research evidence would you cite concerning factors that might bias or distort such testimony? What guidelines would you offer to investigators trying to obtain unbiased testimony from possible child victims?

was that before presenting pictures of suspects to the eyewitnesses, the police let it be known that the suspect might be a priest. Father Pagano was the only suspect wearing a clerical collar, and the witnesses' memories may have been strongly affected by this information (Rodgers, 1982; Tversky & Tuchin, 1989). Whatever the factors involved, only a turn of events as dramatic as a Hollywood script prevented what could have been a grave miscarriage of justice.

Laboratory experiments have shown that eyewitnesses' reports can be strongly affected by information conveyed in interrogators' questions. In one study, subjects watched slides of an auto accident. Half of the subjects were shown slides with a stop sign at the street corner; the others were shown scenes with a yield sign. During questioning about what they had seen, half of the subjects were asked misleading questions that implied that a yield sign rather than a stop sign had been present. The subjects then viewed slides that contained either a stop sign or a yield sign and were asked which they had originally seen. Seventy-five percent of the subjects who had not been asked the misleading question correctly identified what they had seen. Only 41 percent of those who had subtly been given misleading information correctly identified the original slide, however. The rest chose the slide that was consistent with the misleading question (Loftus & others, 1978).

Results like these have raised concerns about the reliability of eyewitness testimony. Recent evidence suggests that children may be especially susceptible to memory distortions produced by misleading questions and information (Ceci & others, 1987; Doris, 1991). In one experiment, children ranging in age from 3 to 12 years listened as an experimenter read a story about a girl who got a stomach ache from eating eggs too fast. The children were then asked questions about the story. In an experimental group, however, children were first asked a misleading question: ''Do you remember the story about Loren, who had a headache because she ate her cereal too fast?'' As you can see in Figure 10.27, children at all ages recalled the story quite well when they were not asked a misleading question. However, the misleading question clearly promoted errors in recall, especially in the younger children. ▼

Some cognitive psychologists believe that post-event information can permanently alter a witness's original memory so that the original memory can never again be retrieved (Loftus & others, 1978; Tversky & Tuchin, 1989). Others are not certain that the original memory is permanently altered (Bekerian & Bowers, 1983; McCloskey & Zaragoza, 1985). But all agree that eyewitness reports can be significantly influenced by postevent information.

Basic research on memory has greatly expanded our understanding of the processes that underlie encoding, storage, and retrieval of memories. The Enhancing Human Performance feature explores the practical implications of this knowledge for improving memory.

Figure 10.27 *Effects of misleading questions on recall of a story by children of various ages. The effect was greater on young children than on older ones. (Data from Ceci & others, 1987).*

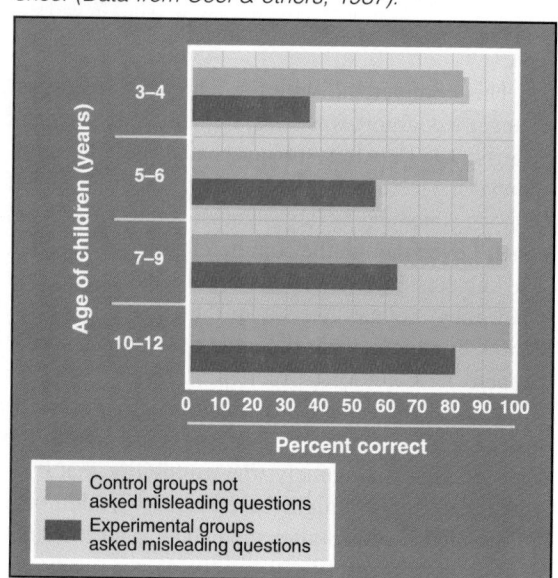

As we have seen repeatedly in our discussion of memory processes, what we get out of memory depends in part on how we put the information there in the first place. Perhaps the most important principle in memory improvement is that the more we are able to link pieces of information in a *meaningful* way with other items in memory, the more efficiently we will be able to access the interconnected memory network and retrieve what we want to remember (see Figure 10.28). A second and related principle is that the more time and effort we spend relating new information to other items in memory (and in the environment) that can serve as retrieval cues later on, the more likely we are to be able to remember the new information. Let us translate these two principles into concrete memory-enhancement techniques.

Find Ways to Make the New Information Personally Meaningful

Memory is formed by the processing of information, and its persistence depends on the depth of processing to which the stimulus is subjected. If a stimulus is analyzed at a shallow sensory level, according to its physical features, the resulting memory will be fragile and easily forgotten. If the stimulus is analyzed at a deeper level, according to its semantic features, and if it is enriched by associations or images, the resulting memory will be more durable and more likely to be remembered. At progressively deeper levels of analysis, more meaning is extracted from the stimulus.

Assuming all this is true, one of the most useful things you can do is find ways to create memory "hooks" on which you can hang new information. For example, nothing is more meaningful to you than yourself and your own experiences. Thus, when you are reading this text, do not simply try to memorize the principles and facts in a rote fashion. Instead, actively relate them to yourself and to experiences you've had so as to give them additional meaning.

(© SIDNEY HARRIS/AMERICAN SCIENTIST MAGAZINE)

Figure 10.28 *One way to remember information is to recode it into a more meaningful form. Not many of us would choose the recoding shown here, but for an Einstein, it might be a very effective one.*

Research has shown that even examples not related to oneself can enhance the meaningfulness of material. For example, subjects in one study read a 32-paragraph essay about a fictitious African nation. Of the 32 paragraphs in the essay, all contained a topic sentence giving the main idea of the paragraph; but eight paragraphs also contained three sentences giving examples; eight others contained two examples; another eight contained only one example; and eight had no examples at all. Subjects were tested for recall of the main ideas after reading the essay. The results are shown in Figure 10.29. As you can see, the more the information was elaborated on and made meaningful by examples, the better the main ideas were recalled (Palmere & others, 1983).

Another key to making information more meaningful is to organize it in some way. This principle leads to several concrete suggestions. When using a textbook like this one, make sure you understand how the information is organized.

Before you begin reading a chapter, study the outline to determine how the material is logically developed. Then read the summary at the end of the chapter to get an additional overview of the material you will be reading about—a "preview of coming attractions."

One of the best ways to impose organization on information is through outlining. Outlining forces you to arrange the main ideas in a hierarchical fashion, with main ideas above associated subordinate ones. The hierarchical structure can then be used as a plan that aids retrieval of each item in the hierarchy. Earlier, we reviewed research showing that organized material is retained better and that hierarchical organization of ideas is especially effective (see Figure 10.17). This is one of the reasons each chapter in this book ends with a summary organized in outline form. Most importantly, organizing the information you are learning keeps you actively thinking about and processing the material, enhancing storage in long-term memory.

Deep and meaningful processing is also enhanced through the use of the "directed questions" study method recommended in the Enhancing Human Performance feature of Chapter 1. Each time you go over your list of questions and attempt to answer them, you are reexposing yourself to the material that you are trying to master. Moreover, you are repeatedly associating a retrieval cue (the question) with the information, forging an ever-stronger associative link between the items in memory and the retrieval cue that can later be used to trigger them. The concepts of encoding specificity and transfer-appropriate processing account for the effectiveness of this approach.

One final organizational device that can be very effective is the *acronym,* a word formed from the first letters of words to be remembered. Generations of students have used HOMES as an aid to remembering the Great Lakes (Huron, Ontario, Michigan, Erie, and Superior) and ROY G. BIV (for red, orange, yellow,

▶ **Figure 10.29** *Number of main ideas recalled from paragraphs in an essay as a function of the number of examples provided. (Data from Palmere & others, 1983).*

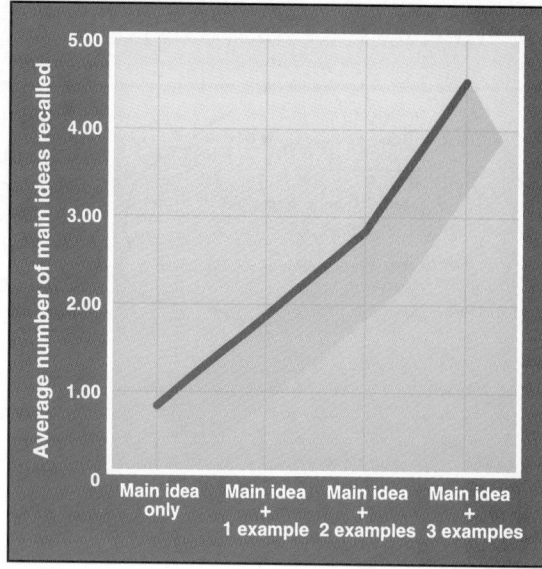

green, blue, indigo, and violet) as an aid to remembering the order of hues in the visible spectrum. Acronyms allow us to chunk information into meaningful and memorable units. A related method is to make up a sentence with words whose first letters correspond to those of words in a list you are trying to memorize. I can still remember learning the order of musical notes in grade school with the sentence "Every good boy does fine." Your own ingenuity can enrich your use of these devices. (Some of the more obscene sentences used by generations of medical students to memorize the names of physiological structures are legendary, but not printable here.)

Use Imagery for Encoding and Retrieval

Cyrus the Great, king of Persia, is said to have known the name of every man in his army. Closer to home, perhaps you have been impressed with the feats of memory experts who are able to remember the names of 100 or more people in an audience after hearing them only once, or marveled at the waitress at a party who can take orders from 20 people without notes and then recall perfectly what each person ordered when she returns with the drinks and food.

People like these do not have "photographic memories," but they usually have mastered some very effective memory strategies. Such feats are often performed with the aid of **mnemonic devices** (memory aids) that use imagery. With a little practice, almost everyone can learn to use imagery as a highly effective encoding and retrieval method. Images can be splendid cognitive hooks on which to hang information that you wish to remember. Why? Recall that the dual-coding principle suggests that visual images create a second memory code that can be combined with a verbal code to give us a double-barreled encoding and retrieval mechanism.

One very simple strategy is to use imagery to make a name more memorable by associating it with a related image. For example, when you are introduced to a person, try to form an image related to the person's name. If you meet Percy, you might form an image of him carrying a large purple purse. When you see him again, retrieving the image should help you remember his name. Waitresses like the one described above often report that they visualize a person holding the drink he or she has ordered or form an image that is associated with the drink. For example, a man who has ordered a margarita might be imagined as having turned light green. As one waitress remarked, "After a while, customers start looking like drinks" (Bennett, 1983, p. 165).

A very effective imagery-based mnemonic device was developed by the ancient Greek orators to remember their long speeches. The method is now known as the **method of loci** (*loci* is Latin for "places"). The orator would take an imaginary walk along a familiar path, associating one idea he wanted to express with each distinctive object along the path. Later, he could retrace his steps during his talk and remember the ideas in sequence. In like manner, if you wanted to remember a shopping list, you could take an imaginary walk through your home and form a highly distinctive image linking a particular place or object with an item on the shopping list. For example, if your list included eggs, tomatoes, and a hairbrush, you might imagine walking into your living room and seeing two sunny-side-up eggs sizzling on your coffee table, a giant tomato perched on your lamp, and Elvis Presley sitting in your favorite chair brushing his hair.

Is the method of loci effective? For a data-based answer, refer to Figure 10.30, which shows the average number of words from a list of 32 recalled by subjects who were instructed to use the method of loci and by a control group that tried to learn the word list by rote memory (Crovitz, 1971).

Distribute Learning over Time

In the preceding chapter, we noted the tendency of some students to delay studying until shortly before a test and then to "cram" for the test. This kind of highly concentrated learning is called **massed practice.** Its alternative is repeated but less intense preparation over a longer time, a procedure known as **distributed practice.**

In preparing for a test to which you can devote 8 hours of study, are you better off with one marathon study session or four 2-hour sessions spread out over several days? A good deal of research suggests that you will retain more with the distributed practice (Smith & Rothkopf, 1984; Underwood, 1970). Based on what we already know, we can suggest several reasons why this might be true. First, distributed practice provides more opportu-

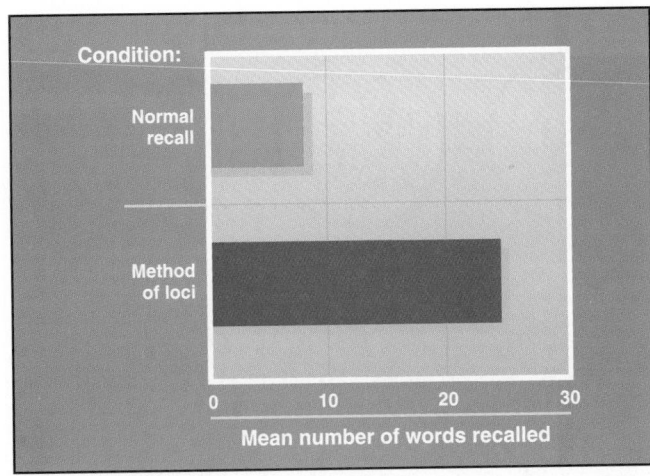

Figure 10.30 *The value of the method of loci is shown in the average recall of a list of 32 works by subjects who were instructed to use the method of loci and by similar subjects given normal recall instructions. (Data from Crovitz, 1971).*

nities for information processing and memory formation. It is also more efficient because fatigue and anxiety are less likely to interfere with learning. Finally, coming back to the material on several occasions gives you better feedback on what you have forgotten, providing you with the opportunity to devote extra time and effort to what you have not yet mastered. For all of these reasons, a study plan that provides for distributed practice is worth developing. However, the final study period should occur as close as possible to test time to minimize interference from later cognitive activities.

Make Use of Situational Retrieval Cues

Up to now we have focused on how to develop effective internal retrieval cues, such as associated ideas and mental images. However, you can also tip the retrieval odds in your favor by building situational retrieval cues into your preparation. One simple way of doing this is to do at least some of your studying in the place where you are going to take a test, finding times when classes are not in session there. This will help associate some of the environmental cues with the information you are learning. You can go a step further and actually link particular objects in the environment with items of information that you are going to recall. As a student, I did this quite frequently, and I was pleasantly surprised on several occasions during tests when a piece of information I couldn't recall returned to mind when I focused on the specific part of the room (for example, the loudspeaker in the left corner) that I had associated with that information. Like other students, I learned that in the memory game, you do well to take advantage of every psychological principle that might give you an edge. Theories of memory provide concrete suggestions for memory improvement, and, as the psychologist Kurt Lewin proclaimed years ago, "There's nothing so practical as a good theory."

Forgetting

Some very bright people have been known for memory failures, or "absent-mindedness." The eminent French writer Voltaire began a passionate letter "My Dear Hortense" and ended it "Farewell, my dear Adele." The splendid absent-mindedness of Canon Sawyer, an English nobleman, once led him, while welcoming a visitor at the railroad station, to board the departing train and disappear (Bryan, 1986).

Most of us would at times (especially around final exam periods) like to have a photograpic memory that could retrieve everything. We seldom stop to think what a curse this could be. The Russian psychologist A. R. Luria (1968) described a man who was tyrannized by his seeming inability to forget anything. Almost any retrieval cue would unleash a flood of trivial memories that dominated consciousness and made concentration and abstract thinking very difficult. Forgetting can also serve a protective function, dulling the hurtful experiences of the past. How often have you heard someone say, "If only I could forget!"

How we forget is nearly as interesting a scientific question as how we remember, and it has long been the topic of psychological theory and research. Important clues about the answers to this question emerged in the earlier discussion of how we encode, store, and retrieve information. Let us apply these principles to forgetting.

Encoding Failures

If memory is in some respects like a giant library, then one reason for an inability to remember is that the book was never put on the shelf. Many memory failures result from failure to encode the information and insert it into long-term memory. This is understandable, given the billions of stimuli that enter the sensory registers every day.

Much of what we sense we never process deeply enough to commit to memory. For example, if you live in the United States, you have undoubtedly looked at many thousands of pennies in your lifetime. Can you draw a rough picture of everything that is on the side with the face? If not, can you recognize which of the pennies in Figure 10.31 is the real thing?

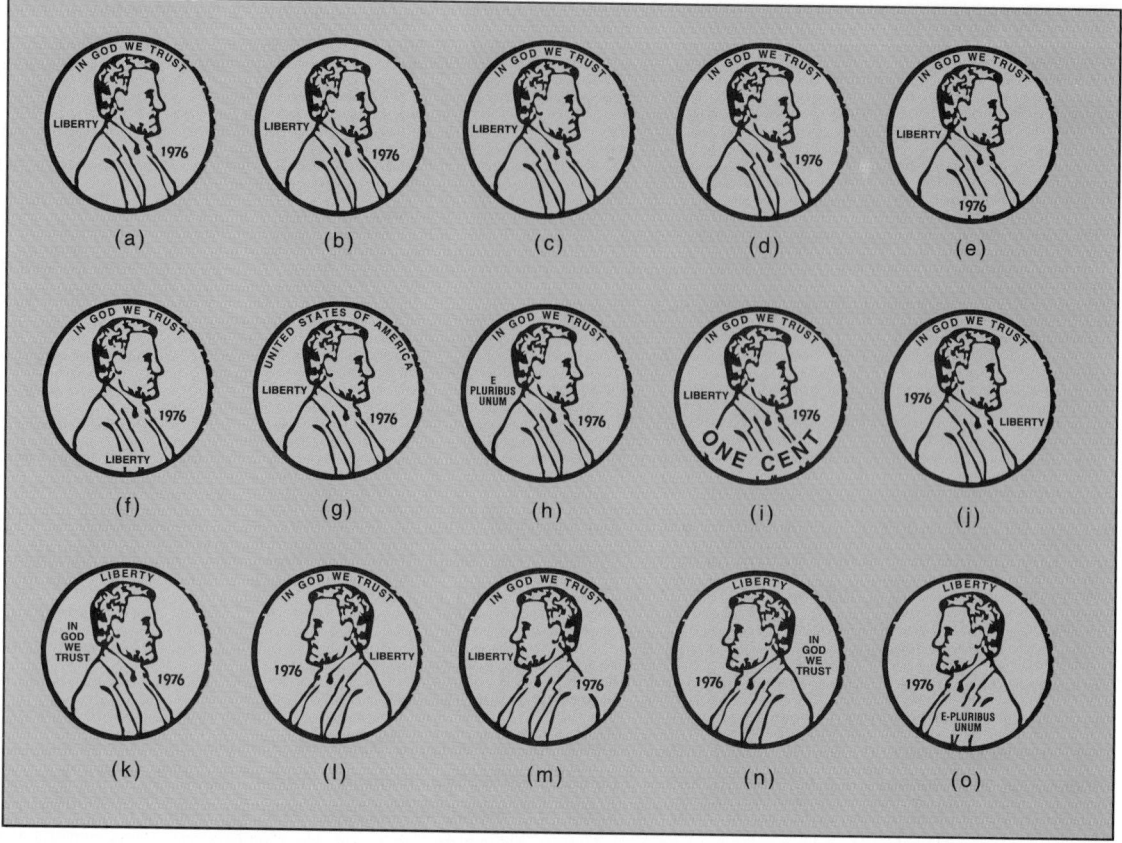

If you are like most people, you will have difficulty doing so (Nickerson & Adams, 1979). The reason is that the details of the penny's appearance are not very meaningful to us, nor are they essential for distinguishing between pennies and other coins. For those reasons, most of us do not encode these features, no matter how often we look at pennies in the course of our daily lives.

Decay and Interference

Other factors that may underlie forgetting involve the processes of storage and retrieval. One of the earliest explanations for forgetting was the **decay theory.** The notion was that with time and disuse, the physical *memory trace* in the nervous system may simply fade away. The decay theory soon fell into disfavor, mainly because scientists did not understand the physical basis of memory and there was no way of measuring the physical decay of the memory trace, let alone specifying what and where it was. Another difficulty with decay theory is its prediction that the longer the interval between learning and recall, the less should be recalled. In many cases this is true, but there are also instances in which it is not. For example, subjects who are retested twice may recall material on the second test that they could not remember on the first. This phenomenon is called **reminiscence,**

and it is clearly inconsistent with a decay of the memory trace over time (Greene, 1992).

Another venerable theory is **interference theory,** the notion that memories sometimes cannot be retrieved because other information in memory interferes with the retrieval process. This theory has a great deal of experimental support, and many cognitive psychologists view interference as the primary reason for retrieval failures.

Two types of interference, proactive and retroactive, are particularly important. **Proactive interference** occurs when material learned in the past interferes with recall of material learned later. **Retroactive interference** is the opposite: Here, newly acquired information interferes with the ability to recall information learned earlier (see Figure 10.32).

I have painful recollections of such interference. I took Spanish in high school and French in college. I found that my earlier learning of Spanish sometimes interfered with my recall of French, especially when the phrases were similar (proactive interference). Later on, I tried to tutor a friend in Spanish, only to find that my recent study of French interfered with my recall of the Spanish I had learned earlier (retroactive interference).

The more similar two stores of information are, the more likely it is that interference will occur. One would probably experience little interference of either type in the recall of highly dissimilar material, such as French and mathematical formulas.

Retroactive interference may be minimized by reducing the number of thoughts and experiences that could interfere with recall. One way of doing that is by going to sleep immediately after studying. This was shown in a classic study in which subjects learned lists of nonsense syllables, then tried to recall them after being either asleep or awake for varying periods up to 8 hours (Jenkins & Dallenbach, 1924). As Figure 10.33 shows, having been asleep resulted in better recall at every time interval, and essentially no loss of recall occurred in the sleepers after 2 hours. Note that a simple decay theory would have predicted equal forgetting for the two groups.

Finally, we should note that sometimes previous learning actually facilitates the learning of new material, a process known as **positive transfer.** Thus, it is quite possible that earlier learning of one foreign language will actually help you learn another, perhaps by teaching you how to learn a new language or by enriching your language-related associative networks. Like interference, positive transfer is likely to be greater if the two tasks are fairly similar to one another.

Motivated Forgetting

Psychodynamic theorists suggest yet another reason for some forgetting. They maintain that recall may be actively prevented by defensive cognitive operations that protect us from anxiety-arousing memories.

In his therapy sessions, Sigmund Freud often observed that his patients eventually remembered traumatic or anxiety-arousing events that had long seemed "forgotten." For example, one of his patients suddenly remembered with great shame that while standing beside her sister's coffin, she had thought, "Now my brother-in-law is free to marry me." Freud concluded that the thought was so shocking and anxiety arousing that it was immediately pushed down into the unconscious mind by the defense mechanism of *repression,* there to remain until it was uncovered years later during psychoanalysis. We will consider repression in greater detail in Chapter 14.

A similar, but more exaggerated, process is thought to occur when people suffer amnesia after a traumatic event. Likewise, the massive dissociation that seems to occur in cases of multiple personality renders large numbers of memories inaccessible to the various personalities.

Physiological Influences

Ultimately, the processes of encoding, storage, and retrieval reflect complex biochemical activities in the nervous system. It follows that events that affect these biochemical processes can result in forgetting (Gormezano & Wasserman, 1992). For example, one well-documented effect of electroconvulsive therapy, a treatment for depression in which brief electric current is applied through the scalp, is memory loss for events that occurred just prior to the neural disruption caused by the shock. This phenomenon is known as **retrograde amnesia** (Weiner & Coffey, 1988). Although the precise mechanism for the amnesia is not yet understood, it is clear that some sort of disruption of memory storage or retrieval occurs.

Clues about the biological bases of memory can also be gleaned from the study of disorders that rob people of memory capabilities. For example, Alzheimer's disease affects about 2.5 million elderly

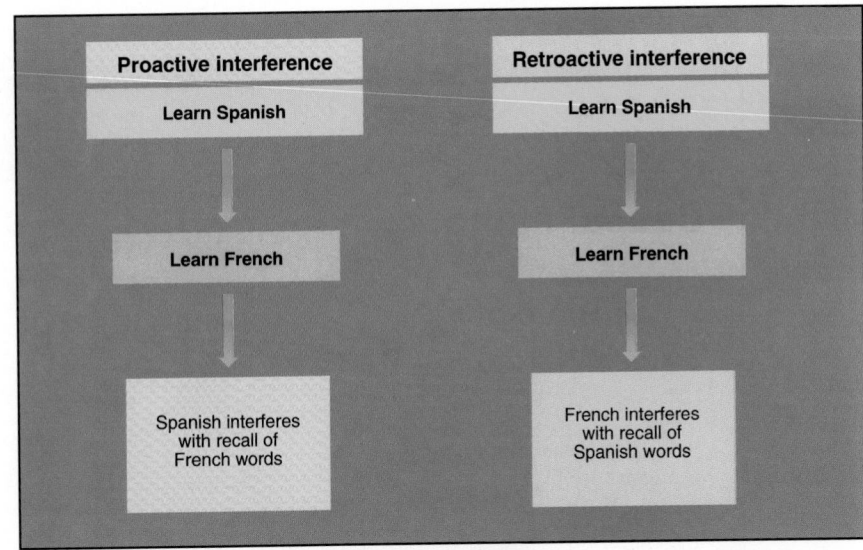

Figure 10.32 *Interference is a major reason for forgetting. In proactive interference, old memories interfere with retrieval of new ones; in retroactive interference, newer memories interfere with the retrieval of older ones.*

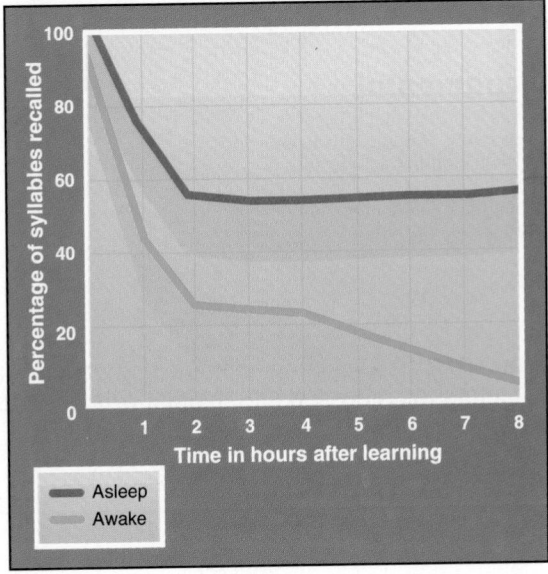

Figure 10.33 *In this study, recall in subjects who stayed awake after learning a list of nonsense syllables and were tested after varying time intervals was compared with recall in subjects who slept for varying periods after learning the syllables and were retested upon being awakened. The superiority of the subjects who slept was attributed to the relative absence of retroactive interference. (Jenkins & Dallenbach, 1924).*

Forgetting:
Factors Suggested by Theory and Research

$B=f(P,E)$

Causal Factors

Biological
- Inadequate protein kinase activity
- Damage to hippocampus, amygdala, cerebellum, cerebral cortex, and other memory areas
- Low levels of acetylcholine and other neurotransmitters involved in memory, as in Alzheimer's disease

Cognitive
- Encoding failures
- Inadequate elaborative rehearsal
- Failure to access retrieval cues
- Reconstructive processes that alter original memory

Intrapsychic
- Repression or defensive distortion of anxiety-arousing memories

Environmental
- Stimulus overload that interferes with encoding, storage, or retrieval
- Other vivid stimuli that interfere with encoding process
- Learning that results in proactive or retroactive interference

Forgetting

Forgetting is a function of interacting personal and environmental causal factors. These factors may vary and may interact with one another in particular ways, depending on the person and the situation.

adults in the United States. One of the cardinal features of the disorder is severe memory loss. Recent research suggests that the memory loss may be due to a decline in the operation of several neurotransmitter systems, especially the acetylcholine system (Kimble, 1992). Acetylcholine is known to play a central role in synaptic transmission in several areas of the brain involved in memory, and disruption of this transmitter system may underlie the devastating loss of memory functions that occurs in Alzheimer's patients.

The causes of forgetting are many and varied. The accompanying Understanding Causes feature summarizes some of the interacting factors we have discussed.

S U M M A R Y

Research Approaches to Memory

● Memory refers to the processes that allow us to record experiences and to retrieve that information later.

● Among the methods used to measure memory are recall, cued recall, recognition, and relearning (savings). These are explicit, or direct, measures of memory. Implicit (indirect) methods disguise the testing of memory.

Perspectives on the Nature of Memory

● Memory can be approached from a number of perspectives. We can study different kinds of memory (such as episodic, semantic, and procedural memory). We can also take an information processing approach and examine the processes (encoding, storage, and retrieval) involved in remembering. Finally, we can explore the architecture, or structure, of memory.

● Episodic memory is memory for events. Semantic memory is our store of information about the world and about language. Procedural memories are learned skills. Declarative, or explicit, memory includes episodic and semantic memory, which can be verbalized, whereas procedural memory is termed nondeclarative, or implicit, memory.

● From an information processing perspective, memory involves three important processes: encoding of information so that it can be incorporated into memory; storage of the information in the ''memory bank''; and later retrieval of the information from memory.

● Architectural approaches to memory consider its structure. The most popular architectural conception of memory divides it into three components: sensory registers, which receive information from the senses; a short-term (or working) memory, which can hold a limited amount of information for about 30 seconds, and a long-term memory, which permanently stores information.

● The sensory registers hold information from the senses for a very brief period, at most a few seconds. The iconic store is the visual sensory register, and the echoic store the auditory register.

● Short-term (working) memory can hold about seven items of information for perhaps 30 seconds, and longer if maintenance rehearsal is carried out. Elaborative rehearsal of information in short-term memory, to give it meaning and to connect it with other things we know, can result in transfer of the information to long-term memory.

● Long-term memory is considered a limitless store of information. The content of long-term memory depends on how information in short-term memory has been encoded. Interactions between the short- and long-term stores are shown in the serial position curve, which demonstrates a primacy effect based on long-term memorization and a recency effect based on short-term memory for recently processed material.

The Physiology of Memory

● Studies of brain-injured people support the notion that episodic, semantic, and procedural memory are distinct systems, for many such people show memory loss in only one system, while the others are left intact. The medial temporal lobe memory system, which includes the hippocampus and adjacent cortex, seems to be an important part of the declarative (episodic and semantic) memory system, whereas the cerebellum has been implicated in procedural learning in animals.

● Recent research indicates that complex biochemical changes in synaptic networks constitute the physiological basis of memory formation. Studies with the sea snail *Aplysia* show that classical conditioning is accompanied by biochemical changes within neurons and actual structural changes that result in more transmitter activity and the development of a more sensitive synaptic connection between neurons.

Encoding and Organization in Memory

● Information is encoded in memory in a number of ways, including verbal codes, imagery codes, and motor codes.

● Verbal encoding includes the use of concepts, schemas, and scripts. When people encode information, they typically do so in terms of the meaning of the information.

● Semantic networks are networks of associated ideas and concepts. Recalling any item in the network is assumed to prime other items and increase the likelihood that they will be recalled.

● According to the dual-coding concept, images can provide a second set of retrieval cues for verbally encoded memories. Schemas are used in imagery coding just as they are in verbal coding. Some people claim to code images with photographic detail and clarity, but this eidetic imagery seems to be a very rare phenomenon.

● Procedural memory often involves motor codes that allow specific responses to occur without conscious control. The repetitive practicing of a motor response to a particular stimulus is one method whereby motor codes and procedural memories are established.

Retrieval of Memories

● Retrieval cues are means whereby information is retrieved from long-term memory. These cues may be internally produced or they may be external cues from the environment.

● A deep level of processing involving elaborative rehearsal provides more retrieval cues and increases the likelihood that a memory will be retrieved.

● Distinctiveness provides unique retrieval cues and can produce vivid and detailed flashbulb memories.

● Encoding specificity refers to the extent to which cues present at recall were also present when the information was originally encoded and can therefore serve as effective retrieval cues. Transfer-appropriate processing occurs when the processing of information is similar to the kind of processing that will be required when the memory is retrieved. Context-dependent, state-dependent, and mood-congruent memories illustrate the potential usefulness of external and internal retrieval cues.

● Memory for events is largely a reconstructive process that can be affected by information processed between the original experience and the recall of the event. This has raised questions about factors, such as misleading questions, that could affect the memories of eyewitnesses to crimes.

● Memory abilities can be enhanced by measures, including mnemonic devices, that increase meaning and enrich the network of associations in which the information is embed-ded. Distributing learning over time and associating contextual cues with the information can also facilitate recall.

Forgetting

● Memory failures can occur for a number of reasons. One is a failure to encode the information and insert it into long-term memory.

● Once information is in long-term memory, it can be forgotten. At one time, it was thought that physical memory traces simply decayed with disuse, but today the concept of interfer-ence is more influential. Proactive interference occurs when material learned earlier interferes with retrieval of information learned later; conversely, retroactive interference occurs when recently learned material interferes with retrieval of information learned earlier. It is also possible that previous learning can enhance later learning, a phenomenon known as positive transfer.

● Psychodynamic theorists suggest that forgetting of anxiety-arousing material may occur through a process of motivated forgetting, or repression.

KEY TERMS AND CONCEPTS

architectural concepts (p. 302)
chunking (p. 304)
concept (p. 310)
context-dependent memory (p. 317)
cued recall (p. 299)
decay theory (p. 324)
declarative memory (p. 301)
distributed practice (p. 322)
dual coding (p. 312)
duplex theory of memory (p. 316)
echoic store (p. 304)
eidetic imagery (p. 313)
elaborative rehearsal (p. 305)
encoding (p. 301)
encoding specificity principle (p. 317)
episodic memory (p. 301)
flashbulb memory (p. 316)
iconic store (p. 303)
interference theory (p. 324)

levels of processing (p. 316)
long-term memory (p. 302)
maintenance rehearsal (p. 305)
massed practice (p. 322)
medial temporal lobe memory system (p. 307)
memory (p. 298)
method of loci (p. 322)
mnemonic devices (p. 322)
mood-congruent recall (p. 318)
nondeclarative, or implicit, memory (p. 301)
nonsense syllables (p. 298)
positive transfer (p. 325)
primacy effect (p. 306)
priming (p. 312)
proactive interference (p. 324)
procedural memory (p. 301)
recall (p. 299)
recency effect (p. 306)

recognition (p. 299)
reconstructive memory (p. 318)
relearning (p. 299)
reminiscence (p. 324)
retrieval (p. 301)
retrieval cues (p. 315)
retroactive interference (p. 324)
retrograde amnesia (p. 325)
schema (p. 311)
script (p. 312)
semantic memory (p. 301)
semantic network (p. 312)
sensory registers (p. 302)
serial position curve (p. 306)
short-term, or working, memory (p. 302)
state-dependent memory (p. 318)
storage (p. 301)
subjective organization (p. 311)
transfer-appropriate processing (p. 317)

SUGGESTED READINGS

Baddeley, A. D. (1982). *Your memory: A user's guide.* New York: Macmillan. A highly readable and lavishly illustrated treatment of memory, with many practical suggestions for improving memory.

Greene, R. L. (1992). *Human memory: Paradigms and paradoxes.* Hillsdale, NJ: Erlbaum. A description of the major research methods that have been used to study human memory and stimulate the development of theories.

Loftus, E., & Ketcham, K. (1991). *Witness for the defense: The accused, the eyewitness, and the expert who puts memory on trial.* New York: St. Martin's Press. Memory researcher Elizabeth Loftus describes her experiences as an expert legal witness who attempts to raise questions about the accuracy of eyewitness identification testimony.

Squire, L. R. (1987). *Memory and brain.* New York: Oxford University Press. A fascinating description by a leading researcher of the linkages that are being found between brain mechanisms and memory.

Reasoning, Problem Solving, and Intelligence

11

CHAPTER OUTLINE

When you think of Hawaiian skies, what comes to mind? For many of us, the words evoke images of bright blue skies with fluffy clouds, an occasional rainbow, and warm tropical breezes. For the crew and passengers of a United Airlines flight in February, 1989, however, the skies over Maui became a terrifying setting in which the limits of human resourcefulness were tested, with survival at stake.

On a routine flight 20,000 feet above the Pacific Ocean, the metal surface at the front of the plane suddenly ripped away from the rest of the aircraft, leaving the flight deck and forward passenger compartments exposed to the air. Eleven passengers were sucked from the airliner to their deaths. The sudden alteration in the physical characteristics of the plane meant that it could not be flown normally. The captain, an experienced pilot, needed to develop a mental model of the plane in its changed form in order to control it and keep it from plunging into the ocean. Thanks to his experience and his knowledge of the principles under which the aircraft normally responded to its controls, the captain quickly recognized what needed to be done, formulated a plan for doing it, and then executed the appropriate actions. The captain and the first officer could not communicate with one another verbally because of the noise from the engines and the roar of the wind, so they used hand signals to coordinate their activities. Through perfect teamwork, they were able to land the aircraft safely at an auxiliary airfield, a feat that was labeled by one aeronautical engineer as "astonishing" (see Figure 11.1).

Incidents like this illustrate the power of human reasoning and problem-solving abilities. The aviators used their memories and reasoning powers quickly and effectively under conditions of extreme stress. Yet the basic mental operations they used to solve this life-and-death challenge were really no different from many of the mundane reasoning and problem-solving activities that you and I engage in each day.

Although human beings are physically puny and relatively defenseless in comparison with some other species, we dominate our world because we think better than other animals do. In the language of the cognitive scientist, we have remarkable abilities to create *mental representations* of the world and to manipulate these mental representations so as to move from problem to solution (Simon, 1990). Mental representations take a variety of forms, including images, ideas, concepts, and principles, all of which are stored in semantic memory.

The most primitive way of solving problems is through *trial and error,* in which one solution after another is tried until the problem is solved. Most of the time, however, people solve problems by developing solutions in their minds before applying them

Figure 11.1 *The successful conclusion of United Airlines Flight 118 was a tribute to the power of human reasoning and problem-solving abilities.*

in the world. For example, if you decide to build yourself a bookcase, you are unlikely to nail or screw boards together at random in the hope that the finished product will serve your purposes. Instead, you will develop mental representations of what the finished product should look like. These will likely include a visual image as well as general principles for successful construction which are likely to be expressed in linguistic terms (for example, "Give the shelves enough support to hold up the heavy books" or "Build from the bottom up").

Cognitive science is in large part the study of how mental representations are formed, manipulated, and translated into action (Hunt, 1989). Thus, a fundamental concern of the cognitive scientist involves how people reason and solve problems. In this chapter, we explore these cognitive skills.

As we all know, people differ in their abilities to reason and to solve problems. Colloquially, we say that some people are more "intelligent" than others. However, as we shall see, this is too simplistic a notion. In many cases, who is "smarter" depends on what sort of problem needs to be solved and how a person thinks about, or *frames,* the problem. Therefore, let us first consider the basic cognitive elements that underlie reasoning and problem solving themselves. Then we will examine reasoning and problem solving, as well as some major sources of error in these activities. Finally, we will explore the nature and origin of individual differences in the wide range of cognitive skills that are included in the term *intelligence.*

Concepts and Propositions

Thinking includes a wide range of mental activities. Basically, thinking may be called the internal ''language of the mind,'' but a moment's reflection suggests that there is more than one language. One mode of thought takes the form of verbal sentences that we seem to ''hear'' in our minds. This is called **propositional thought** because it expresses a proposition, or statement. Another thought mode, **imaginal thought,** consists of images, particularly visual ones that we can ''see'' in our mind. There may also be a third mode, **motoric thought,** which relates to mental representations of motor movements. All three of these modes of thinking enter into our abilities to reason, solve problems, and engage in the many forms that ''intelligent'' thinking can take.

A proposition is a statement that expresses a fact. ''College students are intelligent people'' is a proposition. So is ''Dogs are animals.'' All propositions consist of concepts—such as *college students, intelligent people, dogs,* and *animals*—that are combined in a particular way. As we saw in Chapter 10, concepts form the basic units of semantic memory. They are a means of placing objects, activities, abstractions (*liberal* and *conservative,* for example), and events in broader categories whose members have essential features in common. Categorization has important psychological effects, for it influences how we tend

to think about, and react to, members of a conceptual category. As we shall see, this has important implications for reasoning and problem solving, because how we state propositions about a problem or decision can influence how we try to solve the problem or reason through to a decision (Anderson, 1991).

How do we acquire the many concepts we have? Although some of them, especially those relating to time and space, may be innate, most are learned. Some of this learning occurs through explicit instruction, in which someone defines the central features that are shared by every member of a particular class. For example, you have learned that all propositions are made up of concepts that are joined together to make a statement. Learning also occurs through personal experiences in which we note the similarities in features among various objects or events.

Many of our concepts are difficult to define explicitly. For example, you are quite familiar with the concept *vegetable,* yet you might be hard-pressed to come up with an explicit definition of what a vegetable is. According to Eleanor Rosch (1978), many of our concepts have no firm boundaries. Instead, they are defined by the most typical and familiar members of the class. These are called **prototypes.** Rosch suggests that we often decide which category something belongs to by its degree of resemblance to the prototype (see Figure 11.2).

Consider the following questions: (1) Is a sparrow a bird? (2) Are penguins birds? (3) Are bats birds? According to the prototype view, you should have come to a quicker decision for the first question than for the last two. Why? Because a sparrow fits most people's *bird* prototype (and, in fact may *be* some people's prototype) better than a penguin (which is a bird though it lacks some essential prototypic features, like the ability to fly) or a bat (which flies but is not a bird). Experiments measuring speed of response have found that it does indeed take most people longer to decide whether penguins or bats are birds (Rips & others, 1974).

Figure 11.2 *Which of the following are birds? The speed with which you make the decision is based on the extent to which the creature conforms to your prototype of the concept "bird."*

(a)   (b)   (c)   (d)   (e)

The use of prototypes is perhaps the most elementary method of forming concepts. The prototypic approach requires only that we note similarities among objects. Thus, children's early concepts are based on prototypes of the objects and people they encounter personally. They store these in long-term memory, then decide if new objects they encounter are similar enough to the prototype to be a "Mommy," a "cookie," a "doggie," and so on (Smith & Zarate, 1992). Because prototypes may differ as a result of personal experience, there is considerable room for arbitrariness and individual differences in prototypic concepts.

Combining concepts, as noted, results in propositions. One general rule of combination is that propositions contain one concept that is a subject and another that is a predicate. Thus, in our example, *students* is the subject, and *are intelligent people* is the predicate (see Figure 11.3). Propositions, in turn, can be combined into complex thoughts that govern our attempts to reason and solve problems. As we explore the complexities of reasoning and problem-solving, the central role of concepts and propositions will be demonstrated repeatedly.

■ ■

Reasoning and Problem Solving

Two types of reasoning underly many of our attempts to make decisions and solve problems. In **deductive reasoning,** we reason from general principles to a conclusion about a specific case. In **inductive reasoning,** we start with specific facts and try to develop a general principle. The distinction will become clear as we discuss these two kinds of reasoning, as will the points at which both deductive and inductive reasoning can go awry.

Deductive Reasoning

A person reasons deductively when he or she begins with a set of **premises**—or facts assumed to be true—

and determines what they imply about a specific situation. Deductive reasoning is the basis of formal mathematics and logic. Logicians regard it as the strongest and most valid form of reasoning, because the conclusion cannot be false *if* the premises (factual statements) are true. Thus, to use the classic deductive argument, or syllogism, if all men are mortal (major premise), and if Socrates is a man (minor premise), then Socrates is mortal (conclusion). More formally, the underlying deductive principle may be stated:

> If you have a proposition *if X then Y,* and an *X* occurs, then you can infer *Y.*

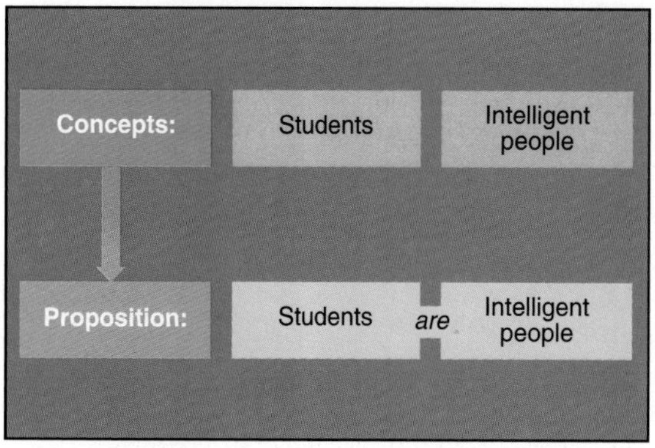

"Simple deduction, my dear Watson." Generations of Sherlock Holmes readers have marveled at the master detective's powers of reasoning. Here is one simple example, taken from the story *Silver Blaze* (Doyle, 1892). In the story, Holmes and Watson are greeted by a barking dog when they arrive at the scene of the crime. They are told that there was a burglary the previous night. Holmes disagrees. Because the dog did not bark the previous night, Holmes concludes that the burglary must have been an inside job. His reasoning is as follows.

1. A burglar is a stranger.
2. If a stranger comes, the dog barks.
3. The dog did not bark.
4. Therefore a stranger did not come.
5. Therefore a burglar did not come.

Stumbling Blocks in Deductive Reasoning

Holmes's argument, though impeccably logical, may not be typical of problem solvers in general. Research has shown that people often have considerable difficulty in applying deductive logic (Markowitz & Nantel, 1989; Rips, 1988). The difficulties occur at several points in the reasoning process. Analyzing these failures tells us much about human reasoning processes and weaknesses.

Failure to Map the Problem. People have trouble translating from a real-world situation to a precise logical notation. Formally, this is called **mapping the problem** into a logical form. In the Holmes story, as it has been stated here, all the relevant information (Statements 1 through 3) and only that information is provided. But in many real-world situations, we are faced with a mass of facts, and we have to decide which ones to consider at all. Robert Sternberg (1988) has called this process **selective encoding.** He has conducted a number of studies showing that people often fail to solve problems because they fail at the selective encoding step. That is, they simply don't

Figure 11.3 *Concepts are the building blocks of thinking and reasoning. They can be combined into propositions to create both simple and complex thoughts, and the propositions can serve as the basis for deductive reasoning.*

consider the relevant information. Instead, they focus on irrelevant information that leads them astray. Consider, for example, the following problem. As you solve it, analyze the mental steps you take, and do not read on until you have decided on an answer.

> Your drawer contains 19 black socks and 13 blue socks. Without turning on the light, how many socks do you have to pull out of the drawer to be sure you have a complete set?

As you solved the problem, did you take into account the fact that there were 19 black socks and 13 blue ones? If so, you—like many of Sternberg's Yale University subjects—made the problem much more difficult by focusing on a factor that is irrelevant. All that matters is how many *colors* of socks there are. It doesn't matter if there are a thousand socks of each color; once you have selected any *three* of them, you are bound to have at least two of the same color.

Failure to Apply Deductive Rules. People have even more trouble with the second step, that of solving the problem in the formal language of deductive reasoning. Even when people have learned to use general problem-solving methods, such as formal logic, they tend to think of them as methods to be used only in certain situations. Probably the best example of this is the way that people use mathematics, which is a special kind of formal logical system. A great many problems *can* be stated mathematically, but people generally do not *use* mathematics in many of these situations.

This point was illustrated in a recent experiment that has important implications for education. Students in high school mathematics classes usually learn how to deal with arithmetic-progression problems. These are problems in which a variable is set at an initial value and then is increased by a constant amount per interval for a number of intervals. An example is "If your bank account had $1,000 to start and you put in $100 every month for 10 months, how much would you have at the end?" Arithmetic-progression problems arise in a number of settings, ranging from arithmetic to cooking to physics. In physics classes, they can take the form of constant-acceleration problems. An example is "If your car was going 30 miles an hour and you accelerated at 5 miles per hour per minute for 5 minutes, how fast would you be going at the end?"

Both math and physics students learn the same problem-solving strategies. However, students in physics classes learn to solve arithmetic-progression problems only as they apply to physics. In contrast, students in mathematics classes practice on arithmetic-progression problems drawn from a variety of areas. Now suppose that physics students are

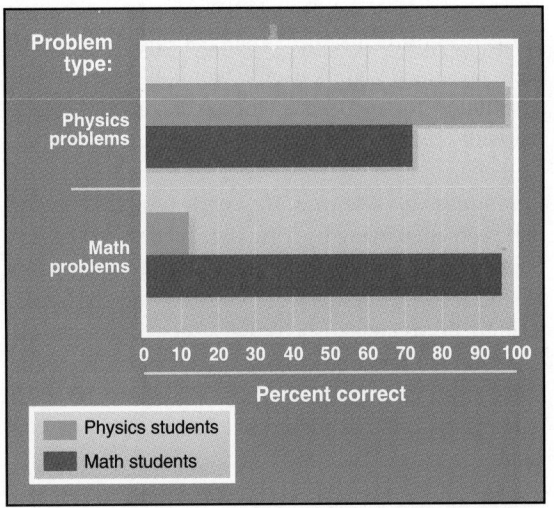

Figure 11.4 *Percentage of arithmetic-progression problems solved by students who were trained to use the same equations, either as a type of mathematics or as a tool in solving physics problems. The specificity of the physics students' previous use apparently interfered with their ability to generalize what they knew to mathematics problems. (Data from Bassok & Holyoak, 1989).*

presented with the problems from a mathematics class, while students from the mathematics class are presented with physics problems for the first time. Will math and physics students be equally skillful at "plugging in" the correct problem-solving methods?

Figure 11.4 shows the results of one experiment (Bassok & Holyoak, 1989). Clearly, the mathematics students had less trouble solving the physics problems than the physics students had solving the mathematics problems, even though exactly the same formal deductive system is used in each case.[1] Because the mathematics students had practiced recognizing when to use the problem-solving method in a variety of different situations, they quickly applied it to the physics problems. The physics students had learned only to use it on physics problems, and they simply failed to apply their knowledge in the novel math situations.

Belief Bias. People often abandon logical rules in favor of their own personal beliefs. For example, in one study, college students were asked to judge if the conclusions followed logically from syllogisms like the following:

> All things that are smoked are good for the health.
> Cigarettes are smoked.
> Therefore, cigarettes are good for the health.

Now, the conclusion *does* follow logically from the premises, even though the first statement is not true. Yet students frequently claimed it did not follow because they disagreed with the major premise (the first statement). They exhibited **belief bias;** their cor-

---

[1] In each case, the appropriate formula is $Y = B + (a)D$, where B is the original value, D is the amount added, and (a) is the number of times it is added, providing Ys of $2,000 and 55 mph, respectively, for the two problems given above.

rect beliefs about the harmful effects of smoking got in the way of their logic. When the same syllogisms were presented with nonsense words like *ramadians* substituted for *cigarettes,* the errors in logic were markedly reduced (Markowitz & Nantel, 1989).

Limitations of Working Memory. Another reason that problem solving by formal deduction can be difficult is that the bookeeping required can simply overwhelm working memory. It is very easy to show this. Arithmetic, as noted, is a formal system of deduction. The rules are summed up in the tables of addition and multiplication for single digits, which we have all memorized. But try computing 1,784 x 49,417 in your head!

Failure to map problems correctly, failure to apply deductive rules, the influence of personal beliefs, and limitations of working memory all interfere with the use of deductive reasoning. Given all these difficulties, how do people solve deductive problems at all? The answer seems to be that we often skirt formal logic in favor of less precise problem-solving methods that apply to specific situations. In the words of the cognitive scientist, we use *problem-solving schemas* to overcome the limitations of a small working memory.

Problem-Solving Schemas as a Substitute for Deduction

Problem-solving schemas are methods for solving specialized classes of problems. We have learned a great many of them, from schemas for cooking dinner or getting acquainted with a person we've just met to schemas for solving arithmetic-progression problems. Problem-solving schemas are similar in many respects to forms that we fill out in our minds, not unlike the do-it-yourself tax computation forms that millions of taxpayers purchase. If the form applies, fill in the blanks and the answer will be obvious.

Another example of a schema is used in the Understanding the Causes of Behavior features in this book. Psychologists use this schema when they want to summarize and understand the factors that influence a given kind of behavior: "Direct your search in terms of biological, environmental, cognitive, and intrapsychic determinants and their interactions." One reason for exposing you to this feature again and again is to give you a useful schema for analyzing the causes of behavior that you can carry with you from your psychology course.

To illustrate the important role played by schemas, let us consider two problems that have been used in studies of deductive reasoning. The first is the *four-cards problem.* Imagine that the four cards shown in Figure 11.5*a* are placed in front of you. As you can

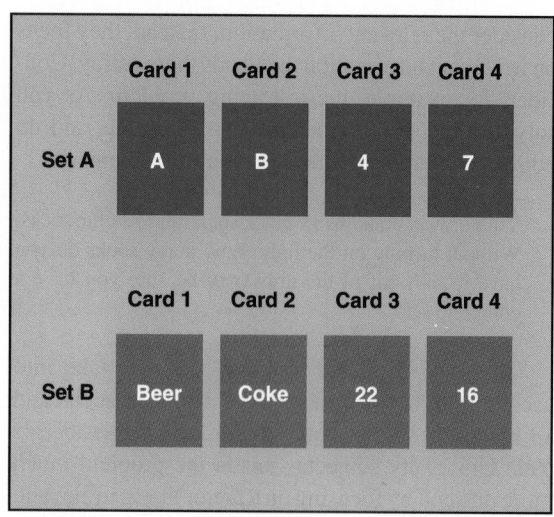

➤ **Figure 11.5** *Two versions of the four-cards problem. Each card has a letter on one side and a number on the other. In Set A, what is the smallest number of cards that you could turn over to test the rule "If the card has a vowel on one side, it has an odd number on the other side?"*

see, each card has a single letter written on one side and a number on the other side. You are told that the following rule *may* apply to the cards: "If the card has a vowel on one side, then it has an odd number on the other side." Your task is to choose the smallest number of cards that you could turn over to determine whether the rule is valid. Now, which cards should you turn over to make this determination? (Please write your answer in the margin; we'll come back to it later.)

Now, let us try another problem, which we will call the cholera problem. Imagine that you are a passport inspector in an Asian country. You are told: "In order to control the spread of disease, examine people's visas. If the visa has REQUEST ENTRY on the front be sure that VACCINATED is stamped on the back."

Four visas are placed on a table in front of you. The entries on the visas are:

REQUEST ENTRY   NOT ENTERING   VACCINATED NOT VACCINATED

Which ones should you turn over? Decide before reading on.

Now, the answers to the problems: On the four-cards problem, you should turn over the A to see if there is an odd number on the other side and the 4 to make sure that there is *not* a vowel on the other side. (If the 4 has a vowel on the other side, the rule is disconfirmed.) On the cholera problem, the answer is that you should turn over the REQUEST ENTRY card and the NOT VACCINATED card.

By now, you may have recognized that the four-cards problem and the cholera problem are logically the same. But they are not at all the same psychologically. Figure 11.6 shows the results from a study in which Chinese students in Hong Kong and U.S. students in Michigan attempted to solve either the four-cards or the cholera problem. The cholera problem was clearly the easier one for the Chinese students to solve, whereas the U.S. students found both problems equally difficult. Why?

The cholera problem is phrased as a "permission" problem, meaning that if someone has met the precondition for an action (being vaccinated), he or she is permitted but not required to perform the action (entering the country). The Hong Kong students knew this, since the problem statement was similar to a regulation that had recently been enforced by the Hong Kong immigration authorities. Therefore, all they had to do was to plug in their existing schema. The U.S. students had no such experience.

Perhaps the Michigan students would do as well as the Hong Kong students did if the problem was relevant to a permission schema that U.S. students understand. To test this hypothesis, U.S. students were shown the cards in Figure 11.5b. They were told that each card had a person's age on one side and what that person was drinking on the other side. Now, the statement to be evaluated was, "If a person is drinking beer, then he or she must be over 19." Given this problem, the U.S. students did as well as the Hong Kong students had done on the cholera problem (Griggs & Cox, 1982).

If formal logic is used to solve the four-cards, cholera, and drinking problems, they should be equally difficult to solve; the cards A, REQUEST ENTRY, and BEER correspond to one another, and so do 7, NOT VACCINATED, and 16. But people often don't use formal logic in approaching such problems. Instead they use schemas that work in restricted situations. Doing so requires less effort, for relying on schemas changes the process of problem solving from the development of an elaborate deductive structure in working memory to the selection of one of many schemas in long-term memory. This is precisely what people are good at. Our working memories are limited, but our long-term memories have unlimited capacity. Schema-based reasoning may not be an elegant method of problem solving, but it is one that draws on a strength of the human mind.

The Role of Schemas in Expertise

Schemas can help explain what it means to be an expert. One of the best examples is the expert chess player; masters and grand masters far exceed the playing ability of even the brightest novices. Similar phenomena can be observed in almost every field. The

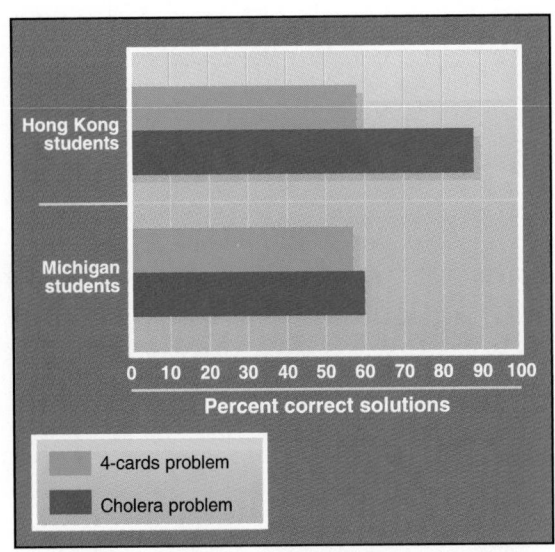

Figure 11.6 *Percentages of students from Hong Kong and from Michigan who solved the four-cards and cholera problems. (Data from Cheng & Holyoak, 1985, Experiment 1).*

airline incident described at the beginning of the chapter demonstrated why commercial airline pilots with 10 or 20 years of experience are generally, and correctly, considered better pilots than novices. Likewise, dentists with a great deal of experience inspire greater confidence from their patients than do dental students who are about to begin work with drills held in trembling hands.

Dentistry, chess playing, and piloting aircraft are very different activities. Nevertheless, researchers have found that there is a common theme underlying almost all expert problem solving (see Figure 11.7). Experts (a) have developed a great many schemas to guide problem solving in their field; and (b) are much better than novices at recognizing when each schema should be applied. We can illustrate this by considering some experiments on reasoning in physics, a notoriously difficult college subject.

Michelene Chi and her colleagues at the University of Pittsburgh compared the problem-solving processes of professional physicists (professors and advanced graduate students) with those of undergraduates who had completed courses in introductory physics (Chi & others, 1988). In all cases both the physicists and the undergraduates, in some sense, "knew enough" to solve the problems they were given. However, the way that they attacked the problems showed how important it is to frame the problem correctly. The experts stated problems in terms of abstract principles, such as "Newton's second law." In contrast, the novices tended to use descriptions that referred to the surface characteristics of the problem, such as "sliding blocks." This difference in descriptions is *not* just a matter of using expert-sounding

Figure 11.7 *Regardless of the field of endeavor, experts differ from novices primarily in their knowledge of problem-solving schemas and when to apply them.*

words. When a problem is described in terms of physical laws, the description itself suggests a schema for problem solving.

Cognitive psychologists have seen the same sort of expert-novice contrast in virtually every field of human endeavor that they have studied (Chase & Simon, 1973; Chi & others, 1988; Lesgold, 1988). Other studies have shown that even among novices, those who approach problems in terms of underlying principles are more effective problem solvers than those who do not try to use principles (Hardiman & others, 1989).

Consider again what this difference in schema application means in terms of what we know about human memory. As we have seen, human long-term memory is quite good. Experts, because they rely on learned schemas, depend on their long-term memory capacity, and they are able to quickly analyze a problem and select the retrieval cues needed to retrieve from memory and apply the appropriate schema. In contrast, novices who haven't yet learned specialized schemas must use general problem-solving methods that force them to solve problems in working memory, on the space-limited "blackboard of the mind" (New-

ell & Simon, 1972). In so doing, they tax their working memories—the weakest link in the human mind.

Inductive Reasoning and Problem Solving

Inductive reasoning is a different mode of reasoning than deduction. In our daily lives, we use it quite often to derive general principles or conclusions. Instead of reasoning from the general rule to the specific case—or deducing what the facts must be, given the assumptions—we reason from specific instances to general conclusions.

Medical diagnosis is one example of inductive thinking. A patient appears with headache, a fever, and dizzy spells. Does the patient have influenza? Or blood poisoning? Or some rare disease, like parrot fever? To make a medical diagnosis, a physician has to proceed from the specific symptoms to a general diagnostic category that includes the patient's complaints and can account for the symptoms in this specific case.

Scientists who discover general principles, or laws, as a result of observing a number of specific instances use a process of induction. If enough apples fall on our heads, we may conclude that there exists a general force that pulls objects toward the earth. Inductive reasoning is also very important in real-life decision making, where we are often presented with facts and asked to draw a conclusion. We will see that people reason inductively by fitting the present situation into a schema—asking "have we seen this sort of problem before?" This works well enough most of the time; but as we shall see, it can lead to certain errors.

An important distinction between deductive and inductive reasoning lies in the certainty of the results. As noted earlier, deductive conclusions are certain to be correct, given that the premises are true. In contrast, inductive reasoning leads to *likelihood* rather than certainty. That is, if we reason flawlessly, it may be improbable that our conclusion is wrong, but the possibility of error (as in a medical diagnosis) remains.

Stages of Inductive Problem Solving

Inductive problem solving proceeds through four stages (see Figure 11.8). First, we must arrive at some understanding of the nature of the problem. Next, we generate hypotheses, or problem-solving strategies, that seem applicable to the problem as we see it. Third, we test the hypotheses or potential problem solutions by trying them out. Fourth, we evaluate the usefulness of the problem-solving strategies by assessing their effectiveness. Our effectiveness at each of these stages determines our success in solving the problem.

Understanding, or Framing, the Problem. Most of us have had the experience of feeling totally frustrated in our attempts to solve a problem. We may even think that the problem is unsolvable. Then someone suggests a new way of looking at the problem and the solution suddenly becomes obvious. Let us consider the following problem, illustrated in Figure 11.9:

Train A leaves Baltimore for its 50-mile trip to Washington D.C. at a constant speed of 25 miles per hour. At the same time, train B leaves Washington, bound for Baltimore at the same speed of 25 miles per hour. A crow who has ingested a large dose of amphetamine leaves Baltimore at the same time as train A, flying toward Washington at a speed of 60 miles per hour. When the crow encounters train B, it turns and flies back to train A, then instantly reverses its direction and flies back to train B. The supercharged bird continues this sequence until trains A and B meet midway between Baltimore and Washington. The question: What is the total distance the bird will have traveled in its excursions between trains A and B?

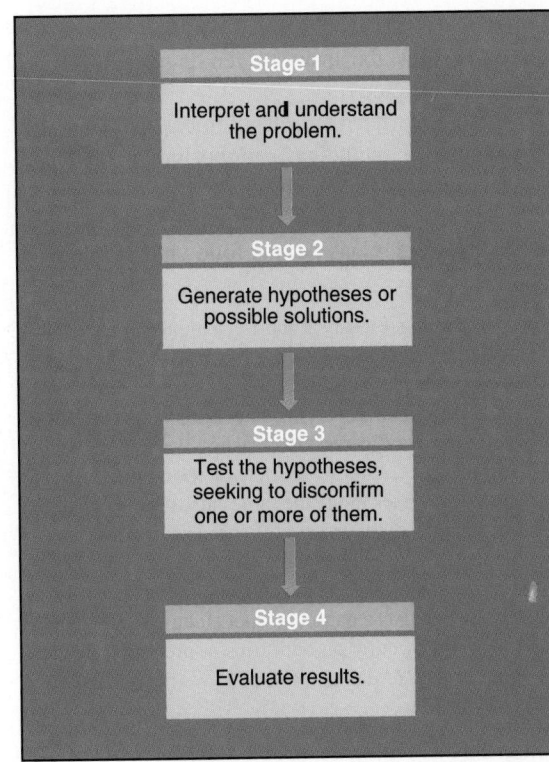

◀ **Figure 11.8** *Stages of inductive problem solving.*

Stage 1
Interpret and understand the problem.

Stage 2
Generate hypotheses or possible solutions.

Stage 3
Test the hypotheses, seeking to disconfirm one or more of them.

Stage 4
Evaluate results.

Try to solve this problem before reading on.

Many people approach the problem as a *distance* problem. They try to compute how far the bird will fly during each segment of its flight between trains A and B. (I have seen pages of computations done to solve the problem in this way.) But suppose you approach the problem by asking how long it will take the trains to meet? The crow will have flown the same period of time at 60 miles per hour. Now that you have reframed it as a *time* problem, the problem be-

Figure 11.9 *The bird and the trains. A crow flies back and forth between the two trains, which are approaching one another at the speeds indicated. How far will the bird have traveled by the time the trains meet at the center of the 50-mile route? (The answer appears on page 363).*

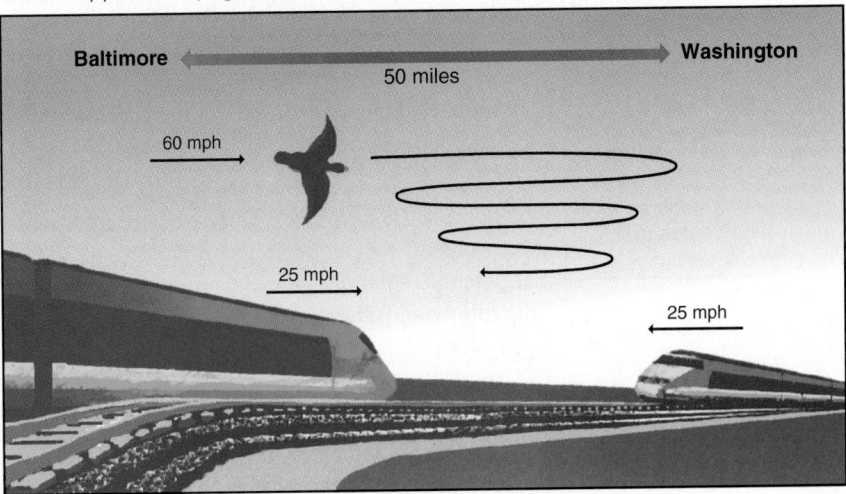

Baltimore ◀————— 50 miles —————▶ Washington

60 mph

25 mph

25 mph

comes much easier to solve. (You can check your solution against the answer given on page 363 at the end of the chapter.)

As noted earlier, there are a number of "languages of the mind," including a propositional mode, an imagery mode, and a motor mode. One of these may be more effective than others in approaching a particular problem. Consider the following problem:

> One morning, exactly at sunrise, a monk began to climb a mountain. A narrow path, a foot or two wide, spiraled around the mountain to a temple at the summit. The monk ascended at varying rates, stopping many times along the way to rest. He reached the temple shortly before sunset. After several days at the temple, he began his journey back along the same path, starting at sunrise and again walking at variable speeds with many pauses along the way. His average speed descending was, of course, greater than his average climbing speed. Prove that there exists a particular spot along the path that the monk will occupy on both trips at precisely the same time of day. (Adams, 1974, p. 4)

In trying to solve this problem, many people begin in a propositional mode. They may even try to write out a set of equations, a strategy that could result in the filling of even more scrap paper than the crow-problem strategy just described. But suppose you approach the problem not in a propositional mode but in a visual mode? All you need to do is *visualize* the upward journey of the monk superimposed on the downward journey. No matter what their respective speeds or how frequent their pauses, there is bound to be a place along the path where the two monk images meet. This proves that there is a spot that the monk occupied on both trips at exactly the same time of day. (Fortunately, you don't have to know where the spot is in order to solve the problem as stated.)

As we can see, the initial understanding of the problem is a most important step to a successful solution. If we set up, or frame, the problem inaccurately, we can easily be led into a maze of blind alleys and ineffective solutions. If we frame it accurately, we at least have a chance to generate an effective solution. Framing can also affect the way we regard the alternatives and the choices we make. ▼

Generating Hypotheses. Once we have interpreted the problem, we can begin to formulate hypotheses, or potential solutions. Ideally, we might proceed in the following fashion:

1. Determine what explanations will be considered. This is called *establishing the initial hypotheses.*
2. Determine which of these explanations are consistent with the evidence that has so far been observed. Rule out any explanations that do not fit the evidence.

We will call this *evaluating the hypotheses against the evidence.*

Testing the Hypotheses. Consider the hypotheses that remain. Is there any test that should give one result if one hypothesis is true and another result if another hypothesis is true? If so, make that test and evaluate the hypotheses again in light of the evidence from that test. This is called *testing the hypotheses.* It is essentially what scientists do when they design experiments. Note that the important thing is that a test is designed to *rule out* hypotheses, not to demonstrate that they are true.

With these steps in mind, let us look again at the Sherlock Holmes problem. As it was described earlier, this was a deductive problem. But I did not describe the whole story; I just described the deductive part. Here is the more general setting:

The valuable racehorse Silver Blaze has disappeared, and the head groom has been found dead on the moors. The stable boy sleeps in a room in the stable. A watchdog barked at Holmes when he and Watson entered the stable. Who took the racehorse?

1. Who could possibly have done it? A mysterious stranger might have entered (hypothesis 1). A member of the household might have done it (hypothesis 2). Or evil witches might have magically spirited the horse away (hypothesis 3).

Holmes doesn't even consider hypothesis 3. In fact, hypothesis 3 was not part of the original story. I have included it to make a point: Some hypotheses are never examined because they are considered so unlikely that they aren't worth thinking about. This is itself a decision, and people can make a mistake by failing to consider all possible explanations at the outset.

2. The horse is gone. Either hypothesis 1 or hypothesis 2 fits this fact. However, there is no apparent reason why an insider would have stolen the horse, so Holmes (and everyone else) initially considers it most likely that a burglar entered.

3. Is there any piece of evidence that is required by hypothesis 1 and not by hypothesis 2, or vice versa? Yes, there is. Based on his own experience with the dog, Holmes reasons that if a mysterious stranger entered, the dog would have barked. Holmes asks the stable boy if he heard anything in the night. New evidence is obtained: The dog did not bark during the night. Assuming that the stable boy's report is accurate, Holmes then applies deductive reasoning to decide that the theft was, indeed, an inside job. "Elementary, my dear Watson."

Failure to generate diverse hypotheses as possible solutions can prevent effective problem solving. For example, try to solve the matchstick problems in Figure 11.10. To do so, you need to consider some unconventional strategies. Specifically, you need to override aspects of how the matches are presented in Figure 11.10—namely, as two-dimensional objects and as boxes of uniform size. The solutions, which are shown on page 363, become obvious once these constraints are abandoned.

Abraham Luchins (1942) demonstrated another barrier to effective problem solving: a tendency to stick to solutions that have worked in the past. Figure 11.11 shows a series of problems that Luchins gave subjects to solve. Here is the first problem:

Suppose you have a 21-cup jug, a 127-cup jug, and a 3-cup jug. Drawing and discarding as much water as you like, how will you measure out exactly 100 cups of water?

This problem is followed by the remaining six problems in Figure 11.11. Solve all of the problems.

As you worked the problems, you probably discovered that they all were solvable by the same formula, namely $B - A - 2C =$ desired amount. However, by applying the successful formula used on problems 1 through 5, you may have missed even easier solutions for problems 6 and 7, namely $A - C$ for 6 and $A + C$ for 7. If so, you, like Luchins's subjects, were blinded by the **mental set** you had developed by working the earlier problems. Luchins found that most subjects readily used the simple solutions to problems 6 and 7 if they had not done problems 1 through 5 first. Studies of mental set have shown how easy it is to become fixated on one particular approach if we enjoy some degree of success with that approach.

Evaluating Results. The final stage of inductive problem solving is to evaluate the problem solutions. As we saw in the water jars problems, even solutions that prove successful may not be the easiest or the best. Thus, effective problem solvers will ask themselves after the solution of a problem, "Would there have been an easier or more effective way to accomplish the same objective?" The answer to this question can lead to the establishment of additional problem-solving schemas, which may be applicable to future problems.

In science, checking results is an integral part of the scientific method. One way results are checked is through *replication* of findings. Unfortunately, many exciting discoveries do not stand up to the test of replication. One fairly recent example is the reported discovery of a means for inducing cold fusion—that is, the fusing of atomic nuclei at relatively low temperatures—which promised to revolutionize the field of physics. Unfortunately, this discovery could

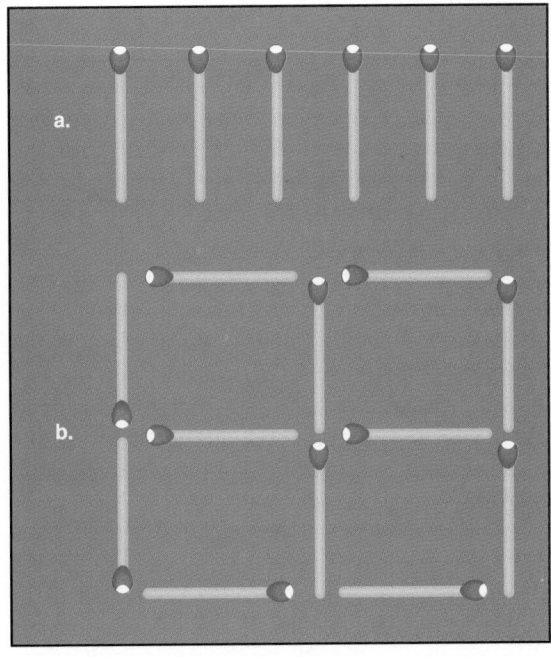

Figure 11.10 *Matchstick problems. (a) Arrange the six matchsticks into four equilateral triangles so that each side is equal in length to the match. (b) Arrange a dozen matchsticks to form four squares as shown. By moving only two matches, make seven squares. (The answer appears on page 363).*

not be verified by other investigators. Many discoveries in psychology have met a similar fate. However, remember that the search for truth involves discovering what is not true as well as what is true. In fact, as the earlier emphasis on disconfirming hypotheses might suggest, it may be more important to know that something is *not* true, a point we will return to presently.

The Use (and Misuse) of Heuristics

Two important strategies for problem solving are algorithms and heuristics. **Algorithms** are formulas or

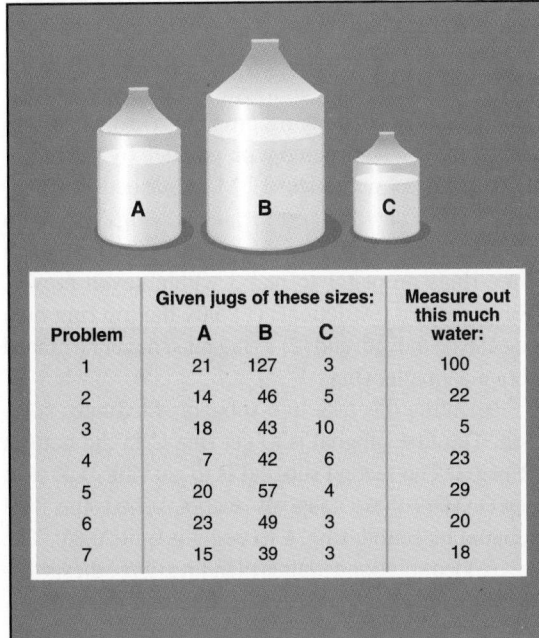

Figure 11.11 *Luchins's water jars problems. Using containers A, B, and C with the capacities shown in the table, how would you measure out the volumes indicated in the right-hand column? You may discover a general formula that fits all seven problems.*

	Given jugs of these sizes:			Measure out this much water:
Problem	A	B	C	
1	21	127	3	100
2	14	46	5	22
3	18	43	10	5
4	7	42	6	23
5	20	57	4	29
6	23	49	3	20
7	15	39	3	18

procedures that automatically generate correct solutions. Mathematical formulas are algorithms; if you use them correctly, you will always get the correct answer. Another algorithm is that if the letters of a word are scrambled in random order to produce an anagram like TERALBAY, then the word can be discovered by a process in which the letters are recombined in all possible combinations.

This last algorithm illustrates one potential problem: Algorithms may be very time-consuming to apply in some situations. In this case, for example, the drawback is that eight letters can be rearranged in 40,320 different ways. We may therefore decide to use a **heuristic,** or rule-of-thumb strategy. In this case, we might try out only consonants in the first and last positions.

Heuristics are mental shortcuts. They are not rules that always provide correct solutions but rather are general strategies that experience has taught us to apply to particular situations. In using these strategies, we typically compare the present facts with some general schema that seems to apply to the present situation.

Problem-Solving Heuristics

Several heuristics serve as general problem-solving strategies. One of them is **means/ends analysis** (Newell & Simon, 1972). This strategy involves identifying differences between the present situation and one's desired state, or goal, and then making changes that will reduce these differences.

Means/ends analysis often results in the application of another heuristic, **subgoal analysis.** People attack a large problem by formulating subgoals, intermediate steps toward a solution. This strategy is an important part of formal goal-setting programs that have proved to be highly effective (Cervone, 1992; Locke & Latham, 1990).

The value of setting subgoals can be seen in the Tower of Hanoi problem, depicted in Figure 11.12. This is a very challenging problem. (In fact, it was one of the tasks mastered with practice by the brain-damaged amnesic patient H. M. described in Chapter 10. However, he never recalled having worked on it.) The terminal goal for this problem is to move all three rings on peg 1 to peg 3 within seven moves. There are two restrictions: (1) only the top ring on a peg can be moved, and (2) a ring must never be placed above a smaller ring.

Breaking this task into subgoals facilitates solution. The first subgoal is to get ring C to the bottom of peg 3. The second subgoal is to get ring B over to peg 3. With these subgoals accomplished, the final subgoal of getting ring A to peg 3 is quite easy. The seven-step solution requires planning (hypothesis formation), checking, and revising hypotheses—all pro-

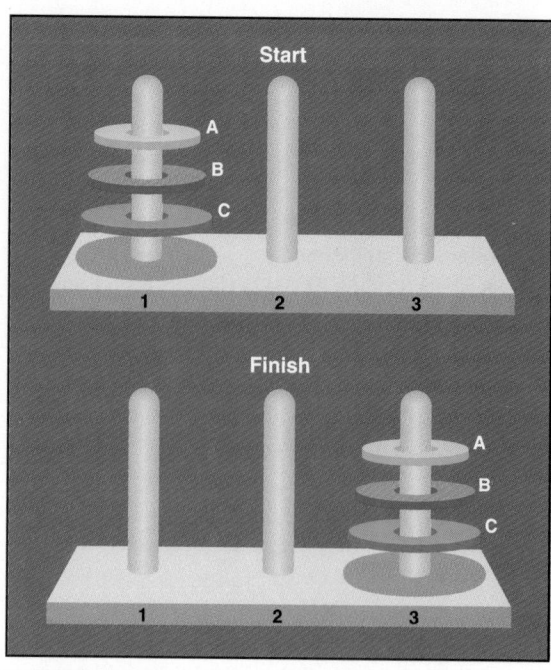

Figure 11.12 *The Tower of Hanoi problem. The object is to move the rings one at a time from peg 1 to peg 3 in the smallest number of moves possible. (It can be done in seven moves.) Only the top ring on a peg can be moved, and a large ring can never be placed on top of a smaller one. (The answer appears on page 363).*

cesses discussed previously. Can you solve the problem? The seven-step sequence of moves is presented on page 363.

Heuristics enter not only into problem-solving strategies but also into judgments and decisions. As we shall see, they can also contribute to errors in judgment.

Uncertainty, Heuristics, and Decision Making

Decision making always occurs in the context of uncertainty; otherwise, there really isn't a decision to be made. In the final analysis, we are always concerned with questions of likelihood, either in formulating a hypothesis, evaluating the evidence, or drawing the conclusion. Since we seldom know what the exact probabilities are, we tend to apply certain heuristics to form judgments of likelihood. Two of these rules of thumb, the representativeness heuristic and the availability heuristic, underlie much of our inductive decision making, and their misuse results in many of our errors. Their role in decision making has been studied extensively by Amos Tversky and Daniel Kahneman (1980, 1982).

The Representativeness Heuristic. An earlier section discussed the importance of prototypes in concept formation. We use the **representativeness**

heuristic to infer how similar something is to our prototype for a particular concept, or class, and therefore how likely it is to be a member of that class.

Suppose that you are given the following description of a young woman.

> Linda is 31 years old, single, outspoken, and very bright. She majored in philosophy. As a student, she was deeply concerned with issues of discrimination and social justice, and she also participated in antinuclear demonstrations.

Rate the likelihood that each of the following hypotheses is true. Use 1 to indicate the most likely statement, 8 to indicate the least likely statement, and any number between 2 and 7 to indicate the likelihood of the second most likely statement.

_____1. Linda is active in the feminist movement.
_____2. Linda is a bank teller.
_____3. Linda is active in the feminist movement and is a bank teller.

Figure 11.13 shows the likelihood estimates that college students attached to each statement (Tversky & Kahneman, 1982). There is a bias toward hypothesis 1, which is not surprising. However, the significant fact is that hypothesis 3 is favored over hypothesis 2. But this *cannot* be correct. Why not? Because everyone who is both a feminist and a bank teller is also ''just'' a bank teller. Furthermore, any person is more likely to be a bank teller than a bank teller *and* a feminist—or for that matter, a bank teller *and* anything else. This illustrates what Tversky and Kahneman termed the **conjunction fallacy,** a violation of the logical principle that the conjunction, or combination, of two events cannot be more likely than either event alone.

Note that you were asked to develop a set of hypotheses about Linda, which is the first step in the inductive reasoning process. What we seem to do in forming hypotheses is to rely on the representativeness of the evidence—the extent to which it is consistent with, or representative of, an existing prototype. This can be a useful way to make a quick judgment, but it may blind us to other evidence, such as the actual probability that the hypothesis holds.

Tversky and Kahneman believe that the reason people make the sort of mistake they did about Linda is that they confuse representativeness with probability. Linda represents our prototype for a feminist bank teller more than she fits our prototype for a bank teller. Therefore, the former is (we think) more likely than the latter. Notice how this argument fits with the ideas about memory discussed in Chapter 10. The description of Linda as ''outspoken'' and ''concerned with issues of discrimination and social justice'' serves a priming function; it activates the components

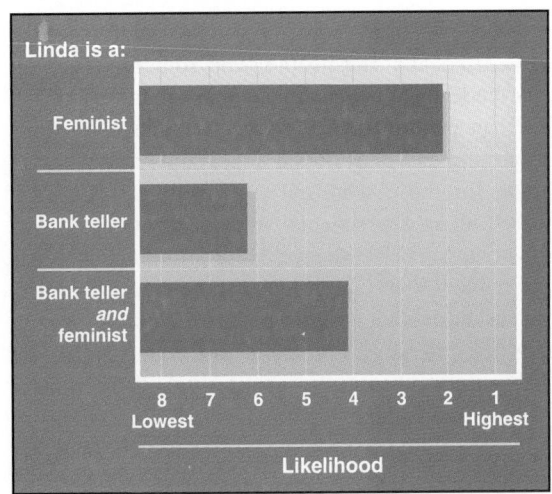

Figure 11.13 *Mean likelihood judgments made by subjects on the basis of the description of Linda cited in the text. (Data from Tversky & Kahneman, 1982).*

in memory that are associated with the concept *feminist,* so it is hard to think of Linda without thinking of a feminist. On the other hand, there is nothing in Linda's description that would activate the concept *bank teller.* Thus, if Linda is to be a bank teller at all, we think she must be a feminist bank teller.

It may well be that we sometimes confuse representativeness with probability. But why shouldn't we? Our minds are built to organize experiences and ideas into classes, or concepts, on the basis of shared characteristics, and the existence of these concepts makes it easy to judge representativeness. This probably works well enough in most circumstances even though, as we have seen, it can sometimes lead to error.

Belief Bias and the Availability Heuristic. Now let us look at another step of the induction process, evaluating the evidence for a hypothesis. Ideally, our determination of how well a hypothesis fits the evidence should not be affected by how much we either believe in the hypothesis or want it to be true. Unfortunately, this is not the case. People are discouragingly able to ignore evidence that doesn't fit in with what they believe, a phenomenon known as the *belief-bias effect.* One reason is a strategy known as the **availability heuristic,** which leads us to base our decisions on the availability of information in memory. If something readily comes to mind, we may consider it more commonplace than it is. For example, recent memorable events, such as the terrorist bombing of an airliner, are readily accessible to memory, and they tend to make people feel that they could suffer a similar fate (Fiske & Taylor, 1991). After several such terrorist acts in the mid-1980s, U.S. and Canadian tourism declined sharply in Europe for nearly a year. Instead of going to Europe, people chose to drive to vacation spots in North America, a decision that, on statistical grounds, actually increased the likelihood of death.

The availability heuristic can be a useful tool for advertisers and salespeople, who sometimes exploit our tendency to believe that events are more likely if we can picture them vividly. The image of one's mourning and debt-ridden dependents is a stock in trade for those who sell life insurance (Cialdini, 1988). In an experimental study, Larry Gregory and his coworkers (1982) gave out promotional materials for cable TV to one group of potential subscribers and asked another group to picture themselves watching first-run movies on cable and saving money on babysitters. The second group, with these images readily accessible in memory, were twice as likely to subscribe as those given the written promotional materials.

The impact of the availability heuristic on erroneous probability judgments has been shown in virtually every field, including psychology (Dawes & others, 1989). For example, clinical psychologists have been shown to grossly overestimate correlations between certain personality traits and certain behaviors (for example, the tendency for paranoids to see eyes looking out at them when they are shown inkblots), when in fact such correlations are quite low or nonexistent (Chapman & Chapman, 1969). One reason is that the clinicians can vividly recall one or more cases in which the personality trait and the behavior were linked while failing to remember the many instances in which the two were unrelated. Much the same can be said of physicians and many other professional judges.

Confirmation Bias. We now move to the last step in the inductive reasoning process, obtaining new evidence. Rationally, we ought to test our ideas by seeking evidence that will disconfirm them, rather than solidifying our ideas by looking for evidence that supports them. The reason is that the most informative piece of evidence we can obtain is one that rules out a hypothesis or causes us to change our ideas. However, people are often unwilling to challenge their cherished beliefs. Instead, they are prone to fall into a trap called **confirmation bias:** They tend to look for evidence that will confirm what they currently believe rather than looking for evidence that tests their beliefs.

To illustrate this, please turn back to page 334 and reread the description of the four-cards problem and the solution you chose. When you were asked "What cards should you turn over?" you were in effect being asked "What new evidence do you need?" The hypothesis to be tested was "If there is a vowel on one side of the card, then there is an odd number on the other side." We *test* this proposition by examining cards that have even numbers on one side. We *confirm* the proposition by examining cards that have vowels or odd numbers on one side. What

people given the four-cards problem do is quite clear. Study after study has shown a strong tendency toward confirmation bias; people tend to look at the card with the odd number to see if it has a vowel on the other side, even though this is a totally uninformative choice (Wason & Johnson-Laird, 1972). Whether it has a vowel or not is irrelevant to the proposition. What did you do?

The principles illustrated in the laboratory study of the four-cards problem undoubtedly apply to real-life situations as well. It has been shown in many social situations (Fiske & Taylor, 1991). For example, William Swann and his coworkers (1992) have shown in a series of experimental studies that people have a strong tendency to seek, elicit, and recall feedback from others that confirms their beliefs about themselves and to avoid and "forget" evidence that disconfirms these self-beliefs. We will review the social aspects of confirmation bias in Chapter 19. They point to the same conclusion as the four-cards problem: People find it difficult to test and challenge their ideas. They want to see them confirmed.

Imagery and Thought

The examples so far have stressed propositional thinking, through which we solve problems by mentally manipulating something like an algebraic language or internal sentences. While propositional thinking is a useful model for much human thought, it doesn't cover all that people do when they solve problems. As in the example of the monk's trips up and down the mountain, we can carry out some problem solving better by manipulating internal visual images than by manipulating internal logical statements. Recent research on the nature of imagery has revealed that the mental operations associated with internal imagery resemble in some important ways the perceptual operations applied to external visual scenes. First, there is physiological evidence for this conclusion. Studies using the PET scan with radioactively labeled deoxyglucose have shown that when subjects are given problems that require the use of visual imagery (for example, "Imagine a kangaroo. Are its back legs shorter than its front legs?"), the occipital cortex, where visual processing is carried out, becomes more active (Tye, 1992). Let us also consider some experimental evidence.

For an example of imagery-based problem solving, refer to Figure 11.14, which shows three pairs of figures used in a *mental rotation experiment* (Shepherd & Cooper, 1982). Try to decide which of these pairs contain two views of the same figure, seen from different orientations, and which contain two nonidentical figures. Do not continue reading until you have made your judgments.

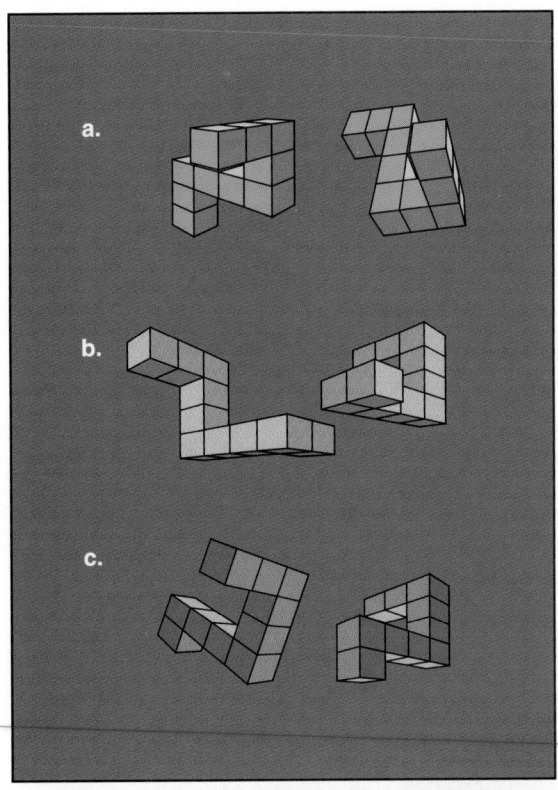

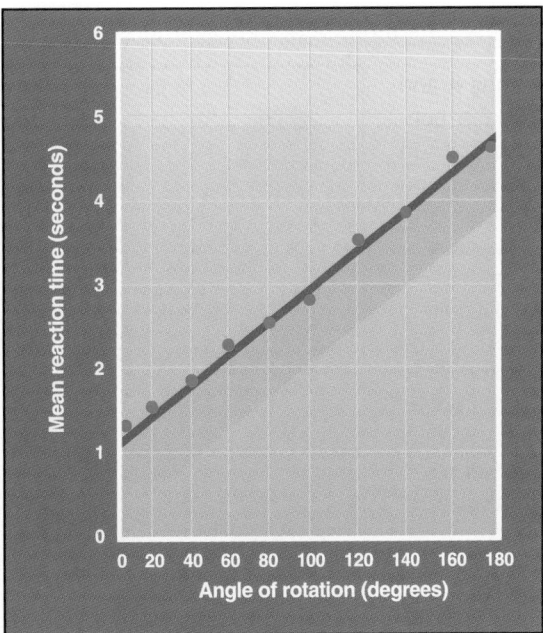

Figure 11.15 *The time required to judge whether rotated figures are the same or different is a linear function of how many degrees the figures must be rotated "in the mind's eye." (Shepard & Cooper, 1982).*

Figure 11.14 *A mental rotation task used in the study of imagery-based thinking. Which of the pairs consist of identical figures viewed from different orientations? (The answer appears on page 363.) (Shepard & Cooper, 1982).*

Now, the answer. The top two pairs are different views of the same figure; the bottom pair consists of a figure and its mirror image. The interesting question is this: How long do you think it took you to make each decision? If you are like most subjects, your data resemble those shown in Figure 11.15. Studies have shown that the time required to decide whether two figures are identical increases in a linear fashion with the amount of rotation required to "mentally" turn one figure into the same orientation as the other. For example, an 80-degree rotation requires twice as long a decision time as a 40-degree rotation.

The importance of this finding is the clue it gives us about what must be occurring in the brain. A linear function like the one in Figure 11.15 would be produced if there were a "little wheel" inside your head that turned the visual image in working memory to the same orientation as the other figure. Now, of course, the idea of a little wheel is silly. What is not at all silly is the discovery that there is a correspondence between the mental processes that operate on images inside your mind and the physical processes that would operate if you were rotating the figures in the external world. This is an important notion, because it means that internal visual images represent physical operations in the external world. However, we must remember that imaginal representations, like propositional ones, are manipulated in working memory. Therefore, this mode of thinking, like propositional reasoning, is limited by the fact that the working memory can only hold an internal representation of limited size.

We have covered a great deal of ground in this discussion of thinking. To conclude the discussion, let us extend what has been discussed to some practical guidelines for increasing creative problem-solving skills.

GUIDELINES FOR CREATIVE PROBLEM SOLVING	ENHANCING HUMAN PERFORMANCE

One of the practical benefits of research on reasoning and problem solving is increased knowledge of how effective and creative problem solvers think and how they approach problems. As suggested in the discussion of the nature of expertise, one of the most valuable resources we can have is experience and training that we can bring to bear on a problem. In some ways, there is no substitute for knowledge and experience, for it provides heuristics and problem-solving schemas that can be very useful. On the other hand, one of the marks of creativity is the ability to break out of conventional schemas when the occasion demands it and engage in **divergent thinking,** the generation of novel ideas or variations on ideas that diverge from the norm (Guilford, 1959). In part, this means refusing to be constrained by convention or traditional approaches to the problem.

Such constraints can be difficult to overcome, as we saw earlier in the matchstick and water jars problems. Consider, for example, the nine-dot problem in Figure 11.16. The task is this: Without lifting your pencil from the paper, draw no more than four *straight* lines that will pass through all nine dots.

Many people have difficulty solving this problem. Did you? If so, it is probably because you imposed an unnecessary constraint on yourself and tried to stay within the boundary formed by the dots. This is the "traditional" way to approach the problem. But nothing in the statement of the problem forced you to do so. Two different solutions to the problem are shown on page 363.

Creative problem solvers are often able to ask themselves questions like the following to stimulate divergent thinking (Brown, 1989; Osborn, 1963):

- What would be some new ways to use this? How else could it be used if I modified it in some way?
- What could I add to or subtract from it to make it helpful to me?
- What would work instead? Would another approach work better?
- Could I rearrange its parts in some way? Could I modify the sequence in which things are done?
- Do the elements remind me of anything else? What else is like this?

Try some of these questions in approaching another problem. Look at the objects in Figure 11.17. Figure out how you could use these objects to mount a candle on the wall and light it so that you could study for your next exam if the power went out. Again, the solution is on page 363.

Solving the candle problem requires using some of the objects in the figure in unconventional ways. People are often prevented from doing so by **functional**

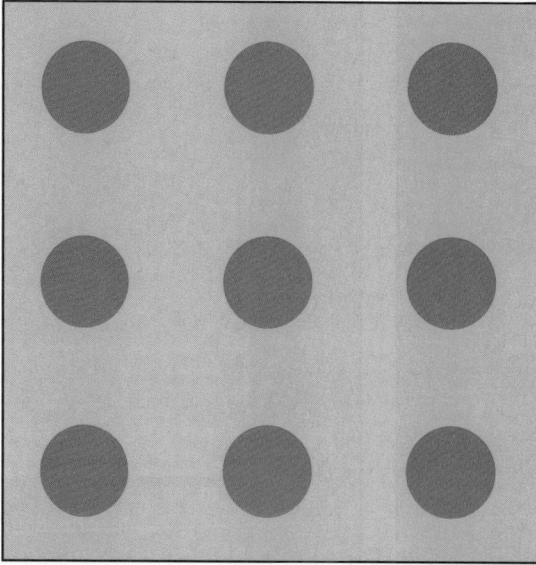

Figure 11.16 *Without lifting your pencil from the paper, draw no more than four straight lines that will pass through all nine dots. (The answer appears on page 363).*

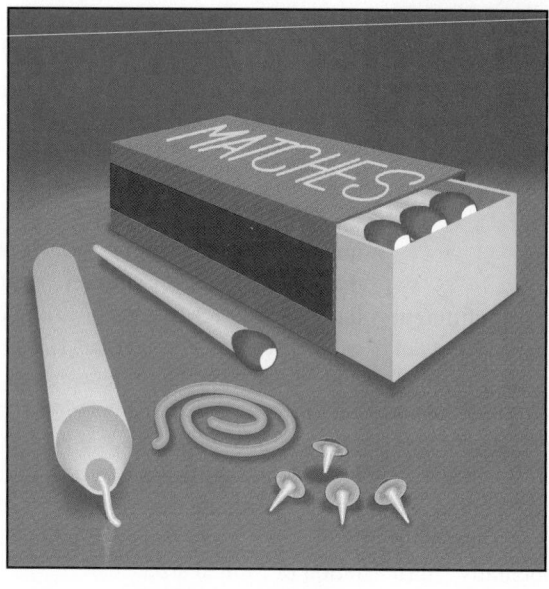

Figure 11.17 *Using these objects, find a way to mount the candle on a wall so it functions like a lamp. (The answer appears on page 363).*

fixedness—the tendency to be so fixed in their perception of the proper function of an object or procedure that they are blinded to new ways of using it.

Sometimes, creative solutions to problems seemingly appear out of the blue, suddenly popping into the problem solver's mind in a flash of insight after the problem solver has temporarily given up and put the problem aside. **Incubation** is the name given to this phenomenon; it is as if the problem is "incubating" at a subconscious level. Many great inventions and scientific insights have occurred in this manner. For example, August William Kekule's discovery of the ring structure of the benzene molecule occurred as he dozed before the fire after many hours of wrestling unsuccessfully with the problem:

I turned my chair to the fire and dozed. Again the atoms were gamboling before my eyes. This time, the smaller groups kept modestly in the background. My mental eye, rendered more acute by repeated visions of this kind, could not distinguish larger structures, of manifold conformation; long rows, sometimes more closely fitted together; all twining and twisting in snake-like motion. But look! What was that? One of the snakes had seized ahold of its own tail, and the form whirled mockingly before my eyes. (Cited in Koestler, 1964).

Kekule's experience, together with accounts of other creative insights, suggests that sometimes the best approach when we are stymied by a problem is to put it aside and gain a bit of psychological distance from it. Perhaps this allows mental sets and other biases to dissipate somewhat, permitting a new idea to emerge.

Evaluating Solutions

Generating ideas is not enough to ensure creative problem solving. At least one of the ideas has to be a useful and practical one. To evaluate how good the ideas are, we must shift from divergent thinking to **convergent thinking,** in which we narrow the alternatives, much as we do in choosing the correct answer on a multiple-choice test (Guilford, 1959). But how do we know which solutions are best? Here are some questions we might ask ourselves:

■ Will the solution work, and work better than conventional approaches to the problem?

■ Is it feasible? Can it be implemented, given the resources and means available?

■ What will be the costs in time, effort, and money of implementing the solution? Do the benefits justify these costs? Are there less costly solutions?

■ Is the solution compatible enough with human nature that people will make use of it? (If it requires significant changes in normal behavior patterns, people—including yourself—may resist it no matter how wonderful a solution it is.)

■ What are the consequences if the idea doesn't work? Do the potential gains justify the risks involved?

■ Are present conditions ripe for this solution? How long will it take to implement? Will conditions change between now and the completion of implementation in any ways that might affect the usefulness and feasibility of the solution?

■ How can I get feedback on how well the solution is working once I implement it? Can I avoid confirmation bias and be honest with myself if the solution is not working? Do I have an alternate plan to try if needed?

As you can see, creative problem solving involves many of the principles discussed earlier. We see the operation of means/ends reasoning, the testing of hypotheses, and the need to overcome biases that may cause us to overestimate or underestimate the likelihood of certain outcomes. Here are some other general problem-solving guidelines suggested by the previous discussion:

1. When you first see a problem, ask yourself if you know some problem-solving schema that you can use to solve it. If you haven't solved exactly this sort of problem before, have you solved a similar one? Maybe the schema for solving a similar problem can be modified to solve this one. (The principle involved is that our long-term memories are better than our working memories.)

2. If you are testing your ideas, really test them! Try to find evidence that would disconfirm your ideas, not evidence that confirms what you already believe. (The principle is that you should be aware of your bias toward confirming your cherished hypotheses.)

3. In particular, if you are asked if statement X is true, see if you can imagine situations in which X would be false. This is the principle described in item 2 applied to the special case of evaluating the truth of a statement.

4. Beware of confusing representativeness with frequency. The bird that is "a little big" for a sparrow and exactly the right size for the rare Patagonian warbler is probably—a big sparrow.

5. Make use of the means/ends problem-solving heuristic. Ask yourself what you are trying to accomplish, what the present state of affairs is, and what means you have for reducing the discrepancy.

6. Don't be afraid to use pencil and paper. Orderly notes can substitute for our rather limited working memories.

7. Be aware of your own range of cognitive abilities, and use them. Many problems can be attacked by a variety of strategies—imagery, verbal representations, analogies, and the like. Find a technique that works for you. Learn to use your own strengths as a problem solver.

Artificial Intelligence: Computer Models of Human Thought

Many modern theories of human thinking are based on the computer metaphor. Chapter 10 discussed the influence of the computer-based information processing model on the ways cognitive scientists think about memory in terms of encoding, storage, and retrieval processes. The idea behind the ''mind as computer'' metaphor is that although human brains are not at all like computer circuits, human mental processes can be understood (at least partially) according to many of the concepts used to explain how certain computer programs solve problems (Hunt, 1989; Simon, 1990).

In the 1960s, two cognitive scientists, Allen Newell and Herbert A. Simon, argued that a psychological theory of thinking ought to be stated as a computer program that, when run, would produce ''thought products'' like those of a human. This simple yet elegant idea helped usher in the era of **artificial intelligence,** computer programs designed to simulate human problem-solving processes and thereby perform sophisticated tasks while expanding our understanding of human thinking.

Newell and Simon (1972) developed a program, called the General Problem Solver (GPS), that could

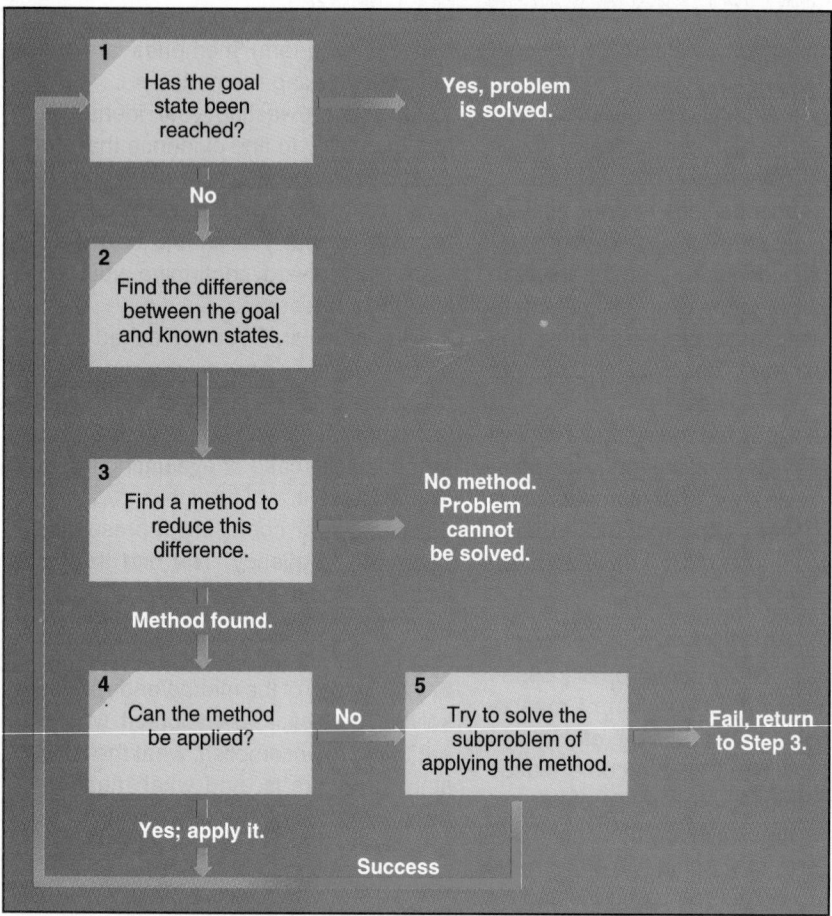

Figure 11.18 *The sequence of operations used by the General Problem Solver, which uses the method of means/ends analysis. This program, developed by Allen Newell and Herbert Simon (1972) illustrates the artificial intelligence approach to modeling human thinking—in this case, means/ends problem solving.*

1 Has the goal state been reached?

Yes, problem is solved.

No

2 Find the difference between the goal and known states.

3 Find a method to reduce this difference.

No method. Problem cannot be solved.

Method found.

4 Can the method be applied?

No

5 Try to solve the subproblem of applying the method.

Fail, return to Step 3.

Yes; apply it.

Success

At the practical level, we have seen the development of artificial intelligence programs that reproduce the thinking patterns of experts in various fields (see Figure 11.19). For example, the widely used medical program MYCIN was built to model the thought processes of several gifted medical diagnosticians (Lipkin, 1988; Shortcliffe, 1983). Suppose a patient complains of extreme fatigue, nausea, and headaches. MYCIN begins by reviewing the patient's symptoms and medical history, then reasons backward to the most likely causes of the symptoms. To do so, it searches its own large information base and, if the search is not successful in reaching the desired end state, requests more information from a consulting physician. The new information can be incorporated into its reasoning processes. The program then lays out the reasoning for its suggested diagnosis, as well as a treatment plan. Other expert systems are being used in the sciences, in industry and business, and even in space, where artificial intelligence systems help astronauts monitor, diagnose, and correct problems in their spacecraft (Lipkin, 1988).

Critics of the computer metaphor claim, quite correctly, that the human mind is so complex that even the most sophisticated of artificial intelligence models leave many aspects of thinking unexplained. It is important to remember, however, that a model does not have to be complete or even correct to be scientifically useful. Its true scientific value lies in its ability to foster new understanding and to stimulate research that advances knowledge. On both counts, artificial intelligence research is making important contributions.

solve problems using means-end analysis, which, as we have seen, compares the present state of affairs with a desired goal state and then considers various means of changing the present situation to the desired one. Figure 11.18 is a sketch of how the program worked. The figure itself is an example of a flow chart, because it shows the flow of computational steps the GPS followed.

Computer models of human thought and problem solving have become much more sophisticated over the years, but not even the most ardent advocate of computer simulation believes that existing artificial intelligence programs capture the amazing complexity of human cognitive processes. For one thing, the human mind engages in **parallel processing,** carrying out a bewildering array of different functions—sensing, making plans, labeling emotions, and so on—at the same time. Most computers engage in **serial processing** of a single sequence of actions. They can process in this way with blinding speed, but they are not capable of the kinds of parallel processing in which humans engage. Nor are computers capable of creativity, feelings, and learning, as humans are.

So far, we have considered general principles of human thinking, reasoning, and problem solving. Yet it is apparent to all of us that there are important individual differences in cognition. Clearly, we don't all think the same way, nor do we all think equally well. In the study of intelligence, to which we now turn, we focus on the nature, the measurement, the meaning, and the causes of these individual differences in cognitive skills.

■ ■

Intelligence

Is it true that some people are *generally* more "intelligent" than others? If so, can we measure these differences and use the measures to predict success and failure in real-life settings? What is the nature of intelligence? What factors are responsible for the differences that we observe in people's cognitive skills? These and related questions have inspired more than a century of scientific research, and attempts to answer them have had an enormous influence on our culture.

It may surprise you to learn that after a century of research and theorizing, there is still no universally accepted definition of intelligence, nor is there agreement on whether there is one general form or a number of different forms of intelligence. In the pages to follow, we shall see why. In the meantime, however, we will use as our working definition of intelligence the following: **Intelligence** is a *concept* that refers to individual differences in the ability to acquire knowledge, to think and reason effectively, and to deal adaptively with the environment. This definition is general enough to encompass some of the finer distinctions that we will encounter later.

The Measurement of Intelligence

The first scientific studies of intelligence were conducted in England in the late 19th century by Sir Francis Galton. Galton was highly influenced by the theory of evolution developed by his cousin, Charles Darwin. In his book *Hereditary Genius,* Galton (1869) reported his research on eminence and genius within certain families across generations. These studies convinced him that people who were successful in society had inherited mental constitutions that made them more fit for thinking than their less successful counterparts. Galton was an avowed hereditarian, and he dismissed the fact that the successful people he studied almost invariably came from privileged environments.

Galton attempted to demonstrate a biological basis for eminence by showing that people who were more socially and occupationally successful were also more "fit" as determined by a variety of tasks thought to measure the efficiency of the nervous system. He developed measures of reaction speed and sensory acuity and even measured the size of people's skulls on the grounds that skull size reflected brain size and hence intelligence.

Galton was unsuccessful in relating his measures of nervous system efficiency to socially relevant measures of mental ability, such as success in school or occupation. In the process of his research, Galton nevertheless made two important contributions. First, he invented the correlation coefficient to measure the magnitude of relations between measures. Second, he created an interest in the measuring of mental abilities, setting the stage for the pioneering work of Alfred Binet.

Binet's Mental Tests

The modern intelligence testing movement began at the turn of the century, when the French psychologist Alfred Binet was commissioned by France's minister

🔺 **Figure 11.19** *Artificial intelligence programs that reproduce the thought patterns and problem-solving procedures used by experts are now widely used in science, medicine, and industry.*

of public education to develop the test that was to become the predecessor of all modern "intelligence tests." Unlike Galton (with whom he had trained), Binet was interested in solving a practical problem rather than supporting a theory. Certain children seemed unable to benefit from normal public schooling. (Today we would refer to these children as "mentally retarded" or "cognitively disabled.") Educators wanted an objective way to identify these children as early as possible so that some form of special education could be arranged for them.

In developing his tests, Binet made two assumptions about intelligence. The first was that mental abilities develop over time, so that adults are more mentally competent than children and older children are generally more competent than younger children. The second assumption was that the rate at which people gain mental competence is a characteristic of the person and is fairly constant over time. If this is true, then a child who is less competent than expected at age 5 should also be lagging at age 10.

These assumptions dictated Binet's method of test development. He asked experienced teachers what sorts of problems children could solve at ages 3, 4, 5, and so on up through the school years. He then used their answers to develop a "standardized interview" in which an adult examiner posed a series of questions to a child to determine whether or not the child was performing at the correct mental level for his or her age (see Table 11.1). The result of the testing was a score called the **mental age.** For instance, if a

Table 11.1 Sample Problems from the Stanford-Binet

Age 3—Child should be able to:	Point to objects that serve various functions such as "goes on your feet." Name pictures of objects such as *chair, flag*. Repeat a list of 2 words or digits—for example, *car, dog*.
Age 4—Child should be able to:	Discriminate visual forms such as squares, circles, and triangles. Define words such as *ball* and *bat*. Repeat 10-word sentences. Count up to 4 objects. Solve problems such as "In daytime it is light; at night it is . . ."
Age 6—Child should be able to:	State the differences between similar items such as a *bird* and a *dog*. Count up to 9 blocks. Solve analogies such as "An inch is short; a mile is . . ."
Age 9—Child should be able to:	Solve verbal problems such as "Tell me a number that rhymes with tree." Solve simple arithmetic problems such as "If I buy 4 cents worth of candy and give the storekeeper 10 cents, how much money will I get back? Repeat 4 digits in reverse order.
Age 12—Child should be able to:	Define words such as *skill* and *muzzle*. Repeat 5 digits in reverse order. Solve verbal absurdities such as "One day we saw several icebergs that had been entirely melted by the warmth of the Gulf Stream. What is foolish about that?"

Source: Terman & Merrill (1972).

child of 8 could solve problems at the level of the average 10-year-old, the child would be said to have a mental age of 10.

The concept of mental age was subsequently expanded to provide an **intelligence quotient,** or **IQ.** The IQ was originally based on the ratio of mental age to chronological age, according to the following formula:

IQ = (Mental age/chronological age) × 100.

Thus, a child who was performing at exactly his or her age level would have an IQ of 100. In our previous example, the child with a mental age of 10 and a chronological age of 8 would have an IQ of (10/8) × 100 = 125. A 12-year-old with a mental age of 16 would also have an IQ of 125, so the two children would be comparable in intelligence even though their ages differed. Thus, the IQ formula provides a *relative* score, indicating how well a person does on the tests compared with others. It is *not* a measure of an absolute quantity, like height or weight.

Today's tests no longer use the concept of mental age. Instead, a process of **standardization** is carried out in which the test questions are administered to a large **norm group** that represents a cross-section of the population. In the case of children's tests, a norm group is selected for each age level of interest. The norm group's performance provides a set of **test norms** against which an individual can be compared.

Today's tests are scored in such a way that the scores can be interpreted in reference to a bell-shaped curve known as a *normal distribution.* (This distribution and its statistical properties are described in detail in Appendix A, which follows Chapter 20.) Because the normal distribution has known statistical properties, we can specify what percentage of the population will score higher than a given score. Thus, as you can see in Figure 11.20, an IQ score of 100 cuts the distribution in half, with 50 percent of the population scoring above and 50 below this midpoint.

The relative nature of the IQ has important implications for interpreting the meaning of scores. Consider two people, one with an IQ of 150 and another with an IQ of 75. Because the scores are computed *relative* to a population norm, it makes no sense whatsoever to say that the first person is "twice as intelligent" as the second. What *can* be said is that in a sample of 1,000 people we would expect that only one person would have a score higher than 150, while 994 people would have a score higher than 75. Table 11.2 shows the percentage of people who are expected to score higher than a given IQ score.

Binet's tests were very successful because both of his assumptions were proven accurate. The fact that mental competence increases from childhood to adulthood is obvious. The second assumption, that intelligence is a stable characteristic, is also correct, provided that the person being tested is not too young. Intelligence tests on very young children are notoriously unstable. The correlation between two tests taken by the same individual, once at age 3 and again at age 40, is approximately .30. However, the correlation between IQ at age 9 and age 40 is in the .70 to .80 range (McCall, 1977).

Lewis Terman, a professor at Stanford University, revised Binet's test for use in the United States. Terman's revision became known as the Stanford-Binet test. By the mid-1920s, it had been widely accepted in North America, and the Stanford-Binet (which is periodically revised) remains in wide use today. Somewhat later, a major competitor emerged in the form of the Wechsler scales.

The Wechsler Scales

The Stanford-Binet contained a preponderance of verbal items, and it yielded a single IQ score. David Wechsler believed that intelligence should be measured as a group of different but related verbal and nonverbal abilities. He therefore developed intelligence tests for adults and for children that measured a range of different intellectual skills. In 1939, the Wechsler Adult Intelligence Scale (WAIS) appeared, followed by the Wechsler Intelligence Scale for Children (WISC) in 1955. More recently (1967), a preschool version, the Wechsler Preschool and Primary Scale of Intelligence (WPPSI) was developed. Like the Stanford-Binet, the Wechsler scales are regularly revised. Today, the Wechsler tests (WAIS–R and WISC–R, where R means ''revised'') are the most widely used intelligence tests in the United States.

The Wechsler tests consist of a series of subtests that fall into two classes; Verbal Tests and Performance Tests. Table 11.3 describes the Wechsler's Verbal and Performance subtests and provides sample items. Three different IQs are yielded by the test: a Verbal IQ based on the sum of the Verbal subscales; a Performance IQ based on the Performance subscales; and a Full-Scale IQ based on all of the scales.

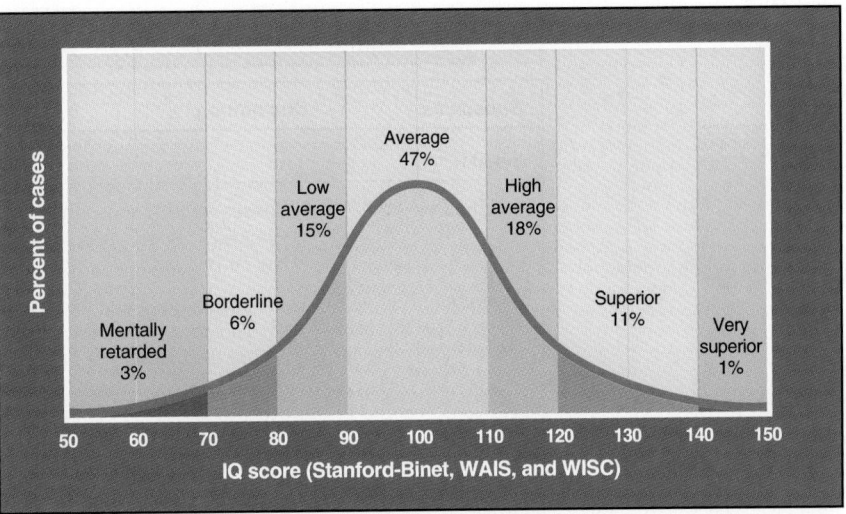

Figure 11.20 *Intelligence tests yield a normal, or bell-shaped, distribution of IQ scores. The mean of the distribution is set at 100, and each 16 points equal one standard deviation above and below that mean. Common descriptive labels are shown relative to the bell-shaped distribution. The range of scores from 90 to 110 is labeled* average *and includes nearly half of the population.*

For some purposes, it is useful to distinguish between the Verbal IQ, which is based only on the verbal tests, and the Performance IQ, based only on the performance tests. In other situations, the Full-Scale IQ, based on all tests, is used to describe the examinee. One can also plot a profile of the scores on each of the 11 subtests to assess an examinee's pattern of intellectual strengths and weaknesses.

Group Tests of Aptitude and Achievement

Intelligence tests like the Stanford-Binet and the Wechsler scales are administered to an individual by a trained tester. They typically take as long as 2 hours to administer and are therefore impractical for large-scale personnel screening. This presented a problem in World War I, when the U.S. Army was expanded very rapidly. In response to the need to screen recruits for mental competence, a group of psychologists under the direction of Robert M. Yerkes, a Yale professor, developed the *Army Alpha* test—the first *group intelligence test*. In group tests, examinees respond to written questions rather than to verbal ones asked by an examiner. The now-familiar multiple-choice format is often used. Statistical studies showed that a recruit's score on a Binet-type test could be predicted reasonably well from his score on the Army Alpha.

The success of the Army Alpha test spurred the development of other group tests of intellectual competence. These include the Educational Testing Service's Scholastic Aptitude Test (SAT), which is widely used to select college applicants in the United

Table 11.2 Approximate Percentages of the People in the Population Expected to Score Higher than Selected Scores on the Binet and Wechsler Scales.

IQ Score	Percent of Population Scoring Higher
70	97%
80	89%
90	76%
100	50%
110	26%
120	11%
130	3%

Table 11.3 Verbal and Performance Subscales of the Wechsler Scales of Intelligence.

Subscales	Description
Verbal	
Information	Assesses general knowledge. "Who was Thomas Jefferson?" (WISC-R) "How far is it from New York to Paris?" (WAIS-R)
Comprehension	Tests understanding of reasons for doing things. "Why should we use zip codes when mailing letters?" (WISC-R) "Why do people buy fire insurance?" (WAIS-R)
Arithmetic	Tests mathematical reasoning abilities. "Dick had 13 pieces of candy and gave away 8. How many did he have left?" (WISC-R) How many hours will it take to drive 240 miles at the rate of 30 miles an hour?" (WAIS-R)
Similarities	Measures abstract reasoning ability. "In what way are corn and macaroni alike?" (WISC-R) "In what way are wood and cotton alike?" (WAIS-R)
Digit span	Tests attention and rote memory. "Listen carefully, and when I am through, say the numbers after me: 2-5-1-8-4-6."
Vocabulary	Tests ability to define increasingly difficult words. "What do we mean by protect?" (WISC-R) "What does formulate mean?" (WAIS-R)
Performance	
Digit symbol	A timed test in which specific symbols associated with numbers must be written in blank boxes below the numbers. Tests speed of learning and fine motor skills.
Picture completion	Pictures of objects with missing parts (e.g., a calendar with the name of the month missing) are shown. Subject must detect what part is missing. Tests visual alertness and visual memory.
Block design	Tests ability to perceive and analyze patterns by having subject recreate complex geometric designs with painted blocks.
Picture arrangement	Tests social understanding through a series of comic-strip pictures that must be arranged to tell a coherent story.
Object assembly	A timed test that assesses ability to deal with part–whole perceptual relationships by means of puzzle pieces that must be put together to form a complete object.

States, and the Armed Services Vocational Aptitude Battery (ASVAB), presently used to screen recruits for the U.S. Armed Services.

The use of written tests in personnel selection highlighted an issue that Binet had faced and that, as we shall see, continues to plague test developers. Should we test a person's abstract "aptitude for learning," or should we test what a person already knows? Consider an example. In selecting applicants for college, we could either give students an **achievement test** designed to find out how much they have learned in high school or present them with an **aptitude test,** in which they must react to new, puzzle-like problems that supposedly depend less on prior learning, and measures the applicant's potential for future learning and performance.

The argument for achievement testing is that it is usually a good predictor; after all, past performance is often the best predictor of future performance. The argument against achievement testing is that it assumes that everyone has had the same chance to learn the material being tested. In the college selection example, if there are marked differences in the quality of the high schools the applicants have attended, a person's test score could depend on whether that person went to a good school rather than on his or her ability to learn.

The argument for aptitude testing is that it is "fairer," since aptitude tests are supposed to depend less on prior knowledge than on a person's ability to react to the problem presented on the test. The argument against aptitude testing is that it is difficult to construct a test that is independent of prior learning. When such a test is constructed, it may require a sort of "ability to deal with puzzles" that is not very relevant to success in situations other than the test.

As we shall see, most intelligence tests are a combination of achievement and aptitude measures. This fact has raised major scientific and social issues concerning the meaning of test scores and the usefulness of the measures for describing mental competence and predicting performance in nontest situations.

Predictive Validity of Test Scores

Intelligence tests were originally developed to predict performance in other situations. Their ability to do so successfully is termed their **predictive validity.** An ideal test would perfectly predict performance on some **criterion,** or outcome measure, such as academic or job performance. For instance, a college selection test like the SAT would have high validity if scores were highly related to future college grade-point averages. If a test were a perfect predictor, its scores would have a correlation of 1.00 with the criterion measure. At the other extreme, a test would have no predictive validity if one could not make any prediction about college grades from test scores. Statistically, we would say that there was a correlation of .00 between the test score and the criterion measure.

How well do intelligence tests predict academic success? In practice, the correlations are neither + 1.00 nor .00. They fall somewhere in between, with maximum correlations in the + .50 to + .60 range for high school students and in the + .40 to + .50 range for college students (Aiken, 1991). These correlations are of about the same magnitude as the correlation between height and weight. In general, then, people who score well on the tests *tend* to do well academically. Intelligence measures also predict performance in the military and on the job fairly well (Barrett & Depinet, 1991). Studies of job performance find correlations of .20 to .50 between test scores and job performance across a range of different occupations (Hartigan & Wigdor, 1989). In a summary of many studies, an average correlation of .45 was found between intellectual ability and job proficiency (Hunter & Hunter, 1984). Generally, it appears that intelligence tests are better at predicting academic success (which requires the kinds of cognitive skills they measure) than job success, which may require other skills. In either case, however, they are far from perfect predictors, indicating that other characteristics are also important contributors to performance.

The modest level of predictive accuracy of intelligence tests may leave you uncomfortable. Consider the comparison of intelligence and school grades with height and weight. In both cases, the correlations are about + .50. Would you let a tailor design a $600 suit of clothes on the basis of your height alone? Similarly, can we justify decisions about such things as college admissions and rejections on the basis of similar cor-

relations? From the individual's point of view, test inaccuracies are disquieting. The courts have agreed, ruling that testing for employee selection is acceptable only when the tests measure specific abilities that are clearly and directly related to the job in question (Wigdor & Garner, 1982).

But now let us look at the problem from the broader view of the college, industry, or government. These social institutions are more interested in the broad, long-term usefulness of prediction than in accuracy in the individual case. The costs arising from extended training of employees who do not succeed, educational failures, and inefficient performance, though perhaps small on an individual basis, can be huge on a national basis. In 1976, the economic costs of *not* using tests were estimated at $13.5 billion (Hunter & Schmidt, 1982). This figure reflects the fact that the number of erroneous decisions increases when methods other than tests are used in making decisions. For example, decisions made on the basis of interviews alone are less accurate than decisions based on interviews and test scores (Guion & Gibson, 1988). Allowing for inflation and the growth of the economy, the 1993 cost of not testing must be close to $25 billion.

So we have a paradox of sorts. We have two types of decisions: individual and institutional (Cronbach, 1990). From the individual's viewpoint, the tests are inaccurate enough to justify people's concern when decisions about their lives are made on the basis of test scores. From the viewpoint of societal institutions, though, the test scores are accurate enough to be a useful guide for assigning jobs and educational opportunities, and the consequences of not using the tests can be very expensive. Like many other controversies in our society, this one revolves around partially incompatible individual and societal needs. The only way to reduce this incompatibility and satisfy both sets of needs is to develop tests that have much greater predictive accuracy and to take into account personality, motivational, experiential, and interest variables that combine with cognitive skills to influence performance.

The Nature of Intelligence

So far in this chapter, the term *intelligence* has been used as if there were general agreement on its meaning. However, as noted earlier, that is not the case, particularly among scientists who study mental skills. One approach that has cropped up from time to time is to skirt the conceptual issue of the nature of intelligence and simply define intelligence as "whatever it is that intelligence tests measure." However, this definition satisfies very few people, and it is no answer at all for those who want to understand the nature of the mental processes that lie behind individual differences in test scores and achievement behaviors.

Attempts to understand the factors that underlie "intelligent" behavior have taken two major forms. The *psychometric approach* attempts to specify *what* the structure of intellect is and, more specifically, how many different classes of mental ability underlie test performance. Is intelligence a single dimension of general mental competence, or is it a collection of specific abilities? A newer approach, the *cognitive psychology approach,* studies *why* there are individual differences in mental competence, focusing on the specific thought processes that underlie mental competencies.

The Psychometric Approach: The Structure of Intellect

Psychometrics is the statistical study of psychological measuring instruments. The psychometric approach to the nature of intelligence focuses on the nature and number of abilities that underlie individual differences in performance on intelligence tests. One of the major tools used by psychometric researchers is *factor analysis,* which analyzes patterns of correlations between test scores to discover clusters of measures that correlate highly with one another but not with measures in other clusters. When such clusters, or *factors,* are found, the investigator tries to decide what common underlying ability accounts for the high correlations. For example, if we were to find that a group of tests were highly correlated with one another and that the tests all required subjects to solve mathematical problems, we might conclude that the underlying factor was "mathematical reasoning ability." (A more extensive discussion of factor analysis can be found in Appendix A.)

Psychometric theorists have disagreed sharply on the nature of intelligence. Some, whom we might term the "groupers," tend to regard intelligence as a general ability that cuts across all of what we would call thinking. At the other extreme are the "splitters," who regard intelligence as a set of specific abilities to do different types of thinking.

Spearman's g Factor. The psychometric argument for intelligence as a general ability was first advanced by the British psychologist Charles Spearman (1923), who pioneered the use of factor analysis. He observed that school grades in very different subjects, such as English and mathematics, were almost always positively correlated but that the correlations were not perfect. Spearman found the same to be true for different types of Binet intelligence test items, such as vocabulary questions, arithmetic reasoning problems, and ability to construct puzzles.

Faced with this pattern of results, Spearman concluded that intellectual performance is determined partly by "general intelligence," (usually indicated by the symbol *g*) and partly by whatever special abilities might be required to perform that particular task. For instance, Spearman would argue that your performance in a mathematics course would partly depend on your general intelligence and partly on your specific ability to learn mathematics. Spearman also contended that since the general factor—the **g factor**—was so important on virtually all tasks, it constituted the most important aspect of intelligence.

Thurstone's Primary Mental Abilities. Spearman's conclusion was soon challenged by L. L. Thurstone of the University of Chicago. Where Spearman had been impressed by the fact that scores on different mental tasks are correlated, Thurstone was impressed by the fact that the correlations are less than perfect. Thurstone concluded that human mental performance depends on seven distinct abilities, which he called **primary mental abilities,** or *factors of the mind.* These are listed in Table 11.4. Thurstone also maintained that performance on any mental task is more influenced by the specific abilities relevant to that task than by any underlying *g* factor. Following Thurstone's lead, some other investigators claimed to have found more and more factors. One prominent theorist maintained that there were over a hundred measurable mental abilities (Guilford, 1967).

One of the reasons that Spearman and Thurstone differed in their conclusions may have been that they looked at somewhat different populations. Spearman reached his conclusion by examining data from English children of low to moderate intelligence in government-supported schools. Thurstone examined the test scores of students at major U.S. universities. Subsequent research has shown that mental abilities are most highly correlated in young children and in less intelligent populations, such as those studied by Spearman. In young adults, especially those above average in intelligence, mental abilities are less highly correlated. Thus, it is understandable that, faced with different patterns of results, Spearman and Thurstone could reach different conclusions concerning the general versus specific nature of intelligence.

Table 11.4 Thurstone's Seven Primary Mental Abilities	
Ability Name	**Description**
S—Space	Reasoning about visual scenes
V—Verbal comprehension	Understanding verbal statements
W—Word fluency	Producing verbal statements
N—Number facility	Dealing with numbers
P—Perceptual speed	Recognizing visual patterns
M—Rote memory	Memorization
R—Reasoning	Dealing with novel problems

There are some trends that are found in almost every population. The clearest of these is a distinction between the ability to deal with verbal information and the ability to deal with spatial-visual problems, such as the one shown in Figure 11.21. These appear to be two relatively distinct abilities, and Thurstone's notion of separate mental abilities is most accurate when we contrast verbal reasoning with reasoning about spatial-visual images.

An interesting added fact emerges in study after study. For some reason not yet understood, the ability to do mathematical reasoning is related to visual-spatial rather than verbal reasoning. This is somewhat surprising, since mathematics, like language, uses symbols. Nevertheless, the findings are quite clear. In fact, the more difficult the mathematical area, the stronger the dependence on visual-spatial reasoning.

Crystallized Versus Fluid Intelligence. What we currently know about the nature of mental abilities suggests a position intermediate between Spearman's general intelligence and Thurstone's factors of the mind. An intermediate model originally developed by Raymond Cattell (1971) and subsequently extended by John Horn (1985) accounts for the facts quite well. This model is shown in Figure 11.22.

First, Horn and Cattell distinguish between spatial–visual reasoning and other types of reasoning. They then break down Spearman's general intelligence into two correlated but not identical abilities. The first, **crystallized intelligence,** is the ability to apply previously learned knowledge to current problems. It involves verbal reasoning and factual knowledge. In fact, vocabulary and information tests are good measures of crystallized intelligence.

Cattell and Horn's second general factor is **fluid intelligence,** which they define as the ability to deal with novel problem-solving situations for which personal experience does not provide a solution. Cattell and Horn argue that over our life spans we progress from using fluid to using crystallized intelligence. This makes sense in terms of problem-solving schemas, discussed earlier. As experience makes us more "expert," we have less need to approach each situation as a new problem. Cattell, Horn, and many other investigators have shown that over the adult years performance on tests of fluid intelligence declines, while performance on tests of crystallized intelligence ("wisdom") improves. However, since fluid intelligence is used to establish crystallized intelligence, it is not surprising to find that there is a moderate correlation (about .50) between the two.

Distinctions between fluid and crystallized intelligence are now appearing in revisions of traditional intelligence tests. Figure 11.23 diagrams the components of the most recent version of the Stanford–Binet. The subtests combine to give scores on three

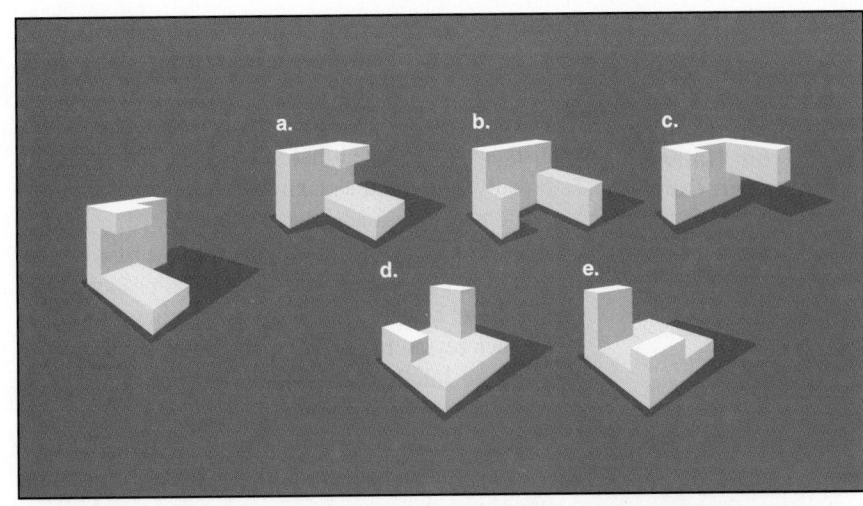

Figure 11.21 *Spatial–visual skills are assessed with problems like this one. Which of the five objects on the right is the same as the object on the left? (The answer appears on page 363).*

second-order factors. One is a short-term memory factor. The other two are fluid and crystallized ability factors that are based on the third-order verbal, quantitative and abstract-visual reasoning factors (Thorndike & others, 1986). These second-order factors in turn combine for a composite score that is assumed to reflect the general factor (g).

Figure 11.22 *The structure of general intelligence, according to Cattell and Horn, includes an important distinction between crystallized and fluid intelligence.*

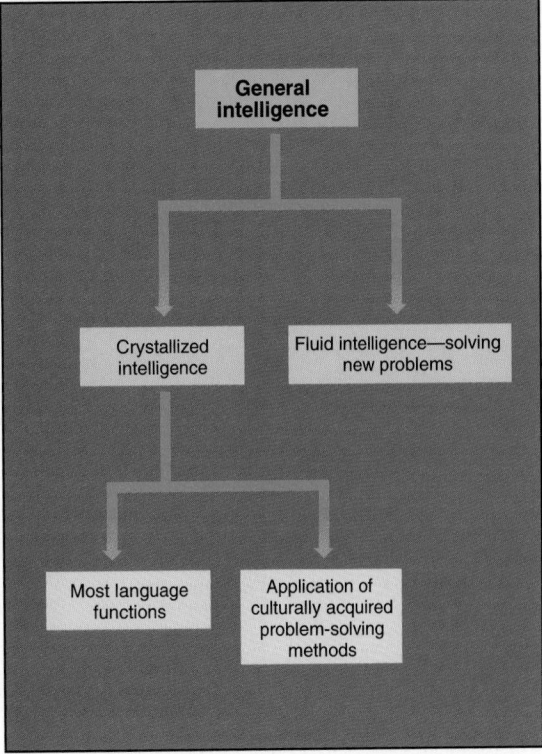

Gardner's Theory of Multiple Intelligences. All of the notions of intelligence we have so far discussed have viewed intelligence as forms of mental competence. However, laypersons and some psychologists have suggested that intelligence may be more broadly conceived as taking a variety of forms that relate to different adaptive demands.

Among the psychologists, Howard Gardner (1983) has been one of the most vocal proponents of this view. Drawing on the work of others as well as his own research, Gardner has advanced a **theory of multiple intelligences,** which includes six distinct varieties of intelligence: (1) linguistic, (2) mathematical, (3) visual-spatial, (4) musical (the ability to perceive pitch and rhythm), (5) bodily-kinesthetic (the ability to control body movements and skillfully manipulate objects, as might be personified in a great ballerina or athlete or in a skilled surgeon), and (6) personal (the ability to insightfully understand ourselves and others). As we have seen, the first three abilities are measured by existing intelligence tests; but the other three are not. Indeed, some of Gardner's critics insist that these abilities are not really part of intelligence. However, Gardner replies that the form of intelligence that is most highly valued within a given culture depends on the adaptive requirements of that culture. ▼ In Gardner's view, Albert Einstein, Michael Jordan, and a "street-smart" gang leader exemplify different forms of intelligence that are highly adaptive within their respective environments (see Figure 11.24). Gardner further believes that these six classes of abilities require the functioning of separate but interacting modules in the brain. He bases his argument on studies of brain damage, which often leaves some abilities devastated while sparing others, and on the characteristics of *idiot savants.* These people are intellectually disabled in a general sense, yet they exhibit striking skills in specific areas, such as the ability to memorize hundreds of television commercials word-for-word after hearing them only once or the ability to mentally compute mathematical problems such as the square root of 2,349,867 × 43,978.

Gardner's approach is provocative and controversial because it goes far beyond traditional conceptions of intelligence. His forceful arguments for broadening the definition of intelligence may stimulate the development of measures to assess the less traditional abilities, resulting in an increase in predictive power beyond the school environment.

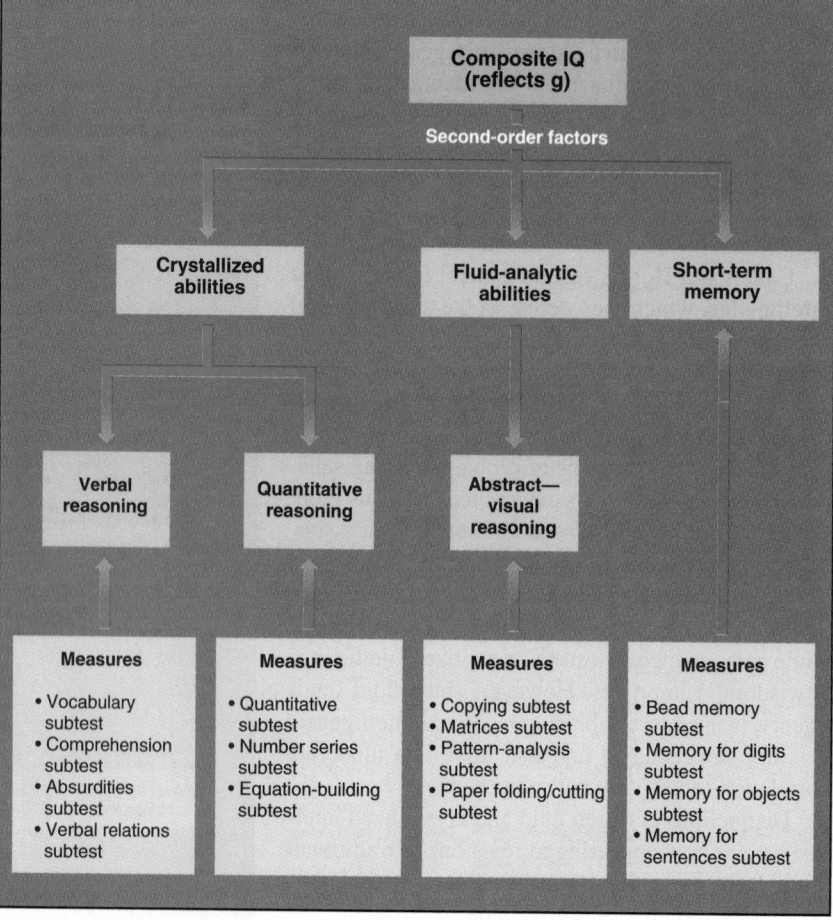

▶ **Figure 11.23** *A hierarchical theory of intelligence forms the basis for the latest revision of the Stanford–Binet. The composite score is assumed to measure a general intelligence factor* (g). *The second-order factors reflect the Horn-Cattell distinction between fluid and crystallized intelligence, which in turn comprise third-order reasoning factors. A separate memory factor is also measured by various Stanford–Binet tests. (Based on Thorndike & others, 1986).*

Composite IQ (reflects g)

Second-order factors

Crystallized abilities — **Fluid-analytic abilities** — **Short-term memory**

Verbal reasoning — **Quantitative reasoning** — **Abstract— visual reasoning**

Measures
• Vocabulary subtest
• Comprehension subtest
• Absurdities subtest
• Verbal relations subtest

Measures
• Quantitative subtest
• Number series subtest
• Equation-building subtest

Measures
• Copying subtest
• Matrices subtest
• Pattern-analysis subtest
• Paper folding/cutting subtest

Measures
• Bead memory subtest
• Memory for digits subtest
• Memory for objects subtest
• Memory for sentences subtest

Figure 11.24 *According to Gardner, these people are exhibiting specific forms of intelligence that are not measured on traditional intelligence tests.*

Cognitive Psychology Approaches: The Process of Intelligent Thinking

Psychometric theories of intelligence are statistically sophisticated ways of describing *how* people differ from one another. What psychometric theories don't do is explain *why* people vary in these ways. **Cognitive process theories** try to do so by relating the types of individual variation described in the psychometric approach to the models of cognition presented in the first part of the chapter. This approach, based on modern cognitive science, regards individual differences in performance as a manifestation of individual differences in elementary psychological processes. Recall that this was the logic behind Galton's early attempts to relate thinking ability to speed of reaction and sensory acuity.

A leading proponent of the cognitive processes approach to intelligence is Robert Sternberg (1985). His **triarchic theory of intelligence** has three subtheories. One of them, the *componential subtheory*, describes the specific cognitive processes that contribute to intelligent behavior (see Figure 11.25). Three components are described: *metacomponents, performance components,* and *knowledge acquisition components.*

Metacomponents are higher-order executive processes used to plan and regulate task performance. They include processes that we discussed earlier in the chapter: identifying problems, formulating hypotheses and strategies, testing them logically, and evaluating performance feedback. Sternberg believes that the metacomponents are the fundamental sources of individual differences in intelligence, although the other two components also contribute. He finds that more intelligent subjects spend more time framing a problem and developing strategies than do less intelligent subjects.

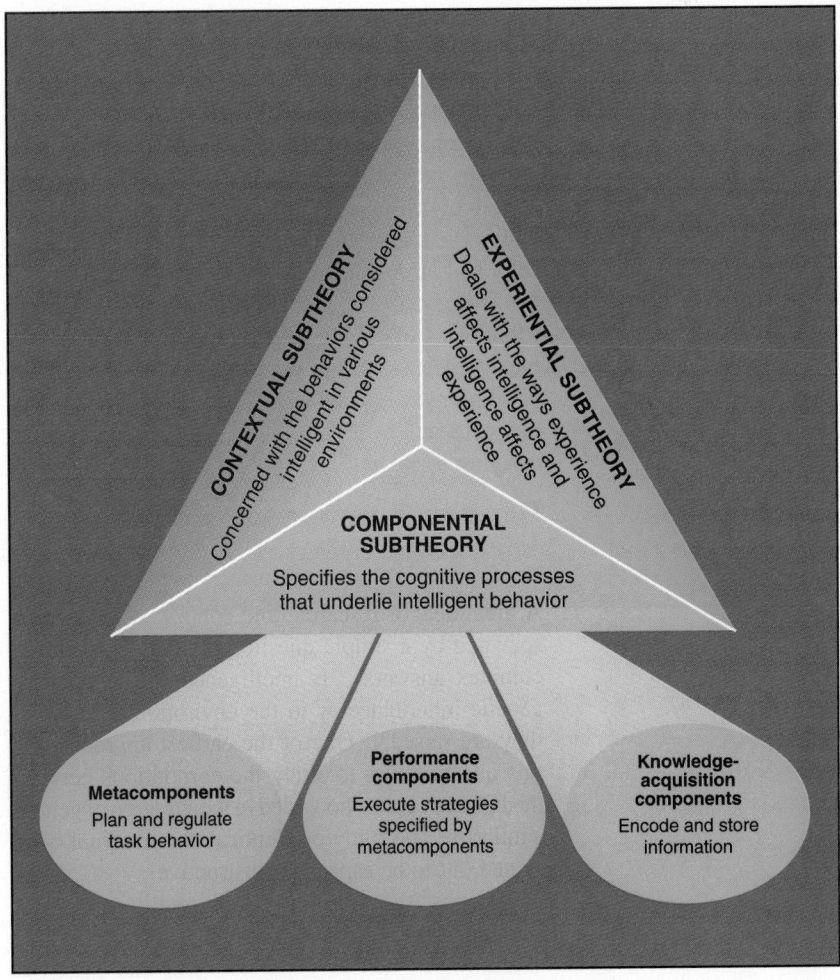

Figure 11.25 *Sternberg's (1985) triarchic theory of intelligence contains contextual, experiential, and componential subtheories. The componential subtheory deals with the specific cognitive processes assumed to underlie intelligent behavior, and it illustrates the current interest of cognitive psychology in underlying processes.*

The second-level components, *performance components*, are the actual mental processes used to perform the task. They include perceptual processing, retrieving appropriate memories and schemas, and making responses. The third-level components are *knowledge-acquisition components,* which allow us to learn from our experiences, store information in memory, and combine new insights with previously acquired information.

Sternberg's theory contains two other subtheories, which address the social and experiential contexts of intelligence. The *contextual subtheory* deals with intelligent behavior as it relates to the individual's culture and environment. Sternberg (1986) has suggested that environmental demands contribute to three different forms of intelligence: (1) the academic problem-solving skills assessed by intelligence tests; (2) the practical–social intelligence needed to cope with everyday demands and to manage oneself and other people effectively; and (3) the creative intelligence needed to deal adaptively with novel problems. However, Sternberg is not willing to extend his notion of intelligence into the musical and bodily-kinesthetic realms espoused by Gardner (Sternberg, 1989).

Finally, the *experiential subtheory* explores relations between experience and intelligence. Sternberg emphasizes two factors as being essential to intelligent behavior. The first is the ability to deal effectively with novel tasks and situations. The second is the ability to handle familiar tasks automatically and effortlessly.

The psychometric approach has made major contributions to our understanding of the structure of intelligence and continues to do so. Now, cognitive psychology is leading us in a new direction in which the focus will be on understanding the processes underlying intelligent behavior.

Heredity, Environment, and Intelligence

A great deal of research (and controversy) has been spawned by a simple question that has exceedingly complex answers: "Is intelligence due to people's genetic inheritance or to the environment in which they are raised?" One of the earliest approaches to this question was to study the correlations between the IQs of people who varied in their degree of genetic similarity. The study of identical and fraternal twins turned out to be especially instructive.

Suppose that intelligence was totally determined by genes. (No one thinks that it is, but examining the extreme view can be instructive.) In this case, two individuals with exactly the same genes would have identical test scores. This means that the correlation between the test scores of identical (*monozygotic*) twins would be +1.00. Nonidentical brothers and sisters share only half their genes. Therefore, the correlation between the test scores of siblings should be substantially lower. Note that this logic holds for nonidentical (*dizygotic*) twins as well, since they are simply siblings who happen to be the same age. Extending the argument, the correlation between a parent's test scores and his or her children's scores should be about the same as that between siblings, since a child inherits only half of his or her genes from each parent.

What do the actual data look like? Table 11.5 summarizes the results from many studies. As you can see, the correlations between the test scores of identical twins are substantially higher than any other correlations. In fact, the correlation for identical twins reared together is about as high as when a particular person is tested twice with the same intelligence test. High correlations occur regardless of whether the twins were raised together or apart. Identical twins separated early in life and reared apart are of special interest because they have identical genes but different environments. The correlation for identical twins raised apart is higher than the figure for nonidentical twins raised together and nearly as high as that for identical twins reared together (Bouchard & others, 1990). This is very strong evidence that genes do play an important role in intelligence.

Notice, however, that the figure for twins raised together *is* higher than the figure for twins raised apart. The same thing is true for siblings raised together and raised apart. This rules out an entirely genetic explanation. Although genetic constitution seems to be an important factor in determining intelligence-test scores, it probably accounts for only 50–70 percent of the variance in intelligence scores in the U.S. population today (Bouchard & others, 1990; Plomin & Rende, 1991). This figure reflects the *heritability* of intelligence. Environment counts, too. How genetics and environment may interact is the topic of the following feature.

Table 11.5 Correlations in IQ for People Who Live Together and Apart

Relationship	Median Correlation
Identical twins reared together	.86
Identical twins reared apart	.75
Nonidentical twins reared together	.57
Siblings reared together	.45
Siblings reared apart	.21
Parent–offspring reared by parent	.36
Parent–offspring not reared by parent	.20
Adopting parent–offspring	.19
Adopted children reared together	.02

Source: Data from Bouchard & McGue, 1981; Bouchard & others, 1990; Scarr, 1992.

Clearly, genetic factors and environmental factors combine to influence intelligence. Recognition of this fact is helping to silence the nature versus nurture controversies of the past. Increasingly, theorists are asserting that the most important scientific question is not whether heredity or environment is more important but rather how the two interact. A key concept in our understanding of genetic–environmental interactions is the **reaction range.** The reaction range for a genetically influenced trait is the range of possibilities that the genetic code allows. Thus, to say that intelligence is genetically influenced does not mean that intelligence is fixed at birth. Instead, it means that an individual inherits a range for intelligence that has upper and lower limits. Environmental effects will then determine where the person falls within these genetically determined boundaries. In other words, each of us has a range of intellectual potential that is jointly influenced by our genetic inheritance and the opportunities our environment provides (and we choose to take advantage of).

According to the reaction range concept, a person who is raised in a home and an educational environment that nurture the development of cognitive skills should have abilities near the top of his or her reaction range. Conversely, a person with the same reaction range who is raised in a culturally and educationally deprived environment may be expected to fall near the lower limit of the range. At present, genetic reaction ranges cannot be measured directly, and it is not known whether their sizes differ from one person to another, but studies of IQ gains associated with environmental enrichment and adoption programs suggest that the ranges could be as large as 15 to 20 points on the IQ scale (Dunn & Plomin, 1990). If this is indeed the case, then one person may have a range of potential IQs from 85 to 105, another from 100 to 115, and so on. This means that the influence of environmental factors on intelligence could be highly significant.

Some of the practical implications of the reaction range concept are illustrated in Figure 11.26. First, consider the cases of Persons *B* and *H*. They have identical reaction ranges, but *B* develops in a very deprived environment and *H* in an enriched environment with many cultural and educational advantages. *H* is able to realize her innate potential and has an IQ that is 20 points higher than *B*'s. Now compare Persons *C* and *I*. *C* actually has greater intellectual potential than *I*

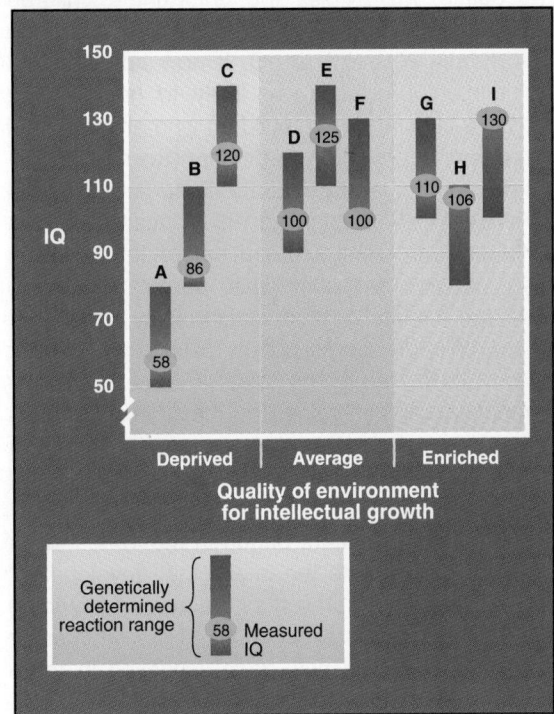

Figure 11.26 *Reaction ranges, environment, and intelligence. Genetic endowment is believed to create a reaction range within which environment exerts its effects. Enriched environments are expected to allow a person's intelligence to develop to the upper region of his or her reaction range, whereas deprived environments may limit intelligence to the lower portion of the range. Where intelligence is concerned, the reaction range may cover as much as 15–20 points on the IQ scale.*

but ends up with a lower IQ as a result of living in an environment that does not allow that potential to develop. Finally, note Person *G*, who was born with high genetic endowment and reared in an enriched environment. His resultant IQ of 110 indicates that he did not take advantage of either his innate or his environmental advantages. This serves to remind us that intellectual growth depends not only on genetic endowment and environmental advantage but also on other personal characteristics, such as interests and motivation, that affect how much we take advantage of our genetic and environmental endowments.

Effects of Environmental Enrichment

If the concept of reaction range is a valid one, then we ought to find that environmental enrichment programs can enhance intellectual abilities. They can, to varying degrees. In a classic study begun in the 1930s, H. M. Skeels (1966) followed the intellectual development of a group of supposedly "retarded," or cognitively disabled, children living in an orphanage in Iowa. Some of the children were transferred to a larger home for the cognitively disabled, where they were exposed to an enriched environment. After 4 years in their new home, the children had gained an average of 30 IQ points. Meanwhile, the unfortunate children who had remained in the impoverished orphanage lost nearly 20 points in IQ. It now appears that enrichment programs are likely to have strong positive effects only on children who are removed from very deprived environments (Scarr, 1992).

In another study, Sandra Scarr and Richard Weinberg (1976) studied 99 African-American children who were adopted before they were a year old and raised by white parents of above-average income and education. They found that these children scored about 15 IQ points higher than did a group of underprivileged African-American children raised by their biological parents. Their mean IQ of 110 was similar to that of white children adopted into similarly advantaged families.

Project Head Start, begun in the 1960s in an attempt to stimulate the intellectual development of underprivileged preschool children by providing them with learning experiences in their homes or in preschools, has now been assessed in more than 1,500 studies (Darlington, 1986; Lee & others, 1988). Although the difference in IQ between Head Start children and controls is neither large nor enduring (perhaps because the intervention does not occur early enough in the child's life), the Head Start children do better academically and are less likely to drop out of school. They also score higher on standardized tests of reading and arithmetic, are less likely to require remedial classes, and by age 15 are more likely to hold after-school jobs.

Figure 11.27 *Intervention programs like Head Start seem to have their strongest effects when they occur early in the child's life and help parents create a more stimulating home environment.*

Taken together, then, studies of enriched and deprived environments indicate that both are capable of influencing intellectual growth. Grossly deprived environments seem to stunt intellectual growth. Enrichment programs seem to be most effective when they are carried out early in a child's life and when the parents are taught and encouraged to provide intellectual stimulation for the child (Darlington, 1986).

Do Genes Affect the Environment?

The results of a large-scale University of Minnesota study of identical and fraternal twins who were reared together and apart have led Thomas Bouchard and his coworkers (1990) to conclude that up to 70 percent of the variance in intelligence in this population is accounted for by genetic factors. This might suggest the conclusion that genes directly determine intelligence to a large extent. However, the investigators suggest another possibility: The identical twins raised apart are so similar because their identical genotypes influence the environments they create for themselves through their inherited behavioral tendencies. That is, the environment and the experiences it provides may well be the *proximal,* or immediate, cause of most psychological variance, as the behaviorists have always claimed. However, the more remote, or *distal,* cause of those very experiences may be inherited temperamental, emotional, and cognitive differences that influence the parenting behaviors children elicit, the experiences they seek out, how they perceive and think about their experiences, and their individual responses to their life events (Plomin & Rende, 1991; Scarr, 1992).

The notion that our individual experiences and our cognitive and behavioral responses are important to our psychological development is supported by a surprising finding: Study after study indicates that being raised in the same family environment has negligible effects on how similar siblings are in intelligence and other psychological traits (Bouchard & others, 1990; Plomin & Rende, 1991). It seems to be the *nonshared,* or individualistic, environment that is important, and behavior geneticists are entertaining the intriguing hypothesis that genes influence development largely by influencing the character, selection, and ways of thinking about and reacting to individual experiences—in other words, that the correct formula may be *nature via nurture* (Bouchard & others, 1990, p. 228).

Racial Differences in Intelligence

Some of the most long-standing and bitter debates in psychology have concerned the existence and meaning of racial differences in intelligence. This is not surprising, because genetic effects are sometimes erroneously thought to imply that intelligence is fixed at birth. Discussions of differences in intelligence between ethnic groups touch on deeply held notions of social equality. To make matters worse, the evidence does not warrant any simple conclusion.

Everyone agrees on certain facts. In the late 20th century, there are consistent racial differences in the average intelligence test scores of members of different racial and national groups. National comparisons indicate that Japanese children have the highest mean IQ in the world. Their mean score of 111 places 77 percent of Japanese children above the mean scores of U.S. and European children (Lynn, 1982). Within the United States, significant racial differences also exist. Asian Americans test somewhat above the white norms, especially on tests related to visual-spatial and mathematical reasoning. The results for Hispanic citizens are mixed. Also, there is some evidence that test scores differ between subgroups of Asian and Hispanic origin. African Americans score, on the average, about 15 IQ points below the white American average (Aiken, 1991; Kaplan, 1985). This, of course, does not mean that all African Americans test lower than all whites; some score as high as the highest-scoring whites. Nevertheless, the difference is large enough to have serious consequences. Only about 15 to 20 percent of whites score below the mean for African Americans.

Keep in mind that these findings apply to test scores, which are the standard operational definition of the construct *intelligence*. Concerns have been expressed that these tests have been written to require knowledge of the white culture. Therefore, it is argued, the tests validly indicate the intelligence of a white person but do not validly measure the intelligence of an African American. Verbal comprehension tests, in particular, are questioned because they are typically written in standard American English.

The argument that the test "isn't fair" can be couched in two ways. One is that intelligence tests underestimate the mental competence of African Americans because the tests are culturally biased. The other is that the test scores are not indicative of how well African Americans can perform in real-life educational and vocational settings. Defenders of the tests as valid indicators of mental competence dispute both versions of the unfairness argument. First, they point out that racial differences appear throughout intelligence tests, not just on those items that would, on their face, appear to be culturally biased (Jensen, 1980). Second, they argue that if the tests were not

fair for African Americans in the predictive sense, then the tests should not predict this group's performance as well as they predict white performance. More precisely, the correlation between African-American test scores and criterion variables, such as school grades and performance in job settings, should be lower than the correlation between white test scores and criterion variables. This does not seem to be the case; most studies find that the tests predict African-American performance as well as they predict white performance (Barrett & Depinet, 1991; Hartigan & Wigdor, 1989). Thus, the tests seem to tap the cognitive skills required for criterion performance equally well for both racial groups.

The next argument about racial differences is a rather different one. The argument tentatively accepts the differences in measures of mental abilities as being real and then asks why they exist. Here, we return to the nature–nurture controversy.

There is no question that a discouragingly high proportion of African-American children in the United States are raised and schooled in situations that do not lead to the development of good reasoning skills. It has also been shown that early childhood education and aggressive programs to improve schooling can have positive long-term effects on cognitive skills, particularly when parents are heavily involved (Darlington, 1986). Moreover, social changes over the past 20 years that have provided African Americans with greater access to educational and vocational opportunities have coincided with a progressive reduction in differences between African Americans and white Americans on reading and mathematics achievement tests in grades 1 through 12, as well as on the SAT (Linn, 1989). People who are impressed by these facts believe racial differences on intelligence tests are due to environmental differences that could be changed.

The key role played by the quality of the environment may be illustrated by an example from plant genetics (see Figure 11.28). Suppose that a farmer has two fields, one with fertile soil and the other barren. The farmer randomly takes corn seed from a bag containing several genetic varieties and plants them in the two fields. When the seeds mature into plants, we will observe that within both fields, the plants vary in size. This variation is attributable to genetic factors. However, it will also be observed that the plants in the fertile field are, in general, larger than those that grew in the barren soil. That difference is due to environmental factors.

A similar case can be made for IQ differences between various human populations. That is, the *between*-group differences could be due to environmental differences even if, *within* each population, all variation were due to genetic differences (Eysenck & Kamin, 1981).▼ In truth, however, where measured

The heritability of a characteristic refers to how much of the variation within a group of people can be attributed to genetic differences. Heritability is one of the most misunderstood concepts in psychology. To say that the heritability of intelligence is 50–70 percent does *not* mean that genetic factors are responsible for 50–70 percent of an individual's intelligence, with the remaining 30–50 percent being due to environment. Heritability refers strictly to variations in intelligence *within* a group of people; and heritability estimates differ from study to study, depending on how similar or dissimilar people are in their genetic endowment and in the environments in which they live. It is also very important to emphasize that heritability estimates do not allow us to conclude that differences in intelligence *between* groups of people (such as racial or socioeconomic groups) are 50–70 percent due to genetic differences. Unfortunately, a misunderstanding of the fact that heritability addresses only variation within groups has caused even some psychologists to erroneously conclude that the high heritability of intelligence means that genetic factors account for most group differences in intelligence.

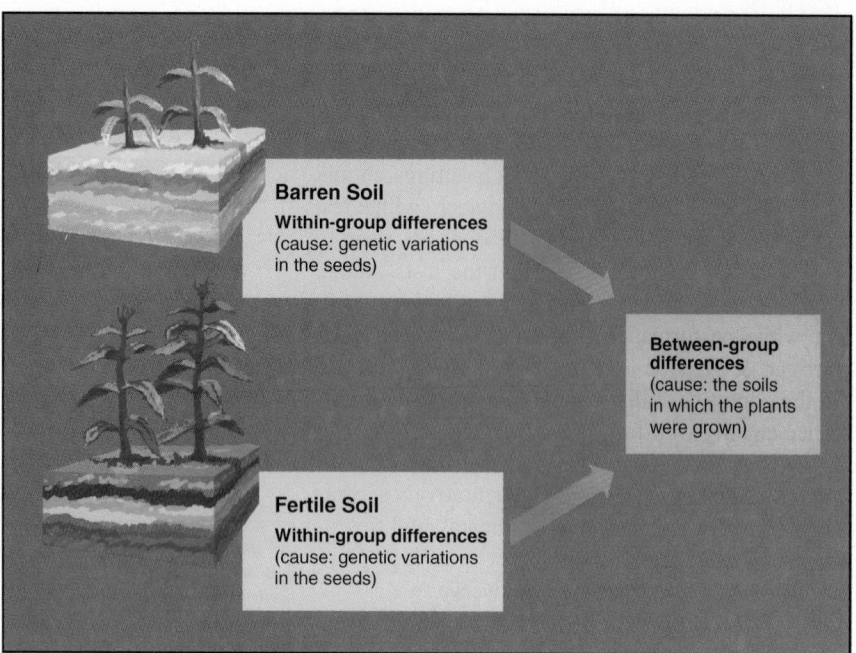

Figure 11.28 *The interaction of heredity and environment is shown in this agricultural analogy. Seeds planted in a fertile field will be, on the average, larger than those planted in poor soil. This between-groups variability is attributable to environment. Within each field, however, plants will also differ in size as a result of genetic factors. Applied to intelligence, this analogy indicates how between-group differences could result from environmental factors despite the fact that intelligence has a strong genetic component.*

directly, gene differences are often greater *within* racial groups than *between* them.

Again, however, saying that cognitive abilities are genetically influenced does *not* mean that they cannot be changed. It would be quite reasonable to believe that genetic factors contribute to group differences in intelligence *and* to believe that the mental competencies of disadvantaged children could be raised by appropriate educational, social, and health-improvement programs. In fact, as we have seen, there is already considerable evidence that such programs can work. Thus, from a social policy perspective, the question of genetic differences is far less important than the fact that intelligence is not a fixed, unchangeable personal quality. It is, instead, a set of cognitive skills that can be enhanced or depressed by the type of environment within which children develop, just as the growth of seedlings can be influenced by the soil in which they are planted.

Gender Differences in Cognitive Skills

Men and women, of course, differ in physical attributes and reproductive function. They also differ in their ability to perform certain types of intellectual tasks. The gender differences lie not in levels of general intelligence but rather in the patterns of cognitive skills that men and women exhibit. Although these ability differences are not necessarily large ones, they have been reported quite consistently by researchers (Hampson & Kimura, 1992).

Figure 11.29 summarizes the most consistent differences. Men, on average, *tend* to outperform women on certain spatial tasks. As a group, men are also more accurate in target-directed skills, such as throwing and catching objects, and they tend to perform slightly better on tests of mathematical reasoning. Women, on the other hand, perform slightly better on tests of perceptual speed, verbal fluency, and mathematical calculation and on precise manual tasks requiring fine motor coordination (Hampson & Kimura, 1992). Keep in mind, however, that men and women also vary considerably among themselves in all of these skills.

Explanations for these gender differences have emphasized both biological and environmental factors. The environmental explanations typically focus on the socialization experiences that males and females have as they grow up, especially the kinds of sex-typed activities that boys and girls are steered into. Until relatively recently, for example, boys were far more likely to play sports that involved throwing and catching balls, which might help account for their general superiority in this ability.

Biological explanations have increasingly focused on the effects of hormones on the developing brain. As discussed in Chapter 4, these influences begin shortly after conception when, during a critical period, the sex hormones (androgens and estrogens) establish sexual differentiation. The hormonal effects go far beyond reproductive characteristics. They alter brain organization and appear to extend to a variety of behavioral differences between men and women, including aggression and problem-solving approaches (Becker & others, 1992). One bit of evidence for hormonal influences is that fluctuations in hormonal levels are related to fluctuations in task performance in women. High levels of estrogen relate to improved performance on some of the ''feminine'' abilities in Figure 11.29 and declines in performance on some of the ''male'' ones (Kimura, 1992).

Meanwhile, researchers continue to search for subtle brain differences between men and women, and a number have been found that might help account for cognitive ability differences (Hampson & Kimura, 1992). Again, however, we must remember that the differences in ability are slight *average* differences and that men and women differ individually in the physical characteristics of their brains (Breedlove, 1992). Thus, the task of establishing gender-related brain–behavior linkages is not an easy one.

If the gender differences in abilities can be attributed to the role of sex hormones in organizing brain function, we might ask why the differences exist in the first place. One answer is that evolutionary pressures have helped shape these abilities and their biological underpinnings. Noting that in primitive societies, men were responsible for planning travel, hunting, and defending the group against predators and enemies, whereas women gathered food near the camp, made clothing, and cared for the children, gender researcher Doreen Kimura offers the following speculation:

> Such specializations would put different selection pressures on men and women. Men would require long-distance route-finding ability so they could recognize a geographic array from different orientations. They would also need targeting skills. Women would require short-range navigation, perhaps using landmarks, fine-motor capacities carried on within a circumscribed space, and perceptual discrimination sensitive to small changes in the environment or in children's appearance and behavior (Kimura, 1992, p. 125).

Widespread interest in the nature of gender differences in cognitive abilities and in the reasons why they might exist will continue to stimulate research on biological factors, on environmental factors, and on the larger question of how they might interact to influence group differences in intellectual abilities.

Extremes of Intelligence

Because of the many genetic and environmental influences on intelligence, there are individuals at both ends of the intelligence distribution who have exceptional mental abilities. At the low end are those labeled mentally retarded; at the upper end are the intellectually gifted.

The Cognitively Disabled

Approximately 3 to 5 percent of the U.S. population, or about 10 million people, are classified as mentally retarded, or cognitively disabled. The American Psychiatric Association has devised a four-level classification system that characterizes cognitive disability as mild, moderate, severe, and profound on the basis of IQ scores. Table 11.6 describes these classifications and their behavioral correlates. As you can see, the vast majority are mildly disabled, obtaining IQs between about 50 and 70. Most of the mildly disabled are capable of living in the mainstream of society, given appropriate support. They are capable of marrying and holding jobs. Progressively greater environmental support is needed as we move toward the profoundly disabled range, where institutional care is usually required.

Mildly disabled children can attend school, but they learn more slowly than other children, and they have difficulties with tasks requiring reading, writing, memory, and mathematical computations. Many of

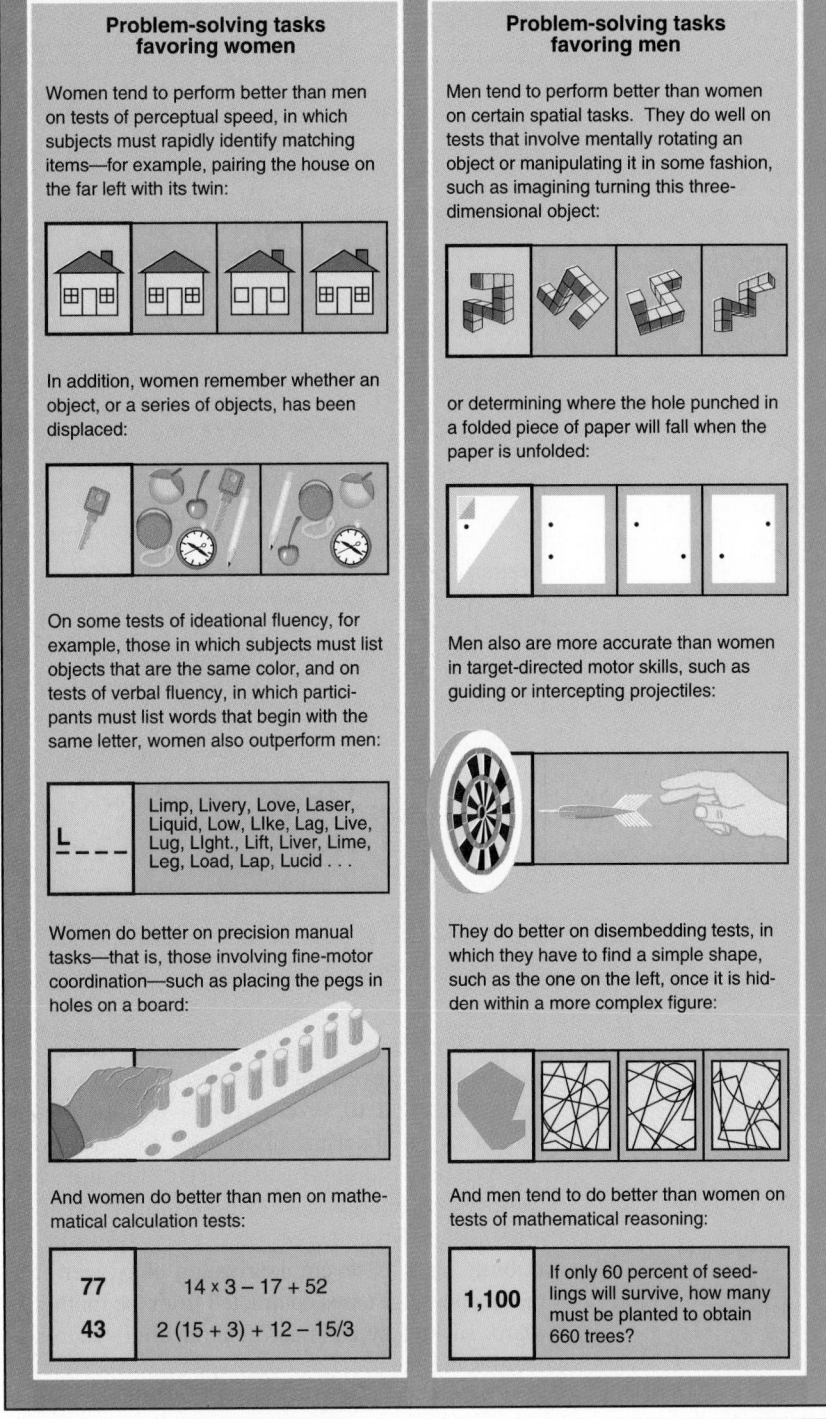

Figure 11.29 *Gender differences in cognitive abilities that have been reported in the scientific literature. (Kimura, 1992).*

their difficulties result from poorly developed problem-solving strategies of the type discussed in this chapter. They often have difficulties reasoning, planning, and evaluating feedback from their efforts.

Cognitive disability has a variety of causes, some genetic, some biological, and some experiential. About 25 percent of cases have known biological

Table 11.6 Behavioral Characteristics of Cognitively Disabled People Throughout the Life Span

Type	Characteristics From Birth to Adulthood		
	Birth through Five	Six through Twenty	Twenty-one and Over
Mild (IQ 53–69)	Often not noticed as delayed by casual observer but is slower to walk, feed him- or herself, and talk than most children.	Can acquire practical skills and master reading and arithmetic to a third- to sixth-grade level with special education. Can be guided toward social conformity.	Can usually achieve adequate social, vocational, and self-maintenance skills; may need occasional guidance and support when under unusual social or economic stress.
Moderate (36–52)	Noticeable delays in motor development, especially in speech; responds to training in various self-help activities.	Can learn simple communication, elementary health and safety habits, and simple manual skills; does not progress in functional reading or arithmetic.	Can perform simple tasks under sheltered conditions; participate in simple recreation; can travel alone in familiar places; usually incapable of self-maintenance.
Severe (20–35)	Marked delay in motor development; little or no communication skill; may respond to training in elementary self-help, such as self-feeding.	Usually walks, barring specific disability; has some understanding of speech and some response; can profit from systematic habit training.	Can conform to daily routines and repetitive activities; needs continuing direction and supervision in protective environment.
Profound (below 20)	Gross disability; minimal capacity for functioning in sensorimotor areas; needs nursing care.	Obvious delays in all areas of development; shows basic emotional responses; may respond to skillful training in use of legs, hands, and jaws; needs close supervision.	May walk, need nursing care, have primitive speech; usually benefits from regular physical activity; incapable of self-maintenance.

Source: Adapted from Kagan & Haveman, 1972.

causes. For example, *Down's syndrome*—characterized by slanted eyes, stubby limbs, thin hair, a short neck, and mild to severe mental retardation—is caused by an abnormal division of the 21st chromosome pair. More than a hundred different genetic causes of retardation have been identified (Shaffer, 1989). Retardation can also be caused by accidents at birth, such as severe deprivation of oxygen (anoxia), and by diseases contracted from the mother *in utero,* such as syphilis and fetal alcohol syndrome. Despite this range of potential biological causes, however, the vast majority of cases (75–80 percent) lack a clear biological cause. These cases may be due to undetectable organic factors, extreme environmental deprivation, or to a combination of the two.

Whatever the cause of the disability, educators are aware that except in the most profound cases, cognitive and social skills can be improved. In the past, "retarded" children were typically placed in special education classes that isolated them from other children and featured a diluted curriculum. The results of special education were disappointing in terms of both academic and social development (Cole & Cole,

1989). Placement in such classes also tended to increase the stigma attached to the label *retarded*. Presently, federal law mandates that such children be given individualized instruction in the "least restrictive environment." This has led to the practice called **mainstreaming,** which allows many children to attend school in regular classrooms (see Figure 11.30). Mainstreaming has accelerated the academic achievement of cognitively disabled children and has increased their acceptance and integration into the normal peer environment (Gaylord-Ross, 1990). Mainstreaming is part of a growing awareness of the needs and potentials of retarded individuals of all ages—an awareness reflected in a growing emphasis on teaching them the social and problem-solving skills that will help them to adapt to the demands of everyday living.

The Gifted

At the other end of the intellectual spectrum are the gifted. Like the cognitively disabled, the gifted are often the victims of stereotypes that depict them as

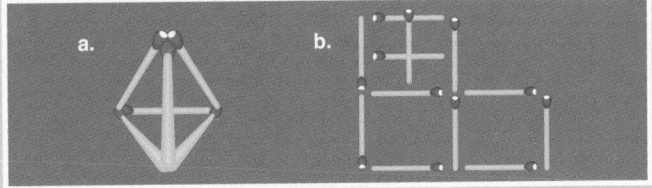Figure 11.30 *The practice of mainstreaming has allowed children of low intelligence to function in normal classrooms, resulting in better academic and social outcomes for them.*

eccentric and socially maladjusted. One of the first studies to challenge this stereotype was conducted by Lewis Terman of Stanford University, who helped develop the Stanford-Binet test. Terman identified some 1,500 California children who had an average IQ of 150 and began an extensive study of them that has continued for over 60 years. Terman found these children to be above average not only in intelligence but also in height, weight, strength, physical health, emotional adjustment, and social maturity. They continued to exhibit high levels of adjustment throughout their adolescent and adult years. By midlife, they had authored 92 books, 2,200 scientific articles, and 235 patents. Their marriages tended to be happy and successful ones, and they seemed well adjusted psychologically. In essence, the gifted children became gifted and happy adults (Holahan, 1984; Sears, 1977).

Like children at the other end of the competence continuum, gifted children often need special educational opportunities. They may become bored in regular classrooms and even drop out of school if they are not sufficiently challenged (Fetterman, 1988). Many states now require every school district to have an accelerated program for the gifted. Unfortunately, this has sometimes resulted in the practice of "ability tracking," which segregates students by aptitude level and denies nongifted students opportunities for educational enrichment. The Carnegie Council on Adolescent Development (1989) warned that, carried to an extreme, academic tracking may widen the achievement gap between the gifted and others while decreasing social integration within the school. Schools should institute integrated programs that provide for the needs of all students and recognize that giftedness is a combination of many traits in addition to intelligence.

Answers to Problems in Text

Figure 11.9   Baltimore and Washington are 50 miles apart. The trains are traveling at the same speed (25 mph). Hence, they will meet at the halfway point, which is 25 miles, after 1 hour of travel time. Since the crow is flying at 60 mph, it will have flown a total of 60 miles when the trains meet.

Figure 11.10   Answers to the matchstick problems:

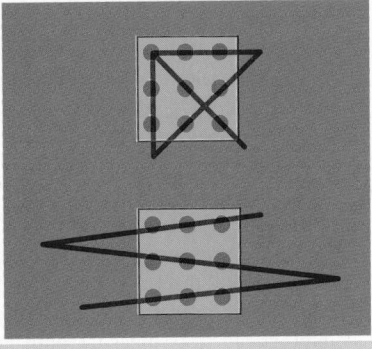

Figure 11.12   Sequence of moves: **A** to **3**, **B** to **2**, **A** to **Z**, **C** to **3**, **A** to **1**, **B** to **3**, **A** to **3**.

Figure 11.14   The objects in pairs: **a** and **b** are the same. Those in **c** are different.

Figure 11.16   Here are two solutions to the dot problem:

Figure 11.17   Solution to the candlestick problem:

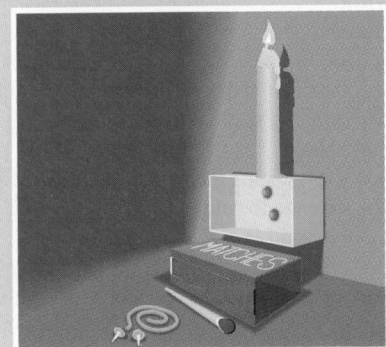

Figure 11.21   Object **b** is the same.

Concepts and Propositions

● Concepts are classes that share certain characteristics. Many concepts are based on prototypes, the most typical and familiar members of a class. How much something resembles the prototype determines whether the concept is applied to it.

● Propositional thought involves the use of concepts, in the form of statements having subjects and predicates.

Deductive Reasoning

● In deductive reasoning, we reason from general principles to a conclusion about a specific case. Deduction is regarded as the strongest and most valid form of reasoning, because the conclusion cannot be false *if* the premises are true.

● Unsuccessful deductive reasoning can result from (a) failure to map the problem in its logical form, often as a result of faulty selective encoding; (b) failure to apply the appropriate deductive reasoning rules, particularly in novel situations; (c) belief bias; and (d) too much dependence on limited working memory.

● Problem-solving schemas, or heuristics, are rule-of-thumb methods for solving specialized classes of problems. They are stored in long-term memory and can help overcome the limitations of working memory. Unlike the rules of deduction, they are not guaranteed to lead to a correct conclusion.

● Expertise in a given area consists largely in having acquired a range of successful problem-solving schemas through training and practical experience, as well as knowing when to apply each schema.

Inductive Reasoning and Problem Solving

● Inductive reasoning involves reasoning from a set of specific facts or observations to a general principle. It proceeds through a number of steps: (1) understanding the nature of the problem, (2) establishing initial hypotheses, (3) testing the hypotheses against existing evidence to rule out hypotheses that do not apply, and (4) evaluating results.

● Several biases can interfere with the process of induction. Some of them involve the misapplication of heuristics. The representativeness heuristic is the tendency to judge evidence according to whether it is consistent with an existing schema. The availability heuristic is the tendency to base conclusions on what is currently available in memory. This heuristic contributes to the belief-bias effect, the tendency to ignore evidence that doesn't fit our

beliefs. Finally, humans have a marked confirmation bias, a tendency to look for facts to support hypotheses rather than to disprove them.

● Problem solving is often facilitated by the application of learned schemas. In some situations, however, divergent thinking is needed for generating novel ideas or variations on ideas. Functional fixedness, which can blind us to new ways of using an object or procedure, can interfere with creative problem solving. In some cases, a period of incubation permits problem solving to go on at a subconscious level while giving the problem solver psychological distance from the problem.

● Convergent thinking narrows alternative solutions to the one that seems most likely to succeed. Practical considerations must be taken into account.

Intelligence and Its Measurement

● Intelligence is a concept that refers to individual differences in the ability to acquire knowledge, to think and reason effectively, and to deal adaptively with the environment.

● The first attempts to relate social and intellectual competence to measures of elementary abilities were made by Galton. They were largely unsuccessful.

● Alfred Binet constructed the first intelligence test to identify students for special instruction. Lewis Terman of Stanford University later revised the test, and the Stanford-Binet test is still widely used with children.

● The IQ is a relative measure that indicates where the person falls within the normal distribution of IQ scores derived in the process of standardization. The concept of mental age introduced by Binet is no longer used.

● The Wechsler scales, separately developed for adults, children, and preschoolers, are the most widely used individual intelligence tests. They consist of a series of verbal and performance subscales that yield separate verbal and performance IQs, as well as a full-scale IQ.

● The success of the Army Alpha test has stimulated the development of other group tests, such as the Scholastic Aptitude Test. An aptitude test is designed to measure potential for future learning and performance, whereas achievement tests are designed to measure what one has already learned. In practice, most intelligence tests measure both aptitude and achievement.

● Predictive validity refers to how well test scores predict other outcomes, or criteria. IQ is a better predictor of academic success than of job success, which often requires abilities that are not measured by the tests.

The Nature of Intelligence

● The psychometric approach attempts to specify what the structure of intellect is and, more specifically, how many different classes of mental ability underlie test performance. A newer approach, the cognitive science approach, focuses on the specific thought processes that underlie mental competencies.

● Spearman believed intelligence was determined both by specific cognitive abilities and a general intelligence (g) factor that constituted the core of intelligence. Thurstone disagreed, viewing intelligence as a set of specific abilities. Thurstone's position is best supported by observed distinctions between verbal and visual–spatial abilities.

● Cattell and Horn have differentiated between crystallized intelligence, based on the ability to apply previously learned knowledge to current problems, and fluid intelligence, the ability to deal with novel problem-solving situations for which experience does not provide a solution. Cattell and Horn argue that over our life spans, we progress from using fluid to using crystallized intelligence.

● Gardner has suggested that there are separate and distinct forms of intelligence, including linguistic, mathematical, spatial, musical, bodily–kinesthetic, and personal intelligence. He believes that these are based in separate (though frequently interacting) modules in the brain.

● Cognitive process theories of intelligence have focused on the elementary information-processing abilities that contribute to intelligence. Sternberg's triadic theory of intelligence includes a componential subtheory that addresses the specific cognitive processes that underlie intelligent behavior.

Heredity, Environment, and Intelligence

● Intelligence is determined by interacting hereditary and environmental factors. Heredity establishes a reaction range. Environment affects what point within that range will be reached.

● Studies of enriched and deprived environments indicate that both are capable of influencing intellectual growth. Enrichment programs seem to be most effective when they are carried out early in a child's life and when the parents are taught and encouraged to provide intellectual stimulation for the child.

Racial Differences in Intelligence

● Racial differences in intelligence have been one of the most controversial topics in psychology. Such differences in intelligence test scores continue to occur, but the relative contributions of genetic and environmental factors are still in question.

Extremes of Intelligence

● Mental retardation can be caused by a number of factors. Biological causes are identified in only about 25 percent of cases. Cognitive disability can range from mild to profound. The vast majority of disabled individuals are able to function in the mainstream of society, given appropriate support.

● Lewis Terman's study of gifted children indicated that these individuals tended to be well adjusted and to have happy and productive adulthoods. Today, special educational curricula for the gifted are mandated in many states, but the "ability tracking" that sometimes results has been a source of controversy.

KEY TERMS AND CONCEPTS

achievement test (p. 350)
algorithm (p. 339)
aptitude test (p. 350)
artificial intelligence (p. 345)
availability heuristic (p. 341)
belief bias (p. 333)
cognitive process theories (p. 355)
confirmation bias (p. 342)
conjunction fallacy (p. 341)
convergent thinking (p. 345)
criterion (p. 351)
crystallized intelligence (p. 353)
deductive reasoning (p. 332)
divergent thinking (p. 344)
fluid intelligence (p. 353)
functional fixedness (p. 344)

g factor (p. 352)
heuristics (p. 340)
imaginal thought (p. 331)
incubation (p. 344)
inductive reasoning (p. 332)
intelligence (p. 347)
intelligence quotient (IQ) (p. 348)
mainstreaming (p. 362)
mapping the problem (p. 332)
means/ends analysis (p. 340)
mental age (p. 347)
mental set (p. 339)
metacomponents (p. 355)
motoric thought (p. 331)
norm group (p. 348)
parallel processing (p. 346)

predictive validity (p. 351)
premise (p. 332)
primary mental abilities (p. 352)
problem-solving schemas (p. 334)
propositional thought (p. 331)
prototype (p. 331)
psychometrics (p. 352)
reaction range (p. 357)
representativeness heuristic (p. 340)
selective encoding (p. 332)
serial processing (p. 346)
standardization (p. 348)
subgoal analysis (p. 340)
test norms (p. 348)
theory of multiple intelligences (p. 354)
triarchic theory of intelligence (p. 355)

SUGGESTED READINGS

Gilovich, T. (1991). *How we know what isn't so: The fallibility of human reasoning in everyday life.* New York: Free Press. An analysis of pitfalls in reasoning, including the heuristics discussed in this chapter, with guidelines on how to avoid faulty reasoning.

Halpern, D. F. (1989). *Thought and knowledge: An introduction to critical thinking.* Hillsdale, N.J.: Erlbaum. A book that focuses on the findings of psychological research on thinking and reasoning, with its implications for thinking more productively.

Linn, R. L. (1989). *Intelligence: Measurement, theory, and public policy.* Urbana: University of Illinois Press. An informative overview of current theories of intelligence, the measurement of intelligence, and implications for public policy.

12 Motivation

he midafternoon sun sifted through the haze above the stadium as the finishers in the Olympic women's marathon entered the stadium and ran their final laps around the field. Many of the competitors tottered on the brink of exhaustion, spurred on only by their competitive pride. One of them, Gabriella Andersen-Scheiss of Switzerland, seemed beyond mere exhaustion, however. She wobbled and nearly fell as she entered the stadium, then lurched blindly along the red running track, her head hanging at a grotesque angle to one side, her body nearly doubled over in agony. Olympic officials ran to her side to remove her from competition, but the semiconscious athlete waved them away and, as a crowd of nearly 100,000 spectators sat transfixed, shuffled step by step toward the finish line, then collapsed after crossing it (see Figure 12.1).

Andersen-Scheiss recovered from her state of exhaustion, and although she won no Olympic medals, she became a heroine in the eyes of her fellow competitors and a worldwide audience. No one who witnessed her grim determination to finish the race will soon forget it, nor will they doubt the power of motivation to stretch the boundaries of human effort.

In many ways, the barriers to goal attainment that confronted Mary Whiton Calkins were far more formidable than the bodily exhaustion that Anderson-Scheiss faced. Although today more than half of the students entering doctoral programs in psychology are women, that was not always the case. When Wellesley College was established in 1870, the founder decided to hire women as faculty at the all-women institution. Unable to find a woman to teach psychology, he hired Calkins, who had a B.A. in classics, and promised to pay for her doctoral education in psychology. However, he found that doctoral training in psychology, as in other sciences, was closed to women. Finally, Harvard grudgingly allowed Calkins to attend its graduate courses, although it would not at first allow her to officially register for them. Calkins, showing great drive and determination, proved herself to be a brilliant student, and she eventually completed all of the requirements for the Ph.D. However, the Harvard administration, while acknowledging her status as the top student in the program, refused to grant her a Harvard Ph.D. because she was a woman. Instead, they offered her a doctorate from Radcliffe College, the recently established undergraduate college for women. Calkins rejected this discriminatory offer, and she never received the doctorate she so richly deserved. Nonetheless, she returned to Wellesley and forged a distinguished scientific career in cognitive and personality psychology. In 1905, she became the first woman president of the American Psychological Association (Furumoto, 1979).

The concept of motivation is central in our attempt to understand behavior and its causes. The word *motivation* comes from the Latin word meaning "to move." Psychologists use the concept of motivation to help explain how internal factors seem to move animals and people toward certain goals. The nature of the goal, or **incentive,** toward which behavior seems to be directed—for example, food, water, success, or control over others—determines the label that we attach to the motivational state—hunger, thirst, achievement motivation, or a need for power (McClelland, 1988; Weiner, 1992). Our opening examples illustrate two different manifestations of the drive to succeed. As the cases of Gabriella Andersen-Scheiss and Mary Calkins illustrate, motivated behavior is often vigorous in nature, and it may persist over long periods of time. We therefore define **motivation** as an internal process that influences the direction, persistence, and vigor of goal-directed behavior.

■ ▢

Motivation: A Biopsychosocial Phenomenon

In no area of psychology has the value of different perspectives on behavior been more evident than in the study of motivation. The range of motives that affect behavior is so great that some of them are bound to be particularly relevant to each perspective (see

Figure 12.2). The perspectives also focus our attention on a variety of causal factors that influence the various motivational states. Thus, motivation has biological, psychological, and social foundations.

The Biological Perspective: Drives, Pleasure, and Evolutionary Factors

We begin with the biological perspective because some of our most basic needs have biological foundations. Without food, water, oxygen, warmth, and the other things that satisfy basic bodily needs, we could not survive. Without a biologically based sex drive, no species could continue to exist. Therefore, the study of the internal and external processes related to the arousal and reduction of biological needs has long been a major focus of psychological theory and research. Major advances have occurred in our understanding of how the nervous and endocrine systems are involved in the regulation of internal states, as well as how such states affect behavior. As we shall see, the biological perspective has also provided valuable insights into certain human problems related to motivation, such as the problem of obesity.

Biological researchers have also sought to understand the nature of need satisfaction and reward. The satisfaction of needs, be they biological needs or psychological ones, generates feelings of pleasure and well-being. These subjective states are thought to be produced by biochemical events in the brain, particularly the release of neurotransmitters such as the endorphins and dopamine in certain brain regions (Kimble, 1992; Pert, 1986). An understanding of the mechanisms of need gratification and pleasure is being sought within the biological perspective.

Evolutionary psychology is exerting an increasingly strong influence on the study of motivation. The fact that many motivated behaviors are instrumental to survival and to opportunities to pass on genes to succeeding generations has led some theorists to suggest that many behaviors—even social ones—may be influenced by genetic factors and may serve evolutionary purposes (Buss, 1991; Cosmides & Tooby, 1987). For example, a recent study of the factors that men and women in 37 cultures find most important in selecting mates revealed not only cultural differences but also universal preferences that were consistent with an evolution-based hypothesis. For women, the most important factors were the ability of the man to provide materially for the family and to protect them, attributes that would help ensure their well-being and survival. For men, the important factors related to the physical attributes of the woman and her ability to bear children, factors that would increase the likelihood of healthy offspring (Buss & others, 1990). Evolutionary theorists suggest that many motives and behaviors that we consider "psychological" may have evolutionary underpinnings that express themselves through the actions of genes.

The Behavioral Perspective: Learning and Environment

If the behavioral perspective makes you think of rats running through mazes to obtain food, it may surprise you to learn that some radical behaviorists have urged that we do away with the concept of motivation entirely. B. F. Skinner, for example, claimed that studying "fictional motives" gives us an illusory understanding of behaviors that can only be truly understood in reference to externally observable stimuli and responses. Skinner believed that psychologists need not muddy their thinking with an internal motivational concept like "hunger" when they can study the effects of an observable and controllable variable like "hours of food deprivation."

Despite Skinner's extreme view, many behavioral psychologists continue to study motivation. For many years, learning and motivation were virtually inseparable in behavioral research because the events that enhanced learning by serving as reinforcers frequently seemed to be related to the reduction of drives like hunger (Berlyne, 1978). Indeed, for a time, some learning theorists argued that all reinforcement involves some kind of biological drive reduction (Hull, 1951). As subsequent research showed, that does not seem to be the case. People often seem to behave so as to *increase* rather than decrease drive levels, as when they take hair-raising rides on roller coasters, seek out sexually arousing films, and engage in high-stakes gambling.

Most modern theorists give motivational variables a prominent place in their theories of how learning occurs, and much current research is focusing on brain mechanisms of reward and punishment (White & Milner, 1992). The concept of motivation also helps to account for fluctuations in performance after learning has occurred; when motivation is low, performance of well-learned behaviors often falls off as well. Finally, as we shall see, some important social motives, such as achievement and power, seem to be learned, and the expression of even innate biological needs like hunger can be modified in important ways by learning (McClelland, 1988).

The behavioral perspective also stresses the importance of environmental stimuli in motivating and directing behavior. Even biological needs are strongly influenced by environmental factors, including the cultural context in which the motives are aroused and satisfied.

The Cognitive Perspective: Expectancy, Value, and Possible Selves

The cognitive perspective on motivation emphasizes the influence of mental processes on goal-directed behavior. One influential cognitive approach to motivation is known as **Expectancy × value theory** (Brehm & Self, 1989; Weiner, 1992). According to this theory, the direction and intensity of goal-directed behavior are jointly determined by the strength of the person's expectation that particular behaviors will lead to a goal and by the value the individual places on that goal. Goal-directed behavior will be strongest and most persistent if the goal is highly valued and if there is a high expectation that the behavior will result in goal attainment. For example, a person who greatly values academic success and expects that hard study will lead to such success will study more than someone who does not have the same value and/or the same expectancy. If value, expectancy, or both are low, the behavior either will not occur at all, or its strength and persistence will be greatly reduced.

The Hidden Costs of Reward: Intrinsic and Extrinsic Motivation

The cognitive approach to motivation raises a number of interesting issues not considered by the behavioral perspective. For example, what might happen if Jennie, who already loves to read (has **intrinsic motivation** for the activity), is given money or some other extrinsic reward for time spent reading? From a behavioral point of view, the added **extrinsic motivation** for reading should increase her total motivation to read. But what happens if the extrinsic reward is later withdrawn? Will Jennie still enjoy reading for its own sake?

Perhaps not. One cognitive theory holds that extrinsic rewards can sometimes undermine and even reduce intrinsic motivation. According to the **overjustification hypothesis,** the crucial factor is our changing interpretation of *why* we perform the behavior. If we come to attribute our behavior to the presence of the external reward rather than to our liking for the activity, our desire to perform the behavior will decrease if the reward is withdrawn; we will become "unmotivated." In one study, children who already spent a great deal of time drawing with felt-tipped markers were suddenly offered certificates for doing so. As long as the certificates were given, the amount of time spent in drawing remained high.

Many psychologists assume that intrinsic motivation is preferable to extrinsic motivation. However, a critical thinker will ask, "In what ways is intrinsic motivation superior?" The Lepper and Greene study showed that intrinsically motivated children spent more time drawing. It said nothing about the quality of their performance, though. We should be concerned about whether people learn and perform at a higher level when their intrinsic motivation is increased.

Louise Parker and Lepper (1992) addressed this issue. They attempted to enhance the intrinsic motivation of elementary school children to learn computer graphics programming. In the control condition, the lessons required the children to draw lines connecting geometric figures, find their way through mazes, or construct geometric designs on the screen. To enhance intrinsic motivation in the experimental condition, exactly the same tasks were embellished with fantasy contexts involving astronauts landing on a series of planets, pirates seeking buried treasure, and a detective negotiating a maze of secret passages in an evil wizard's castle. The fantasy condition was regarded as more fun (more intrinsically motivating), and the children in this condition learned the programming commands faster and performed better. Thus, intrinsic motivation does seem to increase learning and task performance. What educational implications do these results have? How do they relate to the effects of meaningfullness on memory discussed in Chapter 10?

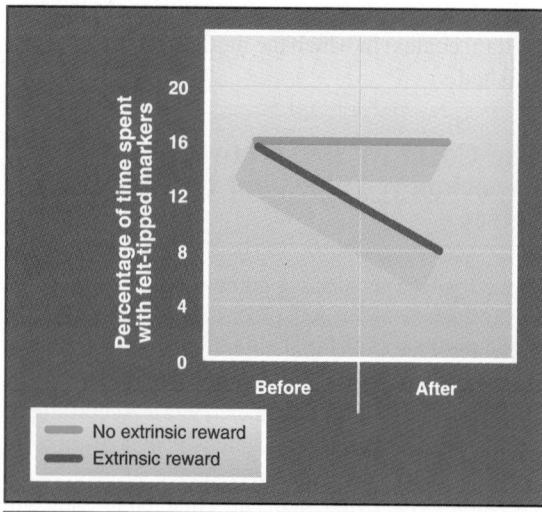

▲ **Figure 12.3** *The ability of extrinsic reinforcers to reduce intrinsic motivation is shown in the decreased amount of time children spent drawing after an extrinsic reinforcer was withdrawn. (Data from Lepper & Greene, 1978).*

But when they stopped receiving certificates, the children decreased their drawing by 50 percent; and as Figure 12.3 shows, they subsequently spent less time drawing than children who had received no external reward (Lepper & Greene, 1978). Similar effects have been observed in sports. Dean Ryan (1980) asked college football players to rate themselves on their enjoyment of the game. Football players who were attending college on athletic scholarships—and were therefore, in a sense, being financially compensated for playing football—gave themselves lower ratings of enjoyment than nonscholarship players. For the scholarship athletes, apparently, the sport had become more work than play. ▼

Does this mean that we should never use extrinsic reinforcers? Not at all. A key factor is how extrinsic rewards are used. When offered as a means of informing people that they are doing well rather than simply as inducements to perform the behavior, extrinsic rewards can increase feelings of competence and intrinsic motivation (Deci & Ryan, 1987). Then, even if the rewards are later withdrawn, intrinsic motivation may continue to motivate the behavior.

Possible Selves as a Motivating Force

Many goals lie in the future, and our fears and anticipations of what might occur help direct our behavior toward those goals. Undoubtedly, you occasionally reflect on what your life will be like after you complete your education and establish a new lifestyle. There are probably future events that you fear as well.

Hazel Markus and her coworkers have linked cognition with motivation in their concept of possible

selves (Cross & Markus, 1991; Markus & Nurius, 1986). As noted in Chapter 5, **possible selves** represent our ideas of what we might become or what we are afraid of becoming; they are the cognitive manifestations of enduring goals, aspirations, fears, and threats. Hoped-for possible selves might include the successful self, the creative self, the thin self, the loved and admired self, or the powerful self, whereas dreaded possible selves could include the alone self, the unemployed self, the alcoholic self, or the unloved self. Possible selves help link the past self, the present self, and the potential future self. The past provides information about our potential, which is translated into hopes and aspirations for the future.

According to Markus, possible selves function as incentives for future behavior, and they direct behavior toward desired goals and away from feared consequences. Personal development can be viewed as a process of acquiring and then achieving or resisting certain possible selves (Cross & Markus, 1991; Ryff, 1991). Achieving or failing to achieve significant possible selves provides a basis for self-pride or self-deprecation as well (Cervone, 1992).

In research with college students, Markus and Nurius (1986) found evidence for a good deal of cognitive activity related to past and possible selves. About 35 percent of the students indicated that they frequently thought about what they were like in the past, and 65 percent reported that they often thought about themselves in the future. Table 12.1 shows subjects' reports of their conceptions of present and possible selves.

The concept of possible selves seems compatible with the expectancy × value model discussed earlier. The value attached to specific possible selves and our expectations of how we might attain or avoid them should provide valuable insights into our motives and goal-directed behavior.

The Psychodynamic Perspective: The Motivational Underworld

A major focus of psychodynamic theorists is the motivational underworld of unconscious wishes and conflicts. Much of human behavior is seen as a product of a never-ending battle between unconscious motives struggling for release and the psychological defenses used to keep them under control. The following case described by psychoanalyst Charles Brenner (1974) illustrates a psychodynamic interpretation of unconscious motives and defenses.

A college student returned to his family's home at the end of the academic term and found no one there. He had a vivid daydream in which he imagined that his mother and younger sister had been killed. He reported feeling absolutely no emotion during or after the daydream and could not understand why. Here is Brenner's analysis of the reason:

> The patient was alone in the house after his return from college. . . . These and other circumstances forcibly reminded the patient of the time when his mother had gone to the hospital for delivery and when the patient had felt very alone. What had happened after the mother's return had been even worse. She had turned from the patient and focused her affection on the new baby, a girl. From that time on, the patient felt unwanted and unloved. But rage was dangerous, since being a "bad boy," he learned, would lead all the more to being abandoned by mother, who used to punish him by putting him in a dark closet when he had an angry outburst, or later on, by refusing to talk to him. . . . When the patient came home to an empty house he reacted with memories of that earlier time when his sister was born and was overcome by jealousy, longing, and rage. He could not banish completely all his frightening and guilt-ridden reactions. He did imagine that his mother and sister had been killed. At the same time, however, he denied that it was his own wish to kill them—in his fantasy, the deed had been done by others—and he did ward off any feelings of either pleasure or unpleasure at the idea that they had been killed. There was no conscious trace of either, any more than there was a conscious trace of sexual wishes toward mother, or of memories of such wishes and the past experiences connected with them (p. 536).

Freud believed that because Western society discourages the direct and unbridled expression of impulses, particularly sex and aggression, the energy from these internal drives is often disguised and expressed as behaviors that are more socially acceptable. He called this process **sublimation.** For example, aggressive impulses may be channeled into a successful career as a boxer, a soldier, a trial attorney, or, in today's world, a political campaign manager.

Maslow's Hierarchy of Needs: A Humanistic Perspective

The concern of humanistic theorists with the ultimate meaning of human existence and with the struggle of the individual toward self-actualization has extended the study of motivation beyond the biological and social focuses of the other perspectives. The humanistic theorist Abraham Maslow (1970) distinguished between **deficiency needs,** which are concerned with the individual's physical and social survival, and **growth needs,** which motivate the person to develop his or her full potential as a human being. Maslow viewed growth needs as the highest expression of human motivation, and he argued that they have not received the attention they deserve from psychologists.

Table 12.1 Percentages of College Students Who Endorsed Self-Descriptive Items Relating to Perceived Current Self and Possible Selves

Item	Question	
	Does this describe you now?	Have you ever considered this a possible self?
Personality		
Happy	88.0	100.0
Confident	83.8	100.0
Depressed	40.2	49.6
Lazy	36.2	48.3
Lifestyle		
Travel widely	43.6	94.0
Have lots of friends	74.6	91.2
Be destitute	4.5	19.6
Have nervous breakdown	11.1	42.7
Physical		
Sexy	51.7	73.5
In good shape	66.7	96.5
Wrinkled	12.0	41.0
Paralyzed	2.6	44.8
General abilities		
Speak well publicly	59.0	80.3
Make own decisions	93.2	99.1
Manipulate people	53.5	56.6
Cheat on taxes	9.4	17.9
Others' feelings toward you		
Powerful	33.3	75.2
Trusted	95.7	99.1
Unimportant	12.8	24.8
Offensive	24.8	32.5
Occupation		
Media personality	2.2	56.1
Owner of a business	1.4	80.3
Janitor	2.6	6.8
Prison guard	0.0	4.3

Source: Markus & Nurius, 1986, p. 959.

Maslow suggested that human needs can be arranged in a hierarchy with the most necessary requirements for survival at the bottom and the most profound expressions of human potential at the top (see Figure 12.4). A given need does not appear until the needs below it have been satisfied. Thus, the basic needs, such as physiological and safety needs, must be satisfied before other, higher-level needs can be attended to. This makes perfect sense—a person who does not have enough to eat or whose safety is threatened in some other way cannot afford the luxury of contemplating beauty and truth. Self-preservation has to come before self-actualization. Even people who have reached the higher levels can quickly tumble back down if circumstances change and their lower-level needs are no longer being met. One's creative inclinations may fade quickly in the face of starvation or physical danger.

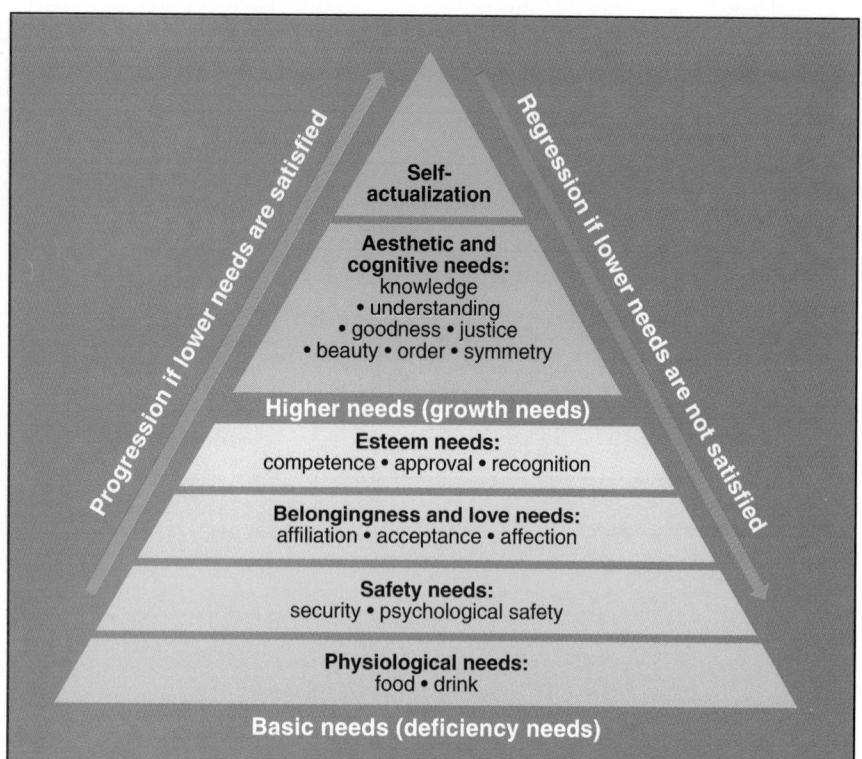

Figure 12.4 *Maslow's need hierarchy extends upward from basic biological needs to self-actualization, the highest of human motives. Maslow believed that in order for the higher growth needs to direct behavior, the deficiency needs lower in the hierarchy must be satisfied.*

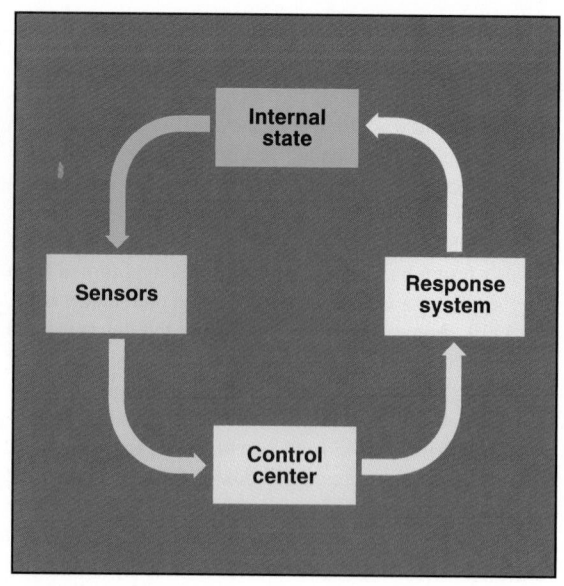

Figure 12.5 *The internal environment of the body is regulated by homeostatic mechanisms, which require sensors for detecting changes, a response system to restore equilibrium, and a control center that receives input from the sensors and regulates the response system.*

Maslow's theory is perhaps the most inclusive of all the theories we have considered. It deals with the full range of human motives, from those that are the focus of the biological and behavioral approaches to the growth needs, which are not considered by any of the other perspectives. Maslow's theory has influenced fields ranging from philosophy to business, where it has been the basis for attempts to increase employee self-actualization, job satisfaction, and creativity (Aamodt, 1991).

We next turn to the motivational states and traits that are the primary focus of psychological theory and research. We first consider one of our most basic biological needs, hunger. Then we examine needs for stimulation and sexual motivation. Finally, social motives for achievement and power are considered. The chapter ends with a discussion of motivational conflict and its resolution.

Hunger

Your body consists of complex and interrelated biological systems. A delicate balance is required within these systems to ensure survival. **Homeostasis** is the regulatory process that maintains this balance.

Homeostasis requires a sensory mechanism for detecting changes in the internal environment, a response system that can maintain equilibrium, and a

control center that receives information from the sensors and activates the response systems (see Figure 12.5). The control center functions like the thermostat in a furnace or air-conditioning unit. If the thermostat is set at a fixed temperature, or *set point*, significant temperature changes in either direction are detected by the sensor. The control unit then turns on the furnace or air conditioner until the sensor indicates that the set point temperature has been restored and then turns it off.

The maintenance of a stable internal state can involve learned behavioral adjustments as well as innate physiological adjustments. When your body temperature becomes too high, for example, the innate physiological adjustment of perspiration helps to cool you. Behavioral adjustments may include looking for a shady place to sit, turning on the air conditioner, or getting something cold to drink.

One of our basic homeostatic motives is the need for food intake. Although the motivational state we call hunger is rooted in basic tissue needs, psychological factors can strongly influence eating behavior.

The Regulation of Eating

How does your body signal that it needs food? Perhaps the most common and noticeable signals are those familiar "hunger pangs" that come from muscular contractions of your stomach wall. Is this the body's signal to eat? In an early experiment that showed an uncommon devotion to the cause of knowledge, the physiologist A. L. Washburn swallowed a balloon. When it reached his stomach, the balloon was inflated and hooked to an amplifying device to record his stomach contractions. With the balloon in his stomach, he pressed a key every time he felt hungry (see Figure 12.6). Washburn found that his stomach contractions did indeed correspond with subjective feelings of hunger (Cannon & Washburn, 1912).

Early physiological theories of hunger proposed that stomach contractions are triggered when receptors in the stomach signal that it is empty and that eating stops when these receptors report that the stomach is full. However, it was later found that feelings of hunger as well as the normal regulation of eating continue even if all nerves leading from the stomach to the brain are cut (Brown & Wallace, 1980). Thus, stomach contractions undoubtedly play a role in the complex processes that regulate food intake, but they cannot be the whole story. We now know that there are additional environmental, cognitive, and internal feedback systems, all of which help to regulate food intake by signaling control centers in the central nervous system.

Neural Control

The brain seems an obvious place to look for these control centers. But where in the brain? One possible lead was provided by medical case histories of people who experienced difficulties in weight regulation after injuries to the hypothalamus (Gazzaniga & others, 1979). Two specific regions of the hypothalamus seemed particularly important. The *lateral* area, located near the sides of the hypothalamus, appeared to stimulate eating behavior, whereas the *ventromedial* area, located near the center of the hypothalamus, seemed to inhibit eating behavior (see Figure 12.7).

Animals whose lateral hypothalamic areas are damaged or surgically destroyed often refuse to eat. In fact, they will actually starve if not forced to take food. They gradually recover from this condition, but they never completely return to normal. Their weight remains lower than it was before the lateral area was damaged.

Quite the opposite effect occurs when the ventromedial hypothalamus is destroyed. Now, instead of animals who undereat, we have animal gluttons who begin to eat huge quantities of food. In a short time they double or triple their body weight and then level off at a very high weight (see Figure 12.8).

As a result of findings like these, researchers at first thought that the lateral and ventromedial hypothalamic areas were the "on-off," or "eating" and "satiation," control centers they had been seeking. However, the true story is more complicated than that. It now appears that fibers from many widely separated areas of the brain funnel through the hypothalamus

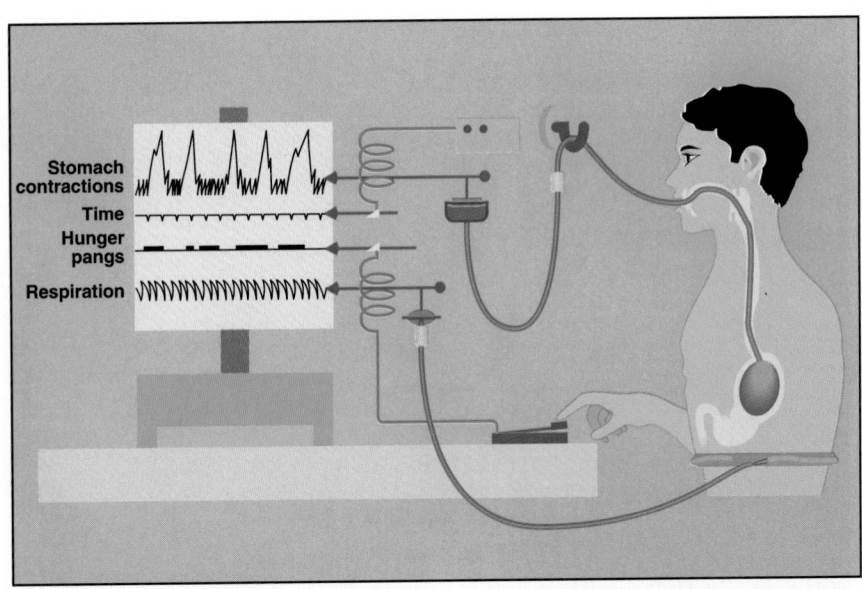

Figure 12.6 *To study the relation of stomach contractions to hunger pangs, A. L. Washburn swallowed a balloon and inflated it in his stomach. A machine recorded stomach contractions by amplifying changes in the pressure on the balloon, and Washburn pressed a telegraph key every time he felt a hunger pang.*

and then spread out again when they leave the hypothalamus. Researchers began to discover that the effects of lesions in the hypothalamic regions could be duplicated with lesions in other locations extending all the way from the brain stem to the frontal lobes (Schwartz, 1984). The dramatic results that occur in the hypothalamic regions appear to stem from the cutting of these tracts rather than from damage to any particular "centers" in the hypothalamus; the same results occur wherever you cut the tracts. Thus, many

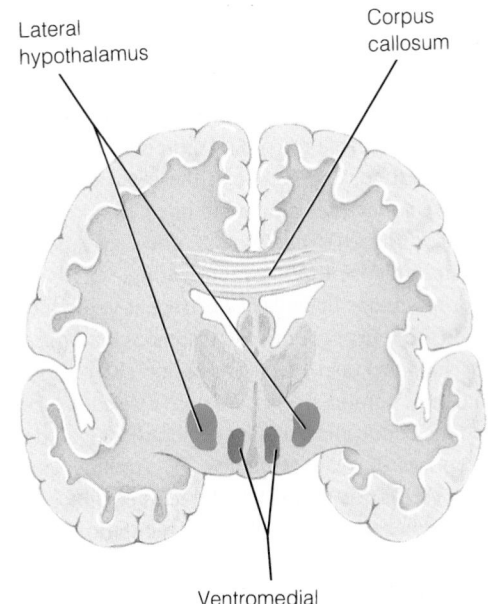

Figure 12.7 *The lateral and ventromedial hypothalamus, shown in this cross section of the brain, have been studied extensively and were at one time thought to be the "start" and "stop" centers for eating. That has proven to be an oversimplification, but the hypothalamus nonetheless is thought to play a role in the regulation of food intake.*

Figure 12.8 *Damage to the ventromedial hypothalamus affects regulation of eating behavior. This rat more than tripled its body weight by overeating after its ventromedial area was destroyed.*

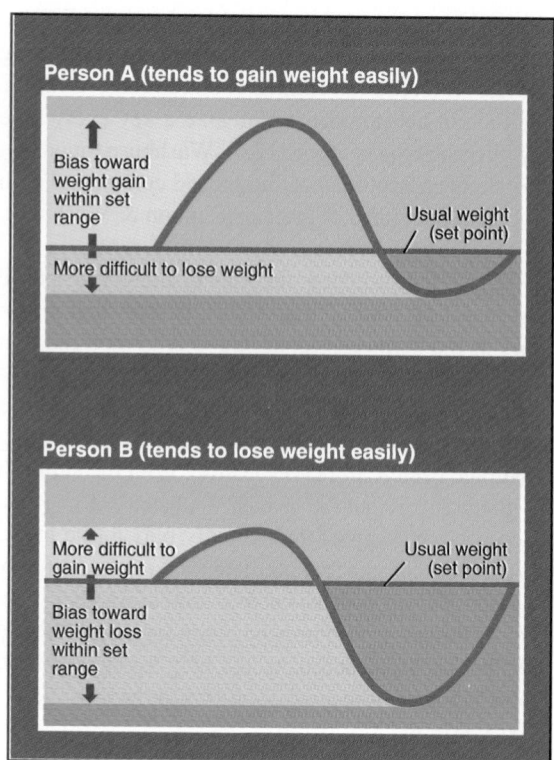

Figure 12.9 *Body weight is regulated within a range around one's usual weight. Individuals differ, however, in the location of the set point within the set range. Person A thus finds it easy to gain weight but difficult to lose it. Person B finds it hard to gain weight but easy to lose weight.*

widely separated parts of the brain seem to be involved in the regulation of eating (Logue, 1991).

Chemical Control

Chemical factors are now known to play a central role in the regulation of food intake. When we eat, enzymes in the saliva, stomach, and small intestine break the food down into sugars, amino acids, and fats. Sugar and amino acids are carried by the bloodstream to the liver and brain (Sherwood, 1992). There, sensors provide feedback to the nervous system about the amount of glucose and other nutrients in the blood. The important role played by **glucoreceptors** in the small intestine, the liver, and the brain is suggested by the fact that after glucose is injected into a hungry animal, it refuses to eat. On the other hand, decreases in blood glucose levels trigger eating.

Some major discoveries of recent years have involved the role of chemical substances known as *peptides* in many aspects of behavior (Kimble, 1992; Whalen & Simon, 1984). We have already encountered the endorphins, a class of peptides related to the perception of pain (Chapter 7). Another peptide, **cholecystokinin (CCK),** has received much recent attention because of its role in the regulation of eating. Released by the intestine, the pancreas, and neurons in the brain, CCK stimulates receptors in several brain regions and decreases eating. It is a leading candidate for the "stop" mechanism formerly thought to reside in the ventromedial hypothalamus (Logue, 1991).

Set Point Theory

Returning to the thermostat analogy, one popular way of viewing the regulation of eating is in terms of an internal standard, or **set point,** around which body weight is regulated. According to one theory, the major cause of obesity is an abnormally high set point (Stunkard, 1982). Wide individual differences exist among individuals' normal set points. Indeed, it may be more useful to think of body weight as being regulated within a "set range" rather than around a single set point (see Figure 12.9). Our weight normally varies with such conditions as diet and sleep changes, exercise or weight training, and processes like menstruation, pregnancy, and aging.

Different regulatory systems may be involved in correcting deviations above and below the usual weight range (Schwartz, 1984). Hence, some people may easily gain a great deal of weight before regulatory mechanisms swing into action, yet tolerate only a relatively small loss before their control systems are activated (Figure 12.9a). Conversely, others might find it easy to lose a lot of weight but hard to gain much (Figure 12.9*b*). The reasons for these differences are not clear, but they add another layer of complexity to the puzzle of weight regulation.

Obesity

In humans, obesity is usually defined as a body weight more than 20 percent over the average for a given height and body build. Figure 12.10 provides a body mass index, derived by dividing body weight (in kilograms) by the square of one's height (in meters). (The chart in Figure 12.10 has been converted to pounds and inches to make it easier to use.) The body mass index is highly correlated with body fat, and obesity is defined as having a body mass index exceeding 30 kg/m (Bray, 1978). By this definition, more than 30 percent of all Americans are obese. Obesity is not only stigmatized in the ''thin is in'' culture of the 1990s, but it also contributes to diabetes, high blood pressure, and heart problems. Therefore, many overweight people are highly motivated to lose weight.

Evaluation of many weight loss methods indicates that almost any overweight person can lose weight. But losing weight is far easier than keeping it off. Few people can maintain a significant weight loss for as long as one year (Grinker, 1982). An unfortunate fact about obesity is that being fat primes people to stay fat or to become fatter, in part by altering body metabolism, body chemistry, and energy expenditure (Logue, 1991). Because of these alterations, it often takes fewer calories to keep people overweight than it did to get them fat in the first place. An overweight person who complains, ''But I hardly eat a thing'' may well be telling the truth.

When people gain weight, the fat cells in their bodies become larger. The larger a fat cell becomes, the greater is its ability to store fat and become still larger (Salans & others, 1968). Moreover, overweight people tend to have higher basal levels of insulin in their bodies than people of normal weight. A higher insulin level increases fat storage because it speeds the entry of sugar into fat cells and the conversion of sugar into fat. Insulin also causes people to feel hungry. Thus, fat people not only are more likely to experience hunger but also are primed to make and store more fat.

Metabolism is the body's rate of energy (or caloric) utilization. About two-thirds of the energy we normally use goes to support the resting, or *basal* metabolism—the metabolic work of the body cells, which goes on continuously. Fat tissue is less active metabolically—it uses less energy—than lean tissue. Therefore, metabolism can be directly lowered as lean tissue is replaced by fatty tissue during weight gain. This may be one reason why some overweight people require fewer calories to maintain a high level of body

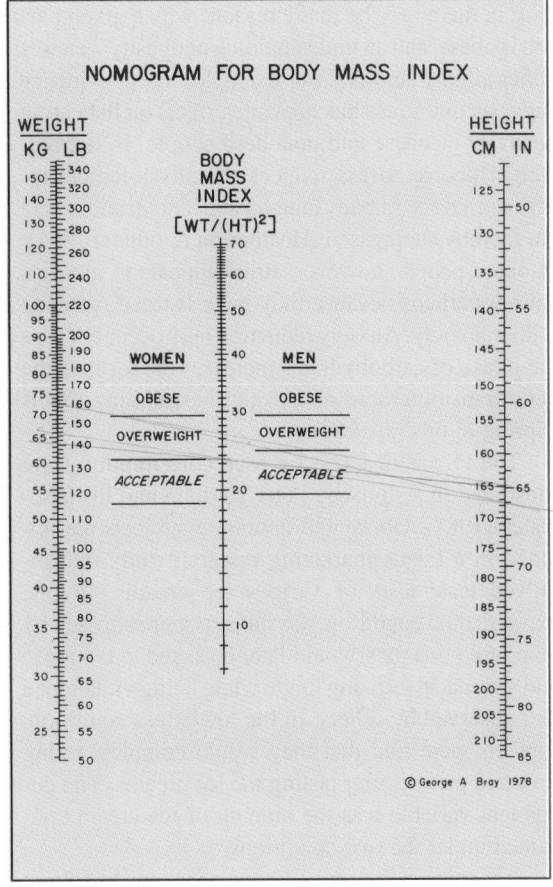

Figure 12.10 *This chart provides a measure of body mass, which correlates about +.75 with body fat measures. To determine your body mass index, place a ruler between your body weight on the left and your height on the right. The point where the ruler crosses the body mass index column provides a rough measure of your body mass. (Bray, 1978).*

weight than people who are gaining the same weight for the first time.

Many people respond to unwanted weight gain by going on diets. Ironically, the practice of dieting also slows down the basal metabolism, because the body responds to food deprivation with decreased energy expenditure. Moreover, this energy-saving metabolic slowdown becomes more pronounced with each weight loss attempt, as if the body has learned to respond more efficiently to new periods of food deprivation (Wooley & others, 1979). Thus, the repeated dieting that many overweight people engage in may actually contribute to their obesity by slowing down their metabolic processes, and new programs designed to help people stop dieting are now being tested (Polivy & Herman, 1992). Finally, obesity tends to reduce physical activity and exercise (which *can* help keep one's weight down), so that overweight people burn fewer calories and thus retain more fat. All in all, it appears that once obesity has developed, a variety of physical and metabolic factors serve to maintain or enhance weight gain and to make permanent weight loss difficult.

But obesity is more than simply a physical problem. Eating behavior is regulated by complex interactions between genetic, physiological, cognitive, social, learning, and psychodynamic factors. For this reason, there may be many reasons why a given person is obese, and an understanding of obesity's causes defies simple answers. For example, recent evidence suggests that stress has opposite effects on the eating behavior of obese and nonobese people. In normal-weight people, stress reduces the physiological reactions that accompany hunger, and hunger and eating are thereby suppressed (Heatherton & others, 1991). In obese people, however, stress appears to increase eating, perhaps because they have learned to eat to reduce anxiety. Anxiety reduction may occur because the intake of carbohydrates increases the level of the neurotransmitter serotonin, which has calming effects (Spring & others, 1987).

The effects of stress on food consumption were illustrated in a study by Peter Herman and his associates (1987). Obese and nonobese subjects participated in a bogus marketing research study that involved taste tests of various ice creams. In one experimental condition, the subjects were stressed by being told that they would later be asked to compose and sing an advertising jingle while being videotaped and observed by others. In the low-stress condition, subjects were told that they would complete rating forms in private after tasting the ice creams. The dependent variable was the amount of ice cream consumed under the two conditions.

As shown in Figure 12.11, the obese and nonobese subjects reacted differently to the two stress conditions. The nonobese subjects ate significantly less ice cream under the high-stress condition. In contrast, the obese subjects greatly increased their consumption of ice cream under high stress.

Another environmental factor that affects eating in some obese individuals is the presence of food-related external cues. Every weight category includes **cue-responsive** people who are highly responsive to the sights and sounds of food and who react to these cues with a rise in insulin level that increases sensations of hunger (Rodin, 1985). Obese individuals who are cue responsive face an additional burden in their attempt to control their food intake.

Eating Disorders: Anorexia and Bulimia

Obesity can have negative physical, social, and psychological consequences; however, there are two other eating disorders whose symptoms are so severe that they are regarded as clinical disorders. Anorexia nervosa and bulimia occur primarily among young women, and both involve abnormal concerns with body size, a morbid fear of becoming fat, and a distorted image of what constitutes normal body size (Garfinkel, 1992; Wilson & Walsh, 1991). Anorexics and bulimics frequently view themselves as fat, even though they may be severely underweight (Altabe & Thompson, 1992; Hadigan & Walsh, 1991).

Victims of **anorexia nervosa** have an intense fear of losing control over their eating, and they severely restrict food intake to the point of self-starvation. Many anorexics lose more than 25 percent of their body weight. Although they are preoccupied with food, they develop what amounts to an eating phobia, which can become a life-threatening condition (see Figure 12.12). The death in 1982 of the singer Karen Carpenter was attributed to the fatal strain that anorexia nervosa placed on her heart.

Anorexia frequently has its onset during adolescence, shortly after the start of menstruation. Personality studies indicate that anorexics are often perfectionists who become easily depressed when they do not live up to lofty self-standards, including distorted standards concerning an acceptably thin body (Garfinkel & Garner, 1982).

Bulimia is sometimes called the "binge–purge syndrome." In contrast to anorexics, who successfully restrict food intake, bulimics indulge in uncontrolled overeating, which is often followed by self-induced vomiting or overdoses of laxatives to eliminate the food they have consumed (Mitchell, 1987). Some bulimics have reportedly consumed up to 55,000 calories at a single sitting—roughly equivalent to 16 pounds of food. More commonly, they consume 2,000 to 3,000 calories of high-calorie food. The vast majority of bulimics (90–95 percent) are females (Carlat & Camargo, 1991).

Unlike anorexics, bulimics are not necessarily underweight; many are of normal weight and some are

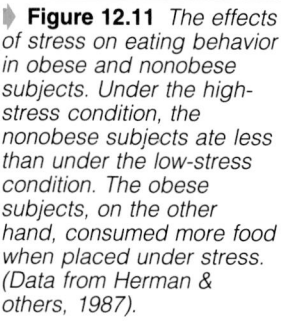

Figure 12.11 *The effects of stress on eating behavior in obese and nonobese subjects. Under the high-stress condition, the nonobese subjects ate less than under the low-stress condition. The obese subjects, on the other hand, consumed more food when placed under stress. (Data from Herman & others, 1987).*

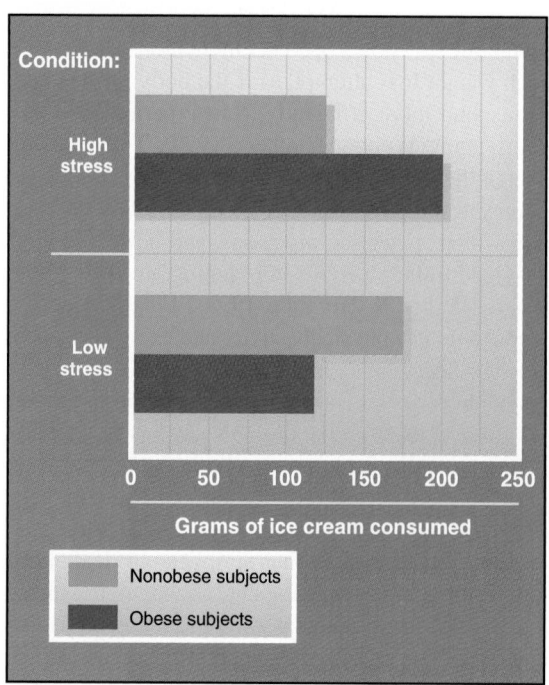

Condition:

High stress

Low stress

0   50   100   150   200   250

Grams of ice cream consumed

Nonobese subjects
Obese subjects

even obese. Nonetheless, the drastic measures they take to expel food from their bodies following binging can produce severe physical consequences, including gastric problems, ulcers, and acute chemical imbalances that can be life-threatening. Surveys have indicated that 10 to 15 percent of college females may exhibit the symptoms of bulimia, and the incidence among all American women is estimated to be 1 to 5 percent (Mitchell, 1987; Schlesier-Stropp, 1984).

High levels of depression and anxiety characterize bulimics, as do obsessive preoccupations with food and a distorted body image that causes them to see themselves as overweight even when they are not. Many bulimics seem to lack a stable sense of personal identity and feelings of self-sufficiency (Strober & Humphrey, 1987). Binging is often triggered by life stress, and it is followed by guilt and self-contempt. The purging may be a means of reducing depression and anxiety triggered by the binging (Rosen & Leitenberg, 1982).

Theories about the causes of bulimia have spanned the physiological and sociocultural domains (Strober & Humphrey, 1987). On the sociocultural side, both bulimics and anorexics may be casualties of our society's emphasis on slimness as a requisite of feminine attractiveness (Brownell, 1991). Miss America contestants, the female models in advertisements, and women appearing in Playboy centerfolds are significantly thinner now than they were in the 1950s and 1960s, and they typically weigh at least 20 percent less than the average American woman (Garfinkel & Garner, 1982). This could influence women's conceptions about what constitutes an acceptable figure.

On the biological side, twin studies indicate a higher concordance rate for bulimia among identical twins (83 percent) than among fraternal twins (27 percent), suggesting a possible genetic predisposition (Fichter & Noegel, 1990). Another biological theory links bulimia with a deficit in the neurotransmitter serotonin. A shortage of serotonin would increase susceptibility to anxiety and depression and could produce a craving for carbohydrates, which, as we saw earlier, increase the level of serotonin in the brain (Bruch, 1973; Fava & others, 1989).

Two other factors may foster the purging side of the disorder. First, the consistent pairing of foods with vomiting may make the foods conditioned stimuli for nausea, thereby increasing the likelihood of vomiting. In one study, bulimics reported sudden feelings of nausea after eating sweet foods like those they tend to consume during binging (Broberg & others, 1990). A second factor that may increase purging is a loss of taste sensitivity caused by the stomach acids that are expelled into the mouth during vomiting. This loss of sensitivity may make the normally unpleasant taste of vomit more tolerable and increase willingness

Figure 12.12 *Victims of anorexia may literally starve themselves. Here, the singer Karen Carpenter is shown shortly before her death from anorexia-induced heart failure.*

to use this method of purging. Recent studies have shown that bulimics do indeed have poorer sensitivity for salty, bitter, sweet, and sour substances (Rodin & others, 1990).

Successful treatment of bulimia frequently requires that women resolve the unrealistic self-standards about body image and femininity that tyrannize its victims (Root & others, 1986). Another goal of psychological treatments is to teach clients coping skills that will help them deal more successfully with the anxiety surrounding eating and gaining weight (Leitenberg & others, 1984; Wolf & Crowther, 1992). However, treatment of bulimia may also need to take into account the conditioned nausea and reduced taste sensitivity that apparently develop as part of the disorder.

It is clear, then, that even so "biological" a motive as hunger is really a product of complex interactions among physiological, environmental, cognitive, and intrapsychic factors. Although it satisfies a basic biological survival need, eating behavior is strongly influenced by mental processes and by the environment as well. The determinants of what, how, and when we eat are far from being totally understood.

■ ■

Sensory Needs

There is a good deal of evidence that animals seek out stimulation and prefer stimulus novelty, change,

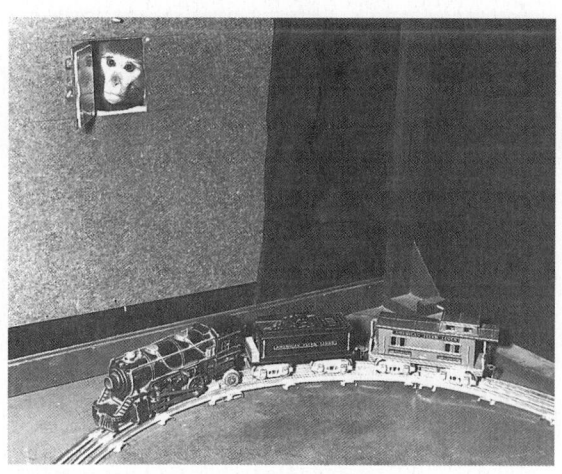
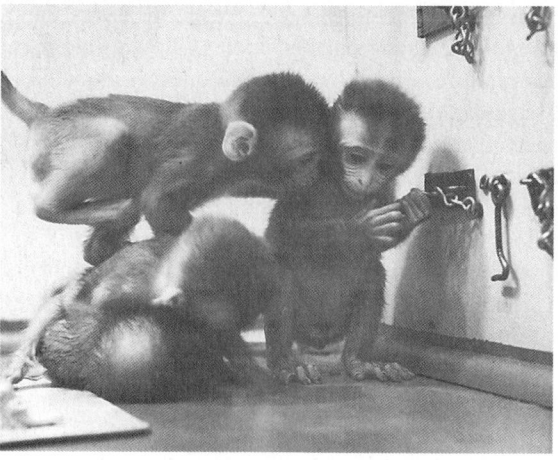

and complexity (Berlyne, 1978). Why else would rats who are thoroughly familiar with a maze quickly explore new sections that are added to the maze network, even if they have been consistently fed somewhere else? How else can we explain why rats and other mammals will learn to press a lever when the only consequence is a brief increase in illumination and why monkeys confined in a box will repeatedly push open a heavy spring door just to see what is happening on the other side (Butler, 1954)? In a classic series of experiments performed at the University of Wisconsin, Harry Harlow (1950) showed that monkeys will spend hour after hour working on mechanical puzzles, even if they receive no tangible reward for doing so (see Figure 12.13).

Humans also seem to have innate needs for activity, exploration, and manipulation. Although these sensory needs have no direct bearing on the maintenance of biological homeostasis, as hunger and thirst do, they still seem to be an important part of human nature. Anyone who has taken small children to an expensive gift store and seen a sign that says, "If they break it, you've bought it" knows how common these exploratory needs are in humans from infancy on.

People differ in their inclinations to seek out stimulation and novelty. Some people prefer a relatively nonstimulating and calm environment, while others seek out adventure, danger, and excitement (see Figure 12.14). Observation of these individual differences prompted Marvin Zuckerman (1979, 1991) to develop a psychological test to measure the **sensation-seeking motive** and to study its effects on behavior. Here are some items from Zuckerman's 22-item Sensation-Seeking Scale. For each of the following sets of statements, choose the alternative that is more characteristic of you.

1. A. I prefer people who are calm and even tempered.
   B. I prefer people who are emotionally expressive, even if they are a bit unstable.
2. A. The most important goal of life is to live it to the fullest and experience as much of it as you can.
   B. The most important goal of life is to find peace and happiness.
3. A. I would like a job which would require a lot of traveling.
   B. I would prefer a job in one location.
4. A. A good painting should shock or jolt the senses.
   B. A good painting should give one the feeling of peace and security.
5. A. I enter cold water gradually, giving myself time to get used to it.
   B. I like to dive or jump right into the ocean or a cold pool.

Note that each item forced you to choose between one alternative that implied novelty, change, or excitement and another that implied the opposite. The test is scored for the number of sensation-seeking alternatives that are endorsed. Research over nearly two decades has shown that scores on this measure are related to numerous behaviors (Zuckerman, 1991; Zuckerman & others, 1980).

People who score high on the Sensation-Seeking Scale tend to enjoy engaging in physically risky activities such as skydiving, motorcycle riding, fire fighting, and scuba diving. Such activities seem less risky to high sensation seekers than to low sensation seekers. High sensation seekers also tend to be interested in gambling, to bet more, and to prefer higher odds against them. The tendency to experiment with drugs is also related to sensation seeking, and there is some evidence that high sensation seekers prefer the more stimulating drugs like amphetamines and LSD. Low sensation seekers are more likely to prefer "downers," such as sedatives and marijuana.

▲ **Figure 12.14** *People differ widely in their sensation-seeking motivation. Some prefer the sedate life, while others seek thrills and excitement.*

Among adolescents, high sensation seekers of both genders are more likely to use illicit drugs, engage in sexual activity, and perform illegal actions such as stealing and destroying property (Newcomb & McGee, 1991). Zuckerman has suggested that it is important to steer high sensation seekers into socially acceptable activities such as sports, where their needs for excitement and stimulation can be satisfied in a more desirable manner.

Among college students, high sensation seekers of both genders report engaging in a wider range of heterosexual activities with more partners. Sensation seeking in married women correlates positively with self-ratings of sexual responsiveness, frequency of masturbation, preferred frequency of intercourse, reports of multiple orgasms, and a preference for sleeping in the nude.

High sensation seeking seems to offer some protection against life stress. Perhaps because of their preference for a calm and predictable environment, low sensation seekers are more likely to experience psychological distress in the face of negative life changes (Smith & others, 1978). Similarly, a positive relation was found between life stress and subsequent injuries among male and female high-school athletes, but only for those who were low in sensation seeking (Smith & others, 1992). For high sensation seekers, life stress was unrelated to injury, suggesting that they are more capable of tolerating negative life changes.

Zuckerman believes that sensation seeking has a biological basis. In support of this hypothesis, EEG recordings of cortical responses have indicated that the cortical evoked responses of high sensation seekers adapt more quickly to a constant stimulus. In other words, the stimulation loses its effect quickly. High sensation seekers also need higher levels of stimu-

lation to maintain evoked cortical responses. Low sensation seekers have stronger cortical responses to weak stimuli, indicating their greater sensitivity to stimulation (Zuckerman, 1991). These differences may reflect different optimal or desired levels of stimulation, and they may mirror the ease with which high sensation-seekers experience boredom and low sensation seekers experience overstimulation.

Sensory needs have important effects on how individuals adapt to the environment. It seems likely that they can also find expression in sexual and social motives, to which we now turn.

Sexual Motivation

Unlike food and drink, sex does not represent a survival need for individuals. One can easily die from hunger or thirst, but no one is known to have died from celibacy. On the other hand, if satisfying the hunger drive were as complicated as satisfying sexual needs, many people would be much thinner. Perhaps no aspect of human behavior provokes as much moral and legal controversy, as many conflicting beliefs, and as much personal conflict as sexuality does. As a powerful motivator that satisfies both biological and psychological needs, sexuality is a topic of central importance in the psychology of motivation.

Sexual Behavior: Patterns and Changes

Because sexual expression has always been laced with moral and legal issues, the scientific study of sexuality was slow to evolve. The first large-scale attempts to

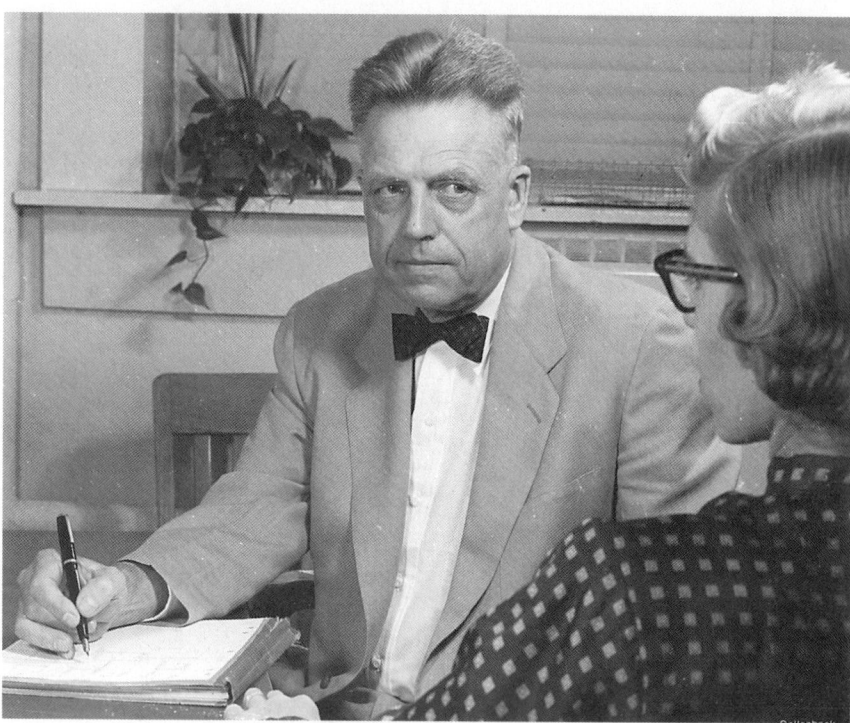

Figure 12.15 *Alfred Kinsey conducts one of the more than 11,000 intensive interviews carried out during his survey of human sexual behavior.*

study and describe human sexual behavior were begun in the late 1930s by Alfred Kinsey and his colleagues at Indiana University. The first Kinsey report, *Sexual Behavior in the Human Male* (Kinsey & others, 1948), presented a highly detailed statistical analysis of the sexual activities of 5,300 American males ranging in age from 10 to 90. In personal interviews that lasted about 2 hours, the men were asked nearly 300 questions about their sex lives. A companion volume, *Sexual Behavior in the Human Female* (Kinsey & others, 1953), was the result of similar interviews with 5,940 American women (see Figure 12.15).

Although they appeared more than a generation ago, the Kinsey reports are still considered the most comprehensive scientific surveys of sexual behavior ever undertaken. More recently, several other large-scale survey studies have appeared (Hite, 1976, 1981, 1988; Hunt, 1974; Sarrel & Sarrel, 1980; Wolfe, 1980). In combination with numerous smaller surveys, these studies provide a broad overview of sexual behaviors, attitudes, and experiences and allow us to see how sexual practices and attitudes have changed over the years.

Kinsey and his coworkers generated a tremendous amount of data. Table 12.2 highlights a number of these results, which attracted much attention in a society that until then had virtually no scientific information about sexual behavior.

Although differences in sample characteristics and data collection methods must be kept in mind, a comparison of the Kinsey figures in Table 12.2 with the results of more recent surveys suggests several notable changes in sexual behavior. For example, it appears that the percentage of people who engage in masturbation has not changed much but that those who masturbate begin doing so at a younger age and do so more frequently.

More profound changes in sexual behavior seem to have occurred in the areas of premarital sex and the practice of oral–genital stimulation (Wade & Cirese, 1992). The practice of oral–genital stimulation has increased rather dramatically at every level of education since the days of Kinsey. One large survey study found that about 80 percent of single males and females between the ages of 25 and 34 and about 90 percent of married persons under 25 engaged in oral–genital stimulation (Hunt, 1974). By the time they are 19, about 60 percent of all females in the United States have had intercourse (Zelnick & others, 1981). Among married persons between the ages of 18 and 24, the percentage who had had premarital intercourse was reported in the 1970s to be as high as 95 percent for males and 81 percent for females (Hunt, 1974). However, there is evidence that the sexual revolution of the 1960s and 1970s may be

Table 12.2 Some Notable Findings From the Kinsey Surveys

1. Masturbation. Over all age groups, 92 percent of the males and 58 percent of the females had masturbated to orgasm at least once in their lives. By age 20, 82 percent of the males and 33 percent of the females had done so. There was wide variaton in the frequency with which both males and females masturbated.

2. Premarital intercourse. Forty-eight percent of all the married women in the sample had had sexual intercourse before marriage. About 25 percent of the 20- and 21-year-old unmarried women reported that they were not virgins. Among men, 85 percent reported premarital sex experiences. The figures ranged from 98 percent among males with no high school education to 68 percent among college graduates.

3. Extramarital sex. Twenty-six percent of the married women and about 50 percent of the married men reported having had extramarital sexual affairs.

4. Oral–genital stimulation. Fifty percent of the college-educated men, but fewer than 5 percent of those with grade school educations engaged in cunnilingus (oral stimulation of the female genitals). Fellatio (oral stimulation of the male's genitals) was reported by slightly over 40 percent of the women, but most had done so infrequently.

5. Female orgasm. Among married women, slightly fewer than half reported experiencing orgasm always or almost always during intercourse; 28 percent said they never experienced orgasm.

6. Homosexual relationships. Of the males interviewed, 37 percent had engaged in at least one homosexual relationship to the extent of having orgasm. Thirteen percent of the females reported similar experiences.

Source: From Kinsey & others, 1948; Kinsey & others, 1953.

cooling a bit. A recent comparative study of college women indicated that the percentage of women who reported having sexual intercourse at least once a month had dropped from 51 percent in the late 1970s to 37 percent in the mid-1980s (Gerrard, 1987). This may herald a return to more conservative sexual attitudes and practices, inspired in part by fear of AIDS and other sexually transmitted diseases, and in part by an increased cultural emphasis on depth of relationships (Wade & Cirese, 1992). ▼

Organizational and Activational Effects of Sex Hormones

Interactions between the endocrine and nervous systems play an important role in sexual development, motivation, and behavior. As in the case of hunger, the hypothalamus is a key actor in sexual motivation and behavior, and its crucial role in regulating and responding to hormonal secretions has become increasingly apparent.

The hypothalamus controls the activity of the pituitary gland, which in turn influences the secretion of *leuteinizing hormone (LH)* into the bloodstream.

LH is important because it controls the rate at which the masculine sex hormones (**androgens**) and the female sex hormones (**estrogens**) are secreted. Actually, androgens and estrogens circulate in the bloodstreams of both males and females, but their relative concentrations differ in the two genders.

The sex hormones have two sets of effects: organizational and activational. The *organizational effects* direct the development of male and female sex characteristics and behaviors (Breedlove, 1992). These effects, which begin to occur in the womb 6 to 8 weeks after conception and are virtually permanent, center around the genetically programmed presence or absence of testosterone, the most important of the androgens. If testosterone is present in sufficient quantities, the brain is programmed to develop a male pattern of neural activation. As part of this pattern, the hypothalamus begins to stimulate the continuous release of testosterone from the testes when the male reaches puberty. If testosterone is not present in sufficient quantities in *utero*, the hypothalamus begins at puberty to stimulate the release of estrogens from the ovaries on the cyclic basis that represents the female menstrual cycle (see Figure 12.16).

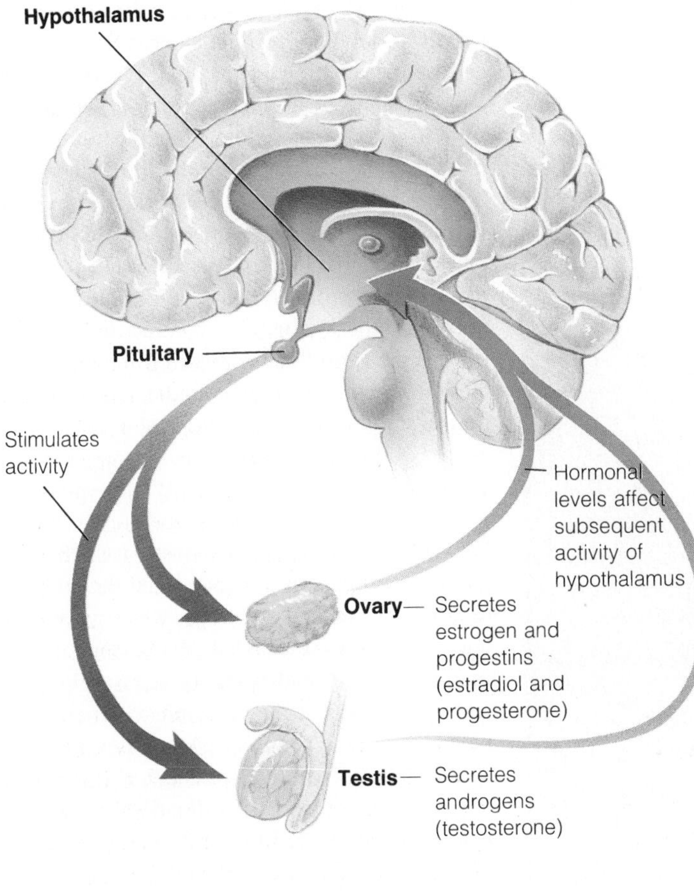

◀ **Figure 12.16** *The hypothalamus and the pituitary gland regulate sex hormones. The hypothalamus stimulates the pituitary gland, which controls the secretion of estrogens by the ovaries and testosterone by the testes. Levels of these hormones in the blood provide feedback to the hypothalamus.*

Hypothalamus

Pituitary

Stimulates activity

Hormonal levels affect subsequent activity of hypothalamus

Ovary — Secretes estrogen and progestins (estradiol and progesterone)

Testis — Secretes androgens (testosterone)

▼
Thinking Critically About the Validity of Sex Surveys

The great strength of the survey approach to sexual behavior can be quickly stated: Although people don't usually let scientists into their bedrooms, they are often willing to fill out a questionnaire or submit to an interview. However, if survey results are to be applied to the general population, the survey should be based on a representative sample in which important characteristics such as age, sex, educational level, and ethnicity exist in the same proportions as in the larger population. This factor should enter into our critical evaluation of a sex survey's results. Unfortunately, no sex survey has come close to obtaining a truly representative sample. In Kinsey's surveys, rural groups and lower educational levels were underrepresented, as were children and people over 50 years of age. Most respondents were white volunteers. In later surveys, a major problem has been the refusal of a great many people to participate. In even the largest surveys, which presented data obtained from as many as 106,000 people, refusal rates have ranged from 80 to 99 percent. All of these studies, then, have the problem of self-selection. It is possible that the people who agreed to provide information may be different in their attitudes and behavior from those who declined to participate. This does not mean that the data are not useful or important, but it does mean that there are limitations to the conclusions that we can draw about other segments of the population.

The *activational effects* of hormones involve the stimulation of sexual desire and behavior. Such effects are more evident in nonhuman animals than in humans. In the animal kingdom, mature males have a relatively constant secretion of sex hormones, and their readiness for sexual behavior is largely governed by the presence of activating stimuli in the environment. In contrast, hormone secretions in female animals follow a cyclic schedule, and female animals are sexually receptive only during periods of high estrogen secretion (that is, when they are "in heat"). Removal of the ovaries eliminates sexual behavior in such animals. Human females may also experience stronger sexual urges during the periods of peak estrogen secretion that occur during ovulation, but their sexual motivation depends far less on hormonal control than that of animals (Harvey, 1987). Women may experience high sexual desires at any time, and sexual desire can continue and sometimes even increase after menopause, when estrogen levels greatly decrease.

Although normal short-term hormonal changes have relatively little effect on human sexual behavior, the surge of sex hormones that occurs at puberty results in increased sexual motivation for most people. If the hormonal increase is prevented, as in the case of men (*castrati*) who were castrated as prepubertal boys to preserve their soprano voices for Italian opera during the 18th and 19th centuries, normal development of mature sex characteristics and sexual desire does not occur (Peschel & Peschel, 1987). To a lesser extent, the decreased secretion of sex hormones that accompanies aging also results in decreased sexual activity, but there is also considerable variability in sexual desire and behavior among older people because of the important role of learning and psychological factors in mature sexuality.

The Human Sexual Response

In 1953, a gynecologist, William Masters, and his research associate Virginia Johnson began a landmark study that greatly increased scientific knowledge about the body's complex responses during sexual activity (see Figure 12.17). For more than 10 years, Masters and Johnson studied the sexual responses of 694 men and women under controlled laboratory conditions. In all, about 10,000 sexual episodes were monitored. While the volunteer subjects engaged in masturbation, intercourse, and other sexual activities, many of their physiological responses were measured. By putting a camera into a transparent penis-shaped case, Masters and Johnson were even able to film vaginal and uterine reactions during simulated intercourse. Their findings were published in a book entitled *Human Sexual Response* (Masters & Johnson, 1966).

Masters and Johnson found that most people go through a basic four-stage physiological response pattern of excitement, plateau, orgasm, and resolution (see Figure 12.18). The initial *excitement* response to sexual stimulation is vaginal lubrication in the female and penile erection in the male. In the second, or *plateau,* stage, heart rate, respiration, and muscle tension all increase as sexual excitement builds toward its climax, which occurs in the third stage, *orgasm.* As orgasm begins, the penis begins to throb in rhythmic contractions. Semen collects in the urethral bulb and contractions of the bulb and penis project the semen out of the penis. In females, orgasm involves rhythmic muscular contractions of the outer third of the vagina and the uterus. In both sexes, muscles throughout the body contract, and there is a temporary state of high physiological arousal.

It is important to note that the *experience* of orgasm involves more than simply these physiological responses. Relatively little association has been found between physiological responses (which are quite similar from person to person) and the intensity and duration of orgasmic feelings, which vary considerably (Bohlen, 1986; Kaplan, 1986). Genital responses may be the physical basis for orgasm, but the subjective elements of the orgasmic experience seem to be governed by people's perceptions and attitudes toward themselves, their partners, and the activity.

In males, orgasm is ordinarily followed by the *resolution* phase, during which physiological arousal decreases rapidly and the genital organs and tissues return to their normal condition. During the resolution phase, males enter a **refractory period** during which

◆ **Figure 12.17** *William Masters and Virginia Johnson carried out pioneering research on the physiology of the human sexual response.*

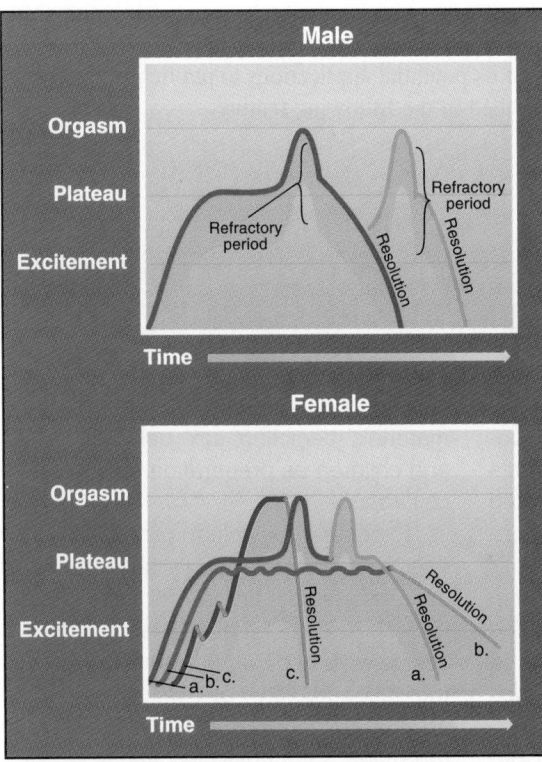

Figure 12.18 *Masters and Johnson discovered a four-phase pattern of sexual response: excitement, plateau, orgasm, and resolution. These figures show male and female sexual response cycles. The darker lines indicate common patterns of response and the lighter colored lines indicate variations. In males, after one and sometimes two orgasms, there is a refractory period during which no further response is possible. Pattern b in females shows a plateau stage with no orgasm, and pattern c shows an orgasm with no preceding plateau stage. (Masters & Johnson, 1976).*

they are temporarily incapable of another orgasm. Females may have two or more successive orgasms before the onset of the resolution phase, but most women experience only one.

Some of Masters and Johnson's research findings contradicted popular beliefs. For example, despite Freud's assertion that female orgasms produced through direct stimulation of the clitoris were "immature," Masters and Johnson found no detectable physiological differences between these orgasms and orgasms brought about by vaginal penetration.

Cultural and Environmental Influences on Sexuality

The human expression of sexuality is heavily influenced by cultural, social, and relationship contexts. These contexts confer on sex much of its psychological meaning, and they also help to determine the forms that sexual expression takes. To understand sexuality from a psychological viewpoint, we must consider the social forces that shape sexual attitudes and behavior.

We do not need to look far to appreciate the role of social factors in human sexuality. Compare your attitudes toward sex with those of your parents and grandparents. As we saw in our look at survey studies, many current sexual practices differ greatly from those of only a generation or two ago.

The role of cultural learning comes into even sharper focus when we go beyond our own culture and examine others. For example, childhood sexuality is frowned upon and suppressed in our culture, but in some other cultures it is not only permitted but encouraged. In the Marquesas Islands in French Polynesia, for example, families sleep together in one room, and children have ample opportunity to observe sexual activity. When a baby boy is distressed, Marquesan parents may masturbate the child. Both boys and girls begin to masturbate at age 2 or 3, and most of them engage in casual homosexual contacts during their youth. When they reach adolescence, an adult of the opposite sex carefully instructs them in sexual techniques by having intercourse with them (Suggs, 1962).

While Americans are clearly not as sexually permissive as the Marquesans, we are not nearly as repressive as the inhabitants of an island off the coast of Ireland. Sex is a taboo topic among these people, and nudity is abhorred. Only infants are allowed to be completely naked, and adults feel embarrased if they are even seen barefoot. The genders are separated from early childhood until marriage, which typically occurs in the mid-thirties for males and in the mid-twenties for females. Sexual jokes are unknown in this society, and sexual anxiety and revulsion are so intense that dogs and other animals are customarily beaten if they are caught licking their genitals. Interviews with members of these very different cultures revealed that in contrast to Marquesan women, who customarily experience orgasm in sexual interactions, sexual climaxes among the women of the Irish island community are virtually unknown (Messenger, 1971).

Thus, what is considered proper, moral, desirable, and normal varies enormously from culture to culture. Moreover, while each society has standards of sexual conduct, which are often enforced by moral and legal sanctions, there can also be important differences within cultures. Our own culture includes enormously diverse viewpoints about sexuality. One important area of current controversy concerns the effects of exposure to erotic stimuli. Because sexuality in humans is affected so strongly by exposure to sexually arousing environmental stimuli, concerns have arisen that certain types of materials might stimulate deviant sexual and violent acts. Such concerns have been reinforced by news accounts of pornographic materials found in the homes of sexual offenders and by the claims of the mass murderer Theodore Bundy that violent pornography helped stimulate his murderous attacks on women. Psychologists have responded to the need for more scientific information concerning the effects of pornography by conducting numerous research studies. The current status of such research and its potential applications to public policy are described in the following feature.

ENHANCING HUMAN PERFORMANCE

PUBLIC POLICY DECISIONS ABOUT PORNOGRAPHY AND SEXUAL VIOLENCE

In 1961, the following resolution was entered into the *Congressional Record* by a subcommittee investigating sexually explicit materials:

There is a black plague sweeping the nation more devastating than the one that ravaged Europe in the Middle Ages. Its principal victims are children and adolescents, although like its ancient predecessor, it destroys adults as well. . . . Those concerned declare that no act of subversion planned by the Communist conspiracy could be more effective in shredding the Nation's moral fabric than the lethal effect of pornography. (August 29, 1961)

As we all know, there is still great concern and controversy about the effects of pornography on those who are exposed to it. Yet the findings of more than a dozen studies in the 1960s suggested that—although exposure to sexually explicit novels, magazines, and movies temporarily increases arousal and allows people to learn sexual responses through modeling—the effects on subsequent sexual activity are quite limited and temporary. Based on such evidence, the Presidential Commission on Obscenity and Pornography concluded in 1969 that no reliable connection had been demonstrated between pornography and criminal acts.

To many respected authorities, the issue of how pornography affects people seemed pretty much settled 20 years ago. But now an important new issue has arisen: While nonviolent pornography may have little effect on people, what about pornography that depicts rape, sexual exploitation, and episodes in which partners inflict pain on one another? What about kiddie porn, which features sex with children, and the so-called "snuff movies," in which the sex act ends with what

is claimed to be a real murder? One authority has suggested that violent pornography may create a climate in which "acts of sexual hostility directed against women are not only tolerated but ideologically encouraged" (Brownmiller, 1975, p. 444). Such concerns have stimulated research which may assist those who are called upon to make public policy decisions in an area where emotion often outstrips knowledge.

Several studies suggest that exposure to violent sexual stimuli may have at least temporary negative effects (Malamuth & Donnerstein, 1983). At the University of Manitoba, Neal Malamuth showed two groups of men a slide show of a rape based on photos taken from a pornography magazine. One group heard a sound track that described the woman as being terrified and forcibly raped. The other group heard a sound track in which the woman agreed to have sex.

Physiological measures revealed that both groups of men experienced high levels of arousal while they watched the episode. The subjects were then asked to create the most sexually arousing fantasies they could. Those who had been exposed to the violent rape version reported more sexual fantasies of a violent nature. Since deviant sexual fantasies have frequently been shown to be associated with sexually deviant behavior (MacCulloch & others, 1983), the fact that exposure to violent pornography can stimulate such fantasies merits concern and further study. Moreover, in a recent in-depth study of convicted rapists, 33 percent of the offenders stated that they purposely used films depicting rape and the fantasies they aroused as part of their preparation to rape women (Marshall, 1988). In the same study, 53 percent of a sample

of child molesters reported that they used materials depicting sex between adults and children as preparation for molesting children.

Exposure to violent rape films also seems to enhance men's acceptance of false beliefs about rape—for example, the view that many women have an unconscious wish to be raped—and to increase the acceptability of sexual violence against women (Linz, 1988). Even more unsettling is the possibility that such stimuli may arouse aggressive impulses. At the University of Wisconsin, Edward Donnerstein and Leonard Berkowitz (1981) studied the effects of erotic and sexually violent films on actual aggression against a woman. Male subjects were randomly divided into four groups. One group saw a nonsexual film of a talk show. The second group was shown an erotic film in which a young couple made love. The films seen by the other two groups were violently erotic depictions of a woman being physically and sexually assaulted by two men. In one of these films, the woman resisted at first but then became a willing sexual participant; in the other, the victim was shown suffering during the entire experience.

In a supposedly unrelated second experiment, all of the male subjects then interacted with a female accomplice of the experimenter. Half of these interactions were designed to make the men angry. After interacting with the woman, the subjects were given the opportunity to aggress against her by giving her electric shocks as punishment for errors made on a learning task she was performing.

As shown in Figure 12.19, exposure to the nonviolent erotic film did not increase aggression above the level in the neutral film condition, but the violent

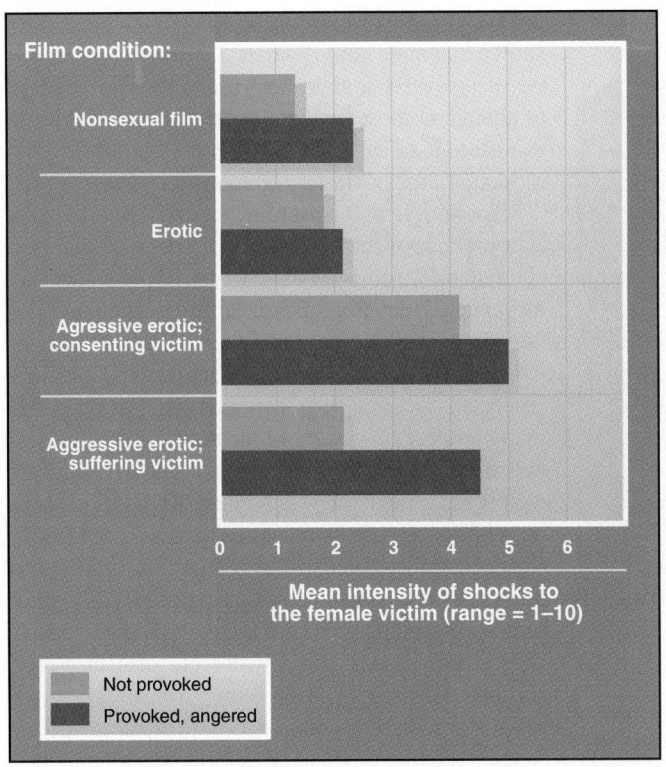

Film condition:

Nonsexual film

Erotic

Agressive erotic;
consenting victim

Aggressive erotic;
suffering victim

0 1 2 3 4 5 6

Mean intensity of shocks to
the female victim (range = 1–10)

Not provoked
Provoked, angered

Figure 12.19 *After seeing an aggressive erotic film in which the female victim did not appear to suffer, both angered and nonangered male subjects showed greater aggression against a female. After seeing an aggressive erotic film in which the female victim did appear to suffer, angered subjects showed almost equally high levels of aggression, although nonangered subjects did not. An erotic film without violent content did not increase later aggression. (Data from Donnerstein & Berkowitz, 1981).*

erotic films did. Among the subjects who had seen the suffering rape victim, only those who were later angered by the female accomplice gave her higher levels of shock. But subjects who had seen a rape victim who ultimately "enjoyed" the experience gave high levels of shock whether or not they had been angered.

Overall, experimental studies indicate that exposure to violent pornography at least temporarily weakens men's restraints against violence toward women, encourages sexually calloused attitudes (for example, that women are sexual objects), and increases the stated willing- ness of men to engage in rape if there were no chance of their being caught (Donnerstein & others, 1987). The strongest and most consistent effects occur with exposure to "slasher" films, in which brutal violence (typically murder) is portrayed in a sexual context. Studies that have tested the effects of such films have consistently found an increase in antisocial and degrading attitudes toward women and an increased acceptance of rape (Linz, 1988).

The causes of sexual abuse and aggression are undoubtedly complex, and we must be careful not to oversim- plify matters by attributing them solely to the effects of pornography. It is also important to note that because of ethical constraints, no experimental study has tested the effects of violent pornography on actual sexual aggression toward women, nor is it ethically possible to do so. Although more research is clearly needed, the existing evidence does suggest that there is legitimate cause for concern about the impact of violent pornography on sexual motivation and behavior. This body of evidence has stimulated two major public policy recommendations by a group of psychologists who do research on violent pornography (see Zillmann & Bryant, 1989).

The first recommendation is to curtail the availability of violent erotica. Proponents of this action believe that the common good outweighs individual rights to produce or view materials that may stimulate perverse or injurious behavior (Sears, 1989). The second recommendation is to develop educational programs that will counter the myths (for example, that women secretly wish to be sexually dominated by men) that are conveyed by violent erotica (Fisher & Barak, 1989; Linz & Donnerstein, 1989). Proponents of this approach cite experimental evidence that information debunking rape myths promotes long-term rejection of the myths on the part of males (Linz & Donnerstein, 1989). They believe that strong messages against coercive sexual practices may promote sexual attitudes in males that help reduce "date rape" and other sexual crimes against women.

Sexual Orientation

Motivation influences not only the strength and persistence but also the direction of goal-directed behavior. The direction of sexual motivation is expressed in **sexual orientation.** Most people are heterosexual in their orientation; their sexual desires and behaviors are directed toward members of the opposite sex. According to studies in both Europe and the United States, about 4 percent of men and about 1 percent of women are exclusively homosexual in their orientation, and perhaps 5 percent of adults are actively bisexual, having sexual relationships with both males and females (Ellis & Ames, 1987; Masters & others, 1988). The rather wide variations that exist in sexual orientation have stimulated efforts to identify the causal factors that influence these differences (McWhirter & others, 1990).

As noted above, not all people who engage in homosexual behavior are exclusively homosexual. Kinsey (1953) proposed a continuum of sexual orientation that ranged from exclusively heterosexual behavior and interest to an exclusively homosexual orientation (see Figure 12.20). In between these extremes are several categories of bisexuals. Research

Figure 12.20 *The factors that contribute to the development of one's sexual orientation are an important focus of current research.*

evidence supports the existence of this type of continuum. In one large-scale study of homosexual men and women in San Francisco, it was found that many of the subjects shared nonsexual activities and interests with heterosexuals and had social and sometimes sexual involvements with the opposite sex. One-third of the women and one-fifth of the males had been in at least one heterosexual marriage (Bell & Weinberg, 1978).

Kinsey's surveys indicated that by age 55, about half of his male subjects had had some type of homosexual contact. About 4 percent of Kinsey's white males were exclusively homosexual, and another 10 percent were primarily homosexual for at least 3 years between the ages of 16 and 65. The proportion of female homosexuals was about one-third to one-half as large as that of males, but according to Kinsey and other surveys, about 25–30 percent of all women have a homosexual experience at some point in their lives (Masters & others, 1988).

A person's sexual orientation is the product of numerous interacting factors, many of which are not yet understood. One conclusion that seems fairly clear is that sexual orientation is neither freely chosen nor easily changed. In an attempt to understand the causal factors that influence sexual orientation, many researchers have focused on the antecedents of homosexual orientation. However, as research evidence has accumulated, theory after theory about the origins of homosexuality has fallen, unsupported, by the wayside.

The simple, single-cause theories were the first to fall. One of the earliest biological theories was that homosexual and heterosexual males differ in their levels of adult sex hormones. But many studies have shown that male homosexuals do not have lower levels of testosterone than heterosexuals, and attempts to change homosexual tendencies with injections of testosterone failed to do so or actually intensified homosexual urges (Masters & Johnson, 1979).

Another set of theories has viewed homosexuality as a product of the environment. For example, psychodynamic theorists have suggested that male homosexuality develops from family relationships involving a weak ineffectual father and a domineering or seductive mother with whom the boy identifies (Bieber & others, 1962). Another suggestion is that many homosexuals were seduced by adult homosexuals as children, thus diverting their sex drives toward members of their own sex (Giese & Schmidt, cited in Schmidt, 1978). A recent behavioral explanation suggests that a homosexual orientation may be the product of a classical conditioning process in which same-sex stimuli are associated with early sexual urges, thus endowing them with erotic properties. According to this theory, in early-maturing children who are still interacting with same-sex peers, adolescent sexual urges are likely to be associated with members of one's own gender and may thus result in the development of homosexual preferences (Storms, 1981).

All of the social–environmental theories have taken a scientific beating in recent years. Environmental explanations were called into question by the results of an extensive study of nearly 1000 homosexual and over 500 heterosexual men and women in the San Francisco area (Bell & others, 1981). In individual interviews, the subjects were asked more than 200 questions about their childhood, adolescent, and adult years. Many of these questions were inspired by various social–environmental theories of homosexuality. The investigators searched in vain for a common pattern of early experiences that would differentiate the two groups. They concluded:

> No particular phenomenon of family life can be singled out, on the basis of our findings, as especially consequential for either homosexual or heterosexual development. You may supply your sons with footballs and your daughters with dolls, but no one can guarantee that they will enjoy them. What we seem to have identified . . . is a pattern of feelings and reactions within the child that cannot be traced back to a single social or psychological root. (pp. 191–192).

In all of the responses, there was only one consistent difference: The homosexual men and women felt that they were somehow different from others of their gender, even in childhood.

Given the shortcomings of adult hormonal and environmental explanations for the development of sexual orientation, recent theories have begun to home in on genetically programmed events that might predispose one toward a homosexual or heterosexual orientation (Bailey & Pillard, 1991; Ellis & Ames, 1987). Research by J. Michael Bailey and Richard Pillard (1991) suggests a possible genetic link. They questioned 167 gay men who had either an identical twin, a fraternal twin, or an adoptive brother. Bailey and Pillard found that the closer the genetic relationship, the higher the concordance rate for homosexuality. Fifty-two percent (29 of 56) of the gay men's identical twin brothers were also gay, compared with concordance rates of 22 percent (12 of 54) and 11 percent (6 of 57) for the fraternal twins and adoptive brothers, respectively.

How might genetic factors influence sexual orientation? One theory focuses on the critical period between the second and sixth months in utero, when the brain's neural and hormonal control systems develop as feminine or are diverted toward masculinity by secretion of testosterone by the fetus. If the fetal androgen–estrogen levels are in the masculine range, it is theorized, the person will develop with a preference for female sex partners; if it is in the feminine range, the person will be predisposed to prefer masculine partners.

A variety of factors can interfere with the typical process of neural and endocrine system development in a genetic male or female. These include genetic instructions that fail to trigger a proper androgen–estrogen balance, certain drugs that can interfere with androgen secretion, and strong stress experienced by the mother during pregnancy (Ellis & Ames, 1987). These prenatal hormonal events do not in themselves *determine* that a person will be heterosexual or homosexual, but they may produce a readiness to learn some sexual preference and behavior patterns easier than others, given certain life experiences.

Genetic factors program not only hormonal events but also the development of brain structures. A hint that there may be brain differences between homosexual and heterosexual men comes from a study by Simon Levay (1991). Examining the brains of deceased homosexual men, heterosexual men, and heterosexual women, LeVay found that a small structure in the hypothalamus that is known to regulate sexual behavior was about the same size in the homosexual men as in the women, but only half as large as in the heterosexual men. These results must be viewed with caution until they are replicated in other samples. Furthermore, the relation between sexual orientation and the size of the structure is correlational, and it is possible that the brain difference between the homosexual and heterosexual men is a result of homosexuality rather than its cause.

A biological basis for homosexuality could help account for the fact that sexual orientation seems extraordinarily difficult to change once it emerges, as well as for the failure to find a single pattern of causal factors in homosexuality. It would also confirm the belief held by many homosexuals that their sexual orientation is due to biological factors and is therefore involuntary (Furnham & Taylor, 1990). However, at present, the causes of homosexuality—and for that matter, of all sexual preferences—remain an intriguing mystery.

Whatever one's sexual orientation may be, romantic love fuels the deepest and most meaningful forms of sexual expression. The pens of poets and perhaps your own experiences indicate that passionate love can be one of the most powerful of motivators. In the following feature, we consider the notion that love truly does embrace ''body and soul.''

PSYCHOBIOLOGICAL INTERACTIONS

Passionate Love: The Interaction of Cognitive and Physiological Factors

Some motivational states have a strong emotional component (Lazarus, 1991). One prime example occurs in the intense motivational state known as passionate love.

In contrast to feelings of liking or respect, passionate love can occur with startling suddenness. We may find ourselves experiencing a depth of feeling that seems far beyond most others, and we ride an emotional roller coaster that ranges from ecstasy in the presence of the other person to heartsickness and longing when the person is absent. Sexual desires and fantasies are a common part of this state of passionate love.

Recent attempts to understand passionate love have focused on the interaction of cognitive and physiological components (Berscheid, 1984; Hatfield & Rapson, 1987). According to these viewpoints, we experience passionate love because our culture has taught us to label strong physiological arousal as "love" under certain conditions. Let us analyze the nature of these body-mind-environment interactions.

North Americans grow up in a culture that believes in the concept of love, and they are exposed to love themes from childhood. Fairy tales contain many stories in which a woman meets Prince Charming and they fall in love, get married, and live happily ever after. Movies, novels, and soap operas reinforce this fairy-tale scenario. By adolescence, many are eagerly awaiting the glories of love; and research suggests that the more a person thinks about love, the more likely she or he is to have the experience (Tesser & Paulhus, 1976).

In addition to beliefs and expectations about love, according to these theories, passionate love requires the presence of someone to love and the experiencing of strong physiological arousal. If we experience high arousal in the presence of someone whom we appraise as attractive and desirable, we may well conclude that we are "falling in love." Once we label our feelings as love, we become even more attentive to features that make the other person "lovable." Thus, the physiological and cognitive components of passionate love tend to enhance one another.

This approach to understanding love has some interesting implications. One is that emotional arousal that occurs for some other reason could sometimes be misinterpreted as love. This phenomenon is known as **transfer of excitation** (Zillmann, 1984). The key requirement for such transfer is that the arousal be attributed at least in part to the presence of the romantic other. There is research evidence to support the idea of transfer of excitation.

For example, consider an experiment designed to determine if fear-produced arousal could be misperceived as sexual arousal. Male subjects were approached by either a male or a female experimenter as they crossed over one of two bridges in Vancouver, Canada. The "arousing" bridge was the Capilano Suspension Bridge, a narrow 450-foot-long structure that wobbles and sways on cables 230 feet above a deep ravine and rushing river (see Figure 12.21). The other bridge was a broader and much lower concrete bridge over the same river. After their encounters on the bridges, the subjects were asked to write stories in response to a series of pictures. When the researchers analyzed the content of the stories, they found that sexual themes occurred only in the stories of subjects who had encountered the female experimenter on the suspension bridge.

The subjects were also told that they could contact the experimenter later if they wished additional information about the experiment. The calls that were later received were mainly from the

◄ **Figure 12.21** *The Capilano Suspension Bridge provided the setting for a study on transfer of excitation. Male subjects who encountered a female experimenter on this wobbling bridge indicated greater sexual arousal and attraction, presumably because they attributed the arousal produced by being on the bridge to the characteristics of the woman.*

subjects who had encountered the female on the wobbly suspension bridge. The researchers concluded that sexual desire and attraction toward a member of the opposite sex were increased by the arousal produced by being on the suspension bridge (Dutton & Aron, 1974). Similar results have been found when arousal is produced by physical exercise rather than fear (White & Kight, 1984). Thus, transfer of excitation seems a realistic possibility.

The cognitive–arousal theory of passionate love seems to account for a number of common observations and experiences. For example, people sometimes experience rapid alternation between intense love and hatred. This shift may occur when the high arousal is suddenly relabeled as anger rather than love because of something that happens in the relationship. As another example, people's feelings of love sometimes increase when the other person plays "hard to get" or even rejects the lover. This may occur because frustration increases arousal, which is then mislabeled as even more intense love (Hatfield & Rapson, 1987).

Passionate love can be a rather fleeting phenomenon, as noted by a 16th century sage, who observed, "the history of a love affair is the drama of its fight against time" (cited in Berscheid, 1983). Unlike milder positive feelings such as liking, passionate love seems distressingly unstable. Research on the time course of romantic love in American marriages suggests that passionate love tends to cool to a "warm afterglow," contentment, and affection (Blood & Blood, 1978). Why should this be?

One possible explanation for the fading of passion is offered by the **opponent-process theory** of motivation (which should not be confused with the opponent-process theory of color vision discussed in Chapter 6). Richard Solomon (1982) believes that the nervous system is constructed so that whenever any emotional response (*A*) occurs, its opposite (*B*) is spontaneously triggered shortly afterwards to return the system to a neutral state of homeostasis. For example, if a stimulus triggers elation, then the nervous system generates its opposite (depression), and vice versa. This may occur through the action of neurotransmitter substances in the brain, some of which produce the pleasure state and others the negative state that restores homeostasis (Pert, 1986). From this point of view, every cloud has a silver lining, and every silver lining is surrounded by a cloud.

Solomon hypothesizes some important differences between the *A* and *B* states. He assumes that they differ in their intensity, the speed with which they develop, and their persistence. Upon initial exposure to the stimulus (Figure 12.22*a*), the *A* process (whether it is a positive or a negative state) develops quickly. The *B* state is delayed somewhat and is not as strong, but when it occurs, it cancels out part of the *A* state. When the stimulus is removed, the *A* state dissipates quickly, but the *B* state fades away more slowly. Thus, if *A* is a positive emotion, such as passion, the negative *B* state will cancel out part of *A* while the stimulus is present and then will produce a temporary "downer" after the stimulus (for example, a love partner) leaves. This state of torment following separation is familiar to all lovers.

With repeated exposure to the loved one, however, an important thing happens: The *A* state remains unchanged, but the *B* state increases in intensity (Figure 12.22*b*). *B*'s greater relative strength has the effect of canceling out more of the *A* state and thereby producing a more neutral emotional response. In the case of passionate love, this implies that with repeated exposures to the object of passion, the opponent processes should begin to reduce the original feelings of in-

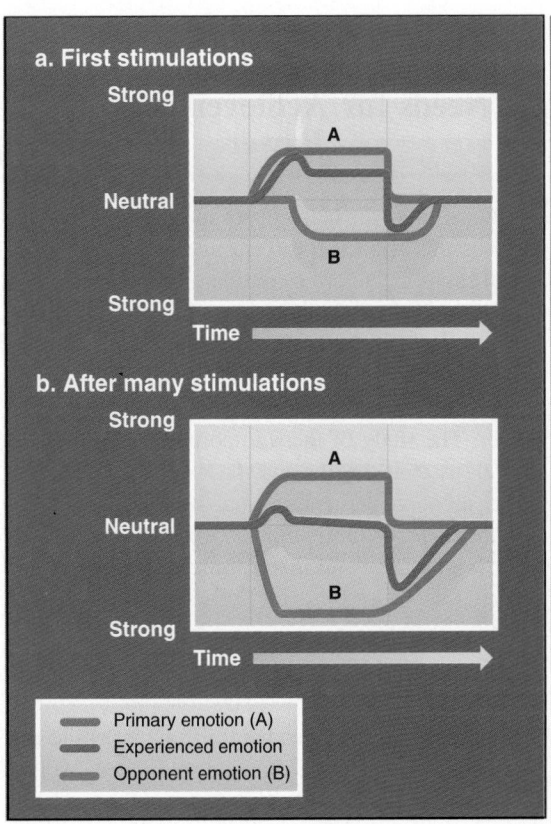

a. First stimulations

Strong

Neutral

Strong

Time

b. After many stimulations

Strong

Neutral

Strong

Time

Primary emotion (A)
Experienced emotion
Opponent emotion (B)

Figure 12.22 *Opponent processes change emotional experience over time. Whenever an emotional response such as passion (A) occurs, an opponent emotion (B) emerges to restore homeostasis. The experienced emotion is the difference between the two states. With repeated experiences, the opponent process becomes stronger, cancels out more of the primary emotion, and produces a stronger rebound effect. In the case of passionate love, this process is thought to result in a cooling of passion over time. (Adapted from Solomon, 1982).*

tense love, joy, and euphoria so that interaction with the loved person comes to be associated with the "cooler" feelings of contentment and comfort (see Figure 12.23).

It follows from what we know about the course of passionate love that we should relish it while it lasts. If a love relationship is to endure, however, it needs a more stable foundation than passion alone. Research suggests that similar attitudes and values, a sense of commitment to the other person, and the ability to share innermost thoughts and feelings provide a basis for the trust, faithfulness, and friendship that can sustain and even increase love for another after passion has cooled (Brehm, 1992; Sternberg, 1988).

Figure 12.23 *The blossoming and decline of passionate love. Current theories of passionate love emphasize relations among physiological, cognitive, cultural, and stimulus factors. One mechanism proposed to account for the often transitory nature of passionate love involves opponent processes, which, over time, dampen the intense passion of the earlier stage, resulting in a "warm afterglow" of contentment and affection.*

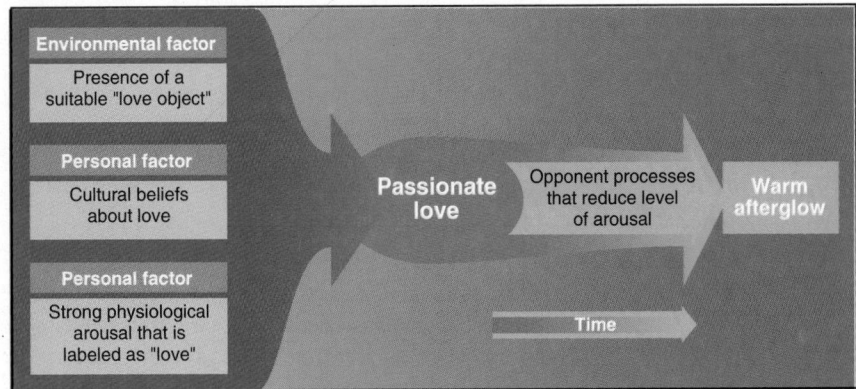

Environmental factor
Presence of a suitable "love object"

Personal factor
Cultural beliefs about love

Personal factor
Strong physiological arousal that is labeled as "love"

Passionate love

Opponent processes that reduce level of arousal

Warm afterglow

Time

Social Motivation: Needs for Achievement and Power

Biological motives help ensure our survival, but the motives that we acquire from interactions with our social environment often dominate our personal functioning and help to establish our individual identities. People show wide individual differences in the vigor and persistence of behaviors directed toward such social goals as affiliation, approval, achievement, and power. The study of these important social motives as well as their origins and the ways in which they affect thought, perception, and behavior is an important focus of motivational research. Two of the most important social motives are achievement and power.

Figure 12.24 *Pictures like this are used to elicit stories that can be scored for achievement motivation.*

Achievement-Related Motives

College students are often painfully aware of the emphasis our society places on achievement, as well as the fierce competition that characterizes the academic atmosphere on many campuses. Americans are internationally regarded as being preoccupied with competition and success. Small wonder, then, that the need for achievement and its origins have received more attention from U.S. researchers than any other learned social motive. **Need for achievement** is defined as the desire to compete successfully with standards of excellence (McClelland & others, 1953).

Measuring Need for Achievement

Much of the research on achievement motivation has used a measurement technique devised by David McClelland, John Atkinson, and their associates (McClelland & others, 1953). Subjects are shown a series of pictures like the one in Figure 12.24 and asked to make up a story about each of them. The story is supposed to answer the following questions:

1. What is the situation—that is, who are the people and what are they doing?
2. What has led up to this situation—that is, what has happened in the past?
3. What is being thought? What is wanted? By whom?
4. What will happen? What will be done?

It is assumed that in interpreting the pictures, people project their own needs onto the characters in the story. The content of the stories is then analyzed according to a well-defined scoring system for achieve-

ment themes. Here is an example of a story that would receive a high need-for-achievement score:

> This young man is sitting in school, but he is dreaming about the day when he will become a doctor. He comes from a poor family that cannot afford to send him to medical school and is worried about where the money will come from, but he is determined to make it. He is thinking about how he will work so hard that he will be the top student in his medical school class. Even though he is not brilliant, he will study and work harder than anyone else. He goes on to become one of the top medical researchers in the world and helps find a cure for cancer.

This story would receive a low score:

> The boy is daydreaming about how much he hates being in school and how much he would like to get out of that classroom. He wanted to drop out last year, but his parents are forcing him to go. He would like to run away from home and just take it easy on a tropical island. However, he is doomed to be in the rat race the rest of his life.

One advantage of this measurement technique is that it can be applied not only to stories written in response to the standard pictures but to any written material. As we shall see, researchers have analyzed written documents from various eras to study historical changes in achievement motivation (McClelland, 1988).

Behavioral Correlates of Need for Achievement

Individuals with a high need for achievement are ambitious, enjoy competitive situations, and are persistent in their attempts to solve problems. They are also better able to pass up immediate gratification for future reward. Achievement motivation scores are sometimes, but not always, positively related to academic grades and IQ. College students with high achievement motivation do best in courses that they perceive as relevant to their future careers, and they tend to seek out and enter more prestigious occupations than do individuals with lower achievement motivation (Heckhausen, 1991). In terms of occupation, those involved in sales and marketing tend to have the highest achievement motivation scores. On a less positive note, there is some evidence that very high need for achievement is associated with a higher-than-average death rate from ulcers and hypertension (Heckhausen & others, 1985).

In people with high achievement motivation, the motive is engaged and affects behavior only when situational factors arouse it. In order for achievement motivation to be aroused, the person must (a) perceive himself or herself as personally responsible for the outcome, (b) perceive some risk of not succeeding, and (c) receive performance feedback (Koester & McClelland, 1990). In experimental situations, people with a high need for achievement generally outperform individuals with low achievement motivation when the experimenter places great stress on excellence of performance, but not under relaxed conditions (McClelland, 1985). Likewise, in work settings, people with a high need for achievement are more successful than those with low achievement motivation, but only when they work for firms that are especially achievement oriented. Subjects low in need for achievement work harder when they are told that a task is easy; those high in achievement motivation work harder when told the task is difficult (Kukla, 1975). People high in achievement motivation also enjoy games and other activities more when they are competing against others, whereas such competiton decreases the enjoyment of those low in achievement motivation (Epstein & Harackiewicz, 1992).

Risk-taking behavior also is related to achievement motivation. Subjects with a high need for achievement prefer intermediate rather than extremely high or low risks (Atkinson & Birch, 1978). For example, on a ring-toss task, "highs" tend at first to select an intermediate distance to toss the rope ring at the peg, a distance from which the task is a challenge and success is uncertain. This pattern seems to extend to real-life areas as well. Young adults who are high in achievement motivation tend to choose college majors and vocations of moderate difficulty (Isaacson, 1964; Morris, 1966).

Achievement motivation has been shown to be related to measures of national accomplishment as well as to individual achievement. In a series of correlational studies, achievement imagery in children's story books was related to national economic growth. The researchers reasoned that the level of concern for achievement in children's books reflects the motivational level of the adults in the country at that time, as well as the values that are being transmitted to children.

The results of one analysis are shown in Figure 12.25. Achievement motivation scores derived from content analysis of second- and fourth-grade school readers corresponded closely to the number of patents issued per million population in the United States between 1810 and 1950 (de Charms & Moeller, 1962).

Cultural Differences in Achievement Motivation

Social motives express themselves within a cultural context, and the values of a culture can influence the forms a motive takes. As we saw in Chapter 1, an important cultural dimension is individualism versus collectivism (Triandis, 1989). Individualistic cultures like those in North America stress personal achievement, whereas cultures that nurture collectivism, such as those in China and Japan, emphasize the goals of the group. Individualism and collectivism might therefore be expected to produce two different kinds of achievement motivation, and it appears that they do (Markus & Kitayama, 1991; Yang, 1986).

Individualism fosters a motive in which the person strives for personal achievement and is driven by

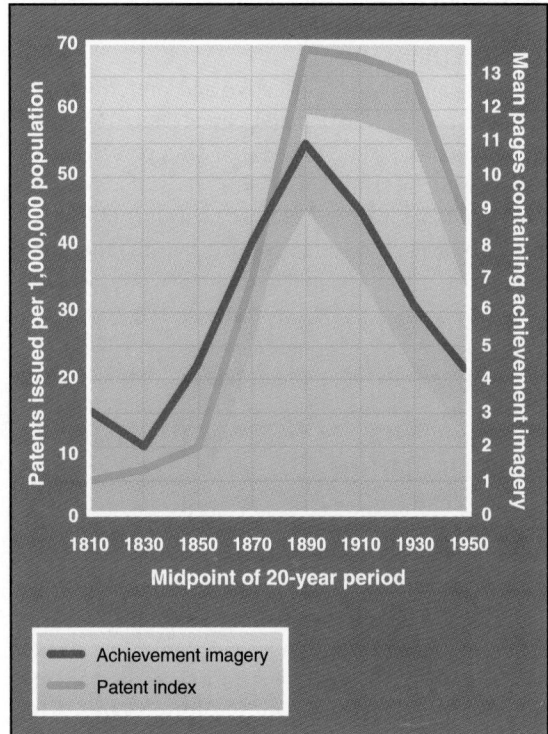

Figure 12.25 *Relation between achievement imagery found in children's stories and number of patents per million population issued in the United States between 1810 and 1950. (de Charms & Moeller, 1962).*

Figure 12.26 *In Japan, achievement motivation generally shows itself as a desire to conform to the expectations of the social group and to contribute to the attainment of group goals. Demanding but caring managers and leaders are highly effective because they foster a sense of obligation that causes workers to work very hard.*

internalized standards of excellence. It is a stable attribute of the person that has little to do with the group as a whole. On the other hand, in collectivist societies like Japan and China, achievement motivation is part of the desire to fit into the family and social group, meet its expectations, and work for its goals. When the specific achievement goal is met, the intense achievement motivation formerly evident may appear to vanish (Bond, 1986).

In Japan, the most effective and preferred managers are people who demand a great deal from workers while at the same time expressing personal concern for them (Hayashi, 1988). It is the personal attachment to the manager and the ensuing obligation to him or her (and to the company itself) that most strongly motivates people to do their work (Misumi, 1985; see Figure 12.26). In contrast, Western workers' achievement strivings are oriented toward the goals of personal attainment and individual recognition (Heckhausen & others, 1985).

Fear of Failure

It is important to distinguish between two very different achievement-related motives, both of which can cause people to appear success-oriented. The first is the positive desire to achieve success that we have been discussing; the second is a negative fear of failure. People high in **fear of failure** work hard not because they yearn for ''the thrill of victory'' but because they dread ''the agony of defeat.''

Fear of failure is typically measured by questionnaires that assess the amount of anxiety experienced in achievement situations. Table 12.3 presents items from two performance anxiety questionnaires, one specific to tests, the other to competitive sports.

Studies on the development of need for achievement and fear of failure indicate that positive achievement motivation develops when parents encourage and reward independence and achievement but do not punish failure (Heckhausen & others, 1985; Koestner & McClelland, 1990). Fear of failure seems to develop when successful achievement is taken for granted by parents but failure is punished. As a result, the child learns to dread the possibility of failing (Weiner, 1980, 1992).

In contrast to people who are motivated to achieve, people who fear failing try to avoid feelings of failure by taking either extremely high risks (where no one can truly expect to succeed) or extremely low risks (where success is all but assured). Their performance deteriorates under pressure to achieve because of the disruptive effect of anxiety, which makes it difficult to process information effectively and attend to the task requirements (Sarason & Sarason, 1990). In sports, this is the athlete who ''chokes'' under pressure (Smith & Smoll, 1990).

Thus, people may be driven toward success or away from failure. We need to know which of these needs is motivating them in order to understand and predict their achievement behavior.

The Power Motive

Many people have high **power motivation**—the need to exert control over the lives of others and to gain positions of prestige and dominance. Like the need to achieve, the need for power can be measured through content analysis of stories (Winter, 1988). Subjects' scores are based on the number of phrases and verbal images that describe impact on or control over other people. These images may involve actions that range from strong, aggressive, and forceful (ordering, threatening) to subtle and socially acceptable (helping, advising, inspiring).

David McClelland (1975) suggested that there are actually two kinds of power motivation. One kind is oriented toward winning out over adversaries. People with this kind of power motivation see life as a jungle in which the strongest survive by destroying or eliminating their foes. In every social interaction someone wins and someone loses.

The other kind of power motive is more socialized. It involves exercising power for the benefit of others and helping to further group goals by exercising social influence (see Figure 12.27). Individuals with this type of motivation may hesitate to be obvious in seeking power because they realize that the overt quest for power for power's sake may be frowned on by society. Perhaps that is why some politicians prefer to be "called" to public service rather than to actively seek an office.

Behavioral Correlates of the Power Motive

Some of the behavioral characteristics of people whose need for power is high have been identified. Male college students with a high need for power hold office in organizations more often, write more letters to university newspapers, and more frequently get elected to important university committees. They are also more likely to play vigorous competitive sports (or at least watch them), to read magazines like *Playboy*, and to watch adventure programs on television (Winter & Stewart, 1978).

Men with high power needs tend to buy material goods that are advertised as prestigious. They prefer highly maneuverable cars, "which give the driver the impression of total control over the vehicle, the road, and, presumably, other drivers" (Winter, 1973, p. 446). People with high power needs are often skilled at manipulating other people and social situations to their advantage. One finding that may relate to these social influence skills is that men who scored high on power motivation in college had wives 10 years later whose levels of career involvement were lower than those of the wives of males with low power needs (Winter & others, 1977). Need for power is also related to the tendency of men to be physically abusive toward their intimate partners (Mason & Blankenship, 1987).

It appears that male power fantasies can be aroused by alcohol, but the nature of the power fantasies is affected by the amount of alcohol the man drinks. Small amounts increase the frequency of socialized power thoughts, but larger amounts promote fantasies about personalized power that often involve exploitative sexual and aggressive behavior (McClelland & others, 1972).

In one intriguing series of studies, the power motivation of U.S. presidents was measured by content analysis of their inaugural addresses (Winter, 1987). Presidents with high power motivation scores, such as John F. Kennedy and Ronald Reagan, tended to be active and fond of their job, and they liked to display themselves publicly. They were also more likely than other presidents to be the targets of assassination attempts, perhaps because of this fondness for self-display.

According to some theorists, a high need for power is a way of compensating for a sense of inferiority or powerlessness as a child. Research suggests, however, that many adults who have a high

Table 12.3 Sample Items from Scales Designed to Measure Fear of Failure in Two Achievement Domains

Reactions to Tests

1. I feel distressed and uneasy before tests.
2. Before taking a test, I worry about failure.
3. While taking a test, I feel tense.
4. During a difficult test, I worry whether I will pass it.
5. Thoughts of doing poorly interfere with my concentration during tests.

Sport Anxiety Scale

1. I am concerned about choking under pressure.
2. I have lapses in concentration during competition because of nervousness.
3. My stomach gets upset before or during competition.
4. I am concerned that I may not do as well in competition as I should.
5. I sometimes find myself trembling before or during a competitive event.

Sources: Sarason, 1984; Smith & others, 1990.

need for power felt powerful, not inferior, when they were younger (Winter & Stewart, 1978). They are often first-born children who were rewarded by their parents when they exercised control over various aspects of their lives, including their younger siblings and their peers.

Gender and Power Motivation

Do men and women differ in power motivation? In our culture, women have traditionally had less access to formal power than have men. Thus, many people believe that women have lower power motivation than men, or that their power needs are expressed by being nurturant and making others dependent on them

▲ **Figure 12.27** *This child is exhibiting the socialized rather than the antisocial type of power motivation.*

"And I hereby swear that should my quest for the secret of superstrength be successful, I shall use this power only for good."

DRAWING BY LORENZ: © 1975 THE NEW YORKER MAGAZINE

Figure 12.28 *Responsibility training may help channel power motivation in socially desirable directions in both males and females.*

(Miller, 1976). However, an analysis of power motivation data collected from men and women over the past 20 years challenges these traditional views (Winter, 1988).

Winter found that in stories written in response to pictures, women expressed as much power motivation as men. He also found that power motivation was related to socialized power behaviors (office holding, seeking prestigious careers, and displaying oneself in order to impress others) in the same manner in women and men. However, women's power motivation was *not* related to the more impulsive antisocial forms of power, such as drinking and aggression. At first, this seemed like a major sex difference, but further analyses showed otherwise. For *both* men and women, ''responsibility training'' in the form of having cared for a younger sibling or having children of one's own eliminated relations between need for power and the less desirable forms of power behavior (see Figure 12.28). This finding suggests that for both genders, socialization experiences involving responsibility for others may help channel power motivation into more desirable forms of power striving, such as leadership and positive impact on others. The fact that women in our culture tend to have more responsibility training than men apparently fosters the more benign variety of power motivation shown by women.

Motivational Conflict

Motives energize and direct behavior toward goals. But as we all know, goals are not always compatible with each other. For example, achievement and affiliation motives may clash when a choice has to be made between studying and attending an enjoyable party. The result is **conflict.** Conflict places us in a motivational bind; we must forego one goal in order to attain another. It also takes a toll on our well-being and behavioral efficiency. Motivational conflict is related to anxiety and depression, physical illness, and the tendency to think a great deal about the conflicting strivings but not act on them (Emmons & King, 1988).

In the 1930s, Kurt Lewin (1935) suggested that conflicts can be described in terms of two opposed tendencies: approach and avoidance. When something attracts us, we tend to approach it; when something repels or frightens us, we tend to avoid it. Different combinations of approach and avoidance tendencies can produce three basic types of conflict (see Figure 12.29).

The first type of conflict involves opposition between two attractive alternatives and is therefore called an **approach–approach conflict.** Selecting one alternative means losing the other. Conflict is at its greatest when both alternatives are equally attractive and very important. A woman who wants to pursue an advanced degree in medicine but also wants to have a family and spend a great deal of time with her children faces an approach–approach conflict.

The reverse of this dilemma is the **avoidance–avoidance conflict,** in which a person is faced with two undesirable alternatives. You may recently have experienced such a conflict if you had to choose between studying a subject you find terribly boring and

Figure 12.29 *Three basic types of conflict result from incompatible motives: approach–approach; avoidance–avoidance, and approach–avoidance.*

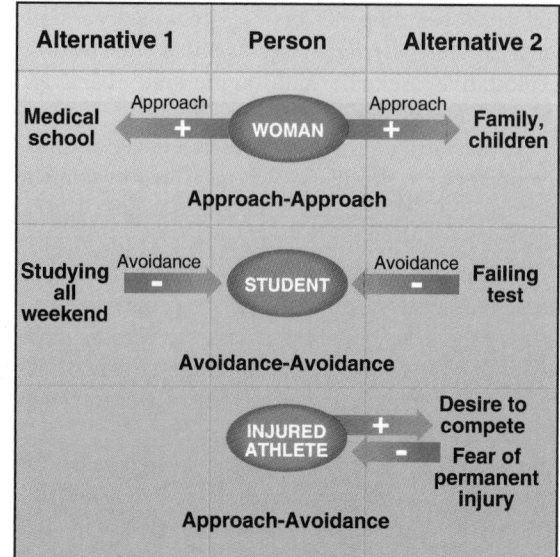

failing an exam. People faced with an avoidance–avoidance conflict often try to escape from the situation (perhaps by dropping the course). When they cannot escape, they tend to vacillate between one threat and the other.

In **approach–avoidance conflicts,** a person is both attracted to and repelled by the same goal. These are sometimes the most difficult conflicts of all to resolve: A person is driven toward a sexual affair but is inhibited by guilt and by moral values and beliefs. An injured athlete wants to take a pain-killing drug so that she can play in an important game but realizes that she may be risking permanent injury if she does so.

Neal Miller (1959) has provided an analysis of approach–avoidance conflicts that is illustrated in Figure 12.30. According to Miller, both the tendency to approach a desired goal and the desire to avoid it grow stronger as we get nearer to the goal. A critical factor, however, is that the avoidance tendency usually increases in strength *faster* than the approach tendency does. Thus, the maximum conflict in an approach–avoidance situation occurs where the two strength-of-motivation lines, or gradients, cross; there, the approach and avoidance tendencies are equal in strength. At this point, we may stop, retreat, approach again, and continue to vacillate in a state of conflict.

Approach–avoidance dilemmas can be resolved in favor of the approach tendency by increasing the motivation to approach, by decreasing the tendency to avoid, or both. Sometimes, without realizing it, people behave in ways that resolve the conflict in favor of avoidance. For example, the person described above whose conflict involves a tempting sexual affair may ''unwittingly'' start an argument with the person he or she desires. The negative feelings resulting from the argument may reduce the approach tendencies enough so that an affair is no longer such a temptation. Psychodynamic explanations of behavior often focus on the ways in which people resolve conflicts, some of which lie beyond their awareness.

Some methods of coping with motivational conflict can be maladaptive. Irving Janis and Leon Mann (1978) have described four defective patterns of coping and decision making. The most common is **defensive avoidance**. The decision maker procrastinates, shifts responsibility for the decision to someone else, and generally avoids coming to grips with the decision. A second defective pattern is **defensive vigilance**. The decision maker becomes upset, frantically searches for a way out of the dilemma, and makes impulsive choices without considering other

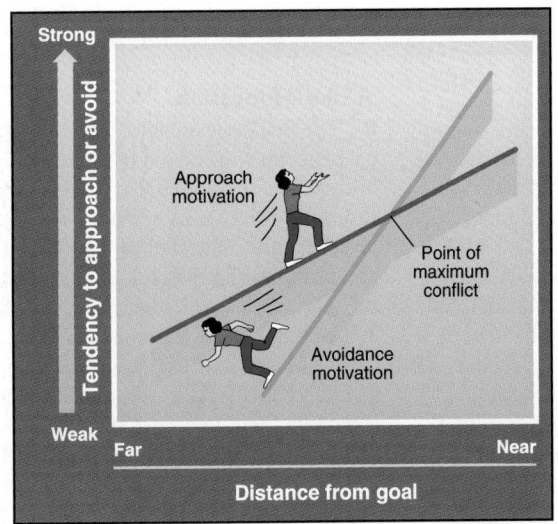

Figure 12.30 *According to Neal Miller's analysis of approach–avoidance conflicts, both the tendency to approach and the tendency to avoid grow stronger as one moves closer to the goal. However, the tendency to avoid increases faster than the tendency to approach. Maximum conflict is experienced where the two gradients cross, because at this point the opposing motives are equal in strength.*

alternatives. In **unconflicted adherence,** the decision maker keeps on doing whatever he or she has been doing, ignoring information about possible negative consequences. The fourth defective strategy, **unconflicted change,** involves an uncritical adoption of whatever new course of action occurs to the person or is recommended by someone else.

In recent years, psychologists have been developing procedures to help people make effective decisions under motivational conflict. One promising approach is derived from the expectancy × value framework discussed earlier. In this procedure, clients are helped to identify the alternative courses of action available to them and the positive as well as negative consequences that might result from each. They then assign numerical values to each consequence in terms of how likely it is to occur (expectancy) and how positive or negative it is (value). These scores can be multiplied to produce an expectancy × value score for each pair of decision alternatives. The person can use this score as a basis for making a rational decision (Janis, 1982). Although this method cannot help people avoid the conflict produced by competing motives, it can help them learn how to approach such situations in a more adaptive fashion.

We have now considered a wide range of human motives. Motivation is one of the most common ways of explaining behavior, yet we have seen that motives themselves have a variety of interacting causes, some biological, some cognitive, some intrapsychic, and others environmental. Moreover, satisfying our motives or failing to do so produces many of our emotional responses (Lazarus, 1991a). In Chapter 13, we consider the closely related topic of emotion.

Perspectives on Motivation

- Motivation is an internal process that influences the direction, vigor, and persistence of goal-directed behavior. Motivation is influenced by biological, cognitive, intrapsychic, and environmental factors.
- The biological perspective studies the external and internal processes related to the arousal and reduction of biological needs; it also investigates the physiological bases of pleasure and the possible role of evolutionary factors in motivation. Behaviorists examine relations between motivation and learning, as well as how learning is involved in acquiring motives. Examples of the cognitive perspective's contributions include the expectancy × value theory, the study of how extrinsic rewards can undermine intrinsic motivation, and the notion of possible selves. Psychodynamic theorists are particularly interested in the role of unconscious motivation in behavior, while humanistic theorists like Maslow stress the importance of higher order growth needs.

Hunger

- Our biological needs are directed at maintaining a stable internal environment and are governed by control centers that respond to deviations from certain set points. Where hunger is concerned, much research has centered on the hypothalamus, but it now appears that many widely separated parts of the brain are involved in the regulation of eating. Chemicals, such as peptides, are known to play a vital role in the regulation of food intake.
- Research on obesity has shown that several factors, including increased fat-cell size and insulin secretion, lowered basal metabolism, and lowered activity level, combine to increase the difficulty obese people have in achieving and maintaining weight loss. Stress tends to reduce the food intake of nonobese people but to increase food intake in the obese.
- Anorexics and bulimics both show a preoccupation with food intake and a distorted body image. Both disorders can have life-threatening consequences.

Sensory Needs

- Both animals and humans tend to seek out novelty and an optimal level of stimulation. Studies of individual differences in the sensation-seeking motive have shown that the strength of this motive is related to a variety of human behaviors, including risk taking, drug use, and sexual activities.

Sexual Motivation

- The first large-scale survey studies of sexual behavior were begun by Alfred Kinsey and his associates in the 1930s. Comparison of the results of recent surveys with Kinsey's suggests that the greatest changes are increases in premarital sex and in oral–genital stimulation.
- Hormones have both organizational and activational effects on sexual behavior. In their organizational role, hormones are crucial in the development of male and female sexual characteristics, and they also influence sexual behavior. Activational effects on sexual desire and behavior are less evident in humans than in animals, but they are clearly seen at puberty and, to a lesser degree, with aging.
- Masters and Johnson measured physiological responses during thousands of sexual episodes and reported a four-stage response pattern consisting of excitement, plateau, orgasm, and resolution. Psychological factors contribute to the subjective experience of orgasm.
- Culture plays a large part in how people express sexual drives and how they feel about sex. Research on the effects of pornography suggests that exposure to nonviolent pornography has no long-term effects on behavior but that the viewing of sexual violence may stimulate deviant sexual fantasies in men as well as increases in males' aggression toward women.
- Kinsey suggested that sexual orientation in the population exists on a continuum from exclusively heterosexual to exclusively homosexual. No single biological, social, or psychological cause for the development of a homosexual orientation has been discovered. Recent interest has focused on the possible effect of prenatal hormones on the potential to develop a particular orientation. It appears that genetic factors may affect sexual orientation by influencing prenatal hormonal events and possibly by producing physical differences in the brain.
- Recent theoretical attempts to understand passionate love have emphasized relations between cognitive and physiological processes. The experiencing of strong arousal in the presence of a suitable person is viewed as the core of passionate love. The fact that passionate love tends to cool to a "warm afterglow" over time has been explained in terms of the opponent-process theory. Factors that increase intimacy and commitment seem to increase the likelihood that love will endure even when passion wanes.

Social Motivation: Needs for Achievement and Power

- Achievement motivation can be measured by analysis of the content of stories told by subjects in response to pictures. People high in achievement motivation perform better than people low in achievement motivation when the situation stresses competition and standards of excellence. They prefer moderate risks and tasks that increase in difficulty over time.
- Culture can influence the forms that achievement motivation takes. In individualist cultures, achievement motivation is a stable trait that involves attempts to meet internal standards of excellence. In collectivist cultures, it takes the form of a desire to fulfill responsibilities to the family and other social groups and may vanish when the group goals have been attained.
- An important distinction exists between achievement motivation and fear of failure, which is a negative motive aimed at avoiding failure rather than at achieving success for its own sake. People high in fear of failure tend to perform more poorly in achievement situations because of the disruptive effects of anxiety.
- The need for power seems to take two forms: winning out over rivals and achieving positive group goals through social influence. The traditional belief that people high in power motivation are compensating for feelings of inferiority or powerlessness as children has not been well supported by research.
- Men and women do not differ in power motivation scores. In both genders, responsibility training seems to channel power motivation away from negative or impulsive power behaviors and into socially desirable forms.

Motivational Conflict

- Three basic varieties of conflict are approach–approach, avoidance–avoidance, and approach–avoidance. According to Miller, in approach–avoidance conflicts, the desire to avoid the goal and the desire to approach it grow stronger as we get closer to the goal, but the avoidance motivation increases in strength faster than the approach motivation.
- Psychologists have developed programs designed to help people avoid several maladaptive forms of decision making and make more rational decisions based on the expectancy × value framework when faced with motivational conflict.

KEY TERMS AND CONCEPTS

androgens (p. 381)
anorexia nervosa (p. 376)
approach–approach conflict (p. 394)
approach–avoidance conflict (p. 394)
avoidance–avoidance conflict (p. 395)
bulimia (p. 376)
cholecystokinin (CCK) (p. 374)
conflict (p. 394)
cue-responsive individuals (p. 376)
defensive avoidance (p. 395)
defensive vigilance (p. 395)
deficiency needs (p. 371)

estrogens (p. 381)
expectancy $\times$ value theory (p. 369)
extrinsic motivation (p. 369)
fear of failure (p. 392)
glucoreceptors (p. 374)
growth needs (p. 370)
homeostasis (p. 372)
incentive (p. 367)
intrinsic motivation (p. 369)
metabolism (p. 375)
motivation (p. 367)
opponent-process theory (p. 389)

overjustification hypothesis (p. 369)
possible selves (p. 370)
power motivation (p. 392)
refractory period (p. 382)
sensation-seeking motive (p. 378)
set point (p. 374)
sexual orientation (p. 385)
sublimation (p. 371)
transfer of excitation (p. 388)
unconflicted adherence (p. 395)
unconflicted change (p. 395)

SUGGESTED READINGS

Kelley, K., & Byrne, D. (1991). *Human sexual behavior*. Englewood Cliffs, N.J.: Prentice-Hall. A comprehensive overview of this important area of human motivation, written by two leading researchers.

McWhirter, D. P., Sanders, S. A., & Reinisch, J. M. (Eds.) (1990). *Homosexuality/heterosexuality: Concepts of sexual orientation.* An authoritative volume from the Kinsey Institute series featuring papers by leading researchers and clinicians on what is currently known about the biological, environmental, intrapsychic, and cognitive factors that affect sexual orientation.

Reeve, J. (1992). *Understanding motivation and emotion*. Ft. Worth: Harcourt Brace Jovanovich. A broad overview of theories, concepts, and research results concerning motivation and its linkages with emotion.

Weiner, B. (1989). *Human motivation.* Hillsdale, N.J.: Erlbaum. An informative and engaging book written primarily from a cognitive perspective and covering the entire range of human motivation. Its discussion of achievement-related motives is especially good.

13 Emotion

There is an inner warm glow, a radiant sensation; I feel like smiling; there is a sense of well-being, a sense of harmony and peace within. . . . I think about beautiful things; I feel safe and secure. . . . My movements are graceful and easy; I feel especially well coordinated. . . . There is a sense of being more alive, I am excited in a calm way. . . . There is a particularly acute awareness of pleasurable things, their sounds, their colors, and textures. . . . I'm optimistic and cheerful; the world seems basically good and beautiful.

I feel empty, drained, hollow, understimulated, undercharged, heavy, loggy, sluggish; I feel let down, tired, sleepy; it's an effort to do anything. I have no desire, no motivation, no interest. . . . I feel sorry for myself; I want to withdraw, disappear, draw back, be alone, away from others, crawl into myself; everything seems useless, absurd, meaningless; I feel as if I'm out of touch, can't reach others; my body wants to contract. . . . I have no appetite; there is a heaviness in my chest; there is a lump in my throat; I can't smile or laugh; it's as if I'm suffocating.

These descriptions of contrasting emotional experiences—happiness and depression—come from interviews with more than 12,000 people who were asked to describe various feelings (Davitz, 1970). It is obvious from the descriptions that emotions are complex internal states with many elements. There are physical components ("an inner warm glow," "tired," "sleepy," "lump in my throat"), thoughts ("sense of harmony and peace within," "everything seems useless"), and behavioral expressions of the feeling ("I feel like smiling," "I can't smile or laugh").

Life without emotion would be strange indeed. The experiences of love, anger, joy, fear, and other emotions are a central part of our conscious lives. No account of psychology would be complete without a consideration of how and why we feel as we do. Modern-day psychology's emphasis on the study of emotion echoes a timeless fascination—expressed in songs, paintings, stories, poems, and scholarly treatises—with human feelings.

There are good reasons to learn more about emotions. First, we cannot completely understand ourselves or our relations with others without taking account of the emotional reactions that occur in our lives and the emotional exchanges that help define our social relationships. When interpersonal relationships are good, they can be a source of intense pleasure and fulfillment. But when they are conflicted, they can produce intense misery, anger, and fear. Moreover, dysfunctional emotional reactions are causal factors in many physical and psychological disorders, as we shall see in Chapters 15 and 16.

Given the central role that emotion plays in happiness and well-being, it is easy to understand why people want to deal more effectively with their feelings and, to whatever extent possible, attain greater control over them. People spend an enormous amount of time and money in the pursuit of emotional control. They pray, exercise, see psychotherapists, study Eastern mysticism, and take drugs, all in an attempt to understand and self-regulate their emotions.

We all intuitively know what emotions feel like, but intuition is not enough for science. Because emotions involve complex interactions between environment, mind, body, and behavior, the biological, behavioral, cognitive, and intrapsychic perspectives all have made important contributions to our current understanding of emotion, and all have prescriptions for how we might gain greater control of our feelings.

The Nature and Functions of Emotions

An **emotion** may be defined as an innate and acquired predisposition to respond cognitively, physiologically, and behaviorally to certain internal and external events that relate to important goals or motives. This definition is a broad one whose implications require a consideration of the nature, structure, and functions of emotions. Let us begin by considering how emotions relate to motivation.

Relations Between Motivation and Emotion

The concepts of motivation and emotion have always been closely linked, and the dividing line between them is not always clear (Carlson & Hatfield, 1992; Reeve, 1992). One reason is that motivation and emotion both involve states of arousal, and they both can impel organisms to action. By triggering action tendencies (for example, flight in the case of fear and attack in the case of anger), emotional states often seem to have motivational properties. Conversely, the energizing aspect of a motivational state often has emotional qualities, as when a motivational trait like fear of failure results in the emotional response of anxiety in an achievement situation (Rothblum, 1990).

Richard Lazarus (1991a) believes that there is always a link between motives and emotions, because "without a goal and personal stake in a transaction [with the environment], an encounter will not generate an emotion. . . . The concept of motivation helps us understand what makes an adaptational encounter personally relevant and a source of harm or benefit, hence emotional" (pp. 820, 824). Thus, we often react emotionally when our motives are gratified or frus-

trated, and we are likely to become most emotional when an encounter relates to goals that are very important to us (see Figure 13.1). Indeed, the descriptions of emotion with which the chapter began might well describe "the thrill of victory" and "the agony of defeat."

One distinction between motivation and emotion made by some theorists is that motives operate more like internal *stimuli* that energize and direct behavior toward some goal or incentive, whereas emotions are basically reactions, or *responses,* to certain events (Mandler, 1984; Scherer, 1988). As we shall see, emotions are indeed integrated response patterns that are programmed in part by innate biological factors and in part by learning experiences.

The Functions of Emotions

Emotions have a number of important functions in helping us adapt to the world. First, they signal that something important is happening, and they rouse us to action. Indeed, emotions may be regarded as a set of action tendencies that involve cognitive, physiological, and behavioral elements linked together and triggered by particular events that have significance for the organism and its well-being (Izard, 1990; Lazarus, 1991b). In an evolutionary sense, some emotions are part of an emergency arousal system that once increased the chances of survival by energizing, directing, and sustaining adaptive behaviors. Probably the most basic of these behavioral tendencies, seen in virtually all species, is fighting or fleeing when confronted by perceived threat or danger. The physiological arousal that is so central to the emotions of anger and fear energizes and intensifies such behaviors. Other emotions, such as sadness, relief, and contentment, may involve an integrated pattern that includes a decrease in arousal and behavioral intensity.

Emotions are also important modes of communication. They communicate something to others about our internal state and intentions. These signals influence the responses of others, including their emotional responses (see Figure 13.2). To social creatures like us, emotional messages are important guides to behavior, and some of people's responses to emotional signals may result from innate predispositions. Consider, for example, responses to another's distress. As early as 1 to 3 days after birth, human infants respond to the crying of another infant with crying of their own, and infants under 2 years of age respond to their mother's real or simulated signs of distress with efforts to help or comfort the mother (Sagi & Hoffman, 1976; Zahn-Waxler & others, 1979, 1992). Studies with adults have also shown that expressions of sadness and distress evoke empathy and helping behavior from others (Izard, 1989).

Emotions add color to our world of experience, and like colors, they cover a wide spectrum. More than 550 words in the English language refer to various emotional states (Averill, 1980). Despite their diversity, however, emotions seem to share some common features. First, because they involve organism–environment transactions, all emotions are responses to particular situations. Second, an emotional response is always the result of some perceptual interpretation of the situation and of its meaning and significance. Third, there is a state of physiological or bodily change; we become physically "stirred up," as in fear or anger, or experience decreased arousal, as in depression. Finally, there are certain behavior tendencies. Some of these are *expressive* behaviors (for example, smiling or crying). Others are *instrumental* behaviors, ways of reacting to the stimulus that aroused the emotion (for example, by attacking or running away). These behavioral features of the emotional response have an innate basis, but they may nevertheless differ from person to person and, as we shall see, from culture to culture because they can be modified somewhat by learning.

Figure 13.3 illustrates the general relationships among these five primary components: (1) the *eliciting stimuli,* the events that arouse the emotion; (2) the person's *cognitive appraisal,* or interpretation of the situation, which gives it meaning; (3) *physiological arousal;* (4) *expressive behaviors,* such as facial expressions and clenched fists; and (5) *instrumental behaviors,* which are designed to accomplish some goal related to the emotion. For example, an insulting remark may evoke in the person who has been insulted a cognitive appraisal that he or she has been unfairly demeaned, an increase in physiological arousal, a clenching of jaw and fists, and a verbal attack on the other person. Of special significance are the relations between cognitive and physiological factors. As the two-way arrows indicate, these components appear to influence one another. Recent findings suggest that certain expressive behaviors, such as facial responses, also share a two-way relation with cognitive appraisals (Adelmann & Zajonc, 1989; Ekman & others, 1990).

As Figure 13.3 indicates, personality and motivational factors can also affect emotion. They do so by influencing what situations people expose themselves to and how they think about those situations, as well as their physiological and behavioral responses. For example, as we saw in Chapter 12, people differ in the strength of their sensation-seeking motivation. Someone high in this motive might seek out and experience emotions of fear and exhilaration by engaging in a stimulating activity like skydiving (Zuckerman, 1991). In contrast, people low in sensation-seeking motivation would have a total aversion to jumping out of an airplane, even *with* a parachute on.

Like motivational factors, personality variables can predispose people to experience certain kinds of emotions. For example, one study showed that when exposed to positive and negative events, extraverted people were likely to experience strong positive emotions in response to the positive events but tended not to have strong negative emotional reactions to negative events. In contrast, people high in the personality trait of neuroticism showed low-level positive emotional responses to positive events and strong negative responses to negative events (Larsen & Ketelaar, 1991).

■ ■
Components of Emotion

In an era of increasing interest in body–mind relations, emotion has become an area of significant research activity and theory development. Much of the

◄ **Figure 13.2** *Emotional responses communicate our internal states, and they can influence the responses of others, thereby providing the aid, comfort, or assistance we need.*

current work in emotion focuses on how the various components in Figure 13.3 function and how they relate to one another. Keeping in mind the fact that these components interact with one another as part of the total emotional response, let us consider each of the components in turn.

Eliciting Stimuli

Emotions do not occur in a vacuum. They always have objects. We cannot simply be angry, fearful,

◄ **Figure 13.3** *Components of emotion, showing the relations between eliciting stimuli, cognitive appraisal processes, physiological arousal, expressive behaviors, and instrumental behaviors. Note the reciprocal (two-way) causal relations that are thought to exist among the appraisal, physiological arousal, and expressive behavior components. Individual differences in motivation and personality can affect any of the five primary components.*

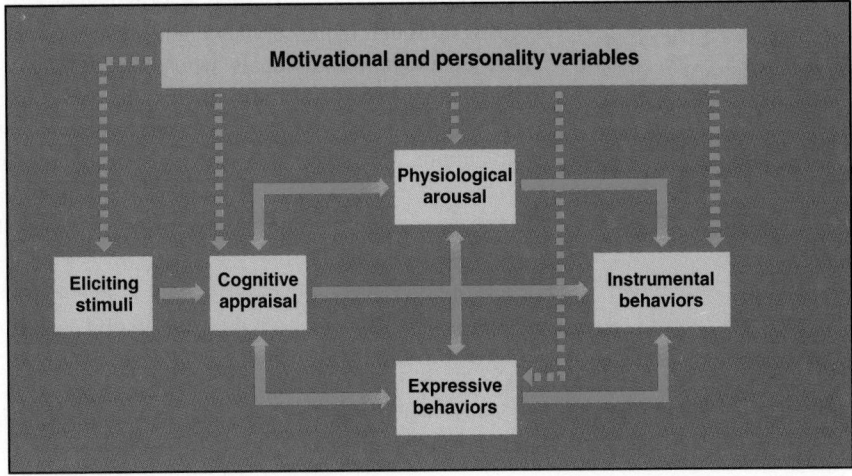

proud, or in love. We are angry *at* something or someone; fearful or proud *of* something; in love *with* someone. Moreover, the stimuli that trigger emotional responses are not always external; they can be internal stimuli in the form of images and memories. Most of us can work up a state of anger by simply recalling or imagining a painful injustice or insult from the past.

Usually we can identify the eliciting stimuli, but not always. Sometimes people feel anxious or "down in the dumps" without being sure why. As we shall see, some emotional responses are triggered more or less automatically with little or no conscious awareness on our part.

Richard Lazarus believes that each emotion has its own specific *relational theme,* or person–environment relation, which involves harms in the case of negative emotions and benefits in the case of positive ones:

> [A]ll of us have had the experience of (a) being slighted or demeaned (for anger), (b) facing existential threats (for anxiety), (c) experiencing irrevocable loss (for sadness), (d) transgressing a moral imperative (for guilt), (e) failing to live up to an ego ideal (for shame) . . . (j) making acceptable progress toward achieving a goal (for happiness), (k) experiencing enhancement of one's self, or one's social worth, by being credited for a highly valued object or accomplishment (for pride). (1991a, p. 826)

Albert Bandura (1983) has also identified eliciting stimuli, focusing in particular on the emotion of anger. According to Bandura, four major classes of events evoke anger: verbal threats or insults, physical assaults, blocking or thwarting of goal-directed behavior, and deprivation of a reward.

Learning plays an important role in how easily particular objects or people will arouse emotions. On the broadest level, cultures have different standards for defining the good, the bad, and the ugly. Physical features that provoke sexual arousal and feelings of infatuation in one culture, such as ornamental scars or rings through the nose, may elicit feelings of disgust in another. Individuals whose emotional responses to particular stimuli differ widely from the norms of their culture may be viewed as deviant. In our culture, for example, such deviance occurs in fetishists, for whom inanimate objects like shoes or handbags are eliciting stimuli for high levels of sexual arousal.

Biological factors may also affect which classes of stimuli have the greatest potential to arouse emotions. For example, the concept of *preparedness* suggests that people may be biologically primed to experience fear in response to certain stimuli, such as heights, snakes, or spiders. As we saw when we re-

viewed the research on preparedness in Chapter 9, fear responses can be more easily conditioned to some stimuli, such as snakes, than to others, such as flowers (Hygge & Öhman, 1978).

Psychodynamic theorists point out that intrapsychic factors may predispose us to react emotionally to certain stimuli that do not generally evoke that emotion in others. For example, anger that has been stored up since childhood may be released if a situation activates the relevant internal conflict. They also point out that psychological defenses sometimes result in a transformation of one emotion into another, more acceptable one. Thus, anger may be transformed into sadness or sexual feelings into fear so as to keep the person unaware of the "true" feelings.

The Cognitive Component

Cognitions are involved in virtually every aspect of emotion. They can elicit emotional responses, they are present in our interpretation of what emotion we are experiencing, and they influence how we express our emotions and act on them. An event may evoke pleasure or distress, depending on how it is appraised. For example, physically painful fatigue experienced by a marathon runner who is training for the Olympics may elicit feelings of satisfaction instead of distress if the runner appraises the pain as evidence that her body is being well conditioned for the important races that lie ahead. Similarly, sexual stimulation may evoke anger, fear, or disgust instead of pleasure if it is deemed inappropriate or unwanted.

Cognitive Appraisal

"Men are disturbed not by things, but by the views they take of them" (Epictetus, A.D. 60).

As you think, so shall you feel. As Epictetus's statement shows, this principle was known long before modern-day psychologists explored its implications in their concept of **cognitive appraisal**. Emotions are always responses to our perceptions of the eliciting stimuli. The act of perception involves attaching meaning to sensations, and our thoughts, judgments, and interpretations create the psychological reality to which we respond. For example, recent research has shown that the strongest predictors of personal happiness are cognitive rather than environmental. Numerous studies on the factors that predict life satisfaction, or *subjective well-being,* reveal that people's appraisals of their current life situations in comparison with others' circumstances, their own past circumstances, and their future aspirations are more important than objective factors like status, income, and marriage in determining how happy they are. Personal happiness is apparently to be found not in material goods but rather in one's state of mind (Myers, 1992; see Figure 13.4).

While all perceptions involve subjective interpretations of reality, the appraisals involved in emotional behavior are especially *evaluative* and *personal;* they relate to what we think is desirable or undesirable for us or for the people we care about (Lazarus, 1991b). It is important to note that we do not need to be consciously aware of the appraisals that underlie emotional responses. Some appraisals are unconscious, involving little more than the transformation of sensory input into a perception that is capable of evoking the emotional response (Lazarus, 1991a; Zajonc, 1984). After all, infants, who have no formal language, can still experience emotions. As our cognitive abilities develop, appraisals are more likely to become tied to language, whether or not we are consciously aware of their content (Izard & Malatesta, 1987).

The ability of thoughts to elicit emotional reactions has been well established in laboratory research. In one study, subjects' physiological responses were recorded while they simply read sentences that expressed anxiety (for example, "This is awful. . . . I'm getting tense"), depression ("There is nothing to look forward to"), or no emotion ("Los Angeles is south of San Francisco"). Subjects also rated their moods. The anxiety sentences were associated with increased physiological arousal and higher ratings of anxiety, while the depressive sentences triggered lowered arousal and higher ratings of depressed mood (Orton & others, 1983). In fact, the reading and imagining of written statements of this type so dependably create emotional responses that this technique has become a commonly used procedure for studying the effects of emotions in laboratory studies.

The idea that emotional reactions are triggered by cognitive appraisal rather than external situations helps to account for the fact that different people (or even the same person at different times) can have very different emotional reactions to the same object or person. Statements like "I have a new attitude toward her now" or "I've decided what's really important in life" reflect changes in appraisals of certain situations or people.

Beliefs and Emotions

Cultural learning and individual life experiences help to shape our appraisals. A clinical psychologist, Albert Ellis, suggests that some commonly held beliefs are irrational and self-defeating because they lead to unnecessary emotional distress (Ellis & Grieger, 1977). Perhaps the most basic of these core beliefs is that "it is terrible, awful, and catastrophic when things and people (including ourselves) are not the way we demand that they be." The two key ir-

⬥ **Figure 13.4** *Research has shown that the emotion of personal happiness is to be found not in material wealth, but in people's appraisals of the positive aspects of their lives in comparison with past circumstances and the lives of others.*

rational elements in this idea, according to Ellis, are that (1) things are seldom awful and catastrophic (they are more likely to be merely annoying and frustrating) and (2) it is self-defeating to turn our preferences and wants into *demands* and dire necessities. People who think in this manner tend to overreact with strong negative emotions (anger, depression, fear) when things or people are not exactly the way they "should" be. Four other irrational beliefs that Ellis has linked to emotional disturbance are listed in Table 13.1.

According to Ellis, cognition plays a central role in all emotional responses, not just negative ones. His

Table 13.1 Irrational Beliefs Responsible for Eliciting Maladaptive Emotional Responses According to Ellis

Irrational Idea		Emotional Reaction
1. It is a dire necessity for an adult to be loved by everyone for everything he or she does.	→	Anxiety and depression when someone disapproves or does not accept one.
2. One should be thoroughly competent, successful, and achieving in all possible respects.	→	Fear, self-anger, shame, and feelings of worthlessness if one fails in any way.
3. Certain people are wicked and villainous when they do not behave as we demand that they do, and they should be severely punished.	→	Anger or hatred when others behave in ways that one does not approve of.
4. If something is or may be threatening, we should be terribly upset about it.	→	Maladaptive and excessive worry, which may interfere with ability to handle the potential problem.

Source: Adapted from Ellis & Grieger, 1977.

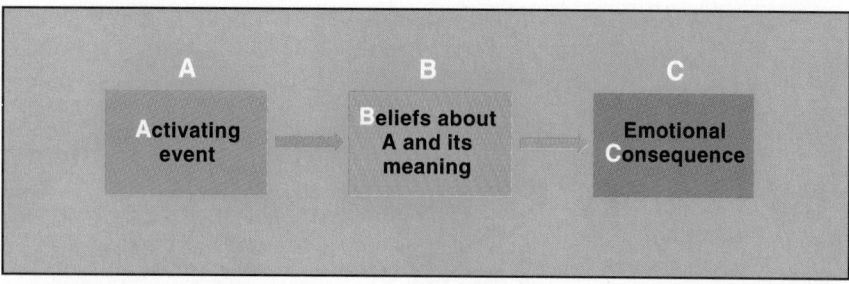

Figure 13.5 *Albert Ellis's ABC theory of emotion states that eliciting stimuli, or activating events (A), result in emotional consequences (C) because of the person's beliefs (B) about the meaning of the antecedents. In other words, situations do not cause emotional responses; rather, beliefs, or self-statements, are the true causes.*

ABC theory of emotion has three elements (see Figure 13.5). A is the activating event, and C is the emotional consequence that we experience. Most people believe that A causes C (e.g., "When he belittled me, *that* really made me angry"). In reality, Ellis maintains, A does not cause C directly. The cause is actually B, our beliefs about A. These beliefs, or self-statements, are the key to understanding how we in

Figure 13.6 *The limbic system plays a key role in emotion. The amygdala is involved in the organization of emotional responses.*

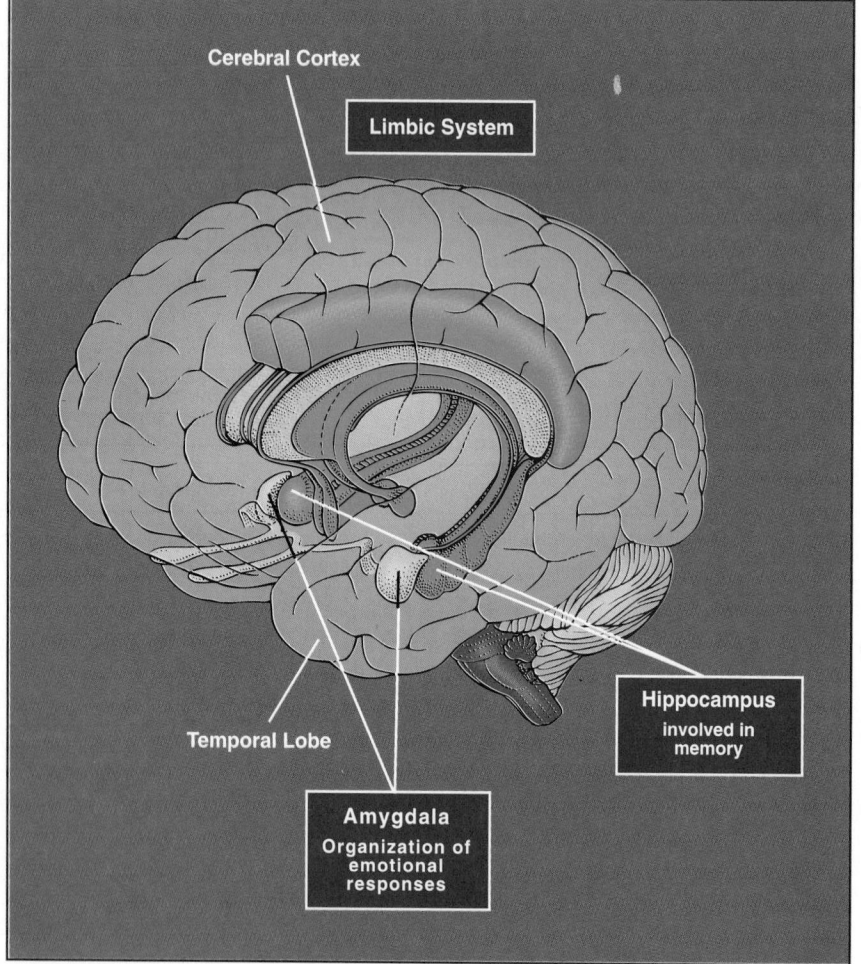

large part create our emotions. As we shall see, our self-statements are also important keys to gaining greater control over our emotions.

The Physiological Component

Perhaps the most immediately noticeable aspect of emotional experience is the physiological arousal that results when our feelings are "stirred up." Many parts of the body are involved in emotional arousal, but certain areas of the brain, the autonomic nervous system, and the endocrine system are especially significant in producing the physiological arousal that we identify with emotion.

Brain Structures and Neurotransmitters

The brain's involvement in emotion is complex, and many aspects are not well understood. It is clear, however, that the hypothalamus, as well as the amygdala and other subcortical structures known collectively as the **limbic system** play a major role (Kimble, 1992). These structures are shown in Figure 13.6. Electrical stimulation of certain areas of these structures produces unrestrained aggression, and an animal stimulated in this way will growl at and attack anything that approaches it. Destruction of the same sites produces an absence of aggression, even if the animal is provoked or attacked. Other areas of the hypothalamus and limbic system show the opposite pattern: lack of emotion when they are stimulated and unrestrained emotion when they are removed (Thompson, 1988).

Emotional reactions of varying kinds and intensities seem to color most of our interactions with the environment, and a look at the course of neural pathways in the brain may explain why. Incoming neural messages from all the senses pass through one or more of the limbic structures known to be involved in emotion: the amygdala, the hippocampus (which may store relevant memories), and part of the hypothalamus. Messages going down from the cortex also pass through these structures.

Although the details are only now beginning to unfold before the probing eyes of brain researchers, the ebb and flow of various neurotransmitter substances appear to activate the emotional programs that reside in the brain. Dopamine activity, for example, appears to underlie some of the pleasurable emotions, and endorphins may also play a role (White & Milner, 1992; Wise & Rompre, 1989). It appears that serotonin plays a role in anger, as does norepinephrine. When certain serotonin-rich tracts in the brains of cats were electrically stimulated, the animals showed intense rage (Bloom & Lazerson, 1988). Despite these linkages, however, it is unlikely that specific brain substances will be found to produce specific emotions. When the final story of the brain and emotion can at last be told, it will undoubtedly feature complex interactions between chemical molecules and systems of brain structures.

For a long time, brain researchers focused primarily on subcortical regions like the hypothalamus and limbic system. But the importance of the cerebral cortex is now being emphasized as well, as it must be if cognition is an important part of the emotional response system (Thompson, 1988; Tomkins, 1991). The cortex has many connections with the hypothalamus and limbic system, so that subcortical and cortical regions are in constant communication with one another. Moreover, cognitive appraisal processes surely involve activities in the cortex, where the mechanisms for language and complex thought reside. Cognitive and physiological processes controlled by various regions of the brain are so intimately related in emotion that all of these neural structures must be taken into account if we are to understand emotional reactions.

Hemispheric Activation and Emotion

Given the degree of specialization in the left and right cerebral hemispheres, might we expect their functioning to underlie different emotions as well? An increasing body of scientific data suggests an affirmative answer to this question.

As is so often the case, the first findings were derived from clinical observations. In Italy, clinically depressed patients were being given electroshock treatments to either the right or the left hemisphere. The electric current temporarily disabled the hemisphere to which it was applied. With the left hemisphere knocked out (allowing the right to dominate), the patients had a "catastrophic" reaction, wailing and crying until the shock effects wore off. When shock was applied to the right hemisphere, quite a different reaction occurred: They seemed happy and sometimes euphoric. A similar pattern of emotions was noted in patients in whom one hemisphere had been damaged by lesions. Left hemisphere damage, particularly in the frontal lobe, accentuated negative emotions like depression; right frontal damage was linked to indifference or euphoria (Gainotti, 1972).

These findings suggested that left-hemisphere activation might underlie certain positive emotions and right-hemisphere functioning negative ones. Recent studies by Richard Davidson of the University of Wisconsin and Nathan Fox of the University of Maryland have provided additional evidence for differential hemispheric activation during positive and negative emotions (Davidson & Fox, 1988; Fox & Davidson, 1991). EEG measures of frontal lobe activity have

shown that when subjects are experiencing positive emotions as a result of recalling pleasurable experiences or watching a happy film, the left hemisphere is relatively more active. In contrast, when sadness or other negative emotions are evoked, the right hemisphere becomes relatively more active. This pattern seems to be innate. Infants 3 to 4 days old show a similar pattern of hemispheric activation when given sucrose solutions, which evoke positive reactions, or a citric acid solution, which apparently disgusts them (Davidson & Fox, 1988).

A similar pattern of right hemisphere activation has been found in 10-month old infants who show a tendency to become distressed. Davidson and Fox (1989) measured resting electrical activity in infants while their mothers were present. Then the mother abruptly left the room. About half of the infants reacted to separation from their mothers with distress and crying. The others did not. Davidson and Fox were interested in whether the brain activation patterns that they measured during the baseline period would predict which infants would later respond with distress. As Figure 13.7 shows, the infants who became distressed had relatively greater right-hemisphere activation *before* mother left (even though behavioral ratings of the criers and noncriers during this baseline period indicated no notable differences in outward emotional expression). In contrast, these infants with the more placid temperaments had relatively greater activity in the left hemisphere. It thus appears possible that temperamental differences among infants might be linked to individual differences in the electrochemical activity of the two hemispheres.

On the basis of the evidence linking hemispheric activity with positive and negative states, Fox and Davidson (1991) have proposed a developmental model of emotion. They suggest that the left and right frontal regions of the brain are the respective sites for "approach" and "avoidance/withdrawal" tendencies, which are the underlying bases for positive and negative emotions. At birth, the approach and avoidance tendencies are expressed as interest and disgust. With increased interhemispheric communication and other maturational changes, more complex emotions, such as fear, jealousy, and sadness appear, reflecting an interaction or blending of activity in the two hemispheres. ▼

Autonomic and Hormonal Processes

You are afraid. Your heart starts to beat faster. Blood is drawn from your stomach, and digestion slows to a crawl as the blood flow to your muscles and the surface of your skin is increased. You breathe harder and faster to get more oxygen. Your blood sugar level is elevated, producing more nutrients for your mus-

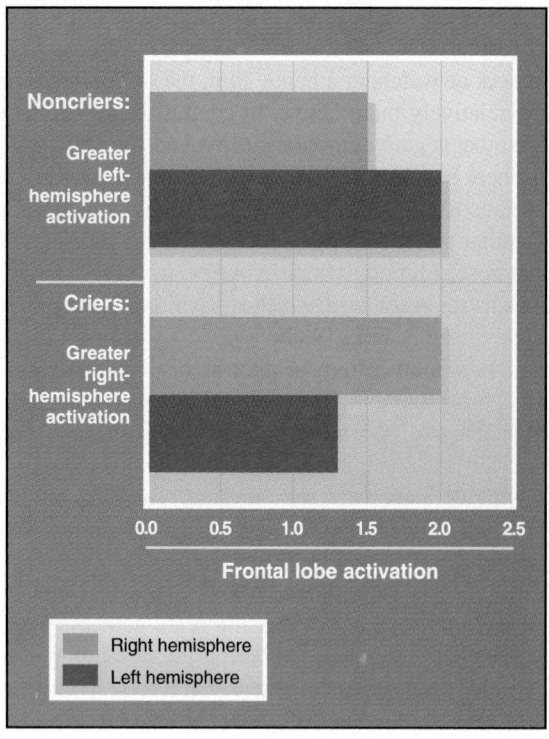

Figure 13.7 *Resting activation of the left and right frontal hemispheres differed in infants who later reacted with distress or no distress when their mothers left. The criers showed relatively greater right hemisphere activation, the noncriers greater left hemisphere activation. (Davidson & Fox, 1989).*

Noncriers:

Greater left-hemisphere activation

Criers:

Greater right-hemisphere activation

0.0   0.5   1.0   1.5   2.0   2.5

Frontal lobe activation

▢ Right hemisphere
▢ Left hemisphere

cles. The pupils of your eyes dilate to let in more light so you can see the danger better. Your skin perspires to keep you cool and to flush out waste products created by extra exertion. Your muscles tense, ready for action.

Some theorists call this state of arousal the **fight-or-flight response** (see Figure 13.8). The arousal is produced by the activity of the sympathetic branch of the autonomic nervous system and by hormones from the endocrine system. The sympathetic nervous system produces its effects within a few seconds by directly stimulating body organs. The endocrine system pumps stress hormones such as adrenaline into the bloodstream. These hormones produce physiological effects like those triggered by the sympathetic nervous system, and their presence in the blood can keep the body aroused for a considerable length of time.

We have already seen that hemispheric activation underlies positive and negative emotions. Do different emotions produce different patterns of autonomic nervous system arousal as well? After 30 years of research using increasingly sophisticated measures of physiological arousal, the answer is still not totally clear. Many investigators have concluded that specific emotions, especially the more complex ones like jealousy and tenderness, do not result in distinct patterns of arousal (Mandler, 1984). Recent evidence suggests that autonomic patterns do differ somewhat in certain basic emotions, but the differences are rather subtle. For example, the heart rate increases in both fear and anger, but there are differences in where the blood gets pumped. Anger causes more blood to flow to the hands and feet, whereas fear reduces blood flow to these areas (Ekman & others, 1983). (Thus, we now have scientific support for the colloquial notion of "cold feet.") Recently, it was also discovered that the temperature of the forehead is associated with positive and negative feelings; cooling is associated with pleasant states and warming with unpleasant states (Zajonc & others, 1989). Whether such differences in blood flow can be detected by people in a manner that would contribute to their experience of specific emotions is an unanswered question (Adelmann & Zajonc, 1989).

The role of physiological arousal in emotion has another layer of complexity: People differ from one another in their patterns of general arousal (Lacey & Lacey, 1970). For example, we don't all show the same pattern of bodily arousal when we are afraid. If our physiological responses were recorded, some of us would show marked changes in heart rate or blood pressure but only minor changes in other responses, such as muscle tension and respiration. Others would show different patterns. Researchers have learned that no single physiological measure is appropriate for all subjects; it is important to measure as many autonomic indicators as possible.

The **polygraph,** an instrument that can measure a wide range of physiological responses, has been a valuable research tool for many years. Because people have less control over physiological responses than over many other behaviors, the polygraph is regarded by some as a nearly infallible means of establishing whether or not someone is telling the truth. However,

Figure 13.8 *An important part of many emotional responses is the physiological arousal state that mobilizes the body to respond with the fight-or-flight response.*

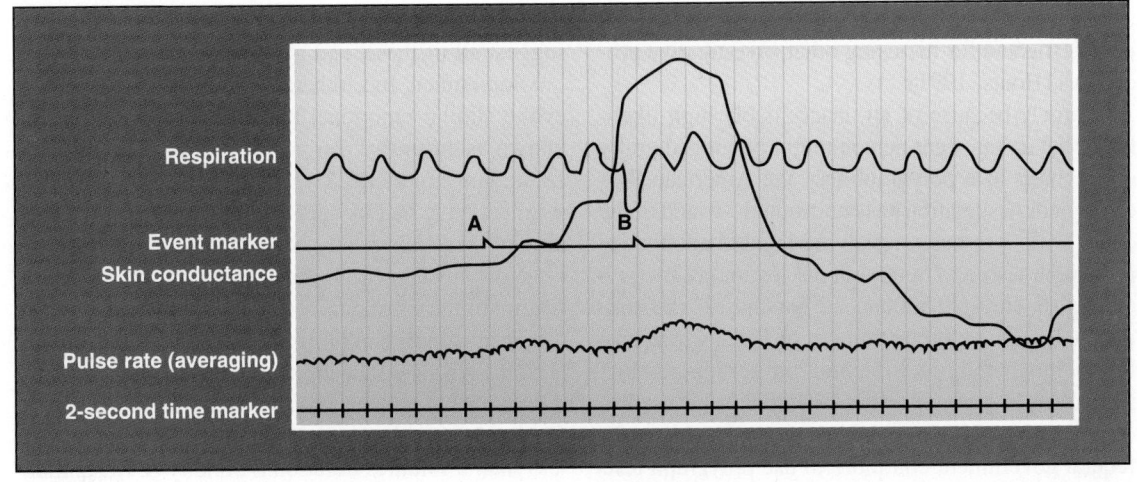

(a)

(b)

Figure 13.9 *The polygraph records physiological changes that are part of emotional responses* (a). *Between points A and B, an emotionally loaded question was asked. Within 2 seconds, the effects of the question were visible in the subject's respiration, skin conductance, and pulse rate. Does this mean he was lying? In part b a polygraph test is carried out.*

this approach to detecting "lying" has some definite shortcomings.

Use of the polygraph as a "lie detector" is based on the fact that emotional arousal is accompanied by certain physiological responses. Figure 13.9 is a portion of a polygraph record showing measures of respiration, electrical skin conductance (which increases in emotion due to sweat gland activity), and heart rate. Polygraph examiners compare physiological responses to critical questions relating to the activities of interest with responses to control questions. In this case, note the changes that occurred on the autonomic measures when an emotionally loaded question was asked (point A to point B).

This emotional response does not necessarily mean that the subject was lying, and herein lies one major problem with polygraph tests. Innocent people may appear guilty when doubt, fear, or lack of confidence increase the activity level of the autonomic nervous system. As David Lykken, a leading critic of the lie detector has noted, "polygraph pens do no special dance when we are lying" (1981, p. 10). People being tested, can also "beat" the polygraph by biting their tongues or contracting their anal sphincters when control questions are asked, producing an arousal response to those questions as well, or by distracting themselves by counting backward by sevens each time the examiner asks a question. William Casey, former director of the CIA, used to delight in his ability to fool the lie detector (Carlson & Hatfield, 1992). A prison convict named Fred Fay, who had been falsely convicted of murder partly on the basis of a polygraph test that indicated he was guilty, became an expert at defeating polygraph tests. On one occasion, he coached 27 fellow inmates who were scheduled for polygraph tests. All of the inmates told Fay they were guilty of the relevant crimes; yet after only 20 minutes of instruction, 23 of the 27 inmates managed to beat the polygraph (Lykken, 1981). In

reality, then, there is no such thing as an infallible lie detector.

This conclusion is supported by research in which experienced polygraph examiners are given the polygraph records of suspects known to be either innocent or guilty on the basis of other evidence and are asked to decide the guilt or innocence of the suspects. The results of these investigations show that the examiners often do quite well in identifying the guilty, with an accuracy rate of 80–98 percent (Honts & Perry, 1992). However, they do less well in identifying the innocent, with anywhere from 10 to 55 percent of the innocent suspects being judged guilty by the experts (Honts & Perry, 1992; Kleinmuntz & Szucko, 1984b; Lykken, 1984). These results call into question the adage that an innocent person has nothing to fear from a polygraph test. On the other hand, the test may be useful for narrowing the number of suspects who can be investigated further using other investigative procedures (Honts, 1991).

Largely because of an unacceptably high likelihood that an innocent person might be judged guilty on the basis of a polygraph test, the American Psychological Association has contributed ''friend of the court'' briefs in cases involving legal challenges to polygraph testing. Congressional testimony by psychologists strongly influenced passage of the Employee Polygraph Protection Act of 1988, which prohibits most nongovernmental polygraph testing. Moreover, polygraph tests alone cannot be used to convict people of crimes in most states. However, the federal government continues to use polygraph tests in internal criminal investigations and in national security screening. Their use for hiring and security clearance decisions has been shown to lack validity (Honts, 1991).

The Behavioral Component

So far, we have examined the situational, cognitive, and physiological components of emotion. We now turn to the all-important behaviors that are part of emotional responses. Because both expressive and instrumental behaviors are externally observable, they are easier to study scientifically than the more hidden elements of emotion that we already considered.

Expressive Behaviors

A child is dying. His frail body, ravaged by leukemia, grows weaker each day. His family, consumed with pain and dread, awaits the inevitable.

> Early one evening Ben's breathing became gradually more shallow. With his parents and sister gently holding him, Ben died. Still holding her brother's hand and through a torrent of tears, Sandy broke the eerie silence that followed.
> ''I can't believe Ben's gone, that he's not here. Why did he have to die? It's not fair!''
> ''It isn't fair, Sandy. It's not fair at all. Go ahead and cry for Ben because you love him and because it's the only thing that makes any sense.''
> For several minutes they sat with Ben's body, all saying their silent goodbyes. A huge part of their world had come to an end. Things would never be the same again (Garfield, 1979, p. 317).

Although we can never directly experience another person's feelings, we can often infer that someone is angry, sad, fearful, or happy on the basis of his or her emotional displays, or **expressive behaviors.** What emotions was Sandy experiencing as she held her brother's lifeless hand? Grief? Anger?

Disbelief? Her verbal behavior and her tears might suggest all of these, and perhaps others.

Sometimes, too, others' emotional displays can evoke similar emotional responses in us, a process known as **empathy.** Perhaps when you read this account, you experienced some of the feelings the family must have had by identifying with their loss and moving psychologically closer to them.

Not only are expressive behaviors an important feature of the emotional response, but they also serve as social stimuli that influence the behavior of others (Lazarus, 1984). Indeed, people can make broad interpersonal judgments with a high degree of accuracy from videotaped samples of expressive behaviors of less than 5 minutes duration (Ambody & Rosenthal, 1992). Because expressive behaviors play an important role in the regulation of social behavior, their origins and features have been an important topic of research and theory for many years.

Evolution and Emotional Expression. Where do emotional expressions come from? One answer is offered from the biological perspective. In a classic work, *The Expression of Emotions in Man and Animals* (1872/1965), Charles Darwin argued that emotional displays are products of evolution and that they developed because they contributed to species survival. Darwin emphasized the basic similarity of emotional expression from lower animals to humans. For example, both wolves and humans bare their teeth when they are angry. As Darwin explained it, this behavior makes the animal look more ferocious and thus decreases its chances of being attacked and perhaps killed in a fight. Darwin did not maintain that all forms of emotional expression are innate, or unlearned, but he believed that many of them are.

As an example of the adaptive significance of innate emotional displays, consider the effects of a baby's crying and smiling on adults. Parents report feeling irritated, annoyed, disturbed, distressed, sympathetic, and unhappy when their babies cry. Physiological arousal also increases in the presence of a crying infant (Frodi & others, 1978). Adults generally respond to crying infants with caretaking responses that have obvious survival value for the infant. On the other hand, a smiling infant is likely to increase parents' feelings of love and caring, thereby increasing the chances that the child's needs will be satisfied.

Not only Darwin but also some modern theorists stress the evolutionary significance of emotional expression (Izard, 1984; Plutchik, 1980; Tomkins, 1991). The expression of certain emotions (for example, rage and friendliness) is similar across a variety of cultures, suggesting that certain **fundamental emotional patterns** are wired into the nervous system. Other emotions are seen as resulting from some combination of these innate emotions. The fundamental emotional patterns proposed by three leading evolutionary theorists—Carroll Izard, Silvan Tomkins, and Robert Plutchik—are shown in Table 13.2.

Infant Emotions. The filming and study of facial movements in infants indicate that they bring certain emotional expressions into the world with them and that several others appear soon afterward. Facial expressions of pain, interest, and disgust, as well as the newborn smile, are present at birth. The social smile appears at 3 to 4 weeks, sadness and anger at about 2 months, and fear by 6 or 7 months (Izard & Malatesta, 1987). Each of these facial expressions communicates a distinct message to the caregiver about the infant's internal states, and they form the basis for social interaction. Infants' expressions of the positive emotions attract caregivers' attention and contribute to parent–infant attachment. The expressions of negative emotions guide caregivers in their attempts to alleviate stress and satisfy momentary needs. Research shows that mothers can distinguish their infants' expressions of pain, anger, and sadness and that they respond differently to each one (Huebner & Izard, 1988).

One argument for the existence of innate expressive patterns is that children who are blind from birth seem to express emotions in the same ways that sighted children do (Eibl-Eibesfeldt, 1973). Again, however, it is important to emphasize that the evolutionary view does not assume that *all* emotional expressions are innate, nor does it deny that innate emotional expressions can be modified or inhibited as a result of social learning.

Facial Expressions of Emotion. Most of us have a fair degree of confidence in our ability to "read" the emotions of others. Although many parts of the body can communicate feelings, we tend to concentrate on what the face tells us. Most lower animals have relatively few facial muscles, so they are limited in their facial expressions of emotion. Only monkeys, apes, and humans have enough well-developed facial muscles to produce large numbers of expressions.

Interest in the study of facial expressions has been spurred by the development of sophisticated measurement procedures, such as the **Facial Action Coding System (FACS).** Developed by Paul Ekman and Wallace Friesen of the University of California, San Francisco, the FACS requires a trained observer to dissect an observed expression in terms of all the muscular actions that produced it (Ekman & Friesen, 1978). The system is so complex that it takes about 100 minutes to score each minute of observed facial expression (Ekman & others, 1988).

Common lore has it that the eyes are particularly good sources of information about what is being felt:

Table 13.2 Fundamental or Primary Innate Emotions Proposed by Three Leading Evolutionary Theorists

Carroll Izard	Silvan Tomkins	Robert Plutchik
Anger	Anger	Anger
Fear	Fear	Fear
Joy	Joy	Enjoyment
Disgust	Disgust	Disgust
Interest	Interest	Anticipation
Surprise	Surprise	Surprise
Contempt	Contempt	
Shame	Shame	
	Sadness	Sadness
	Distress	
Guilt		
		Acceptance

Source: Based on Izard (1989); Tomkins (1991); and Plutchik (1986).

"If looks could kill;" "the look of love;" "there's red-hot anger in his eyes;" "her eyes twinkled with amusement." Research tells us, however, that other parts of the face are at least as important, if not more so. In fact, it appears that different emotions are expressed through different parts of the face.

In one experiment, judges first agreed on the emotions being expressed in a set of 32 posed facial photographs. Each photograph was then cut into three parts—a brow–forehead part, an eyes part, and a mouth part. These partial photos were shown to a group of subjects, who were asked to rate each in terms of six emotions: anger, fear, happiness, surprise, sadness, and disgust. The results showed that different parts of the face provided the best cues for recognizing the various emotions. The eyes provided the most important cues for fear and sadness, but the mouth was the major cue for happiness and disgust, while the forehead was the best indicator of surprise. Anger appeared to be a more complex emotion; observers required information from all facial areas to recognize it accurately (Boucher & Ekman, 1975).

Although facial expressions can be valuable cues for judging emotion, people show learned differences in their facial expressions of emotion. Fortunately, we usually have more than facial cues on which to base our judgments. We usually know something about the situation to which the person is reacting, and this seems to be a particularly important basis for judgment. Many experiments have shown that subjects' accuracy and agreement in labeling emotions from pictures is considerably higher when the pictures show a background situation. For example, if a woman is crying, is she crying because of sadness or because of happiness? A background showing her being declared the winner of a lottery will result in a different emotional judgment than one showing her at a graveside.

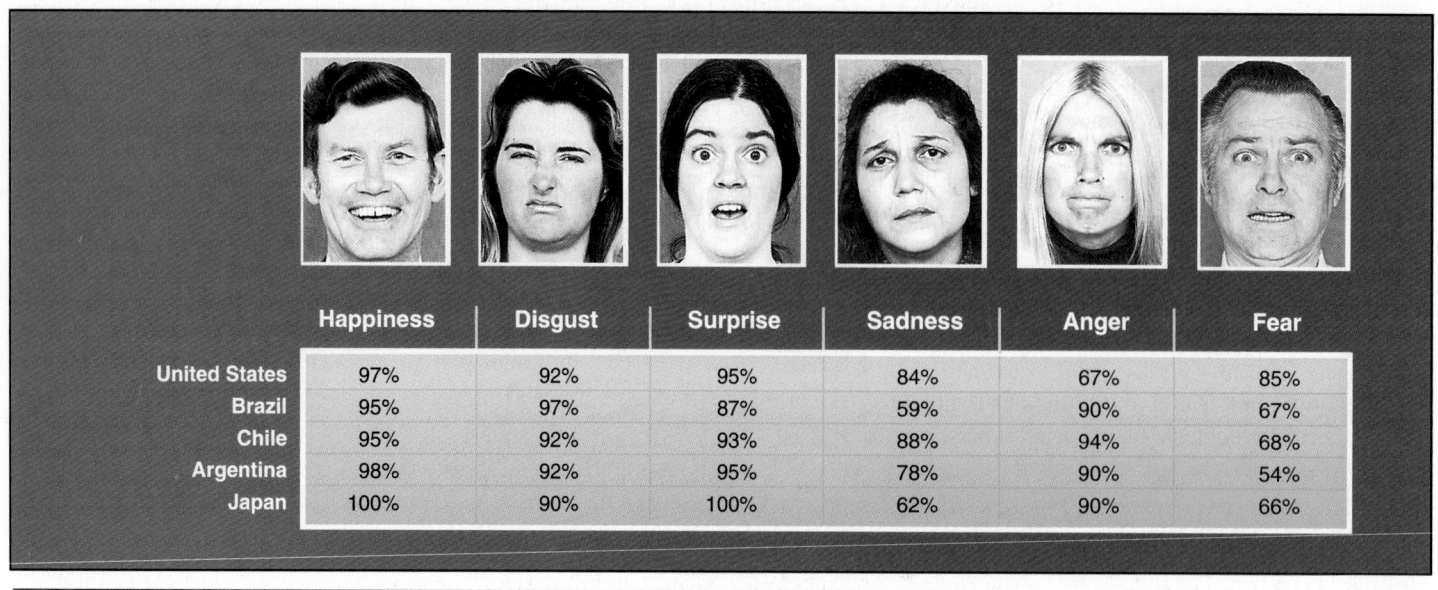

	Happiness	Disgust	Surprise	Sadness	Anger	Fear
United States	97%	92%	95%	84%	67%	85%
Brazil	95%	97%	87%	59%	90%	67%
Chile	95%	92%	93%	88%	94%	68%
Argentina	98%	92%	95%	78%	90%	54%
Japan	100%	90%	100%	62%	90%	66%

Figure 13.10 *Percentage of agreement in judgments of facial expressions of emotion by subjects in five different cultures. (Ekman, 1973).*

It is interesting to note that across many cultures, women have proven to be more accurate judges of emotional expressions than men (Ekman, 1982; Zuckerman, 1976). Perhaps the ability to accurately read the emotions of others has some adaptive evolutionary significance for women, whose traditional role within many cultures has been to care for others and attend to their needs (Buss, 1991). It is also possible that this ability results from cultural encouragement of women to be sensitive to the emotions of others and to express their feelings openly. However, men who work in professions such as psychology, psychiatry, drama, and art are as accurate as women are (Rosenthal & others, 1974).

What of Darwin's claim that certain facial expressions are universal indicators of specific emotions? Darwin himself observed facial displays in many cultures during more than 30 years of world travel, and he became convinced that there are universal expressions. More recently, Paul Ekman and his coworkers (1987) and Carroll Izard (1977) have approached this question by investigating how much people in different cultures agree on the emotions being expressed in facial photographs. The results of one such study are shown in Figure 13.10. Researchers have consistently found high (but not perfect) levels of agreement across a variety of cultures.

In other studies, they have found that the FACS can readily detect differences between real expressions of an emotion and faked ones (Ekman & others, 1988). Can you tell which smile in Figure 13.11 is the real smile of happiness? A hint: Real smiles of pleasure involve the muscles that orbit the eye as well as the muscles that pull up the corners of the lips. This smile has been termed the *Duchenne smile*, after

the French anatomist who identified it on the basis of extensive studies of facial musculature (Ekman & others, 1990). There are also cross-cultural similarities in the ability to discriminate between real and faked emotions.

Cultural Factors and Display Rules. Some expressions of emotion, such as the Duchenne smile, seem to be the same all over the world. However, the culture we grow up in also strongly influences what form our emotional expressions take.

Certain gestures. body postures, and physical movements can convey dramatically different meanings in different cultures. For example, using our familiar upright thumb gesture while hitchhiking in certain regions of Greece and Sardinia could result in decidedly negative consequences. In those parts, an upright thumb is the equivalent of a raised middle finger in our culture (Morris & others, 1979). As another example, being spat on is a sign of contempt in most cultures. Yet the Masai tribe of Africa traditionally considered being spat on a great compliment, particularly if the person doing the spitting was a member of the opposite sex (Thomson, 1887).

Do emotional expressions differ across cultures in the same way that gestures do? Apparently, to some extent, they do. A number of theorists, including Silvan Tomkins (1991), Paul Ekman (1971), and Carroll Izard (1989), have proposed that not only innate factors but also cultural display rules shape emotional expression. As we have already seen, there is strong evidence that certain emotions are expressed in much the same way in all cultures, suggesting that such expressions are innate. But the **display rules** of a culture dictate when and how such emotions are to

be expressed. For example, some Asian cultures, such as the Japanese, are more subdued in their expression of emotion in public settings than Americans are.

An experiment by Ekman, Wallace Friesen, and Phoebe Ellsworth (1972) illustrates cultural commonalities and differences in emotional expression. Japanese and American students viewed a highly stressful film in private, not knowing that their facial expressions were being videotaped by a hidden camera. Their expressions were coded by means of the facial affect scoring technique that measures the movement of muscles in various regions of the face. The measurement procedure yields frequency and duration scores for six emotions: happiness, anger, sadness, surprise, fear, and disgust.

Analysis of the facial displays showed no differences between the Japanese and American students for any of the emotions; they reacted emotionally and expressed their emotions in much the same way. Afterward, however, the students were individually interviewed concerning their reactions to the film. The American students were interviewed by an American, the Japanese by a Japanese interviewer. Again, their facial expressions were photographed by a hidden camera. When these facial expressions were coded, major differences were found between the Americans and the Japanese. During the interview, the Japanese masked their feelings and presented a happy face throughout. In contrast, the Americans clearly registered their disgust and anxiety; their facial expressions closely mirrored those photographed as they watched the stressful movie. The study demonstrates the roles that biology and culture play in emotional expression. Biological universals are evident in how people "naturally" respond emotionally, but cultural display rules can influence when, where, and how people express their feelings.

Instrumental Behaviors

Emotional responses are often "calls to action," requiring some sort of response to the situation that aroused the emotion. A highly anxious student must find some way to cope with an impending test. A mother angered by her child's behavior must find a nondestructive way to get her point across. A basketball player attempting a game-winning free throw must concentrate and shoot the ball with a fluid motion despite a high level of emotional arousal. These are **instrumental behaviors** directed at achieving some goal.

Emotional Arousal and Performance.

It is sometimes assumed that high levels of emotional arousal enhance performance. Athletic teams sometimes try to "psych themselves up" for important games. A coach who is highly effective at locker-room pep talks may get his team so aroused that it will almost literally run through the walls to get at the "enemy." Yet we also know that a team can get too "high." After his team had shot very poorly and lost an important tournament game, a college basketball coach explained, "Our kids were so high for this game that they grew five thumbs on each hand." But another coach who lost in the same tournament accounted for his team's poor performance by saying, "We had no intensity. We were completely flat."

Clearly, then, arousal can be either too high or too low. In many situations, the relation between emotional arousal and performance seems to take the shape of an upside-down, or inverted, U (Smith & Smoll, 1990). As physiological arousal increases up to some optimal level, performance improves. But beyond that optimal level, further increases in arousal impair performance. It is thus possible to be either too "flat" or too "high" to perform well.

Figure 13.11 *One of these smiles reflects true happiness; the other is faked. Can you tell which is which? Recent research using the FACS indicates that it is very difficult to fake emotions. The photo on the left shows a Duchenne smile; note the activity of the muscles around the eyes as well as those that raise the corners of the lips. The expression in photo on the right contains a hint of disgust because of the slight raising of the upper lip. (Ekman & others, 1988).*

The Role of Task Difficulty. There is yet another factor that must be taken into account: the complexity of the task. The optimal level of emotional arousal depends on how difficult or complex the task is. A very high level of arousal may help us to perform a simple task, such as running, but might interfere with performance on a more complex task, such as taking a difficult examination or performing a complex gymnastics routine.

This relation between optimal arousal and task difficulty was recognized early in the history of experimental psychology and formalized as the **Yerkes–Dodson law** (Yerkes & Dodson, 1908). The Yerkes–Dodson law has two parts. First, it states that for every task, there is an optimal level of arousal for maximum performance. (This is the inverted U curve just discussed.) Second, it states that the more difficult the task is, the lower is the optimal level of arousal for maximum performance.

These two principles are illustrated in Figure 13.12. Note that the inverted U relation applies for all three tasks and that the more difficult the task, the lower the optimal arousal level. One other feature of Figure 13.12 is worth noting: Performance drops off less at high levels of arousal for the simple task than for the others. In fact, even the highest levels of arousal can enhance performance of very simple tasks. Sometimes the results are quite astounding. In one case, a 102-pound mother in a highly distraught state reportedly lifted up the front end of a panel truck in order to free her child, who was trapped under one of its wheels (Honolulu *Star-Bulletin,* January 6, 1980). Laboratory studies have produced nothing so dramatic as this anecdotal account, but they too have shown that high levels of arousal can enhance performance on simple tasks such as lifting and running (Smith & Smoll, 1990).

For complex tasks, the relation between arousal and performance is different. High emotionality can interfere with attentional and information processing requirements of such tasks, and muscle tension can interfere with the skillful execution of complex movements. The harmful effects of anxiety on the performance of a highly complex task was demonstrated in a sport psychology study by Robert Weinberg and Marvin Genuchi (1980). The setting was an intercollegiate golf tournament. The tendency of the competitors to experience anxiety during matches was measured by questionnaire before the tournament began, and players who were low, moderate, and high in competition anxiety were identified. Although the three groups of golfers were similar in ability, the researchers found that their golf scores differed sharply during the anxiety-arousing tournament rounds. On the first day of competition, the average performance of the low-anxiety group was five strokes better than the performance of the high-

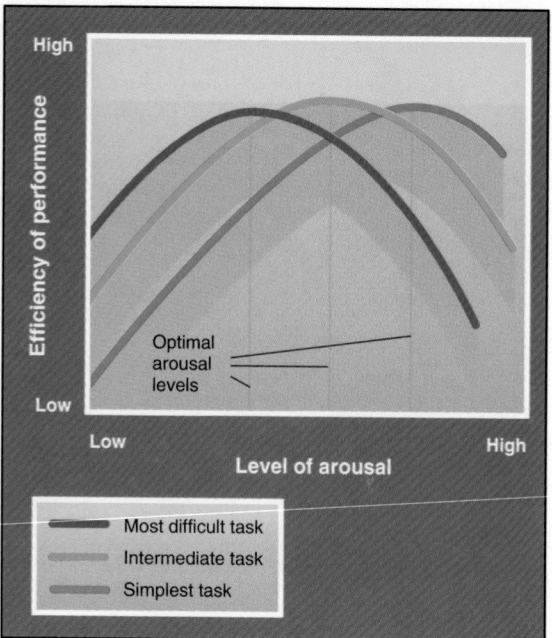

(a)

(b)

⬆ **Figure 13.12** *The Yerkes–Dodson law states that the relation between arousal and performance takes the form of an inverted U, with performance declining above and below an optimal arousal level (a). The law further states that the more difficult or complex a task is, the lower is the optimal level of arousal for performing it. For example, a complex activity like golf probably has a much lower optimal level than one like sprinting (b).*

anxiety group. On the last day of the tournament, the difference between the two groups rose to nearly seven strokes. The moderate-anxiety group had intermediate scores. These results indicate that high levels of anxiety are especially likely to impair performance on a highly complex and difficult motor task, such as golf. High anxiety also impairs performance on complex mental tasks, such as taking college tests (Sarason & Sarason, 1990).

The components of emotion provide important clues to the causal determinants of emotional states. As we have seen, biological, environmental, cognitive, and intrapsychic factors can play important roles. The determinants discussed thus far are applied to the emotion of anger in the accompanying Understanding Causes feature (page 414). As the feature emphasizes, the causal factors in anger (like those in other emotions) interact with one another in complex ways. We now turn to these all-important interactions.

Interactions Among the Components of Emotion

Speculations concerning how the environmental, cognitive, physiological, and behavioral components of emotion relate to one another have given rise to several prominent theories of emotion. We now consider several classical and contemporary theories, showing how they have influenced research.

The James–Lange Theory

Consider the following statement:

> Common sense says . . . we meet a bear, are frightened, and run; we are insulted by a rival, are angry, and strike. The hypothesis here to be defended says that this order of sequence is incorrect . . . and that the more rational statement is that we feel sorry because we cry, angry because we strike, afraid because we tremble (James, 1890/1950, p. 451).

This statement, made by William James in 1890, ushered in more than a century of research and theory concerning relations among the cognitive, physiological, and behavioral components of emotion. At about the same time that James advanced his theory, a Danish psychologist named Carl Lange reached the similar conclusion that body reactions form the basis for our labeling and experiencing of emotions. The two theorists differed, however, in their notions of which bodily responses were important. Lange restricted his emotional determinants to cardiovascular responses,

whereas James thought that any combination of somatic and autonomic responses, including cardiovascular ones, could produce the experiencing of different emotions.

The James–Lange theory is the historical precursor of today's **somatic theory of emotion** (Papanicolaou, 1989). This theory holds that when people encounter an emotion-arousing stimulus, their bodies react instantaneously with physiological arousal, expressive behaviors, and instrumental behaviors. Any or all of these bodily (somatic) responses give rise to the experience of emotion. In other words, we know we are afraid or in love only because our bodily reactions tell us so (see Figure 13.13).

The Cannon–Bard Theory

It wasn't long before the James–Lange theory was challenged. In 1927, a physiologist, Walter Cannon, noted that people's bodies do *not* respond instantaneously to an emotional stimulus; several seconds may pass before signs of physiological arousal appear. Yet they often experience the emotion immediately. This would be impossible according to the James–Lange theory.

In place of the James–Lange theory, Cannon and L. L. Bard advanced their own. The **Cannon–Bard theory** proposed that the thalamus, a major relay station for sensory input, plays a key role in both emotional experience and physiological arousal. According to Cannon and Bard, when an emotion-arousing situation is encountered, the thalamus simultaneously

Figure 13.13 *Two early theories of emotion continue to influence current-day theorizing. The James–Lange theory holds that the experience of emotion is caused by somatic feedback and physiological arousal. According to the Cannon–Bard theory, the thalamus receives sensory input and simultaneously stimulates physiological responses and cognitive awareness.*

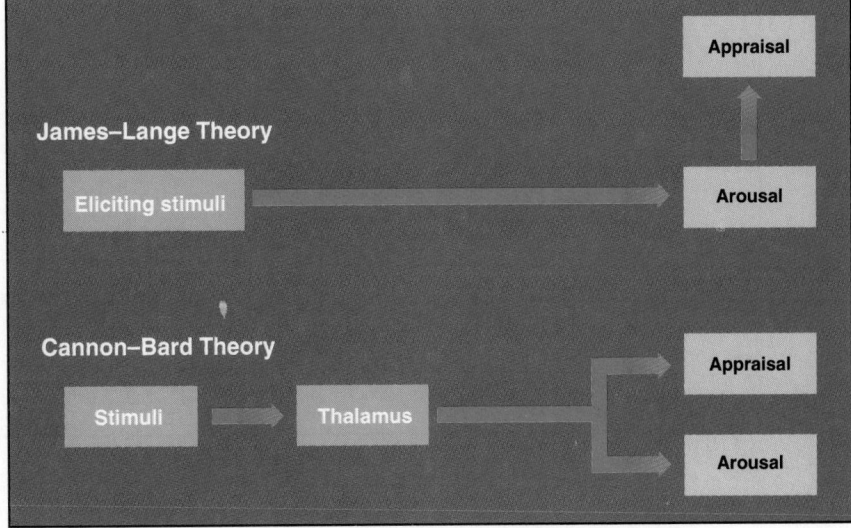

Anger:
Factors Suggested by Theory and Research

$B = f(P, E)$

Causal Factors

Biological
- Cortical activities involved in appraisal
- Activation of limbic system structures involved in anger
- "Angry" facial expressions that trigger emotional response
- Relative activation of the left hemisphere (negative emotions)

Cognitive
- Appraisal of being intentionally hurt by another
- Conviction that a person or situation ought to be different
- Belief that someone deserves to be hurt or punished

Intrapsychic
- Angry responses to immediate need-frustration or hurt
- Release of stored anger related to past conflicts or unmet needs
- Defensive transformation of other impulses (e.g., sexual) into anger

Environmental
- Environmental obstacles to goal attainment or need satisfaction
- Physical or verbal attack by another
- Cultural learning of when and how to display anger
- Past reinforcement or lack of punishment for anger displays

Anger

Anger is a function of interacting personal and environmental causal factors. These factors may vary and may interact with one another in particular ways, depending on the person and the situation.

sends messages to the cerebral cortex and to the body's internal organs (see Figure 13.13). The message to the cortex produces the experience of emotion, and the one to the internal organs produces the physiological arousal. Thus, neither cognition nor arousal causes the other; they are independent responses to stimulation from the thalamus.

According to the James–Lange theory, people should not experience emotion unless they receive feedback from their bodies' reactions to eliciting stimuli. In contrast, the Cannon–Bard theory maintains that the experiencing of emotions results from signals sent from the thalamus to the cortex. Is there any situation that would provide a test of how necessary feedback from the body is?

In fact, there is. People with severed spinal cords receive no sensory feedback from the body areas below the injury. If emotional experience is produced by body responses, as the James–Lange theory maintains, then these individuals should experience little in the way of emotions. In a University of Illinois study, Kathleen Chwalisz, Ed Diener, and Dennis Gallagher (1988) interviewed and administered measures of emotional experience to subjects who had sustained spinal injuries. For comparison, the same measures were administered to subjects with other handicaps that did not affect autonomic feedback, and to a group of nonhandicapped subjects. As shown in Figure 13.14, the subjects with spinal injuries did not differ from the other two groups in the intensity with which they reportedly experienced either positive or negative emotions. Other analyses showed no differences in the intensity of emotions experienced by subjects with high and low spinal injuries, whose injury sites caused them to differ in the amount of bodily feedback they could receive. Moreover, subjects with spinal injuries reported that they frequently experienced very intense emotions—sometimes emo-

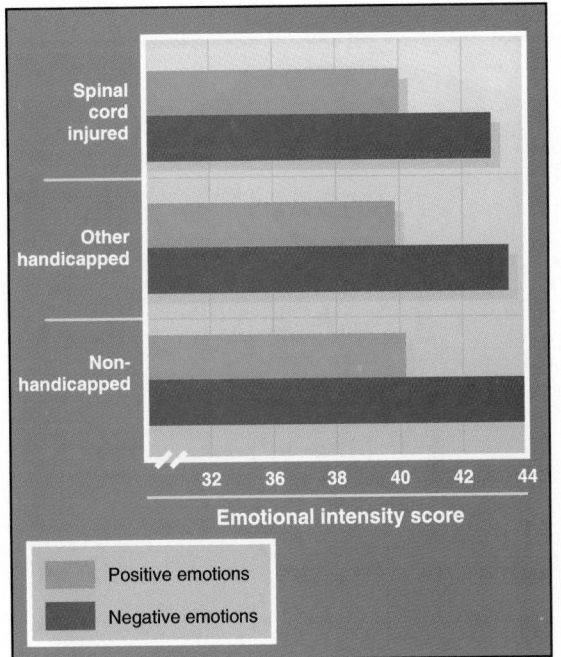

Figure 13.14 *Intensity of positive and negative emotions reported by subjects with spinal injuries, by handicapped subjects with no spinal damage, and by nonhandicapped subjects. The lack of differences casts doubt on the assertion that feedback from physiological arousal is essential for the experiencing of normal emotional responses. (Data from Chwalisz & others, 1988).*

tions more intense than those they had experienced before their injuries. These results appear to cast doubt on the claim that arousal feedback from the body is absolutely necessary in order for people to experience intense emotions.

Arousal feedback, however, is not the only kind of body feedback considered important by the somatic theory. While it appears that emotions can occur in the absence of autonomic feedback, the somatic theory has attracted renewed interest as a result of recent findings that another form of body feedback—that provided by the actions of the facial muscles—may exert an important influence on emotional experience. We explore this new evidence in the following feature.

PSYCHOBIOLOGICAL INTERACTIONS

The Facial Feedback Hypothesis

To many psychologists, the James–Lange theory seemed until recently to be little more than a historical curiosity. There was little evidence that different emotions had different patterns of autonomic arousal that could tell people what emotion they were experiencing. Moreover, studies done with animals in the 1920s showed that even if the nerves leading from the internal organs of the body were severed so that the brain received no feedback from them, the animals continued to exhibit emotional responses.

All but forgotten in the wave of findings that cast doubt on the necessity of autonomic arousal was the possible role of muscular movements, including those of the face. Like autonomic responses, facial muscles also feed messages to the brain when they are activated, and they are active even in patients with spinal injuries who may receive no sensory input from below the neck. We have seen evidence suggesting that certain facial muscle patterns are almost universally linked to different emotions. Could facial expres-

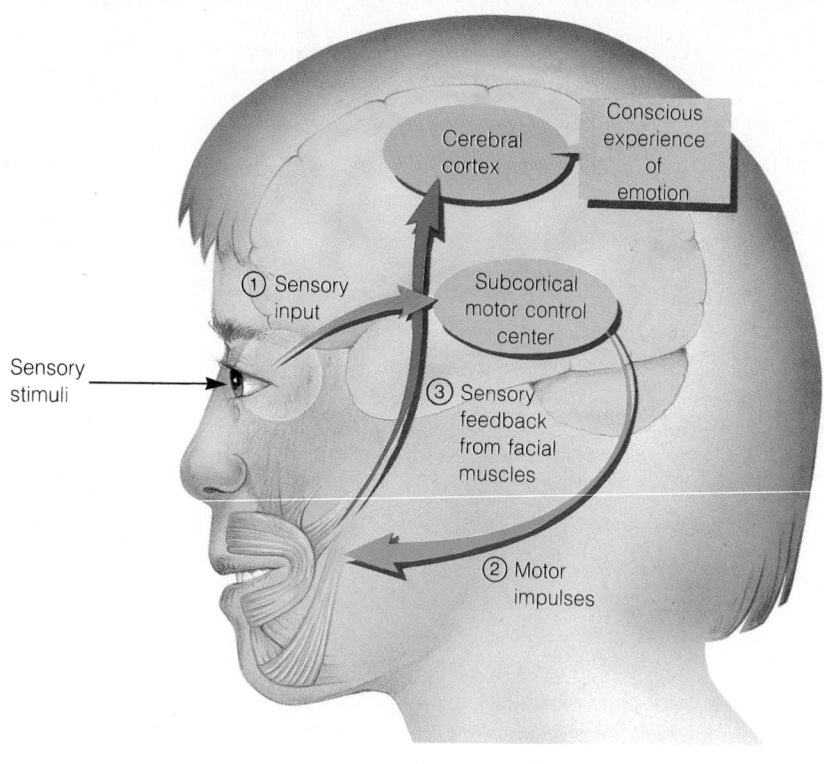

Sensory stimuli

① Sensory input

Cerebral cortex

Conscious experience of emotion

Subcortical motor control center

③ Sensory feedback from facial muscles

② Motor impulses

Figure 13.15 *The facial feedback hypothesis of emotional activation. Sensory input to subcortical motor control areas evokes facial expressions, whose sensory feedback to the cerebral cortex results in the subjective experience of the particular emotion.*

sions be part of innate emotional "programs" triggered in the limbic system or other subcortical areas by certain eliciting stimuli? If so, then sensory feedback from the facial muscles to the cortex might play a key role in the type and intensity of emotion that we experience (Izard, 1981; Tomkins, 1982, 1991). This notion of how body may affect mind is known as the **facial feedback hypothesis.**

A schematic representation of the facial feedback hypothesis is shown in Figure 13.15. According to the theory, sensory input from the eliciting stimuli (which may come either from the external environment or from an internal thought or image) is routed directly to the subcortical areas of the brain that control facial movements. These centers immediately send signals to the facial muscles. Sensory feedback from the movements of the facial muscles is then routed to the cerebral cortex, which produces the conscious experience of the emotion. To return to James's example of the bear, the facial feedback hypothesis says that

we are frightened partly because the automatic expression of terror that appears on our faces when the bear approaches sends signals to the cortex that are interpreted there as fear.

Recent research has shown that feedback produced by facial muscles can produce the three effects shown in Figure 13.16 (Adelmann & Zajonc, 1989). First, facial expressions can arouse specific emotional reactions. Second, they can affect physiological arousal through feedback sent to the autonomic nervous system. Finally, they can increase or decrease the intensity of emotion that is subjectively experienced.

Positive or negative emotional responses can be triggered by contraction of specific facial muscles. Especially significant are studies in which subjects do not know that they are activating muscles used in specific expressions. Such studies rule out the possible role of demand characteristics (page 49). Demand characteristics might result from requests to produce smiles, frowns, or some other expression, which would tell subjects what kinds of emotional ratings were expected of them.

In one such study, Fritz Strack and his co-workers (1988) found that subjects rated themselves as feeling more pleasant when they held pens in their teeth, which activates muscles used in smiling, than when they held the pens with their lips, which activates muscles involved in frowning

Figure 13.16 *Documented effects of facial feedback on other aspects of the emotional response system. Facial feedback stimuli can elicit specific emotional experiences, can increase or decrease physiological arousal, and can intensify or reduce the intensity of emotional experiences.*

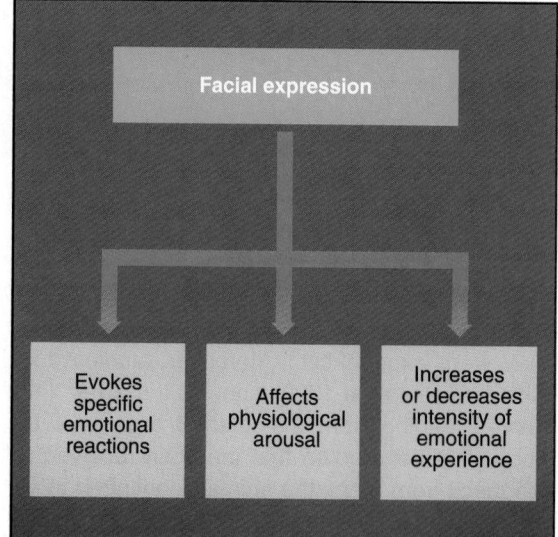

Facial expression

Evokes specific emotional reactions

Affects physiological arousal

Increases or decreases intensity of emotional experience

(see Figure 13.17). (Try this yourself and see if the actions influence your feelings.) Strack and his coworkers also showed that facial expressions can increase or reduce emotional intensity. Subjects rated cartoons as funnier while holding pens in their teeth than while holding pens with their lips.

In another study, Robert Zajonc and his colleagues compared the subjective experiences of subjects who pronounced different phonemes, such as *ee* and the German *ü*. Saying the *ee* sound, which activates muscles used in smiling, was associated with more pleasant feelings than saying the *ü* sound, which activates muscles involved in negative facial expressions (Zajonc & others, 1989). Photographers seem to know what they are about when they force us to say "cheese." (Perhaps they should also do so later when they hand us picture proofs that are less than flattering.)

In a study that involved posed expressions, subjects were exposed to either pleasant or unpleasant odors while being instructed to assume either pleasant or unpleasant facial responses. The facial reactions increased or decreased the subjects' emotional responses of liking or disgust to the two classes of odors, depending on whether they were consistent or inconsistent with the odors (Kraut, 1982).

Facial expressions can affect not only subjective experiences of emotion, but also physiological arousal. Paul Ekman and his coworkers (1983) asked experienced actors to assume facial expressions associated with six different emotions and measured their physiological responses. Three different subgroups of emotions were identified based on physiological measures: Poses of happiness, surprise, and disgust were linked with lowered heart rate; poses of fear and sadness produced high heart rate and low skin temperature; and poses of anger were accompanied by high skin temperature and high heart rate. This finding suggests that facial responses may have important linkages with the autonomic nervous system.

What is the nature of the feedback from the face to the brain, and how might the feedback trigger emotional experience? One recent suggestion is the **vascular theory of emotional feedback** (Adelmann & Zajonc, 1989; Zajonc, 1985). In the study by Zajonc and his coworkers described earlier, the phonemes (such as *ee*) that activated muscles involved in smiling produced not only pleasant feelings but also cooling of the forehead as measured by temperature sensors. The phonemes (for example, the German *ü*) that activated muscles involved in negative facial expressions evoked negative emotions and also raised fore-

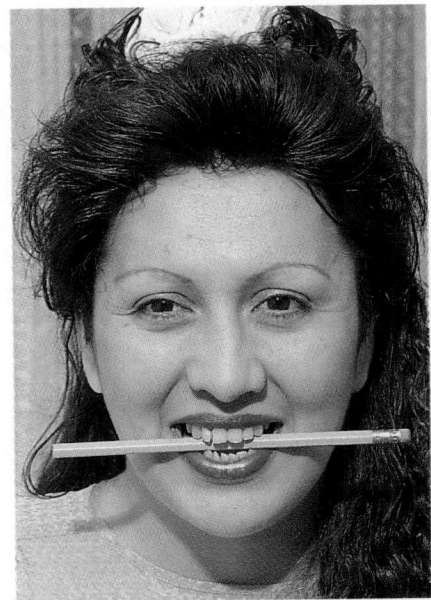 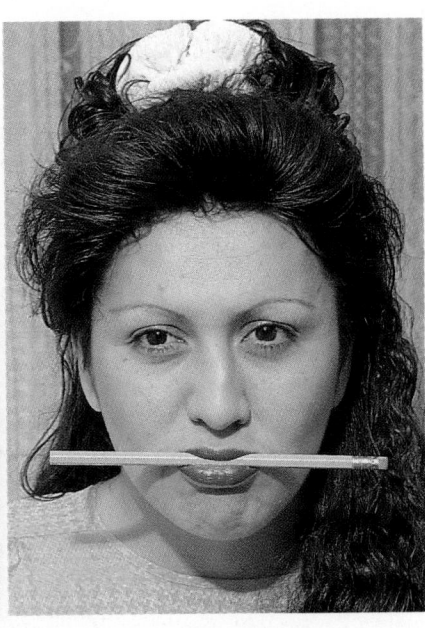

(a)   (b)

➤ **Figure 13.17** *Holding a pen in the teeth* (a) *so as to activate the muscles used in smiling evokes more pleasant feelings than holding the pen in one's lips* (b), *which activates muscles used in frowning. This finding provides support for the facial feedback hypothesis.*

head temperature. Zajonc's vascular theory holds that facial muscles can affect blood flow and possibly blood temperature, and that changes in the temperature of blood entering the brain may affect the synthesis and release of a number of different neurotransmitters, thereby affecting subjective experiences of emotion. Though highly speculative at this point, the vascular theory is testable and, if supported by future research, may help explain how body and mind are linked in the realm of the emotions.

One additional link between facial expression and brain activity has recently been reported. Richard Davidson, who studies hemispheric differences in positive and negative emotions, teamed up with Paul Ekman, who studies facial expressions, in a study of relations between hemispheric activity and facial expressions (Davidson & others, 1990; Ekman & others, 1990). The researchers simultaneously filmed facial expressions and recorded EEG responses in the two hemispheres of the brain as subjects watched films designed to produce positive and negative emotions. The positive films showed animals at play, whereas the negative ones showed a leg being amputated and closeups of a third-degree burn victim. As predicted, facial expressions of happiness—particularly the Duchenne smile described earlier—were accompanied by relatively greater left hemisphere activation in the cerebral cortex. Facial expressions of disgust were accompanied by relatively greater cortical activation in the right hemisphere.

A convincing body of evidence has emerged to support the existence of emotion-specific physiological patterning that involves the somatic, autonomic, and central nervous systems. It appears that there is indeed a physiological response system activated by specific classes of eliciting stimuli. Occurring with these physiological events are cognitive processes that define the meaning of the eliciting stimuli and give rise to the subjective experience of the emotional state. We now turn to interactions between physiological and cognitive factors.

Cognitive Appraisal Theories: Interactions Between Cognition and Arousal

Nowhere are mind–body interactions more obvious than in the emotions, where thinking and feeling are intimately connected. For the past quarter-century, a dominant theme in the study of the emotions has been the ways in which cognitions and physiological arousal interact. If you will refer back to Figure 13.3, you will see this interaction represented as a two-way causal link in which cognitive appraisals can trigger physiological arousal and arousal can in turn influence appraisal. Thus, an appraisal of danger triggers the physiological arousal pattern associated with fear, and feedback from that arousal contributes to subsequent appraisals of the situation and the associated feeling state (Lazarus, 1991b).

Two of the most important figures among the cognitive theorists are Richard Lazarus and Stanley Schachter. Lazarus has strongly emphasized the link between cognitive appraisal and arousal. Indeed, he insists that *all* emotional responses require some sort of appraisal:

> The fundamental premise is that in order to survive, animals (humans particularly) are constructed biologically to be constantly evaluating (appraising) their relationship with the environment with respect to significance for well-being. ... *If* a person (or animal) appraises his or her relationship with the environment in a particular way, *then* a specific emotion, which is tied to the appraisal, always results; and *if* two persons make the same appraisal, *then* they will experience the same emotion regardless of the actual circumstances. We are built this way, and presumably our neural makeup makes these appraisals and the emotions they generate reside somehow in our collective mind (Lazarus, 1991a, p. 825).

The appraisal itself need not be a conscious thought; it may be some instantaneous perception that does not enter conscious awareness. Once the appraisal has elicited the arousal response, this response may feed back into the ongoing appraisal process (see Figure 13.18).

In a very influential theory advanced in the 1960s, Stanley Schachter also emphasized links between cognition and arousal, but he was particularly concerned with the question of how we know what we are feeling. To him, the two major aspects of emotional experience are the *quality* of the emotion (that is, the label we attach to it) and the emotion's perceived *intensity*. Schachter's **two-factor theory of emotion** states that the intensity of physiological arousal tells people *how strongly* they are feeling something but they *label* emotions as fear, anger, love, or whatever on the basis of the situation they are in (Schachter, 1966). This notion underlies the theory of passionate love reviewed in Chapter 12, which states that the experience of passion is likely to occur when people experience physiological arousal in the presence of suitable partners (Carlson & Hatfield, 1992).

At the time Schachter formulated his theory, there was far less evidence than there is now that emotions may have specific response patterns, such as those identified by facial feedback theorists. Schachter thus assumed that physiological arousal was basically the same for all emotions and that perception of environmental cues must therefore be the basis for the labeling of the emotion being felt. Although there is now more evidence for physiological differentiation among emotions, Schachter was probably correct in his assertion that environmental cues can serve as an important source of information about what we are feeling. In Schachter's theory, as in the one developed by Lazarus, cognition and arousal are therefore highly interrelated. Figure 13.18 provides a summary of Schachter's two-factor theory.

If appraisal and arousal affect one another in the ways these theories suggest, some intriguing possibilities arise. For instance, if we can influence appraisals, we should be able to modify physiological arousal. Conversely, if we can influence arousal, we should be able to affect cognitive appraisals of the situation. In other words, we should find the two-way influence between cognition and arousal shown in the model of emotion presented in Figure 13.3. Let us turn to some research that tests these propositions.

Manipulating Appraisal to Influence Arousal

In their development of the cognitive appraisal theory, Lazarus and his colleagues at the University of California, Berkeley, were particularly concerned with how appraisal can influence physiological arousal. In one classic study, they showed subjects an anthropology film entitled *Subincision in the Arunta,* which depicts in vivid detail a puberty rite during which the penises of aboriginal boys are cut with a jagged flint knife. The film typically elicits a high level of stress in viewers.

To study the effects of appraisal on the intensity of the physiological stress response, the researchers tried to influence the subjects' appraisals by experimentally varying the film's sound track. Four different sound tracks were used: The ''trauma'' sound track emphasized the pain suffered by the boys, the danger of infection, the jaggedness of the flint knife, and other unpleasant aspects of the operation. The ''denial'' sound track was just the opposite; it denied that the operation was excessively painful or traumatic and emphasized that the boys looked forward to entering adulthood by undergoing the rite and demonstrating their bravery. The ''intellectualization'' sound track, also designed to produce a more benign appraisal, ignored the emotional elements of the scenes and focused on the traditions and history of the tribe. In a ''silent'' control condition, the film was shown without any sound track at all.

The amount of physiological arousal (measured by increased skin conductance caused by sweat gland activity) exhibited by subjects in the four appraisal conditions was the dependent variable. As shown in Figure 13.19, the sound tracks produced markedly different levels of arousal. The trauma sound track resulted in the highest arousal, and silence turned out to be more arousing than either denial or intellectualization, presumably because silence left people free to make their own negative appraisals (Speisman & others, 1964). The denial and intellectualization soundtracks were apparently effective in making the subjects' appraisals more benign, resulting in lower levels of arousal. This study, as well as the one described earlier in which subjects read ''emotional'' sentences to themselves, confirm that what we tell ourselves about external situations influences the level of arousal that we experience.

Manipulating Arousal to Influence Appraisal

Appraisals influence arousal. Is the reverse also true? It is conceivable that arousal could affect our appraisal of situations by giving us feedback on how our bodies are responding and causing us to wonder why we are becoming aroused. To study this possibility, research-

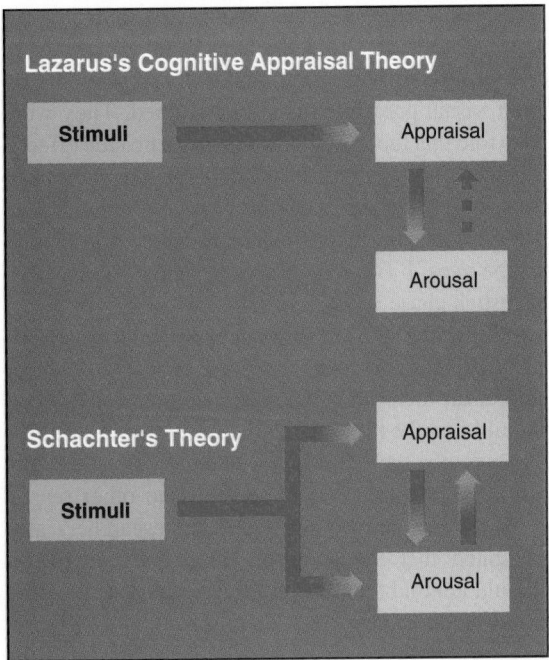

Figure 13.18 *The cognitive appraisal theory of Richard Lazarus holds that cognitive appraisal processes stimulate emotional arousal, which may then affect subsequent appraisals. Stanley Schachter's two-factor theory also focuses on the interactive role of cognition and arousal. Schachter emphasized the role of appraisals of the environment in our labeling of the emotions we experience.*

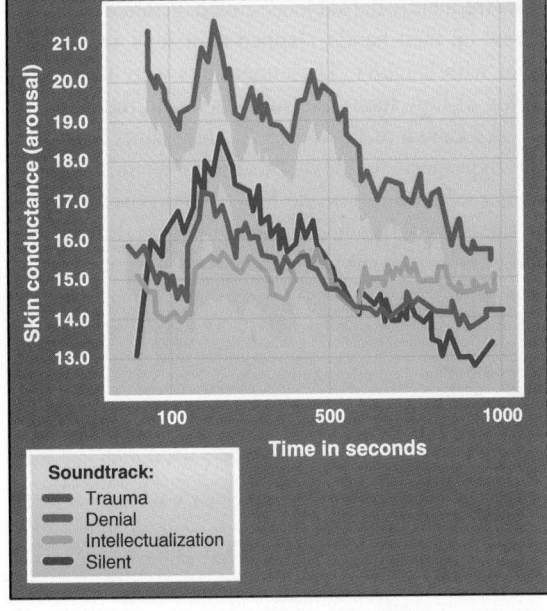

Figure 13.19 *Appraisal influences arousal. Subjects who viewed a film showing a tribal subincision rite in vivid detail exhibited different levels of physiological arousal, depending on the sound track that accompanied the film. (Speisman & others, 1964).*

ers must influence arousal directly in some way. Perhaps the easiest way to do this is with drugs, but it must be done in such a way that subjects are unaware that their arousal is being caused by the drugs. They have to believe that their arousal is being caused solely by the external situation they are appraising.

In an experiment in Stanley Schachter's laboratory (Schachter & Wheeler, 1962), the researchers directly manipulated arousal by injecting subjects with either epinephrine to increase arousal, a tranquilizer to decrease arousal, or a placebo control substance. To hide from the subjects the fact that they

As we have seen, emotion researchers have been very interested in how cultural learning might affect emotional responses. Thinking critically about this issue should prompt us to ask what specific processes or mechanisms could produce such differences. Robert Mauro, Kaori Sato, and John Tucker (1992) have proposed three mechanisms. First, people from different cultures may evaluate, or appraise, an event differently from one another, leading to different emotional responses. Thus, what is a humorous pratfall in one culture may be a source of disgrace in another. Second, people from different cultures may appraise the event in the same way, but the appraisals may call for different emotional responses. Thus, in one culture, a person who has harmed another may experience guilt only if he or she intended harm, whereas in another culture, personal intent may not be required in order for a person to feel guilty. Finally, the way in which the emotion is outwardly expressed may differ even where the situations and appraisals are identical. For example, the grief experienced as the result of a loved one's death may be expressed with wailing in one culture and stoic silence in another. These three mechanisms make possible many learned cultural variations in emotional experience and expression.

were being given drugs that would affect their arousal, the experimenters told the subjects that they were being injected with a vitamin so that its effects on their visual perception could be studied. They were also told that the injection would have no side effects. Then, while presumably waiting for the vitamin to take effect, the subjects were shown a short movie "to provide continuous black and white stimulation to the eyes." The movie was a comedy film with a slapstick chase scene.

Schachter and his associate, Wheeler, hypothesized that if the level of emotional arousal influences appraisal, then the subjects aroused by epinephrine should find the film funnier than the control subjects. Presumably, they would attribute their arousal to the film, because they would know of no other reason why they should be aroused. The researchers also reasoned that the subjects given the tranquilizer should not find the film very funny, because the drug would reduce their level of arousal.

Subjects were observed while they watched the movie by raters who were unaware of which subjects had received which injections. The raters recorded how frequently the subjects smiled, grinned, laughed, threw up their hands, slapped their legs, or doubled over with laughter. These measures were used as an index of how funny the subjects found the film.

As shown in Figure 13.20, the results supported the hypothesis that level of arousal would influence subjects' appraisal of the film. The aroused subjects in the epinephrine group found the film funnier than the tranquilized subjects did, and the placebo control

➡ **Figure 13.20** *Level of arousal can influence environmental appraisals. Subjects were injected with either epinephrine, a tranquilizer, or a placebo to affect arousal and then were shown a humorous film. The amount of amusement they displayed varied with their state of arousal. (Schachter & Wheeler, 1962).*

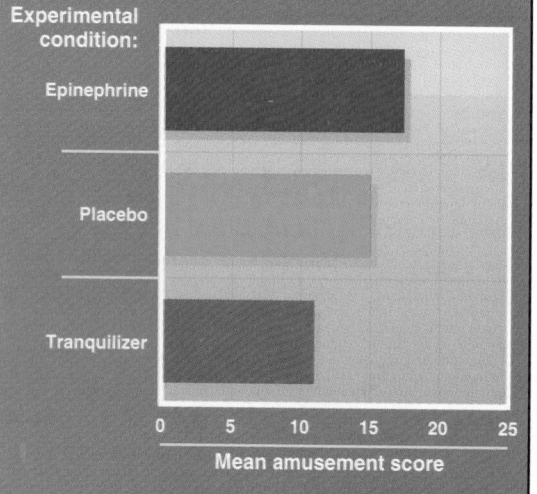

group was in the middle. It appears that as long as one attributes one's arousal to the external situation, arousal cues can affect appraisal. Note that this is basically the same "transfer of excitation" principle that was discussed in relation to passionate love in Chapter 12.

Cultural Influences on Cognitive Appraisal

We have already seen that there are strong cross-cultural similarities in the expression of basic emotions like fear, anger, and disgust. However, we found that cultural learning may also influence how emotions are expressed. ▼

Like theorists who study emotional expression, those who study cognitive appraisal and its role in emotion have looked for cross-cultural similarities and differences. Several of these theorists have suggested that there are a small number of universal dimensions of appraisal. These dimensions include pleasant–unpleasant, benign–dangerous, able to cope–unable to cope, compatability of behavior to social rules, controllable–uncontrollable, degree of personal responsibility for events, certainty–uncertainty, and conduciveness of the situation to goal attainment (Scherer, 1984; Smith & Ellsworth, 1985). Are these dimensions of appraisal indeed consistent across cultures? Are possible cultural differences in appraisal related to differences in the subjective experience of emotions? These are the questions that have recently been explored by appraisal researchers.

In these studies, respondents in a variety of cultures have been asked to recall events that evoked certain emotions, then to answer questions about how they appraised the situations on dimensions like those described above. In one study involving 27 countries, the researchers found marked cross-cultural similarities in the appraisals of events that evoked joy, fear, anger, sadness, disgust, shame, and guilt (Wallbott & Scherer, 1988).

A more recent study by Robert Mauro and his coworkers (1992) led to a similar conclusion. The researchers compared the appraisal–emotion links in a sample of 973 subjects from the United States, Japan, Hong Kong, and the People's Republic of China. They found a number of cultural differences in the frequency with which various emotions were experienced. For example, American subjects reported feeling happiness, pride, and hope more frequently than Japanese subjects. The Japanese, in turn, reported more frequent feelings of shame and regret than did the Hong Kong subjects. In contrast, virtually no cultural differences were found in linkages between type of appraisal and emotion. The few cultural differences that emerged primarily involved perceived personal responsibility for events. For example, Americans had to feel a high degree of personal control over an outcome in order to feel pride, whereas the Asian subjects (particularly the Japanese) did not. This pattern may reflect the individualistic culture of the United States, which emphasizes personal striving to attain individual goals. The Japanese and Chinese cultures stress collectivism, where individual attainment is less important than collective action taken to achieve group goals. It appears that pride can be experienced in the achievement of such goals regardless of who in the group is most responsible for goal attainment (Mauro & others, 1992).

Cross-cultural research on appraisal and emotion is painting a consistent picture: There seems to be a set of "primitive" appraisals that universally evoke certain emotions. On the other hand, cultural differences may well exist on more complex dimensions of appraisal, such as perceived personal responsibility and compatability of one's behavior with social norms. Whatever cultural differences may exist, however, it seems clear that within each culture, certain appraisals are strongly linked to specific emotional responses (Mauro & others, 1992; Wallbott & Scherer, 1988).

Associative Networks Involving Emotion

Chapter 10 discussed how concepts or units of knowledge are linked in memory as networks (see page 312). This model from cognitive psychology is now being applied to emotion as well (Berkowitz, 1990). The basic idea is that each network is made up of associated groups of ideas, emotional responses, and behavioral tendencies. An example of such a network is shown in Figure 13.21.

It is assumed that activation of any element in a network tends to call forth the elements associated with it. Thus, a particular idea may evoke associated memories, feelings, and behaviors, particularly if the network's associations are strong ones. Consider, for example, the description given by a subject in a facial feedback experiment of what happened when he was instructed to frown and clench his teeth, activating the facial muscle component of the anger response network:

When my jaw was clenched and my brows down, I tried not to be angry but it just fit the position. I'm not in an angry mood but I found my thoughts wandering to things that made me angry, which is sort of silly I guess. I knew I was in an experiment and knew I had no reason to feel that way, but I just lost control (Laird, 1974, p. 480).

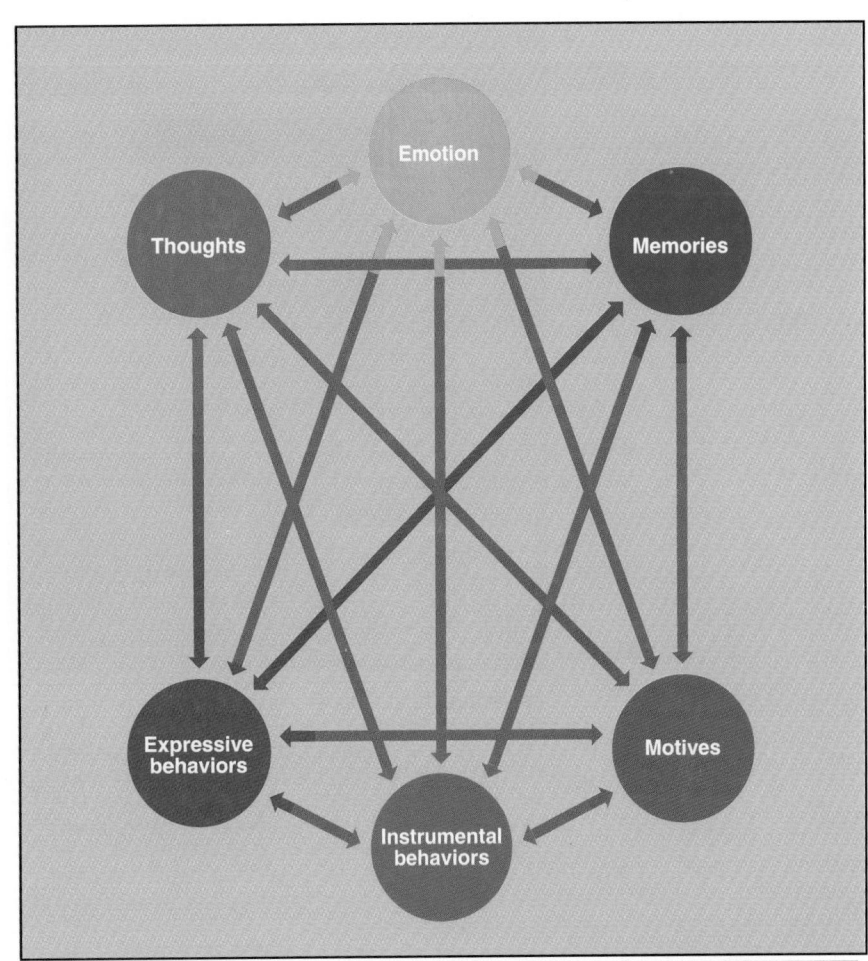

Figure 13.21 *Networks involving cognitive, physiological, and behavioral elements and organized by associative links are a new way of looking at emotion. The network theory holds that activation of any part of the network also can stimulate associated parts.*

Leonard Berkowitz (1990) has used the associative model to account for the formation of anger. He suggests that any frustrating event can produce a *priming effect* that activates the network of ideas, feelings, and behavioral tendencies that define anger. Those individuals in whom aggressive ideas are strongly related to anger and to aggressive behavioral tendencies are most likely to be stimulated to behave aggressively when they become angry.

Most of us have first-hand knowledge of how our moods can affect our thinking. When we are feeling happy, we tend to think "good thoughts" and see the world in a positive light. But when we are feeling sad, the world can seem like a pretty bleak place. In a series of experiments, Gordon Bower (1981) showed that memory can be strongly and selectively influenced by mood, as the associative network theory would predict. Bower created happy and sad moods in his subjects by having each of them imagine happy or sad scenes while they were hypnotized. The subjects also learned two lists of words, one while they

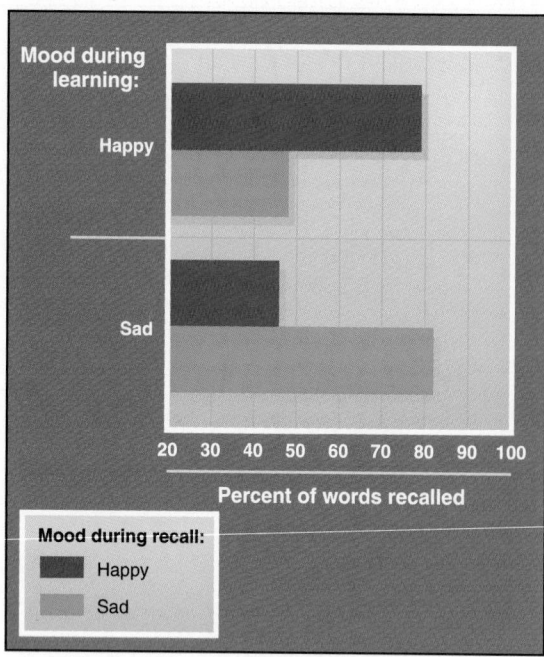

Mood during learning:

Happy

Sad

20 30 40 50 60 70 80 90 100

Percent of words recalled

Mood during recall:

Happy

Sad

◆ **Figure 13.22** *Memory is affected by the match between the mood experienced during learning and the mood existing during recall. Subjects recalled more words when the mood they were experiencing during the recall phase of the experiment was the same as the mood present when the material was originally learned. (Adapted from Bower, 1981).*

were feeling happy and another while they were feeling sad. Later, the subjects were hypnotically returned to their happy and sad moods and asked to recall the two lists of words. As Figure 13.22 shows, subjects recalled more words when the recall mood and the learning mood were the same. When the moods were different, less than half of the words were recalled. This phenomenon is called **mood-congruent memory,** (a type of state-dependent memory) and it helps explain several commonly observed phenomena. For example, people in a relationship are often able to do a fine job of dredging up all the negative events of the past when they are angry, while seemingly losing sight of positive experiences. In contrast, feelings of passionate love may help block out memories of past problems in the relationship.

Does the same mood-congruence principle apply to people who experience certain emotions on a stable day-to-day basis? To find out, Michael Greenberg and Aaron Beck (1989) compared clinically depressed patients with a group of patients suffering from chronic anxiety and a control group of psychiatric patients who were not suffering from either depression or anxiety. The patients were asked to read a list of adjectives. Some of the adjectives were relevant to depression (*inadequate, gloomy, hopeless*) and others were anxiety-related (*nervous, erratic, frightening*). The

subjects were asked to indicate which adjectives applied to them, to the world, and to the future. Later, the patients were given a surprise quiz and were asked to write down as many of the adjectives as they could recall.

The results of chronic states of depression and anxiety on memory are shown in Figure 13.23. As you can see, the depressed patients recalled more of the depressive adjectives, and the anxious patients remembered more of the anxiety-related ones. This pattern of results might help explain one of the ways in which these emotional responses are chronically maintained in people who suffer from them. Depressed people seem to have a general tendency to remember depressing events particularly well, whereas those who suffer from anxiety seem to remember the frightening stimuli they encounter. Emotion thus seems to help steer our thinking in much the same way that thinking steers our emotions. How we feel influences our perceptions and cognitions.

Unconscious Influences on Emotion

Emotions play a central role in personality functioning, and intrapsychic theories of personality have had a great deal to say about how emotions develop, are expressed, and are defended against. In Freud's psychodynamic theory, for example, emotions and instincts are tightly intertwined. According to Freud, conscious emotions are usually pale shadows of the fiery instincts that struggle for release from the unconscious depths of the mind. However rich and varied our emotional lives might be, they are products of defensive processes that distort and temper the underlying sexual and aggressive instincts. In his novel, *Heart of Darkness,* Joseph Conrad (1902/1947) provides a chilling description of what a glimpse into the instinctual cauldron might be like:

> I tried to break the spell—the heavy mute spell of the wilderness—that seemed to draw him to its pitiless breast by the awakening of forgotten and brutal instincts, by the memory of gratified and monstrous passions. This alone, I was convinced, had driven him to the edge of the forest, to the brush, towards the gleam of fires, the throb of drums, the drone of weird incantations; this alone had beguiled his unlawful soul beyond the bounds of permitted aspirations. . . . But his soul was mad . . . it had looked within itself, and by heavens! I tell you, it had gone mad. (pp. 585–586)

Freud had several important insights about the processing of emotional information that are now being borne out by research into information processing in the brain. He suggested that there is both conscious and unconscious processing of emotional information and that much emotional content might

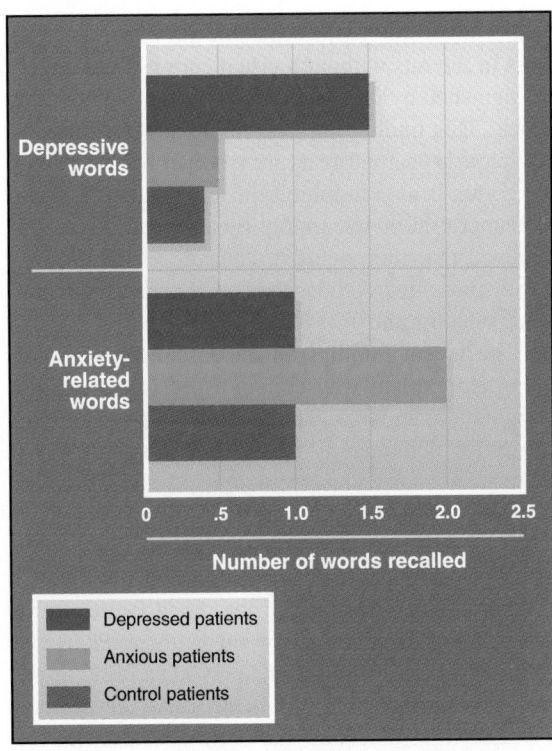

Figure 13.23 *Differences among depressed patients, patients suffering from anxiety, and a control group of patients suffering from neither depression nor anxiety in their recall of depression-relevant and anxiety-relevant words. Consistent with the associative linkages model, the depressives recalled more depression-relevant words, whereas the anxiety patients tended to remember more anxiety-relevant words. (Data from Greenberg & Beck, 1989).*

be processed in a manner that is not accessible to the conscious mind. Thus, what we *think* we feel may not be what we "really" feel at a deeper and inaccessible level.

For many years, experimental psychologists found Freud's notion of the unconscious mind unacceptable from a scientific perspective. However, the past decade has seen a virtual explosion of research on unconscious processing of information. A considerable body of evidence now suggests that unconscious mental processes, though far less sophisticated than those proposed by Freud, do exist (Bruner, 1992; Greenwald, 1992). Even stimuli that do not register in awareness can produce some degree of learning, and memories and other aspects of consciousness can be dissociated from one another (the most extreme examples occurring in multiple personality disorders). How might this happen?

Some possible answers are beginning to emerge from brain research. Joseph LeDoux (1986, 1992) has provided anatomical evidence that the brain is arranged so that key aspects of emotional life can operate largely independent of thought. The new evi-

dence suggests that certain emotional reactions occur before the cerebral cortex has had time to fully interpret what is causing the reaction. LeDoux's animal research on the neural pathways involved in processing emotional information suggests that three structures—the thalamus, the limbic system (particularly the amygdala), and the cerebral cortex—are parts of two parallel and somewhat independent systems for the activation of emotion. One system involves the conscious processing of information, and the other operates largely independent of thought.

The model of emotion suggested by LeDoux is shown in Figure 13.24. The key player in this model is the amygdala, a structure in the limbic system. The amygdala plays a central role in organizing the physiological and behavioral components of emotional responses. The thalamus, as we saw in Chapter 3, operates like a giant switchboard, routing sensory input to the appropriate areas of the brain. When the thalamus receives signals from the eyes, ears, and other sensory organs, it transmits the information to the cortex, where the sensory input is organized as perceptions and evaluated by the "thinking," or linguistic, part of the brain. This is where the thoughts

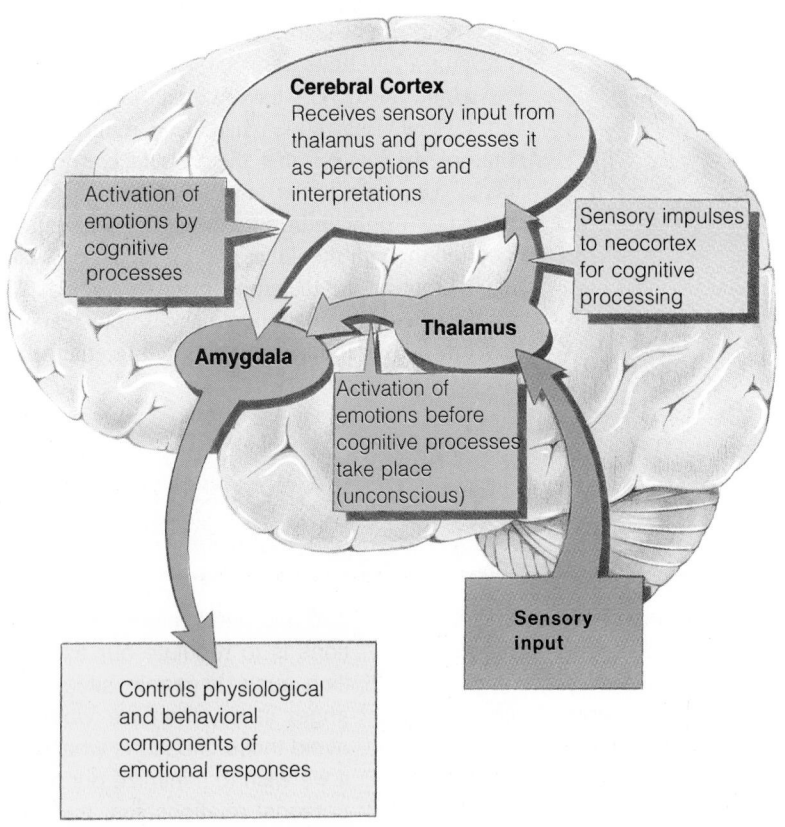

Figure 13.24 *Parallel processes may produce conscious and unconscious emotional responses at about the same time. LeDoux's research suggests that sensory input to the thalamus can be routed directly to the amygdala in the limbic system, producing an "unconscious" emotional response before cognitive responses evoked by the other pathway to the cortex can occur.*

and evaluations that constitute cognitive appraisal occur. Signals are then sent to the amygdala from the cortex to activate the rest of the emotional response pattern.

LeDoux's major discovery was that there are also neural pathways directly from the thalamus to the amygdala. This means that the amygdala can also receive direct inputs from the senses before the information reaches the cortex. Emotions can therefore be triggered before the brain has had time to register what is being responded to. LeDoux suggests that this mechanism (which is the only emotional mechanism in more primitive species, like birds and reptiles), has survival value because it enables the organism to react with great speed. In humans, this primitive appraisal process frees the cortex from the need to evaluate each and every stimulus for its emotional meaning. The amygdala may thus act as sort of an unconscious filter for incoming information. It can react immediately; and shortly afterward, information arrives from the cortex with a more carefully processed cognitive interpretation of the situation. This may be what occurs when we see a shape that looks like a snake and jump out of the way, only to realize an instant later that the object is a rope.

One intriguing finding from LeDoux's laboratory is that fears can be learned without conscious activity (LeDoux, 1989). Rats were classically conditioned to fear a light (the CS) by having it paired with electric shock. The visual cortex had been removed from some of the rats, so that their visual cortex never "saw" the CS. These animals, like intact ones, learned to fear the light, suggesting that learning had occurred through the direct pathway from the visual relay station in the thalamus to the amygdala. This mechanism may explain how unconscious fears can be learned. But another notable finding emerged as

well: Unlike the learned fears in the intact rats, the fears in the rats without a visual cortex could not be extinguished by presentation of the light without the shock. This finding led LeDoux to suggest that unconsciously learned fears may be permanent unless the cortex is able to inhibit the amygdala as a result of reappraisal or relearning. Freud would agree; he believed that the cognitive changes (insights) produced through psychoanalysis are necessary to reverse unconscious fears.

The recent findings on unconscious processing may help explain why certain aspects of our emotional lives can be puzzling. While some emotional memories undoubtedly reach consciousness, many more are not consciously remembered but may nevertheless lead to actions. LeDoux's discoveries have led Richard Lazarus (1991c) to suggest that people are capable of having two simultaneous emotional reactions to the same event, a conscious one occurring as a result of cortical activity and an unconscious one created by direct input to the amygdala. This might help explain instances in which people are puzzled by behavioral reactions that seem at odds with the emotion they are consciously experiencing: "I don't know why I acted as if I were angry. I felt very warm and friendly."

We have covered a good deal of what is known about emotions and the factors that influence them. Because emotions contribute so richly to psychological well-being, most people wish not only to understand feelings but also to gain greater personal control over them so that they can maximize the positive ones and minimize the negative ones. To that end, let us translate the research results we have reviewed into some practical guidelines for emotional self-regulation.

 **ENHANCING HUMAN PERFORMANCE**

SELF-REGULATION OF EMOTIONS

As we have seen, emotional episodes involve interactions among eliciting stimuli, cognitive appraisals, physiological responses, and behaviors. Each of these components can be the focus of efforts directed at the self-regulation of emotion (Masters, 1991; Mayer & others, 1991).

Controlling Eliciting Stimuli

Certain stimuli can trigger either positive or negative emotions. It therefore follows

that one basic means of controlling emotions is to regulate our exposure to eliciting cues. If certain situations generate anger in us, then we would do well to avoid those situations whenever possible if we wish to minimize our anger. In interpersonal relationships, for example, certain topics of discussion can trigger arguments, recriminations about past misdeeds, and escalating anger. Learning to avoid these kinds of communications and to deal with the relationship is-

sues in more adaptive ways can be a key to reducing the potential for destructive anger. In contrast, research shows that people are generally happiest when they are engaged in leisurely, involving, and challenging pursuits (Csikszentmihalyi, 1990). The most consistent states of happiness seem to be produced by active leisure activities and relaxed involvement in meaningful relationships rather than by either passive nonactivity or frantic activity in search of the "good life" (Myers,

1992). An obvious key to maximizing feelings of contentment and happiness is to expose yourself to those situations that make you feel good, such as those just mentioned. Yet it is surprising how many people get so bound up in other activities that they stop making time for the things they enjoy most. Ironically, research has shown that when people are depressed, they are most likely to stop doing the very things that might make them feel better (Lewinsohn & others, 1985). The point to be emphasized is that our own behavior helps create the situations that make us happy or unhappy, and an important first step in controlling eliciting stimuli is a realization of this fact.

Cognitive Control Over Emotion

Cognitive appraisal processes play a central role in generating emotional responses. Lazarus, Ellis, and other cognitive theorists tell us that perhaps the most powerful means of regulating our feelings is by controlling how we think about situations (eliciting stimuli) and about ourselves. Ellis (1962) in particular has emphasized that a relatively small number of core beliefs that most people never bother challenging lie at the root of most of the internal self-talk that triggers negative feelings. We tell ourselves that we *must* achieve and be approved of in virtually every respect if we are to consider ourselves worthwhile people; that it is *terrible, awful, and catastrophic* when life or other people are not the way we demand that they be; that people who do not behave as we wish are *bad* and therefore deserving of punishment. These and other ideas have the power to generate anxiety, despair, and anger. When people begin to think differently, their feelings can change dramatically. Here is an example of a cognitive about-face reported by one of Ellis's clients:

I'm beginning to see now what you mean by not blaming others for their mistakes and wrongdoings. My mother called me the other day—the first time in a year that she has dared to do so, after I gave her a real piece of my mind the last time I spoke to her—and she started going on as usual, after first being nice for a few minutes, about how I wasn't getting anywhere in life, how terrible it was that I was still going for

psychotherapy, and all that kind of jazz. I began, as usual, to feel my temperature rising and I was all set to tell her off again.

But then I said, as you have been teaching me to do, "What am I telling *myself* to make me get so angry at this poor woman? *She's* not making me mad; *I* am." And I could see right away that I was telling myself that she shouldn't be the nagging, bitchy type of woman that she is and has always been. So I said to myself, "All right: *why* shouldn't she be the way she is and has always been?" And of course, just as you keep pointing out, I couldn't find any good reason why she shouldn't be exactly as she is. For there isn't any such reason. Sure, it would be nice if she were approving, and calm, and everything else. But she isn't. And she's not going to be. And I don't *need* her to be, in order to get along well in the world myself.

Well, as soon as I saw *that*, all my anger against the old gal of course vanished. I tried, just as an experiment, to work it back up again, to get angry at her all over. But I couldn't make it. Instead, I was very nice to her—much to her surprise, you can imagine!—and even invited her to my home for Christmas dinner—which I haven't done or even thought of doing for years now (Ellis, 1962, p. 185).

Studies of the thought processes that seem to produce contentment and happiness suggest that we often create happiness by comparing our present circumstances with those of people who are worse off than we are or with circumstances in our past that were worse for us than our present ones (Diener, 1984; Myers, 1992). "Counting our blessings" might seem to be a rather simplistic approach to feeling good, but it seems to be highly effective for many people. In part, the disposition to be happy seems to be fueled by a mental set to see the good in our lives and in other people (Carlson & Hatfield, 1992). This does not mean that happy people deny or ignore problems but rather that they tend to appraise them as challenges and opportunities rather than as threats and catastrophes (Lazarus, 1991b). Once again, we are reminded of Epictetus's words, written centuries ago: "As you think, so shall you feel."

Muscular and Autonomic Control

We turn now to the autonomic and muscular responses that are part of the emotional response system. The ability to

control these responses should enhance emotional self-regulation. Darwin (1872/1965) was well aware of this potential:

The free expression by outward sign of an emotion intensifies it. On the other hand, the repression, as far as this is possible, softens our emotions. He who gives way to violent gestures will increase his rage; he who does not control the signs of fear will experience fear in a greater degree. (p. 365)

William James (1890/1950) echoed Darwin's principle of self-regulation 18 years later:

If we wish to conquer undesirable emotional tendencies in ourselves, we must assiduously, and in the first instance, go through the outward movements of those contrary dispositions which we prefer to cultivate. (p. 463)

Darwin's and James's suggestion that emotions may be controlled through the regulation of bodily responses has attracted new attention, especially among researchers who are exploring the facial feedback hypothesis and other aspects of expressive behavior. It may indeed be possible to willfully control expressive behavior and thereby influence emotions in a goal-directed fashion (Izard, 1990).

There is experimental evidence that how we choose to appear can affect emotions. John Lanzetta and his colleagues (1976) asked some men and women subjects to pretend that they were receiving intensely painful shocks (to deceive another subject) and asked other subjects to hide their feelings. The subjects who pretended to receive intense shocks rated the mild shocks they actually received as more painful and also had more intense autonomic responses to the shocks. We can add to this result the findings obtained in facial feedback studies in which expressive movements of the face were shown to affect emotional experience by evoking the other elements of the emotional response system. Finally, postural responses as well as facial responses may affect emotions. For example, many sport psychologists urge athletes to remain calm and to appear self-assured no matter how badly things are going (Williams, 1993). While these suggestions are usually made in the service of intimidating one's opponent and depriving the opponent of the psychological boost that a display of discouragement might provide, it is also possible that the recommended actions directly affect the emotional state of the athlete. If we act confident and poised, we may increase our feelings of confidence and poise. In support of this notion, Sandra Duclos and her coworkers (1989) found that when subjects were asked to adopt postures characteristic of fear, anger, and sadness, they rated themselves as correspondingly more fearful, angry, or sad.

We might add to the statement, "As you *think,* so shall you feel" a corollary that states, "As you *act,* so shall you feel." This would perhaps be an overstatement in most cases. Occasionally, however, acting a part may evoke such strong feelings that the actor, in a sense, becomes the part. The actor Kirk Douglas reported such an experience (see Figure 13.25):

> I was close to getting lost in the character of Van Gogh in "Lust for Life." I felt myself going over the line, into the skin of Van Gogh. . . . Sometimes I had to stop myself from reaching my hand up and touching my ear to find out if it was actually there.
>
> It was a frightening experience. That way lies madness. . . . I could never play him again (Lehmann-Haupt, 1988, p. 10).

Control can be exercised not only over muscle responses involved in facial

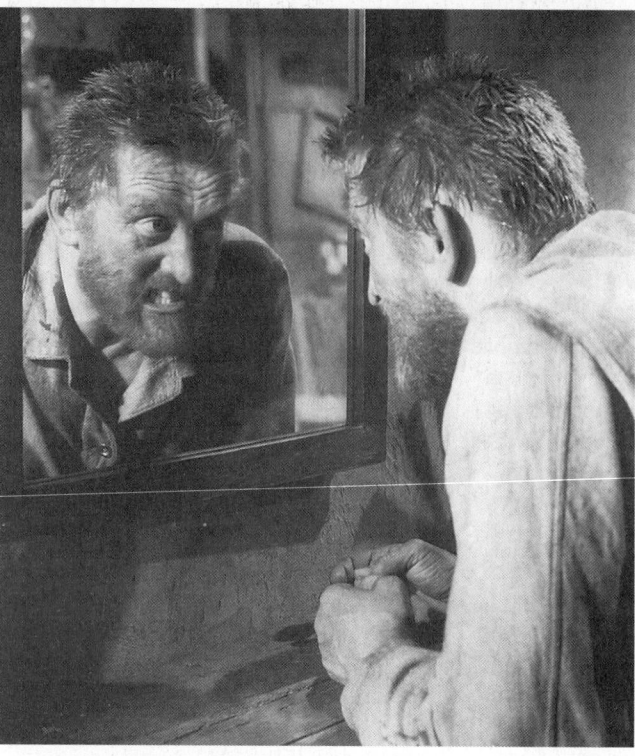

Figure 13.25 *Kirk Douglas, shown playing Vincent Van Gogh in the movie* Lust for Life, *reported that by virtue of behaving like Van Gogh, he at times lost the ability to separate himself from the character. This exemplifies the fact that voluntary expressions, postures, and actions can affect emotions.*

expression and postures but also over the physiological arousal responses that are a central part of many emotions. There is now considerable evidence that by using voluntary relaxation, deep breathing, and meditation, people can learn to control physiological arousal and gain control over such states as anxiety and anger (Izard, 1990; Morris, 1991). Because relaxation is incompatible with arousal, the ability to willfully relax and calm the body produces, in the previously quoted words

of William James, "the contrary disposition which we prefer to cultivate." In Chapter 15, we will consider some of these techniques in greater detail.

It is clear that, as intense and perplexing as emotions might sometimes be, we need not be helpless in their grip. Much has been learned about emotion through scientific research, and we can use these principles to produce for ourselves a more gratifying and fulfilling emotional life.

SUMMARY

The Nature and Functions of Emotions
- Emotions are innate and acquired predispositions to respond cognitively, physiologically, and behaviorally to certain internal and external events that relate to important goals and motives.
- Emotions and motives are intimately related because emotions are responses to threats to or achievement of personal goals. Both emotions and motives can result in physiological arousal.
- Emotions further our well-being in several ways: by rousing us to action, by helping us

communicate with others, and by eliciting empathy and help.

Components of Emotion
- The primary components of emotion are the eliciting stimuli, the person's cognitive appraisal of the situation, physiological arousal, and expressive and instrumental behaviors. Individual differences in personality and motivation affect the experience and expression of emotion, as do cultural factors.
- Although innate factors can affect the eliciting properties of certain stimuli, learning can

also play an important role in determining the arousal properties of stimuli.
- The cognitive component of emotional experience involves the evaluative and personal appraisal of the eliciting stimuli. The ability of thoughts to elicit emotional arousal has been demonstrated clinically and in experimental research.
- Our physiological responses in emotion are produced by certain areas of the brain, including the hypothalamus, the limbic system, and the cortex, and by the autonomic and endocrine systems. Recent studies suggest that

negative emotions reflect greater relative activation of the right hemisphere, whereas positive emotions are related to relatively greater activation in the left hemisphere.

- The validity of the polygraph as a "lie detector" has been questioned largely because of the difficulty of establishing the meaning of physiological responses.
- The behavioral component of emotion includes expressive and instrumental behaviors. Different parts of the face are important in the expression of various emotions. The accuracy of people's interpretation of these expressions is enhanced when situational cues are also available. Based in part on similarities in facial expression of emotions across widely separate cultures, evolutionary theorists propose that certain fundamental emotional patterns are innate. They agree, however, that cultural learning can influence emotional expression in important ways.
- According to the Yerkes–Dodson law, there is an optimal level of arousal for the performance of any task. This optimal level varies with the complexity or difficulty of the task; complex tasks have lower optimal levels.

Interactions Among the Components of Emotion

- Several past and present theories posit causal relations among emotional components.

The James–Lange/somatic theory maintains that we first become aroused and then judge what we are feeling. The Cannon–Bard theory proposes that arousal and cognition are simultaneously triggered by the thalamus. Cognitive appraisal theory states that appraisals trigger emotional arousal. According to Schachter's two-factor theory, arousal tells us how strongly we feel, while cognitions derived from situational cues help us to label the specific emotion.

- The facial feedback hypothesis, derived from the James–Lange/somatic theory, states that feedback from the facial muscles associated with innate emotional displays affects cognitive and physiological processes. Recent evidence provides support for the theory.
- There appears to be a reciprocal, or two-way, relationship between the cognitive and physiological components of emotion. It is possible to manipulate appraisals and thereby influence level of arousal, and arousal changes can also affect appraisal of the eliciting stimuli. Cross-cultural research indicates considerable agreement across cultures in the basic appraisal dimensions that evoke basic emotions, but also some degree of variation in more complex appraisals.
- Several theorists have applied the concept of associative networks to emotion. The networks consist of associated groups of ideas,

emotional responses, and behavioral tendencies. This idea receives support from studies of state-dependent memory, which have shown that recall is better when the moods that exist under conditions of learning and recall are the same.

- Psychodynamic theorists hold that emotions are subdued or altered manifestations of underlying instincts and that they can sometimes operate unconsciously. Recent psychobiological research suggests that unconscious emotional reactions may indeed occur because of structural characteristics of the brain.
- Theory and research provide bases for enhancing self-regulation of emotion. Self-regulation may be achieved through conscious control of exposure to eliciting stimuli and by modification of cognitions, control of physiological arousal, or regulation of expressive behaviors.

SUGGESTED READINGS

Carlson, J. G., & Hatfield, E. (1992). *Psychology of emotion*. Ft. Worth: Harcourt Brace Jovanovich. An outstanding summary of theory and research in emotion containing many interesting examples and practical applications.

Lazarus, R. S. (1991). *Emotion and adaptation*. New York: Oxford University Press. A monumental work in which Lazarus reviews and

distills his own work and that of others to arrive at a new statement of cognitive appraisal theory.

Myers, D. (1992). *Well-being: Who is happy—and why*. New York: William Morrow. An engaging and informative review of the research on subjective well-being, together with suggestions for increasing personal happiness.

Tomkins, S. S. (1991). *Affect, imagery, and consciousness. Volume 3: Anger and fear*. New York: Springer. A fascinating account of the evolutionary origins of these basic emotions and how they can be modified by cognitive and experiential factors.

14 Personality

CHAPTER OUTLINE

T he young couple walked slowly through the park, oblivious to the droplets of rain that were beginning to fall. They had come to this place often in the past, and many memories of a budding romance still lingered among its trees and along its paths. A year ago, before they each went away to separate colleges, they would have been walking hand in hand. Now they walked several feet apart.

Lisa spoke first. "Tom, it's just not right with us since we've gotten back from school. We used to be so compatible, but now it seems as if we can't agree on anything. I don't feel as if I've changed much, but you seem like a different person."

They walked in silence for several minutes before Tom spoke. "I still love you, Lisa, and I do want to work out our problems. But I guess my personality has changed a lot. In fact, sometimes I wonder who I really am these days. Since getting away from home, I've had lots of experiences in college that have affected how I feel about things and how I relate to people. I guess I feel that I'm growing in a lot of ways, but some of the changes I see make me feel as if I'm adrift, searching for the real me."

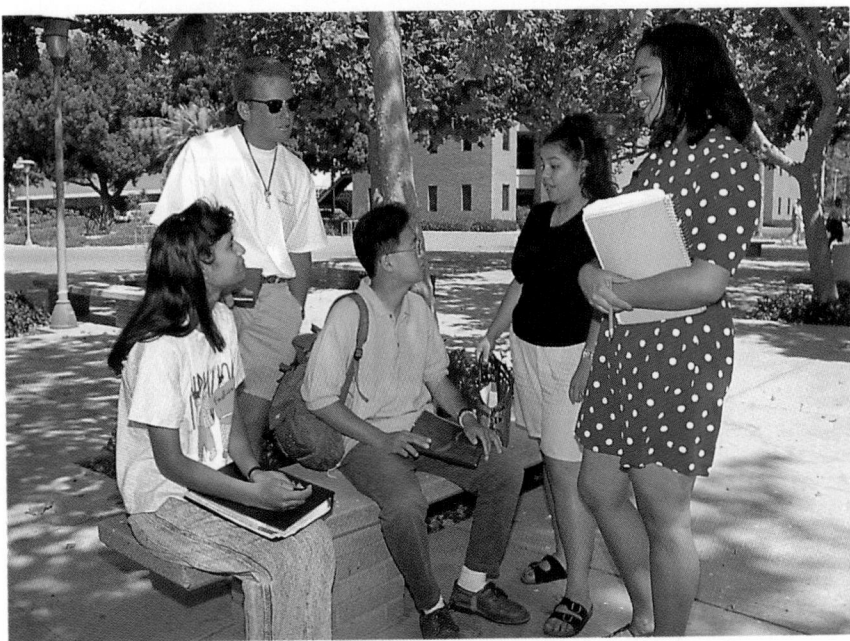

Figure 14.1 *Personality plays a major role in how we relate to others, and judgments about personality are among the first we form when we meet someone for the first time.*

Perhaps you have occasionally experienced feelings like Tom's. But most of the time you probably feel more like Lisa—that there is a core of self-identity that remains relatively constant over time. The concept of personality is relevant to both consistency and change in behavior. Personality lies at the heart of our attempts to know and to understand ourselves and other people.

Few, if any, topics in psychology have received as much attention as has personality. As an area of inquiry, personality has attracted many theorists and researchers who have devoted their careers to expanding knowledge about the factors that produce individual identities. In this chapter, we focus on and evaluate some of the major conceptions of personality that have arisen in the quest to understand the individual. We also discuss the major methods used by psychologists to measure individual differences in personality.

What Is Personality?

When they begin to study personality theories, students are sometimes puzzled and confused by the diversity of viewpoints about the nature of personality. As one pair of observers noted, "it seems hard to believe that all the theorists are talking about the same creature, who is now angelic and now depraved, now a black-box robot shaped by reinforcers and now

a shaper of its own destiny, now devious . . . and now hardheadedly oriented to solid reality" (Stone & Church, 1968). An analysis of what personality is and what it is not may help to account for the diverse conceptions of personality that we will encounter in this chapter.

Because it is a noun, the term *personality* is used as if it were a *thing,* something that people *have.* We speak of *the* personality, *her* personality, and so on, as if it were something real and concrete, like a muscular body, red hair, and freckles. But personality is *not* a thing. It has no existence apart from behavior. Personality is a concept, or *construct,* that arises from the observation of certain types of behaviors. For example, when we say someone has a "good" personality or a "lousy" one, we mean that the person customarily behaves in ways that are either pleasing or displeasing to *us.*

Once we realize that personality is a construct drawn from observable behaviors, we are ready to consider why people invented the concept of personality, why it occupies such an important place in psychology, and what kinds of behaviors it includes.

The concept of personality arises from the fascinating spectrum of human individuality. If everyone thought and behaved in exactly the same way, it would be a pretty dull world, and there would be no need for a construct like personality. The starting point for the concept of personality is the observation that people differ in meaningful ways in how they think, feel, and behave. As one group of theorists has

"Sure, I remember you—the chubby kid in English class who never went anywhere without his slingshot."

(Drawing by James Estes; © 1982 by The Wall Street Journal)

noted, each of us is in certain respects like all other people, like some other people, *and* like no other person who has lived in the past or will exist in the future (Kluckhohn & Murray, 1953). The concept of personality is part of an attempt to account for those differences that contribute to our *individuality* as thinking, feeling, and behaving humans.

Another common observation is that people seem to show some degree of *consistency* in their behavior over time and across different situations (see Figure 14.2). All of us seem to have predispositions to behave in certain ways so that our behavior is somewhat

Figure 14.3 *Perceived characteristics of behaviors viewed as reflecting an individual's personality.*

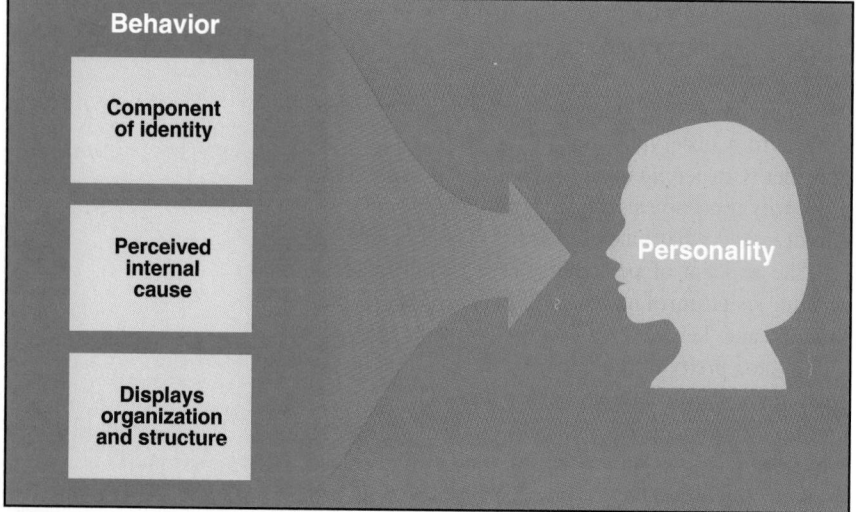

predictable even under changing circumstances. From this perceived consistency comes the notion of *personality traits,* which describe an individual's characteristic ways of responding to his or her world. Combining these notions of individuality and consistency, we may define **personality** as *the distinctive and relatively consistent ways of thinking, feeling, and acting that characterize a person's responses to life situations.*

To fully appreciate how personality enters into attempts to describe and understand human individuality, we need to travel one step further and consider the characteristics of the behaviors that define personality. In a thoughtful analysis of the concept of personality, Leon Levy (1971) identified three key characteristics.

First, the behavior serves as a *component of identity.* That is, it helps to establish the identity of the person as distinct from others. Jason's eye color tells us little about his psychological identity, but the fact that he frequently "blows up" at others does.

Second, the cause of the behavior is seen as residing primarily in the person rather than in the immediate situation; it has a *perceived internal cause.* A behavior that can clearly be attributed to situational factors gives us little information about what a person is like as an individual. If Kristen stands up and cheers wildly during an exciting football game along with 50,000 other people, the behavior is less likely to be viewed as a reflection of her personality than if the same behavior occurs during a funeral service.

Third, behaviors that reflect personality are viewed as having *organization and structure.* When the many behaviors of a person seem to "fit together" in a meaningful fashion, we find it convenient to attribute them to an inner "personality" that guides and directs behavior. Thus, we might conclude that much of Brad's behavior is understandable in terms of a driving ambition to achieve power and recognition. His behaviors seem to fit like the pieces of a puzzle within the template provided by this central aspect of his personality.

You may already have noticed that all three of the conditions Levy set down for inferring personality from others' behaviors involve perceptual judgments of those behaviors (see Figure 14.3). It is also evident that these perceptions can vary according to the behaviors being observed, the situation in which the person is behaving, and the personal characteristics of the observer. Levy thus concludes that it makes more sense to regard personality judgments as a product of our perceptions of behavior than as something existing within the person being observed. Viewing personality as a product of perception helps us to understand why we can sometimes disagree with others about what someone's personality is like and why we may sometimes feel that others have a mistaken image of what we are like. Moreover, because psychologists and psychiatrists are perceivers too, we can appreciate why there are so many different theories of personality and why theorists can become so committed to their own perspectives for viewing and understanding human individuality.

As we consider the various theories of personality, it is important to keep in mind that their components are constructs, just as personality itself is. In the following pages we will encounter a variety of constructs from personality theories, such as introversion–extraversion, id, ego, superego, anxiety, personal constructs, expectancies, and the self. All of these constructs are products of the theorists' cognitive processes, invented by them to describe behavior and explain its causes. They are not real, concrete things.

Every formal theory consists of a network of constructs and a set of principles or "laws" that explain how the constructs are related to one another. As we regard these theories, we will be concerned less with their *truth* than with their *usefulness* as scientific theories. As discussed in Chapter 2, a theory is scientifically useful to the extent that it (1) provides a comprehensive framework into which known facts can be incorporated, (2) allows us to predict future events with some precision, and (3) stimulates the discovery of new knowledge. Each theory that we encounter will be evaluated in terms of these scientific standards.

The five perspectives that have guided us throughout the book—biological, psychodynamic, humanistic, cognitive, and behavioral—have all provided rich insights about personality. We begin, however, with a tradition that goes back even farther than the traditional theories, although it has links with all of them. The **trait approach** to personality is concerned with identifying, describing, and measuring the dimensions of thought, feelings, and behavior that define the individuality we see in people.

Years ago, the trait theorist Gordon Allport and an associate went through the English dictionary and painstakingly identified and counted all of the words that could be used to describe personal traits. The result: a gigantic list of 17,953 words (Allport & Odbert, 1936). Obviously, it would be impractical if not impossible to describe people in terms of where they fall on some 18,000 dimensions. The trait theorist's goal is to condense the behavioral descriptors into a manageable number of basic traits that can capture the individuality we see in personality (John, 1989).

Two major approaches have been taken to defining what Allport (1937) called "the building blocks of personality." One approach has been to propose single traits (for example, "dominance," "friendliness," and "dependability") that seem to be of central importance from an intuitive or theoretical point of view and that incorporate a wide range of specific behaviors.

A more systematic approach uses the statistical tool of **factor analysis** to identify clusters of specific behaviors that are correlated with one another so highly that they can be viewed as reflecting a basic dimension, or trait, on which people vary. For example, you might find that some people who are very talkative and sociable also like parties and excitement, dislike solitary activities like reading, and constantly seek out new acquaintances. Others are retiring, reserved, like quiet activities, and enjoy being alone. These behavioral patterns define a factor that we might term *extraversion–introversion*. At one end of the dimension are highly extraverted behaviors, and at the other end are highly introverted behaviors (see Figure 14.4). Presumably, each of us can be placed at some point along this dimension in terms of our customary and relevant behavior patterns. (If you wish to know more about the logic and method of

The Trait Approach: Mapping the Constructs of Personality

What are the key behavioral predispositions that define individual identities? This is the question addressed by the trait perspective on personality. The goal of trait theorists is to describe the basic classes of behavior that define personality, to devise ways of measuring individual differences in these components of identity, and to use these measures to account for and predict a person's behavior in various types of situations.

The starting point for the trait researcher is behavior. But here, we have an embarrassment of riches.

Figure 14.4 Factor analysis allows researchers to reduce many behaviors to a smaller number of basic dimensions, or factors. A factor comprises behaviors that are highly correlated with one another and are therefore assumed to have common psychological meaning. Here, we see the kinds of behaviors that might fall on the two ends of the introversion–extraversion dimension. The two groups of behaviors are negatively correlated with one another.

Introversion	Dimension (factor)	Extraversion
• Retiring • Reserved • Enjoys being alone • Likes solitary activities • Does not attend parties		• Outgoing and talkative • Wants many friends • Enjoys parties • Dislikes solitary activities • Dominates social situations

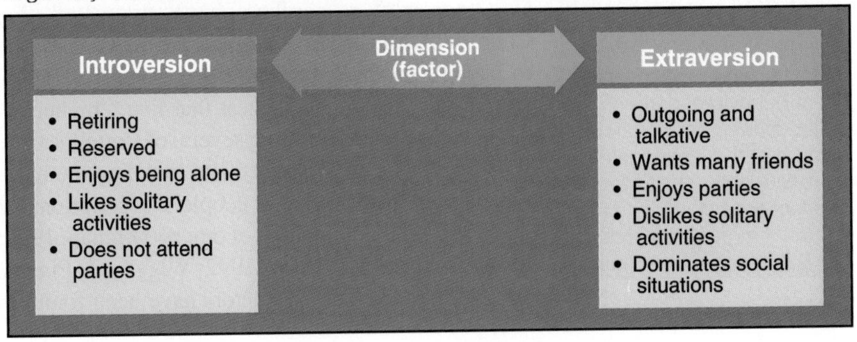

The Big Five factors have emerged consistently in factor analyses of trait ratings and self-descriptions. However, we should remember that trait names are concepts. One challenge to the Big Five, known as the **semantic similarity hypothesis,** links the Big Five to semantic networks of associated concepts like those discussed earlier in relation to memory (Chapter 10, p. 312). Could it be that the Big Five reflect nothing more than clusters of words that have common meanings (for example, *sociable, outgoing*) rather than clusters of behavioral traits that actually occur together in the real world? Thinking critically about this question, Sampo Paunonen and his coworkers (1992) reasoned that if the Big Five factors emerged when nonverbal descriptors of behaviors were used, doubt would be cast on the semantic similarity explanation. Accordingly, they devised a nonverbal personality questionnaire that consisted of pictures of people engaging in many different social behaviors and asked groups of subjects in Canada, Finland, Germany, and Poland to rate the extent to which they engaged in those behaviors. When the ratings were factor-analyzed, five factors corresponding to the Big Five emerged in all four cultures. The authors concluded that the Big Five factors represent consistent behavioral patterns that occur cross-culturally and that the languages of the four cultures studied reflect the behavioral patterns that people witness in themselves and others.

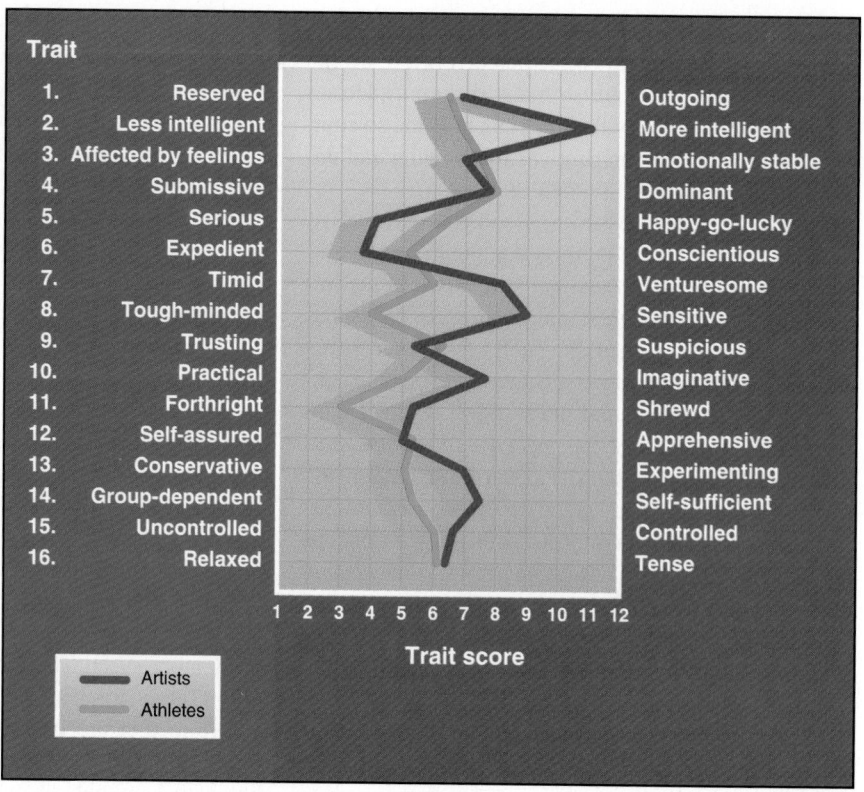

▶ **Figure 14.5** *Cattell identified 16 basic personality traits through factor analysis. Here, we see personality profiles (mean scores) for Olympic athletes and creative artists on the 16PF, the test developed by Cattell to measure the traits. (Cattell, 1965).*

factor analysis, you will find a discussion of this approach in Appendix A at the back of the book.)

How many basic personality traits are there? This is where trait theorists disagree. Because the mathematical technique of factor analysis can be used and interpreted in different ways, trait theorists have cut up the personality pie into smaller or larger pieces. For example, Raymond B. Cattell (1965, 1990) spent many years collecting data on the behaviors of thousands of people. He asked people to rate themselves on numerous behavioral characteristics and also got ratings from people who knew the subjects well. His factor analysis revealed 16 basic behavior clusters, or traits, that to him define the structure of personality. Cattell's personality factors are shown in Figure 14.5. Using this information, Cattell went on to develop a widely used personality test called the 16 Personality Factor Questionnaire (16PF) to measure individual differences on each of the dimensions and thereby provide a comprehensive personality description.

Other trait researchers have suggested that Cattell's 16 dimensions may be more than are needed to capture the basic structure of personality. Many factor analytic studies suggest that five "higher order" factors, each including several of Cattell's more specific factors, may be adequate to define the basic dimensions that appear in people's descriptions of their own behavior and that of others (Digman, 1990; McAdams, 1992; McCrae, 1992; Wiggins & Pincus, 1992). The identical five factors have been found in

diverse North American and European cultures (Paunonen & others, 1992). The so-called **Big Five personality factors** are shown in Table 14.1. Proponents of this model suggest that when a person is placed at a specific point on each of these five dimensions by means of a psychological test, behavior ratings, or direct observations of behavior, the essence of his or her personality has been captured (McCrae & John, 1992). ▼

Your reaction to this statement may be one of skepticism, since it seems that there must be more to individuality than can be captured by only five dimensions. However, recall from Chapter 6 that the incredible number of hues that humans can discriminate is based on the differential activity patterns of only three types of cones. Thus, even as few as five personality dimensions can reflect enormous variations in the pattern of people's behavioral tendencies.

One goal of trait theorists is to describe the basic structure of personality. But another is to be able to predict real-life behavior on the basis of a person's traits. Even if a limited number of general traits like the Big Five seem adequate to describe important features of personality, it is entirely possible that more specific traits like Cattell's would be better for predictive purposes, since they would be more likely to capture nuances of behavior within particular situations. To address this issue, Bryan Mershon and Richard Gorsuch (1988) studied the ability of scores derived from the 16PF to predict real-life outcomes like choice of occupation, job performance and promotions, marijuana smoking, and the development of psychological disorders. For 16 different samples of subjects, they scored the 187 items of the 16PF in two different ways. First, they calculated the standard 16 scores shown in Figure 14.5. Then they scored the test for six broader factors, five of which corresponded to the Big Five. Finally, they correlated the two sets of scores with the specific behaviors they were trying to predict so as to compare the predictive accuracy of the Big Five scores with the standard 16 scores. They found that although the Big Five factors were able to predict the behaviors to a moderate degree, the 16 factors were far superior in their predictive power. In fact, they did, on average, about twice as well. It thus appears that more specific behavioral traits are better for predictive purposes. More precisely, broad traits may do a better job of predicting behavior across a whole range of situations, but specific traits may do best in specific situations that call for the behaviors measured by narrower traits.

The Issue of Consistency: Traits, Situations, and Behavior

Because they are enduring behavioral predispositions, traits are expected to show some degree of stability over time and across situations. The research literature on stability over time shows evidence for both stability and change. Indeed, stability of personal characteristics may itself be an important individual difference variable; some people seem to show less personality change over time than others (Caspi & Bem, 1990). Some personality dimensions also tend to be more stable than others. For example, introversion–extraversion, as well as temperamental traits such as emotionality and activity level, tend to be quite stable from childhood into adulthood and across the adult years (Eysenck, 1990; McCrae & Costa, 1990; Zuckerman, 1991).

Certain kinds of thought patterns may also be fairly stable. For example, Melanie Burns and Martin Seligman (1989) studied the diaries and letters that elderly people had written approximately 50 years earlier. The letters and diaries were analyzed for the tendency to respond either optimistically or pessimistically to positive and negative life events. The elderly subjects also completed a questionnaire that measured their current optimistic–pessimistic tendencies. Although little consistency over time was shown for dealing optimistically or pessimistically with positive events, there was a notable tendency for people who had been pessimistic 50 years earlier in response to negative events to still be pessimistic when negative events occurred. The authors suggested that this tendency to be pessimistic might con-

Table 14.1 The Big Five Personality Factors and The Lower Level Trait Dimensions They Incorporate

Big Five Factors	Lower Order Traits
Extraversion/Surgency	Talkative *versus* silent Frank, open *versus* secretive Adventurous *versus* cautious Sociable *versus* reclusive
Agreeableness	Good-natured *versus* irritable Not jealous *versus* jealous Mild, gentle *versus* headstrong Cooperative *versus* negativistic
Conscientiousness	Fussy, tidy *versus* careless Responsible *versus* undependable Scrupulous *versus* unscrupulous Persevering *versus* quitting, fickle
Emotional Stability	Poised *versus* nervous, tense Calm *versus* anxious Composed *versus* excitable Emotionally stable *versus* moody, unstable
Culture/Openness	Artistically sensitive *versus* artistically insensitive Intellectual *versus* unreflective, narrow Polished, refined *versus* crude, boorish Imaginative *versus* simple, direct

Source: Based on Digman, 1990; Goldberg, 1990; McCrae & John, 1992.

stitute an enduring risk factor for depression, low achievement, and physical illness, and they are presently studying such linkages.

Across time, personality shows both a degree of stability and some capacity for change. The same appears to be true across situations. Because behavior always results from a person interacting with a situation, we would be foolish to expect people to behave in the same manner from situation to situation. Indeed, people even show variability in their behavior across situations relevant to so central a trait as honesty. In a classic study done in the 1920s, Hugh Hartshorne and Mark May (1928) tested the honesty of thousands of children. The children were given opportunities to lie, steal, and cheat in a number of different settings—at home, in school, at a party, and in an athletic contest. The rather surprising finding was that "lying, cheating and stealing as measured by the test situations in this study are only very loosely related . . . Most children will deceive in certain situations but not in others" (p. 411). More than a half-century later, Walter Mischel (1984) reported similar findings for college students on the trait of "conscientiousness." A student might be highly conscientious in one situation (for example, coming to work on time) without being conscientious in another (turning in class assignments on time).

Four factors make it difficult to predict on the basis of personality traits how people will behave in particular situations. First, situations differ in their power to evoke certain behaviors. Personality traits will not be very useful in helping us predict who will run from a burning building, since most people will do so regardless of personality differences. Traits may influence behavior more strongly in ambiguous situations, such as a relaxed group setting, where there are many behavioral options and where it is not obvious how one should behave. Second, we must remember that personality traits interact with other traits as well as with situational factors. This melding of behavioral predispositions accounts for the incredible richness we see in personality, but it also provides challenges to the psychologist who wants to predict behavior. When two or more traits, such as honesty, dominance, and agreeableness, influence a behavior, our ability to predict on the basis of only one of the traits is bound to be quite limited (Ahadi & Diener, 1989). Third, consistency across situations seems to be governed by how important a given trait is for the person. A person for whom honesty is a central component of the self-concept may show considerable stability in honest behaviors across situations, since feelings of self-worth may be linked to living up to moral standards regardless of the circumstances (Kenrick & Funder, 1991). Finally, all current personality measures are imperfect measuring devices, and this also limits their predictive power.

The stability and distinctiveness that we see in personality comes not from the fact that we and others behave the same way in every situation, but rather from the fact that we exhibit an *average* amount of extraversion, emotional stability, agreeableness, and other traits across *many* different situations (Epstein, 1983; Kenrick & Funder, 1988). Personality researchers need to define the relevant characteristics of both the situation and the person if they wish to understand more about these interactions between personality traits, situations, and behavior.

Evaluating the Trait Approach

Despite differences of opinion concerning the nature and number of basic personality dimensions, trait theorists have made an important contribution by focusing attention on the value of identifying, classifying, and measuring stable, enduring dispositions.

Several issues confront personality psychologists who are committed to a trait approach. One is the need for more agreement about the number of basic traits needed for arriving at comprehensive personality descriptions (Briggs, 1989). As we have previously seen in our discussion of intelligence, there seem to be two camps: ''splitters,'' who believe that many specific traits are needed to get at a person's individuality, and ''lumpers,'' who prefer working

with a small number of basic traits, such as the Big Five. More research is needed on the optimal number of traits for predicting behavior in specific classes of situations. The research described earlier comparing the Big Five factors with Cattell's 16 factors is a promising step in that direction.

As noted, interactions between personal and situational characteristics must be considered in predicting behavior. There is a strong movement in personality psychology toward the study of such interactions (Carson, 1989; Kenrick & Funder, 1991). This is a positive development for the trait perspective, since it places a premium on identifying and measuring the personal traits that influence how people interpret and respond to situations.

Finally, more attention must be paid to how traits interact with one another to affect various behaviors if we are to capture the true complexities of personality (Ahadi & Diener, 1989; Choca & others, 1992; Smith & others, 1990). All too often, researchers try to make specific predictions on the basis of a single measured personality trait, without taking into account other personality factors that might also influence the behavior in question. This approach sells short the complexity of personality.

In evaluating the trait perspective, it is important that we remember the distinction between description and explanation. To say that someone is outgoing and fun-loving because she is high in extraversion is merely to describe the behavior with a trait name, not to understand the nature of the inner disposition and how it operates. Traditionally, the trait perspective has been more concerned with describing the structure of personality and predicting behavior than with understanding the psychological processes that produce the traits (McAdams, 1992). The descriptive contributions of the trait perspective are very important, but the next crucial task is to understand how biological, psychodynamic, cognitive, and environmental factors combine to affect the components of identity that we call personality. With that task in mind, we now turn to theories of personality that have been concerned with understanding how inner dispositions and environmental factors interact to produce human individuality.

The Biological Perspective: Evolutionary and Physiological Foundations

More than 2,000 years ago, the Greek writer Theophrastus asked: ''Why is it that while all Greece lies under the same sky and all the Greeks are educated alike, yet we all have characters differently consti-

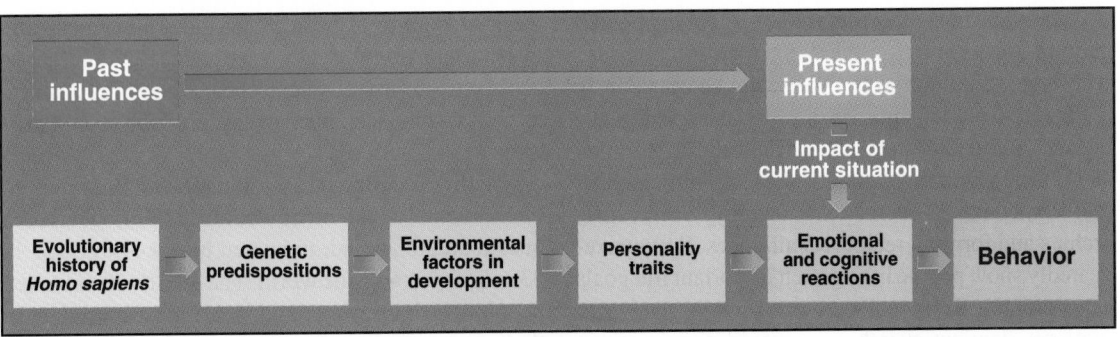

Figure 14.6 *Evolutionary theorists maintain that the factors that influence a personality behavior may stretch from the distant past to the present.*

tuted?'' Theophrastus, like many writers since, speculated that character, or personality, is physically based. The Greek physician Hippocrates sought to account for differences in personality in terms of the balance among four natural body fluids, or **humors:** black bile, blood, yellow bile, and phlegm. He hypothesized, for example, that people characterized by an overabundance of phlegm are sluggish, listless, and apathetic—a legacy expressed in our modern description of such people as *phlegmatic.*

Over the years, many speculations have been offered concerning the biological basis of personality. These have had intuitive appeal, for it is clear that even newborns differ in characteristics such as activity level and fussiness and that people differ from one another in many biological respects. Today, there remains great interest in discovering which biological processes are most relevant to human individuality and how they might interact with social influences, culture, and other factors that affect the organization of personality. A growing body of research suggests that biological hypotheses will lead to valuable information about human personality.

Evolutionary Personality Theory

Current behavior patterns are influenced by a range of determinants, some from the past and some in the present. As Figure 14.6 shows, some of the factors that affect personality are thought by sociobiologists and other evolutionary theorists to lie in the evolution of our species (Buss, 1991; Gangestad, 1989; Tooby & Cosmides, 1990). Let us begin by examining this evolutionary approach to personality.

Psychological Mechanisms and Strategies

The aim of evolutionary psychology is to identify psychological mechanisms and behavioral strategies as evolved solutions to the problems of adaptation faced by our species over millions of years. No behavior can occur in the absence of **biologically-based mechanisms** that receive input from the environment, process the information, and respond to it. These

mechanisms are, according to the evolutionary perspective, established through a process of natural selection (Buss, 1991). The mechanisms may be broad ones, such as a biological capacity to learn through operant conditioning or to reason inductively, or they may be more numerous and specific, each suited to the solution of a specific kind of adaptive problem, such as how to find a mate or form a group. These more limited mechanisms dedicated to solving specific problems are called **domain-specific mechanisms** (Tooby & Cosmides, 1990).

Evolutionary personality theory also seeks to identify **evolved behavioral strategies** for solving specific problems that face the human species. These strategies, made possible by the underlying psychological mechanisms, are cognitive, motivational, emotional, and behavioral in nature. According to David Buss (Figure 14.7), an evolutionary personality theorist, they exist in our species because they have helped humans achieve two overriding goals: physical survival and reproduction of the species (Buss, 1991).

Figure 14.7 *David Buss is a leading contributor to evolutionary personality theory.*

Many specific goals, such as achievement, power, gaining affection from others, forming relationships with others, and nurturing others, can be traced back to these two fundamental species-enhancement goals, because in one way or another they aid in survival and reproduction. So can two other sets of behaviors that mark human interactions: forming social hierarchies and forming reciprocal alliances. Surveys repeatedly show people listing such important life goals as graduating from college, getting jobs and promotions, dominating other people in certain ways, and making friends and winning lovers (Emmons, 1990). An evolutionary theorist might say that because favorable positions in social hierarchies have always provided advantages in obtaining survival resources such as food and lodging, as well as better mating opportunities, status striving is likely a major species-specific goal of humans. Likewise, the ability to form cooperative relationships is an important survival and reproductive mechanism, and so we should expect it to be heavily ingrained in human nature (Buss, 1991).

The master goals of survival and reproduction may require different subgoals and strategies for men and women. For example, women are limited in the number of eggs they can produce in their period of fertility, whereas men produce millions of sperm daily. Given these differences, the genetic survival of a female would depend on her success in finding a mate who could provide the resources to protect her and the offspring he fathered; she would not wish to squander her limited supply of eggs. For the male,

the important thing would be to find a mate capable of bearing offspring. His most valuable clues about a mate would be physical ones suggesting fertility, as well as physical attractiveness, which would promote sexual activity.

With this rationale in mind, David Buss and an international cadre of coworkers (1990) devised a questionnaire and administered it to 9,474 people in 33 cultures around the world. The questionnaire asked people which characteristics were most important to them in a mate. Despite their cultural and geographic diversity, females placed greatest emphasis on wealth and ambition, whereas males were more sensitive to youth, attractiveness, and fertility. Finding a mate who is a good provider was more important to females than to males in 36 out of the 37 groups, and physical attractiveness (which increases sexual interest) was more important to males than to females in all 37. In all 37 groups, males preferred young women, and women older men (see Figure 14.8).

Obviously, these findings do not prove the existence of an innate mechanism and strategy that differs in men and women. It could be that in most cultures, women are denied independent access to resources and therefore select the most practical remaining option. Nonetheless, the findings do not rule out the possibility of an evolutionary mechanism that is a remnant of ages past.

Evolution and the Big Five Personality Factors

Earlier, we discussed the Big Five personality factors. These personality dimensions have been found with remarkable consistency across many cultures, contexts, and data sources (Digman, 1990). Could they possibly have an evolutionary basis?

David Buss (1991) suggests that the Big Five may be so widely found because they are the most important psychological factors in our adaptive social landscape:

> They provide information for answering adaptively important life questions: Who is high or low in the social hierarchy? . . . Who will make a good member of my coalition? Who possesses the resources that I need? Who will share their resources with me? With whom should I share my resources? Who can I go to for advice? . . . With whom should I mate? Whom can I trust? . . . I hypothesize that people have evolved psychological mechanisms sensitive to individual differences in others that are relevant to answering these critical questions. (p. 472)

As a species, humans typically live in groups. Groups provide many benefits, but also some risks, such as intergroup competition and aggression and depletion of resources. Buss suggests that because

➤ **Figure 14.8** *Evolutionary theorists have predicted what factors men and women should find important in selecting mates based on principles of natural selection. Does this picture illustrate or challenge their hypothesis?*

other humans create many of the problems to which we must adapt, natural selection favored those who could detect Big Five differences in others and use this information to further his or her reproductive and survival goals. These discernments remain with us as part of our biological heritage.

The Origins of Individual Differences

So far, we have discussed evolutionary pressures that create the commonalities that constitute "human nature." But personality theory is most concerned with individual differences among people. How does evolutionary theory account for these differences?

Personality dispositions can be regarded as adaptive strategies. Although the underlying mechanisms that produce the strategies may be universal products of evolution, interactions with the environment can strongly affect the particular strategies that emerge. These environmental influences may have their impact at either the group or the individual level. For example, groups that live in hostile and dangerous environments may become more cautious in pursuing resources such as food, because caution enhances the chances of survival. In contrast, a group that lives in a benign environment with unlimited food supplies may be expected to be quite assertive and even reckless in pursuing those resources.

As individuals, each of us grows up in a unique environment, and there are many opportunities for this environment to affect our behavior. Obviously, the environment cannot change our genotype (our specific genetic structure), but it does interact with it to produce physical and psychological consequences for us and resultant changes in behavior (Scarr, 1992).

For example, all of the developmental factors discussed in Chapters 4 and 5 would be considered valid by evolutionary theorists. Moreover, given an environment with particular demands or opportunities, gender differences in male and female behavior tendencies could conceivably be reversed. They would emphasize, however, that environmental factors operate not on a "blank tablet" organism but rather on one who comes equipped with biobehavioral mechanisms that are products of natural selection and human evolutionary history. Thus, no behavior can be produced without underlying mechanisms, and no mechanism operates in a vacuum; it operates in response to an environment.

Evolution and Culture

From an evolutionary perspective, culture reflects human adaptation to particular environments, and culture provides important environmental input to evolutionary mechanisms. Consider, for example, how children are raised. We ought to find differences between cultures but also some commonalities based on evolutionary pressures. In a large-scale multicultural study of child-rearing practices in 93 societies, striking support was found for three hypotheses derived from evolutionary theory and intended to account for the reproductive roles of men and women (Low, 1989). First, boys are more commonly trained to show bravery, aggression, and self-reliance than girls (see Figure 14.9). Second, in societies that permit males to mate with several women, training in competitive striving was particularly pronounced. Finally, across cultures, girls were trained to be more responsible, obedient, and sexually restrained than boys.

Figure 14.9 *Cross-cultural research has shown that, consistent with the hypothesis that gender roles are based on processes of natural selection, boys are trained to be brave and self-reliant in the vast majority of cultures.*

These socialization practices were seen as both reflecting and reinforcing evolution-based mechanisms and strategies.

Evolutionary theory traces personality predispositions into the distant past. Any innate mechanisms of the types proposed by these theorists would have to be passed on in the genes. However, one need not take an evolutionary perspective to study genetic factors. The field of behavior genetics traces the influence of genetic factors on complex behaviors (Plomin & Rende, 1991). Recent research in behavior genetics indicates that important foundations for personality development reside in the genes we inherit. Let us examine these genetic linkages more closely.

PSYCHOBIOLOGICAL INTERACTIONS

Behavior Genetics and Personality

As discussed earlier, a number of approaches have been used to study the influence of genetic factors in humans, including studies of the degree of resemblance among family members and comparisons of monozygotic (identical) and dizygotic (fraternal) twins. Twin studies are particularly useful because they compare the degree of resemblance between monozygotic twins, who have identical genetic makeup, and dizygotic twins, who do not (Rowe, 1989). On a great many psychological characteristics, identical twins have been shown to be more similar, suggesting a role for genetics. However, the issue is clouded a bit by the possibility that identical twins may also have more similar environments than fraternal twins because they are more similar in appearance, size, and other physical characteristics.

The ideal solution to this problem would be to compare identical and fraternal twins who were reared together with identical and fraternal twins who were separated early in life and reared apart. If the identical twins who were reared in different families were as similar as those reared together, a powerful argument could be made for the role of genetic factors. Moreover, this research design would allow us to divide the total variation among individuals on each personality trait into three components: (1) variation attributable to genetic factors; (2) variation due to shared family factors; and (3) variation attributable to other factors, including individual life experiences. The relative influence of these sources of variation could be estimated by comparing correlations between personality test scores of the various groups of twins (Plomin & Rende, 1991; Scarr, 1992).

Several studies using this design with different personality measures have now appeared (Bouchard & others, 1990; Pederson & others, 1988; Tellegen & others, 1988). The studies have shown that identical twins are far more similar in personality than fraternal twins, and it makes little difference whether they were reared together or in different families. Indeed, contrary to what many personality psychologists would expect, the overall family environment had little influence on personality differences in these studies.

The results of one of the studies, conducted by Auke Tellegen and his colleagues at the University of Minnesota, is shown in Table 14.2. As you can see, genetic factors account for 40 to 50 percent of the variance in scores on the traits measured, and the general family environment accounts for little variance in any of the traits. However, the individual's *unique* environmental experiences, such as his or her relationships with parents and peers, account for considerable personality variance.

The results of these and other twin studies provide powerful evidence for the influence of genetic

Table 14.2 Estimates of the Percentages of Variance in 14 Personality Traits Attributable to Genetic Factors, the Family Environment, and Unique Environmental Factors*

Trait	Genetic	Familial Environment	Unique Environment
Well-being	.48	.13	.39
Social-potency	.54	.10	.36
Achievement	.39	.11	.50
Social closeness	.40	.19	.41
Stress reaction	.53	.00	.47
Alienation	.45	.11	.54
Aggression	.44	.00	.56
Control	.44	.00	.56
Harm avoidance	.55	.00	.45
Traditionalism	.45	.12	.43
Absorption	.50	.03	.47
Positive emotionality	.40	.22	.38
Negative emotionality	.55	.02	.43
Constraint	.58	.00	.42

*Note: The variance estimates are based on a comparison of the degree of personality similarity in identical and fraternal twins who were reared together or apart.

Source: Data from Tellegen & others, 1988.

factors on personality, but they also leave plenty of room for the influence of individual life experiences. Let us consider some ways in which the two sets of factors might interact.

Interactions between Genetic and Environmental Factors

Although we know that heredity and environment jointly influence the development of personality, it is not clear exactly how the two interact. Our genotype is established long before we enter our social environment, so the environment clearly does not change our genetic makeup. On the other hand, our genotype might influence the experiences we have and how we respond to those experiences (Plomin & Rende, 1991; Scarr & McCartney, 1983). How might this occur?

Figure 14.10 shows three ways in which genotype might influence experience. First, genetically based characteristics may influence how people respond to the early environment created by their parents and others. For example, highly intelligent parents frequently have bright children, since intelligence has a strong hereditary component (Loehlin & others, 1988). If, because of their own interest in intellectual pursuits, the parents provide an intellectually stimulating environment with many books and educational toys, the child's own intellectual growth is likely to be stimulated. The resulting bright child is thus a product both of the genes shared with her parents and of her ability to profit from the environment they provide (Scarr, 1992).

A second genetic influence on the environment is the **evocative influence.** That is, genetically influenced traits may evoke certain responses from others. Some children are very sociable and outgoing, a temperamental trait that appears to have

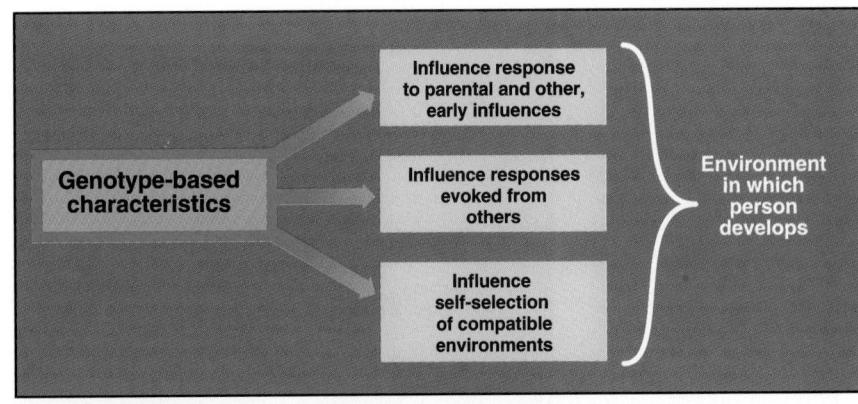

Figure 14.10 *Three ways in which a person's genotype can influence the nature of the environment in which the person develops.*

a genetic basis (Kagan, 1989). Such children are likely to evoke friendly social responses from others and create for themselves an environment in which their sociable tendencies are reinforced and strengthened (Bandura, 1989; Kagan, 1989).

Finally, genetically influenced traits are likely to affect the specific environments people seek out. That is, people seek out environments that are compatible with their personality traits. Thus, a large, aggressive boy may be attracted to football and other contact sports, whereas a shy introverted one is more likely to choose solitary activities. These different social environments may, in turn, have very different effects on subsequent personality development.

Within the biological perspective, we once again find interactions between person and environment. How people respond is influenced by both biological factors and experience, and these factors combine in ways that are just beginning to be understood.

Eysenck's Biological Dimensions of Personality

When we discussed trait approaches, we noted that there are ''splitters'' who posit many basic traits and ''lumpers'' who favor a smaller number. Hans J. Eysenck (Figure 14.11), one of Britain's leading psychologists, is the ultimate example of a lumper, for he maintains that personality can be understood in terms of only two basic dimensions, which blend together to form all of the more specific traits. Further, he believes that both of these dimensions have biological bases (Eysenck, 1990).

Eysenck's two-dimensional model of personality is shown in Figure 14.12. The basic dimensions of *introversion–extraversion* and *stability–instability* intersect at right angles (meaning that they are statistically independent, or uncorrelated), and the secondary traits shown in the circle reflect varying combinations of these two primary dimensions. Eysenck believes that differences in **introversion–extraversion** reflect a person's customary level of physiological arousal in the nervous system. Extreme introverts are chronically overaroused, so they avoid more stimulation. In contrast, extreme extraverts are chronically underaroused, so they seek out as much stimulation as they can get.

Figure 14.11 *Hans Eysenck believes that several major dimensions of personality are biologically based.*

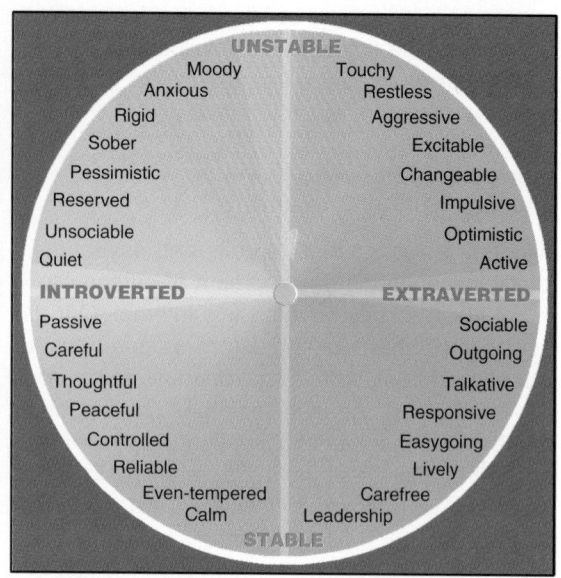

UNSTABLE

Moody · Touchy
Anxious · Restless
Rigid · Aggressive
Sober · Excitable
Pessimistic · Changeable
Reserved · Impulsive
Unsociable · Optimistic
Quiet · Active

INTROVERTED · EXTRAVERTED

Passive · Sociable
Careful · Outgoing
Thoughtful · Talkative
Peaceful · Responsive
Controlled · Easygoing
Reliable · Lively
Even-tempered · Carefree
Calm · Leadership

STABLE

Figure 14.12 *Eysenck's two major dimensions of personality, introversion–extraversion and stability–instability, are assumed to combine to form the more specific traits shown in the figure. The two basic dimensions are thought to reflect individual differences in nervous system functioning. (Eysenck, 1967).*

Stability–instability reflects not a person's customary level of arousal but the suddenness with which shifts occur. Unstable people have a hair-trigger nervous system that shows quick and sudden shifts in arousal, whereas stable people show more gradual shifts. In some of his writings, Eysenck has called this dimension **neuroticism,** for he has found that people with extremely unstable nervous systems tend to experience emotional problems that require clinical attention.

According to Eysenck, introverts need to avoid stimulus overload because their nervous systems are particularly sensitive to excitation. Their higher levels of cortical arousal make introverts more attentive to details, and so they don't need a great deal of stimulation from outside; a little goes a long way. The typical introvert is introspective, is socially distant except with certain intimate friends, keeps feelings tightly under control, and seldom behaves in an angry or aggressive manner. Extraverts, on the other hand, have a chronically low level of cortical arousal. They need powerful or frequent stimulation to achieve an optimal level of cortical arousal and excitation. The extravert seeks social contacts and physical arousal, likes parties, takes chances, and is assertive.

A closer look at Figure 14.12 shows how the basic introversion–extraversion dimension interacts with the stable–unstable dimension. When emotionally stable, the extravert is a carefree, lively person who tends to seek out leadership roles, whereas unstable extraverts tend to be touchy, aggressive, and restless.

The stable introvert tends to be calm, reliable, and even-tempered, but the unstable introvert tends to be rigid, anxious, and moody. Thus, different mixtures of the two basic dimensions can produce quite different personality patterns.

Eysenck believes that the two basic dimensions have a genetic basis, and a growing body of evidence from twin studies supports this view (Loehlin & others, 1988; Pederson & others, 1988). Eysenck thus concludes that although personality is strongly influenced by life experiences, the manner in which people respond to those experiences may be at least partially programmed by biological factors.

Evaluating the Biological Perspective

With the exception of Eysenck's theory, the biological perspective has up to now been primarily concerned with determining the extent to which genetic and other biological factors affect personality. As yet, little is known about how such factors operate and, in particular, how they interact with social and environmental factors. This seems destined to be the next objective of the researchers who work in this intriguing area (Davidson, 1991; Plomin & Rende, 1991).

The evolutionary approach to personality has stimulated considerable discussion and a renewed emphasis on cross-cultural studies. As David Buss (1991) points out, however, the evolutionary approach is more concerned with the causes of personality than with a description of personality. And as critics of the approach point out, even when studies (such as the ones on male–female differences described earlier) yield results that are consistent with evolutionary hypotheses, one cannot rule out other explanations, because there is no way to control the process of human evolution and study its effects. Nonetheless, it is clear that genetic factors are very important determinants of personality, and the possibility that some of these genetic factors may have an evolutionary basis is an intriguing one.

We now consider perspectives on personality that have been especially concerned with its inner workings, beginning with the highly influential psychodynamic perspective.

■ ▭ Psychodynamic Theories

Historically, the psychodynamic perspective has had a powerful influence on both theory and research in personality. Sigmund Freud's theory of psychoanalysis heralded the beginning of modern personality theory; and a century after his initial speculations about the role of unconscious factors and the crucial role of early childhood experiences, his ideas continue to influence Western thought.

Freud's controversial theory also attracted many critics who disagreed strongly with his conception of human nature. Some of these critics went on to develop new theories that also advanced the study of human personality. Erik Erikson, whose psychosocial stages of personality development were discussed in Chapters 4 and 5, was one such theorist. Others included Carl Jung and Alfred Adler.

Sigmund Freud's Psychoanalytic Theory

Sigmund Freud (1856–1939) lived most of his life in Vienna, where he attended medical school with the intention of becoming a medical researcher. He was particularly interested in the workings of the brain, and a pivotal event in his life occurred when he was awarded a fellowship to study in Paris with the famous French neurologist Jean Charcot. Charcot was treating patients who suffered from **conversion hysteria,** a disorder in which physical symptoms such as paralysis and blindness appeared suddenly and with no discernable physical cause. In treating these patients, Freud discovered that their symptoms were often related to painful memories and feelings that seemed to have been pushed out of awareness. When his pa-

tients were able to recall these traumatic memories and impulses, many of which were sexual or aggressive in nature, their symptoms frequently disappeared or improved markedly.

These observations convinced Freud that there exists an unconscious part of the mind that exerts great influence on behavior. Freud began to experiment with various techniques to unearth the buried contents of the unconscious mind, including hypnosis, free association (saying whatever comes to mind, no matter how trivial or embarrassing), and dream analysis. He also conducted an extensive self-analysis based on his own dreams, which he believed to be an escape valve for the release of repressed material from his unconscious mind. In 1900, he published his first book, *The Interpretation of Dreams.* The book sold only 600 copies in its first 6 years, but his revolutionary ideas began to attract new followers. They also evoked scathing criticism from a Victorian society that was not ready to regard the human being as a seething cauldron of sexual and aggressive impulses.

Freud based his theory on careful clinical observations and constantly sought to expand it (see Figure 14.13). Very much a scientist, Freud formulated specific hypotheses about the people he treated and tested them by making predictions about what should happen in therapy. He constantly revised and modified

Figure 14.13 *Sigmund Freud's influence extends far beyond the boundaries of psychology into art and literature; indeed, he is considered one of the most influential thinkers of recent centuries. In the background is the office in Vienna where Freud treated his patients and did much of his writing.*

his ideas as he gathered new data, and he never viewed his theory as a finished product (although some of his disciples did). Over time, psychoanalysis became (a) a theory for personality, (b) a method for studying the mind, and (c) a method for treating psychological disorders.

Psychic Energy and Mental Events

Freud's conception of personality as an energy system was based on the hydraulic models of 19th-century physics, which emphasized exchanges and releases of physical energy. According to Freud, psychic energy is generated by instinctual drives and constantly presses for discharge. Equilibrium in the psychic energy level is maintained by either direct or indirect discharges of impulses. For example, a buildup of energy from sexual instincts may be discharged directly in sexual intercourse or indirectly through such diverse behaviors as sexual fantasies, farming, and painting.

Psychic energy powers the mind, whose contents may be conscious, preconscious, or unconscious. Freud considered the conscious, preconscious, and unconscious to be actual areas of the mind. As we saw in Chapter 8, the **conscious** mind consists of mental events that we are presently aware of. At this moment, for example, I am aware of the words that I am typing on my computer screen and my internal image of what I want to tell you in this section. The **preconscious** is one step removed from consciousness. It contains memories, thoughts, feelings, and images that we are unaware of at the moment but that can be recalled. A friend's telephone number, a date learned in history class, and memories of your 16th birthday are all likely to reside in the preconscious mind.

Because we are aware of their contents, we are likely to see the conscious and preconscious areas of the mind as the most important ones. According to Freud, however, these areas are tiny in comparison with the **unconscious,** a dynamic realm of wishes, feelings, and impulses that lies beyond our awareness. Only when impulses from the unconscious are discharged in one way or another, such as in dreams, overt behavior, slips of the tongue, or neurotic symptoms, does the unconscious reveal itself. For example, a young man proclaimed his love for his fiance by whispering, ''I love you, Marcia.'' The only problem was that his fiance's name was Amy. Freud would probably have concluded that the slip of the tongue is a sign that the young man's feelings for Marcia, his previous romantic partner, are still there, buried in his unconscious mind. Psychoanalysts believe that such verbal slips are holes in our armor of conscious control and expressions of our true feelings (Westen, 1990).

The Structure of Personality

Freud divided the personality into three structures: id, ego, and superego. These three structures interact intimately with one another, but each has its own separate characteristics.

The **id** exists totally within the unconscious mind (see Figure 14.14). It is the innermost core of the personality, the only structure present at birth, and the ultimate source of all psychic energy. Freud described the id as ''a chaos, a cauldron of seething excitations'' (Freud, 1900/1964, p. 73). It has no direct contact with reality and functions in a totally irrational manner. The id operates according to the **pleasure principle:** It seeks immediate gratification or release, regardless of rational considerations and environmental realities. If sexual tensions build up, for example, it seeks immediate sexual satisfaction, regardless of the circumstances.

The id cannot directly satisfy itself by obtaining what it needs from the environment because it has no contact with the outer world. Therefore, in the course of development, a new structure develops out of the id. The **ego** is in direct contact with reality, and it works to satisfy the demands of the id without jeopardizing the individual's survival in society. Because the ego is an outgrowth of the id, it receives all its energy and power from the id and never becomes totally independent of it. The ego functions primarily at a conscious level, and it operates according to the **reality principle.** It tests reality to decide when and under what conditions the id can safely discharge its impulses and satisfy its needs. For example, the ego would seek sexual gratification within a consenting

Figure 14.14 *Relation of the id, ego, and superego to the conscious, preconscious, and unconscious areas of the mind.*

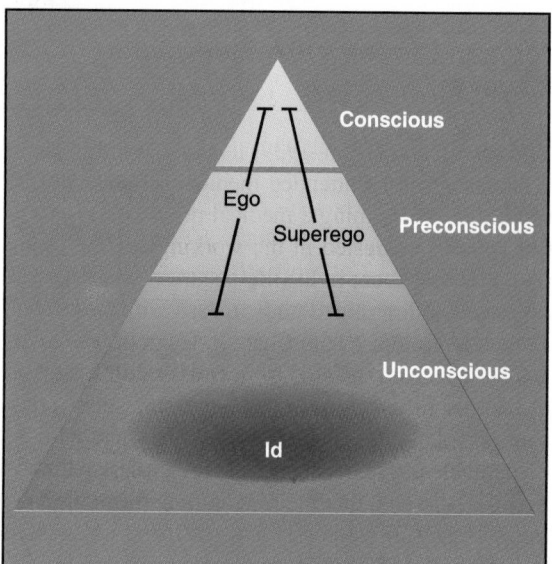

relationship rather than allowing the pleasure principle to dictate an impulsive sexual assault on the first person who happened by. The logical decision-making functions of the ego has led to its nickname, "the executive of the personality."

The third and last personality structure to develop is the **superego,** the moral arm of the personality. It contains the traditional values and ideals of the society that have been communicated to the child by parents and others. This communication occurs chiefly through the use of rewards and punishments that teach the child what is "right" and what is "wrong." These values are taken on as the person's own through the process of **internalization.** With the development of the superego, self-control is substituted for external control. Thus, the superego might cause a person to experience intense guilt over sexual activity even within a consenting relationship because it has internalized the idea that sex is "dirty."

Like the ego, the superego strives to control the instincts of the id. However, unlike the ego, the superego is irrational. The ego simply tries to postpone instinctual gratification until conditions are safe and appropriate; but the superego, in its blind quest for perfection, tries to block gratification permanently, particularly of those sexual and aggressive impulses that are condemned by society. For the superego, moralistic goals take precedence over realistic ones, regardless of the potential cost to the individual. Thus, intense guilt generated by the superego might prevent a person from enjoying sexual activity even within marriage.

Conflict, Anxiety, and Defense

The dynamics of personality involve a continuing struggle between instincts and drives in the id struggling for release and counterforces generated by the ego and superego to contain them. Observable behavior is the product of this continuing struggle (Nye, 1992).

As the "executive of the personality," the ego is squarely in the eye of the storm. When the ego is confronted with impulses that threaten to get out of control or with dangers from the environment, the result is **anxiety,** an increase in tension that, like physical pain, serves as a danger signal and motivates the ego to deal with the problem at hand. In many instances, the anxiety can be reduced through realistic coping behaviors, as when a person who is extremely angry at another decides to work out the problem through rational discussion instead of a physical assault. However, when realistic strategies are ineffective in reducing anxiety, the ego may resort to another line of defense, one that involves the denial or distortion of reality. The intrapsychic strategies, or **defense mechanisms,** that make this possible are

constructed by the ego to allow the release of impulses from the id in disguised forms that will not conflict with conditions in the external world or with the prohibitions of the superego.

Psychoanalysts believe that **repression** is the most basic defense mechanism and the primary means by which the ego "keeps the lid on the id." Repression is often described as motivated forgetting. It is an active process in which the ego uses some of its energy to prevent anxiety-arousing memories, feelings, and impulses from entering consciousness. Repressed thoughts and wishes remain in the unconscious striving for release, but they may be expressed indirectly, as in slips of the tongue or in dreams.

Freud's interest in defense mechanisms centered around the role of repression. Although he discussed other defenses in his work, it was his daughter Anna Freud, also a psychoanalyst, who defined and described the variety of defense mechanisms that psychologists think of today. Table 14.3 lists, defines, and illustrates a number of the defense mechanisms.▼

The defense mechanisms are one aspect of ego functioning that occurs at an unconscious level (Knapp, 1988). People are usually unaware that they are using self-deception to ward off anxiety. Almost everyone uses these defense mechanisms at times, but those who use them excessively in place of more realistic approaches to dealing with problems are considered maladjusted. For example, a person who constantly represses unpleasant feelings is cutting off a very important aspect of experience. She may have difficulty dealing with problems because she is so out of touch with her emotions that in her eyes, no problem exists; she may even develop a conversion hysteria, in which the repressed feelings are released in the form of physical symptoms.

The Dissenters: Neoanalytic Theories

Freud's ideas were so powerful and controversial that they generated disagreement even within his inner circle of disciples. The **neoanalysts** are a group of psychoanalytically oriented theorists who disagree with certain aspects of orthodox psychoanalysis.

Most of the neoanalysts have two basic criticisms of Freudian theory. One criticism is that the theory does not give social and cultural factors a sufficiently important role in the development and dynamics of personality. In particular, many critics attacked the psychosexual theory of development discussed in Chapter 4, and some of Freud's own followers eventually came to feel that he stressed infantile sexuality at the expense of other important determinants of personality (Kurzweil, 1989). The second major criticism is that Freud laid too much emphasis on the

▼
Thinking Critically About Gender Differences in the Use of Defense Mechanisms

Consider the defense mechanisms described in Table 14.3. Based on what you have learned about gender differences and their causes, would you predict that men and women would differ in the defense mechanisms they favor?

Research has, in fact, revealed such differences. Using the Defense Mechanism Inventory, a measure that asks subjects how they would likely respond to a variety of situations involving interpersonal conflict, David Levit (1992) found that adolescent males (ages 14–19) reported more use of "externalizing" defenses, such as projection and displacement, which involved the outward expression of aggression. In contrast, adolescent girls scored higher in "internalizing" defenses, such as turning anger inward toward the self. Other studies suggest that females tend to use more repression, denial, and reaction formation than males do. If these differences are real, how would you explain their origin based on (a) Freud's theory of sex-role development through resolution of the Oedipal and Electra complexes (Chapter 4, p. 121) and (b) social learning formulations of sex-role development (Chapter 4, p. 130)?

Table 14.3 Ego Defense Mechanisms

Defense Mechanism	Description	Example
Repression	An active defensive process through which anxiety-arousing impulses or memories are rendered unconscious.	A person who was sexually abused in childhood develops amnesia for the event.
Denial	A person refuses to acknowledge anxiety-arousing aspects of the environment. The denial may involve either the emotions connected with the event or the event itself.	A man who is told he has terminal cancer refuses to consider the possibility that he will not recover.
Displacement	An unacceptable or dangerous impulse is repressed, then directed at a safer substitute target.	A man who is harrassed by his boss experiences no anger at work, then goes home and abuses his wife and children.
Intellectualization	The emotion connected with an upsetting event is repressed, and the situation is dealt with as an intellectually interesting event.	A person who has been rejected in an important relationship talks in a highly rational manner about the interesting unpredictability of love relationships.
Projection	An unacceptable impulse is repressed, then attributed to (projected onto) other people.	A woman with strong repressed desires to have an affair continually accuses her husband of being unfaithful to her.
Rationalization	A person constructs a false but plausible explanation or excuse for an anxiety-arousing behavior or event that has already occurred.	A student caught cheating on an exam justifies the act by pointing out that the professor's tests are unfair and, besides, everybody else was cheating, too.
Reaction Formation	An anxiety-arousing impulse is repressed, and its psychic energy finds release in an exaggerated expression of the opposite behavior.	A mother who harbors feelings of hatred for her child represses them and becomes very oversolicitous and overprotective of the child.
Sublimation	A repressed impulse is released in the form of a socially acceptable or even admired behavior.	A man with strong hostile impulses becomes an investigative reporter who ruins political careers with his stories.

events of childhood as determinants of adult personality. Neoanalytic theorists agree that childhood experiences are important, but some of them, such as Erik Erikson, believe that personality development continues throughout the life span as individuals confront problems that are specific to particular stages in their lives.

Alfred Adler and Carl Jung were members of Freud's inner circle who left orthodox psychoanalysis to establish their own schools of thought (see Figure 14.15). Adler's position is known as **individual psychology.** In contrast to Freud's assertion that behavior is motivated by inborn sexual and aggressive instincts and drives, Adler insisted that humans are inherently social beings who are motivated by **social interest,** the desire to advance the welfare of others. Adler's conception of human nature was much more optimistic than Freud's, for he viewed humans as

creatures who relate to others, cooperate with them, and place general social welfare above selfish personal interests. Freud, on the other hand, often seemed to view people as animals caged by the bars of civilization. Adler also postulated a general motive of **striving for superiority,** which drives people to compensate for real or imagined defects in themselves and to strive to be ever more competent in life.

Like Adler, Carl Jung was Freud's friend and associate before he broke away and developed his own theory, **analytical psychology.** Jung disagreed with several aspects of Freud's theory, particularly its emphasis on sexuality. Jung also expanded Freud's notion of the unconscious in unique directions. For example, he believed that humans possess not only a **personal unconscious** based on their life experiences but also a **collective unconscious** which consists of memories accumulated throughout the entire history

Figure 14.15 *Carl Jung (1875–1961) and Alfred Adler (1870–1937) were associates of Freud who broke away and established highly influential neoanalytic theories. Jung is shown on the left, Adler on the right.*

of the human race. These memories are represented by **archetypes,** inherited tendencies to interpret experiences in certain ways. Archetypes find expression in symbols, myths, and beliefs that appear across many cultures, such as the image of a God, an evil force, the hero, the good mother, and the quest for unity and completeness in personality. Indeed, some of Jung's notions bear resemblances to those of the modern evolutionary theorists discussed earlier, who also believe we carry in our genes remnants of our evolutionary history that influence how we perceive, think, and act.

Evaluating Psychoanalytic Theory

Freud's most notable contributions were his recognition of the influence of unconscious motives and conflicts and his emphasis on the importance of childhood experiences in personality development. His theory of personality evolved largely from his experiences in treating psychiatric patients, and it has had a major role in attempts to understand and treat behavior disorders. (We discuss these contributions in Chapters 16 and 17.)

Freud's emphasis on the unconscious was scorned by a Victorian society that emphasized rationality and condemned as unscientific by generations of personality psychologists with a behaviorist orientation. However, research over the past 20 years has vindicated Freud to some extent by showing that nonconscious mental and emotional phenomena do indeed occur (Greenwald, 1992; Kihlstrom, 1990).

Unconscious priming of memories, subliminal perception, unconscious emotional responses, and unconscious learning have been described in previous chapters. To be sure, the nonconscious processes that have been experimentally demonstrated are by no means as sophisticated as those described by Freud (Greenwald, 1992). Nonetheless, it seems clear that much mental and emotional activity can go on outside of our awareness and that such processes can affect our cognitive, emotional, and behavioral responses. Whether these nonconscious processes, being studied largely within the cognitive perspective, are as powerful as those described by Freud remains to be seen.

Despite the doubts of Adler, Jung, and others concerning Freud's emphasis on childhood experiences, the traditional psychoanalytic approach to the early years of life remains influential. There is increasing evidence that individual life experiences in childhood have powerful effects on later behavior. For example, seductive or abusive parents can scar some children for the rest of their lives. On the other hand, a warm, supportive home environment can help a child to develop self-confidence and the ability to enjoy life (Caspi, 1989).

Although it has had a profound influence in psychology, psychiatry, and other fields, psychoanalytic theory has been criticized on scientific grounds. Many of Freud's constructs are ambiguous and difficult to operationally define and measure. How, for example, can we measure the strength of an individual's id impulses and defenses? Moreover, because very different (even opposite) behaviors can result from the same impulse because of the operation of various defense mechanisms, it is hard to make specific behavioral predictions. For example, suppose we predict on the basis of psychoanalytic theory that a person will behave aggressively, and the subject behaves instead in a loving manner. Is the theory wrong, or is the aggression being masked by the operation of a defense mechanism such as reaction formation? The difficulties in operationally defining psychoanalytic constructs and in making clear-cut behavioral predictions mean that many aspects of psychoanalytic theory are untestable, and this detracts greatly from its scientific usefulness. One of the greatest scientific challenges psychologists have faced is studying psychoanalytic constructs under controlled conditions. Let us consider an example.

In an ingenious series of experiments, Lloyd Silverman (1983) used subliminal presentations of stimuli in an attempt to evoke the unconscious wishes and conflicts that psychoanalysts view as central motivators of behavior. Usually, in this research method, sentences or phrases considered relevant to the unconscious process of interest are presented by means of a tachistoscope for .04 second—too quickly to be consciously perceived but long enough to be processed by the perceptual system. In several experiments, attempts have been made to demonstrate the presumed role of unresolved Oedipal concerns (especially unconscious guilt about desires to kill the father and possess the mother) in male college students. After performing a dart-throwing task to give a baseline measure of accuracy, subjects were randomly divided into two groups for the presentation of the subliminal stimuli. The critical stimuli were "Beating Dad is OK" (intended to reduce Oedipal conflict) and "Beating Dad is wrong" (intended to arouse it). In several experiments, Silverman and his coworkers found that subjects who received subliminal exposure to "Beating Dad is wrong" showed a significant deterioration in their dart-throwing accuracy, whereas "Beating Dad is OK" was followed by either no performance decrease or an increase in accuracy.

These results attracted a great deal of attention when they were reported, but other researchers tried to replicate them without success (Heilbrun, 1980). Other investigators have attacked the logic behind the experiments. According to psychoanalytic theory, males can resolve the Oedipal conflict in different ways, one of which is by identifying with the aggressor (father). Theoretically, a male who internalized his father's aggression could actually improve on an aggressively toned task like dart throwing when Oedipal dynamics were activated by the subliminal stimuli (Balay & Shevrin, 1988). Thus, it would be difficult to predict on the basis of psychoanalytic theory whether a given subject's task performance should increase or decrease when the subliminal messages were presented. This is a huge shortcoming from a scientific perspective. For a scientific theory to be useful, it must be capable of being *disproven.* A problem with psychoanalytic theory is that any conceivable observation can be explained after the fact, and it is hard to think of observations that would not be possible from the perspective of Freud's theory.

To counter these criticisms, psychoanalytic researchers have had to invent increasingly sophisticated research designs. For example, Howard Shevrin (1988) and his coworkers at the University of Michigan have been conducting extensive psychodynamic evaluations of patients, using interviews and psychological tests to assess their personality dynamics. On the basis of these intensive personality work-ups, critical words that relate specifically to the symptoms and presumed underlying conflicts of each subject are identified and then presented subliminally to the subject while event-related potentials are measured in the brain. The researchers have found that the critical words evoke a specific pattern of electrical responses in the brain, a pattern that other stimuli do not evoke. Is it possible that these responses reflect an activation of brain processes related to the subjects' psychological problems? If the answer to this question is yes, then these findings may represent a major research breakthrough in the study of psychoanalytic phenomena.

It is to be hoped that the coming years will see a narrowing of the gap between the psychoanalyst and the experimentalist so that the rich ideas of psychoanalysis can be subjected to more rigorous scientific scrutiny.

The Humanistic Approach

Psychoanalysis is an intrapsychic theory because it focuses on the interplay among mental forces that are assumed to influence behavior. Another group of theories about the inner workings of personality almost totally rejects the assumptions of psychoanalytic theorists. Instead of viewing the human as driven by irrational and destructive impulses, humanistic theorists emphasize the individual's creative potential and inborn striving for personal growth.

Abraham Maslow, the humanistic theorist whose hierarchy of needs we encountered in the study of motivation, stressed the importance of self-actualization. By **self-actualization,** Maslow meant self-fulfillment and the complete realization of one's potential, the "highest" of the needs in his need hierarchy (see Chapter 12). While Jung, Adler, and others have used the concept in passing, contemporary humanistic psychologists see self-actualization as the core of human development and creativity. The characteristics attributed to self-actualized people included self-acceptance, an ability to perceive reality without defensive distortion or "blind spots," independence, spontaneity in thought and behavior, a good sense of humor, creativity, an abiding concern for the welfare of the human race, a deep appreciation of the basic experiences of life, and an ability to establish deeply intimate and satisfying relations with a few people (Valle & Halling, 1989).

Carl Rogers's Self Theory

Carl Rogers was one of the most influential of the humanistic theorists (see Figure 14.16). Rogers emphasized the unique moment-to-moment character of reality. He viewed behavior not as a reaction to external stimuli but as a response to the individual's perceptions of those stimuli (Rogers, 1951). Because no one else can directly know our perceptions, Rogers maintained that no one can explain our behavior more expertly than we ourselves can.

Rogers's conception of human nature was an optimistic and positive one. He believed that the forces that direct behavior are within us and that, when they are not distorted by social conditions, these forces can be trusted to direct us toward self-actualization.

The central concept in Rogers's theory is the self. Rogers theorized that at the beginning of their lives, children cannot distinguish between themselves and their environment. As each child interacts with the world, a portion of his or her perceptual, or *phenomenal,* field gradually becomes differentiated as the self. Rogers defined the **self** as an organized, consistent set of perceptions of and beliefs about oneself (Rogers, 1959). Once the self-concept has been formed, one has a tendency to maintain it, and any experience that is inconsistent with it, including one's own behaviors, is a **threat** which generates anxiety. Well-adjusted individuals can respond to threats adaptively by modifying their self-concepts so that the experiences fit, or are *congruent with,* the self. However, other people choose to deny or distort the experiences to remove the incongruence, a strategy that can lead to problems in living.

For example, suppose that an important part of a young man's self-concept is that he is so charming and handsome that every woman finds him irresistible. He meets a young woman whom he finds very attractive but who shows a total lack of interest in him. This incongruence between his self-concept and his experience produces a threat and anxiety because his basic view of himself is challenged. He could react adaptively by modifying his self-concept to acknowl-

Figure 14.16 *Carl Rogers (1902–1987) was interested in using personal exploration as a vehicle for self-actualization.*

edge that he is not, after all, irresistible to all women. On the other hand, he might resolve the incongruence by distorting reality. He might deny the woman's lack of interest ("She's just playing hard to get"), or he might distort his perception of the woman ("She would have to be crazy not to go for me—thank heaven I found out in time").

At the other extreme, consider a young man who believes that he is totally unattractive to women. If a desirable woman expresses interest, he might revise his self-concept, but it is often as difficult for people with negative self-concepts to accept success as it is for those with unrealistically positive self-concepts to accept failure. Thus, he might also find it necessary to give a congruent explanation. ("She just feels sorry for me because I'm so ugly. She's just trying to be nice. She doesn't really like me.") Such interpretations will surely help the young man maintain his negative image of himself. Indeed, a recent study showed that when people with firmly-held negative self-views find themselves with spouses who appraise them favorably, they tend to withdraw from the marriage (Swann & others, 1992).

Adjustment refers to the degree of congruence between self-concept and experience (see Figure 14.17). The more rigid and inflexible people's self-concepts are, the less open they will be to accepting incongruous experiences and the more maladjusted they will become. If there is a significant degree of incongruence between self and experience, the de-

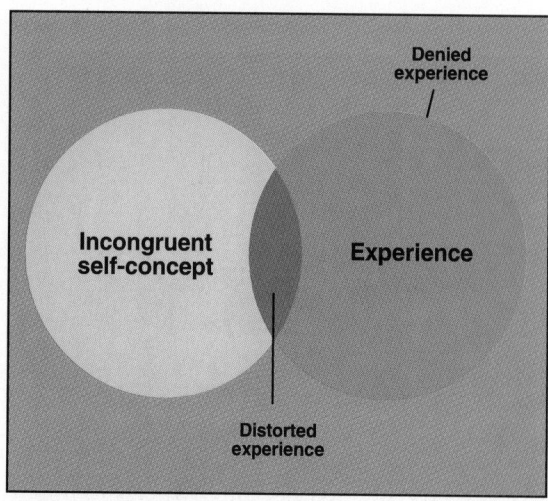

Figure 14.17 *Rogers defined psychological adjustment in terms of the degree of congruence between self-concept and experience. Maladjustment occurs when a person faced with incongruities between self and experience distorts or denies reality to make it consistent with the self-concept.*

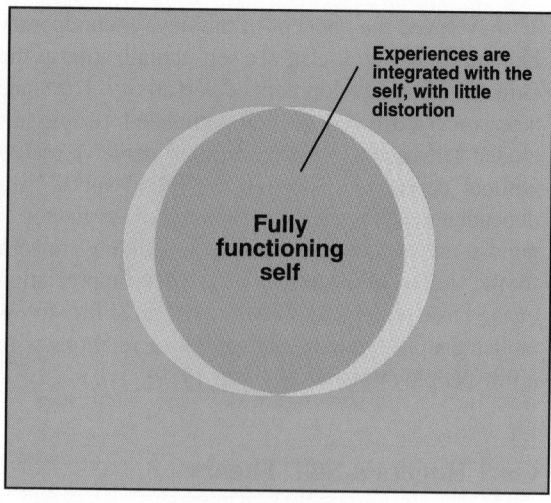

Figure 14.18 *In Rogers's view, extremely well-adjusted, or fully functioning, people integrate experiences into the self with minimal distortion, so that they have great integrity and are able to profit fully from their experiences.*

fenses used to deny and distort reality may collapse, and the individual may experience extreme anxiety and a disorganization of the self-concept.

Rogers worked with individuals who fell everywhere along the continuum from adjustment to maladjustment. Toward the end of his career, he became particularly interested in working with relatively well-adjusted individuals who wanted to grow into what he defined as **fully functioning persons** (see Figure 14.18). As Rogers viewed them, fully functioning persons do not hide behind masks or adopt artificial roles. They feel a sense of inner freedom, self-determination, and choice in the direction of their growth. They have no fear of behaving spontaneously, freely, and creatively. They can accept inner and outer experiences as they are, without modifying them defensively to suit a rigid self-concept or the expectations of others. Thus, a fully functioning unmarried woman would be able to state quite frankly that her career is more important to her than a role as wife and mother if she truly felt that way, and to act comfortably on those feelings.

Evaluating Humanistic Theories

The psychodynamics that interest theorists like Rogers differ markedly from those discussed by psychoanalysts. Instead of impulses, defenses, and unconscious processes, humanists speak of self-expression, creativity, and individual growth. People are inherently good and will actualize themselves if their environments do not interfere with their innate tendency to become all that they can be. In contrast,

Freud believed that the environment provides the controls that keep people's inherently destructive nature in check.

Humanistic theorists are especially concerned with the individual's subjective experiences. What matters most is how people view themselves and the world (Nye, 1992). Some critics believe that the humanistic point of view is limited because it relies too much on individuals' reports of their personal experiences. For example, psychoanalytic theorists maintain that accepting what a person says at face value may easily lead to erroneous conclusions because of the always-present influence of unconscious factors. Some critics also believe that it is very difficult to make precise behavioral predictions on the basis of certain humanistic concepts. For example, they argue that it is impossible to define an individual's actualizing tendency except in terms of the behavior that it supposedly produces.

Humanism may indeed seem nonscientific in its emphasis on subjective experience. Carl Rogers recognized the need for scientific research, however (Rogers, 1959). One of his most notable contributions was a series of ground-breaking studies on the process of self-growth that can occur in psychotherapy. To measure the effectiveness of psychotherapy, Rogers and his coworkers focused on the discrepancy between clients' ideal selves (what they would like to be) and their real selves (their perceptions of what they are actually like). The studies revealed that when clients first enter therapy, the discrepancy is typically large, but it gets smaller as therapy proceeds, suggesting that therapy may help the client to become more self-accepting and perhaps also more realistic. By analyzing tape recordings of therapy sessions, Rogers and his coworkers also discovered therapist characteristics that either aid or impede the process of self-actualization in therapy. This research will be described in Chapter 17.

By giving the self a central place in his theory, Rogers helped stimulate a great deal of research on the self-concept (Fiske & Taylor, 1991). For example, self-esteem (how positively or negatively we feel about ourselves) has been the focus of much recent research. Self-esteem is clearly a personality trait of overriding importance. Indeed, it may be the most important component of personal well-being, happiness, and adjustment (Epstein, 1990; C. A. Smith, 1991). Many studies have shown that people with high self-esteem are less susceptible to social pressure, have fewer interpersonal problems, achieve at a higher and more persistent level, and are more capable of forming satisfying love relationships (Baumeister, 1991; Cheek, 1989). In contrast, people with a poor self-image are more prone to psychological problems like anxiety and depression, to physical illness, and to poor social relationships and underachievement (Higgins, 1987).

Rogers suggested that people have a need to regard themselves positively, and research has indeed revealed a strong and pervasive tendency to gain and preserve a positive self-image. These processes are known as **self-enhancement** (Brown, 1991; Tesser, 1988). As Rogers suggested, people have a variety of strategies for preserving their self-images, and sometimes these strategies, like Freud's defense mechanisms, involve the denial and distortion of reality. However, in contrast to Rogers's belief that such distortions occur primarily in maladjusted people, research has shown that they actually characterize most people. Moreover, there is evidence that, if they are not taken to an extreme, positive self-biases may actually help to maintain and increase feelings of psychological well-being (Brown, 1991; Greenwald, 1989).

Several self-enhancement strategies have been identified. For example, people show a marked tendency to attribute their successes to their own abilities and effort but to attribute their failures to environmental factors. Furthermore, most people rate themselves as better than average on virtually any socially desirable characteristic that is subjective in nature (Steele, 1988). For example, most business people and politicians rate themselves as more ethical than the average, and the majority of high-school students rate themselves in the top 10 percent in their ability to get along with others. Even people who have been hospitalized after causing auto accidents rate themselves as more skillful than the average driver (Pyszczynski & Greenberg, 1987). Indeed, as evidence on self-serving biases in self-perception continues to accumulate, researchers are concluding that positive illusions of this sort are the rule rather than the exception in well-adjusted people and that these self-enhancement tendencies are in large part successful in maintaining people's positive self-concepts (Taylor & Brown, 1988). Much of this research reflects the legacy left by Rogers.

■ ▢

Cognitive and Cognitive–Behavioral Theories

Like psychodynamic and humanistic theories, cognitive approaches to personality emphasize the role that mental life plays in behavior. However, cognitive theorists focus less on people's unconscious processes and self-concepts and more on their conscious information processing tendencies. These theorists are most interested in how people interpret situations and formulate plans for action. Cognitive theorists might say that each of us is his or her own personality theorist, with unique assumptions and views of the world that guide our lives. Understanding our individuality requires that we know something about these personal theories.

We now consider two cognitive approaches to personality. The first is George Kelly's vision of people as personal scientists who try to understand, predict, and control the events in their lives. The second is Albert Bandura's attempt to integrate cognitive and behavioral perspectives into a more encompassing social–cognitive theory.

George Kelly's Personal Construct Theory

A theory developed by George Kelly is the clearest example of a purely cognitive perspective on personality (see Figure 14.19). According to Kelly, people's primary goal is to make sense out of the world, to find personal meaning in it. When they are unable to do so, they experience uncertainty and anxiety. To achieve understanding, they try to explain and understand the events of their lives, and they test this understanding in the same way scientists do: by attempting to anticipate, to predict. Kelly's primary interest was how people construct reality by sorting the persons and events in their lives into categories. Kelly termed these categories **personal constructs.**

All perception involves categorizing. Even when we see something we have never seen before, we categorize it as "something I have never seen before." From birth, stimuli are categorized, given meaning, and reacted to in terms of the categories, or

► **Figure 14.19** *George Kelly (1905–1966) developed his personal construct theory in the 1940s and 1950s while serving on the faculty of Ohio State University.*

personal constructs, into which they are placed. Every person has his or her own pattern of preferred personal constructs (such as "good," "bad," "successful," "powerful," and so on), which vary in personal importance. By understanding these constructs, the rules an individual uses to assign events to categories, and his or her hypotheses about how the categories relate to one another, Kelly believed that we can understand the person's psychological world.

Personal constructs, like scientific constructs, must have operational definitions, or *referents.* For example, what does a person mean when he or she uses the category *trustworthy?* What kinds of behaviors fit into that construct? We need either examples of behaviors that the individual would label as trustworthy or a statement of the person's standards for considering someone trustworthy to understand the meaning of the construct for that person.

The same event can be categorized, or perceived, in entirely different ways by different individuals. For example, suppose that two lovers break up. One observer may construe the event as "simple incompatibility"; another may think that one person was "jilted" by the other; another might describe the breakup as the "result of parental meddling"; another might call it "a terrible development"; and a fifth might see it as "a blessing in disguise."

Rather than evaluating alternative constructions according to whether or not they were "true" (which we cannot know), Kelly examined the consequences of construing in particular ways. For example, if one of the people in the broken relationship interpreted what happened as "being rejected," Kelly would try to discover the consequences for the person of construing the situation in that way. If the construction led to bad outcomes or predictions, such as the conclusion that "No one will ever love me, and I'll never get involved again," then the task would be to find a more useful alternative (for example, "I am someone who hasn't found the right person yet but who will if I keep trying"). Kelly saw psychotherapy as a way of demonstrating to clients that their constructions are hypotheses rather than facts. Once clients realize this, they can be encouraged to test their constructs so that the maladaptive ones can be replaced by more useful ones.

In order to help clients experiment with new viewpoints and behaviors, Kelly developed a technique called **fixed-role therapy.** He wrote role descriptions for his clients that differed from their typical views of themselves. For example, a shy person might be asked to play the role of a more confident and assertive person for two or three days, to think and act like a confident person. Kelly and the client would practice the role within the therapy setting to be certain that the client had command of the required behaviors and the view of the world that a confident individual would have. Kelly hoped that by trying out the new role, the client might gain a first-hand appreciation for the ways in which different constructions and behaviors can lead to more satisfying life outcomes. Kelly suggested that the willingness to experiment with new roles and ways of thinking can help all of us to develop in ways that enhance our lives.

Albert Bandura's Social Cognitive Theory

The psychology of learning has had a pervasive influence in American psychology, and this influence has extended to the area of personality. Many of our behaviors, particularly those that fall within the realm of personality, are acquired through learning. The behavioral perspective views personality as a set of learned behaviors and attempts to specify the conditions under which particular patterns of behavior are developed, maintained, and changed.

For radical behaviorists like John Watson and B. F. Skinner, personality had no place within a scientific psychology; they rejected any reference to unobservable processes occurring within the individual. They regarded internal "personality" processes as "explanatory fictions" that deflect attention from the true causes of behavior, which to them resided in the external environment and the past learning history of the person. An operant approach to behavior involves careful and precise measurement of the individual subject's behavior as it is affected by observable environmental conditions. Skinnerians believed that their approach was more likely to isolate the variables that cause behavior to develop and change than an approach that attributes behavior to the internal workings of an unobservable "personality."

A newer and less radical behavioral approach that has attracted many adherents is Albert Bandura's **social cognitive theory** (Bandura, 1986, Cervone & Williams, 1992). Although it also focuses on environmental causes of behavior, this approach differs from the Skinnerian position in emphasizing the importance of the cognitive processes that mediate between stimulus and response. Bandura believes that humans are more than passive responders to external stimuli and that there is a need to understand the interplay between what people think about, on the one hand, and the environmental conditions under which particular personality patterns are developed, maintained, and changed, on the other. Although he agrees that people learn much of their behavior as a result of positive reinforcement, punishment, and other consequences, Bandura also believes that complex cognitive processes play important roles in human personality. For example, people can solve problems symbolically ("in their heads") without having to resort to actual trial and error because they can foresee the consequences of their behavior. Thus, you can imagine how people are likely to react to various statements you might make in a social situation. As I write this book, I am constantly asking myself questions like, "Will the reader understand this concept if I present it in this way?" and making self-statements like, "I think they'll find this study interesting." These cognitive events govern my behavior even though environmental rewards (or punishments) will not occur until I find out how students and professors have responded to my efforts.

Cognitive processes also allow people to encode observations of others' behaviors and consequences and store them in memory. In other words, as we have seen, people often acquire complex social behaviors through observational learning or modeling (see Figure 14.20). As mentioned in Chapter 9, observation alone is sufficient for learning, but whether or not observers subsequently perform a behavior depends on the consequences that the model experiences and on the observers' expectations about the consequences they would experience if they performed the behavior. Thus, a shy person may observe and even admire an extravert who can easily engage others in conversation and yet may not perform the same be-

◆ **Figure 14.20** *According to Bandura's social cognitive theory, many of the behaviors that constitute personality are at least partially acquired through modeling.*

haviors because he believes, "That would never work for me."

Like other learning theorists, Bandura believes that behavior is strongly influenced by the consequences it produces. However, he points out that rewards and punishments may be either external or self-administered, and he places strong emphasis on the importance of self-reinforcement and self-punishment. In some cases, powerful self-administered consequences may override external consequences. For example, we saw in the case of Holy Hubert, the campus evangelist described in Chapter 9, that behaviors that are unrewarded or even punished by others may be maintained by self-approval. Bandura (1989) has become interested in **self-regulation** of behavior through internal, as opposed to external, reinforcement and punishment. He believes that attention to such processes may contribute to our understanding of moral development. Social cognitive theory has also focused on the development of techniques through which people lacking in behavioral self-control can be helped to acquire self-regulation skills that increase personal control of their thoughts, emotions, and behaviors.

Bandura believes that the question of whether behavior is more strongly influenced by personality factors or by the person's environment is basically a meaningless one. For Bandura, the person, the person's behavior, and the environment all influence one another in a pattern of two-way relationships that he calls **reciprocal determinism** (see Figure 14.21). For

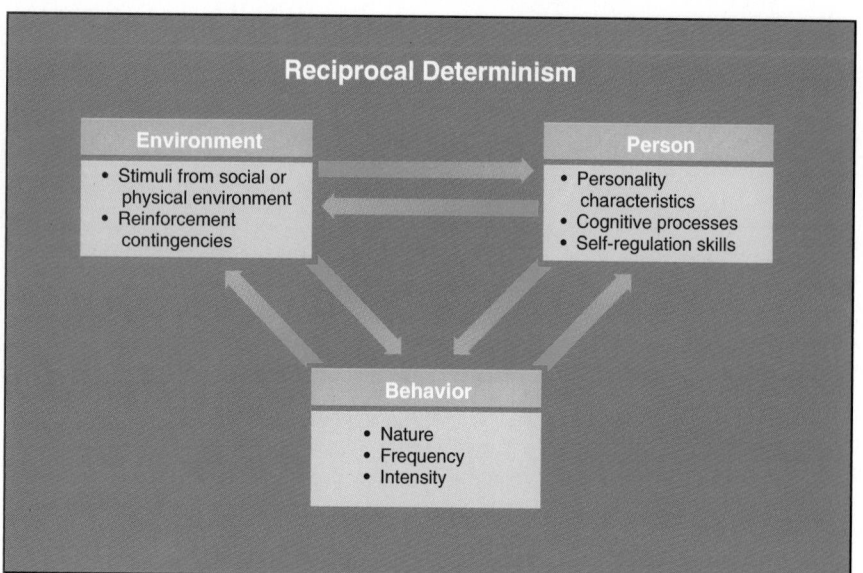

Reciprocal Determinism

Environment
- Stimuli from social or physical environment
- Reinforcement contingencies

Person
- Personality characteristics
- Cognitive processes
- Self-regulation skills

Behavior
- Nature
- Frequency
- Intensity

Figure 14.21 *A key concept in social cognitive theory is reciprocal determinism, in which characteristics of the person, the person's behavior, and the environment all affect one another in reciprocal, or two-way causal relations.*

example, the trait of extraversion will be expressed in outgoing social behaviors (person influences behavior). These outgoing behaviors are likely to evoke positive responses from others (behavior influences

environment) that strengthen the person's extraverted trait and behavior tendencies even more (environment influences person and behavior). Bandura's theory of behavior echoes the many descriptions in this book (including this chapter's Psychobiological Interactions feature) of instances in which personal characteristics influence the environment and the environment influences the person.

An important factor in how people regulate their lives is their sense of **self-efficacy,** their beliefs concerning their ability to perform behaviors that will yield desired outcomes. People whose self-efficacy is high have confidence in their ability to perform those behaviors needed to overcome obstacles and satisfy needs. According to Bandura, anxiety occurs when self-efficacy is low in a situation in which the person could suffer physical or psychological harm (Bandura, 1989).

The most effective method for boosting self-efficacy is *performance accomplishment.* Consequently, Bandura emphasizes the need to create environmental settings that maximize opportunities for personal accomplishment. Parents need to help their children gain mastery over important features of their environment. Teachers need to do the same thing. The following feature provides guidelines for increasing self-efficacy, and thereby increasing self-esteem.

ENHANCING HUMAN PERFORMANCE

INCREASING SELF-EFFICACY

What makes us expect that we can perform the behaviors needed to achieve our personal goals? A good deal of research has been done on the factors that govern self-efficacy (see Figure 14.22). Four important sources of information that can increase or decrease self-efficacy have been identified: performance experiences, observational learning, verbal persuasion, and emotional arousal (Bandura, 1986; Cervone, 1992). The first important determinant is our past performance in similar situations, particularly our successes and failures. A second source of information comes from observing others' behaviors and their outcomes. For example, if you observe a person similar to yourself accomplish something, then you are likely to believe that if you perform those same behaviors, you will also succeed. Third, self-efficacy can be increased or decreased by what others

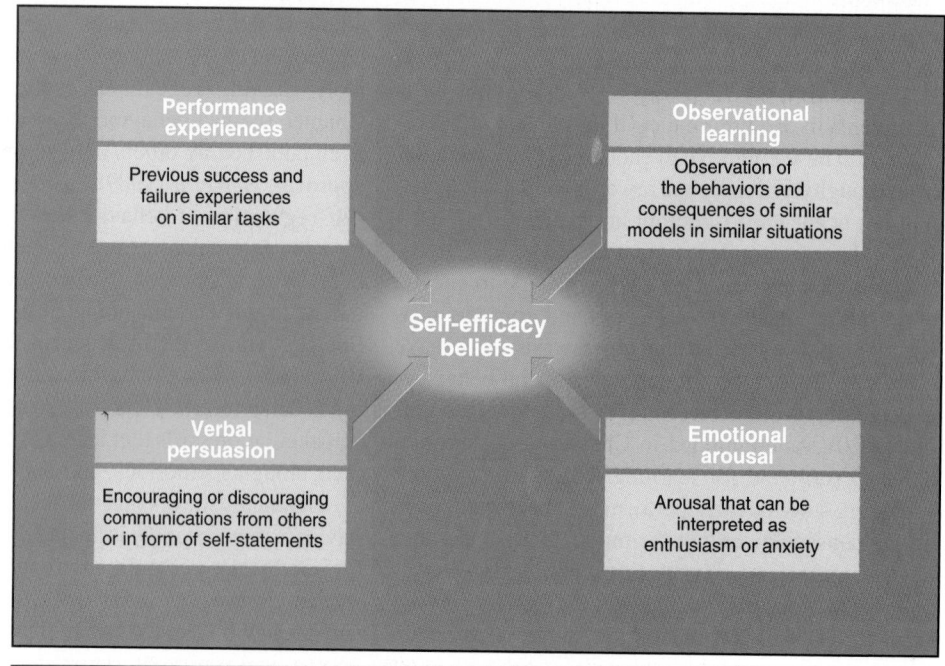

Performance experiences
Previous success and failure experiences on similar tasks

Observational learning
Observation of the behaviors and consequences of similar models in similar situations

Self-efficacy beliefs

Verbal persuasion
Encouraging or discouraging communications from others or in form of self-statements

Emotional arousal
Arousal that can be interpreted as enthusiasm or anxiety

Figure 14.22 *Sources of information that affect self-efficacy beliefs.*

tell us about our capabilities or by what we tell ourselves. Finally, high emotional arousal that is interpreted as anxiety tends to decrease self-efficacy.

By far the most important determinants of self-efficacy are personal accomplishments (Maddux, 1991). Therefore, we focus here on how you can increase your own success experiences through systematic goal setting and the mastery experiences that result.

Self-efficacy relates in part to goals that we wish to attain. When we succeed in reaching a particular goal, our self-efficacy in relation to that goal increases. When we learn coping skills that can be applied to many areas of our lives, our general sense of personal efficacy tends to increase (Smith, 1989). Fortunately for us, there exist some highly effective principles for systematic goal setting that can increase our chances for success (Locke & Latham, 1990). Goal setting, done correctly, is a powerful tool for personal development. Highly successful people have usually mastered the skills involved in setting challenging and realistic goals, figuring out what they have to do on a day-by-day basis to achieve them, and making the commitment to do what is required. As they achieve each goal they have set, they become more skillful and increase their sense of personal efficacy.

An enormous amount of research has been done on the factors that make goal-setting programs most effective (Locke & Latham, 1990). Here are some guidelines derived from that research:

1. *Set specific, behavioral, and measurable goals.*
The first step in changing some aspect of your life is to set a goal. The kind of goal you set is very important, because good goals encourage us to work harder, enjoy success, and increase self-efficacy.

Specific and fairly narrow goals have been shown to be far more effective than general "do your best" goals (Locke & Latham, 1990). A goal such as "improving my tennis game" is less likely to be helpful than "increasing the percentage of serves I put in play by 20 percent." The latter goal refers to a specific behavior that you can focus on and measure.

One of the most important aspects of goal setting is to be able to measure

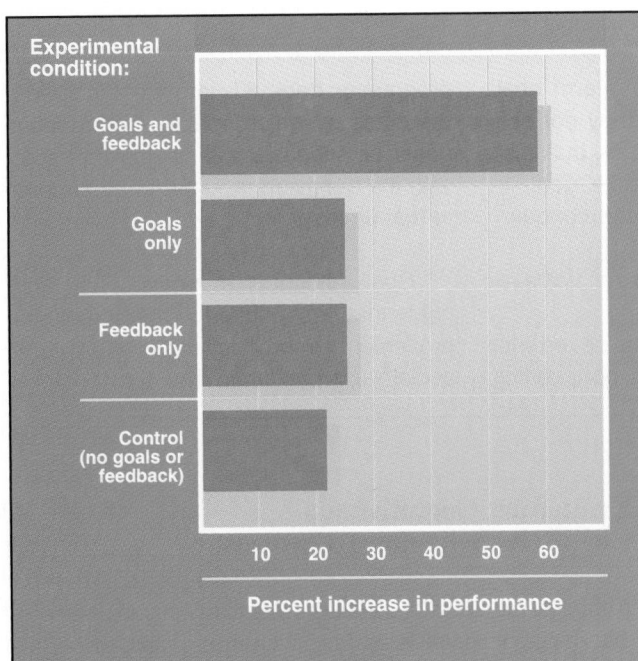

◀ **Figure 14.23** *The effects of improvement goals and performance feedback on performance improvement on a grueling bicycling task. Clearly, the combination of explicit goals and performance feedback resulted in the greatest improvement in performance. (Data from Bandura & Cervone, 1983).*

progress toward the goal. This was shown in a study by Bandura and Daniel Cervone (1983) in which subjects worked on a strenuous bicycle-pedaling task over a number of trials. Two experimental variables were manipulated: (1) whether the subjects were given specific improvement goals and (2) whether the subjects were given feedback on their performance on the previous trial. The dependent variable was the speed and power with which they pedaled. As shown in Figure 14.23, the subjects who had both goals and feedback showed by far the greatest improvement. Thus, it is very important to find a way to measure your progress toward the goal so that you get performance feedback and can see your improvement.

2. *Set performance, not outcome, goals.*
Many of our goals relate to outcomes in the future, such as "getting an A in this course." You are more likely to achieve such goals if you use the means–ends strategy discussed in Chapter 11 and think about what specific things you must do to achieve that outcome goal. Performance goals (what one has to do) work better than outcome goals because they keep the focus on the necessary behaviors. A performance goal might be "read the book and outline the lecture notes for one hour each day." Achievement of this performance goal can also be measured, giving you constant feedback. Many peo-

ple focus on outcome goals and forget what has to be done on a day-to-day basis to achieve them. It has been said that there are three kinds of people: those who wait for things to happen, those who *make* things happen, and those who wonder what happened.

3. *Set difficult but realistic goals.*
Moderately difficult goals challenge and motivate us and give us a sense of hope. When reached, they increase self-efficacy. Easy goals do not provide a sense of accomplishment, and extremely difficult goals do not provide the success experiences we need.

4. *Set positive, not negative, goals.*
Chapter 9 discussed the advantages of positive reinforcement over punishment. Working toward positive goals, such as "getting a B," is better than avoiding a negative consequence, as in "not flunking." Again, positive goals keep you focused on the positive steps that you need to take to achieve them.

5. *Set short-range as well as long-term goals.*
Short-range goals are important because they provide the opportunity for immediate mastery experiences, and they keep you working positively. A long-term goal like "graduating with honors" can easily be broken into a series of subgoals that you can be working toward right now. Short-term goals are like the steps on a

staircase leading to the long-term goal. As they are accomplished, they not only provide mastery experiences but also lead you toward your ultimate goal. In reaching any goal, "divide and conquer" is a cliché that works.

6. *Set definite time spans for achievement.*

It is said that the road to hell is paved with good intentions. To keep a goal-setting program on track, it is important to specify the dates by which specific performance goals or subgoals will be met, together with the behaviors needed to attain them in that time span.

Goal setting is a motivational technique that has resulted in remarkable improvements in productivity in many work, social, and academic settings (Locke & Latham, 1990). Moreover, for purposes of increasing self-efficacy, it has the added advantage of providing the repeated mastery experiences that are the most powerful sources of efficacy information.

Evaluating Cognitive and Cognitive–Behavioral Theories

Although the effort to develop personality theories that integrate cognitive and behavioral principles is a relatively recent trend, the progress that has been made is encouraging. In the past decade, cognitive–behavioral theorists like Bandura have paid increasing attention to personality variables that determine how individuals give "meaning" to situations. As cognitive theorists emphasize, people are active as interpreters of information and also as planners, decision makers, and doers. Recent attempts to specify the personal variables, such as self-efficacy expectancies, that influence an individual's responses to situations are a major step toward understanding person–situation interactions.

Another recent trend that seems promising concerns overlap between the psychoanalytic and cognitive perspectives (Horowitz, 1988). Recently, cognitive psychologists have done research on what a Freudian might call unconscious information-processing (Greenwald, 1992; Kihlstrom, 1990). As earlier chapters have shown, this work suggests that people can process and respond to internal and external stimuli that are not in conscious awareness. It may be that despite the subjective experience of being in conscious control of feelings and thoughts, decisions and actions, people are piloted far more than they know by the unconscious mind. Although it may be difficult to draw the precise border between conscious and nonconscious, researchers are fascinated by what that elusive line means for the understanding of behavior (Mandler, 1988).

Personality Assessment

If I were to point out a woman you have never met and give you one week to provide a complete personality description of her, what would you do?

Chances are, you would seek information in a variety of ways. You might start by interviewing the person and finding out as much as you could about her. Based on your knowledge of the theories we have discussed, what questions would you ask? Would you ask about early childhood experiences and dreams? About how the person sees herself and others? About how the person customarily feels and responds in various situations? Would you be interested in the kinds of traits embodied in the Big Five or in Eysenck's dimension of introversion–extraversion? Your answers to these questions and your other assessment decisions reflect your own theory of what is important in describing personality.

You probably would not be content simply to interview the woman. You might also decide to interview other people who know her well and get their views of what she is like. You might even ask them to rate her on a variety of traits such as those listed in Table 14.1 or Figure 14.5, and you could ask the person you are studying to rate herself on the same measures to see how well the two sets of measures agree.

Finally, you might decide that it would be useful to observe how the person behaves in a variety of situations. You would want to observe her in such a way that you got as "natural" and characteristic a sample of her behavior as possible. This information, together with that obtained from the person and from those who know her best, might provide a reasonable basis for a personality description.

The goal of the professional personality assessor is, like yours, to decide which personality characteristics are to be measured and then to find ways to obtain a sample of behavior—either from the person who is being assessed or from other people—that is useful in describing personality and in predicting the behavior of that person. Figure 14.24 shows the major methods used to assess personality characteristics. As you can see, psychologists use some of the same methods you might have chosen: the interview; trait ratings and behavior reports; and behavioral assessment, or direct observation and measurement of the person's behavior. In addition, they have developed several different types of psychological tests, including objective self-report measures and projective tests, such as those involving the perception of inkblots or pictures. Finally, physiological measures are also used to measure various aspects of personality, such as emotional reactivity and levels of cortical arousal.

Reliability and Validity of Personality Measures

The task of devising valid and useful personality measures is anything but simple, and it has taxed the ingenuity of psychologists for nearly a century. Before describing these various methods for assessing personality, we should understand the characteristics that a personality measure must have in order to be useful from either a scientific or a practical perspective.

First, personality measures need to be reliable. **Reliability** refers to consistency of measurement, and its several aspects are summarized in Table 14.4. If we assume that we are measuring a stable personality trait, then scores on our measure should be stable, or consistent, over time. This type of measurement consistency is defined as **test–retest reliability,** and it is assessed by administering the measure to the same subjects on two occasions separated in time. The scores obtained on the two administrations should correlate highly (between .75 and .90).

Another form of reliability, **internal consistency,** has to do with the consistency of measurement *within* the measure itself. For example, if we assume that the questions on a 30-item questionnaire are all measuring anxiety, then the individual items should correlate with one another. Thus, we ought to be able to randomly select any two sets of 15 items and score them as separate tests. People's scores on the two subtests should be highly correlated with one another.

Finally, **interobserver reliability** refers to consistency of measurement between different investigators using the measure. For example, observers who are counting the number of times particular behaviors occur during a videotaped interview should have very similar if not identical scores.

Validity is the second critical characteristic of personality measures. Validity refers in general to how well an assessment device actually measures what it is designed to measure. As in the case of reliability, there are several types of validity. **Content validity** refers to whether the measure asks about the major classes of behavior that comprise the construct of interest. For example, if we believe that anxiety involves both worry and physiological arousal, then our measure of anxiety should have questions that ask about both of these aspects of anxiety.

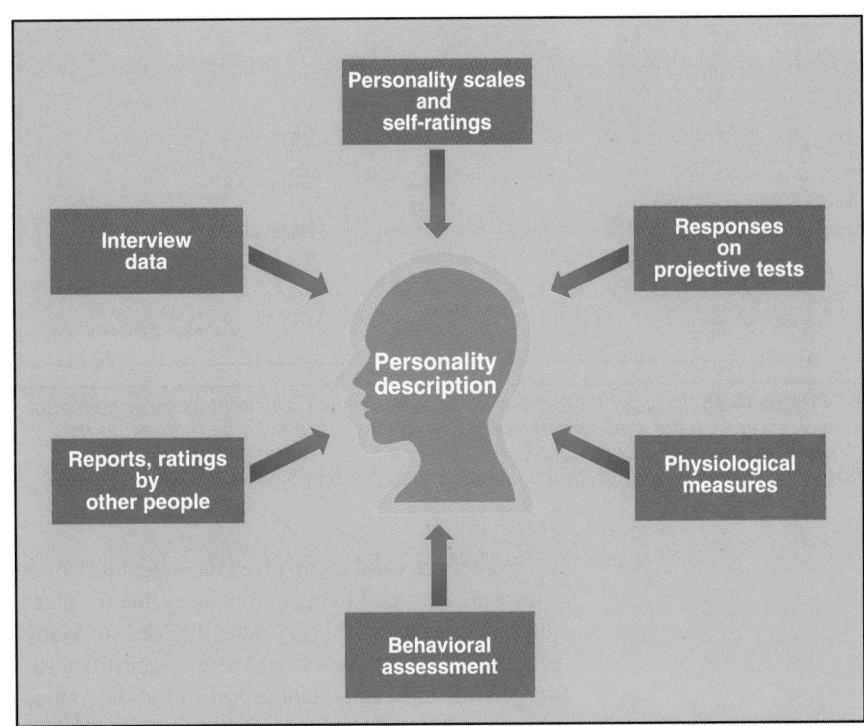

▲ **Figure 14.24** *A variety of approaches can be used to assess the constructs of personality.*

Criterion-related validity is the ability of scores on a measure to predict some present or future behavior, or criterion, relating to the trait or characteristic being measured. Such validity is very important for practical use of tests. Thus, scores on the college entrance examination you took were designed to predict the criterion of grades in college. A measure of need for power might be used to predict the criterion of seeking political office.

Table 14.4 Types of Reliability and Validity for Personality Measures

Types of Reliability	Meaning and Critical Questions
Test–retest reliability	Are scores on the measure stable over time?
Internal consistency	Do all of the items on the measure seem to be measuring the same thing, as indicated by high correlations among them?
Interobserver reliability	Do different raters or scorers agree on their scoring or observations?
Types of Validity	
Content	Do the questions or test items relate to all aspects of the construct being measured?
Criterion-related validity	Do scores on the test predict some present or future behavior or outcome assumed to be affected by the construct being measured?
Construct validity	To what extent is the assessment device actually measuring the construct of interest?

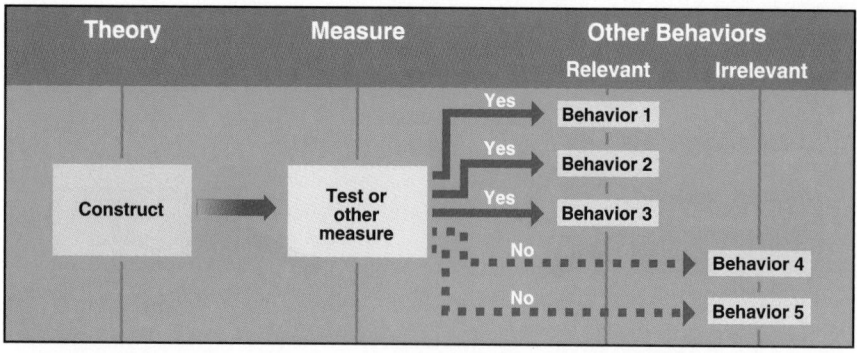

Theory | Measure | Other Behaviors
Relevant | Irrelevant

Construct → Test or other measure

Yes → Behavior 1
Yes → Behavior 2
Yes → Behavior 3
No ┈┈┈> Behavior 4
No ┈┈┈> Behavior 5

⬅ **Figure 14.25** *In order for a measure of a personality construct to show construct validity, scores on the measure must relate to behaviors viewed as relevant to the construct (in this case, behaviors 1, 2, and 3) and must not relate to behaviors assumed to be irrelevant to the construct (in this case, behaviors 4 and 5).*

Construct validity involves the extent to which a measure designed to operationally define (or measure) a construct in a theory actually does so. Many personality psychologists believe that construct validity is the most important aspect of validity, since it permits the testing of personality theories (Hogan & Nicholson, 1988; Ozer, 1989). If a measure has high construct validity, it can be used to test hypotheses derived from the theory.

The construct validity of a measure is assessed through research. A measure will be judged to have high construct validity if it (1) relates to other behaviors in the manner predicted by the theory and (2) does *not* relate to behaviors that have nothing to do with the construct. Suppose the example shown in Figure 14.25 relates to a test designed to measure the construct of anxiety. We can see that the test relates as the theory says it should to three behaviors that should be affected by anxiety—say, physiological arousal, lowered performance, and avoidance of the feared situation. On the other hand, scores on the measure are unrelated to behavior 4, perhaps a measure of extraversion that the theory considers irrelevant to anxiety, and behavior 5, a measure of the tendency to deny difficulties such as anxiety even if we have them. Evidence of this kind would indicate that the anxiety measure had high construct validity for measuring individual differences in anxiety.

Having considered the measurement standards by which psychological tests are evaluated, let us now turn to the kinds of measures that are used to assess personality variables.

Interviews and Behavioral Observation Approaches

Interviews and observations are the oldest methods of assessment. Long before the invention of writing, people undoubtedly made judgments about others by observing them and talking with them. Observation and interviewing are similar in that both involve observing verbal and nonverbal behavior and drawing conclusions from the observations. They differ in that interviewers interact directly with the person being observed, whereas behavioral observers normally do not. Although the presence and characteristics of the interviewer may affect how the person responds in ways that can affect the validity of the information obtained, interviewers have greater opportunity to obtain information about a person's thoughts, feelings, and other internal states, as well as information about past behavior.

The Interview

An old adage says that if we want to know something about a person, we should simply ask him or her. The appeal of this adage is reflected in the fact that practitioners in all the theoretical perspectives use interviews to assess personality (see Figure 14.26). Their interviewing techniques range from informal conversational exchanges (**unstructured interviews**) to well-organized series of specific questions designed to elicit specific information (**structured interviews**).

Good interviewers do not limit their attention to what an interviewee says; they also look at how he or she says it. They note interviewees' general appearance and grooming, their voice and speech patterns, the content of their statements, and their facial expressions and posture.

The interview is valuable for the direct personal contact it provides, but it has some limitations, particularly from a research standpoint. For example, it is difficult to measure everything that goes on in an interview, although the use of videotaping now makes it possible to go back and analyze both verbal and nonverbal behavior in greater detail than was previously possible. A second limitation is that the validity of the information obtained in an interview depends on the interviewee's desire to cooperate and his or her knowledge and ability to report what the interviewer is trying to assess. The person being interviewed may not understand the questions or may resist the purpose behind the interview. Some interviewees may be defensive and may hesitate to discuss personal opinions, attitudes, and concerns openly. Interviewers must estimate the degree to which the desire of some interviewees to distort facts or to present themselves in a socially desirable light may invalidate some or all of their responses.

Sometimes interviewers observe behaviors that clients are unaware of themselves, as in the following incident:

> During the interview she held her small son on her lap. The child began to play with his genitals. The mother,

without looking directly at the child, moved his hand away and held it securely for a while. . . . Later in the interview the mother was asked what she ordinarily did when the child masturbated. She replied that he never did this—he was a very "good" boy. She was evidently entirely unconscious of what had transpired in the very presence of the interviewer (Maccoby & Maccoby, 1954, p. 484).

Despite its limitations, the face-to-face interview is obviously essential for certain purposes. A clinical psychologist needs to observe and converse with someone who is being considered for admission to a mental hospital. A personnel specialist who wants to fill a top management position must interview those being considered for the job. The interview may also provide an opportunity to establish a good working relationship with a person and increase the validity of other personality measures, such as tests and questionnaires.

Behavioral Assessment

Personality psychologists can sometimes directly observe the behaviors they are interested in rather than asking people about them. **Behavioral assessment** procedures can provide highly reliable and valid information about how frequently and under what conditions certain classes of behavior occur (see Figure 14.27). Coding systems representing the behavioral categories of interest are constructed, and observers are trained in these systems until they show high interobserver reliability in their use (Haynes, 1990).

Observing and recording behavior in different settings allows assessors to identify stimulus situations that give rise to specific types of behavior. For example, behavioral assessors reporting on a young child who is having problems in school do not simply say "Jerry is disruptive." Instead, they try to answer such questions as "What does Jerry do that causes disruption? What events precede and follow his disruptive behavior?" Once they have identified a specific type of response, the next question is "How often and under what conditions does the response occur?" Answers to these questions can be particularly important not only in measuring individual differences in people's personality characteristics but also in assessing the kinds of person–behavior–environment interactions described by Bandura's reciprocal determinism.

Personality Scales

The most widely used method for assessing personality in both research and clinical work is the personality scale, or questionnaire. Personality scales include standard sets of questions, usually in a true–false or multiple-choice format. Their advantages in-

Figure 14.26 *The interview is one of the most widely used methods of obtaining information about personality, for it provides a great deal of behavioral information in addition to the verbal responses of the person being interviewed.*

clude the ability to collect data from many people at the same time, the fact that all people respond to the same items, and ease of scoring. Their major disadvantage is the possibility that people will choose not to answer the items truthfully, in which case their scores will not be valid reflections of the trait being measured.

Personality scales are constructed in two major ways. The most common method is the **rational–**

Figure 14.27 *In behavioral assessment, carefully trained observers code behaviors and the circumstances under which they occur. Here a psychologist codes interactions between children and their parents.*

theoretical approach. Here, items are based on the theorist's conception of the construct he or she wants to measure. For example, to develop a measure of self-esteem, we would ask ourselves what people high and low in self-esteem would be likely to say about themselves. We might write items such as the following:

Item	Answer Key
I usually think of myself as a very worthwhile person.	True
I am a basically good person.	True
I consider myself a success in life.	True
There are a lot of things about myself that I would like to change.	False

The second major approach to selecting items is the **empirical approach.** In this method, items are chosen because they differentiate between groups of people already known on other bases to differ in the personality characteristic of interest. To develop a self-esteem measure using the empirical approach, we would find one group of people who are known, perhaps on the basis of interviews, to be very high in self-esteem and another group known to be low in self-esteem. Then we would administer a set of items to the subjects and identify items answered differently by the two groups, regardless of the items' content. These discriminating items would constitute our self-esteem scale.

The empirical approach was used in the development of the **Minnesota Multiphasic Personality Inventory (MMPI)** (Hathaway & McKinley, 1989), the most widely used personality instrument. It was originally designed to provide an objective basis for classifying different types of psychiatric patients. The recently revised MMPI-2 consists of 567 statements to be answered true or false. The items vary widely in content; some are concerned with attitudes and emotions, others relate to overt behavior and symptoms, and still others refer to the person's life history. The following sample items suggest the diversity of MMPI-2 statements.

- I believe there is a God.
- I would rather win than lose a game.
- I am worried about sex matters.
- I believe I am being plotted against.
- I believe in obeying the law.
- Everything smells the same.

The MMPI-2 consists of 10 *clinical scales* and three *validity scales* (see Table 14.5). The validity

Table 14.5 The Validity and Clinical Scales of the Minnesota Multiphasic Personality Inventory-2 (MMPI-2) and the Behavioral Characteristics Associated with High Scores on the Scales

Scale	Abbreviation	Behavioral Correlates
Validity scales		
Lie	L	Lies or is highly conventional
Frequency	F	Exaggerates complaints, answers haphazardly
Correction	K	Denies problems
Clinical scales		
Hypochondriasis	Hs	Expresses bodily concerns and complaints
Depression	D	Is depressed, pessimistic, guilty
Hysteria	Hy	Reacts to stress with physical symptoms, lacks insight into negative feelings
Psychopathic deviate	Pd	Is impulsive, in conflict with the law, involved in stormy relationships
Masculinity, femininity	Mf	Has interests characteristic of stereotypical male or female sex roles
Paranoia	Pa	Is suspicious, resentful
Psychasthenia	Pt	Is anxious, worried, high-strung
Schizophrenia	Sc	Is confused, disorganized, disoriented, and withdrawing from others
Hypomania	Ma	Is energetic, active, restless
Social introversion	Si	Is introverted, timid, shy, lacking self-confidence

scales are used to evaluate the validity of the person's responses to the test. Most of the clinical scales are made up of items that were answered differently by various categories of psychiatric patients than by persons not diagnosed as having a psychiatric disorder. Responses on the MMPI-2 are scored in relation to a number of keys. These scores are then plotted on a graph, or profile sheet, that reflects the degree to which the individual deviates from the "normal" group (see Figure 14.28). A high score on any scale indicates that the individual's responses to its items were similar to those of the particular type of psychiatric patients whose responses were used to construct the scale.

The clinical scales are designed to measure personality deviations such as schizophrenia, depression, and psychopathic personality. The validity scales are designed to measure people's tendencies to lie, to "fake bad," or to place themselves in a socially desirable light. For example, if you marked "true" to items like the following, your responses would be somewhat suspect, and your scores on several of the clinical scales would be adjusted upward to "correct" for your defensiveness:

■ I like everyone, even loud-mouthed, obnoxious people.
■ I have never been jealous of the good fortune of another.
■ I am always kind and thoughtful.

On the basis of findings gathered over nearly 50 years, MMPI-2 users believe that its scales are useful not only for diagnosing psychological disorders but also for describing the personality characteristics of people who do not display such symptoms. The test is also widely used as a screening device in industrial and military settings.

Projective Tests

Freud's emphasis on the importance of unconscious factors stimulated attempts to devise methods for assessing such personality phenomena. Since, by definition, people are unaware of the contents of the unconscious, they cannot report them on questionnaires. A different approach was needed, and the projective hypothesis provided the basis for several widely used measures. The **projective hypothesis** holds that if a person is presented with a stimulus whose meaning is not clear, the meaning the person attributes to the stimulus will have to come partly from within. The person's interpretation may thus reflect the projection of inner needs, feelings, and ways of viewing the world onto the stimulus.

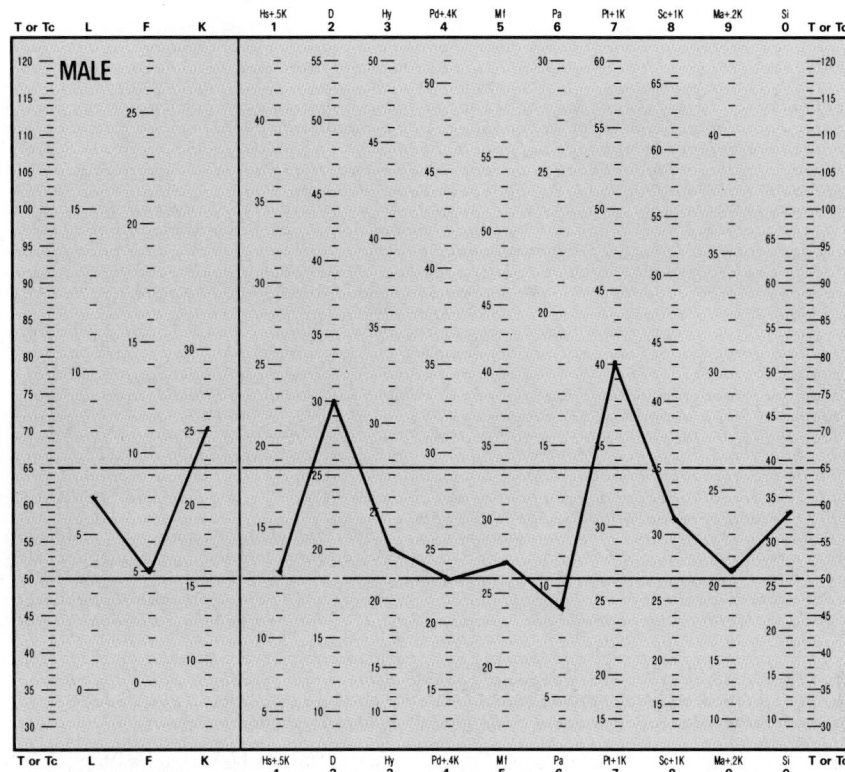

◆ **Figure 14.28** Scores on the MMPI–2 scales are recorded on a personality profile sheet. Scores above 65 are clinically significant. This person's profile indicates clinically significant levels of depression (D) and anxiety (Pt), as well as a tendency to present a defensively positive impression (high K).

Perhaps the following apocryphal story will help illustrate the rationale for projective techniques. During the administration of a set of Rorschach inkblots, a man saw nothing in the inkblots except sex organs and people engaging in sexual relations. After the last card, the tester exclaimed, "I've never in my entire career seen anyone so obsessed with sex as you seem to be." The man responded indignantly, "What do you mean, *I'm* obsessed with sex? *You're* the one with all the dirty pictures!"

The two most widely employed **projective tests**—the Rorschach inkblots and the Thematic Apperception Test—are based on psychodynamic theories and are used to assess unconscious processes.

Rorschach Inkblots

There are 10 **Rorschach inkblots.** Subjects are shown each one and asked, "What does this look like? What might it be?" (see Figure 14.29). Examiners write down the responses word for word. They also carefully note subjects' behavior during testing, including gestures, mannerisms, and expressed attitudes. They categorize and score responses in terms of the kinds of objects reported, the

features attended to (for example, the whole blot, colored portions, tiny details), and the emotional tone associated with particular types of responses (Erdberg, 1990). Interpretations made by Rorschach examiners are often based on what the responses seem to symbolize. For example, people who see peering eyes and threatening figures in the inkblots are likely to be viewed as projecting their own paranoid fears and suspicions into the stimuli.

Research on the validity of traditional Rorschach ''signs'' has been quite discouraging, with many of them demonstrating no validity whatsoever (Aiken, 1989). Despite these bleak results, many psychodynamic clinicians have maintained their faith in the usefulness of the instrument, insisting that there is no better way of gaining insight into the unconscious processes in which they are interested.

Thematic Apperception Test

The **Thematic Apperception Test (TAT)** was developed in the 1930s by Henry Murray of Harvard University. It consists of 30 pictures, including a blank card that requires the person to describe a scene. The pictures were obtained from paintings, drawings, and magazine illustrations. Although they are more ambiguous than most photographs, they have much more structure than inkblots. Subjects are told to describe what is going on in each scene, what the characters are thinking and feeling, and what the outcome of the situation will be.

Descriptions of personality written on the basis of the TAT usually deal with such topics as the following:

1. The subject's behavior in the testing situation.
2. Characteristics of the subject's words or phrases.
3. Kinds of fantasies that the subject talks about.
4. Personal relationships depicted in the stories.
5. Inferences about conscious and unconscious needs of the subject.
6. The subject's perception of the environment.
7. Emotional tone of the stories.
8. Outcomes of the stories.
9. Common themes that run through the stories.
10. Degree to which the stories reflect control over impulses and contact with reality.

The TAT has proved to be a useful clinical and research instrument. You may recall from Chapter 12 that this method has been used by researchers to measure motivational variables such as need for achievement and need for power. Indeed, it appears to be the most valid measure of these needs (McClelland, 1988).

Cognitive Assessment

Assessing the thoughts and ideas that pass through people's minds is a relatively new development. It has received impetus from the cognitive approach to personality and from the growing evidence that thought processes and the content of thinking are related to emotions and behavior. The difference between normal and abnormal behavior can frequently be explained by the thoughts that preoccupy the individual.

Cognitive assessment provides information about adaptive and maladaptive aspects of people's thoughts and the role that their thoughts play in planning, decision making, and interpreting reality. Cognitive assessment can also provide information about thoughts that precede, accompany, and follow maladaptive behavior and can be useful in measuring the effects of treatment procedures designed to modify these thought patterns (Beck & Freeman, 1990).

Cognitive assessment can be carried out in a variety of ways. ''Beepers'' have been used as signals for subjects to record their current thoughts at certain times of the day (Csikszentmihalyi, 1990; Singer, 1988). Questionnaires have been developed to sample thoughts that follow an upsetting event.

Cognitive assessment is useful not only in providing data for researchers but also in helping people keep track of their own thoughts. We are often not aware of how frequently we think about particular, often unwanted, ideas as we engage in our daily activities.

Personality Theory and Personality Assessment

The nature and organization of thoughts, feelings, and bodily processes and their relationships to behavior are what personality theories are all about. Researchers obtain information about these aspects of people's lives through the use of the various assessment techniques. A researcher's theoretical perspective influences what assessment approach he or she is likely to use. Projective techniques are favored by psychoanalytic theorists because the way people respond to tests like the Rorschach and TAT resembles the free association method that Freud advocated. Assessments of the self-concept and personal aspirations are used by humanistic theorists to measure people's current self-perceptions and goals (Wylie, 1989). Cognitive theorists ask people to list or describe their thoughts either orally or through a paper-and-pencil questionnaire. Social cognitive theory leads researchers to use behavioral assessments and to ask people to rate their expectations about what will happen in the future and how well they will do in particular situations. Paper-and-pencil inventories like the MMPI are favored by trait theorists. Relations between theoretical perspectives and assessment approaches are shown in Table 14.6.

While particular theoretical perspectives seem to lend themselves to certain assessment approaches, the connections between theory and assessment are not hard and fast. One reason for this is that it is not immediately obvious what is the best way to assess characteristics like repression, personal constructs, and the self-concept. In order to resolve this important issue, we need clearly defined theoretical constructs, effective instruments to assess the constructs, and criteria for validating the assessment devices. As we enter a second century of systematic approaches to the study of personality, recent advances in both theory and assessment promise new progress in understanding and measuring the components of identity that constitute personality.

Table 14.6 Assessment Techniques Associated with the Major Theoretical Approaches to Personality

Theoretical Approach	Assessment Techniques
Trait	Personality scales to measure the relevant dimensions of personality
Biological	Personality scales; psychophysiological measures
Psychoanalytic	Clinical interviews and projective tests to assess unconscious dynamics, conflicts, and defenses
Humanistic	Client-centered interviews and self-concept questionnaires to assess real self and ideal self
Cognitive	Interviews and a test devised by Kelly to assess personal constructs; cognitive assessment through interviews and self-report questionnaires; use of beepers to sample thoughts
Social cognitive	Interviews to obtain reports of learning experiences; behavioral assessment techniques; questionnaires to assess self-efficacy

S U M M A R Y

What Is Personality?

● The concept of personality arises from observations of individual differences and consistencies in behavior. Personality is not a thing but a concept, or construct, used in reference to certain behaviors. The term *personality* is applied to behaviors that are perceived to be components of identity, to be internally caused, and to have organization and structure. Because all these conditions are perceptual, personality may be regarded as a perceptual phenomenon rather than something concrete that exists within the person being described.

● Personality theories consist of systems of constructs and series of propositions that specify how the constructs are related to one another. To be scientifically useful, a theory's constructs must be capable of operational definition. Theories have three basic functions: (1) to organize existing knowledge, (2) to allow prediction of future events, and (3) to stimulate the discovery of new knowledge.

The Trait Approach

● Trait theorists try to identify and measure the basic dimensions of personality. They disagree concerning the number of traits needed to adequately describe personality. Cattell suggested 16 basic traits; other theorists insist that as few as 5 may be adequate. Prediction studies indicate that the larger number of more specific traits may be superior for prediction of behavior in specific situations.

● Traits have not proved to be highly consistent across situations, and they also vary in stability over time. The degree of consistency shown varies among individuals and may also vary for different traits, depending on the importance of the trait for the individual and the power of situations to evoke particular responses. It is also important to remember that traits interact not only with situations but with one another.

The Biological Perspective

● Evolutionary theories of personality attribute some personality dispositions to genetically controlled mechanisms based on natural selection.

● Recent studies comparing similarities in identical and fraternal twins reared together or apart indicate that genetic factors account for as much as half of the variance in personality test scores, with individual experiences accounting for the rest. Surprisingly, the general family environment seems to account for very little variance.

● Genetic factors may help influence the environment in which a person develops by influencing reactions to the early environment created by parents and others, by affecting the ability of people to evoke particular responses from others, and by influencing the environments that people select for themselves.

● Eysenck's theory posits two major dimensions of personality, introversion–extraversion and stability–instability, both of which are assumed to have biological bases.

Psychodynamic Theories

● Freud's psychoanalytic theory views personality as an energy system. Personality dynamics involve modifications and exchanges of energy within this system. Mental events may be conscious, preconscious, or unconscious.

● Freud divided the personality into three structures: id, ego, and superego. The id is irrational and seeks immediate instinctual gratification on the basis of the pleasure principle. The ego operates on the reality principle, which requires it to test reality and to mediate between the demands of the id, the superego, and reality. The superego is the moral arm of the personality.

● The dynamics of Freudian personality functioning involve a continuous conflict between impulses of the id and counterforces of the ego and superego. When dangerous id impulses threaten to get out of control or when danger from the environment threatens, the result is anxiety. In order to deal with threat, the ego may develop defense mechanisms, which are used to ward off anxiety and permit instinctual gratification in disguised forms.

● Neoanalytic theories incorporated many of Freud's basic ideas but stressed the importance of social rather than sexual determinants of personality development and functioning.

The Humanistic Approach

● Humanistic theories emphasize the subjective experiences of the individual and thus deal with perceptual and cognitive processes.

● Carl Rogers's theory postulates an innate tendency toward self-actualization. Central importance is attached to the role of the self. Experiences that are incongruous with the established self-concept produce threat and may result in a denial or distortion of reality. Rogers described a number of characteristics of the fully functioning person. His theory helped stimulate a great deal of research on the self-concept. This research indicates the prevalence of self-enhancement tendencies, which seem to contribute to people's adjustment.

Cognitive and Cognitive–Behavioral Theories

● George Kelly viewed people as scientists whose major goal is to understand, predict, and control their world. His cognitive theory emphasizes how people mentally create their own reality by means of the personal constructs they use to categorize the events and persons in their world.

● Bandura's social cognitive theory is concerned with how social relationships, learning mechanisms, and cognitive processes jointly contribute to behavior. Learning experiences affect people through the influence of thought. Bandura is concerned with the role of internal self-regulation in guiding behavior, and in the role of self-efficacy, people's beliefs concern-

ing their ability to perform behaviors that will yield desired outcomes.

Personality Assessment

● Methods used by psychologists to assess personality include the interview, behavioral assessment, physiological measures, personality scales, and projective tests. An increasing interest in cognitive assessment is emerging as well.

● In order to be useful measures of personality traits, assessment devices must be reliable and valid. Especially important are criterion-related validity (how well the device predicts other behaviors) and construct validity (how well the device measures the construct it is assumed to measure).

● The major approaches to constructing personality scales are the rational–theoretical approach, in which items are written on an intuitive basis, and the empirical approach, in which items that discriminate between groups known to differ on the trait of interest are used.

● Projective tests present ambiguous stimuli to subjects. It is assumed that in order to interpret the stimuli, the subjects must project internal processes onto them. The Rorschach inkblot test and the Thematic Apperception Test are the most commonly used projective tests.

● Cognitive assessment is used to measure individuals' thought contents.

KEY TERMS AND CONCEPTS

analytic psychology (p. 444)
anxiety (p. 443)
archetypes (p. 445)
behavioral assessment (p. 457)
Big Five personality factors (p. 432)
biologically-based mechanisms (p. 435)
cognitive assessment (p. 460)
collective unconscious (p. 444)
conscious (p. 442)
construct validity (p. 456)
content validity (p. 455)
conversion hysteria (p. 441)
criterion-related validity (p. 455)
defense mechanism (p. 443)
domain-specific mechanisms (p. 435)
ego (p. 442)
empirical approach (p. 458)
evocative influence (p. 439)

evolved behavioral strategies (p. 435)
factor analysis (p. 431)
fixed-role therapy (p. 450)
fully functioning person (p. 448)
humors (p. 435)
id (p. 442)
individual psychology (p. 444)
internal consistency (p. 455)
internalization (p. 443)
interobserver reliability (p. 455)
introversion–extraversion (p. 439)
Minnesota Multiphasic Personality Inventory (MMPI) (p. 458)
neoanalytic theory (p. 443)
neuroticism (p. 440)
personal construct (p. 449)
personality (p. 430)
personal unconscious (p. 444)

pleasure principle (p. 442)
preconscious (p. 442)
projective hypothesis (p. 459)
projective tests (p. 459)
rational–theoretical approach (p. 458)
reality principle (p. 442)
reciprocal determinism (p. 451)
reliability (p. 455)
repression (p. 443)
Rorschach inkblots (p. 459)
self (p. 447)
self-actualization (p. 446)
self-efficacy (p. 452)
self-enhancement (p. 449)
self-regulation (p. 451)
semantic similarity hypothesis (p. 432)
social cognitive theory (p. 451)
social interest (p. 444)

stability–instability (p. 440)
striving for superiority (p. 444)
structured interview (p. 456)
superego (p. 443)

test–retest reliability (p. 455)
Thematic Apperception Test (TAT) (p. 460)
threat (p. 447)
trait approach (p. 431)

unconscious (p. 442)
unstructured interview (p. 456)
validity (p. 455)

SUGGESTED READINGS

Aiken, L. R. (1989). *Assessment of personality.* Boston: Allyn & Bacon. A comprehensive overview of the major tests and measures used to assess personality. The author discusses the backgrounds and characteristics of the various tests and measurement approaches and critically evaluates their reliability and validity.

McAdams, D. P. (1990). *The person: An introduction to personality psychology.* Ft. Worth: Harcourt Brace Jovanovich. A comprehensive and well-written overview of the field of per-

sonality. The text provides many interesting biographical facts about the various theorists as well as a well-integrated treatment of representative research.

Nye, R. D. (1992). *Three psychologies: Perspectives from Freud, Skinner, and Rogers* (4th ed.). Pacific Grove, Calif.: Brooks/Cole. This critically acclaimed book presents a brief but engaging overview of the major ideas of these important theorists, as well as their real-world implications.

Pervin, L. A. (Ed.). (1990). *Handbook of personality: Theory and research.* New York: Guilford Press. For the student looking for an advanced, in-depth treatment of the topics covered in this chapter and many others as well, this is an outstanding resource. The 27 chapters, written by experts in their fields of specialization, provide an overview of the entire field of personality.

15 Stress, Coping and Well-Being

■□

C H A P T E R   O U T L I N E

N early 50 years after the horror of the Holocaust, psychological scars remain for many of the Jewish survivors of the Nazi concentration camps. Long-term follow-up studies paint a consistently negative picture of their adjustment (Krystal, 1968; Nadler & Ben-Shushan, 1989; Ryn, 1990). Psychological tests and interviews indicate that most of them are still troubled by high levels of anxiety and recurrent nightmares about their traumatic concentration camp experiences. Many who lost their families continue to experience sudden fear that something terrible will happen to their spouses or children whenever they are out of sight. Depression and crying spells are also common, as are feelings of insecurity and difficulties in forming close relationships.

Priscilla, now 15, had anything but an idyllic childhood. She grew up in an impoverished inner-city home with an alcoholic father who sexually abused her and her younger sister. Her mother was twice hospitalized with ''nervous breakdowns.'' When Priscilla was 7 years of age, her father called his family together in the living room and told them, ''You drove me to this.'' He then put a gun to his head and committed suicide as they watched. From that time on, Priscilla had to work after school to help support the family. Her mother became increasingly disturbed and sometimes beat her.

Considering her background, we might expect Priscilla to be an unhappy, maladjusted child. Instead, she is a delightful and popular young woman who is president of her high school class, a talented singer, and an honor student. Children like her have been termed ''invulnerable'' or ''resilient'' youngsters (Garmezy, 1983; Werner & Smith, 1982). What allows them to rise above the stressful environments in which they developed?

At age 34, Walter Chadwick was already a millionaire. His meteoric rise to the top at a Wall Street investment firm was the product of relentless work, a constant struggle to meet nearly impossible time demands, a hostile impatience with anything or anyone who caused delays in getting things accomplished, and an inability to relax and enjoy his young family. Unbeknownst to Chadwick, his family, and his associates, a silent killer gathered strength within his apparently healthy body. The killer struck late one evening as Chadwick worked feverishly to complete a project. The night janitor in his office building found him slumped over his uncompleted report, the victim of a fatal heart attack.

The enterprise of living involves a constant confrontation with demands, some produced by our environment and some of our own making. Our psychological and physical well-being depends on complex interactions among environmental demands, the personal and environmental resources that we have to deal with them, and the individual vulnerabilities that place us at particular risk when we are confronted with certain kinds of demands.

The cases just described raise interesting questions about the many ways in which demands, resources, and vulnerabilities interact. How is it that some victims of catastrophe, such as the Holocaust victims mentioned earlier, are scarred for life by their experiences, while others, like Priscilla, somehow rise above the traumatic demands they encounter? What kinds of relations exist between lifestyle and personality variables, such as those exhibited by Walter Chadwick, and susceptibility to diseases? Did Chadwick's behavior place him at risk for a heart attack? If so, could anything have been done to help him change his lifestyle? On a more general level, what can be done to increase the physical and psychological well-being of people by making them more resilient to the impact of stress? These are just a few of the questions we will consider as we explore the linkages among stress, coping, and well-being.

The Nature of Stress

Stress has been defined in various ways by theorists and researchers. Some have defined stress in terms of *stimuli,* or events, that place strong demands on us. These situations are frequently termed **stressors.** We are using the term *stress* in this ''stimulus'' fashion when we make statements such as, ''I've got a lot of stress in my life right now. I have three exams next week, somebody stole my winter coat, and my car just died.''

Stress has also been conceptualized as a *response* having cognitive, physiological, and behavioral components. This use of the term is typified in statements such as, ''I'm feeling a lot of stress, I'm all tensed up, I can't concentrate because I'm really worried, and I've been flying off the handle all week.''

A third way of viewing stress combines the stimulus and response definitions. Here, stress is viewed as a person–situation interaction, or, more formally, as a *transaction* between the organism and the environment (Lazarus, 1989, 1991). This way of viewing stress acknowledges the fact that features of the situation and characteristics of the person combine to influence how a particular stressor affects a person. The transactional conception of stress forms the basis

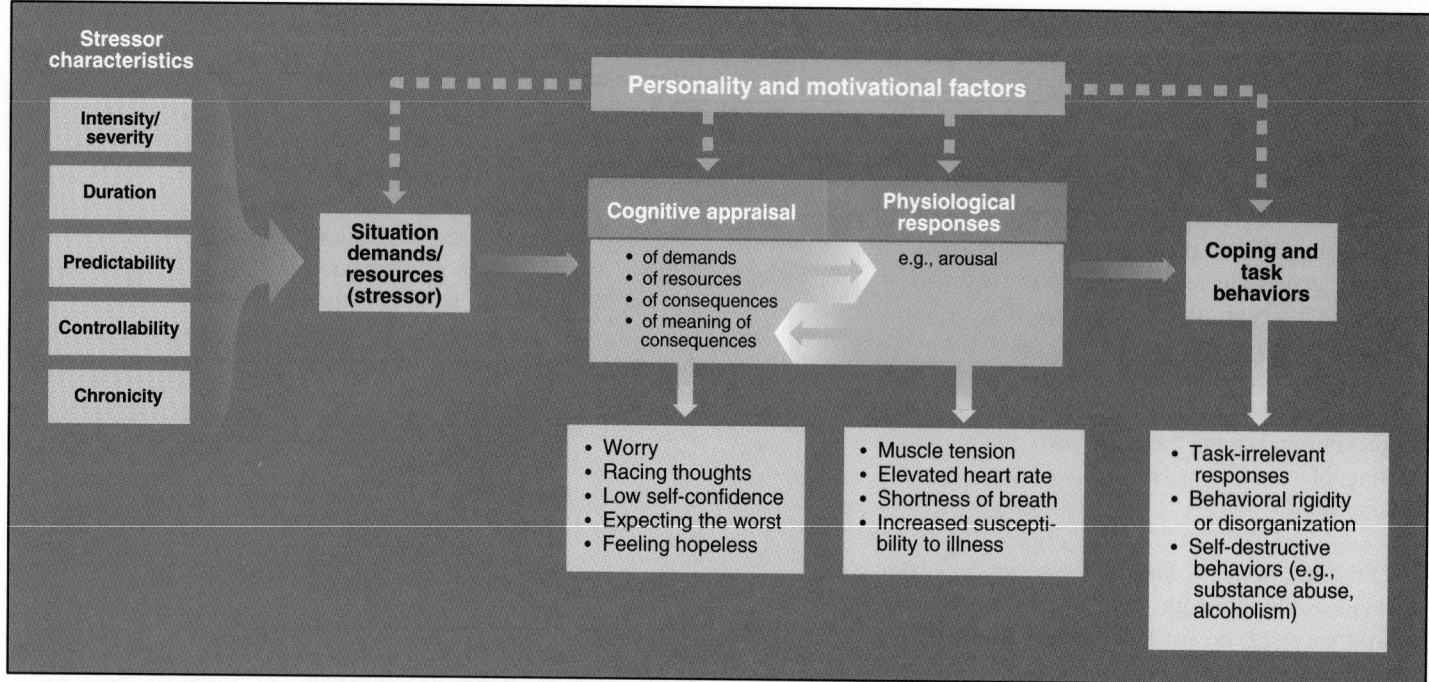

Stressor characteristics

- Intensity/severity
- Duration
- Predictability
- Controllability
- Chronicity

Personality and motivational factors

Situation demands/resources (stressor)

Cognitive appraisal
- of demands
- of resources
- of consequences
- of meaning of consequences

Physiological responses
e.g., arousal

Coping and task behaviors

- Worry
- Racing thoughts
- Low self-confidence
- Expecting the worst
- Feeling hopeless

- Muscle tension
- Elevated heart rate
- Shortness of breath
- Increased susceptibility to illness

- Task-irrelevant responses
- Behavioral rigidity or disorganization
- Self-destructive behaviors (e.g., substance abuse, alcoholism)

Figure 15.1 *Stress involves complex interactions among situational factors, cognitive appraisal processes, physiological responses, and behavioral attempts to cope with the situational demands. Personality and motivational factors may influence all of these components. The lower panels show potential cognitive, physiological, and behavioral stress responses that can interfere with well-being.*

for the model shown in Figure 15.1. The figure summarizes five basic components of stress:

1. The dimensions on which stressors can vary.
2. The cognitive appraisal processes involved in judgments about the stressor, about one's ability to cope with it, and about its potential consequences and personal meaning.
3. The physiological responses that are triggered by certain types of appraisals and that, in turn, influence the ongoing appraisal process.
4. Behavioral responses that constitute attempts to cope with the stressful situation.
5. Personality and motivational variables, which influence the situations people encounter, as well as how they think, feel, and behave.

In the lower part of the figure, some of the maladaptive cognitive, physiological, and behavioral features of the stress reaction are shown. This framework, which integrates the situational, cognitive, physiological, and behavioral aspects of stress within one model, will guide our exploration of the nature and consequences of stress.

Stressors

All stressors, whether physical or psychological, have one thing in common: They place **demands** on the organism. One useful way of looking at stressors involves the balance between the demands of the situation and the **resources** available to the organism to cope with those demands (Lazarus & Folkman, 1984; Neufeld, 1989). The degree of balance or imbalance between demands and resources helps determine how stressful a situation or life event is likely to be. With this in mind, let us consider some of the important dimensions along which life events vary.

Life Event Dimensions

Perhaps the most obvious way in which life events differ is in how positive or negative they are. Most people think of stressors as negative events, but not all theorists have agreed with this interpretation. Instead, some have suggested that *any* event that requires adaptation, whether it is a positive life change or a negative one, should be considered a stressor; to them, what is important is the degree of *adaptation* that is required (Holmes & Rahe, 1967; Selye, 1976). From this perspective, getting married or winning a lottery might be more stressful than having major problems with one's boss because the positive events might actually require more adaptation.

The controversy concerning whether both positive and negative events serve as stressors has generated a large body of research (L. Cohen, 1988). Most studies have found that only negative events are related to negative outcomes, such as psychological

distress and physical illness. Indeed, it appears that in some cases, positive events can actually help cancel out the stressful effects of negative events (Reich & Zautra, 1988). These findings have reinforced the tendency of most theorists to regard stressors as negative life events.

Another dimension that has received a great deal of attention is the severity of the stressor (see Figure 15.2). **Microstressors,** or **daily hassles,** are the everyday annoyances we encounter at school, on the job, and in our family relations (Lazarus & Folkman, 1984; Kohn & others, 1991). They include such things as commuting in rush-hour traffic, encounters with unpleasant or inconsiderate people, and waiting in long lines. Events that can have strong impacts and long-term consequences, such as the death or loss of a loved one, career failure, failure to be accepted into medical or professional school, or being a victim of a violent crime, constitute **major life events.** Finally, some events have such a profound impact that they are labeled **catastrophic life events.** These include natural disasters, acts of war, and concentration camp confinement. These events often occur unexpectedly and affect large numbers of people. All three classes of events—microstressors, major events, and catastrophic events—can have significant negative impacts on psychological and physical well-being.

Because of their traumatic nature, catastrophes tend to have the most visible, severe, and long-term effects. As we have already seen, victims of the Holocaust are still suffering aftereffects nearly 50 years later. Natural disasters can also have dramatic and widespread effects. In the 7 months following the 1980 eruption of Mount St. Helens, the number of people seeking mental health services for stress-related illnesses doubled, emergency room visits rose 34 percent, and deaths increased by 19 percent in the nearby town of Othello, Washington (Adams &

Adams, 1984). Anthony Rubonis and Leonard Bickman (1991) confirmed the negative psychological aftermath of natural disasters by combining the results of 52 separate studies of catastrophic floods, hurricanes, and fires. In the wake of disaster, they found an average increase of 17 percent in rates of psychological disorders such as anxiety and depression.

Major life events and microstressors can also affect well-being, although the consequences are generally not so immediate and dramatic as in catastrophes. Major life events have frequently been found

Figure 15.2 *Life events vary from catastrophic events to major events and microstressors ("daily hassles").*

to be related to both psychological and physical outcomes, and microstressors can accumulate over time and take a toll on health and well-being (Neufeld, 1989; Weinberger & others, 1987). Peter Kohn and his coworkers (1991) found substantial relations between daily hassles experienced over the past month and college students' reports of psychological discomfort, minor physical ailments, and psychiatric symptoms such as anxiety and depression over the same period.

Several other characteristics of events have been identified as important. These include the suddenness with which the event occurs, its duration, its chronicity (that is, whether it recurs frequently), and its predictability and controllability. In general, events over which the person has little or no control, which occur suddenly and unpredictably, and which confront a person over a long period of time seem to take the greatest toll on physical and psychological well-being (Lazarus & Folkman, 1984; Taylor, 1991).

Measurement of Life Events

In order to study linkages between life events and well-being, researchers have devised **life event scales** to quantify the amount of life stress that a person has experienced over a given period of time (for example, the last 6 months or the past 2 years). In 1967, Thomas Holmes and Richard Rahe published the Social Readjustment Rating Scale (SRRS) for this purpose. The SRRS listed 43 life events, each associated with a scaled **life change unit** value based on the ratings of many judges concerning the degree of adjustment required by the event. Holmes and Rahe defined stress purely in terms of the amount of adjustment or adaptation required by a given life change; they did not

distinguish between positive and negative events. A sample of items from the SRRS is presented in Table 15.1. A respondent would check each event that he or she had experienced during a specified period, and a life stress score—the total of the life change units associated with those events—would be calculated.

For over a decade, the SRRS was the most widely used measure of life change. It demonstrated consistent, though modest, statistical relations with a variety of medical and psychological measures, indicating that people who had experienced a great deal of life change were more susceptible to future psychological or health problems. Nevertheless, many researchers were dissatisfied with the failure of the SRRS to distinguish between positive and negative events. Moreover, they suggested that a given event, such as a "business readjustment," could constitute a major life change for one person and a minor one for another. For these reasons, a new generation of life event scales has largely replaced the SRRS in life stress research.

An example of one such scale is shown in Table 15.2. This scale requires the subject to indicate not only whether a particular event occurred but also (a) whether the event was a positive or a negative one, (b) whether it was a major event (defined as having a significant and long-term impact on the person's life) or a "day-to-day" event, and (c) what emotional impact the event had at the time it occurred (Smith & others, 1990). The scale includes a total of 197 events that were reported by college students (Compas & others, 1987), and it yields many different event scores, all of which can be related to medical or psychological outcome measures. Thus, a researcher can derive scores for the number and impact of positive minor and positive major events, for negative minor and negative major events, total positive and total negative events, and total change (the total number or impact of all events endorsed). Moreover, additional information can be obtained. For example, subjects can be asked to rate the predictability, controllability, and duration of each event they experienced, permitting an analysis of these factors as well.

How well do life event scales actually predict medical and psychological outcomes? Some researchers find the answer to this question discouraging, since the relations between life event scores and outcome measures are typically quite modest. In **prospective studies,** in which the life event measure is obtained at one time and the outcome measure at a later time, typical correlations between negative life events and outcome measures fall in the .20 to .30 range (L. H. Cohen, 1988; Rodin & Salovey, 1989). As noted in Chapter 2, squaring a correlation coefficient indicates what percentage of the variance on one measure can be accounted for by differences on the other. Squaring the .20 to .30 correlations suggests that only about 4 to 9 percent of the variance in med-

Table 15.1 Items from the Holmes-Rahe Social Readjustment Rating Scale

Life Event	Life Change Units
Death of spouse	100
Divorce	73
Marital separation	65
Jail term	63
Marriage	50
Being fired	47
Retirement	45
Sex difficulties	39
Gaining of a new family member	39
Change in number of arguments with spouse	35
Son or daughter leaving home	29
Outstanding personal achievement	25
Change in residence	20
Vacation	13

Source: Holmes & Rahe, 1967.

Table 15.2 Sample Items from a Scale That Assesses the Nature and Impact of Life Events

Experience	Happened in Last 6 Months?		Good or Bad?		"Day-to-day" or "Major"		Emotional Response at the Time		
Parents discover something you didn't want them to know	No	Yes	Good	Bad	Day-to-day	Major	Slight	Moderate	Strong
Pressures or expectations by parents	No	Yes	Good	Bad	Day-to-day	Major	Slight	Moderate	Strong
Receiving a gift	No	Yes	Good	Bad	Day-to-day	Major	Slight	Moderate	Strong
Having plans fall through (not going on a trip, etc.)	No	Yes	Good	Bad	Day-to-day	Major	Slight	Moderate	Strong
Losing job (quitting, getting fired, laid off, etc.)	No	Yes	Good	Bad	Day-to-day	Major	Slight	Moderate	Strong
Making honor roll or other school achievement	No	Yes	Good	Bad	Day-to-day	Major	Slight	Moderate	Strong
Making love or sexual intercourse	No	Yes	Good	Bad	Day-to-day	Major	Slight	Moderate	Strong
Having a good talk with a professor or other adult	No	Yes	Good	Bad	Day-to-day	Major	Slight	Moderate	Strong
Something good happens to a friend	No	Yes	Good	Bad	Day-to-day	Major	Slight	Moderate	Strong
Work hassles (rude customers, unpleasant jobs, etc.)	No	Yes	Good	Bad	Day-to-day	Major	Slight	Moderate	Strong
Exercising	No	Yes	Good	Bad	Day-to-day	Major	Slight	Moderate	Strong

Source: Scale used in Smith & others, 1990.

ical or psychological outcome measures can be attributed to differences in life events. Again, however, we must remember that negative events are only one part of the life stress equation. As we shall see, characteristics of the person who experiences the life events, as well as the amount of social support available to the person, must also be taken into account in predicting medical and psychological outcomes. For example, knowing only the traumatic life events she had experienced, few of us would have predicted that Priscilla, the resilient young woman described at the beginning of the chapter, could have achieved such a positive psychological outcome.

Responses to Stressors

Having considered the stimulus characteristics of stressors, we now consider stress as a response of the organism to these situational demands. Like the emotional responses we considered in Chapter 13, the stress response has cognitive, physiological, and behavioral components.

Cognitive Appraisal Processes

We respond to situations as we perceive them. The starting point for the stress response is therefore the person's appraisal of the situation and of its implications for him or her. As Figure 15.1 indicates, four aspects of the appraisal process are of particular significance: (1) appraisal of the demands of the situation, (2) appraisal of the resources available to cope with it, (3) judgments of what the consequences of the situation could be, and (4) appraisal of the meaning that the outcome might have for the person.

Let us apply these appraisal steps to a real-life situation. You are about to have an important interview for a job you would very much like to have. According to one stress researcher, Richard Lazarus (1991a), you will first appraise this situation as benign, neutral/irrelevant, or threatening in terms of its demands and its significance for your well-being, a process that he terms **primary appraisal.** How demanding is this situation for you, and what is going to be required of you? Is the interviewer a supportive person or a threatening one?

At the same time, you will be appraising your perceived ability to cope with the situation—that is, the resources available to deal with it. Lazarus calls this step **secondary appraisal.** Coping resources include your knowledge and abilities, your verbal skills, and your social resources, such as people who will give you emotional support and encouragement. If you believe that the situational demands greatly exceed your resources, you will likely experience stress.

You will also take into account the potential consequences of failing to cope successfully with the situation, including both the seriousness of the consequences and the likelihood that they will occur. Appraising the consequences of failing as very costly and very likely to occur can evoke the stress response.

Finally, the psychological meaning of the consequences may be related to your basic beliefs about yourself or the world. Certain beliefs or personal standards can make people vulnerable to particular types of situational demands. For example, if your feelings of self-worth depend on how successful you are in situations like this one, you may regard doing poorly on the interview as evidence that you are a worthless failure. In contrast, people who define their self-worth in other ways might regard the same consequence as irrelevant to their self-regard.

It is worth noting that distortions and mistaken appraisals can occur at any of the four points in the appraisal process, causing inappropriate stress responses. People may exaggerate the seriousness of the situation, they may underestimate their own resources, they may "catastrophize" about the potential consequences, or they may have irrational beliefs that give inappropriate meaning to the consequences (see Figure 15.3). Realizing that appraisal patterns can differ from person to person in many ways helps us understand why there is so much individual variation in how people respond to the same event or situation, and it also helps us understand why some people are particularly vulnerable to certain types of demands.

Physiological Responses

As we saw when we studied emotion, cognitive and physiological events are intimately related. As soon as appraisals are made, the body responds to them. Although appraisals begin the process, appraisals and physiological responses mutually affect one another, since autonomic and somatic feedback can affect our **reappraisals** of how stressful a situation is and whether our resources are sufficient to cope with it. To use Bandura's term, they exhibit *reciprocal determinism.* Thus, if you find yourself trembling as you enter the interview room, you may appraise the situation as even more threatening than you did initially.

The body's physiological stress response involves both the nervous system and the endocrine (hormonal) system (see Figure 15.4). Through a variety of central nervous system pathways, including paths from the cortical and subcortical areas involved in appraisal, the autonomic nervous system and the endocrine glands are triggered into action. Activity in the sympathetic nervous system increases heart rate and respiration, releases fat from the body's stores, and diverts blood to the muscles that may be needed to fight or to flee. The sympathetic nervous system also stimulates the secretion of stress hormones known as **catecholamines,** which include epinephrine and norepinephrine, from its own neurons and from the adrenal medulla. These substances enter the bloodstream, travel throughout the body, and increase the general level of physiological arousal. A second important endocrine reaction involves the secretion of stress hormones known as **corticosteroids,** the most notable of which is **cortisol.** These stress hormones are secreted from another part of the adrenal gland, the adrenal cortex, through stimulation of the pituitary gland by the hypothalamus. Corticosteroids have a variety of effects on the body, some beneficial, some perhaps not. For example, cortisol reduces the activity of the immune system as part of its function of controlling inflammation. The problem is that it does so whether or not there is actual tissue injury in the body (Calabrese & others, 1987). It also appears that cortisol is secreted at higher levels when events are appraised as threats than when they are perceived as controllable or as challenges (Dienstbier, 1989).

One of the most important historical figures in the study of the body's response to stress was the endocrinologist Hans Selye. As he experimented with many different kinds of stressors, including electric shock, heat and cold, surgical trauma, and physical restraint, Selye observed a common physiological response to stress which he termed the **General**

Figure 15.3 *"Catastrophizing" about the personal implications of failure experiences may have drastic behavioral consequences.*

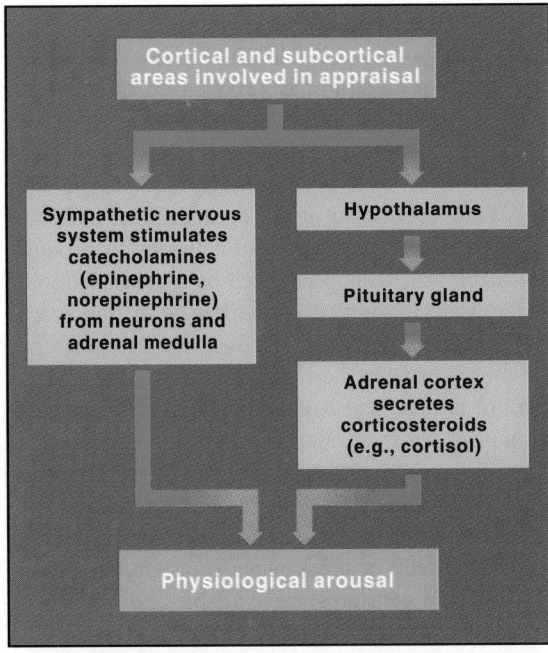

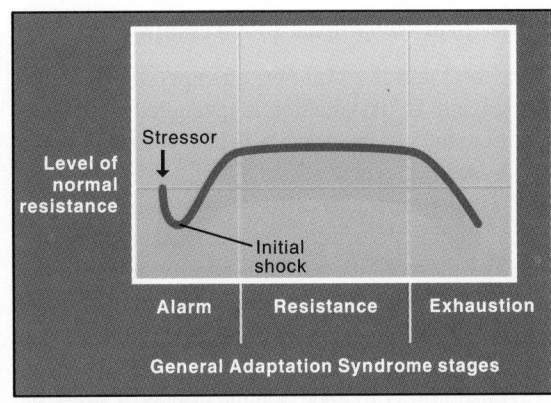

Figure 15.4 *The body's response to stress is a state of physiological arousal produced by the autonomic nervous system and stress hormones from the endocrine glands.*

Figure 15.5 *Hans Selye described the General Adaptation Syndrome. When a person is exposed to a stressor, the body's resistance is temporarily reduced by a state of shock until the alarm reaction mobilizes the body's resources. During the stage of resistance, stress hormones maintain the body's defensive changes, and the body signs characteristic of the alarm reaction virtually disappear. But if the stress persists over a long time, the body's resources become depleted, and exhaustion occurs; the organism can no longer cope and is highly vulnerable to breakdown. (Selye, 1976).*

Adaptation Syndrome (GAS). The GAS consists of three phases, which Selye called *alarm, resistance,* and *exhaustion* (see Figure 15.5).

In response to a physical or psychological stressor, the initial **alarm** reaction occurs because of the sudden activation of the sympathetic nervous system, and the organism exhibits an immediate increase in physiological arousal. In its attempt to maintain homeostasis, the body responds with the second stage, resistance. During **resistance,** the body's resources are mobilized by an outpouring of stress hormones. The resistance stage can last for a relatively long time, but the body's resources are being depleted during this stage. If the stress persists too long, the body's physical resources may become completely depleted, causing the final stage of **exhaustion,** in which there is extreme vulnerability to disease and, in some cases, collapse and death. Selye believed that whatever system of the body is weakest will be the first to be affected. One common manifestation of the GAS is familiar to students who deal successfully with the rigors of the end of the academic term and final exams, only to become ill as soon as the stressors end and vacation begins.

The General Adaptation Syndrome has provided a useful framework for exploring the effects of stress on both physical and psychological well-being (see Figure 15.6). As we shall see, there is little question that prolonged stress can result in physical and psychological deterioration. A physical mobilization system sculpted by evolution to help organisms deal with life-threatening physical stressors may not be as adaptive for dealing with psychological stressors. As one medical authority noted, ''Stone Age physiological and biochemical responses to emotion have become inappropriate in a Space Age setting, and can pave the way to psychosomatic diseases'' (Carruthers, 1981, p. 239).

Figure 15.6 *The General Adaptation Syndrome has been applied to psychological reactions to traumatic and prolonged stress.*

Behavioral Responses to Stressors

Behavioral responses involve attempts to respond to the demands of the situation as perceived by the person. In many instances, these demands require that a person perform a task of some kind.

Task performance is affected by a number of factors, including the specific demands imposed by the task and the person's skills in relation to those demands. Obviously, skilled people generally perform at a higher level than unskilled people. But stress can impair the performance of even highly skilled people.

A useful way to approach the effects of stress on performance involves the balance between **task-relevant responses** and **task-irrelevant responses.** This balance is affected not only by the skill level of the person but also by the stress response itself. At low levels of stress, performance may be enhanced because the stress increases task-relevant responses, such as greater attentiveness to the task, stronger persistence in meeting its demands, and greater effort. As the stress response increases, however, task-irrelevant cognitive and physiological responses may begin to interfere with performance.

Task-irrelevant cognitive responses include the tendency to worry about the consequences of not performing well and to focus on one's predicament rather than on the task at hand. Irwin and Barbara Sarason (1990) have found that students suffering from test anxiety frequently forget facts that they know, make silly mistakes as a result of not reading questions carefully, and have difficulty concentrating on the test itself because of their internal preoccupations.

Physiological arousal may produce task-relevant or task-irrelevant responses. On motor tasks, for example, increased arousal may result in greater effort and more vigorous task-relevant responses. However, as noted in relation to the Yerkes–Dodson Law, the relation between arousal and quality of performance often takes the form of an inverted U (see Figure 13.12 on page 412). That is, performance improves with increasing arousal up to an optimal level and then begins to deteriorate as arousal begins to produce task-irrelevant responses, such as increased tremor and muscle tension, that interfere with fine motor coordination. The Yerkes–Dodson law also states that the more complex the task is, the lower will be the level of arousal that begins to negatively affect performance. An increasing level of arousal would be expected to produce task-irrelevant responses sooner where the tasks require fine motor coordination.

Sports is an excellent real-life setting in which to study the effects of stress on performance, since good performance measures are available and athletes at all levels experience stress to varying degrees. Moreover, several new measures have been developed that permit the measurement of individual differences in the cognitive and physiological aspects of the stress response (Martens & others, 1990; Smith & others, 1990). These measures contain separate scales for cognitive anxiety (such as worry and intrusive thoughts) and somatic anxiety (muscle tension, heart-pounding, and other arousal responses). Damon Burton (1988) administered one such measure to 80 elite amateur swimmers who were competing in the National Sports Festival. He then related their cognitive and somatic anxiety scores to their performance during the swimming meet. As you can see in Figure 15.7, cognitive and somatic anxiety produced different results. Physiological arousal bore the familiar inverted-U relation to performance. Cognitive anxiety, however, exhibited a linear (straight-line) relation to performance; the more athletes experienced worry and other task-irrelevant cognitions, the worse they performed. Although the forms of their relations to performance are somewhat different, the results show clearly that both the cognitive and physiological components of the stress response can interfere with task performance when they reach high levels.

Before concluding our discussion of stress and performance, we should note one aspect of the appraisal process that seems quite important. Demanding situations may be appraised as either *threats* or *challenges.* Situations appraised as threats appear more likely to trigger task-irrelevant responses, such as worry and excessive levels of arousal. On the other hand, when situations are appraised as challenges, the motivational and emotional responses that result seem to trigger predominantly task-relevant responses (Lazarus & Folkman, 1984; Patterson & Neufeld, 1989). This may be one reason why certain individuals are able to "rise to the occasion" under stressful

Figure 15.7 *Relations between elite competitive swimmers' performance and their pre-event cognitive and somatic anxiety. Each point represents a swimmer's performance and anxiety score, and the lines represent the mathematical function that best fits the data pattern. (Burton, 1988).*

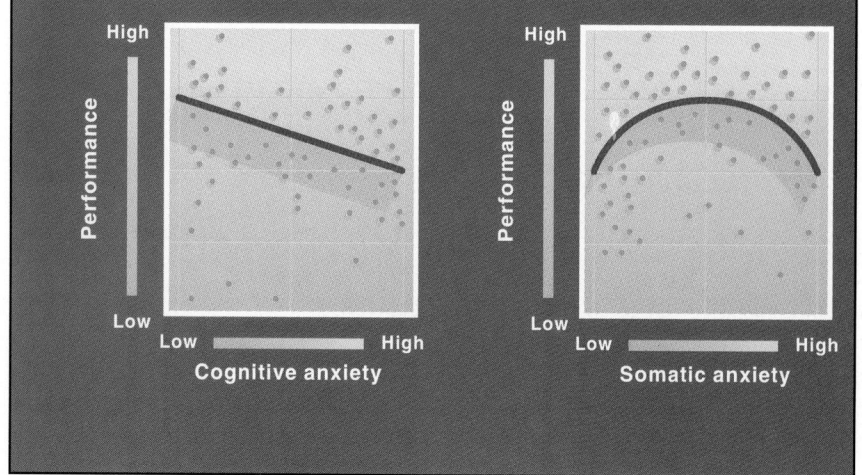

conditions. Many champion athletes who are able to respond with peak performances in pressure-packed competitive situations say that they appraise these situations as challenges or opportunities to excel rather than as threats. They welcome the pressure and demands that can cause other athletes to "choke" (Dorfman & Kuehl, 1989; Smith, 1992).

Stress and Well-Being

Findings from hundreds of studies indicate that stressful events and the ways in which individuals respond to them play a major role in both psychological and physical well-being. Before considering the specific coping responses, resources, and vulnerabilities that affect the outcomes of stressful encounters, we examine the general impact of stress on psychological distress, on illness, and on the phenomenon known as burnout.

Stress and Psychological Well-Being

During the past two decades, few topics in psychology have received as much attention as the effects of life stress on psychological well-being, as well as the situational and personal factors that make people vulnerable or resilient to the impact of stressors. As we shall see, many questions have been answered, but some basic ones remain.

Catastrophic Life Events

Disasters can occur suddenly and without warning. These catastrophic life events tend to be so traumatic that they exert a noticeable and substantial impact on most people. In some instances, the effects are extremely long-lasting, as in the case of the Holocaust survivors. Similar long-lasting symptoms have been found among soldiers who were captured and held as prisoners of war. Forty years after World War II, a random sample of Australian soldiers who had been held in Japanese prison camps was compared with a sample of non-POW soldiers. The former POW's were more depressed and had more stomach ulcers (Tennant & others, 1986). A similar study of World War II American POW's revealed that after 20 years, about one-third had fully recovered, one-third still had mild psychological symptoms, and one-third still had moderate to severe symptoms (Kluznik & others, 1986).

Studies of people who have been exposed to traumatic life events have revealed a syndrome known as **post-traumatic stress disorder.** Three major symptoms define the disorder. First, the person relives the trauma recurrently in "flashbacks," in dreams, and in fantasy. Second, the person becomes numb to the world and avoids stimuli that remind him or her of the trauma. Finally, the person experiences symptoms of anxiety, arousal, and distress that were not present before the trauma (Task Force on DSM IV, 1991). In addition, the person may experience extreme guilt about surviving the catastrophe when others did not.

The catastrophe that brings about a post-traumatic stress reaction need not be experienced by a mass of people, as occurs in wars and natural disasters; it can be an individual experience. The trauma of being raped is perhaps the most common such catastrophe in modern American society. The following description graphically depicts the trauma that can accompany rape:

> Rape can be the most terrifying event in a woman's life. The sexual act or acts performed are often intended to humiliate or degrade her: bottles, gun barrels and sticks may be thrust into her vagina or anus. She may be compelled to swallow urine or perform felatio with such force that she thinks she might strangle or suffocate; her breasts may be bitten or burned with cigarettes. In many instances, her hope is to save her life—not her chastity. Her terror may be so overwhelming that she urinates, defecates, or vomits. If she escapes without serious outward signs of injury, she may suffer vaginal tears or infections, contract venereal disease, or be impregnated. For months or years afterward, she may distrust others, change residence frequently, and sleep poorly. Friends and families may blame or reject her (National Institute of Law Enforcement and Criminal Justice, 1978, p. 15).

The aftermath of rape can be nearly as traumatic as the incident itself. Many victims experience a form of the post-traumatic stress disorder known as the **rape trauma syndrome** (Burgess & Holmstrom, 1974). The initial reaction of most women is a strong display of fear, anxiety, self-blame, or anger, although some victims mask their inner turmoil with a controlled external appearance. For months or even years after the rape, victims may feel nervous and may fear retaliation by the rapist. Many victims change their place of residence but continue to have nightmares and to be frightened when they are alone, outdoors, or in crowds. Victims frequently report decreased enjoyment of sexual activity long after the rape, even when their ability to have orgasms is not affected (Holmes & St. Lawrence, 1983; Masters & others, 1988). In one long-term study of rape victims, one quarter of the subjects felt that they had not recovered psychologically at the end of a 6-year period following the rape (Meyer & Taylor, 1986).

The importance of prompt psychological intervention after disasters has become increasingly evident, and psychologists have been called on to design

▲ **Figure 15.8** *The need to treat the psychological wounds suffered by disaster victims and workers is receiving increasing attention from psychologists.*

programs and provide services for those who have experienced catastrophic events. For example, when an airliner crashes, traumatic consequences occur not only for the victims and survivors themselves but also for their friends and families, for the disaster workers who must confront scenes of incredible carnage, for emergency coordinators who must make decisions and deal with all aspects of the disaster under highly stressful conditions, and for the people who provide emotional assistance to victims and the bereaved (Williams & others, 1988). All of these survivor groups may experience long-term psychological difficulties as a result of their experiences during and after the disaster (see Figure 15.8). Even highly experienced disaster workers are often unprepared for what they experience at a crash site. The trauma of collecting body parts, some from small children, and witnessing hundreds of mangled bodies can devastate even the most "macho" fireman or police officer (Keating, 1987). In the aftermath of a crash in San Diego that claimed 144 lives, a group of psychologists set up a crisis intervention program for disaster workers that lasted for 6 weeks. The workers were allowed to openly discuss their traumatic experiences and were taught coping responses, such as relaxation and thought control, to control their emotions. Interventions like this one may help prevent the development of post-traumatic stress disorder by allowing workers to share and work through their experiences in a supportive atmosphere.

Major and Minor Life Stressors: Causal Issues

No one doubts that catastrophic events have a negative psychological impact. Fortunately, the majority

of stressors that people experience are not catastrophic. How do these more typical but less serious stressors affect psychological well-being?

Although many studies have found substantial correlations between both major and minor negative events and psychological distress, the meaning of these relationships is by no means clear. The major problem lies in unraveling the causal linkages between events and psychological consequences. For example, a consistent finding is that the more negative life events people have experienced, the more likely they are to report symptoms of anxiety, depression, anger, and other distressing psychological reactions (Holahan & Moos, 1990; Monroe & Peterman, 1988). However, the interpretation of these relations is open to question because the studies are correlational in nature.

Assume, for example, that we find a high positive correlation between the number of major negative events reported by subjects (as measured by life change scores) and the subjects' scores on a measure of depression. We might be tempted to conclude that their current depressed state is the result of the stressful events they have experienced. However, other interpretations are entirely possible. Two other causal possibilities are shown in Figure 15.9.

Possibility 2 is that differences in levels of depression cause differences in the reporting of negative life events. That is, depressed people may be more likely to remember negative things that have happened to them or simply to view more events as negative, resulting in higher negative life change scores. Another way in which depression might cause higher life change scores is by actually causing more negative events in people's lives because of the self-defeating behaviors that depression produces. For example, it is well documented that depressed people tend to evoke negative reactions from others (Coyne & others, 1991; Joiner & others, 1992).

Possibility 3 is that some third variable causes both negative life events and depressed moods. A general trait of neuroticism (the tendency to experience negative emotions and to behave in self-defeating ways) might be one such factor. People who are high in neuroticism tend to get themselves in a great many stressful situations through their maladaptive behaviors, and they also tend to experience depression and anxiety (Eysenck, 1989). In line with this hypothesis, Johan Ormel and Tamar Wohlfarth (1991) found in a longitudinal study of Dutch adults that initial scores on a neuroticism scale were related to both the number of stressful events the subjects later reported and the amount of psychological distress they complained of in the succeeding 6 years. They also found that the relation between stressful life events and psychological distress during any given period of the study was strongest for subjects

474   PSYCHOLOGY

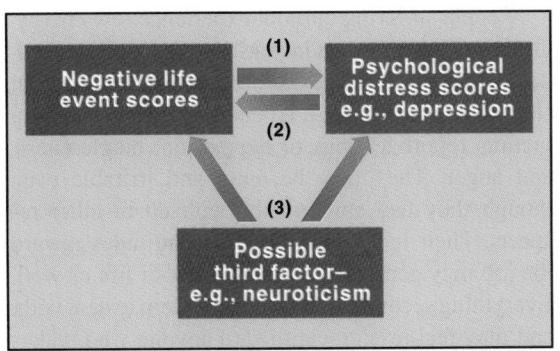

Figure 15.9 *Statistical relations between stressful life events and psychological distress may reflect a number of different causal relations: (1) stressful life events may cause distress; (2) distress may cause higher stressful life event scores; or (3) a third factor, such as neuroticism, may cause both distress and high life change scores.*

who were high in neuroticism. Thus, we again confront the principle stressed earlier: Stressful life events are part of a network of causal relations that involve ongoing transactions between people and situations. It appears that stressful life events can function as both cause and effect (Cohen & Edwards, 1989; Epstein & Katz, 1992).▼

Stress and Illness

Traditionally, medical researchers have sought to understand the causes of disease and illness purely in terms of biological processes and the action of external disease agents such as viruses and bacteria. That view of illness is rapidly being supplanted by a biopsychosocial orientation that attempts to understand physical well-being in terms of interacting biological, psychological, and social systems.

It is now widely acknowledged that in combination with other psychological factors, stress can play a crucial role in the entire spectrum of physical illnesses, from the common cold to cancer, heart disease, and sudden death (Cohen & Williamson, 1991; Taylor, 1991). The interactions are by no means simple ones, however, for when we speak of stress responses, we are referring to life events and also to their interactions with personality factors, coping styles, biological vulnerabilities, environmental factors, and lifestyle behaviors.

Intrapsychic factors can play an important role in the stress equation. For example, one study examined personality factors such as chronic anxiety, depression, and anger in relation to five important diseases: coronary heart disease, asthma, ulcers, arthritis, and headaches (Friedman & Booth-Kewley, 1987). In all, data from 217 separate samples were combined through a statistical procedure known as **meta-analysis** to study relations between the per-

sonality factors and the diseases. All of the diseases were significantly related to anxiety and depression; and coronary heart disease, asthma, and arthritis were also related to anger. Although the correlations were relatively modest (generally in the .20 range) they compare favorably with correlations involving other medical risk factors. For example, high serum cholesterol levels and smoking correlate with coronary heart disease at about that same magnitude (Friedman & DiMatteo, 1989).

Life events have also been linked to various physical disorders. For example, several studies have shown that people who have recently lost their spouses are more likely to die of heart disease, an outcome that may be due to the stress of bereavement (Kaprio & others, 1987). In several prospective studies, stressful life events have been linked to an increased likelihood of developing cancer later on (Skylar & Anisman, 1981). A traumatic life event may also worsen an already existing medical condition, as in the following case of a 7-year-old African-American girl with sickle-cell anemia.

> This little girl was bused to a new elementary school in a white neighborhood of Chicago. She and other black children were met with cries by angry whites to "go back to where you belong!" The little girl was quite upset by the incident. After some time at the school she went to the principal's office crying and complaining of chest pains. She died later that day in the hospital, apparently from a sickle-cell crisis brought on by stress. As she died, she kept repeating "go back where you belong" (Friedman & DiMatteo, 1989, p. 169).

The aspect of the stress response that relates most immediately to illness is the physiological component (although this is, in turn, affected by appraisals). In the case of coronary heart disease, for example, attention has focused on stress-produced neuroendocrine activity. As noted earlier, an important part of the stress response involves the secretion of catecholamines and corticosteroids by the adrenal gland. These hormones affect the activity of the heart and arteries, and excess secretions may damage the lining of the arteries. The stress hormones also affect the metabolism of fats and hence the fatty substances that can be deposited in the arteries to form blockages (Kimble, 1992; Taylor, 1991).

Neuroendocrine responses also appear to affect the functioning of the immune system. Although the exact mechanisms are not completely understood, there is growing evidence that the stress response can weaken immune functioning and thereby increase people's susceptibility to a variety of disorders, including respiratory illnesses, heart disease, and cancer (Rodin & Salovey, 1989; Taylor, 1991). In one lon-

▼
Thinking Critically About the Person–Situation Distinction in Stress Research

In research on links between life stress and measures of personal adjustment, how important is it to identify stressors in a manner that is independent of the personality characteristics of the people who are the targets of the stressors? Some researchers are concerned that people's level of psychological adjustment may influence both the number of stressors they produce in their lives and the number of physical and psychological symptoms they manifest. In critically thinking about this issue, Seymour Epstein and Lori Katz (1992) reasoned that it might be important to distinguish between self-produced and externally produced stressors. Accordingly, judges divided life-change items into those that people likely contributed to or caused themselves (for example, arguments with a roommate) and those caused by external sources (for example, course examinations). They found that self-produced stressors occurred far more frequently and were more strongly related to measures of physical and psychological symptoms than externally produced stressors. They concluded that an important goal of stress management programs should be to teach people how they produce many of their own stressors and how they can reduce this source of stress in their lives.

gitudinal study, lymphocyte counts were assessed in arthritis patients over a 3-month period, during which time the subjects also completed measures of stressful life events, coping effectiveness, and psychological distress. Major negative events and microstressors, as well as psychological distress, were associated with lymphocyte changes that increase susceptibility to illness (Zautra & others, 1989).

Linkages between stress and the immune system suggest the possibility that stress sometimes affects susceptibility to illness by weakening the body's natural defenses against disease entities. In other instances, such as in certain **psychophysiological disorders,** the link between stress and illness is more direct. For example, peptic ulcers are caused by an excessive outpouring of stomach acids, and such secretions can be caused by emotional states such as anxiety and anger (Taylor, 1991).

Burnout

During the past decade, a stress-related phenomenon known as **burnout** has received increasing theoretical and research attention (Cherniss, 1980; Pines & Aronson, 1981; Smith, 1986). In the human service professions, staff burnout has been identified as a critical problem that can be debilitating to workers, detrimental to clients, and costly to agencies. The consequences of burnout are no less serious in business, educational, and sport settings.

Burnout is a reaction to chronic stress that affects physical and psychological well-being, as well as work performance. Burnout involves psychological, emotional, and sometimes physical withdrawal from an activity or profession in response to excessive stress or dissatisfaction. When burnout occurs, a previously enjoyable activity becomes an aversive source of stress. A once-dedicated social worker, for example, may literally have to drag himself or herself to work. Ironically, the most dedicated and idealistic members of a profession may be most susceptible to burnout once they begin to fall victim to the chronic stress they experience on the job (Pines & Aronson, 1981).

People suffering burnout experience low energy, chronic fatigue, and an increased susceptibility to illness. They may feel exhausted during the day yet sleep poorly at night. At an emotional level, burnout victims report feelings of depression, helplessness, and anger. They may be tense and irritable even though they feel emotionally depleted in other respects. Their increasingly negative attitudes toward the job may generalize to other areas of life as well. Everything seems like too much for them to deal with, and they feel resentment toward anyone who makes demands. Their behavior can become rigidly inflexible or even disorganized, resulting in decreased efficiency, inconsistent performance, and interpersonal behaviors that alienate others. At extreme levels, inappropriate behavior and withdrawal may result.

Figure 15.10 shows the situational, cognitive, physiological, and behavioral features that have been identified in research on burnout. As in the case of other consequences of stress, burnout is the product of complex interactions between the person and the environment. Situations present demands, but their ultimate impact on the person depends in large part on how the person copes with these demands. We now consider the decisive role of coping strategies.

Coping With Stress

My courage sank, and with each succeeding minute it became less possible to resist this horror. My cue came, and on I went to that stage where I knew with grim certainty I would not be capable of remaining more than a few minutes. . . . I took one pace forward and stopped abruptly. My voice had started to fade, my throat closed up and the audience was beginning to go giddily round'' (Aaron, 1986, p. 24).

This description of "stage fright" was given not by a novice actor in his first play, but by Sir Laurence Olivier, considered by many to be the greatest actor of his generation (see Figure 15.11). Few people are

Figure 15.10 *A possible consequence of chronic job- or activity-related stress is burnout. Research has identified some of the situational, cognitive, physiological, and behavioral components of the burnout syndrome. (Smith, 1986).*

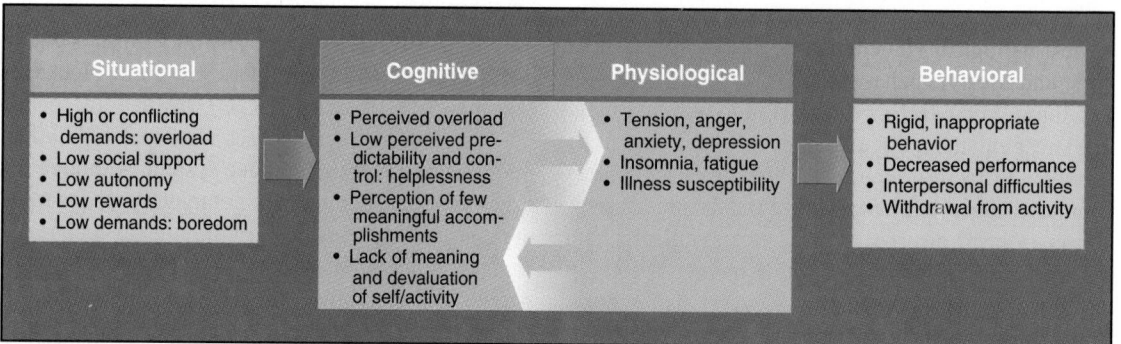

 **Figure 15.11** *The renowned actor Sir Laurence Olivier suffered extreme stress before every performance, yet was able to apply coping skills that resulted in award-winning performances once he was onstage.*

aware that for most of his career, Olivier experienced a private hell before every performance. His audiences saw only what happened once he stepped onto the stage: another flawless performance. Olivier had a remarkable ability to purge the terror from his mind, relax his body, and concentrate fully on his role once showtime arrived (Aaron, 1986).

There are countless ways in which people might respond to a stressor, and a great deal of research has been directed at identifying the primary classes of coping responses. Scales and interview techniques have been developed to measure individual differences in coping preferences and to relate them to measures of well-being.

Recent findings indicate that coping strategies can be divided into three general classes (Carver & others, 1989; Folkman & Lazarus, 1988). **Problem-focused coping strategies** are attempts to confront and directly deal with the demands of the situation or to change the situation so that it is no longer stressful. As shown in Figure 15.12, problem-focused coping includes such behaviors as planning, problem solving, and other activities directed at mastering the situation. Examples include studying for a test, going directly to another person to work out a misunderstanding, and signing up for a course in time management in order to deal with time pressures.

Emotion-focused coping strategies are directed not at dealing with the situation but rather at managing the appraisal and physiological components of the stress response. As shown in Figure 15.12, emotion-focused coping can take a variety of forms. Some of them involve appraising the situation in a manner that minimizes its emotional impact while others involve directly venting or controlling emotional arousal. Thus, a student might decide to deal with anxiety about an upcoming test by going to a party and forgetting about it. A person might deal with the stress from an interpersonal conflict by denying that any problem exists. Informed that he has a terminal illness, a man might simply accept grim reality, realizing that there is nothing that can be done to change the situation. Some forms of emotion-focused coping (such as controlling tension with relaxation or challenging irrational ideas that are causing disturbance) can be quite adaptive. In contrast, many of the defense mechanisms discussed in the preceding chapter may be regarded as emotion-focused coping responses that are capable of creating problems (Holmes & McCaul, 1989).

A third class of coping strategies involves seeking **social support**—that is, turning to others for assistance and emotional support in times of stress. Thus, the man with the terminal illness might choose to join a support group for the terminally ill, and the student might seek help in preparing for the test. As we shall see, support from other people can be invaluable in helping us cope with the impact of stressors.

The tendency to favor one coping strategy over another is influenced by many factors, one of which seems to be gender roles. Although men and women both use problem-focused coping, men are more likely to favor it as the *first* strategy they use when they confront a stressor (Ptacek & others, 1992). On

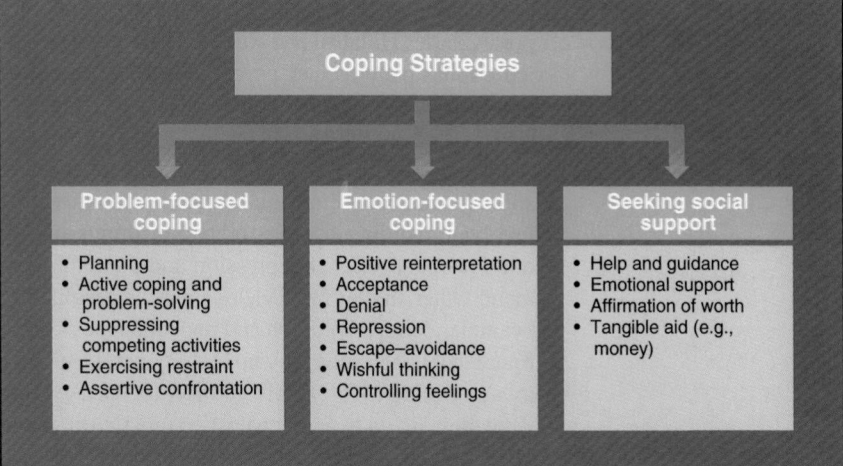

Figure 15.12 *Coping strategies fall into three general categories: (1) problem-focused coping, consisting of active attempts to respond to situational demands; (2) emotion-focused coping, directed at minimizing emotional distress; and (3) seeking or accepting social support.*

Problem-focused coping	Emotion-focused coping	Seeking social support
• Planning • Active coping and problem-solving • Suppressing competing activities • Exercising restraint • Assertive confrontation	• Positive reinterpretation • Acceptance • Denial • Repression • Escape–avoidance • Wishful thinking • Controlling feelings	• Help and guidance • Emotional support • Affirmation of worth • Tangible aid (e.g., money)

the other hand, women are more likely than men to seek social support (Billings & Moos, 1984; Pearlin & Schooler, 1978; Ptacek & others, 1992). This finding is consistent with the fact that women tend to have larger support networks and higher needs for affiliation than men (Kessler & others, 1985; Wong & Csikszentihalyi, 1991). Women also appear somewhat more likely than men to report using emotion-focused coping (Carver & others, 1989; Pearlin & Schooler, 1978).

This general pattern of sex differences is consistent with the socialization that boys and girls traditionally experience. As we saw in Chapter 4, boys are pushed to be more independent, assertive, and self-sufficient, whereas girls are expected to be more emotionally expressive, supportive, and dependent (Eccles, 1991; Lytton & Romney, 1991). It therefore makes sense that men would have a general tendency to favor problem-focused coping strategies and that women would use more emotion-focused coping and social-support seeking.

Effectiveness of Coping Strategies

If you were to hazard a guess, which of the three general classes of coping strategies would you expect to be most generally effective? Whenever I ask this question in my class, the majority of students vote for problem-focused coping. This response is understandable, for most of us initially approach problems with the attitude, that if something needs fixing, we should fix it. This mastery-oriented philosophy is instilled in many of us beginning in early childhood and carries with it the need to view ourselves as competent and able to act effectively to control almost any situation. Moreover, we are often told to ''face our feelings'' and not run away from them, suggesting that emotion-focused coping may be a less adaptive way of dealing with stress.

What does the research literature tell us about this issue? In general, the findings come down on the side of problem-focused coping and seeking social support. Charles Holahan and Rudolf Moos (1990) studied coping patterns and psychological outcomes in more than 400 California adults over a one-year period. They found that problem-focused coping methods were associated with stable adjustment to stressors. In contrast, emotion-focused strategies that involved avoiding feelings or taking things out on other people predicted depression and poorer adjustment. Other studies have yielded similar results. For example, Zahava Solomon and his colleagues (1989) found that Israeli soldiers who had a general tendency to use avoidant forms of emotion-focused coping were more likely to develop post-traumatic stress disorders when exposed to combat. In general, in both children and adults, and across a wide variety of different types of stressors, those emotion-focused coping strategies that involve avoidance, denial, and wishful thinking seem to be related to less effective adaptation. In contrast, problem-focused coping seems to be related to better emotional adjustment in the face of stressors (Folkman & Lazarus, 1988; Revenson & Felton, 1989; Vitaliano & others, 1989). But there are some qualifying factors, one of which is the amount of control we have over the stressors.

Controllability and Coping Efficacy

Despite the evidence favoring problem-solving coping, it is important to note that attempts to change the situation are not always the most adaptive way to cope with stress. A key factor in the effectiveness of coping strategies is the amount of control that people have over stressful situations. When we cannot influence or modify a situation, problem-focused coping may do us little good. In such cases, emotion-focused coping may be the most adaptive approach we can take; for even if we cannot master the situation, we may be able to prevent or control maladaptive emotional responses to it (Auerbach, 1989; Taylor, 1991). Of course, reliance on emotion-focused coping is likely to be maladaptive if it prevents us from acting to change situations in which we actually *do* have control.

A study by Thomas Strantz and Stephen Auerbach (1988) demonstrated the effective role that emotion-focused coping can play in adapting to stressful situations in which there is very limited personal control. As part of a training program conducted by the Federal Bureau of Investigation, airline employees who might be future victims of hijackings were given the opportunity to participate in an exercise in which they were abducted by FBI agents posing as terrorists and held hostage for 4 days under very realistic and stressful conditions.

Before their abduction, the subjects were randomly assigned to two experimental conditions and a control condition. In one condition, subjects were instructed in problem-focused techniques that hostages can use to actively deal with and modify the situation. They were shown how to interact with captors and maintain a facade of dignity and composure through appearance and behavior. They also learned ways of supporting one another nonverbally and communicating with one another through use of the prisoner-of-war tap code, as well as methods for gathering intelligence while in captivity.

Training for the second experimental group focused on the emotional reactions the hostages would be likely to experience and techniques they could use to directly minimize their stress responses. These emotion-focused techniques included deep breathing, muscular relaxation, stopping unwanted thoughts, and generating pleasant fantasies. Hostages in the control condition were given no coping skills training.

At various points during their captivity, the hostages completed self-report measures of emotional distress and psychiatric symptoms. In addition, the adaptiveness of their behavior was coded by trained observers.

Both the subjects trained in problem-focused coping methods and those trained in emotion-focused ones fared better than the untrained control subjects on both the self-report and the behavioral measures. However, subjects who had received instruction in emotion-focused coping adapted better to the largely uncontrollable conditions of captivity than did subjects who had received problem-focused coping instruction (see Figure 15.13).

An important principle to remember is that no coping strategy or technique is equally effective in all situations. Instead, effectiveness depends on the characteristics of the situation, the appropriateness of the technique, and the skill with which it is carried out. People are likely to adapt most effectively to the stresses of life if they have mastered a variety of coping techniques and know how and when to apply each most effectively. In other words, coping skill and flexibility are keys to good adjustment. The importance of controllability in the choice of techniques recalls the wisdom in the theologian Reinhold Niebuhr's famous prayer that asks for the courage to change those things that can be changed, the forbearance to accept those that cannot be changed, and the wisdom to discern the difference.

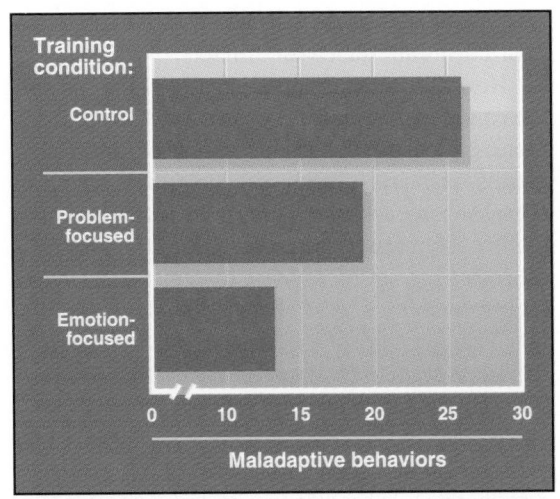

Figure 15.13 *Behavioral ratings of adjustment to the stress of captivity by airline personnel given instruction in problem- or emotion-focused coping techniques prior to their abduction by FBI agents posing as terrorists. The control group received no coping skills instruction. Higher scores indicated more disturbed behaviors. (Data from Strantz & Auerbach, 1988).*

Vulnerability and Protective Factors

The same stressful life event may have very different effects on different people, and it may even affect the same person in different ways at different times. Some individuals seem able to tolerate extremely demanding stressors over a long period of time; others appear to quickly fall prey to even relatively minor stressors. **Protective factors** are environmental or personal resources that help people cope more effectively with stressful events. They include social support and personality factors such as coping skills. In contrast, **vulnerability factors** increase people's susceptibility to stressful events. They include lack of a support network, poor coping skills, tendencies to become anxious, and other factors that reduce stress resistance.

Certain life conditions in and of themselves can increase people's vulnerability to subsequent stress-

ors. If one has recently been subjected to a great deal of stress, for example, it may take only a very light straw to break the camel's back. Vulnerability may also be increased by biological factors, such as a highly reactive autonomic nervous system; by certain personality characteristics, such as low self-esteem; or by poorly developed coping skills. Some people are vulnerable to a wide range of stressful situations; others are particularly sensitive only to certain types of situations, such as those involving loss or a threat to self-esteem.

Although we will consider them individually, it should be kept in mind that protective and vulnerability factors can interact with one another in complex ways, helping to produce the diversity we see in people's resiliency in the face of stress.

Physiological Toughness

People exhibit individual differences in how they respond physiologically to stressors. Richard Dienstbier (1989) has described a physiological response pattern that seems to be an important protective factor.

As noted earlier, two different hormonal systems are activated as part of the body's response to stressors. The sympathetic nervous system stimulates the adrenal medulla to secrete catecholamines such as epinephrine; and it releases another catecholamine, norepinephrine, from its own nerve endings. Meanwhile, the adrenal cortex secretes corticosteroids, such as cortisol. Both catecholamines and corticosteroids mobilize the body to deal with the event, but their effects are somewhat different.

How a situation is appraised affects the extent to which the two hormonal systems are activated. The arousal produced by events appraised as positive results primarily from catecholamine secretion (Frankenhauser & others, 1980). In contrast, cortisol tends to be released in response to events appraised as threats but not in response to demands appraised as pleasurable or as challenges (Ursin, 1978). As noted earlier, cortisol's effects last much longer, and its effects seem to be more damaging than those produced by the catecholamines except when the catecholamines are secreted at high levels over a long period of time. For example, cortisol has a stronger role than the catecholamines in bringing about the fatty deposits in the arteries that lead to heart disease (Herd, 1986). Cortisol also suppresses immune system activity, whereas catecholamine secretion enhances immune system activity (Calabrese & others, 1987; Solomon & others, 1986). Thus, cortisol seems to play an important role in the negative effects that stress can have on the body.

To support his concept of physiological toughness, Dienstbier has brought together an impressive body of research with both animals and humans which suggests that the body's ability to cope with stress is enhanced by a particular pattern of endocrine responses. This **physiological toughness** pattern consists of (1) a low resting level of cortisol and low

levels of cortisol secretion in response to stressors and (2) a low resting level of catecholamines such as epinephrine and norepinephrine but a quick and strong catecholamine response to stressors. The catecholamine surge is followed by a quick decline in arousal when the stressor is over (see Figure 15.14). This hormonal pattern seems to provide maximum short-term mobilization of resources to deal with the stressor but prevents the eventual depletion of catecholamines and the wear and tear on the body that Selye identified with the exhaustion phase of the General Adaptation Syndrome (Dienstbier, 1989).

Can physiological toughness be increased, or "trained," by exposure to stress? The answer seems to be yes. Animal research has shown that exposure to intermittent physical stressors early in life can make organisms more physiologically and behaviorally resilient in the face of later stress (Weiss, 1975). Perhaps certain patterns of early stress also contribute to the resiliency shown by "invulnerable" children like Priscilla, the young woman described at the beginning of the chapter (Garmezy, 1983). To this point, no research has been conducted on the physiological response patterns of such children. For now, however, there is good reason to believe that one's customary physiological response pattern when confronting stressors can be either a protective factor or a vulnerability factor.

Social Support

One of the most important environmental resources that people can have is the knowledge that they can rely on others for help and support in a time of crisis. The essence of social support seems to be not so much the number of people in our social networks but rather the conviction that somebody values and cares about us and is ready to help if we need it (Sarason, 1990). Furthermore, feelings of social support consist of the general conviction that we can get support from others if we need it as well as the expectation of support in our most significant relationships, such as with a parent or a best friend (Pierce & others, 1991).

A growing body of research has identified social support as a strong protective factor against stress. In contrast, social isolation is an important vulnerability factor (see Figure 15.15). The devastating effects of loneliness and social isolation on physical well-being are suggested by studies in the United States, Finland, and Sweden involving more than 37,000 people who were followed carefully over periods of up to 12 years (House & others, 1988). The 10 to 20 percent of people who said they had no one with whom they could share their private feelings, as well as those who had close contact with others less than once a week, appeared to be at significant physical risk. So-

▶ **Figure 15.14** *Physiological toughness consists of a pattern of low baseline levels of catecholamines and cortisol, low cortisol elevations in response to stressors, and a quick and strong catecholamine response to stressors followed by a fast return to baseline after the stressors are withdrawn. Increased vulnerability to stressors occurs with the opposite pattern.*

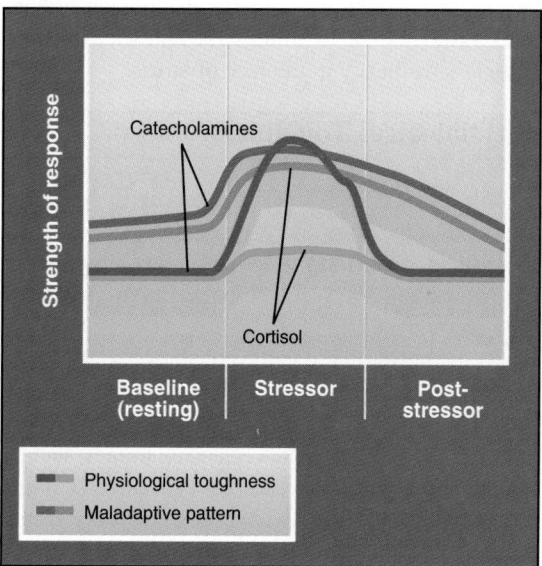

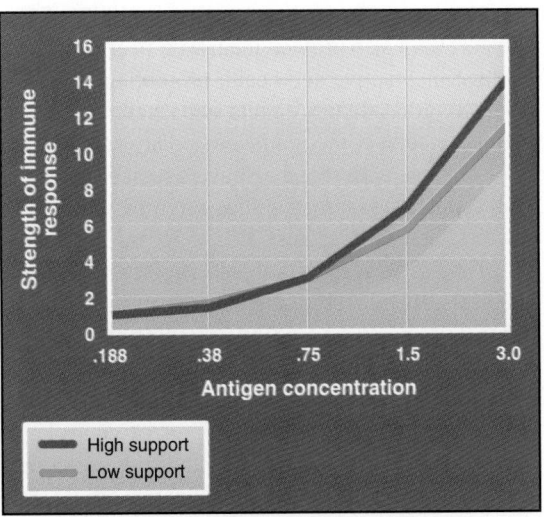

Figure 15.16 *Relation of social support to immune function in spouses of cancer patients. T cell formation in response to antigens was greater in subjects high in social support, indicating stronger immune system functioning. (Baron & others, 1990).*

Figure 15.15 *Loneliness and social isolation place people at risk for both psychological and physical disorders.*

cial isolation proved to be as great a risk factor for death as smoking, high blood pressure, high cholesterol levels, obesity, or lack of physical exercise. Indeed, after controlling for the effects of these medical risk factors, as well as age and physical health, the researchers found that those with few or weak social ties were twice as likely to die during the period of the study as were those with strong ties.

Social support can also affect recovery from stressful medical interventions. James Kulik and Heike Mahler (1989) studied the recovery patterns of married men who had undergone coronary bypass surgery. They found that patients who were frequently visited by their spouses required less pain medication, were discharged from the coronary intensive care unit sooner, and were ultimately able to go home sooner than patients who received few or no visits from their spouses. In another study, males who had had heart attacks or coronary bypass surgery were followed closely over a one-year period. Those who reported high levels of social support and intimacy in their lives experienced less psychological distress and fewer cardiac symptoms during their recovery periods (Fontana & others, 1989). Many other studies have shown that social support provides relief from psychological distress in people confronting stressful life events (Holahan & Moos, 1986, 1990; Rodin & Salovey, 1989).

There is even evidence that social support enhances immune system functioning under stress.

Robert Baron and his coworkers (1990) studied the spouses of cancer patients undergoing treatment at the University of Iowa hospital. The spouses completed a social support measure on which they rated the degree to which their social relationships were providing them with guidance, assurance of personal worth, emotional support, and social connectedness. On the basis of this measure, they were divided into high-support and low-support groups. They were then injected with increasing concentrations of an antigen that stimulates T cell activity in the immune system. At each antigen concentration, T cell concentration was measured in blood samples. As shown in Figure 15.16, the immune systems of the spouses who rated themselves high in social support produced more T cells, particularly at high levels of the antigens, indicating stronger functioning of the immune system. These results are consistent with others in indicating that people who have high levels of social support are more disease-resistant when they are under stress (House & others, 1988).

Recent theoretical analyses of social support have suggested a number of ways in which it may enhance physical and psychological well-being (S. Cohen, 1988). Two classes of effects have been identified: (1) *direct effects* on physical and psychological well-being that occur even when people are not experiencing stress and (2) *buffering effects* that help protect people from the impact of stressors.

In terms of direct effects, people who feel that they are part of a social system may experience a greater sense of identity and meaning in their lives, which in turn results in greater psychological well-being and enhanced immune system functioning

How a given source of
stress affects people may
depend on the sources of
support and gratification
available in other areas of
their lives. For example,
are women who have
partners and family in-
volvement more or less
susceptible to job stress?
To answer this question,
Rosalind Barnett, Nancy
Marshall, and Judith
Singer (1992) did a 3-year
longitudinal study of 403
social workers and nurses,
obtaining yearly measures
of job satisfaction and
psychological distress (including anxiety, depres-
sion, and unhappiness). In
women with intimate part-
ners and those with chil-
dren, no relation was
found between job stress
and psychological dis-
tress. In contrast, job
stress was directly related
to psychological distress
in women who were un-
partnered, childless, and
career focused. The re-
searchers concluded that
rewards associated with
intimate relationships and
family roles help protect
women from the negative
effects of job stress. However, a critical thinker
might wonder if the
women studied tended to
have positive family relationships. Is it possible
that unsatisfying family relationships might make
working women even
more susceptible to stress
on the job? The answer to
this question awaits fur-
ther research.

(S. Cohen, 1988; Rodin & Salovey, 1989). Social support may also provide them with peer pressure to engage in adaptive and health-promoting behaviors, such as good dietary habits and exercise. Finally, being embedded in significant social networks provides people with social resources such as assistance and support, and it may reduce exposure to other risk factors such as loneliness. ▼

The **buffering hypothesis** suggests that social support can play a significant role in buffering the impact of negative events by providing aid that helps eliminate or reduce stressors. Social support also helps people feel that they have the backing of others, and this can increase their feelings of control over stressors. Finally, true friends can bring social pressure to bear so that people do not cope with stressors in maladaptive ways (for example, through alcohol or drug use). Any of these buffering effects can significantly reduce the impact of stressful life events.

In a series of studies, James Pennebaker (1990) has found that one of the benefits of close relationships is the opportunity to disclose painful experiences and feelings. Talking about our problems can be therapeutic. Pennebaker and his colleagues invited 33 Holocaust survivors like those described at the beginning of the chapter to come in and talk about their horrible experiences. Many discussed these experiences in greater detail than ever before and even showed friends and families videotapes of what their experiences were like. Those who were the most disclosing had the most improved health 14 months later (Pennebaker & others, 1989). Pennebaker also found

that writing about personal traumas can help by allowing people to deal with the pain of the event instead of blocking it out. Volunteers who did this had fewer health complaints during the ensuing 4 to 6 months (Pennebaker, 1990).

Let us return to the case of Priscilla, described at the beginning of the chapter. How was she able to overcome her traumatic childhood? In studies of children who grow up under horrendous conditions, yet somehow rise above them, the buffering effects of social support are evident (Garmezy, 1983; Werner & Smith, 1982). Summarizing the findings of her 30-year longitudinal study of such children, one psychologist, Emmy Werner, noted, "Without exception, all of the children who thrived had at least one person that provided them with consistent emotional support—a grandmother, an older sister, a teacher or a neighbor" (*New York Times,* October 13, 1987, p. C11). The support and encouragement they received apparently helped to blunt the impact of the terrible stressors they experienced in their daily lives. For Priscilla, that person was a teacher who cared enough to befriend and encourage her during her childhood years.

Self-Efficacy

One of the most significant appraisals that we make when confronted with a stressor involves how much personal control we think we have over the situation (Neufeld & Patterson, 1989). Small wonder, then, that self-efficacy—the conviction that we can perform the

⟶ **Figure 15.17a** *Training women in self-defense techniques had positive and lasting effects on their sense of self-efficacy and reduced their sense of personal vulnerability and their anxiety about the possibility of being attacked. No significant changes occurred during a baseline period (Pre₁ and Pre₂) that preceded training, but positive effects were observed after training and at a 6-month follow-up. (Ozer & Bandura, 1990).*

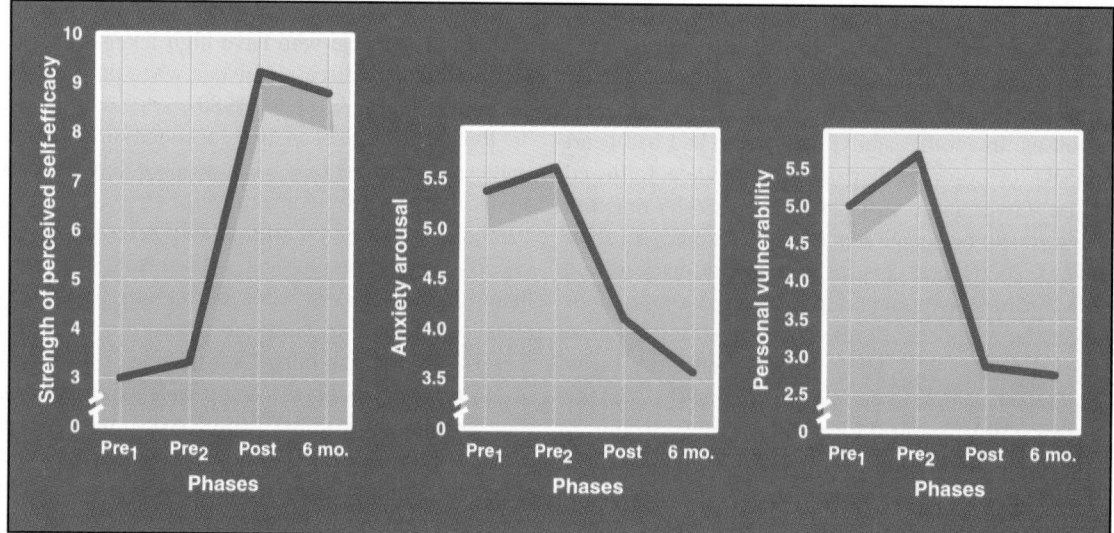

behaviors necessary to produce a desired outcome—has emerged as a highly potent protective factor (Bandura, 1989). Even events that are appraised as extremely demanding may generate little stress if they are also appraised as controllable or manageable.

Self-efficacy can be enhanced in a number of ways (Bandura, 1986). As noted in Chapter 14, the most effective way to build a sense of efficacy is through mastery experiences. Performance successes enhance self-efficacy; failures undermine it. People can also increase efficacy expectancies by observing others cope successfully and through social persuasion and encouragement from others (''You can do it!''). Finally, experiencing a low level of physiological arousal in the face of a stressor can convey a sense of strength and ability to cope.

A potential stressor faced by all women is the possibility of being raped, and many women are distressed by their sense of helplessness in physically defending themselves against a rapist. Elizabeth Ozer and Albert Bandura (1990) assessed changes in self-efficacy, perceived vulnerability, and anxiety about being assaulted in groups of women who participated in a self-defense class designed to teach them how to protect themselves against an unarmed assailant. During the 5-week course, the women were shown various ways of escaping or disabling an attacker, and they practiced them during simulated attacks by male assistants who wore protective gear (see Figure 15.17b). The women observed and encouraged one another, and they were verbally assured that such protective measures could be highly effective.

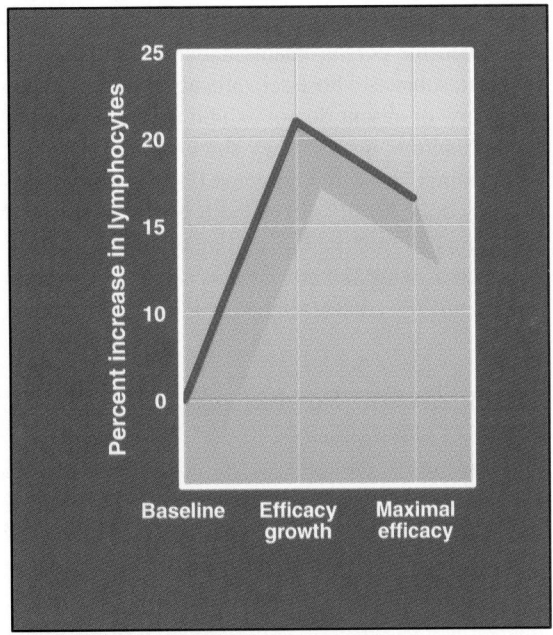

Figure 15.18 *Feelings of self-efficacy increase immune system functioning. An increase in lymphocytes occurs as self-efficacy increases while subjects successfully confront a phobic object, and they remain at a level higher than the baseline after coping self-efficacy has reached its maximal level. (Data from Wiedenfeld & others, 1989).*

Figure 15.17b *Self-defense classes like this can have positive effects on women's self-efficacy.*

The effects of the program on self-efficacy, anxiety about being raped, and perceived personal vulnerability to rape were assessed during a no-treatment control phase before the classes began, at the end of the program, and again 6 months later. As Figure 15.17a indicates, the program clearly affected all of these outcome measures; increases in self-efficacy were accompanied by reduced anxiety and reduced feelings of personal vulnerability. Although the women who took the class continued to view women in general as vulnerable to being raped, they viewed themselves as less vulnerable as a result of mastering the self-protective skills.

Self-efficacy has profound effects not only on performance and cognitions but also on physiological functioning. When people are confronted with threats and distrust their coping efficacy, they exhibit accelerated heart rate, increased blood pressure, and increased catecholamine secretion (Bandura & others, 1985). Their immune system functioning is also impaired, probably as a result of endorphin release (Bandura & others, 1988; Cohen & Levine, 1989). Furthermore, recent findings indicate that when people experience an increase in self-efficacy while confronting a stressful situation (in this case, a phobic object), a marked *increase* in immune function occurs (Wiedenfeld & others, 1992). As Figure 15.18 indicates, immune function is at its peak while efficacy is growing, but it remains at a higher level than baseline when the person attains maximum efficacy. In contrast, subjects whose self-efficacy development is very slow or absent do not exhibit the increased immune function; instead, they show lowered immune functioning. These findings leave little doubt that self-efficacy dramatically affects both psychological and physiological functioning, and they point to the importance of other factors, such as social support and skill acquisition, that are known to affect self-efficacy.

Optimism and Pessimism

Attribution is the process of making judgments about the causes of events or behaviors. Recent research has shown that people have stable tendencies to make particular kinds of attributions concerning positive and negative events. Of particular current interest is a **pessimistic explanatory style** in which negative events are attributed to personal deficits that will never change. For example, a pessimistic explanatory style in a student who has just been turned down for a date might take the following form: ''She turned me down because I'm ugly and uninteresting, and my unattractiveness will always keep me from developing a relationship.'' In contrast, optimists respond to negative events with a conviction that they will handle the situations successfully in the future. Explanatory style is measured by means of either self-report scales or content analysis of written or verbal materials (Burns & Seligman, 1991).

Recent research indicates that pessimistic people are at greater risk for helplessness and depression when they confront stressful events. They are also at increased risk for illness and death. In one study, infectious illnesses and number of doctor visits were counted over a one-year period for undergraduates who had optimistic and pessimistic explanatory styles as measured by means of a questionnaire. Pessimists had about twice as many illnesses and made about twice as many visits to doctors as did optimists (Peterson & Seligman, 1987). In another study, women who came to the National Cancer Institute for treatment of breast cancer were followed for 5 years. On the average, pessimists died sooner than optimists even where the physical severity of the disease was the same at the beginning of the 5-year period (Levy & others, 1989).

Longitudinal studies suggest that pessimists may suffer more illnesses over their lifetimes and die younger. Members of the Harvard classes of 1939–1944 have been followed since leaving college (they are now in their 70s). At age 25, their explanatory styles were determined on the basis of questionnaires. Since that time, they have had physical checkups every 5 years. The data strongly suggest that pessimism at age 25 predicts poorer health beginning at about age 45 (Peterson & others, 1988). Whether we consider pessimism a personality characteristic or a cognitive style, it appears that a pessimistic explanatory style constitutes a risk factor that affects both psychological and physical well-being.

Chapter 14 discussed Bandura's concept of reciprocal determinism, which emphasizes that personal characteristics, behavior, and the environment affect one another in a network of two-way causal relations. Where stress and vulnerability are concerned, this concept is exemplified in the case of the Type A personality.

PSYCHOBIOLOGICAL INTERACTIONS

Type A Personality and Coronary Heart Disease: An Example of Person–Behavior–Environment Interactions

Stress has long been suspected as a potentially important risk factor in coronary heart disease (CHD). CHD accounts for two thirds of all cardiovascular deaths, claiming about 650,000 victims per year in the United States. About one fourth of all CHD deaths occur in people less than 65 years of age.

CHD occurs when fatty deposits known as *plaque* partially or totally obstruct one or more of the three arteries that circulate blood within the heart. The obstructions reduce or cut off the supply of blood to various portions of the heart, and two major forms of CHD may appear as a result.

In *angina pectoris,* people suffer from periodic chest pains caused by an insufficient supply of blood to the heart. Even more serious is *myocardial infarction,* or "heart attack," which results from a major reduction in the heart's blood supply.

Certain people seem especially prone to heart problems. Is there a CHD-prone personality? Two heart specialists, Meyer Friedman and Ray Rosenman (1974), have concluded that there is. They have described a behavior pattern, called **Type A,** that seems to be associated with increased risk of coronary disease. The Type A pattern is said to have been discovered by an upholsterer who came to repair the chairs in the office of a physician who specialized in treating heart attack victims. The upholsterer noticed an unusual wear pattern: The chairs were worn at the front of the seat, not the back, indicating that the patients were constantly sitting on the edges of their seats and moving about during their appointments.

The upholsterer's observation typifies many of the behaviors seen in Type A personalities. Type A people are apt to live under great pressure and to be demanding of themselves and others. Their behaviors include rapid talking, moving, walking, and eating. They have an exaggerated sense of time urgency and become very irritated at delays or failures to meet their deadlines. Many of them are workaholics who tend to schedule more and more activities in less and less time and try to do several things at once. Figure 15.19 shows a page from the appointment book of a Type A person who later died of a heart attack. Type A people are also characterized by high levels of competitiveness and ambition, as well as aggressiveness and hostility when things get in their way. They stand in sharp contrast to *Type B* persons, who are more relaxed, more agreeable, and have far less sense of time urgency (Strube, 1989). Walter Chadwick, the heart attack victim described in the chapter opening, fits the Type A pattern.

The most valid measure of Type A behavior seems to be a structured interview in which the interviewer asks a number of questions and observes the manner in which the interviewee responds. The speed, volume, and tenseness of the individual's words are noted, as are gestures, posture, and body movements. Voice analysis is also sometimes used (Roskies & others, 1989). Several questionnaires have also been developed to assess Type A characteristics, but the interview measure is most consistently related to CHD (Rodin & Salovey, 1989).

Several large-scale prospective studies suggest that Type A personality is a risk factor for CHD in the population at large. In the *Western Collaborative Study,* which began in 1960, 3,200 working men who had no history of CHD were followed for 8.5 years. Men who had been judged Type A by the structured interview technique had 2.2 times as much CHD as people judged Type B. Even when other physical risk factors, such as obesity and smoking, were taken into account, Type A men still had double the risk for CHD (Rosenman & others, 1975).

In the *Framingham Heart Study,* more than 1,600 healthy men and women were followed for 8 years after being classified as either Type A or Type B. White-collar Type A men's risk of developing CHD was almost three times that of white-

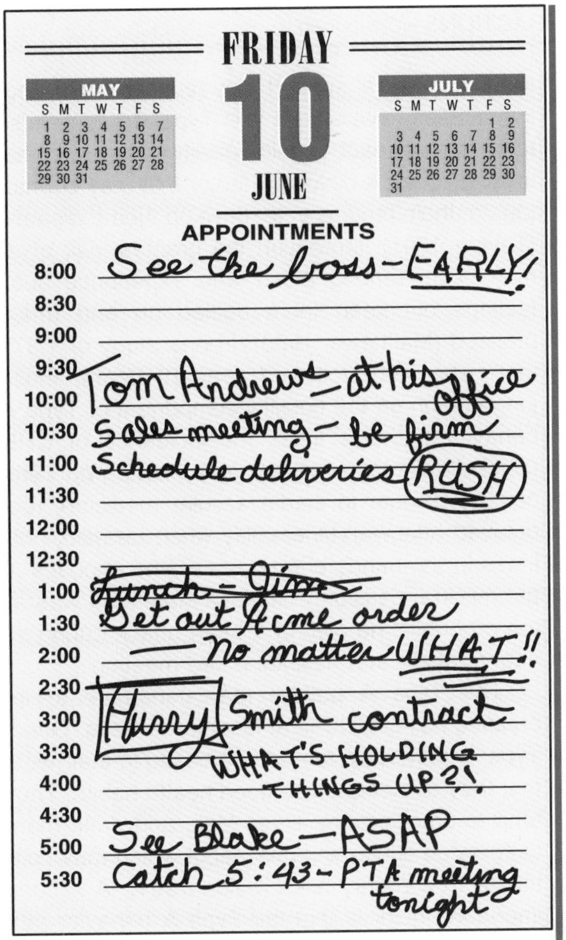

Figure 15.19 *Type A people experience a continuous sense of time urgency and feelings of irritable impatience. The owner of this appointment book died of a heart attack shortly after the date on this schedule. (Carver & Scheier, 1988).*

collar Type B men, and Type A women's risk was twice that of Type B women (Haynes & others, 1980). However, although the Type A pattern predicts risk of CHD within the general population, it has not been shown to have predictive value in high-risk groups (that is, for people who smoke, have high blood cholesterol levels, and do not exercise) or in very-low-risk populations (that is, people who have good health habits and no familial history of CHD) (Cohen & Reed, 1985; Shekelle & others, 1985).

Recent research indicates that not all components of the Type A pattern increase vulnerability to CHD. CHD does not appear to be linked to the fast-paced, time-conscious lifestyle or to high ambition. Rather, the crucial component of Type A seems to be negative emotions, particularly the anger associated with the aggressive temperament of Type A (Booth-Kewley & Friedman, 1987; Friedman, 1991). A particular type of hostility may be especially important—namely, a cynical hostility marked by suspiciousness, resentment, frequent anger, distrust, and antagonism (Barefoot & others, 1989). This aspect of Type A people's behavior is likely to alienate others and reduce the amount of social support they receive. Physiological studies have shown that Type A people also tend to overreact physiologically to events that arouse anger, a biological factor that may contribute to their tendency to develop heart disease (Taylor, 1991). Moreover, the greatest risk of all may occur among those who experience such feelings but keep them bottled up and unexpressed (Matthews, 1988). In one study of 1,877 men who were followed over 10 years, those judged high on the hostility component of Type A behavior had five times the incidence of CHD (Shekelle & others, 1985). John Hunter, an 18th-century pioneer in cardiovascular medicine, recognized his own vulnerability when he said, "My life is in the hands of any rascal who chooses to put me in a passion." Hunter's statement was all too prophetic; he died of a heart attack during an angry debate at a hospital board meeting.

The Type A pattern may contribute to increased risk of CHD in at least three ways. Often, Type A individuals are so engrossed in their work that they do not practice good health habits. They tend to smoke more, sleep less, and drink more caffeinated drinks and milk, all of which may contribute to coronary risk (Taylor, 1991). A second important factor is that the Type A behavior pattern virtually guarantees that the individuals who exhibit it will encounter many stressful situations, such as time pressures of their own making and barriers that anger them. Finally, physiological studies of Type A individuals indicate that their autonomic and endocrine systems are highly reactive when they confront such stressors. In Selye's terms, Type A people spend much of their time in the alarm and resistance stages of the General Adaptation Syndrome, and their chronic physiological arousal may be an important contributor to the eventual development of heart disease.

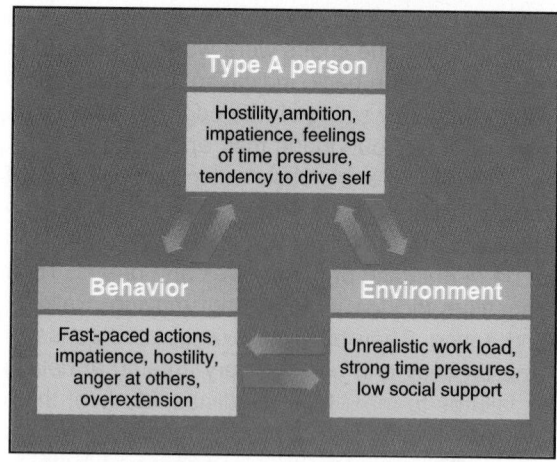

Figure 15.20 *Reciprocal determinism and the Type A behavior pattern. Personal factors, behaviors, and the environment all interact in two-way causal relations.*

Bandura's notion of reciprocal influence between person, behavior, and environment certainly applies to Type A personalities (see Figure 15.20). Their personality characteristics cause them to behave in ways that are virtually guaranteed to create a stressful environment, to which they then overrespond physiologically and emotionally.

In concluding, I should note that the Type A pattern may not be all bad. A 13-year longitudinal study showed that Type A men were more likely than Type B men to have heart attacks but also more likely than Type B men to recover from them (Ragland & Brand, 1988). One reason may be that their hard-driving nature gives them the tools to adhere to demanding rehabilitation programs that increase the chances of recovery. Thus, the very personality characteristics that place them at risk for CHD may also help them recover from their heart attacks.

Interacting Causal Factors in Vulnerability

Although we have examined stress, resources, and vulnerabilities separately, it is clear that these factors interact in important ways to affect well-being. Thus, certain combinations of these factors may be necessary in order for physical well-being to be affected. One example of interacting causal factors comes from a study of athletic injuries. In a prospective study of 451 high school athletes, it was found that neither life stress, nor low social support, nor poor coping skills alone were related to subsequent injuries. However, a particular combination of these three vulnerability factors placed athletes at significant risk of injury (see Figure 15.21). Athletes who had high levels of life stress, low levels of social support, and poor coping skills were twice as likely to be injured during the season as athletes showing any other combination of these three factors (Smith & others, 1990).

The fact that causal factors may interact in this manner increases the difficulty for the researcher who wants to identify people whose well-being is at risk.

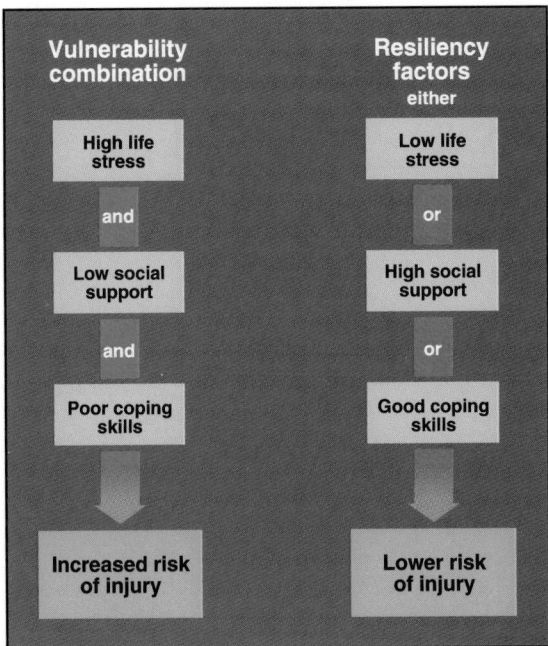

Figure 15.21 *The interaction of psychosocial causal factors in producing vulnerability to athletic injuries. The combination of three vulnerability factors—high life stress, low social support, and poor coping skills—doubled the risk of injury. The absence of any one of the vulnerability factors reduced the risk of injury. (Data from Smith & others, 1990).*

It would be easy for any study to leave out a piece of the causal puzzle by failing to take account of some risk factor that is in fact important when combined with other variables.

As we have seen, a variety of causal factors, including biological processes, cognitive factors, intrapsychic variables, and environmental factors, can increase vulnerability to stress. The *Understanding Causes* feature on page 488 summarizes the personal and environmental factors we have discussed.

■ ■

Stress Management

Because of the toll that stress takes on people's physical and psychological well-being, much effort has gone into the development of methods for reducing stress. The model of stress that we have used throughout this chapter suggests that stress reduction could be directed at any of the model's five major components. Thus, we can reduce stress by instituting changes in the *situation* that make it less demanding. In industry, for example, psychological consultants have worked with employees and management to decrease situational sources of job stress, such as shift

changes, unrealistic time demands and production schedules, relationship problems between workers and supervisors, and environmental stressors such as excessive noise, heat, and pollutants (Stokols, 1992). Second, as we shall see, we can help people make changes in the *cognitive appraisal* process that can trigger the rest of the stress response. Third, people can learn effective ways to control their *physiological arousal*. Fourth, we can help people develop *behavioral skills* that allow them to deal with situational demands more effectively. We saw one example of this in the FBI program for airline employees at risk for terrorist activities. Finally, in instances where the stress response is a product of severe personality problems, it may be necessary to intervene with psychological treatment designed to modify these factors.

We will postpone our discussion of major personality change until Chapter 17. For now, we will consider stress management approaches that are designed to enhance coping skills.

Cognitive Coping Skills

Stressful situations cannot always be altered, and so another approach to stress management is to help people acquire coping skills. Many coping skills programs are directed at the cognitive appraisal and physiological arousal components of the stress response (Meichenbaum, 1985; Smith & Rohsenow, 1989). Thus, people are taught to modify aspects of their appraisals that lead to inappropriate emotional responses and are also taught ways of directly controlling physiological arousal responses (see Figure 15.22).

Modifying dysfunctional appraisals, or developing cognitive coping skills, can be a highly effective stress management approach. Two major tech-

Figure 15.22 *Coping skills training programs employ a variety of approaches to develop cognitive and physiological coping responses that can be used to reduce or prevent stress.*

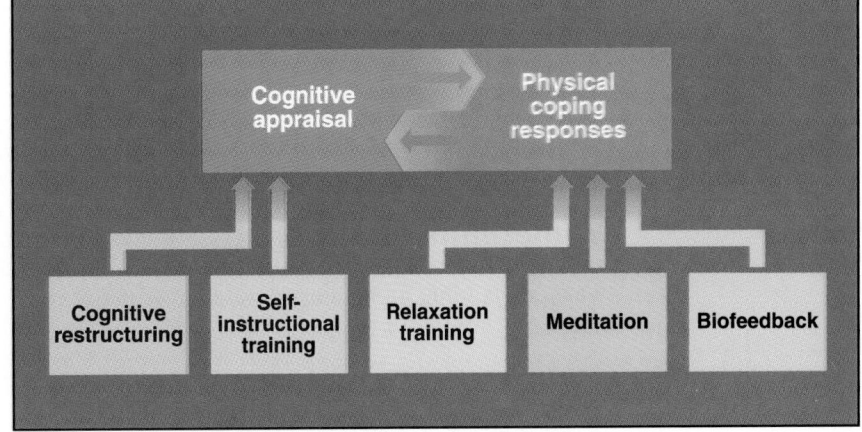

Causal Factors

Biological
- High physiological reactivity to stressors
- Long-lasting catecholamine and corticosteroid response (low physiological toughness)
- Weak body system(s) (diathesis)

Cognitive
- Low self-efficacy beliefs
- Pessimistic explanatory style
- Unreasonable self-standards that create perfectionistic demands
- Irrational beliefs that create disturbance

Intrapsychic
- Tendency to use denial, wishful thinking, and avoidance coping responses
- Personality conflicts that make certain situations threatening
- Type A personality pattern (cardiovascular disease)

Environmental
- Negative life events of high severity, duration, chronicity, and/or low predictability, controllability
- Low levels of social and environmental support

Vulnerability to Stress

Vulnerability to Stress is a function of interacting personal and environmental causal factors. These factors may vary and may interact with one another in particular ways, depending on the person and the situation.

niques can be used to modify appraisals. **Cognitive restructuring** is directed at discovering and replacing irrational, distorted, or self-defeating appraisals related to demands, resources, consequences, or the personal meaning of consequences. Subjects are taught to "tune in" to their thought patterns during stressful situations and to be especially attentive to exaggerated appraisals of how serious the situation is ("catastrophizing") and to irrational ideas such as those suggested by Albert Ellis (see Table 13.1). The benefits of successful cognitive restructuring are evident in the following case:

> Whenever I find myself getting guilty or upset, I immediately tell myself that there must be some silly sentence that I am saying to myself to cause this upset; and almost immediately . . . I find this sentence . . . [T]he sentence invariably takes the form of "Isn't it terrible that . . . " or "Wouldn't it be awful if . . . " And when I look at and question these sentences and ask myself, "*How* is it really terrible that . . . ? or "*Why* would it actually be awful if . . . ?" I always find that it isn't terrible or wouldn't be awful, and I get over being upset very quickly. . . . I can hardly believe it, but I seem to be getting to the point, after so many years of worrying over practically everything and thinking I was a slob no matter what I did, of now finding that *nothing* is so terrible or awful, and I now seem to be recognizing this *in advance* rather than after I have seriously upset myself (Ellis, 1962, pp. 31–32).

A somewhat different approach to changing cognitions is **self-instructional training** (Meichenbaum, 1985). Rather than attacking irrational ideas that cause disturbance, subjects learn to "talk to themselves" in ways that will help them cope more effectively at four critical stages of the stressful episode: (1) preparing for the stressor, (2) confronting the stressor, (3) dealing with the feeling of being overwhelmed, and (4) appraising coping efforts after the stressful situation. Table 15.3 provides examples of self-instructions that can be used at these stages of the coping process.

Skills for Controlling Arousal

Coping skills training can also help people control their physiological responses in stressful situations. The most common approach is training in muscle relaxation, which provides a means of voluntarily reducing or preventing high levels of arousal. Most muscle (somatic) relaxation training techniques are based on **progressive muscle relaxation,** which involves tensing and relaxing of the muscles (Jacobson, 1938). People can generally learn to control their muscle tension within about a week of practice, providing themselves with an effective means of controlling arousal.

Table 15.3 Examples of Self-Statements Learned in Self-Instructional Training to Enhance Performance and Minimize Emotional Responses at Various Phases of the Coping Process

Phase of Coping Process	Self-Statements
Preparing for the Stressor	• What do I have to do? • I can work out a plan to deal with it. • Remember, stick to the issues and don't take it personally. • Stop worrying. Worrying won't help anything.
Confronting and Handling the Stressor	• As long as I keep my cool, I'm in control of the situation. • I can meet this challenge. This tenseness is just a cue to use my coping exercises. • Don't think about stress, just about what I have to do. • Take a deep breath and relax. Ah, good.
Coping with the Feeling of Being Overwhelmed	• Keep my focus on the present. What is it I have to do? • Relax and slow things down. • Don't try to eliminate stress totally; just keep it manageable. • Let's take the issue point by point.
Evaluation and Self-Reinforcement	• OK, what worked and what didn't? • I handled it pretty well. • It didn't work, but that's OK. I'll do better next time. • Way to go! You did it!

Source: Meichenbaum, 1985.

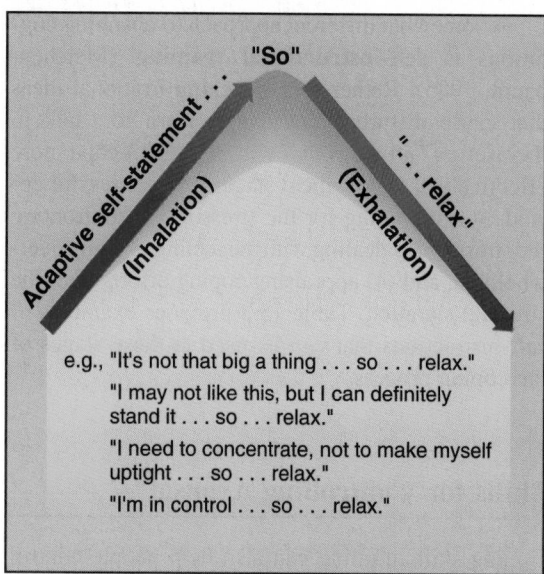

e.g., "It's not that big a thing . . . so . . . relax."

"I may not like this, but I can definitely stand it . . . so . . . relax."

"I need to concentrate, not to make myself uptight . . . so . . . relax."

"I'm in control . . . so . . . relax."

Figure 15.23 *This integrated coping response, acquired through cognitive restructuring, self-instructional training, and relaxation training, provides a means of controlling appraisals and physiological arousal when incorporated into the breathing cycle. During the exhalation phase, the person applies the skill of relaxation to control arousal. (Smith & Rohsenow, 1989).*

Meditation is another means of reducing physiological arousal, but its value seems to be as a general stress reducer and a means of producing a relaxed mental state; it does not appear to be as effective as relaxation training in dealing with situational stressors (Pagano & Warrenburg, 1983; Smith & Rohsenow, 1989). Finally, biofeedback techniques involving visual or auditory feedback from the muscles may be effectively used when the goal is relaxation of specific muscles, such as the forehead and scalp muscles involved in tension headaches (Blanchard & Andrasik,

1985). However, relaxation training is a less expensive and more effective approach to general body relaxation (Nigl, 1984).

Cognitive and relaxation coping responses can be combined into an **integrated coping response,** as shown in Figure 15.23. The coping elements are integrated into the breathing cycle, giving the person a coping response that can be quickly applied and modified as needed during a coping sequence. Statements learned through cognitive restructuring or self-instructional training accompany inhalation, and the relaxation response occurs during exhalation. Use of this integrated response has been shown to increase self-efficacy, reduce negative emotional states, and improve task performance in both sports and academic test situations (Crocker, 1989; Smith & Nye, 1989).

Stress management methods have been applied to several high-risk populations, including Type A men. Ethel Roskies and her coworkers (1989) used relaxation training and cognitive interventions with healthy Type A men and achieved marked positive changes in their Type A behavioral patterns. However, the researchers were not able to demonstrate changes in the men's exaggerated physiological responses to stressors. Perhaps, though, the cognitive and behavioral changes that occurred in the Type A men will help reduce the number of stressful situations they create for themselves.

The demonstrated benefits of physiological control of arousal through relaxation techniques warrants special attention to these procedures. Therefore, the following feature provides a program that will enable you to learn progressive relaxation and a widely used meditation technique, both of which have demonstrated their effectiveness in stress management (Benson & Klipper, 1976; Davidson & Schwartz, 1976; Morris, 1991).

ENHANCING HUMAN PERFORMANCE

SOMATIC AND COGNITIVE RELAXATION SKILLS

Richard Davidson and Gary Schwartz (1976) distinguished between **somatic relaxation** (relaxation of the body) and **cognitive relaxation** (relaxation and clearing of the mind). They suggested that muscle relaxation techniques are primarily somatic techniques, whereas meditation techniques are ideally suited for cognitive relaxation (although they may produce physical relaxation as well). Both techniques can be very effective in en-

hancing stress management and performance under stress. The somatic relaxation approach can be used in any stressful situation to quickly reduce arousal without interfering with other behaviors. It is used as part of the integrated coping response described earlier. The meditation technique can be used for general relaxation and physical rejuvenation (Benson & Klipper, 1976).

Progressive Muscle Relaxation

It is recommended that you practice somatic relaxation exercises at least once a day until you have mastered them. The exercises will initially require about 15 minutes of practice, but as you master the technique, the time required will become progressively shorter. Practice in a quiet atmosphere while sitting up in bed or in a comfortable chair or sofa.

1. Get as comfortable as possible. Loosen clothing, and do not cross your legs. Take a deep breath, let it out slowly, and become as relaxed as possible.

2. While sitting comfortably, bend your arms at the elbow. Now make a hard fist with both hands, and bend your wrists downward while simultaneously tensing the muscles of your upper arms. This will produce a state of tension in your hands, forearms, and upper arms. Hold this tension for 5 seconds and study it carefully. Then slowly let out the tension halfway while concentrating on the sensations in your arms and fingers as the tension decreases. Hold the tension at the halfway point for 5 seconds, and then slowly let the tension out the rest of the way and let your arms rest comfortably in your lap. Concentrate carefully on the contrast between the tension you have just experienced and the ensuing relaxation, which deepens as you voluntarily relax the muscles for an additional 10–15 seconds. As you breathe normally, concentrate on those muscles, and give yourself a mental command to "relax" each time you exhale. Do this for 7 to 10 breaths.

3. Tense the calf and thigh muscles in your legs. You can do this by straightening your legs while pointing your toes downward. Hold the tension for 5 seconds, then slowly let it out halfway. Hold at the halfway point for an additional 5 seconds, and then slowly let the tension out all the way and concentrate on relaxing the muscles as completely as possible. Again, pay careful attention to the feelings of tension and relaxation as they develop. Finish by giving the muscles a mental command to relax each time you exhale (7 to 10 times), and concentrate on relaxing them as deeply as possible.

4. Cross the palms of your hands in front of your chest, and press them together so as to tense the chest and shoulder muscles. At the same time, tense your stomach muscles hard. As before, hold the tension for 5 seconds, and then slowly let the tension out halfway, focusing on the decreasing levels of tension as you do so. Hold again for 5 seconds at the halfway point, and then slowly let the tension out completely. Again, perform the breathing procedure, and give a mental command to deepen the relaxation in your stomach, chest, and shoulder muscles.

5. Arch your back, and push your shoulders back as far as possible so as to tense your upper and lower back muscles. (Be careful not to tense these muscles too hard.) Repeat the procedure of slowly releasing the tension halfway, then all the way. Finish by performing the breathing and mental command as you relax your back muscles as deeply as possible.

6. Tense your neck and jaw muscles by thrusting your jaw outward and drawing the corners of your mouth back. Release the tension slowly to the halfway point, hold for 5 seconds, and then slowly release all the tension in these muscles. Let your head droop into a comfortable position and your jaw slacken as you concentrate on relaxing these muscles totally with your breathing exercise and mental command. (You can also tense your neck muscles in other ways, such as by bending your neck forward, backward, or to one side. Experiment to find the way that's best for you. Tense your jaw at the same time.)

7. Wrinkle your forehead and scalp upward to tense those muscles. Hold the tension for 5 seconds, release it halfway for an additional 5 seconds, and then relax completely. Focus on relaxing your forehead and scalp muscles, and use your breathing and the associated mental command to deepen relaxation.

8. While sitting in a totally relaxed position, take a series of short inhalations, about one per second, until your chest is filled and tense. Hold this for about 5 seconds, then exhale slowly while repeating silently the word "relax." Most people can produce a deeply relaxed state by doing this. Repeat this exercise three times.

9. Finish off your relaxation practice by concentrating on breathing comfortably into your abdomen (rather than into your chest area). Simply let your abdomen fill with air as you inhale, and deepen your relaxation as you exhale. Abdominal breathing is far more relaxing than breathing into the chest.

The Benson Meditation Technique

The cognitive relaxation technique developed by Herbert Benson is a generalized version of a variety of Eastern and Western religious, cultic, and lay meditation practices (such as yoga and Transcendental Meditation). Four basic components, though not universal, are common to such techniques: (1) a quiet environment; (2) a comfortable position, typically sitting upright in a chair; (3) a mental device or word on which the meditator focuses to shift attention from the external environment; and (4) a passive attitude in which whatever occurs in consciousness is allowed to occur but the meditator attempts to maintain attention to the mental device being used. The procedure itself is quite simple and can be learned very quickly:

1. Sit quietly in a comfortable position.
2. Close your eyes.
3. Deeply relax all your muscles, beginning at your feet and progressing up to your face. Keep them relaxed.
4. Breathe through your nose. Concentrate on your breathing. As you breathe out, say the word *ONE* silently to yourself. Breathe easily and naturally, each time repeating *ONE* as you exhale.
5. Continue for 10 to 20 minutes. You may open your eyes to check the time, but do not use an alarm. When you finish, sit quietly for several minutes, at first with your eyes closed and later with your eyes open. Do not stand up for a few minutes.
6. Do not worry about whether you are successful in achieving a deep level of relaxation. Maintain a passive attitude and permit relaxation to occur at its own pace. When distracting thoughts occur, try to ignore them by not dwelling on them and return to repeating *ONE*. With practice, the response should come with little effort. Practice the technique once or twice daily, but not within 2 hours after any meal, since the digestive processes seem to interfere with the elicitation of the relaxation response.

SUMMARY

The Nature of Stress

● Stress has been conceptualized by various theorists as a stimulus; as a response having cognitive, physiological, and behavioral components; and as a person–situation interaction, or a transaction between the person and the environment.

● A useful model of stress specifies interactions among situational factors, cognitive appraisal processes, physiological responses, and behavioral attempts to cope. Personality and motivational variables are assumed to influence all of these factors. This model by its nature predicts individual differences in response to stressors.

● Stressors are events that place physical or psychological demands on organisms. The stressfulness of a situation is defined by the balance between demands and resources. Life events can vary in terms of how positive or negative they are, as well as in predictability, controllability, chronicity, and other dimensions that affect their impact.

● Catastrophic life events, major life events, and microstressors can all affect physical and psychological well-being. However, their impact depends on interactions between situational and individual factors.

● Cognitive appraisal processes play an essential role in people's responses to stressors. People appraise the nature of the demands, the resources available to deal with them, their possible consequences, and the personal meaning of these consequences. Distortions at any of these levels can result in inappropriate stress responses.

● The physiological response to stressors is mediated by the autonomic and endocrine systems and involves a pattern of arousal that mobilizes the body to deal with the stressor. Selye described a General Adaptation Syndrome, which includes the stages of alarm, resistance, and exhaustion.

● Adequacy of task performance under stressful conditions depends on the balance between task-relevant and task-irrelevant responses, some of which are generated by physiological arousal. Appraising demands as challenges or opportunities seems to elicit primarily task-relevant responses.

Stress and Well-Being

● Catastrophic events can affect both psychological and physical well-being. The posttraumatic stress disorder includes reliving of the trauma, numbness and avoidance of stimuli associated with the trauma, and symptoms of anxiety, arousal, and distress. One variant of this disorder is seen in the rape trauma syndrome. Psychological intervention may be very useful in helping people who have experienced catastrophic events to avoid the development of the disorder.

● Measures of both major negative life events and microstressors are associated with negative physical and psychological outcomes, but the correlations tend to be modest in prospective studies because of the importance of individual differences in responding to such events. Causal linkages may be difficult to identify.

● Burnout is a response to chronic stress. The cognitive, physiological, and behavioral consequences of burnout may lead to psychological and physical withdrawal from an activity or job and may negatively affect both performance and well-being.

Coping with Stress

● Three major ways of coping with stressors are problem-focused coping, emotion-focused coping, and seeking social support.

● Problem-focused coping and seeking social support generally relate better to adjustment than emotion-focused coping. However, the outcome of a coping strategy depends on its appropriateness to the situation and the skill with which it is carried out. In situations involving low personal control, emotion-focused coping may be the most appropriate and effective strategy.

Vulnerability and Protective Factors

● People differ in their physiological responses to stressors. Physiological toughness —a pattern involving low resting levels of catecholamines and cortisol, low cortisol elevations during confrontations with stressors, and a quick and strong catecholamine response to stressors that returns quickly to baseline— appears to serve as a protective factor.

● Social support is an important protective factor for people who are confronting stressors. Such support has both direct and buffering effects that help people cope with stress.

● Self-efficacy is another protective factor. High self-efficacy is produced by performance successes, modeling and social persuasion, and experiencing low arousal in the presence of a stressor. Self-efficacy enhances performance, results in lowered physiological arousal, and appears to enhance immune functioning.

● A pessimistic explanatory style appears to place people at risk for both physical and psychological disorders. Optimists live longer than pessimists, and they have fewer illnesses and less depression.

● The Type A behavior pattern is associated with increased risk of coronary heart disease in the general population. The aspect of Type A behavior that appears to increase risk is negative emotional responses, particularly anger and hostility. Bottling up such feelings appears to increase the risk still further.

● The interaction of causal factors in vulnerability to stress is demonstrated by the finding that life stress predicts increased risk of injury only in athletes that also have both low levels of social support and poor coping skills.

Stress Management

● Stress management may be accomplished at the situational level; as in programs to reduce job stress by changing aspects of the job.

● Stress management can also be accomplished through coping skills training. Cognitive restructuring and self-instructional training can be used to develop cognitive coping responses; and relaxation training, meditation, and biofeedback can be used to develop greater control of physiological arousal.

KEY TERMS AND CONCEPTS

alarm (p. 471)
attribution (p. 484)
buffering hypothesis (p. 482)
burnout (p. 476)
catastrophic life event (p. 467)
catecholamines (p. 470)

cognitive relaxation (p. 490)
cognitive restructuring (p. 489)
corticosteroid (p. 470)
cortisol (p. 470)
daily hassle (p. 467)
demand (p. 466)

emotion-focused coping strategy (p. 477)
exhaustion (p. 471)
General Adaptation Syndrome (GAS) (p. 471)
integrated coping response (p. 490)
life change unit (p. 468)

life event scale (p. 468)
major life event (p. 467)
meta-analysis (p. 475)
microstressor (p. 467)
pessimistic explanatory style (p. 484)
physiological toughness (p. 480)
post-traumatic stress disorder (p. 473)
primary appraisal (p. 469)
problem-focused coping strategy (p. 477)

progressive muscle relaxation (p. 489)
prospective study (p. 468)
protective factor (p. 479)
psychophysiological disorder (p. 476)
rape trauma syndrome (p. 473)
reappraisal (p. 470)
resistance (p. 471)
resource (p. 466)
secondary appraisal (p. 469)

self-instructional training (p. 489)
social support (p. 477)
somatic relaxation (p. 490)
stress (p. 465)
stressor (p. 465)
task-irrelevant responses (p. 472)
task-relevant responses (p. 472)
Type A behavior pattern (p. 484)
vulnerability factors (p. 479)

S U G G E S T E D   R E A D I N G S

Friedman, H. S. (1991). *The self-healing personality: Why some people achieve health and others succumb to illness.* Ft. Worth: Harcourt Brace Jovanovich. A timely and interesting description of biological and psychological factors that enhance health or make people disease-prone.

Kleinke, C. L. (1991). *Coping with life challenges.* Pacific Grove, Calif.: Brooks/Cole. A useful book containing many practical pointers for learning effective coping skills for dealing with a wide range of stressful life events.

Lazarus, R. S., & Folkman, S. (1984). *Stress, appraisal, and coping.* New York: Springer. A classic and highly interesting book that discusses stress and coping from a perspective very similar to the one used in this chapter.

Taylor, S. E. (1991). *Health psychology* (2nd ed.). New York: McGraw-Hill. A comprehensive and authoritative textbook that includes an extensive discussion of the health-related effects of stress and coping. The book also contains a detailed description of research and intervention with the Type A personality.

16 Psychological Disorders

■ ◻

C H A P T E R   O U T L I N E

Sarah was in the shopping mall when it first happened. Suddenly, she felt her heart pounding, grew weak and shaky, and experienced an indescribable sense of doom. She was sure she was either going to die or become insane on the spot. Gathering all her strength, she made it to her car and drove home. Now, after several such incidents, she is afraid to leave her house.

Mark has been depressed for several years, but things are even worse now. He feels totally inadequate and inferior. The future looks hopeless, and he cannot sleep at night. During the day, he can barely function, and his moods alternate between deadening depression and intense anxiety. A friend has suggested that he seek professional counseling, but Mark is convinced that he has slipped too deeply into the black hole of despair to ever feel good again. He wonders how long he wants to go on living in his private hell.

"One day, I just knew that the aliens had taken over the bodies and minds of our next door neighbors and that they were plotting to destroy me because I had discovered them. Not long afterward, I began feeling tingling sensations in my body and realized that they had some sort of death ray trained on my house. I called the FBI, but they told me that I should talk to my doctor about my situation. They're in on it too, you know. It was then that I knew I had to protect myself. So I did the only reasonable thing. I got a gun and started shooting back. When the police came, they sided with the aliens instead of me. So that's how I ended up here in the hospital."

These three distressed people could very well live in your city, or even in your neighborhood. In 1991, the National Institute of Mental Health (NIMH) released the results of the largest study ever undertaken to assess the incidence of psychological disorders in the United States (Robins & Regier, 1991). The NIMH Epidemiologic Catchment Area Study, originally commissioned in 1980, involved more than 18,500 people selected at random in five areas of the United States. All of the respondents underwent detailed psychiatric interviews.

The results of the study suggested that the incidence of psychological disorders is much higher than previously assumed. Projections from the study indicated that during any given 6-month period, nearly one in five Americans will suffer from a major mental disorder, and that nearly a third of Americans will suffer at least one major psychological disorder during their lifetimes.

Other facts emerging from recent research paint an equally grim picture (Comer, 1992; Sarason & Sarason, 1993):

- This year, over a million students will withdraw from college because of emotional problems.
- One adolescent commits suicide every 90 seconds.
- More than 30 million Americans will have alcohol-related problems during their lives, and alcohol abuse costs the U.S. economy about $117 billion a year.
- Fifty million people experience mild to moderate depression, and another 2 million suffer from serious depression.
- Valium and other drugs used for the treatment of anxiety are among the most frequently prescribed drugs in the United States.

Figure 16.1 shows some of the results from the NIMH study (Robins & Regier, 1991). But these statistics, impressive though they may be, do not capture the intense suffering that they reflect. Indeed, they may be only the tip of the iceberg. They cannot communicate the confusion and terror felt by the schizophrenic patient whose world is disintegrating and makes no sense anymore. They cannot convey the intense personal misery of a depressed person who is

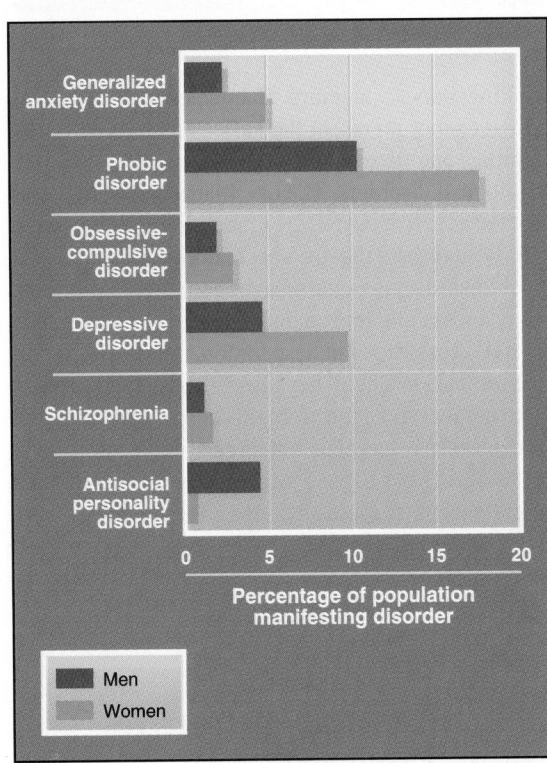

◀ **Figure 16.1** *Results from the NIMH Epidemiologic Catchment Area Study show the percentages of men and women who have experienced various types of psychological disorders at some time in their lives. (Data from Robins & Regier, 1991).*

Figure 16.2 *Among the famous people throughout history who suffered from psychological disorders was Abraham Lincoln. Lincoln suffered from periodic episodes of severe depression.*

sinking into a quagmire of hopelessness. Statistics alone cannot represent the suffering endured by the families and friends of those who are victims of psychological disorders. The psychiatric interviews conducted as part of the NIMH Epidemiologic Catchment Study suggested that the vast majority of people with such disorders as acute schizophrenia, major depression, and debilitating anxiety disorders live their lives in quiet suffering and desperation, never seeking out the professional help they need. This chapter is therefore not just about the problems of someone else. The impact of psychological disorders strikes almost all of us during our lives. If we ourselves do not at some point encounter more stress than we are able to cope with, a family member, a friend, or an acquaintance may do so.

Historical Perspectives on Psychological Disorders

From the dawn of human existence, people have tried to comprehend unconventional, self-defeating, and bizarre behaviors. The pages of history are filled with accounts of prominent people who suffered from psychological disorders (see Figure 16.2). For example, Tamerlane, the 14th-century Mongol conquerer of much of central Asia and Europe, was particularly fond of building pyramids out of human skulls. One of his creations reportedly contained 40,000 of them. The 18th-century French philosopher Jean-Jacques Rousseau developed marked paranoid symptoms in the latter part of his life. He was obsessed with fears of secret enemies and thought that Prussia, England, France, the king, the priests, and others were waging a secret war against him. During the time he was composing his requiem, Mozart was convinced he was being poisoned. John Stuart Mill made remarkable intellectual contributions despite suffering from severe depression. Abraham Lincoln also suffered several bouts of suicidal depression and on one occasion was so depressed that he failed to show up for his own wedding (Fieve, 1976).

These dysfunctional behaviors did not go unnoticed. Human society has explained and responded to abnormal behavior in different ways at different times, based on its values and assumptions about human life and behavior. At various times, behavior disorders have been viewed as the work of gods or demons, as physical diseases, as the result of psychological conflicts, as learned maladaptive behaviors, and as a product of the ways in which we perceive our world.

The Demonological Perspective

The belief that abnormal behavior is caused by supernatural forces goes back a long way. The ancient Chinese, Egyptians, and Hebrews attributed deviance to the work of the devil. As early as 800 B.C., Homer maintained that when behavior got out of control, punishment should be used to drive the evil spirits out. Another ancient "treatment" was based on the notion that bizarre behavior reflected an evil spirit's attempt to escape from a person's body. In order to "release" the spirit, a procedure called **trephination** was carried out. A sharp tool was used to chisel a hole in the skull about 2 centimeters in diameter (see Figure 16.3). It is likely that in many cases, this procedure did indeed result in the elimination of abnormal behaviors, as well as all others.

In the later Middle Ages, religious dogma held that disturbed people either were possessed involuntarily by the devil or had voluntarily made a pact with the forces of darkness (see Figure 16.4). Two Dominican monks were commissioned in the late 15th century to write the *Malleus Maleficarum,* or *The Witch's Hammer,* a manual for hunting and disposing of witches. The book justified the destroying

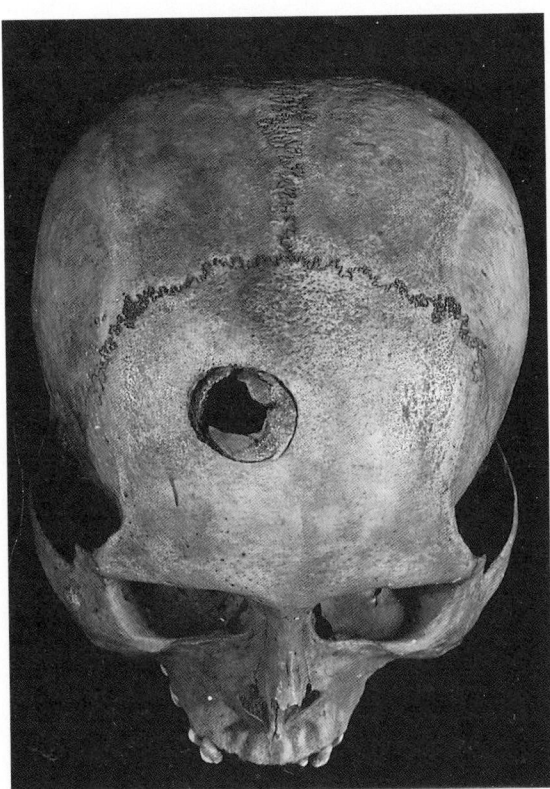

Figure 16.3 *An early treatment for disordered behavior was trephination, in which a hole was chiseled through the skull to release the evil spirit thought to be causing the abnormal behavior. Some people survived the operation; in this case, healing of the skull is evident around the hole. (American Museum of Natural History).*

Figure 16.4 *This painting by Francisco José Goya reflects the widespread belief that disordered people were possessed by the devil. Sabbath portrays the weekly gathering of Satan and the witches he possessed. (Scala/Art Resource, New York).*

of witches on theological grounds and told how to detect them (for example, red spots were a sign that a person had a pact with the devil). During the next 200 years, it is estimated that more than 100,000 people with behavior disorders were identified as witches, hunted down, and executed on this basis.

Early Biological and Psychological Views

Despite the recurrent influence of the demonic perspective, other voices presented alternative ideas about the causes of abnormal behavior. About the 5th century B.C., the Greek physician Hippocrates suggested that mental illnesses are diseases just like physical disorders. He insisted that people with disordered behavior were sick, not possessed by evil spirits. Hippocrates believed that the site of illness was the brain, which he saw as the organ of the mind. Hippocrates was the first to suggest that a mental or behavioral disorder could be caused by a physical dysfunction, a belief that is now reflected in the biological perspective on psychological disorders.

Around the same time, Plato suggested that abnormal behavior resulted when people's reason was overcome by their emotions, a view represented in today's cognitive perspective.

In the 4th century A.D., St. Augustine became interested in the causes of disordered behavior. He advocated soul-searching, introspection, and insight, thus foreshadowing the intrapsychic perspective that would arise some 1,500 years later. Augustine also emphasized the importance of Christian charity toward these troubled people, a notion that was sadly ignored during the later era of the witch hunts.

The Asylums

In the 16th century, coexisting with the witch hunt mentality was the idea that the insane should be segregated from the rest of society. This idea ushered in the era of insane asylums, where disordered people were locked up to isolate them from others (see Figure 16.5). One of the most notorious of the asylums was the Hospital of St. Mary of Bethlehem in London, where King Henry VIII had a balcony built so that the aristocracy could come and be entertained by viewing the bizarre behavior of the patients. The scenes they witnessed were the source of the word

bedlam, a term derived from the name of the Bethlehem Hospital.

A turning point in the treatment of disordered people occurred when Philippe Pinel took over an asylum in Paris in 1792. Pinel advocated some revolutionary ideas: Abnormal behavior is caused by stress; the inmates are people just like us who have been damaged by their social environments; if we remove the chains and create a benign and kind environment, they will respond. Pinel directed that the patients in his hospital be unchained and that the hospital quarters be renovated to make them more pleasant (see Figure 16.6). Although Pinel did not develop specific therapeutic procedures beyond the benign environment he created, his ideas gave impetus to the more humane treatment of the psychologically disturbed.

Early Medical Approaches

In the 17th century, an emerging medical science began to resurrect Hippocrates's idea that physical dis-

orders might cause mental illness. In 1653, Johann Weyer published a treatise declaring that those who were being burned and tortured as witches were actually suffering from physical disorders that caused their mental symptoms. He was accused by the clergy of being Satan himself, but his ideas endured, and Weyer is now called the Father of Psychiatry.

By the 1800s, attempts were being made to extend medical diagnoses to mental disorders by specifying both a cause for the disorder and a treatment for it. The biological emphasis was given impetus by the discovery that **general paresis,** a disorder characterized in its advanced stages by mental deterioration and bizarre behavior, resulted from massive brain deterioration caused by syphilis. This was a breakthrough, the first demonstration that a psychological disorder was linked to an underlying physical malady.

Today, the biological perspective continues to guide researchers seeking the causes of abnormal behavior. As we shall see, genetic factors have been shown to be involved in a number of behavior disorders, and a focus of great current interest is the role of brain processes and neurotransmitters in abnormal behavior.

Psychological Perspectives

In the early 1900s, Sigmund Freud's theory of psychoanalysis emerged as a new way of looking at deviant behavior. Psychoanalytic theory was the first theory to explain behavior and mental disorders in terms of the individual's emotional history. As we saw in Chapter 14, Freud believed that both normal and abnormal behavior result from the interactions of the id, ego, and superego. According to psychoanalytic theory, abnormal behavior occurs when the ego is not able to deal successfully with the instincts of the id, the moral demands of the superego, or the realistic demands of the world. Many problems of maladjustment are caused by unresolved conflicts from childhood that make the person vulnerable to certain kinds of life events. These situations arouse anxiety, and the person tries to cope by using defense mechanisms such as repression, projection, reaction formation, and displacement. Inappropriate or extreme use of the defense mechanisms results in maladaptive patterns of behavior that are called **neuroses.** In some instances, the anxiety caused by these unresolved conflicts may become so great that the person is unable to deal with reality. The break with reality and the severe psychological disorders that can develop under these circumstances are called **psychoses.**

Intrapsychic factors are also emphasized by humanistic theorists. According to humanists like Carl Rogers and Abraham Maslow, forces in the family and in society often prevent people from developing self-acceptance and damage their self-esteem. People who do not hold themselves in high regard are prone to develop psychological problems under stressful conditions.

The behavioral perspective views disordered behaviors not as a reflection of intrapsychic factors but rather as learned responses. In other words, it is the behaviors themselves that are the problem, not factors within the individual. Both adaptive and maladaptive behavior patterns are learned in exactly the same ways: through classical conditioning, operant conditioning, and modeling. The behavioral perspective has profoundly influenced our understanding of how environmental factors help shape both normal and abnormal behavior. Furthermore, the behavioral perspective is an optimistic one, for it emphasizes that if maladaptive behaviors are learned, they can also be unlearned under appropriate environmental conditions. In Chapter 17, we will see that this assumption has resulted in a number of highly effective behavioral treatments.

A final perspective that has strongly influenced current conceptions of abnormal behavior is the cognitive perspective. Cognitive theorists emphasize the important role played by people's thoughts and perceptions about themselves and the environment. Theorists like Albert Ellis and Aaron Beck have identified maladaptive and self-defeating thought patterns that are linked to a number of different disorders, such as depression and anxiety. From this psychological perspective, the key to understanding many maladaptive behaviors is to isolate the specific thought patterns, beliefs, and attitudes that underlie them.

The five modern perspectives on abnormal behavior—biological, psychodynamic, humanistic, behavioral, and cognitive—all lead to different ideas about the causes and the treatment of behavior disorders. As we shall see, all of these perspectives have been useful in identifying the multiple causal factors that may be involved in abnormal behavior.

Defining and Classifying Abnormal Behavior

So far, we have discussed historical and contemporary accounts of abnormal behavior without actually defining what is meant by the term. The most literal definition of *abnormal* is "deviation from the normal level of functioning." By this definition, however, both the disturbed individual and the exceptionally well-adjusted person would be "abnormal." Since we are concerned here with the maladjusted end of

➤ **Figure 16.6** *Philippe Pinel, one of the first of the mental hospital reformers, supervises the unchaining of inmates in the asylum he directed.*

the adjustment continuum, let us explore what is involved in judgments of negative behavioral abnormality.

What is "Abnormal?"

Defining what is normal and what is abnormal is not as easy as it might at first appear. Judgments about where the line between normal and abnormal should be drawn differ depending on the time and the place. A century ago, a father who disciplined his child with a vicious beating would have been regarded as quite normal. Today, the same person might be regarded as a psychologically disturbed child-abuser. In the 1940s, a woman who decided to forsake marriage and children in favor of a career in engineering would have been seen by many segments of society, including some psychologists and psychiatrists, as deviant and possibly in need of psychotherapy. Today, most people would regard the woman's choice as a valid one.

Despite the arbitrariness introduced by time and place, there are certain constant criteria that seem to govern decisions about abnormality. These are sometimes referred to as the three Ds, and one or more of them seem to apply to virtually any behavior regarded as abnormal. Specifically, the behavior in question is likely to be (1) *distressing* to the person or to others with whom he or she interacts; (2) *dysfunctional,* maladaptive, or self-defeating; and (3) regarded as socially *deviant* in a negative sense.

First, we are likely to label behaviors as abnormal if they are intensely *distressing* to a person or to other people. Individuals are often viewed as having a behavior disorder when they are anxious, depressed, dissatisfied, or otherwise seriously upset, either about themselves or about their environment. This is particularly the case if they seem to have little control over these reactions. Personal distress is neither necessary nor sufficient to define abnormality, however. For example, some seriously disturbed mental patients are so out of contact with reality that they seem to experience little distress, and yet their behaviors are considered very abnormal. Conversely, almost all of us experience suffering as a part of our lives. We are all likely to grieve over the death of a loved one with the same degree of misery that is experienced by a clinically depressed person, and yet this behavior in and of itself should not be considered abnormal.

Most behaviors that are labeled as abnormal are *dysfunctional* either for the individual or for society. On an individual level, behaviors that interfere with a person's ability to work and to conduct satisfying relations with other people are likely to be seen as maladaptive and self-defeating. To the extent that an individual is unable to control such behaviors, he or she is likely to be seen as disturbed. Sometimes, behaviors are labeled as abnormal because they interfere with the well-being of society. But even here, the standards are not cut and dried. For example, is a terrorist who plants a bomb in a school building psychologically disturbed or simply a criminal?

The third criterion for abnormality is based on society's judgments of the *deviance* of a given behavior. Within every society, conduct is regulated by **norms,** behavioral rules that specify how people are expected to behave. Some norms are explicitly codified as laws, and violation of these norms defines criminal behavior. Other norms, however, are far less explicit. For example, it is generally expected in our culture that one should not carry on animated conversations with people who are not present and should not face the rear of the elevator staring intently into the eyes of one's fellow passengers. (You might try engaging in the latter behavior if you want to see an elevator empty out quickly.) The sociologist Thomas Scheff (1966) refers to these less explicit norms as **residual rules** and points out that violations of this class of norms are particularly likely to be viewed as reflecting psychological disturbance, especially if the violations cannot be attributed to environmental causes. Behaviors that are attributed to personal or internal factors, that seem irrational and unpredictable, and that make others uncomfortable are especially likely to be seen as indicative of psychological disorder.

To summarize, both personal and social judgments of behavior enter into judgments of what is abnormal, and therefore it is quite possible for abnormality to differ from individual to individual, from culture to culture, and from time to time. Nonetheless, as a working definition, we might define **abnormal behavior** as behavior that is personally distressful, personally dysfunctional, or so culturally deviant that other people judge it to be inappropriate or maladaptive. Having developed this general definition of abnormality, we now consider how such behavior is classified and diagnosed.

Diagnosis of Abnormal Behavior

Labeling an individual as abnormal tells us very little about the nature of the person's problems because the label is so broad. It does not tell us whether the person is anxious, depressed, hallucinating, delusional, having physical problems, addicted to drugs, or suffering from any of hundreds of possible problem behaviors.

Classification is essential to any science, be it medical or behavioral. In abnormal psychology, classification is a necessary first step toward introducing order into discussions of the nature, causes, and treatment of such behavior and communicating about behavior disorders in meaningful ways (Millon, 1991).

The DSM

The diagnostic classification system most widely used in the United States is the **DSM**—the *Diagnostic and Statistical Manual of Mental Disorders.* Introduced in 1952 by the American Psychiatric Association, the DSM has undergone significant revisions since then. The revised third edition of the DSM (DSM-III-R) was published in 1987 and contains over 200 specific diagnostic labels (American Psychiatric Association, 1987). The DSM is currently undergoing another revision, and DSM IV is scheduled to appear sometime between 1993 and 1995 (Task Force on DSM IV, 1991).

The original DSM gave brief, general descriptions of various disorders, from which clinicians tried to select the appropriate diagnoses. These vague categories resulted in very low reliability, or diagnostic agreement among clinicians. Studies often showed that when different clinicians diagnosed the same patients, they agreed in less than 50 percent of the cases. Partly in an attempt to improve the reliability of the system, the revised DSM contains detailed lists of observable behaviors that must be present in order for a diagnosis to be made. For example, Table 16.1 shows the behavioral criteria for a diagnosis of major depression. These specific criteria have increased diagnostic agreement across categories to over 70 percent; but obviously, there is still room for improvement (Nelson-Gray, 1991).

Earlier versions of DSM led to diagnoses in which each individual was given one label that described his or her major clinical problem (for example, anxiety neurosis or paranoid schizophrenia). Reflecting a new emphasis on person–situation interactions, DSM now assesses an individual's behavior according to five different dimensions, or **axes.** Axis I contains 16 major mental disorders defined on the basis of specific behavioral criteria. Axis II includes ingrained, inflexible aspects of personality that may influence the client's behavior and response to treatment (personality disorders), as well as specific developmental disorders, such as mental retardation or other impairments in social or intellectual development (see Table 16.2). Individuals can be diagnosed as having disorders on both axes, as in the case of a person who suffers from major depression (an Axis I disorder) but also shows a long-standing tendency to be highly suspicious of the motives of others (an Axis II paranoid personality disorder).

In the preceding chapter, we saw that an individual's well-being is influenced by the interacting factors of stress, resources, and vulnerabilities. The three remaining axes (III through V) of DSM take these factors into account in an attempt to specify resources and vulnerabilities that might be related to the diagnosed disorder and that could influence the person's potential for further breakdown and response to treatment. Axis III describes physical disorders that may be relevant, such as a history of heart attacks or chronic illnesses. Axis IV takes into account the severity of psychosocial stressors (such as divorce, the loss of a job, or the death of a spouse) in the recent past that may have contributed to the clinical problem and that may influence the course of treatment. The clinician rates the severity of psychosocial stress on a scale ranging from 1 (none apparent) to 6 (catastrophic). Finally, Axis V addresses the individual's coping resources by providing an estimate of the highest level of adaptive functioning shown in occupational activities, social relationships, and leisure activities during the past year. This rating is made on a scale ranging from highly effective functioning to total inadequacy in almost all areas of functioning. The ratings of psychosocial stress and adaptive functioning can have important implications for assessing the person's risk for further breakdown as well as planning treatment. Figure 16.7 shows how the five axes contribute to an overall diagnosis.

Because of its specific behavioral emphasis as well as its focus on both personal and situational factors, the current DSM is a major improvement over earlier versions. However, much additional research is being carried out in a series of field trials designed to evaluate the reliability of diagnoses based on the current DSM as well as the validity of its diagnostic categories. The validity question relates to whether these categories actually describe similar behavioral clusters that have common causes and respond in a fairly uniform fashion to specific forms of treatment.

Table 16.1 DSM Criteria for the Diagnosis of a Major Depressive Disorder

At least five of the following symptoms have been present during the same two-week period and represent a change from previous functioning:

1. Depressed mood most of the day, nearly every day
2. Markedly diminished interest or pleasure in all, or almost all, activities most of the day, nearly every day
3. Significant weight loss or weight gain when not dieting or decrease or increase in appetite nearly every day
4. Insomnia or hypersomnia (excessive sleeping) nearly every day
5. Psychomotor agitation or retardation nearly every day
6. Fatigue or loss of energy nearly every day
7. Feelings of worthlessness or excessive or inappropriate guilt nearly every day
8. Diminished ability to think or concentrate, or indecisiveness, nearly every day
9. Recurrent thoughts of death (not just fear of dying), recurrent suicidal ideation without a specific plan, or a suicide attempt or a specific plan for committing suicide

Source: American Psychiatric Association, 1987.

In colloquial terms, a validity question might take the form, ''Is there such a disorder as a mixed anxiety–depressive disorder?''

Beyond questions of reliability and validity lie important issues that relate to the very process of diagnosis and are of concern to many psychologists. Diagnostic labels can have important consequences for people who receive them.

Critical Issues in Diagnostic Labeling

Although some means of classifying abnormal behaviors is necessary for both scientific and practical reasons, it is important that we realize that all clas-

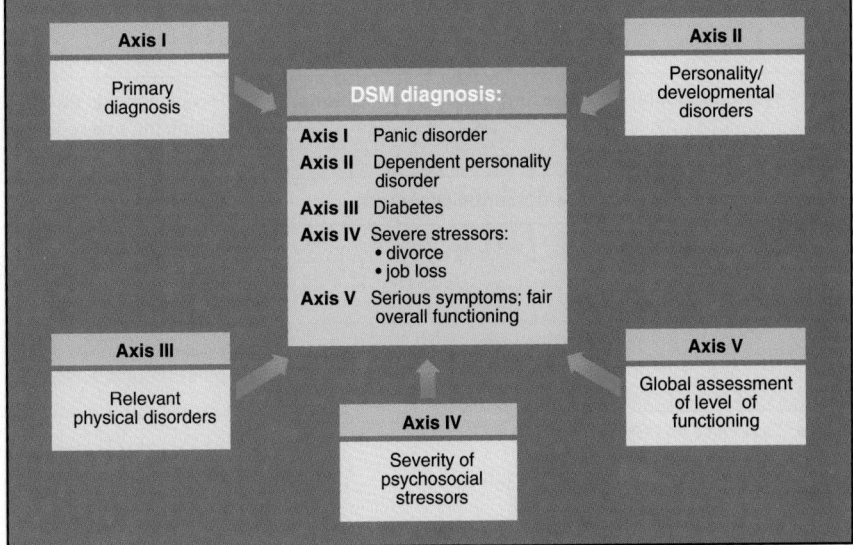

Figure 16.7 *The DSM uses a multiaxial classification system that takes into account the individual's psychiatric symptoms, physical status, life stressors, and level of current and recent functioning.*

Table 16.2 The Major Categories of Behavior Disorders in Axis I and II of DSM

Axis I: Major Mental Disorders	Description
1. Disorders arising in childhood or adolescence.	Problems such as hyperactivity, abnormal aggressiveness, childhood fears, frequent bedwetting or soiling, or other deviations from normal social and behavioral development that are first identified in childhood or adolescence.
2. Organic mental disorders.	Transient or permanent problems caused by physical deterioration of the brain due to disease, aging, or chemical causes.
3. Substance abuse disorders.	Personal and social problems associated with the use of psychoactive substances, such as alcohol, heroin, or other drugs.
4. Schizophrenic disorders.	Severe disorders of thinking, perception, and emotion that involve loss of contact with reality and disordered behavior.
5. Paranoid (delusional) disorders.	Problems involving false beliefs (delusions) of being persecuted or being exceptionally important without the bizarre quality of the delusions that occur in schizophrenic disorders.
6. Psychotic disorders not classified elsewhere.	Severe mental problems involving loss of reality contact that have not lasted long enough (six months) to be categorized as schizophrenia, or disorders that combine schizophrenic-like symptoms with those from other disorders, such as depression.
7. Mood disorders.	Severe disturbances of mood, including depression and mania (extreme elation and excitement).
8. Anxiety disorders.	Disorders involving intense, frequent, or inappropriate anxiety, but no loss of reality contact. Includes phobias, generalized anxiety reactions, panic disorders, and obsessive–compulsive disorders.
9. Somatoform disorders.	Physical symptoms, such as blindness, paralysis, or pain, which have no physical basis and are assumed to be caused by psychological factors. Also, excessive preoccupations and worry about health (hypochondriasis).
10. Dissociative disorders.	Psychologically caused problems of consciousness and self-identification, including multiple personality disorders and amnesia.
11. Sexual disorders.	Problems involving the inability to function sexually or enjoy sexuality (sexual dysfunctions) and deviant sexual behaviors, such as child molestation and arousal by inappropriate objects (fetishes).
12. Sleep disorders.	Problems involving the sleep cycle, such as insomnia, sleepwalking, narcolepsy, or severe and recurrent nightmares.
13. Factitious disorders.	False physical or behavioral symptoms that are voluntarily produced, apparently in an attempt to play the role of a patient.
14. Impulse control disorders.	Compulsive stealing, gambling, fire setting, or other behaviors characterized by an inability to control impulses.
15. Adjustment disorders.	Failure to adjust satisfactorily to stressful life events or developmental transitions, such as divorce, financial problems, leaving home, or retirement.
16. Psychological factors affecting physical conditions.	Psychosomatic disorders, in which psychological factors cause or increase physical symptoms that reflect actual body damage (e.g., peptic ulcers, high blood pressure).
Axis II: Personality and Developmental Disorders	Description
1. Personality disorders.	Lifelong rigid and inappropriate patterns of responding that are maladaptive for the person or for others. May be diagnosed with or without an accompanying Axis I diagnosis.
2. Specific developmental disorders.	Problems involving abnormal development, such as mental retardation, as well as other problems, such as reading difficulties and speech problems.

Source: Task Force on DSM IV, 1991.

sification is the product of human invention. Classifying is a matter of making generalizations about observations and lumping together phenomena that seem similar to one another. There is no guarantee that the resulting classification system adequately captures "reality." This is an important point, because the classification system can have profound effects on the judgments we make about people and their behavior. Moreover, the labels that we attach to behaviors and to people on the basis of a classification system can in turn profoundly influence them and the courses of their lives, for important social, legal, and personal consequences can result from psychiatric diagnosis.

We should never lose sight of the fact that diagnosis is merely a verbal label applied to a defined set of behaviors. These categories *describe;* they do not explain. Thus, schizophrenic behavior is not explained by labeling someone schizophrenic. We also need to keep in mind that the label describes the *behavior* and not the person. Unfortunately, however, once a label has been assigned, it becomes all too easy to accept the label as an accurate description of the individual rather than of the behavior. It then becomes difficult to look at the person's behavior objectively, without preconceptions about how he or she will act. It is also likely to affect how we will interact with that person. Consider for a moment what your reaction might be to discovering that your next-door neighbor has been diagnosed by professionals as a "sexual psychopath." It would be surprising if this label did not influence your perceptions and interactions with that person, whether or not the label was accurate. This phenomenon has been demonstrated experimentally with both laypersons and professional psychologists. These subjects were asked to make judgments about people after watching identical videotaped interviews. Subjects who had been told that the person had a history of psychological disturbance rated the person and his or her behavior much more negatively than did subjects who were not given such information (Langer & Abelson, 1974).▼

Psychiatric diagnoses can have important legal consequences as well. As we shall see in Chapter 17, individuals who are judged to be dangerous to themselves or others may be involuntarily committed to mental institutions under certain circumstances. When so committed, they lose some of their civil rights, and they may be detained indefinitely if their behavior does not improve.

The law tries to take into account mental disorders in individuals accused of crimes. An accused person judged too disturbed to understand the nature of the legal proceedings may be regarded as not competent to stand trial and institutionalized until judged competent.

Competency refers to a defendant's state of mind at the time of a judicial hearing. **Insanity,** a far more controversial issue, relates to the presumed state of mind of the defendant at the time the crime was committed. Under current law, when people are judged to have been so severely impaired at that time that they lacked the capacity either to appreciate the wrongfulness of their acts or to control their conduct, they may be declared not guilty by reason of insanity. It should be noted that *insanity* is a legal term, not a psychological one.

Despite the fact that the insanity plea is entered only twice in every 1,000 felony cases and that in 85 percent of those cases the prosecution agrees that the person was indeed insane, the insanity defense has become a hotly debated topic. One stimulus for this debate was the acquittal of John Hinckley, who attempted to assassinate President Ronald Reagan in 1981 (see Figure 16.8). In 1992, Jeffrey Dahmer, accused of the grisly murders and mutilations of 15 men, also entered a plea of not guilty by reason of insanity. The defense contended that no sane person could have committed the shocking acts that Dahmer freely admitted. In this instance, the insanity plea was rejected, and Dahmer was found guilty.

A critical difference in the two cases was an important change in the legal requirement for proving sanity or insanity. At the time Hinckley was tried, the law required the prosecution to prove that Hinckley was sane. They could not do so beyond a reasonable doubt, and Hinckley was acquitted. Partly in response to Hinckley's acquittal, the law was changed, and the burden of proof was shifted to the defense. Dahmer's attorneys were not able to prove that their client was insane at the time he committed the crime.

In an attempt to balance concern about a defendant's mental status and need for treatment with punishment for crimes, Canada and an increasing number of U.S. jurisdictions have adopted a verdict of *guilty but mentally ill* (Comer, 1992; Sarason & Sarason, 1993). This verdict imposes a normal sentence for a crime but sends the defendant to a mental hospital for treatment. If the defendant is considered recovered before the end of the sentence, he or she is sent to prison to serve the remainder of the sentence.

The issues that revolve around diagnostic labeling are not easy to resolve, and they have important implications for both the mental health professions and society at large. These issues clearly deserve the attention they are receiving from contemporary psychologists.

Having considered issues of diagnosis, we now move to the disorders, themselves. First, however, you should be aware of a common phenomenon that in medical schools is termed "medical students' disease." When people read descriptions of disorders, whether physical or psychological, they often see

▼
Thinking Critically About Self-Fulfilling Consequences of Diagnostic Labels

Diagnostic labels may have effects that go beyond how other people respond to those who are labeled; they may also play a role in actually creating psychological disorders (Wright, 1991). When an individual becomes aware that a psychiatric label has been applied by a professional, he or she may accept the new identity implied by the label and develop the expected role and outlook. This can be very harmful, because psychiatric diagnostic labels often carry degrading and stigmatizing implications. Applying the label to oneself may transform one's social identity, and the effects on morale and self-esteem can be devastating. Moreover, one may despair of ever changing, and therefore give up attempts to deal with the life circumstances that may be responsible for one's problems. In this way, the expectations that accompany a label may result in a self-fulfilling prophecy, a situation in which one's expectations cause to happen what one expects will happen. For these reasons, the attachment of such labels deserves our careful consideration.

↞ **Figure 16.8** *Both John Hinckley (left), who shot Ronald Reagan and his press secretary, and the mass murderer Jeffrey Dahmer (right) pleaded not guilty by reason of insanity. Hinckley won his plea, whereas Dahmer's was rejected. These cases focused considerable attention on the insanity defense.*

some of those symptoms or characteristics in themselves. In the case of psychological disorders, this is quite understandable. We all experience problems in living at various times, and we may react to them in ways that bear similarities to the reactions you will now be reading about. Seeing such a similarity does not necessarily mean that you have the disorder. On the other hand, if you find that maladaptive behaviors like those described here are interfering with your happiness or effectiveness, then you should not hesitate to seek help in changing these behaviors. Some guidelines for doing so are presented in Chapter 17.

■ ▭

Anxiety Disorders

All of us have experienced anxiety, that state of tension and apprehension that is a natural response to threat. For some people, however, the frequency and intensity of anxiety responses interfere with daily life. What is unusual about anxiety disorders is not the experiencing of anxiety; **anxiety disorders** are unusual because the amount or duration of anxiety is out of proportion to the situation or object that triggers it.

Anxiety responses have three basic components: (1) *subjective feelings* of tension and apprehension, a sense of impending danger, and a feeling of inability to cope; (2) *physiological responses,* including increased heart rate and blood pressure, muscle tension, rapid breathing, nausea, dry mouth, diarrhea, and frequent urination; and (3) *behavioral responses,* such

as avoidance of the situation and impaired motor performance.

Anxiety disorders take a number of different forms, including phobic disorders, generalized anxiety disorders, panic disorders, and obsessive–compulsive disorders. According to the recent NIMH Epidemiologic Catchment Area Study, anxiety disorders affect 17.6 percent of Americans during their lifetimes and 7.3 percent at any one time (Robins & Regier, 1991). We now consider the various forms that these disorders can take.

Phobic Disorder

Phobias are strong and irrational fears of certain objects or situations. People with phobias realize that their fears are out of all proportion to the danger involved, but they feel helpless to deal with these fears (see Figure 16.9). Instead, they make strenuous efforts to avoid the phobic situation or object. In our society, the most common phobias are **agoraphobia** (fear of crowds and open spaces), social phobias, and three classes of specific phobias: (1) fear of animals; (2) fear of inanimate objects, such as dirt, heights, flying, water, or the like; and (3) fear of illness, injury, or death.

Agoraphobia accounts for 50 to 80 percent of the phobics who refer themselves for treatment. Agoraphobics avoid being in crowds, traveling, or going into open spaces. In extreme cases, they may have an irrational fear of leaving the familiar setting of the home, and agoraphobics have been known to be housebound for years at a time. The following account, by a professor whose agoraphobia almost com-

Figure 16.9 *Phobias can be highly debilitating. This person has such a severe fear of heights that he cannot climb more than a few feet above the ground without experiencing intense anxiety.*

may avoid any outdoor setting where a spider might possibly be encountered. As we learned in Chapter 9, successful avoidance responses are negatively reinforced by anxiety reduction and thus become stronger over time. After a while, these avoidance responses may be very difficult to overcome, even if the underlying fear itself has not increased.

The degree of impairment produced by a phobia depends in part on the degree to which the phobic stimulus is customarily encountered in the individual's normal round of activities. For example, fear of flying is a common phobia that, according to a survey made by the Boeing Company, occurs in some 25 million Americans. Fear of flying may be a relatively minor inconvenience for a person who never needs to travel by air, but it may be a debilitating condition for an executive who has to travel frequently. Some people simply refuse to fly even at great personal inconvenience. One celebrated example is John Madden, former coach of the Oakland Raiders and now a prominent TV football analyst, whose fear of flying forces him to commute from coast to coast in a motor home (see Figure 16.10).

Generalized Anxiety Disorder

pletely confined him to the campus where he taught, illustrates the terror that agoraphobics can experience.

> Let me assume that I am walking down University Drive by the lake. I am a normal man for the first quarter of a mile; for the next hundred yards I am in a mild state of dread, controllable and controlled; for the next twenty yards in an acute state of dread, yet controlled; for the next ten, in an anguish of terror that hasn't reached the crisis of explosion; and in a half-dozen steps more I am in as fierce a panic of isolation from help and home and of immediate death as a man overboard in mid-Atlantic or on a window-ledge far up in a skyscraper with flames lapping his shoulders. . . . It is as scientific a fact as any I know that my phobic seizures at their worst approach any limits of terror that the human mind is capable of in the actual presence of death in its most horrible forms. That I have never fainted away or died under them is due to two factors: first, my physical vitality, and second, my skill in devising escapes—psychic surrogates, deflections of attention, or actual retreat to safety—before the exhausting surge has torn me to pieces. But more than once the escape has been at all but the last moment (Leonard, 1927, pp. 321–323).

An important aspect of the phobic reaction is the avoidance behaviors people learn in order to avoid the phobic object. Thus, a person with a spider phobia

On initial assessment, Dr. J., who is manifestly tense, complains of never being entirely free of a sense of impending disaster, although he cannot further specify the nature of this anticipated catastrophe. The thought

Figure 16.10 *Many people suffer from a fear of flying. One famous figure is John Madden, formerly a professional football coach and currently a television analyst, who travels to his weekly assignments (sometimes separated by thousands of miles) in this specially equipped motor home.*

of being involuntarily terminated from his envied position on the cardiology team, earlier a source of intense anxiety, has "on one or two occasions lately," he acknowledges, provided him momentary feelings of relief. He notes a number of signs of autonomic hyperarousal that he experiences on virtually a daily basis, emphasizing in particular excessive sweating, which has become a source of embarrassment. He is medicating himself for persistent attacks of diarrhea. He complains of an inability to attain a refreshing level of sleep even on those rare occasions when he can count on a few uninterrupted off-duty hours, and his very few waking "leisure" hours are filled with restless irritability (Carson & others, 1988, p. 195).

Dr. J is suffering from a **generalized anxiety disorder,** a chronic state of diffuse, or "free-floating," anxiety that is not attached to specific situations or objects. In such cases, the anxiety may last for months on end with the signs almost continuously present. Emotionally, the person feels jittery, tense, and constantly on edge. Cognitively, he or she expects something awful to happen but doesn't know what. Physically, he or she experiences a mild chronic emergency reaction. Dr. J sweats, his stomach is usually upset, he has diarrhea, and so forth.

As we might expect, this disorder can markedly interfere with daily functioning. The person may find it hard to concentrate, to make decisions, and to remember commitments. Figure 16.11 shows the incidence of various emotional and cognitive–behavioral symptoms in the generalized anxiety disorder.

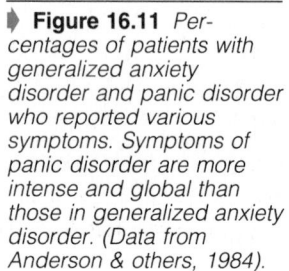
▶ **Figure 16.11** *Percentages of patients with generalized anxiety disorder and panic disorder who reported various symptoms. Symptoms of panic disorder are more intense and global than those in generalized anxiety disorder. (Data from Anderson & others, 1984).*

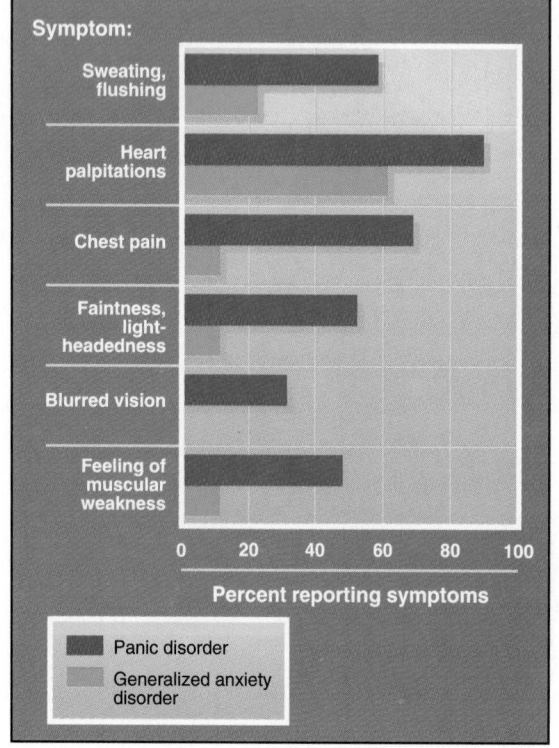

Panic Disorder

In contrast to generalized anxiety disorders, which involve chronic tension and anxiety, **panic disorders** occur suddenly and unpredictably, and they tend to be much more intense (see Figure 16.11). The symptoms of panic attacks are extreme and terrifying, and it is not unusual for victims to feel that they are dying (Barlow, 1988). The following case typifies a panic attack:

> My heart was beating so hard and fast it would jump out and hit my hand. I felt like I couldn't stand up—that my legs wouldn't support me. My hands got icy and my feet stung. There were horrible shooting pains in my forehead. My head felt tight, like someone had pulled the skin down too tight and I wanted to pull it away.... I couldn't breathe, I was short of breath. I literally got out of breath and panted like I had run up and down the stairs. I felt like I had run an eight-mile race. I couldn't do anything. I felt all in; weak, no strengh. I can't even dial a telephone (Laughlin, 1967, p. 92).

In many cases, panic attacks occur out of the blue and in the absence of any identifiable stimulus. It is this unpredictable quality that makes panic attacks so mysterious and terrifying to their victims. The impact that the attacks can have on the victim's life is illustrated in the following case:

> As the attacks continued, Ms. Watson began to dread going out of the house alone. She feared that while out she would have an attack and would be stranded and helpless. She stopped riding the subway to work out of fear she might be trapped in a car between stops when an attack struck, preferring instead to walk the 20 blocks between her home and work. Social and recreational activities, previously frequent and enjoyed, were severely curtailed because an attack might occur, necessitating an abrupt and embarrassing flight from the scene. When household duties and the like required brief driving excursions, she surreptitiously put these off until she could be accompanied by one of the children or a neighbor (Adapted from Spitzer & others, 1983).

Many cases of agoraphobia start with an initial panic attack. Eventually, the person becomes so afraid of having an attack, especially in a public place, that he or she begins to stay closer and closer to home.

Panic disorders with or without agoraphobia tend to appear in late adolescence or early adulthood and affect about 1 percent of the population. Even more common are occasional panic attacks. In one survey of Canadian students, 34 percent reported having had at least one panic attack in the previous year (Norton & others, 1985).

Obsessive–Compulsive Disorder

A thirty-eight-year-old mother of one child had been obsessed by fears of contamination during her entire adult life. Literally hundreds of times a day, thoughts of being infected by germs would occur to her. Once she began to think that either she or her child might become infected, she could not dismiss the thought. The constant concern about infection resulted in a series of washing and cleaning rituals that took up most of her day. Her child was confined to one room only, which the woman tried to keep entirely free of germs by scrubbing it—floor to ceiling—several times a day. Moreover, she opened and closed all doors with her feet, in order to avoid contaminating her own hands (Rachman & Hodgson, 1980).

The woman was diagnosed as having a severe **obsessive–compulsive disorder.** Such disorders consist of two components; obsessions and compulsions. **Obsessions** are repetitive thoughts, images, or impulses that invade consciousness, are often abhorrent to the person, and are very difficult to dismiss or control. The woman just described was tyrannized by thoughts and images of contamination, for example. **Compulsions** are repetitive behavioral responses—like the woman's cleaning rituals—that can be resisted only with great difficulty (see Figure 16.12). Compulsions are often responses to obsessive thoughts and function to reduce the anxiety associated with the thoughts.

Obsessions of clinical proportions differ from more typical and harmless recurring thoughts in three ways: (1) obsessions are unwelcome and intrude on consciousness; (2) they arise from within, not from an external stimulus; and (3) they are very difficult to control. People with normal recurring thoughts can think of something else and distract themselves. In contrast, obsessives have great difficulty in suppressing the troublesome thoughts.

Compulsions are also extremely difficult to control. If the person does not perform the compulsive act, he or she may experience tremendous anxiety, perhaps even a panic attack. Like phobic avoidance responses, compulsions appear to be strengthened through a process of negative reinforcement because they allow a person to avoid anxiety.

Causal Factors in the Anxiety Disorders

Anxiety is a complex phenomenon having physiological, cognitive, intrapsychic, and behavioral facets which can interact with one another in many ways. We now consider these factors.

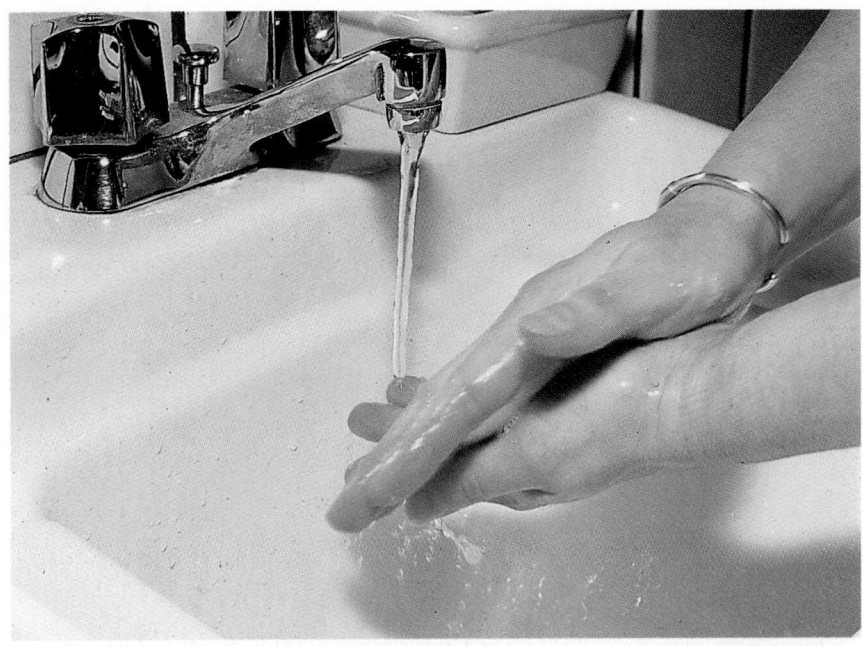

Figure 16.12 *This person has a hand-washing compulsion that compels her to wash her hands nearly 50 times a day. Failure to do so results in intense anxiety.*

Biological Factors

The search for biological processes associated with the anxiety disorders has focused on several neurotransmitters in the brain. The research has been guided in part by the fact that certain antianxiety and tranquilizing drugs are effective treatments for many forms of anxiety. These drugs include Valium and Librium, which belong to a family called the **benzodiazapines.** Research on how these drugs work has revealed that they attach to receptor sites tailored for a natural transmitter substance called *GABA* (gama-aminobutyric acid). GABA is an inhibitory transmitter substance that reduces activity in parts of the brain that are responsible for arousal. Some researchers believe that abnormally low levels of GABA, or an inadequate number of GABA receptor sites on their neurons, may cause some people to have abnormally reactive nervous systems that give rise to generalized anxiety responses. Such people may also be easily conditioned to produce phobias.

Panic disorders may have a different biochemical basis. Many people who suffer from panic attacks appear to be abnormally responsive to lactic acid, a natural substance produced by the body during stress. A full-blown panic attack can be produced by injections of sodium lactate, and PET scans of brain activity in panic disorder patients shows that lactate injection results in a marked increase in blood flow in right hemisphere areas known to be involved in negative emotional responses (see Figure 16.13). Peo-

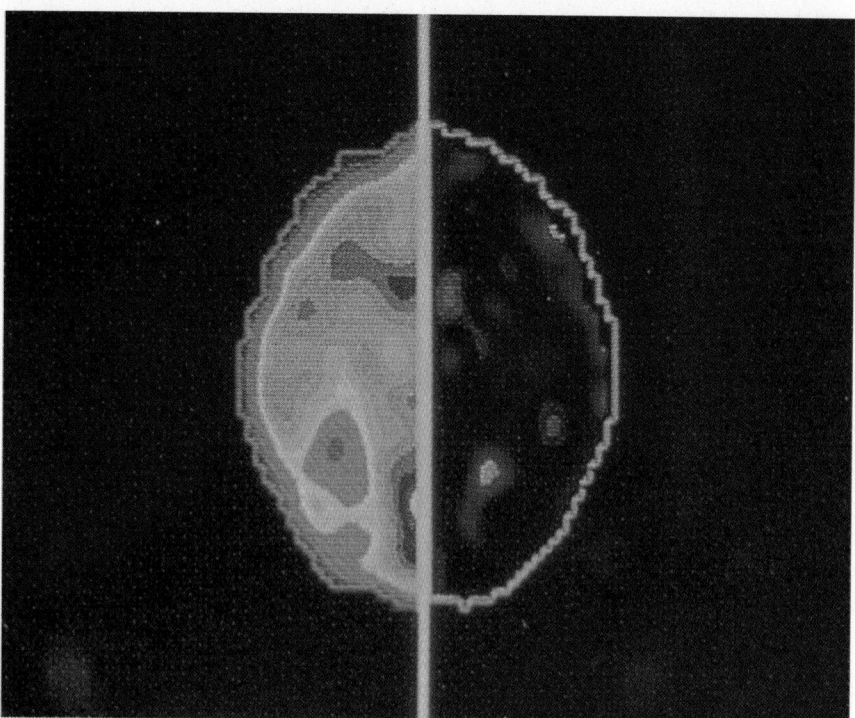

ple who do not suffer from panic disorders do not show this response (Barlow, 1988).

Another piece of evidence that the various anxiety disorders may have different biochemical bases is the recent finding that panic and obsessive–compulsive disorders respond better to antidepressant drugs than to antianxiety medication (Comer, 1992; Levinthal, 1990). This finding suggests that certain forms of anxiety may be biochemically related to depression, and it might help explain the fact that many depressed people experience anxiety as well (Clark & Watson, 1991; Zinbarg & others, 1992). In fact, one notion is that anxiety and depression have a common core of generalized affective (emotional) distress termed **negative affectivity** (Watson & Clark, 1992). Anxiety adds to this core a state of physiological over-arousal, whereas depression involves reduced positive affect.

Vulnerability to anxiety disorders may well be increased by genetic factors. Studies of identical and fraternal twins raised together and apart indicate that about 50 percent of the variance in self-reported tendency to experience anxiety is attributable to genetic factors (Tellegen & others, 1988). Where clinical levels of anxiety are concerned, monozygotic twins have a concordance rate of about 40 percent for anxiety disorders, compared with a 4 percent concordance rate in dizygotic twins (Carey & Gottesman, 1981). Although such findings indicate a genetic predispo-

sition, the concordance rate even in identical twins is a long way from 100 percent, indicating the importance of environmental factors as well.

Intrapsychic Factors

Anxiety is a central feature of psychoanalytic conceptions of abnormal behavior. From this perspective, anxiety results from conflicts involving the id, the ego, the superego, and the environment. Freud distinguished among three different varieties of anxiety. **Objective anxiety** results from realistic environmental threats or dangers and is usually labeled fear. The other two kinds of anxiety result from the threatened breakthrough of id impulses. **Neurotic anxiety** occurs when the impulses threaten to overwhelm the ego's defenses and explode into action. **Moral anxiety,** or guilt, stems from fear of punishment by the superego for morally unacceptable impulses. For Freud, neurotic and moral anxieties resulting from unconscious conflicts were the primary causes of abnormal behavior.

How anxiety is dealt with by the ego's defense mechanisms determines the form of the anxiety disorder, according to psychoanalytic theorists. In phobic disorders, the anxiety is displaced onto some external stimulus that has symbolic significance in relation to the underlying conflict. For example, in one of Freud's most celebrated cases, a little boy named Hans suddenly developed a fear of horses and the possibility of being bitten. To Freud, the powerful horse represented Hans's father, and the fear of being bitten symbolized Hans's unconscious fear of being castrated by his father if he acted on his sexual impulses toward his mother.

Obsessions and compulsions are also ways of handling anxiety. The obsession is symbolically related to, but less terrifying than, the underlying impulse; and the compulsion is a way of "taking back," or undoing, one's unacceptable urges, as when an obsession about dirt and compulsive handwashing are used to deal with one's "dirty" impulses. Finally, generalized anxiety and panic attacks are thought to occur when one's defenses are not strong enough to control or contain anxiety.

Humanistic theorists view anxiety disorders differently. For Carl Rogers, anxiety resulted when the self-concept and experience were discordant and the self-structure was threatened. For example, an immoral action by a person who considers herself a highly moral individual would be expected to threaten her self-concept and generate considerable anxiety. Anxiety is also produced by marked discrepancies between a person's perceived self and his or her ideal self, which defines the person's conditions for being worthwhile. In support of this hypothesis, Timothy Strauman (1992) found that discrepancies between college students' conceptions of what they are like and what they *ought* to be like were associated with persistent anxiety.

Humanistic theorists also believe that people's fear of taking true responsibility for their choices and lives is a universal source of anxiety, and they point to fear of eventual death and "nonbeing" as a terrifying source of existential anxiety that may be displaced into other forms of anxiety that are easier to deal with.

Cognitive Factors

As we saw when we considered the role of cognitive factors in emotion, appraisal processes play a key role in anxiety as well as other emotions. Cognitive theorists like Albert Ellis and Aaron Beck stress the role of maladaptive thought patterns and beliefs. Among the most important cognitive distortions are tendencies to exaggerate the amount of threat in the environment and to underestimate one's resources or ability to cope with situational demands. Anxiety-disordered people "catastrophize" about demands and magnify them into threats, anticipate that the worst will happen, and feel powerless to cope effectively (Clark, 1988; Ellis, 1962).

The cognitive perspective has recently begun to focus on panic disorders (Craske, 1991; Zinbarg & others, 1992). David Barlow (1991) and David Clark (1988) both suggest that panic attacks result from catastrophic misinterpretations of normal anxiety symptoms, such as heart palpitations, dizziness, and breathlessness. The panic-disordered person appraises these as signs that a heart attack or a psychological loss of control is about to occur, and these catastrophic appraisals produce a full-blown state of panic (see Figure 16.14). Michelle Craske and her coworkers (1991) found that helping panic patients to modify such appraisals in favor of more benign interpretations of their bodily symptoms (for example, "It's only anxiety, not a heart attack") resulted in a marked reduction in panic attacks.

Anxiety as a Learned Response

From the behavioral perspective, the anxiety disorders are viewed as a product of learning. Both classical conditioning and modeling may be involved in the learning of anxiety. Some fears are acquired as a result of traumatic experiences that result in a classically conditioned fear response. Others are learned through vicarious experience; for example, televised reports of the death and devastation that resulted from the 1989 San Francisco earthquake were very frightening to many adults and children in other areas of the country and evoked fears about potential earthquakes there as well. Conditioned anxiety responses may also be generalized to other situations, and a widening range of stimuli may become capable of evoking anxiety.

Once anxiety is learned, either cues from the environment or internal cues can trigger the anxiety response. In the case of phobic reactions, the cues tend to be external ones relating to the feared object or situation. In panic disorders, on the other hand, the anxiety-arousing cues tend to be internal ones, such as bodily sensations (for example, one's heart rate) or cognitive images (Craske, 1991).

As we saw in Chapter 9, people are highly motivated to avoid or escape the aversive emotional response of anxiety. Here, operant conditioning enters the picture. Behaviors that are successful in reducing

⬤ **Figure 16.14** *Current cognitive explanations of panic attacks depict a process in which normal manifestations of anxiety are appraised catastrophically, ultimately resulting in a full-blown panic attack.*

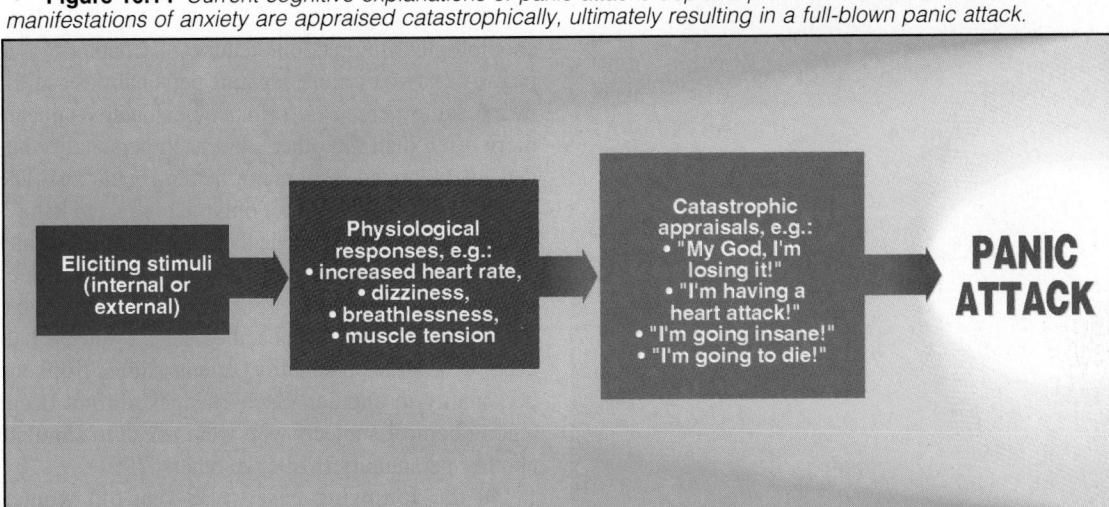

anxiety, such as compulsions and the avoidance responses of the phobic, are strengthened through a process of negative reinforcement. Because these responses successfully alleviate anxiety, they prevent extinction of the classically conditioned anxiety response.

The behavioral perspective has played a major role in the understanding of anxiety responses, particularly phobic and compulsive disorders. As we shall see in Chapter 17, behavioral explanations of anxiety have also resulted in a number of effective approaches to treating these problems.

■ ▬ ▬
Dissociative Disorders

In Chapter 8, the concept of dissociation was discussed at some length. As that discussion pointed out, there is considerable evidence that cognitive functions can dissociate, or split off, from one another even under conditions of normal functioning. Abnormal extremes of such dissociations are found in the dissociative disorders.

➡ **Figure 16.15** *In 1980, a Florida park ranger found a woman naked and starving in the wilderness. Unaware of her identity and in an apparent fugue state, the woman was hospitalized as Jane Doe. Five months later, the woman was recognized by her mother when she was interviewed by David Hartman on the television show* Good Morning America. *The 34-year-old daughter had been missing for 7 years and was reunited with her family shortly thereafter.*

Ordinarily, personality has unity and coherence, and its facets are integrated so that people act, think, and feel with some degree of consistency. Memory plays a critical role in this integration. Memory connects past with present, and it provides a sense of personal identity that has a past, a present, and a future.

Dissociative disorders involve a breakdown of this integration in which people experience a significant alteration in memory or identity. Three forms that such disorders can take are psychogenic amnesia, psychogenic fugue, and multiple personality disorder.

In **psychogenic amnesia,** a person responds to a stressful event with extensive but selective memory losses. Some people can remember nothing about their pasts. Others can no longer recall specific events, people, places, or objects, although other contents of memory remain intact. The memory losses almost always involve episodic memory, whereas semantic and procedural memories are generally unaffected. In one case, for example, a motorist who had killed a pedestrian experienced complete amnesia for the accident and for the events that surrounded it, while retaining his occupational and linguistic skills (Cameron, 1963).

Psychogenic fugue is a more dramatic disorder in which a person loses all sense of personal identity, gives up his or her customary life, and wanders to a new faraway location and begins to establish a new identity. Usually, the fugue is triggered by a highly stressful event or trauma, and it may last from a few hours or days to several years (see Figure 16.15). Some adolescent runaways have been found to be in a fugue state, and fugue victims have been known to marry another spouse and start a new career (Loewenstein, 1991). Typically, the fugue ends when the person suddenly recovers his or her original identity and "wakes up," mystified and distressed at being in a strange place under strange circumstances.

Multiple personality disorder is the most striking of the dissociative disorders. As noted in the Psychobiological Interactions feature of Chapter 8 (see page 247), two or more separate personalities coexist in the same person. A primary personality appears more often than the others, but each personality has its own integrated set of memories and behaviors. The personalities can differ not only mentally and behaviorally but also physiologically. One personality may have an allergy, for example, whereas another does not. In one recent study, ophthalmologists were able to measure shifts in visual acuity and eye-muscle balance as multiple personality patients shifted from one personality to another. Such changes did not occur among control subjects who were asked to simulate another personality (Miller & others, 1991).

In the following case, a 38-year-old woman named Margaret was admitted to a hospital with paralysis of her legs following a minor car accident. During the course of her interview, the woman, a member of an ultrareligious sect, reported that she often heard a strange voice inside her threatening to "take over completely." The physician suggested that she let the voice "take over."

> The woman closed her eyes, clenched her fists, and grimaced for a few moments during which she was out of contact with those in the room. Suddenly she opened her eyes and one was in the presence of another person. Her name, she said, was "Harriet." Whereas Margaret had been paralyzed, and complained of fatigue, headache, and backache, Harriet felt well and she at once proceeded to walk around the room unaided. She spoke scornfully of Margaret's religiousness, her invalidism, and her puritanical life, professing that she herself liked to drink and "go partying" but that Margaret was always going to church and reading the Bible. . . . At length, at the interviewer's suggestion, Harriet reluctantly agreed to "bring Margaret back" and after more grimacing and fist clenching, Margaret reappeared paralyzed, complaining of her headache and backache, and completely amnesic for the brief period of Harriet's release from her prison (Nemiah, 1978, pp. 179–180).

Dissociative reactions seem almost invariably to be responses to stress. Psychoanalytic theorists believe that dissociative disorders represent extreme repression of painful memories and impulses. As noted in Chapter 8, childhood sexual abuse is reported by a great many people with multiple personality disorder. In addition to having experienced harsh trauma in early childhood, they have a striking tendency to go into spontaneous hypnotic trances to escape stress, and some theorists believe that they create the other personalities in such trances in order to cope with situational demands.

Behavioral theorists have suggested that the dissociative disorders may be understood as learned responses that are elicited by anxiety and reinforced by anxiety reduction. Thus, amnesia may represent an example of avoidance learning in which the loss of memory is an operant response that is reinforced by anxiety reduction, and multiple personality disorder may represent a means of avoiding or escaping stress by invoking the presence of another identity (Comer, 1992). At present, these are reasonable hypotheses, but only that.

Conflict, anxiety, and other emotional problems involve the functioning of the body, and we should therefore not be surprised that what people think and what they feel can have dramatic effects on their bodies. The powerful influence of psychological states is shown in psychophysiological disorders.

PSYCHOBIOLOGICAL INTERACTIONS

Psychophysiological Disorders

Medical science has long recognized the central role that psychological factors can play in diseases of the body. One category of physical diseases with a strong psychological component are the **psychophysiological disorders.** Such a disorder is diagnosed if there is known physical pathology present *and* if psychologically meaningful events preceded and are judged to have contributed to the development or worsening of the condition. A dramatic example is presented by the following case, in which *stigmata,* symbolic marks on the skin, were produced by the reliving of a psychological trauma.

> Since childhood, Steven had suffered from nightmares and sleepwalking. On one occasion, he was hospitalized for an infection. In order to prevent his sleepwalking while in the hospital, Steven's hands were bound tightly behind his back and he was restrained with straps while he slept. He awoke one night from a nightmare and was terrified to be tied down. After struggling with his bonds, he was able to free himself and escape from the hospital. He returned several hours later.

> Ten years later, Steven was hospitalized in an attempt to cure his sleepwalking. One evening his nurse found him having a nightmare and struggling violently on his bed as he tried to free his hands, held behind his back, from an imaginary bond. He again left the hospital, his hands still held behind his back. When he returned after awakening, his nurse noticed deep welts, as might be made by a rope, on his arms. Steven could not explain where they came from. The marks were visible for nearly three days.

> To test the hypothesis that the marks resulted from a reliving of his traumatic experience of ten years earlier, Steven's physician gave him a hypnotic drug and asked him to relive that experience. While reliving the experience, Steven writhed violently on the couch and welts began to appear on each forearm. Gradually these marks deepened and blood began to appear along their course. As shown in [Figure 16.16], the marks were still visible the next day (Moody, 1946).

Psychophysiological disorders are different from **conversion disorders,** in which psychological factors produce a physical symptom, such as blindness, numbness, pain, or paralysis. In con-

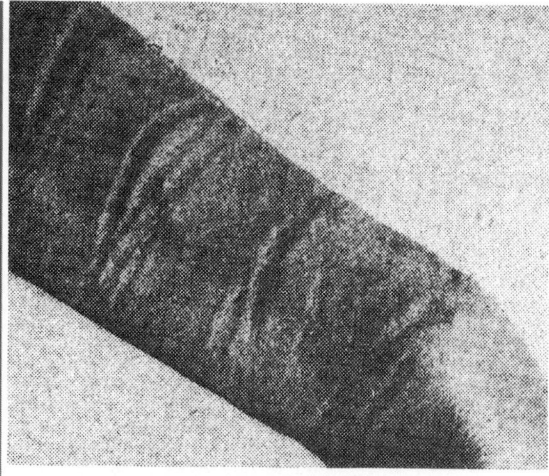

Figure 16.16 *The rope marks produced by the reliving of his traumatic experience were still visible on Steven's arm the following day. (Moody, 1946).*

version disorders, no physical cause can be found; the causal factors are purely psychological, and the symptom is usually a symbolic expression of an underlying conflict. Thus, a soldier about to go into combat may suddenly develop blindness for which no physical cause can be found. In contrast, psychophysiological disorders are produced by interacting psychological and physiological factors that produce actual tissue damage of some kind.

The study of psychophysiological illnesses has given rise to the **diathesis–stress model.** According to this model, psychophysiological disorders are products of the constitutional strength or

weakness of various organ systems (diathesis) and the psychological disturbance experienced (stress). In a person with a weak organ, minimal stress may cause a breakdown of the organ; in a person with a strong constitution, great stress may be required to cause a breakdown.

Among the most researched of the psychophysiological disorders are peptic ulcers. Ulcers are formed when the mucous membrane of the stomach or small intestine is eroded by an oversecretion of stomach acids, especially those containing *pepsin,* which decomposes protein. More than 2 million Americans have peptic ulcers, and about 5,000 die from them each year (Rosenhan & Seligman, 1989). People who secrete excess digestive juices, people with a weak mucous defense against acid, and people whose stomach lining regenerates slowly may generally be more susceptible to ulcers (the diathesis). The stress portion of the equation is found in the fact that anxiety, anger, and some other psychological states can drastically increase the secretion of hydrochloric acid and pepsin into the stomach (Friedman & DiMatteo, 1989; Taylor, 1991).

Environmental stressors can increase the risk of psychophysiological disorders in people with vulnerable organs. High rates of peptic ulcer development are found among people in occupations that produce high levels of stress (see Figure 16.17). For example, air traffic controllers have twice the ulcer rate of matched control groups, and controllers who work in airports with a great deal of traffic have twice the ulcer rate of those who work in airports with less traffic (Cobb & Rose, 1973). We must keep in mind, however, that these are correlational data, and it is possible that ulcer-prone people tend to choose stressful jobs.

Is there an ulcer-prone personality type? The psychoanalyst Franz Alexander (1950) believed that there is. Based on clinical observations of ulcer patients, Alexander concluded that an unconscious conflict of dependency versus independence predisposes men to develop ulcers. He maintained that the ulcer patient has a deep-seated wish to be loved and nurtured like a child; but at the same time, these motives give rise to guilt and shame and are rejected by the adult ego. To avoid displaying the dependency of an infant, which he considers shameful, the ulcer-prone person puts on a mask of exaggerated self-sufficiency, driving ambition, and inappropriate displays of strength. This works as long as his dependency needs are not rearoused; but when these needs are aroused, the conflict is intensi-

Figure 16.17 *People with highly stressful occupations tend to have a higher incidence of ulcers.*

fied, and the person responds with gastric over-secretion, producing ulcer symptoms. Although research has indicated that this personality pattern is indeed frequently found among ulcer patients, the theory seems to apply only to men and not to women (Alexander & others, 1968). More research is clearly needed to isolate personality variables that may contribute to the development of ulcers. At any rate, psychophysiological disorders serve to illustrate once again the intimate linkages between mind and body.

Depressive Disorders

Almost everyone has experienced depression, at least in its milder forms. Loss and pain are inevitable parts of life, and when they occur, most of us feel blue, sad and discouraged, and apathetic and passive. The future looks bleak, and some of the zest goes out of living. Such reactions are normal; researchers have repeatedly found that at any given point in time, 25 to 30 percent of college undergraduates are in the throes of some of these feelings (Rosenhan & Seligman, 1989). The feelings usually fade away fairly quickly after the event has passed or as the person becomes accustomed to the new situation, and they do not call for a diagnosis of depressive disorder. In clinical depression, on the other hand, the frequency, intensity, and duration of depressive symptoms are out of proportion to the person's life situation (Oatley & Jenkins, 1992). Thus, a person might respond to a minor setback or loss with a lengthy and intense depressive reaction (see Figure 16.18).

Although depression is widely regarded as a disorder of mood, there are actually four sets of symptoms in depression. In addition to the mood, or *emotional* symptoms, there are *cognitive* symptoms, *motivational* symptoms, and physical, or *somatic* symptoms (see Figure 16.19).

When depressed people are asked how they feel, they most commonly report sadness, misery, feelings of hopelessness and helplessness, loneliness, worry, anxiety, and feelings of worthlessness. Almost as pervasive as these negative feelings is a loss of the ability to experience pleasure. There is a numbing of the joy of living, and activities that used to bring satisfaction and happiness feel dull and flat. As depression increases in severity, a loss of interest begins to spread through practically everything the person does. Pleasure derived from recreation, hobbies, family, and other relationships diminishes. Even biological pleasures, such as eating and sex, lose their appeal.

Cognitive symptoms are also a central part of depression. Depressed people often have low self-esteem (Coyne & others, 1991). They believe that they are inferior, inadequate, and incompetent. When failures occur, depressed people tend to blame themselves; when failure has not yet occurred, they imagine that it will and that it will be caused by their inadequacies. Depressed people almost always view the future with great pessimism and hopelessness.

Motivational symptoms in depression involve an inability to get started and perform behaviors that might produce pleasure or accomplishment. A depressed student may be unable to get out of bed in the morning, let alone go to class or study. Everything seems too much of an effort. In extreme depressive reactions, the person may have to be prodded out of bed, clothed, and fed. Severe depression may also be accompanied by **psychomotor retardation,** in which movements slow down and the person walks or talks slowly and with excruciating effort.

Depression affects not only mood, thought, and behavior but also the body. Loss of appetite is common, and weight loss often occurs in moderate and severe depression. (In mild depression, however, weight gain sometimes occurs as a person eats compulsively.) Sleep disturbances are also common. Depressed people may have trouble getting to sleep, or they may fall asleep but then awaken and not be able to get back to sleep the rest of the night. Sleep dis-

Figure 16.18 *The most notable emotional feature of depression is profound sadness.*

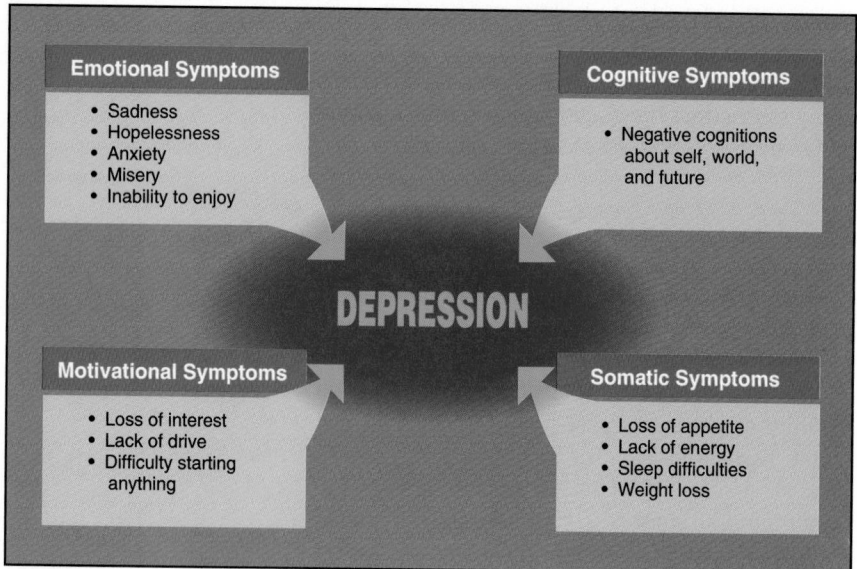

Figure 16.19 *Depression involves emotional, cognitive, motivational, and somatic features.*

turbance and weight loss lead to fatigue and weakness. Depressed people also may lose interest in sex, and men frequently experience difficulties in getting or maintaining an erection, whereas women often experience a lack of arousal.

The symptoms of self-reproach and hopelessness that we have discussed are graphically illustrated in the following exchange between a therapist (Th.) and a patient (Pt.):

> Th.: Good morning, how are you today?
> Pt.: (Pause) Well, okay I guess, Doctor. . . . I don't know, I just feel sort of discouraged.
> Th.: Is there anything in particular that worries you?
> Pt.: I don't know, Doctor . . . everything seems to be futile . . . nothing seems worthwhile any more. It seems as if all that was beautiful has lost its beauty. I guess I expected more than life has given. It just doesn't seem worthwhile going on. I can't seem to make up my mind about anything. I guess I have what you would call the ''blues.''
> Th.: Can you tell me more about your feelings?
> Pt.: Well . . . my family expected great things of me. I am supposed to be the outstanding member of the family . . . they think because I went through college everything should begin to pop and there's nothing to pop. I . . . really don't expect anything from anyone. Those whom I have trusted proved themselves less than friends should be.
> Th.: Oh?
> Pt.: Yes, I once had a very good girlfriend with whom I spent a good deal of time. She was very important to me . . . I thought she was my friend but now she treats me like a casual acquaintance (tears).
> Th.: Can you think of any reason for this?
> Pt.: Yes, it's all my fault. I can't blame them—anybody that is . . . I am not worthy of them (Carson & others, 1988, p. 289).

Incidence of Depression

At this moment, about 1 in 20 Americans is severely depressed (Robins & Regier, 1991). Statistically, the chances are 1 in 10 that you will have a depressive episode of clinical proportions at least once in your lifetime. Data from the NIMH Catchment Area Study indicate that depression is on the rise in younger groups, with the onset of depression increasing dramatically in the 15-to-19-year-old group (Burke & others, 1991). If you were born after 1960, you are 10 times more likely to have at some time been clinically depressed than are your grandparents, even though they have lived much longer (Seligman, 1989). The reasons for this striking increase are not totally clear, but we will consider one possible explanation later.

Women appear to be twice as likely as men to suffer depressive disorders (McGrath & others, 1992; Nolen-Hoeksema, 1988). Studies of people being treated for depression as well as community epidemiological studies consistently show this sex difference, but the reasons for it are not completely clear. Both biological and cultural explanations have been offered. Biological theories suggest that genetic factors, biochemical differences in the nervous system, or the monthly premenstrual depression that many women experience could increase vulnerability to depressive disorders. In contrast, environmental theories focus on possible cultural causes. One suggestion is that the traditional sex role expectation for females in our culture is to be passive and dependent in the face of stress or loss. Thus, women may be more willing to express depressive symptoms than men because helplessness is more consistent with the female sex role (Rosenhan & Seligman, 1989).

No age group is exempt from depression. It appears in infants as young as 6 months who have been separated from their mothers for prolonged periods, and recent research using sensitive tests of depression have revealed a rate of depressive symptoms in children and adolescents as high as the adult rate (Blumberg & Izard, 1985).

The Course of Depression

Most people who suffer depressive episodes never seek treatment. What is likely to happen to such people? Perhaps the one positive thing that can be said about depression is that it usually dissipates with time. After the initial attack, which comes on suddenly about three-quarters of the time, depression seems to last an average of about 3 months in outpatients. In more severely depressed people who require hospitalization, depression may last twice as long. Complete recovery from the episode occurs in 70 to 95 percent of depressed people (Rosenhan & Seligman, 1989).

Once a depressive episode has occurred, one of three patterns may follow. In perhaps half of all cases, depression will never recur. Many other cases show a second pattern: recovery with recurrence. On the average, these people will remain symptom-free for perhaps 3 years before experiencing another depressive episode of about the same severity and duration. The time interval between subsequent episodes of depression tends to become shorter over the years (NIMH, 1984). Finally, about 10 percent of people who have a major depressive episode will not recover and will remain chronically depressed (see Figure 16.20).

Causal Factors in Depression

No single cause has been found for depression. It is clear that in many instances, depression involves a variety of interacting causes stemming both from the person and from the environment.

Biological Factors

Both genetic and neurochemical factors have been linked to depression. The strongest evidence for genetic factors comes from studies of the incidence of depression in adoptive versus biological relatives of depressed patients. Among adopted people who developed depression, biological relatives were found to be eight times more likely than adoptive relatives to suffer from depression (Wender & others, 1986).

Comparison of concordance rates in identical and fraternal twins reinforces the conclusion that genetics are involved. Identical twins have a concordance rate of about 67 percent compared with a rate of only 15 percent for fraternal twins (Gershon & others, 1989). Overall, it is clear that having a depressed family member increases the risk for depression, but the precise genetic basis for this increased risk awaits more evidence. What is likely inherited is a predisposition to develop a depressive disorder, given certain kinds of environmental factors such as significant losses and low social support (Plomin & Rende, 1991).

Given the critical role of brain neurotransmitters in virtually all behaviors, it is not surprising that much current work is focusing on the possible role of brain chemistry in depression (Depue & Iacono, 1989). One influential theory holds that depression is a disorder of motivation caused by deficiencies in a family of neurotransmitters, the **biogenic amines,** which include norepinephrine, dopamine, and serotonin. The biogenic amines play important roles in neurotransmission within several subcortical brain regions

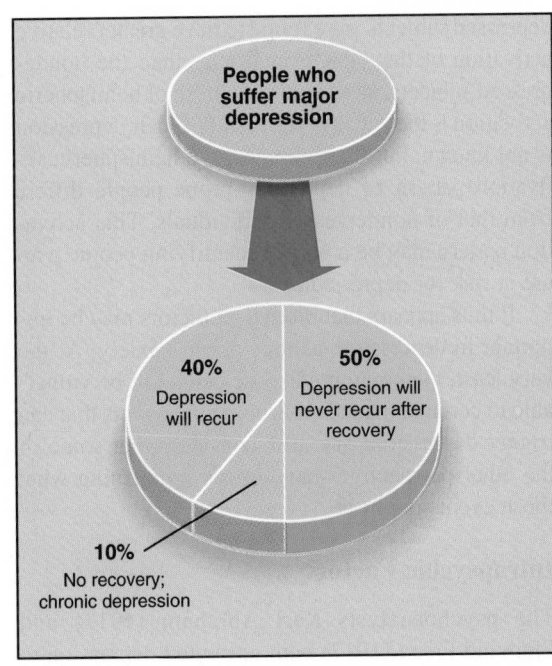

Figure 16.20 *Course of outcome following a major depressive episode. About half never have a recurrence, a sizable proportion do have a recurrence, and about 10 percent suffer chronic depression.*

known to be important sites for reward (White & Milner, 1992). These neurotransmitters appear to be centrally involved in the experiencing of pleasure, as well as in the activation of goal-directed behavior. When the biogenic amines are failing to function at a high enough level, neural activity in these systems is thought to be reduced, resulting in the lack of pleasure and loss of motivation that characterizes depression.

One important line of evidence in support of the biogenic amine theory is that several highly effective groups of antidepressant drugs operate by increasing dopamine activity in the brain. One group of antidepressant drugs, called **tricyclics,** blocks the reuptake of the transmitters into the cell bodies so that more of the substances remain in the synapse to activate the receptor neurons. This results in a higher level of neural activity in the crucial reward-activation system and a marked improvement in depressive symptoms. Another group of antidepressant drugs, called **MAO inhibitors,** prevents the enzyme MAO (monoamine oxidase) from deactivating the amine transmitters, allowing them to continue stimulating the critical neural systems that underlie positive mood and goal-directed behavior.

Chapter 13 reviewed evidence that positive emotions are associated with relatively greater left-hemisphere activation and negative emotions with greater right-hemisphere activity. These findings have been applied to the study of depression by Jeffrey Henriques and Richard Davidson (1990). They compared previously depressed subjects with subjects who had no history of depression. None of the subjects were currently depressed. The previously depressed subjects were found to have greater relative activation of the right frontal lobe than the nondepressed subjects. Whether this pattern of hemispheric activation is the cause or the result of their depression is not known, but it appears that the hemispheric activation pattern of depression-prone people differs from that of nondepressed individuals. This activation pattern may be a way of identifying people who are at risk for depression.

It thus appears that biological factors may be important in depression, as they are in anxiety. At the very least, they may predispose people to be vulnerable to certain types of environmental events that can trigger depression. We now consider what some of the other perspectives have to say concerning what those events might be.

Intrapsychic Factors

The psychoanalysts Karl Abraham (1911) and Sigmund Freud (1917) both attributed depression to anger turned inward upon the self. Abraham and Freud viewed many, if not all, depressions as reactions to events that are symbolically meaningful to a person because the person lost or was rejected by someone he or she deeply loved earlier in life, particularly in childhood (see Figure 16.21). The depressive feels rage at having been disappointed. Furthermore, the intense love the depressive felt is not transferred to another person, but is fused with the

self as the ego incorporates the lost person as part of the depressive's own identity.

Psychoanalysts believe that this process creates an intrapsychic vulnerability mechanism for later depression. Subsequent losses and rejection reactivate the original loss and cause the depressive's rage to be turned again toward the original love object, which is now fused with the depressive's own ego. This turning in of anger produces symptoms of low self-esteem, public self-accusation, irrational feelings of guilt, and in the most extreme cases, suicide. Thus, the original rage continues to exert an influence, and the person becomes especially vulnerable to real or symbolic losses throughout life.

Were he alive today, Freud would surely point to research by the English sociologists George Brown and Terrill Harris (1978) to support his theory of early loss. Brown and Harris interviewed women in London and found that the rate of depression among women who had lost their mothers before age 11 and who had also experienced a severe recent loss was almost three times higher than the rate of depression among women who had experienced a similar recent loss but had not lost their mothers before age 11. More recent research has shown that death of the father while a child is young is also associated with a greatly increased risk of later depression (Barnes & Prosen, 1985).

The humanistic theorist Carl Rogers (1959) viewed depression as a product of perceived failure to measure up to the ideal self. This notion received support from a recent study by Timothy Strauman (1992), who obtained measures of people's self-perceptions and their ideal selves. He found that feelings of depression were indeed related to the size of the discrepancy between the current self and the ideal self.

In an attempt to explain the dramatic increase in depression among people born after 1960, Martin Seligman (1989) has offered some suggestions that are consistent with the humanistic perspective. Seligman believes that the "me" generation, with its overemphasis on individuality and the need for personal control, has sown the seeds of its own depression. Because people define their self-worth in terms of individual attainment and have fewer commitments to traditional values of family, religion, and the common good, they are likely to react much more strongly to failures, to view them as reflecting their own inadequacies, and to experience a sense of meaninglessness in their lives. Seligman notes:

> But surely one necessary condition for meaning (assuredly not sufficient) is the attachment to something larger than oneself. ... To the extent that it is now difficult for young people to take seriously their relationship with God, to care about their relationship with

▶ **Figure 16.21** *Early catastrophic losses are thought by psychoanalysts to increase vulnerability to later depressive disorders.*

the country, or to be part of a large and abiding family, meaning in life will be very difficult to find. The self, to put it another way, is a very poor site for meaning . . . so individualism without commitment to the commons produces depression and meaninglessness on a massive scale (Seligman, 1989, p. 94).

Cognitive Factors

The cognitive approach to understanding depression has become one of the most influential perspectives. Two of the central figures in this area are Aaron Beck and Martin Seligman. Both have focused on the distortions and faulty beliefs that cause the depressed person to view the self, the world, and the future negatively. We now examine these two theories more closely.

Beck's Cognitive Theory. According to Beck, depressed people victimize themselves through their own thought processes. Depressives believe that they are defective, worthless, and inadequate. They also believe that whatever happens to them is bad, and that the negative things that are happening now will

continue because of their personal defects (Clark & others, 1989). These thought patterns seem to occur automatically, and many depressives indicate that they are impossible to control (Wenzlaff & others, 1988). The depressive's dim views of self, the world, and the future form a **cognitive triad** of negative beliefs reinforced by selective memory for past events. Depressed people tend to recall most of their failures and few of their successes (Haaga & others, 1991; Pyszczynski & others, 1991).

Beck (1976) believes that systematic errors in logic characterize the thinking of depressives and maintain their depressive triad. These faulty and self-defeating logical patterns, presented in Table 16.3, ensure that depressives will continue to feel bad even when things are in reality not going badly for them.

A final cognitive pattern that helps produce and maintain depression is what Beck calls a **depressive attributional pattern.** *Attribution* refers to the process whereby people interpret the causes of events in their lives. As noted in the discussion of self-enhancing tendencies in Chapter 14, most people tend to take personal credit for the good outcomes in their

Table 16.3 Systematic Errors of Logic Thought to Characterize People with Depression

Systematic Logical Errors	Description	Example
Arbitrary inference	Drawing an unfavorable inference or conclusion about oneself when there is little or no evidence to support it.	A paper is returned to a student with a grade of A but no comments by the professor. The student concludes, "She doesn't like me and probably thinks my work is not very good."
Selective abstraction	Focusing on one insignificant detail while ignoring the more important features of a situation.	An office worker is praised lavishly by the boss for his work. In the course of the conversation, the boss suggests he need not make an additional copy of his work any more. In spite of all the positive feedback, the worker's conclusion is, "The boss is not happy with what I am doing."
Overgeneralization	Drawing global conclusions about abilities or worth on the basis of a single fact.	A person goes on a blind date that does not go particularly well. This one experience convinces her that no one will ever be attracted to her and that she is doomed to a life without a love relationship.
Magnification and minimization	Evaluating negative and positive outcomes to one's disadvantage, with bad outcomes magnified and good ones minimized.	A person feels very depressed at the end of a day in which he has received a major sales award from his company but has also lost a rather insignificant sale.
Personalization	Incorrectly taking blame or responsibility for events that are unintended or beyond one's control.	A man blames himself for being a poor father and becomes depressed after a cancellation of his air flight from another city results in his missing his son's birthday party.

Source: Based on Beck, 1976.

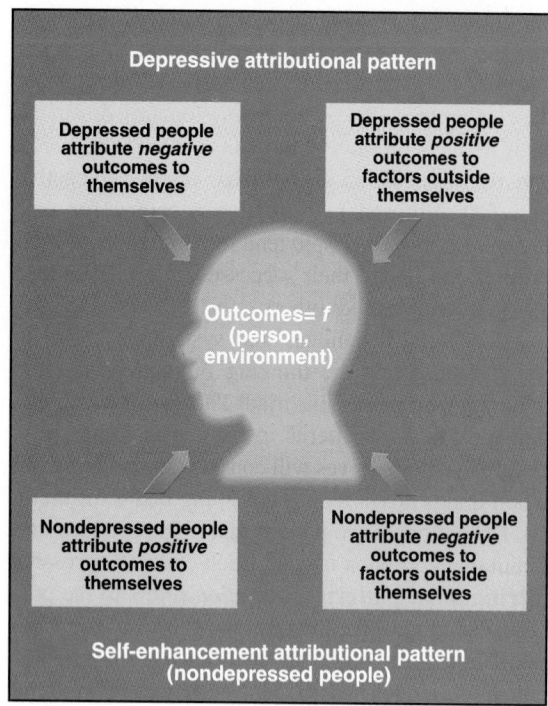

Depressive attributional pattern

Depressed people attribute *negative* outcomes to themselves

Depressed people attribute *positive* outcomes to factors outside themselves

Outcomes= *f* (person, environment)

Nondepressed people attribute *positive* outcomes to themselves

Nondepressed people attribute *negative* outcomes to factors outside themselves

Self-enhancement attributional pattern (nondepressed people)

lives and to blame their misfortunes on factors outside of themselves, thereby maintaining and enhancing their self-esteem. According to Beck, depressed people do exactly the opposite: They interpret successes or other positive events as being due to factors outside the self while attributing negative outcomes to personal factors (see Figure 16.22). Beck believes that this attributional pattern of taking no credit for successes but blaming themselves for failures serves to maintain depressed people's low self-esteem and their conviction that they are worthless failures. Quite literally, they can't win!

The logical errors and the depressive attributional pattern might lead us to expect that depressed people are less accurate in evaluating events than people who are not depressed. Surprisingly, however, some studies suggest that this is not the case. In fact, the situation may be quite the opposite. In one study of social competence, depressed patients rated themselves more accurately than did other psychiatric patients or normal controls, all of whom tended to overrate themselves in a self-enhancing fashion. Most interesting of all was the finding that as the depressed patients improved, they became more self-enhancing and less realistic about their impact on other people (Lewinsohn & others, 1980). Depressed people may have low self-esteem, but this low self-evaluation may not always be a distortion. Sometimes it may be an accurate and sober assessment of reality. As Freud once noted, ''it may be, so far as we know, that he (the depressive) has to be ill before he can be accessible to a truth of this kind'' (Freud, 1917/1957, p. 246). It may be that many nondepressed people main-

tain their positive feelings (and, perhaps, avoid depression) through self-enhancing illusions about the self, the world, and the future (Brown, 1991; Taylor & Brown, 1988).

Seligman's Learned Helplessness Hypothesis. Seligman's **learned helplessness hypothesis** states that depressive deficits are produced when people expect that bad events will occur and that there is nothing they can do to prevent or cope with them. Seligman suggests that chronic and intense depression occurs as the result of negative attributions that are *personal, stable,* and *global.* Thus, people who attribute negative events in their lives to factors such as low intelligence, physical repulsiveness, or an unlovable personality tend to believe that their personal defects will render them helpless to avoid negative events in the future, and they are therefore at risk for depression.

One set of findings from learned helplessness studies is particularly intriguing. In rats, learned helplessness produced by unavoidable aversive stimulation is accompanied by a depletion in the brain of norepinephrine, one of the biogenic amines whose underactivity has been linked to human depression (Weiss & others, 1976). Seligman suggests that learned helplessness expectancies, even in animals, may produce biochemical effects that underlie depression.

Learning and Environmental Factors

Depression has a vicious-cycle quality about it. As people become depressed, they lose the motivation to engage in activities that previously provided them with pleasure, which in turn deepens their depression. Peter Lewinsohn and his colleagues (1985) have noted that depression is initially triggered in many cases by a loss or some other punishing event or by a drastic decrease in the amount of positive reinforcement that the person receives from his or her environment. As the depression begins to take hold, the person stops performing behaviors that previously provided reinforcement, such as hobbies and socializing. Moreover, his or her behavior becomes punishing to others, since depressed people—who constantly seem to ask for reassurance, and then question its sincerity when it is given—are no fun to be around (Coyne & others, 1991). Indeed, research has shown that depressed people tend to make those who come in contact with them feel anxious, depressed, and hostile. Eventually, these other people begin to lose patience with the depressed individual, failing to understand why the person doesn't ''snap out of it.'' This diminishes social support still further and may eventually cause the depressed person to be abandoned by those who are most important to him or her (Joiner & others, 1992).

Behavioral theorists believe that in order to begin feeling better, depressed people must break into the vicious cycle by initially forcing themselves to engage in behaviors that are likely to produce some degree of pleasure. Eventually, positive reinforcement effects will begin to counteract the depressive feelings, undermine the feelings of helplessness that characterize depression, and increase feelings of personal control over the environment.

Environmental factors may also underlie the fact that depression tends to run in families. Constance Hammen and her colleagues (1992) studied the family histories of depressed people and concluded that one reason for this generational link may be that children of depressed parents experience poor parenting and many stressful experiences as children. As a result, they may fail to develop good coping skills and a positive self-concept. They are therefore vulnerable later in life to stressful events that can trigger depressive reactions.

Clearly, depression is a complex phenomenon having multiple causes that interact in a circular fashion. Thus, biological and intrapsychic predispositions may increase people's vulnerability to stressful life events. These events may trigger depressive cognitions, which induce depressed mood (or perhaps may trigger depressed mood, which arouses depressive cognitions). The behavioral responses to the depressive cognitions and mood intensify the depression and are likely to create more environmental stress, which can in turn maintain or increase biochemical events in the brain that underlie depression. The pieces of the puzzle are many, and sorting them out is a challenging task for researchers.

Many depressed people at one time or another consider suicide as a way to escape from the unhappiness of their lives. We now examine suicide, its causes, and what can be done to prevent this tragic event.

UNDERSTANDING AND PREVENTING SUICIDE

ENHANCING HUMAN PERFORMANCE

Suicide ranks ninth among the causes of death in the United States. Between 20,000 and 35,000 people end their lives each year, and 10 times that number attempt suicide. Suicide is now the second most frequent cause of death (after accidents) among high school and college students, and statistics suggest that it is on the rise in this age group (National Center for Health Statistics, 1991; see Figure 16.23). The death of a young person who will never fulfill all of his or her promise is an especially terrible tragedy. An understanding of the factors that increase the risk of suicide and guidelines for preventing suicide may increase your effectiveness should you encounter a potentially suicidal person.

Women make about three times as many suicide attempts as men, but men actually succeed in killing themselves three times more often than women. The higher rate of suicide attempts in woman may be due to a higher incidence of depression, whereas the higher completed suicide rate in men seems related to their choice of much more lethal meth-

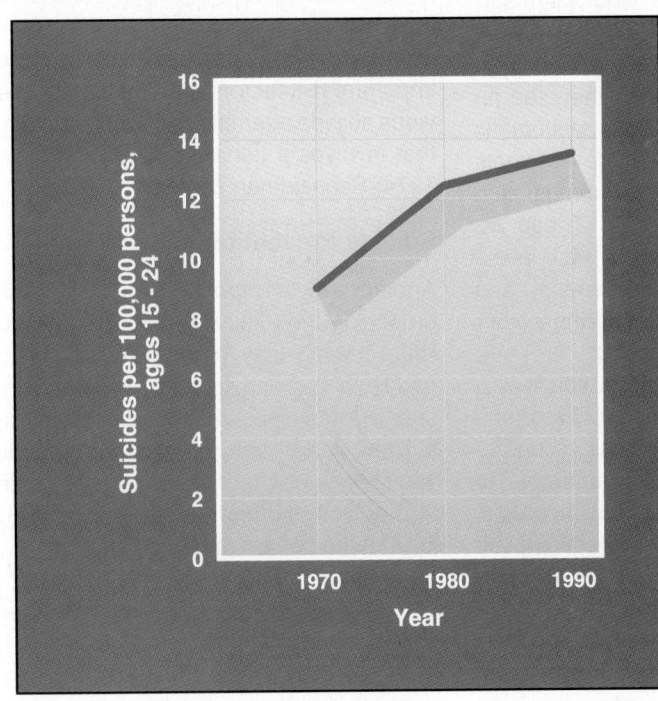

▼ **Figure 16.23** *Suicide rate per 100,000 persons aged 15–24. A suicide rate increase of 51 percent occurred in this age group between 1970 and 1990. (Data from National Center for Health Statistics, 1991).*

ods, such as shooting themselves or jumping off buildings (Rosenhan & Seligman, 1989). The suicide rate for both men and women is higher among those who have been divorced or widowed. Women who commit suicide tend to be motivated by failures in love relationships, whereas men tend to be motivated by failure in their occupations (Shneidman, 1976).

Depression is one of the strongest predictors of suicide. About 15 percent of clinically depressed individuals will eventually kill themselves. This rate is 22 to 36 times higher than the rate for the general population. An estimated 80 percent of suicidal patients are significantly depressed.

Surprisingly, suicide often occurs as a depressed person seems to be emerging from depression. For example, Ernest Hemingway shot himself to death shortly after being released from a hospital when his depression improved. The lifting of depression may provide the energy needed to complete the act without affecting the individual's underlying cognitions of hopelessness and despair.

Motives for Suicide

There appear to be two fundamental motivations for suicide: the desire to end one's life (sometimes referred to as the desire for **surcease)** and **manipulation** of other people. Those who wish surcease have basically given up. They see no other way to deal with intolerable emotional distress, and in death they see an end to their problems. In one systematic study, 56 percent of suicide attempts were classified as having been motivated by the desire for surcease. These attempts were accompanied by high levels of depression and hopelessness, and they tended to be more lethal than other suicide attempts (Beck, 1976).

The second primary motivation for suicide is manipulation. **Parasuicides** (suicide attempts that do not end in death) are often cries for help or attempts to coerce people to meet one's needs. Thus, they are attempts to manipulate others. Trying to prevent a lover from ending a relationship and trying to dramatize one's sufferings are manipulative motives. Manipulative suicide attempters tend to use less lethal means (such as drug overdoses or wrist-slashing) and to make sure help is available. In the study cited earlier (Beck, 1976), 13 percent of the suicide attempts were classified as

manipulative. The remaining 31 percent combined the two types of motivation. In these cases, the attempters were not certain whether they wished to live or die. In this undecided group, the more hopeless and depressed the individual, the stronger the surcease motivation for the suicide attempt (Beck & others, 1979).

Warning Signs for Suicide

The best predictor of suicide attempts in both genders is a threat of suicide, and such threats should always be taken seriously. One of the myths about suicide is that people who talk about suicide don't actually commit suicide. A high proportion of suicide attempts—perhaps 80 percent—are preceded by some kind of warning. Sometimes the warning is an explicit statement of intent, such as "I don't want to go on living" or "I won't be a burden much longer," and sometimes the warning is quite vague, as when a person expresses hopelessness about the future. At other times, the signs of distress or hopelessness are behavioral ones, such as withdrawing from others or from favorite activities, giving away treasured possessions, or taking unusual risks. Other important risk factors are a history of previous suicide attempts and a detailed plan that involves a lethal method (Farberow, 1974; Schneidman & others, 1970).

Suicide Prevention

Another myth about suicide is that broaching the topic with a potentially suicidal person may prompt the person to carry out the act. In truth, the best first step if you suspect that someone may be suicidal is to ask the person directly whether he or she is considering suicide: "Have you thought about ending your life?" If the person responds affirmatively, try to find out if he or she has a plan or a time table in mind. Your ultimate goal should be to help the person to get help from qualified professionals as soon as possible, but there are also some immediate steps you can take that may be helpful.

Many suicidal people feel alone in their misery. It is important to provide so-

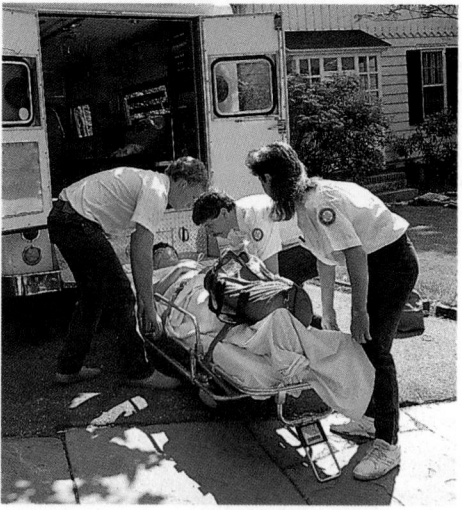

cial support and empathy at this critical juncture. An expression of genuine concern can pave the way for other potentially helpful interventions. For example, a frank discussion of the problem that is foremost in the person's life can be helpful. The suicidal person often feels totally overwhelmed by life, and a focus on a specific problem may help the person to understand that it is not unsolvable and that it need not cloud his or her total perception of life.

When people are distressed and hopeless, their time orientation tends to narrow, and they have difficulty seeing beyond their current distress. Try to help the person see his or her present situation within a wider time perspective and to consider positive possibilities that might exist in the future. In particular, discuss with the person the reasons for continuing to live and focus on any doubts the person might have about electing suicide. For example, if the person indicates that his or her family will suffer greatly from the suicide, adopt this as one of your arguments for a different solution to the problem. Many suicidal people would like to feel that they do not have to commit suicide. Capitalize on such feelings.

If a person is suicidal, stay with him or her and seek professional assistance. Most cities have suicide prevention centers that offer 24-hour services, including telephone and direct counseling. These centers are usually listed under *suicide* or *crisis* in the phone book.

Bipolar Disorders

Not all people who suffer from mood disorders experience only depression. For people who suffer from **bipolar disorders,** the symptom picture includes episodes of both mania and depression or, in a smaller number of cases, mania without depression. Because the depressive symptoms that occur in bipolar disorder resemble those of unipolar depression, we will focus on the mania component of the disorder. Like depression, mania presents four sets of symptoms: emotional, cognitive, motivational, and somatic.

The mood of an individual in a manic state is expansive, euphoric, and elevated. However, irritability may occur very quickly if the manic individual is thwarted in his or her ambitions. Manic cognitions tend to be highly grandiose. A person in a manic state does not believe there are limits to his or her ability and does not recognize the negative consequences that may ensue when his or her plans are carried out. At a motivational level, manic behavior is hyperactive. The manic engages in frenetic activity, be it in work, in sexual relationships, or elsewhere. Speech is rapid or pressured, as if the person must say as many words as possible in the time allotted. With all this flurry of activity comes a greatly lessened need for sleep. Manic people may go for several days without sleeping, until exhaustion inevitably sets in and the mania slows down.

The onset of a manic episode is usually quite sudden, and the euphoric mood, grandiose and racing thoughts, and frenetic acts stand in marked contrast to the person's usual functioning. This is illustrated in the following case:

Robert B., 56 years old, was a dentist who for most of his 25 years of dental practice provided rather well for his wife and three daughters. Mrs. B. reported that there had been times when Robert displayed behavior similar to that which preceded his hospitalization, but that this was the worst she had ever seen him.

About two weeks prior to hospitalization, the patient awoke one morning with the idea that he was the most gifted dental surgeon in his tri-state area; his mission then was to provide service for as many persons as possible so that they could benefit from his talents. Consequently, he decided to enlarge his 2-chair practice to a 20-chair one, and his plan was to reconstruct his two dental offices into 20 booths so that he could simultaneously attend to as many patients. That very day he drew up the plans for this arrangement and telephoned a number of remodelers and invited them to submit bids for the work.

Toward the end of that day he became irritated with the "interminable delays" and, after he attended to his last patient, rolled up his sleeves and began to knock down the walls of his dental offices. When he discovered that he couldn't manage this chore with the sledge hammer he had purchased for this purpose earlier, he became frustrated and proceeded to smash his more destructible tools, washbasins, and X-ray equipment. He justified this behavior in his own mind by saying, "This junk is not suitable for the likes of me; it'll have to be replaced anyway."

He was in perpetual motion and his speech was "overexcited." [When Robert was later admitted to a hospital] he could not sit in his chair; instead he paced the office floor like a caged animal (Kleinmuntz, 1980, pp. 309–310).

In contrast to unipolar depression, which occurs more frequently in women, bipolar disorder affects men and women equally. Bipolar disorder also appears to have a stronger genetic basis than unipolar depression. In the general population, the lifetime risk of developing a bipolar disorder is 1 percent. In contrast, however, 50 percent of patients with bipolar disorder have a parent, grandparent, or child with the disorder. The concordance for bipolar disorder is 5 times as high in identical twins as in fraternal twins. Researchers are working to find out exactly how bipolar disorder is genetically transmitted.

One prevalent biological theory of manic disorder is that it involves an *overproduction* of biogenic amines, producing a symptom picture exactly opposite that seen in depression. Significantly, lithium chloride, the drug most frequently used to calm manic disorders, works by decreasing the amount of amine transmitters at the synapses of the motivational activation system in the brain (Depue & Iacono, 1989).

Schizophrenic Disorders

Of all the behavior disorders, schizophrenia is the most serious and the most puzzling. Although there are many theories of schizophrenia and thousands of research studies, a complete understanding of this disorder continues to elude us.

The term **schizophrenia** was introduced by the Swiss psychiatrist Eugen Bleuler in 1911. Literally, the term means "split mind." This term has often led people to confuse schizophrenia with multiple personality disorder or with a Dr. Jekyll–Mr. Hyde phenomenon, but that is not what Bleuler had in mind when he coined the term. Instead, Bleuler intended to suggest that certain psychological functions, such as thought, emotion, and behavior, which are joined together in normal people, are somehow split apart in schizophrenia. Thus, thoughts are jumbled and confused, emotional responses are absent or inappropriate, and behavior may be inappropriate, bizarre, or disorganized.

Characteristics of Schizophrenia

According to the DSM, a diagnosis of schizophrenia requires evidence that a person misinterprets reality and exhibits disordered attention, thought, and perception. In addition, withdrawal from social interactions is common, communication is strange or inappropriate, personal grooming may be neglected, and behavior may become disorganized.

The thought disorder that is the central feature of schizophrenia often includes delusions or hallucinations. **Delusions** are false beliefs that are sustained in the face of evidence that normally would be sufficient to destroy them. A schizophrenic may believe that his brain is being turned to glass by ray guns operated by his enemies from outer space, for example, or that God is a special agent of his. The first is a *delusion of persecution,* the second a *delusion of grandeur.* **Hallucinations** are false perceptions that have a compelling sense of reality. Auditory hallucinations, typically voices speaking to the patient, are most common, although visual and tactile hallucinations may also occur (see Figure 16.24).

Several aspects of the thought disorder were described by a schizophrenic during a period of recovery:

> The most wearing aspect of schizophrenia is the fierce battle that goes on inside my head in which conflicts become unresolvable. I am so ambivalent that my mind

can divide on a subject, and those two parts subdivide over and over until my mind feels like it is in pieces, and I am totally disorganized. At other times, I feel like I am trapped inside my head, banging against its walls, trying desperately to escape while my lips can utter only nonsense. . . . Recently, my mind has played tricks on me, creating The People inside my head who sometimes come out to haunt me and torment me. They surround me in rooms, hide behind trees and under the snow outside. They taunt me and scream at me and devise plans to break my spirit. The voices come and go, but The People are always there, always real (*New York Times,* March 18, 1986, p. C12).

The emotional responses of schizophrenics can also be highly inappropriate, as in the following case:

> [T]he psychologist noted that Carl "smiles when he is uncomfortable, and smiles more when in pain. He cries during television comedies. He seems angry when justice is done, frightened when someone compliments him, and roars with laughter on reading that a young child was burned in a tragic fire. He grimaces often" (Rosenhan & Seligman, 1989, p. 369).

Categorizing Schizophrenias

Schizophrenia has cognitive, emotional, and behavioral facets that can vary widely from case to case. There is now general agreement that rather than treating schizophrenia as a single disorder, it makes sense to refer to a number of different subtypes (Task Force on DSM IV, 1991). The most recent version of DSM differentiates among five different subtypes of schizophrenia: *paranoid, disorganized, catatonic, undifferentiated,* and *residual.* The major features of these subtypes are described in Table 16.4.

Schizophrenic reactions can also be categorized in two other ways, both of which relate to likelihood of recovery and possible causal factors more strongly than the categories in Table 16.4 (Comer, 1992; Fenton & McGlashan, 1991b). The first differentiation relates to the *onset* of symptoms. **Acute** schizophrenic reactions are characterized by a rapid onset of very intense symptoms. Often, the reaction can be linked to a highly stressful life event. In contrast, **chronic** schizophrenics manifest a rather gradual onset of the disorder and a long history of difficulties and social withdrawal. The symptoms are seldom as dramatic as in the acute reactions, but the difficulties seem more deeply ingrained and resistant to change. Acute disorders tend to have a better prognosis than chronic ones, since the person has been well adjusted in the past.

Another way of categorizing schizophrenic reactions is based on the *nature* of the symptoms (Task Force on DSM IV, 1991). One type of schizophrenia

▶ **Figure 16.24** *The artist William Blake, who suffered from hallucinations himself, captures the terror and agony that they can produce in* Unizen.

Table 16.4 Major Subtypes of Schizophrenic Disorders According to the DSM

Major Subtypes of Schizophrenia	Description
Paranoid Type	The most prominent features in paranoid schizophrenics are delusions of persecution, in which they believe that others mean to harm them, and delusions of grandeur, in which they believe they are enormously important. Suspicion, anxiety, or anger may accompany the delusions, and hallucinations may also occur in this subtype.
Disorganized Type	The central features are confusion and incoherence, together with a particularly severe deterioration of adaptive behavior. Fragmentary hallucinations and delusions may be present, but the disorganization of thought is so extreme that it is difficult to communicate with them. Their behavior often appears silly and childlike, and their emotional responses are highly inappropriate. These people are usually unable to function on their own.
Catatonic Type	The central feature is a striking motor disturbance ranging from muscular rigidity to random motor activity. Catatonics may exhibit a *waxy flexibility* in which their limbs can be molded into grotesque positions that they will maintain for hours. Catatonics sometimes alternate between stuporous states in which they seem oblivious to reality and agitated excitement during which they can be dangerous to others.
Undifferentiated Type	This category is for people who exhibit some of the symptoms and thought disorders of the above categories but do not have enough of the specific criteria to be diagnosed in those categories.
Residual Type	This category is used for schizophrenics whose symptoms have lessened in intensity but are still present in a reduced or residual form. After two years, the residual type is labeled *chronic.*

is characterized by **positive symptoms,** such as delusions, hallucinations, and disordered speech and thinking. These symptoms are called positive because they represent pathological excesses of normal processes. The second type features **negative symptoms**—normal reactions that seem to be missing—such as lack of emotional expression, loss of motivation, and an absence or poverty of speech. The distinction between positive and negative subtypes seems to be an important one. In one large follow-up study of previously hospitalized schizophrenics, negative symptoms were far more likely to be associated with a long-term history of poor functioning prior to hospitalization and with a poor outcome following treatment (McGlashan & Fenton, 1992). The same investigators found that the positive symptoms associated with a diagnosis of paranoid schizophrenia were associated with good functioning prior to breakdown and a better prognosis for eventual recovery (Fenton & McGlashan, 1991a, 1991b).

Causal Factors in Schizophrenia

Schizophrenia afflicts only 1 to 2 percent of the population, yet schizophrenic patients occupy about half of all psychiatric hospital beds in the United States (Robins & Regier, 1991). Many other schizophrenics barely function as homeless ''street people'' in large cities. Because of the seriousness of the disorder, the fact that it afflicts adolescents and young adults, and the many years of anguish and incapacitation that its victims are likely to experience, schizophrenia is perhaps the most widely researched of the behavior disorders. Although we are a long way from a complete understanding of this perplexing disorder, there is a growing consensus that schizophrenia results from a biologically based vulnerability factor that is set into motion by environmental and intrapsychic events (Fowles, 1992; Gottesman, 1991).

Biological Factors

Technical advances in the neurosciences have provided breakthroughs in knowledge about brain mechanisms that may underlie the schizophrenias. Brain-scanning devices have made it possible for researchers to look into the brains of schizophrenic patients and study neural processes as they occur. Special attention has focused on structural differences in the brains of schizophrenics and on biochemical differences involving neurotransmitter substances.

CAT scans and magnetic resonance imaging, which reveal the structural characteristics of the brain, have indicated a number of structural anomalies. First, 20 to 50 percent of the schizophrenics studied by various investigators show mild to moderate enlargement of the **ventricles,** cavities or canals in the brain

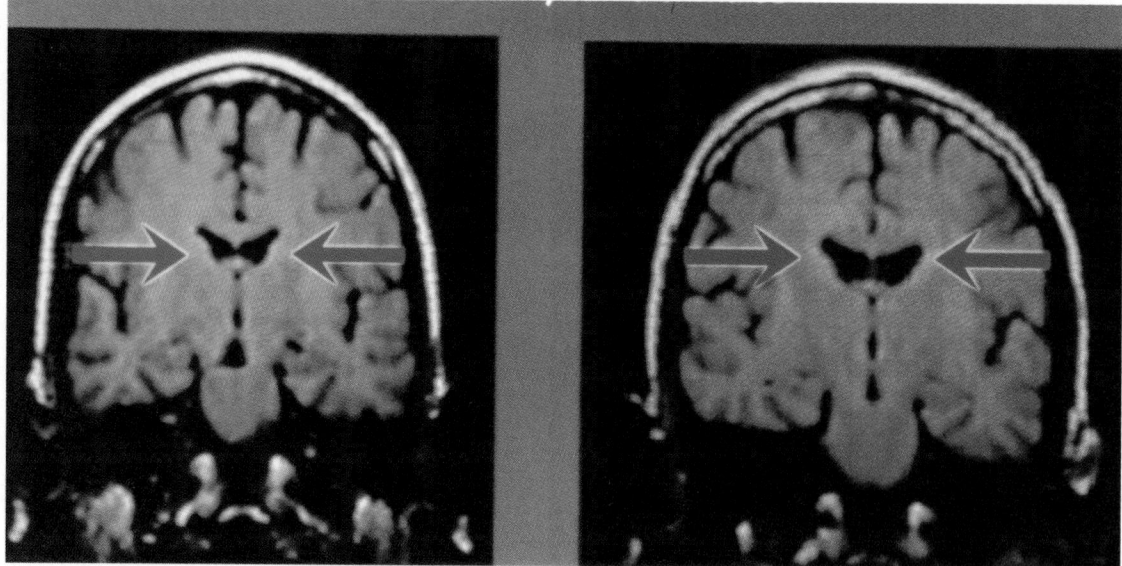

Figure 16.25 *The brain scan on the right illustrates the enlarged ventricles (butterfly-shaped cavities) that are frequently found in schizophrenic patients, particularly those who exhibit negative symptoms.*

that contain cerebrospinal fluid (see Figure 16.25). A second structural difference is brain atrophy, a general loss or deterioration of neurons in the cerebral cortex and limbic system, which occurs in 20 to 35 percent of schizophrenic patients (Jernigan & others, 1991). Both of these structural differences are more common in schizophrenics who have chronic disorders or who exhibit the negative symptom pattern. As we have seen, these schizophrenics have a poorer chance of recovery than those with acute schizophrenia or those with the positive symptom pattern. The latter groups tend not to show brain abnormalities. One suggestion is that the brain abnormalities result in a reduction of brain tissue that ordinarily supplies needed neurotransmitters or that carries out activities critical for normal adjustment (Andreasen, 1988; Fowles, 1992).

Aided by the development of the PET scan, which permits researchers to measure ongoing biochemical processes in the brain, many investigations of neurotransmitter systems are being carried out. Evidence has emerged that schizophrenia may involve over-activity of the dopamine transmitter system. Dopamine is a major excitatory transmitter substance in areas of the brain that regulate emotional expression, motivated behavior, and cognitive functioning (White & Milner, 1992). The **dopamine hypothesis** states that the symptoms of schizophrenia are produced by overactivity of the dopamine system. In support of this hypothesis, researchers point to evidence that schizophrenics have more dopamine receptors on neuron membranes than nonschizophrenics and that these receptors seem to be overreactive to dopamine stimulation (Black & others, 1988; Wong & others, 1986). Additional evidence comes from the finding that the effectiveness of antipsychotic drugs used to treat schizophrenic symptoms is directly related to their effectiveness in blocking dopamine receptors by

binding to them (Creese & others, 1976). These drugs are especially effective in reducing positive symptoms, such as hallucinations and delusions. Some researchers therefore suggest that the positive symptom subtype of schizophrenia may have a biochemical basis, whereas the negative symptom subtype may be based on structural abnormalities in the brain (Holmes, 1991).

The biological findings concerning schizophrenia are intriguing. However, more research is needed to confirm the findings and to establish precisely how the phenomena described relate to the symptoms of the disorder. Do they cause the disorder, for example, or are they caused by it? Moreover, future research is almost certain to reveal other possible physiological bases for the complex disorders of schizophrenia.

Whatever the physiological vulnerability that places some people at risk for schizophrenia, there is strong evidence that it is influenced by genetic factors. First, schizophrenia is more prevalent in the relatives of schizophrenics. As noted earlier, the risk of developing schizophrenia is 1 to 2 percent in the general population. However, if one parent or a brother or sister (except an identical twin) has been diagnosed as schizophrenic, the risk rises tenfold (Gottesman, 1991). If both parents or an identical twin is schizophrenic, the risk increases dramatically to about 50 percent. Figure 16.26 shows a remarkable phenomenon, a set of identical quadruplets, all of whom developed schizophrenia.

One might argue that increased risk for schizophrenia results from highly similar disturbed environments shared by genetically identical twins, but that explanation is called into question by other findings from adoption studies. Children of nonschizophrenic biological parents who are adopted in infancy by parents who eventually become schizophrenic do *not* show an increased risk of developing the disorder. In contrast, children who have a schizophrenic biological parent but are raised by normal adoptive parents are as likely to develop schizophrenia as if they had remained with their biological parents (Gottesman, 1991). These findings all suggest the importance of genetic factors; but again, genetics do not by themselves account for the development of schizophrenia. If they did, the concordance rate in identical twins would be 100 percent, not 50 percent. Let us therefore consider other factors.

Intrapsychic Factors

Freud and other psychoanalytic thinkers viewed schizophrenia as a retreat from unbearable stress and conflict. For Freud, schizophrenia represented the ultimate example of the defense mechanism of **regression,** in which a person retreats to an earlier and more secure stage of psychosocial development in the face of overwhelming anxiety and in the absence of more mature defenses to cope with it. He viewed schizophrenia as a regression back to the oral stage of infantile development, where hallucinations and delusions represent the unchecked activities of the id (see Figure 16.27). Other psychoanalysts, focusing on the interpersonal withdrawal that is an important feature of schizophrenia, view the disorder as a retreat from an interpersonal world that has become too stressful to deal with. Thus, psychodynamic theories view schizophrenia as a break with a reality that has become terrifying because it arouses powerful unresolved conflicts from childhood that the ego cannot handle. The ego therefore begins to disintegrate and retreats to an infantile level of development.

Environmental Factors

As intrapsychic theories would suggest, stressful life events seem to play an important role in the emergence of schizophrenic behavior. These events tend to cluster in the 2 or 3 weeks preceding the ''break,'' when the acute signs of the disorder appear (Day & others, 1987). Stressful life events seem to interact with vulnerability factors, which may have a biological or an intrapsychic basis. A highly vulnerable person may require little in the way of life stress to reach the breaking point (Fowles, 1992).

The family has been the target of much speculation concerning the origins of schizophrenia, and there has been a long search for parent or family characteristics that might define the **schizophrenogenic family.** It has been difficult to find a family pattern that causes schizophrenia, however, as we might expect on the basis of the finding, discussed earlier, that children of biologically normal parents who are raised by schizophrenic adoptive parents do

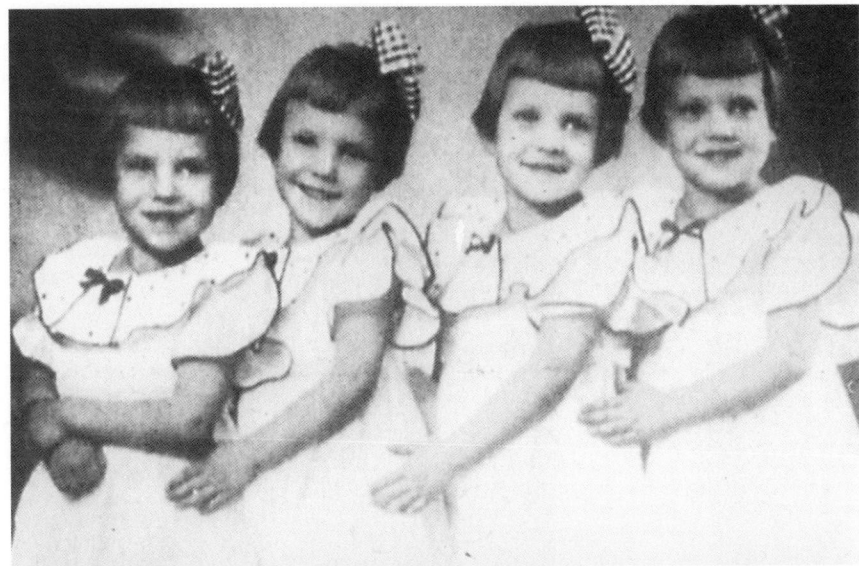

⬆ **Figure 16.26** *The Genain quadruplets, whose family tree contained several disordered people, all developed schizophrenia during their adolescent and young adult years. They have been studied for most of their adult lives at the National Institute of Mental Health. The quadruplets show remarkable similarities in abnormal brain functioning and in their patterns of behavior. (National Institute of Mental Health).*

not show an increased risk of developing schizophrenia. Although persons with schizophrenia often come from families with problems, the nature and seriousness of those problems are not different from those of families in which nonschizophrenics are raised. This does not mean that family dynamics are not important; rather, it may mean that a biological vulnerability factor must be present in order for stressful familial events to cause their damage.

Recently, researchers have identified a family pattern termed **negative expressed emotion** that seems to promote relapse in formerly hospitalized schizophrenics who return home. Families high in negative expressed emotion make critical comments about the

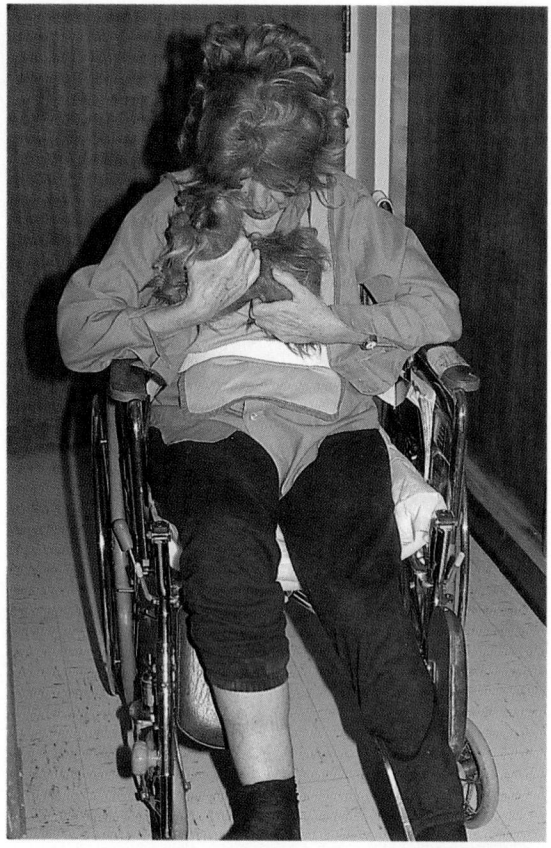

patient and one another, express strong hostility toward the patient for what he or she *is* rather than what he or she does, and tend to be intrusively overinvolved in the patient's life (Leff & Vaughn, 1985). As one parent said, ''I've tried to jolly him out of it and pestered him into doing things. Maybe I've overdone it, I don't know'' (Hooley, 1985, p. 134). Expressed emotion can be reliably rated during visits with the family. Patients who return to homes that are rated as high in negative expressed emotion are 5 times more likely to suffer a relapse and be rehospitalized (Hogarty & others, 1986; Leff & Vaughn, 1985).

Cognitive Factors

Cognitive theorists have focused on the thought disorder and other cognitive impairments that are a central feature of schizophrenia. Many of these theorists believe that schizophrenics have a defect in the attentional mechanism that filters out irrelevant stimuli, so that they are overwhelmed by both internal and external stimuli. Thus, sensory imput becomes a chaotic flood, and irrelevant thoughts and images flash into consciousness. The stimulus overload produces distractability, thought disorganization, and the sense of being overwhelmed by disconnected thoughts and ideas. As one schizophrenic noted, ''everything seems to come pouring in at once . . . I can't seem to keep anything out'' (Carson & others, 1988, p. 329).

Schizophrenics may respond to their disorganized cognitive world either by attending to nothing at all or by focusing their attention totally on one stimulus (perhaps an image that becomes a hallucination) to the exclusion of all others. Likewise, their language can become incomprehensible because they cannot focus their attention and therefore spin off on new thoughts before they finish communicating the previous ones. The stream of language often seems to reflect word associations that are based on rhymes or other associations rather than meaning. Consider the following conversation between a psychologist and a hospitalized schizophrenic:

> After two weeks, the psychologist said to him: ''You hide a lot. As you say, you are wired precisely wrong. But why won't you let me see the diagram?''
>   Carl answered: ''Never, ever will you find the lever, the eternalever that will sever me forever with my real, seal, deal, heel. It is not on my shoe, not even on the sole. It walks away'' (Rosenhan & Seligman, 1989, p. 369).

Schizophrenia is a broad and complex disorder that seems to involve disruptions of biological functioning, cognitive processes, intrapsychic functioning, and environmental events. None of these classes of causal agents can account for all of the dimensions of this perplexing disorder. Taken together, however, they help us to organize the many factors that may contribute to an understanding of schizophrenia. These factors are summarized in the accompanying Understanding Causes feature.

Personality Disorders

Chapter 15 stressed the importance of flexibility in coping with environmental demands. **Personality disorders** represent inflexible and maladaptive ways of thinking, feeling, and behaving. People with personality disorders tend to cope with the environment through inappropriately rigid and uniformly applied strategies that have marked their adjustment patterns over a long period of time. The inflexibility of people with personality disorders results in difficulties in situations that require behaviors other than their favored ones. A person cannot always be dependent, self-centered, aggressive, or suspicious without encountering difficulties. When people with disorders characterized by such traits are faced with situations in which their typical behavior patterns do not work, unresolved conflicts tend to reemerge, they are likely to intensify their inappropriate ways of coping, and

Causal Factors

Biological
- Genetically based vulnerability factor
- Overactivity of the dopamine neurotransmitter system
- Possible cortical atrophy, producing negative symptoms

Cognitive
- Defect in attentional filter, producing overstimulation and thought disorder

Schizophrenia

Intrapsychic
- Severe regression to an early stage of psychological development in response to severe anxiety
- Interpersonal withdrawal from a traumatic social environment

Environmental
- Stressful life events in period preceding schizophrenic break
- Family pattern of expressed negative affect
- Possible traumatic early family experiences and social rejection

Schizophrenia is a function of interacting personal and environmental causal factors. These factors may vary and may interact with one another in particular ways, depending on the person and the situation.

Table 16.5 The DSM Axis II Personality Disorders and Their Major Features

DSM Axis II Personality Disorder	Major Characteristics
Paranoid Personality Disorder	An unwarranted tendency to interpret the behavior of other people as threatening, exploiting, or harmful
Schizoid Personality Disorder	Indifference to social relationships and a restricted range of experiencing and expressing emotions
Schizotypal Personality Disorder	Odd thoughts, appearance, and behavior and extreme discomfort in social situations
Antisocial Personality Disorder	Severe irresponsible and antisocial behavior beginning in childhood and continuing past age 18
Borderline Personality Disorder	Pattern of severe instability of self-image, interpersonal relationships, and mood
Histrionic Personality Disorder	Excessive emotional reactions and attention seeking
Narcissistic Personality Disorder	Grandiose fantasies or behavior, lack of empathy, and oversensitivity to evaluation
Avoidant Personality Disorder	Extreme social discomfort and timidity
Dependent Personality Disorder	Extreme submissive and dependent behavior
Obsessive–Compulsive Personality Disorder	Extreme perfectionism and inflexibility
Passive–Aggressive Personality Disorder	Indirect aggression toward others

their emotional controls may break down (Millon & Everly, 1985).

Table 16.5 briefly describes the personality disorders categorized in Axis II of the DSM. We concentrate here on two disorders that are currently receiving considerable attention, namely, the borderline and antisocial disorders.

Borderline Personality Disorder

The borderline personality disorder has become the focus of intense interest among clinical researchers because of its chaotic effects on those who suffer from the disorder, their families, and their therapists. The disorder may occur in 3 to 5 percent of the general population (Clarkin & others, 1992; Frances & Widiger, 1986). About two thirds of those diagnosed are women.

Before 1980, the term *borderline* referred to an intermediate level of disturbance between neurotic and psychotic. Now, however, **borderline personality disorder** refers to a collection of symptoms characterized primarily by serious instability in behavior, emotion, identity, and interpersonal relationships. Borderline individuals have intense and unstable personal relationships and experience chronic feelings of intense anger, loneliness, and emptiness, as well as momentary losses of personal identity. They are inclined to engage in impulsive behavior such as running away, promiscuity, binge eating, and drug abuse, and their lives are often marked by re-

petitive self-destructive behaviors, such as suicide attempts that seem designed to call forth a "saving" response from other people in their lives (see Figure 16.28).

The complex nature of the borderline disorder is shown in the following case:

A 27-year-old woman was married and had two small children. She had had a stormy adolescence, having been forced into sexual relations with a brother 6 years her senior whom she at first idolized and later feared. Their relationship continued until just before she left home for college, when she told her parents of it. In the ensuing emotional turmoil, she made a gesture of suicide (overdose of aspirin) but was not hospitalized. . . . Outwardly flirtatious, although inwardly shy and ill at ease, she felt intensely lonely and went through a period of mild alcohol abuse and brief sexual affairs in an effort to cope with her anxiety and sense of inner emptiness. At age 19, she married a classmate and dropped out of school.

Fairly at ease in the first years of her marriage, she became anxious, bored, and given to fits of sadness and tearfulness after the birth of her second child. Her mood fluctuated widely from hour to hour and day to day, but negative feelings were greatly intensified on the 3 or 4 days before her period. Her husband had grown less attentive as the family expanded, in response to which she became increasingly irritable, provocative, and at times abusive (smashing plates, hurling insults). Her husband began to carry on an extramarital relationship, which she eventually discovered. At that point, she became seriously depressed, lost sleep and appetite, began to abuse alcohol and sedatives, and made several gestures of suicide, including one instance of cutting her wrist. On two occasions she hid for several nights in motels without informing anyone where she was (Stone, 1986, p. 210).

Borderlines tend to have chaotic personal histories marked by interpersonal strife, abuse, and inconsistent parenting. This history is sometimes reflected in their earliest memories. In one study, borderlines and normals were asked to describe their earliest memories in life. When the researchers analyzed the content of the memory reports, they found that the borderlines reported significantly more events in which someone had treated them in a malevolent manner or had injured them emotionally or physically (see Figure 16.29). They also viewed potential helpers as far less helpful (Nigg & others, 1992).

The chaos that marks the lives of borderline patients extends to their relationships with their psychotherapists. They are considered among the most difficult clients to treat because of their clinging dependency, their irrational anger, and their tendency to engage in manipulative suicide threats and gestures. Many borderline individuals eventually do kill themselves, either by miscalculation or by design (Linehan & others, 1991).

Antisocial Personality Disorder

The antisocial pattern is the most widely studied of the personality disorders. In the past, individuals with this disorder have been referred to as *psychopaths* or *sociopaths,* and they are among the most interpersonally destructive and emotionally harmful individuals in our society. Males outnumber females three to one in this group.

Perhaps the most notable symptom of the **antisocial disorder** is a lack of anxiety and guilt. Antisocial personalities are often said to lack a conscience and to have a predatory attitude toward others. Because they do not have the restraints that are typically provided by guilt and anxiety, antisocial people tend to be impulsive and unable or unwilling to delay gratification of their needs.

Another central characteristic of antisocials is a shallowness of feelings and a lack of emotional attachments to other people. Although antisocial individuals often verbalize feelings and commitments, their behaviors indicate otherwise (see Figure 16.30). They often appear to be very intelligent, and they tend to have well-developed verbal and social skills, as well as the ability to rationalize their inappropriate behavior so that it appears reasonable and justifiable. Because of these abilities, they are often able to talk their way out of trouble. One researcher who wanted

Figure 16.28 *The character Alex (played by Glenn Close) in the movie* Fatal Attraction *exhibited many features of a severe borderline personality disorder.*

to study antisocial personalities attracted them with the following classified ad:

Wanted: Charming, aggressive, carefree people who are impulsively irresponsible but are good at handling people and at looking after number one. Send name, address, phone, and short biography proving how interesting you are to. . . (Widom, 1983, page 72).

A final characteristic of people with antisocial personalities is their perplexing failure to profit from punishment. Probably because of their lack of anxi-

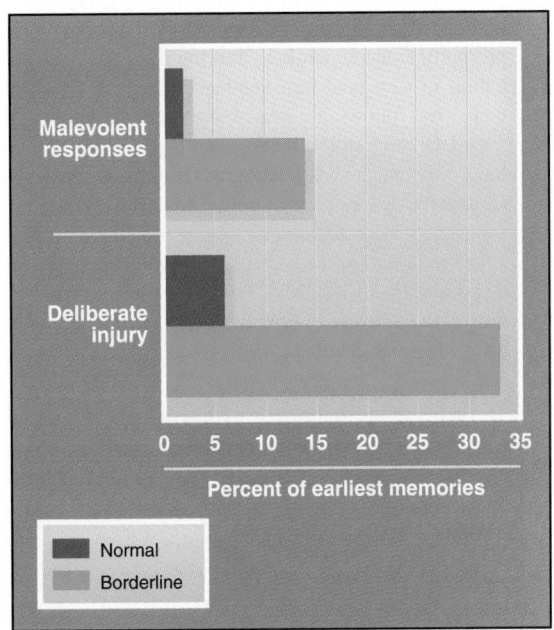

Figure 16.29 *Percentage of earliest memories of borderline disordered and normal subjects that contained themes of malevolent responses from others or behaviors by others that inflicted deliberate emotional or physical injury on the subjects. (Data from Nigg & others, 1992).*

Figure 16.30 *The mass murderer Theodore Bundy exhibited many features of the antisocial personality, including a charismatic personality and an ability to injure others without remorse or guilt.*

ety, these individuals are not deterred by punishment from engaging in self-defeating or illegal acts again and again. In addition, their lack of anxiety and guilt increases the likelihood that they will carry out impulsive and seemingly senseless acts. This pattern was illustrated in the case of Gary Gilmore, who was diagnosed as having an antisocial personality disorder prior to his execution in 1977.

> Gilmore had been released from prison only six months earlier, after serving time for armed robbery. He promptly violated parole by leaving the state. His probation officer gave him another chance. But shortly thereafter, following a heated argument with his girlfriend, Gilmore stole a stereo. Once again, he persuaded the police not to bring charges. Gilmore himself described the next events: ''I pulled up near a gas station. I told the service station guy to give me all his money. I then took him to the bathroom and told him to kneel down and then I shot him in the head twice. The guy didn't give me any trouble but I just felt like I had to do it'' (Spitzer & others, 1983, p. 68).

In order to be diagnosed as having an antisocial personality disorder, a person must be at least 18 years of age. However, the diagnostic criteria also require substantial evidence of antisocial behavior before the age of 15, including such acts as habitual lying, early and aggressive sexual behavior, excessive drinking, theft, vandalism, and chronic rule violation at home and school.

Causal Factors in Personality Disorders

Because the personality disorders are relatively new to the DSM, researchers know less about what factors may cause them than about causal factors in some other disorders. The greatest amount of research has been done on the antisocial personality disorder, which has been studied for many years under its former name, psychopathy. We therefore focus on this disorder to illustrate the interaction of biological and psychological factors.

Biological Factors

Biological research on the antisocial personality disorder has focused on both genetic and physiological factors that may underlie the maladaptive behavioral pattern. The genetic studies have focused on concordance rates for criminal behavior among identical twins and fraternal twins. Consistently higher rates of concordance have been found among identical twins (Holmes, 1991). In one study, a concordance rate of 69 percent for criminality was found in 216 monozygotic pairs, compared with a 33 percent concordance rate among 214 dizygotic pairs (Christiansen, 1977).

Another set of studies focused on children who had been adopted at an early age. The criminal records of adopted children were compared with those of both their biological parents and their adoptive parents. The sons of biological fathers who had no record of criminal behavior showed a low incidence of criminal behavior themselves, regardless of whether their adoptive fathers were criminal offenders. The criminal rate was nearly double for the sons of biological fathers who had criminal records and adoptive fathers who did not, clearly suggesting the operation of genetic factors. However, the rate of criminality in the sons was even greater when both the biological and the adoptive fathers were criminals, underscoring the combined influence of heredity and environment on criminality. These sons probably inherited the tendency toward criminality from their biological fathers and learned criminal behaviors from their adoptive fathers (Cloninger & Gottesman, 1987).

How might genetic factors predispose individuals to engage in antisocial behavior? One clue might lie in the relative absence of anxiety and guilt that seems to underlie many of the behaviors in the antisocial disorder. Many researchers have suggested that the physiological basis for the disorder might lie in some dysfunction in brain structures that govern emotional arousal, resulting in a chronically unaroused state. Supporting this hypothesis is the finding that a substantial proportion of antisocial individuals have abnormal EEG patterns. Many of them show positive spiking in their brain waves—sudden and brief bursts of brain-wave activity thought to reflect a dysfunction in the brain's limbic system, which controls emotional regulation, particularly fear. Thus, dysfunctions in arousal and emotional regulation may underlie many of the phenomena observed in the antisocial personality disorder (Holmes, 1991; Rosenhan & Seligman, 1989).

Intrapsychic Factors

Traditional psychoanalytic theories have provided two explanations for the development of antisocial personality disorder. First, using Freud's structural model of personality, some theorists have suggested that persons with the disorder lack anxiety and guilt because they did not develop an adequate superego. In the absence of a well-developed superego, the restraints on the id are reduced, resulting in impulsive and hedonistic behavior. The failure to develop a strong superego is thought to be the result of inadequate identification with appropriate adult figures because these figures were either physically or psychologically unavailable.

Another psychoanalytic explanation suggests that the impulsive and hedonistic behaviors displayed by antisocial people are due to the fact that their psychological development has been arrested, or *fixated,* at an early stage of psychosexual development because their needs for love, support, and acceptance were not satisfied by their parents. From this perspective, the antisocial person, despite his or her smooth social veneer, is still psychologically an infant who cares only for instant gratification of needs.

Learning and Cognitive Factors

Learning explanations for the development of antisocial behaviors focus on classical conditioning, op- erant conditioning, and modeling. Where classical conditioning is concerned, it is suggested that persons with the disorder lack anxiety because their ability to develop classically conditioned emotional responses is somehow impaired. Thus, even when they are punished, they do not develop the conditioned fear responses that are assumed to make punishment work. In support of this hypothesis, a number of experiments have shown that individuals diagnosed as psychopaths show a marked deficit in their ability to learn avoidance responses when shock is used to punish incorrect responses on a learning task (Schachter & Latané, 1964). Cognitively, they fail to think about or anticipate the negative consequences of their acts, so that cognitive processes do not serve their normal inhibitory and control functions.

Modeling influences may also play an important role. Many studies have shown that antisocial individuals tend to come from homes in which parents exhibit a good deal of aggression and are quite inattentive to children's needs. This might furnish role models for both aggressive behavior and disregard for the needs of others, and these modeling influences could in turn influence the aggression and lack of concern for others that is so evident in the antisocial person's behavioral pattern (Bandura, 1986).

We have now examined a wide range of psychological disorders, all of which represent failures to adapt successfully to the demands of living. No mere descriptions can capture the pain, the loneliness, and the terror that these disorders can produce in their victims and in those who care about them. In the next chapter, we focus on what can be done to ease the suffering produced by psychological disorders.

S U M M A R Y

Historical Perspectives on Psychological Disorders

- Psychological disorders have often been attributed to demonic possession or witchcraft. At various times throughout history, however, alternative explanations have been offered that are historical precursors to today's biological, psychodynamic, humanistic, behavioral and cognitive perspectives. The perceived causes of abnormal behavior have influenced the ways in which cultures have dealt with deviant behavior.

Defining and Classifying Abnormal Behavior

- Abnormality is largely a social judgment. Behavior that is judged to reflect a psychological disorder typically is (1) distressing to the person or to other people; (2) dysfunctional, maladaptive, or self-defeating; and (3) socially deviant in a way that arouses discomfort in others and cannot be attributed to environmental causes.
- The major psychiatric classification system in the United States is the DSM. The sys- tem has more than 200 specific diagnostic categories, and diagnosis involves five different axes: (1) the major disorder, (2) personality or developmental disorders that might also be present, (3) relevant physical disorders, (4) severity of psychosocial stressors, and (5) highest level of recent adaptive functioning.
- Among the important issues in psychiatric diagnosis that are currently being researched are the reliability and validity of the diagnostic categories and the potential negative effects of labeling on perceptions and self-perceptions.

Legal implications of competency and insanity judgments are also receiving attention.

Anxiety Disorders

● The anxiety disorders include phobic disorders (irrational fears of specific objects or situations), generalized anxiety disorder, panic disorder, and obsessive–compulsive disorder (which involves uncontrollable and unwelcome thoughts and repetitive behaviors).

● The biological perspective on anxiety focuses on the possible roles of genetic and biochemical factors in anxiety. At a biochemical level, some findings suggest that panic disorders may be different biochemically from other anxiety reactions and may be more strongly related to depression.

● Psychoanalytic theorists believe that anxiety results from the inability of the ego's defenses to deal with conflicts involving the id and the superego. Humanistic theorists focus on incongruities between the self and experience, as well as on the fears connected with taking responsibility for our lives.

● The cognitive perspective stresses the role of cognitive distortions, including the tendencies to magnify the degree of threat and danger and to misinterpret normal anxiety symptoms in ways that can evoke panic.

● The behavioral perspective views anxiety as a learned response established through classical conditioning or vicarious learning. The avoidance responses in phobias and compulsive disorders are seen as operant responses that are negatively reinforced through anxiety reduction.

Dissociative Disorders

● Dissociative disorders involve losses of memory and personal identity. The major dissociative disorders are psychogenic amnesia, psychogenic fugue, and multiple personality disorder.

Psychophysiological Disorders

● Psychophysiological disorders involve actual bodily damage that is caused or worsened by psychological factors.

● According to the diathesis–stress model, interactions between organic weaknesses and life stresses are causal factors in psychophys-

iological disorders. Peptic ulcers are an example of a disorder that has been interpreted within a diathesis–stress framework.

Depressive Disorders

● Depression has four sets of symptoms: emotional, motivational, cognitive, and somatic.

● Women have a much higher incidence of depression than men. Although depression is found in all age groups, including infants, a recent increase has been found in people under the age of 30.

● Both genetic and neurochemical factors have been linked to depression. One prominent biochemical theory links depression to underactivity of the biogenic amine neurotransmitters (norepinephrine, dopamine, and serotonin). Drugs that relieve depression increase the activity of these transmitters.

● Psychoanalytic theorists view depression as anger turned against the self in reaction to unresolved past losses.

● Cognitive theorists like Aaron Beck emphasize the cognitive triad (negative feelings about the self, the world, and the future), systematic errors in logic, and a depressive attributional pattern in which negative outcomes are attributed to personal causes and successes are attributed to situational causes. Seligman's theory of learned helplessness suggests that attributing negative outcomes to personal, stable, and global causes fosters depression.

● The behavioral approach focuses on the vicious cycle in which depression-induced inactivity and aversive behaviors reduce reinforcement from the environment and thereby increase depression still further.

● Surcease and manipulation are the two major motives for suicide. Suicide potential increases if the person has a lethal plan and a past history of parasuicide.

Schizophrenic Disorders

● Schizophrenia is a severe disorder featuring disordered thinking, poor contact with reality, flat or inappropriate emotion, and disordered behavior. The thought disorder often includes delusions (false beliefs) or hallucinations (false perceptions).

● Schizophrenias have been categorized in a number of ways. The DSM lists five subcat-

egories: paranoid, disorganized, catatonic, undifferentiated, and residual. Other categorizations relate to onset of symptoms (acute versus chronic) and nature of symptoms (positive versus negative). Acute onset and positive symptoms predict a better outcome.

● There is strong evidence for a genetic predisposition to schizophrenia that makes some people particularly vulnerable to stressful life events. The dopamine hypothesis states that schizophrenia involves overactivity of the dopamine system, resulting in too much stimulation.

● Psychoanalytic theorists regard schizophrenia as a profound regression to a primitive stage of psychosocial development.

● Stressful life events often precede a schizophrenic episode. Negative expressed emotion is a family variable related to relapse among formerly hospitalized schizophrenics.

● Cognitive theorists focus on the thought disorder that is central to schizophrenia. One idea is that schizophrenics have a defect in their attentional filters, so that they are overwhelmed by internal and external stimuli and become disorganized.

Personality Disorders

● Personality disorders are rigid, maladaptive patterns of behavior that characterize an individual's behavior over a long period of time. They fall on Axis II of the DSM.

● The borderline personality disorder features serious instability in behavior, emotions, interpersonal relations, and personal identity, as well as impulsive self-destructive behaviors. The antisocial personality disorder involves lack of caring for others, lack of negative emotions like anxiety and guilt, and the tendency to repeat destructive patterns of behavior because of impulsivity and failure to be inhibited by fear of punishment.

● Research on the antisocial disorder suggests that genetic and physiological factors that result in underarousal may contribute to the disorder's causes. Psychoanalysts view the disorder as a failure to develop a superego or as a fixation at an early childlike stage of development. Learning explanations focus on the failure of punishment to inhibit maladaptive behaviors and exposure to aggressive, uncaring models.

KEY TERMS AND CONCEPTS

abnormal behavior (p. 500)
acute (p. 522)
agoraphobia (p. 504)
antisocial disorder (p. 529)
anxiety disorders (p. 504)
axis (p. 501)
benzodiazapines (p. 507)
biogenic amine (p. 515)
bipolar disorder (p. 521)
borderline personality disorder (p. 528)
chronic (p. 522)
cognitive triad (p. 517)
competency (p. 503)
compulsion (p. 507)
conversion disorder (p. 511)
delusion (p. 522)
depressive attributional pattern (p. 517)
diathesis–stress model (p. 512)
dissociative disorder (p. 510)

dopamine hypothesis (p. 524)
DSM (p. 500)
generalized anxiety disorder (p. 506)
general paresis (p. 498)
hallucination (p. 522)
insanity (p. 503)
learned helplessness hypothesis (p. 518)
manipulation (p. 520)
MAO inhibitor (p. 515)
moral anxiety (p. 508)
multiple personality disorder (p. 510)
negative affectivity (p. 508)
negative expressed emotion (p. 525)
negative symptom (p. 523)
neurosis (p. 498)
neurotic anxiety (p. 508)
norm (p. 500)
objective anxiety (p. 508)
obsession (p. 507)

obsessive–compulsive disorder (p. 507)
panic disorder (p. 506)
parasuicide (p. 520)
personality disorder (p. 526)
phobia (p. 504)
positive symptom (p. 523)
psychogenic amnesia (p. 510)
psychogenic fugue (p. 510)
psychomotor retardation (p. 513)
psychophysiological disorder (p. 511)
psychosis (p. 498)
regression (p. 525)
residual rule (p. 500)
schizophrenia (p. 521)
schizophrenogenic family (p. 525)
surcease (p. 520)
trephination (p. 496)
tricyclic (p. 515)
ventricles (p. 523)

SUGGESTED READINGS

Craske, M. G., & Barlow, D. H. (1991). *Mastery of your anxiety and worry.* New York: Graywind Publications. Two of the leading researchers on the treatment of anxiety disorders describe a variety of cognitive–behavioral strategies for maladaptive anxiety problems, including phobias and panic.

Holmes, R. M., & DeBurger, J. (1987). *Serial murder.* Newbury Park, Calif.: Sage. A fascinating glimpse into the minds of people who are capable of committing mass murders and into the psychological disorders that enable them to do so.

Sarason, I. G., & Sarason, B. R. (1993). *Abnormal psychology: The problem of maladaptive behavior* (7th ed.). Englewood Cliffs, N.J.: Prentice-Hall. A classic textbook in abnormal psychology that presents an in-depth treatment of all of the major psychological disorders.

Sheehan, S. (1982). *Is there no place on earth for me?* Boston: Houghton Mifflin. The poignant and tragic story of a woman who endured 17 years as a schizophrenic patient and underwent treatment in numerous mental health facilities.

17

Treatment of Psychological Disorders

■□

CHAPTER OUTLINE

I n this poignant account, written by a person who has suffered from schizophrenia for much of his life, we see that even in this most serious of all behavior disorders, humans can reach out and help one another.

I fought my way through Harvard in the midst of psychosis and "spaciness." . . . There is no doubt in my mind that therapy helped me get through school. My freshman year and the first half of my sophomore year (until my first hospitalization) I was involved in supportive therapies with two different therapists who seemed to offer day-to-day support that was well-intentioned but was not enough. It was the combination of support and learning to understand why I thought the way I did, why I felt so bad, that gave me the strength to finish school.

For so long I wondered why my therapist insisted on talking about my relationship with him. He was not my problem; the problem was my life—my past, my fears, what I was going to do tomorrow, how I would handle things, sometimes just how to survive. . . . I took a long time, but finally I saw why it was important to explore my relationship with my therapist—it was the first real relationship I had ever had: that is, the first I felt safe enough to invest myself in. I rationalized that it was all right because I would learn from this relationship how to relate to other people and maybe even one day leave behind the isolation of my own world. . . . I often felt at odds with my therapist until I could see that he was a real person and he related to me and I to him, not only as patient and therapist, but as human beings. Eventually I began to feel that I too was a person, not just an outsider looking in on the world.

Medication or superficial support is not a substitute for the feeling that one is understood by another human being. For me, the greatest gift came the day I realized that my therapist really had stood by me for years and that he would continue to stand by me and help me achieve what I wanted to achieve. With that realization, my viability as a person began to grow. I do not profess to be cured—I still feel the pain, fear, and frustration of my illness. I know I have a long road ahead of me, but I can honestly say that I am no longer without hope ("A Recovering Patient," 1986, pp. 68–70).

This chapter explores the many approaches that are being taken to treat psychological disorders. It is concerned not only with a description of the various therapeutic approaches but also with the critical issue of their effectiveness. Although first-person reports like that offered by the "recovering patient" suggest that many people derive considerable benefit from psychotherapy, psychologists demand much more in the way of evidence. Nearly 40 years of research on psychological treatments, using increasingly sophisticated research methodologies, have taught us that the question of efficacy is a tremendously complex one that has no simple answers. Yet, as we shall see,

much has been learned about the effectiveness of these various therapeutic approaches and about some of the factors that influence treatment outcome.

The Helping Relationship

The basic goal of all treatment approaches is to help people change maladaptive, self-defeating thoughts, feelings, and behavior patterns so that they can live happier and more productive lives. Although this goal may be approached in a wide variety of ways, the common core of psychological treatment is a helping relationship between a *client* and a helping professional, or *therapist.* Most psychologists prefer the term *client* to the term *patient,* which connotes a person who is a passive recipient of treatment. In contrast, most forms of psychological treatment emphasize the role of the client as an active participant who has primary responsibility for the ultimate outcome of therapy.

As the remarks of the "recovering patient" suggest, the importance of the relationship between client and therapist cannot be overemphasized (Derlega & others, 1991; Teyber, 1992). Within that helping relationship, therapists use a variety of treatment techniques in an attempt to promote positive changes in the client. These techniques vary widely, depending on the therapists' own theories of cause and change, and they may range from biomedical approaches (such as administering psychoactive drugs) to a wide range of psychological treatments. Thus, the treatment of psychological disorders combines a special and often intense interpersonal relationship between client and therapist with a set of therapeutic procedures designed to promote specific kinds of changes in the client. Both of these elements, relationship and techniques, are important to the success of the treatment enterprise (see Figure 17.1).

Research suggests that a majority of people with mental health problems first seek help not from mental

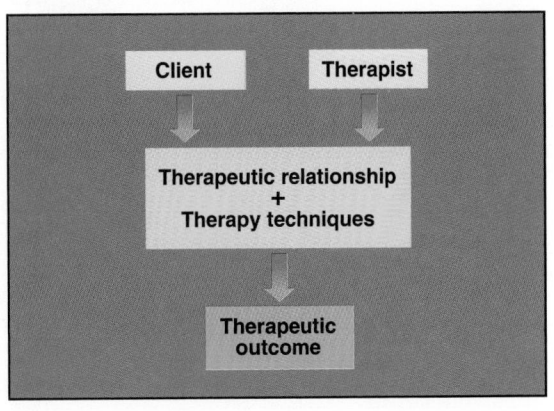

Figure 17.1 *The process of therapy involves a relationship between a client and a therapist, who applies the techniques dictated by his or her approach to treatment.*

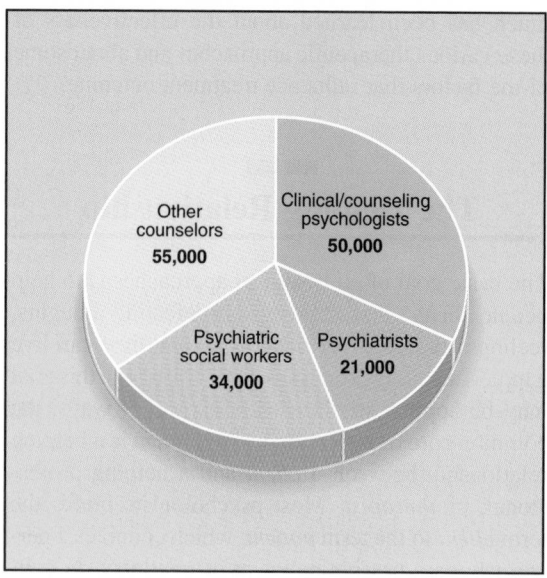

◗ **Figure 17.2** *Estimated numbers of psychologists, psychiatrists, psychiatric social workers, and other counselors who provide psychotherapy in the United States. (Data from Hunt, 1987).*

Other counselors
55,000

Clinical/counseling psychologists
50,000

Psychiatric social workers
34,000

Psychiatrists
21,000

percent of Americans have sought psychological counseling from professionals at some point in their lives, a dramatic rise from the 13 percent who had done so in the mid-1950s (Meredith, 1986). These people receive treatment from more than 150,000 mental health professionals (see Figure 17.2).

Mental health professionals fall into several categories. Counseling and clinical psychologists make up one group. These psychologists have received 5 or more years of intensive training and supervision in a variety of psychotherapeutic techniques as well as training in research and psychological assessment techniques. Mental health services are also provided by psychiatrists, medical doctors who specialize in psychotherapy and in drug therapy and other medically oriented treatments. In addition to psychologists and psychiatrists, a number of other professionals provide treatment. These include psychiatric social workers, who often work in community agencies; marriage and family counselors, who specialize in problems arising from family relations; pastoral counselors, who tend to focus on spiritual issues; and abuse counselors, who work with substance and sexual abusers and their victims. These professionals typically receive master's degrees based on 2 years of highly focused and practical experience.

health professionals but from family members, physicians, acquaintances, and members of the clergy. In recent years, self-help groups that address particular problems, such as bereavement, sexual victimization, and addictive behaviors, have become increasingly widespread. It is estimated that nearly 7 million Americans participate in such groups (Jacobs & Goodman, 1989).

Often, these sources of psychological support are not enough, and to an increasing degree, distressed people are seeking help from professional counselors and therapists. Recent surveys indicate that nearly 30

Having briefly reviewed the nature of therapy and the cast of characters who provide it, we now consider the therapeutic approaches that have developed within the major perspectives on human behavior. Figure 17.3 provides an overview of the therapies we will consider.

◗ **Figure 17.3** *An overview of the major treatment approaches to the behavior disorders, organized according to the five major perspectives on behavior.*

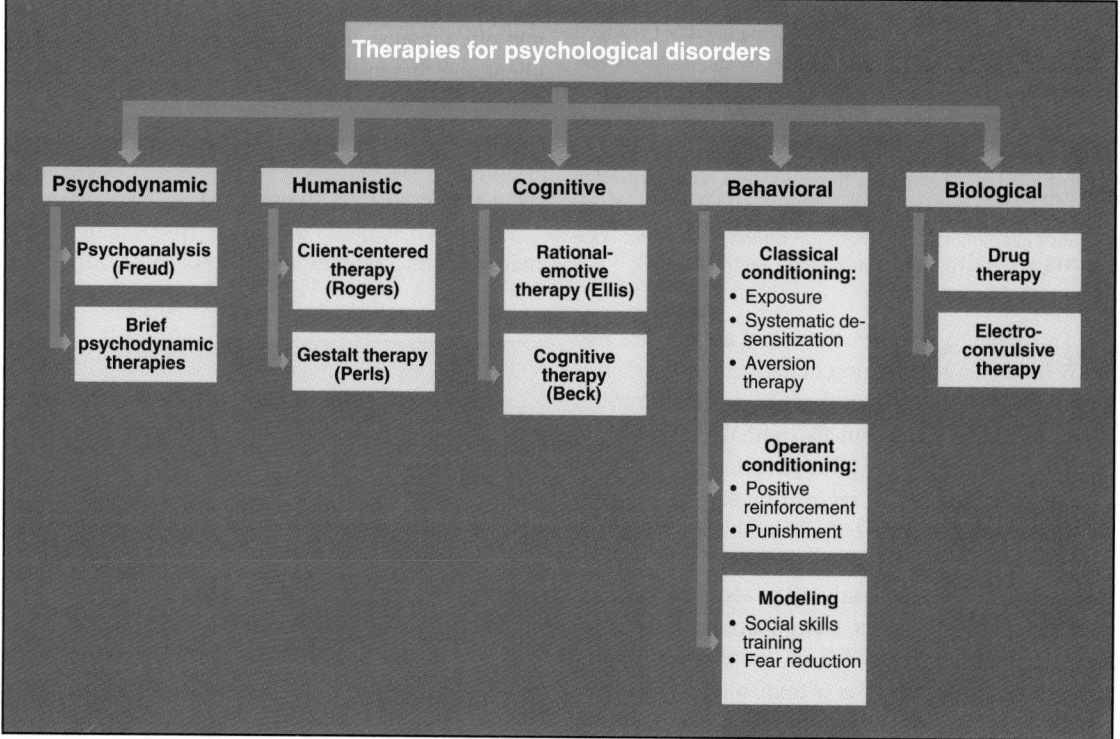

Therapies for psychological disorders

Psychodynamic
- Psychoanalysis (Freud)
- Brief psychodynamic therapies

Humanistic
- Client-centered therapy (Rogers)
- Gestalt therapy (Perls)

Cognitive
- Rational-emotive therapy (Ellis)
- Cognitive therapy (Beck)

Behavioral
- Classical conditioning:
  • Exposure
  • Systematic de-sensitization
  • Aversion therapy
- Operant conditioning:
  • Positive reinforcement
  • Punishment
- Modeling
  • Social skills training
  • Fear reduction

Biological
- Drug therapy
- Electro-convulsive therapy

Psychodynamic Psychotherapies

The psychodynamic approach to psychotherapy focuses on internal conflicts and unconscious factors that underlie maladaptive behavior. Although there are many different psychodynamic therapies today, the historical roots of psychodynamic approaches are to be found in Sigmund Freud's development of psychoanalysis. The term *psychoanalysis* refers not only to the theory of personality developed by Freud but also to the specific approach to treatment that he developed. Although both the theory and the techniques of therapy were later modified both by his followers and by those who defected to pursue rival approaches, the psychodynamic principles underlying Freud's approach continue to exert a major influence even today.

Psychoanalysis

Psychoanalysis developed out of Freud's medical practice, where he began to treat patients who suffered from conversion disorders—paralysis and other physical symptoms that had no physical basis. Freud became convinced that not only conversion symptoms but all maladaptive ways of dealing with impulses and with significant others were reflections of neurotic conflicts learned primarily in childhood as a result of faulty interactions with parents and other adults. The goal of psychoanalysis is to help clients develop greater ego control through conscious awareness of, or **insight** into, the maladaptive patterns and their underlying dynamics. Such awareness permits the client to adjust his or her behavior more appropriately to the current situation, rather than continuing to repeat the old maladaptive routines learned in childhood. As the client repeatedly encounters, or **works through,** buried conflicts as they manifest themselves both in and outside of therapy, the psychic energy that was previously devoted to keeping the id–ego–superego conflicts under control can be released and redirected to more adaptive ways of living.

Free Association

Freud originally used hypnosis in an effort to help clients recapture and relive the traumatic experiences that fostered their problems. Eventually, Freud gave up hypnosis in favor of a new technique called **free association.** He believed that mental events are meaningfully associated with one another and that in the constant stream of thoughts, memories, images, and feelings we all experience, there are clues to the contents of the unconscious. Freud therefore asked his clients to recline on a couch and to verbally report all thoughts, feelings, or images that came to aware-

Figure 17.4 *In classical Freudian psychoanalysis the client reclines on a couch, with the analyst sitting out of the client's view.*

ness in an often-rambling stream of associations (see Figure 17.4). Freud sat out of sight behind the client. Because the influence of external factors was minimized, the client's thought processes were determined primarily by internal factors.

The analyst does not expect that free association will necessarily lead directly to unconscious material but rather that it will provide clues concerning important themes or issues. For example, a client's stream of thoughts may suddenly stop after she has mentioned her father, suggesting the possibility that she was approaching a "loaded" topic that activated repressive defenses.

Free association is also used as a method for the interpretation of dreams. As noted in Chapter 8, psychoanalysts believe that dreams express impulses, fantasies, and wishes that the client's defenses keep unconscious during waking hours. However, even in dreams, defenses usually disguise the threatening material to protect the dreamer from the anxiety that the material might evoke. In dream interpretation, the analyst tries to help the client search for the unconscious material contained in the dreams. One means of doing so is to ask the client to free-associate to each element of the dream and thus try to help the client arrive at an understanding of what the symbols in the dream really represent.

Resistance

Although the client has come to the therapist for help, the client also has a strong unconscious investment in maintaining the status quo. After all, the client's problems result from the fact that certain unconscious conflicts are so painful that he or she has resorted to maladaptive defensive patterns in order to deal with them. These defensive patterns emerge in the course of therapy as **resistance,** which involves largely unconscious maneuvers that hinder the process of therapy. Resistance may be manifested in many different ways. For example, a client may experience difficulty in free-associating, may ''forget about'' a therapy appointment, or may avoid talking about certain topics. Resistance is a sign that anxiety lurks nearby and that sensitive material is being approached. An important task of analysis is to explore the reasons for resistance, both to promote insight and to guard against the ultimate resistance: the client's decision to drop out of therapy prematurely.

Transference

As noted earlier, the analyst sits out of view of the client and reveals nothing to the client about himself or herself. Nonetheless, clients will eventually begin to project onto the ''blank screen'' of the therapist important characteristics and feelings related to their underlying conflicts. **Transference** occurs when the client begins to react in an irrational fashion to the analyst as if he or she were an important figure from the client's past life. Transference is one of the most important processes in psychoanalysis, and it takes two basic forms. *Positive transference* occurs when a client transfers feelings of intense affection or love to the analyst, whereas *negative transference* involves irrational expressions of anger, hatred, or disappointment. Trained analysts are prepared for such reactions, and they use them to help the client get in touch with repressed feelings and understand where the feelings come from and what they represent. Analysts believe that until transference reactions are analyzed and resolved, there can be no full resolution of the client's problems.

In the following excerpt from a psychoanalytic session, a client traces her transference reaction to its source and then recognizes the operation of similar reactions in other relationships. In the process, she stitches together a tangled web of feelings, memories, symbolic associations, and dream content.

> *Client:* I don't want to like you. I'd rather not like you.
>
> *Therapist:* I wonder why?
>
> *Client:* I feel I'll be hurt. Liking you will expose me to being hurt.
>
> *Therapist:* But how *do* you feel about me?
>
> *Client:* I don't know. I have conflicting emotions about you. Sometimes I like you too much and sometimes I get mad at you for no reason. I often can't think of you, even picture you. . . . Yes, I don't want to like you. If I do, I won't be able to help myself. I'll get hurt. But why do I feel or insist that I'm in love with you?

> *Therapist:* Are you?
>
> *Client:* Yes. And I feel so guilty and upset about it. At night I think of you and get sexual feelings and it frightens me.
>
> *Therapist:* Do I remind you of anyone?
>
> *Client:* Yes. (Pause) There are things about you that remind me of my brother. (Laughs) I realize this is silly.
>
> *Therapist:* MmHmm.
>
> *Client:* My brother Harry, the one I had the sex experiences with when I was little. He made me do things I didn't want to. I let him fool with me because he made me feel sorry for him.
>
> *Therapist:* Do you have any of the same feelings toward me?
>
> *Client:* It's not that I expect that anything will really happen, but I just don't want to have feelings for you. I never liked doctors or dentists, especially dentists. The other day I had to go to a dentist. My mind was filled with crazy thoughts.
>
> *Therapist:* MmHmm.
>
> *Client:* These crazy things come into my mind and make no sense. I made this dental appointment and I thought of the drill going into my tooth. Then I thought of the drill being an eggbeater. Later I went to the movies and in a cartoon I saw eggs. I didn't realize my attitude toward eggs has always been wrong. As a child my mother scolded me for frying eggs and burning them. Then the day before I went to the dentist, I got nervous. I then pictured eggs being cooked, and then I had a picture of a raw egg and realized the white of the egg looked like seminal fluid and I got sick. It's like this fluid can kill me. I remember my brother wanted to have sex with me when I was a child. He said he had this fluid in him and it would poison him if he didn't get it out. I let him fool with me. Then he told me about people putting it in their mouth. It disgusted me, made me sick. I have dreams of my mouth being smashed and my teeth falling out. The whole thing seems to be connected with sex.
>
> *Therapist:* But what about your feelings for me?
>
> *Client:* I know it's the same thing. I'm afraid of you taking advantage of me. If I tell you I like you, that means you'll make me do what *you* want.
>
> *Therapist:* Just like Harry made you do what he wanted.
>
> *Client:* Yes. I didn't want to let him do what he did, but I couldn't help myself. I hated myself. That's why. I know it now because there is no reason why I should feel you are the same way. That's why I act that way with other people too. . . . I don't like to have people get too close to me. I think wrong about that. When I was little my sister used to take advantage of me too. But the most of it was my brother. The whole thing is the same as happens with you. It's all so silly and wrong. You aren't my brother and the other people aren't my brother. I never saw the connection until now (Wolberg, 1967, pp. 660–661).

In this interchange, we see elements of both positive and negative transference based on an important past relationship. We also see a string of significant free associations to other events and objects that occur as the client focuses on her reactions to the analyst.

Interpretation

How can analysts help clients to detect and understand resistances, the meaning of dream symbols, and transference reactions? The analyst's chief therapeutic technique for these purposes is interpretation of the material the client presents. An **interpretation** is any statement by the therapist that has the intent or function of providing the client with new information. An interpretative statement confronts clients with something that they have not previously admitted into consciousness: "It's almost as if you're angry with me without realizing it."

Depth of interpretation refers to the psychological distance between the client's current awareness and the therapist's apparent awareness of what is occurring (Speisman, 1959). For example, an analyst might simply restate or clarify something the client has been saying. This would be a relatively shallow interpretation. At increasingly deeper levels, interpretations may also deal with recurrent patterns of behavior, with possible feelings underlying those behaviors, or even with the hypothesized unconscious conflict that is being defended against. The latter would be considered a "deep" interpretation. Offering deep interpretations is considered poor technique because, even if they are correct, they are so far removed from the client's current awareness that they cannot be informative or helpful. A general rule in psychoanalytic treatment is to interpret what is already near the surface. This is one reason why psychoanalysis may require years of treatment even after the analyst fully understands the causes of the client's problems. It is the client who must eventually arrive at the insights.

Brief Psychodynamic Therapies

Classical psychoanalysis, as practiced by Freud and by a relatively small number of contemporary analysts, is an expensive and time-consuming process. In classical psychoanalysis, it is not unusual for a client to be seen five times a week for 10 years or more. Many therapists consider this level of commitment both impractical and unnecessary. Their conclusion is supported by studies in which researchers and clients rated the degree of improvement at the end of therapy as a function of the total number of sessions. As Figure 17.5 indicates, most of the therapeutic effects occurred within 26 sessions.

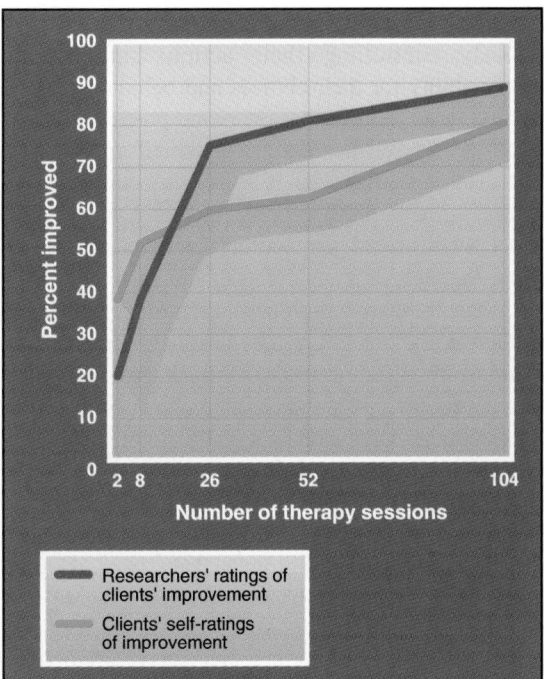

Figure 17.5 *Clients' improvement (based on researchers' and clients' ratings) in relation to the number of sessions of psychotherapy the clients received. These data suggest that most improvement occurs within the first 26 sessions. (Howard & others, 1986).*

Brief psychodynamic psychotherapies also emphasize understanding the maladaptive influences of the past and relating them to current patterns of self-defeating behavior. In these briefer therapies, the therapist and client are likely to sit facing one another, and conversation typically replaces free association. Clients are seen once or twice a week rather than daily, and the goal is typically limited to helping the client deal with specific life problems rather than attempting a complete rebuilding of the client's personality. Treatment may be completed within 30 sessions or less (Wells & Gianetti, 1990). Therapists also tend to take a much more active role, with greater emphasis on interpreting and providing encouragement and guidance. Moreover, the therapy is more likely to focus on the client's current life situations than on past childhood experiences; specifically, the therapy is likely to focus less on childhood sexual themes and more on how current deep-seated feelings of insecurity, inferiority, or anxiety create problems in relating to others and leading a productive life. Many of these brief therapies utilize basic concepts from psychoanalysis as well as many of the psychoanalytic methods just discussed, but they employ them in a more focused and active fashion (Garfield, 1989).

Humanistic Psychotherapies

In contrast to psychodynamic theorists, who view behavior as a product of unconscious processes, humanistic theorists view humans as capable of consciously controlling their actions and taking responsibility for their choices and behavior. These theorists also believe that everyone possesses inner resources for self-healing and personal growth and that disordered behavior reflects a blocking of the natural growth process. This blocking is brought about by distorted perceptions, lack of awareness about feelings, or a negative self-image.

When these assumptions about human nature are applied to psychotherapy, they inspire treatments that are radically different from psychoanalysis. Humanistic psychotherapy is seen as a human encounter between equals. The therapist's goal is to create an environment in which clients can engage in self-exploration, discover their true identities as people, and remove the barriers that block their natural tendencies toward personal growth. These barriers often result from childhood experiences that fostered unrealistic or maladaptive standards for self-worth. When people try to live their lives according to the expectations of others rather than in terms of their own desires and feelings, they often feel unfulfilled and empty, and unsure about who they really are as people.

In contrast to psychoanalytic therapies, humanistic approaches focus primarily on the present and future instead of the past. Therapy is directed at helping clients to become aware of feelings as they occur rather than to achieve insights into the childhood origins of the feelings.

▶ **Figure 17.6** *"Psychotherapy is the releasing of an already existing capacity in a potentially competent individual, not the expert manipulation of a more or less passive personality."—Carl Rogers*

Client-Centered Therapy

The best-known and most widely used form of humanistic therapy is the **client-centered** (now sometimes called *person-centered)* approach of Carl Rogers (1959, 1980), who is shown in Figure 17.6. In the 1940s, Rogers began to depart from psychoanalytic methods in favor of an approach that emphasized the client's own drive toward growth, or self-actualization. He became convinced that the important "active ingredient" in therapy is the relationship that exists between client and therapist, and he began to focus his attention on what kind of therapeutic environment seemed to be most effective in fostering self-exploration and personal growth. Rogers's experiences as a therapist convinced him that three important and interrelated attitudes on the part of the therapist were of critical importance. He termed them unconditional positive regard, empathy, and genuineness.

Unconditional positive regard is communicated when the therapist shows clients that he or she genuinely cares about them and accepts them as persons. The therapist expresses a willingness to listen to clients and to accept what is said, without judgment or evaluation. The therapist also communicates a sense of trust in clients' ability to work through their problems. In part, this sense of trust is communicated in the therapist's refusal to offer advice or guidance.

A second critical therapeutic attitude is **empathy.** The therapist must communicate to the client a willingness and ability to view the world through the client's eyes. In a good therapeutic relationship, the therapist comes to sense the feelings and meanings experienced by the client and communicates this understanding to the client. The therapist does this by **reflecting** back to the client what he or she is communicating—perhaps rephrasing something the client has just said in a way that captures the meaning and emotion involved.

The third important attribute is **genuineness.** There must be consistency between the way the therapist feels and the way he or she behaves. A therapist must be open enough to honestly express feelings, whether positive or negative. In the case of negative feelings, this may seem to be contradictory to the attribute of unconditional positive regard; but that is not necessarily the case. Indeed, the most striking demonstrations of both attributes occur when a therapist can express displeasure with a client's behavior while at the same time communicating acceptance of the client as a *person.* For example, a therapist might say, "I feel frustrated with the way you handled that situation because I want things to work out better than that for you."

When therapists can express these three critical therapeutic attributes, they create a situation in which the client feels accepted, understood, and free to explore basic attitudes and feelings without fear of being judged or rejected. Rogers believed that within such a relationship, clients experience the courage and freedom to grow.

In the following excerpt from one of Rogers's therapy sessions, the three therapeutic attitudes we have just discussed are exhibited:

Client: I cannot be the kind of person I want to be. I guess maybe I haven't the guts or the strength to kill myself, and if someone else would relieve me of the responsibility or I would be in an accident, I—just don't want to live.

Therapist: At the present time things look so black that you can't see much point in living. (Note the use of empathic reflection and the absence of any criticism.)

Client: Yes, I wish I'd never started this therapy. I was happy when I was living in my dream world. There I could be the kind of person I wanted to be. But now there is such a wide, wide gap between my ideal and what I am. . . . (Notice how the client responds to reflection with more information.)

Therapist: It's really tough digging into this like you are and at times the shelter of your dream world looks more attractive and comfortable. (Reflection.)

Client: My dream world or suicide. . . . So I don't see why I should waste your time—coming in twice a week—I'm not worth it—what do you think?

Therapist: It's up to you. . . . It isn't wasting my time. I'd be glad to see you whenever you come, but it's how you feel about it. . . . (Note the genuineness in stating an honest desire to see the client and the unconditional positive regard in trusting her capacity and responsibility for choice.)

Client: You're not going to suggest that I come in oftener? You're not alarmed and think I ought to come in every day until I get out of this?

Therapist: I believe you're able to make your own decision. I'll see you whenever you want to come. (Trust and positive regard.)

Client: (Note of awe in her voice.) I don't believe you are alarmed about—I see—I may be afraid of myself but you aren't afraid for me. (She experiences the therapist's confidence in her.)

Therapist: You say you may be afraid of yourself and are wondering why I don't seem to be afraid for you. (Reflection.)

Client: You have more confidence in me than I have. I'll see you next week, maybe. (Rogers, 1951, p. 49)

[The client did not attempt suicide.]

Rogers believes that as clients experience a constructive therapeutic relationship, they exhibit increased self-acceptance, greater self-awareness, enhanced self-reliance, increased comfort with other relationships, and improved life functioning. As we shall see, there is a substantial body of research evidence indicating that therapists' characteristics do indeed have a strong effect on the outcome of psychotherapy (Phares, 1992; Teyber, 1992). Therapy is most successful when the therapist is perceived as genuine, warm, and caring (Parloff & others, 1986; Strupp, 1989).

Gestalt Therapy

A far different humanistic approach to treatment was developed by Frederick S. (Fritz) Perls, a European psychoanalyst who was also trained in gestalt psychology (see Figure 17.7). As noted in Chapter 7, which discussed perception, the term *gestalt* ("organized whole") refers to perceptual principles through which people actively organize stimulus elements into meaningful "whole" patterns. Ordinarily, in whatever we perceive, whether external stimuli, ideas, or emotions, we concentrate on only part of our whole experience—the *figure*—while largely ignoring the background against which the figure appears. For people who have psychological difficulties, that background includes important feelings, wishes, and thoughts that are blocked from ordinary awareness because they would evoke anxiety. Like Rogers, Perls believed that people have an inherent tendency toward self-actualization but that they can be blocked from achieving their potential when they cut off important aspects of their experience.

Figure 17.7 *"If the patient can become truly aware at every instant of himself and his actions on whatever level—fantasy, verbal, or physical—he can see how he is producing his difficulties and he can solve them in the present, in the here and now."—Fritz Perls*

Gestalt therapy is often carried out in groups, and gestalt therapists have developed a variety of unconventional techniques to help clients get in touch with various aspects of themselves. In the *empty-chair technique,* for example, a client is asked to imagine that an empty chair nearby holds a significant person in his or her life. The client talks to this person, trying to express his or her innermost feelings. The client may then sit in the "empty" chair and act the part of the other person, perhaps gaining greater insight into how that other person experiences him or her. A client may also use the empty chair to talk to particular aspects of the self, perhaps a part that he or she is ashamed of. This may help the client to confront hidden feelings and accept these feelings as part of his or her total makeup.

Gestalt therapists also focus a great deal on "body language" to help clients get in touch with their feelings. For example, this client has just indicated that he is feeling angry, but he is not sure why.

Therapist: Will you address that resentment to somebody?

Client: Mother, I resent you . . . everything about you.

Therapist: Specify your resentment.

Client: I . . . I resent you for making me dependent on you.

Therapist: Tom, how is your voice?

Client: It's . . . it's a whine.

Therapist: Will you own your voice? Take responsibility?

Client: I . . . I'm whining . . . I'm whining.

Therapist: Do that. Whine to your mother, and experience yourself doing that.

Client: (Whining voice; reaching out with hands) Mother . . . please . . . please let me go . . . please turn me loose.

Therapist: Tom, how are your hands?

Client: What do you mean?

Therapist: As you whine to your mother again, try to develop an awareness of what you experience in your hands.

Client: (Hands are retroflected claws; implores) Mother, please let me go . . . please . . . please!

Therapist: Be your hands. Give your hands a voice and speak to her.

Client: (Leaves left hand palm up; turns right hand over in clawlike deportment; looks at hands) Mother . . . I'm . . . I need you, and I resent you. (Begins on own, clawing movements with right hand)

Therapist: Speak as your experience of your hands, and frame a statement of your existence.

Client: (Continues with left hand palm up, right hand in clawing motion) Mother . . . I . . . I need and want

support and control from you, but I resent you, and I'm clawing you.

Therapist: Tom, I don't hear you in your words. Will you change *but* to *and?*

Client: (Left hand in seeking attitude; right hand clawing) Mother . . . (a sob) . . . Mother . . . I need you (bursts into tears and sobs) . . . and I (screams) *resent you!!*

Therapist: Will you begin to specify your resentment?

Client: (With appropriate affect, begins enumerating resentments, appreciations, and regrets) (Dublin, 1976, pp. 139–140).

Gestalt therapists emphasize the humanistic value of being true to oneself and not abandoning one's own values and desires because of the "shoulds" imposed by others. Nowhere is this value (which some critics regard as selfish egocentrism) expressed more strongly than in Perls's memorable credo:

> I do my thing, and you do your thing. I am not in this world to live up to your expectations. And you are not in this world to live up to mine. You are you and I am I. And if by chance we find each other, it's beautiful. If not, it can't be helped (Perls, 1972, p. 70).

Despite their common commitment to humanistic principles, Rogers and Perls differed sharply in their attitudes toward doing research on humanistic therapies. Rogers was committed to research that would help identify the factors that contribute to therapeutic success, and he was a pioneer in tape-recording therapy sessions and analyzing them to study what went on in therapy. In contrast, Perls had a strongly anti-scientific attitude that kept him and his followers from doing systematic research on the effectiveness of gestalt therapy. As a result, the influence of the gestalt movement, despite the potentially powerful techniques that it inspired, seems to be waning.

Cognitive Therapies

Many behavior disorders involve maladaptive ways of thinking about oneself and the world. Cognitive approaches to psychotherapy focus on the role of irrational and self-defeating thought patterns, and therapists who employ this approach try to help clients discover and change the thinking that underlies their problems (Vallis & others, 1991).

In contrast to psychoanalysts, cognitive therapists do not emphasize the importance of unconscious psychodynamic processes. They do, however, point out that because our habitual thought patterns are so well practiced and ingrained, they tend to "run off" almost automatically, so that we may be only minimally aware of them and may simply accept them as reflecting "reality." Thus, clients often need help in identifying the beliefs, ideas, and self-statements that trigger maladaptive emotions and behaviors. Once identified, these cognitions can be challenged and, with practice and effort, changed.

Albert Ellis and Aaron Beck are the most influential figures in the cognitive approach to therapy. Originally trained as psychoanalytic therapists, both Ellis (a psychologist) and Beck (a psychiatrist) became disenchanted with the time-consuming process of analytic therapy and with what they regarded as disappointing results. In 1962, Ellis published a landmark book, *Reason and Emotion in Psychotherapy,* in which he identified a number of irrational ideas that cause emotional disturbance and advocated a therapeutic frontal assault on these cognitions. Some years later, Beck published *Cognitive Therapy and the Emotional Disorders* (1976), which outlined ways of changing the logical errors in thinking that characterize the thought patterns of clients suffering from depression and other forms of emotional disturbance. Beck's contributions to the treatment of depression have made his cognitive therapy the psychological treatment of choice for that disorder in the eyes of many clinicians. More recently, cognitive therapy has been extended to the treatment of anger and anxiety disorders, with equally encouraging results (Beck, 1988; Craske & others, 1991; Zinbarg & others, 1992).

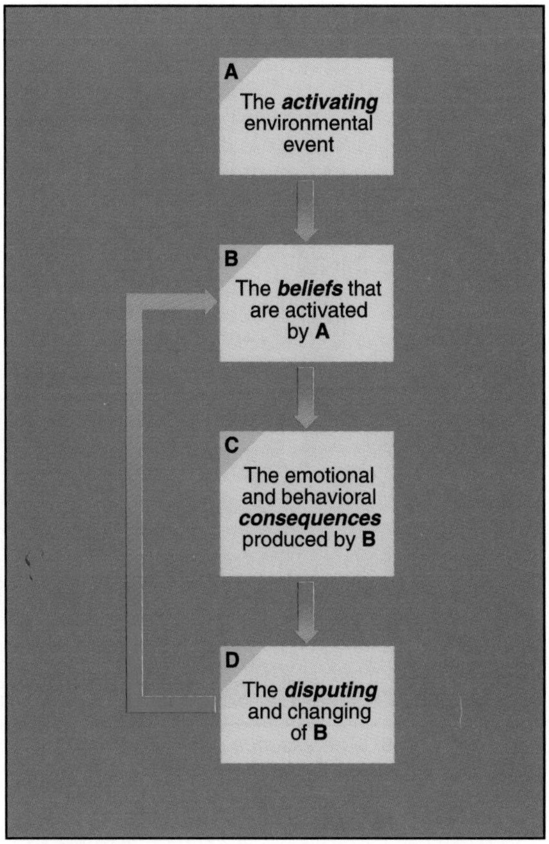

Ellis's Rational–Emotive Therapy

Ellis's theory of emotional disturbance and his **rational-emotive therapy** are embodied in his ABCD model (see Figure 17.8). As noted in Chapter 13, A stands for the *activating event.* B stands for the *belief system* that underlies the way in which a person appraises the event. C stands for the emotional and behavioral *consequences* of that appraisal. Finally, D is the key to changing maladaptive emotions and behaviors: *disputing,* or challenging, an erroneous belief system.

Ellis points out that people are accustomed to viewing their emotions (Cs) as being caused directly by events (As). Thus, a young man who is turned down for a date may feel depressed and rejected. However, Ellis would insist that the woman's refusal is not the reason for the emotional reaction. Rather, that reaction is caused by the young man's belief that "in order to be a worthwhile person, I *must* be loved and accepted by virtually everyone, especially those I consider important." If the young man does not want to feel depressed and rejected, this irrational belief (irrational in the sense that we do not need to always be loved and accepted in order to be worth-

▲ **Figure 17.8** *Albert Ellis's ABCD model describes his theory of the cause—and cure—of maladaptive emotional responses and behaviors. In therapy, the goal is to discover, dispute, and change the client's maladaptive beliefs.*

while human beings) must be countered by a more rational interpretation (for example, "It would have been nice if she had accepted my invitation, but I don't need to turn it into a catastrophe or act as if no one will ever go out with me").

Ellis's confronting style, as well as the manner in which he ferrets out irrational elements of clients' thinking, are typified in the following exchange (see Figure 17.9). The client has just told Ellis that he is depressed because he doesn't have a purpose in life and that he sees no way out of his dilemma. Ellis attacks an irrational idea that underlies many instances of emotional disturbances: the belief that one *should, must,* or *ought to* be a certain way and that it is horrible and catastrophic if these *self-demands* are not met.

Therapist: You're perfectly able, as I said, to think—to stop giving up. That's what you've done most of your life; that's why you're disturbed. Because you refuse to think. And let's go over it again. . . .

Client: You mean, why do I feel that way?

Therapist: No, no. It's a belief. You feel that way because you believe that way.

Client: Yes.

Therapist: If you believed you were a kangaroo, you'd be hopping around, and you'd *feel* like a kangaroo.

Figure 17.9 *"The essence of effective therapy according to [rational–emotive therapy] is full tolerance of people* as individuals *combined with a ruthless campaign against their self-defeating ideas. . . . These can be easily elicited and demolished by any scientist worth his or her salt; and the rational–emotive therapist is exactly that: an exposing and nonsense-annihilating scientist."*—Albert Ellis

Whatever you *believe,* you feel. Now, I'm forgetting about your feelings, because we really can't change feelings without changing beliefs. So I'm showing you: you have two beliefs—or two feelings, if you want to call them that. One, "It would be better if I had a purpose in life." Do you agree? [Client nods] Now that's perfectly reasonable. That's quite true. We could prove it. Two, "Therefore, I *should* do what would be better." Now those are two different statements. They may seem the same, but they are vastly different. Now, the first one, as I said, is sane. Because we could prove it. It's related to reality. We can list the advantages of having a purpose—for almost anybody, not just for you.

Client: [calm now, and listening intently to T's explanation]: Uh-huh.

Therapist: But the second one, "therefore, I *should* do what would be better" is crazy. Now, why is it crazy?

Client: I can't accept it as a crazy statement.

Therapist: Because who said you *should?*

Client: I don't know where it all began! Somebody said it.

Therapist: I know, but I say that whoever said it was screwy!

Client: [laughs] All right.

Therapist: How could the world possibly have a *should?*

Client: Well, it does.

Therapist: But it *doesn't!* You see, that's what emotional disturbance is: believing in *shoulds, oughts,* and *musts* instead of *it would be betters.* That's exactly what makes people disturbed! (Ellis, 1979, p. 208).

The rational–emotive therapist introduces the client to common irrational ideas (see Table 17.1) and then trains the client to ferret out the irrational ideas that underlie his or her maladaptive emotional responses. One approach is for the client to stop when becoming upset and say, "*I* am creating this upset. What must I be telling myself in order to make myself feel this way?" With the therapist's assistance, the client learns to logically challenge irrational ideas and develop rational alternatives. These alternatives can be used to prevent or control maladaptive responses the next time an activating event occurs. An example of a rational alternative might be: "I may not like this situation, but I can definitely stand it even if I can't change it. No sense upsetting myself."

Clients are given homework assignments in analyzing and changing self-statements. They are also required to place themselves in difficult situations and practice control over their emotions by using the new self-statements. For example, a shy person might be required to go to a party. By learning and practicing cognitive coping responses, clients eventually modify underlying belief systems in ways that facilitate adjustment.

Beck's Cognitive Therapy

As a therapist, Beck is more gentle and less confronting than Ellis (see Figure 17.10). Yet the goal of his **cognitive therapy** is the same: to point out errors of thinking and logic that underlie emotional disturbance, such as those discussed in Chapter 16 (see Table 16.3, page 517), and to help clients identify and reprogram their overlearned "automatic" thought patterns. In treating depressed clients, a first step is to identify the thoughts that trigger depression, as in the following example:

A mother of three reported that her depression was at its worst at breakfast time each morning as she was preparing breakfast for her children. She was unable to explain this until she was taught to record her thoughts in writing as they occurred. As a result, she discovered that she consistently compared herself with her mother, whom she remembered as irritable and argumentative in the morning. When her children misbehaved or made unreasonable requests, the patient often thought,

Table 17.1 Some Irrational Ideas that Cause Disturbance, Together with the More Rational Alternatives that Might be Offered by a Rational-Emotive Therapist

Irrational Belief	Rational Alternative
It is a dire necessity that I be loved and approved of by virtually everyone for everything I do.	Although we might *prefer* approval to disapproval, our self-worth need not depend on the love and approval of others. Self-respect is more important than giving up one's individuality to buy the approval of others.
I must be thoroughly competent and achieving in order to be worthwhile. To fail is to be *a failure.*	As imperfect and fallible human beings, we are bound to fail from time to time. We can control only effort; we have incomplete control over outcome. We are better off focusing on the process of doing rather than on demands that we do well.
It is terrible, awful, and catastrophic when things are not the way I demand that they be.	Stop catastrophizing and turning an annoyance or irritation into a major crisis. Who are we to *demand* that things be different from what they are? When we turn our preferences into dire necessities, we set ourselves up for needless distress. We had best learn to change those things we can control and accept those that we can't control (and be wise enough to know the difference).
Human misery is externally caused and forced on one by other people and events.	Human misery is produced not by external factors but rather by what we tell ourselves about those events. We feel as we think, and most of our misery is needlessly self-inflicted by self-defeating thought patterns.
Because something deeply affected me in the past, it must continue to do so.	We hold ourselves prisoner to the past because we continue to believe philosophies and ideas learned in the past. If they are still troubling us today, it is because we are still propagandizing ourselves with irrational nonsense. We *can* control how we think in the here and now and thereby liberate ourselves from the "scars" of the past.

"Don't get angry, or they'll resent you," with the result that she typically ignored them. With increasing frequency, however, she "exploded" at the children and then thought, "I'm worse than my mother ever was. I'm not fit to care for my children. They'd be better off if I were dead" (Beck & others, 1979).

More recently, Beck's cognitive approach has been applied with considerable success to the treatment of anxiety-based disorders, including panic disorders (Michelson & Marchione, 1991). In one study, David Barlow and his colleagues (1989) applied cognitive therapy to attack the tendency of panic-disordered clients to "think themselves into" a true panic by misinterpreting ordinary anxiety cues as indications that a catastrophic and possibly fatal panic attack is about to occur. The clients were trained through cognitive therapy to stop catastrophizing and to tell themselves that they were simply experiencing anxiety. After 15 sessions, 85 percent of the treated clients were free of panic attacks over a 2-week period, compared with only 30 percent of clients in a control group for whom treatment was delayed. A recent 2-year follow-up indicated that the therapeutic gains had been largely maintained (Craske & others, 1991).

As research identifies the critical cognitive factors that frequently underlie clinical problems, cognitive therapy approaches are being developed for an in-

creasing range of behavior disorders. As we shall see, cognitive therapy is also being combined with other therapeutic techniques to form highly effective treatment "packages" that combine the benefits of various techniques (Hollon & others, 1991).

Figure 17.10 *"The formula for treatment may be stated in simple terms: The therapist helps the patient to identify his warped thinking and to learn more realistic ways to formulate his experience."—Aaron Beck*

Behavioral and Cognitive–Behavioral Therapies

In the 1960s, behavioral approaches emerged as a dramatic departure from the assumptions and methods that characterized psychoanalytic and humanistic approaches to psychotherapy. The new practitioners of **behavior therapy** denied the importance of inner dynamics. Instead, they insisted that (1) behavior disorders are basically learned patterns just as normal behaviors are, and (2) these maladaptive behaviors can be unlearned by application of principles derived from animal research on classical conditioning and operant conditioning. Behaviorists demonstrated that learning procedures derived from laboratory studies could indeed be applied to change the behaviors of schizophrenics, to effectively treat anxiety disorders, and to modify many child and adult behavior problems that seemed resistant to traditional therapy approaches.

By the early 1970s, a new revolution had overtaken the radical behaviorism of the 1960s as many behavior therapists began to incorporate cognitive concepts into their behavioral techniques (Mahoney, 1974). The contributions of Ellis and Beck, as well as the philosophical conviction that the human being is too complex and too cognitive to be regarded as a stimulus–response organism, resulted in the development of a **cognitive–behavioral approach.** This approach sought to retain the scientific rigor of radical behaviorism while broadening the focus of therapy to include not only externally observable behaviors but also internal responses such as thoughts and images. Today, the cognitive–behavioral approach is the dominant one among behavior therapists.

When we considered learning in Chapter 9, we focused on three important types of learning processes: classical conditioning, operant conditioning, and modeling. We now consider therapy techniques based on each of these forms of learning.

Classical Conditioning Procedures

Classical conditioning procedures have been used in two major ways. First, they have been used to reduce anxiety responses. Second, they have been used in attempts to establish an aversion to a particular class of stimuli, such as alcoholic beverages or inappropriate sexual objects. The most commonly used classical conditioning procedures are exposure therapies, systematic desensitization, and aversion therapy.

Exposure: (Flooding)

From a behavioral point of view, phobias and other fears result from classically conditioned emotional responses. The conditioning experience is assumed to involve a pairing of the phobic object with an aversive unconditioned stimulus (UCS). As a result, the phobic stimulus becomes a conditioned stimulus (CS) that elicits the conditioned response (CR) of anxiety. According to the two-factor learning theory discussed in Chapter 9, avoidance responses to the phobic situation are then reinforced by anxiety reduction (operant conditioning based on negative reinforcement). Thus, a person who is injured in an automobile accident may find herself afraid to ride in a car. Moreover, each time she avoids exposure to cars, her avoidance response is strengthened through anxiety reduction.

According to this formulation, the most effective way to reduce the fear is through a process of classical extinction of the anxiety response, which consists of exposing the client to the feared CS in the absence of the UCS while preventing the avoidance response from occurring. This is the theoretical basis for the **exposure** approach (Marks, 1991; Zinbarg & others, 1992). The client may be exposed to real-life stimuli or may be asked to imagine scenes involving the stimuli. These stimuli will, of course, evoke considerable anxiety, but the anxiety will extinguish in time if the person remains in the presence of the CS and the UCS does not occur. This therapeutic approach is sometimes termed **flooding,** since the client is "flooded" with anxiety-arousing stimuli and anxiety during the exposure.

Exposure has proved to be a highly effective technique for extinguishing anxiety responses in both animals and humans (Thyer & others, 1988). In one study, agoraphobics with multiple phobias were treated. The researchers used an exposure therapy that required the clients to confront feared situations such as driving alone and going into crowded shopping centers. Both before and after the exposure therapy, each client was assessed on a series of real-life performance tasks. For example, an agoraphobic who feared being in public might be asked to go and stand in a long check-out line in a crowded supermarket.

The results of the study are shown in Figure 17.11. Before treatment, the phobics were able to pass only 27 percent of the performance tasks. After treatment, they were able to perform 71 percent of the tasks. Moreover, this improvement was maintained at follow-ups ranging from 3 months to 2 years. Finally, the treatment effects generalized to transfer phobias—that is, phobias that were not directly treated (Williams & others, 1989). These are extremely encouraging results, since agoraphobics are difficult to treat with nonbehavioral methods. Moreover, there is considerable evidence that clients can administer exposure techniques to themselves, under a therapist's direction, with high success rates (Marks, 1991).

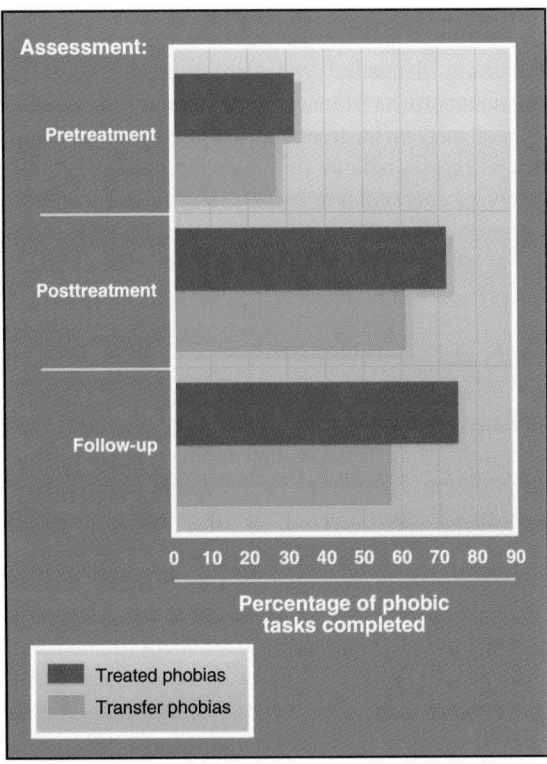

Assessment:

Pretreatment

Posttreatment

Follow-up

0 10 20 30 40 50 60 70 80 90

Percentage of phobic tasks completed

■ Treated phobias
▨ Transfer phobias

Figure 17.11 *Effects of exposure therapy on treated phobias and untreated (transfer) phobias in agoraphobics. Each subject suffered from an average of 10 phobias. Both treated and transfer phobias improved, and the improvement was maintained at follow-up. (Data from Williams & others, 1989).*

Although exposure techniques are quite effective in reducing anxiety, they do result in high levels of anxiety for the client during treatment. For this reason, before using exposure therapy, many behavior therapists prefer to try another deconditioning technique—systematic desensitization—which results in minimal anxiety during treatment.

Systematic Desensitization

In 1958, Joseph Wolpe published a highly influential book entitled *Psychotherapy by Reciprocal Inhibition.* In the book, Wolpe introduced a new learning-based treatment for anxiety disorders and presented impressive data on outcomes for 100 phobics he had treated with the technique. Within a decade, **systematic desensitization** became the most popular treatment for phobias and other anxiety-based disorders. It remains a widely used treatment today; and in many controlled studies, its success rate in treating a wide range of phobic disorders has been 80 percent or better (O'Leary & Wilson, 1987; Phares, 1992).

Wolpe viewed anxiety as a classically conditioned emotional response. His approach to treatment was to gradually expose clients to a *hierarchy* of stimuli—

that is, stimuli that are progressively more anxiety arousing. At the same time, he prevented anxiety from occurring by establishing an incompatible response, such as relaxation (hence the term *reciprocal inhibition*). In this way, the ability of the stimuli to evoke anxiety was gradually diminished. The procedure was based on the concept of **counterconditioning,** in which a new response is conditioned to the stimuli that formerly evoked an unwanted response.

The first step in systematic desensitization is usually to train the client in the skill of voluntary muscle relaxation, using an approach similar to that described in the Enhancing Human Performance feature of Chapter 15 (p. 490). Relaxation is incompatible with anxiety, so the client who can relax voluntarily can be exposed to anxiety-arousing stimuli without feeling anxious.

Next, the client is helped to construct a hierarchy of 10 to 15 scenes relating to the fear. The hierarchy is carefully arranged in roughly equal steps from low-anxiety scenes to high-anxiety ones. For example, a hierarchy for a person with a fear of heights might range from standing on a step stool to looking down from the top of a high building or walking across a wobbly suspension bridge above a deep canyon. A hierarchy that was used to desensitize a student having high test anxiety is presented in Table 17.2.

In the desensitization sessions, the therapist deeply relaxes the client and then asks the client to vividly imagine the first scene in the hierarchy (the least anxiety-arousing one) for several seconds. When the client can imagine that scene for increasingly longer periods without experiencing anxiety, the therapist proceeds to the next scene. The goal is to prevent anxiety from occurring and to countercondition relaxation to the stimulus cues.

Desensitization can also be accomplished through controlled exposure to a hierarchy of real-life situations (for example, actually standing on a step stool or walking across the suspension bridge while voluntarily relaxed). Many therapists prefer this approach, because it involves the actual stimuli of interest, whereas there is sometimes concern whether therapy effects based on imagined situations will generalize to real-life situations. On the other hand, the therapist has greater control over stimulus exposure in the imagery-based procedure and is better able to ensure that the client will not experience strong anxiety during the procedure. Both approaches to desensitization seem highly effective in reducing anxiety (Barlow, 1988).

Aversion Therapy

For some clients, the goal is not to reduce anxiety, but to actually condition it to a particular stimulus in order to reduce deviant approach behaviors. In

Table 17.2 A Stimulus Hierarchy Used in the Systematic Desensitization Treatment of a Highly Test-Anxious College Student

Scene 1.	Hearing about someone else who has a test.
Scene 2.	The instructor announcing that a test will be given in 3 weeks.
Scene 3.	Instructor reminding the class that there will be a test in 2 weeks.
Scene 4.	Overhearing classmates talk about studying for the test, which will occur in 1 week.
Scene 5.	Instructor reminding class of what it will be tested on in 2 days.
Scene 6.	Leaving class the day before the exam.
Scene 7.	Studying the night before the exam.
Scene 8.	Getting up the morning of the exam.
Scene 9.	Walking toward the building where the exam will be given.
Scene 10.	Walking into the testing room.
Scene 11.	Instructor walking into room with tests.
Scene 12.	Tests being passed out.
Scene 13.	Reading the test questions.
Scene 14.	Watching others finish the test.
Scene 15.	Seeing a question I can't answer.
Scene 16.	Instructor waiting for me to finish the test.

aversion therapy, a stimulus that is attractive to a person and stimulates deviant or self-defeating behavior (the CS) is paired with a noxious UCS in an attempt to condition an aversion to the CS. For example, aversion treatment for alcoholics may involve injecting the client with a nausea-producing drug (the UCS), then having him or her drink alcohol (the CS) as nausea (the UCR) develops. Similarly, pedophiles (child molesters) have undergone treatment in which strong electric shock is paired with slides showing children similar to those the offenders sexually abused (see Figure 17.12). Measures of penile blood volume in response to the slides can be compared before and after treatment to assess the treatment's effectiveness (Sandler, 1986). This is done by attaching a physiological recording device to the penis.

Aversion therapies have been applied with variable results to a range of disorders. In one study of 278 alcoholics who underwent aversion therapy, 190 (63 percent) were still abstinent a year after treatment had ended. Three years later, a third of the patients

were still abstinent, an impressive result given the traditionally high relapse rate in chronic alcoholics (Wiens & Menustik, 1983). Unfortunately, however, treatment effects from aversion therapies often fail to generalize from the treatment setting to the real world. Some experts believe that aversion therapy is most likely to succeed if it is part of a larger treatment program in which the client also learns coping skills for avoiding relapses (Marlatt & Gordon, 1985).

Operant Treatments

The term **behavior modification** refers to treatment techniques that involve the application of operant conditioning procedures in an attempt to increase or decrease a specific behavior. These techniques may use any of the operant procedures for manipulating the environment that were discussed in Chapter 9: positive reinforcement, extinction, negative reinforcement, or punishment. The focus in behavior modification is on externally observable behaviors, and measurement of the behaviors targeted for change occurs throughout the treatment program. This measurement allows the therapist to track the progress of the treatment program and to make modifications if behavior change begins to lag.

Behavior modification techniques have been successfully applied to many different behavior disorders, and they have yielded particularly impressive results when applied to populations that are difficult to treat with more traditional therapies, such as chronic hospitalized schizophrenics, profoundly disturbed children, and mentally retarded individuals. Here, we consider the use of positive reinforcement and punishment in two of these populations.

Positive Reinforcement

One of the dangers of long-term psychiatric hospitalization is the gradual loss of social, personal-care, and occupational skills needed to survive outside the hospital. Such deterioration is common among chronic schizophrenic patients who have been hospitalized for an extended period. Verbal psychotherapies have very limited effects in rebuilding such skills.

In the 1960s, Teodoro Ayllon and Nathan Azrin (1968) introduced the **token economy,** a revolutionary approach to the behavioral treatment of hospitalized schizophrenics. The token economy is a system for strengthening desired behaviors—such as personal grooming, appropriate social responses, housekeeping behaviors, working on assigned jobs, and participation in vocational training programs—through positive reinforcement. A specified number of plastic tokens is given for performance of each desired behavior. The tokens act as generalized reinforcers; they can be redeemed by the patients for a wide range of tangible reinforcers, such as a private room, exclusive rental of a radio or television set, selection of personal furniture, freedom to leave the ward and walk around the grounds, recreational activities, and items from the commissary, such as candy and cigarettes.

In the token economy that Ayllon and Azrin established at Anna State Hospital in southern Illinois, the tokens proved highly effective in increasing desired behaviors in patients who rarely performed them under normal circumstances. For example, Figure 17.13 shows how quickly the introduction of tokens increased work behavior on two jobs, one a preferred job and the other a nonpreferred job.

The long-term goal of token economy programs is to get the desired behaviors started with tangible reinforcers so that eventually they come under the control of social reinforcers and self-reinforcement processes, which will be needed to maintain them in the world outside the hospital. When this begins to occur, the tokens can be phased out (Kazdin, 1982).

Token economy programs are expensive to institute because of the training, time, and effort required in order for the hospital staff to observe and reinforce the actions of each patient. However, such programs have produced encouraging results in a number of studies. For example, one token economy program was carried out over a 4-year period with severely disturbed schizophrenic patients who had been hospitalized an average of more than 17 years. During the course of the program, 98 percent of the patients from the behavioral treatment program were able to be released from the hospital (most to shelter-care facilities in the community), compared with only 45 percent of a control group of similar patients who had received the normal hospital treatments (Paul & Lentz, 1977). These results indicate that positive reinforcement techniques can be an effective approach to treating even the most chronic and disordered clinical populations.

Therapeutic Use of Punishment

In the eyes of most psychologists, punishment is the most distasteful way to control behavior. Therefore, before using punishment therapeutically, they ask themselves two important questions: (1) Are there alternative, less painful approaches that might be effective? (2) Is the behavior to be eliminated sufficiently injurious to the individual or to society to justify the severity of the punishment?

Sometimes, the answers to these questions lead to a decision to use punishment. For example, some

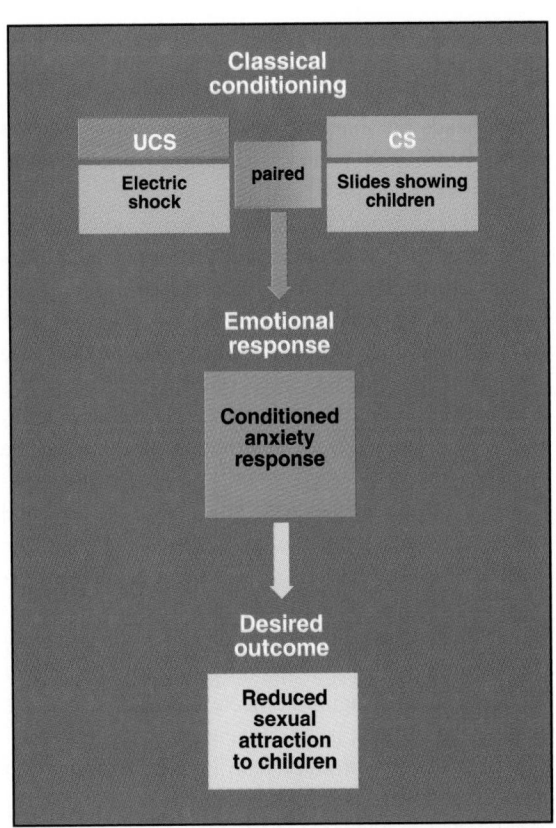

Figure 17.12 *The classical conditioning that occurs in aversion therapy is illustrated in the treatment of a pedophile who receives electric shocks when pictures of children are presented. The goal of the treatment is the development of a conditioned anxiety response that reduces the sexual attractiveness of children.*

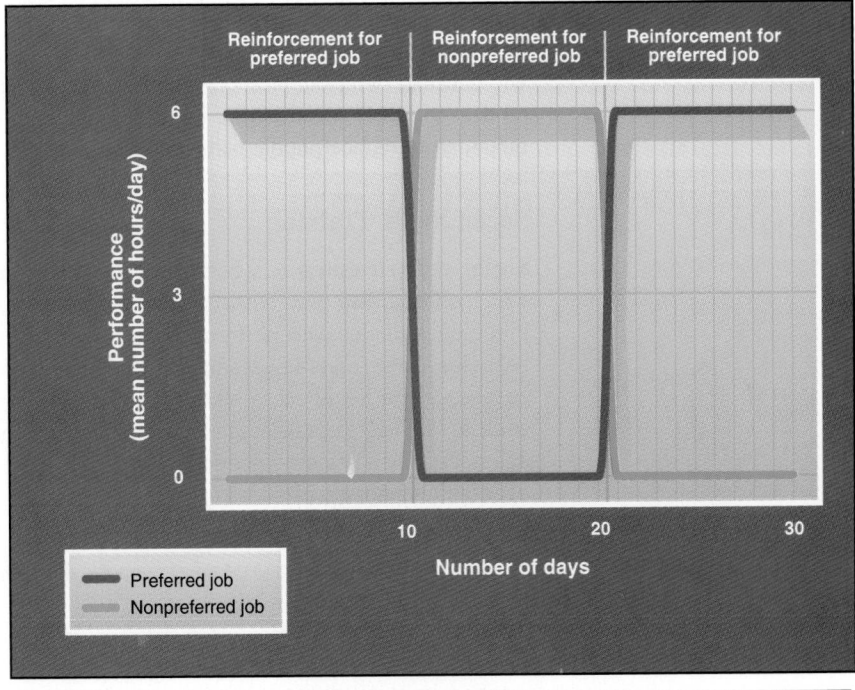

Figure 17.13 *Average number of hours hospitalized schizophrenic patients worked per day on a job they preferred and a job they did not prefer when tokens were used as reinforcement. Note how quickly behavior is influenced by the reinforcement contingency. (Ayllon & Azrin, 1965).*

of the most startling self-destructive behaviors imaginable occur in certain severely disturbed children. Such children may strike themselves repeatedly, bang their heads on sharp objects, bite or tear pieces of flesh from their bodies, or engage in other self-mutilating behaviors.

O. Ivar Lovaas (1977), a UCLA psychologist who pioneered the use of operant conditioning techniques in the treatment of such children, has been successful in eliminating severe self-destructive behavior with a limited number of contingent electric shocks. One 7-year-old boy had been self-injurious for 5 years and had to be kept in physical restraints. During one 90-minute period when his restraints were removed, he struck himself more than 3,000 times. During treatment, shock electrodes were attached to the boy, and he was given a painful electric shock each time he struck himself. Only 12 shocks were needed to virtually eliminate the self-destructive behavior. In another case, 15 shocks eliminated self-destructive behavior in a severely disturbed girl with a history of banging her head against objects. No one is quite sure why electric shock is effective in suppressing behaviors that already produce pain in such children, but this short-term punishment (always requiring the knowledge and consent of the parents) has been successfully used after all else had failed.

Therapeutic Use of Modeling

Modeling is one of the most important learning processes in humans, and modeling procedures have been used to treat a variety of behavioral problems. We will consider two examples, one involving the use of models to teach social skills, the other employing modeling to reduce phobic behavior.

Social Skills Training

Social skills training is a behavioral technique in which clients learn new skills by observing and then imitating a model who performs a socially skillful behavior. In the following example, a therapist served as a model for his client, a socially anxious college student who had great difficulty in asking women for dates. The client began by pretending to ask for a date over the telephone:

> *Client:* By the way (pause), I don't suppose you want to go out Saturday night?
>
> *Therapist:* Up to actually asking for the date you were very good. However, if I were the girl, I might have been offended when you said, "By the way." It's like asking her out is pretty casual. Also, the way you posed the question, you are kind of suggesting to her that she doesn't want to go out with you. Pretend for the moment

I'm you. Now, how does this sound: There's a movie at the Varsity Theatre that I want to see. If you don't have other plans, I'd very much like to take you.

> *Client:* That sounded good. Like you were sure of yourself and like the girl, too.
>
> *Therapist:* Why don't you try it? (Masters & others, 1987, p. 100).

Social skills training is applicable to a wide variety of populations, including normal individuals who have minor deficits in social skills, delinquents who need to learn how to respond adaptively to negative peer pressures, and even hospitalized schizophrenics, who need to learn social skills in order to function adaptively outside the hospital. It is often used in conjunction with other psychological or biological treatments.

Modeling in the Treatment of Phobias

Albert Bandura and his colleagues introduced a highly effective method for reducing phobic behaviors which he called **participant modeling.** In this therapy, a phobic person observes a fearless model engage in a hierarchy of responses involving progressively closer contact with the feared object. At each step, the client tries to imitate the model's behavior. For example, in a study involving snake phobias, the model first approached the snake's cage, then encouraged the phobic individual to do likewise. Then the model touched the snake on its tail, and the phobic was encouraged to do the same. Eventually, the model actually picked up the snake fearlessly and let it crawl over her lap, reassuring the client that the snake was harmless.

In this study, the participant modeling condition was compared with three other conditions: (1) a symbolic modeling condition in which phobic subjects watched a videotape of the model performing the behaviors but did not participate themselves, (2) a systematic desensitization condition in which the subjects imagined themselves performing the behaviors, and (3) a no-treatment control condition. As shown in Figure 17.14, the participant modeling condition was by far the most effective treatment condition, and even the symbolic modeling condition was as effective as desensitization (Bandura & others, 1969).

Research has demonstrated that the key factor underlying the effectiveness of both social skills training and participant modeling is the increase in self-efficacy that the procedures produce. When subjects come to believe that they are capable of performing the desired behaviors, they succeed in doing so (Bandura, 1986; Cervone, 1992). The observation of successful models can be a very potent factor in increasing self-efficacy.

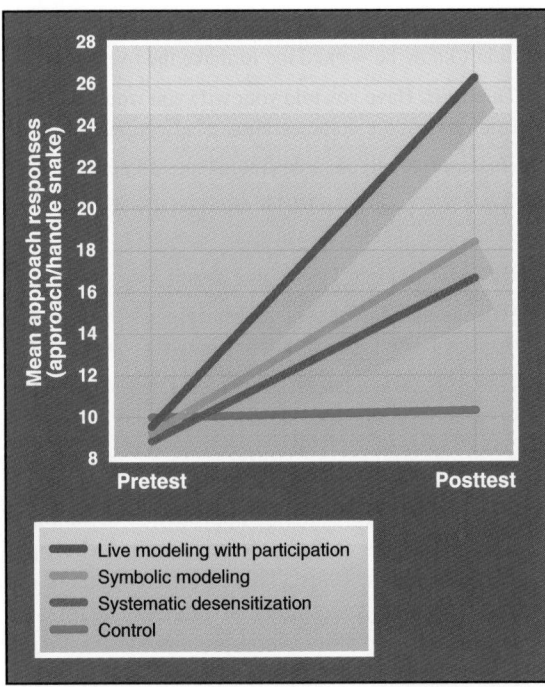

Figure 17.14 *Comparison of participant modeling with symbolic modeling, systematic desensitization, and an untreated control condition. The outcome measure, or dependent variable, was the phobic subjects' ability to approach and handle snakes. (Bandura & others, 1969).*

Group, Family, and Marital Therapies

Most of the therapeutic approaches we have discussed can be carried out with groups of clients as well as with individuals. Treatment of clients in groups first became popular in the military during World War II, when therapists were in short supply. However, it was soon discovered that in addition to being an economical use of therapists' time, group approaches offered many unique benefits of their own. Within a group, clients can experience acceptance, support, and a sense of belonging. They soon see that other people also struggle with problems, a realization that helps to counter feelings of isolation and deviance. Within the group context, clients can observe how others approach problems, and the interpersonal relations that develop within the group can be a training ground for learning new interpersonal skills. Furthermore, clients can gain insight into how they are perceived by others. Sometimes they learn about themselves through the experiences of others, as in the following instance:

Jerry, a competent business executive, was puzzled by the statements of others in an early session, and he

remarked, ''I look at myself with some strangeness because I have no friends, and I don't seem to require friends.'' In a later session when he heard Beth, a married woman, talking of a remoteness she felt between herself and her husband and how much she craved a deeper and more communicative relationship, his face began to work and his jaw to quiver. Roz, another member of the group, seeing this, went over and put her arm around him and he broke into literally uncontrollable sobs. He had discovered a loneliness in himself of which he had been completely unaware and from which he had been well defended by an armor-plated shell of self-sufficiency (Adapted from Rogers, 1970, p. 109).

Therapy groups typically include six to eight clients and a single therapist. What the therapist does and how the group operates depend on the therapist's theoretical orientation. Psychoanalytic group therapy focuses on achieving insight into unconscious conflicts and defenses as they express themselves in the group setting. Clients learn how their current ways of relating to others are being affected by conflicts and trauma suffered in significant relationships in the past. Humanistic therapists are more concerned with the here and now of immediate experience. Humanistic **encounter groups** and gestalt therapy groups aim for greater awareness of personal feelings and the ability to express them honestly and directly. Behavioral group therapy is more likely to focus on learning and practicing specific coping skills within the group and receiving group suggestions for dealing with problems.

Family Therapy

Family therapy had its roots in the clinical observation that many clients who had shown marked improvement in individual therapy—often in institutional settings—suffered relapses when they returned home and began interacting with their families. This observation led to an important concept in the field of psychotherapy—namely, that the disorder shown by the ''identified patient'' is only a symptom of a pathological set of relationships within the family system, and that permanent change in the client requires that the entire family system be the focus of therapy (Minuchin, 1974). Family therapists therefore try to help the family understand how it functions and how its unique patterns of interactions contribute to the problems of one or more members (see Figure 17.15).

In one family, an anorexic 14-year-old girl was the identified patient. However, as the therapist worked with the family, he saw a competitive struggle for the father's attention and observed that the girl, Laura, was able to compete and get ''cuddly'' affection from her father only when she presented herself to him as a ''sick'' person. To bring the hidden dy-

Figure 17.15 *Family therapists focus on the total pattern of family interactions, and they include the entire family in treatment.*

namics out into the open, the therapist worked at getting the family members to express their desires more directly—in words instead of through hidden behavioral messages. In time, Laura became capable of expressing her need for affection directly to her father, and her anorexia disappeared (Aponte & Hoffman, 1974).

Marital Therapy

Today's soaring divorce rate is a stark reflection of the difficulties that exist in many marriages. Nearly half of all first marriages end in divorce, and the divorce rate is even higher among people who remarry (Brody & others, 1988). Couples frequently seek marital therapy because they are troubled by their relationship or because one or both are contemplating separation or divorce. Typically, the therapist works with both partners together, and therapy focuses on clarifying and improving the interactions between them. Research has shown that happily married couples differ from distressed couples in that they talk more to one another, keep channels of communication open, show more sensitivity to each other's feelings and needs, and are more skilled at solving problems (Gottman & Levinson, 1992). Marital therapy focuses on improvement in these areas.

Distressed couples frequently have faulty communication patterns, as demonstrated in the following case:

> *Husband:* She never comes up to me and kisses me. I am always the one to make the overtures.
>
> *Therapist:* Is this the way you see yourself behaving with your husband?

Wife: Yes, I would say he is the demonstrative one. I didn't know he wanted me to make the overtures.

Therapist: Have you told your wife you would like this from her—more demonstration of affection?

Husband: Well, no. You'd think she'd know.

Wife: No, how would I know? You always said you didn't like aggressive women.

Husband: I don't, I don't like *dominating* women.

Wife: Well, I thought you meant women who make the overtures. How am I to know what you want?

Therapist: You'd have a better idea if he had been able to *tell* you (Satir, 1967, pp. 72–73).

One of the most promising approaches to helping distressed couples is **behavioral marital therapy** (Gurman & others, 1986). This cognitive–behavioral approach combines a number of elements relating to behavioral change into a comprehensive treatment package. Couples are helped to identify the problem behaviors in their marriages, as well as the conditions that maintain them. They also receive training in communication skills, problem solving, and conflict resolution. Finally, they negotiate behavioral contracts that will provide more rewards and fewer punishments in their relationships. For example, the husband might contract to spend quiet conversational time with his wife each night. She, in turn, may elect to help him with the yard work on weekends so that they have time to go out for dinner on Saturday evenings. The goal is to give the couple the skills needed to reduce marital distress and to make their relationship more mutually rewarding.

A recent 4-year follow-up study comparing behavioral marital therapy with an insight-oriented approach suggests that the addition of an insight orientation might increase the efficacy of marital therapy. The effects of the two therapies did not differ at the end of treatment or at a 6-month follow-up, but after 4 years the insight-oriented approach proved markedly superior. Thirty-eight percent of the couples who had gone through behavioral marital therapy had divorced, compared with only 3 percent of those who had worked on achieving insight into the unconscious reasons for their difficulties (Snyder & others, 1991). This study suggests the wisdom of combining the best features of different therapy approaches.

Sexual problems frequently contribute to marital difficulties, and they create unhappiness and disrupt intimate relationships for unmarried people as well. Because psychological factors play a central role in such problems, the development of psychological methods of treatment has been an important therapeutic advance. We explore these treatments in the following feature.

Sex may be a perfectly natural biological function, but for most people it is not naturally perfect. Virtually everyone's ability to achieve high levels of arousal, to experience intense orgasms, and to give sexual pleasure fluctuates from time to time. Some people, however, experience difficulties in sexual performance or enjoyment to such an extent that they are said to suffer from a **sexual dysfunction.** Such difficulties are not at all uncommon. In one study of 100 well-educated couples, 80 percent of whom claimed to have happy marriages, 40 percent of the men reported problems with getting or maintaining an erection or with ejaculating too quickly. More than 60 percent of the women reported difficulties in becoming aroused or in reaching orgasm, including 15 percent who never reached orgasm (Frank & others, 1978).

In perhaps 10 to 20 percent of cases, sexual dysfunction results directly from physical factors. In the remainder, psychological factors play a central role. The most common sources of sexual difficulties are negative emotional responses such as anxiety, revulsion, guilt, and anger, all of which are incompatible with sexual arousal. Negative emotional responses may be elicited by the immediate situation, or they may have their origins in past traumatic sexual experiences, in faulty beliefs and attitudes, in conflicts with the partner, or in personality disturbances. For example, some people have learned to cognitively appraise sex in general or certain sex practices as "dirty," immoral, or perverted, resulting in guilt, revulsion, or anxiety rather than arousal (Walen, 1980).

Another important set of appraisals involve self-perceptions of performance during sexual activity. Many people are self-conscious about how well they are performing and satisfying their partner. If they perceive themselves as not performing or responding adequately, they experience **performance anxiety.** Performance anxiety is a frequent contributor to erectile difficulties and premature ejaculation in men (Masters & others, 1988). Similarly, some women are troubled that they cannot have (or do not want) more than one orgasm. People with unrealistic standards can easily form unnecessary perceptions of failure that can seriously undermine their sexual adjustment. In sexual disorders, we see another example of how psychological and biological factors can influence one another.

The publication of Masters and Johnson's *Human Sexual Inadequacy* in 1970 had a major impact on the treatment of sexual dysfunction. Previously, these disorders had been treated with traditional "talking" therapies, with relatively limited success. The Masters and Johnson program strongly influenced today's cognitive–behavioral sex therapy approaches, in which the couple, not the "patient," is usually the focus of treatment (Wincze & Carey, 1991). The couple is seen together, often by a male and female therapist team, and the couple works in partnership to increase sexual satisfaction. For example, through sex education and cognitive approaches designed to change faulty beliefs and attitudes, sex therapists try to modify negative appraisals that interfere with sexual functioning. Therapists also encourage open verbal and nonverbal communication between the partners. Specific "homework" assignments are given to help couples learn to more effectively stimulate one another, to become more aware and appreciative of their sexual sensations, and to overcome fears and inhibitions. A kind of behavioral shaping procedure is used in which the couple moves gradually from nonthreatening sexual interactions like hugging toward more involved exchanges that terminate in intercourse. The aim is to reduce anxiety so that it does not interfere with sexual functioning while increasing the amount of sexual pleasure the couple experiences. These general principles are illustrated in the treatment of orgasmic dysfunction in women and premature ejaculation in men.

In the treatment of **orgasmic dysfunction**—inability of a woman to experience orgasm despite adequate sexual stimulation—the first step is an exploration of the woman's beliefs and attitudes about sex and an attempt to modify dysfunctional ones through sex education or cognitive therapy approaches. When the woman is ready, she is instructed to begin exploring her body in private, focusing on the sensations that result, and to stimulate herself through masturbation. As she becomes more comfortable with her body and its stimulation, her partner begins to participate in these sessions and helps her to explore new sensations at her own pace and choosing. Much time is spent in "pleasuring" through kissing and tactile stimulation, with no attempt at intercourse. There is also a strong emphasis on the woman's clear communication of her reactions and desires to her partner. As the woman becomes more comfortable with stimulation and arousal, the couple moves gradually toward full sexual relations. Through these mind–body procedures, cognitions and anxiety that could interfere with sexual arousal and eventual orgasm are directly confronted and eventually eliminated.

Treatment of **premature ejaculation**—the consistent inability to control or postpone ejaculation long enough to experience or share sexual enjoyment—involves gradually intensified pleasuring of the man by his partner. Here, however, the goal is to train the man to experience high levels of arousal without ejaculating. Over time, the woman increases her stimulation of the man. Any time the man signals that he is about to ejaculate, his partner inhibits ejaculation by firmly squeezing the penis just under the rim or at the base for 3 to 4 seconds. This *squeeze technique* permits the man to experience progressively longer and more intense stimulation without ejaculating. From a conditioning standpoint, the association between

sexual arousal and quick ejaculation is being reduced, resulting in greater control of ejaculation. From a cognitive viewpoint, self-efficacy in controlling ejaculation is being established.

After treating 432 clients suffering from premature ejaculation and 730 cases of female orgasmic difficulties, Masters and Johnson (1970) reported that only 2 percent of the men and about 24 percent of the women failed to improve. Other sex therapists who have used the same techniques with less favorable success rates have criticized Masters and Johnson for not being clearer on exactly how they defined success and failure (Zilbergeld & Evans, 1980). Nevertheless, these techniques seem far superior in their effectiveness to more traditional approaches, such as intensive psychotherapy (Wade & Cirese, 1992; Wincze & Carey, 1991). By focusing on the critical interactions between mind and body, modern sex therapies offer new hope to the many people who suffer sexual dysfunctions.

Evaluating Psychotherapies

We have now considered a variety of psychotherapeutic approaches. If you were to choose a form of therapy for yourself, which would it be? Would it make any difference which approach you chose? What factors would influence the effects of that therapy on your life?

These personal questions mirror some of the questions psychologists ask about psychotherapies. They want to know which approaches are most effective, what kinds of problems are best treated with each approach, and what it is about each type of treatment that produces the observed effects. These are exceedingly complex questions. Indeed, the most basic question—"Does psychotherapy work?"—is today viewed as a gross oversimplification of a much more involved question: "Which types of therapy, administered by which kinds of therapists to which kinds of clients having which kinds of problems, produce which kinds of effects?" The complexity of this question helps explain why many questions remain unanswered after nearly a half century of psychotherapy research involving hundreds of studies. Nonetheless, for many reasons, these questions demand answers. Selecting and administering the most appropriate kind of intervention is vital in human terms. It is also im-

portant for economic reasons. Many millions of dollars are spent each year on psychological treatments, and an increasing share of these costs is being paid by so-called third parties, such as insurance companies and government agencies. As the costs rise, those who bear the financial burden increase their demands for accountability and for demonstrations that the treatments are useful.

Designing good psychotherapy research is one of the most challenging tasks in all of psychology, because there are so many variables that cannot be completely controlled. In contrast to laboratory studies, in which the experimental conditions can be highly standardized, therapist–client interactions are by their nature infinitely varied. Another difficulty involves measuring the effects of psychotherapy. Figure 17.16 shows some of the typical ways of measuring change. These measures differ in the outcome variable assessed (emotions, thoughts, or behaviors) and in the source of the data (the client, the therapist, or other informants). One perplexing problem is that different combinations of these outcome measures may produce different results. Which indexes of change are most important or valid? A behaviorist will insist that direct observations of behavior are the best measures, whereas a psychodynamic therapist may be most interested in how clients feel and what they have learned about the childhood roots of their problems. When one set of measures indicates improvement, another

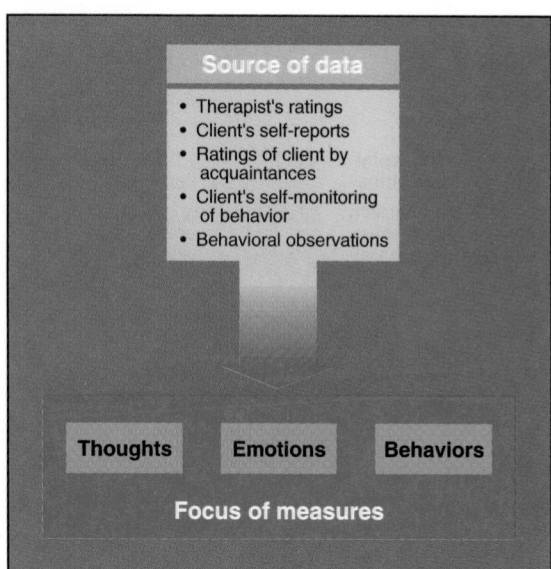

Figure 17.16 *The measures used to assess the outcome of psychotherapy may come from a variety of data sources, and they may measure different aspects of the client's functioning.*

indicates no change, and a third suggests that the client is worse off than before treatment, how should we evaluate the effects of the therapy? These are just a few of the vexing issues that can arise in therapy research.

Meta-Analysis: a Look at the Big Picture

Because individual psychotherapy studies differ considerably in client characteristics, therapist variables, the way in which treatments are administered, and outcome measures, it is difficult to draw definite conclusions about effectiveness from any one study. However, statisticians have developed a technique known as **meta-analysis** that allows researchers to combine the results of many studies into an **effect size** statistic that represents a common measure of treatment effectiveness. The effect size statistic can tell researchers what percentage of subjects who have received therapy have a more favorable outcome than that of the *average* control subject who has not received therapy. The procedure can be used to combine studies of different kinds of treatments.

In the first large-scale study of its kind, Mary Ann Smith and Gene Glass (1977) used meta-analysis to combine the effects of 375 studies of psychotherapy involving 25,000 clients and 25,000 control subjects. These studies differed in many ways, but they all compared a treatment condition with a control con-

dition. The question was whether, overall, therapy subjects improved more than control subjects. The results of the meta-analysis indicated that the average therapy subject had a more favorable outcome than 75 percent of the untreated subjects. We would expect a figure of 50 percent if therapy had no effect. Smith and Glass therefore concluded that therapy does indeed have positive effects.

What about differences among therapies? Smith and Glass broke down their meta-analysis in terms of many of the therapies we have considered in this chapter. As shown in Figure 17.17, psychodynamic, client-centered, and behavioral approaches were similar in their effectiveness, and all of them seemed to yield somewhat more positive effects than gestalt therapy. Again, however, remember that the studies lumped together differ in many ways, including the nature and severity of the problems that were treated, the outcome measures that were used, and the quality of the methodology. Other psychotherapy researchers have pointed out that combining good studies with less adequate ones can produce misleading results (Kazdin, 1986). They insist that only the best studies should be combined in meta-analyses.

To make results easier to interpret, recent meta-analyses have tended to focus on studies that are directed at particular behavior disorders and that use the same outcome measures. For example, Keith Dobson (1989) performed a meta-analysis of 28 cognitive therapy studies involving clients suffering from

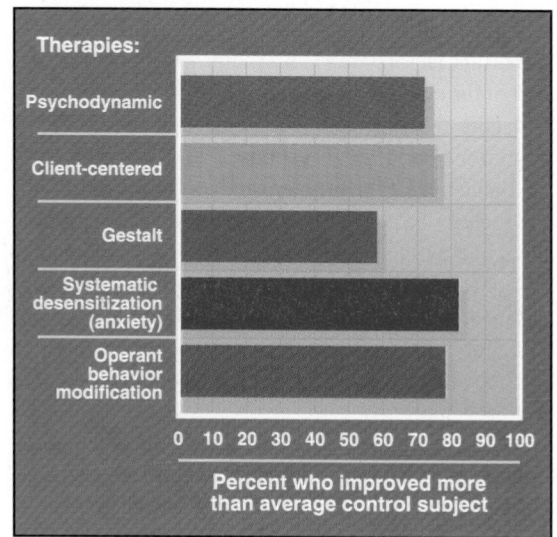

Figure 17.17 *The Smith and Glass meta-analysis of 375 studies of psychotherapy outcome yielded effectiveness data on various types of psychotherapy. The bars indicate the percentage of treated subjects who improved more than the average control subject. (Data from Smith & Glass, 1977).*

depression. All of the studies had used as an outcome measure the Beck Depression Inventory (Beck, 1967), a client self-report instrument that assesses the physical, cognitive, motivational, and mood symptoms of depression. Dobson found that the average cognitive therapy client showed more improvement than 98 percent of the controls who received no treatment. They also showed greater improvement than 70 percent of clients who received drug therapy and 68 percent of clients who underwent psychodynamic or behavioral therapy. These results reinforce the opinion of many clinicians that cognitive therapy may be the psychological treatment of choice for depression.

Factors Affecting the Outcome of Therapy

Clearly, not everyone who enters therapy profits from it. There is even evidence that some clients may get worse as a result of treatment (Lambert & others, 1986). What, then, are the factors that influence the outcome of treatment?

Three sets of factors have been the focus of research designed to answer this question—namely, *therapist* variables, *technique* variables, and *client* variables (Beutler, 1991). These three sets of factors combine to affect the nature of the treatment that the client experiences (see Figure 17.18). To this point, investigators have tended to study these three classes of variables in isolation rather than in combination, so we are not yet sure exactly how they interact. However, we can draw some conclusions about which components of each seem most important.

Where client variables are concerned, the most important factors are (1) a general willingness on the part of the client to invest himself or herself in therapy and take the risks required to change maladaptive cognitions, emotional responses, and behavior, and (2) the nature of the problem and its degree of fit with the therapy being used. For example, specific problems like phobias may respond best to a specifically tailored anxiety-reduction treatment like systematic desensitization, whereas a more global problem, such as a search for self-discovery and greater meaning in life, may respond better to a psychodynamic or client-centered approach.

Despite dramatic differences in the techniques they employ, various therapies tend to enjoy similar success rates. This finding has led many experts to conclude that there are certain *common factors* in all therapies that make them therapeutic. These include faith in the therapist and the belief on the part of clients that they are receiving help, a more plausible explanation for their problems and an alternative way of looking at themselves and their problems, and a trust-

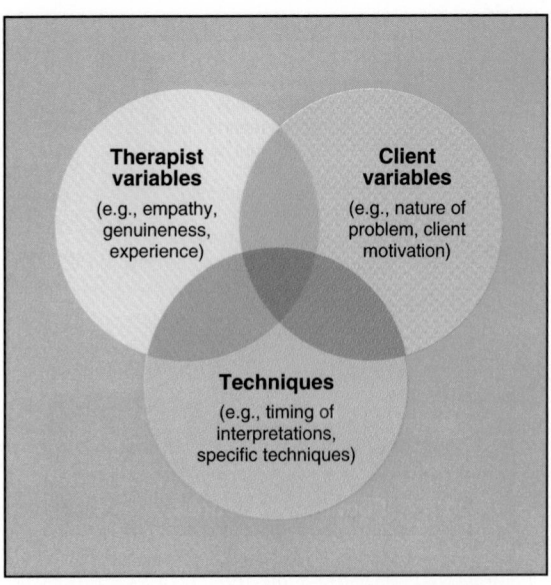

Figure 17.18 *Research on factors that influence therapy outcome has focused on three sets of interacting variables: client factors, therapist factors, and technique factors.*

ing and caring relationship with the therapist (Strupp, 1989). The most important common factor in therapy outcome may well be the quality of the relationship that the therapist is able to establish with the client (Garfield & Bergin, 1986; Lafferty & others, 1989; Strupp, 1989). Carl Rogers's emphasis on the importance of therapist qualities such as empathy, unconditional acceptance of the client as a person, and genuineness has been borne out in a great many studies (Beutler & others, 1986). The establishment of an empathic, trusting, and caring relationship forms the foundation upon which the specific techniques employed by the therapist can have their most beneficial effects. Regardless of the approach to therapy that has been studied, differences in therapists' abilities to form a caring and supportive relationship seem directly related to the effectiveness of the techniques they employ (Derlega & others, 1991; Orlinsky & Howard, 1986).

This does not mean that as long as a therapist has a good relationship with a client, it does not matter what therapy techniques are used or how they are used. It does matter. In psychoanalytic therapy, for example, the correctness of the interpretations made by the therapist, as measured by expert ratings, was positively related to treatment outcome in a large-scale study at the University of Pennsylvania (Crits-Christoph & others, 1988). Likewise, in an intensive analysis of the audiotaped therapy sessions of 21 psychotherapists, Enrico Jones and coworkers (1988) found that the most effective therapists adjusted their techniques to the specific needs of their

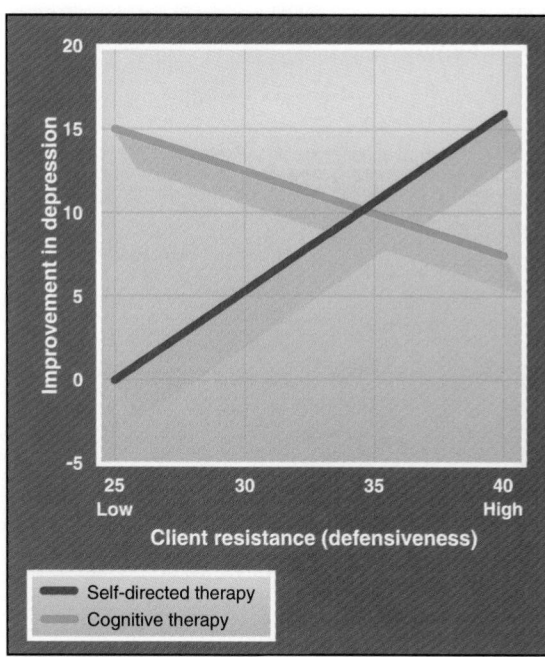

Figure 17.19 *An interaction between client characteristics and mode of treatment that influenced the outcome of psychotherapy. Clients low in resistance profited more from cognitive therapy than from a self-directed therapy for depression. In contrast, clients with high resistance potential (high defensiveness) profited more from the self-directed treatment than from cognitive therapy, which requires closer interaction with a therapist. (Data from Beutler & others, 1991).*

clients. They concluded that "general relationship factors, such as therapeutic alliance, are closely bound with the skillful selection and application of psychotherapeutic techniques" (p. 55).

More research is needed on how client characteristics interact with specific therapies to affect outcomes. In one demonstration of such an interaction, Larry Beutler and his coworkers (1991) compared cognitive therapy for depression with a self-directed treatment in which depressed clients were given guidance through selected reading materials and received occasional supportive telephone calls from their therapists. The researchers found that clients whose psychological test scores predicted that they would be resistant in therapy did better with the self-directed treatment than with cognitive therapy, whereas the reverse was true for clients who were low in resistance (see Figure 17.19). Beutler suggests that such data can be used as the basis for selecting clients for particular kinds of therapy, thereby increasing the likelihood that the clients will benefit from treatment.

The complexities of psychotherapy pose a formidable challenge for the psychotherapy researcher. As the "active ingredients" of psychotherapy are identified in future research, it will be possible to

make treatment approaches more effective and to learn more about the factors that make human relationships therapeutic.

Biological Approaches to Treatment

We have already seen that biological factors play an important role in many varieties of abnormal behavior. Thus, an alternative to psychological treatment is a direct biological approach designed to alter the brain's functioning. However, it would be a mistake to believe that such an approach is "purely" biological, for changes in the brain are likely to affect psychological processes such as cognitions and emotions.

Drug therapy and electroconvulsive therapy (ECT) are the two general approaches most likely to be used by therapists who have a biological orientation. Of these, the various drug therapies are by far the more common, and they are used for a wide variety of behavior disorders. ECT is now used primarily in the treatment of severely depressed individuals when drug treatment does not seem to be effective. Both drug therapy and ECT may be used in conjunction with psychotherapy, or they may be used alone.

Drug Therapies

Discoveries in the field of *psychopharmacology* (the study of how drugs affect cognitions, emotions, and behavior) have revolutionized the treatment of the entire range of behavior disorders. Perhaps the most dramatic effects of drug therapy have occurred in the treatment of severely disordered people, permitting many of them to function outside of the hospital setting.

Each year in the United States alone, more than 200 million prescriptions are filled for drugs that affect mood, thought, and behavior (Lickey & Gordon, 1991). The drugs commonly prescribed for the treatment of anxiety disorders, schizophrenia, and depression comprise three major categories: antianxiety drugs (the minor tranquilizers); antipsychotic drugs (the major tranquilizers); and antidepressant drugs.

Antianxiety Drugs

Surveys have shown that more than 15 percent of Americans between the ages of 18 and 74 use antianxiety or tranquilizing drugs such as Valium, Xanax, and Librium. Between 15 and 20 percent of the people who visit physicians represent the "worried well," who do not have clear physical disorders that might explain their tension and anxiety symptoms.

Some physicians routinely prescribe antianxiety medication for such patients; about 90 percent of the prescriptions for antianxiety drugs are written by general practitioners (Lickey & Gordon, 1991). These drugs are designed to reduce anxiety as much as possible without affecting alertness or concentration. Sometimes, antianxiety drugs are used in combination with other therapies to help clients cope successfully with fear-arousing situations. A temporary reduction in anxiety from the use of a drug may allow a client to enter anxiety-arousing situations and learn to cope more effectively with them.

One drawback of antianxiety drugs is the fact that psychological and physical dependence can result from their long-term use. As with any other addictive drug, people who have developed physiological dependence on tranquilizers can experience characteristic withdrawal symptoms, such as intense anxiety, nausea, and restlessness when they stop taking them (Grilly, 1989). A recently introduced antianxiety drug, Buspar, is slow acting, has fewer fatiguing side effects, and seems to have less potential for abuse (Julien, 1991).

Antipsychotic Drugs

The revolution in drug therapy for severe psychological disorders began around 1950, when it was accidentally discovered that reserpine, a drug derived from the root of the snakeroot plant, calmed psychotic patients. This discovery resulted in the development of the **major tranquilizers** used today to treat schizophrenic disorders. In the early 1950s, a synthetic antipsychotic drug was created. Known as **chlorpromazine,** and sold under the trade name Thorazine, it was the first of a group of drugs known as the phenothiazines, whose effects on schizophrenic symptoms were similar to reserpine's but did not cause the latter's undesirable side effects, such as depression and lowered blood pressure.

The primary effect of the phenothiazines is to block the action of dopamine, a neurotransmitter whose overactivity is thought to be involved in schizophrenia. These drugs can have dramatic effects on the positive symptoms of hallucinations and delusions; they have little effect on the negative symptoms of apathy and withdrawal. Antipsychotic drugs are now so widely used that nearly all schizophrenic patients living in the United States, Canada, and Western Europe have received them at one time or another. In fact, it is common practice to recommend that the medication be continued indefinitely once the individual has returned to the community (Carpenter & Heinrichs, 1983). The phenothiazines have created a revolution in the treatment of schizophrenia, not only allowing many patients to be released from hospitals but also reducing the need for padded cells, straitjack-

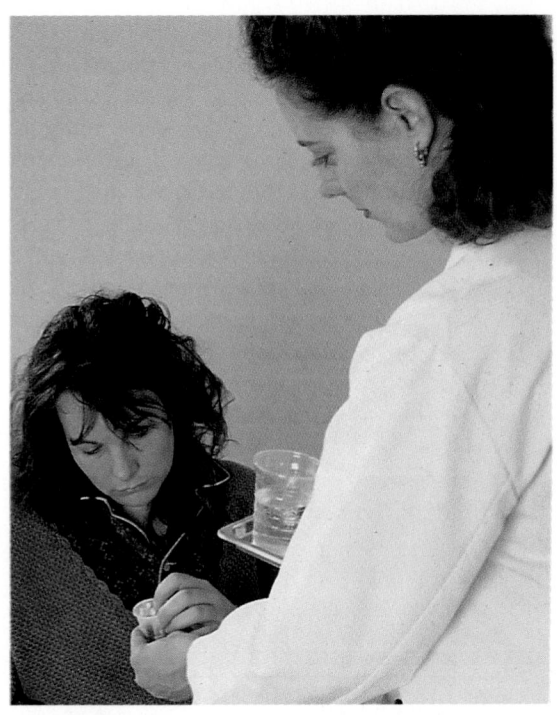

Figure 17.20 *Antipsychotic drugs have revolutionized the treatment of severely disturbed individuals, allowing many of them to leave mental hospitals.*

ets, and other restraints that were used to control the behavior of hospitalized patients (see Figure 17.20).

But these drugs are not perfect. One of the most serious side effects is a severe movement disorder known as **tardive dyskinesia** (Kane, 1992). Uncontrollable and grotesque movements of the face and tongue are especially prominent in this disorder, and sometimes the patient's arms and legs flail uncontrollably. Tardive dyskinesia can be more debilitating than the psychotic symptoms that prompted the drug treatment, and it appears to be irreversible once it develops. One prospective 4-year study revealed a tardive dyskenesia rate of 18.5 percent in young adults and 31 percent in those over 55 who were taking antipsychotic medications (Saltz & others, 1991). Researchers are attempting to develop new drugs that can control schizophrenic symptoms without producing the devastating symptoms of tardive dyskinesia.

Antipsychotic drugs can often be used effectively in conjunction with psychotherapy. For example, drugs may be used to bring psychotic symptoms under control so that other approaches, such as social skills training, family therapy, and group therapy, can be applied to maintain the initial improvement.

Antidepressant Drugs

There are two major groups of antidepressant drugs: **tricyclics** (Elavil) and **monoamineoxidase (MAO)** inhibitors (Nardil). These drugs apparently increase the availability of the neurotransmitters norepinephrine and serotonin, whose lowered level of activity is related to depression. Drugs from the tricyclic group are usually tried first, because their side effects are not as severe as those of the MAO inhibitors. The latter can cause dangerous elevations in blood pressure when taken with certain foods, such as cheeses and some types of wine. One disadvantage of both drug groups is that their positive effects do not begin until 3 or 4 weeks after treatment has begun. Why it takes so long for the drugs to affect mood and behavior is a mystery, because norepinephrine and serotonin levels in the brain are increased almost immediately when the drugs are taken. Like the antianxiety and antipsychotic drugs, antidepressant drugs are often used in combination with some type of psychotherapy or behavior therapy.

A newly developed antidepressive drug, Prozac, received enthusiastic early reviews because it reduces depressive symptoms rapidly and also seems to reduce obsessive–compulsive symptoms (Lickey & Gordon, 1991). However, there are disquieting reports that some patients on Prozac have developed serious side effects, such as intense suicidal impulses (Teicher & others, 1990). Obviously, more thorough evaluations of Prozac's effects are warranted.

Electroconvulsive Therapy

Another biologically based treatment, **electroconvulsive therapy (ECT),** was based on the observation of a Hungarian physician that schizophrenia and epilepsy rarely occur in the same person. The physician suggested that seizure induction might therefore be useful in the treatment of schizophrenia. Two Italian physicians, Ugo Cerletti and Lucio Bini, began to treat schizophrenic patients by attaching electrodes to their skulls and inducing a seizure by means of an electric current administered to the brain. When ECT was first introduced in the 1930s, it was applied to a wide range of disorders, though research now suggests that it cannot relieve anxiety disorders and it is of questionable value for schizophrenic patients (Weiner & Coffey, 1988). However, ECT can be useful in treating depression, especially when there is a high risk of suicide. In such cases, the use of antidepressant drugs may be impractical, because they will likely take several weeks to begin reducing the depression. In contrast, the effects of ECT can be immediate.

Dramatizations of ECT in the mass media have portrayed a barbaric procedure, and this portrayal was perhaps deserved in the beginning. When ECT was first introduced, a wide-awake patient was strapped to a table, electrodes were attached to the patient's

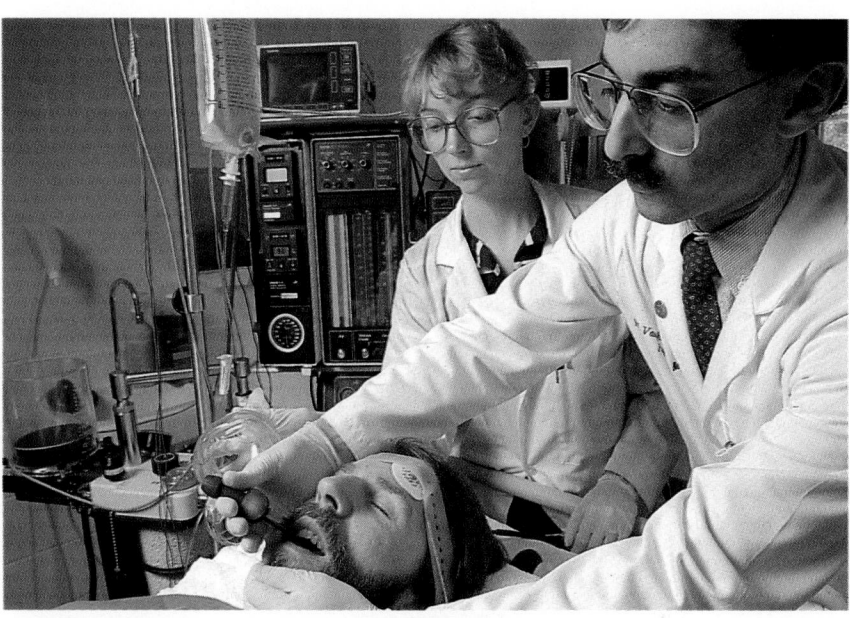

◆ **Figure 17.21** *A depressed patient is prepared for electroconvulsive therapy. The patient has been sedated and given a muscle relaxant to prevent bone fractures from occurring during the convulsions that will be produced by the half second of shock delivered to the brain.*

scalp, and roughly 100 volts of electricity was applied to the brain, producing violent convulsions and momentary unconsciousness. Sometimes, the seizures were so violent that patients fractured their arms or legs.

Today, however, the procedure is different (see Figure 17.21). A patient is first given a sedative and a muscle relaxant to prevent injuries from convulsions. The patient is then placed on a well-padded mattress, and electrodes are attached to his or her head. The duration of the shock is less than a second, causing a seizure of the central nervous system. There is little observable movement in the patient, other than a twitch of the toes and a slight facial grimace. The patient wakes up 10 to 20 minutes after ECT, possibly with a headache, sore muscles, and some confusion. Recently, scientists have been able to calibrate the amount of current a patient needs so that treatments can be individualized, and research is being carried out to determine whether certain drugs can reduce seizure-induced confusion and amnesia.

ECT has many critics, despite its effectiveness in alleviating major depression. Critics note that even where the effects are dramatically positive, the possibility of a depressive relapse is high. Concerns have been raised about the safety of ECT because in some instances permanent memory loss has been reported, and there are also concerns about possible cumulative brain damage when ECT is used repeatedly. Today, the number of ECT treatments is limited to less than 10, but in the past, many patients received numerous treatments. One person who suffered a tragic outcome was the author Ernest Hemingway.

In December 1960, Hemingway underwent 11 shock treatments at the Mayo Clinic in Rochester, Minnesota. Three months later he was back for another series. His friend and biographer, A. E. Hotchner, described him at that time: "Ernest was even more infuriated with these treatments than the previous ones, registering bitter complaints about how his memory was wrecked and how he was ruined as a writer." Hotchner quotes Hemingway: "What these shock doctors don't know is about writers and such things as remorse and contrition and what they do to them. What is the sense of ruining my head and erasing my memory, which is my capital, and putting me out of business? It was a brilliant cure but we lost the patient." One month after the second series of ECT treatments, Hemingway committed suicide (Friedberg, 1975, pp. 25–26).

Steps have been taken to increase the safety of ECT, and available scientific evidence suggests that ECT is an acceptably safe treatment today, especially since the introduction of a modified procedure in which electrodes are placed on only one side of the head (Martin, 1986). Recent magnetic imaging studies of the brains of patients who received brief pulse treatment to both sides of the brain revealed no evidence of brain damage (Coffey & others, 1991). After reviewing both sides of the issues, the American Psychiatric Association (1990) concluded that this therapy should be regarded as a useful procedure under the right circumstances and has published guidelines for its use. ECT is now being increasingly accepted as the preferred treatment for major depression in patients who cannot take or do not respond to medication. More than 100,000 patients may currently be receiving ECT in the United States alone. Studies of ECT and the mechanisms involved in its action—which are currently unknown—may yield insights into the causes of depression and other disorders.

Mind, Body, and Therapeutic Interventions

The impact of drug and electroconvulsive therapies on psychological disorders illustrates once again the important interactions between biological and psychological phenomena. In the final analysis, both psychological and biological treatments affect the functioning of the brain in ways that can change disordered thoughts, emotions, and behavior. For example, Lewis Baxter and his coworkers (1992) used PET scans to study cortical brain metabolism changes in patients who were being treated for obsessive–compulsive disorders with either behavior therapy or drug therapy. Those patients who showed improvement in their obsessive–compulsive behaviors exhibited a specific pattern of changes in brain activity, regardless of which treatment they had received. Clients who did not improve did not show the changes in brain activity. Thus, different forms of therapy, whether "psychological" or "biological" in nature, may result in similar changes at a neurological level and, ultimately, at a behavioral level.

Although there may be conflicting theories concerning the causes of behavior disorders, there need be no conflict in the combined use of psychological and biological approaches to alleviating them. Thus, a client who suffers from depression might be treated with a combination of cognitive therapy designed to change faulty belief systems, behavioral treatment to increase behaviors that might produce pleasure, and antidepressant medication to control the depression and give the psychological treatments a better chance to work.

An important consideration to keep in mind is that biological treatments, however effective they may be in modifying some disordered behaviors in the short term, do not teach the client coping skills that might be used to deal with stressful life situations. Many therapists believe that one of the major benefits of psychological treatments is their potential not only for helping clients to deal with current problems but also for increasing their personal resources so that they might enjoy a higher level of personal adjustment and life satisfaction in the future.

We have now considered a wide spectrum of approaches to treating abnormal behavior. The accompanying Understanding Causes feature summarizes the mechanisms for therapeutic change that are emphasized by the various psychological and biological approaches.

■ ▢

Psychological Disorders and Society:
Challenges for the 1990s

For nearly four months, 18 year old Mark Huston cloistered himself in his dark upstairs bedroom. In the final weeks, he refused to bathe or change his clothes and ate nothing but a molding chocolate cake he kept hidden under his bed. Mark's mother knew her son needed help, and she called the local mental health agency in the hope her son could be hospitalized. They replied that under state laws they could do nothing because Mark was not "gravely disabled," which they interpreted to mean that he might die within 24 hours.

This was not the first time she had called the mental health facility. A month earlier, Mark had come downstairs to watch the movie "Psycho." When Mrs. Huston told him he could not watch the movie, he produced a

Causal Factors

Biological
- Changes in neurotransmitter systems and brain function produced by drug treatment, ECT, or environmental events

Cognitive
- Identification, challenging, and displacement of faulty belief systems or thought patterns
- Decreased discrepancy between perceived and ideal self
- Increased self-efficacy
- Increased openness to current experiences and feelings

Intrapsychic
- Insight into unconscious needs and conflicts
- Development of more adaptive defenses against anxiety
- Analysis of relationship with therapist (transference)
- Use of well-timed interpretations by therapist

Environmental
- Positive therapeutic climate created by the therapist
- Extinction of maladaptive emotional responses (exposure) or conditioned aversions to positive stimuli (e.g., alcohol)
- Operant conditioning of adaptive behaviors
- Exposure to adaptive modeled behaviors

Therapeutic Behavior Change

Therapeutic Behavior Change is a function of interacting personal and environmental causal factors. These factors may vary and may interact with one another in particular ways, depending on the person and the situation.

large butcher knife and put it to her throat. He laid down the knife only after she pleaded with him for several minutes. Trembling and crying, she called the mental health professionals and pleaded that they come and evaluate Mark. They informed her that since he had put the knife down voluntarily, he did not present an immediate danger to her and therefore could not be committed. It was not until Mark assaulted his brother and attacked a police officer who came to the home that he was jailed and later committed to a state mental hospital for treatment (Based on the *Seattle Times,* January 11, 1989).

Police were about to arrest Robert Friedman for begging for dimes in front of a downtown bus station when he pleaded, ''Don't take me in. I'm not broke.'' He then opened a briefcase containing more than $24,000 in small bills. A few days later he was committed to a private mental hospital by a judge who said he was protecting Friedman from thugs who might steal his money. Friedman's lawyer protested the commitment, telling the judge that his client had a singular obsession with saving money and that he had accumulated his small fortune by saving his wages for 31 years and living in an inexpensive apartment. He worked as a stenographer and presented·no evidence of a mental disorder.

Within four months, Friedman saw half his life savings eaten up by the hospital fees and treatment ordered by the court. His lawyer claimed that Friedman had deteriorated markedly, and he added, ''If he didn't have that money when he was panhandling, he'd be a free man today. He was committed on the possibility he would be mugged, beaten and robbed, and instead, he's locked up, filled with drugs and his money is taken gradually instead of in one clean sweep'' (Based on the *Chicago Tribune,* August 1, 1975).

Most of us would probably agree that what happened to Mark Huston and his family and to Robert Friedman represent failures of the mental health system. Yet these sad stories are only the tip of a massive iceberg that represents a national crisis. The system simply is not effectively serving the needs of those afflicted with behavior disorders or of society as a whole. This chapter closes with a discussion of some of the dilemmas and challenges posed by society's response—and lack of response—to those who are labeled mentally ill.

Institutional Treatment

Since the days of the asylums, much of the treatment of severe behavior disorders has been carried out in institutional settings. In the United States, a national network of nearly 300 state-funded mental hospitals was built between 1845 and 1945. Many private facilities were also built.

Patients enter mental hospitals through a process of **commitment.** Many commitments are voluntary, but in some instances, people are subject to the more controversial process of *involuntary commitment.* Although commitment standards and procedures vary from state to state, involuntary commitment usually requires more than the mere presence of a diagnosed behavior disorder. The person must also be judged to be (1) dangerous to self or others; (2) gravely disabled to the point of being unable to provide for his or her basic physical needs; (3) unable to make responsible decisions about hospitalization; and (4) in need of treatment or care in a hospital.

In recent years, concerns about civil rights have made long-term involuntary commitments more difficult to achieve. Many states provide for a formal hearing with legal representation, and some permit a jury trial if the person requests it. Once a person is committed, the state must periodically petition for continued involuntary commitment. If it fails to do so, the person is free to leave the hospital.

The issues that surround involuntary commitment are vexing ones. On the one hand, we must be concerned about people being unnecessarily deprived of their liberties, as Robert Friedman apparently was. On the other, we must keep in mind that the welfare of people like Mark Huston and his family may be seriously threatened if disturbed people do not receive needed treatment.

Concerns about Hospital Treatment

The number of patients being treated in public mental hospitals increased steadily from about 250,000 in 1920 to more than 500,000 in 1950 (see Figure 17.22). By 1955, half of all hospital beds in the United States were occupied by psychiatric patients. However, it was readily apparent to mental health experts that although there were some high-quality institutions, many public mental hospitals were not fulfilling their intended role as treatment facilities. They were overcrowded, understaffed, and underfinanced. Many of them could provide little more than minimal custodial care and a haven from the stresses and demands of the outer world.

Sociological analyses of mental hospitals by Erving Goffman (1961) and Thomas Scheff (1966) introduced a new concept and a set of new concerns. The **hospitalization syndrome** describes a frequent effect of hospitalization on people who already have negative self-concepts and uncertainties about social roles and responsibilities. In the process of being committed to a mental hospital, these people are legally certified as incompetent; and once admitted to the hospital, they are placed in ''sick'' and ''helpless'' social roles. In custodial institutions, their social and work skills may atrophy through disuse, and technological changes may render their occupational skills obsolete. In the final stages of the syndrome, the patients sink passively into a chronic sick role in which passive dependence and "crazy" behavior are not only tolerated, but expected. The patients have now lost the self-confidence, motivation, and skills needed to reenter and adapt to the outside world, and they are likely to prefer the sheltered environment of the hospital and to have little chance of surviving outside it.

The Deinstitutionalization Movement

By the 1960s, the stage was set for a new approach to the treatment of behavior disorders. Concerns about the inadequacies of mental hospitals and about the hospitalization syndrome, together with the ability of antipsychotic drugs to "normalize" patients' behavior, moved the primary focus of treatment from the hospital to the community.

In 1963, Congress passed the Community Mental Health Centers Act, which provided for the establishment of one mental health center for every 50,000 people. Community mental health centers are designed to provide comprehensive mental health care for their local communities. Their major function is to provide outpatient psychotherapy and drug treatment so that clients can remain in their normal social and work environments. They also arrange for short-term inpatient care, usually at a local general hospital, when clients are acutely disturbed. Many have crisis centers and telephone "hot lines" to respond to emergency situations encountered by people in the community. Finally, community mental health centers provide education and consultation for their communities. For example, staff members may provide drug education programs to local schools or educate police officers on how to deal with seriously disturbed people they might encounter in the line of duty.

Deinstitutionalization seemed to offer something for everyone. Hospital administrators supported the move because it would enable them to offer more intensive and better treatment to a smaller patient population. Patients would benefit from remaining in their social and occupational environments and being treated with minimal disruption of their lives and no loss of civil liberties. Many politicians found the reduced costs of outpatient care very attractive. Finally, many mental health professionals were convinced that highly effective treatment programs could be developed in community settings (Kiesler, 1982).

The impact of deinstitutionalization on the treatment of behavior disorders has been quite dramatic. Figure 17.22 shows the marked exodus from mental hospitals that has occurred since 1955. According to the National Institute of Mental Health, 77.4 percent of all patients were being treated as inpatients in public and private hospitals in 1955. By 1983, the inpatient figure had shrunk to 27.1 percent. As Figure

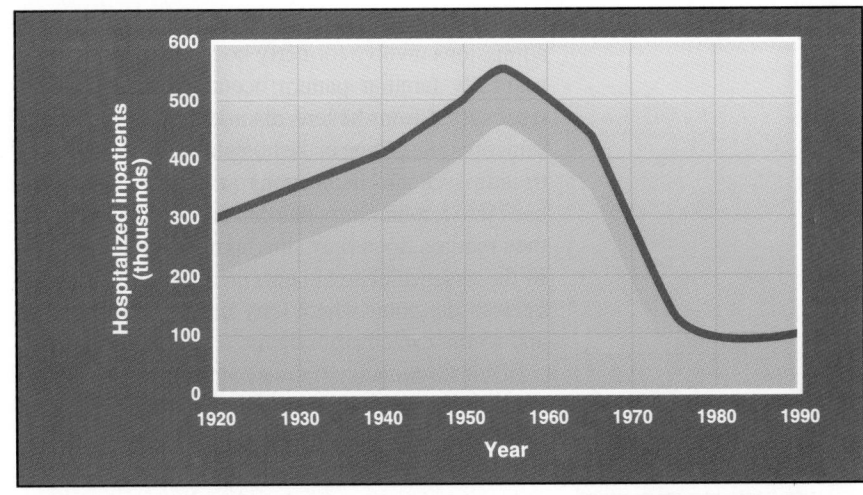

Figure 17.22 *The inpatient population in public mental hospitals increased steadily until 1955, when drug therapies and the trend toward deinstitutionalization combined to effect a sharp decline in the number of hospitalized patients. (Data from National Institute of Mental Health, 1992).*

17.23 indicates, the average length of hospitalization for patients having severe (typically schizophrenic) disorders has also decreased markedly.

For the reasons cited above, the concept of community treatment is a good one. However, its success is predicated on the availability of high-quality mental health care for deinstitutionalized patients in community clinics, half-way houses, sheltered workshops, and other community facilities. When these facilities are available, deinstitutionalization can work. Unfortunately, however, many communities never were able to fund the needed facilities, and the 1980s saw cutbacks in federal funding of community mental health centers. The result is that many patients are being released into communities that are not prepared to care for their needs. This has resulted in a **revolving door phenomenon** involving repeated re-

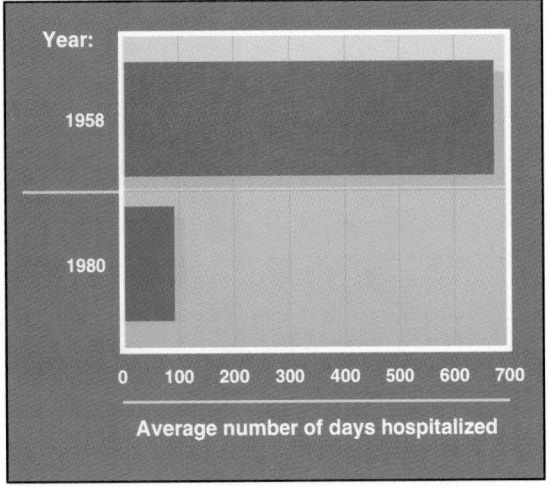

Figure 17.23 *Average length of psychiatric hospitalization at Veterans Administration Hospitals in 1958 and 1980. (Data from National Institute of Mental Health, 1992).*

hospitalizations. Nearly three-fourths of all hospital admissions involve formerly hospitalized patients. A tragically familiar pattern occurs in many patients who suffer from severe disorders such as chronic schizophrenia. Once in the hospital, they respond well to antipsychotic medications and are soon released back into a community that cannot offer them the care they require. Soon they stop taking their medication. In the absence of treatment, their condition deteriorates to the point where they must be hospitalized, and so the cycle begins again.

Deinstitutionalization also appears to have helped create a growing population of disturbed and homeless people who have nowhere to go for help. In some states with large urban populations, the largest mental patient wards exist not in hospitals but on city streets. A report in the state of Washington indicated that for every inpatient who occupied a bed in a state mental hospital on a given night, two mentally disturbed homeless people spent the night on the streets of Seattle, Tacoma, or Spokane (*Senate Health Care and Corrections Committee*, 1988).

Deinstitutionalization can work only if we as a society have the will to make it work. Only time will tell if the needed financial resources will be made available to slow the revolving door and provide the help so desperately needed by the many people who are being left without treatment and without hope.

Up to now, we have focused entirely on what can be done to help people once they have developed a behavior disorder. Successful treatment is one way to reduce the toll of human suffering produced by failures to adapt. Another way, however, is to try to prevent the development of disorders through psychological intervention. In terms of economic, personal, and societal costs, it may indeed be the case that "an ounce of prevention is worth a pound of cure."

Preventive Mental Health

As we have seen repeatedly, behavior results from the interaction of personal and environmental factors. Vulnerability factors may be either personal or situational in nature. Thus, prevention can be approached from two perspectives. **Situation-focused prevention** is directed at reducing or eliminating the environmental causes of behavior disorders. For example, many cities have created recreational and athletic programs for disadvantaged inner-city youngsters in an attempt to provide them with a highly supportive "family" atmosphere and thereby counteract the dangers of gang membership and the pressures to enter the world of drugs and antisocial behavior (see Figure 17.24).

The personal side of the equation is addressed by **competency-focused prevention,** which is designed to increase personal competencies and coping skills. One program using this approach was designed to help people deal with the stresses that accompany divorce. Divorced people are overrepresented among those who develop alcoholism, experience depression, make suicide attempts, and seek therapy. During the 6 months following separation, divorced people in the program received counseling and training in practical skills, such as how to deal with the stresses of separation and with issues involving children. Compared with newly separated people who did not participate in the program, the participants reported

▶ **Figure 17.24** *Inner-city youth programs meant to counteract environmental pressures toward deviant and antisocial behavior illustrate primary prevention programs.*

less fatigue, anxiety, and physical illness, as well as greater coping ability (Bloom & others, 1982).

Prevention may be carried out at different times in the developmental history of a behavior disorder. From this perspective, there are three major kinds of prevention programs: primary, secondary, and tertiary. **Primary prevention** includes measures aimed at preventing the occurrence of disorders in people who may be at risk for developing them. Both of the programs just described involve primary prevention.

Secondary prevention is designed to reduce the intensity, duration, or disability resulting from an already existing condition. For example, crisis intervention programs carried out by means of short-term crisis therapy or telephone hot lines are designed to help people who are experiencing acute stresses cope with them so as to reduce the likelihood of a more permanent disorder (see Figure 17.25).

Tertiary prevention is aimed at enhancing the rehabilitation process. We have seen in the revolving door phenomenon what can occur when patients are released from the hospital with no aftercare to help them maintain their treatment gains. Day hospitals, halfway houses, and sheltered workshops can help recently released mental patients with the transition back into the community and provide the support needed to reduce the likelihood of relapse. One community study showed that only 16 percent of patients who received aftercare required rehospitalization in the 6 months following their release, compared with

47 percent of those who did not receive aftercare in the community (Glasscote, 1978). ▼

One of the great scientific and political challenges for psychology is to find ways to increase personal effectiveness, happiness, and the common good of the human family. The social need for prevention will continue to be a major stimulus for objective research on the causes of behavior disorders and on ways of modifying these causal factors.

◀ **Figure 17.25** *Crisis intervention programs can help prevent acute life stress reactions from developing into more permanent behavior disorders.*

GUIDELINES FOR SEEKING PSYCHOLOGICAL TREATMENT

ENHANCING HUMAN PERFORMANCE

No one is immune to problems in living. Every day, all of us do the best we can to balance our personal and social resources against the demands created by our life circumstances. All of us also have certain vulnerabilities, and if environmental demands and our vulnerabilities combine to exceed our resources, we may experience psychological problems for which professional assistance would be helpful. Here are some general guidelines for seeking such help and profiting from it.

Help may be sought at a school counseling center, at a community agency, or from a professional in private practice. The counseling center is a good place for a student to start, for it can provide either help or an appropriate referral to a reputable mental health professional.

How expensive is treatment? It is often offered free or at a nominal fee at a campus facility (see Figure 17.26). Community agencies typically have a sliding fee scale based on the client's income. Thus, financial considerations need not be a barrier to seeking professional assistance. A private practitioner may charge a fee similar to that charged by doctors, dentists, and attorneys, perhaps exceeding $100 per 50-minute session. The prospective client should always ask beforehand about the fee.

Suppose you are choosing a therapist. What should you look for? It is important that your therapist be fully trained and licensed. Ask the therapist about his or her degree, license, training, and therapeutic orientation and the problems in which he or she specializes. This chapter

has provided an overview of the major theoretical orientations, and one or more of them may be especially attractive to you.

As this chapter has emphasized, the relationship between client and therapist is of the utmost importance. You will want to feel that the therapist with whom you are working can create a good working relationship with you. Personal warmth, sincere concern, and empathy are important characteristics. Some clients prefer to work with a therapist of a particular gender, depending on the nature of the personal issues that have caused them to seek counseling. You should like and feel comfortable with your therapist, and you should feel at ease with the methods the therapist uses. Under no circumstances should your therapeutic relationship in-

◆ **Figure 17.26** *Professional assistance with problems in living is available at campus-based counseling centers like this one.*

volve physical intimacy of any kind, and if a therapist ever makes inappropriate advances, a client should immediately terminate treatment with that therapist and notify the state psychological association. Such conduct is a serious breach of professional ethics and cannot be condoned under any circumstances.

In the course of therapy, it is not unusual for clients to examine some of their personal values and to change some of them. One question that has interested researchers is how the degree of similarity between the client's and the therapist's values is related to the outcome of treatment. Timothy Kelly and Hans Strupp (1992) found that the most positive therapeutic outcomes were achieved when the client and therapist were neither very similar nor very dissimilar in values. They concluded that high similarity may result in a failure to explore value-related issues that should be explored, whereas high and conspicuous dissimilarity may interfere with the building of a good therapeu-

tic relationship. One exception to this general rule may occur in the area of religious values. It appears that clients who have strong and committed religious values may profit most from a therapy that supports those values and uses them to help change problem behaviors. Thus, L. Rebecca Probst and her coworkers (1992) found that religious clients profited more from a cognitive therapy that sometimes used religious principles to counter irrational beliefs than from a nonreligious cognitive therapy.

You and your therapist should have explicit, agreed-on goals for the treatment program. If therapy proceeds well, you will experience beneficial changes in your thoughts, feelings, and behaviors that indicate movement toward these goals. It may take some time for these changes to occur, however, since long-standing personal vulnerabilities are not easily changed, and significant change seldom occurs overnight. If you do not see any progress after several months, or if you

seem to be functioning less well than before, you should discuss your progress with the therapist. You must entertain the possibility that your lack of progress is due to resistance on your part (Teyber, 1992). Resistance is indicated by signs like the following:

1. You feel anxious when going to your treatment session, particularly if you have recently begun to discuss some sensitive issues.
2. You find yourself unable to find topics to discuss during your sessions or feel inclined to hide things from your therapist.
3. You find yourself having intense and unexplainable negative feelings toward your therapist.
4. You forget therapy appointments or find yourself canceling them in favor of other commitments.

Obviously, resistance is not the only barrier to therapeutic progress. You should not expect miracles, but it is best to review your progress with your therapist and come to a common view of what has been occurring in therapy. It is possible that the therapist is more satisfied with your progress than you are.

If you continue to be dissatisfied with your progress or with the therapeutic relationship, you may at some point decide to terminate it. This should not prevent you from seeking help from another therapist.

Entering a helping relationship is a courageous step, and resolving problems in living may involve taking risks and experiencing pain. However, many clients look back on the pain and risks and feel that the process has been a valuable one that has enabled them to live happier lives than they could otherwise have.

The Helping Relationship

- Therapy is the product of three sets of interacting factors: a client, a therapist, and a set of specific techniques administered within the therapeutic relationship.
- Therapies are administered by many types of mental health professionals, including clinical and counseling psychologists, psychiatrists, psychiatric social workers, and counselors.

Psychodynamic Psychotherapies

- The goal of Freudian psychoanalysis is to give clients insight into the unconscious dynamics that underlie their behavior disorders so that their egos can deal realistically with the environment.
- The chief means for promoting insight in psychoanalysis is the therapist's interpretations of free associations and dream content, resistance, and transference reactions.
- Brief psychodynamic psychotherapies have become increasingly popular alternatives to lengthy psychoanalysis. Their goal is also to promote insight, but they tend to focus more on current life events.

Humanistic Psychotherapies

- Humanistic psychotherapies attempt to liberate the client's natural tendency toward self-actualization by establishing a growth-inducing therapeutic relationship.
- Rogers's client-centered therapy emphasizes the importance of three therapist characteristics: unconditional positive regard, empathy, and genuineness.
- The goal of gestalt therapy is to remove blockages to clients' awareness of the wholeness of immediate experience by making them more aware of their feelings and the ways in which they interact with others.

Cognitive Therapies

- Ellis's rational–emotive therapy and Beck's cognitive therapy focus on discovering and changing maladaptive beliefs and logical errors of thinking that underlie maladaptive emotional responses and behaviors.

Behavioral and Cognitive–Behavioral Therapies

- Behavioral treatments based on classical conditioning include exposure to the CS to promote extinction, systematic desensitization, and aversion therapy, which is designed to establish a conditioned aversion response to an inappropriate stimulus that attracts the client.
- Operant procedures have been applied successfully in many behavior modification programs. The token economy is a positive reinforcement program designed to strengthen adaptive behaviors in hospitalized patients. Punishment has been used to reduce self-destructive behaviors in disturbed children.
- Modeling is an important component of social skills training programs. It has also been used in participant modeling programs to reduce fears.

Group, Family, and Marital Therapies

- Group approaches offer clients a number of advantages, including opportunities to form close relationships with others, to gain insights into how they interact with others and are perceived by them, and to observe how others approach problems.
- Family therapy is based on the notion that individuals' problems are often reflections of dysfunctional family systems. Such systems should be treated as a unit.
- Marital therapies help couples to improve their communication patterns and resolve difficulties in their relationships. In behavioral marital therapies, couples receive communication skills training and negotiate behavioral contracts to increase positive exchanges in their marriages.
- Cognitive–behavioral sex therapies based on the techniques developed by Masters and Johnson have proved successful in treating male and female sexual dysfunctions. In these treatments, the couple is treated as a unit.

Evaluating Psychotherapies

- Three sets of interacting factors affect the outcome of treatment: client characteristics (including the nature of the problem), therapist characteristics, and therapy techniques.
- Meta-analysis is a method for combining the results of many studies into an effect size statistic. One large-scale meta-analysis of treatment outcome studies indicated that therapy subjects improved more than about 75 percent of control subjects, and that various therapies seemed to differ little in effectiveness.

- Many therapy researchers have concluded that the most important common factor in the success of various therapies is the quality of the relationship that the therapist establishes with the client. The three characteristics suggested by Rogers—empathy, unconditional positive regard, and genuineness—seem to be particularly important.

Biological Approaches to Treatment

- Drugs have revolutionized the treatment of many behavior disorders and have permitted many hospitalized patients to function outside institutions.
- Effective drug treatments exist for anxiety, schizophrenia and depression. Some of these drugs have undesirable side effects, and tranquilizing drugs can be addictive.
- Electroconvulsive therapy is used less frequently than in the past, and its safety has been increased. It is used primarily to treat severe depression, particularly when a threat of suicide exists.

The Community and Disordered Behavior

- The introduction of drug therapies that normalize disturbed behavior, as well as concerns about the hospitalization syndrome, have helped to stimulate a move toward deinstitutionalization—the treatment of people in their communities.
- Research has shown that deinstitutionalization can work when adequate community treatment is provided. Unfortunately, the needed facilities have not been funded, resulting in a "revolving door" of release and rehospitalization, as well as a new generation of homeless people who live in the streets and do not receive needed treatment.
- Prevention programs may be classified as either situation-focused or competency-focused, depending on whether they are directed at changing environmental conditions or personal factors. Another classification system involves the timing of treatment. Primary prevention is designed to prevent problems in people who are at risk but are not yet exhibiting problems. Secondary prevention is designed to reduce the consequences of already existing conditions. Tertiary prevention is aimed at enhancing the rehabilitation of people who have undergone treatment.

aversion therapy (p. 548)

behavioral marital therapy (p. 552)

behavior modification (p. 548)

behavior therapy (p. 546)

chlorpromazine (p. 558)

client-centered therapy (p. 540)

cognitive-behavioral approach (p. 546)

cognitive therapy (p. 544)

commitment (p. 562)

competency-focused prevention (p. 564)

counterconditioning (p. 547)

effect size (p. 555)

electroconvulsive therapy (ECT) (p. 559)

empathy (p. 540)

encounter group (p. 551)

exposure (flooding) (p. 546)

free association (p. 537)

genuineness (p. 540)

gestalt therapy (p. 542)

hospitalization syndrome (p. 552)

insight (p. 537)

interpretation (p. 539)

major tranquilizers (p. 558)

meta-analysis (p. 555)

monoamineoxidase (MAO) inhibitor (p. 558)

orgasmic dysfunction (p. 553)

participant modeling (p. 550)

performance anxiety (p. 553)

premature ejaculation (p. 554)

primary prevention (p. 565)

rational–emotive therapy (p. 543)

reflecting (p. 540)

resistance (p. 538)

revolving-door phenomenon (p. 563)

secondary prevention (p. 565)

sexual dysfunction (p. 553)

situation-focused prevention (p. 564)

social skills training (p. 550)

systematic desensitization (p. 547)

tardive dyskenesia (p. 558)

tertiary prevention (p. 565)

token economy (p. 548)

transference (p. 538)

tricyclic (p. 558)

unconditional positive regard (p. 540)

working through (p. 537)

SUGGESTED READINGS

Gay, P. (1990). *Reading Freud: Explorations and entertainments.* New Haven, Conn.: Yale University Press. This fascinating series of essays on Freud provides insights into the mind of this genius and into the factors that influenced the development of his theory and his therapeutic methods.

Phares, E. J. (1992). *Clinical psychology: Concepts, methods, and profession* (4th ed.). Pacific Grove, Calif.: Brooks/Cole. A comprehensive and readable overview of the field of clinical psychology, with chapters on research methods, assessment, and all of the major approaches to treatment.

Teyber, E. (1992). *Interpersonal process in psychotherapy: A guide for clinical training* (2nd ed.). Pacific Grove, Calif.: Brooks/Cole. This informative book, written for the beginning therapist, is a good introduction to the aspects of the therapeutic relationship that seem to facilitate psychotherapy. The book provides an overview of what goes into becoming a psychotherapist.

Social Influences On Behavior

18

CHAPTER OUTLINE

The prison was a living hell. Hidden behind their mirrored sunglasses, the guards asserted their total authority and power over the prisoners. The guards' permission was required to do virtually anything, including going to the toilet.

It wasn't long before the prisoners rebelled. The disturbance was quickly and efficiently put down by the guards. Cruelty now became the order of the day. The guards began to do roll calls in the middle of the night to disrupt the prisoners' sleep and to assert their power. Prisoners were forced to do push-ups, sometimes with a guard's foot pushing down on the prisoner's back. The guards stretched routine 10-minute lineups into hour-long ordeals filled with verbal abuse (see Figure 18.1). They refused to allow the prisoners bathroom privileges during the night and forced them to use containers in their cells.

For their part, the prisoners became increasingly passive, helpless, and depressed. They hated the guards, but they were powerless against them. After a few days, one of the prisoners cracked emotionally. Soon afterward, another broke down. Before long, the smelly, demoralized prisoners became what the guards imagined them to be—objects of scorn and abuse.

This prison was not in some Central American country. It was not in Iraq, in the Gulag, or on Devil's Island. The prisoners were not hardened criminals, nor were the guards sadistic psychopaths. Instead, this prison was in the basement of the Psychology Building at Stanford University, and the guards and prisoners were intelligent, well-adjusted college students who had been carefully screened beforehand. The warden of the Stanford County Prison was Philip G. Zimbardo, a prominent social psychologist, who watched in disbelief and horror as scenes of callous inhumanity unfolded before him.

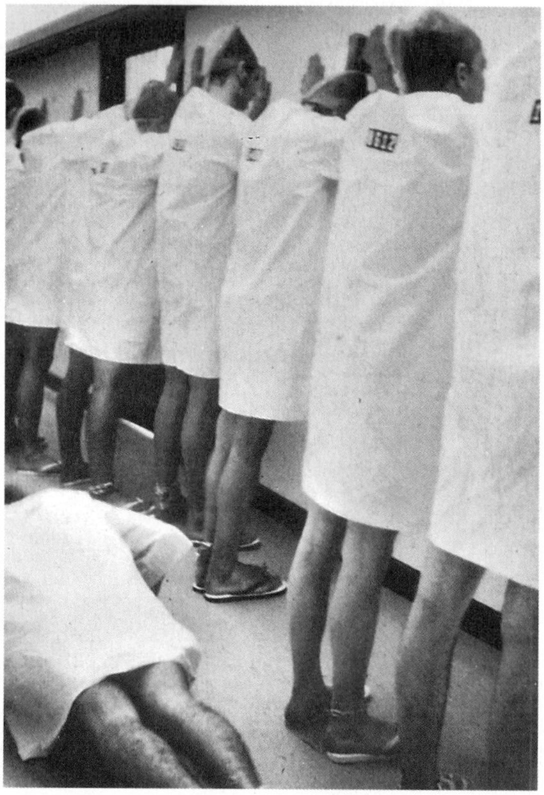

What had begun as a 2-week simulation study of prison life had to be stopped after only 6 days. So powerful was the experience for both the prisoners and the guards that Zimbardo and his associates held several sessions with the participants to help them work through their emotional reactions, and they maintained contact with each student over the following year to ensure that the negative effects of the prison simulation did not persist.

What happened to transform these normal college students into people they themselves would not have recognized a week earlier? What goes on in a social setting that can transform the typical behavior of college peers so dramatically that they become dehumanized enemies? Before the disbelieving eyes of the researchers, a simulation in which two groups of people had been asked to take on temporary roles as prisoners and guards became a nightmarish social reality that called forth extreme and uncharacteristic behaviors. As one of the guards later recalled, "I was surprised at myself. . . . I made them call each other names and clean out the toilets with their bare hands. I practically considered the prisoners cattle, and I kept thinking: 'I have to watch out for them in case they try something'" (Zimbardo & others, 1973, p. 42).

Zimbardo recalls, "In the end, I called off the experiment not only because of the horror I saw out there in the prison yard, but because of the horror of realizing that I could have easily traded places with the most brutal guard or become the weakest prisoner, full of hatred at being so powerless that I could not eat, sleep, or go to the toilet without the permission of authorities" (Zimbardo, 1972).

As social beings, we belong. We spend our lives embedded in social systems that exert profound influences on our thoughts, emotions, attitudes, and behavior. In this chapter, we examine the forces of influence at work in the social environment.

Figure 18.1 *During the Stanford prison study, prisoners were forced to stand in lineups like this one for long periods. The prisoner doing the push-ups is being punished by the guards for moving during the lineup. (Courtesy of Philip G. Zimbardo).*

■ ▢

Social Norms and Roles: The Rules of the Game

As our lives unfold, most of us function in many social systems. First, we are part of a family. Later, we become immersed in the social systems of the neighborhood peer group, the schools we attend, perhaps sport teams and the military, college groups like fraternities and sororities, business and occupational groups, and newly formed families resulting from our own marriages. In all of these systems, we occupy particular positions known as social roles.

A **social role** may be defined as a pattern of behavior that characterizes a particular position in a social system and is expected of a person who occupies that position. Certain behaviors are socially programmed into the roles of mother, father, student, police officer, and minister, for example. At any given time, we occupy a number of different roles. Because the appropriate behavior patterns for these roles may differ and may even conflict with one another, considerable behavioral flexibility may be required to meet the demands of these different roles. One role may require us to be deferent and submissive; another may demand that we be assertive and directive. The concept of roles is therefore a useful one in helping us to understand how situational demands cause people's behavior to vary from situation to situation.

The "rules of the game" that regulate social behavior are called **social norms.** Social norms are expectations shared by the members of a group about how they should think, feel, and behave. They are the cement that binds social systems together and allows them to function more or less harmoniously.

Norms differ in their explicitness. The most explicit ones are written down as formal laws. Others are implicit, and perhaps even unspoken; yet they, too, may function as powerful regulators of social interaction. For example, you may have had the experience of feeling an unwelcome pressure to repay a favor. If so, you were probably feeling the influence of the widely held **norm of reciprocity,** which specifies that a person who has been helped should "pay back" the helper or giver. People who don't ask for or accept favors because they "don't want to feel obligated" are usually trying to avoid the consequences of this norm. On the other hand, what we term *ingratiation* often takes the form of doing nice things for others so that they feel a sense of obligation to reciprocate (see Figure 18.2).

Social norms and social roles are intimately related to one another. The norms associated with social roles specify how the person occupying that role is expected to think, feel, and behave, as well as how others are expected to respond in return (see Figure 18.3). These norms can influence behavior so strongly that they may compel a person to behave in a totally uncharacteristic manner. The Zimbardo prison study may be a dramatic example of this. Once the college students began to occupy the roles of prisoner and guard, the norms associated with those roles seemed to take over, resulting in a destructive pattern of social interactions. The prisoners and guards had been selected because of their psychological "normality"

Figure 18.2 *The norm of reciprocity in action. By giving passersby flowers as gifts, Hare Krishnas increase the likelihood that the potential donors will feel pressure to comply with requests for donations.*

and randomly assigned to their roles. Nevertheless, the social norms of a system organized around the concepts of crime and punishment came to control and regulate their behavior. The power of the norms seemed to override the previously acquired values, ethics, and personality characteristics of the subjects. As one of the prisoners later reported, "I began to feel that I was losing my identity. The person I call (subject's real name) . . . was distant from me, was remote, until finally I wasn't that. I was Number 416—I was really my number" (Zimbardo, 1972).

Although few of us are likely to find ourselves in such an extreme situation, all of us will find ourselves in new roles that are foreign to us. Exposure to new roles is a major way in which personality develops and changes. Indeed, this is precisely why many psychotherapists try to get their clients to experiment with new social roles as a way of encouraging them to change their maladaptive patterns of social interaction.

Development of Norms

Social psychologists define **reference groups** as groups whose standards and beliefs a person identifies with and accepts. The earliest reference group for most of us is the family. Within the family, an important part of the socialization process is the passing on of attitudes, values, and rules of conduct. The norms that are important to the family and to its social roles are communicated verbally (for example, "Al-

Figure 18.3 *The norms associated with social roles specify how people in those roles are expected to behave and how others are expected to behave toward them.*

ways treat others as you want them to treat you," "In this family, we have a strong work ethic") and through the modeling of role-appropriate behaviors by other family members (for example, being kind to others and working hard). Many of these early lessons on the nature of social reality may remain intact throughout a person's life.

As we develop, however, reference groups beyond the family become important to us and may even override the earlier family influences. A study by Theodore Newcomb (1963) demonstrates this point. In 1935, Newcomb had conducted extensive interviews with the freshman class at Bennington College, an expensive and exclusive college for women. Most of the freshmen were daughters of wealthy and highly conservative New England families, and they shared

their families' conservative attitudes. In contrast, junior and senior students as well as the faculty at Bennington tended to have extremely liberal political beliefs.

Newcomb was interested in how much the attitudes of the freshmen women would change as a result of their college experiences. He predicted that students whose primary reference group shifted from their families to their college peers and professors would become more politically liberal. This is exactly what he found (see Figure 18.4). In contrast, students who remained very attached to their families maintained their conservative beliefs, but they were less popular and less involved in campus life.

In 1960, Newcomb again interviewed the women. He found that the attitudes formed through association with the liberal college reference group were just as enduring as those formed through close attachments to the family. Women who had become more liberal during their college years continued to be liberal and had tended to marry extremely liberal men. Those who remained conservative had married men whose attitudes were similar to their own.

In a classic social psychology study, Muzafer Sherif (1935) observed the process by which group members establish a common norm as they interact over time. To do so, he needed a situation in which prior experience provided little basis for judgment. He found this in a phenomenon known as the **autokinetic effect.** When subjects are presented with a stationary pinpoint of light in an otherwise pitch-dark room, the light appears to move about erratically. Sherif first asked male subjects to make individual judgments concerning how far the light moved. Their judgments varied widely; some saw the light move only a few inches, while others judged it to have moved several feet. Over time, each subject's judg-

Figure 18.4 *Theodore Newcomb's study of Bennington girls showed what a powerful influence the college reference group can have on attitudes and viewpoints.*

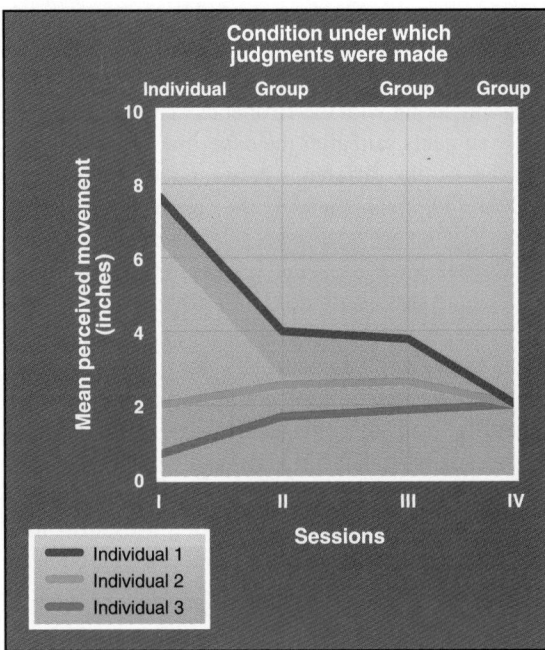

Figure 18.5 *In Sherif's experiments on the development of group norms, individuals' autokinetic judgments began to converge when they were made in the presence of two other subjects. Each mean is based on 100 judgments per session. The figure shows what occurred in one of the three-person groups. (Based on Sherif, 1935).*

ments tended to fall within a relatively narrow range as an individual judgment norm was established.

Then Sherif put subjects together in groups of three and asked them to make their judgments in front of the others. What occurred over time was a clear convergence of individual judgments toward a group norm, as shown in Figure 18.5. It is interesting to note that the group norm was not the simple average of the original judgments. Sherif found that personal characteristics and degree of social dominance affected the final group norm. For example, a subject who made extreme judgments with considerable force and self-confidence could pull the other members' judgments toward his, although even he would tend to compromise a bit toward their judgments. In contrast, the person with the most deviant initial judgments could move in the direction of the majority, as in the group represented in Figure 18.5.

After a group norm is established, what do you suppose happens if the subjects make additional autokinetic judgments by themselves? Do they revert to their original judgments once they are alone again, or do they maintain the group norm? Sherif found that even when the subjects were separated, they continued to follow the norm established by the group. Most of the subjects had taken on the norm as their own.

Conformity

Of course, norms can influence behavior only if people conform to them. Without **conformity**—the adjustment of individual behaviors, attitudes, and beliefs to a group standard—we would have social chaos. Consider what would happen in supermarket checkout lines, outside movie theaters, and in crowded rest rooms if people did not conform to the norm of forming a line and waiting their turns. Conformity to social norms is the stitching that holds the fabric of society together. It is no accident, therefore, that all social systems exert considerable pressure on their members to conform. Often, the process is so subtle and gradual that we fail to recognize it as it occurs (see Figure 18.6).

The pressures become more obvious when we fail to conform and begin to violate norms. ▼ If we violate the explicit norms we call laws, we are labeled as criminals and punished. Violation of the more subtle and unspoken norms (for example, the norm that we not hold animated conversations in public with people who are not present) may be grounds for being labeled mentally ill. Indeed, the various behavior disorders described in Chapter 16 all involve violations of certain social norms. In a variety of ways, people who are labeled as emotionally disturbed do not live up to widely accepted social expectations. Their behavior is therefore judged abnormal.

Why People Conform

Conformity occurs for a variety of reasons. One important underlying motive is to obtain the rewards that come from being accepted by other people and at the same time to avoid rejection by the group. This factor seemed to be important in the attitude shifts shown by the Bennington women who identified with and sought the approval of the older students and the faculty. A second reason for conforming stems from the desire to understand the world so that we can respond effectively to it (Biener & Boudreau, 1991). In this case, the actions of others serve as information on how to get along, how to survive. Either or both of these factors may influence conformity in a given situation. Both were probably at work in a series of famous experiments on conformity conducted by Solomon Asch (1951, 1956).

In these experiments, groups of seven to nine college students were told that they were going to take part in an experiment on visual discrimination. Their task was to match a line with one of three comparison lines. In each case, one comparison line was the same length while the other two were obviously longer or shorter.

Only one member of the group was actually a subject. The rest were accomplices of the experi-

Figure 18.6 *Although the teen-age years are often viewed as a time of rebellion and nonconformity, teenagers actually conform highly within their peer groups.*

menter. The group members were seated around a table and were called on in order. The real subject was always next to last. The confederates gave previously agreed on answers, which were sometimes correct and sometimes incorrect. If the subject's answer disagreed with their obviously incorrect answers, they did not act surprised but continued to respond in an unemotional way.

When the majority gave the same incorrect answers, the effect was striking. In a control group, in which no incorrect answers were given, only 5 percent of the subjects made errors. But in the experimental condition, at least 76 percent made one or more errors by going along with the erroneous majority. Many of these subjects said after the experiment that they felt puzzled by the difference between their perceptions and the judgments made by the unanimous majority. After several trials, subjects began to have doubts about their own eyesight, judgment, and ability to understand the instructions (see Figure 18.7). Even the subjects who did not conform expressed doubts about their own judgment.

It is easy to see how conformity influences behavior in everyday life (see Figure 18.8). For example, many students in high school and college are subjected to group pressures concerning such things as clothing, the importance of high grades, drug use, and sexual behavior. Being a member of a group can result in conformity to attitudes that characterize the group even for a group member who disagrees initially. Studies have shown that if a group makes a majority decision, individuals in the group who disagreed with the majority during earlier discussions tend to shift their viewpoints so that they conform more closely to that of the majority (Worth & others, 1987).

But does the majority always rule? What happens if a determined and united minority opposes the group norm in a consistent and confident fashion? The results of numerous studies suggest that there is an important distinction to be made between *public conformity* and *private conformity* (Shaver, 1987). When confronted by a majority that appears to be wrong, as in the Asch studies, many people conform publicly while maintaining their private convictions. And when a determined and consistent minority calls their

Figure 18.7 *In one of Asch's conformity experiments, seven students are being asked to judge which of three lines is the same length as another line. Subject number 6 (from the left) has just heard the preceding five subjects (all of whom are accomplices of the experimenter) make the same incorrect judgment. As he prepares to answer, note the look of bewilderment on his face. (Asch, 1955).*

Figure 18.8 *The kind of conformity demonstrated in the Asch experiments can be found in a variety of settings.*

"Well, heck! If all you smart cookies agree, who am I to dissent?"

(Drawing by Handlesman; © 1972 The New Yorker Magazine, Inc.)

views into question, people tend to change or at least question their views on a private level even though they are less likely to conform publicly to the minority view (Maass & Clark, 1984). If the minority view is presented a number of times, the dissenting information may cause a reassessment of the entire issue by majority members (Nemeth & others, 1990). Thus, a determined minority with a credible point of view may exert more influence on the beliefs and judgments of other group members than is immediately and publicly apparent. The characteristics of effective minority influences seem to be investment in their points of view, ability to remain independent in the face of group pressure to conform, consistency of viewpoint over time, and willingness to keep an open mind (Moscovici, 1985). When these conditions exist, the majority sometimes comes to conform to the will of a determined minority (Biener & Boudreau, 1991).

▲ **Figure 18.9** *Aftermath of the Jonestown mass suicide. This shocking event helped to rekindle interest in extreme forms of thought control and conformity.*

The Outer Limits of Conformity: The Psychology of the Cult

In the oppressive heat of the Guyanese jungle, the Reverend Jim Jones gave his last command. In response, over 900 of his followers walked to the galvanized iron buckets, dipped out cupfuls of a fruit drink laced with cyanide, and drank the lethal potion. Mothers fed the drink to their children, and husbands gave it to their wives. In a matter of minutes, the village of Jonestown was littered with the corpses of its inhabitants (see Figure 18.9).

One of the most striking and bizarre episodes of this or any other century, the Jonestown incident evoked the questions "Why?" and "How?" throughout the world. How could one man, no matter how powerful and charismatic, exert such total domination over the lives of his followers? How can we account for the extraordinary degree of conformity seen in Jones's People's Temple and in the other religious cults that have attracted more than 3 million members in the United States alone?

Some observers of the cult phenomenon have concluded that the motivation to be controlled must lie within the converts themselves. But the view that the converts are social misfits who seek in cults the group involvement denied them by the rest of society is not supported by research on cult converts. To be sure, people who become cult converts are often struggling to gain a sense of self-identity, to pursue idealistic goals, or to find a sense of personal meaning in their lives (Schwartz & Kaslow, 1981). Yet these people seldom seek out cults. Rather, cult members encounter them largely by chance at a time when they are particularly open to offers of friendship and "answers" to their questions. The group treats recruits

with warmth, openness, and concern; and recruits hear testimonials from members about the joy, peace, and love they have experienced by devoting their lives to the goals of the cult. The unrelenting pace of the indoctrination allows the recruits little opportunity to critically evaluate what they are experiencing. The indoctrination technique is designed to lower resistance while instilling guilt, uncertainty, and confusion. The answer to the guilt and confusion, of course, is to reject one's former life and join the cult. Eventually, converts are told that they must break all ties with the past, including family and acquaintances. Thus, the success of cult recruiting seems to stem from an interaction between characteristics of recruits that increase their vulnerability and highly effective social influence techniques that establish the cult as the converts' new and powerful reference group (see Figure 18.10).

Once converts begin to conform and behave according to the dictates of the group, new forces come to bear. As we shall see, there is considerable evidence that if people see themselves freely behaving in a particular manner, their attitudes will tend to become consistent with their behavior (Olson & Zanna, 1991). Thus, cult members who forsake family and friends, give all worldly possessions to the cult, and go out seeking to convert others will logically conclude that they subscribe totally to the cult's belief system (Baumeister, 1986). That belief system can become the new "social reality" for the cult's members, particularly if the group isolates itself from other aspects of society.

⬤ **Figure 18.10** *A cult can elicit extreme levels of conformity from its members by capitalizing on their needs for acceptance and a sense of purpose and by establishing the cult as a powerful reference group. Here members of a religious cult celebrate a mass wedding ceremony.*

This is exactly what Jim Jones's People's Temple did when it left San Francisco and went to Guyana. In a new and strange land, the cult members increasingly depended on one another to define correct beliefs and conduct. When Jones proclaimed that suicide was the only correct course of action and some of the true believers moved to the poison vats and began to consume the liquid, the stage was set for mass conformity (Cialdini, 1988). Jones's genius was not in effecting "mass hypnosis" but in setting up social conditions that maximized pressures to conform to the beliefs and actions of the cult.

In the final analysis, then, conformity is a two-edged sword. On the one hand, a certain amount of conformity is needed if social systems are to function. On the other hand, conforming to social norms can result in destructive consequences, as we have seen in the Zimbardo prison study, in the Jonestown incident, and in Milgram's studies of obedience to authority described in Chapter 2. It remains for each person to decide when conformity spells destructive consequences for the individual or the group.

Deindividuation: Conditions that Weaken Social Restraints

In New York City's Spanish Harlem, a Puerto Rican handyman sat perched on a ledge for an hour while a crowd of nearly 500 people on the street below shouted at him in Spanish and English to jump. As the cries of "Jump!" and "Brinca!" rang out, police managed to rescue the man.

What would prompt people to encourage a distraught human being to end his life? We have seen that social norms and roles help to bring order to social behavior. Now we consider a form of social influence that leads to a loss of social restraints.

The social psychologist Leon Mann (1981) analyzed newspaper reports of 21 cases in which crowds of people were present when a person threatened to jump off a building. In 10 of the cases, the news accounts reported that the crowd had encouraged the person to jump. Mann found that this was most likely to occur when the crowd was large, when the incident occurred after dark, and when the victim was above the 12th floor and thus distant from the crowd.

All of these conditions help to create anonymity. In the 19th Century, Gustave LeBon, a French physician who became fascinated with the psychology of mob violence, suggested that the anonymity that exists in mobs leads to a loss of personal identity and the weakening of restraints. Immersed in a mob, people may engage in behaviors that they would not consider performing as individuals. Social psychologists have labeled this state **deindividuation** (Festinger & others, 1952).

Recent analyses of deindividuation suggest that the key to this phenomenon is the loss of self-awareness that can occur under certain conditions (Diener, 1980; Prentice-Dunn & Spivey, 1986). In order to regulate our own behavior, we need a moment-by-moment awareness of our feelings, values, and behavior. Such factors as anonymity (the knowledge that we are not identifiable), heightened emotional arousal, a focus of attention outward rather than inward, and immersion in a group with a common purpose can lead to a sharp reduction in personal awareness. The result is a drastic weakening of restraints and a lowered ability to engage in rational control of behavior. Thus, a study of extreme aggression in lynch mobs found that as the size of lynch mobs increased, the anonymity of individual members became greater, personal accountability and self-attention decreased, and more savage atrocities were committed against the victims (Mullen, 1986; see Figure 18.11).

The factors thought to be involved in deindividuation are shown in Figure 18.12. This theoretical model was tested in an experiment in which subjects were permitted to behave aggressively toward another person (an accomplice of the experimenters) by supposedly delivering electric shocks (Prentice-Dunn & Rogers, 1982). The subjects' private self-awareness and their public self-awareness were manipulated in the experiment. To increase their private self-awareness, the researchers instructed some subjects to pay close attention to their thoughts and feelings. They told others to concentrate on the situation rather than on themselves, a directive designed to decrease their private self-awareness. To enhance public self-awareness, the experimenters told some of the subjects that they would meet the victim after the experiment for a discussion of the shocks and that the shock levels they administered would be recorded. Finally, the researchers attempted to reduce the public self-awareness of other subjects by telling them that they would not meet the victim and that their behavior would not be monitored.

Both before and after delivering shocks to the accomplice, subjects completed a questionnaire designed to measure their subjective feelings of deindividuation. This permitted the experimenters to determine whether shifts in self-awareness produced deindividuation and whether, in turn, this state increased aggression. The results showed that reductions in both private and public self-awareness enhanced aggression. However, the subjective sense of deindividuation was produced only when private self-awareness was reduced. Finally, the researchers found that the more intense the experience of deindividuation was, the more electric shock was administered. It thus appears that conditions that decrease private self-awareness can result in deindividuation and its consequences.

Returning for the moment to the Stanford prison study, we can see that a number of conditions were present that might be expected to enhance deindividuation in the guards: No names were ever used. Guards had to be called ''Mr. Correctional Officer.'' All wore identical uniforms and reflecting sunglasses that prevented eye contact. They were unaware that their behavior was being monitored. These factors have led Zimbardo to conclude that deindividuation may have been a key factor in the cruelty exhibited by the guards.

Can deindividuation be counteracted? The knowledge that social psychologists have gained about its nature and causes suggests a number of possible an-

Figure 18.11 *Deindividuation can lead to a loss of restraint that enables people to engage in ordinarily taboo behaviors. Studies of mobs indicate that the size of the mob is related to the level of atrocities committed against the mob's victims.*

tidotes. One is to take steps to reduce anonymity. In the late 1960s, for example, reports of police brutality during civil disturbances decreased drastically in cities where police were equipped with large name plates. Similarly, authorities have found that one way to reduce crowd violence is to convince crowd members that the proceedings are being photographed or videotaped. Measures that reduce emotional arousal and that prompt people to focus on themselves rather than totally on the external event may also be effective. Finally, restoring internal restraints by appealing to people to examine their own attitudes and values or by threatening punishment may help to counter deindividuation.

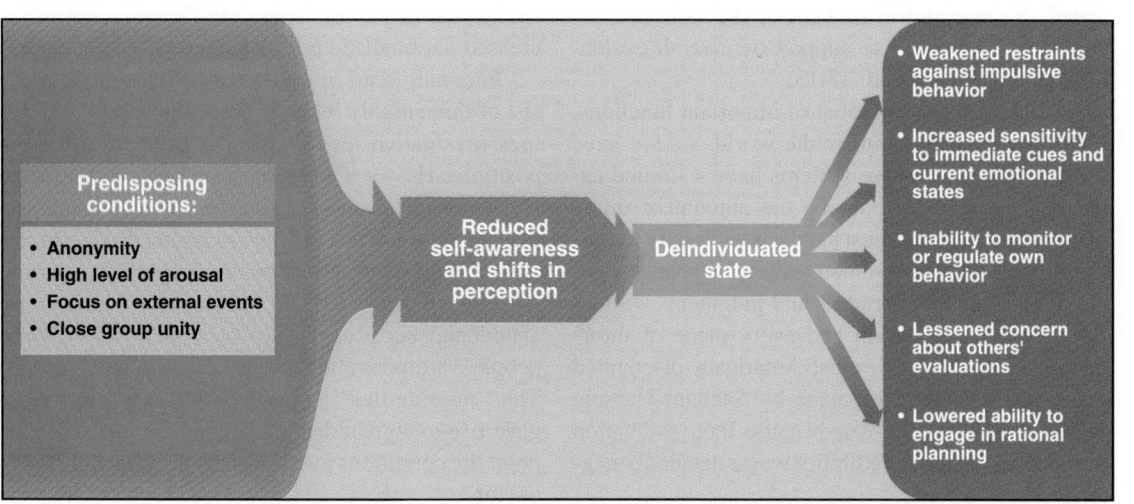

Figure 18.12 *Certain environmental factors (such as anonymity and immersion in the group) lead to reduced self-awareness and the accompanying shifts in perception that constitute deindividuation. Deindividuation, in turn, produces several important effects, such as a weakening of internal restraints against impulsive behavior. (Diener, 1980).*

As we have seen, a variety of social forces lead to conformity and compliance with the desires of others. Important targets of attempts to influence people are their attitudes and the behaviors these attitudes are assumed to affect.

■ ▫

Attitude Formation and Change

In 1935, Gordon Allport, a prominent personality and social psychologist, called attitude "social psychology's most indispensable concept" (p. 798). We might arrive at similar conclusions in our daily lives. Most of us tend to focus a good deal on people's attitudes in our attempts to understand and predict their behavior.

Social psychologists have used the concept of attitude to explain such diverse phenomena as consumer behavior, political activities, prejudice, human sexuality, organizational behavior, and the self-concept (Brown, 1991; Olson & Zanna, 1991). Understandably, then, a great deal of the theorizing and research related to social influences on behavior has focused on the factors that affect the formation and changing of attitudes.

Attitude is a rather broad and imprecise term as it is used in everyday life; so let's pin it down a bit. Today, many social psychologists define an **attitude** as an evaluative reaction, stored in long-term memory, that is attached to categories of people, objects, issues, and events. Thus, our attitudes vary primarily along a positive–negative, agree–disagree, or like–dislike dimension. An attitude is represented in memory by (1) an object label (for example, "liberals," "Arabs," "junk foods," "me") and rules for applying that label, (2) a positive or negative evaluative reaction to the object, and (3) a knowledge or belief structure supporting that evaluation (Greenwald, 1990; Tesser & Shaffer, 1990). The knowledge or belief structure may contain elements that are themselves positive and negative, but the elements are combined cognitively to support the overall evaluative reaction (see Figure 18.13).

Attitudes serve a number of important functions. First, they help to simplify the world. As we have seen, people's cognitive systems have a limited capacity. One way of reducing the amount of information these systems must handle is to classify things. Classifying along an evaluative dimension helps people to make quick appraisals and judgments without having to consider each and every piece of information received. Thus, most Americans discounted many of the statements made by Saddam Hussein during the 1991 Gulf War because their evaluation of the Iraqi leader's credibility was a decidedly negative one.

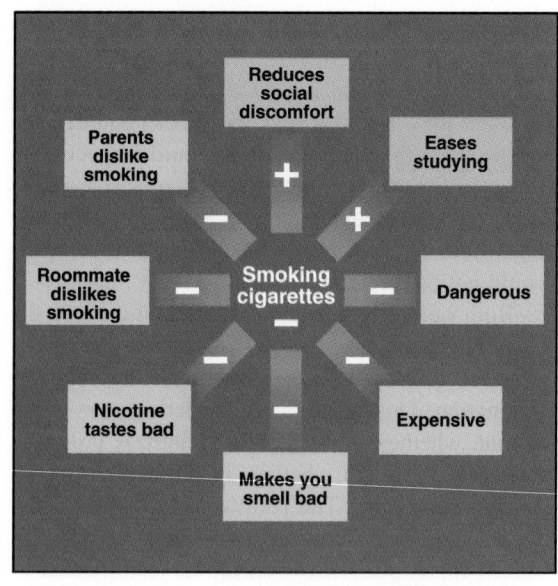

◀ **Figure 18.13** *The cognitive and affective components of a person's attitude toward smoking. Around the attitude object (smoking) are cognitive components related to smoking. The plus and minus signs show the positive and negative affect associated with each of the cognitions. The minus sign in the center indicates the resulting overall negative attitude toward smoking cigarettes. (Adapted from Sears & others, 1985).*

Second, the knowledge or belief structure supporting an evaluation helps people organize their thoughts, memories, and actions toward the object. Thus, exposure to new facts about Hussein and the dangers he might pose in the future within the context of already-negative beliefs about him made many people in the coalition countries ever more supportive of waging war against Iraq. Finally, many attitudes are held in service of what is perhaps the most important attitude object, the self. As we shall see, many attitudes are used to define and to maintain self-worth. Thus, the successful early days of the Gulf War against the negatively appraised Hussein evoked increased nationalistic pride among many Americans.

For many years, it was assumed that attitudes consist of three highly related components: beliefs, feelings (evaluative responses), and behavioral predispositions. However, research has shown that how we feel is not necessarily related to what we think and that the thought and feeling components of attitudes do not necessarily predict our behavior. Indeed, some critics have suggested that the concept of attitude be abandoned because of the weak linkages between people's attitudes and their behavior (Wicker, 1969). The "missing link" between attitudes and behavior gave rise to a great deal of research designed to pinpoint the conditions under which attitudes predict behavior.

Attitudes and Behavior

In the 1930s, the sociologist Richard LaPiere (1934) took a young Chinese couple on a 10,000-mile automobile trip during which they visited 250 restaurants and hotels throughout the United States. At the time, prejudice against Asians was very widespread, yet the couple was refused service only once. Later, LaPiere wrote back to all of the places they had visited, asking if they would provide service to Chinese patrons. More than 90 percent of those who responded stated that they would not. Clearly, there was a marked discrepancy between these people's stated prejudicial attitudes and their earlier behavior.

LaPiere's study was not the only one to call the assumption of attitude–behavior consistency into question. In 1969, Allen Wicker reviewed all of the existing research on the topic and concluded that there was little evidence that attitudes predict behavior. Subsequent research has tempered Wicker's conclusion and has helped identify the conditions under which attitudes do predict behavior.

It is important to remember that attitudes are only one of many variables that may affect behavior in a given situation. Some of the variables at work are, like attitudes, internal. These include personality variables, motivational factors, and **subjective norms**—that is, our beliefs about what others think we should do. In the influential **theory of reasoned action** developed by Martin Fishbein and Icek Ajzen (1980), attitudes and subjective norms act in combination to influence behavioral intentions, and it is these intentions that ultimately affect how people behave (see Figure 18.14).

Other variables that reduce attitude–behavior consistency are situational in nature. We have already discussed some of the ways in which social pressures toward conformity, compliance, and obedience may

lead people to behave in ways that are at odds with their inner convictions. For example, research indicates that high school students' future decisions regarding marijuana use can be predicted more accurately from the number of their friends who use marijuana than from their stated attitudes toward smoking marijuana (Andrews & Kandel, 1979).

The power of internal or external factors may easily override the influence of attitudes in a given instance, thus making it appear that attitudes have no effect on behavior. Therefore, attitude–behavior relations are likely to be strongest when other possible influences on behavior are minimized.

Another lesson from research on attitude–behavior relations is that general attitudes do far better at predicting general *classes* of behavior than at predicting specific behaviors. For example, Fishbein and Ajzen (1974) examined the relation between attitudes toward religion and 70 different religious behaviors. They found almost no relation between positive religious attitudes and any one of the behaviors (for example, praying before meals or attending services each week); the average correlation was only +.15. However, when they combined the 70 behaviors into a single index of religious behavior and related this index to attitude, the correlation rose dramatically to +.71. Squaring this coefficient indicated that religious attitudes accounted for about half of the variance in religious behaviors as a whole.

Fishbein and Ajzen offer an additional caveat. They find that measuring attitudes toward specific behaviors results in higher correlations than measuring attitudes toward objects. For example, Andrew Davidson and James Jaccard (1979) found that women's attitudes toward "using birth control pills within the next 2 years" predicted their actual use of birth control pills much better than their general attitudes toward birth control. LaPiere might thus have found stronger attitude–behavior correspondence if he had

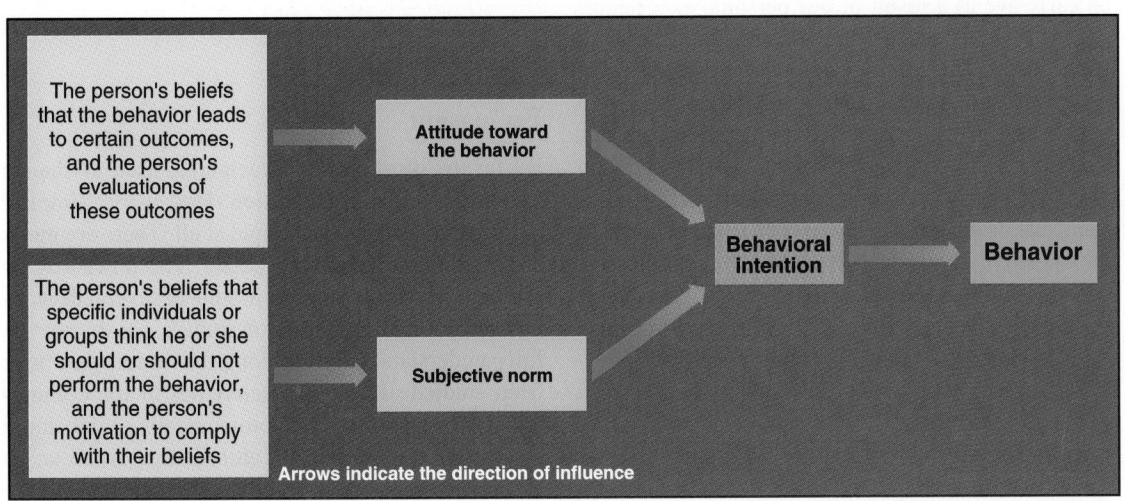

Figure 18.14 *The theory of reasoned action asserts that how people behave is influenced by their behavioral intentions, which in turn are influenced by their attitudes and subjective norms and the relative importance of the attitudes and norms. (Adapted from Ajzen & Fishbein, 1980).*

The person's beliefs that the behavior leads to certain outcomes, and the person's evaluations of these outcomes

Attitude toward the behavior

The person's beliefs that specific individuals or groups think he or she should or should not perform the behavior, and the person's motivation to comply with their beliefs

Subjective norm

Behavioral intention

Behavior

Arrows indicate the direction of influence

asked the restauranteurs and innkeepers whether they would serve a young, well-dressed, attractive Chinese couple accompanied by an American professor rather than asking them about their attitudes toward serving Asians in general.

Finally, the strength of an attitude and the person's present awareness of it affects the magnitude of attitude–behavior relations. Research has shown that attitudes are stronger, more stable, and more predictive of behavior when they are formed through direct personal experience with the attitude object rather than through secondhand, indirect information (Brehm & Kassin, 1990). Deeply held attitudes are also more likely to appear frequently in people's awareness and therefore to be taken into account when they act. However, less strongly held attitudes have been found to be potent predictors of behavior when investigators have called them to mind by asking people to think carefully about their views or by questioning them repeatedly about their attitudes (Powell & Fazio, 1984; Snyder & Swann, 1976).

It is clear that, depending on the conditions, the relations between attitudes and behaviors can range from no relation at all to a high degree of correspondence. And the relations between attitudes and behavior do not travel in only one direction. There is a less obvious but equally important causal relation between attitudes and behavior that moves in the opposite direction: *Actions can influence attitudes.* We will look more closely at this linkage later, in the discussion of attitude change.

Having considered the nature and functions of attitudes and how they relate to behavior, let us now consider how they are formed—and changed—as people interact with their social worlds.

Attitude Formation

We are not born with attitudes. They develop from an early age as a result of our personal experiences with attitude objects and the information we receive from others. The central role of learning in the formation of attitudes makes all of the learning principles discussed in Chapter 9 relevant to their development. Thus, classical conditioning accounts for some of our attitudes, and advertisers spend nearly $100 billion each year on advertising that associates their products with positive stimuli such as soothing music, pleasant colors, wealth and success, and sexually attractive people (Aamodt, 1991). In contrast to these positive associations, associating objects or people with negative stimuli (including such negatively toned words as "bad" and "lazy") can create negative attitudes toward the objects (Krosnick & others, 1992; Kuykendall & Keating, 1990).

Operant conditioning also contributes to the development of attitudes. Our personal experiences predispose us to form positive attitudes toward objects that provide rewarding outcomes and negative attitudes toward objects that produce punishing consequences. People may acquire a lifelong negative attitude toward an academic subject in which they once failed, a factor that seems to underlie the negative attitudes of some "math haters." Likewise, our social environments (including parents, peers, and reference groups) provide reinforcement and punishment, usually in the form of approval or disapproval, for the expression of certain attitudes. As we saw earlier, this seemed to be a factor in the liberalization of many of the Bennington women (Newcomb, 1963).

Modeling is also an extremely potent process in the development of attitudes. As early in life as we are capable of processing such information, we observe our parents and other people modeling particular attitudes. They show us (or tell us) what we should believe, how we should feel, and how we should behave toward the objects of our attitudes.

Other experiential bases of attitude formation are even more subtle. One, described in Chapter 13, is the **mere exposure effect.** This refers to people's tendency to evaluate a stimulus more positively after they have been exposed to it a number of times. Many stimuli, including Chinese characters, songs, foods, and people, seem subject to the mere exposure effect (Zajonc, 1980). How often have you had a negative initial reaction to a new style of clothing, then found yourself actually wearing (and liking) it after a period of exposure?

Attitude Change

Many of our attitudes change over time as we are exposed to new social influences. The factors that underlie attitude change have long been a subject of fascination for social psychologists—and for the many people who would like to influence the attitudes and behaviors of others.

Persuasion

By far the most common technique used to change attitudes is simple persuasion. However, "simple" persuasion is not really simple at all. There are many approaches to persuading others. The processes involved are so complex that, in spite of several decades of research and hundreds of studies, we do not yet fully understand them. Among the factors that have been studied are the characteristics of the communicator, the form of the communication, and, more recently, the nature of the attitude that is the target of change.

Communicator Characteristics. In the 1950s, a Yale University research group began to study systematically the role of the communicator in the process of persuasion. They identified **credibility**—how believable the communicator is—as a critical characteristic. They also found that credibility has two major components: expertise and trustworthiness. The most effective persuader is one who appears to be an expert in the area he or she is talking about and who appears to be presenting the truth in as unbiased a manner as possible. Physical attractiveness and status add to the credibility effect, but all of these communicator characteristics tend to dissipate with time, probably because the source becomes separated in our minds from the message (Chaiken, 1987).

Communication Characteristics. In trying to persuade someone, is it more effective to present only one side of the issue or to present the opposition's arguments as well and then try to refute them? The relative effectiveness of *one-sided* and *two-sided* arguments seems to depend on the audience's existing attitude toward the position the persuader wants them to take and on their awareness that there are two reasonable sides to the issue. One-sided arguments are most effective for audiences who agree with the message or who are ignorant of the other side of the issue. But two-sided messages are more effective with people who disagree with the message or who are aware that there are two sides to the issue. Such people are likely to perceive a one-sided argument as biased and to construct counterarguments against it, as well as to question the persuader's credibility. Two-sided arguments that acknowledge and refute the arguments against the persuader's position seem more fair and discourage the audience from formulating counterarguments. The latter consideration is important, because evidence indicates that people's attitudes are more resistant to change when they have formulated the belief structures underlying the attitudes, including counterarguments against the opposing position (Petty & Cacioppo, 1986).

Nature of the Attitude. The function or purpose an attitude serves for an individual may determine which kind of persuasive message will be most effective in changing it. Attitudes are formed for a variety of reasons, such as pursuit of rewards, reality testing, and ego defensiveness. The relative contribution of emotion and cognition to an attitude's formation may be associated with particular motivational pressures. For example, attitudes formed in the service of understanding the world may have a stronger cognitive component. In contrast, attitudes formed in the service of need satisfaction or maintenance of self-esteem may have a stronger emotional component (Edwards, 1990).

Murray and Karen Millar (1990) proposed that when we attack another person's attitude with an argument that collides with the basis for the attitude, whether cognitive or emotional, the persuasive communication is more likely to threaten the individual and promote self-protective counterarguments. Accordingly, they proposed that attitudes based strongly on emotion might be more susceptible to factual or rational (that is, cognitive) communications than to emotional appeals, whereas attitudes based strongly on cognition should be more susceptible to communications emphasizing emotion. To test this hypothesis, they classified subjects' attitudes toward various beverages as either primarily cognitive or primarily emotional on the basis of the reasons subjects gave for liking or disliking the beverages. For example, ''I hate the taste of that beverage'' would be classified as emotional, whereas ''the drink is low in calories and high in vitamins'' would be classified as cognitive. Next, the researchers presented counter-communications that were either rational or emotional in nature, and the changes in subjects' attitudes toward the beverages were then measured. As you can see in Figure 18.15, the hypothesis was confirmed; emotionally based attitudes changed more in response to rational counterarguments, whereas cognitively based attitudes were altered more by emotional communications. In a subsequent experiment, the Millars found that subjects produced more counterarguments against persuasive communications that attacked the primary basis (cognitive or emotional) for their attitudes, and they remembered fewer

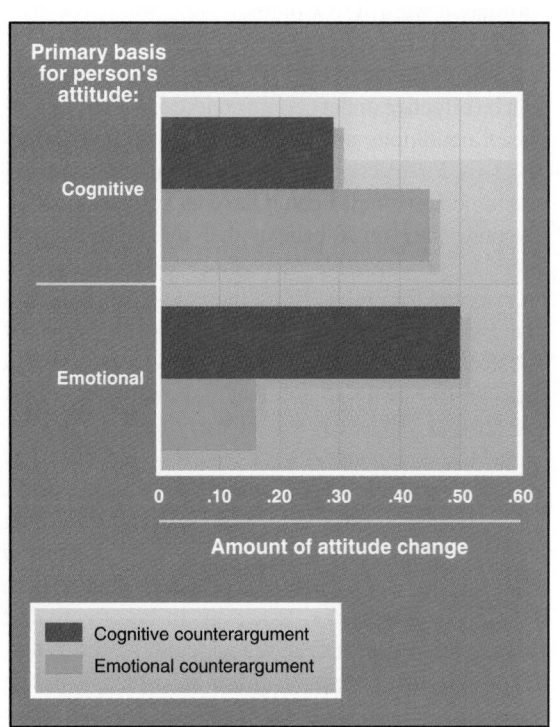

Figure 18.15 *The effect of cognitive or emotional counterattitudinal communications on preexisting attitudes that had either a primarily cognitive or a primarily emotional basis. Emotion-based attitudes were changed more by cognitive arguments, whereas cognitively based attitudes were affected more by emotional counterarguments. (Data from Millar & Millar, 1990).*

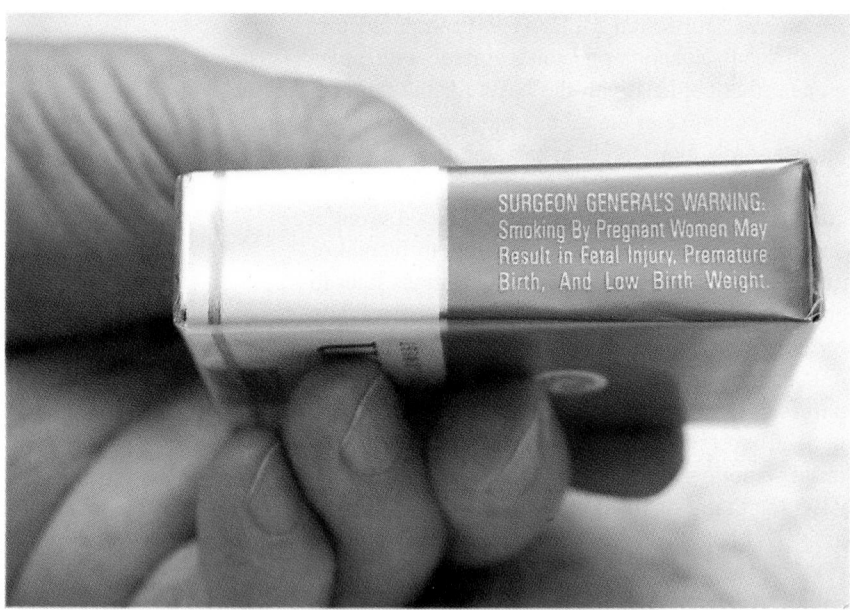

Figure 18.16 *Fear appeals are a very common approach to changing attitudes and influencing behaviors. Under certain conditions, they can be quite effective.*

elements of the messages that argued against their attitudes in such instances.

Persuading Through Fear. Many attempts to change attitudes and behaviors are specifically designed to operate by arousing fear (see Figure 18.16). We are told that smoking will increase our chances of developing lung cancer and that not wearing seat belts will increase our chances of dying in an auto accident. We are warned that if we do not change our attitudes toward the use of fossil fuels, we will destroy our habitat. Do such appeals work?

Ronald Rogers (1983) believes that fear appeals can be effective under certain conditions. Four belief-based conditions must be met for maximum effectiveness. First, people must believe that a feared event could occur ("Yes, I could have an auto accident"). Second, they must believe that the consequences could be very aversive ("I could be killed, paralyzed, or crippled for life"). Third, they must conclude that there is an effective way to reduce the likelihood of the feared consequence ("Using a seat belt would help protect me in an accident"). Finally, they must see themselves as capable of carrying out the self-protective behavior without incurring terrible costs or inconvenience ("It's easy enough to buckle up").

Arousing a realistic level of fear and providing concrete behavioral guidelines for avoiding the feared consequence can be an effective way to change both attitudes and behavior. However, to be effective, it is very important that the message not be too frightening and that people be given an effective means of coping with the fear. Otherwise, they may reduce

their anxiety by denying the message or the credibility of the communicator, leaving little chance that either attitude or behavior will change (Jepsen & Chaiken, 1986).

"Inoculation" Against Persuasion. Is it possible to make people more resistant to future attempts to change their attitudes? William McGuire (1985) suggests that it is indeed possible to "inoculate" people against persuasive attempts through a special form of two-sided argument. The procedure involves stating weak counterarguments to people's positions and then refuting the counterarguments in a convincing fashion. For example, young athletes might be told: "A person trying to get you to use steroids might tell you that once you bulk up, you can stop the steroids and keep the muscle bulk. In fact, scientific studies show that you'll lose the bulk pretty quickly." This method can be highly effective in strengthening people's attitudes not only because it makes their positions look even more credible but also because it stimulates them to come up with additional counterarguments of their own. If people are presented only with one-sided arguments favoring their positions, McGuire claims, they develop little resistance to persuasive attacks. Thus, parents or governments that do not permit exposure to opposing viewpoints tend to foster attitudes that are as rigid as glass but that are just as easily shattered if they are finally hit with convincing counterarguments.

Changing Attitudes by Changing Behavior: Cognitive Dissonance and Self-Perception Theories

As noted earlier, behaviors can affect attitudes. We saw one striking example of this in Zimbardo's prison experiment. As the guards slipped into their roles and began mistreating the prisoners, their attitudes toward their charges became increasingly more negative until they regarded them as little more than animals. There are many additional examples of positive and negative attitude changes brought about by changes in behavior, both in the everyday world and in the pages of social psychology research journals. Let us consider several examples of the latter type. We'll start by imagining that you are a participant in one of the most famous studies in the annals of social psychology.

You volunteer for an experiment and arrive at the laboratory, where you are asked to perform two simple motor tasks. The first consists of filling a tray with spools, emptying the tray, then starting over, again and again. The second consists of turning 48 pegs stuck into holes a quarter turn, then repeating the process endlessly. After 30 minutes, you are probably wondering what you did to deserve your present fate. At this point, the experimenter enters the room, thanks

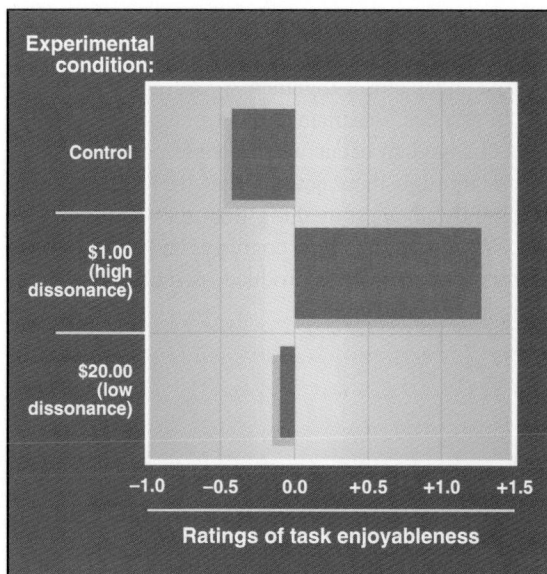

Experimental condition:

Control

$1.00 (high dissonance)

$20.00 (low dissonance)

−1.0   −0.5   0.0   +0.5   +1.0   +1.5

Ratings of task enjoyableness

Figure 18.17 *Results of the experiment by Festinger and Carlsmith. The more positive ratings of the boring tasks by the $1 group were interpreted as evidence that the subjects in this group had reduced their cognitive dissonance by bringing their evaluations of the tasks in line with their behavior. The $20 group was assumed to have little if any dissonance; the somewhat negative attitude of these subjects was no different from those of subjects who had not lied about the tasks. (Data from Festinger & Carlsmith, 1959).*

you for your participation, and asks if you will act as his research assistant and help him with the next subject. This subject is in a different experimental condition, which requires that she enter with a "positive attitude" about the task. All you have to do is tell the subject that the tasks are highly interesting and lots of fun. The experimenter offers to pay you $1 for essentially lying to the next subject. (This is the actual experimental manipulation; there is also a group offered $20 and a control group that simply performs and then rates the tasks.) You agree to do so. Afterward, you go to the Psychology Department office to collect your money. There, you are asked to fill out a "routine" form. One of the questions asks how interesting you found the tasks in the experiment. (This is the dependent variable measure in the study.) How would you rate the tasks? Would you rate them more positively or less positively than if you had received $20?

The actual results of the experiment, conducted by Leon Festinger and J. Merril Carlsmith (1959), are shown in Figure 18.17. If you behaved like the other "assistants" who were paid $1, you would have rated the tasks as more interesting than if you had received the larger reward of $20. But why? The answer to this question was offered by Festinger and Carlsmith

in a theory that has had an enormous impact on social psychology.

According to Festinger's (1957) **theory of cognitive dissonance,** people strive for consistency in their thoughts, feelings, and actions. People's cognitions include their knowledge about their own behavior. When two or more of a person's cognitions contradict one another (such as the person's attitude and his or her knowledge of how he or she has behaved), the person experiences the state of tension or discomfort that Festinger calls *dissonance,* and is motivated to reduce this dissonance. One way to return to a state of cognitive consistency is to change the attitude so that it is consistent with the behavior.

In the experiment described above, it is reasonable to assume that most of the subjects perceived themselves as basically moral people. Yet they knew that they had lied to another person about the interest level of the tasks. This discrepancy should produce dissonance. The theory predicts that people will change one of their cognitions or add more cognitions to reduce such a discrepancy. The subjects who received the large reward could justify their behavior on the basis of the cash incentive ("After all, who wouldn't tell a little lie for $20?"), and there was little reason for them to change their attitude toward the boring tasks. Those who had lied for only $1 could not justify their behavior on the basis of their monetary gain. However, there was another way out for them: If they were to convince themselves that the tasks were actually enjoyable, then they wouldn't have been lying after all, and the dissonance would be removed. This could account for their more positive attitudes toward the tasks.

Later research has shown that cognitive dissonance is only produced by attitude-discrepant behavior if the person views the behavior as freely chosen, as in the experiment just described. Otherwise, he or she can attribute the behavior to coercion or other external demands. Moreover, dissonance is most likely to be produced when the behavior has some negative consequence for others, when the person has a feeling of personal responsibility for the unpleasant consequences, and when these consequences were foreseeable at the time the person elected to engage in the behavior. These facts have led Claude Steele (1988) to suggest that the driving force behind dissonance is not simply inconsistencies between cognitions, but rather, discrepancies that threaten self-worth. From Steele's perspective, the inconsistency between the moral self-image of Festinger and Carlsmith's subjects and the knowledge that they had just lied for no good reason threatened their self-esteem and motivated them to find a way to deny the implication that they were liars.

Dissonance theory has inspired many researchers to attempt to change attitudes by inducing people to engage in attitude-discrepant behaviors. For example, several studies have shown that when subjects are induced to make speeches or to write essays that advocate positions opposite to their own, their attitudes actually shift in the direction of the speech or essay they have produced (Croyle & Cooper, 1983). In such instances, it appears as if *saying* is believing! This principle of *counterattitudinal advocacy* is occasionally used by mediators in labor disputes. The mediators ask company executives and labor leaders to switch roles for a time and present each others' arguments in the hope that the exercise will help bring the two sides closer together.

In essence, dissonance theory suggests that attitude change can occur when people persuade themselves through their actions that they actually feel differently about something than they thought they did. We now explore how cognitive and physiological factors may interact to produce such change.

PSYCHOBIOLOGICAL INTERACTIONS

Cognitive and Physiological Processes in Self-Persuasion

A key assumption in Festinger's theory of cognitive dissonance is that an aversive state of physiological arousal is produced by the perception of an attitude–behavior discrepancy. Steele's theory (1988) also posits a physiologically produced state of discomfort. Both theorists agree that the desire to reduce the aversive physiological state of dissonance is the motivational force in the process whereby people convince themselves that their attitudes are actually consistent with their behavior. The assumption that dissonance represents an interaction between psychological and physiological factors has received a great deal of research attention.

Perhaps the first question is whether people who are engaging in attitude-discrepant behavior actually experience heightened physiological arousal. The answer is yes. In a recent study by Mary Losch and John Cacioppo (1990), subjects who were known to have negative attitudes toward the use of painful electric shock in psychological experiments were induced to generate arguments in favor of the greater use of such shock procedures in experiments at their school. Recall that attitude change typically occurs in such studies only when subjects freely choose to perform the attitude-discrepant behavior, a condition that should maximize dissonance. Losch and Cacioppo found that subjects who freely chose to generate arguments against their own attitudes showed significantly higher levels of physiological arousal than did subjects who were simply ordered to do so as part of an experimental procedure. Moreover, as predicted by dissonance theory, the more highly aroused subjects in the low-choice condition also showed greater subsequent attitude change in the direction of favoring greater use of shock.

If unpleasant physiological arousal produced by dissonance motivates attitude change, then measures that reduce arousal should reduce such attitude change. Alcohol consumption is one possible candidate for such a measure, since this depressant drug dampens physiological reactivity (see Chapter 8). Claude Steele and his coworkers (1981) asked college students to write an essay favoring a large increase in tuition at their university. Immediately after writing the essay, some of the students were allowed to consume small amounts of alcohol in what they believed to be another experiment, supposedly a marketing study on the taste qualities of several brands of vodka and beer. These subjects showed no subsequent change in their originally negative attitude toward the tuition increase, whereas the subjects who did not consume alcohol shifted toward favoring the tuition hike. Steele suggested that people may sometimes consume alcohol in order to "drink their (dissonance-produced) troubles away."

Let us take this line of reasoning a step further. What happens if people experience negative arousal following attitude-discrepant behavior but attribute it to something else? Will attitude change still occur?

To answer this question, Mark Zanna and Joel Cooper (1974) invited subjects to participate in a study of a drug's effects on subsequent learning. All subjects were given a placebo, but some of them were told that the immediate side effects of the pill might be feelings of tension. A second group was told that the side effect would be feelings of relaxation, and a third group (the control group) was told nothing about side effects. The subjects in the two experimental groups were then told that although the side effects could occur quickly, the effects on learning would not occur for some time. In the meantime, they were asked to write a counterattitudinal essay under either a low-choice or a high-choice condition. Later, their attitude change was measured.

The attitude change results are presented in Figure 18.18. As usual, the low-choice condition yielded no attitude change, presumably because it produced no dissonance. Of greatest interest, however, is what occurred in the high-choice condition. Here, we see that subjects who had been told that the pill might produce feelings of tension showed no attitude change. Why might this be? Zanna and Cooper suggested that these subjects attributed the dissonance-produced unpleasant feelings to something external (the pill) and therefore were not motivated to reduce the discomfort by adjusting their attitude to fit their behavior. In contrast, the subjects in the relaxation side effects condition were especially likely to attribute discomfort to their own uneasiness with their attitude-discrepant behavior, and their motivation to reduce their dissonance was especially strong. Accordingly, these subjects showed the greatest shift in attitude. This result suggests another important factor in dissonance-produced attitude change: Dissonance-induced arousal may not be enough to bring about change; a person must view arousal as being produced by the attitude-discrepant behavior (Olson & Zanna, 1991).

Despite the evidence that physiological arousal plays a central role in dissonance, not all theorists believe that it is the major factor promoting behavior–attitude consistency. Daryl Bem's (1972) **self-perception theory** holds that we make inferences about our attitudes in much the same way that we make inferences about the attitudes of other people: by observing how we (or they) behave. Particularly when our attitudes are unclear to us, we observe our behaviors and then infer what our attitudes must be. Self-perception theory assumes that a state of dissonance-produced arousal is not needed to explain attitude change; we simply need to observe what we do in order to infer what we think and how we feel.

How can we resolve the differing explanations offered by dissonance theory and self-perception theory? Is physiological arousal *always* necessary to produce self-generated attitude change, as dissonance theory suggests? It now appears that both dissonance theory and self-perception theory may be correct, but under different circumstances (Fazio & others, 1977; Tesser & Shaffer, 1990).

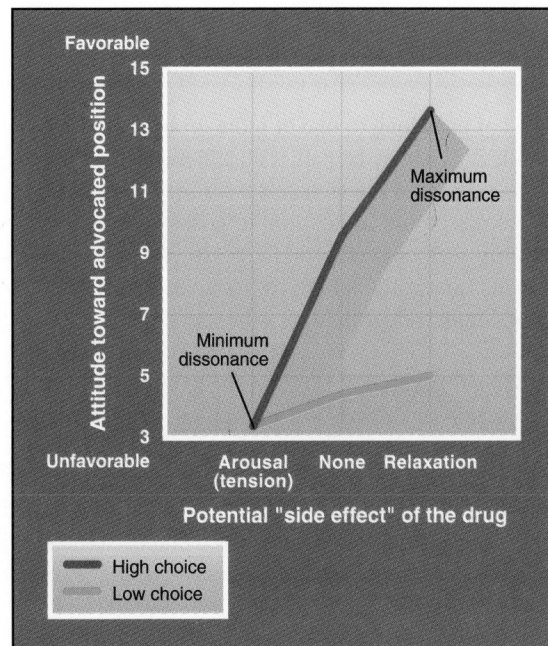

Figure 18.18 *Subjects' attitudes toward an advocated position contrary to their original attitudes as a function of their degree of choice and what they were told concerning the side effects of the drug they had supposedly been given. When subjects presumably attributed their dissonance-produced discomfort to the drug (arousal side effect condition), no attitude change occurred even in the high-choice condition. (Data from Zanna & Cooper, 1974).*

Self-perception theory appears adequate to account for behavior-produced attitude changes where people's attitudes are unclear to them or where their behaviors do not appear to be very discrepant with their attitudes or to threaten their self-worth. In such cases, there is no reason to expect a marked increase in arousal. On the other hand, dissonance theory better explains instances in which people's behaviors openly contradict their clearly defined attitudes, particularly when they view the behaviors as hurtful or morally wrong in some way. In these cases, it is likely that people do experience an aversive state of arousal that they are motivated to reduce.

In any case, we are led to the same conclusion: Behaviors can influence attitudes, and powerful processes of self-persuasion account for some attitude changes. As one social psychologist has observed, "If social psychology has taught us anything during the last twenty-five years, it is that we are likely not only to think ourselves into a way of acting, but also to act ourselves into a way of thinking" (Myers, 1990, p. 40).

Group Dynamics

Most of us belong to one or more groups besides our families. You may be part of an athletic team, a social club, a group of housemates, a sorority or fraternity, or a work group. In addition to groups that you voluntarily seek out and join, there are groups to which you automatically belong by virtue of your religion, your ethnic background, or other personal characteristics.

Social psychologists think of **groups** as having two major characteristics. First, their members usually recognize some degree of connection, or affiliation, with one another. Second, there are interdependent, or interlocking, roles within the group, so that the behavior of each group member somehow affects what happens to the group as a whole (Paulus & Garcia, 1991).

A group is distinguished from an **aggregate**, which is merely a collection of people who have only an accidental or trivial relationship. On the first day your psychology class met, it was probably more an aggregate than a group. By this time, however, it is likely that certain groups or subgroups have formed, particularly if students have been studying together or working on joint projects.

People join groups for many reasons. They may be attracted to some of the members, or they may like the group's activities. Joining a group is sometimes a way to gain certain privileges or to make useful contacts. Sometimes, people join groups because of the social support they offer their members. Finally,

► **Figure 18.19** *Groups may take a variety of measures to enhance group cohesion.*

groups may come together to work collectively on solving a problem or attaining a common goal (Paulus & Garcia, 1991).

Once formed, groups can differ along a number of important dimensions. One of these is *group composition*—that is, the size of the group and the characteristics of its members. A second important dimension is the **cohesiveness** of the group. The spirit of closeness in a group—or the lack of one—can have important consequences. For example, more than one athletic team with gifted personnel has failed to reach its potential because it lacked cohesiveness. It is no accident that experienced coaches devote considerable effort to "team building" (see Figure 18.19).

Group characteristics can interact in complex ways, and to some extent each group is as unique as the individuals in it. Nonetheless, the study of how groups function and how effectively they perform has a long tradition in social psychology. We will focus on three particularly important areas: (1) group influences on task performance, (2) decision-making in groups, and (3) social power and leadership.

Group Influences on Task Performance

One of the major reasons people form groups is to solve problems and perform tasks. Many tasks are simply too complex or too physically demanding to be accomplished by one person. Moreover, it is frequently assumed that, because of their ability to call on the expertise of several persons, groups can turn out a better product. The assumption that two (or three or four) heads are better than one underlies the use of "brainstorming" sessions in some organizations.

On the other hand, you've probably heard *camel* defined as "a horse designed by a committee" and that "too many cooks spoil the broth." In other words, the dynamics that operate in certain groups can actually impair task performance. We now consider some of the factors that enhance or interfere with group productivity.

Social Facilitation

One of the earliest studies of social influence was performed by Norman Triplett (1898). Triplett, an avid bicyclist, carefully studied the records of the League of American Wheelmen. The league kept records on three kinds of bicycle races: unpaced, in which a person ran against a clock; paced, in which the racer was accompanied by a pacing vehicle that stayed slightly ahead; and competition, in which people raced against each other. Triplett's statistical analyses showed that racing times were fastest for groups in competition, next fastest for paced races, and slowest for races against the clock. He suggested that the presence of others had an energizing effect on performance. This effect came to be known as **social facilitation.**

Although Triplett's data indicated that performance was enhanced in the presence of others, other studies showed that the presence of others sometimes had quite the opposite effect. Task performance was sometimes much poorer in the presence of an audience than when subjects performed in private.

In 1965, Robert Zajonc advanced a theory to explain why the presence of others has such variable effects. Zajonc suggested that the major factor in audience effects is physiological arousal, or *drive*. The presence of an audience can increase motivation to perform well or anxiety about performing poorly. The resulting arousal energizes behavioral tendencies and increases their vigor.

We come now to the key principle in accounting for enhanced or impaired behavior. Arousal has the strongest energizing effects on *dominant* responses, the ones that are most likely to occur in a given situation. Thus, Zajonc's **drive theory of social facilitation** predicts that the presence of others will lead to improved performance when the dominant response is the correct one. This is likely to be the case when the task is a very simple one, such as running, or when the correct response has been learned very well. In contrast, an increase in arousal will result in impaired performance when the dominant responses are incorrect ones. This is especially likely when tasks are difficult, complex, or poorly learned; in such situations, many other response tendencies compete with the performance of the correct response. These predictions are shown in Figure 18.20. Note that the term *social facilitation* is applied whether performance is enhanced or impaired. What is being facilitated by increased arousal is not performance but dominant responses.

Predictions derived from social facilitation theory have been widely supported, even in such animals as cockroaches, rats, and fruit flies (Zajonc, 1980). For example, cockroaches escape more quickly from a beam of light if other cockroaches are present and the escape response is a simple one, such as running straight ahead into a dark bottle. However, if the trail to the bottle is a winding one (resulting in a more complex task for a cockroach), then the presence of other cockroaches results in poorer performance.

Social psychologists have found social facilitation effects in many settings. They have even wandered into such unlikely places as pool halls to test social facilitation theory. James Michaels and his colleagues identified pairs of players who were either above average or below average in ability by watching the action in the pool room of their college's student union. Then, teams consisting of four observers sauntered over to the tables and watched the pairs play. The researchers predicted that the presence of an audience would increase the performance of the accomplished players, whose energized dominant responses were likely to be correct, while decreasing the performance of the less skilled players. This is exactly what happened (Michaels & others, 1982).

The practical implications of social facilitation theory are quite clear: The best way to ensure that performance will be enhanced by increased arousal is to overlearn the correct responses through practice, practice, and more practice.

Social Loafing: Many Hands Make Light the Work

In the 1920s, Max Ringelman, a French agricultural engineer, asked men to pull as hard as they could on a rope attached to a meter that measured the force they exerted. Not surprisingly, the amount of force increased as group size increased. What was surpris-

---

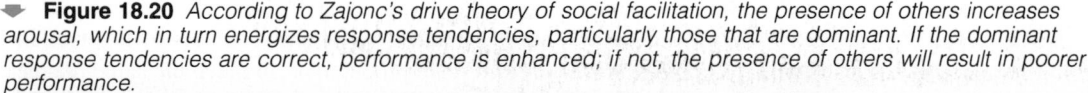

Figure 18.20 *According to Zajonc's drive theory of social facilitation, the presence of others increases arousal, which in turn energizes response tendencies, particularly those that are dominant. If the dominant response tendencies are correct, performance is enhanced; if not, the presence of others will result in poorer performance.*

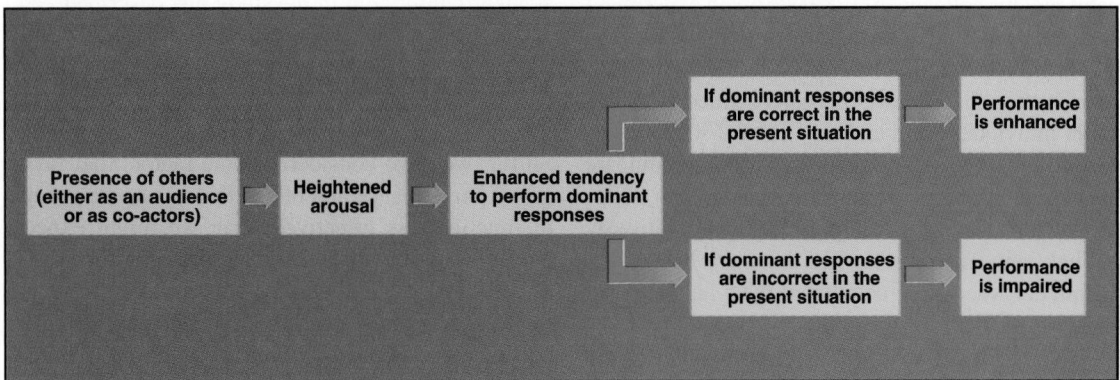

ing, however, was that the *average* amount of effort applied by each individual dropped rather dramatically as group size increased. Thus, while a man pulling alone exerted an average pull of 63 kilograms, the average force dropped to 53 kilograms in groups of three and to 31 kilograms in groups of eight.

At first glance, Ringelman's finding might seem puzzling in view of the previous discussion of social facilitation. After all, the task is a very simple one that should be enhanced by any increase in arousal resulting from the presence of others. But, instead of social facilitation, we find **social loafing.** Why does working on a task with several others appear to reduce individual effort?

One possible answer is presented by the **theory of social impact,** advanced by Bibb Latané and his colleagues (Latané & others, 1979). According to this theory, any social pressure directed toward a group is diffused, or divided, among its members. Thus, as group size increases, each individual feels under less pressure to comply or to put forth maximum effort. When people are working together on a task, they may also tend to believe that their individual efforts are less essential (Kerr & Bruun, 1983). The net result of social loafing can be an appreciable loss in group productivity.

Social loafing has important consequences in many arenas, including the courtroom. Some states require that juries have 12 members, while others require only 6. In one experiment, mock trials were conducted using either 6- or 12-person juries. As social impact theory would predict, the larger juries did a poorer job; they were less responsive to the strength of evidence against the defendant, suggesting that they did not inspect the evidence as critically. When the evidence against the accused was strong, fewer of the 12-person juries voted for conviction (see Figure 18.21); when the evidence was weak, the larger juries were less likely to vote for acquittal (Valenti & Downing, 1975).

It should be possible to reduce social loafing by making individual performance within the group identifiable so that it is harder to conceal mediocre effort. To study the role of identifiability, Kip Williams and his colleagues (1989) set up an experiment with the Ohio State University swimming team. The men's squad was divided into four teams of four swimmers each. All swimmers were timed in a 100-meter individual event and also swam 100 meters as part of a relay race. It was thus possible to compare the individual and group performances of each swimmer. The researchers manipulated identifiability by publicly announcing relay lap times for half of the swimmers when they completed their laps and not announcing them for the others.

The results of the experiment are shown in Figure 18.22. For swimmers whose relay lap times were not

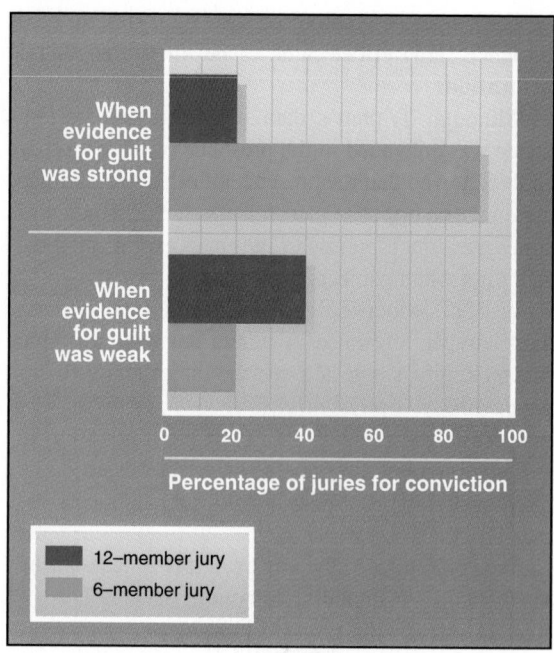

Percentage of juries for conviction

- ■ 12–member jury
- ■ 6–member jury

Figure 18.21 *The possibility of a social loafing effect is shown in these results from mock jury trials. The verdicts of the smaller, 6-person juries are more consistent with the strength of the evidence, suggesting that the larger, 12-person juries did not inspect the evidence as critically. (Data from Valenti & Downing, 1975).*

announced, and whose identifiability was thus low, relay times were slower than individual times, indicating a social loafing effect. Under the condition of high identifiability, however, relay times were actually faster than individual times, suggesting not only that social loafing was overcome but also that the group situation provided an additional social incentive for maximum effort. Although the time differences identifed in the figure may appear small, they are large enough to spell the difference between victory and defeat in an actual swim meet.

Many successful coaches have developed methods for identifying and publicly displaying individual contributions to team performance. These methods are designed to tip group processes in favor of increased team productivity in much the same manner as identifiability did in the study just described.

When Are Groups More Productive than Individuals?

So far, we have considered some factors that favor group performance and others that can cause groups to function less effectively than we might expect. Under what circumstances do groups perform more effectively than individuals working alone? As we might expect, the answer to this question is complex and seems to depend on both the nature of the task and the characteristics of the group.

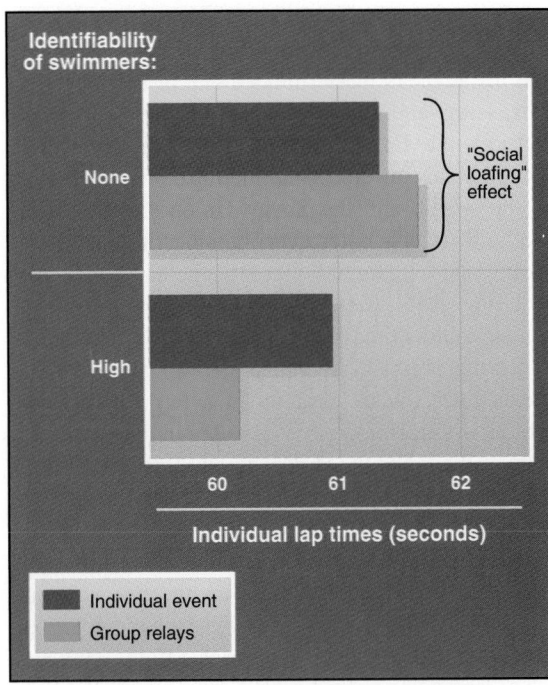

Identifiability
of swimmers:

None

High

"Social
loafing"
effect

60   61   62

Individual lap times (seconds)

■ Individual event
■ Group relays

⬥ **Figure 18.22** *Social loafing and an antidote. Under conditions of low identifiability, collegiate swimmers had slower times in relays than in individual laps. Increasing identifiability by announcing the lap time of each member of the relay team not only eliminated the social loafing effect but actually enhanced relay performance. (Data from Williams & others, 1989).*

On a purely physical task, such as pulling a car out of a ditch, group performance should be better than any individual's, despite the possibility of social loafing. On problem-solving tasks, groups frequently develop better solutions than individuals do (Hellriegel & others, 1989). Groups provide more opportunities for errors to be corrected as well as a greater likelihood that the skills or information needed to solve a complex problem will be available.

Groups are usually more effective than individuals at performing tasks or solving problems that can be subdivided easily. Such tasks also tend to reduce social loafing, because each person's contribution is fairly obvious. On tasks that cannot be subdivided, the group usually performs at the level of its most gifted member if the task is simple and the solution is obvious to everyone once that member proposes it (Baron & Byrne, 1991). In some situations, however, group processes may actually interfere with the activities of a gifted individual, resulting in poorer performance. For example, a gifted person may feel reluctant to make suggestions in a group whose members make it clear that they do not want any one person to "run the show." The social interchanges that go on within groups often cause them to work more slowly than individuals do.

Another factor that has been carefully studied is similarity among group members. Whether similarity helps or hinders group performance depends on the nature of the task and on the characteristics the group members share. A group composed of similar people might very well be more cohesive (since perceived similarity causes attraction), but similarity might also produce "blind spots" that would not exist in a more varied group (Raven & Rubin, 1983). We will see one example of this when we discuss the phenomenon of groupthink.

Group Decision Making

Many key decisions are made by groups. Governments function largely through committees and panels. Large corporations are run by boards of directors who shape company policy. The fate and even the lives of defendants rest in the hands of juries. Social psychologists, noting the importance of group decision-making processes, have devoted much study to them (Castellan, 1993). We will consider two important aspects of this work: group polarization and groupthink.

Group Polarization

One reason that important decisions are frequently entrusted to groups is that they are assumed to be more conservative and thoughtful than individuals and less likely to "go off the deep end." Is this assumption correct? Research testing the assumption has provided an answer that you should be used to by now: "It all depends."

It seems to depend primarily on the group's initial position on an issue. There is a strong tendency for groups to assume more extreme positions on issues on which they agree following discussion of the issues, a phenomenon known as **group polarization** (Mackie, 1986; Paulus & Garcia, 1991). If the group is generally conservative to begin with, its final opinions or attitudes will likely be even more conservative (see Figure 18.23). If the group members are generally liberal, their attitudes after discussion will be even more liberal.

Decisions of judges in real court situations seem to be affected by polarization. One study compared decisions in civil liberties cases made by three federal judges acting as individuals with decisions made by those same three judges acting as a panel. The judges all tended to be slightly liberal in the area of civil liberties, and 30 percent of their individual decisions were liberal. But when they served together on the panel, 65 percent of their collective decisions were liberal (Walker & Main, 1973).

Why does group polarization occur? One possibility is that when individuals are attracted to a group,

"And I say one bomb is worth a thousand words."

(Drawing by Dan Frandon; © 1980 The New Yorker Magazine.

Figure 18.23 *Group polarization of opinion or attitude is a common consequence of group discussions. The opinions of the individual members become more extreme if supported by the rest of the group.*

they are motivated to hold more strongly the attitude valued in the group so as to gain the group's approval or maintain a favorable self-image (Myers, 1990). Thus, polarization would be especially likely to occur in cohesive groups or in groups composed of similar individuals (Mackie & Cooper, 1984). Another factor may be that during group discussions, people hear arguments supporting their positions that they had not previously considered. These additional supporting arguments will tend to make the initial positions seem even more valid, resulting in a shift to a more extreme conviction (Burnstein, 1983).

Groupthink

In June 1972, police arrested five men who had broken into the offices of the Democratic National Committee at the Watergate complex in Washington, D.C. The investigation that followed brought the Nixon administration to its knees and resulted in the president's resignation.

During the inquiry, President Nixon and his inner circle of advisors made a series of critical decisions, each of which got them into deeper trouble. Afterward, H. R. Haldeman, the president's chief advisor, said, "Too many foolish risks were taken. Too little judgment was used at every stage to evaluate the potential risks versus the gains." Nixon himself later said, "I have sometimes wondered whether, if we had spent more time on the problem at the outset, we might have handled it less stupidly" (Janis, 1982, p. 216).

Lest we mistakenly conclude that only Republican administrations do stupid things, we need only recall another fiasco, this one carried out by the Kennedy administration. In 1961, John F. Kennedy and his advisors masterminded one of the most embarrassing and disastrous ventures in American history—the Bay of Pigs invasion of Cuba. The United States suffered a humiliating defeat in the eyes of the world, and the Soviet Union gained a firm foothold in Cuba. Later, every member of the advisory group found it hard to believe that he had gone along with the plan. Kennedy himself later wondered, "How could we have been so stupid?"

Irving Janis (1983) thinks he knows how. Janis has analyzed what went on in a large number of groups whose deliberations resulted in disastrous decisions, including the Watergate and Bay of Pigs misadventures. Out of his analyses has come the concept of groupthink.

Groupthink tends to occur under stressful conditions in highly cohesive groups that are so committed to reaching a consensus that each member suspends his or her critical judgment. Group members are prepared to go along with any proposal advanced by the leader or by the majority of the group. To remain loyal, the group's members stick with the policies and courses of action to which the group has committed itself even when it becomes clear that these are not working out well and that there are alternatives. Any group member who expresses reservations about the group's policies is faced with immediate and direct pressure to stop "rocking the boat." *Mind guards* in the group protect members from information that might threaten the group's consensus and complacency. Under these conditions, even highly intelligent people may stop thinking independently, abandon their consideration of moral principles, and stop considering alternatives. An *illusion of unanimity* in the group reinforces all the other groupthink processes (see Figure 18.24). The model of groupthink advanced by Janis is shown in Figure 18.25. Let us apply this model to another disaster.

In the morning hours of an unusually cold Florida day, the Challenger space shuttle lifted off into the air above Cape Canaveral. Seconds later, before the horrified eyes of the crew's families, space program officials, and a national television audience, the shuttle exploded, showering flaming wreckage into the Atlantic. The disaster had far-reaching consequences for the space program, and serious questions were soon raised about the decision process that had led NASA to proceed with the launch. This decision process was called "seriously flawed" by the presidential commission that investigated the circumstances surrounding the Challenger disaster.

The commission's investigation showed that engineers who had designed the shuttle's rocket boosters and orbiters had strongly opposed the launch because of dangers posed by the subfreezing weather. The

"All those in favor say 'aye'."
   "Aye."   "Aye."
      "Aye."   "Aye."   "Aye."

(Drawing by H. Martin: © 1979 The New Yorker Magazine Inc.)

Figure 18.24 *The process of groupthink may produce an illusion of unanimity in a group that is cohesive and committed to a consensus.*

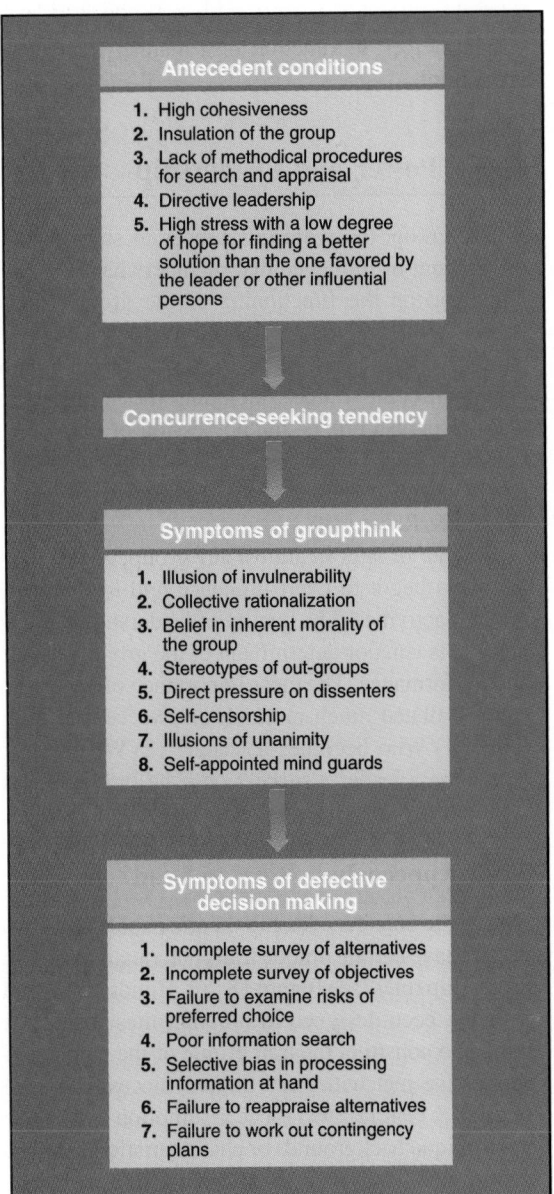

Antecedent conditions

1. High cohesiveness
2. Insulation of the group
3. Lack of methodical procedures for search and appraisal
4. Directive leadership
5. High stress with a low degree of hope for finding a better solution than the one favored by the leader or other influential persons

Concurrence-seeking tendency

Symptoms of groupthink

1. Illusion of invulnerability
2. Collective rationalization
3. Belief in inherent morality of the group
4. Stereotypes of out-groups
5. Direct pressure on dissenters
6. Self-censorship
7. Illusions of unanimity
8. Self-appointed mind guards

Symptoms of defective decision making

1. Incomplete survey of alternatives
2. Incomplete survey of objectives
3. Failure to examine risks of preferred choice
4. Poor information search
5. Selective bias in processing information at hand
6. Failure to reappraise alternatives
7. Failure to work out contingency plans

Figure 18.25 *The antecedents, characteristics, and consequences of groupthink as it relates to decision making. (Based on Janis, 1983).*

engineers feared that the cold would make the rubber seals at the joints too brittle to contain the hot gasses from the rocket. A memo from the president of the company that manufactured the booster rockets warned that it was a "jump ball" whether the seal would hold and that a catastrophe would result if it did not. Almost to the moment of the launch, the engineers pleaded with NASA officials to delay it.

The sequence of decisions that led NASA officials to go ahead with the launch despite the engineers' warnings has all the signs of groupthink. The program had suffered several delays, and NASA was determined not to have yet another one. The nation was waiting, and the launch had considerable fanfare, partly because of the presence of a public-school science teacher among the crew members. Clearly, an illusion of invulnerability existed among the NASA officials who were committed to the launch. To foster an illusion of unanimity, a key NASA executive polled only management officials, excluding the engineers from the final decision-making process on the grounds that "we have to make a management decision" (Magnuson, 1986). Finally, thanks to a process of mind guarding, the NASA official who gave the final go-ahead was never informed of the concerns expressed by the engineers. And so, with all the confidence spawned by the process of groupthink, NASA sent the doomed Challenger on its mission.

Can groupthink be counteracted or prevented? Janis thinks that it can. He suggests that leaders inform their group about the nature, causes, and consequences of groupthink. The leader should remain im-

partial during discussions and should regularly encourage and reward critical thinking and even disagreement among group members. Several outside planning and evaluation groups with different leaders should be set up to prevent the formation of an insulated inner circle. At each stage of the group's deliberations, members should be encouraged to state any doubts they might have, and the group should review alternative courses of action.

After the Bay of Pigs fiasco, President Kennedy incorporated several of these techniques into his cabinet decision-making process. The same group of advisors subsequently handled the 1962 Cuban missile

As we have seen on several occasions, traditional sex roles tend to place women in a passive, unassertive, and subordinate role in relation to men. If people act upon these stereotypes, we should expect to find evidence that women tend to choose social influence strategies that are associated with a lower status. We should also find that departures from these stereotypic strategies evoke negative reactions. There is research evidence to support both of these predictions. In one study, men and women involved in intimate heterosexual relationships were asked how they got their partners to comply with their wishes. Women were more likely to report using indirect strategies such as dropping hints, being especially affectionate, and pouting. In contrast, men tended to report using assertive and direct strategies, such as telling their partners what they wanted and negotiating directly with them (Falbo & Peplau, 1980). Other research shows that the use of assertive strategies by women in their relationships with men tends to evoke negative reactions. Except in their child-rearing role, women tend to be derogated for using direct power over males (Biener & Boudreau, 1991). Do these findings conform to your own observations and experiences?

crisis in a much more effective way. Thus, groups can be helped to function in a manner that avoids groupthink.

Social Power and Leadership

In any group, there are differences in status and in the amount of influence that members have on each other and on the functioning of the group. **Social power** is the ability to influence others to behave in particular ways. Such power may come from a number of different sources, including the ability to reward or punish others, the possession of knowledge or skills needed by the group, and the particular social role a person occupies, such as teacher or parent (Raven & Rubin, 1983). ▼

Sooner or later in almost any group, one or more members begin to exert influence and to direct the group's activities. The quality of leadership that they provide is a major determinant of the group's morale and performance. The clear importance of leadership has stimulated much research on two central questions: (1) Who becomes a leader? (2) What factors determine a leader's success once he or she has assumed that role?

Trait Approaches: Born to Lead?

One of the oldest leadership theories holds that some people have certain unique traits that qualify them for leadership roles (see Figure 18.26). Hundreds of studies have been designed to pinpoint these traits. Attempts to construct the trait profile of the "great person" have met with very limited success, however (Paulus & Garcia, 1991). The assumption that leaders have unique backgrounds or characteristics that make them fundamentally different from followers has not been well supported. Indeed, most people who are rated as good leaders are also rated as good followers. A second assumption, that leadership is a general attribute that gives the individual the ability to lead in all situations, also has not held up well. Research shows that different group members are likely to emerge as leaders in different situations, depending on what knowledge or skills are needed to lead the group toward a goal.

Although no unique cluster of "leader" traits appears to exist, there is evidence that certain personality characteristics may be associated with the tendency to assume leadership positions. In one study, the personality test scores of more than 2,000 political leaders who served as delegates or alternates to their parties' U.S. presidential conventions were compared with scores of the general public. As a group, the political leaders were higher than average in self-confidence, dominance, and need for achievement;

and they were lower than average in the tendency to seek emotional support from others and to engage in self-criticism (Constantini & Craik, 1980). However, there was a great deal of variability in the personality test scores of the leaders, and many of them did not fit this mold. Thus, although relations do exist between personal traits and leadership, trait theories cannot fully explain why certain people become leaders.

Leadership Styles: The Contingency Model

During the 1950s and 1960s, several important studies were conducted to observe and classify leadership behaviors. Two major styles of leadership emerged. One style, which was called *initiating and directing,* is oriented toward organization and task accomplishment. The second, labeled *consideration,* is relationship oriented and includes behaviors aimed at increasing morale, motivation, and group satisfaction (Bales & Slater, 1955).

A currently influential theory of leadership is the **contingency model** advanced by Fred Fiedler of the University of Washington (Fiedler, 1978; Fiedler & Garcia, 1987). Fiedler argues that the effectiveness of both task- and relationship-oriented leadership styles is dependent, or *contingent,* on the nature of the leadership situation—most specifically, on its *favorableness.* A highly favorable leadership situation is one in which the leader's relations with the members are very good, the task is clear and well-defined, and the leader's power to direct the group is acknowledged and accepted by the members. An unfavorable situation is one in which the group dislikes or is not willing to follow the leader, the task is uncertain or ambiguous, and/or the group members question the leader's right to power.

Fiedler maintains that task-oriented leaders are most effective when the situation is either very unfavorable or very favorable. In an unfavorable situation, there is often confusion, hostility, and uncertainty, and the task oriented leader's skills in organizing and directing can bring order from chaos. In a favorable situation, relations between leader and member are already good, and so the task-oriented leader can concentrate on completing the task. Fiedler asserts that relationship-oriented leaders function best in situations of moderate favorability, where the task is somewhat clear and the leader can use his or her interpersonal skills to increase group satisfaction and morale (see Figure 18.27).

Predictions derived from the contingency model have been supported in a great many studies with groups ranging from tank crews to store staffs (Fiedler & Garcia, 1987). The contingency model, unlike the great-person theory, takes the characteristics of both

Figure 18.26 *Trait theories of leadership search for common characteristics in prominent leaders like these. As the diversity among these leaders might suggest, researchers have had difficulty finding a common pattern of traits.*

the leader and the leadership situation into account. Thus, it provides another example of how individual and situational influences interact to affect behavior.

■ ▬ Social Impact of the Physical Environment

Relatedness to the physical environment is another aspect of belonging. As we shall see, even under the normal conditions of everyday life, the physical environment in which we live influences our social behavior and psychological well-being in important ways. The field of **environmental psychology** deals

with some of the most important issues confronting society, including crowding, pollution, environmental planning, and other factors that affect the quality of our lives (Stokols, 1992).

Crowding

It is estimated that three centuries ago, the population of the entire world was 500 million people. By 1850, it had grown to about 1 billion; and by 1970, to over 3 billion. Each day, the earth gains about 200,000 people. At that rate, the population of our planet will double every 35 years. Although the rate of population growth has slowed in the United States, Canada, China, and Europe, it continues largely unabated in some of the poorest and most underdeveloped nations.

Figure 18.27 *In Fiedler's contingency model of leadership, a leader's effectiveness is jointly determined by the leader's primary leadership goals and the favorableness of the situation. Leaders who are primarily task oriented (left) are more effective in highly unfavorable or highly favorable situations, whereas relationship-oriented leaders (right) are more effective in moderately favorable situations.*

If human beings were scattered uniformly over the land areas of the earth, each person would have about 10 acres of land to live on. For many reasons, however, people have congregated in urban areas, many of which have serious problems of uncontrolled growth. In densely populated areas like New York's Manhattan Island, there are up to 70,000 people per square mile (see Figure 18.28).

Many theorists are convinced that the crowding that has become typical in the world's urban areas has negative effects on personal and social behavior. This belief has stimulated a great deal of research on how crowding affects behavior and well-being.

Calhoun's Behavioral Sink

John Calhoun (1962) built an ideal environment for rats, supplying them with abundant food, water, and nesting materials (see Figure 18.29). As the rats multiplied in their physical Utopia, Calhoun was able to study how they adapted to increasingly crowded living conditions.

If the growth pattern that occurred early in the study had continued, Calhoun could have expected a population of over 5,000 living rats at the end of his 27 months of observation. But after that early period of rapid growth, the population stabilized at about 150 adults. This stablilization was due to an extraor-

dinarily high rate of infant mortality as the rats' behavior became increasingly pathological. Many females were unable to carry their pregnancies to full term, and others did not survive the delivery of their litters. Still others abandoned their litters or even ate them. Aggression was common, and the sexual behavior of the males became pathological. Some males became totally disinterested in sex; others mounted virtually any other animal, whether it was a female, a male, or an infant. Some rats became hyperactive and constantly dashed about, while others became withdrawn and came out to eat only when the others were asleep. Calhoun was so struck by the deterioration of social and sexual behavior that he coined the term **behavioral sink** to describe the pathological environment that developed as conditions became increasingly crowded.

Effects on Humans: Density versus Crowding

The dramatic effects observed by Calhoun, as well as those noted by other researchers who studied animals in their natural environments, stimulated a good deal of research on how crowding affects humans. Some of the early studies were correlational in nature, relating population density in various cities with indices of physical and social health, such as mortality rates, fertility rates, juvenile delinquency, crime, and admissions to mental hospitals. Although correlations between density and measures of social pathology were often found, the interpretation of these findings was clouded by the fact that socioeconomic factors were also related to density. It is usually the poorest people who live in the most crowded conditions. Thus, it is possible that other things that go along with being poor, and not density itself, were the important factors. Recent studies have attempted to control for the influence of socioeconomic factors. These studies indicate that there are indeed relations between density and poor mental health, poor social relationships, and poor child care (Cohen & others, 1986).

The inherent difficulties in establishing causal relations in correlational studies gave rise to experimental studies in which density was carefully defined in terms of number of square feet per person. In these studies, people were placed in rooms of varying sizes with varying numbers of other people. Such studies have shown that density can result in negative emotional states, including dislike for both the situation and others in the situation, particularly in males. Density also results in higher levels of physiological arousal when subjects are kept in experimental settings for hours at a time (Stokols & Baron, 1991). A number of studies have shown that density can lead to poorer task performance, particularly when inter-

▶ **Figure 18.28** *There is considerable evidence that for many people the experience of crowding is a stressful one that influences physical and psychological well-being.*

Figure 18.29 *John Calhoun stands in one of the animal universes he constructed to study the effects of population density in rats.*

action among subjects is required (Heller & others, 1977). Furthermore, exposure to density appears to produce aftereffects on later task performance. For example, subjects placed in high-density situations later show less persistence in solving puzzles than subjects exposed to low-density experimental conditions (Stokols, 1992).

But experimental studies indicated that physically defined density was not the only factor at work. Sometimes density had negative effects, and sometimes it didn't. Moreover, subjects in the same experiment often seemed to be affected differently by physical density.

These observations led to an important distinction between density and crowding (Paulus, 1980; Stokols, 1978). **Density** refers to physical conditions—that is, how many people per square foot occupy an area. **Crowding** refers to a negative psychological experience related to density. Density does not necessarily result in the experience of crowding. For example, people often pack themselves into football stadiums and rock concerts and find that the high density adds to their pleasure.

What leads to the experience of crowding? Daniel Stokols (1976, 1978) has summarized five sets of factors suggested by various theorists: social overload, behavior constraint, unwanted interaction, interference, and ecological concerns (see Table 18.1). Each of these factors gives rise to different ways of coping with the experience of crowding, ranging from withdrawal, to attempts to cooperate, to aggression.

This approach is clearly a more comprehensive and useful way of understanding the complexities of crowding, because it takes into account the fact that crowding depends on how the individual interprets the situation and its personal implications as well as on the physical variable of density. It also takes into account individual differences in personality, motivation, and background (for example, having grown up in a large city versus having grown up in a small farm community) that might influence whether a person experiences a situation as crowded. Personality characteristics may be particularly important. For ex-

Table 18.1 Theoretical Perspectives on Factors that Result in the Experience of Crowding and Coping Mechanisms Used to Avoid or Reduce Crowding

Theoretical Perspective	Critical Causes of Experience of Crowding	Primary Coping Mechanisms
Social overload	Excessive social contact, too much social stimulation	Escape stimulation, resist low priority interactions, withdraw
Behavior constraint	Reduced behavioral freedom	Pursue aggressive behavior, leave situation, coordinate actions with others
Unwanted interaction	Excessive, uncontrollable, or unwanted contact with others	Withdraw, organize small primary groups
Interference	Disruption or blocking of goal-directed behavior	Create structure, pursue aggressive behavior, escape
Ecological concerns	Scarcity of resources	Defend group boundaries, exclude outsiders

Source: Adapted from Stokols, 1976, 1978.

ample, people who are high in the need to affiliate with others report feeling less stressed and crowded in a densely packed college dorm than do those lower in the need to affiliate (Miller & others, 1981).

A study by India Fleming, Andrew Baum, and Linda Weiss (1987) illustrates the usefulness of taking into account both density and the psychological experience of reduced control. These researchers studied urban residents who lived on city blocks that were equivalent in physical density (number of residents) but that differed in whether they contained stores. Since stores increase the number of people who visit the block and make regulation of social interactions more difficult, the researchers predicted that residents of streets having stores would perceive more crowding and less social and personal control over their environments. This hypothesis was confirmed in the residents' responses to questionnaires. The study also showed that the people who lived on the blocks having stores reported significantly higher levels of stress and depressive symptoms and had higher levels of stress hormones in their systems. Finally, the researchers measured the ability to tolerate frustration by recording the amount of time residents from the two kinds of blocks spent on a difficult test requiring them to find figures embedded in drawings. As shown in Figure 18.30, the high density–low control residents showed more frustration and far less persistence. It thus appears that the experience of crowding increases stress and lowers behavioral efficiency.

Noise

Like crowding, the experience of noise is partly subjective. The crescendos from a rock band may be music to one person but noise to another. Because noise is, by definition, aversive, it increases arousal and is stressful. Noise also causes people to feel less in control of their environment (Bell & others, 1990).

David Glass and Jerome Singer (1972) conducted a series of experiments to test the effects of noise on physiological and psychological responses. Subjects were exposed to 108 decibels of noise (approximately as loud as an automobile horn at 3 feet or a jet plane at 500 feet overhead) for 9 seconds per minute over a period of 25 minutes. The subjects had strong physiological responses to the initial blasts but then seemed to adapt rather well. During this phase of the experiment, subjects worked on a series of arithmetic and word problems. Subjects exposed to noise made more errors at first than did control subjects not exposed to noise. But here, too, they adapted, and their task performance was soon as good as that of the control subjects.

So far, the results sound like a monument to the human's ability to adapt to stress. But there is more. Glass and Singer also tested for aftereffects of the noise. In the second phase of the experiment, the experimental and control subjects were given more mental tasks. This time, the subjects who had been exposed to the noise performed more poorly. They also became more easily frustrated. This finding parallels the findings described earlier concerning the delayed effects of density on task performance. It appears that, although people may be surprisingly capable of adapting to noise while it is present, there may be longer term effects on their ability to perform. This seems to be particularly true if they feel powerless to predict or control the noise (Sherrod & others, 1977).

Let us consider one additional study on noise that was carried out in the real-life environment of the classroom. Sheldon Cohen and his associates (1986) compared children who attended a noisy school near the Los Angeles International Airport with comparable children from quieter schools. The children from the noisy school had higher blood pressure than the other children and were also less successful at solving puzzles. Even more striking was their tendency to give up trying to solve the puzzles. This suggested to the researchers that the time spent in the noisy setting may have produced a kind of learned helplessness in the children (see Figure 18.31).

We might expect that children from the noisy school would have learned ways of coping with the distractions caused by airliners passing overhead. However, this was not the case. These children were actually more distractible than the children from the

Figure 18.30 *Effects of the chronic stress resulting from crowding on the task persistence of urban residents. Those who lived on blocks with stores showed poorer frustration tolerance while working on a difficult embedded-figures task. (Data from Fleming & others, 1987).*

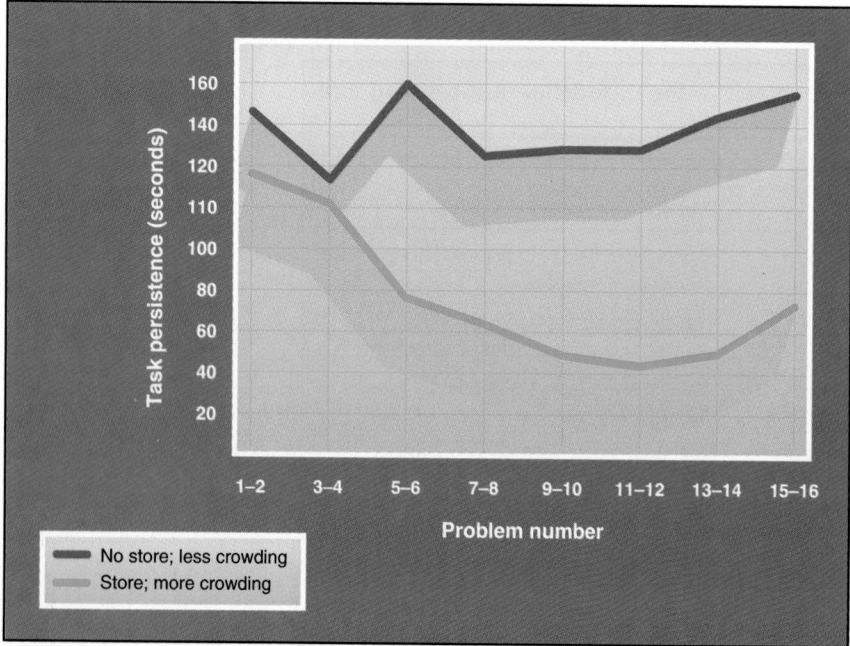

quiet schools, and distractions interfered more with their performance. The researchers also found that the longer the children had been in the noisy school, the greater were the differences between them and the other children in blood pressure, performance, lack of persistence in solving problems, and distractibility. Finally, in a follow-up study done a year later, after 43 percent of the noisy classrooms had been modified to reduce noise levels, the researchers found that the children in these rooms were *still* more distractable than the children from the quiet schools (Cohen & others, 1986). It thus appears that people are unable to completely adapt to the negative effects of noise pollution even after they have left the noisy situation.

In addition to crowding and noise, we currently face other critical environmental issues, including air pollution, energy shortages, the potentially disastrous consequences of nuclear accidents, littering and vandalism, and threats to the scenic environment. Does psychology have anything to contribute to the solution of these environmental problems?

It would seem that psychology has a great deal to offer. Human behavior is responsible for most of the threats to our environment, and human behavior is therefore likely to provide most of the ultimate solutions. Principles of learning, motivation, perception, attitude formation, decision making, and social interaction help explain how the problems arose, and they can suggest specific ways in which the problems might be solved. The application of psychological principles to the improvement of our physical and social environments is one of the ways in which the field of psychology can contribute to the quality of both human and nonhuman life.

⬆ **Figure 18.31** *Research has shown that being subjected to intense noise over a long period affects the physiological, cognitive, and behavioral functioning of school children.*

Recognizing and Resisting Social Influence

In this chapter, we have considered many ways in which our behavior is influenced by the social environment, as well as the psychological principles that underlie these influences. In closing, let us translate some of those principles into concrete suggestions for recognizing and resisting unwanted attempts at influence.

TACTICS OF SOCIAL INFLUENCE AND HOW TO RESIST THEM

ENHANCING HUMAN PERFORMANCE

We live in an era of unprecedented attempts to influence us to vote, to donate, to buy, to behave, to believe (see Figure 18.32). In his book *Influence* (1988), the social psychologist Robert Cialdini analyzes many of the principles discussed in this chapter and shows not only how they can be used as tactics of influence but also how we can learn to resist their power over our decisions and actions.

One tactic of influence uses the norm of reciprocity. We have seen how the unwritten rule to repay others' favors is used by cults and charitable agencies to produce feelings of indebtedness, setting the

stage for a request for something in return. The free food or drink samples you are offered at the local supermarket are another example: People often buy a product they don't really want just to avoid the feeling of being a freeloader. Moreover, the force of the norm of reciprocity is so strong that people will often give more in return than they originally received. I once saw a businessman thank a member of a religious cult who pinned a flower to his lapel in an airport concourse, give the cult member a $10 bill, then throw the flower away at the first opportunity.

The norm of reciprocity can also be used to gain concessions in bargaining situations. One tactic, known as the *door-in-the-face technique,* is to make an extreme demand that is likely to be summarily rejected. Having had the door slammed in his face, the bargainer now moves to a less extreme position, indicating to the other person that since he is willing to compromise, the least she can do is reciprocate. This produces strong pressure on the other person to make a concession, one that she would not have made originally. In one illustration of this principle, Cialdini and his colleagues

◆ **Figure 18.32** *Attempts to influence us are common and important parts of our social lives.*

(1975) approached college students and asked them to commit several hours per week for the next 2 years to working as a counselor with juvenile delinquents. Not surprisingly, virtually everybody refused. The students were then immediately asked if they would be willing to make a much smaller commitment: a one-time agreement to chaperone a group of delinquents on a trip to the zoo. Fifty percent of the subjects complied with this smaller request, compared with only 17 percent of a control group who had not been approached with the larger request.

The norm of reciprocity places tremendous pressure on people to comply with requests. How does one counter the pressure? Cialdini suggests that the preferred defense is not to resist the initial gift or favor. Instead, accept the "favor"; or in the case of the door-in-the-face technique, be prepared to respond with noncompliance to the request that follows the initial concession. Viewing these influence techniques as tricks reduces the pressure to comply.

The earlier discussion of cognitive dissonance noted that the need for consistency can place strong pressures on people to comply. One of the most effective persuasive ploys is to induce people to

"voluntarily" engage in some behavior that is consistent with a behavior that will later be requested of them. For example, some auto dealers have the customer, rather than the salesperson, write up the sales agreement. Another example involves contests in which consumers are invited to write brief essays on why they like a particular product; these contests are designed to get people to search for reasons why the product would be a good one to buy later. Fraternity and sorority initiations induce people to do something effortful, which tends to increase a group's attractiveness by bringing the initiates' attitudes in line with the amount of effort they have expended to join the group. A final example is the technique of *lowballing,* sometimes used by salespeople. A low cost is quoted, but once the customer has agreed to the purchase, hidden charges are added on or a mistake in calculations is found that will increase the cost. The frequent success of this ploy is due to the commitment the customer has already made to purchase the product. Having made that commitment, people may find it easy to rationalize the added "minimal" costs in view of the "great deal" they have made. Similarly, salespeople are taught to try to sell

the most expensive part of a package first, then the less expensive add-ons. A salesperson who has sold a customer an expensive suit can pretty easily induce the person to buy an expensive tie to go with it. It would be much more difficult to sell the tie first and then try to sell the suit.

The principle of social reality was mentioned in relation to cults. For example, Jim Jones's followers depended only on each other in defining correct beliefs and conduct. As a result, they followed one another like lambs to the slaughter. This principle can be especially powerful in ambiguous situations, where the correct course of action is not clear. In such situations, people tend to look to others for cues concerning what is "right." Persuaders use this principle to encourage compliance by informing people that many other individuals (the more the better) have already complied. Thus, people circulating petitions often make sure that completed pages of the petition are clearly visible. The best defense against this ploy is sensitivity to when it is being used in a counterfeit manner and recognition that the actions of similar others should not be the sole basis for decisions.

The discussions of persuasive communications touched on another mechanism of influence—authority. People are socialized to respond positively to authority, and to the extent that a person can demonstrate expertise and trustworthiness, his or her power to induce compliance is increased. This principle underlies ads in which an obviously knowledgeable person like a race car driver recommends a particular automobile, motor oil, or gasoline. In defending ourselves against the pull of authority, we need to assess the expertise and the trustworthiness of the person and then ask ourselves if compliance is in our best interest.

A final tactic is the "reverse psychology" by which a persuader tells someone that he or she may not be able to do what the persuader wants the person to do. For example, the persuader may emphasize the scarcity of a commodity being offered. If the persuasion target can be convinced that there is a limited opportunity to obtain a product or comply with a request, the likelihood of compliance will be increased. In part, the power of scarcity stems from the fact that people have learned that things that are difficult to obtain are typically more valuable. This is also a reason why materials that are censored often increase in desirability. It used to be said that the surest route to having a best-selling book was to make sure it was banned in Boston. Several years ago, the rock group Two Live Crew enjoyed a period of unprecedented popularity when an attempt was made to censor their material on the grounds of obscenity. If people are told they can't have something, their sense of personal freedom is threatened, and their desire for the forbidden thing tends to increase (Brehm & Kassin, 1990).

The best defense against any tactic of social influence is awareness of its power and recognition of when it is being brought to bear. Knowledge can help us use social psychological principles more effectively both to influence others and to protect ourselves from influence attempts that are not in our best interests.

S U M M A R Y

Social Norms and Roles

● Social roles are positions in a social system. Certain patterns of behavior characterize given roles and are expected of persons who occupy the roles. Social norms are rules or expectations shared by the members of a group about how group members should think, feel, and behave. Roles and norms are intimately related.

● Social norms are learned in the process of socialization. A person's reference groups are particularly important sources of the norms the person adopts.

● People conform in order to be accepted by others and to learn certain behaviors that are adaptive. Nonconformity involves the violation of social norms, and such behavior may result in negative sanctions, as in the case of criminal behavior and ''mental illness.''

● In extreme cases, people may adopt new beliefs and values as a result of intense persuasion. Cults frequently succeed in converting people by weakening previous ties and establishing the cult as the person's new reference group.

● Deindividuation is a temporary lowering of restraints that can occur when a person is immersed in a group. Recent theoretical analyses have focused on the role of reduced private self-awareness in producing deindividuation.

Attitudes and Behavior

● Today, many social psychologists define *attitude* as an evaluative reaction, stored in long-term memory, that is attached to categories of people, objects, issues, and events.

● Attitudes and behavior are not necessarily related. Attitudes are most predictive of behavior when (1) the role of situational influences is minimized, (2) the attitude is used to predict classes of behavior, rather than single behaviors, (3) attitudes toward performing certain behaviors, rather than attitudes toward an

object are measured, and (4) the attitude is a strong one acquired through personal experience and present in personal awareness.

● Attitudes are largely products of social learning. Classical conditioning, operant conditioning, modeling, and mere exposure have all been implicated in their development.

Attitude Change

● The effectiveness of persuasive communications is influenced by communicator characteristics (especially credibility) and the nature of the communication. Whether one-sided or two-sided communications will be more effective depends on the nature of the audience. Recent evidence suggests that emotion-based attitudes are more susceptible to rational counterarguments, whereas cognitively based attitudes are more susceptible to emotional counterarguments.

● Fear-arousing communications may be highly effective if they do not arouse excessive fear, if they provide behavioral guidelines for avoiding the feared consequence, and if they convince the person that he or she is capable of carrying out the prescribed behavior.

● People can be ''inoculated'' against future persuasive communications through a procedure wherein they are exposed to weak counterarguments, which are then refuted in a convincing fashion.

● People's attitudes may change when they freely engage in behaviors that are inconsistent with the attitudes. Cognitive dissonance theory assumes that people are motivated to maintain consistency in their thoughts, feelings, and actions. They may reduce perceived inconsistencies between attitudes and behavior by changing the attitudes to fit the behavior.

● There is evidence that dissonance produces physiological arousal and that conditions that prevent arousal or cause it to be attributed to factors other than behavior prevent attitude change from occurring.

● Self-perception theory, offered as an alternative to cognitive dissonance theory, may account for attitude changes that occur when attitude–behavior discrepancies are not large or when people's attitudes are unclear to them.

Groups

● Groups differ from aggregates in that group members recognize some degree of affiliation with each other and interdependent roles exist within groups.

● Groups can vary on a number of important dimensions, including composition and cohesiveness.

Group Influences on Task Performance

● Social facilitation refers to enhanced or reduced performance in the presence of an audience. Zajonc's drive theory of social facilitation states that the presence of an audience increases arousal, which in turn energizes behavior. When dominant response tendencies are correct, the arousal helps to improve performance; when they are incorrect, performance suffers.

● Social impact theory attributes social loafing—the reduction of individual effort that occurs in a group—to diffusion of social pressure, which decreases feelings of personal responsibility and accountability. Identifying individual contributions to the group effort helps reduce social loafing.

● Groups are more effective than individuals at performing tasks that can be subdivided easily. Also, there are more opportunities for errors to be corrected in a group and a greater chance that at least one person will have the skills and knowledge necessary to carry out the group's tasks. In some cases, however, group processes can make a group less effective than an individual.

Group Decision Making

● There is a strong tendency for groups to become more polarized in their opinions and attitudes following group discussions. This is believed to occur because people in groups desire the approval of other group members and because they are likely to hear new supportive arguments during group discussions.

● Groupthink occurs when cohesive groups become so committed to reaching a consensus that their members suspend their critical judgment and support any proposal advanced by the leader or by a majority of the group. The group shares an illusion of unanimity and is effectively blinded to erroneous courses of action and to alternatives.

Social Power and Leadership

● Although a few traits are loosely associated with leadership, the nature of the group and the nature of the task seem more important in determining who will assume a leadership role.

● Fiedler's contingency model states that the effectiveness of leadership depends on the match between leadership style and the favorableness of the situation. Task-oriented leaders function more effectively than relationship-oriented leaders when the situation is highly favorable or highly unfavorable, whereas relationship-oriented leaders perform better under moderately favorable conditions.

The Social Impact of the Physical Environment

● Relations have been found between crowding and various indices of physical and social pathology in both animals and humans. Laboratory studies have sometimes showed crowded experimental conditions to be related to negative emotional responses and lowered task performance.

● A useful distinction has been made between density and crowding. Density relates to the physical environment, whereas crowding is a subjective experience that depends on the individual's appraisals, needs, and personal characteristics.

● Like crowding, noise is a subjective experience. Research has shown that exposure to noise can lower task performance (though the effects are sometimes delayed), can increase physiological arousal, and can be perceived as stressful. Studies of children exposed to high levels of noise have shown negative effects that persist even after the noise has been reduced.

Recognizing and Resisting Social Influence

● The most effective tactics of social influence take advantage of the norm of reciprocity, needs for cognitive consistency, manipulation of social reality, appeals to authority, and perceived scarcity. Awareness of when these principles are being employed can increase resistance to them.

KEY TERMS AND CONCEPTS

aggregate (p. 586)
attitude (p. 578)
autokinetic effect (p. 572)
behavioral sink (p. 594)
cognitive dissonance theory (p. 583)
cohesiveness (p. 586)
conformity (p. 573)
contingency model of leadership (p. 592)
credibility (p. 581)
crowding (p. 595)

deindividuation (p. 576)
density (p. 595)
drive theory of social facilitation (p. 587)
environmental psychology (p. 593)
group (p. 586)
group polarization (p. 589)
groupthink (p. 590)
mere exposure effect (p. 580)
norm of reciprocity (p. 571)
reference group (p. 571)

self-perception theory (p. 585)
social facilitation (p. 587)
social loafing (p. 588)
social norm (p. 571)
social power (p. 592)
social role (p. 571)
subjective norm (p. 579)
theory of reasoned action (p. 579)
theory of social impact (p. 588)

SUGGESTED READINGS

Baron, R. A., and Byrne, D. (1991). *Social psychology: Understanding human interaction* (6th ed.). Boston: Allyn and Bacon. A general social psychology textbook that discusses the major areas in the field and is very current in its coverage of social psychological theory and research.

Cialdini, R. B. (1988). *Influence: Science and practice.* An engaging description of tactics of social influence and how they can be defended against.

Fisher, J. D., Bell, P. A., and Baum, A. (1988). *Environmental psychology* (3rd ed.). New York: Holt, Rinehart, & Winston. An updated book covering many areas of theory, research, and application in environmental psychology.

Social Interaction 19

I t is said that our existence as humans centers around two key relationships: the relationship we have with ourselves and our relationship with others. In this chapter, we focus on these two relationships and how they affect one another. As social beings, we love and we hate, we help and we hurt one another. We shall see that many of the psychological principles discussed in earlier chapters help explain the broad spectrum of human social relationships.

Social Perception

Social relationships exist among virtually all animal species. In humans, cognitive processes play a central role in these interactions. Perception of the stimuli we confront, including those in our social environment, is an active, constructive process. Because our social interactions involve transactions between ourselves and at least one other person, they are influenced by our perceptions of both ourselves and others. Thus, many of the concepts discussed in previous chapters on perception, cognition, development, and personality reappear in our study of human social behavior.

The Self and Social Behavior

For each of us, in an important sense, the self is the center of the social universe. Theorists like Carl Rogers have pointed out that once the self-concept is formed, self-appraisals help shape our actions and reactions toward other people. Moreover, the self's very existence is largely a product of social interactions.

What is the "me" we call the self? One currently popular answer utilizes a concept that we encountered in our earlier discussion of memory and cognition: the schema. According to Hazel Markus (1977), the cognitive components of the self-concept are **self-schemas,** which contain information, memories, and beliefs about the self. Thus, a person may regard herself as dependent or independent, overweight or underweight; loving or hostile; attractive or unattractive; loved or unloved; black, white, or Asian; and so on, depending on what descriptors are relevant to her view of herself in the current situation (Nurius & Markus, 1991). Moreover, people think not only about their current selves but also about **possible selves**—the selves they might become, would like to become, or would dread becoming (Markus & Nurius, 1986).

Once formed, self-schemas, like other schemas, can exert powerful influences on the processing of information that is relevant to them (Schlenker & Weigold, 1992). For example, people remember information better if it is relevant to their self-schemas, a phenomenon known as the **self-reference effect** (Fiske & Taylor, 1991). In one experiment, subjects were asked to decide if a series of trait names (for example, *timid, logical, helpful*) were true of them. Other subjects were asked to make judgments unrelated to the self, such as whether the words had the same meaning, length, or sound as another word. Later, the subjects were given a surprise test to measure recall of the trait names. As you can see in Figure 19.1, the subjects who had made self-relevant judgments recalled more of the words. Furthermore, they were especially likely to recall names they had judged to be true of themselves (Rogers & others, 1977).

In addition to influencing recall of past events, self-schemas help determine which stimuli are selected for attention; and they serve as filters that can cause people to disregard information that is not consistent with their self-schemas (Brown, 1991). In this way, schemas can be self-perpetuating and resistant to change. Later, we shall see how this principle, when applied to schemas about certain groups, can help to perpetuate stereotypes and prejudices.

Development of Self-Schemas

The origins of the self arise early in life when infants develop an awareness that they are separate from the

Figure 19.1 *The self-reference effect on memory. By far the highest level of recall of adjectives occurred when the adjectives had been evaluated earlier in relation to the self. (Data from Rogers & others, 1977).*

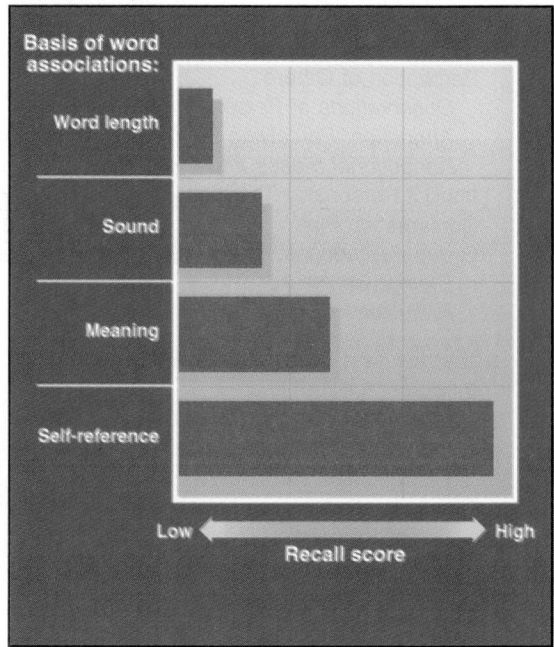

Basis of word associations:

Word length

Sound

Meaning

Self-reference

Low — Recall score — High

environment. From this point on, social experiences play a major role in the development of self-schemas. Several social processes are particularly important, including reflected appraisals, social comparison, and self-perceptions (see Figure 19.2).

One way we know who we are is by others' reactions to us. Such feedback allows us to infer how these others view us and feel about us. This idea is captured in the concept of the *looking-glass self,* proposed by the sociologist Charles Cooley (1902). The looking-glass self is like a mirror reflecting the inferred reactions of others. Today's psychologists use the term **reflected appraisals** to denote self-judgments based on our perceptions of how others appraise and evaluate us. The way others respond to us when we are children is thought to be particularly influential, because at that time, we have little information about who we are. This is why childhood relations with parents and peers can play such a strong role in shaping self-schemas.

Social comparison is a second important process in self-schema development (Suls & Marco, 1991; Wills, 1991). At a relatively early age, children begin to compare themselves with other children, and this process continues throughout life. This is quite natural, since it is difficult for people to judge their traits and abilities in any absolute sense. It follows, then, that our self-schemas depend in part on whom we compare ourselves with. For example, college students who viewed photographs of extremely attractive people subsequently rated themselves as less physically attractive than did another group of subjects who had viewed pictures of physically unattractive people (Brown & others, 1992). Social comparison may also account for the fact that the siblings of gifted children sometimes view themselves as inadequate in the areas where their siblings excel, even though they may actually be average or above average (Fiske & Taylor, 1991).

Finally, processes of **self-perception** contribute to the formation of self-schemas. We observe our own behavior and infer our attitudes and traits from it. Sometimes, however, we mistakenly attribute our actions to our own characteristics because we fail to recognize the power of situational factors. For example, some of the students who served as guards in Zimbardo's prison experiment were disturbed afterward by how they had behaved. Zimbardo felt the need to reassure them that they were not bad people, but simply normal people who had responded to powerful social norms (Zimbardo, 1972).

Self-Presentation: The Self on Display

"Who are you in your own eyes?" "Who are you to those who know you?" If you are like most people, the answers to these two questions may differ to some

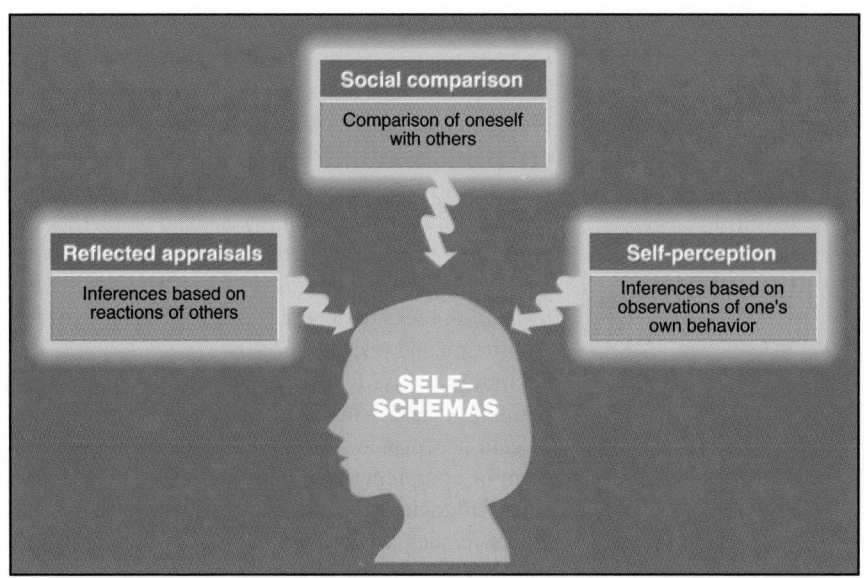

Figure 19.2 *Self-schemas are based on several sources of information.*

degree; your private self may be somewhat different from your public self. **Self-presentation** refers to the process by which people regulate their verbal and nonverbal behavior so as to project certain impressions of themselves (DePaulo, 1992; Schlenker & Weigold, 1992). There are two primary motives for self-presentation: The first is to convey an image to others, and the second is to confirm our own self-image (see Figure 19.3).

In **strategic self-presentation,** our projection of self is designed to shape others' impressions of us in

Figure 19.3 *Self-presentations not only influence others' perceptions but also can serve to verify and reinforce one's own self-concept.*

"I can't say I like the looks of that bunch."
(Drawing by Dana Fradon; © 1971 The New Yorker Magazine, Inc.)

Consistency (self-verification) theories like Festinger's and Rogers's say that people strive for consistency between self-concept and experience, whereas the self-enhancement model maintains that people are motivated to enhance their self-views and feel good about themselves. These two theories lead to different predictions of what will happen when people who are low in self-esteem receive positive feedback about themselves. According to consistency theories, such feedback should be anxiety- or dissonance-arousing because it is inconsistent with the negative self-concept. In contrast, the self-enhancement model predicts that people with poor self-esteem have especially strong self-enhancement needs and should be gratified by such feedback. Yet according to William Swann and his coworkers (1992), both needs are operative, and the dissonance created by positive feedback to a person low in self-esteem may at least partially cancel out the positive feelings created by self-enhancement. Thus, in this instance, one motive (consistency) is frustrated; the other (enhancement), gratified. According to this dual-motive view, the worst state of affairs should occur when people who are high in self-esteem receive strong and convincing negative feedback, because both the need for consistency and the need for self-enhancement are frustrated.

order to evoke some desired reaction from them. The ultimate goal of strategic self-presentation is to gain power and influence over the behavior of others, even if the interpersonal commodity we are seeking is the opportunity to be weak and dependent. For example, people who employ the strategy of *supplication* manipulate others by appearing weak and helpless, thus prompting help and dominance from others. In contrast, the person who uses the strategy of *self-promotion* seeks to appear competent and to win the admiration and respect of others. *Intimidation* is the attempt to arouse fear by presenting a dangerous or punitive facade, whereas *ingratiation* is the attempt to gain acceptance from others by doing favors for them or complimenting them. All of these interpersonal strategies are designed to display the self to others in such a way that the desired reaction from them seems appropriate.

Self-presentation has a second important function, that of **self-verification** (Swann & others, 1992). In this case, the most important audience is oneself, and the underlying motivation is to confirm existing self-schemas. This may be regarded as another manifestation of the need for cognitive consistency—in this case, consistency between our self-images and our reflected appraisals of how others react to us. For example, a person who views himself as weak and dependent and who behaves in such a helpless fashion that he evokes dominant and helpful behaviors from others gets interpersonal feedback that is consistent with his self-schema of being weak and helpless. For people who are high in self-esteem, positive self-presentations serve to maintain and enhance positive feelings about the self. Not surprisingly, one of the fastest ways to rile people is to tell them that they are not what they believe themselves to be. Challenges to self-schemas are often met with considerable resistance because of people's general need for self-consistency. ▼

Self-Monitoring: Stylistic Differences in Self-Presentation Motives

Everyone engages in strategic self-presentation to some extent, but there are wide individual differences in the tendency to do so. According to Mark Snyder (1987), differences in the tendency to regulate one's social behavior to meet the demands of social situations are manifested as a personality trait called **self-monitoring.** Snyder and his colleagues have developed a scale to measure differences in self-monitoring. Some of the items are shown in Table 19.1.

High self-monitors are very aware of how they are behaving and are highly sensitive to social cues that signal the rules for appropriate action. They have a repertoire of strategic self-presentation skills, and

they pride themselves on their ability to fit into any social situation. High self-monitors may elect to act in ways that are inconsistent with their inner convictions and feelings if the situation demands it. They are better than low self-monitors at detecting when others are lying, indicating their skills at discerning the interpersonal gestures required for successful self-presentation (Krauss & others, 1976). They also attend closely to surface qualities such as physical attractiveness and social status not only in choosing people to associate with but even in evaluating consumer goods. High self-monitors prefer ''image'' products, and experiments have shown that they respond to advertising based on social status (''Heineken—you're moving up'') more than to advertising that emphasizes quality (''Heineken—you can taste the difference'') (DeBono & Snyder, 1989; Zuckerman & others, 1988).

In contrast, low self-monitors either are not motivated or do not have the interpersonal skills needed to act as social chameleons. Instead, they express themselves consistently from one situation to another, exhibiting what they regard as their true inner selves. Their self-presentations seem geared to the motive of self-verification instead of strategic self-presentation, and they personify the expression ''what you see is what you get.''

As ''I–thou'' relationships, social interactions are a joint product of how we view ourselves and how we view other people. As we shall see, some of the same principles that govern self-perception also govern perception of others.

Perception of Others

Our responses to other people depend on our understanding of who they are and why they behave as they do. Achieving understanding of others is no easy task, but it is a critically important one that involves a variety of psychological processes.

Figure 19.4 provides an overview of the major processes involved in social perception, a task that can be likened to solving a puzzle. The processes begin with a perceiver, who relies on incomplete and sometimes conflicting information in forming an impression of another person. The impression is based on characteristics of the person, the nature of the situation, and the person's behavior in that situation. The perceiver then makes *attributions,* or inferences, about the causes of the person's behavior. Attributional judgments contribute to impressions about the individual's personal characteristics. Once formed, personal impressions, like the self-schemas discussed earlier, are subject to biases that favor confirmation of the impressions. Finally, perceptions may cause the perceiver to respond to the other person in a manner that results in a self-fulfilling prophecy.

Observations of Persons and Situations

Personal Appearance.   One of the first pieces of information we receive when we meet a person is that individual's physical appearance. Can we judge a book by its cover?

Whether or not we can, there is considerable evidence that we try. In one study, Karen Dion and her coworkers showed University of Minnesota students a series of photographs of males and females that varied in physical attractiveness, then asked the students to rate these people on several dimensions. The highly attractive people of both genders were rated more positively on personality traits, and raters expected these people to have more success and personal happiness in their future lives (Dion & others, 1972). Subsequent research has repeatedly confirmed people's tendency to form more favorable first impressions of both adults and children who are physically attractive, even though correlational studies have shown that, in fact, physical attractiveness is virtually unrelated to other positive traits (Feingold, 1992).

Other physical features are also used in making judgments. For example, adults who have baby-faced features—a combination of large round eyes, a large forehead, smooth skin, and a rounded chin—are perceived as warm, naive, weak, honest, and submissive (Berry & McArthur, 1986). People with high-pitched voices are assumed to have other childlike attributes as well (Montepare & McArthur, 1987). However, surface characteristics like these can lead social perceptions astray. One example occurred in a New York subway in 1986 when four teenagers approached Bernhard Goetz and demanded money. Within seconds, he pulled out a gun and shot them all. Asked why they had picked on Goetz, one of the teenagers

Table 19.1 The Self-Monitoring Scale

To find out whether you are high or low in self-monitoring, answer each statement true or false as it applies to you. Give yourself one point for each true response to items 4, 5, 6, 8, 10, 12, 17, and 18 and each false response to items 1, 2, 3, 7, 9, 11, 13, 14, 15, and 16. The average score among North American college students is about 10; a score of 7 or below or 13 or above places you in the lower or upper 25 percent, respectively.

1. I find it hard to imitate the behavior of other people.
2. At parties and social gatherings, I do not attempt to do or say things that others will like.
3. I can only argue for ideas which I already believe.
4. I can make impromptu speeches even on topics about which I have almost no information.
5. I guess I put on a show to impress or entertain others.
6. I would probably make a good actor.
7. In a group of people I am rarely the center of attention.
8. In different situations and with different people, I often act like very different persons.
9. I am not particularly good at making other people like me.
10. I'm not always the person I appear to be.
11. I would not change my opinions (or the way I do things) in order to please someone or win their favor.
12. I have considered being an entertainer.
13. I have never been good at games like charades or improvisational acting.
14. I have trouble changing my behavior to suit different people and different situations.
15. At a party I let others keep the jokes and stories going.
16. I feel a bit awkward in company and do not show up quite as well as I should.
17. I can look anyone in the eye and tell a lie with a straight face (if for a right end).
18. I may deceive people by being friendly when I really dislike them.

Source: Snyder & Gangestad, 1986.

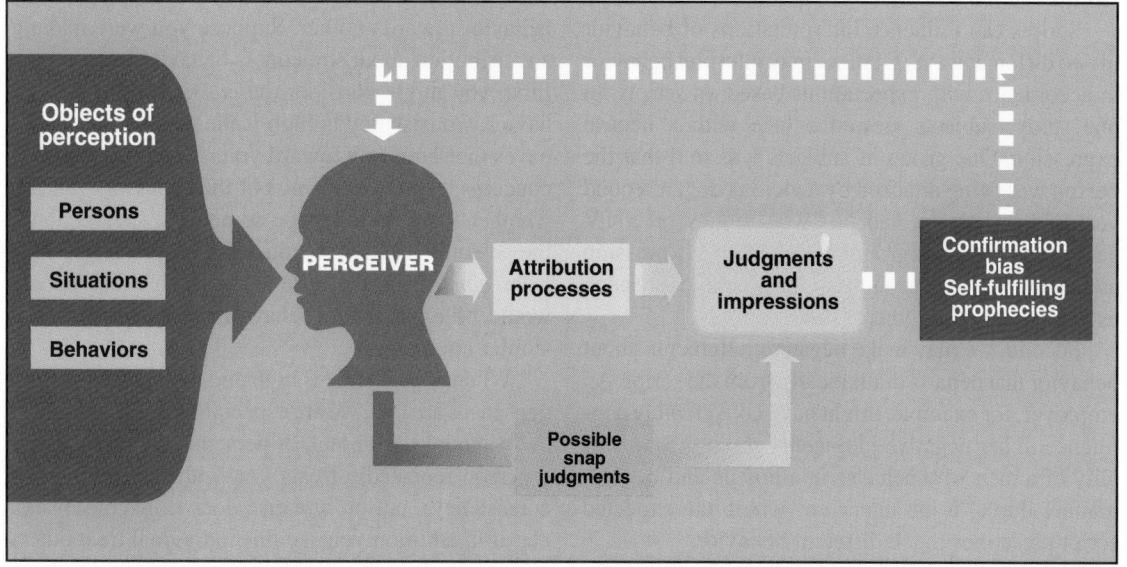

Figure 19.4 *Processes involved in social perception. Social perception begins with observations of persons, behaviors, and situations. Sometimes, these initial perceptions result in snap judgments; at other times, perceivers make attributions about the causes of behavior and integrate them into their judgments. Once made, the judgments are subject to confirmation biases and may result in self-fulfilling prophecies by influencing behavior.*

➤ **Figure 19.5** *Appearances can be deceiving. Baby-faced individuals are typically viewed as submissive, gentle, and warm. It is not surprising, therefore, that New Yorkers were shocked when David Berkowitz, the notorious "Son of Sam," was arrested in 1977 for the serial killings of six innocent people. They expected a face that matched the savagery of the crimes.*

said, "He looked soft" (Johnson, 1987). See Figure 19.5 for another exception.

Situational Scripts. The situation in which behavior occurs can provide valuable clues about a person's characteristics. Just as we have schemas about ourselves and about particular classes of people, we have schemas about situations. As discussed in Chapter 11, familiar situations have associated with them *scripts* based on the norms associated with the situations. Scripts tell us how people are *supposed* to behave in job interviews, on a first date, at funerals, and so on.

Scripts can influence interpretations of behavior in two different ways. First, we may interpret behavior in accordance with expectations based on scripts. In one study, subjects viewed a face with a neutral expression. One group of subjects was told that the person was being attacked by a vicious dog; a second was told the person had just won money on a TV game show. The first group rated the facial expression as fearful, but the second rated the same expression as happy (Trope & others, 1988).

Second, we may make negative judgments about behavior that departs dramatically from the script. An employer, for example, might have considerable confidence in her negative judgments about the personality of a man who behaves in a hostile and boorish manner during a job interview, where the expected script prescribes much different behavior.

Attribution: Perceiving the Causes of Behavior

Let us return for a moment to a study described in Chapter 2. Stanley Milgram's study of obedience to authority was inspired by the Nuremberg trials, where Nazis accused of terrible atrocities claimed that they were not inherently evil people but instead were "only following orders." You will recall that when Milgram created a social situation in which ordinary people were ordered to administer painful electric shock to another person, supposedly as part of a learning experiment, the majority of subjects obeyed.

How can we account for such behavior? Were these weak and callous people who didn't have the courage to stand up to an authority figure, or were they truly "ordinary people" whose inner dispositions were overwhelmed by powerful situational forces? In attempting to answer this question, we are engaging in the process of **attribution,** whereby we assign causes to both our own and others' behavior.

Fritz Heider (1958), the father of attribution theory, maintained that attempts to understand why people behave as they do typically involve either personal attributions or situational attributions. **Personal attributions** are inferences that a behavior is caused by characteristics of the individual, such as personality traits, abilities, or attitudes. The Nuremberg war crimes tribunal, which convicted the Nazi defendants of war crimes, attributed their behavior to personal factors that made them morally responsible for their actions. Milgram interpreted the behavior of his subjects quite differently: He claimed that they were not evil people but rather victims of overwhelming situational forces. He was making **situational attributions** for their "blind obedience."

How do we go about deciding whether a behavior is caused by personal or situational factors? Harold Kelley (1973) suggested that three factors are particularly important in attributions concerning a person's behavior toward another. Suppose you were making an attribution about someone's behavior toward you. First, you might consider the *consistency* of the behavior. Consistency is high if the person always behaves the same way toward you. A second judgment concerns the *distinctiveness* of the behavior—that is, whether there seems to be something special about the person's reaction to you. Finally, you might consider *consensus,* the extent to which other people would be expected to behave in this manner under similar conditions.

When consistency is high and distinctiveness and consensus are low, we are especially likely to attribute the behavior to internal, or personal, causes. Thus, if a person repeatedly treats you with contempt (high consistency), but no one else does (low consensus), and if in addition you see this individual treat others

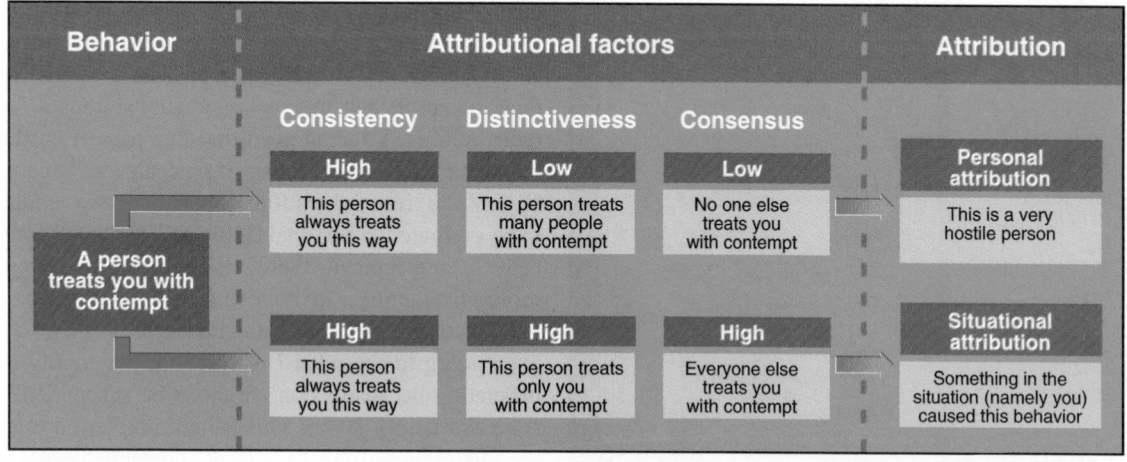

Behavior	Attributional factors			Attribution
	Consistency	**Distinctiveness**	**Consensus**	
	High	**Low**	**Low**	**Personal attribution**
A person treats you with contempt	This person always treats you this way	This person treats many people with contempt	No one else treats you with contempt	This is a very hostile person
	High	**High**	**High**	**Situational attribution**
	This person always treats you this way	This person treats only you with contempt	Everyone else treats you with contempt	Something in the situation (namely you) caused this behavior

◆ **Figure 19.6** *Factors that influence personal and situational attributions include consistency, distinctiveness, and consensus. When consistency is high, then low distinctiveness and low consensus result in personal attributions, whereas high distinctiveness and high consensus result in situational attributions. (Low-consistency behaviors, not shown here, are typically attributed to transient conditions rather than to stable personal or situational factors.)*

in the same manner (low distinctiveness), then you are likely to attribute the behavior to a personal trait of the contemptuous person.

In contrast, if consistency, distinctiveness, and consensus are all high, then we are particularly likely to attribute the behavior to situational causes. Thus, if everyone else also treats you with contempt (high consensus) and the person in question treats only you in this manner (high distinctiveness), then you may be forced to attribute the person's behavior to a factor external to him or her (namely, something about you). These judgmental patterns and the attributions they encourage are shown in Figure 19.6.

Attributional Biases and Distortions

A question may have already occurred to you. Do people really expend the effort (or do they have sufficient information) to take consistency, distinctiveness, and consensus factors into account? A considerable amount of research shows that people often do make thoughtful attributions in the way that Kelley suggests (Baron & others, 1991). But people also are, in a sense, *cognitive misers* (Ross & Nisbett, 1991). That is, they often take mental shortcuts, make snap judgments, and hope for the best. Examples of this appeared in the discussion of judgmental heuristics, such as availability and representativeness, in Chapter 11. In social judgments, as in other judgments, this tendency can result in attributional errors. More than three decades of research have highlighted some widespread biases in the attributions people make.

The Fundamental Attribution Error. If social psychology has taught us anything over the years, it is the profound power the social environment can

have over our behavior. Perhaps the reason why so many people are surprised by findings like those in Milgram's obedience studies is that we have a striking tendency to overestimate the role of personal factors and to underestimate the impact of the situation when explaining the behavior of others. This tendency is so strong and pervasive that it has been termed the **fundamental attribution error** (Ross, 1977).

The tendency to make personal attributions when explaining others' behavior occurs even when people are aware of situational factors. For example, subjects in one experiment were given the task of assigning the position that other subjects were to argue when they gave a speech on a controversial issue. Despite this clear influence that the observers had over the nature of the speech, they tended to attribute the arguments to the speakers' own attitudes on the issue (Gilbert & Jones, 1986). Findings like these have led Daniel Gilbert (1989) to suggest that the attribution process actually has two stages. At the first stage, people automatically make a personal attribution for another's behavior. A second, more effortful, stage may follow at which they take situational factors into account and perhaps adjust their original personal attribution.

Why does the fundamental attribution error occur? One reason may be that in observing others' actions, people focus on the actions and fail to take adequate account of the situation. Another possibility is that this attributional bias is, at least in part, the product of a cultural emphasis on the autonomous and responsible individual. If this is the case, then we might expect to find less of this bias in cultures that emphasize adherence to defined social roles, like that of India. Support for this notion comes from a study by J. G. Miller (1984) in which American and Indian

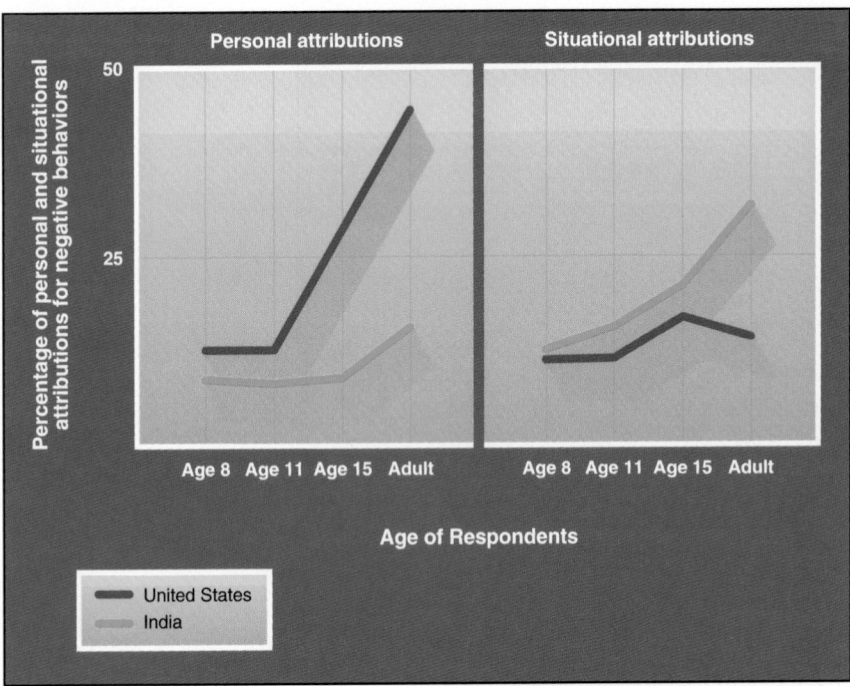

Figure 19.7 *Personal and situational attributions made about others' negative behaviors by Americans and Asian Indians of varying ages. With increasing age, Americans increased in their tendency to make personal attributions, whereas Indians actually increased in their tendency to make situational attributions from adolescence to adulthood. Similar findings occurred for positive events. Is the fundamental attribution error largely a Western phenomenon? (Data from Miller, 1984).*

subjects of varying ages explained the causes of others' positive and negative behaviors. As you can see in Figure 19.7, with increasing age came a tendency for Americans to make more personal attributions and fewer situational ones, while Indian subjects made more situational attributions.

The Actor–Observer Effect. The fundamental attribution error is half of an even broader phenomenon known as the **actor–observer effect.** We have already seen that people tend to make personal attributions in explaining others' behavior. The other half of the actor–observer effect occurs when people make judgments about their own behavior. In such judgments, they tend to emphasize the role of situational rather than personal factors. In one striking example, college students were presented with a request to commit a burglary. Whether they agreed or refused, the students tended to attribute their behavior to compelling factors in the situation, such as how convincing the requestor was. In contrast, other subjects who read about the students' decisions attributed their behavior to personal traits of honesty or dishonesty (West & others, 1975).

Self-Serving Bias. The actor–observer attributional pattern does not hold in all situations. A self-

enhancement factor is sometimes at work as well. In general, as earlier chapters have pointed out, people show a tendency to make personal attributions for their successes but to invoke situational causes for their failures. You can even find this pattern on the sports pages. In one analysis of postgame statements by athletes, researchers found that successes tended to be attributed to personal factors (''We played great defense and hung in there''), whereas losses were more frequently attributed to external factors (''Everything they shot was going in'' or ''I'm not even going to say what I think about the quality of officiating because I don't want to be suspended'') (Lau & Russell, 1980). This pattern is referred to as the **self-serving bias,** because it apparently operates to protect self-esteem (Ross & Nisbett, 1991). The self-serving bias allows us to take credit for our successes and disown our failures, thereby protecting or enhancing our self-esteem. But this tendency is not universal; as discussed in Chapter 16, depressed people frequently show the opposite pattern, a factor that helps keep them depressed.

Implicit Personality Theories

On the basis of our social interactions and the knowledge we gain about ourselves and others, all of us develop our own informal theories about what different types of people are like. These **implicit personality theories** contain our beliefs about how various traits and behaviors are related to one another. One widely held hypothesis has already been demonstrated in the findings that physically attractive people are seen as being more positive in other ways. Because our implicit personality theories help us ''fill in the blanks'' about other people, we may allow a single piece of information to strongly influence our impression of another.

We do not give each piece of information equal weight, however. In a classic experiment, Solomon Asch (1946) told one group of subjects that another person was ''intelligent, skillful, industrious, warm, determined, practical, and cautious.'' Other subjects were given the same descriptors, except that the word *warm* was replaced with *cold.* The subjects were then asked to write a fuller description of the stimulus person. Asch found that those who were given the description with the word *warm* in it tended to write more favorable descriptions of the person and to ascribe more socially desirable traits to him than did those who received the information that the person was cold. When Asch repeated the experiment, this time substituting the words *polite* and *blunt* for *warm* and *cold,* there were few differences in the character sketches (see Table 19.2). Asch concluded that warmth and coldness are **central traits,** since they

Table 19.2 Central and Peripheral Traits In Person Perception. Effect of Describing a Person as Either Warm vs. Cold or Polite vs. Blunt on Other Characteristics Attributed to Him

Experimenter's Description of Stimulus Person	Percentage of Subjects who Attributed Other Traits to Stimulus Person*				
	Sociable	Happy	Good-natured	Wise	Generous
Warm	77%	90%	94%	65%	91%
Cold	13%	34%	17%	25%	8%
Polite	71%	75%	87%	30%	56%
Blunt	48%	65%	56%	50%	58%

*The numbers represent the percentage of subjects who attributed the other characteristics to the stimulus person. Obviously, warm vs. cold exerted a stronger effect than polite vs. blunt, suggesting that it is a central trait dimension.

Source: Data from Asch, 1946.

strongly affect other judgments of the stimulus person, whereas bluntness and politeness are **peripheral traits** that color other judgments very little.

Confirmation Bias

The discussion of problem solving in Chapter 11 described how **confirmation bias** keeps people from testing their hypotheses and beliefs by looking for disconfirming evidence. Accordingly, once people have formed an impression about another, they tend to seek, interpret, and even create information that supports that impression. In one study illustrating this confirmation bias, subjects watched a videotape of a 9-year-old girl named Hannah and were asked to judge her academic potential. Half of the subjects were told that Hannah came from an upper-middle-class environment and that both of her parents were professional people. Other subjects were told that Hannah came from a poor neighborhood and that both of her parents were blue-collar workers. On the videotape, the girl performed at an average level, answering some difficult questions and missing some others. Although all the subjects had seen the same performance, the subjects who thought Hannah came from an affluent setting rated her higher in ability than did those who thought she came from a disadvantaged background (Darley & Gross, 1983).

Confirmation bias can have an important influence on human interactions, as we see in the case of self-fulfilling prophecy. A **self-fulfilling prophecy** occurs when people's impressions or expectations lead them to behave toward others in a way that evokes the expected behaviors and confirms the original impressions (see Figure 19.8). In one demonstration of this process, Robert Rosenthal and Lenore Jacobson (1968) told elementary school teachers that a new psychological test had indicated that certain

children could be expected to demonstrate a large intellectual growth spurt during the next year. The identified children had actually been chosen at random by the experimenters. Eight months later, the researchers readministered intelligence tests and found that the children they had identified as "late bloomers" had actually shown substantial IQ gains. Apparently, these children had received more encouragement and personal attention from their teachers and had improved their intellectual skills as a result. This "Pygmalion in the classroom" effect has been shown in a significant number of other studies as well, and it has important educational implications. It seems that in the classroom, as elsewhere, what you expect is often what you get (Rosenthal, 1985).

Figure 19.8 *The self-fulfilling prophecy operates as a three-step process that transforms expectations into reality. The perceiver's expectations influence how he or she behaves toward the target person. In response to the perceiver's behavior, the target person behaves in a manner that confirms the original expectations.*

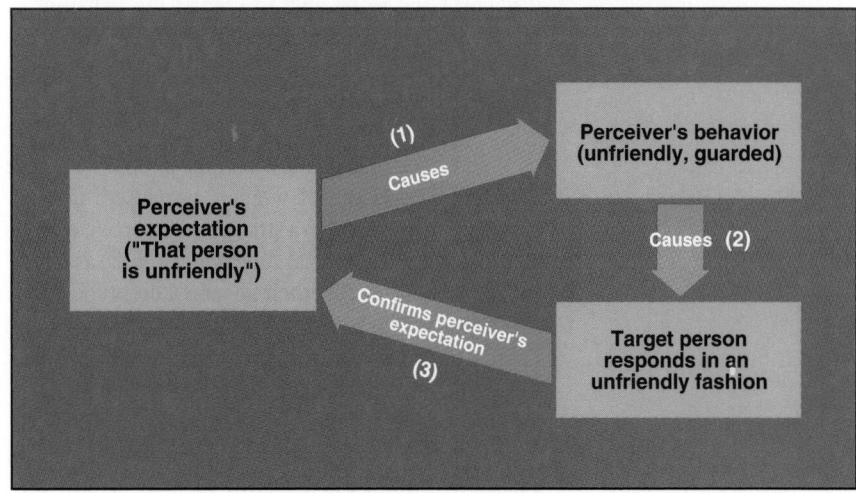

Group Perceptions: Stereotypes and Prejudice

The social perception principles we have explored thus far apply to people's perceptions of groups as well as their perceptions of individuals. For example, social schemas are often applied to groups in the form of stereotypes, and such stereotypes can sometimes foment prejudice.

Stereotypes

Stereotypes are schemas that associate certain characteristics with a defined group. In a sense, they are implicit personality theories that are applied to a particular group. They reflect people's normal perceptual tendency to sort objects into groups rather than to treat each object as unique. Thus, people sort others into groups based on gender, race, age, nationality, economic status, and other characteristics. Such grouping has the adaptive function of helping people to form impressions quickly, predict the behavior of others to some extent, and adjust their behavior appropriately (Smith & Zarate, 1992).

The dark side of stereotyping is that people's schemas may be inaccurate and may cause them to treat others in a manner that is inappropriate or discriminatory. People have a pronounced tendency to regard members of *outgroups*—groups to which they do not belong—as being more similar to one another than members of *ingroups*—groups to which they do belong. As a result of this tendency, people are quick to respond to an individual from an outgroup simply as a member of that group and to be blinded to characteristics of the individual that depart from the stereotype.

One reason for that blindness is the now-familiar theme of cognitive consistency. Just as self-schemas resist disconfirmation, so do schemas about groups. Motivated by the general need to make sense out of the world and to be able to predict the behavior of others, people sometimes resist or explain away information that is inconsistent with group schemas. One of the ways they do so is by creating *subcategories* into which exceptions to their general stereotypes can be placed. For example, people who have a stereotyped image of women as passive and dependent may respond to a strong and assertive woman by placing her in a special subcategory, such as "feminist," thereby leaving their general stereotype intact. The process of creating subcategories makes it more difficult for people's stereotypes to be changed through contact with exceptions to the rule.

Prejudice

Prejudice, defined as negative feelings toward persons based solely on their membership in certain groups, is one pernicious form of stereotyped thinking. Prejudice involves "prejudgment" of individuals based on their group status, and it may also involve a negative judgment of a group based on exposure to one or a few individuals from the group who have negative or threatening qualities. Negative emotional reactions are attached to the schema associated with the group, and these can result in a tendency to behave in a discriminatory fashion toward members of the group. One of the most tragic consequences of prejudice is that the targets of discrimination may eventually come to accept the negative stereotype themselves, resulting in lowered self-esteem, feelings of hopelessness, and even self-rejection (Zimbardo & Leippe, 1991).

What psychological forces foster prejudice? Two major theories have been advanced. The first, known as **realistic conflict theory,** links prejudice to competition for valued resources. In its original form, this theory stated that prejudice arises when the individual's material resources are threatened by an outgroup. However, years of research have resulted in a revision of the theory. It now appears that prejudice results not from a perceived personal threat but from a threat to one's ingroup. Among white Americans, for example, anti–African American feelings are not related to personal gains and losses but to the belief that white people as a group are in danger of falling behind (Bobo, 1988).

What is so important about the ingroup? **Social identity theory** provides one possible answer. According to this theory, the self-concept has two components, a personal identity and a group identity based on ingroup memberships (Tajfel & Turner, 1986). Thus, people can enhance self-esteem either through personal accomplishment or through association with groups that are successful. Associated with this is a tendency to take pride in one's ingroup and to belittle outgroups. A recent study showed that this tendency extends even to evaluation of nonsense syllables that are randomly associated with ingroups or outgroups. Subjects were exposed to lists of nonsense syllables such as *yof* and *xeh*. On each trial, a nonsense syllable appeared on one side of a screen and a word on the other. Some of the words had ingroup connotations (*us, we,* or *ours*), whereas others had outgroup connotations (*them, they,* or *theirs*). Control syllables were paired with words that had no group connotations (*he, she, me*). After a number of exposures to the syllables, the subjects rated each of them on a pleasantness–unpleasantness scale. Figure 19.9 shows the results. The ingroup-associated nonsense syllables were rated as most pleasant and the outgroup-associated as most unpleasant (Perdue & others, 1990).

Once people identify with a group, the group's successes have great power to fulfill esteem-

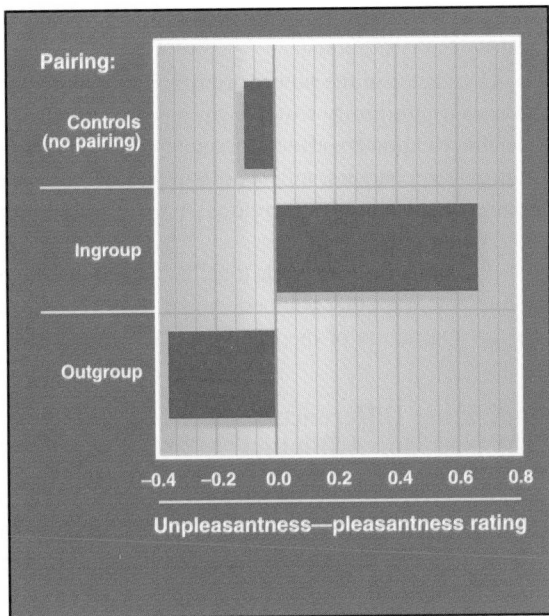

Figure 19.9 *Effects of pairing nonsense syllables with ingroup- or outgroup-associated words on the judged pleasantness or unpleasantness of the nonsense syllables. (Perdue & others, 1990).*

Pairing:

Controls (no pairing)

Ingroup

Outgroup

-0.4 -0.2 0.0 0.2 0.4 0.6 0.8
Unpleasantness—pleasantness rating

Figure 19.10 *As shown by Americans' responses to military success during the 1991 Persian Gulf War, identification with a winner can produce powerful ego gratification.*

enhancement needs. For example, a study conducted at seven major universities revealed that people tend to bask in the reflected glory of their athletic teams (Cialdini & others, 1976). The researchers simply counted the number of school sweatshirts worn on the Mondays following football games. They found that significantly more sweatshirts were worn on the Mondays after victories than on the Mondays after defeats and that the larger the margin of victory, the greater the number of shirts worn. Similarly, nationalistic pride and support for "our troops" peaked in the United States during the military successes of the 1991 Persian Gulf War (see Figure 19.10). The pervasive nature of the need for self-enhancement might well explain why prejudice is increased by perceived threats to the ingroup. One current example is a wave of "Japan-bashing" based at least in part on that country's perceived threat to the economic well-being of the United States.

■ ▢
Attraction and Close Relationships

When people are asked to identify the most important aspect of their lives, many reply that it is their friendships and close relationships with others. Caring about others and being cared about in return are central concerns for most of us. It is not surprising, there-

fore, that the factors that influence the formation and course of positive relationships have long been a focus of psychological research.

Numerous questions have been posed: What factors influence whether we will be attracted to another person? Do birds of a feather flock together, or do opposites attract? Once formed, how do some relationships grow from acquaintanceships into close and intimate relationships? What happens to make some intimate relationships deteriorate and end? How do people cope with the deterioration or loss of a close relationship? We now consider these and other questions relating to positive relationships.

Interpersonal Attraction

Attraction is the first phase of most close relationships. During the attraction phase, the social perception processes just discussed result in an impression about the other person, a degree of liking or disliking, and a decision about whether to pursue the relationship further. Interpersonal attraction is affected by a number of factors, some involving one's own characteristics, some involving those of the other person, and some relating to situational factors.

Situational Factors: Proximity and Familiarity

The single most important situational factor is physical proximity (see Figure 19.11). The sheer distance

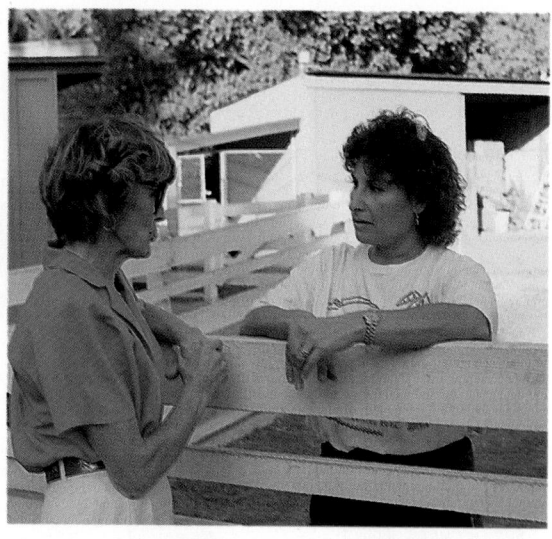

Figure 19.11 *One influential determinant of attraction is simple proximity of people to one another.*

between two people strongly affects the likelihood that they will form a relationship. Of course, proximity does not determine what the quality of the relationship will be: Familiarity can breed contempt as well as friendship. Overall, however, physical proximity has a positive influence on attraction. For example, an observational study by Leon Festinger and his coworkers (1950) revealed that residents of a large apartment building for married students were most likely to form friendships with those who lived on the same floor. Studies of classrooms in which students were seated alphabetically found that friend-

Figure 19.12 *During stressful or ambiguous situations, such as the San Francisco earthquake, people may be inclined to affiliate in order to reduce uncertainty through social comparison of their perceptions and reactions with those of others.*

ships were most likely to develop among students seated near one another.

One factor in the power of proximity may be the increased familiarity fostered by repeated exposure. The **mere exposure effect,** encountered several times in previous chapters, tells us that repeated exposure to almost any stimulus increases a person's liking for it (Zajonc, 1980).

Proximity brings people together and allows them to interact. From that point on, attraction is influenced by the interaction of their personal characteristics.

Individual Differences: The Need for Affiliation

People differ both in the strength of their desire to relate to others and in their reasons for wanting to affiliate. Wide differences have been found in the *need for affiliation*—the tendency to seek out relationships with others. In a college classroom, students who score high on a measure of this motive make more friends during the semester than students who score low (Byrne & Greendlinger, 1989). In a recent study, high school students wore "beepers" over a one-week period. Approximately every two hours, they were signalled by the experimenter to complete a series of questions concerning their present thoughts, wishes, and activities. Subjects who had scored high on a measure of affiliation motivation were more likely than others to report that they wished they were with others and were less likely to report that they wanted to be alone. They also were more likely to report thinking about their friends. Moreover, girls high in affiliation motivation were actually with friends more of the time, but this difference was not found for boys (Wong & Csikszentmihalyi, 1991).

What do people want from affiliations with others? Craig Hill (1987, 1991) suggests that four basic motives underlie the desire to affiliate. First, people may affiliate to reduce uncertainty through *social comparison.* During the San Francisco earthquake of 1989, many residents of the city found themselves bonding to strangers, partly to reduce the uncertainty they were feeling about the situation (Humphriss, 1989; see Figure 19.12). Other motives for affiliation include getting *positive stimulation,* obtaining *emotional support,* and gaining *attention* from others. Table 19.3 contains sample items from the Interpersonal Orientation Scale that Hill developed to measure the various forms of affiliation motivation.

Characteristics of Others

To whom are we attracted, and why? Answers to this question have isolated a number of key variables and the psychological processes that underlie their effects on people's feelings toward others.

Physical Attractiveness. We have already seen that physical attractiveness influences people's judgments about others. We might therefore expect that this variable would exert a strong effect on attraction, and it does. Physically attractive people seem to attract others for a number of reasons. First, as mentioned earlier, the ''what is beautiful is good'' stereotype leads people to expect that attractive people also have other desirable traits (Feingold, 1992). Actually, this can indeed be the case where social skills and self-confidence are concerned, because attractive people often have a history of being treated well by others—a good example of the self-fulfilling prophecy discussed earlier. Moreover, we may buttress our own feelings of self-esteem by associating with people who are widely viewed as attractive; we are indeed judged by the company we keep, or date. Thus, it is not surprising that both men and women respond more favorably to attractive dating partners and that people who are high in self-monitoring are especially likely to gravitate toward attractive people (Richardson, 1991; Snyder & others, 1985).

Lest you conclude that attractiveness is the key to happiness, we should note some interesting findings about physical attractiveness. First, physical attractiveness during the college years is unrelated to life satisfaction in middle age (Berscheid & others, 1972). Second, physically attractive people do not necessarily have the highest levels of self-esteem (Major & others, 1984). In fact, great attractiveness is sometimes linked with self-doubt, possibly because highly attractive individuals may attribute the positive responses of others solely to their ''surface'' beauty rather than to their inner personal qualities (see Figure 19.13).

Although we might tend to be most attracted initially to the ''beautiful people,'' we are, in fact, most likely to end up in close relationships with others who are similar to ourselves in attractiveness. Studies of the physical attractiveness of dating, engaged, and married couples support this **matching hypothesis,** and several possible reasons for this phenomenon have been suggested (Baron & Byrne, 1991; Feingold, 1988). One explanation, based on the norm of reciprocity, is that we regard beauty as a kind of commodity or resource to be exchanged in a relationship and therefore tend toward an equitable, or ''fair,'' arrangement in terms of attractiveness. Another possibility is that the most attractive match up first and are ''taken,'' then the next most attractive, and so on, until only the least attractive are available to match up with one another (Kalick & Hamilton, 1988).

Similarity and Attraction. All of us have heard the adage ''opposites attract.'' However, there are few cases in which conventional wisdom is so mistaken.

Table 19.3 Hill's Interpersonal Orientation Scale

The scale is designed to measure the strength of four types of affiliation motives. The sample items suggest four reasons for affiliating with others.

Reasons for Affiliation	Sample Item from Interpersonal Orientation Scale
Emotional support	I usually have the greatest need to have other people around me when I feel upset about something.
Positive Stimulation	I think being close to others, listening to them, and relating to them on a one-to-one level is one of my favorite and most satisfying pastimes.
Attention	I often have a strong desire to get people I am around to notice me and appreciate what I am like.
Social comparison	I find that I often have the desire to be around other people who are experiencing the same thing I am when I am unsure of what is going on.

Source: Based on Hill, 1987.

One of the strongest and most consistent findings in the psychological literature is that perceived *similarity,* not dissimilarity, increases attraction. People seem most attracted to others who are similar to them in a variety of ways, including personality characteristics and behaviors (Byrne & others, 1986; Griffin & Sparks, 1990). The strongest effects of similarity

Figure 19.13 *Marilyn Monroe's striking beauty was in a sense a curse, since she reportedly attributed people's positive responses to her appearance rather than to her more basic personal qualities. Her unhappy and insecure life ended tragically in suicide at age 36.*

occur in relation to attitudes, beliefs, and values. Attraction to people with dissimilar attitudes is low to begin with and decreases still further over time (Rosenbaum, 1986; Neimeyer & Mitchell, 1988). In contrast, perceived similarity in attitudes and values is positively related to attraction in both short-term and long-term relationships.

Donn Byrne and his coworkers (Byrne & Nelson, 1965; Byrne & others, 1986) have directly manipulated attitude similarity in the laboratory by askng subjects to complete an attitude questionnaire on a variety of topics and then providing them with a questionnaire completed by a stranger who differs from them on varying proportions of the attitude statements. Byrne has found that attitude similarity is related to attraction to the stranger in such a consistent manner that it is possible to write a precise mathematical formula (technically, a *regression equation*) to predict attraction responses on the basis of the proportion of similar attitudes (see Figure 19.14). This similarity–attraction relation is found not only for American college students but also for subjects in Mexico, India, and Japan who ranged from 4th-graders to retirees.

Why is attitude similarity so attractive? One suggestion is that it provides us with interpersonal rewards of reassurance and self-confirmation. In contrast, disagreement threatens our view of the world (Byrne & Clore, 1971). Another explanation is that most of us want to be liked and accepted by others, and similarity signals to us that the other person is probably going to like us. We therefore reciprocate with liking for the other person (Condon & Crano, 1988). In contrast, dissimilarity serves as a warning that the other person will dislike us, and we reciprocate with dislike (Aronson & Worchel, 1966). Whatever the cause of the relation between similarity and attraction, however, it seems clear that the data are most consistent with another old adage: "Birds of a feather flock together."

Close Relationships

Some of our relationships go no further than initial attraction, indifference, or repulsion. Others proceed to a deeper level of intimacy and commitment. What factors determine the development of close relationships?

Social Exchange: Relationship Economics

Social exchange theory, proposed by John Thibaut and Harold Kelley (1967), suggests that the movement toward closeness is governed by the balance of rewards and costs experienced in a relationship. Rewards include companionship, emotional support in times of stress, and satisfaction of other needs. Costs can include time, money, and effort spent to maintain the relationship, suffering in times of conflict, and the passing up of other relationship opportunities (Kelley, 1979).

Rewards and costs do not occur in a psychological vacuum. The balance of rewards and costs (that is, the **outcome**) experienced in the relationship is evaluated in terms of two standards. The first standard, known as the **comparison level,** is the balance of rewards and costs a person has grown to expect in relationships, based on both personal experiences and observations of others' relationships. According to Thibaut and Kelley, the relation between outcome and comparison level determines the degree of *satisfaction* in a relationship. Outcomes that meet or exceed the comparison level are satisfying; those that fall below this standard are dissatisfying.

However, even a satisfying relationship may not last, because there is another important standard of comparison: what a person can expect to get out of alternative relationships or life circumstances. Comparison of outcomes with this standard, known as the **comparison level for alternatives,** determines the degree of *commitment* to the relationship. Thus, a person may elect to leave a satisfying relationship if something even better is available in another relationship. On the other hand, some people remain committed to relationships that are basically unsatisfying to them (including those involving physical or psy-

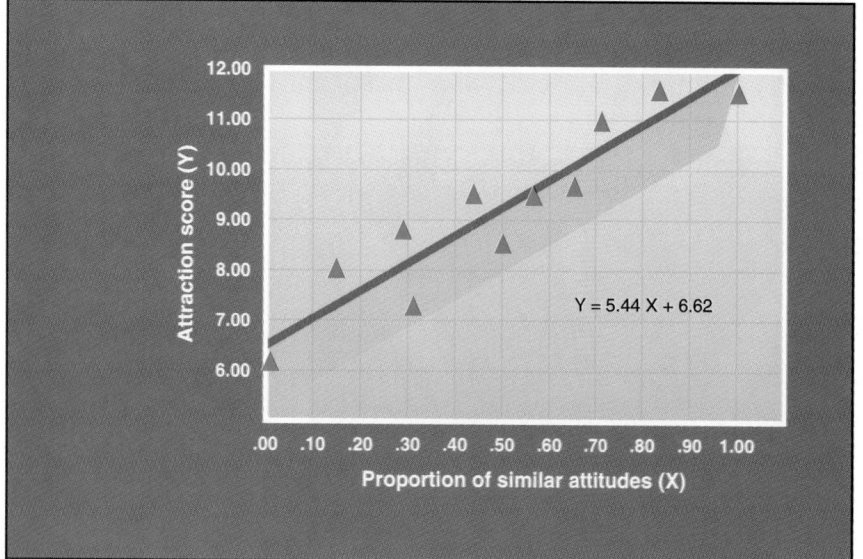

Figure 19.14 *The attitude similarity–attraction relation. In the formula, Y is the score measuring attraction toward the stranger and X is the proportion of similar attitudes. The triangles are data points provided by groups of actual subjects, and the line is the result predicted by the formula. (Byrne & Nelson, 1965).*

$$Y = 5.44\ X + 6.62$$

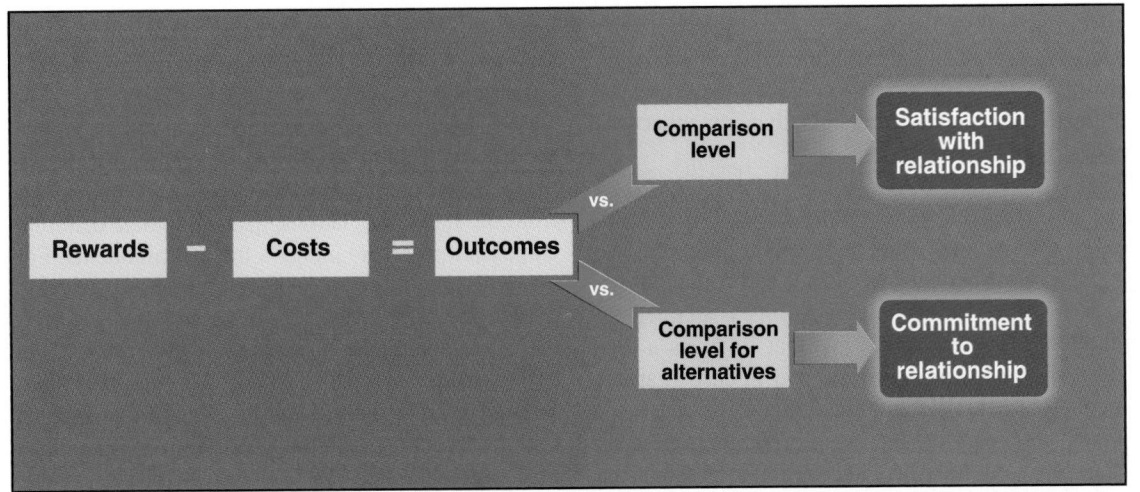

Figure 19.15 *According to Thibaut and Kelley's social exchange theory, rewards minus costs equal the outcome of a relationship. Comparison of outcomes with two standards, the comparison level and the comparison level for alternatives, determines the degrees of satisfaction and commitment in the relationship.*

chological abuse) because the alternatives seem even worse.

From the perspective of social exchange theory, then, the balance of rewards and costs, considered in relation to the two standards of comparison, determine the degrees of satisfaction and commitment to a relationship. These relations are shown in Figure 19.15.

Self-Disclosure and Social Penetration

According to Irwin Altman and Dalmas Taylor (1973), the authors of **social penetration theory,** relationships progress from superficial exchanges to more intimate ones as people begin to give more of themselves to one another. Their exchanges become both broader, involving more areas of their lives, and deeper, involving more intimate and personally meaningful areas. As shown in Figure 19.16, exchanges progress from a narrow and shallow sliver to a broader and deeper wedge. The social penetration process may involve a greater sharing of possessions or physical intimacy, but the most important commodity of all may be the sharing of innermost thoughts and feelings with another in the act of **self-disclosure.**

Research results support the importance of self-disclosure in strengthening relationships. More extensive and intimate self-disclosure is associated with greater emotional involvement in friendships and in dating relationships and greater satisfaction in marital relationships (Hendrick, 1989; Miller, 1990; Rubin & others, 1980). However, the relation between self-disclosure and intimacy is reciprocal. That is, self-disclosure fosters intimacy, and intimacy and trust encourage self-disclosure (Miller, 1990).

Intimacy and Love

Some close relationships develop into intimacy. Although intimate relationships come in a variety of forms, all involve at least one of the following three components (Brehm & Kassin, 1990):

1. *Emotional attachment,* most often involving feelings of affection and love.
2. *Interdependence* between the partners, each of whom relies on the other's assistance to satisfy psychological needs.
3. *Fulfillment of psychological needs* of the partners, such as needs for intimacy and support.

Varieties of Love

"How do I love thee? Let me count the ways." This insight on the part of the poet Elizabeth Barrett Browning is echoed in attempts by poets, theologians,

Figure 19.16 *According to the theory of social penetration, as a relationship deepens, the partners increase the breadth of their exchanges (including self-disclosure) and the depth of their intimacy. (Brehm & Kassin, 1990).*

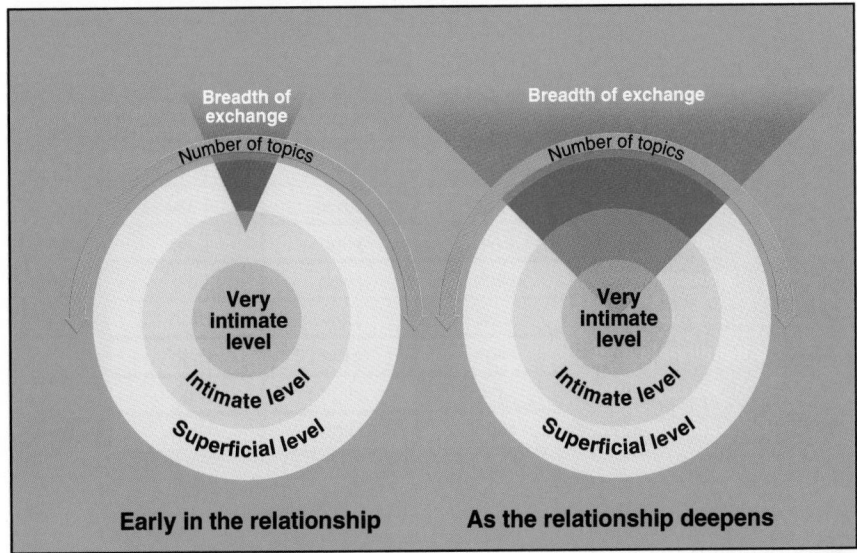

novelists, philosophers, and psychologists to count the ways people can love another. Apparently, there are a great many ways. The word *love* has more entries in *Bartlett's Famous Quotations* than any other term except *man* (Levinger, 1988).

Passionate and Companionate Love. One of the oldest differentiations made in social psychology is the distinction between passionate and companionate love (Hatfield, 1988). *Passionate love* is an intensely emotional and absorbing love that involves a high level of physiological arousal and intense yearning for the partner. (We examined this form of love in the Psychobiological Interactions feature of Chapter 12). **Companionate love** involves an affectionate relationship marked by deep caring about the partner's well-being and happiness and a commitment to being there for the other (Caspi & Herbener, 1990; Hatfield, 1988). It lacks the emotional intensity of passionate love, but it is more stable and enduring. Passionate love sometimes evolves into companionate love over time (Metts & others, 1989).

Sternberg's Triangular Model. Robert Sternberg (1988) has proposed a somewhat more complex three-dimensional model of love. The three points of his triangular model are intimacy, commitment, and passion. Sternberg defines *intimacy* as the closeness two people feel toward one another and the extent to which they value one another, count on one another in time of need, and share their possessions and themselves with one another. *Commitment* is the decision to remain in the relationship and the labeling of the re-

lationship as a love relationship. *Passion* includes feelings of romance, as well as physical and sexual attraction.

Sternberg has done more than simply add one more component to the passionate–companionate distinction. The complexity of Sternberg's model arises from the fact that relationships can involve different combinations of the model's three components. For example, the liking that occurs in a close friendship is high in intimacy but low in passion and commitment. Companionate love is high in intimacy and commitment but low in passion. Figure 19.17 describes the eight varieties of love (actually, seven plus nonlove) that are thought to result from combinations of the three factors.

The Lee–Hendricks Model: Six Styles of Love. The sociologist John Alan Lee (1973) proposed a model featuring six basic "styles" of love. Drawing on Lee's work, Clyde and Susan Hendrick (1986) constructed scales to measure people's perceptions of their love relationships (see Table 19.4). Research using the Styles of Love Scale has demonstrated that these styles do appear to exist and that they affect the character of love relationships. As a group, males score higher than females in both passionate and game-playing love. Females, in turn, score higher in friendship, logical, and possessive love. College couples tend to agree with one another in the kinds of love they report in their relationship. Passionate and selfless love are positively related to satisfaction with the relationship, whereas game-playing love predicts low satisfaction. A follow-up study of couples over several years indicated that those who remained together were most likely to be simultaneously high in passionate love and low in game-playing love (Hendrick & others, 1984, 1988).

An Attachment Approach to Love Relationships. So far, we have looked at a number of different ways of characterizing love relationships. These typologies are basically descriptive in nature; they do not explain why people love in particular ways. Phillip Shaver and his coworkers (1988) have approached this question from the perspective of **attachment style.** They assume that the type of attachment formed with parents in early childhood expresses itself in later intimate relationships. You may recall that the discussion of attachment in Chapter 4 described three primary attachment patterns: secure, avoidant, and anxious–ambivalent. Table 19.5 shows how these patterns manifest themselves in adult relationships.

In a large-scale study, the researchers found that adults' recollections of their relationships with their parents related to their current experiences and feelings in romantic relationships. It seems clear that a pattern of secure early attachments in which the child

Figure 19.17 *According to Sternberg's triangular theory of love, intimacy, passion, and commitment in various combinations form seven distinct love relationships (plus nonlove, where all are low).*

	Intimacy	Passion	Decision and commitment
Nonlove	Low	Low	Low
Liking	High	Low	Low
Infatuated love	Low	High	Low
Romantic love	High	High	Low
Empty love	Low	Low	High
Companionate love	High	Low	High
Fatuous love	Low	High	High
Consummate love	High	High	High

felt loved and accepted is related to the most positive outcomes. Regrettably, this category included only 56 percent of a sample of more than 600 adults. The rest were divided between the two categories of insecure attachment (avoidant and anxious–ambivalent). Those who reported avoidant attachment with their parents (feelings of rejection) were uncomfortable with closeness as adults, and they found it difficult to trust and self-disclose to their partners. They reported experiencing jealousy and emotional extremes in their love relationships. The anxious–ambivalent types, who reported both positive and negative feelings toward their parents, were characterized by a desire to merge completely with their partners while at the same time fearing abandonment by the partners. They reported experiencing strong sexual attraction and love at first sight, followed by obsessive preoccupations and concerns about the relationship and whether it would last.

The attachment model seems to offer researchers the potential for investigating the roots of love within a developmental perspective. It may well be that in the patterns of close relationships, the child is truly the parent of the adult.

■ ■ ■

Prosocial Behavior: Helping Others

The Kitty Genovese incident, described in Chapter 2, was a shocking example of a failure to help a woman who was savagely attacked and murdered outside her New York apartment. Although many of the victim's neighbors heard the screams and watched from their windows, no one came to her aid, and the police were not even summoned until she was dead.

In sharp contrast, we often read of heroic acts of bravery and self-sacrifice. One example occurred on a January night in 1982 when an airliner crashed into the frigid waters of the Potomac River in Washington, D.C. A man who was himself injured stayed near the wreckage, trying to help other victims to safety. When a life ring was thrown to him from a helicopter, he passed it on to others who were more badly injured than he. By the time the helicopter returned to assist him, he had died beneath the icy waves.

Helping behavior comes in many forms. It characterizes the entire lifestyle of people like Mother Teresa, whose devotion to the poor of Calcutta is well known. Less visible are the approximately 90 million adult Americans (about half of the adult population) who voluntarily participate in charitable activities each year (Clary & Snyder, 1991). The impact of such acts on the lives of the afflicted, the oppressed, and

Table 19.4 Lee's Six Styles of Love and Items from the Styles of Love Scale Developed by Hendrick and Hendrick to Measure Them

Basic Love Styles	Sample Items Measuring Each Style
1. Passionate love (*Eros*)	My lover and I were attracted to each other immediately after we first met.
	My lover and I became emotionally involved rather quickly.
2. Game-playing love (*Ludus*)	I have sometimes had to keep two of my lovers from finding out about each other.
	I can get over love affairs pretty easily and quickly.
3. Friendship love (*Storge*)	The best kind of love grows out of a long friendship.
	Love is really a deep friendship, not a mysterious, mystical emotion.
4. Logical love (*Pragma*)	It is best to love someone with a similar background.
	An important factor in choosing a partner is whether or not he [she] will be a good parent.
5. Possessive love (*Mania*)	When my lover doesn't pay attention to me, I feel sick all over.
	I cannot relax if I suspect that my lover is with someone else.
6. Selfless love (*Agape*)	I would rather suffer myself than let my lover suffer.
	Whatever I own is my lover's to use as he [she] chooses.

Note: Lee's (1988) formal names for the six styles of love are listed in parentheses.

Source: Hendrick & Hendrick, 1986.

Table 19.5 Attachment Styles in Adult Relationships

Question: Which of the following best describes your feelings?

A. I find it relatively easy to get close to others and am comfortable depending on them and having them depend on me. I don't often worry about being abandoned or about someone getting too close to me.

B. I am somewhat uncomfortable being close to others; I find it difficult to trust them completely, difficult to allow myself to depend on them. I am nervous when anyone gets too close, and often, love partners want me to be more intimate than I feel comfortable being.

C. I find that others are reluctant to get as close as I would like. I often worry that my partner doesn't really love me or won't want to stay with me. I want to merge completely with another person, and this desire sometimes scares people away.

The first type of attachment style is described as "secure," the second as "avoidant," and the third as "anxious/ambivalent."

Source: Shaver & others, 1988.

the needy cannot be measured, but it must be enormous.

What factors determine whether we will offer help to others? What are the motives for giving help when we do so? Are there ways to increase **prosocial behavior,** actions intended to assist other people? These questions have stimulated considerable re-

Figure 19.18 *Scenes like this are commonplace in large cities. Do they reflect callous indifference or the operation of social psychological factors that inhibit helping behavior?*

search during the past two decades. The answers have not only practical consequences but also profound implications for our conceptions of human nature.

Unresponsive Bystanders: Why Don't They Help?

Let us begin with the vexing question raised by the Kitty Genovese incident. Why do people often fail to assist victims who are clearly in distress (see Figure 19.18)? Perhaps the following scenario will provide some suggestions:

> As you walk along a city street, an elderly man ahead of you staggers and then slumps to the sidewalk. You wonder what is wrong with him. Is he sick? Drunk? Having a heart attack? Setting you up for a mugging? As you try to figure out what is happening, you look around to see if you are alone or if there are others nearby. If others are around, you look to see how they are reacting. Do they seem concerned? Is anyone else coming to help? You might say to yourself, "OK, stay cool. Don't make a fool of yourself by acting panicky. There are others around. They don't seem too concerned, so it mustn't be anything too serious. Besides, if I don't help, someone else will—someone who knows what to do. It's not my responsibility."

This monologue captures the essence of four important processes that can foster a decision to intervene or not to intervene. These factors include *social comparison, diffusion of responsibility, potential costs,* and *self-efficacy.* Let us see how they apply to this situation.

Like many emergency situations, this one is somewhat ambiguous. What is happening to the man? How

serious is his condition? In making such judgments, the process of social comparison, mentioned earlier, can be very important. If other people are present, you may compare your reactions with theirs and use these cues to decide whether the situation is serious enough to warrant intervention. In a culture where it is fashionable to "stay cool," social comparison processes may cause us to mistakenly interpret an emergency as a matter of little concern and fail to react to it. Interestingly, as suggested in Chapter 2, some of Kitty Genovese's neighbors stated later that they interpreted the failure of someone else to intervene as an indication that they were witnessing nothing more than a "lover's quarrel" that didn't warrant their "butting in" (Darley & Latané, 1968).

In a laboratory demonstration of the same phenomenon, similar to a study mentioned in Chapter 2, a male subject and a male confederate (the experimenter's accomplice) were completing experimental questionnaires when a female experimenter suddenly put her hand to her head, moaned softly, and staggered to the doorway of an adjoining room. She lurched inside, and there was a loud crash as she fell and upset a table. Then there was silence, except for occasional gasps and moans. For half the subjects, the confederate appeared totally unconcerned and returned nonchalantly to filling out his forms. For the other half, he registered alarm and concern but did not move to help the "lady in distress." As shown in Figure 19.19, the confederate's degree of demonstrated concern markedly affected the likelihood that the subject would eventually go to the aid of the experimenter. Apparently, an expression of concern by the confederate helped the subject confirm his own interpretation that the situation was indeed an emergency that required intervention (Smith & others, 1973).

The presence of other people can also alter the level of responsibility a person feels for helping the victim. If you were the only person present in the situation described earlier, then the total responsibility for helping would fall on you. But if others were also present, there would be a diffusion of responsibility through the group so that no one person would feel responsible. It is not surprising, therefore, that you might think, "If I don't help, someone else will." In the Kitty Genovese incident, many of the bystanders who did interpret the incident as an emergency failed to intervene because they were certain that someone *must* already have called the police (Darley & Latané, 1968).

Not the least of a person's concerns in such a situation are the potential costs of intervening (Dovidio & others, 1991). In the scenario involving the elderly man, concerns were expressed about the possibility of being set up for a mugging. Such concerns can have a strong basis in reality. In one tragic example, three employees of CBS went to the aid of

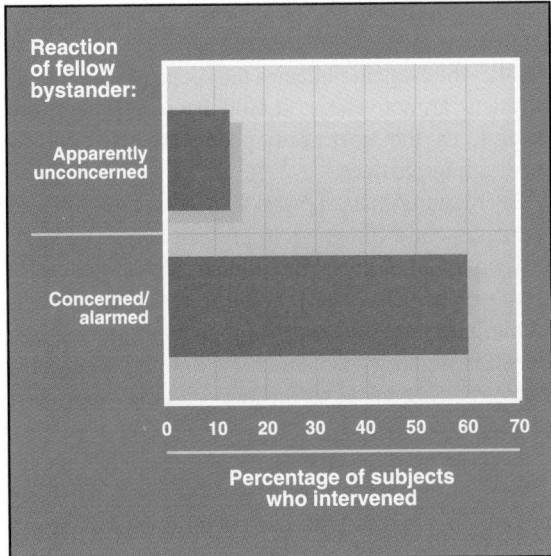

Figure 19.19 *Social comparison and helping behavior. The figure shows the influence of a fellow bystander's degree of expressed alarm and concern on the percentage of subjects who went to help a woman in distress. (Data from Smith & others, 1973).*

a woman who was being attacked in a parking garage. The assailant turned out to be a hired killer who turned his gun on the rescuers and killed them as well as the woman who was his original target (Hammer, 1987).

Potential costs include not only possible physical danger but also negative social consequences. There is the possibility that a person will appear foolish to others by trying to help inappropriately. Thus, it is not surprising that you might think, ''Don't make a fool of yourself by acting panicky.''

Even if you decided that the situation was an emergency and that you should help, whether or not you actually did so would depend on the fourth factor, your self-efficacy in dealing with the situation. If others are present, there may indeed be ''someone who knows what to do.'' Perhaps there is someone with medical knowledge and experience who can tell what is wrong with the man and knows how to help him. Sometimes, we fail to help because we simply don't know how or because we do not believe that we can help effectively.

Figure 19.20 shows how these four processes influence the string of decisions that result in helping or not helping in a potential emergency. The factors just discussed suggest that the adage ''there's safety in numbers'' may not always be true when it comes to getting help. A victim may be better off if there is only one other person present to help, for the presence of others may give false social comparison cues, may diffuse perceived responsibility for helping, may suggest that someone else could help more effectively,

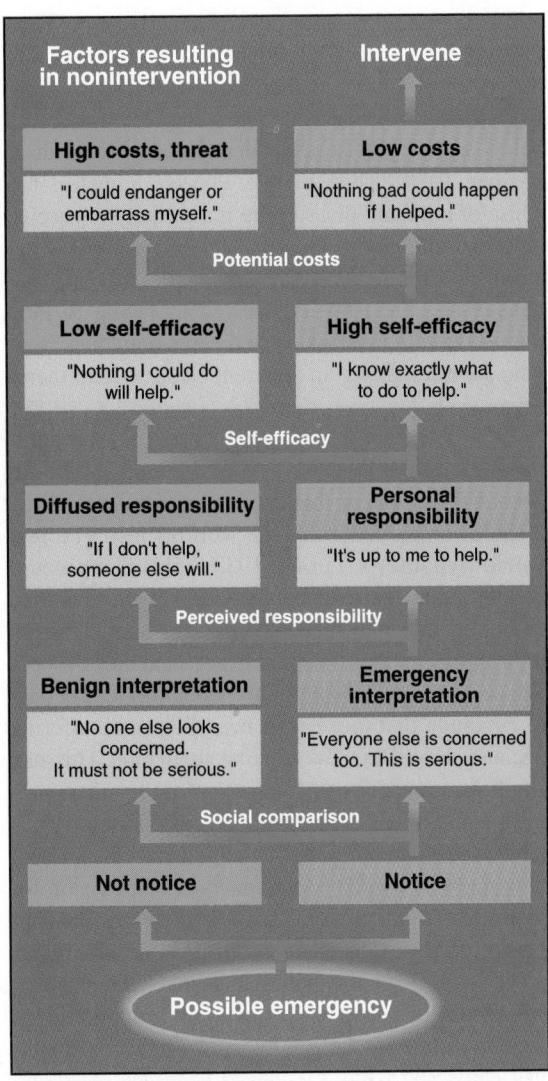

Figure 19.20 *Four factors—social comparison, perceived responsibility, self-efficacy, and potential costs—have been shown to affect decisions to help in a potential emergency.*

or may arouse anxiety about acting inappropriately. Any of these factors could reduce the probability that someone in the group will help.

Characteristics of the Needy: Whom Do We Help?

Are some people more likely to receive help than others? Research as well as everyday observations indicate an affirmative answer to this question. Which characteristics of needy people affect helping behavior?

Attributions and the Just World Hypothesis

Once we decide that a person needs help, the attributions we make concerning the source of the problem influence whether or not we actually help. When the problems of needy people are viewed as being due to factors beyond their control, they are more likely to receive help than when they are viewed as being responsible for their needy state (Schmidt & Weiner, 1988). Thus, people who are homeless because of a natural disaster are more likely to receive help than those who are seen as being homeless because of their unwillingness to work. In nonemergencies, people who are viewed as trying to help themselves are more likely to receive help than those who are not making an apparent effort to help themselves.

A problem, of course, is that attributions regarding the cause of a person's need for help can be inaccurate. One factor that can lead attributions astray is the common belief that the world is just. The **just world hypothesis** (Lerner, 1980) holds that because people want to believe that the world is fair (and that, by implication, they themselves will be treated fairly), they tend to believe that people get what they deserve and deserve what they get. This belief may lead people to conclude that those who need help are suffering because they somehow deserve their fate. This can result in a tendency to blame victims for their predicaments, to see their difficulties as due to controllable factors, and to refuse to help them. This process may underlie some people's lack of compassion for victims of AIDS: If something this terrible has happened to them, then clearly they must deserve it.

The irony of the belief in a just world is that sometimes the most needy of victims may end up receiving the least help. This is one of the tragedies that can result from a tendency to blame disadvantaged individuals and groups for their plight.

Other Victim Characteristics

Physical attractiveness seems to affect a host of social and psychological reactions to other people. Does it also affect the likelihood of getting help?

The answer seems to be yes. Consider the following scenario: You enter a phone booth in an airport and find a completed application form for graduate school that has been left behind. With the application is a photograph of the person and a stamped addressed envelope. Do you help by putting the materials in the envelope and dropping them in a mailbox? Would your helpfulness be affected by how attractive the person in the picture is?

If you are like the 442 men and 162 women who actually encountered this situation in a large municipal airport, the attractiveness of the person might well influence your behavior. Peter Benson and his coworkers (1976), who had planted the materials in the telephone booths, found that applications with pictures of physically attractive men and women were more likely to be mailed than applications accompanied by pictures of unattractive candidates. This result, which again indicates the social advantages of physical attractiveness, should be somewhat troubling to us; the most needy people are often not the most attractive ones.

Perceiving that a person in need is similar to us increases our willingness to provide help. The similarity may be in dress, in attitudes, in nationality, or in other characteristics (Dovidio, 1984). The effects of similarity are not surprising, given the strong link between similarity and attraction. Similarity may also make it easier for us to identify with the victim and his or her plight.

As the norm of reciprocity, discussed in Chapter 18, might lead us to expect, we also are more likely to help people who have been helpful to us and even people who are perceived as helpful but with whom we have had no personal contact. Thus, people in helping professions, such as nurses, are more likely to receive help than those in nonhelping occupations, such as bookkeepers (Yinon & Dovrat, 1987).

Why Do People Help?

We now come to perhaps the most interesting question of all: What factors might underlie the desire to help others?

Helping as a Sociobiological Phenomenon

Humans are not the only animals that engage in helping behavior. Sociobiologists have proposed that in all species, helping behavior is a mechanism for ensuring the survival of the gene pool by increasing the likelihood that the helper's offspring and relatives will survive (Buck & Ginsburg, 1991). Many examples of helping behavior among both kin and non-kin can be found in the animal kingdom (see Figure 19.21). For instance, adult birds will pretend to be injured in order to lead predators away from their young. Soldier termites use their own bodies to protect other termites against intruders. Field studies of primates have identified some striking examples of protective behaviors. One investigator observed a male baboon watching two juveniles playing on a ledge below. Suddenly, a rock was dislodged and began to fall toward the juveniles. The male grabbed the rock and held it in place, releasing it only after the juveniles were out of harm's way (Rushton, 1989).

From the sociobiological perspective, helping occurs as a relatively automatic response to certain social situations, such as the distress of a child or of someone who is similar to the helper (and who is therefore especially likely to have some genes like the helper's). The helper in such situations may seem

Figure 19.21. *Sociobiologists view helping behavior as a means of ensuring survival of the gene pool.*

to be acting selflessly; but always, the gene's selfish interests are being served. Indeed, one sociobiologist, J. Phillipe Rushton, believes that helping behavior has a genetic basis, citing evidence that identical twins are more similar in the behavioral trait of helpfulness than siblings or fraternal twins (Rushton, 1989).

Social Learning: Norms and Self-Reinforcement

According to the behavioral perspective, the roots of helping lie buried in people's individual social learning histories. In the course of development, people are exposed to models who are helpful, as well as to the norms of the society. They are then rewarded with approval when they behave in accordance with social norms and punished when they do not. Eventually, they internalize the norms as their own.

One social norm that is relevant to helping is the norm of reciprocity, discussed earlier. Many of us have learned that we should do unto others as they do unto us—or, in the words of the Golden Rule, as we would *like* them to do unto us. One derivative of the norm of reciprocity is the just world principle described earlier (Batson & Weeks, 1991). Applied to oneself, this principle suggests that people should expect to get what they deserve, or reap as they sow. Thus, it may sometimes motivate helping by causing people to believe that if they help others, they will deserve better outcomes themselves. In one test of

this idea, Miron Zuckerman (1975) found that students who believed in a just world, compared with students who did not, gave other students more help before a test. After the test, they no longer gave more help. Zuckerman speculated that those who had a strong belief in a just world helped others more before the exam to make themselves more deserving of a high grade.

Another important social norm is the *norm of social responsibility.* This norm states that people should help others and contribute to the welfare of society. Helping is one of many possible expressions of this norm in social behavior.

Once people internalize the norms and values of their society, a powerful internal process of *self-reinforcement* can maintain the relevant behaviors in the complete absence of external reinforcement. Thus, people experience self-reinforcement in the form of pride and self-praise when they engage in behaviors they consider laudable, such as helping. Many people report that they experience great personal satisfaction (sometimes called the *helper's high*) by contributing to charities and helping others, even when no one else knows what they have done. In fact, people can most easily attribute their helpfulness to inner goodness when there is no external reward for helping. Conversely, they experience self-punishment in the form of guilt or regret when they act in ways that violate norms of ''rightness.''

Empathy and Altruism

The self-reinforcement hypothesis reflects the view that all actions on behalf of others, regardless of how noble they appear, are ultimately motivated by some form of self-benefit. Is there no basis for true and selfless **altruism,** the desire to increase the welfare of another without concern for oneself? C. Daniel Batson believes that altruism does indeed exist, though he does not claim that true altruism motivates all, or even most, helping behaviors.

According to Batson, the basis for altruism is **empathy,** the ability to put oneself in the place of another and to share what that person is experiencing (Batson, 1991). Researchers can manipulate empathy by making subjects believe that they are either similar or dissimilar to another person, the idea being that they will find it easier to put themselves in the place of someone who is similar to them.

In one experiment designed to demonstrate the existence of selfless altruism, subjects' empathy was manipulated in this manner (Batson & others, 1981). Then each male subject was told that either he or another person would receive painful electric shocks in an experiment on task performance under unpleasant conditions. By a coin flip, the other person (actually a female confederate) was designated as the

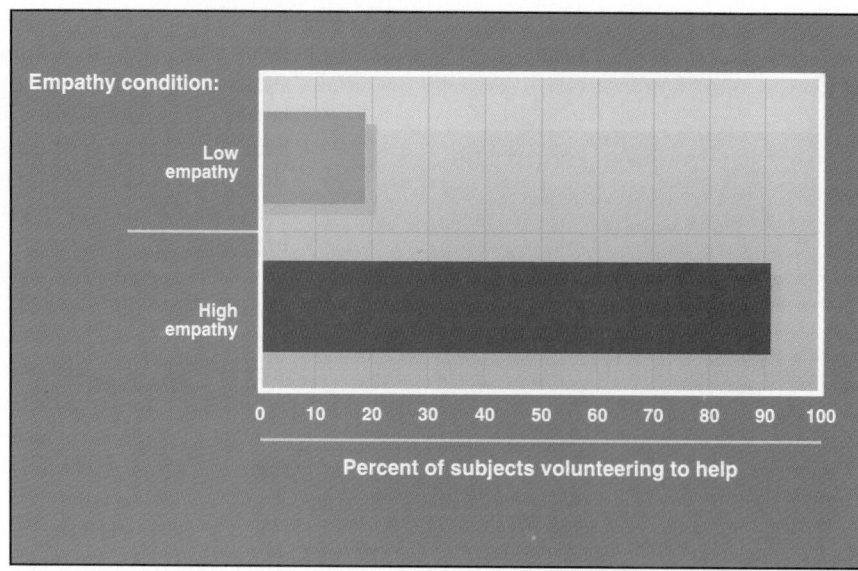

The answer to the question "Why do people do good deeds for one another?" can provide you with insights into your conception of human nature. You have read about several explanations of altruism—sociobiological, social learning, Batson's altruism explanation, and Cialdini's negative state relief model. Which seemed most credible to you? How does this judgment reflect your own philosophical views of human nature? Are good deeds an expression of an inherently good being, a reflection of God's goodness manifested in us, a product of a *tabula rasa,* or "blank tablet," that has been conditioned to respond to social norms, the actions of a basically selfish being who acts only to maximize pleasure and minimize discomfort, or the behaviors of a creature driven to act in the genetic self-interest of the species? What answers to this question would be given by the major perspectives on behavior discussed in Chapter 1 (biological, behavioral, cognitive, psychodynamic, and humanistic)?

▶ **Figure 19.22** *Effects of empathy on willingness to volunteer to receive electric shock in place of another. In this case, empathy was manipulated in terms of perceived similarity. (Data from Batson & others, 1981).*

performer and the subject as an observer. This procedure was designed to convey to subjects that they could easily have been in the learner's predicament. When the experiment began, the performer expressed great fear of the electric shock because she had nearly been electrocuted as a child. At this point, the subject was told that he could leave after watching only two trials or, if he wished, could change places with the performer, thereby saving her from the trauma of being shocked.

According to the empathy–altruism hypothesis, we should expect highly empathic subjects to be more likely to help; low-empathy subjects should elect to escape and thereby protect themselves from both the trauma of shock and the unpleasantness of having to watch the subject being shocked. As Figure 19.22 shows, that is exactly what happened.

A challenge to Batson's conclusion that people can be altruistic was soon issued by Robert Cialdini

and his colleagues (1987) in the form of the **negative state relief model.** Cialdini argued that the reason people in the high-empathy condition helped was to relieve their distress at seeing a similar person suffer, not to selflessly promote the welfare of the other person. Although Cialdini believes that helping has the egoistic function of relieving one's own distress, he agrees with Batson that empathy is an important factor in helping behavior. Nonetheless, the larger philosophical issue of whether people are by nature altruistic or egoistic remains unanswered at this time. ▼

Understanding the reasons people help can provide valuable clues to the practical question of how helping behavior can be increased in a world filled with people who need help. The following feature considers this question.

ENHANCING HUMAN PERFORMANCE

INCREASING THE LIKELIHOOD AND EFFECTIVENESS OF PROSOCIAL BEHAVIOR

We live in a world filled with needy people. Sadly, their needs frequently go unmet because others who are in a position to help fail to do so. What can be done to increase prosocial behavior? Psychological research on the personal and situational factors that influence helping behavior suggests a number of potentially useful approaches to enhancing the per-

formance of prosocial behaviors that can have positive outcomes for both doer and recipient. Enhancement here entails increasing both the likelihood and the effectiveness of helping behaviors.

The importance attached to empathy by many theorists suggests that developing feelings of connectedness with others may make people more likely to help.

In line with this hypothesis, Margaret Clark and her coworkers (1987) found that people who feel a sense of connectedness with others in their environment were more likely to experience a need to be socially responsible and to help others than those who did not feel connected to their communities. Later, we will see how this principle was applied in an attempt to increase blood donorship.

Several studies indicate that if we want to increase helping behavior, we should be sure that people are exposed to helpful models, particularly in the mass media. Children seem particularly influenced. In one study, 6-year-old children were shown an episode of "Lassie" containing a rescue scene. Other children were shown a "Lassie" episode or a "Brady Bunch" episode that contained no helping behavior. Later, as the children played a competitive game, they heard the sound of some puppies who seemed to be in distress. Despite the fact that going to the aid of the puppies interfered with the chance to win an attractive prize, children who had been exposed to the prosocial program with the rescue scene spent nearly twice the amount of time trying to free the puppies—about 93 seconds, compared with 45 to 50 seconds in the other two conditions (Sprafkin & others, 1975).

In another experiment, disadvantaged youngsters who watched episodes of the public television program "Mister Rogers' Neighborhood" subsequently became more helpful in their preschool than those who watched neutral or aggressive programs (Stein & Friedrich, 1972). A survey of nearly 200 studies of the effects of prosocial TV on children's behavior indicated that such programs have a strong positive effect on prosocial behavior—an effect about twice as strong as the negative effects violent TV shows have on aggressive behavior (Hearold, 1986). These results suggest that it would be socially valuable to have more programs showing prosocial behavior and lauding those who perform good deeds.

Exposure to helpful models was part of a nationwide program designed to increase blood donations among high-school students (Sarason & others, 1991). Students in 66 high schools watched an experimental audiovisual program that

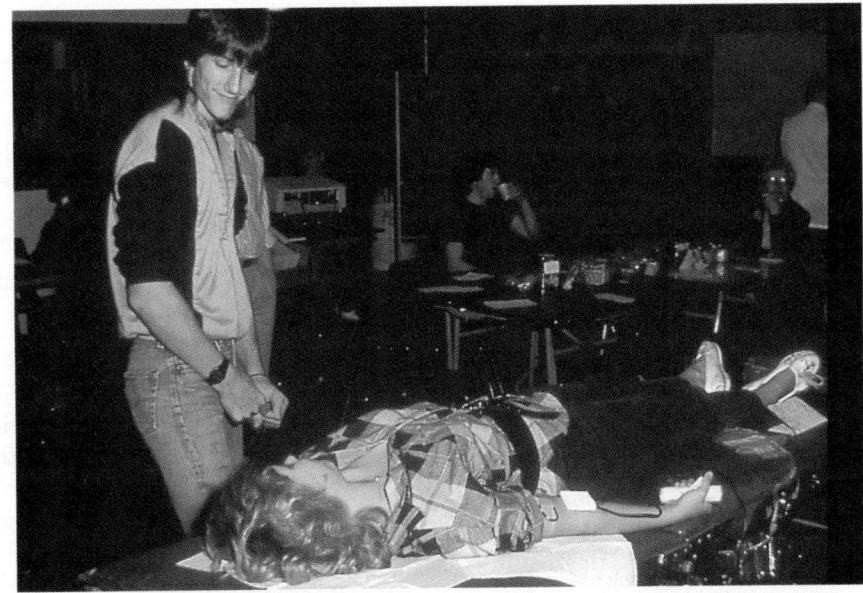

Figure 19.23 *Exposure to displays showing other high-school students giving blood resulted in a substantial increase in students' donor behavior in a national study. (Courtesy of Irwin G. and Barbara R. Sarason).*

showed high-school donors giving blood. The scenes emphasized membership in an important group (teen-age blood donors) and the virtues of saving the lives of other people in the community (see Figure 19.23). A control condition included the standard appeal for blood from the local blood bank. The results showed that the experimental program resulted in a 16.9 percent increase in blood donations when compared with the most compelling appeal the blood banks had been able to develop. With blood shortages reaching critical levels in many communities, an increase in blood donations of this magnitude could have a significant social impact.

In the preceding pages, you have read about the social and cognitive factors that can prevent people from intervening to help someone in distress. Would knowing about these factors increase your tendency to help if you came upon an ambiguous emergency situation? To answer this question, Arthur Beaman and his coworkers (1978) exposed college students to a lecture or a film about the decision-making process involved in bystander intervention (refer to Figure 19.20). Control group subjects did not receive this information. Two weeks later, the subjects suddenly came upon a person (actually a research confederate) sprawled in a hallway on another part of campus. The subjects were observed to see if they would help the victim. More than half of the subjects who had learned about the factors that inhibit helping rendered assistance, compared with only about one fourth of the control group subjects.

Thus, we have in the case of prosocial behavior another instance in which knowledge gained in basic research can be applied in a way that, by enhancing human performance, can make a real difference in someone's life. Indeed, in some cases, it can mean the difference between life and death.

Hostility and Aggression

Interpersonal attraction, intimate relationships, and helping represent the bright side of human relationships. There is, of course, another side. Our great capacity to love and help one another cannot totally mask the fact that we are the most destructive creatures ever to inhabit the earth. Our penchant for violence is perhaps the greatest threat to our survival as a species. Here are just a few stark reminders of a world threatened by our capacity to hurt one another:

- Over 800,000 violent crimes are committed against Americans every year.
- Every 23 minutes, someone is murdered in the United States; every 6 minutes, a woman is raped; every 48 seconds, a man, woman, or child is assaulted.
- If you are between the ages of 17 and 24, your chances of being a homicide victim are twice as great today as they would have been in 1961.
- Between 1984 and 1989, the number of children arrested for murder more than doubled. Children under 18 now make up more than 10 percent of all homicide arrests. In some neighborhoods, two out of three youths carry lethal weapons.
- The total destructive force unleashed by all the armies during World War II was about 3 megatons (equivalent to 3 million tons of TNT). Today, the nations of the world have an estimated 15 *thousand* megatons of destructive power at their fingertips. If this power were unleashed, nuclear weapons the size of the one dropped on Hiroshima could rain down on us at a rate of one every 3 seconds for 40 days and 40 nights.

In humans, **aggression** may be defined as any form of behavior that is *intended* to harm another person. Thus, unintentional harming of another is not considered to be aggressive behavior. A distinction is often made between **hostile aggression,** which springs from anger, and **instrumental aggression,** where gaining some other benefit, such as power or

material goods, provides the primary motive to harm another.

If human aggression had a single cause, perhaps we would be more successful in controlling it. But like most human behavior, aggression is very complex, and so are its causes. As we shall see, biological, environmental, cognitive, and intrapsychic factors contribute to our understanding of when and why people behave aggressively.

Biological Factors in Aggression

The biological perspective looks for causes of aggression in evolutionary history, in genetic factors, and in the workings of the brain and the physiology of the body.

Evolutionary and Behavior Genetic Viewpoints

The biologist Konrad Lorenz (1966) argued that aggression is instinctive in human beings as well as in other animals. The critical difference, he believed, is that most lower animals have developed internal, genetically based controls against killing members of their own species. Usually, these controls involve ritualized behaviors that signal submission and allow the submissive animal to escape unharmed (see Figure 19.24). But people often fail to respond to signs of submission from their fellows. Lorenz believes that, because human beings are physically rather harmless creatures in comparison with many predatory animals, they did not develop genetically based inhibitions and controls against killing their own kind. Hence, once they began to use their brains to construct weapons, there was nothing to curb their acquired deadliness except the thin veneer of societal prohibitions.

From an evolutionary standpoint, aggressiveness has been important to the development and survival of the human species (Zillmann, 1984). Prehistoric humans survived by becoming hunters, and evolutionary psychologists have suggested that human aggressiveness can be traced to this prehistoric adaptation. Obviously, aggressiveness was also important in competing successfully for resources, in defending territory, and in surviving, both individually and for the purpose of passing one's genes on to the next generation (Rushton, 1989). It is ironic that a form of behavior that may have figured so prominently in humankind's past survival has now become the problem that most endangers its future survival. As the biologist Loren Eiseley has written, ''The need is now for a gentler, a more tolerant people than those who won for us against the ice, the tiger, and the bear'' (1946, p. 140).

Figure 19.24 *In the animal kingdom, submissive behavior patterns help prevent killing among members of the same species.*

There is no compelling scientific evidence that human beings have an innate aggressive instinct that programs them to respond violently to specific stimuli, as some animals do. Genetic factors do appear to play a more general role in aggressive behavior, however (Baron & Richardson, 1991; Loehlin, 1992). Evidence comes from findings that identical twins are more similar in their aggressive and dominant behavior patterns than are fraternal twins (Plomin & Rende, 1991). This is the case even if the identical twins are raised in different homes with presumably different social environments (Bouchard & others, 1990). However, behavior geneticists also remind us that where social behavior is concerned, genetic factors never operate in isolation; they always interact with environmental factors.

The Brain and Aggression

Many attempts have been made to locate and study areas of the brain involved in aggressive behavior. Several structures deep in the brain—in the limbic system and the hypothalamus—are involved in triggering and inhibiting such behavior. Surgical destruction of these areas can produce either extremely tame or very aggressive animals, and electrical stimulation of specific regions can cause an animal to viciously attack and kill other animals (Flynn, 1975). Certain kinds of brain damage or disorders can produce violent and unpredictable behavior in humans, too. During one 8-month period, a total of 45 people appeared at Massachusetts General Hospital complaining of violent impulses. About a quarter of these patients had symptoms of neurological disorders (Lion, Bach-y-Rita, & Ervin, 1969). In the majority of individuals who behave aggressively, however, there is no evidence of brain damage.

Temperament and Aggression

Another biological factor that has been studied in relation to aggression is temperament. Anyone who has observed babies knows that temperamental differences are present from birth, and there is little doubt that these differences are biologically determined (Kagan, 1989). Some babies can be charitably described as "difficult," and this characteristic is related to later aggressive behavior in both childhood and adolescence (Bates, 1982; Olweus, 1980). Here again, however, there is probably an interaction between a biologically based characteristic and the environment. It is hard for parents to react to crabby and obnoxious children with warmth and approval. Hostility and at times outright dislike expressed by parents may contribute to the further development of anger and hostility in a child predisposed to be difficult (Bates, 1982).

Although biological factors can contribute to aggression, learning experiences and features of the environment combine with biological factors in critically important ways. We turn now to some environmental influences.

Environmental Influences: Social Learning of Aggression

The behavioral perspective emphasizes the importance of social learning processes in the development of aggressive behaviors and in their expression. The behavioral approach to the study of aggression involves an analysis of the following elements:

Present stimulus conditions and previous learning → Aggressive behavior → Consequences of aggression → Probable future behavior

Aggression as Learned Behavior

The cornerstone of the behavioral perspective is the influence of past consequences on present behavior. Behaviors that have led to positive outcomes in the past are more likely to recur in the future, while behaviors that have had negative consequences are less likely to be repeated. Following this assumption, it seems obvious that people who are rewarded for aggressive behaviors are more likely to behave aggressively.

Research with both animals and humans supports this prediction. Numerous studies have shown that formerly nonaggressive animals can be trained to become vicious aggressors if conditions are arranged so that they are consistently victorious in fights with weaker animals. Conversely, if conditions are arranged so that an animal is defeated in its early battles, it becomes extremely submissive. Moreover, the younger an animal is when it first suffers repeated defeats, the more submissively it will react to attacks by other animals (Zillmann, 1979).

The rewarding of aggression affects people in much the same way. In one study of 4-year-old nursery-school children, the investigators recorded a total of 2,583 aggressive acts and their consequences. Children became increasingly aggressive when their aggressive behavior produced positive outcomes for them (as when an aggressive act resulted in another child's giving up a desired toy). Those whose aggressive behavior was unsuccessful or who experienced unpleasant consequences were less likely to be aggressive in the future (Patterson & others, 1967). A particularly ominous finding was that about 80 percent of the aggressive behaviors were rewarding for the aggressor.

In some social groups, aggressive behavior receives a great deal of social support and provides aggressors with important rewards. Consider the following statement made by a youth involved in a gang killing: "If I would of got the knife, I would have stabbed him. That would have gave me more of a build up. People would have respected me for what I've done and things like that. They would say, 'There goes a cold killer' " (Yablonsky, 1962, p. 8).

Observation of Aggressive Models

There is a great deal of evidence that aggressive behavior can be learned simply by observation of others' behavior (Baron & Richardson, 1991). Whether or not the observer later performs the behavior depends in part on the consequences he or she has observed. A child who sees a model deliver an exotic karate chop is more likely to imitate the aggression if he or she sees the model being rewarded in some way (or at least not being punished). But regardless of what happens to the model, the child will probably have learned the aggressive behavior, and if you offer him or her a reward for reproducing it, chances are the child will be able to do so. This principle was illustrated in the "Bobo doll" experiment by Bandura (1965) described in Chapter 9 (p. 288). Recall that children who were exposed to an aggressive model were more likely to spontaneously imitate the behaviors if the model was not punished. But virtually all the children clearly had learned the behaviors regardless of the consequences to the model, as shown when they were asked to reproduce it.

Exposure to aggressive models can set the stage for later aggression. Many studies have shown that aggressive and delinquent children tend to have parents who frequently model aggressive behavior (Bandura, 1973; Baron, 1977). Parents who abuse their children frequently have been abused themselves as children, which also suggests the possibility of modeling effects (Straus & others, 1980).

Modeling can be accomplished through description as well as through direct demonstration. News accounts of criminal activities often provide detailed information about how antisocial behaviors are performed. Not surprisingly, media reports of a sensational crime are often followed by a series of "copycat" crimes (Bandura, 1986).

Media Violence and Aggressive Behavior

A good deal of public attention and debate have focused on the possible role of televised violence in the learning of aggressive behavior. This issue has been the subject of scientific investigation for over two decades, and there is now substantial evidence that exposure to television and movie violence is related to the tendency of both children and adults to behave aggressively (Liebert & others, 1989). For example, using data collected over a 22-year period, Leonard Eron (1987) found that amount of televised violence observed at age 8 was related to seriousness of criminal activity engaged in by age 30 (see Figure 19.25). Eron concludes that there is a reciprocal relation between televised violence and aggression. That is, observed violence increases aggressiveness, and aggressiveness in turn increases enjoyment of media violence.

Even playing violent video games results in at least short-term increases in aggressive behavior in

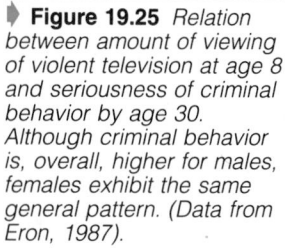 **Figure 19.25** *Relation between amount of viewing of violent television at age 8 and seriousness of criminal behavior by age 30. Although criminal behavior is, overall, higher for males, females exhibit the same general pattern. (Data from Eron, 1987).*

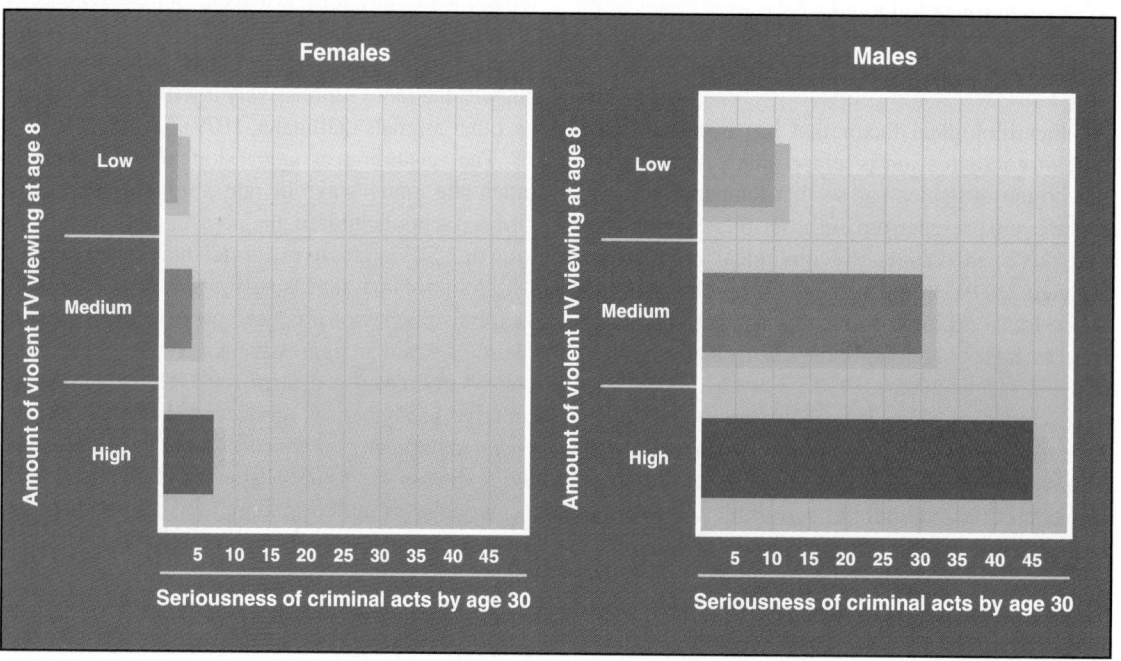

young children (Schutte & others, 1988). And, as we saw in Chapter 12, recent studies indicate that viewing violent pornography depicting rape and physical abuse increases the tendency of males to act aggressively against women (Zillmann & Bryant, 1989). Nonviolent pornography does not appear to increase aggressive behavior.

It appears that television and the movies (and perhaps even video games) can indeed function as "schools for violence." They can exert their effects through a number of psychological mechanisms (see Figure 19.26). First, observers may learn new aggressive behaviors through modeling. Second, observation of aggression (especially by the "good guys," with whom people tend to identify) may reduce inhibitions against aggression by suggesting that aggression is a typical or permissible way of solving problems or attaining goals. Third, a steady diet of observed violence can desensitize people to violence and the suffering of victims so that it no longer disturbs them. Any or all of these processes could increase the likelihood of acting aggressively (O'Neal, 1991).

Cognitive Processes in Aggression

How people perceive and interpret situations and the actions of others helps to determine how they behave. Aggression is prompted by people's perceptions that they have been provoked in some way and that the provocation was intended. This *perceived intentionality* provides a basis for blame, for hostility, and for possible retaliation.

Through their thought processes, people can create enemies and justify aggression toward them. Such cognitive processes may allow even a person with appropriate moral standards to commit unspeakable acts of aggression, even terrorist acts (Bandura, 1988). For example, by blaming a person or group for real or imagined wrongs, people can create an image of a hated enemy fully deserving of aggression. Before and during wars, participants on both sides tend to view themselves and their adversaries in black-and-white terms, developing a "diabolical enemy image" and a "moral self-image" (White, 1968). The adversary becomes the incarnation of evil, and one's own side is regarded as the defender of all that is right and good (see Figure 19.27). These extreme images help people to justify aggression and to see their victims as having brought the suffering on themselves.

A variety of other cognitive measures may be used to reduce guilt reactions and thereby weaken inhibitions against aggressive behavior. For example, people sometimes minimize the seriousness of their own actions through *comparison with enemy acts*

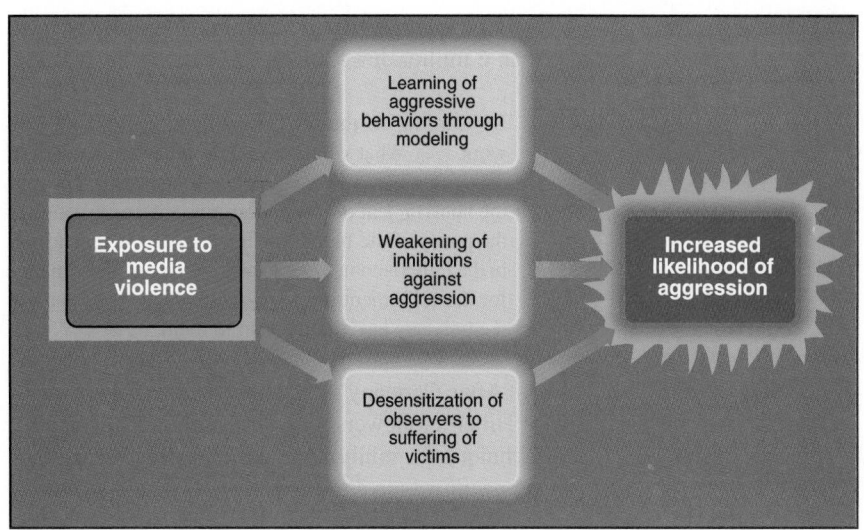

Figure 19.26 *Exposure to televised violence may increase the tendency to engage in aggressive behavior in several ways.*

that are viewed as even more repulsive. Each side in the seemingly endless struggle between Arabs and Jews in the Middle East has justified its escalating brutality by pointing to "acts of terrorism" committed by its adversary.

The *appeal to moral principles* also helps to minimize guilt and self-condemnation (Schlenker & Weigold, 1992). The pages of history are filled with accounts of brutal acts performed in "holy wars" and "moral crusades." Here is Adolf Hitler's justification

Figure 19.27 *The "diabolical enemy" image is illustrated in this cartoon depicting Iran's Ayatollah Khomeini during a period of strained relations between the U.S. and Iran.*

for a policy that was to result in the murder of more than 6 million Jews:

> By warding off the Jews, I am fighting for the Lord's work . . . . What we have to fight for is the security of the existence and the increase of our race and our people, the nourishment of its children, and the preservation of the purity of the blood, the freedom and independence in the fatherland in order to enable our people to mature for the fulfillment of the mission which the Creator of the universe has allotted also to them.

After Germany's defeat in World War II, many of Hitler's followers found themselves using another technique for minimizing guilt: *displacement of responsibility* onto another person. Nazi war criminals as well as American soldiers involved in atrocities during the Vietnam War disclaimed personal responsibility for their acts by displacing it onto those in command: "It wasn't my idea. I was only following orders."

A related method of minimizing guilt is *diffusion of responsibility*. If a decision is made by a group, no single individual needs to feel totally responsible for the consequences. Sometimes the diffusion of responsibility can enable a group (for example, a lynch mob) to commit an act of violence that no individual within the group would commit alone.

Another self-justifying cognitive mechanism is *dehumanization*. If victims are stripped of all human qualities, the aggressor can treat them as objects rather than as individuals with hopes, sensitivities, and feelings. Often the process involves attaching demeaning labels, such as "gooks," "savages," or "the Great Satan," to the victims so that they can be viewed as

members of a despised group rather than as individual human beings. Figure 19.28 summarizes cognitive processes that can promote aggression.

Psychodynamic Factors in Aggression

Psychodynamic theorists look to individual differences in personality for the causes of aggression. According to psychoanalytic theory, for example, human aggression is an outgrowth of the continuous conflict between unconscious impulses and the defenses developed by the ego to keep them in check. Freud believed that behavior is largely directed toward satisfying inborn biological drives, one of which is aggression. But how does one go about releasing aggressive impulses in a world in which people are made to feel guilty and fearful about their violent desires? Freud's answer was that defense mechanisms help to control our unacceptable impulses and to channel them in socially acceptable ways. He noted that there are many disguised forms for aggressive impulses, such as competitive sports, law enforcement, debate, and hunting.

Overcontrolled Hostility

What if people's defenses become so rigid that they cannot express their aggressive impulses even in indirect or disguised forms? Will the unreleased pressures build up to an explosion point? In some cases, the answer appears to be yes.

Aggressive acts are often committed by individuals who have a history of violent behavior, but some of the most shocking and brutal crimes are committed by those who are described by the psychologist Edwin Megargee (1966) as having **overcontrolled hostility.** These people show little immediate reaction to provocations. Instead, they repress, or bottle up, their anger; and over time, the pressure to aggress builds up. At a critical point, their rigid defenses shatter, and they erupt into violence that is often extreme and brutal. Often, the provocation that triggers their destructive outburst is trivial. For example, one overcontrolled 10-year-old boy with no previous history of aggression stabbed his sister more than 80 times with an ice pick after she changed the channel during his favorite television show. After the aggressive outburst, such people revert to their former passive state, appearing again as unassertive individuals quite incapable of violence (Quinsey & others, 1983).

The Habitually Violent

Psychodynamic theorists have also sought to understand persons for whom aggression has become a lifestyle. Such individuals, far from being overcontrolled, use aggression as their primary means of

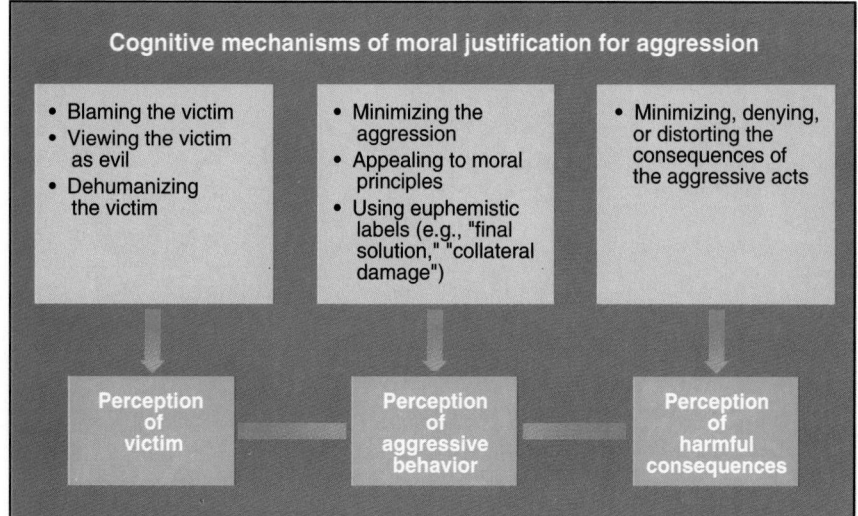

◄ **Figure 19.28** *Cognitive mechanisms of moral justification for aggression. According to Bandura, these cognitive mechanisms allow people to excuse the behavior, deny personal responsibility, minimize the consequences of the actions, and blame the victim. (Adapted from Bandura, 1988).*

Cognitive mechanisms of moral justification for aggression

- Blaming the victim
- Viewing the victim as evil
- Dehumanizing the victim

- Minimizing the aggression
- Appealing to moral principles
- Using euphemistic labels (e.g., "final solution," "collateral damage")

- Minimizing, denying, or distorting the consequences of the aggressive acts

| Perception of victim | Perception of aggressive behavior | Perception of harmful consequences |

achieving their goals and dealing with interpersonal problems. According to Hans Toch (1992), who carried out intensive psychological studies of these *violence-prone* people, they fall into four fairly distinct personality patterns. *Self-defenders* behave aggressively out of intense fear of others. They consistently view others as wanting to harm them, and they regard their aggression as a legitimate way of protecting themselves. A second type, *self-indulgers,* have an infantile view of the world and seem to think that others exist solely to satisfy their every need. When others fail to cater to their whims, they feel betrayed and strike out in blind fury. A third violence-prone group, *bullies and sadists,* derive pleasure from harming others. They seek out victims who are relatively defenseless, and signs of submission from their victims cause them to engage in even more cruelty. (For Lorenz, these people would exemplify a lack of internal inhibitions against aggression in the presence of submissive signals.) Finally, *self-image*

compensators behave aggressively as a result of feelings of insecurity and low self-esteem. Successful aggression shores up their poor self-images and demonstrates their power to others. Such people are extremely sensitive to signs that they are being laughed at or belittled, and they often respond to such perceptions with unprovoked attacks.

Megargee's and Toch's findings illustrate different ways in which personality factors can result in aggressive behavior. They also show that similar behaviors can have completely different underlying causes.

For a number of years, investigators pursuing various perspectives worked somewhat independently in studying the determinants of aggression. There have, however, been several attempts to integrate what is known into more general theories. The following feature explores two attempts to integrate biological and psychological causes of aggression.

PSYCHOBIOLOGICAL INTERACTIONS

Arousal, Cognition, and the Modified Frustration–Aggression Hypothesis

One of the oldest psychological explanations for aggression is the **frustration–aggression hypothesis.** According to this view, *frustration,* defined as anything that interferes with goal-directed behavior, arouses a drive to engage in aggressive behavior. In its original form, the frustration–aggression hypothesis held that (1) frustration inevitably leads to aggression and (2) all aggression is the result of frustration (Dollard & others, 1939).

Both of these sweeping assertions have since been disproved. Frustration does not always result in aggression; it can lead to other reactions, such as despair, resignation, or nonaggressive ways of dealing with the frustration. Moreover, not all instances of aggression result from frustration; sometimes, people behave aggressively to obtain power over others or to acquire things they want.

Several recent formulations have broadened the original frustration–aggression hypothesis in useful ways. In his **cognitive–neoassociationistic model,** Leonard Berkowitz (1990) attributes aggressive behavior not merely to frustration but to a wider range of *aversive events,* which include virtually any unpleasant occurrence. Aversive events automatically trigger *negative affect,* including not only frustration but also such varied arousal states as depression, fear, and discomfort. Negative affect, in turn, automatically and simul-

taneously evokes two *primal response tendencies:* fight and flight (or, more specifically, the tendencies to behave aggressively and to escape). Citing evidence that depression, grief, physical discomfort, and other negative states result in angry feelings, Berkowitz suggests that negative affect evokes anger and other elements of an *associative network* that includes thoughts and memories related to anger as well as behavioral tendencies to be aggressive. This is why "persons who feel bad for one reason or another—whether they have a toothache, are very hot, are exposed to foul smells or an unpleasant noise, or are just very sad or depressed—are likely to be angry, have hostile ideas and memories, and to be aggressively disposed" (Berkowitz, 1990, p. 496). In a similar manner, the negative affect arouses feelings, thoughts, memories, and behavioral tendencies toward flight from the aversive event. Whether anger or flight predominates depends on the thoughts, memories, and behavioral tendencies evoked by the present situation as well as the person's past learning history. Some individuals, like the habitually violent people described by Toch, have strong associative links that include many aggressive thoughts, memories, and compelling behavioral tendencies to strike out at others.

For Berkowitz, there are two important stages in the process of responding to an aversive event

Figure 19.29
*Berkowitz's cognitive–
neoassociationistic model
of aggression.*

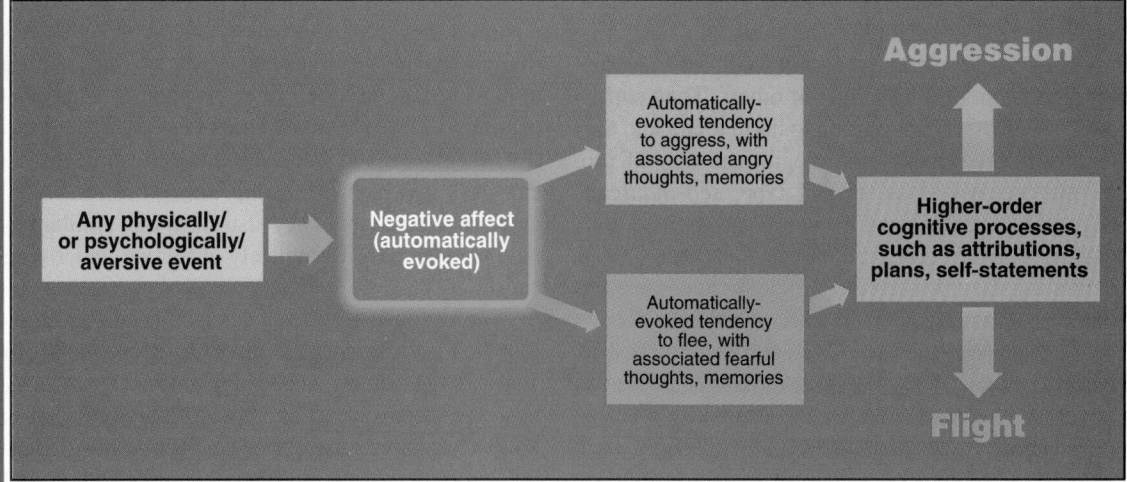

(see Figure 19.29). The first is the automatic triggering of negative affect by the aversive event. This process involves little, if any, cognition. But once the associative network is triggered by the negative affect, cognitive appraisals, attributions, self-statements, and other higher order cognitions help determine whether aggression occurs. Personality and psychodynamic factors are also part of the network of memories and thoughts, and they may be triggered as well. Berkowitz's reformulation of the frustration–aggression hypothesis thus integrates situational, physiological, cognitive, and psychodynamic factors into a more complex and sophisticated theoretical framework for understanding aggression.

Another formulation concerned with physiological–psychological interactions is Dolph Zillmann's (1979) notion of **excitation transfer.** According to this theory, any residual arousal left over from a preceding event may be attributed to one's current emotional response. Thus, anger may sometimes be perceived as more intense than it actually is, thereby increasing the likelihood of aggression. For example, suppose a person who has just worked out has an argument with another person. If some residual arousal remains from the workout, this residual arousal could be added to the arousal evoked by the argument. Zillmann has found in his research that people's beliefs about the intensity of their anger can strongly influence their level of aggressive behavior, even if these beliefs are inaccurate. Once again, therefore, we see an illustration of the complex ways in which mind and body interact.

This chapter's Understanding Causes feature provides an overview of biological, environmental, cognitive, and psychodynamic factors in aggression.

In this chapter and the previous one, we have explored the social context of behavior and have again seen how personal and environmental factors interact.

Identifying important causal factors in behavior gives psychologists a basis for applying behavioral principles to many real-life settings in social institutions. In the final chapter, we will explore some of the important frontiers of applied psychology.

Aggression:
Factors Suggested by Theory and Research

$B=f(P,E)$

Causal Factors

Biological
- Evolution: Natural selection of aggressive behaviors that enhanced species survival
- Genetic contribution to individual differences in aggressiveness
- Activity of neural and biochemical control systems in the brain
- Physiological arousal from negative affect

Cognitive
- Attribution of malevolent intent to those who provoke or frustrate
- Blaming of victims for "bringing it on themselves"
- Diabolical enemy image and moral self-image
- Beliefs that aggression is the best solution and that it will be effective

Intrapsychic
- Ability to sublimate and defend against hostile impulses
- Sudden breakthrough of impulses, as in overcontrolled hostility
- Personality dynamics that produce habitual aggression
- Aggression as self-verification of "tough" self-concept

Environmental
- Environmental frustrations and provocations
- Past history of reinforcement and punishment for aggressive behavior

Aggression

Aggression Is a function of interacting personal and environmental causal factors. These factors may vary and may interact with one another in particular ways, depending on the person and the situation.

The Self and Social Behavior

- The self is an organizing force in social interactions. It consists of a set of self-schemas that contain information, memories, and beliefs about oneself. Once formed, self-schemas can exert powerful influences on the processing of information that is relevant to them. For example, there is a tendency toward maintenance of self-schemas through selective information processing.
- Reflected appraisals, social comparison, and self-perception of behavior all play roles in the development of self-schemas.
- Self-presentation functions to project certain information to others so as to elicit desired behavior (strategic self-presentation) as well as to confirm one's own self-image (self-verification). Self-monitoring reflects the tendency to change one's behavior in accordance with the demands of the situation.

Perception of Others

- Perception of others involves the processing of both personal and situational information. Physical appearance influences judgments of other traits. So do other central traits, such as warmth or coldness.
- Attribution refers to perception of the causes of behavior. According to Kelley, consistency, distinctiveness, and consensus combine to affect our attributions.
- A number of attributional biases have been identified. One is the fundamental attribution error, the tendency to attribute the behavior of others to personal factors. The actor–observer effect refers to the tendency to attribute one's own behavior to situational factors and to attribute others' behavior to dispositional factors. The self-serving bias is the tendency to attribute one's successes to personal factors and one's failures to situational factors.
- Social judgments often exhibit confirmation bias, the tendency to attend to or favor information that supports the judgments. This may at times result in self-fulfilling prophecies.

Stereotypes and Prejudice

- Stereotypes are schemas that associate certain characteristics with a group; they may blind us to group members' individual characteristics. Stereotypes also reflect confirmation bias, and subcategorization may preserve them in the face of conflicting information.
- One of the negative effects of prejudice is that the targets of prejudice may come to accept the negative stereotypes associated with their group.
- It appears that prejudice results not from a perceived personal threat, as realistic conflict theory suggested, but from a threat to one's ingroup.

Attraction and Close Relationships

- Among the factors that influence interpersonal attraction are physical proximity, need to affiliate, physical attractiveness, and perceived similarity.
- Social exchange theory suggests that close relationships are governed by the balance of rewards and costs (that is, the outcomes) experienced in the relationship. Outcomes are compared with two standards, the comparison level and the comparison level for alternatives, to determine satisfaction and commitment, respectively. Social penetration theory emphasizes increases in self-disclosure and sharing of resources as relationships deepen.
- Several important distinctions have been made between kinds of love. One is the distinction between passionate and companionate love. Lee and the Hendricks have identified six different varieties of love, whereas Sternberg has identified seven varieties in terms of combinations of intimacy, commitment, and passion. Recently, attachment theory has also been applied to adult love relationships.

Prosocial Behavior: Helping Others

- Several psychological factors, including social comparison, diffusion of responsibility, perceived costs, and self-efficacy, influence bystander intervention in emergencies. These factors may reduce the likelihood of intervention when more than one bystander is present.
- Other factors that influence helping behavior are the belief in a just world, the attractiveness and perceived similarity of the victim, and the norm of reciprocity.
- Prosocial behavior has been explained in terms of sociobiology, social learning of norms and self-reinforcement, and the operation of altruism. Whether true altruism actually exists is a topic of current controversy.
- Exposure to helpful models has proved to be an effective means of increasing prosocial behavior in both children and adults. Moreover, being informed about the factors that prevent helping in emergencies seems to make people more resistant to their influence.

Hostility and Aggression

- Human aggression is behavior intended to harm another person. A distinction has been made between hostile aggression based on anger and instrumental aggression, which is a means to some other end.
- The biological perspective stresses the role of evolutionary forces, genetic processes, brain mechanisms, and temperament in aggression.
- Social learning theorists have demonstrated that aggressive behavior is learned through both direct reinforcement and exposure to aggressive models. Exposure to violence by means of the mass media appears to increase aggressive behavior through a number of processes, including observational learning of aggressive responses, reduction of inhibitions against aggression, and desensitization to the suffering of victims. The relation between media violence and aggression may be a reciprocal one, with observation of violence increasing aggressiveness, and aggressiveness increasing the enjoyment of media violence.
- Cognitive processes are also important determinants of aggression. Aggression is enhanced by such cognitive processes as blaming victims, displacing and diffusing responsibility, and dehumanizing victims.
- Psychodynamic theorists search for personality processes that increase aggression. Studies of overcontrolled individuals who suddenly erupt into violence and of people who are habitually violent point to a variety of psychodynamic processes that can lead to violent behavior.
- Recent formulations, including Berkowitz's cognitive–neoassociationistic reformulation of the frustration–aggression hypothesis and Zillmann's concept of excitation transfer, have emphasized interactions among physiological, cognitive, personality, and environmental variables.

actor–observer effect (p. 608)
aggression (p. 624)
altruism (p. 621)
attachment style (p. 616)
attribution (p. 606)
central trait (p. 608)
cognitive–neoassociationistic model of
   aggression (p. 629)
companionate love (p. 616)
comparison level (p. 614)
comparison level for alternatives (p. 614)
confirmation bias (p. 609)
empathy (p. 621)
excitation transfer (p. 630)
frustration–aggression hypothesis (p. 629)
fundamental attribution error (p. 607)

hostile aggression (p. 624)
implicit personality theory (p. 608)
instrumental aggression (p. 624)
just world hypothesis (p. 620)
matching hypothesis (p. 613)
mere exposure effect (p. 612)
negative state relief model (p. 622)
outcome (p. 614)
overcontrolled hostility (p. 628)
peripheral trait (p. 609)
prejudice (p. 610)
personal attributions (p. 606)
prosocial behavior (p. 617)
realistic conflict theory (p. 610)
reflected appraisals (p. 603)
self-disclosure (p. 615)

self-fulfilling prophecy (p. 609)
self-monitoring (p. 604)
self-perception (p. 603)
self-presentation (p. 603)
self-reference effect (p. 602)
self-schema (p. 602)
self-serving bias (p. 608)
self-verification (p. 604)
situational attributions (p. 606)
social comparison (p. 603)
social exchange theory (p. 614)
social identity theory (p. 610)
social penetration theory (p. 615)
stereotype (p. 610)
strategic self-presentation (p. 603)

SUGGESTED READINGS

Baron, R. A., & Richardson, D. R. (1991). *Human aggression* (2nd ed.). New York: Plenum. A good overview of current theories and research findings relating to aggression.

Clark, M. S. (Ed.) (1991). *Prosocial behavior.* Newbury Park, Calif.: Sage. An outstanding collection of discussions by leading researchers and theorists of anthropological, biological, and sociological approaches to such topics as altruism, volunteerism, the effects of helping on the helper, and methods for increasing prosocial behavior.

Fiske, S. T., & Taylor, S. E. (1991). *Social cognition* (2nd ed.). New York: McGraw-Hill. A classic high-level treatment of a wide range of topics in social cognition. It includes major sections on the self, stereotypes, and prejudice.

20 Applied Psychology: Themes and Directions

CHAPTER OUTLINE

When Lisa Powell was a doctoral student doing laboratory research on human learning and memory, she had little indication that her career path would take her far from her laboratory and into a variety of real-world settings. As she now recalls, "I was interested primarily in theoretical issues and basic research that would answer the theoretical questions. What I failed to appreciate was the incredible number of practical problems that can be solved by applying those principles and research findings."

Powell's life as a college professor is embellished by a number of consulting relationships in which she applies her knowledge of human learning and research methods to the development and evaluation of new programs. "For example, I'm part of an educational team that is using principles of learning and memory to design a new program for Hispanic and Asian children who do not speak English. The program will gradually phase in the use of English in their course work so that they learn not only the course content but also a new language."

"Another of my pet projects is with a major industrial corporation trying to retrain its work force to use new high-tech equipment so that the corporation can remain competitive in today's marketplace. As part of that transition, we are evaluating various ways of redesigning jobs to increase both work satisfaction and productivity. It's a fascinating and challenging task."

As a former college gymnast, Powell is well aware of the importance of psychological factors in sport performance, and she has found a way to combine her knowledge of psychology with her love of athletics. "The baseball immortal Ty Cobb once said that the most important part of the player's body is above the neck, and I think there's a lot of truth in that. For the past two years, I've been working with our school's gymnastics and basketball teams, and I've designed a program that helps them learn important psychological skills like stress management, goal setting, concentration, and visualization. I enjoy working with the athletes, and many of them have improved their performance by learning these skills."

Since psychology's earliest days, the application of psychological principles to practical problems has been an important goal, and this objective continues to inspire the day-to-day activities of psychologists like Lisa Powell. We have seen many examples of psychological applications in preceding chapters. For example, perceptual principles were applied to uncovering the illusion that caused mysterious airline crashes at night, leading to remedies that should prevent similar tragedies in the future. Principles of learning are finding application in many areas, including improved teaching techniques, clinical interventions,

and the expansion of individual freedom through self-regulation strategies. People are being helped to improve their memories and problem-solving skills, thanks to advances in cognitive psychology. Humanistic concepts are being used to help people establish more satisfying relationships with others and find greater self-acceptance and meaning in their own lives. Technological advances in the biological areas of psychology are being applied in countless ways, including the diagnosis and treatment of deviant behavior and disorders of the nervous system (Stricker, 1992). Psychological principles are also being applied to the design of more livable environments. This chapter highlights some of the applications of psychological principles and methods in education, business and industry, the law, sports, and medicine (see Figure 20.1).

As we have seen repeatedly, close connections exist between basic psychological research and the application of psychological principles. Ideally, an application, or intervention, should be based on a body of scientific evidence or on a theory that specifies how the application should be designed (Stricker, 1992). Once implemented, the results of the intervention should be scientifically evaluated. Evaluation provides new scientific data from an applied setting and also tests the adequacy of the theory. Unexpected or disconfirming results may indicate that the theory needs revision (Chen, 1990). Thus, theory, research, and intervention are intimately involved in a network of reciprocal, or two-way, interactions; all three elements can affect one another (see Figure 20.2).

Program evaluation involves a set of scientific procedures that can be used in both planning and appraising social interventions. In a sense, every social intervention can be considered an experiment of sorts, with an outcome that is often uncertain. We begin by considering the role of program evaluation in social experimentation and reform. Specifically, we look at one of the most important social challenges of our time: multiracial education.

Program Evaluation: Designing and Appraising Social Experiments

We live in an era of rapid social change. Many of our social institutions are in a state of crisis. Our economic system has suffered from spiraling inflation and a massive national debt. Our educational system is under fire from every side as it struggles to deal with increased enrollments, discipline and dropout problems, and mounting evidence that students are not learning basic academic skills. Industry is beset with lagging productivity, difficulties in competing with

(a)

(b)

(c)

Figure 20.1 *Psychological theories and research find application in a variety of social systems.*

foreign competition, and widespread feelings of dissatisfaction and alienation among workers. A tidal wave of dissatisfaction with our social institutions, together with demands that new answers be found to nagging social and economic problems, has had strong political repercussions. New approaches to both old and new problems are being taken, and we await answers to the critical question of how successful the new approaches will be.

In a sense, programs designed to deal with society's problems may be viewed as social experiments having independent and dependent variables (Campbell, 1969). The interventions are like independent variables; they are designed to have an effect on people, situations, or problems. The behavioral or social indicators used to evaluate the impact of the interventions are like dependent, or outcome, variables. But while the similarities between social programs and scientific experiments are evident, it is equally obvious that the complexity of the settings and the number of uncontrollable factors that exist in social experiments far exceed anything that the laboratory experimenter has to contend with.

How do we know whether a social program works or not? Can we measure its effects, both intended and unintended, and isolate the reasons for its success or lack of success? Do the benefits of the program outweigh its costs? Is the program the most efficient way to use limited resources? These are the kinds of questions that are the focus of the growing area of program evaluation.

Designing Evaluation Research

An increasing number of psychologists are applying their scientific skills to designing and measuring the impact of social programs. The challenge to evaluate such programs is rooted in the realization that past programs have often been misguided, poorly con-

ducted, and ineffective. Program evaluators—including policy makers, planners, funding agencies, and program staff—need to know if a program is reaching the target population, if it is being conducted in the specified manner, and if it is working well enough to justify the costs involved (Heller, 1990).

More than most other research, evaluation studies deal with highly sensitive areas. Decisions about budgets, program retention, personnel assignments, and program changes often hinge on the outcome of an evaluation. Needless to say, the people involved in a social program can be threatened by an evaluation of what they are doing. It is critically important that an atmosphere of trust surround the evaluation and that the results be presented as a way of improving services rather than as criticisms of what people have done (Love, 1991).

The points in an intervention program at which evaluation might occur are shown in Figure 20.3. The figure also shows the process by which the intervention program is designed. In the design process, research may first be done on the nature and extent of the perceived problem and a decision made on what the specific objectives of the program should be. This is a critical point for later evaluations, because in order to assess a program's impact, the program must have a set of specific goals that can be operationally defined and measured. The objectives may be social–behavioral goals, such as an increase in reading scores or a decline in nutritional deficiencies among disadvantaged children; community goals, such as an increase in the use of public transportation; or physical goals, such as a decrease in vandalism in parks. It must be decided specifically to whom the program will be targeted and how the specific outcome measures will be collected.

During the program design stage, preliminary, or *formative evaluations* can help to determine whether the design and the manner in which it will be implemented are likely to promote the program's objective. Evaluation experts may be of great help during the planning stage. For example, few educational programs have had the positive impact and longevity of the television program "Sesame Street." This did not occur by accident. Before "Sesame Street" went on the air, over a year and a half of careful planning and research was done to measure the audience appeal of possible program formats. Appeal was a vital ingredient if "Sesame Street" was to reach and keep its audience, particularly children from disadvantaged backgrounds. Small groups of children were brought to the Children's Television Workshop studios to view proposed programs and segments of programs (see Figure 20.4). The taped program segments were presented on a television monitor while on an adjoining wall slides showing various scenes and objects of interest to children were projected. To assess interest value, observers measured the proportion of time the children viewed the program rather than the slides. It was thus possible to relate the content or format of the program to the amount of attention that it attracted from the test audience. The findings led to decisions to accept or reject certain versions of programs, and they also provided important information about features that did or did not attract the attention of economically disadvantaged children. The program's producers later concluded that these formative evaluations contributed to the ultimate success of the program in attracting and holding its audience (Reeves, 1970).

Frequently, however, program evaluators do not enter the picture until a program is already underway. At the point of *outcome evaluation*, they collect the data needed to determine whether the program is

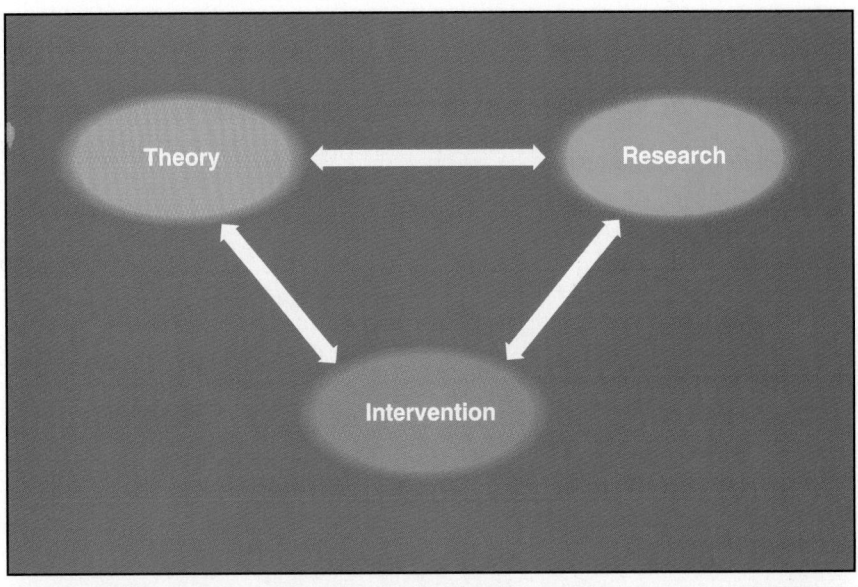

Figure 20.2 *Theory, research, and intervention are intimately related. Applied interventions are inspired by existing theories and research results. They, in turn, can provide data that suggest new basic research and that either support psychological theories or inspire revisions.*

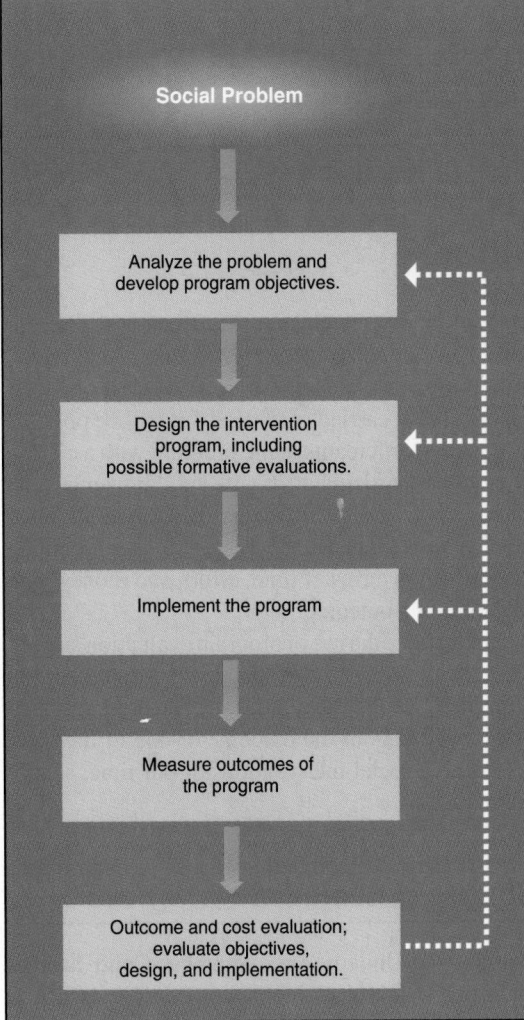

Figure 20.3 *The major steps in the design and evaluation of a program. On the basis of the social problem in question, measurable objectives are defined, a program is designed and implemented, and its outcome is evaluated. Program evaluation may also occur at any of the intermediate steps and may have implications for the appropriateness of the program's objectives, its design, or the way it is being carried out.*

⬆ **Figure 20.4** *The success of "Sesame Street" is due in part to careful formative evaluations designed to determine the attractiveness of various program formats to children.*

achieving some movement toward its goals. The outcome data may help pinpoint strengths or weaknesses in the program's objectives, in its design, or in the way it is being carried out. Ideally, it will be possible to compare participants in the program with a control group of nonparticipants or with similar people in an alternative program. To assess the program's cost-effectiveness, evaluators compare the costs of running the program in terms of time, effort, and money with the program's outcome.

To illustrate the use of program evaluation, as well as some of the difficulties encountered in working in a complex social system, let us consider what is currently known about the outcome of one of the most far-reaching social interventions of our time: school integration.

Evaluating the Effects of Multiracial Education

In 1954, the United States Supreme Court handed down one of its most momentous decisions in the case of *Brown v. Board of Education.* The Court ruled that school segregation based solely on race is a violation of the constitutional rights of racial minorities. Of major importance was testimony given by several psychologists who stated that segregation had harmful effects on the self-esteem and academic achievements of African Americans and that it contributed to racial prejudice and hostility (Stephan, 1991).

The Court's decision ushered in one of the most controversial social reforms in U.S. history. Forty years later, conflict and occasional violence continue to erupt over issues like "racial balance" and busing. Here, obviously, is a program that demands scientific evaluation. Has desegregation achieved its goals of reducing prejudice, increasing the self-esteem of minorities, and enhancing their school achievement?

The approach to answering these questions seems fairly clear-cut. We need to find good measures of prejudice, self-esteem, and school achievement. Then we can compare minority pupils and white pupils in desegregated schools with similar students in segregated schools. Another feasible approach would be to administer self-esteem, prejudice, and achievement measures to minority children before and after they enter desegregated schools, see what kinds of changes occur, and compare these with changes in children who remain in segregated schools over the same period of time. These two basic approaches to evaluating the effects of desegregation programs have characterized much of the research done since the 1950s. But the results have been far from conclusive, and they have often conflicted with one another. Walter Stephan (1990) reviewed more than 80 evaluation studies of desegregation programs involving African-American and white children. Taken at face value, they suggest the following conclusions about the immediate effects of desegregation:

1. Desegregation in and of itself does not seem to reduce racial prejudice. In fact, it is more likely to increase prejudice than to decrease it among white students. Among African-American students, prejudice toward whites was more likely to decrease than to increase, but some increases in prejudice were also found.
2. Desegregation does not appear to have a positive effect on the self-esteem of African-American children. Indeed, many of the studies provided evidence of lowered self-esteem among African-American children in desegregated schools.
3. In the area of school achievement, the results of desegregation are somewhat more positive. The reading achievement level of African Americans was found to be higher in desegregated schools than in segregated ones in about 30 percent of the studies reviewed, but mathematics performance did not increase in desegregated schools.

Thus, the short-term impact of desegregation was not very encouraging. But what about longer term effects? Until recently, it was impossible to study long-term effects because it took time for graduates of desegregated schools to go on to college and enter the work force. Studies now being done on long-term effects suggest a more optimistic picture. They indicate that African Americans who attended integrated schools are more likely to graduate from high school and attend college. Once in college, they achieve higher grades and are more likely to complete their college education than are African-American students who attended segregated schools. They also tend to work in a wider range of jobs (including professional occupations) and in desegregated environments. Finally, they are more likely to live in integrated neighborhoods and to send their own children to integrated schools (Braddock, 1985; Stephan, 1990).

Thus, the long-term effects of school desegregation seem more in accord with social scientists' predictions than the short-term effects. Nonetheless, attempts to evaluate multiracial educational programs have shown that many factors can influence outcomes. For example, the degree of racial balance in the classroom appears to make a difference, at least in the lower grades. African-American children seem to achieve best when they constitute more than a small minority and less than a large majority of the total student population. Unfortunately, many studies have not taken the degree of racial balance into account, or the number of different racial groups in the school, which could account for some of the inconsistent findings. Other factors that should be considered include the racial composition of the school prior to desegregation, whether integration was voluntary or forced, the attitudes of the school staff and the community toward integration, the socioeconomic levels of white and minority students, and the methods of instruction (Weinstein, 1991). Until these and other factors are evaluated more thoroughly, we are likely to be left with inconclusive and conflicting outcomes.

Another limitation of desegregation evaluation studies is that they have focused almost exclusively on *outcome*. We need to know more about the ongoing behavioral *processes* that occur among school personnel and students during desegregation programs, for these undoubtedly play key roles in the programs' outcomes.

In an attempt to study the process of integration, one evaluation team carefully observed and recorded over time the events that occurred in a newly integrated middle school (Schofield & Sagar, 1979). Their observations suggest some reasons why we cannot depend on simple mixing of racial groups in the school setting to increase positive interracial attitudes and social interaction. For example, they found that official desegregation can shortly be followed by resegregation in the school setting. Minority students may be placed in specific classes, gym periods, or "learning tracks" designed for the educationally disadvantaged. Hispanics, African Americans, Asians, Native Americans, and whites may cluster in separate social groups, with little interaction between the groups and a resulting tendency toward intergroup hostility. The competitive atmosphere that exists in the traditional classroom is another serious problem. Minority students are sometimes poorly equipped by their previous educational experiences to compete successfully. In such a situation, resentment, withdrawal, behavior problems, and lowered self-esteem are not at all surprising.

Evaluations of Cooperative Learning Programs

Scientific evidence on the outcomes of school desegregation indicates that forced integration by itself is not the ultimate solution to interracial problems. Getting youngsters of different races and ethnic backgrounds into the same school is a start, but what happens after they get there is critically important. As newer and more carefully conducted evaluation studies of traditional school integration programs have begun to isolate some of the factors that counteract the intended effects of desegregation, alternative approaches have begun to be developed and evaluated. One promising approach, known as **cooperative learning,** is intended to increase mutually rewarding interactions among students by replacing competition with cooperation.

Cooperative learning programs were inspired in part by a classic social psychology field study known as the Robber's Cave experiment (Sherif & others, 1961). The study was carried out at a summer camp for preadolescent boys in Oklahoma. The boys were divided into two groups, which chose to call themselves the Eagles and the Rattlers. At first, the groups got along well, but when the experimenters began to pit them against one another in a series of competitive contests, deep intergroup hostility and discriminatory practices emerged. The researchers then attempted to restore harmony, but they soon learned that simply increasing contact between the groups only increased the level of hostility and distrust. They finally succeeded in reducing the hostility by placing the children in situations in which the two groups were forced to cooperate with each other to accomplish important common goals like repairing the water supply system and towing a truck to get it started. In these situations, the boys were *mutually interdependent,* needing each other to attain common goals.

Could the same principle be applied to increase racial harmony? An attempt to introduce mutual interdependence into the classroom is the **jigsaw program,** developed by the social psychologist Elliot Aronson and his colleagues (Aronson & others, 1978). Drawing in part on Sherif's work, they created a classroom procedure in which children must cooperate rather than compete in order to succeed. The goals of the program were clearly specified: (1) to increase cooperative interactions among children of different racial groups, (2) to increase interpersonal attraction among the children, (3) to increase the children's enjoyment of school, (4) to increase the self-esteem and performance of the children, particularly minority children, and (5) to increase the children's empathy with one another.

The approach involves creating multiracial groups of five or six children. The groups are assigned to prepare for an upcoming test on, for example, the life of Abraham Lincoln. Within the groups, each child is given a "piece" of the total knowledge to be learned. For example, only one child has information about Lincoln's early childhood. In order for the group members to pass the test, they must fit their knowledge pieces together as if they were working a jigsaw puzzle. Each child must share his or her piece of knowledge with the rest of the group.

To prepare for his or her contribution to the group, each child joins a second multiracial group composed of children from the various groups who are to learn corresponding pieces of information (for example, information on Lincoln's early childhood). The members of this second group work together to prepare for their presentations to their own groups. They teach one another and rehearse their presentations together. When the children return to their own groups, each

has mastered his or her prized information on Lincoln's life. The children learn to listen to one another and to help each other prepare for the test. Each student functions both as a resource and as a recipient of help from his or her classmates. The children soon learn that the only way they can be successful is to work together and help one another. They learn to appreciate one another and to feel appreciated by the other group members (see Figure 20.5).

The effects of the jigsaw technique and other cooperative learning programs have been carefully evaluated in hundreds of classrooms, and the results are encouraging (Slavin, 1990; Weinstein, 1991). Children's liking for one another generally increased, and this increased liking crossed racial boundaries. Prejudice decreased among both white and minority children. Scores on tests of self-esteem increased for both whites and minorities, as did school achievement. Achievement gains were particularly pronounced for minority students. In one study, minority children increased their performance by almost one letter grade after only 2 weeks of jigsaw participation (Lucker & others, 1977). Measures of school enjoyment also increased for all racial groups. Finally, the jigsaw method increased children's empathy—their ability to put themselves in another's position and see the world through his or her eyes (Aronson, 1990). Empathy helps to increase mutual understanding and reduce hostility.

Cooperative learning programs show how careful problem analysis and program evaluation can help to identify which aspects of a social system's functioning need change. They also exemplify how research like the Robber's Cave experiment can be used as a basis for designing an intervention program. Reducing competition and replacing it with cooperation has proved to be a key factor in progress toward the intended objectives of multiracial education.

Decades of painful experiences in trying to solve social problems have demonstrated the need for new and innovative approaches in many social institutions. Failures of the past have also shown that common sense and conventional wisdom are not always the best basis for designing social programs. The problems are simply too complex. Decision makers have become increasingly aware that well-designed program evaluations can provide vital information and aid in the design of more effective social experiments.

■ ▪ ▬

Applied Psychology in Business and Industry

Depending on your vocation, you may spend as much as 20 years of schooling in preparation for your life's

Figure 20.5 *The jigsaw classroom, designed by the social psychologist Elliot Aronson, was based on research that showed how conditions of mutual interdependence can reduce intergroup hostility among children.*

work. Then, for perhaps 40 to 50 years, you will devote as much as half of each waking day to work. Your standard of living, your sense of well-being and accomplishment, and your security and prestige will be closely tied to your work.

Because psychological processes like motivation, learning, perception, and personality functioning play key roles in job selection, performance, and satisfaction, the world of work has provided an inviting setting for the application of psychological principles. We will focus on two of these important areas of application. The first involves attempts to improve the functioning of organizations by increasing the satisfaction and productivity of employees. The second area is personnel selection, in which psychological tests and other assessment devices are used in an attempt to place the right people in the right jobs.

Increasing Job Satisfaction and Productivity

In order to be successful, every organization needs people who meet three behavioral requirements. First, they must desire not only to join the organization but to remain in it. Second, they must competently and dependably perform the tasks for which they are hired. Third, at least some of them must go beyond their designated work roles and function in a creative and spontaneous manner that allows the company to move forward in innovative ways (Steers & Porter, 1991).

The past two decades have seen a decline in the competitive standing of the U.S. and Canadian work forces in relation to foreign competitors, most notably Japan. Although there are certainly many factors involved in the higher efficiency and quality of Japanese production systems, special attention has been drawn to differences in work environments in the United States and Japan. Surprisingly, research has shown that Japanese workers are not more satisfied with their jobs than U.S. workers; in fact, they tend to be *less* satisfied (Lincoln, 1989). They are far more committed to their companies, however, and their tendency to spend their entire working careers with one employer contrasts sharply with the high turnover rates in the United States and Canada.

A major reason for the high level of job commitment among Japanese workers is a system that integrates employees into the inner workings of the company. Japanese firms often emphasize the establishment of groups of employees who work closely together on projects and are also involved in quality control of the product (see Figure 20.6). Japanese companies also encourage open communication among employees at all levels and close consultation among workers and management (Ouchi, 1981).

These features of Japanese firms encourage close social interactions and a concern for the good of the company as well as the individual.

Cross-cultural comparisons have fueled an interest in experimentation and innovation among U.S. and Canadian firms and a recognition that worker motivation is a vital factor in both job satisfaction and productivity. Surprisingly, perhaps, research has shown that satisfaction and productivity are not highly related to one another (Steers & Porter, 1991), but low job satisfaction is related to both absenteeism and turnover. Both job satisfaction and productivity reflect work motivation, but they may also be influenced by reward systems (Locke, 1990). Let us, then, consider the motives that underlie work behavior.

Work Motivation

Why do people work, and what do they want from their jobs? The earliest theory of work motivation, advanced by Frederick Taylor (1911), held that workers are basically lazy and are motivated almost entirely by money. In Taylor's model, workers will be satisfied and productive on any job if they are paid enough.

How does Taylor's theory stack up against current knowledge of work motivation? For most people, not very well. For one thing, we know that there are wide individual differences in the motives that drive work behavior. Some people are, as Taylor suggests, motivated almost entirely by monetary considerations. But for most people, other factors are more important. For example, Figure 20.7 shows the results from a Harris survey in which people in diverse occupations were asked what they sought more than anything from a job. Although the traditional features of salary, job

▶ **Figure 20.6** *Japanese work groups foster feelings of mutual responsibility for producing a high-quality product and appear to increase the degree of employee commitment to the company.*

▶ **Figure 20.7** *What
Americans want most from
their jobs. These data are
based on a large sample of
American adults who were
asked to choose the most
important aspect of a job.
(Data from Harris, 1987).*

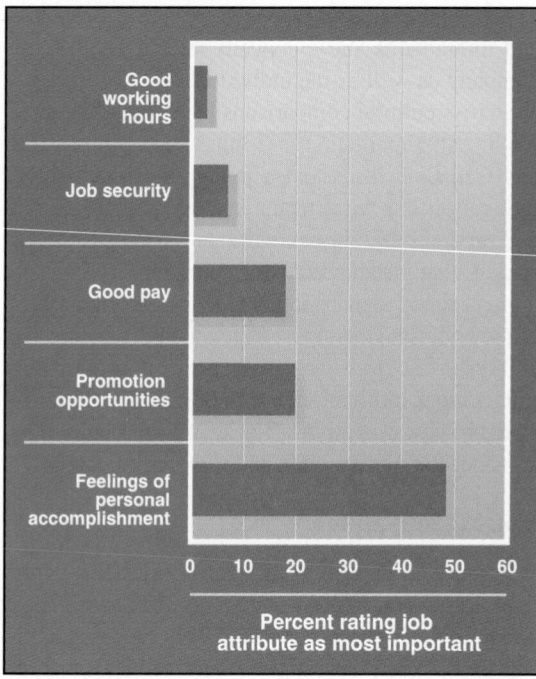

Good
working
hours

Job security

Good pay

Promotion
opportunities

Feelings of
personal
accomplishment

0   10   20   30   40   50   60

**Percent rating job
attribute as most important**

3. *Task significance.* Jobs that have a significant impact on the lives and work of other people either within or outside the organization are more motivating and satisfying.

4. *Autonomy.* Jobs that give employees the freedom to schedule the work and choose the procedures to be used are prized by most employees.

5. *Job feedback.* Obtaining clear and direct feedback about the effectiveness of one's performance increases intrinsic motivation and satisfaction.

Figure 20.8 shows the hypothesized relations among these job characteristics, the psychological states they elicit, and the work outcomes that result (Hackman, 1991).

A successful example of job enrichment occurred at a truck assembly plant owned by Volvo in Sweden. There, assembly lines (which are low on all five of these core dimensions) have been replaced by production teams of 5 to 12 workers. The members of the team elect their own coordinator and decide among themselves how the work will be divided up and distributed. They are responsible for their own quality control. They also have freedom to vary their work and to schedule work breaks, as long as they meet the production standards established by management. Group members can deal directly with other departments in solving problems and obtaining supplies, and they also perform some of the support and maintenance duties formerly carried out by staff and service personnel.

The Volvo experiment has been a successful one resulting in better performance and lower absenteeism and turnover (Wexley & Yukl, 1977). Similar successes have been observed in other occupational settings, including white-collar organizations (Spector & Jex, 1991). Typically, successful job enrichment programs have combined several jobs into a larger job involving a wider variety of skills and have given each employee a natural unit of work so he or she can complete a meaningful task. Increasing workers' autonomy and providing channels for direct performance feedback are other job enrichment strategies.

Job enrichment programs do not always work, however. A well-designed industrial study found that workers achieved the highest performance and were most satisfied with an enriched job only when they desired personal growth and were satisfied with other factors, such as pay and social relationships in the organization. Workers who found their jobs highly motivating but were uninterested in personal growth and dissatisfied with the organization were not as productive (Hackman & Oldham, 1976). Thus, a complex relationship between job structure, employee characteristics, and organizational features must be taken into account in redesigning jobs.

security, and good working hours were cited, the most frequent answer was that the work be meaningful and offer feelings of accomplishment. Other studies have shown that intrinsic rewards relating to feelings of meaningful contribution, personal accomplishment, and mastery are critically important in producing both job satisfaction and productivity. These findings, together with analyses of Japanese business practices, have spurred attempts to design job environments that permit satisfaction of such needs. We now examine several of these innovative approaches.

Job Enrichment

Job enrichment is an approach for redesigning jobs so as to increase intrinsic motivation and job satisfaction. A worker is intrinsically motivated when his or her work helps to fulfill growth needs such as needs for competence, achievement, and self-actualization. Psychologists have been particularly interested in the conditions that make jobs intrinsically motivating. In one large-scale study of seven organizations, it was found that five "core dimensions" of the job were related to the job's intrinsic motivation and the workers' job satisfaction (Hackman & Oldham, 1976).

1. *Skill variety.* Jobs that require a variety of different activities and that involve the use of a number of different talents and skills are more intrinsically motivating and satisfying.

2. *Task identity.* Jobs that require completion of a "whole" product from beginning to end are more motivating and satisfying.

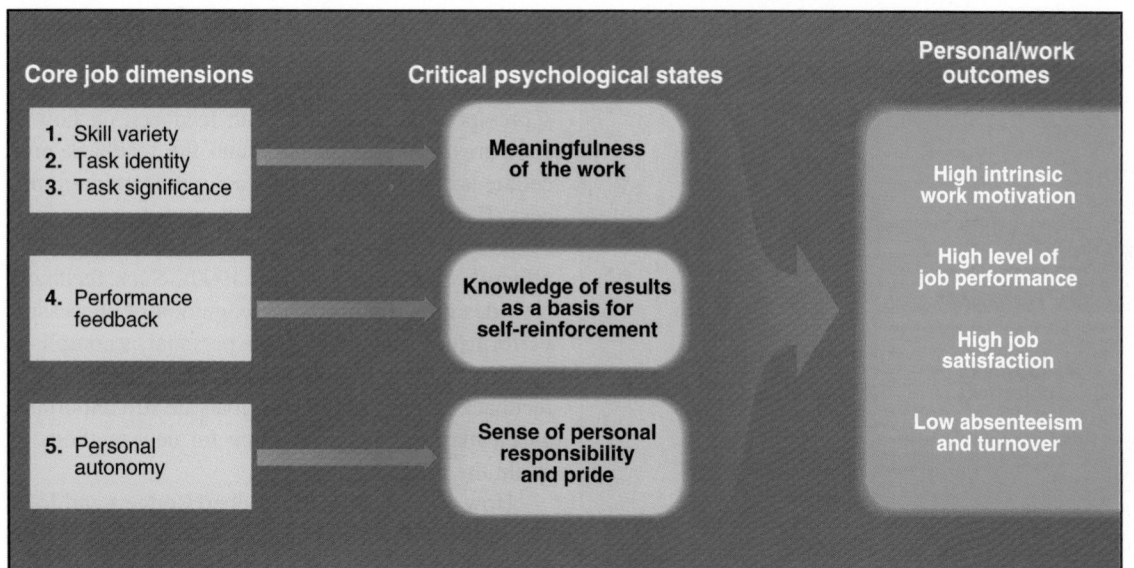

Figure 20.8 *Job characteristics interact with individual differences in the need for personal growth to create three critical psychological states. These states affect performance and job satisfaction. (Based on Hackman & Suttle, 1977).*

Programs Based on Operant Conditioning

The intrinsic motivation principles that underlie job enrichment programs should not lead us to conclude that extrinsic positive reinforcers, such as money, are not effective means of increasing productivity. Programs based on operant conditioning principles make the amount of money a worker earns contingent on how productive the worker is. For example, Union National Bank in Little Rock, Arkansas, has had great success in paying its workers for the number of customers they serve, the number of new accounts they gain, the amount of time taken to balance accounts at the end of the day, and other performance measures (see Figure 20.9). The bank's pay-for-performance program has resulted in a 25-percent increase in the average employee's take-home pay, and the bank's profits have doubled. In North Carolina, Nucor has doubled its productivity by paying steelworkers for the amount of work they complete, and the average worker takes home more than $30,000 per year, compared with an industry average of $27,000 (Aamodt, 1991).

Despite the success of operant conditioning programs in promoting high levels of productivity, concerns have been raised about potential negative effects on job satisfaction and intrinsic motivation. For example, Edward Deci and Richard Ryan (1985) cite evidence that such programs may produce an *over-justification effect* (see Chapter 12), in which the administration of extrinsic reinforcement for intrinsically rewarding behaviors eventually reduces the intrinsic motivation. They urge employers to ensure that jobs are interesting and meaningful and that workers are given as much control as possible in set-

ting reinforcement contingencies so that intrinsic as well as extrinsic motivation will operate.

Goal Setting and Management by Objectives

An approach that combines several of the most effective job enrichment and operant conditioning techniques is known as **management by objectives (MBO).** The cornerstone of MBO is goal setting, an exceedingly powerful motivational technique. In

Figure 20.9 *In programs based on operant conditioning principles, employees' pay is based on specific measures of productivity, such as the number of new accounts opened by bank employees.*

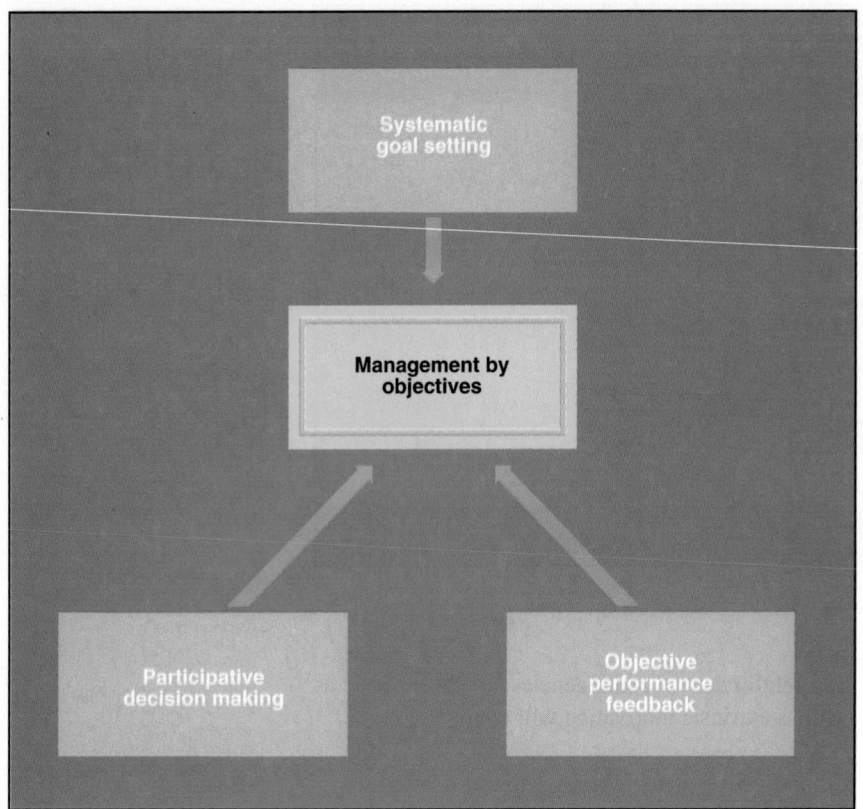

Systematic
goal setting

Management by
objectives

Participative
decision making

Objective
performance
feedback

🔺 **Figure 20.10** *Management by objectives (MBO) programs combine three proven procedures for increasing productivity.*

no's Pizza publishes a ''box score'' with the average delivery and service times for each of its stores in *The Pepperoni Press,* its monthly newsletter. The box scores provide each store with feedback on how it compares with other stores, and the feedback procedure is considered a prime factor in Domino's success (Feuer, 1987).

Without performance feedback, goal setting is not effective (Locke & Latham, 1990). Such feedback provides opportunities for recognition of successful performance and feelings of personal accomplishment in the organization. When goals are not attained, feedback emphasizes that the goals are still important, and it may encourage a search for new methods to attain the goals.

How effective is MBO? Robert Rodgers and John Hunter (1991) performed a meta-analysis of MBO outcome studies carried out in 70 organizations. Increases in productivity were found in 97 percent of the studies, with a highly impressive mean productivity increase of 44.6 percent. However, the researchers also found that the success of MBO programs depended on the extent to which top management supported and actively participated in them (see Figure 20.11). This finding illustrates an important point: Even the most effective intervention program is unlikely to succeed unless the organization is committed to the program and becomes actively involved in carrying it out effectively.

Personnel Selection: Matching People with Jobs

Choosing the right person for the job is an important factor in both job performance and job satisfaction. Because the costs of error in selection decisions can be great in both economic and human terms, many employers try to do the best they can to match work requirements with the aptitudes, interests, values, and personality characteristics of job applicants. Psychologists are often called in to develop scientifically based selection procedures. The goal is to find the most objective, accurate, and cost-efficient ways of matching people with jobs.

Developing and Evaluating Selection Measures

The development of a personnel selection program typically proceeds through a well-defined series of steps, as shown in Figure 20.12. First, the job is analyzed to isolate the traits, abilities, or previous experiences that are likely to contribute to job success (Schmidt & Klimoski, 1991). To obtain this information, a psychologist may interview workers and supervisors, directly observe people performing or

more than 95 percent of the program evaluation studies that have assessed its effects in industry, goal setting has been found to increase productivity (Locke & Latham, 1990). As discussed in Chapter 14, goal-setting is a systematic approach that involves setting explicit long-term and short-term goals and planning a well-specified strategy for achieving the goals. To be most useful, goals should be well-defined, difficult and challenging, and attainable. The goals may be either individual goals or group goals, but they must be clearly specified and must relate directly to outcomes that can be measured.

MBO adds to goal setting two other important components—employee participation in decision making and objective feedback (see Figure 20.10). Employees at all levels of the organization are invited to provide input as to specific goals, the means that will be used to attain them, and any changes that should be made in the goals, the strategies, or the work environment. Participation helps increase involvement and commitment to the goals, thereby enhancing the likelihood that they will be attained.

The third MBO component is objective feedback related to goal attainment. Such feedback is based on objective measures and is given by managers at the end of each evaluation period. For example, Domi-

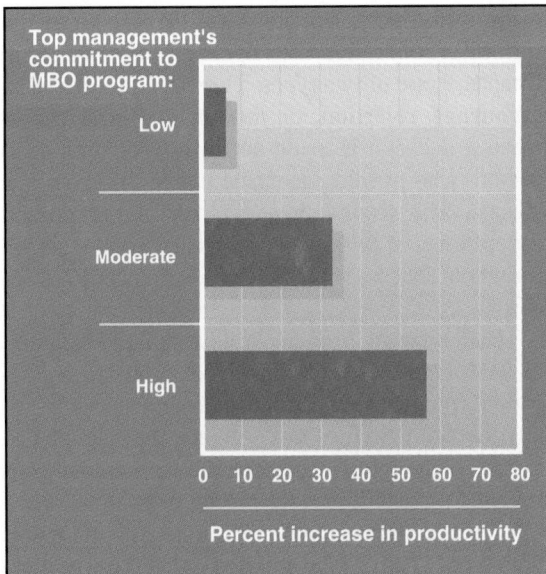

Figure 20.11 *MBO programs can result in large increases in organizational productivity, but the extent to which this occurs depends on the extent to which top management is supportive and participates in the programs. (Data from Rodgers & Hunter, 1991).*

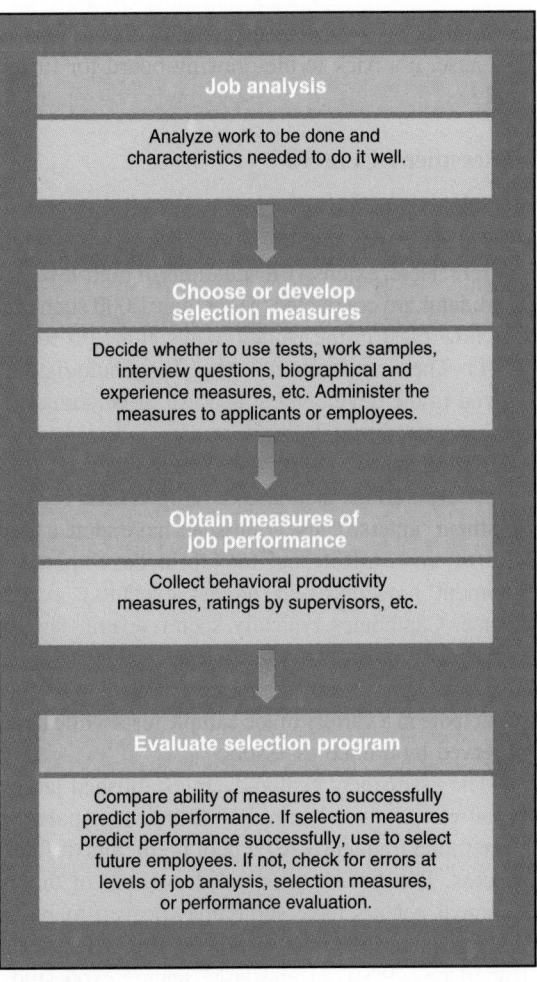

Figure 20.12 *Steps in the development of a personnel selection program.*

being trained for the job, or ask workers to rate the importance of certain skills.

Next, methods for measuring these required characteristics are chosen or developed. A variety of methods may be used, including interviews, psychological tests that measure specific abilities and aptitudes, personality and interest tests, and job samples.

Job samples test the ability of applicants to function successfully in simulations of the actual job situation. For example, in an assessment program designed for Sears, Roebuck and Company to identify managerial potential, raters assessed the ability of applicants to generate ideas and solve problems in group discussions. Applicants were presented with problems like the following *in-basket task:*

> You and the men at your table are members of a staff group that reports to Frank Hastings, Zone Manager of the Mid-Central Zone.
>
> Last Saturday the Exville store manager died of a heart attack. Sunday Mr. Hastings drove to Exville to take a look at the store. He reported the store wasn't in as good a shape as he thought it might be. Mr. Hastings has given each of you a copy of the material found in the manager's in-basket and asked that you come together as a staff group for the purpose of making an analysis of the store and its problems, and then decide upon a series of recommendations that the new manager might follow in rebuilding the Exville store. Together, the analysis and recommendations should form a kind of managerial strategy that could effectively rebuild Exville (Bentz, 1968, p. 98).

Sears found the job sample procedure to be a good predictor of later managerial success. Many companies now use job samples in conjunction with aptitude tests. A job sample constructed for a specific situation is likely to be a somewhat better predictor for that situation than an aptitude test, but the broader aptitude test is more likely to give results that are applicable to many situations. Aptitude tests are also less costly to administer.

Once measures of job-related skills or traits have been selected, their ability to predict job performance is evaluated. Ideally, the measures should not be used to select people for jobs at this point, because they have not yet been shown to predict job success. The best procedure is to administer the measures to many job applicants. Later, the results can be compared with measures of job performance for the applicants who were hired. The stronger the relations between the measures and job performance, the more useful the measures are likely to be in selecting future employees. If the measures do not predict later performance, the researchers can only conclude that errors have been made in the job analysis, in the selection of measures used to predict success, in measuring job performance, or at more than one of these steps. In that case, it's back to the drawing board for further study.

Assessment Centers

Many large business concerns carry out formal managerial selection programs at specialized **assessment centers.** Here, extensive evaluations of high-level job candidates are conducted. More than 1,000 such centers now exist in the United States alone (O'Reilly, 1991). Their staffs include many psychologists involved in the development and use of personnel selection procedures.

Exxon, Sears, and AT&T are examples of prominent corporations that have developed their own assessment centers. These companies have spent a great deal of time, effort, and money in developing assessment procedures to predict executive performance. Candidates typically spend several days at assessment centers. They are given an extensive series of psychological tests, are interviewed at length, and participate in a variety of job sample tests while being observed by trained assessors.

The assessment centers were established largely because supervisors' ratings of management potential were found frequently to be poor predictors of future success. The more sophisticated methods of the assessment centers have sometimes proven to be far more accurate (Gaugler & others, 1987; Schmitt & Robertson, 1990). In one large-scale Exxon study, 400 managers were assessed. When the various test and job sample scores were combined, it was found that 95 percent of those having the highest scores were judged highly successful managers by other measures, while only 21 percent of those with low scores were judged highly successful (Laurent, 1968).

The success achieved by assessment centers is not always this impressive, however. Several meta-analyses of assessment center research have indicated that the centers can vary quite widely in the accuracy of their predictions (Gaugler & others, 1987; Schmidt & others, 1992). The expense involved in operating assessment centers can only be justified when their success rates far exceed those of less expensive methods, such as job interviews, performance ratings made by superiors, and letters of reference (Goldsmith, 1990). Several recent studies indicate that this is not always the case; ratings provided by skilled interviewers as well as scores on general cognitive ability tests can sometimes equal or exceed assessment center scores in predicting job performance (Gatewood & Field, 1990; Schmidt & others, 1992).

Decision Issues in Personnel Selection

No personnel selection procedure, regardless of how sophisticated, can guarantee that errors will not be made. Personnel selection errors, like the errors described in connection with signal detection theory in Chapter 7, are of two types. The first is known as an **erroneous rejection,** or *false negative.* It occurs when a decision is made not to hire or promote a person who would have succeeded if given the chance. The second type of error, an **erroneous acceptance,** or *false positive,* occurs when a person for whom success is predicted fails to meet job standards.

Both types of error can be costly to organizations as well as to the people involved. From an organization's point of view, erroneous acceptances are usually the more glaring errors. In fact, they can be disastrous if the job is important and the company has invested a great deal in the wrong individual.

Clearly, organizations would like to minimize both types of error. The problem is that the procedure most often used to reduce erroneous acceptances—namely, tighter screening and more rigorous hiring or admission standards—is also likely to increase the rate of erroneous rejections. For example, universities that have extremely high admission standards reduce the likelihood of losing students through academic failure but at the same time reject many students who could succeed if given the opportunity.

Attempts to reduce selection errors must take into account the potential costs involved. In some cases, the avoidance of erroneous acceptance is paramount. In the selection of astronauts, for example, the costs involved in picking the wrong person are so extreme that rigid selection standards must be used, even at the cost of excluding candidates who would be successful if chosen.

In contrast, many people believe that the social and personal costs of excluding disadvantaged or minority group members from job entry justify the risk of erroneous acceptances in some situations. This issue becomes especially significant when **cut-off scores** are used in making decisions, so that persons scoring below a certain critical score are rejected. Frequently, these cut-off scores were established in research done with white applicants, and the critical score has been shown to achieve the highest likelihood of correct decisions for that group. The problem is that because of cultural factors and poorer educational opportunities, the average scores of minority groups are often lower. As a result, fewer minority group members are likely to exceed a cut-off score derived from a white sample. However, many studies have shown that tests commonly used in personnel selection are equally valid in predicting job success for minority and white candidates even though the minority groups' range of scores may be lower overall (Schmitt & Robertson, 1990). In other words, an African-American or Hispanic person who scores in the upper 10 percent of his or her racial group is as likely to succeed as a white person who scores in the upper 10 percent of the white group, even though the minority person's actual scores may be lower.

This problem is a complex one that defies simple answers. One procedure that is sometimes used is to establish two separate cut-off scores, one for whites and the other for minorities. But this creates two different standards, which some people find objectionable. It also means that some white candidates will be rejected who actually score higher than some minority applicants who are hired, leading to complaints of reverse discrimination (Schmitt & others, 1992). In many instances, the courts are being called on to settle such issues, but court decisions are unlikely to resolve the controversies concerning the social and personal consequences of selection errors.

<hr>

Psychology and the Law

One of our most important, complex, and fascinating social institutions is the law. The behavioral dramas played out in the criminal justice system have attracted the interest and attention of psychologists for many years. As early as 1906, Sigmund Freud lectured to Viennese judges concerning the applicability of psychological principles to law (Tapp, 1976). During that same period, psychologists in the United States were forging connections between the psychological laboratory and the courtroom. In 1908, Hugo Münsterberg of Harvard's psychology laboratory published a classic book, *On the Witness Stand,* in which he attempted to demonstrate that principles of perception and memory must be considered in evaluating courtroom testimony.

But this initial flirtation between law and psychology did not develop into a meaningful relationship until the 1960s and 1970s, when a new field called **forensic psychology** began to emerge. Partly because the legal system recognized that psychology could make potentially important contributions and partly because many psychologists saw the law as an interesting setting in which to study and apply psychological principles, interactions between law and psychology increased.

The province of law covers a vast terrain, extending all the way from crime prevention to punishment and rehabilitation of offenders. Psychology can be applied in countless areas of law, but we will narrow our attention to three important areas in which psychological principles are being applied. One significant line of research and application concerns evidence provided by eyewitness testimony. A second involves the process of jury decision making. The third concerns the expanding role of the psychologist as an expert witness and communicator of research findings.

Psychology and the Eyewitness

"He's the one I saw!" This statement by a witness has probably resulted in more convictions than any other. Eyewitness identification is usually compelling evidence to a judge or jury. After all, seeing is believing, isn't it?

Not always, unfortunately. In the 1930s, a carefully documented study of 65 criminal prosecutions and convictions of defendants whose innocence was later established beyond a doubt indicated that mistaken identity by eyewitnesses was a major reason for these tragic miscarriages of justice. Mistaken identifications accounted for 29 of the convictions. In 27 of these 29 cases, there was not even a strong resemblance between the innocent person and the guilty party who was later found to have committed the crime (Borchard, 1932). Other studies have confirmed this potential for eyewitness error (Loftus & Ketcham, 1991).

How can our memories betray us so badly? Such mistakes would never occur if memory functioned like a videotape recorder. But, as we saw so clearly in Chapter 10, it doesn't. We must encode and store incoming information, retain it over a period of time, and then retrieve what is left of the stored information when we need it. The memory system may fail at any of these stages. Our encoding may be faulty, our retention may be poor, or we may introduce distortions during retrieval (see Figure 20.13).

▸ **Figure 20.13** *Research on memory has shown that eyewitness accounts can be distorted by a variety of factors, including the identification process itself.*

"Do you swear to tell your version of the truth as you perceive it, clouded perhaps by the passage of time and preconceived notions?"

Drawing by Sidney Harris; © 1989, Trial Diplomacy Journal.

The final stage of retrieval is highly relevant to what happens when a person views a police lineup or mug shots or testifies on the witness stand. Here, reconstructive memory becomes very important. Many studies have shown that how questions are asked can influence what the subject "recalls." In one study, subjects were shown a film of an auto accident. Later, some subjects were asked, "Did you see *the* broken headlight?" Others were asked "Did you see *a* broken headlight?" The former were more likely to say "yes" although no broken headlight had been shown in the film. (Loftus & Zanni, 1975). Such findings have important implications for eyewitness testimony, because they show that memory can be distorted. Memories may actually be modified to make them consistent with the new information that the question provides. To reduce the likelihood of such distortions, the witness should be allowed to report freely on the incident as he or she remembers it before specific questions are asked (Wells & Luus, 1990).

Many eyewitness identifications occur in the context of photo spreads and police lineups. It is now clear that identification tasks can be set up in ways that increase the likelihood that a particular suspect will be identified. In one particularly blatant example, a police lineup set up to identify the perpetrator of a crime known to have been committed by an African-American man contained an African-American man (the police suspect), an African-American woman, and three Caucasian men (Sobel & Pridgen, 1981).

In a sense, a police lineup can be likened to a psychology experiment (Wells & Luus, 1990). The eyewitnesses are the subjects, and the police officer conducting the lineup is the experimenter. Instructions to the eyewitnesses are like instructions in an experimental protocol. The positioning of the suspect in the lineup and the characteristics of other people in the lineup who are known to be innocent are elements of the experimental design. The police officer is likely to have a hypothesis (for example, that Number 3 is the guilty party) and has created a design and procedure to test this hypothesis.

The lineup-as-experiment analogy suggests that the lineup may also be subject to the factors that can contaminate research experiments, such as demand characteristics (stimuli that suggest to subjects how they are expected to respond), experimenter bias, and lack of appropriate control groups. The experimental psychologist's understanding of such factors can be applied directly to reducing errors in police-conducted eyewitness identification procedures.

Let us consider the control group problem. Police have assumed that the presence of innocent parties, or foils, in a lineup is an adequate control for mistaken identifications. Yet research has shown that subjects who did not actually witness the crime for which the lineup is being conducted may have a distinct tendency to pick out the suspect if the foils look less like the stereotypes people have about the appearance of criminals than the suspect does (Doob & Kirschenbaum, 1973). A second problem is that many eyewitnesses have made positive identifications when shown picture spreads or lineups consisting entirely of people known to be innocent (Wells, 1984).

These findings have led to the development of two different control conditions. In the **mock-witness control** procedure, subjects who were not eyewitnesses try to identify a suspect from a lineup or photo spread. This procedure can be used to help create a good lineup in which the people do not differ drastically in their tendency to be perceived as a "criminal type." A second procedure, the **blank-lineup control,** involves showing an eyewitness a lineup composed entirely of innocent foils before showing the witness a second lineup that actually does contain the suspect. Research has shown that this procedure discredits many witnesses who have poor recall or presumably are overeager to identify someone as the culprit; but it does not affect witnesses' ability to identify the perpetrator in the second lineup (Wells, 1984).

A forensic psychologist, Gary Wells (1988), has written a handbook for police based on the results of research on factors that distort or improve eyewitness identifications. The handbook contains many practical suggestions for improving eyewitness identification tasks, and it is now being used in police training centers. Table 20.1 provides a sample of concrete suggestions for the conduct of lineups and photo spreads and relates them to principles of sound experimental design. Wells and other psychologists are also conducting training workshops for judges, police officers, and attorneys on factors that affect eyewitnesses. In this way, knowledge based on psychological research is being translated directly into legal guidelines designed to promote justice.

Psychology and the Jury

To many people, the most fascinating aspect of the U.S. legal system is the process by which juries make decisions. Many aspects of jury functioning are relevant to the concerns of psychologists. Perception, information processing, persuasion, and individual and group decision making, as well as the role of personality factors, all enter into the functioning of juries. We should therefore expect psychologists to be interested in jury behavior and also to have something to say about the many factors that influence the judgments of a jury (see Figure 20.14).

Psychologists have taken two basic approaches to the study of decision making by juries. The more

Table 20.1 Recommendations for Conducting Police Lineups and Photo Spreads*

Examples	Experiment Analogue
1. Witnesses should be separated as soon as possible.	If subjects interact prior to responding to the dependent measure, then their data cannot be analyzed as though they were independent.
2. At no time should a witness be led to believe that the actual perpetrator is in the set of mugshots.	Experimenter protocols should be worded in a way that does not create demands on the subject to respond in a particular way.
3. The officer conducting the photo spread should not be knowledgeable of whom the police suspect in the case.	Experimenters who come into contact with subjects should be kept blind about the condition to which the subject is assigned.
4. If there is more than one witness, the position of the suspect in the photo spread should be changed for each witness.	Stimulus presentation order should be randomized or counterbalanced across subjects.
5. No cues of any kind should be given to the witness concerning whether or not the identified person is the suspect in the case (at least until a statement of certainty is obtained from the witness).	Debriefings regarding the experimenter's hypothesis and related matters should not be given until all dependent measures have been collected.

*The recommendations were derived from a conception of these identification procedures as experiments. The parallel guidelines for experimenters are shown on the right.

Source: Wells & Luus, 1990.

common of the two is the **simulation study,** in which subjects are placed in the role of jurors and asked to make judgments. Subjects may be asked to respond to written case descriptions, videotaped presentations, or actual mock trials. The strength of the simulation approach is the high degree of experimental control that can be achieved. But this approach also has several weaknesses that limit the extent to which findings can be generalized to actual courtrooms. Subjects are often college students rather than a cross-section of the jury population, which consists of registered voters. Moreover, they are responding to an artificial situation in which their decisions have no real effects on the life of the plaintiff or the defendant. Thus, the trade-off is control at the expense of real involvement in the role of juror.

The second and less common approach is to study real juries. This presents different problems to the scientist. Because each trial is unique and because the legal system obviously does not permit psychologists to manipulate variables, it is difficult to determine cause-and-effect relations. But in some instances, the fact that real juries are being studied can outweigh the lack of scientific control.

Sometimes simulations are used to check the validity of more informal observation of actual courtroom situations. Consider the following example. A defendant is being tried for murder. During cross-examination of the defendant, the prosecuting attorney asks, ''Mr. Jones, isn't it true that on five previous occasions in other states, you have been charged with

felonious assault and attempted murder, four times being released because witnesses were afraid to testify, and once having a conviction overturned on a legal technicality?'' The defense attorney leaps to his feet and objects strenuously that the question is irrelevant, immaterial, and an attempt to bias the jury. The judge agrees and instructs the jury to disregard the question.

◆ **Figure 20.14** *The process by which juries make decisions has been a topic of great interest to psychologists.*

Can jurors *really* disregard such information? Many lawyers feel that they cannot and that the information may bias their decisions. To assess this possibility, a simulation study was done in which college students read a description of a murder trial. The evidence against the defendant was either very strong or quite weak. Some of the subjects read trial transcripts in which additional damaging and incriminating evidence resulting from a police telephone tap was presented by the prosecution. Half of the subjects who received this additional evidence were told that the judge had ruled it inadmissible and had instructed the jury to disregard it, while the other half were told that the evidence had been ruled admissible. A control group received the strong or weak evidence without the additional incriminating evidence. After reading the case descriptions, the subjects were asked to render a verdict as if they were jury members.

It was found that when the other evidence against the defendant was strong, the additional incriminating evidence did not increase the number of guilty verdicts whether it had been ruled admissible or not. But when the other evidence was weak, the incriminating evidence exerted a strong effect, even if it had been ruled inadmissible. Figure 20.15 shows that in the weak-evidence condition, there were no guilty verdicts when the additional incriminating evidence was not presented. When the additional incriminating evidence was presented and ruled admissible, 26 percent of the simulated jurors rendered guilty verdicts. But

when it was ruled inadmissible, an even higher 35 percent gave a guilty verdict (Sue & others, 1973). The results of this study support the conclusion of many legal experts that jurors can be biased by inadmissible evidence even when they are told to disregard it. Their desire to see justice done may override the rules of law (Pennington & Hastie, 1990; Wissler & Saks, 1985).

Can anything be done to eliminate such bias? One method that is being tried in several states involves videotaping the actual trial in the absence of the jury. After all evidence has been presented, the opposing attorneys and the trial judge edit out evidence judged to be irrelevant or inadmissible. The jurors then view the edited videotape and deliberate as they would ordinarily. They can also ask to review portions of the tape during their deliberations (McCrystal, 1978). When innovative procedures like videotaped trials are used, psychologists can play an important role in assessing their effects on juries' decision making.

Psychologists as Expert Witnesses

For many years, clinical psychologists have appeared in court as expert witnesses. Typically, they have been asked to testify in criminal insanity cases and to offer their opinions of defendants' mental status based on psychological test results and interviews.

In recent years, psychologists in nonclinical areas have also begun to appear as expert witnesses. Experimental psychologists who are experts on memory have frequently testified about the problems involved in eyewitness identification (Loftus & Ketcham, 1991). Social and developmental psychologists have offered testimony based on research results concerning such issues as busing, racial desegregation, child abuse, the adequacy of product warning labels, and bilingual education. In a United States Supreme Court decision on the minimum allowable jury size, no fewer than 14 of the 32 paragraphs in the opinion cited psychological studies of jury size and decision making that supported the Court's decision (Loftus & Monahan, 1980).

Another issue related to expert testimony concerns the ability of psychologists and others to predict violent behavior. This is an especially important issue because people may be involuntarily committed to mental hospitals, given indeterminate prison sentences, and even executed if they are judged likely to be violent. Yet according to a series of studies of persons released from prisons or mental hospitals, predictions of future violence made by psychiatrists and psychologists were incorrect in 65 to 90 percent of the cases (Monahan, 1981). John Monahan, the psychologist who conducted these studies, has testified in a number of court cases on the arbitrary nature

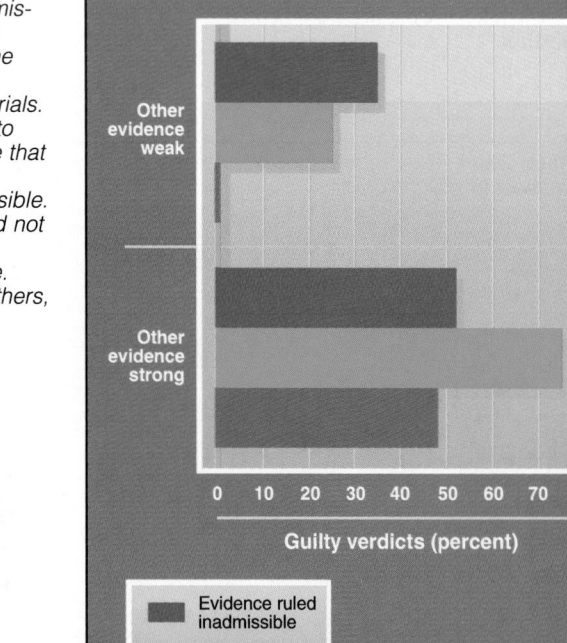

▶ **Figure 20.15** *Inadmissible but incriminating evidence can affect the percentage of guilty verdicts in simulated trials. Jurors were exposed to incriminating evidence that was later ruled either admissible or inadmissible. The control groups did not receive the additional incriminating evidence. (Data from Sue and others, 1973).*

of the prediction of violent behavior in an effort to help ensure the civil rights of individuals who have been judged violence prone (Monahan, 1992).

How helpful can psychologists be to the legal system? Certainly, psychological principles are applicable to many aspects of the criminal justice system, including the training of police officers, the judicial process, sentencing and parole decisions, the rehabilitation of offenders, and the design and operation of humane correctional institutions. Whatever the future holds, it is to be hoped that the developing relationship between psychology and the law will promote both science and justice.

Sport Psychology

At one time, only a few psychologists referred to themselves as *sport psychologists*. Most of these pioneers were clinical psychologists to whom coaches referred athletes who had psychological problems that interfered with their performance. But as awareness grew of the important role of psychological factors in sport, psychologists were increasingly attracted to the study and application of psychological principles in athletics. Psychological researchers have also begun to appreciate sport as an unusually rich ''natural laboratory'' for studying psychological phenomena. If you stop to consider for a moment, most of the topics we have dealt with in this book—perception, learning, cognition, motivation and emotion, development, sex roles, personality, stress, behavior change—have direct relevance to sport and can be studied in the ''real world'' of the sport setting.

One way in which psychologists have recently become involved in sport is as researchers and consultants to youth sport programs. Such programs have frequently been criticized for an overemphasis on winning and competition. Psychologists can help programs create a more positive and less stressful environment that will contribute to the personal growth of child athletes.

Researching and Improving Youth Sport Programs

In the United States alone, about 26 million boys and girls between the ages of 6 and 16 participate in sport programs outside of school (Martens, 1986). The kind of relationship that exists between coaches and athletes is of major importance in determining whether the sport experience is enjoyable and promotes personal growth (see Figure 20.16). Most coaches are volunteers, and while they may be quite knowledgeable about the technical aspects of their particular

Figure 20.16 *Interactions between coaches and child athletes can have a strong impact on the psychological well-being of the child.*

sport, they typically receive little if any training in how to create a positive psychological environment for their young athletes.

Psychologists have recently begun to study how coaching behaviors affect children's attitudes toward their coaches, their sport, their teammates, and themselves (Smith & Smoll, 1991). In the first phase of one large-scale research project, 51 male Little League Baseball coaches were observed during more than 200 complete games. More than 57,000 individual coaching behaviors were coded into 12 different categories (including reinforcement, encouragement, technical instruction, punishment, organizational behaviors, and discipline), and a behavioral profile based on an average of more than 1,100 behaviors was computed for each coach. After the Little League season, 542 of the children who played for the 51 coaches were interviewed in their homes. The young athletes rated how often their coaches had engaged in each category of behavior, and they completed attitude questionnaires about their coaches, their teammates, and their feelings about their experience and about themselves. The measures obtained from the children were then related to the behavioral profiles of the coaches, and clear-cut relations between coaching behaviors and player attitudes were found. Children clearly preferred playing for supportive coaches who gave a good deal of positive reinforcement, responded to mistakes with encouragement and technical instruction instead of criticism, and encouraged team unity and player support for one another. This was particularly the case

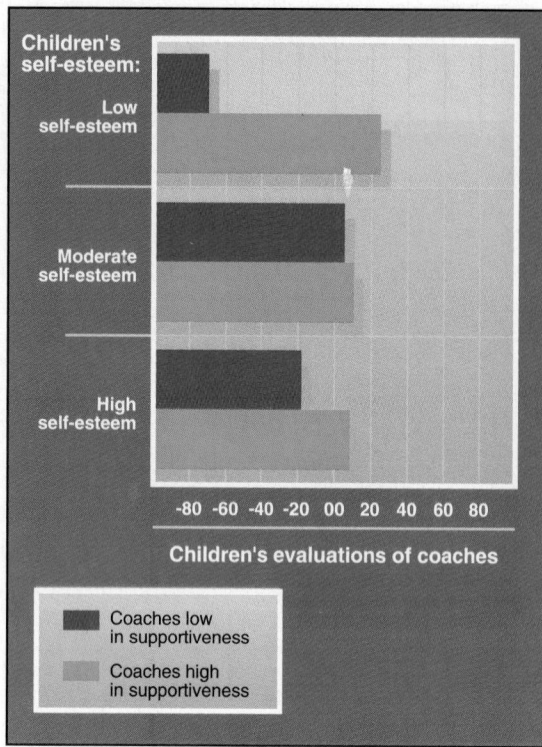

Children's self-esteem:

Low self-esteem

Moderate self-esteem

High self-esteem

-80 -60 -40 -20 00 20 40 60 80

Children's evaluations of coaches

■ Coaches low in supportiveness

▨ Coaches high in supportiveness

Figure 20.17 *Attraction responses of children who were high, moderate, or low in self-esteem to coaches who were high or low in supportiveness and quality of instruction. Consistent with the self-enhancement model, children low in self-esteem were most affected by these differences in coaching behaviors. (Smith & Smoll, 1990).*

for children who were low in self-esteem (see Figure 20.17). As self-enhancement theory (discussed in Chapter 19) would predict, the need for positive feedback from coaches should be especially great among such children because of their strong need to feel more positive about themselves.

Having established relationships between coaching behaviors and children's reactions to their athletic experiences, the researchers' next step was to use these findings to develop a training program for coaches. The 3-hour Coach Effectiveness Training program that evolved is designed to give coaches specific behavioral guidelines for creating a more positive psychological environment for children, as well as to help them become more aware of their behavior. The basic behavioral guidelines are described in Table 20.2.

Several program evaluations have been conducted to test the effectiveness of the training program. In these studies, youth coaches were randomly assigned to either a training group or an untrained control group. The coaches in the training group were presented with the behavioral guidelines. The researchers also demonstrated useful ways of responding to de-

sirable behaviors, mistakes, and misbehaviors, as well as ways in which the coaches could monitor their own behavior more closely. Following the 3-hour preseason training program, the trained and untrained coaches were observed during games, and their behaviors were coded by raters who had no knowledge of the training program. After the season ended, attitude and self-esteem measures were collected from children who played for the two groups of coaches.

The behavioral assessment showed that the trained coaches behaved more in accord with the "positive approach" guidelines than did the control group coaches. Moreover, there were strong differences in the attitudes expressed by their players. The children who had played for the trained coaches more frequently indicated that they had enjoyed playing for the coaches and that they wished to play for them again. They also rated their coaches as better teachers, liked their teammates more, and felt that their coaches and teammates evaluated them more positively. Another important finding was that the children who played for the trained coaches showed an increase in self-esteem scores compared with scores from the previous year. The control group's players showed no change (Smith & others, 1979; Smoll & others, 1993). Apparently, the trained coaches were successful, through their positive approach, in helping their players feel better about themselves.

A recent program evaluation of Coach Effectiveness Training revealed another important benefit of the program. Dropout rates exceeding 30 percent are frequently found in youth sport programs (Gould, 1982). Nancy Barnett and her coworkers (1992) followed up children who had played for trained and untrained coaches to see how many of the children dropped out of sports the following year. They found an extremely low dropout rate among children who had played for the trained coaches (see Figure 20.18). It thus appears that training coaches to create a supportive and pleasant athletic environment helps to achieve the goal of keeping children involved in sports.

Here we see another example of the links between basic research, application, and program evaluation. The basic research on how coaching behaviors affect child athletes provided a scientific basis for designing the training program. Once implemented, the program's effectiveness was assessed through evaluation research.

Psychological Skills Training for Athletes

The crucial role that psychological factors can play in athletic performance is well known to coaches, athletes, and observers of the sport scene. Perhaps the strongest trend in contemporary sport psychology is the development and application of procedures for training athletes in psychological skills that can enhance their performance. This section briefly describes current approaches to psychological skills training.

"Mental Toughness" Training

From youth programs to the professional level, players must cope with the stresses of athletic competition (see Figure 20.19). Because stress can damage athletic performance and reduce enjoyment, a number of psychologists have developed programs to train athletes in coping skills. These programs are designed to give athletes greater control over stress responses and help them keep emotional arousal within manageable limits. Typically, the coping skills taught (like those discussed in Chapter 15) are directed toward the cognitive appraisal and physiological arousal components of the stress response. Athletes are first trained in voluntary muscle relaxation skills. Because relaxation is incompatible with emotional arousal, it can be used to reduce or prevent high levels of arousal. In addition, participants are helped to identify the negative thoughts and ideas (the cognitive appraisals) that elicit their stress responses and interfere with their concentration and attention (Smith, 1992).

In terms of coping skills, a "mentally tough" athlete is one who is able to think in such a way as to keep emotional arousal within manageable limits so that it does not impair performance. Such an athlete can also keep his or her attention on the task at hand under highly adverse conditions. To increase mental toughness, atheletes inclined to react negatively to stress are taught to replace their self-defeating thoughts with self-statements that prevent stress responses and aid concentration, such as "I can do no more than give my best" and "Don't think about anything except what you have to do." Finally, they are shown how to combine the self-statements and the relaxation into the integrated coping response described in Chapter 15. As the athletes inhale, they say to themselves a stress-reducing self-statement; as they slowly exhale, they say "Relax" and concentrate on inducing relaxation.

Practice is essential in the learning of any skill. To provide opportunities for rehearsal, athletes are asked to imagine stressful situations, are helped to experience the emotional response as fully as possible, and then practice reducing the arousal with the integrated coping response. In this manner, athletes eventually learn to almost instantaneously "turn off" intense emotional responses and return to a level of arousal where they perform best. Another rehearsal approach involves introducing stressful elements into practice sessions. For example, a basketball player

Table 20.2 Behavioral Guidelines for Youth Sport Coaches Derived from the Coach Effectiveness Training Program

The basic guidelines in Coach Effectiveness Training are briefly summarized here.

I. Reactions to Player Behaviors and Game Situations

A. *Good plays and effort*
- **Do:** Reward! Do so immediately. Let the athletes know that you appreciate and value their efforts. Reward effort as much as you do results. Look for positive things, reward them, and you'll see them increase. Remember, whether the children show it or not, the positive things you say and do stick with them.

B. *Mistakes and errors*
- **Do:** Encourage immediately after mistakes. That's when the youngster needs encouragement most. Also give corrective instruction on how to do it right, but always do so in an encouraging manner. Do this by emphasizing not the bad thing that just happened but the good outcome that will occur if the athlete follows your instruction (the "why" of it). This will make the athlete positively self-motivated to correct the mistake rather than negatively motivated to avoid failure and your disapproval.
- **Don't:** Punish when things are going wrong. Punishment isn't just yelling at children; it can be any indication of disapproval, tone of voice, or action. Children respond much better to a positive approach. Fear of failure is reduced if you work to reduce fear of punishment.

C. *Misbehaviors, lack of attention*
- **Do:** Maintain order by establishing clear expectations. Emphasize that during a game, all members of the team are part of the game, even those on the bench. Use reward to strengthen team participation. In other words, try to prevent misbehaviors from occurring by using the positive approach to strengthen good behaviors.
- **Don't:** Get into the position of having to constantly nag or threaten your team to prevent chaos. Don't be a drill sergeant. If an athlete refuses to cooperate, quietly remove him or her from the bench for a period of time.
- **Don't:** Use physical measures (for example, doing pushups or running laps) to punish misbehaviors. Doing so will make these activities aversive for athletes by associating them with punishment, a consequence that is not desirable.

The idea is that if you establish clear behavioral guidelines early and work to build team spirit in achieving them, you can avoid having to repeatedly keep control. Remember, children want clear guidelines and expectations, but they don't want to be regimented. Try to achieve a healthy balance.

II. Getting Positive Things to Happen

- **Do:** Give instruction. Establish your role as a teacher. Try to structure participation as a learning experience in which you're going to help each athlete become the best that he or she is capable of becoming. Always give instruction in a positive fashion. Satisfy your athletes' desire to become the best they can be. Give instruction in a clear, concise manner and, if possible, demonstrate skills along with explaining them.
- **Do:** Give encouragement. Encourage effort, don't demand results. Use encouragement selectively so that it is meaningful. Be supportive without acting like a cheerleader.
- **Do:** Concentrate on the game. Be "in" the game with the players. Set a good example for team unity.
- **Don't:** Give either instruction or encouragement in a sarcastic or degrading manner. Make a point, then leave it. Don't let "encouragement" become irritating to the athletes.

Source: Adapted from Smoll & Smith, 1987.

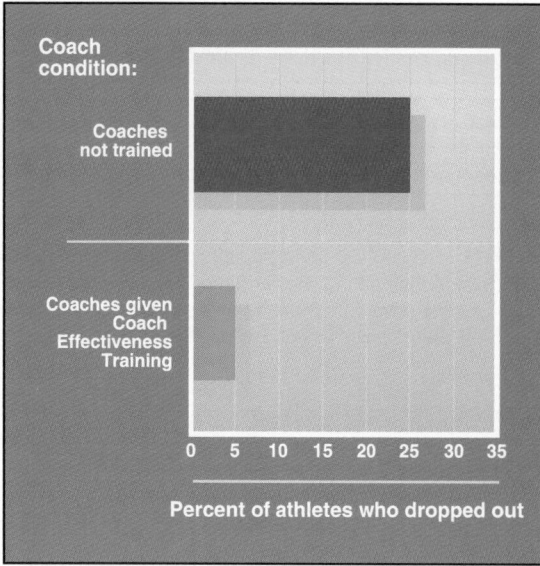

Figure 20.18 *Impact of Coach Effectiveness Training on subsequent dropout rates. Children who were led by trained coaches were far less likely to drop out of organized sports the following year. (Data from Barnett & others, 1992).*

Coach condition:

Coaches not trained

Coaches given Coach Effectiveness Training

Percent of athletes who dropped out

might practice shooting free throws while a tape recording of a screaming crowd is played over loudspeakers and people behind the basket wave their arms and taunt the player. This procedure helps athletes remain focused under stressful conditions.

Coping skills training can be helpful to athletes who have problems coping with stress. College football players who participated in one training program showed significant decreases on measures of pregame anxiety and tension, as well as improved game performance based on coaches' ratings of game films (Smith, 1980). Performance improvement was also shown among elite volleyball players (Crocker & oth-

Figure 20.19 *At all levels, athletes must confront the stresses of athletic competition. Stress management programs are designed to give them the skills to do so successfully.*

ers, 1989). Training in emotional control has become the cornerstone of most psychological skills programs used by sport psychologists (Williams, 1993).

Mental Imagery Techniques

Everyone knows that the most effective way to perfect a skill is through practice. Athletes spend countless hours physically rehearsing their skills. Much interest has arisen concerning the potential value of mental rehearsal of physical responses in the absence of gross muscular movements. Mental rehearsal techniques have been used to improve the performance of skiers, basketball players, gymnasts, and athletes in a variety of other sports (Mahoney, 1989; Murphy, 1992). Many champion athletes have reported using mental rehearsal. Controlled laboratory studies have often, though not always, reported that mental rehearsal improves skills (Landers & Feltz, 1987). Although physical practice is generally more effective, the effects of mental practice on skill improvement are sometimes as great as the effects of an equivalent amount of physical practice (Landers & Pirozzolo, 1991).

Sport psychologists are exploring how and when mental rehearsal techniques can be applied most effectively. For example, *internal imagery,* in which a person focuses on imagined muscle sensations and the visual scene he or she would experience "from the inside," may be more effective than *external imagery,* in which a person takes the perspective of an external observer (Epstein, 1980; Murphy, 1992). It may also be important to tailor the nature and complexity of the imagery to the skill level of the athlete. Imagining the entire sequence of an act may be valuable for the highly skilled athlete, whereas visualizing only one important part of the skilled movement may be more useful for the novice (Noel, 1980). As research on such factors continues to accumulate, mental rehearsal techniques will become more valuable training aids for athletes.

As suggested earlier, the field of sport psychology has attracted numerous psychologists in recent years. Its potential value has also been recognized by college and professional sport organizations. In baseball, for example, only about 5 percent of the athletes who are signed to professional contracts reach the major leagues. For each one who does, the franchise invests about $1.8 million in developmental costs during that player's minor-league career. Realizing that many players fail to reach the big leagues because of psychological factors rather than a lack of physical talent, several organizations, including the Oakland Athletics and the Houston Astros, have incorporated formal psychological skills training into their minor-league player development programs in the hope of helping their athletes maximize their physical talents and increase their chances of reaching the major leagues

(Dorfman, 1990; Smith & Johnson, 1990). These programs have been well received by the athletes, who tend to view the performance-enhancement skills as beneficial. As an example, Table 20.3 shows player ratings of the various components of the Astros' psychological skills program. Similarly positive evaluations have been made of programs offered to U.S. and Canadian Olympic athletes (Murphy, 1990; Orlick, 1989).

Health Psychology: Promoting Healthy Lifestyles

In 1979, the Surgeon General of the United States issued a report entitled *Healthy People* (U.S. Public Health Service, 1979). The report concluded that improvements in the health of Americans were most likely to result from efforts to prevent disease and promote health, rather than from new drugs and medical technologies.

That conclusion is borne out by comparing the leading causes of death in the 1990s with those in 1900. As Figure 20.20 indicates, the leading culprits have changed from influenza, pneumonia, tuberculosis, and gastroenteritis to heart disease, cancer, and strokes. The leading killers of the early 1900s have been largely controlled by medical advances. On the other hand, today's killers are diseases that are strongly influenced by behavioral factors. It is estimated that half the mortality from the 10 leading causes of death can be traced to cigarette smoking, excessive alcohol consumption, insufficient exercise, poor nutrition, use of illicit drugs, failure to adhere to doctors' instructions, and other self-defeating behaviors (National Academy of Sciences, 1982; Taylor, 1991).

Consider, for example, cross-cultural evidence that links a high-fat diet with the incidence of breast cancer in women (Muir & Sasco, 1990; Taylor, 1991). Consistent with findings from animal studies that high-fat diets promote mammary tumors, multicultural studies have shown strong associations between the fat content of the diets of various countries and the incidence of breast cancer. For example, Figure 20.21 compares Japan, where people eat little fat, and the United States, where consumption of fat is extremely high. The role of diet in this relation is supported by findings that Japanese women who have become westernized have shown a dramatic increase in the incidence of breast cancer, whereas those who have adhered to their traditional Japanese diet of fish and rice have not shown this increase (Shimizu & others, 1990). Obviously, dietary habits are behav-

ioral in nature and therefore within the province of psychology.

Recognition of the crucial role of behavior in health maintenance has stimulated the growth of health psychology and its increasing influence on the medical community. The clear need for lifestyle interventions has spurred attempts around the world to

Table 20.3 Psychological Skills Training in Professional Baseball. Anonymous Evaluations of the Usefulness of Skills Taught in the Houston Astros Player Development Program

	Rating			
Procedure	Not helpful	Slightly helpful	Somewhat helpful	Very helpful
Relaxation training	1	3	16	37
Cognitive modification	3	5	17	27
Concentration training	1	3	17	34
Mental rehearsal	1	4	27	20
Goal setting	1	2	17	29

N= 88 professional baseball players.

Source: Smith & Johnson, 1990.

Figure 20.20 *The four leading causes of death in 1900 and 1990. (Data from Sexton, 1979, and the National Center for Health Statistics, 1991).*

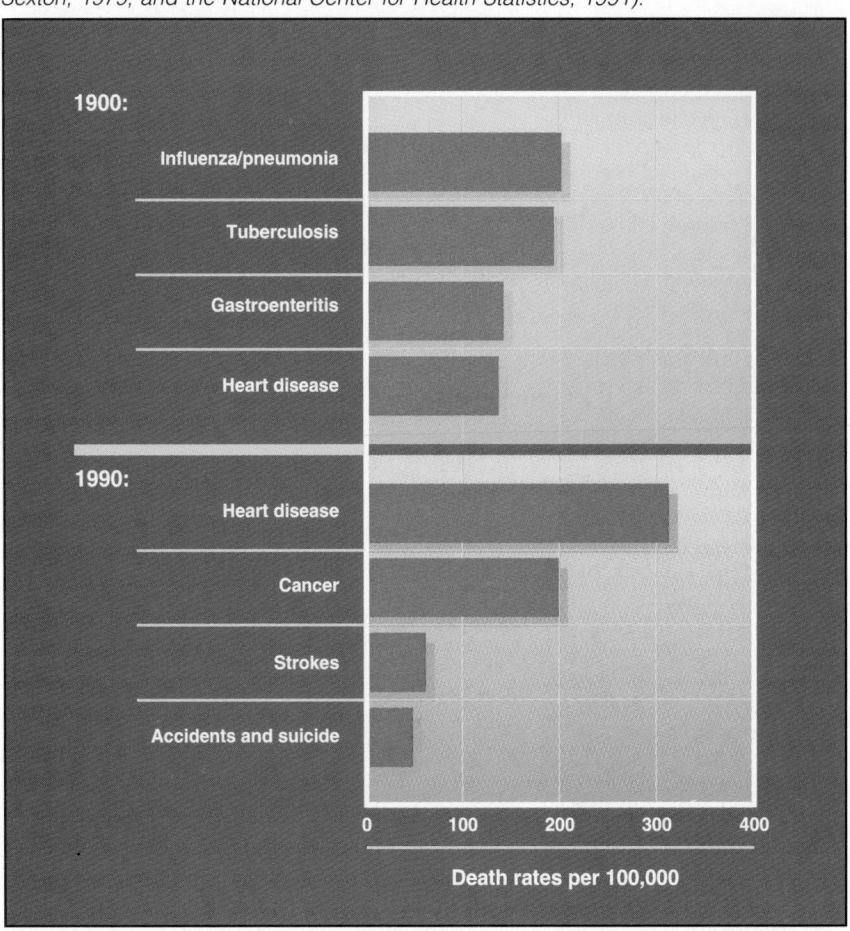

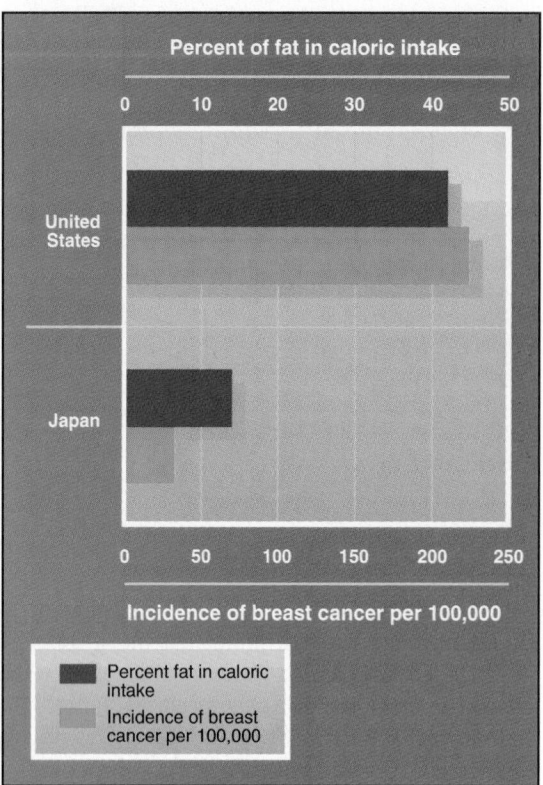

Thinking Critically About Nutritional Claims

A growing emphasis on diet and nutrition has prompted advertisers to emphasize the health-promoting characteristics of their food products. However, as the Center for Science in the Public Interest points out, these claims should be subjected to critical examination. For example, many consumers are unaware that the term *all natural* has no legal meaning. Foods so labeled may contain any number of additives and preservatives. The term *sugar free* refers only to an absence of sucrose, or table sugar. It does not cover glucose, fructose, or sorbitol, which contain just as many calories as sucrose. *Eighty percent lean* means that fully one fifth of the total weight (a significant amount) is fat. Contrary to what advertisers would like consumers to believe, the term *whole wheat* does not mean that the flour is whole grain. Many products carrying this label contain more white flour than the more nutritious whole wheat flour. *Low calorie* means that a food has less than 40 calories per serving and less than 0.4 calories per gram. Ironically, despite its name, Weight Watchers Creamy Italian salad dressing has 100 grams of fat and 100 calories in each two-tablespoon serving. Finally, *enriched* foods are not necessarily nutritious. Such foods have lost nutrients during processing and have had them replaced to some degree (but not necessarily to their preprocessed level). These examples make clear the importance of critical thinking and accurate information in evaluating nutritional claims.

Figure 20.21 *Dietary fat intake and incidence of breast cancer among women aged 45–69 in the United States and Japan. (Data from Muir & Sasco, 1990, and Shimizu & others, 1990).*

promote positive changes in dietary behaviors, exercise, dental practices, alcohol and drug consumption, risky sex practices, and safety behaviors such as the use of automobile seat belts (Stokols, 1992; Taylor, 1991). We now consider two focal areas of this work: exercise promotion and psychology's response to the AIDS crisis.

Exercise

The couch potato lives! (But apparently, not as long.) A sedentary life style is a significant risk factor for a variety of health problems, including coronary heart disease (Rodin & Salovey, 1989; Taylor, 1991). Despite this widely publicized fact, about 70 percent of Americans can be characterized as inactive (Dishman, 1988). As our society has become more sedentary, the effects of reduced exercise have become more apparent. For example, inactivity has helped double the rate of obesity since 1900 despite a 10-percent decrease in daily caloric consumption over the same period (Friedman & DiMatteo, 1989). ▼

Aerobic exercise is sustained activity, such as jogging, swimming, and bicycling, that elevates the heart rate and increases the body's need for oxygen. This kind of exercise has many physiological benefits.

In a well-conditioned person, the heart beats more slowly and efficiently, oxygen is better utilized, cholesterol levels may be reduced, faster adaptation to stressors occurs, and more calories are burned (Dienstbier, 1989; Friedman & DiMatteo, 1989).

Exercise is associated with both physical health and longevity. One study of 15,000 Control Data Corporation employees revealed that those who exercised had 25 percent fewer days of hospitalization than nonexercisers (Anderson & Jose, 1987). Moreover, people who exercise regularly and in moderation live longer. A study that followed 17,000 Harvard undergraduates into middle age revealed that among a group whose members exercised at a moderate level, death rates were one-quarter to one-third lower than the death rates in a less active group. Surprisingly, perhaps, very high levels of exercise were not associated with enhanced health; moderate exercise (burning 2,000 to 3,500 calories per week) on a regular basis produced the best health benefits (Paffenbarger & others, 1986).

Findings like these have inspired interventions designed to promote regular exercise. Typically, these programs have an educational component that provides information on the benefits of regular exercise and the best ways to exercise. They may also include other components of behavior change, such as goal setting, writing explicit contracts that specify an exercise regimen, self-monitoring, and social support. Finally, many programs provide both an exercise program and a setting for implementing it. For example, Johnson & Johnson, the health products company, has a program for employees that includes exercise leaders and on-site exercise, shower, and locker facilities (Nathan, 1984).

Despite the demonstrated benefits of regular exercise, people have a strong tendency to either avoid exercise or discontinue it after a short period. When exercise programs are offered to employees, fewer than 30 percent of them typically elect to participate; and of those who do, fewer than a third continue to be active over a 3-year period (Oldridge, 1984; Taylor, 1991). Drop-out rates of 50 percent within 6 months are quite typical in virtually all exercise programs that have been studied (Dishman, 1988).

What factors predict dropout? As we might anticipate from our discussion of attitude–behavior discrepancies in Chapter 18, attitudes toward physical fitness do not; the attitudes of dropouts are as favorable as those of the people who adhere to their exercise programs. However, low self-efficacy for success in exercising regularly, Type A personality (''Sorry, too busy to exercise''), inflated estimates of current physical fitness, and inactive leisure-time pursuits (such as watching television) all predict dropout (Martin & Dubbert, 1985). The strongest social–environmental factor related to dropout is lack of social support from friends, family, or other exercisers (Feist & Brannon, 1989).

As applied researchers seek the best ways to improve adherence to exercise programs and thereby produce more effective programs, scientific research continues to provide evidence for the benefits of exercise. For example, recent evidence indicates that physical fitness buffers the impact of life stress on physical well-being.

PSYCHOBIOLOGICAL INTERACTIONS

Fitness, Stress, and Health

Chapter 15 introduced the concept of physiological toughness, a pattern of physiological response to stress that reduces the physical wear and tear on the body that can occur when the stress response is intense and prolonged. Dienstbier (1989) suggested that physical exercise might increase physiological toughness and thereby make people more resilient to stress.

As we saw in Chapter 15, life stress places vulnerable people at increased risk for a variety of disorders, ranging from the common cold to coronary heart disease. If fitness increases resiliency to stress, then we ought to find that among people who are experiencing life stress, those who are fit are more likely to stay well.

Several studies suggest that fitness can indeed increase resiliency. For example, Jonathon Brown and Judith Siegel (1988) administered self-report measures of life stress and exercise habits to adolescents. Later, they obtained a report of illnesses experienced since the first assessment. They found that stressful life events were linked to health deterioration among subjects who exercised infrequently but not among those who exercised on a regular basis.

One shortcoming of this study was that the measures of life stress, exercise habits, and illnesses were all self-report measures that could be subject to bias or distortion. Brown (1991b) therefore followed up the first study with another in which both physical fitness and illness were measured in more objective ways. To assess fitness, the researchers had each subject pump an exercise bicycle at maximum force, yielding a measure of aerobic capacity. The subjects also completed a measure of stressful life events. Physical health was defined in terms of number of visits made by each subject to the campus health center over the next 6 months, based on the center's records.

The results of the study, shown in Figure 20.22, supported the role of fitness as a buffer against stress. As in the previous study, life stress was related to illness among subjects who were

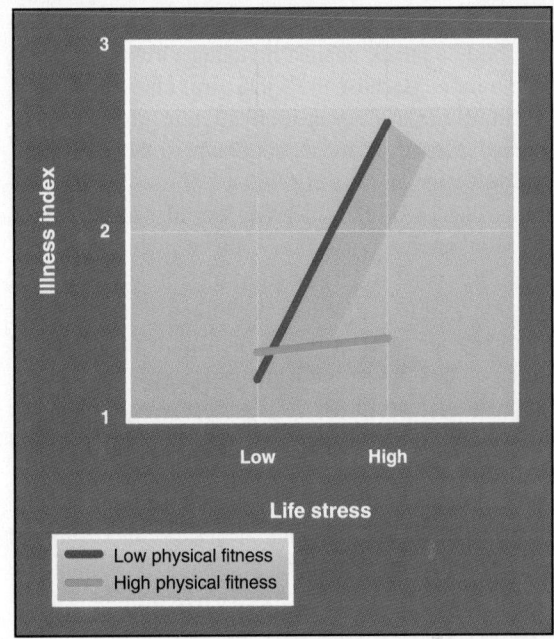

Figure 20.22 *Relation between amount of life stress and illness in physically fit and physically unfit students. No relation between stress and illness is shown in the fit students, indicating that physical fitness is a protective factor against the effects of life stress. (Brown, 1991b).*

low in fitness. In contrast, no relation between stress and illness was found in the physically fit subjects. Those who were physically fit also reported experiencing less psychological distress over the 6-month period.

What are the processes through which fitness increases resiliency to stress? As noted earlier, fitness has positive effects on physiology, making people less biologically reactive to stress. Cognitive factors may also be involved, however. Researchers have found that exercise increases people's general feelings of perceived control, self-efficacy, and mastery, all of which have been shown to increase resiliency to stress (Taylor, 1991). Attentional focus may also be involved, because exercise helps deflect people's attention away from the stressful circumstances of their lives (Brown, 1991b). Exercise is a means of "getting away from it all." Whatever the specific processes involved, it appears that being fit is a state of both mind and body that contributes to staying well, even in the face of stress.

Psychology and the AIDS Crisis

On June 5, 1981, the Centers for Disease Control reported the first case of acquired immune deficiency syndrome (AIDS). In the decade that followed, AIDS grew from an unknown disease into a devastating worldwide epidemic for which there is currently no medical cure. This epidemic threatens to overwhelm our health care delivery and financing systems, our public health structures, and the limits of human compassion.

AIDS is caused by a virus known as the human immunodeficiency virus (HIV). The virus cripples the immune system by killing key cells that coordinate the body's attack against invading viruses, bacteria, and tumors. Because the AIDS virus changes rapidly, vaccines are at present ineffective in preventing its spread. Moreover, the incubation period between initial infection and the appearance of the disease may be as long as 10 years, meaning that an infected person may unknowingly pass the virus to many other people. The major modes of transmission are direct exposure to infected semen and blood through either homosexual or heterosexual contact, the sharing of infected needles in intravenous drug use, and exposure to infected blood through transfusion or in the womb. In 1992, researchers reported evidence that the virus might also be passed on through mothers' milk. Because AIDS is transmitted through specific behaviors, the only existing means of controlling the AIDS epidemic is by changing high-risk behaviors. In this respect, AIDS is as much a psychological problem as a medical one.

Psychologists have been quick to respond to the many aspects of the AIDS epidemic that fall within their areas of expertise. Basic research has focused on the biological mechanisms of AIDS infection, as well as on individual, developmental, social, and community factors that influence high-risk behaviors and their reduction. Basic research findings have been applied in designing prevention programs directed at changing behaviors that result in the spread of the disease (Kelly & others, 1989; Mays & others, 1989). Finally, clinical and counseling psychologists have taken on the formidable task of caring for the mental health needs of potential and actual AIDS victims, their caretakers, and their loved ones.

Prevention Programs

If the AIDS epidemic is to be checked, people must change the behaviors that lead to transmission of the disease. In recent years, principles derived from educational psychology, social psychology, and the psychology of learning have been applied in designing and carrying out prevention programs. Many of these programs have been directed toward the two groups that constitute more than 70 percent of known AIDS cases: homosexual men and intravenous drug users. However, as the disease spreads to heterosexual populations, prevention programs are being directed there as well (Mays & others, 1989). Prevention programs typically are designed to (1) educate people concerning the risks that attend certain behaviors, such as having sex without a condom; (2) provide specific guidelines concerning how these behaviors may be changed; and (3) support and encourage the desired changes.

Some prevention programs have brought about behavioral changes in high-risk groups. For example, in New York City, programs designed to educate drug users about the dangers of sharing hypodermic needles resulted in positive behavior changes (not sharing needles or sterilizing them with bleach) in 54 to 69 percent of the users sampled (Des Jarlais & Friedman, 1988). However, a sizeable proportion of this population remains at high risk.

Similar results have been found in several prevention studies directed at homosexual men. In this high-risk population, a major mechanism of HIV transmission is anal intercourse without use of a condom. In one prevention study (Kelly & St. Lawrence, 1989), 42 homosexual men went through a program that provided them with information on the risks accompanying unprotected intercourse, helped them develop and rehearse strategies for avoiding high-risk situations (such as sexual relations with strangers), and taught them how to be more assertive in refusing to engage in high-risk behaviors such as sexual relations without a condom. A control group of 43 homosexual men did not participate in the program until the first group had completed it. Both groups were assessed before and after the first group went through the program and then were followed for 8 months after completion of the program to assess long-term behavior changes. As shown in Figure 20.23, the program resulted in substantial and lasting changes in the use of condoms during sexual activity, suggesting the potential usefulness of such programs in changing high-risk behaviors. Similar programs are now being directed at the adolescent population, where unprotected heterosexual intercourse is resulting in a surge of new infections (see Figure 20.24).

The effects of psychological intervention programs are not uniformly positive. Research by social psychologists has shown that the success of prevention programs depends in part on the extent to which the individual's social system supports the desired changes. Where the sharing of drug needles is deeply woven into the social fabric of the population or where the use of condoms runs contrary to the values of a given group or individual, people may continue to engage in high-risk behaviors even though they have been informed of the dangers involved (Herdt &

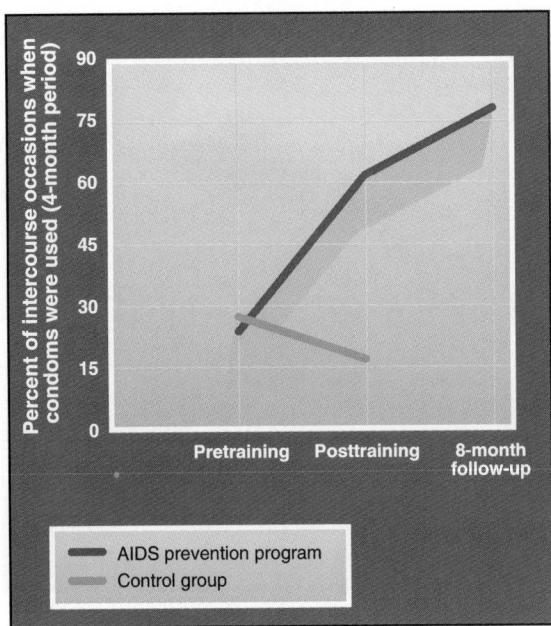

Figure 20.23 *Effects of an AIDS-prevention educational and coping skills program emphasizing condom use among homosexual men. The waiting-list control group eventually received the intervention. (Kelly & St. Lawrence, 1989).*

Figure 20.24 *News that the basketball star Earvin "Magic" Johnson had been infected by HIV was a shocking reminder that AIDS can be transmitted through unprotected heterosexual intercourse. Here, Johnson counsels an audience of young people about the dangers of infection.*

Lindenbaum, 1992). Likewise, within both homosexual and heterosexual populations, and particularly among adolescents and young adults, many individuals continue to have an irrational sense of invulnerability to infection, and this belief contributes to a failure to engage in safe sexual practices (Kelly & others, 1991). Counteracting these barriers to safe sexual behavior is a major challenge for health psychologists.

Clinical Concerns

Mental health needs associated with AIDS have presented a new challenge to clinical and counseling psychologists. The emotional impact of receiving a positive AIDS diagnosis is reflected in the incidence of suicide, which is 36 times higher in males so diagnosed than in the general male population (Marzuk & others, 1988).

Once diagnosed as infected with HIV, a person may well seek professional help for depression or suicidal impulses, grief and loss, family and relationship problems, or issues of impending death. Stress management interventions may be especially helpful to those who are suffering the stress of knowing they have been infected. In one study, a stress management program not only reduced distress among HIV-infected men but also helped reduce their loss of immune functioning (Antoni & others, 1991).

The needs of those who provide professional services to AIDS victims are also receiving attention.

Some clinicians are now working therapeutically with members of their own profession and with other health care professionals who treat AIDS victims, knowing that their fellow helpers are by no means immune to the fear, anger, depression, and emotional exhaustion that can be the fate of those who care enough to counsel AIDS patients.

The AIDS crisis involves complex interactions between body, mind, the environment, and behavior. It demands a response that takes all of these factors into account. As the AIDS epidemic continues to spread in both homosexual and heterosexual populations, new social, political, and economic consequences will emerge as challenges to psychology. In responding to the scientific and social needs that the future will bring, psychology has a unique opportunity to make a difference.

Psychology in a Multicultural Society: Increasing Understanding and Tolerance

Throughout, this book has emphasized the importance of understanding psychological phenomena from a multicultural perspective. As we have seen repeatedly, culture can exert powerful influences on humans' thoughts, motives, feelings, and behavior. This realization has revitalized the field of cross-

▶ **Figure 20.25** *The tragic consequences of multicultural conflict were all too apparent in the 1992 Los Angeles riot, which claimed many lives and resulted in considerable property damage.*

Thinking Critically About "Who I Am"

Try the following exercise: On a sheet of paper, write 20 different statements in response to the question "Who am I?" Respond as if you were giving the answers to yourself rather than someone else, and write your answers in the order they occur to you, without regard to their logic or importance. Please write the answers now, before reading on.

When you have finished, count the number of entries that relate to a social entity, such as your family ("I am a son/daughter"), your religion ("I am a Roman Catholic"), or a group to which you belong ("I am a member of Alpha Cholera fraternity"). Also count the number of entries that relate to individual characteristics (for example, "I am intelligent" or "I am insecure").

This exercise tends to evoke different patterns of response based on the respondent's dominant culture (Brislin, 1988). People from individualistic cultures, such as the United States and Canada, are likely to define their self-identities primarily in terms of individual traits rather than in terms of social groups. In contrast, students who have grown up in collectivist societies, such as Japan and China, are more likely to define their self-identities in terms of the social entities to which they belong. Do your responses conform to this expected pattern?

---

cultural psychology. Indeed, multiculturalism is now being described as a "fourth force" in psychology, the first three having been psychoanalysis, behaviorism, and humanism. As we prepare to enter the twenty-first century, the multicultural nature of our society becomes ever clearer, and diverse cultural groups face the challenge of living harmoniously and productively with one another. Minority populations struggle to retain treasured cultural traditions while at the same time trying to integrate themselves into the dominant culture. ▼

It is clear that we are far from achieving a society that appreciates and tolerates cultural diversity. Racism, prejudice, and discrimination are all too common. The 1992 Los Angeles riots, which left 54 people dead, 2,383 injured, and 5,200 buildings destroyed or seriously damaged, are a grim reminder of the volatile conditions that exist in many urban areas. Most of the victims of the violence in South Central Los Angeles were members of two minority groups, African Americans and Korean Americans, who are struggling to eke out an existence there (see Figure 20.25). Meanwhile, in what was formerly Yugoslavia, a tragic civil war raged in which different cultural groups seemed intent on destroying one another in the name of "ethnic cleansing."

In the United States and Canada, today's crises result in part from the alienation experienced by culturally different individuals and groups. The "melting pot" theory of cultural assimilation seems to have been rejected by both the dominant culture and minority cultures (Locke, 1992). To an increasing extent, the pluralistic nature of our society is being acknowledged and accepted. It is being recognized that methods of dealing with people must take into account the specific needs that spring from the unique char-

acteristics of their own cultural groups. Whether in education, human services, medicine, work settings, or counseling, there can no longer be a single method of interaction based solely on the dominant culture.

Psychology's Potential Contributions

Psychology is in a unique position to contribute to the task of furthering multicultural understanding and tolerance. Understanding cannot possibly occur unless members of diverse cultures know what's on each others' minds, and why. As a research-based science, psychology is in a position to provide scientifically valid information concerning important cultural factors that influence behavior. Ethnic research has provided considerable information concerning the ways in which such factors as cultural background, desire to blend into the dominant culture (degree of acculturation), child-rearing practices, primary values, and other factors influence people in various cultures. These factors may vary widely from culture to culture and can therefore produce striking differences at the level of customary behavior.

One starting point for research on cultural diversity is an analysis of the dominant culture (which, in the United States and Canada, derives largely from Anglo-Saxon themes and values). Although members of a given culture may vary widely in their individual characteristics and may therefore depart in important ways from the typical norms of their cultural group, it is nonetheless possible to identify dominant themes. Several thoughtful analyses of Anglo-Saxon culture have isolated the values and themes shown in Table 20.4 (Locke, 1992; Williams, 1970). As we shall see, minority cultures represented in the United States and Canada differ in important ways from these themes.

A failure to understand the reasons for these differences can breed intolerance and a belief that the members of those groups are deviant or inferior.

Multicultural research can be a challenging enterprise, especially for a person from outside the culture being studied. Such a researcher can answer important questions through discussions with members of the cultural group, direct observations, and participation in the culture itself. In the final analysis, however, this research is probably best conducted by professionals who are members of the cultural groups under study. This is one reason why psychology is a most receptive field for members of minority groups.

In addition to basic research on multicultural issues, psychology has unique contributions to make in applied work aimed at alleviating multicultural problems and encouraging tolerance. Earlier in this chapter, we saw how Sherif's findings on resolving intergroup conflict at Robbers Cave were directly applied to multiracial educational settings in the form of cooperative learning programs. Increased multicultural understanding and tolerance can occur through soundly designed social intervention programs based on psychological principles. As one example, considerable emphasis is now being placed on developing psychologically based programs for teaching educators, medical personnel, police officers, social case workers, counselors, and other professionals from the dominant culture who work with ethnically diverse groups about the cultural backgrounds of those they serve (Locke, 1992; Sue & Sue, 1990). Hopefully, such information will help these professionals more effectively serve members of minority groups. Ethnic awareness programs are also being introduced in elementary schools, high schools, and colleges. Soundly conducted program evaluations can help identify programs that work, as well as the reasons for their effectiveness.

As we saw in Chapter 19, stereotypes, misunderstanding, and prejudice are often based on a lack of realistic information about another group. Let us therefore examine some of the important factors that contribute to the development of ethnic identity and influence the behavior of the members of a given culture. Awareness of such factors would be expected to enhance multicultural understanding and tolerance on the part of those from other cultures.

Understanding the Bases for Cultural Diversity

When immigrants come to another country, they bring with them their own languages, social norms, family structures, child-rearing practices, religious beliefs and practices, and values that characterize their cultures. Once they arrive, they are influenced by the

Table 20.4 Basic Themes and Values of Anglo-Saxon Culture

1. A premium on achievement and success and on "rags to riches" stories.
2. An emphasis on helping others and a traditional sympathy for the underdog.
3. A moral orientation—a concern about what is right and wrong.
4. An emphasis on the practical value of getting things done.
5. A general optimism—a belief that things will get better.
6. Emphasis on the good life and conspicuous consumption.
7. A constant avowal of commitment to equality.
8. A fervent belief in individual freedom and individual responsibility.
9. Esteem for the sciences as a means of mastering the environment.
10. Nationalism and patriotism—strong sense of loyalty to what is "American" (or "Canadian").
11. A strong emphasis on democracy and democratic values.
12. A belief in individual self-actualization—a belief that the group should not take precedence over the individual.
13. Attitudes of racial and ingroup superiority.

Source: Based on Williams, 1970.

environment created by the dominant culture. These two sets of factors can work either together or against each other. The degree to which an immigrant is assimilated into the dominant culture depends both on the immigrant group and on the dominant culture. Sometimes it is the immigrant group that resists acculturation; sometimes it is the dominant group that denies assimilation. In any case, the gap that exists between the dominant culture and the immigrants' culture of origin can create prejudice and intolerance.

Figure 20.26 is based on recent models developed by Locke (1992) and by Sue and Sue (1990) concerning the factors that influence multicultural diversity. As the model suggests, the individual's development is shaped by increasingly larger social entities, beginning with the family and proceeding to the larger social environment of the community and finally to the broader culture which influences both the family and the community.

Transmission of culture occurs first through the family, and important aspects of the culture's values are expressed in child-rearing practices. Let us therefore compare the traditional parenting practices of four minority groups: African Americans, Japanese Americans, Chinese Americans, and Mexican Americans. It is of course important to keep in mind as you read these comparisons that there may be considerable differences within a given culture; we must be careful not to create stereotypes and apply them to all members of a given ethnic group.

In a study of child socialization practices, Allen (1981) found that how African-American parents rear their sons reflects their beliefs that their sons need to learn to be confrontive in a hostile society but also to be selectively agreeable and cooperative. Another researcher concluded that the strict no-nonsense discipline that characterizes many African-American

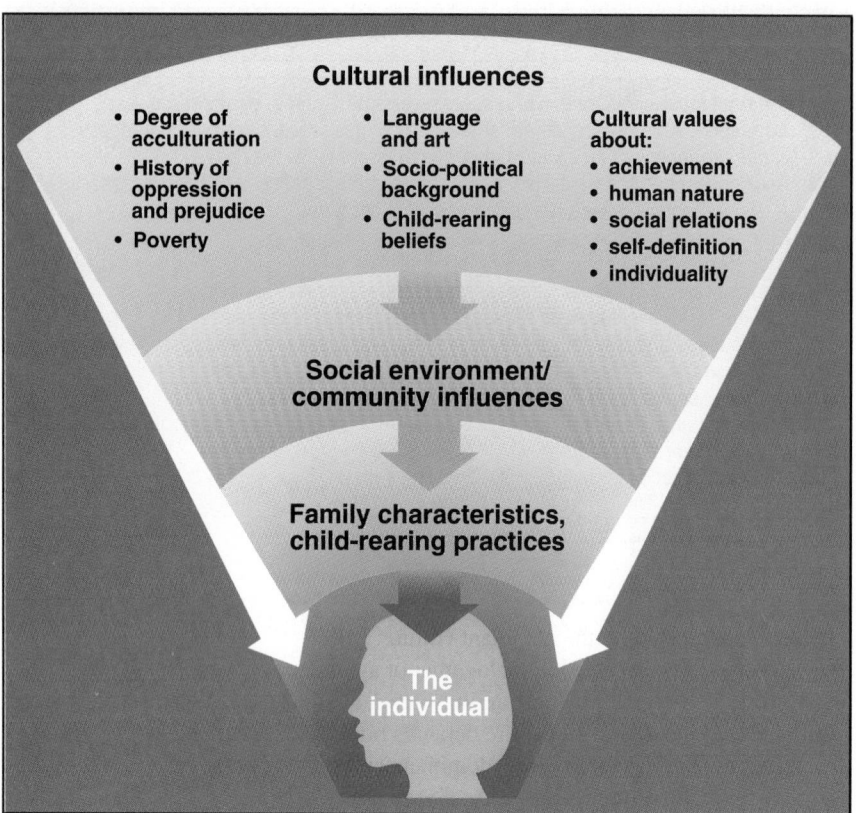

Cultural influences

- Degree of acculturation
- History of oppression and prejudice
- Poverty

- Language and art
- Socio-political background
- Child-rearing beliefs

Cultural values about:
- achievement
- human nature
- social relations
- self-definition
- individuality

Social environment/ community influences

Family characteristics, child-rearing practices

The individual

Figure 20.26 *A model showing important causal factors in multicultural diversity. The prevailing cultural values are transmitted and reinforced by the social environment and the family.*

families helps prepare children for an environment that is covertly, if not overtly, discriminatory against them (Young, 1970). Many research studies challenge the stereotype of the African-American family as matriarchal, showing that fathers take an active role in child rearing and actively support mothers' concerns about the child's successful development (Staples, 1981).

Among Japanese Americans, as in Japan, the mother traditionally has the major responsibility for child rearing (Sue & Sue, 1990). She devotes herself to this task and pushes her children to excel academically. The expression used to describe Japanese mothers is *Kyoiku-Mama,* which translates to "education mommy." In her child-rearing role, the mother reflects the most pervasive values of Japanese society: selflessness, the work ethic, and subservience to the welfare of the group (here, the family). Discipline takes the form of expressing displeasure and appealing to guilt; physical discipline is rarely used. Elders are viewed with great respect, and a strong family system is revered and nurtured. The father's role is less that of a disciplinarian than in almost any Western nation. The child is expected to show nothing less than total respect to the father. The primary obligation of a son is allegiance to his father, even before

his obligation to be a good husband and a good father to his own children.

Among Chinese Americans, the integrity of the family is of utmost importance, and the bond between parent and child is strengthened through genuine affection, the demand for absolute obedience and complete devotion to the parents, and the expectation that, as the child was taken care of by the parents when young, the child will care for the parents when they are old (Sue & Sue, 1990). The avoidance of offending others is emphasized, and family members are expected to suppress feelings that might disrupt family harmony. The behavior of each family member is assumed to reflect on the entire family, and children are expected to behave in a manner that will not embarrass or shame the family. Chinese children tend to be very well behaved, especially in public. Parents use gentle admonishment and encouragement to control their children; to become angry in public would be to "lose face." The primary means by which parents control children is by inducing guilt and shame and appealing to obligation (Sue & Sue, 1990). If children attempt to act independently of their parents' wishes, they are labeled selfish, inconsiderate, and ungrateful. In extreme cases, they may be disowned.

Traditionally, the Mexican-American family is highly child centered while the children are young. Both parents tend to be permissive and indulgent with the younger children, but male children tend to be indulged more than girls (Panitz & others, 1983). Children are assigned tasks according to their age and ability so they will learn responsibility, and their self-esteem is often tied to how well they perform their family responsibilities. A great deal of sex-role training occurs from infancy on, with boys being taught to act more assertively and independently. This trend increases during adolescence; males are given more freedom to come and go as they choose, and females are protected and guarded in their relationships outside the family (Mirande, 1985). In general, less explicit emphasis is placed on academic achievement than in the two Asian groups.

Clearly, the cultural values and child-rearing practices to which members of these four ethnic groups are exposed differ quite markedly, and they may help us to understand some of the personality differences that are likely to be seen among the groups. Again, however, we must remember that within each group, individuals vary. Nonetheless, a greater understanding of the culture of origin can help increase understanding and tolerance.

At a personal level, a greater awareness of your own culture is a good starting point for increased sensitivity to other cultures. Members of a particular culture tend to see their culture as "normal"—as the way people should be. The reality, of course, is that a given culture is only one among many, and every human culture has admirable features that can provide new insights and paths to follow in the enterprise of living.

Multiculturalism encourages people to treat other cultural groups with respect, dignity, and responsibility (see Figure 20.27). If we are to live harmoniously in the pluralistic society of the twenty-first century, a key factor will be the extent to which people from culturally diverse backgrounds can learn to celebrate and value their differences, rather than allowing them to serve as sources of conflict and discrimination. To the extent that psychology as a science and profession can enhance multicultural understanding and tolerance, it will move toward its own goal of promoting human betterment.

■ ■ ■

A Final Word

More than 650 pages ago, we began a journey through the sprawling domain of modern-day psychology. That journey has taken us from the inner recesses of the human mind to the social world in which we spend our lives. We have examined the intricate workings of the brain and the biological processes that underlie our thoughts, feelings, and behaviors. We have achieved greater understanding of the sophisticated cognitive processes that, more than anything else about us, define our humanity. We have also gained insights into the intrapsychic processes that make

Figure 20.27 *The promotion of multicultural understanding and tolerance is a goal to which psychology can contribute in important ways.*

each of us unique. Finally, we have seen how the environment in which we live exerts powerful influences over who we become and how we behave. All of these processes, we have found repeatedly, interact in complex ways to influence our behavior. It is my hope that our shared journey has influenced your conception of human nature, your understanding of yourself and others, and your ability to apply psychological principles and performance enhancement techniques to enrich your life.

S U M M A R Y

Program Evaluation: Designing and Appraising Social Experiments

● Program evaluation is a set of scientific procedures that can be used in both planning and appraising social interventions. In a sense, such interventions can be regarded as experiments; and principles of experimental design can be applied in designing and evaluating interventions.

● School desegregation is an example of a massive social experiment. Evaluation studies indicate rather modest and sometimes negative short-term effects on prejudice and school achievement, but studies of longer term effects are more encouraging.

● Program evaluations have helped to identify some of the reasons why school desegregation programs have not been as successful as anticipated. One factor is the competitive nature of the typical classroom, which often places minorities at a disadvantage. Cooper-

ative learning programs, such as the jigsaw program, are designed to create mutual interdependence rather than competition. These programs have been quite successful in fostering positive interactions among white and minority children and in improving academic achievement by minorities.

Applied Psychology in Business and Industry

● Research has shown that many workers are more highly motivated by intrinsic rewards relating to personal accomplishment and meaningfulness than by extrinsic rewards like money. This has resulted in job enrichment programs designed to make jobs more meaningful. Skill variety, task identity, task significance, autonomy, and performance feedback are factors that increase intrinsic work motivation.

● Programs based on operant conditioning principles make pay contingent on specific indices of job performance. When designed well, such programs result in both increased pay for employees and increased work productivity. Some critics have cautioned that an overemphasis on extrinsic rewards may reduce intrinsic motivation.

● Management by objectives (MBO) incorporates three effective components: systematic goal setting, employee participation in decision making, and systematic performance feedback. MBO programs are highly effective in increasing productivity and satisfaction when top management supports and participates in them.

● Personnel selection procedures generally involve analyzing a job to isolate the traits, abilities, and experiences thought to contribute to job success. Methods for measuring these factors are then developed and tested to determine how well they actually predict job success. In evaluating a selection program, it is important to take into account the organizational and human costs that result from erroneous rejections and erroneous acceptances.

Psychology and the Law

● Psychology is being applied in many areas of the law. Research on eyewitness identification has been applied to improving police lineup and photo spread procedures and in understanding how memory can be biased by the manner in which eyewitnesses are questioned.

● Simulation studies as well as observations of actual juries have allowed psychologists to test hypotheses about decision-making processes in juries. For example, studies have indicated that jurors do not necessarily disregard evidence that is ruled inadmissible.

● Psychologists often appear as expert witnesses in civil and criminal proceedings. They may be called on to make diagnoses and other judgments (for example, in insanity cases). Increasingly, they are also being called on to summarize the results of relevant psychological research on such topics as eyewitness identification, prediction of violence, effects of stress, and bilingual education.

Sport Psychology

● Sport psychology is a growing field. In the area of youth sports, psychologists have studied the effects of adult coaching practices on child athletes and have designed training programs to help coaches create sport environments that promote the psychological growth of children and keep them involved in sport.

● Psychologists have also developed psychological skills training programs designed to enhance performance and reduce the risk of injury. These include stress management and mental imagery programs.

Health Psychology

● Behavior plays a prominent role in health, and health psychologists study the role of behavioral and psychological factors in health and illness. Their applied activities often involve the development of programs to encourage people to pursue healthful behaviors and lifestyles.

● Aerobic exercise has been linked to numerous physical and psychological benefits. Physically fit individuals are more resistant to the negative impact of life stress. Despite the well-known benefits of regular exercise, it is difficult for people to maintain exercise programs, and dropout rates of 50 percent within 6 months are common.

● The AIDS crisis represents a formidable new challenge for psychology. Prevention programs have made inroads into preventing some of the behaviors that increase the risk of AIDS, but many people continue to engage in risky behaviors. Clinical interventions are needed to support AIDS victims, their loved ones, and the persons who care for them.

Psychology in a Multicultural Society: Increasing Understanding and Tolerance

● Through basic research and soundly designed interventions, psychology can make significant contributions to furthering the goal of a multicultural society in which members of diverse ethnic groups live together harmoniously.

● Models of ethnic diversity emphasize the roles played by family environment, the larger social group, and the cultural attitudes and values that are transmitted to members of a given culture. The earliest forms of transmission take place in the family.

KEY TERMS AND CONCEPTS

aerobic exercise (p. 656)
assessment centers (p. 646)
blank-lineup control (p. 648)
cooperative learning program (p. 639)
cut-off score (p. 646)

erroneous acceptance (p. 646)
erroneous rejection (p. 646)
forensic psychology (p. 647)
jigsaw program (p. 640)
job enrichment (p. 642)

job sample (p. 645)
management by objectives (MBO) (p. 643)
mock-witness control (p. 648)
program evaluation (p. 635)
simulation study (p. 649)

SUGGESTED READINGS

Aamodt, M. G. (1991). *Applied industrial/organizational psychology*. Belmont, Calif.: Wadsworth. An interesting and well-written overview of applied programs for increasing productivity and job satisfaction in business and industry. Contains many interesting case examples.

Gregory, W. L., & Burroughs, W. J. (1989). *Introduction to applied psychology*. Glenview, Ill.: Scott Foresman. An interesting overview of applied psychology, including several areas not described in this chapter.

Taylor, S. E. (1991). *Health psychology*. New York: McGraw-Hill. A comprehensive book that describes not only the results of basic research in health psychology but also how this knowledge is being applied to preventing illnesses and enhancing health.

Williams, J. M. (Ed.) (1993) *Applied sport psychology: Personal growth to peak performance* (2nd ed). Palo Alto, Calif.: Mayfield Press. A book containing chapters written by a number of experts in sport psychology. Intended for general audiences, the book describes many aspects of psychological skills training, together with guidelines for enhancing performance.

Statistics in Psychology

■ ▢

A P P E N D I X   O U T L I N E

Descriptive Statistics
  Measures of Central Tendency
  Measures of Variability

The Normal Curve

Statistical Methods for Data Analysis
  A Key Concept: Variance Accounted
    For Correlational Methods

The Correlation Coefficient
Correlation and Prediction
Factor Analysis
Inferential Statistics and Hypothesis Testing

At various points in the text I have briefly described statistical procedures to help you understand the information being presented. This appendix is a more detailed description of statistical methods and focuses primarily on the concepts and reasoning underlying these procedures. Its goal is to help you gain a basic understanding of how psychologists use statistics in their research.

For some students, the prospect of studying statistical procedures initially evokes reactions ranging from disinterest to dread. You will find, however, that you need not be a mathematical genius to grasp the concepts to be presented. In fact, if you can add, subtract, multiply, and divide, you can easily perform basic statistical operations.

Table A.1 Frequency Distribution of Test Anxiety Scores

Test Anxiety Scores	Frequency
30–32	2
27–29	0
24–26	5
21–23	6
18–20	9
15–17	11
12–14	8
9–11	3
6–8	4
3–5	1
0–2	1

a column above each score that shows how frequently the score occurred in the sample of 50 subjects.

Descriptive Statistics

Psychological research often results in a large number of measurements. Data are frequently obtained from many subjects under different experimental conditions, and it is difficult to make much sense out of these data by merely examining the individual scores of the subjects. **Descriptive statistics** allow us to summarize and describe the characteristics of sets, or **distributions,** of scores.

A first step in summarizing a set of scores is to construct a **frequency distribution.** A frequency distribution will show us at a glance how many subjects received each score as well as certain characteristics of the distribution, such as whether there are more high or low scores, whether scores tend to cluster in one region of the distribution or are scattered throughout the distribution, and so on.

Table A.1 shows a frequency distribution of the scores obtained by 50 subjects on a 32-item measure of test anxiety. The frequency distribution tells us that 2 subjects had scores of 30, 31, or 32; none had scores of 27, 28, or 29; 11 had scores of 15, 16, or 17, and so on. Note that the researcher chose to use *intervals* of 3 points (for example, 30–32) rather than to show the number, or frequency, of subjects who obtained each of the 33 possible scores (zero to 32). She could have done the latter if she had wished to break down the scores even further. The number of intervals chosen is somewhat arbitrary, but most frequency distributions seen in the literature contain 10 to 12 categories.

Methods of graphing can give us a pictorial representation of our data. Figure A.1 shows a **histogram** of the test anxiety scores. In a histogram, the scores (in this case, score intervals) are plotted along the horizontal axis, or *abscissa,* while the frequencies are plotted on the vertical axis, or *ordinate.* The result is

Measures of Central Tendency

Frequency distributions and histograms give us a general picture of how scores are distributed. **Measures of central tendency** allow us to describe a distribution in terms of a single score that is in some way typical of the subject sample as a whole. There are three commonly used measures of central tendency—the mode, the mean, and the median.

To illustrate the statistical properties and the methods of computation of these three measures of central tendency, we will examine the salaries of 10 employees of Honest Al's Savings and Loan Corporation, as shown in Table A.2. Our task is to arrive at a single number that somehow typifies the salaries of the group as a whole.

The **mode** is defined as the most frequently occurring score in a distribution. At Honest Al's, the modal salary is $105,000, since it is the only salary received by more than one person. (In a distribution in which no score occurs more than once, there is no mode.) While the mode is easy to identify in a distribution, it is not always the most representative score, particularly if it falls far from the center of the distribution. Clearly, $105,000 is not the "typical" salary of the 10 employees, since 8 of them receive $10,000 or less.

The **mean** is probably the most popular measure of central tendency. It is the arithmetic average, obtained by adding up all the scores and dividing by the number of scores. The statistical formula for computing the mean is as follows:

$$M = \frac{\Sigma X}{N}$$

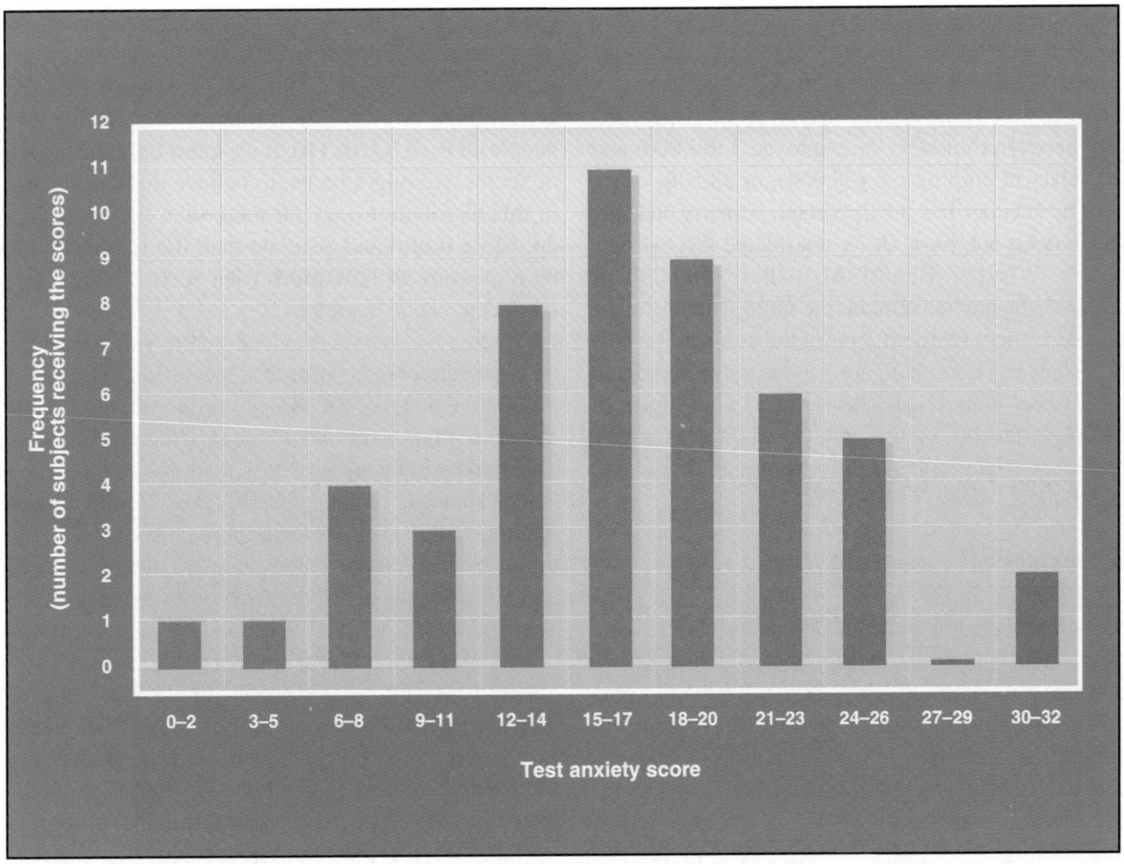

Figure A.1 *Frequency histogram of the test anxiety distribution shown in Table A.1.*

M is the symbol for the mean of the individual scores (X). The Greek letter Σ (sigma) means "the sum," and N denotes the number of scores. To compute the mean of the salaries at Honest Al's, we simply add up the individual salaries, and divide the total by 10, the number of salaries. As shown in Table A.2, the mean salary at Honest Al's is $27,350.

Would you be tempted to go to work for Honest Al upon hearing that "our average salary is $27,350 per year"? Is that figure really representative of the company's salaries? Your negative answer to this question illustrates one of the shortcomings of the mean as a measure of central tendency. The mean can be strongly affected by one or more extremely high or low scores that are not representative of the group as a whole. In this case, the high salaries of Honest Al and his mother raise the mean to a figure nearly three times as great as the salary of the next-highest-paid employee. Thus, in this instance, we cannot consider the mean to be representative of the salaries of Al's employees.

Our third measure of central tendency, the **median,** is defined as that point which divides the distribution in half when the scores are arranged in order from lowest to highest. Exactly half of the scores lie above the median and half below it. If there is an odd number of scores, there will be one score that is exactly in the middle. If there were 11 salaries in Table A.2, the 6th-ranked score would be the median, since

Table A.2 Statistical Properties and Computation of the Mode, Mean, and Median of the Annual Salaries of 10 Employees

Employee	Annual Salary (X)
(1) Honest Al	$105,000
(2) Honest Al's mother	105,000
(3) Johnson	10,000
(4) Thompson	9,500
(5) Jones	9,000
(6) Quiggly	8,000
(7) Brown	7,500
(8) Carter	7,000
(9) Mullins	6,500
(10) Watson	6,000

$N = 10$ $\Sigma = \$273,500$

Mode = The score that occurs most often—in this case, $105,000.

Mean = The arithmetic average, computed by the following formula:

$$M = \frac{\Sigma X}{N} = \frac{273,500}{10} = \$27,350$$

Median = The point above and below which there is an equal number of scores. In this case, because there is an even number of scores, the median is midway between the 5th- and 6th-ranked salaries—that is, $8,500.

STATISTICS IN PSYCHOLOGY **A-3**

five scores would fall above it and five below. In distributions having an even number of scores, the median is halfway between the two middle scores. In our salary distribution, the median is the point halfway between the salary of employee 5 ($9,000) and the salary of employee 6 ($8,000), or $8,500.

The median has an important property that the mean does not have: It is unaffected by extreme scores. Whether Honest Al makes $500,000 or $11,000, the median remains the same. Therefore, the median is more representative of the group as a whole in instances where there are very extreme scores. In the case of Honest Al's firm, the median figure of $8,500 is far more representative of the "average" employee's salary than is the mean figure of $27,370 or the modal salary of $105,000.

Measures of Variability

Measures of central tendency provide us with a single score that typifies the distribution. But in order to describe a distribution adequately, we need to know more. One critical question concerns the amount of variability, or scatter, among scores. Do the scores tend to cluster about the mean, or do they vary widely? **Measures of variability** provide us with answers to this question.

The quickest, but least informative, measure of variability is the **range.** The range is simply the difference between the highest and the lowest score in a distribution. If, in a distribution of 20 IQ scores, the highest IQ is 160 and the lowest is 70, then the range is 90 ($160 - 70 = 90$). But suppose the other 18 people all have IQs of 110. If we knew only the range of scores, we might be led to believe that the scores in this distribution vary far more than they actually do. More useful and accurate than the range would be a measure of how much each score varies from the mean *on the average.*

Such a measure is provided by the **variance** and its close relative, the **standard deviation.** The variance is the mean of the squared differences between each individual score and the mean of the distribution. The standard deviation is the square root of the variance. These definitions probably sound quite intimidating, so let's analyze them more closely by showing how the variance and standard deviation are computed for the distribution of scores in Table A.3.

First we take each score (X) and subtract the mean of the distribution (M) from it. In this manner, we obtain the *deviation,* or distance, of each score from the group mean. The deviation, $X - M$, is represented by a lowercase x. Having obtained the deviation for each score, we next square these deviations and add them up. We then divide by the total number of scores (in this case, 10) to obtain the mean of the squared deviation scores. This is the variance (s^2). The reason we square the deviation scores is to eliminate their

Table A.3 Computation of the Variance and Standard Deviation for Two Distributions of Scores with Identical Means ($M = 10$)

Distribution A			Distribution B		
X (score)	$X - M = x$	x^2	X (score)	$X - M = x$	x^2
12	+2	4	18	+8	64
12	+2	4	18	+8	64
11	+1	1	15	+5	25
11	+1	1	15	+5	25
10	0	0	10	0	0
10	0	0	10	0	0
9	−1	1	5	−5	25
9	−1	1	5	−5	25
8	−2	4	2	−8	64
8	−2	4	2	−8	64
$\Sigma X = 100$	$\Sigma x = 0$	$\Sigma x^2 = 20$	$\Sigma X = 100$	$\Sigma x = 0$	$\Sigma x^2 = 356$
$N = 10$			$N = 10$		
$M = 10.00$			$M = 10.00$		

x (deviation) $= X - M$

s^2 (variance) $= \dfrac{\Sigma x^2}{N} = \dfrac{20}{10} = 2.00$ $\qquad\qquad s^2 = \dfrac{\Sigma x^2}{N} = \dfrac{356}{10} = 35.6$

SD (standard deviation) $= \sqrt{2.00} = 1.414$ $\qquad\qquad SD = \sqrt{35.6} = 5.967$

positive and negative signs. If we simply summed the *x*s, the positive and negative values would always cancel each other out, resulting in $\Sigma x = 0$. We are interested in the *average* deviation of the scores from the mean without regard to direction above or below the mean.

Once we have obtained the variance, we can easily obtain the standard deviation (*SD*) by taking the square root of the variance. Since we squared the deviation scores to compute the variance, we can now get back to the original scale of measurement by taking the square root of the variance. Psychologists tend to prefer the standard deviation over the variance as a measure of variability because the *SD* is expressed in the same unit of measurement as the original (raw) data.

Besides showing how the variance and standard deviation are calculated, Table A.3 illustrates how these measures of variability provide us with important descriptive information. Note that distribution A and distribution B have an identical mean of 10. However, it is clear that there is more variability in B than in A. In fact, calculation of the standard deviations for the two sets of scores shows that the average deviation from the mean of distribution B is more than four times greater than the average deviation from the mean of distribution A.

The Normal Curve

One type of distribution of particular importance in statistics is the **normal curve.** In this bell-shaped, symmetrical curve, 50 percent of the cases fall on each side of the mean. The median and the mode have exactly the same value as the mean. As we move away from the mean, the number of scores steadily decreases. As noted in Chapter 2, the normal curve is important because so many phenomena—weight, height, IQ, and anxiety, to name a few—are distributed in the population in this fashion.

The normal curve is a statistician's delight because it has certain specific and very important properties. Of greatest importance is the fact that in a normal distribution, the standard deviation can be used to divide the distribution into areas containing known percentages of the total sample.

Figure A.2 shows a normal curve and illustrates its statistical properties. In a normal curve, nearly all of the cases fall between 3 standard deviations above and 3 standard deviations below the mean. If we know that a characteristic is normally distributed (as many are), then we can use the statistical properties of the normal curve to deduce more information about the

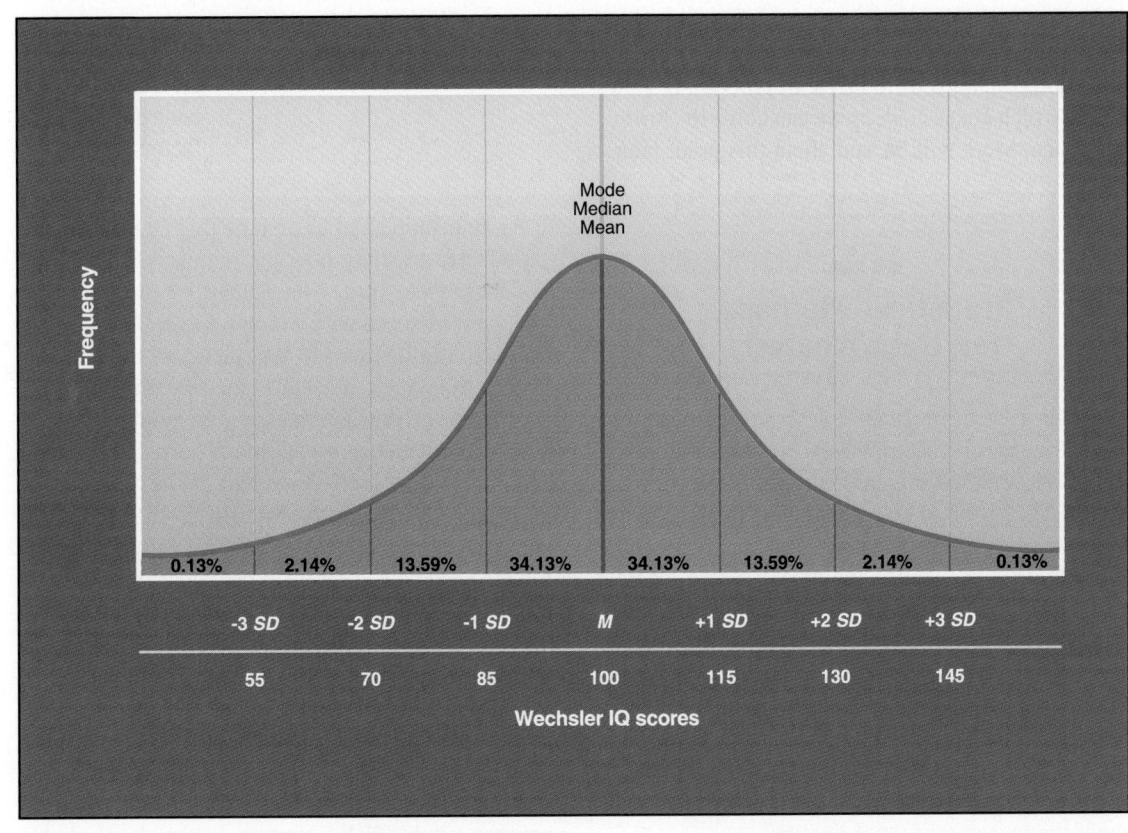

Figure A.2 *The normal curve, showing the percentage of cases falling within each area of the normal distribution and Wechsler IQ scores corresponding to standard deviation (SD) units.*

characteristic. For example, IQ scores as measured by the Wechsler tests (see Chapter 11) are normally distributed, with a mean of 100 and a standard deviation of 15. Knowing this, we can use our knowledge of the normal curve to answer questions like these:

1. What percentage of people have IQs below 115? (Approximately 84 percent—the 50 percent having IQs below 100 plus the 34 percent having IQs between 100 and 115, which is one standard deviation above the mean.)
2. What percentage of people have IQs between 70 and 130? (Approximately 95 percent. These scores are -2 and $+2$ SD from the mean. This area of the curve includes $13.59 + 34.13 + 34.13 + 13.59$ percent of the cases, or 95.44 percent.)
3. What is the probability that a person selected at random from the population will have an IQ of 145 or more? (Approximately one-tenth of 1 percent. The probability corresponds to the area under the curve beyond $+3$ SD, which includes 0.13 percent of the cases.)

The last example points to an important use of the normal curve. We can use it to make probability statements—that is, to estimate the likelihood that a given event will occur. Indeed, the statistical tests described next are methods for arriving at probability statements based on the assumption that the phenomena being investigated are normally distributed. Thus, the normal curve not only mirrors reality in many cases but also helps us to arrive at probability statements, which are as close as we can come to "truth" in science. More will be said about this point later.

■ ▢
Statistical Methods
for Data Analysis

As we have seen, we can use descriptive statistics to summarize the characteristics of sets of data. But psychologists want to do more than simply describe behavior. They want to be able to understand behavior and its causes. From a scientific point of view, the only way to understand behavior is to determine how it is *related* to other things. In psychology, then, scientific understanding involves establishing exactly how a behavioral phenomenon is related to other behaviors, to the characteristics of individuals, and to environmental events. All of the statistical methods described in this section are methods for measuring relations among variables and for drawing inferences about the meaning of those relations.

A Key Concept:
Variance Accounted For

Behavior varies. It varies between individuals, and it varies for the same individual over time. Why does such variation occur? This question is the reason we have a science of psychology. The psychologist's goal is to explain variations in behavior, or **behavioral variance.** For example, an experimenter often wants to know how much of the variation observed in a given behavior—the dependent variable—can be accounted for by differences in some other variable or set of variables—the independent variable. Note that we are now using the term *variance* in a general sense, to refer to total variation, rather than in reference to the specific statistical measure of variation described earlier.

Because the concept of **variance accounted for** is a key one in understanding the rationale for statistical tests, let us look at it more closely. In any research study, the total amount of variation in a behavior or characteristic can be divided into two components: (1) the amount of variance that can be attributed to differences in the independent variables that we have measured or manipulated and (2) the amount of variance that is left over and cannot be accounted for in terms of the factors we have manipulated.

Total variance =	Variance accounted for (due to independent variables)	+	Variance not accounted for (due to random, unmeasured, or uncontrolled factors)

As an example, let us assume that an experiment is conducted to study how the number of other bystanders present (none, one other, or three others) influences the speed with which subjects go to the aid of a person in distress. In this instance, the number of other bystanders present is the experimental (independent) variable and the speed of helping (in seconds) is the dependent variable. The results of this experiment show that 20 percent of the variance in the speed with which subjects help another person in distress can be accounted for in terms of the number of other bystanders present. This means that the experimental, or independent, variable (the number of other bystanders) accounts for one fifth of the total variance in speed of helping. This is shown schematically in Figure A.3. The other 80 percent of the helping variance (the unshaded portion of the circle) is due to other factors that were not controlled in the experiment. Some of this 80 percent is simply **error variance** produced by random factors beyond the control of the experimenter. For example, some subjects may have been tired or preoccupied with personal problems and may thus have responded more slowly than they would have otherwise. The rest of the unexplained variance is the result of factors that *do* systematically affect speed of helping but that the experimenter either does not know about or did not control for in the experimental design. Such variables may include personality characteristics; sex of subject, victim, and other bystanders; nature of the emergency; and so forth. As other independent variables are added in future experiments, the experimenter should be able to increase the size of the shaded area in Figure A.3 by increasing the amount of variance accounted for.

Viewed from this perspective, understanding behavior involves isolating factors that account for behavioral variance. We judge how important a particular variable is by how highly it is related to the behavior of interest and how much variance it helps us account for. As scientific research proceeds, the goal is to discover new variables that account for additional portions of the total variance. To be sure, we can never completely eliminate the random factors that produce error variance. But generally speaking, the more variance we are able to account for, the more understanding we have of the behavior in question.

Correlational Methods

As noted earlier, understanding is achieved in science through identification of relations among events. When variables are related to one another, they are said to *covary*, or vary together in some systematic fashion whereby changes in one variable are associated with changes in the other. The varying together of two sets of measures is known as **correlation.**

This section describes three statistical techniques that assess relations among variables. The **correlation coefficient** provides the psychologist with a numerical index of the strength and direction of the relation between two variables. Another technique, a more complex application of correlational analysis, is *factor analysis.* Factor analysis allows us to reduce a large number of measures to a smaller number of factors—clusters of variables that are highly correlated with one another—and thereby to identify underlying dimensions or variables.

The Correlation Coefficient

Relations among variables can differ in terms of the *direction* of the relation and the *magnitude* of the relation. To illustrate, we will examine the relations shown in the five sets of X and Y scores in Table A.4. In each set, we have a score on variable X and a score

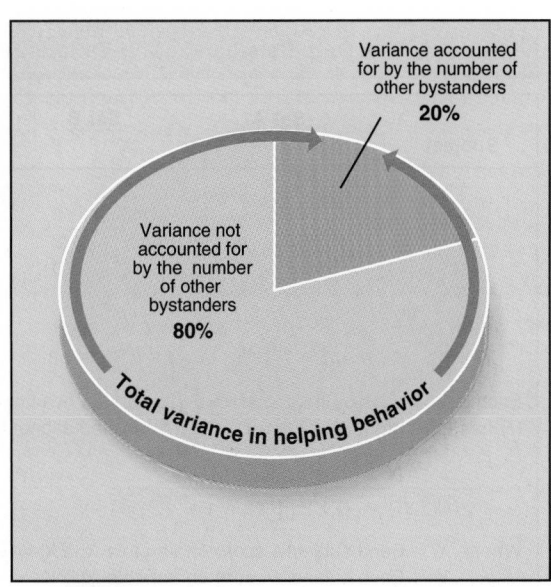

Variance accounted for by the number of other bystanders
20%

Variance not accounted for by the number of other bystanders
80%

Total variance in helping behavior

◀ **Figure A.3** *The total amount of variation in the dependent variable (speed of responding to a person in distress) is represented within the circle. The total variance may be divided into the portion accounted for by the experimental (independent) variable (number of other bystanders) and the larger portion not accounted for by the independent variable.*

on variable Y for each of six individuals. Of interest is the manner in which X and Y scores are related to one another.

In set A, the relation is positive in direction. That is, high scores on variable X are associated with high scores on Y, and low scores on X are associated with low scores on Y. The opposite direction of relation is seen in set E. Here, there is a perfect inverse ordering of scores on X and Y; low scores on X are associated with high Y scores, and vice versa. Thus, in set E, we have a negative relation between X and Y. In set C, the X and Y scores show no tendency to covary in either a positive or a negative direction. They show a zero relation; they are not correlated. Thus, in sets A, C, and E, we see three different types of relations—positive, none (zero), and negative.

The second way in which relations vary is in magnitude, or strength. To illustrate differences in magnitude, let us compare set A with set B and set D with set E. In set A, the Xs and Ys have the same rank order; there is a perfect positive relation. In set B, individuals having high X scores tend to have high Y scores, but the ordering is not as perfect as in set A. In other words, the positive relation is not as strong in magnitude. Likewise, in set D, there is an overall negative relation between X and Y scores, but the magnitude of the relation is less than the perfect negative relation that exists in set E.

Is it possible to be more precise about the magnitude of relations in the sets of measures in Table A.4? There is a statistic, the **product–moment correlation coefficient,** that provides us with a precise numerical index of the direction and magnitude of the relation between two variables.

The product–moment correlation coefficient (designated r) can range in magnitude from − 1.00 to

	Set A		Set B		Set C		Set D		Set E	
Subject	X	Y	X	Y	X	Y	X	Y	X	Y
1	1	2	1	4	1	4	1	6	1	8
2	2	4	2	5	2	8	2	8	2	6
3	3	5	3	2	3	5	3	10	3	5
4	4	6	4	10	4	2	4	4	4	4
5	5	8	5	6	5	6	5	2	5	2
6	6	10	6	8	6	6	6	1	6	1
$N = 6$	$r = +1.00$		$r = +.58$		$r = +.02$		$r = -.75$		$r = -1.00$	

Table A.4 Five Data Sets Illustrating Various Relations That May Exist Between Two Variables

Each set consists of the scores of 6 subjects on two variables, X and Y. The product–moment correlation coefficient (r) has been computed for each set. The computational formula for r is as follows:

$$r = \frac{N\,(\Sigma X_i Y_i) - (\Sigma X_i)\,(\Sigma Y_i)}{\sqrt{[N(\Sigma X_i^2) - (\Sigma X_i)^2]\,[N(\Sigma Y_i^2) - (\Sigma Y_i)^2]}}$$

Where X_i = Each subject's score on variable X; ΣX_i = sum of Xs
Y_i = Each subject's score on variable Y; ΣY_i = sum of Ys
N = Total number of subjects

+1.00. If $r = -1.00$, there is a perfect negative relation between X and Y scores, as in set E of Table A.4. A correlation coefficient of +1.00 signifies a perfect relation, as in set A. Correlations close to 0.00 indicate that there is no systematic relation between the variables, as in set C.

In psychological research, a correlation of −1.00 or +1.00 is very rare, since psychological variables tend to be imperfectly correlated with one another. More typically, correlation coefficients resemble those in sets B ($r = +.58$) and D ($r = -.75$). An important point to remember is that it is the *magnitude,* or size, of the correlation coefficient and not its sign (direction) that indicates how strongly two variables are related to one another. Thus, X and Y are more strongly related in set D ($r = -.75$) than in set B ($r = +.58$), even though the correlation is a negative one in set D.

The correlation coefficient has one very important and useful property that is pertinent to the researcher's goal of accounting for variance. If the product–moment correlation coefficient (the type of coefficient most frequently used) is squared, the squared coefficient (r^2) indicates the amount of variance that the two variables share, or have in common. Stated another way, r^2 tells us how much of the variance in one measure can be accounted for by differences in the other measure. For example, suppose that a correlation of +.50 is obtained between scores on a mechanical aptitude test and grades in an engineering course. Squaring the correlation coefficient—$(.50)^2 = .25$—tells us that 25 percent of the total variance in course grades can be accounted for by differences in mechanical aptitude scores, and vice

versa. The relationship is illustrated in Figure A.4. The more highly two variables are correlated (either positively or negatively), the more common variance they share.

At this point, it is important to note a fact discussed in Chapter 2—namely, that a correlation between two variables does not allow us to conclude that one caused the other. We know only that they are related to one another. If variables A and B are correlated, it is possible that A causes B, that B causes A, or that both A and B are caused by some other variable, C. We cannot infer causality from correlation. If this point is not entirely clear, you may wish to refer to Chapter 2 for a fuller discussion of the issue. (See also Chapter 15, page 475).

Correlation and Prediction

We have seen that correlation coefficients provide us with information concerning the strength and direction of the relation between two variables and give us the basis for determining how much variance is shared by the variables. Correlation coefficients have still another function. They can help us to make predictions. If two variables are highly correlated with one another and we know an individual's score on one variable, then we can predict his or her score on the other variable. The more highly the variables are correlated, the more accurate our predictions will be. In statistical prediction based on correlation, we are thus taking advantage of lawful relations among variables to predict to the individual case.

There are many practical applications for predictions based on correlational analysis. In industry, for

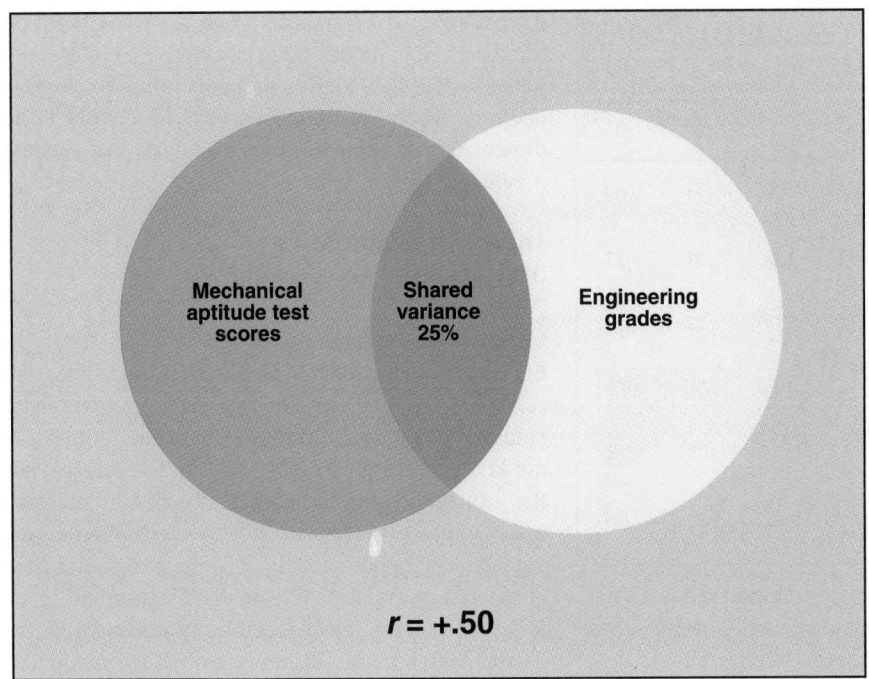

Mechanical
aptitude test
scores

Shared
variance
25%

Engineering
grades

$r = +.50$

Figure A.4 *Squaring the correlation coefficient provides an estimate of the amount of variance shared by two variables. In this instance, r = .50, indicating that 25 percent of the variance in engineering grades can be accounted for by individual differences in mechanical aptitude in this sample.*

example, on-the-job performance is often found to be correlated with scores on various aptitude tests. Personnel managers can therefore use these test scores to predict which of their applicants are most likely to perform well. The more highly the test scores, or **predictor variables,** are correlated with job performance, the more useful is their contribution to accurate prediction.

Factor Analysis

Another important correlational technique is **factor analysis.** The technique provides a tool for reducing a large number of measures to a smaller number of clusters on the basis of correlations among the original measures. Just as chemists can analyze complex chemical compounds to discover the basic elements they consist of, psychologists can use factor analysis to identify the basic dimensions that underlie a large number of measures and to account for the relations among them.

Factor analysis is a highly complex statistical procedure, and we need not be concerned here with its mathematical basis. Our interest is in how psychologists use it as a research tool. As an example, psychologists have long been interested in determining what basic mental abilities people possess. How many are there? Are there hundreds, or are there perhaps only a few basic abilities involved in the performance of many different tasks? What is the nature of these abilities?

Let us assume that, to answer questions like these, a psychologist administers 40 different and varied

tests to a large number of subjects and correlates all of the test scores with one another. She reasons that tests that correlate highly with one another are probably measuring the same underlying ability because the underlying ability that enables people to do well on one such test probably also enables them to do well on the others. Further, if there are groups or clusters consisting of tests that correlate highly with one another but are not correlated with tests in other clusters, then these test clusters probably reflect the operation of different and distinct mental abilities. Thus, from her table of correlations, the psychologist hopes to determine how many test clusters exist and what the clusters reveal about the nature of the underlying abilities.

When each of the 40 test scores is correlated with the other 39 scores, our psychologist will have 1,560 (40 × 39) separate correlation coefficients. She will need to work with only half of the total, because each correlation is repeated (for example, the correlation between variable 1 and 2 is the same as that between 2 and 1). That still leaves 780 correlations. Now, obviously, trying to determine by visual examination which tests cluster together by virtue of their correlation with one another (and lack of correlation with other tests) is a hopelessly complex task with this large number of correlations. In instances like this, factor analysis comes to the rescue, for it is one of the most powerful methods for reducing variable complexity to greater simplicity. In less than a minute, a modern computer can analyze the table of correlations and perform a factor analysis that will tell the psychologist which tests or measures form distinct

Table A.5 Intercorrelations Among Six Ability Tests

Test	1	2	3	4	5	6
1	1.00	.84	.71	.04	.11	-.07
2		1.00	.79	.12	.01	.00
3			1.00	-.05	.12	.08
4				1.00	.69	.74
5					1.00	.92
6						1.00

groupings. The underlying, or unobserved, variables (abilities, in this case) that presumably underlie these groupings are called **factors.**

A highly simplified example illustrates the kind of clustering that we are interested in. Assume that Table A.5 shows the correlations among 6 of the 40 measures. Such a table is called a *correlation matrix.* Since the bottom of the matrix will contain the same correlations as the top, we need concern ourselves only with the upper half, as shown. The correlation coefficients of 1.00 along the diagonal of the matrix reflect the fact that, of course, each variable correlates perfectly with itself.

Examination of Table A.5 indicates the presence of two clear clusters of tests that correlate highly with one another. Test 1 correlates .84 with test 2 and .71 with test 3, while test 2 correlates .79 with test 3. Likewise, test 4 correlates .69 with test 5 and .74 with test 6, while tests 5 and 6 correlate .92. Note also that tests 1, 2, and 3 have very low correlations with tests 4, 5, and 6. This indicates that these two sets of tests are measuring different things. We have thus determined that there are two different factors.

But what are these two groups of tests measuring? This question cannot be answered by the factor analysis. The analysis can only identify the clusters for us. It is up to the psychologist to decide what the underlying factors might be by examining the nature of the tests in each cluster. Suppose, for example, that test 1 measures vocabulary, test 2 measures the ability to construct words out of groups of random letters, and test 3 requires subjects to complete sentences having missing words. Since all of these tasks involve the use of words, the psychologist might decide to call the underlying factor "verbal ability." What she calls the factor is up to her; some other psychologist might decide that a better name for the factor would be "word fluency." The important thing is that we

have reduced six variables to two variables based on the correlations among them and have arrived at some idea of what the underlying factors might be. In psychology, where we frequently wish to identify basic dimensions of behavior, factor analysis has become a valuable tool.

Inferential Statistics and Hypothesis Testing

Correlational research is one way in which we try to understand behaviors by determining what they are related to. Another way of assessing relations is by studying behavioral differences between groups that are known to differ in some way. In some instances, the groups differ in terms of a subject variable such as sex, high versus low anxiety, or schizophrenic versus nonschizophrenic status. These groups are then compared on some behavior that is assumed to be affected by the subject variable. In other cases, the experimenter creates different groups by manipulating some experimental variable. For example, in a study of aggression, subjects may be randomly assigned to one of two groups. One group (the experimental group) is frustrated in some way, while the other group (the control group) is not. Differences in subsequent aggression by the two groups are then measured to determine whether frustration is related to aggression.

In experiments like these, we are typically interested in overall differences between the groups. The question we usually ask is whether the means of the two groups differ enough for us to conclude that the independent and dependent variables are truly related to one another. Methods known as **inferential statistics** allow us to draw conclusions and test hypotheses by telling us how likely it is that observed differences between groups reflect a "real" difference between the groups.

If we have observed a difference, why do we need to ask whether the difference is "real" or not? The reason is that our observations are based on only a sample of people drawn from a larger population. In most instances, of course, researchers do not have access to the entire population of interest (for example, to all schizophrenics and all nonschizophrenic people). They must be satisfied with studying a relatively small sample of subjects. On the basis of results obtained from their samples, they want to generalize to the population as a whole. But do they know that the same difference would occur if they tested every member of the population? Perhaps, for one reason or another, the groups tested were not truly representative of the populations from which they were drawn, and the differences observed were the result of chance alone.

Inferential statistics provide a means of determining how much confidence researchers can have in results obtained from samples by telling them exactly how likely it is that the results occurred by chance alone. In actual practice, they (or their computers) need only perform a series of statistical computations and then consult special tables that tell them the precise likelihood that the differences in their samples do *not* reflect corresponding differences in the populations from which the samples were drawn. This probability is called the **level of statistical significance.** Psychologists typically consider results to be statistically significant only if they could have occurred by chance alone less than 5 times in 100.

The logic underlying tests of statistical significance is related to the earlier discussion of the normal curve and its statistical properties. Recall the following problem, presented earlier in the appendix: If IQ is normally distributed, with a mean of 100 and a standard deviation of 15, what is the likelihood of randomly selecting from the population a person with an IQ of 145 or more? To answer that question, all we had to do was determine what proportion of cases are 3 standard deviations above the mean in a normal distribution. We found that proportion to be about one tenth of 1 percent. Thus, we would expect to randomly select a person with an IQ that high about once in 1,000 times—pretty small odds. With this example in mind, let us consider the logic of statistical inference in greater detail.

Suppose we are interested in the effects of a stress management program on the academic performance of freshman college students who are high in test anxiety. We hypothesize that learning to control anxiety during tests will result in better performance. We randomly assign 40 students who have received high scores on a self-report measure of test anxiety to either an experimental group of 20 subjects who will participate in a stress management program for test anxiety or a control group that will receive no guidance or treatment. All of the students take the same required courses; and at the end of the academic year, we compare the mean grade-point averages of the two groups. We find that the experimental group, which went through the training program, obtains a mean grade point of 3.17 (A = 4.0), whereas the control group has a mean grade point of 2.61. How can we now decide whether the grade-point difference in the two samples reflects a difference in the respective populations (that is, all test-anxious students who might participate in a stress management program and all who do not)?

Suppose we repeated our experiment many times with different samples of high-anxiety subjects. If we did, we would surely find that the means for the two samples would vary in each experiment. The next

time we performed the study, the means might be 2.94 (experimental) and 2.77 (control); the next time, 3.34 and 2.31; the next time 2.89 and 2.83; and so on. Since each of the means would vary with each study, the differences between the means of the experimental and control groups would vary, too. By repeating the experiment a great many times, we could actually create a distribution of mean differences between experimental and control groups, and mathematical theory tells us that this distribution would be a *normal* distribution.

This, then, gives us the key. Because we have a normal distribution, we can assess the likelihood of randomly obtaining any particular difference between our sample means, just as we could arrive at the exact likelihood of randomly selecting a person with an IQ of 145, 92, or 71. But in order to do this, we must know what the mean and standard deviation of our distribution of differences are. One way to determine these values would be to perform our experiment a large number of times. But, fortunately, we can estimate these values on the basis of a single experiment. Here's how it works.

If there were no real difference in grade point between the populations of trained and untrained test-anxious students, and if we repeated our experiment a great many times, then we would expect the average difference between the experimental and control group means to be around zero and to take the form of a normal distribution. The standard deviation of this normal distribution can be estimated from the standard deviations of the two samples, although the mathematics need not concern us here.

Statistical analysis involves testing the **null hypothesis,** which assumes that the difference between two population means is zero and that any observed difference between samples is due to chance. In our hypothetical experiment, we obtained grade-point means of 3.17 for the experimental group and 2.61 for the controls, a difference of +0.51. Let us now suppose that the standard deviation of our distribution of differences between means was estimated on the basis of our samples to be .25. Thus, our obtained difference is slightly more than 2 *SD* above the mean (0) of the null hypothesis distribution. From the properties of the normal curve, we know that more than 95 percent of the cases fall in the area of the curve between −2 *SD* and +2 *SD*. Thus, if the null hypothesis were true, we would expect a difference in means as large as .51 (in either direction from the mean) less than 5 percent of the time on the basis of chance factors. This is another way of saying that our level of statistical significance is less than .05. In view of this fact, we would probably reject the null hypothesis and conclude that there is a real difference in grade point in the two populations. Thus, our experimental hypothesis that the stress management program would result in a higher level of academic performance would be supported. Note that we use the term *supported,* not proven, because we are making an inference based on a probability statement. There is, after all, a 5 percent chance that the null hypothesis is true.

This is one reason why repeating, or replicating, research studies is so valuable. If another study also yields statistically significant results, we can have more confidence that the difference we obtained reflects a real relation between the independent variable (stress management training) and the dependent variable (academic performance). But no matter how many times we repeat the experiment, we can never escape from the world of probability into the world of absolute truth.

SUMMARY

Descriptive Statistics
• Descriptive statistics allow us to summarize and describe the characteristics of whole sets, or distributions, of data. A frequency distribution shows how many subjects received each score and indicates the pattern of scores. Histograms are pictorial representations of frequency distributions.
• Measures of central tendency—the mode, the mean, and the median—describe a distribution in terms of a single score that is typical of the sample as a whole. The mode is the most frequently occurring score in a distribution. The mean is the arithmetic average, while the median is the point that divides the distribution in half. The median is less affected by extreme scores than is the mean.
• Measures of variability tell us how much variation there is among scores. The differences between the highest and the lowest scores in the distribution is the range. The variance and the standard deviation are the most useful measures of variability. The variance is the mean of the squared differences between each score and the mean of the distribution. The standard deviation is the square root of the variance.

The Normal Curve
• A normal curve is a symmetrical, bell-shaped curve. Fifty percent of the cases fall on each side of the mean. The mean, median, and mode all have the same value. The standard deviation can be used to divide the distribution into areas containing known percentages of the total sample. Probability statements are based on the assumption that the phenomena being studied are distributed normally in the population.

Variance Accounted For
• A major goal of psychological research is to determine how much behavioral variance can be accounted for by relations between variables, including experimental manipulations, and how much is due to random, unmeasured, or uncontrolled factors. Random factors that are beyond the experimenter's control produce error variance.

Correlational Methods
• In science, understanding is achieved through the identification of relations among events. Variables that are related covary in some systematic fashion; covariation in two groups of measures is called correlation.
• The correlation coefficient is a numerical index of the direction and magnitude of the relation between two variables. Correlations may be positive, negative, or zero, as well as weak or strong.
• Squaring the correlation coefficient tells us how much of the variance in one measure can be accounted for by differences in the other measure. Although correlation does not allow us to assume causality, correlations are often the basis for predictions.
• Factor analysis allows us to use correlations to reduce a large number of measures to a smaller number of clusters in which the measures are highly correlated with one another and presumably measure the same psychological dimension. Factor analysis only identifies the clusters; the researcher must infer the nature of the underlying factors.

Inferential Statistics and Hypothesis Testing
• Inferential statistics allow us to draw conclusions and test hypotheses because they tell us how likely it is that differences between groups or correlations among variables are the result of chance alone. Inferential statistics are needed because most research is done with samples, and conclusions must be generalized to the population from which the samples were drawn.
• The probability that relations shown among variables do not reflect corresponding relations in the population is called the level of statistical significance. Statistical analysis involves testing the null hypothesis, which assumes that any observed relation is due to chance, or that the difference between the two population means is zero. Inferential statistics yield probability statements, not proof.

KEY TERMS AND CONCEPTS

behavioral variance (p. A-6)
correlation (p. A-7)
correlation coefficient (p. A-7)
descriptive statistics (p. A-2)
distribution (p. A-2)
error variance (p. A-6)
factor (p. A-10)
factor analysis (p. A-9)
frequency distribution (p. A-2)

histogram (p. A-2)
inferential statistics (p. A-10)
level of statistical significance (p. A-11)
mean (p. A-2)
measure of central tendency (p. A-2)
measure of variability (p. A-4)
median (p. A-3)
mode (p. A-2)
normal curve (p. A-5)

null hypothesis (p. A-11)
predictor variable (p. A-9)
product–moment correlation
   coefficient (p. A-7)
range (p. A-4)
standard deviation (p. A-4)
variance (p. A-4)
variance accounted for (p. A-6)

Kerlinger, F. N. (1979). *Behavioral research: A conceptual approach.* New York: Holt, Rinehart and Winston. An excellent introduction to research design and methods with clear, nonmathematical explanations of statistical techniques.

Kimble, G. (1978). *How to use (and misuse) statistics.* Englewood Cliffs, N.J.: Prentice-Hall. A brief text on statistical methods written especially for people with a limited background in mathematics; it includes many practical examples of the use of statistics in psychology.

Pagano, R. R. (1990). *Understanding statistics in the behavioral sciences* (3rd ed.). St. Paul: West. An extremely readable text that covers statistical concepts and methods of computation of commonly used statistical techniques, along with many practice problems; more mathematical than the Kerlinger and Kimble books.

B A User's Guide to the Literature in Psychology

APPENDIX OUTLINE

Reviewing the Psychological Literature
Annual Review of Psychology
Psychological Abstracts and *Thesaurus of Psychological Index Terms*

Social Sciences Citation Index (SSCI)
Books in Print and *PsycBOOKS*
Current Contents

Computer Searches

Psychology is a dynamic, fast-changing science of great breadth. Its lifeblood is a constant flow of new theoretical developments, scientific findings, and applications of psychological principles. Advances in all of these areas are to be found in a voluminous psychological literature that includes some 2,000 periodicals worldwide and up to 1,000 new books each year.

Whether you wish to pursue some topic that has aroused your interest during your reading of this book, complete a term paper on a psychological topic, or review what is currently known about a topic as a beginning step in conducting scientific research of your own, you will find your ability to systematically use the psychological literature an indispensable tool. Many resources are available to you. This appendix will discuss methods and resources that can give you quicker and more effective access to the psychological literature.

Reviewing the Psychological Literature

If you are interested in reviewing the literature on a topic discussed in this text, you may find the citations in this book to be a useful starting point. I have tried to make the book as current and up-to-date as possible, and fully one quarter of the literature cited here is from the 1990s. In general, it is best to start with the most recent works you can find, for the references cited in that article, book chapter, or book will steer you to earlier work on the topic.

Your campus library offers many resources for gathering information about psychological topics. These range from reference materials, journals, and books to computerized systems that can give you access to tremendous amounts of information in minutes. Here are some of the resources that can be particularly useful.

Annual Review of Psychology

Published each year, the *Annual Review of Psychology* contains approximately 20 review chapters on various topics written by eminent psychologists who work in the topic areas. The topics may be as broad as ''Personality: Structure and Assessment'' or as specific as ''The Psychobiology of Reinforcers.'' Both these chapters appeared in the 1992 volume. Each chapter reviews the major developments in the topic area over the past several years and typically contains several hundred recent citations. The authors highlight critical issues, areas needing more research,

and future directions for research. The *Annual Review* can give you a comprehensive overview of an area if it has been covered in a recent edition.

Psychological Abstracts and Thesaurus of Psychological Index Terms

Psychological Abstracts is probably the most widely used resource. The *Abstracts* provide brief summaries of articles from hundreds of journals, as well as doctoral dissertations. The *Abstracts* are published in soft-cover form each month and are typically bound together in hard-cover form at the end of each year by your library. For example, all of the issues published in 1993 comprise Volume 80.

The mass of information in the *Abstracts* is organized in such a way that relevant works can easily be found. Two indexing systems are used to help readers locate relevant articles. First, articles are indexed by topic. Second, they are indexed by author. The topic and author indexes are bound separately. Thus, to search the bound Volume 79 for articles (typically 1991 articles) abstracted in 1992, look for the hard-bound *Subject Index* and *Author Index*. (In the soft-bound issues from the current year, these indexes will be found in each issue.) The topic index will give you the numbers of the abstracts relating to that term. For example, if you looked up the topic *aggression* and found the numbers 6074, 6082, and 8934, you would look up these numbers in the *Abstracts*. The abstracts in each volume are numbered consecutively.

A valuable companion to the topic index is the *Thesaurus of Psychological Index Terms*. The *Thesaurus* is a hierarchically structured vocabulary of approximately 4,750 subject, or index, terms. It can be used to verify and expand the terminology of your search, telling you what other terms your topic might be listed under. Table B.1 shows some of the entries listed under the broad topic *interpersonal interaction*.

The author index of the *Abstracts* can be useful if you know the name of an author who works in the topic area you are interested in. For example, if you are interested in developments in the social cognitive approach to personality, it would be a good idea to look up authors like Albert Bandura, Robert Wood, and Daniel Cervone, who are major contributors to the theory. Often, the abstracts found through the topic index will help you identify authors who work in that topic area.

Each entry in *Psychological Abstracts* will provide you with the author's name and affiliation, the title of the article, the volume and page numbers of the journal where the article can be found, and a 150-word summary of the article. A sample abstract is

Table B.1 An Example of a Topical Category and Its Subcategories in the *Thesaurus of Psychological Index Terms.*

Interpersonal Interaction

Arguments
Assistance
Bargaining
Charitable behavior
Collective behavior
Conflict
Conversation
Cooperation
Double bind interaction
Employee interaction
Eye contact
Friendship
Group discussion
Group participation
Group performance
Interpersonal attraction
Interpersonal communication
Interpersonal incompatibility
Interpersonal influences
Interviewing
Interviews
Job applicant interviews
Male–female relations
Negotiation
Participation
Peer relations
Persecution
Rivalry
Sharing
Social dating
Stranger reactions
Violence
Affection
Codependency intimacy
Popularity
Retaliation

Source: Thesaurus of Psychological Index Terms, pp. 110–111.

shown in Figure B.1. Once you locate the articles of interest, you can go to the original sources and examine their reference lists for earlier articles.

Social Sciences Citation Index (SSCI)

The *Social Sciences Citation Index (SSCI),* published in several volumes each year, gives you three different ways to find references: by topic, by author, and by other authors who have referred to an article of interest. The *SSCI* consists of three separate but related indexes: a topic index called the *Permuterm Subject Index,* an author index called the *Source Index,* and the *Citation Index.*

The *Permuterm Subject Index* will give you the names of authors who published works on the par-

ticular topic during the year in question. You can then look up those authors' names in the *Source Index* to find out where the works were published. Finally, if you know of a particular article on the topic that was published in the past, you can look up that article in the *Citation Index* and find the names of all the authors who cited that article in their work. If they cited it, chances are they have also published on the topic, and you can look up their names in the *Source Index* to locate those more recent references.

Books in Print and PsycBOOKS

Two useful sources that can help you locate relevant books are *Books in Print* and *PsycBOOKS. Books in Print,* which can be found in your library's reference area, contains the titles and authors of every book currently being sold by any publisher. You can look up books by topic or by author. Many libraries have a computerized version of *Books in Print.*

An especially useful guide to the psychological literature is *PsycBOOKS,* which can help you find not only books on the topic of interest but also relevant chapters in edited books.

Current Contents

Current Contents is a periodical that reproduces the tables of contents of a wide range of scientific journals in all the behavioral sciences, including psychology, psychiatry, and sociology. By examining the contents of journals that are relevant to your area of interest, you can gain access to the very latest publications on that topic. In contrast to the reference sources already discussed, which are typically 6 to 12 months behind the publication dates of the articles they cite or abstract, *Current Contents* reproduces the most recent tables of contents of the journals it covers. Thus, *Current Contents* can help keep you on the cutting edge of developments in your area of interest.

As mentioned, a great many psychological journals are covered in *Current Contents.* Table B.2 lists some of the major journals, classifying them in terms of the major topic areas covered in this book.

Computer Searches

The quickest and most efficient way to locate references is to do a computer search. There are two types of searches: on-line searches and cd-rom searches.

On-line searches involve using a computer terminal to gain access to records stored on a central computer at some other location. Your library may

19861. **Mauro, Robert; Sato, Kaori & Tucker, John.** (U Oregon, Eugene) **The role of appraisal in human emotions: A cross-cultural study.** *Journal of Personality & Social Psychology,* 1992(Feb),Vol 62(2), 301-317. —Several theories of emotion propose that emotional responses are largely determined by the way events are appraised. To determine whether the proposed dimensions of appraisal are consistent across cultures, 973 Ss from the US, Japan, Hong Kong, and the People's Republic of China were asked to describe emotional experiences. Few differences between the 3 cultures were observed on the more primitive dimensions (pleasantness, attentional activity, certainty, coping ability, and goal/need conduciveness) and on 2 of the more cognitively complex dimensions (legitimacy and norm/self compatibility). More substantial differences were observed on 3 other complex dimensions (control, responsibility, and anticipated effort). Considerable pan-cultural consistency was also observed in the dimensions of subjective experience of emotion and in the relations between these dimensions and cognitive appraisals.
—*Journal abstract.*

Figure B.1 *A sample entry from the* Psychological Abstracts *(June 1992, p. 2399).*

Table B.2 Selected Psychological Journals

Articles of General Interest	Personality
American Psychologist	*Journal of Personality*
Psychological Science	*Journal of Personality and Social Psychology*
Theoretical and Review Articles	*Journal of Research in Personality*
Psychological Review	*Personality and Social Psychology Bulletin*
Psychological Bulletin	Abnormal Psychology
Contemporary Psychology (book reviews)	*Journal of Abnormal Psychology*
Physiological Psychology	*Archives of General Psychiatry*
Behavioral Neuroscience	*Journal of Nervous and Mental Diseases*
Journal of Neuroscience	*Clinical Psychology Review*
Psychophysiology	Treatment of Psychological Disorders
Neuroscience and Biobehavioral Reviews	*Journal of Consulting and Clinical Psychology*
Psychopharmacology	*Behavior Therapy*
Developmental Psychology	*Cognitive Therapy and Research*
Developmental Psychology	Social Psychology
Child Development	*Journal of Personality and Social Psychology*
Psychology and Aging	*Personality and Social Psychology Bulletin*
Sensation and Perception	*Journal of Experimental Social Psychology*
Journal of Experimental Psychology: Human Perception and Performance	*Journal of Applied Social Psychology*
Perception and Psychophysics	Industrial–Organizational Psychology
Vision Research	*Journal of Applied Psychology*
Learning and Cognition	*Personnel Psychology*
Journal of Experimental Psychology: General	*Journal of Consumer Research*
Journal of Experimental Psychology: Learning, Memory, and Cognition	*Human Factors*
Cognitive Psychology	Health Psychology
Memory and Cognition	*Health Psychology*
Journal of Applied Behavior Analysis	*Journal of Health and Social Behavior*
Motivation and Emotion	*Journal of Behavioral Medicine*
Addictive Behaviors	Sport Psychology
Journal of Personality and Social Psychology	*Journal of Sport and Exercise Psychology*
Motivation and Emotion	*Journal of Applied Sport Psychology*
Archives of Sexual Behavior	*The Sport Psychologist*
Anxiety Research	
International Journal of Eating Disorders	

have access to databases such as *PsycINFO, MEDLINE,* and *ERIC. PsycINFO,* produced by the American Psychological Association, is essentially a computerized version of the *Psychological Abstracts.* When you access an on-line database such as *PsycINFO,* your library (or you) will be charged for the amount of time you spend searching the system. You can electronically "tag" certain abstracts or references and have them printed out in your library. If you own a modem, you can access giant databases like *PsycINFO* from your own home.

Disk-based systems using cd-rom are a recent advance in computerized search systems. Rather than connecting with a computer at some distant site, you use a microcomputer equipped with a cd-rom disk drive to read databases on disk. The most popular cd-rom database for psychology is *PsycLIT. PsycLIT* is a computerized version of *Psychological Abstracts;* both are produced by the American Psychological Association. *PsycLIT* contains citations and abstracts of the world's psychology literature from 1974 to the present. Abstracts from more than 1,300 journals and more than 50 countries appear on the system. The same classification system used in the *Psychological Abstracts* is used in *PsycLIT.* Any of the 4,750 subject terms used to index all articles can be used to locate relevant material. On average, five to six index terms are applied to each article.

It might take hours to search the *Psychological Abstracts* or the *Social Sciences Citation Index* to find the articles you need, but a computer search can condense that time into minutes. All you need to do is enter the index terms you are interested in. In a few

seconds, the computer will search the huge database and select all relevant citations and abstracts. You can then view each abstract, select the ones you are interested in, and print out the abstracts, as well as complete citation information about the articles.

One of the great benefits of a computer search is that you can cross-reference several terms to "home in" on the relevant articles. For example, if you are interested in locating all of the articles published since 1988 that deal with the effects of alcohol ingestion on moral decision making in adolescents, you can ask the computer to select only those articles with a publication date of 1988 or later that contain the index terms *alcohol, moral reasoning,* and *adolescents.* Were you to conduct the same search in the *Psychological Abstracts,* you would have to search through all of the abstracts on alcohol to find the few that dealt with moral reasoning by adolescents.

Computer searches can help you locate not only relevant journal articles but also pertinent books and book chapters. As early as possible in your academic career, you owe it to yourself to learn to use these marvels of the computer age. Your on-campus reference library can provide you with instruction in doing computer searches.

The psychological literature is a vast one, but there are many resources available to help you find the information you need. Learning how to use these resources can save you a great deal of time and effort while ensuring that your information search will be successful and comprehensive.

Careers In Psychology

■ ▢

Psychology is at once a discipline, a science, and a profession. First, it is a discipline, an important topic of study in colleges and universities. It is also a science, a set of methods for conducting research and understanding behavior and its causes. Finally, it is a profession that requires an individual to apply special knowledge and skills in order to solve human problems.

As a career, psychology offers a panorama of varied opportunities. The psychologists you are most likely to encounter function as teachers and perhaps researchers, working in universities, colleges, and high schools. As researchers, psychologists are also employed in government, business, and the military to do basic and applied work. Many other psychologists work as service providers and administrators in mental health clinics, nonprofit organizations, government agencies, hospitals, universities, and businesses. Finally, psychologists with special expertise serve as consultants; they are hired by organizations to evaluate problems and suggest solutions. For example, a consulting psychologist may work with an educational system to devise new ways of improving children's learning and mental health, or she may consult with industry to design an employee evaluation or job enrichment program.

Many psychologists perform more than one of these roles, making for a varied vocational life. For example, I am presently occupying the roles of teacher, researcher, administrator, and consultant. Thus, in addition to my teaching at the University of Washington, I have an active research program in the areas of stress, coping, and performance enhancement. As an administrator, I function as the head of our Social Psychology and Personality Program. As a consultant, I direct a performance enhancement program for a major league baseball organization. I also provide sport psychology consultation to my university's athletic department. I find this range of activities very stimulating, and I can't imagine a profession that I would enjoy more.

As a result of your introductory psychology course (and, hopefully, this book), you may be interested in exploring a possible career in psychology. This Appendix briefly describes the career options available in psychology and the educational background required to perform various functions. It also provides some advice on how to prepare yourself for possible advanced study in psychology.

▬ ▭

Employment Opportunities in Psychology

Chapter 1 (page 6) of this text provided a brief description of the various specialty areas within psychology (Table 1.1) and described the settings in which psychologists work (Figure 1.4). These many specialty areas accommodate people with widely varying interests. For example, you may be interested in working directly with people to help them overcome problems in living. If so, then a career in clinical or counseling psychology may be of interest to you. In either of these fields, you would also have opportunities to do research on the causes and remediation of such problems. On the other hand, you may be more interested in pursuing answers to research questions on topics such as the functioning of the brain, child development, social behavior, learning and memory, or sensation and perception. You will find specialty areas in psychology that deal with all of these topics. As you explore psychology in greater depth, you may find that one or more of its specialty areas conform to your interest pattern. Whether you're interested in human services, education, high technology, management, sports, or any of numerous other fields, you are likely to find psychologists working in that field. A common denominator in the activities of all psychologists is their interest in human or animal behavior and their desire to have a challenging and personally fulfilling career.

Understandably, anyone considering a career wants to know what the employment opportunities are and what kinds of salaries are available. Where salaries are concerned, it is difficult to make any general statement because of the great variety of employment settings in which psychologists work. In addition, salaries are also determined by years of experience, level of expertise and productivity, and amount of advanced training in the field. Nonetheless, some general, or ''ball park,'' figures can be estimated. For example, a new Ph.D. (Doctor of Philosophy) who is hired as a faculty member at a major research institution may begin at a salary of around $40,000 a year for a 9- to 10-month contract (with another 20–22 percent added for summer teaching or summer salary from a research grant or contract). A full professor with 15 to 20 years' experience who is a prominent researcher might well double that salary. Applied psychologists who work in industry probably average about $60,000 a year, while clinical psychologists who offer direct human services probably average $45,000 to $50,000 a year, with some in private practice earning considerably more.

What is the job market like in psychology? The downturn in the economy in the early 1990s has dampened an academic job market that was expected to improve dramatically with projected increases in college enrollments and retirement of current faculty. As a result, the next several years will remain a period of keen competition for faculty positions in academia. In contrast, good opportunities continue to exist in nonacademic settings, such as full-time independent practice and business and industry. Opportunities for psychologists in the public sector may also grow, particularly if federal, state, and local funding is increased for health maintenance and illness prevention and for psychological services to special populations such as the aged and the disadvantaged. I would expect that psychologists with doctoral degrees in clinical, counseling, industrial/organizational, cognitive psychology, and health psychology will have especially good employment opportunities. Moreover, opportunities in all settings, including academic ones, should show notable increases if the economy improves over the next five to seven years.

Training in Psychology

Obviously, many employment possibilities exist for which a degree in psychology is extremely useful. To make an informed vocational choice involving psychology, you must not only evaluate the extent to which your interests and abilities match the various job opportunities but also decide how many years you are willing to commit to your education. Although the doctoral degree is recognized as the basic credential in the profession of psychology, stimulating career opportunities in many different fields are open to students with an education in psychology at the bachelor's and master's level.

Planning a career is rarely a simple, logical, or orderly process. Indeed, many people change their career choices a number of times. Nonetheless, the early college years are a good time to take courses in fields that may interest you and to explore these vocational possibilities personally through volunteer work and part-time jobs. Doing so will help you to focus on vocations that seem right for you in an informed fashion.

Career Options with Bachelor's and Master's Degrees

A bachelor's degree in psychology will not prepare you to become a professional psychologist. However, an undergraduate major can lay a foundation for entry-level employment in business and other settings, particularly if the work in psychology is combined with courses in economics, marketing, or general business. A combination of psychology and education courses could prepare a student to teach psychology in a high school or to work with special populations, such as those with mental disabilities. People in a wide variety of vocations have found that a psychology major proves very useful to them in their work, particularly if their jobs involve working with people. Likewise, many undergraduate students

who are preparing for advanced study in medicine, law, physical therapy, rehabilitation, and other professions choose psychology as a major.

The next degree beyond the bachelor's degree is the master's degree. A master's degree typically involves two years of graduate school training. People with master's degrees in psychology can work in a variety of settings, including community mental health centers, public and private institutions, and schools and businesses. However, career advancement in most areas is limited without the doctoral degree, and individuals with master's degrees often work under the supervision of a doctoral-level psychologist. A master's degree will usually not enable one to obtain a permanent position in a four-year college or a university, and most states will not license individuals with only a master's degree to provide independent psychological services. Nonetheless, such professionals can work in a variety of applied settings, including community mental health agencies and public and private mental and custodial institutions. For example, many master's-level counselors work in programs dealing with special problems such as substance abuse, crisis intervention, child abuse, mental retardation, and vocational rehabilitation. With appropriate training, such individuals can also be employed in industry as personnel selection and training specialists and in school settings, where they may evaluate students with special needs and assist in the planning of appropriate educational programs for such students. Many school psychologists and counselors are individuals with master's degrees and specialized training in educational and school psychology.

Doctoral Training in Psychology

The doctoral degree in psychology opens up many additional career opportunities. At least four years of study beyond the bachelor's degree are usually required to obtain a doctorate. In areas that provide psychological services, such as clinical and counseling psychology, another year for an internship and at least one additional year of supervised practice are required for licensing. Doctoral programs in psychology consist of a series of core courses in various areas of psychology, supervised research training, a general or comprehensive examination that advances the student to doctoral candidacy, and a doctoral dissertation, which consists of a piece of independent research.

In addition to the traditional university-based programs, there are also so-called professional schools that offer the Doctor of Psychology (Psy.D.) degree rather than the traditional Ph.D. or Ed.D. (Doctor of Education). These are often referred to as free-standing programs because they are not affiliated with a university. Professional schools place primary emphasis on training students for professional practice. Their programs feature extensive practical work and little emphasis on research training. Psy.D. programs, which typically offer training in clinical, counseling, or school psychology, usually require three years of coursework and practical experience plus a supervised internship during the fourth year.

Graduate programs differ widely in their admission requirements and in the quality of the training that they offer. In the more applied fields of psychology, *accreditation* is one important indicator of quality. In the areas of clinical, counseling, and school psychology, the American Psychological Association (APA) accredits doctoral programs that meet rigorous standards of training. A listing of accredited programs is published each year in the *American Psychologist.* Graduation from a nonaccredited program does not prevent licensing or employment in most states, but an increasing number of states are requiring graduation from an APA-approved doctoral program for licensing in clinical psychology. Likewise, some employers decline to hire graduates of nonaccredited programs.

All 50 states and the District of Columbia require that psychologists be licensed or certified by a state board in order to offer psychological services on an independent and unsupervised basis. Licensing is based on a careful review of the psychologist's educational background and the passing of rather rigorous written and oral examinations. Before entering a doctoral program, a student who wishes to practice psychology should find out about the status of the institution offering the doctorate. APA-accredited programs meet the standards of every licensing board. Your state's Examining Board for Psychology can provide information on the status of nonaccredited programs. Obviously, it behooves students to investigate the quality of a graduate program carefully before committing themselves to years of training in that program.

Preparation for Graduate Training in Psychology

A career in psychology that allows one to function beyond the level of supervised researcher or human services assistant requires an advanced degree, preferably the doctorate. Graduate school is a very challenging undertaking. High scholastic achievement, the ability to cope with a much heavier workload than at the undergraduate level, and a high level of self-motivation are required. However, if you have good academic ability, are truly committed to a career in psychology, and are willing to put in the effort required, attending graduate school can be a very gratifying experience. In graduate programs at major research institutions, most (if not all) students who are admitted are provided with financial aid in the form of teaching and research assistantships, traineeships, or fellowships. Thus, graduate school need not involve great financial sacrifice.

Admission to a graduate program is based on a number of criteria, including evidence of academic ability, scholarship as an undergraduate, previous involvement in related research or fieldwork, and promise of success in scholarly activity. These qualities are judged primarily on the basis of the applicant's record of academic achievement as an undergraduate, scores on standardized tests such as the Graduate Record Examination and Miller Analogies Test, and letters of recommendation from faculty members at the undergraduate institution.

Because a great many people are interested in graduate study in psychology, gaining entry to graduate school is a challenging enterprise. The average program accepts only about 15 percent of its applicants, and some clinical programs accept fewer than 2 percent. In 1992, for example, the University of Washington received 816 applications for its eight specialty-area doctoral programs, and 33 were accepted. Of the 559 applicants to the clinical psychology program, a total of 9 were accepted. These figures are quite representative of the top graduate programs in the United States. However, there are many high-quality doctoral programs that offer excellent training and are not so difficult to gain admission to. Some students enroll first in a master's program, then apply later to a doctoral program when they have clearly demonstrated their ability to do doctoral-level work. This course of training typically takes one or two years longer than direct entry into a program that offers the doctorate.

You need not have an undergraduate major in psychology to be admitted to a graduate program; however, the bachelor's degree in psychology can provide a strong foundation for the advanced training of graduate school. Although the specifics of the undergraduate major in psychology vary from school to school, the major typically consists of courses in introductory psychology, statistics and research design, experimental psychology, personality, abnormal psychology, learning, social psychology, developmental psychology, physiological psychology, history of psychology, and tests and measurement. In addition, undergraduate preparation in the natural sciences and mathematics is highly desirable in graduate school. A high level of academic performance is required, and students accepted for graduate study in psychology typically have grade point averages that exceed 3.5 (A = 4.0).

Good academic performance is only part of the graduate school equation. Practical experience in the field is also essential. The most important aspects of this practical work involve exposure to the kinds of activities in which you will be engaged during graduate school, such as research and fieldwork.

As early as possible in your college career, you should begin developing relationships with several faculty members in your psychology department who are working in areas of research that are of interest to you. Try to get involved in their research programs, either by volunteering or by taking an independent studies course under their supervision. This will provide you with firsthand experience in research and can help you decide how much you enjoy the research enterprise. The involvement may result in research ideas of your own. You might even be an author or coauthor of an article that is published in a psychology journal or a paper that is presented at a psychology convention. Such an accomplishment would be regarded as noteworthy evidence of scholarly achievement when you applied to graduate school. Moreover, your involvement in one or more research programs gives faculty members the opportunity to write very personalized letters of recommendation for you. These letters weigh heavily in graduate school admissions decisions. Virtually all students who are accepted into top graduate programs have strong letters of recommendation from faculty members who have supervised their research activities at undergraduate institutions.

The same applies to letters received from fieldwork supervisors. If you are interested in service-oriented specialty areas, such as clinical, counseling, or school psychology, you should try to become involved in fieldwork that will give you some exposure and training in those areas. Many undergraduate programs have formal relationships with community agencies that can provide students with fieldwork experiences. For example, many undergraduates get their first clinical experiences as volunteers at crisis clinics or on telephone hotlines. Again, exposure to these experiences can help you decide whether you are truly interested in clinical work.

Several other types of experience can be helpful to you in your undergraduate preparation. For example, many psychology departments sponsor a colloquium series at which invited speakers present their research and ideas. It is a good idea for undergraduate students to attend such colloquia. Another valuable experience is to attend a state or regional psychological association meeting. You can learn a great deal from the presentations; but even more importantly, you will have an opportunity to meet and talk with psychologists who work in a wide variety of settings and who engage in diverse professional activities. If you talk to psychologists about their work, the chances are very good that they will share with you the excitement that they experience in their professional lives. You might also be able to become acquainted with psychologists associated with graduate programs that interest you and gain firsthand information about the "fit" between your interests and their programs. Such contacts could influence later admissions decisions (both yours and theirs).

This appendix has provided a very brief overview of careers in psychology. For more information, I strongly recommend *Careers in Psychology,* a 28-page booklet produced by the American Psychological Association. To obtain a free copy, write to Order Department, APA, 750 First Street, N.W., Washington, D.C. 20002. Another useful APA publication is *Graduate Study in Psychology and Associated Fields,* which provides descriptions of more than 600 programs of study as well as information about graduate education, financial assistance, and requirements for admission to various programs. This book may be available through your university library, student counseling center, or psychology advisory office.

A career in psychology can be a wonderfully fulfilling way to live one's life. I would not trade my job for any other. I hope that I have been able to communicate and share with you my enthusiasm for the field of psychology in the pages of this book.

Glossary

A

ABC theory of emotion Albert Ellis's proposal that emotional consequences (C) are directly evoked not by activating events (A) but by the beliefs (B) that relate to the activating events and their personal meaning.

ablation Surgical removal of parts of the brain to study the effects on behavior.

abnormal behavior Behavior that is personally distressful, personally dysfunctional, and/or so culturally deviant that other people judge the behavior to be inappropriate and maladaptive.

absolute threshold The amount of energy a stimulus must exert before it can be detected 50 percent of the time.

accommodation (1) Adaptation of one's current schemas on the basis of new information. (2) The process by which the lens of the eye changes shape to focus the image of nearby or distant objects on the retina.

acetylcholine (ACh) A chemical transmitter substance, secreted into the synapse, that is involved in stimulating muscle contractions. Also involved in memory.

achievement test Test that measures how much has been learned from past experience.

acquired immunodeficiency syndrome (AIDS) A currently fatal disease that is caused by a virus that cripples the immune system.

acronym A word formed from the initial letter or letters of each of a series of words.

action potential The change in cell polarity that takes place during the passage of a nerve impulse. The membrane becomes permeable to sodium, and sodium ions flow into the interior of the cell.

action potential threshold The level of stimulation capable of evoking the all-or-none action potential, or nerve impulse.

actor–observer effect The tendency to attribute the behaviors of others to dispositional factors and our own behaviors to situational factors.

acute Physical or psychological reactions characterized by a rapid onset and symptoms of an intense nature.

addiction A strong physiological and psychological dependence on a drug with a resulting craving for the drug when it is not available.

additive color mixture Mixture in which the entire color spectrum is produced when red, green, and blue beams of light overlap on a white surface.

adolescence The period extending from the beginning of sexual maturity to the attainment of independent adult status.

adrenal cortex The outer portion of the adrenal gland, which secretes stress hormones and sex hormones.

adrenal glands A pair of endocrine glands, one situated over each kidney. The adrenals secrete epinephrine and norepinephrine, hormones that produce physiological arousal under stress conditions.

adrenaline See *epinephrine.*

adrenal medulla The inner portion of the adrenal gland, which secretes the hormones epinephrine and norepinephrine in response to stimulation from the sympathetic nervous system.

aerobic exercise Sustained activity, such as jogging, swimming, and bicycling, that elevates the heart rate and increases the body's need for oxygen.

aggregate A collection of people who have only an accidental and trivial relationship with one another.

aggression In humans, behavior that is intended to harm another. Hostile aggression is based on feelings of anger or hatred, whereas instrumental aggression has some other objective, such as attainment of power or acquisition of material goods.

agoraphobia Fear of crowds and open places.

alarm The initial phase of the General Adaptation Syndrome, in which the body is mobilized to deal with a stressor.

algorithm Strategy for problem solving that involves applying a standard formula that guarantees a correct solution.

allergy A maladaptive overreaction of the immune system to an antigen.

alpha rhythm A brain wave pattern of 8–12 cps that is characteristic of humans in a relaxed waking state.

altruism The desire to increase the welfare of another without concern for one's own welfare.

amine neurotransmitter system The body's source of a group of short-lived chemical compounds important in transferring a nerve impulse from one neuron to another.

amplitude The height of a sound wave; related to perceived loudness.

amygdala A structure in the limbic system that is involved in the coordination of emotional responses.

anal stage In Freud's theory, the period during the second and third years of life when pleasure becomes focused on the process of elimination and the child is faced with society's first attempt to control a biological urge.

analytic psychology The neoanalytic theory of Carl Jung.

androgen A male sex hormone. The major androgen is testosterone.

anorexia nervosa An eating disorder involving a severe and sometimes fatal restriction of food intake.

antecedent Situational factor or stimulus that affects the occurrence of an operant response when it is present.

antigen A foreign substance to which the immune system responds.

antinoise device Device that analyzes the sound-wave components of unwanted noise and generates a mirror-image sound wave that cancels out the offending noise.

antisocial personality disorder A long-term

maladaptive pattern of behavior in which an individual exhibits a lack of conscience for wrongdoing and a tendency to act out in an impulsive manner that disregards future consequences.

anvil One of the bones in the middle ear that relay the eardrum's vibrations through the oval window and into the fluid-filled cochlea.

anxiety disorder Psychological disorder marked by a high level of actual or inferred anxiety, such as a phobic or compulsive reaction.

aphasia An inability to understand language or to express it.

applied research Systematic application of scientific knowledge and research principles to the solution of practical problems.

approach–approach conflict A conflict in which an individual is simultaneously attracted to two incompatible positive goals.

approach–avoidance conflict A conflict in which an individual is simultaneously attracted and repelled by the same goal.

aptitude test Test that purports to measure an individual's potential for future learning and performance.

aqueous humor A fluid in the eye that nourishes the cornea.

archetype Jung's term for a racially inherited tendency to think and perceive in a certain way. Archetypes are said to exist in the collective unconscious.

architectural concept Description of the structure of memory—for example, as comprising sensory registers, short-term memory, and long-term memory.

artificial intelligence A subfield of cognitive science that develops and explores complex computer models of human mental processes.

assessment center Specialized personnel selection center where candidates for managerial positions are assessed with tests, interviews, and job samples.

assimilation The process whereby new experiences are incorporated into existing schemas without changing the schemas.

association cortex The areas of the cerebral cortex that do not have sensory or motor functions. These areas, which include most of the cortex, are involved in perception, language, and thought.

associative strategy Cognitive pain-control strategy that involves focusing on body sensations in an unemotional manner.

attachment An emotional tie with another person, as shown by young children with caregivers. Attachments may be secure or insecure.

attachment style The notion that the type of attachment formed with parents in early childhood expresses itself in later intimate relationships. The three primary attachment patterns are secure, avoidant, and anxious–ambivalent.

attitude An evaluative reaction to particular categories of people, issues, objects, or events.

attribution The process of making judgments about the causes of behavior or events. The two main classes of attributions are situational and personal (i.e., internal or dispositional).

authoritarian parent Parent who combines hostility and rejection with the placing of restrictions on the child.

authoritative parent Parent who is warm and accepting of the child but places restrictions on his or her behavior.

autoimmune reaction An attack by the immune system on healthy body tissue, as occurs in rheumatoid arthritis.

autokinetic movement The illusion of movement of a light stimulus that a viewer experiences in a darkened room because of undetected eye movements.

automatic processing Mental activities that occur automatically and require minimal or no mental control or awareness; "mindlessness."

autonomic nervous system A division of the peripheral nervous system that directs the activity of the glands and internal organs of the body. It is especially important in emotional behavior.

autonomy In Erikson's theory, the ability to behave independently.

availability heuristic The basing of judgments and decisions on the availability of information currently in memory.

aversion therapy Procedures that condition an aversive response, such as fear or nausea, to stimuli that ordinarily evoke maladaptive approach behaviors.

aversive punishment The suppression of a behavior by making an unpleasant or painful consequence contingent upon the behavior.

avoidance–avoidance conflict A conflict in which an individual must choose between two consequences that he or she wishes to avoid.

avoidance conditioning Operant conditioning in which the organism learns to perform a response in order to avoid an undesirable consequence (a negative reinforcer).

axes The five diagnostic dimensions of the *Diagnostic and Statistical Manual of Mental Disorders* (DSM).

axis In the Diagnostic and Statistical Manual for Mental Disorders (DSM), one of five categories of assessment of an individual's psychological and physical symptoms, life stress, and recent level of adaptation.

axon An extension from one side of the neuron cell body that conducts electrical impulses away from the cell body to other neurons, muscles, or glands.

B

basal metabolic rate The rate at which the resting body converts food into energy. A slowdown during middle adulthood accounts for the tendency to gain weight.

baseline The current level of a behavior under the naturally existing circumstances prior to intervention.

basic mistrust In Erikson's theory, the sense that other people cannot be depended upon for need satisfaction.

basic research Quest for knowledge for its own sake rather than to solve an immediate problem.

basic science Scientific knowledge acquired for its own sake.

basic trust In Erikson's theory, a general sense of trust in other people and the world.

basilar membrane A membrane in the cochlea whose movement stimulates the auditory receptors in the organ of Corti.

B-cell Lymphocyte (immune cell) that matures in the bone marrow.

behavioral assessment The direct observation and measurement of specific behaviors and the conditions that affect them.

behavioral marital therapy A cognitive–behavioral approach to helping married couples improve their relationships by learning communication skills and making behavioral contracts with one another.

behavioral perspective A view that behavior results from an organism's interaction with its environment; the belief that human beings are basically reactors and that the factors controlling human behavior reside in the external environment rather than in the individual. Behavior is determined by how the individual has been conditioned previously and by the stimuli in his or her immediate environment.

behavioral sink Calhoun's term for the pathological patterns of behavior that occurred when animals were placed in overcrowded environments.

behavioral variance Variation in behavior, both among individuals and across situations.

behavior chain In operant conditioning, a sequence of behaviors that are reinforced following the last response in the sequence (chain).

behavior genetics The study of the inheritance of behavioral characteristics.

behaviorism A school of psychology founded by John B. Watson that holds that scientific psychology should focus only on observable stimuli and responses.

behavior modification The direct application of operant conditioning procedures to change maladaptive behaviors.

behavior therapy A set of treatment approaches based on principles of learning.

belief bias The tendency for people's beliefs to override the rules of logic.

benzodiazapine One of a class of tranquilizing drugs, including Valium and Librium.

Big Five factors The global factors of extraversion, agreeableness, conscientiousness, emotional stability, and culture that are assumed by some trait theorists to be the basic dimensions of personality.

binocular cue One of the distance and depth cues that involve the use of both eyes.

binocular disparity The slightly different views of an object seen by the two eyes, which results in depth perception.

biogenic amines Neurotransmitters, including norepinephrine, dopamine, and serotonin, believed to play a role in depression and schizophrenia.

biologically based mechanism According to evolutionary personality theory, an evolved physiological structure that underlies psychological processes.

biological perspective The perspective on behavior that emphasizes the role of biological factors, such as brain processes and genetic determinants.

bipedal locomotion The ability to walk upright on the hind limbs.

bipolar cell One of the second-order cells in the visual system that shares synapses with the rods and cones.

bipolar disorder A disorder that alternates between mania and depression.

blank-lineup control A police lineup procedure designed to screen out eyewitnesses who have poor recall or are too eager to make a positive identification by exposing them to a lineup consisting entirely of innocent people.

blind spot The point at which the optic nerve leaves the eye, resulting in an area with no rods or cones.

blocking A classical conditioning phenomenon in which a previously conditioned CS prevents the establishment of a second stimulus as a CS when the new stimulus is subsequently paired with the UCS.

blood alcohol level The concentration of alcohol in the blood. A level of 0.10 defines legal drunkenness in most states.

blood–brain barrier Specialized cells in the brain that screen out foreign chemicals while letting in substances that neurons need.

borderline personality disorder A personality disorder marked by serious instability in personal relationships, identity, and emotional control.

brain stem The portion of the brain between the spinal cord and the cerebellum, made up of the pons and the medulla. It contains many ascending and descending fibers (including the reticular formation) that connect the higher and lower levels of the central nervous system.

British empiricism A philosophical school that emphasized that all ideas and knowledge are gained through the senses and that empirical knowledge gained through the senses is more valid than knowledge gained through reason.

Broca's area An area of the left frontal lobe of the brain that directs the muscular movements involved in speech.

buffering effect The capacity of certain personal and situational factors to blunt the negative impact of high stress.

bulimia An eating disorder that involves a repeated cycle of binge eating followed by purging of the food.

burnout A reaction to chronic stress that involves emotional distress and psychological (and perhaps physical) withdrawal from an activity or setting.

C

cannabis The hemp plant, from which marijuana is produced.

Cannon–Bard theory The theory that the thalamus responds to emotion-arousing stimuli by sending simultaneous messages to the neocortex and to the viscera and skeletal muscles. The messages to the cortex result in our experience of emotion, whereas those to the muscles and viscera produce actions and physiological responses.

case study An observational technique in which a single individual or group is studied intensively with the goal of discovering a general principle of behavior.

castration anxiety In Freud's theory, the fear of a child experiencing the Oedipal conflict that the father will castrate him in response to the child's erotic feelings toward the mother.

catastrophic life events Unusually stressful events, such as natural disasters, that occur rarely and require unusually demanding adaptations.

catecholamines One of a set of stress hormones that arouse the body, including epinephrine and norepinephrine.

CAT scan See *computerized axial tomography (CAT) scan*.

central fissure A fold in the cerebral cortex that separates the frontal and parietal lobes of the brain.

central nervous system One of the two major divisions of the nervous system; includes all the neurons in the brain and spinal cord.

central trait Asch's term for an important characteristic, such as a person's physical appearance or warmth versus coldness, that affects our overall impression of the person and our judgments of his or her other traits. Peripheral traits do not have this effect.

cephalocaudal principle The tendency for development to proceed from the head to the lower parts of the body.

cerebellum An area of the hindbrain that controls the coordination of motor movement.

cerebral hemisphere The largest part of the human brain, consisting of an outer gray cortex, composed primarily of neuron cell bodies and unmyelinated fibers, and an internal white core, composed primarily of myelinated fibers.

cerebral vascular accident (CVA) See *stroke*.

chlorpromazine A synthetic major tranquilizer used to treat schizophrenia.

cholecystokinin (CCK) A peptide that appears to decrease eating and thereby help regulate food intake.

chromosome One of the threadlike DNA structures that contain the genes.

chronic Long-term in nature. Chronic disorders have a gradual onset and become more or less constant.

chunking The procedure for combining units of information into larger, meaningful units as an aid for memory.

ciliary muscle One of the tiny muscles that change the shape of the lens in the process of accommodation.

circadian rhythm Biological cycle within the body that occurs on a 24-hour cycle.

classical conditioning A procedure in which a formerly neutral stimulus (the conditioned stimulus) comes to evoke a conditioned response by virtue of being paired with an unconditioned stimulus that elicits a similar response (the unconditioned response).

client-centered therapy The approach to psychotherapy developed by Carl Rogers, in which the client is given major responsibility for exploring the self within a supportive and empathic therapeutic relationship.

cochlea The coiled, fluid-filled tubes in the inner ear that contain the auditory receptors.

cognitive appraisal The process of interpreting and attaching meaning to internal or external events.

cognitive assessment methods Self-report methods, such as the use of random beepers, that are used to assess ongoing cognitive activity.

cognitive behaviorism A behavioral approach that incorporates cognitive processes, suggesting that the environment affects behavior through the influence of thought.

cognitive dissonance theory Festinger's theory that people are motivated to reduce the discomfort they experience when two of their cognitions are inconsistent—as when a person changes an attitude to be more consistent with an attitude-discrepant behavior.

cognitive–neoassociationistic model of aggression Leonard Berkowitz's revision and elaboration of the frustration–aggression hypothesis. It states that aggression is caused by negative affect that triggers primal response tendencies as well as associative networks that may inhibit or enhance aggression.

cognitive perspective A view of behavior that emphasizes the role of the individual's thoughts, understandings, interpretations, and ideas about the environment. This point of view emphasizes the ways in which individuals mentally process, evaluate, and respond to stimuli.

cognitive process theory Theory concerned with the specific mental processes that enter into intelligent thinking.

cognitive relaxation Mental relaxation that is free of intruding thoughts, particularly those of an anxiety-arousing or worrisome nature.

cognitive restructuring A cognitive change technique that involves identifying and challenging irrational ideas that cause disturbance.

cognitive therapy A therapy approach, developed largely by Aaron Beck, that focuses on helping clients change maladaptive thought patterns.

cognitive triad Beck's term for depressives' negative views about the self, the world, and the future.

cohesion Emotional closeness and mutual commitment to group goals within a group.

cohort A particular group to which an individual belongs; often describes a group of people the same age who are exposed to the same cultural and historical events.

collective unconscious In Jung's theory, the part of the unconscious mind that contains memories common to the entire human race. Compare with *personal unconscious.*

collectivism A cultural emphasis on the welfare and goals of the group, together with a tendency to define one's identity in terms of the larger social group rather than individual attainments and attributes. Compare with *individualism.*

commitment The voluntary or involuntary process whereby people are confined to mental hospitals.

common region The tendency to group elements together if they are located in the same general area.

companionate love An affectionate relationship characterized by commitment and caring about the partner's well-being; sometimes contrasted with passionate love, which is more intensely emotional.

comparison level In social exchange theory, the level of outcomes that people have come to expect in relationships. The relation between outcomes and the comparison level determines degree of satisfaction with the relationship.

comparison level for alternatives In social exchange theory, the standard for evaluating outcomes in relation to the best possible alternative. The relation between outcomes and this standard determines degree of com-

mitment to the relationship.

compensatory response Physical response that opposes a drug's effects and occurs as part of the body's attempt to restore homeostasis. Compensatory responses underlie tolerance, the tendency to need increasingly larger doses of a drug to produce the original effects.

competency The ability of a defendant to understand legal proceedings at the time of the proceedings.

competency-focused prevention Measures taken to increase personal competencies and resources so as to prevent the development of behavior disorders.

compulsion Repetitive behavioral response that can be resisted only with great difficulty.

computerized axial tomography (CAT scan) A method of scanning the brain with narrow beams of X-rays. The data are analyzed by a computer, which generates a picture of the brain's anatomical features.

concept A mental grouping of similar objects, events, or people.

concrete operational stage In Piaget's theory, the stage of cognitive development, occurring approximately from age 7 to age 12, during which children acquire operations (mental activities that organize and transform information) that permit logical thought about concrete events.

concussion A violent shock or jarring of the brain against the skull that often results in a temporary loss of consciousness.

conditioned reinforcer See *secondary reinforcer.*

conditioned response (CR) In classical conditioning, the response established by the pairing of a conditioned stimulus with an unconditioned stimulus that evokes a similar response.

conditioned stimulus (CS) A neutral stimulus that comes to evoke a conditioned response after being paired with an unconditioned stimulus.

conduction deafness Deafness caused by damage to the bones and membrane that conduct sound waves to the cochlea.

cones Visual receptor cells in the retina that are responsive to hues.

confirmation bias The tendency to look for evidence that will confirm our beliefs and hypotheses, rather than seeking evidence to disconfirm them.

conflict The state that exists when two goals are incompatible or when a goal arouses both approach and avoidance tendencies.

conformity The adjustment of an individual's behaviors, attitudes, and beliefs to a group standard.

confounding The mixing of two or more variables in an experiment so that it is impossible to determine which variable produced the effect.

conjunction fallacy The erroneous judgment that two events occurring together (such as being a feminist lawyer) are more likely than either alone (i.e., being either a feminist or a lawyer).

connectedness A new Gestalt law referring to the tendency to perceive any uniform, connected region as a single unit.

conscious Contents of the mind of which we are currently aware.

consciousness Selective attention to ongoing thoughts, perceptions, and feelings.

consequences In operant conditioning, the events that result from a given behavior.

conservation The principle that properties such as mass, weight, and volume remain the same despite changes in the forms of objects. Piaget believed conservation to be part of concrete operational reasoning.

construct A term or concept that refers to a presumed psychological process and that is operationally defined in terms of stimulus characteristics or subjects' responses.

construct validity The extent to which a test adequately measures a construct derived from a theory.

content validity The extent to which the items on a test sample the various aspects of the construct in question.

context-dependent memory Memories that can be recalled within the original context in which they were formed as the result of situation-specific retrieval cues.

contingency The specific arrangement that exists between a behavior and its consequences.

contingency model of leadership A theory of leadership, advanced by Fiedler, in which leadership performance is a joint function of the motivational orientation of the leader (relationship or task oriented) and the amount of situational control the leader has.

continuous reinforcement schedule A reinforcement schedule in which each response is followed by reinforcement.

control group Subjects in an experiment who do not receive the experimental treatment. The control group is a comparison group used to assess the effect of the conditions to which the experimental group is exposed.

controlled observation Observational research conducted under carefully standardized conditions, frequently in a laboratory setting.

controlled processing Mental processing that requires some degree of volitional control and attentiveness.

contusion bruise Bruising of the brain, a more severe injury than a concussion, usually with longer lasting and more severe effects.

conventional morality In Kohlberg's theory, the middle stages of moral reasoning, in which morality is defined by the standards of the social group.

convergent thinking The process of using information to arrive at a standard correct answer.

conversion disorder Psychologically caused physical symptom for which there is no physical cause.

conversion hysteria Psychological disorder in which a repressed conflict is expressed as a physical symptom for which no physical cause can be found.

cooperative learning program Classroom program designed to create mutual interdependence among pupils, thereby reducing competitive interactions and fostering positive ones.

copulin Vaginal secretion whose odor has sexual arousal properties for males.

cornea The clear outer area of the eye.

corpus callosum A large band of fibers that connects the two hemispheres of the brain and allows them to function as a single unit.

correlation A relation between two classes of events.

correlational research Research that assesses the nature of relations among naturally occurring variables. Correlational data can serve as a basis for prediction, but they do not prove causality.

correlation coefficient A numerical index of the direction (positive or negative) and degree of relation between two variables.

cortical column Vertical arrangements of cells in the visual cortex that are maximally sensitive to specific stimulus features, such as the angle of a line.

cortical projection area The specific areas of the cerebral cortex to which input from the various sensory receptors is directed.

corticosteroid Stress hormones, including cortisol, that are released by the adrenal cortex under stress and have long-lasting effects on the body.

cortisol A stress hormone released by the adrenal cortex.

counterconditioning The conditioning of a new response to a particular class of stimuli that is incompatible with the old response.

covert behavior Internal behaviors or processes, such as thoughts and images, that cannot be directly observed.

credibility The perceived expertise and trustworthiness of a communicator.

criterion (1) A standard of judgment. (2) An outcome that one is trying to predict by means of a test.

criterion-related validity The ability of a test to predict nontest behaviors assumed to be influenced by the personality characteristic measured by the test.

critical period A restricted time period during which an organism must be exposed to certain influences or experiences if normal development is to occur.

cross-cultural psychology An area of study that focuses on cultural determinants of behavior and the comparison of cultures.

cross-sectional design A developmental research design in which different age groups are tested at the same time and compared.

crowding The subjectively negative experience of wanting more space or the presence of fewer people. Compare with *density*.

crystallized intelligence The store of knowledge that an individual has acquired.

cued recall method A memory assessment method in which the subject is presented with a cue that may serve as a retrieval cue.

cue-responsive individual Person whose eating behavior is strongly stimulated by the presence of food-related cues in the environment.

culture The enduring values, beliefs, behaviors, and traditions that are shared by a large group of people and transmitted from one generation to the next.

cumulative recorder A response recorder that measures (and usually graphs) the total number of responses that have been made to that point.

cut-off score Specific test-score value used to select or reject individuals who score above or below the specific cut-off point.

D

daily hassles Minor or everyday stressors that require little adaptation but can accumulate and cause distress.

dark adaptation The process by which visual pigments regenerate so that the visual receptors become more sensitive to low illumination.

data The information, often expressed in numerical form, that results from scientific observation.

decay theory A theory that explains forgetting in terms of gradual fading of the memory trace over time.

decibel A logarithmic measure of sound intensity.

decision criterion In signal detection theory, the shifting judgmental standard for stimulus detection decisions.

declarative memory Memory stores whose content can be verbalized. Includes episodic and semantic memory. Compare with *nondeclarative memory*.

deductive reasoning Reasoning from general principles to a particular case.

deep structure The underlying meaning of a spoken or written sentence.

defense mechanism In psychoanalysis, a mental operation that either suppresses the instincts of the id or allows their release in disguised form.

defensive avoidance A response to motivational conflict in which the person procrastinates and avoids making a decision.

defensive vigilance A response to motivational conflict in which the person becomes upset and tends to make impulsive decisions.

deficiency need In Maslow's theory, one of the needs that ensure survival, such as the need for food or oxygen.

dehumanization The stripping of human qualities from others.

deindividuation A state of reduced self-awareness, self-produced by immersion in a group setting, that fosters emotional arousal and anonymity, during which restraints against unacceptable behaviors are weakened.

delayed sleep syndrome A form of sleep disorder characterized by difficulty in falling asleep.

delta waves Low-frequency brain waves that predominate in Stage 4 sleep.

delusion False belief sustained in the face of compelling negative evidence.

demand The degree of adaptation required of an organism by a particular stressor.

demand characteristic Cues in an experimental situation that give subjects information about how they are expected to behave.

dendrite One of many small fibers that extend from the neuron's cell body and receive electrical messages from adjacent cells, which are then conducted to the cell body.

density The number of people per unit of space (e.g., square foot or square mile) in a given area. Compare with *crowding*.

deoxyglucose A substance that is chemically similar to glucose but not digested by neurons. Radioactive deoxyglucose absorption by neurons can be measured by the PET scan, yielding a measure of the activity occurring in specific brain regions.

dependence The strong desire for a drug when it is not available. In physical dependence, the user experiences physical withdrawal symptoms, which he or she wishes to avoid by taking the drug, whereas in psychological dependence, the user craves the drug because of its pleasurable effects.

dependent variable In experiments, the variable that is measured to determine any changes caused by manipulation of the independent variable.

depressant Drug that reduces neural activity and can reduce feelings of tension and anxiety. Alcohol, barbiturates, and tranquilizers are depressants.

depressive attributional pattern Beck's term for the tendency of depressed people to attribute positive outcomes to situational factors and negative ones to personal factors.

depth of processing The extent to which information in short-term memory is processed through elaborative rehearsal for transfer to long-term memory.

descriptive statistics Statistics used to summarize groups of individual observations, the most common being measures of central tendency and measures of variability.

developmental psychology The scientific study of how, when, and why people change over time.

diathesis–stress model The notion that physical disorders are a joint function of biological organ vulnerability and stress.

dichromat A person with color blindness in either the red–green or the yellow–blue system.

difference threshold (jnd) The minimum difference between stimuli that a subject can detect 50 percent of the time.

differentiation The process by which functions become more specific or separate over time; a principle of development.

diffusion of responsibility A process by which being part of a group lowers each group member's sense of responsibility. It has been used to explain the failure of group members to help in an emergency.

discrimination In classical conditioning, the ability to distinguish between a conditioned stimulus and other, similar stimuli, so that those other stimuli do not elicit the conditioned response. In operant conditioning, the ability to discriminate between conditions in which various consequences will or will not occur or to distinguish between behaviors that will or will not be reinforced or punished.

discriminative stimulus Situational or antecedent stimulus that signals the likelihood that certain consequences will occur if a response is made.

disengagement theory The notion that withdrawal from social relationships by the aged represents a symbolic preparation for death.

display rule Culture-bound rule that dictates when and how emotions are to be expressed.

dissociation A split in consciousness that allows certain experiences, thoughts, and behaviors to occur independently of one another. Perhaps the most dramatic example of dissociation occurs in multiple personality disorder.

dissociative disorder A group of disorders, including psychogenic amnesia, psychogenic fugue, and multiple personality disorder, which involve a major dissociation of cognitive events or memories.

dissociative strategy Pain control strategy that involves distracting oneself from the painful stimulation.

distributed practice Learning that is spread, or distributed, over time. Compare with *massed practice*.

distribution A representation of obtained measures ordered from highest to lowest.

divergent thinking Thinking that departs, or diverges, from the norm, and that may lead to creative solutions.

DNA Deoxyribonucleic acid, a complex molecule in cells that contains genetic information.

domain-specific mechanism Evolution-based biological process suited to the solution of a specific class of environmental challenges, such as the formation of a status hierarchy.

dominant gene A gene that will produce a specific characteristic when it is present. Compare with *recessive gene*.

dopamine One of the group of neurotransmitters called catecholamines.

dopamine hypothesis The hypothesis that schizophrenia is caused by an overactivity of the dopamine transmitter system in the brain.

dorsal root The back-facing portion of the spinal cord that contains sensory nerves.

double-blind procedure An experimental procedure in which neither the subject nor the experimenter knows which experimental condition the subject is in.

dream work In Freudian theory, the process whereby the latent content of a dream (its true dynamics) is transformed into the partially disguised manifest content for defensive purposes.

drive theory of social facilitation A theory developed by Robert Zajonc that explains social facilitation on the basis of arousal produced by audience effects; the arousal energizes dominant response tendencies, either positive or negative.

drug Any substance, other than food, whose chemical action alters the structure or functioning of the body.

DSM The *Diagnostic and Statistical Manual of Mental Disorders,* the major classification system used in the United States.

dual coding The coding of information in both verbal and imaginal memory codes.

duplex theory of memory Theory of memory that views short- and long-term memory as separate stores.

E

eardrum The membrane that helps convert sound waves into fluid waves in the inner ear.

echoic store The sensory register for auditory input, which holds incoming information for a few seconds.

effect size A common measure of treatment effectiveness that indicates what percentage of treated clients improved more than the average untreated client.

ego In psychoanalysis, the part of the personality that is reality based and mediates among the demands of the id for instinctual gratification, the restraints of the superego, and reality.

egocentrism In Piaget's theory, the inability to adopt another's point of view; characteristic of preoperational children.

eidetic imagery Imagery in which stimuli are imagined in "photographic" detail and vividness.

elaborative rehearsal The process of rehearsing material and conferring meaning on it with the intention of remembering it permanently; facilitates transfer of material from short-term to long-term memory through deep processing.

Electra complex In Freud's theory, a conflict during the phallic stage during which a young girl develops erotic feelings toward the father. This conflict is resolved in most cases through identification with the mother.

electroconvulsive therapy (ECT) A treatment for severe depression in which a mild electric current is applied to the brain, producing a seizure similar to an epileptic convulsion. Also known as *electroshock therapy.*

electroencephalograph (EEG) A device used to record the electrical activity of the brain detected through electrodes attached to the scalp. The EEG records the simultaneous activity of millions of neurons.

elicited behavior Behavior evoked by particular stimuli, as in the case of a classically conditioned behavior.

embryo An organism in an early stage of development. In humans, this stage extends from about 2 weeks to 2 months following conception.

emitted behavior Operant behavior initiated by the organism in the presence of certain antecedents.

emotion An innate and acquired disposition to respond cognitively, physiologically, and behaviorally to certain internal and external events that relate to important goals or motives.

emotion-focused coping Coping strategies designed to control negative emotional responses caused by stressful situations.

empathic inference Piaget's term for the process of carefully observing how children approach problems and then attempting to infer how they must have experienced the situation in order to respond as they did.

empathy (1) The ability to put oneself in the place of another and to experience what that person is experiencing. (2) The communication of a therapist's ability to see the world through the client's eyes and to experience the client's emotions.

empirical approach As applied to personality test construction, an approach in which items are chosen because they have been answered differently by groups of subjects who are known to differ on the personality variable of interest.

encoding (1) The process of translating a piece of information into a neural code that can be stored in memory. (2) An interpretive or meaning-conferring process that occurs in the memory process.

encoding specificity principle The notion that retrieval from memory is enhanced by the presence of retrieval cues (or "meanings") that were encoded at the time the information was originally stored in memory.

encounter group Therapy group based on Gestalt principles that involves attempts to help clients experience their feelings and understand their relations with others.

endocrine system The system of glands that secrete hormones into the bloodstream and thereby affect many bodily functions.

endorphins A class of neuropeptides that have pain-reducing qualities similar to those of the opiates; literally, "morphine within."

environmental psychology An area of psychology that deals with the effects of the physical environment on thoughts, feelings, and behavior.

epilepsy A disorder characterized by sudden electrical changes in the brain that produce seizures or changes in consciousness.

epinephrine A hormone secreted by the adrenal glands. Secretion is associated with fear and anger. Also called *adrenaline.*

episodic memory Memory for events and experiences.

erroneous acceptance In personnel selection, an erroneous decision to hire or promote someone who subsequently fails.

erroneous rejection In personnel selection, an erroneous decision not to hire or promote a person who would have succeeded.

error variance Behavioral variations caused by random uncontrolled factors or errors of measurement.

escape conditioning A form of learning in which the organism learns to perform a behavior in order to escape from aversive stimuli.

estrogen Female sex hormone.

evocative influence In behavior genetics, the tendency of genetically influenced traits to evoke certain responses from others and thereby influence the environment.

evolutionary psychology An emerging area of psychology that focuses on how evolutionary factors have influenced the learning and information-processing mechanisms that help humans adapt to their environment.

evolved behavioral strategy In evolutionary personality theory, one of the evolved strategies that have developed through natural selection to enhance survival and the passing on of one's genes.

excitation transfer According to Zillman, the process by which arousal from other sources may combine with anger to enhance the anger and the tendency to aggress.

exhaustion The final phase of the General Adaptation Syndrome, in which the body breaks down because its physical resources have been depleted.

expectancy In cognitive approaches to learning, the organism's cognitive representation of the relations between the occurrence of conditioned and unconditioned stimuli (classical conditioning) or between responses and their consequences under certain conditions (operant conditioning).

expectancy × value theory The theory that goal-directed behavior is jointly influenced by (1) the person's expectancy concerning the likelihood of a certain consequence and (2) how positive or negative the value of that consequence is for the individual.

experimental group The subjects in an experiment who are exposed to the independent variable thought to influence the dependent variable. The subjects' responses are compared with those of the control group, which does not receive the experimental manipulation.

experimenter expectancy effects Experimental effects caused by the experimenter's unintentional cues, which cause the subject to respond in the manner anticipated by the experimenter.

exposure A behavioral treatment in which the client is exposed to anxiety-arousing stimuli so that the anxiety response can be extinguished. Also called *flooding*.

expressive behavior Externally observable expressions of an emotional response.

external validity The extent to which the results of laboratory experiments can be generalized to situations outside of the laboratory.

extinction In classical conditioning, presentation of the conditioned stimulus in the absence of the unconditioned stimulus after classical conditioning has occurred. In operant conditioning, the failure to reinforce a previously reinforced response, resulting in a decreased likelihood of response.

extrinsic motivation Motivation to perform a behavior in order to obtain external reinforcers, such as money or status, rather than because of inherent enjoyment of the behavior.

F

Facial Action Coding System A sophisticated coding system developed by Paul Ekman and his coworkers to measure the facial muscle movements that accompany various emotions.

facial feedback hypothesis The notion that spontaneous facial expressions that occur in response to eliciting stimuli provide feedback to the brain and shape emotional experiences.

factor A cluster of variables that are correlated with one another and are thus assumed to have common psychological meaning.

factor analysis A statistical procedure by which an investigator reduces a large number of behaviors to a smaller number of clusters, or factors.

fast MRI A scanning device that allows researchers to observe changes in blood flow and glucose activity in the brain as they occur through scans taken at short intervals.

fear-avoidance theory of pain A theory that explains the development of chronic pain behavior in terms of a desire to avoid further pain or injury.

feature detector Sensory neuron that responds to specific features of the stimulus, such as its angle, shape, movement, or color.

fetal alcohol syndrome A group of physical and cognitive dysfunctions in a child that were caused by excessive alcohol consumption by the mother during pregnancy.

fetus The developing human from the 2nd month until birth.

fight-or-flight response A state of physiological activation aroused in response to threatening stimuli that facilitates either fighting or fleeing from the threatening agent.

figure–ground relations Perceptual organization in which the focal stimulus is seen as a figure against a background.

fixation In Freud's theory, the arresting of development at a particular psychosexual stage as a result of anxiety or frustration.

fixed-interval schedule A reinforcement schedule in which the first response that occurs after a constant time interval is reinforced.

fixed-ratio schedule A reinforcement schedule in which reinforcement is given after a constant, or fixed, number of responses.

fixed-role therapy A technique developed by Kelly in which clients role-play and then adopt new thinking and behavior patterns

for a time so as to sample the effects of these patterns on their lives.

fixed schedule A schedule of reinforcement in which reinforcement occurs after a constant amount of time or number of responses.

flashbulb memory Vivid memory for highly distinctive or emotion-arousing events.

flooding See *exposure*.

fluid intelligence The ability to deal with novel situations for which previous experience does not provide guidance.

forebrain The portion of the brain that includes the cerebrum, the thalamus, the limbic system, and the hypothalamus.

foreclosure Premature commitment to a personal identity offered by parents or society without the self-exploration that occurs during the moratorium phase.

forensic psychology The area of psychology that involves research or application within the legal system.

formal operations Piaget's 4th stage of cognitive development, often achieved in adolescence, when schemas reach maturity and deductive reasoning makes it possible to solve complex, hypothetical, and combinatorial problems in a systematic way.

fovea A portion of the retina that contains only closely packed cones.

free association In psychoanalysis, the procedure of verbalizing all thoughts that come to mind without censorship.

frequency The number of complete wavelengths that pass a point in a given unit of time. In hearing, related to pitch; in vision, to hue.

frequency distribution A table that shows the number of scores falling into certain intervals ordered from lowest to highest.

frequency theory A theory of pitch perception that holds that at low frequencies, the number of nerve impulses sent to the brain by auditory receptors corresponds to the frequency of the sound wave.

frontal lobe The frontal portion of the cerebral cortex, which controls motor movements and is involved in higher mental activities.

frustration–aggression hypothesis In its original form, a theory that held that all aggression is the result of frustration and frustration inevitably results in aggression. Subsequent research has called both assumptions into question.

fully functioning person Rogers's term for a person who has achieved a high level of self-actualization and whose self is congruent with reality.

functional fixedness The tendency to be fixed in one's perception of how an object or procedure should be used so that one cannot see new ways of using it.

functionalism An early school of American psychology that focused on how animals and humans satisfy needs and solve problems.

fundamental attribution error The tendency to overestimate the importance of personal factors and to underestimate the importance of situational factors when making attributions about the behavior of others.

fundamental emotional pattern One of a presumed set of universal innate emotional responses.

G

ganglion cell One of the visual neurons whose axons form the optic nerve.

gate control theory A theory, proposed by Melzack and Wall, that the spinal cord contains a series of neurological ''gates'' that can be opened or closed by influences from the brain to admit or restrict the flow of nerve impulses from pain receptors to the brain.

gender constancy The understanding on the part of a child that being male or female is a permanent part of a person regardless of alterations in clothing or physical appearance.

gender identity The ability of a child to understand that he or she is either a male or a female.

General Adaptation Syndrome Selye's description of a stress response sequence, which includes alarm, resistance, and exhaustion phases.

generalized anxiety disorder An anxiety disorder in which an individual experiences chronic anxiety that is not related to specific environmental events but occurs generally.

generalized personality disorder A chronic state of diffuse anxiety that is not attached to specific situations or objects.

general paresis A progressive mental and physical disorder caused by syphilis.

generativity In Erikson's theory, a focus on helping better the next generation and society as a whole that typically arises during midlife.

genes The biochemical units of heredity, located on the chromosomes.

genital stage In Freud's theory, the period be-

ginning in adolescence when sexual impulses can be expressed in a mature love relationship with another.

genotype The inherited genetic pattern.

genuineness The ability of a therapist to honestly express his or her feelings to the client.

geon Geometric shape that combines with others to give rise to humans' perception of objects.

Gestalt psychology A German school of psychology that emphasized the natural organization of human perceptions into wholes, or patterns, and the role of insight in solving problems.

Gestalt therapy The humanistic approach to therapy developed by Frederick Perls.

g factor Spearman's general intellectual factor, which is assumed to underlie specific abilities.

glucoreceptor Sensor for blood sugar level. Glucoreceptors are located in the small intestine, the liver, and the brain.

G protein A protein body in the neuron that is activated by the binding of a neurotransmitter to a receptor and that triggers subsequent neuron activities.

graded potential Electrical potential in receptor neurons that is proportional to the intensity of stimulation; must reach a certain level to trigger an action potential.

gray matter Nervous tissue consisting primarily of gray neuron cell bodies.

group A social system in which individuals recognize some degree of connectedness among themselves and occupy interdependent roles.

group polarization The tendency for group members who agree on an issue to become even more extreme in their views following group discussion.

groupthink A mode of thinking in which a highly cohesive group, operating under stressful conditions, becomes so committed to reaching a consensus that each member suspends his or her critical judgment.

growth need In Maslow's theory, a motive toward personal growth and self-actualization.

guilt In Piaget's theory, a pervasive sense that one is not capable of functioning independently and self-sufficiently.

H

hallucination False perception that gives a compelling sense of being real.

hallucinogen Drug that distorts or intensifies

sensory experiences and evokes hallucinations and disordered thought processes. LSD and PCP are hallucinogens.

hammer One of the bones in the middle ear that relay the eardrum's vibrations through the oval window and into the fluid-filled cochlea.

helper T-cell Immune system cell that enhances the activities of other immune system cells.

hertz (Hz) The unit used to measure sound frequency in cycles per second.

heterozygous Having a dominant and a recessive gene for a given characteristic.

heuristic Rule-of-thumb approach to solving problems that involves mental shortcuts but does not guarantee success.

hidden observer Hilgard's term for a dissociated part of a person's consciousness that is aware of experiences, such as pain sensations, that occur when the person is in a hypnotized state but are not apparently experienced by the hypnotized person.

hierarchy In systematic desensitization, a graded list of anxiety-arousing stimuli.

higher order conditioning A classical conditioning phenomenon in which a conditioned stimulus serves as an unconditioned stimulus for classical conditioning of a new conditioned stimulus that is paired with it.

hindbrain The portion of the brain above the spinal cord that contains the pons, medulla, and cerebellum.

hippocampus A structure in the limbic system that appears to be a site for learning.

histogram A bar graph representing a frequency distribution.

homeostasis The maintenance of biological equilibrium, or balance, within the body.

homozygous Having two dominant or two recessive genes for a given characteristic.

hormone A substance secreted by the glands of the endocrine system and carried through the bloodstream to stimulate neurons, muscles, and glands.

hospitalization syndrome The deterioration of motivation, work skills, and social competencies that can occur as a product of the passive role into which mental patients are often placed.

hostile aggression Aggressive behaviors that occur as a result of angry feelings and a desire to harm the victim.

humanistic perspective A view of behavior that emphasizes the freedom and inherent goodness of human nature.

humor One of four body fluids thought by Hippocrates to be the biological foundations of personality differences.

hypercolumns Groups of feature detector columns in the visual cortex that are thought to be basic integrating units for visual input.

hyperopia Farsightedness occurring when the lens does not thicken enough to focus the image of nearby objects directly on the retina.

hypersomnia Sleep disorder, such as narcolepsy, that involves extreme sleepiness or involuntary onset of sleep.

hypnosis A condition of enhanced suggestibility in which some people are able to experience imagined test suggestions as if they were real.

hypnotic susceptibility scales Induction procedures and sets of test suggestions that enable a researcher to obtain a measure of the subject's responsiveness to hypnotic suggestions.

hypothalamus A part of the forebrain consisting of a group of small nuclei lying at the base of the brain; known to be involved in sexual behavior, temperature regulation, sleeping, eating, aggression, and emotional behavior.

hypothesis A predicted relationship between two or more events that is tested in order to assess degree of understanding.

hysteria See *conversion disorder.*

I

iconic store A photographic sensory store for visual information that fades in less than a second.

id In psychoanalysis, the unconscious part of the personality that contains primitive drives that strive for release.

ideal self One's conception of the type of person he or she would like to be.

identification The process of becoming like another in one's personal characteristics, attitudes, and beliefs.

identity crisis Period of emotional upheaval during which an individual is unsure of his or her personal identity.

identity diffusion A formative stage in the process of establishing self-identity during which identity is vague and unclear.

illusion A false or incorrect perception.

imaginal thought Cognitive activity that involves the use of visual or other imagery.

implicit memory See *nondeclarative memory.*

implicit personality theory A belief about how various traits and behaviors are related to one another.

in-basket task A job-sample technique in which an applicant has to inspect items in a manager's ''in-basket'' and make decisions and recommendations based on this information.

incentive Positive or negative environmental stimulus that motivates behavior.

incubation A problem-solving phenomenon in which a solution is presumably facilitated by subconscious factors when the problem is temporarily laid aside.

independent variable The variable that is manipulated in an experiment with the expectation that the manipulation will cause changes in the dependent variable.

individualism A cultural emphasis on the individual rather than the larger social group, together with a tendency for personal identity to be based on individual attainments and attributes rather than group membership. Compare with *collectivism.*

individual psychology Alfred Adler's neoanalytic theory, which stressed striving for superiority.

inductive reasoning Reasoning that proceeds from specific instances to general principles.

indulgent parent Parent who has a warm, accepting relationship with the child while also being very permissive.

industry In Erikson's theory, the positive outcome of the psychosocial crisis in the middle years of childhood, involving a feeling of self-confidence and pride concerning one's achievements.

inferential statistics Statistical procedures used to draw conclusions about data based on probability theory.

inferiority In Erikson's theory, the negative outcome of the psychosocial crisis in the middle years of childhood, involving the child's belief that his or her work and achievements are below par.

information-processing approach An approach to cognitive development that rejects stages in favor of gradual maturation of key cognitive abilities, such as attentional abilities.

informed consent Consent given by subjects after they have been informed about the procedures in an experiment and warned about any risks that might be involved. Experimenters are ethically required to obtain informed consent.

inhibition The process whereby the synaptic activity of a neuron is prevented from occurring.

initiative In Erikson's theory, the third psychosocial stage, in which the positive outcome is a favorable view of one's own desires and actions.

insanity A legal term referring to the inability of a person to understand the wrongfulness of acts and to control his or her conduct at the time a crime was committed.

insight In psychodynamic psychotherapy, awareness of the causes of one's behavior. In Gestalt psychology, the sudden perception of useful relationships that helps solve a problem.

insomnia A sleep disorder involving difficulty in falling asleep or staying asleep.

instinctive drift The tendency for relevant innate behaviors to override a conditioning procedure so that animals cannot readily be conditioned.

instrumental aggression Aggressive acts that are primarily motivated not by anger but by some other reason, such as a desire to gain power or to acquire something.

instrumental behavior Goal-directed behavior that may occur as part of an emotional response.

instrumental conditioning See *operant conditioning.*

integrated coping response A stress-management coping strategy in which stress-reducing thoughts and relaxation responses are tied to the breathing cycle.

integration The coordination of separate elements or structures with one another over time; a principle of development.

integrity In Erikson's theory, a sense of completeness and a feeling that one's life has been worthwhile.

intelligence A concept, or construct, that describes individual differences in the ability to acquire knowledge, to think and reason effectively, and to deal adaptively with the environment.

intelligence quotient (IQ) Originally, the ratio of mental age to chronological age, multiplied by 100. The score is now based on norms established for performance on the items that comprise intelligence tests.

interference theory The notion that people forget not because the memory trace fades but because of interference by earlier or later memories.

internal consistency The extent to which the

items on a personality test correlate with one another, suggesting that they are measuring the same characteristic.

internalization In Freudian theory, the process whereby the values of parents and society are taken on as one's own.

internal validity The ability of an experimental design to isolate the true causes of a given behavior within the experimental situation.

interneuron Neuron that performs an associative function in the nervous system, rather than a sensory or motor function.

interobserver reliability The level of agreement exhibited by different observers who are using the same assessment method to measure the same events or behaviors.

interposition A monocular depth cue by which an object that cuts off part of another object is seen as being nearer to the viewer.

interpretation Any statement by the therapist that is designed to promote insight in the client.

interrater reliability Consistency of scores on a measure among different testers; especially important in the scoring of projective techniques and in behavioral assessment.

interrole conflict The difficulties experienced, particularly by women, as a result of conflicting demands created by career and family.

interval schedule A schedule of reinforcement in which the occurrence of reinforcement is based on the amount of time that has elapsed since the last reinforced response.

intimacy In Erikson's model, the ability to form trusting and caring relationships.

intrapsychic Related to inner personality processes that influence behavior.

intrinsic motivation The motivation to perform a behavior for its own sake.

introspection Process of looking within and verbally reporting subjective experiences.

introversion–extraversion One of Eysenck's two biological dimensions of personality, assumed to reflect a person's customary level of physiological arousal in the nervous system. Also see *stability–instability*.

iris The colored part of the eye.

J

James–Lange theory The theory that people's experience of emotion is caused by the way they respond behaviorally to eliciting stimuli.

jigsaw program A cooperative learning program designed to foster positive interactions among white and minority children by making them depend on one another to complete a school lesson.

job enrichment An approach for redesigning jobs so as to increase the intrinsic motivation and job satisfaction of workers by fostering feelings of mastery and personal accomplishment.

job sample Simulation of an actual job situation that is used in personnel selection programs. An example is the in-basket technique.

just world hypothesis The belief that the world operates according to principles of justice, so that people get what they deserve and deserve what they get.

K

killer T-cell Cell of the immune system that destroys abnormal cells or intruders.

kinesthesis The sense of body position and the movement of muscles and joints.

L

language An organized system of symbols and the rules for combining them that permit the communication of meaning.

language acquisition device (LAD) Chomsky's notion of a biologically innate language acquisition function that requires only exposure to a language in order for language to develop.

language acquisition support system (LASS) System of environmental supports for language acquisition, such as parents talking to children.

latency stage In Freud's theory, the period during the elementary-school years when sexual impulses recede into the background and the child builds social relationships with same-sex peers.

latent content In Freudian theory, the true psychological meaning of a dream.

latent learning Tolman's term for learning in the absence of reinforcement; it is not obvious until reinforcement is introduced into the situation, at which point the learned response occurs.

lateral fissure The folds along the side of the brain that divide the temporal lobes from the frontal and parietal lobes.

law of closure Gestalt law of perceptual organization relating to the tendency to fill in gaps when a stimulus is incomplete.

law of continuity Gestalt law of perceptual organization relating to the tendency to link individual stimulus elements to form a smooth, continuous pattern that makes sense.

law of effect Thorndike's notion that behavior is governed by its consequences.

law of proximity Gestalt law of perceptual organization stating that elements near one another are likely to be perceived as part of the same configuration.

law of similarity Gestalt law of perceptual organization stating that there is a tendency to group similar stimuli together.

leadership style A leader's tendency to be primarily motivated either toward completion of group tasks (task motivated) or toward the enhancing of social relationships within the group (relationship motivated).

learned helplessness hypothesis Seligman's notion that depression is produced by a state of helplessness in which negative outcomes are attributed to personal, global, and stable causes.

learning A change in potential behavior that occurs as a result of experience.

learning trial In classical conditioning, the pairing of a CS with a UCS; in operant conditioning, the occurrence of a response and its consequence.

lens The elastic structure in the eye that changes shape to focus the visual image on the retina.

lesioning A technique for studying the function of particular parts of the brain by destroying tissue.

level of statistical significance An index derived from inferential statistical techniques that estimates the likelihood that the results obtained in a study occurred by chance alone.

levels of processing Levels at which material is elaborated upon and related to other items in memory. According to one theory, the likelihood of recall is based on the levels of processing.

life change unit A measure of the judged amount of adaptation required by a particular life event on the Social Readjustment Rating Scale.

life event scale Questionnaire that measures the number and severity of life events that a person has experienced over a given period of time.

life structure In Levinson's theory of adult

development, the underlying theme in a person's life at any point in time.

limbic system A group of subcortical structures, including the hippocampus and the amygdala, that are involved in memory and in the organization of motivational and emotional responses.

linear perspective A monocular depth cue by which the viewer interprets the convergence of what he or she assumes to be parallel lines as indicating increasing distance, as in the case of railroad tracks.

linguistic relativity hypothesis Benjamin Whorf's hypothesis that one's language determines how one is capable of thinking.

longitudinal design A research design in which the same subjects are retested at different ages so that the course of development can be studied.

long-term memory The relatively limitless and permanent storehouse of the memory system.

lymphocyte White blood cell programmed to provide immune defense against a specific target.

lysergic acid diethlyamide (LSD) A hallucinogenic compound that produces vivid sensory experiences and a possible loss of contact with reality.

M

macrophage Amoeba-like cell of the immune system that consumes debris, viruses, and bacteria.

magnetic resonance imagery (MRI) A method for producing a computer-generated picture of an internal organ by measuring the reactions of atoms to changes in a magnetic field.

mainstreaming The practice of placing children with various disabilities in regular classrooms.

maintenance rehearsal The process of retaining information in short-term memory by repeating the information to oneself, as with a telephone number.

major life event Life event, such as the death of a loved one or the loss of a job, that requires major adaptations.

major tranquilizer Antipsychotic drug used to treat schizophrenia.

management by objectives (MBO) An approach to management that combines the techniques of goal setting, employee participation in decision making, and objective performance feedback in an attempt to increase productivity and job satisfaction.

manifest content In Freudian theory, the disguised content of a dream, the content that the dreamer experiences.

manipulation A motive for suicidal behavior which is designed to control the behavior of other people.

MAO inhibitor One of a class of antidepressant drugs that increase synaptic activity by inhibiting the action of the enzyme monoamineoxidase in the synaptic space.

mapping the problem An important first step in problem solving in which the problem is formulated in some way that facilitates solution.

massed practice Highly concentrated learning over a relatively brief period of time. Compare with *distributed practice*.

matching hypothesis The expectation that people will form close relationships with others who are similar to themselves in physical attractiveness.

maturation An orderly sequence of physical development programmed by genetic factors.

mean The arithmetic average of a group of scores.

means–ends analysis A problem-solving heuristic that involves comparing the current state with a desired state and determining if there are means available to reduce the discrepancy.

measure of central tendency A single score that characterizes the level of performance of a group, such as the mean, median, or mode.

measure of variability An index of how widely the scores in a distribution vary, or the amount of "scatter" that occurs among scores.

medial temporal lobe memory system An area including the hippocampus and associated cortex that is involved in the transfer of information from working to long-term memory.

median The point in a distribution above and below which there is an equal number of values.

medulla A portion of the brain stem that plays a vital role in bodily functions, such as heart rate and respiration. It also contains all the sensory and motor nerve tracts coming up from the spinal cord and descending from the brain.

memory Perceptual and cognitive processes that allow us to record information and retrieve it at a later time.

memory consolidation The physiological processes that result in the neural formation of memories in the brain.

menarche The first menstrual flow, which signals puberty for females.

menopause The loss of fertility and the final menstrual period, resulting from a decline in estrogen and progesterone levels at midlife.

mental age The age level at which a person is able to function intellectually.

mental set The tendency to approach the solution of a problem in a certain way based on past experience.

mere exposure effect The tendency to evaluate a stimulus more favorably after repeated exposure to it.

mesmerism An early name given to hypnotism in honor of Anton Mesmer, who developed hypnotic procedures for curing illnesses, supposedly through magnetic forces that radiated from the planets.

meta-analysis A statistical technique that allows researchers to combine the outcomes of many studies into a single statistic called effect size.

metabolism The rate of energy expenditure by the body.

metacognition Insight into the nature of one's own cognitive processes; the ability to think about one's own thinking.

metacomponent In Sternberg's triarchic theory of intelligence, one of the executive cognitive processes used in understanding and planning solutions to problems.

method of constant stimuli A method used in psychophysics to measure the absolute threshold.

method of loci A mnemonic (memory-enhancing) device by which items to be remembered are associated with particular elements of a familiar place.

microstressor Minor life stress that requires little adaptation but that, when combined with others, can produce distress.

midbrain The stalklike portion of the brain above the pons and medulla that contains sensory and motor tracts as well as the reticular formation.

Minnesota Multiphasic Personality Inventory (MMPI) A frequently used objective measure of personality that consists of a series of clinical scales and three validity scales.

mnemonic device Memory-enhancement strategy, such as the pegword approach or the method of loci.

mock-witness control A procedure, used in designing unbiased police lineups, in which people who did not witness the crime are asked to pick out the guilty party.

mode The most frequently occurring score in a distribution.

modeling Learning through observation and imitation.

monoamine oxidase inhibitors One of a category of drugs used to treat depression.

monochromat A person who is totally color-blind and can only sense the black–white dimension.

monocular depth cue A depth/distance cue that requires the use of only one eye.

mood-congruent recall Recall of material by a person who is in the same mood as when the material was learned. Mood-congruent memories are more easily retrieved.

moral anxiety Freud's term for guilt, or fear of punishment by the superego.

moratorium A period of personal identity development during which a person tries out different roles and values before making a commitment to a particular identity.

morpheme In language, the smallest unit that carries meaning, typically a word or part of a word, such as a prefix.

motion parallax A monocular depth cue by which the nearer of two objects shows greater change in spatial position when the viewer's head is moved back and forth or up and down.

motivation An internal process that affects the direction, vigor, and persistence of goal-directed behavior.

motoric thought Cognitive activity that underlies the execution of motor skills.

motor neuron Neuron involved in the innervation of muscles or glands.

multiple personality disorder A dissociative disorder in which several personalities coexist at the same time within an individual.

myelin sheath The sheath of fatty tissue that covers the axons of many neurons. The sheath serves to increase speed of neural transmission.

myopia Nearsightedness caused when the lens does not become thin enough to focus the image of a distant object directly on the retina.

N

nanometer A measure of the wavelength of electromagnetic (light) stimuli.

narcolepsy A sleep disorder in which the subject suddenly and involuntarily falls asleep.

narcotic Opium or an opium derivative, including morphine, heroin, and codeine; reduces pain and produces intense pleasure.

natural killer cell Immune cell that attacks and kills cancerous or infected cells in the body.

natural selection Process by which characteristics that increase chances of survival are maintained in the species over time; one of Darwin's evolutionary principles.

nature–nurture controversy The long-standing controversy over biological versus environmental determinants of development.

negative affectivity A core state of general distress that characterizes both anxiety and depression.

negative correlation A statistical relation in which high scores on one variable are associated with low scores on the other.

negative expressed emotion A pattern of negative family interactions that is related to relapse among schizophrenic patients.

negative reinforcement A consequence that increases the likelihood of a behavior that results in its removal or avoidance.

negative state relief model Theory that people help others not out of an altruistic need to promote the others' welfare but to relieve their own negative reactions to suffering.

negative symptom Schizophrenic symptom that indicates a deficit in normal functioning, such as lack of emotional expression or motivation.

neglecting parent Parent who combines hostility and rejection toward the child with permissiveness and a lack of limits on behavior. Such a parent is indifferent and uninvolved with the child.

neoanalytic theory One of the personality theories formulated by psychoanalysts who broke away from Freud, such as Jung and Adler.

neonate The newborn child.

nerve deafness Hearing loss caused by damage to the auditory receptors in the inner ear.

nerve impulse A sudden reversal in the polarity of a neuron's membrane voltage, resulting in an electrical impulse that travels the length of the neuron.

neural plasticity The capacity of the nervous system to recover its function following injury.

neuron A nerve cell, consisting of three main parts: the soma, dendrites, and an axon.

neuropeptide Hormone released by the hypothalamus or pituitary gland that affects the functioning of neurons. Among the neuropeptides are the endorphins, which are involved in pain perception.

neurosis A psychoanalytic term referring to a behavioral disturbance that does not involve a loss of contact with reality.

neurotic anxiety Freud's term for anxiety aroused when impulses from the id threaten to break through into behavior.

neuroticism In Eysenck's theory, a heightened conditionability that makes certain people more likely to acquire psychological disorders.

neurotic paradox The tendency for people to engage in self-defeating behaviors that have short-term positive consequences (usually anxiety reduction) but long-term negative ones.

neurotransmitter Chemical substance that crosses the synaptic gap and binds to receptor sites on the receiving neuron to excite or inhibit its activity.

node of Ranvier Site on a myelinated axon at which the myelin is either absent or very thin, enabling impulses to skip from node to node and thus speeding nerve conduction.

nondeclarative memory Procedural memory that cannot be verbalized. Many nondeclarative memories are encoded with motor codes. Also called *implicit memory*. Compare with *declarative memory*.

nonreactive measures Naturally occurring behaviors or environmental effects of behavior that can be used as measures without the subjects' being aware that they are being studied. Also called *unobtrusive measures*.

nonsense syllable Meaningless syllable, typically composed of three or four letters, used in memory studies.

norm Rule for expected and accepted behavior that is shared by the members of a social group.

normal curve A bell-shaped symmetrical curve having known statistical properties.

norm group A sample to which a test is administered so that performance data can be collected and then used to evaluate the standing of other people who take the test in the future.

norm of reciprocity The behavioral rule that holds that we are obligated to repay those who provide us with benefits.

null hypothesis The statistical hypothesis that no difference exists between designated groups or that no correlation exists among measures.

O

objective anxiety Freud's term for realistic fear evoked by environmental dangers.

object permanence The understanding that objects and people continue to exist even when they are out of sight.

obsession Repetitive thoughts, images, or impulses that invade consciousness and cannot be easily controlled.

obsessive–compulsive disorder An anxiety disorder in which an individual is victimized by uncontrollable and repetitive negative thoughts and a tendency to engage in repetitive behaviors in order to avoid anxiety.

occipital lobe The posterior portion of the cerebral cortex; has a primary role in vision.

ocular dominance columns Alternating columns of feature detectors in the visual cortex that represent each eye.

Oedipus complex In Freud's theory, a conflict occurring during the phallic stage when a male child desires the mother sexually and regards the father as a rival. In most cases, the conflict is resolved through identification with the same-sex parent.

operant conditioning A type of learning in which an organism learns to respond to its environment so as to produce certain consequences. Also called *instrumental conditioning*.

operational definition The description or specification of a concept in terms of some observable event that can be measured. An operational definition can take the form of a stimulus or a response definition.

opponent-process theory (1) Solomon's theory that, because of the body's tendency to maintain homeostasis, any emotional response is followed by its opposite, and the latter becomes stronger over time. (2) Hering's theory of color vision. It posits that

three sets of receptors (red–green, blue–yellow, and black–white) are responsible for the perception of all colors.

optic chiasma The point at which optic nerves cross after leaving the eyes, so that one half of each eye's visual field is sent to each cerebral hemisphere.

optic nerve The band of axons that carries information from the visual receptors to the thalamus for further transmission in the brain.

oral stage In Freud's theory, the period during the first year of life in which infants gain primary satisfaction from sucking and chewing.

organ of Corti The structure in the inner ear that contains the hair cells, the auditory receptors.

orgasmic dysfunction Inability of a woman to experience sexual orgasm despite adequate physical stimulation.

orientation columns Cortical columns of feature receptors that respond to the same feature of the stimulus (e.g., the angle of a line).

outcome In social exchange theory, the difference between the rewards attained and the costs incurred in an interpersonal transaction.

outgroup homogeneity bias The tendency to view members of outgroups as being more similar to one another than are members of ingroups.

oval window The vibrating membrane through which the bones of the middle ear transmit sound waves to the inner ear.

overcontrolled hostility Explosive and exaggerated aggression that occurs in passive and rigidly controlled individuals whose defenses suddenly break down in response to a minor provocation.

overjustification hypothesis The notion that intrinsic motivation will decrease if a person attributes his or her performance of a behavior to the availability of extrinsic reinforcers, which are then withdrawn.

overt behavior Behavior that can be directly observed.

P

panic disorder An anxiety disorder in which the individual has sudden and inexplicable episodes of terror and feelings of impending doom accompanied by physiological symptoms of fear.

parallel processing Information processing in which several aspects of a problem are processed simultaneously, as opposed to serially.

parasuicide Suicide attempt that does not end in death.

parasympathetic nervous system The portion of the autonomic nervous system that slows down bodily processes and reduces physiological arousal.

parietal lobe The portion of the cerebral cortex that lies behind the central fissure and contains the body sense projection areas.

parsimony The quality of explaining as much as possible in the simplest possible terms. A standard for the adequacy of a theory.

partial reinforcement schedule A reinforcement schedule in which reinforcement follows some responses but not others.

participant modeling A modeling treatment in which a phobic person observes a model approaching the feared stimulus, then does likewise.

perception The process whereby sensory input is organized, synthesized, and interpreted by the brain.

perceptual constancy The ability to recognize objects under different conditions of stimulation, such as from different angles and under different illumination.

perceptual defense The phenomenon by which perceptual thresholds for anxiety-arousing stimuli are higher than those for nonthreatening ones, presumably as a defense against anxiety.

perceptual schema Information structure that contains the essential features of an object, event, or perceptual phenomenon.

perceptual set A readiness to perceive a particular stimulus or to perceive a stimulus in a particular way.

performance anxiety A term used by sex therapists to refer to anxiety concerning the adequacy of one's sexual performance.

peripheral nervous system One of the two major divisions of the nervous system, made up of all neurons connecting the central nervous system with the muscles, glands, and sensory receptors. This system may be further subdivided into the somatic nervous system and the autonomic nervous system.

peripheral trait Asch's term for a personality characteristic that does not influence judgments of other attributes.

personal attribution Inference that a behavior is caused by characteristics of the individual, such as personality traits, abilities, or attitudes.

personal constructs George Kelly's term for the mental categories people use to construe themselves and the events in their lives.

personality The distinctive and relatively consistent ways of thinking, feeling, and acting that characterize a person's responses to the life situations that he or she encounters.

personality disorder Stable, inflexible, and maladaptive behavior pattern that results in maladjustment.

personal unconscious In Jung's theory, the part of the unconscious mind that is based on individual life experiences. Compare with *collective unconscious.*

pessimistic explanatory style A tendency to attribute negative events to stable personal deficits, producing pessimism for the future.

PET scan See *positron emission tomography (PET) scan.*

phallic stage In Freud's theory, a psychosexual stage that begins at 4 to 5 years of age when children begin to derive pleasure from their sexual organs and begin to experience erotic feelings toward the parent of the opposite sex.

phencyclidine (PCP) A hallucinogenic drug with dangerous side effects, including uncontrolled aggression.

phenotype The expression of the genotype in structure or behavior.

pheromone Natural body substance whose odor is thought to affect sexual motivation and behavior.

phi phenomenon See *stroboscopic movement.*

phobia A strong and irrational fear of an object or situation.

phoneme The smallest distinctive sound unit in a language.

photopigments Molecules in the visual receptors whose chemical changes trigger nerve impulses.

physiological toughness A pattern of endocrine responses, including low levels of cortisol and quick, temporary evocation of catecholamines, that results in increased resistance to the long-term negative effects of stressors.

placebo A substance or treatment having no intrinsic curative power that produces a beneficial effect as a result of a person's expectation or belief that it will be beneficial.

placenta An organ that filters the mother's blood and provides nutrients to the fetus through the umbilical cord.

place theory Theory of pitch perception that holds that sound frequencies are coded in terms of the portion of the basilar membrane that undergoes maximum wave action.

plasticity The ability of the nervous system to reorganize itself following injury.

pleasure principle In Freud's theory, the tendency of the id to strive for immediate gratification of instincts, regardless of realistic constraints.

polygraph A recording instrument that can be used to measure the autonomic components of an emotional response, sometimes used as a purported ''lie detector.''

pons The portion of the brain stem that lies just above the medulla. It contains many ascending and descending fibers that connect the higher and lower levels of the central nervous system, as well as nuclei that carry sensory information to the brain or that are involved in respiration.

population All observations that could be made; the larger group from which a sample is drawn and that the sample is assumed to represent.

positive correlation A statistical relationship in which high values on one variable are associated with high values on the other.

positive reinforcement In operant conditioning, the process of strengthening a behavior by making a positive consequence contingent upon the performance of the behavior.

positive symptoms Schizophrenic symptoms that involve pathological excess. Hallucinations, delusions, and disordered speech are positive symptoms.

positive transfer Process by which new learning is facilitated by previously learned material.

positron emission tomography (PET) scan A method for scanning the living brain to determine the amount of radioactive deoxyglucose absorbed by active neurons.

possible self Markus's term for a self one desires or fears in the future.

postconventional morality In Kohlberg's theory, morality based on internalized standards of justice.

postformal thought Riegel's term for the ability to reason about opposing points of view and accept contradictions and irreconcilable differences.

post-traumatic stress disorder A pattern of symptoms, including flashbacks, emotional numbness, and psychological distress, that recur after the experiencing of traumatic events.

power motivation A motive directed at being in control, having high status, and exerting influence over other people.

preconscious In psychoanalysis, the part of the mind that is not currently conscious but can become conscious with appropriate stimulation.

preconventional morality In Kohlberg's theory, the earliest stages of moral reasoning, in which judgments are based on the rewards or punishments that will result from certain acts.

predictive validity The success with which test scores predict future outcomes, or criteria.

predictor variable A measure used to predict some other measure. For example, SAT scores are predictor variables for college GPA.

prejudice Negative beliefs, feelings, and behavioral tendencies toward members of a particular group based solely on their membership in that group.

premature ejaculation A male sexual dysfunction in which the man is unable to delay ejaculation long enough to give or receive pleasure.

premise A statement of assumed truth in a syllogism.

preoperational stage In Piaget's theory, the stage extending from about age 2 to about age 7, during which the child learns to use language but is unable to manipulate it effectively to think logically.

preparedness In Seligman's view, innate readiness, produced by evolutionary factors, to learn certain associations that have had survival implications in the past.

primacy effect Superior recall for stimuli that are presented at the beginning of a sequence of stimuli.

primary appraisal An individual's instantaneous appraisal of the personal implications of an event, primarily along a good–bad dimension.

primary mental ability In Thurstone's view, one of seven separate mental abilities, or ''factors of the mind,'' on which human mental activity depends.

primary prevention Measures aimed at preventing disorders in people who may be at risk for developing them.

primary reinforcer A positive reinforcer that satisfies a biological need, such as food or water.

primary sex characteristic One of the physical characteristics of men and women that make procreation possible.

priming The process by which the activation of one component of a memory network activates associated elements as well.

prioritizing In time management, the practice of ordering activities in terms of their importance.

proactive interference The process by which previously established memories interfere with the retrieval of more recently established ones.

problem finding A variety of postformal thought that involves posing new questions about the world and trying to discover novel solutions to problems.

problem-focused coping Coping strategies that involve direct attempts to confront and master a stressful situation.

problem-solving schema Mental template for solving a particular type of problem.

procedural memory The store of learned associations between stimuli and responses that allow people to perform skills.

product–moment correlation coefficient A numerical index of the magnitude and direction of relation between two variables.

professional specialization Piaget's term for the application of formal operations within one's particular field of interest.

program evaluation A set of scientific procedures that can be applied in designing programs (formative evaluations) and assessing the effectiveness of programs (outcome evaluations).

progressive muscle relaxation A relaxation training technique that involves tensing and relaxing specific muscles.

projective hypothesis The psychodynamic notion that people's internal needs and conflicts are projected into the environment and influence their perceptions.

projective test Measure of personality that requires people to interpret ambiguous stimuli such as inkblots or pictures.

propositional thought Thought that involves the use of verbal symbols and concepts.

prosocial behavior Behavior designed to enhance the welfare of another individual or group.

prospective study A study in which a variable thought to affect a given outcome is measured at the beginning of the study and used to predict a future outcome.

protective factor Personal or situational factor that reduces the impact of stressors.

prototype The most typical and familiar members of a class.

proximodistal principle The tendency for development to proceed from the body's midline to its extremities.

psychoactive drug Drug that affects consciousness, mood, and behavior.

psychodynamic perspective A view of behavior that focuses on inner causes, such as unconscious factors, motives, and personality characteristics.

psychogenic amnesia Selective loss of memory, usually in response to stress or trauma.

psychogenic fugue Loss of personal identity, possibly involving flight to a faraway place, where a new identity is established.

psychology The scientific study of behavior and its causes.

psychometrics Mathematically based procedures for designing and evaluating psychological tests.

psychomotor retardation A slowing down of physical movements, typically caused by severe depression.

psychoneuroimmunology The study of interactions between psychosocial factors and immune system functioning.

psychophysics The scientific study of relations between the physical characteristics of stimuli and the sensory experiences they evoke.

psychophysiological disorder Disorder in which physical damage to the body is brought about by psychological factors such as stress.

psychosis A psychoanalytic term referring to a severe disorder that involves a loss of contact with reality.

psychosomatic disorder A physical disorder caused or greatly worsened by psychological factors.

puberty The period of rapid physical growth and sexual maturation that marks the onset of adolescence.

punishment A consequence that suppresses a behavior that produces it; may involve either the application of aversive stimuli or the withholding of some normally noncontingent reinforcer.

pupil The circular opening through which light waves enter the eye.

R

radical behaviorism The view that psychology should study only externally observable stimuli and responses, without reference to unobservable internal processes.

random assignment In experiments, the assignment of subjects to experimental and control groups on some random basis in an attempt to rule out systematic differences between the groups.

range The difference between the highest and lowest scores in a distribution.

rape trauma syndrome A post-traumatic stress response to having been raped. See *post-traumatic stress disorder.*

rational–emotive psychotherapy The cognitive approach to therapy developed by Albert Ellis.

rational-theoretical approach An approach to the development of test items in which rational decisions are made as to what kinds of questions should be asked in order to measure a particular characteristic or construct.

ratio schedule A reinforcement schedule in which reinforcement is based on a particular number of responses, which may be either constant or variable.

reaction range The range of possibilities that a genetic code allows for the expression of a genetically influenced trait.

reactivity The possible effect on subjects' behavior of the subjects' awareness that they are being observed or studied.

realistic conflict theory A theory that links prejudice to a perceived threat to one's in-group.

reality principle The ego's tendency to test reality in order to decide when and under what conditions the id can safely discharge its impulses.

reappraisal An ongoing process of appraisal affected by feedback from physiological responses and the outcomes of behaviors.

recall Ability to reproduce information from memory.

recency effect Superior recall for the stimuli to which one has been most recently exposed.

receptor site Specially keyed structure on the surface of a neuron that receives a particular neurotransmitter substance that can stimulate the neuron to activity.

recessive gene A gene whose effect can be

masked by a corresponding dominant gene. It will produce its characteristic only if it is paired with another recessive gene of the same type.

reciprocal causal relations Two-way causal relations, as when a behavior caused by the environment also exerts a causal effect on the environment.

reciprocal determinism Bandura's term for the two-way causal relations between person, behavior, and the environment.

recognition Ability to recognize previously presented information.

recognition-by-components theory Biederman's theory that basic geometric forms, or geons, are combined in a bottom-up fashion to create perceptions of objects.

reconstructive memory The process whereby a person's previous experiences are retrieved not as exact copies of the original experiences but rather in terms of the person's reconstructions of them, which can be affected by later experiences.

reference group A social group whose standards and beliefs an individual identifies with and accepts.

reflected appraisal A person's inferences about how others are perceiving and evaluating him or her, based on their reactions.

reflecting In client-centered therapy, the therapeutic response in which the therapist restates, or ''reflects back,'' something that the client has just said.

reflex A simple innate response to a particular type of stimulus.

refractory period (1) The brief period following an action potential during which a neuron cannot be stimulated. (2) A period following orgasm during which an individual is incapable of sexual performance.

regression A psychoanalytic term for a retreat to an earlier stage of development in response to severe stress.

relapse prevention Procedures designed to teach recovering addicts coping skills that will enable them to avoid relapse.

relaxation response Herbert Benson's term for a generalized state of reduced physiological arousal that accompanies meditation.

relearning method A method for measuring memory in which the reduced time or trials needed to relearn material is measured. Also called *savings method.*

reliability (1) Consistency of measurement across time and among the items that comprise a test and among different people who

score the test. (2) Diagnostic agreement among clinicians.

REM rebound effect The tendency for REM sleep to increase following REM deprivation produced by awakening of subjects during REM sleep.

REM sleep A recurring sleep stage characterized by a Stage 1 EEG pattern, increased physiological arousal, and rapid eye movements. Subjects awakened during REM sleep are especially likely to report that they were dreaming.

representativeness heuristic Inferences about how similar something is to a prototype, or how representative of the prototype it is.

representative sample A sample in which the numbers of individuals from various groups are proportional to the size of these groups in the population. This type of sampling is used by most public opinion polling firms.

repression The most basic Freudian defense mechanism, in which the ego uses some of its energy to keep anxiety-arousing material in the unconscious.

residual rule Scheff's term for a norm that is implicit and whose violation is likely to result in a judgment of mental disturbance.

resistance (1) Largely unconscious maneuvers that prevent clients from dealing with anxiety-provoking material in therapy. (2) The second phase of the General Adaptation Syndrome, in which the resources of the body are continually mobilized by the secretion of stress hormones.

resources An organism's personal and environmental assets for coping with a stressor.

response cost A form of punishment in which an organism is deprived of some reinforcer that is normally not produced by the undesirable behavior, as in fines and groundings.

resting potential The voltage generated by unequal distribution of ions inside and outside the cell membrane when the neuron is in its resting state.

reticular formation A large bundle of neurons in the midbrain that control the activation level of the cortex. It plays a central role in consciousness, attention, and sleep.

retina The rear portion of the eyeball, which contains the visual receptors (rods and cones).

retrieval The process whereby information is brought out of long-term memory storage. Retrieval may be measured by recall, rec-

ognition, or relearning procedures.

retrieval cue Internal or external cue that stimulates the recall of information stored in long-term memory.

retroactive interference The interference of recently established memories with the retrieval of previously established ones.

retrograde amnesia Loss of memory for events that occurred prior to a particular event, such as a trauma, an injury, or electroshock therapy.

reuptake The process whereby neurotransmitters in the synaptic space are taken back into the presynaptic neuron.

revolving door phenomenon The cyclic process of hospitalization, release, and rehospitalization that occurs when mental patients are released into communities that do not have the resources for follow-up care.

rod Visual receptor in the retina that responds to brightness differences only, and not to colors.

role theory of hypnosis Theory that attributes hypnotic phenomena to the subject's immersion in a role comprising his or her beliefs concerning what is experienced by hypnotized people and how they behave.

Rorschach inkblot test A projective technique in which individuals are asked to indicate how inkblots appear to them and why.

S

sample A designated group of subjects from whom data are collected for the purpose of drawing conclusions about the larger population.

savings method See *relearning method.*

schedule of reinforcement See *reinforcement schedule.*

schema A mental structure used to interpret experience.

schizophrenia A severe disorder in which a person exhibits thought disorders, delusions, hallucinations, flat affect, and other severe problems that interfere with his or her maintaining contact with reality.

schizophrenogenic family A family exhibiting a pattern of interactions that might contribute to the development of schizophrenia.

script A cognitive structure that organizes information about specific activities and social interactions.

seasonal affective disorder A depressive disorder produced by a seasonal reduction in light stimulation.

secondary appraisal An individual's appraisal of his or her ability to cope with a stressful event.

secondary prevention Process by which programs attempt to reduce the worsening of already existing disorders.

secondary reinforcer A stimulus that acquires reinforcing qualities by being associated with a primary reinforcer. Also called a *conditioned reinforcer.*

secondary sex characteristics A visible physical characteristic other than genitalia that distinguishes the mature male from the mature female.

selective encoding Encoding process in which some information is taken into account while other information is ignored.

selectivity theory The notion that as people age, they become more selective in relationships and prefer to concentrate on existing relationships rather than forming new ones.

self In Rogers's theory, an organized, consistent set of perceptions and beliefs about oneself.

self-actualization In humanistic theories, an innate tendency to fully actualize one's abilities and potential.

self-control desensitization An approach that considers systematic desensitization to be the learning of a voluntarily applied coping response rather than passive counterconditioning.

self-disclosure The act of revealing information about oneself to another individual.

self-efficacy Bandura's term for the belief that one is capable of performing the behaviors that are required for attaining specific goals.

self-enhancement A general and apparently pervasive tendency to gain and maintain a positive self-image.

self-evaluative process Process by which humans reinforce or punish themselves contingent on certain behaviors that relate to internal standards.

self-fulfilling prophecy The tendency to behave on the basis of our expectations in such a way that our impressions of others or ourselves are confirmed.

self-instructional training A cognitive change technique that involves making specific coping self-statements at various stages of the coping process.

self-monitoring (1) The process of observing and measuring one's own behavior. (2) An individual difference variable that reflects the tendency to regulate social behavior in accordance with the situation (high self-monitoring) or in accordance with internal factors (low self-monitoring).

self-perception theory The theory, advanced by Bem, that people infer their attitudes from their observations of their own behavior.

self-presentation Actions designed to convey a desired impression or personal image.

self-reference effect The tendency to remember information better if it is related to one's self-schemas.

self-regulation In Bandura's social cognitive theory, processes such as self-reinforcement and self-punishment that allow individuals to exert control over their own behavior.

self-schema An organized collection of beliefs and feelings about oneself.

self-selection Condition in which only certain people are willing to participate in a study, leading to a tendency to obtain biased samples.

self-serving bias The tendency to attribute positive outcomes to personal factors and negative ones to situational factors.

self-verification A process by which people behave in ways that support or confirm their self-perceptions.

semantic memory One's organized, relatively stable store of information about the world and one's system of language.

semantic network A semantic memory network based on associations among concepts.

semantics The meaning derived from spoken or written language, or the study thereof.

semantic similarity hypothesis The notion that behaviors that constitute a cluster (as in the Big Five personality factors) may be seen as similar because of verbal similarities among the words themselves rather than similarities among the behaviors.

semicircular canals Curved tubular canals that exist in three planes in the inner ear and are concerned with the sense of equilibrium and motion.

sensation The process whereby stimulus energies are detected and transduced.

sensation-seeking motive A motivational state directed toward intense stimulation, novelty, and excitement.

sensitive period The optimal (but not the only) developmental period during which a particular event can influence subsequent development.

sensorimotor stage In Piaget's theory, the early developmental period (through the first 2 years) during which the child knows the world largely through sensory and motor activities and is incapable of logical thinking.

sensory adaptation The habituation of sensory neurons to a stimulus over time.

sensory neuron Neuron involved in synaptic transmission of impulses from the sense organs.

sensory register The portion of the memory system that receives incoming information from the senses and briefly retains it so that it can be interpreted.

serial position curve Curve showing the tendency of persons learning lists of information to remember items that occur early in the list (*primacy effect*) and late in the list (*recency effect*) better than those in the middle of the list.

serial processing The carrying out of a single sequence of actions, as is typically done by computers.

set point The "normal" value around which a person's weight fluctuates.

sex-role stereotyping Beliefs that it is only natural and fitting for males and females to adhere to traditional sex-role patterns.

sex typing In social learning theories, the process of treating males and females differently, contributing to their gender identity.

sexual dysfunction Difficulties in sexual performance or enjoyment.

sexual orientation The direction of sexual motivation toward members of the same or the opposite sex.

sexual response cycle The biological sequence of sexual responsiveness identified by Masters and Johnson, which involves four stages: excitement, plateau, orgasm, and resolution.

shadowing An experimental situation in which a person receives two or more messages simultaneously and is asked to report on one or more of them. Shadowing has been used to test attentional capacities.

shame In Erikson's theory, the negative outcome of the second psychosocial stage, in which a child becomes dependent and lacks self-confidence.

shaping An operant conditioning procedure that involves first reinforcing a behavior that the organism can already perform and then reinforcing behaviors that increasingly approximate the final desired behavior.

short-term memory The component of the memory system that holds information for perhaps 30 seconds, until it is processed and transferred to long-term memory, maintained through maintenance rehearsal, or displaced by new information. Also called *working memory.*

signal detection theory A theory relating to sensory capabilities that states that stimulus detection is influenced by a variety of psychological factors.

simulation study A research procedure in which an attempt is made to simulate under controlled conditions an actual event, such as a legal trial.

single-blind procedure A research design in which subjects do not know which experimental condition they have been assigned to, but the experimenter does know (raising the possibility of experimenter expectancy effects).

situational attribution Judgment that a behavior is caused not by personal characteristics of the individual but by the situation to which the individual is exposed.

situation-based prevention Measures taken to prevent psychological disorders by altering the environmental factors that contribute to their development.

Skinner box Experimental chamber in which animals learn to perform operant responses, such as bar presses or pecking responses, so that the learning process can be studied.

sleep apnea A sleep disorder characterized by temporary stoppage of breathing during sleep and consequent momentary reawakenings and loud snores.

sleep spindles Periodic bursts of electrical activity that appear in the EEG in Stage 2 sleep.

slow-wave sleep Stages 3 and 4 of sleep, in which the EEG pattern shows large, regular brain waves, indicating synchronization of neural activity in the brain and a deep level of sleep.

social cognitive theory A theory of behavior developed by Albert Bandura that integrates cognitive and behavioral determinants of behavior.

social comparison The act of comparing one's personal attributes, abilities, and perceptions with those of other people.

social exchange theory A theory of interpersonal behavior that holds that social encounters can best be described in terms of exchanges of rewards and costs associated with the relationship.

social facilitation The tendency for people's performance to be either positively or negatively affected by the presence of others because dominant response tendencies are more strongly activated.

social identity theory Theory that holds that the self-concept has two components, a personal identity and an identity based on one's ingroup memberships.

social interest In Adler's theory, the innate desire of people to advance the welfare of other people and society.

social loafing The tendency for individuals to put forth less effort when performing as part of a group than they would if they were working on the task by themselves.

social norm Behavioral expectation shared by members of a social group, that operates as a rule for behavior.

social penetration theory Theory that holds that as a relationship deepens, exchanges (including self-disclosure) become broader and more intimate.

social power The ability to influence others to behave in a particular way.

social role A pattern of behavior that is expected of a person who occupies a particular position in a social system.

social skills training A modeling and role-playing approach to the learning of social skills.

social support The availability of other people who are considered willing and able to provide assistance and support.

soma The cell body of a neuron, which contains its nucleus.

somatic nervous system The portion of the nervous system that involves the musculature of the body.

somatic relaxation Relaxation of the body, particularly the muscles.

somatic theory of emotion One of the theories, such as the James–Lange and facial feedback models, that view emotional experiences as being caused by physiological responses of the body.

spatial frequency filter Neuron in the visual system that codes variations in patterns of light and darkness.

spatial frequency model Theory of visual perception that holds that differences in spatial frequency curves detected by spatial frequency filters are the basis for visual perception of objects.

spinal reflex Innate reflex, involving sensory neurons, motor neurons, and interneurons, that occurs at the level of the spinal cord.

split-brain patient Patient whose corpus callosum has been severed surgically to prevent the spread of a type of epileptic seizure from one side of the brain to the other. Examination of these patients has indicated that the two halves of the brain have somewhat different functions.

spontaneous recovery In classical conditioning, the reappearance of a previously extinguished conditioned response after a period of time has passed following extinction.

stability–instability One of Eysenck's two biological dimensions of personality, involving the suddenness with which shifts in arousal occur in the nervous system. Eysenck has also called this dimension *neuroticism.* (Also see *introversion–extraversion.*

stage A distinct phase within a larger sequence of development in which skills and behavior seem to emerge suddenly and occur in a specific order in virtually all members of a species.

standard deviation A commonly used measure of dispersion. One computes it by finding the difference between each score in a distribution and the mean, squaring and summing the deviations, dividing by the number of observations minus 1, and taking the square root of this value.

standardization The process of developing uniform procedures for administering a psychological test and establishing performance norms for the test.

state-dependent experience Conscious experience that occurs and can be reproduced only in specific states of consciousness, such as under the influence of a drug.

state-dependent memory Superior recall that occurs when one is in a psychological state similar to the state one was in when the material was originally learned.

stereopsis The ability to perceive depth and distance, made possible by the slightly different views provided by the two eyes.

stereotype Schema that associates certain characteristics with a particular group and is generalized to almost all group members.

stimulant Drug that stimulates the central and autonomic nervous systems, resulting in an experienced state of excitement or aroused euphoria. Amphetamines and cocaine are stimulants.

stimulus control Influence exerted by antecedent conditions or discriminative stimuli on operant behaviors.

stimulus generalization The tendency to respond with a conditioned response to stimuli other than the original conditioned stimulus on the basis of the similarity of these stimuli to the continued stimulus.

stirrup One of the bones in the middle ear that relay the eardrum's vibrations through the oval window and into the fluid-filled cochlea.

storage The process by which encoded information is retained in long-term memory.

stranger anxiety The fear of strangers that infants commonly display beginning by about 8 months of age.

strange situation Laboratory procedure designed by Mary Ainsworth in which the observer assesses the quality of attachment by observing a child interact with the parent and a stranger.

strategic self-presentation Behaviors intended to influence others' perceptions of us and to evoke desired behaviors from them.

stress A construct defined (a) in terms of stimuli that place excessive demands on the organism; (b) as a response to those demands that has cognitive, physiological, and behavioral components; or (c) as a transaction between a stressor and an organism that responds to it.

stress-induced analgesia A reduction in sensitivity to painful stimuli that occurs under stress and is believed to be produced by the release of endorphins.

stressor A situation that places excessive demands upon an organism.

striving for superiority Adler's general motive that drives people to overcome limitations in themselves.

stroboscopic movement An illusion of movement created by the timing of illumination of adjacent lights or the presentation of movie frames at a specific frequency. Also called the *phi phenomenon.*

stroke A rupturing of one or more blood vessels in the brain. Also called a *cerebral vascular accident (CVA).*

structuralism An early school of psychology that focused on the analysis of the mind in terms of its basic elements, thought to be sensations.

structured interview An interview in which a specific sequence of questions is asked of all interviewees.

subconscious A state in which a stimulus is not being attended to directly, but is nevertheless being processed automatically.

subgoal analysis The process of solving a problem by reducing the ultimate goal to a series of subgoals which are then pursued.

subjective norm A person's belief about how other people think he or she should behave.

subjective organization In memory, a recoding process by which people impose order on randomly presented events so that they can remember the events better.

sublimation In Freud's theory, the channeling of a taboo impulse into socially desirable behavior.

substance P A neurotransmitter substance in the spinal cord that is involved in the transmission of pain stimulation to the brain.

superego In psychoanalysis, the moral arm of the personality, which strives to suppress the id's drives for gratification.

suppressor T-cell Immune system cell that suppresses the activity of other immune-system cells, serving to turn off or limit immune responses.

surcease Cessation of one's life; a prominent desire among suicidal individuals.

surface structure A linguistic term describing the way in which words are organized in a written or spoken sentence.

symbolic thought Thought using concepts or images.

sympathetic ganglia A chain of cell bodies running along the spinal cord where sympathetic neurons come together in synapses with nerves that fan out to the organs of the body.

sympathetic nervous system The portion of the autonomic nervous system that speeds up bodily processes and increases physiological arousal.

synapse The microscopic space between neurons across which the nerve impulse must pass.

synaptic vessicle Structure in the axon terminal of a neuron that contains neurotransmitters.

synesthesia A condition in which stimuli are experienced not only in the normal sensory modality but in others as well.

syntax Rules for combining words into grammatically correct sentences.

systematic desensitization A counterconditioning approach to treating anxiety in which an incompatible state, such as relaxation, is conditioned to the feared stimulus.

T

tardive dyskinesia A severe motor disorder that can occur as a side effect of the major tranquilizers.

task-irrelevant response Behavior that impedes or interferes with the process of successful coping.

task-relevant response Response that aids in the coping or problem-solving process.

taste bud Structure on the tongue that contains the receptors for the chemical substances that give rise to the sensory experience of taste.

T-cell Immune cell that matures in the thymus. T-cells are of several types: *helper T-cells, killer T-cells,* and *suppressor T-cells.*

TDF gene The specific gene on the Y chromosome that programs a fetus to develop as a male.

tectorial membrane A membrane in the inner ear whose movement stimulates the hair cells (auditory receptors).

telegraphic speech An early speech stage in which the child speaks like a telegram, using mostly nouns and verbs and omitting articles, adjectives, and adverbs.

temperament Characteristic patterns of emotionality and reactions to the environment that are visible early in life and appear to be genetically based.

temporal lobe The portion of the cerebral cortex, behind and below the frontal lobes, that is involved in hearing and other functions.

teratogen Substance, such as a chemical or virus, that can be passed from the mother to the fetus, adversely affecting its development.

tertiary prevention Measures aimed at enhancing the rehabilitation of people who have developed disorders.

test norms Tables of test scores based on a relevant group of subjects (the norm group), which are then used to evaluate and interpret other people's scores on the test.

test–retest reliability Consistency or stability of test scores when the test is administered on two or more occasions.

thalamus A large group of nuclei located above the midbrain; serves as an important sensory relay system.

Thematic Apperception Test A projective test in which people are asked to make up stories in response to pictures.

theory A system of generalizations that specify lawful relations between specific behaviors and their causes.

theory of cognitive dissonance See *cognitive dissonance theory.*

theory of multiple intelligences Gardner's notion that there are six distinct varieties of intelligence: linguistic, mathematical, visual–spatial, musical, bodily–kinesthetic, and personal.

theory of reasoned action A model developed by Fishbein and Ajzen to predict the circumstances under which behavior will be consistent with a given attitude.

theory of social impact Bibb Latané's theory that social pressure directed toward a group is diffused among its members, so that no one feels total responsibility for the success of the group enterprise.

threat In Rogers's theory, discrepancy between self-concept and experience that generates anxiety and motivates the person to reduce the discrepancy.

time out An extinction procedure in which an organism is removed from a situation in which positive reinforcement of a problem behavior can occur.

token economy A behavior modification program designed to strengthen appropriate behaviors by making tokenlike reinforcers contingent on those behaviors.

tolerance Condition in which increasingly larger doses of a drug are required in order for the original effects of the drug to be reproduced; caused by the body's compensatory responses, which counter the effects of the drug.

trait approach An approach to the study of personality that focuses on people's specific patterns of traits and is oriented toward measuring individual differences in traits.

transduction The process whereby sensory systems convert various forms of physical energy into nerve impulses.

transfer-appropriate processing Processing used to retrieve a memory that is of the same type as the processing used to store the memory. Such processing is thought to enhance recall.

transference The therapeutic phenomenon in which the client begins to respond irrationally to the therapist as if the latter were an important figure from the client's past.

transfer of excitation Zillmann's term for the possible misinterpretation of one's state of arousal, as when a person misperceives fear as sexual arousal.

trephination The ancient practice of chiseling a hole in the skull of a disordered person to allow the presumed demon to escape.

triarchic theory of intelligence Sternberg's three-part theory of intelligence. It includes the components that underlie intelligent behavior, the contexts in which intelligence is exercised, and the types of tasks that require intelligence.

trichromat A person capable of experiencing all the hues in the spectrum.

tricyclic One of a category of drugs used to treat depression.

tumor Tissue mass that results from uncontrolled cell growth.

two-factor theory of avoidance learning Learning theory that holds that avoidance learning involves both classical conditioning of fear and the learning of operant avoidance responses reinforced by anxiety reduction.

two-factor theory of emotion Schachter's theory that intensity of physiological arousal provides cues as to how strongly one is experiencing emotion, whereas appraisal of environmental cues tells one which emotion he or she is experiencing.

Type A behavior pattern A behavior pattern, involving a sense of time urgency, pressured behavior, and hostility, that appears to increase the risk of coronary heart disease.

U

unconditional positive regard Unconditional acceptance of a person, regardless of his or her failings or negative behaviors.

unconditioned response (UCR) The response (usually a reflex or innate response) that occurs unconditionally in the presence of a certain stimulus (the unconditioned stimulus) in the absence of previous learning.

unconditioned stimulus (UCS) A stimulus that evokes a particular unlearned response (the unconditioned response).

unconflicted adherence A response to motivational conflict in which a person ignores information and keeps doing what he or she has done before.

unconflicted change A response to motivational conflict in which a person uncritically changes his or her behavior.

unconscious (1) Contents of the mind that are not accessible to consciousness. (2) In psychoanalysis, the part of the mind that is beyond consciousness and contains instinctual drives and repressed material.

uncontrolled observation Observation carried out in a natural setting, which cannot be standardized or controlled.

unobtrusive measures See *nonreactive measures*.

unstructured interview An interview that proceeds spontaneously rather than according to a specific planned sequence of questions.

V

validity (1) The extent to which a test measures the characteristic it purports to measure. (2) The extent to which diagnostic categories capture actual disordered behavior patterns.

variable Any characteristic of a person, animal, or situation that can vary or take on different numerical values.

variable-interval schedule A reinforcement schedule in which reinforcement follows the first response that occurs after an average (but variable) interval following the last reinforced response.

variable-ratio schedule A schedule in which reinforcement is based on an average but variable number of responses.

variable schedule A reinforcement schedule in which reinforcement occurs after a variable amount of time or number of responses.

variance A measure of dispersion. One computes it by finding the difference between each score in a distribution and the mean, squaring and summing the deviations, and dividing by the number of observations minus 1.

variance accounted for The proportion of total behavioral variance that can be accounted for by an experimental manipulation or in terms of the relations among measured variables.

vascular theory of emotional feedback A theory that facial expressions produce changes in blood flow and temperature, which provide feedback to the brain concerning the emotion being triggered by eliciting stimuli.

ventral root The portion of the spinal cord that contains motor nerves.

ventricles Cavities in the brain that contain cerebrospinal fluid.

verbal conditioning A learning procedure for increasing certain classes of verbal responses by making a social reinforcer (such as ''good'' or a nod) contingent on the desired behaviors.

vestibular apparatus An organ in the inner ear that contains receptors for body movement and kinesthesis.

vestibular sense The sense for balance and equilibrium.

visual acuity The ability to sense fine visual detail.

vitreous humor A fluid in the eye that helps the eyeball maintain its shape.

vulnerability factor Personal or situational factor that makes people more susceptible to the negative impact of stressors.

W

Weber's law The principle that two stimuli must differ by a minimum percentage (or ratio) in order for their difference to be perceived.

Wernicke's area An area of the left temporal lobe involved in language comprehension.

white matter Portions of the nervous system made up of myelinated axons.

wish fulfillment In Freudian theory, the partial or complete satisfaction of a psychological need through dreaming or waking fantasy.

working memory See *short-term memory.*

working through In psychodynamic psychotherapy, the repeated encountering and struggle with significant issues during the course of treatment.

Y

Yerkes–Dodson law The hypothesis that for any task there is an optimal level of arousal. An inverted U relation often exists between emotional arousal and task performance, and the optimal level of arousal is lower for complex tasks than for simple ones.

Young–Helmholtz trichromatic theory The classical theory of color vision, which posits the existence of separate cones that respond maximally to red, blue, or green.

Z

zygote A new cell formed by the union of egg and sperm. After about 2 weeks, it becomes an embryo.

References

"A recovering patient" (1986). "Can we talk?" The schizophrenic patient in psychotherapy. *American Journal of Psychiatry, 143,* 68–70.

Aamodt, M. G. (1991). *Applied industrial/organizational psychology.* Belmont, CA: Wadsworth.

Aaron, S. (1986). *Stage fright.* Chicago: University of Chicago Press.

Abraham, K. (1968). Notes on the psychoanalytic investigation and treatment of manic-depressive insanity and allied conditions. In K. Abraham, *Selected papers of Karl Abraham.* New York: Basic Books. (Original work published 1911)

Abrams, D. B., & Wilson, G. T. (1983). Alcohol, sexual arousal, and self-control. *Journal of Personality and Social Psychology, 45,* 188–198.

Ada, G. L., & Nossal, G. (1987). The clonal-selection theory. *Scientific American, 257*(2), 62–69.

Adams, G. R., & Fitch, S. A. (1982). Ego stage and identity status development: A cross-sequential analysis. *Journal of Personality and Social Psychology, 43,* 574–583.

Adams, G. R., Gullotta, T. P., & Montemayor, R. (Eds.). (1992). *Adolescent identity formation.* Newbury Park, CA: Sage.

Adams, J. L. (1974). *Conceptual blockbusting.* Stanford, CA: Stanford Alumni Association.

Adams, P. R., & Adams, G. R. (1984). Mount Saint Helen's ashfall: Evidence for a disaster stress reaction. *American Psychologist, 39,* 252–260.

Adelmann, P. K., & Zajonc, R. B. (1989). Facial efference and the experience of emotion. *Annual Review of Psychology, 40,* 249–280.

Ader, R., & Cohen, N. (1990). The influence of conditioning on immune responses. In R. Ader, N. Cohen, & D. L. Felten (Eds.), *Psychoneuroimmunology II.* New York: Academic Press.

Ader, R., Cohen, N., & Felten, D. L. (Eds.). (1990). *Psychoneuroimmunology II.* New York: Academic Press.

Ahadi, S., & Diener, E. (1989). Multiple determinants and effect size. *Journal of Personality and Social Psychology, 56,* 398–406.

Ahles, T. A., Blanchard, E. B., & Leventhal, H. (1983). Cognitive control of pain: Attention to the sensory aspects of the cold pressor stimulus. *Cognitive Therapy and Research, 7,* 159–178.

Aiken, L. R. (1989). *Assessment of personality.* Boston: Allyn & Bacon.

Aiken, L. R. (1991). *Psychological testing and assessment* (7th ed.). Boston: Allyn & Bacon.

Ainsworth, M. S. (1989). Attachments beyond infancy. *American Psychologist, 44,* 709–716.

Ainsworth, M., Blehar, M. C., Waters, E., & Wall, S. (1978). *Patterns of attachment: A psychological study of the strange situation.* Hillsdale, NJ: Erlbaum.

Ainsworth, M. S., & Bowlby, J. (1991). An etiological approach to personality development. *American Psychologist, 46,* 333–341.

Akerstedt, T. (1988). Sleepiness as a consequence of shift work. *Sleep, 11,* 17–34.

Alan Guttmacher Institute. (1982). *Teenage pregnancy: The problem that hasn't gone away.* New York: Author.

Alcock, J. E. (1990). *Science and supernature: A critical appraisal of parapsychology.* Buffalo, NY: Prometheus Books.

Alcohol, Drug Abuse, and Mental Health Administration. (1990). *Economic costs of alcohol and drug abuse and mental illness: 1985.* Rockwell, MD: National Clearinghouse for Alcohol and Drug Information.

Aldwin, C. M., Levenson, M. R., Spiro, A., III, & Bosse, R. (1989). Does emotionality predict stress? Findings from the Normative Aging Study. *Journal of Personality and Social Psychology, 56,* 618–624.

Alexander, C. N., & Langer, E. J. (Eds.) (1990). *Higher stages of human development: Perspectives on adult growth.* New York: Oxford.

Alexander, F. (1950). *Psychosomatic medicine.* New York: Norton.

Alexander, F., French, T. M., & Pollack, G. H. (1968). *Psychosomatic specificity: Experimental studies and results.* Chicago: University of Chicago Press.

Alexander, R. C., et al. (1992). Search for cytomegalovirus in the postmortem brains of schizophrenic patients using the polymerase chain reaction. *Archives of General Psychiatry, 49,* 47–53.

Alkon, D. L. (1989). Memory storage and neural systems. *Scientific American, 261*(1), 42–50.

Allen, C. T., & Janiszewski, C. A. (1989). Assessing the role of contingency awareness in attitudinal conditioning with implications for advertising research. *Journal of Marketing Research, 26*(1), 30–43.

Allen, W. R. (1981). Moms, dads, and boys: Race and sex differences in the socialization of male children. In L. E. Gary (Ed.), *Black men.* Beverly Hills, CA: Sage.

Allport, G. W. (1935). Attitudes. In C. Murchison (Ed.), *Handbook of social psychology.* Worcester, MA: Clark University Press.

Altabe, M., & Thompson, J. K. (1992). Size estimation versus figural ratings of body image disturbance: Relation to body dissatisfaction and eating dysfunction. *International Journal of Eating Disorders, 11,* 397–402.

Altman, I., & Taylor, D. A. (1973). *Social penetration: The development of interpersonal relationships.* New York: Holt, Rinehart & Winston.

Amato, P. R., & Keith, B. (1991). Parental divorce and the well-being of children: A meta-analysis. *Psychological Bulletin, 110,* 26–46.

Ambady, N., & Rosenthal, R. (1992). Thin slices of expressive behavior as predictors of interpersonal consquences: A meta-analysis. *Psychological Bulletin, 111,* 256–274.

American Psychiatric Assocation. (1987). *Diagnostic and statistical manual of mental disorders* (3rd ed., rev.). Washington, DC: Author.

American Psychiatric Association. (1990). *The practice of ECT: Recommendations for treatment, training, and privileging.* Washington, DC: American Psychiatric Press.

Amsel, A. (1988). *Behaviorism, neobehaviorism, and cognitivism in learning theory: Historical and contemporary perspectives.* Hillsdale, NJ: Erlbaum.

Anderson, D. J., Noyes, R., Jr., & Crowe, R. R. (1984). A comparison of panic disorder and generalized anxiety disorder. *American Journal of Psychiatry, 141,* 572–575.

Anderson, D. R., & Jose, W. S., II. (1987, December). Employee lifestyle and the bottom line: Results from the Stay Well evaluation. *Fitness in Business,* pp. 86–91.

Anderson, J. R. (1980). *Cognitive psychology and its implications.* San Francisco: Freeman.

Anderson, J. R. (1991). The adaptive nature of human categorization. *Psychological Review, 98,* 409–429.

Anderson, T. (1988). The Airport Directors' perspective on disaster planning and mental health needs. *American Psychologist, 43,* 721–723.

Andersson, B. E. (1992). Effects of day-care on cognitive and socioemotional competence of thirteen-year-old Swedish schoolchildren. *Child Development, 63,* 20–36.

Andreasen, N. C. (1988). Brain imaging: Applications in psychiatry. *Science, 239,* 1381–1388.

Andreassi, J. L. (1989). *Psychophysiology: Human behavior and physiological response* (2nd ed.). Hillsdale, NJ: Erlbaum.

Andrews, K. H., & Kandel, D. B. (1979). Attitude and behavior: A specification of the contingent consistency hypothesis. *American Sociological Review, 44,* 298–310.

Antoni, M. H., et al. (1991). Cognitive-behavioral stress management intervention buffers distress responses and immunologic changes following notification of HIV-I seropositivity. *Journal of Consulting and Clinical Psychology, 59,* 906–915.

Antrobus, J. (1991). Dreaming: Cognitive processes during cortical activation and high afferent thresholds. *Psychological Review, 98,* 96–121.

Antrobus, J., Reinsel, R., & Wollman, M. (1984). Dreaming: Cortical activation and perceptual thresholds: More evidence. *Sleep Research, 13,* 101–112.

Apgar, V., & Beck, J. (1972). *Is my baby all right? A guide to birth defects.* New York: Trident.

Aponte, H., & Hoffman, L. (1973). The open door: A structural approach to a family with an anorectic child. *Family Process, 12,* 1–44.

Arena, J. M. (1984, April). A look at the opposite sex. *Newsweek on Campus,* p. 21.

Arlin, P. K. (1984). Adolescent and adult thought: A structural interpretation. In M. L. Commons, F. A. Richards, & C. Armon (Eds.), *Beyond formal operations: Late adolescent and adult cognitive development* (pp. 258–271). New York: Praeger.

Aronson, B., & Worchel, S. (1966). Similarity versus liking as determinants of interpersonal attractiveness. *Psychonomic Science, 5,* 157–158.

Aronson, E. (1990). Applying social psychology to desegregation and energy conservation. *Personality and Social Psychology Bulletin, 16,* 118–132.

Aronson, E., Stephan, C., Sikes, J., Blaney, N., & Snopp, M. (1978). *The jigsaw classroom.* Beverly Hills, CA: Sage.

Asch, S. E. (1946). Forming impressions of personality. *Journal of Abnormal and Social Psychology, 41,* 258–290.

Asch, S. E. (1951). Effects of group pressure upon the modification and distortion of judgment. In H. Guetzkow (Ed.), *Groups, leadership, and men.* Pittsburgh: Carnegie Press.

Asch, S. E. (1956). Studies of independence and conformity: A minority of one against a unanimous majority. *Psychological Monographs, 70,* 9, 416.

Aserinsky, E., & Kleitman, N. (1953). Regularly occurring periods of ocular motility and concomitant phenomena during sleep. *Science, 118,* 361–375.

Ash, P. (1991). A history of honesty testing. In J. W. Jones (Ed.), *Pre-employment honesty testing: Current research and future directions.* Westport, CT: Greenwood.

Aslin, R. N. (1987). Visual and auditory development in infancy. In J. Osofsky (Ed.), *Handbook of infant development* (pp. 5–97). New York: Wiley.

Astin, A. W., et al. (1991). *The American freshman: National norms for fall, 1990.* Los Angeles: American Council on Education and UCLA.

Atchley, R. C. (1976). *The sociology of retirement.* Cambridge, MA: Schenkman.

Atkinson, J., & Braddick, O. (1989). Development of basic visual functions. In A. Slater and G. Bremner (Eds.), *Infant development.* Hillsdale, NJ: Erlbaum.

Atkinson, J. W., & Birch, D. (1978). *An introduction to motivation.* New York: Van Nostrand.

Atkinson, R. C. & Shiffrin, R. M. (1968). Human memory: A proposed system and its control processes. In K. W. Spence & J. T. Spence (Eds.), *Advances in the psychology of learning and motivation: Research and theory* (Vol.2). New York: Academic Press.

Atwood, V. A. (1984). Children's concepts of death: A descriptive study. *Child Study Journal, 14,* 11–29.

Auerbach, S. M. (1989). Stress management and coping research in the health care setting: An overview and methodological commentary. *Journal of Consulting and Clinical Psychology, 57,* 388–395.

Averill, J. A. (1980). A constructivist view of emotion. In R. Plutchik & H. Kellerman (Eds.) *Emotion: Theory, research, and experience.* Vol. 1, *Theories of emotion.* New York: Academic Press.

Axelrod, S., & Apsche, J. (Eds.). (1983). *The effects of punishment on human behavior.* New York: Academic Press.

Ayllon, T., & Azrin, N. H. (1968). *The token economy: A motivational system for therapy and rehabilitation.* New York: Appleton-Century-Crofts.

Babor, T. F., Cooney, N. L., & Lauerman, R. J. (1987). The dependence syndrome concept as a psychological theory of relapse behaviour: An empirical evaluation of alcoholic and opiate addicts. *British Journal of Addiction, 82,* 393–406.

Bach, S., & Klein, G. S. (1957). The effects of prolonged subliminal exposure of words. *American Psychologist, 12,* 397–398.

Bachman, J. G., Johnson, L. D., & O'Malley, P. M. (1987). *Monitoring the future: Questionnaire responses from the nation's high school seniors.* Ann Arbor: Institute for Social Research, University of Michigan.

Baddeley, A. (1982). *Your memory: A user's guide.* Harmondsworth, England: Penguin.

Baddeley, A. (1986). *Working memory.* Oxford: Oxford.

Baddeley, A., & Logie, R. (1992). Auditory imagery and working memory. In D. Reisberg (Ed.), *Auditory imagery.* Hillsdale, NJ: Erlbaum.

Bailey, C. H., & Chen, M. (1992). The anatomy of long-term sensitization in *Aplysia*: Morphological insights into learning and memory. In L. R. Squire, N. M. Weinberger, G. Lynch, & J. L. McGaugh (Eds.), *Memory: Organization and locus of change.* New York: Oxford.

Bailey, J. M., & Pillard, R. C. (1991). A genetic study of male sexual orientation. *Archives of General Psychiatry, 48,* 1089–1096.

Baker, S. L., & Kirsch, I. (1991). Cognitive mediators of pain perception and tolerance. *Journal of Personality and Social Psychology, 61,* 504–510.

Balay, J., & Shevrin, H. (1988). The subliminal psychodynamic activation method: A critical review. *American Psychologist, 43,* 161–174.

Bales, J. (1987, June). House bill outlaws worker polygraphs. *APA Monitor,* p. 17.

Bales, R. F., & Slater, P. E. (1955). Role differentiation in small decision-making groups. In T. Parsons & R. F. Bales (Eds.), *Family, socialization, and interaction process.* New York: Free Press.

Baltes, P. B. (1987). Theoretical propositions of life-span developmental psychology: On the dynamics between growth and decline. *Developmental Psychology, 23,* 611–626.

Bandura, A. (1965). Influence of models' reinforcement contingencies on the acquisition of imitated responses. *Journal of Personality and Social Psychology, 1,* 589–595.

Bandura, A. (1973). *Aggression: A social learning analysis.* Englewood Cliffs, NJ: Prentice-Hall.

Bandura, A. (1986). *Social foundations of thought and action: A social-cognitive theory.* Englewood Cliffs, NJ: Prentice-Hall.

Bandura, A. (1988). Mechanisms of moral disengagement in terrorism. In W. Reich (Ed.), *The psychology of terrorism: Behaviors, world-views, states of mind.* New York: Cambridge.

Bandura, A. (1989). Social cognitive theory. *Annals of Child Development. 6,* 3–58.

Bandura, A., Blanchard, E. B., & Ritter, B. (1969). The relative efficacy of desensitization and modeling approaches for inducing behavioral, affective and attitudinal changes. *Journal of Personality and Social Psychology, 13,* 173–199.

Bandura, A., & Cervone, D. (1983). Self-evaluative and self-efficacy mechanisms governing the motivational effects of goal systems. *Journal of Personality and Social Psychology, 45,* 1017–1028.

Bandura, A., O'Leary, A., Taylor, C. B., Gauthier, J., & Gossard, D. (1987). Perceived self-efficacy and pain control: Opioid and nonopioid mechanisms. *Journal of Personality and Social Psychology, 53,* 563–571.

Banks, W. P., & Krajicek, D. (1991). Perception. *Annual Review of Psychology, 42,* 305–332.

Barber, B. L., & Eccles, J. S. (1992). Long-term influence of divorce and single parenting on adolescent family- and work-related values, behaviors, and aspirations. *Psychological Bulletin, 111,* 108–126.

Barber, J. (1977). Rapid induction analgesia. *American Journal of Clinical Hypnosis, 19,* 138–143.

Barefoot, J. C., Dodge, K. A., Peterson, B. L., Dahlstrom, W. G., & Williams, R. B. (1989). The Cook-Medley Hostility Scale: Item content and ability to predict survival. *Psychosomatic Medicine, 51,* 46–57.

Bargh, J. A. (1984). Automatic and conscious processing of social information. In R. S. Wyer & T. K. Srull (Eds.), *Handbook of social cognition* (Vol. 3). Hillsdale, NJ: Erlbaum.

Barker, R. (1972). The effects of REM sleep on the retention of a visual task. *Psychophysiology, 9,* 107.

Barlow, D. H. (1988). *Anxiety and its disorders: The nature and treatment of anxiety and panic.* New York: Guilford.

Barlow, D. H. (1991) Disorders of emotion. *Psychological Inquiry, 2,* 58–71.

Barlow, D. H., Craske, M. G., Cerny, J. A. & Klosko, J. S. (1989). Behavioral treatment of panic disorder. *Behavior Therapy, 20,* 261–282.

Barnes, D. M. (1990, Spring). Silver Spring monkeys yield unexpected data on brain reorganization. *Journal of NIH Research,* 19–20.

Barnes, G. E., & Prosen, H. (1985). Parental death and depression. *Journal of Abnormal Psychology, 94,* 64–69.

Barnett, N. P., Smoll, F. L., & Smith, R. E. (1992). Effects of enhancing coach-athlete relationships on youth sport attrition. *Sport Psychologist, 6,* 111–127.

Barnett, R. G., Marshall, N. L., & Singer, J. D. (1992). Job experiences over time, multiple roles, and women's mental health: A longitudinal study. *Journal of Personality and Social Psychology, 62,* 634–644.

Baron, R. A. (1977). *Human aggression.* New York: Plenum.

Baron, R. A., & Byrne, D. (1991). *Social psychology: Understanding human interaction* (6th ed.). Boston: Allyn & Bacon.

Baron, R. A., & Richardson, D. R. (1991). *Human aggression* (2nd ed.). New York: Plenum.

Baron, R. M., Graziano, W. G., & Stangor, C. (1991). Social perception and social cognition. In R. M.

Baron, W. G. Graziano, & C. Stangor (Eds.), *Social psychology*. Ft. Worth, TX: Holt, Rinehart & Winston.

Baron, R. S. (1986). Distraction-conflict theory: Progress and problems. In L. Berkowitz (Ed.), *Advances in experimental social psychology* (Vol. 20). New York: Academic Press.

Baron, R. S., Cutrona, C. E., Hicklin, D., Russell, D. W., & Lubaroff, D. M. (1990). Social support and immune responses among spouses of cancer patients. *Journal of Personality and Social Psychology, 59,* 344–352.

Barrett, G. V., & Depinet, R. L. (1991). A reconsideration of testing for competence rather than intelligence. *American Psychologist, 46,* 1012–1024.

Barrett, N. (1987). Women and the economy. In S. E. Rix (Ed.), *The American woman, 1987–1988*. New York: Norton.

Barrett, R. J. (1985). Behavioral approaches to individual differences in substance abuse: Drug taking behavior. In M. Galizio & S. A. Maisto (Eds.), *Determinants of substance abuse treatment: Biological, psychological, and environmental factors*. New York: Plenum.

Barsalou, L. W. (1992). *Cognitive psychology: An overview for cognitive scientists*. Hillsdale, NJ: Erlbaum.

Bartlett, F. C. (1932). *Remembering: A study in experimental and social psychology*. New York: Cambridge.

Baruch, G., Barnett, R., & Rivers, C. (1983). *Life prints: New patterns of love and work for today's woman*. New York: McGraw-Hill.

Bassok, M., & Holyoak, K. J. (1989). Interdomain transfer between isomorphic topics in algebra and physics. *Journal of Experimental Psychology: Learning, Memory, and Cognition, 15,* 153–166.

Bassuck, E. L., Rubin, L., & Lauriat, A. (1984). Is homelessness a mental health problem? *American Journal of Psychiatry, 141,* 1546–1550.

Bates, J. E. (1982, March). *Temperament as a part of social relationships: Implications of perceived infant difficultness*. Paper presented at the International Conference on Infant Studies, Austin, TX.

Batson, C. D., & Weeks, J. (1991). Helping. In R. M. Baron, W. G. Graziano, & C. Stangor (Eds.), *Social psychology*. Ft. Worth, TX: Holt, Rinehart & Winston.

Batson, G. D. (1991). *The altruism question: Toward a social-psychological answer*. Hillsdale, NJ: Erlbaum.

Baudry, M., & Davis, J. L. (Eds.). (1991). *Long-term potentiation: A debate of current issues*. Cambridge, MA: MIT Press.

Bauer, K. E., & McCanne, T. R. (1980). Autonomic and central nervous system responding during hypnosis and simulation of hypnosis. *International Journal of Clinical and Experimental Hypnosis, 28,* 148–163.

Baumeister, R. F. (1986). *Identity*. New York: Oxford.

Baumeister, R. F. (1991). Self-concept and identity. In N. J. Derlega, B. A. Winstead, & W. H. Jones (Eds.), *Personality: Contemporary theory and research*. Chicago: Nelson-Hall.

Baumrind, D. (1967). Child care practices anteceding three patterns of preschool behavior. *Genetic Psychology Monographs, 75,* 43–88.

Baumrind, D. (1980). New directions in socialization research. *American Psychologist, 35,* 639–652.

Baumrind, D. (1983). Rejoinder to Lewis's reinterpretation of parental firm control effects: Are authoritative families really harmonious? *Psychological Bulletin, 94,* 132–142.

Baumrind, D. (1991). Parenting styles and adolescent development. In J. Brooks-Gunn, R. Lerner, & A. C. Petersen (Eds.), *The encyclopedia of adolescence*. New York: Garland.

Bayer, L. M., Buechy, D. W., & Honzik, M. P. (1981). Health in the middle years. In D. Eichorn, J. Clausen, N. Haan, M. Honzik, & P. Mussen (Eds.), *Present and past in middle life*. New York: Academic Press.

Baylor, D. (1987). Photoreceptor signals and vision. *Investigative Ophthalmology and Visual Science, 28,* 34–49.

Beaman, A. L., Barnes, P. J., Klentz, D., & McQuirk, B. F. (1978). Increasing helping rates through information dissemination: Teaching pays. *Personality and Social Psychology Bulletin, 4,* 406–411.

Beck, A. T. (1967). *Depression: Clinical, experimental, and theoretical aspects*. New York: Hoeber.

Beck, A. T. (1976). *Cognitive therapy and the emotional disorders*. New York: International Universities Press.

Beck, A. T. (1988). Cognitive approaches to panic disorder: Theory and therapy. In S. Rachman & J. D. Maser (Eds.), *Panic: Psychological perspectives*. Hillsdale, NJ: Erlbaum.

Beck, A. T. (1991). Cognitive therapy: A 30-year retrospective. *American Psychologist, 46,* 368–375.

Beck, A. T., & Freeman, A. (1990). *Cognitive theory of personality disorders*. New York: Guilford.

Beck, A. T., Rush, A. J., Shaw, B. F., & Emery, G. (1979). *Cognitive therapy of depression*. New York: Guilford.

Beck, S. H. (1982). Adjustment to and satisfaction with retirement. *Journal of Gerontology, 37,* 616–624.

Becker, J. B., Breedlove, S. M., & Crews, D. (Eds.). (1992). *Behavioral endocrinology*. Cambridge, MA: MIT Press.

Bee, H. (1989). *The developing child* (5th ed.). New York: Harper & Row.

Beecher, H. K. (1959). Generalization from pain of various types and diverse origins. *Science, 130,* 267–268.

Beilin, H. (1992). Piaget's enduring contribution to developmental psychology. *Developmental Psychology, 28,* 191–204.

Bekerian, D. A., & Bowers, J. M. (1983). Eyewitness testimony: Were we misled? *Journal of Experimental Psychology: Learning, Memory, and Cognition, 9,* 139–145.

Bekesy, G. von. (1957). The ear. *Scientific American, 230*(8), 66–78.

Bell, A. P., Weinberg, M. S., & Hammersmith, S. K. (1981). *Sexual preference: Its development in men and women*. Bloomington: Indiana University Press.

Bell, P. A., Fisher, J. D., Baum, A., & Greene, T. E. (1990). *Environmental psychology* (3rd ed.). New York: Holt, Rinehart & Winston.

Belsky, J. (1990). *The psychology of aging: Theory, research, and interventions*. Pacific Grove, CA: Brooks/Cole.

Belsky, J., & Rovine, M. J. (1988). Nonmaternal care in the first year of life and the security of infant-parent attachment. *Child Development, 59,* 157–167.

Belsky, J., & Steinberg, L. (1978). The effects of day care: A critical review. *Child Development, 49,* 929–949.

Bem, D. J. (1972). Self-perception theory. In L. Berkowitz (Ed.), *Advances in experimental social psychology* (Vol. 6). New York: Academic Press.

Benbow, C. P. (1988). Sex differences in mathematical reasoning ability in intellectually talented adolescents: Their nature, effect, and possible causes. *Behavioral and Brain Sciences, 11,* 169–232.

Benjamin, L. T., Cavell, T. A., & Shallenberger, W. R. (1984). Staying with initial answers on objective tests: Is it a myth? *Teaching of Psychology, 11,* 133–141.

Bennett, H. L. (1983). Remembering drink orders: The memory skills of cocktail waitresses. *Human Learning, 2,* 157–169.

Bennett, N. G., Blane, A. K., & Bloom, D. E. (1988). Commitment and the modern union: Assessing the link between premarital cohabitation and subsequent marital stability. *American Sociological Review, 53,* 127–138.

Benson, H., & Klipper, M. Z. (1976). *The relaxation response*. New York: Morrow.

Benson, P. L., Karabenick, S. A., & Lerner, R. M. (1976). Pretty pleases: The effects of physical attractiveness, race, and sex on receiving help. *Journal of Experimental Social Psychology, 12,* 409–415.

Bentz, V. J. (1968). The Sears experience in the investigation, description, and prediction of executive behavior. In J. A. Myers, Jr. (Ed.), *Predicting managerial success*. Ann Arbor, MI: Foundation for Research on Human Behavior.

Berg, J. H., & McQuinn, R. D. (1986). Attraction and exchange in continuing and noncontinuing relationships. *Journal of Personality and Social Psychology, 50,* 942–952.

Berk, R. A., & Rossi, P. H. (1990). *Thinking about program evaluation*. Newbury Park, CA: Sage.

Berkowitz, L. (1990). On the formation and regulation of anger and aggression. *American Psychologist, 45,* 494–503.

Berlyne, D. E. (1978). Curiosity and learning. *Learning and Motivation, 2,* 99–175.

Berman, A. L., & Jobes, D. A. (1991). *Adolescent suicide: Assessment and intervention*. Washington, DC: American Psychological Association.

Berndt, T. J. (1982). The features and effects of friendships in early adolescence. *Child Development, 53,* 1447–1460.

Berry, D. S., & McArthur, L. Z. (1986). Perceiving character in faces: The impact of age-related craniofacial changes on social perception. *Psychological Bulletin, 100,* 3–18.

Berscheid, E. (1984). *The problem of emotion in close relationships*. New York: Plenum.

Best, D. L., Williams, J. E., Cloud, J. M., Davis, S. W., Robertson, L. S., Edwards, J. R., Giles, H., & Fowles, J. (1977). Development of sex-trait stereotypes among young children in the United States, England, and Ireland. *Child Development, 48,* 1375–1384.

Best, J. B. (1992). *Cognitive psychology* (3rd ed.). St. Paul, MN: West.

Bettelheim, B. (1943). Individual and mass behavior in extreme situations. *Journal of Abnormal and Social*

Psychology, 38, 417–462.

Beutler, L. E. (1991). Have all won and must all have prizes? Revisiting Luborsky et al.'s verdict. *Journal of Consulting and Clinical Psychology, 59,* 226–232.

Beutler, L. E., Crago, M., & Arizmendi, T. G. (1986). Research on therapist variables in psychotherapy. In S. L. Garfield & A. E. Bergin (Eds.), *Handbook of psychotherapy and behavior change* (3rd ed.). New York: Wiley.

Beutler, L. E., Engle, D., Mohr, D., Daldrup, R. J., Bergan, J., Meredith, K., & Merry, W. (1991). Predictors of differential response to cognitive, experiential, and self-directed psychotherapeutic procedures. *Journal of Consulting and Clinical Psychology, 59,* 333–340.

Bever, T. G., Carroll, J. M., & Miller, L. A. (Eds.). (1984). *Talking minds: The study of language in the cognitive sciences.* Cambridge, MA: MIT Press.

Bickman, L., & Dokecki, P. R. (1989). Public and private responsibility for mental health services. *American Psychologist, 44,* 1133–1137.

Bieber, I., et al. (1962). *Homosexuality.* New York: Vintage Books.

Biener, L., & Boudreau, L. (1991). Social power and influence. In R. M. Baron, W. G. Graziano, & C. Stangor (Eds.), *Social psychology.* Ft. Worth, TX: Holt, Rinehart & Winston.

Bigler, E. D., Yeo, R. A., & Turkeheimer, E. (Eds.). (1989). *Neuropsychological function and brain imaging.* New York: Plenum.

Billings, A. G., & Moos, R. H. (1981). The role of coping responses and social resources in attenuating the stress of life events. *Journal of Behavioral Medicine, 4,* 139–157.

Binet, A. M., & Simon, T. (1905). Méthodes nouvelles pour le diagnostic du niveau intellectuel des anormaux. *L'Anée Psychologique, 11,* 191–224.

Black, D. W., Yates, W. R., & Andreasen, N. C. (1988). Schizophrenia, schizophreniform disorder, and delusional paranoid disorders. In J. A. Talbott, R. E. Hales, & S. C. Yudofsky (Eds.), *Textbook of psychiatry.* Washington, DC: American Psychiatric Press.

Blackwell, C. (1981). Transition to widowhood: A review of the literature. *Family Relations, 30,* 117–127.

Blakemore, C., & Cooper, G. F. (1970). Development of the brain depends on visual environment. *Nature, 228,* 477–478.

Blanchard, E. B., & Andrasik, F. (1985). *Management of chronic headaches: A psychological approach.* New York: Pergamon Press.

Blaney, P. H. (1986). Affect and memory: A review. *Psychological Bulletin, 99,* 229–246.

Block, J. (1981). Some enduring and consequential structures of personality. In A. I. Rabin (Ed.), *Further explorations in personality.* New York: Wiley.

Blodgett, R. (1986, May). Lost in the stars: Psychics strike out (again). *People Expression,* pp. 32–35.

Blood, R. O., Jr., & Blood, M. (1978). *Marriage* (3rd ed.) New York: Free Press.

Bloom, B., Hodges, W., & Caldwell, R. (1982). A preventive program for the newly separated: Initial evaluation. *American Journal of Community Psychology, 10,* 251–264.

Bloom, F. E., Lazerson, A., & Hofstadter, L. (1984). *Brain, mind, and behavior.* New York: Freeman.

Blumberg, S. H., & Izard, C. E. (1985). Affective and cognitive characteristics of depression in 10- and 11-year-old children. *Journal of Personality and Social Psychology, 49,* 194–202.

Blumenthal, J. A., Burg, M. M., Barefoot, J., Williams, R. B., Haney, T., & Zimet, G. (1987). Social support, Type A behavior, and coronary artery disease. *Psychosomatic Medicine, 49,* 331–340.

Bobo, L. (1988). Attitudes toward the black political movement: Trends, meaning, and effects of racial policy preferences. *Social Psychology Quarterly, 51,* 287–302.

Bobvjerg, D., Cohen, N., & Adler, R. (1987). Behaviorally conditioned enhancement of delayed-type hypersensitivity in the mouse. *Brain, Behavior, and Immunity, 1,* 64–71.

Bohannon, J. N. (1988). Flashbulb memories and the space shuttle disaster: A tale of two theories. *Cognition, 29,* 179–196.

Bohlen, J. (1986, February). Quoted in W. Galagher, The etiology of orgasm. *Discover,* pp. 51–59.

Bolles, R. C. (1979). *Learning theory* (2nd ed.). New York: Holt, Rinehart and Winston.

Bond, M. H. (1986). *The psychology of the Chinese people.* New York: Oxford.

Booth-Kewley, S., & Friedman, H. S. (1987). Psychological predictors of heart disease: A quantitative review. *Psychological Bulletin, 101,* 343–362.

Borchard, E. M. (1932). *Convicting the innocent: Errors of criminal justice.* New Haven, CT: Yale University Press.

Bornstein, R. F. (1989). Exposure and affect: Overview and meta-analysis of research, 1968–1987. *Psychological Bulletin, 106,* 265–289.

Bornstein, R. F., Leone, D. R., & Galley, D. J. (1987). The generalizability of subliminal mere exposure effects: Influence of stimuli perceived without awareness on social behavior. *Journal of Personality and Social Psychology, 53,* 1070–1079.

Botwin, M. D., & Buss, D. M. (1989). Structure of act report data: Is the five-factor model of personality recaptured? *Journal of Personality and Social Psychology, 56,* 988–1001.

Bouchard, T. J., Lykken, D. T., McGue, M., Segal, N. L., & Tellegen, A. (1990). Sources of human psychological differences: The Minnesota study of twins reared apart. *Science, 250,* 223–228.

Bouchard, T. J., & McGue, M. (1981). Familial studies of intelligence: A review. *Science, 212,* 1055–1059.

Boucher, J. D., & Ekman, P. (1975). Facial areas and emotional information. *Journal of Communication, 25,* 21–29.

Boudewyns, P. A., Fry, T. J., & Nightingale, E. J. (1986). Token economy program in VA medical centers: Where are they today? *Behavior Therapist, 6,* 126–127.

Bourne, L., Dominowski, R., Loftus, E., & Healy, A. (1986). *Cognitive processes* (2nd ed.). Englewood Cliffs, NJ: Prentice-Hall.

Bower, G. H. (1981). Mood and memory. *American Psychologist, 36,* 129–148.

Bower, G. H., Clark, M. C., Lesgold, M. A., & Winzenz, D. (1969). Hierarchical retrieval schemes in recall of categorized word lists. *Journal of Verbal Learning and Verbal Behavior, 8,* 323–343.

Bower, T. (1989). The perceptual world of the new-born child. In A. Slater & G. Bremner (Eds.), *Infant development.* Hillsdale, NJ: Erlbaum.

Bowlby, J. (1958). The nature of the child's tie to his mother. *International Journal of Psychoanalysis, 39,* 350–373.

Braddock, J. H. (1985). School desegregation and black assimilation. *Journal of Social Issues, 41,* 9–22.

Brady, E. G., & Kendall, P. C. (1992). Comorbidity of anxiety and depression in children and adolescents. *Psychological Bulletin, 111,* 244–255.

Bransford, J. D., & Franks, J. J. (1971). The abstraction of linguistic ideas. *Cognitive Psychology, 2,* 331–350.

Braungart, J. M., Plomin, R., De Fries, J. C., & Fulkes, D. W. (1992). Genetic influence on tester-rated infant temperament as assessed by Bayley's Infant Behavior Record: Nonadoptive and adoptive siblings and twins. *Developmental Psychology, 28,* 40–47.

Bray, G. A. (1978). Definitions, measurements, and classification of the syndromes of obesity. *International Journal of Obesity, 2,* 99–112.

Breedlove, S. M. (1992). Sexual differentiation of brain and behavior. In J. B. Becker, S. M. Breedlove, & D. Crews (Eds.), *Behavioral endocrinology.* Cambridge, MA: MIT Press.

Brehm, J. W., & Self, E. A. (1989). The intensity of motivation. *Annual Review of Psychology, 40,* 109–131.

Brehm, S. S. (1992). *Intimate relationships* (2nd ed.). New York: McGraw-Hill.

Brehm, S. S., & Kassin, S. M. (1990). *Social psychology.* Dallas: Houghton Mifflin.

Breier, A., Schreber, J. L., Dyer, J., & Pickar, D. (1991). National Institute of Mental Health longitudinal study of chronic schizophrenia: Progress and predictors of outcome. *Archives of General Psychiatry, 48,* 239–246.

Briggs, S. R. (1989). The optimal level of measurement for personality constructs. In D. M. Buss & N. Cantor (Eds.), *Personality psychology: Recent trends and emerging directions.* New York: Springer-Verlag.

Briggs, S. R. (1991). Personality measurement. In N. J. Derlega, B. A. Winstead, & W. H. Jones (Eds.), *Personality: Contemporary theory and research.* Chicago: Nelson-Hall.

Brislin, R. W. (1988). Increasing awareness of class, ethnicity, culture, and race by expanding on students' own experiences. In I. S. Cohen (Ed.), *The G. Stanley Hall lecture series* (Vol. 8). Washington, DC: American Psychological Association.

Broadbent, D. E. (1958). *Perception and communication.* London: Pergamon.

Broberg, D. J., Dorsa, D. M., & Bernstein, I. L. (1990). Nausea in bulimic women in response to a palatable food. *Journal of Abnormal Psychology, 99,* 183–189.

Brockhaus, A., & Elger, C. E. (1990). Hypalgesic efficacy of acupuncture on experimental pain in man: Comparison of laser acupuncture and needle acupuncture. *Pain, 43,* 181–185.

Brody, G. H., Neubaum, E., & Forehand, R. (1988). Serial marriages: A heuristic analysis of an emerging family form. *Psychological Bulletin, 103,* 211–222.

Brooks-Gunn, J., & Furstenberg, F. F., Jr. (1989). Adolescent sexual behavior. *American Psychologist, 44,* 249–257.

Brown, A. L., Bransford, J. D., Ferrara, R. A., & Campione, J. C. (1983). Learning, remembering, and understanding. In P. Mussen (Ed.), *Handbook of child psychology: Vol. 3. Cognitive development.* New York: Wiley.

Brown, B. B., Clasen, D. R., & Eicher, S. A. (1986). Perceptions of peer pressure, peer conformity dispositions, and self-reported behavior among adolescents. *Developmental Psychology, 22,* 521–530.

Brown, D. P., & Fromm, E. (1987). *Hypnosis and behavioral medicine.* Hillsdale, NJ: Erlbaum.

Brown, G., & Harris, T. (1978). *Social origins of depression: A study of psychiatric disorder in women.* New York: Free Press.

Brown, J. B. (1991a). Accuracy and bias in self-knowledge. In C. R. Snyder & D. R. Forsythe (Eds.), *Handbook of social and clinical psychology: The health perspective.* New York: Pergamon.

Brown, J. B. (1991b). Staying fit and staying well: Physical fitness as a moderator of life stress. *Journal of Personality and Social Psychology, 60,* 555–561.

Brown, J. B., & Siegel, J. M. (1988). Exercise as a buffer of life stress: A prospective study. *Health Psychology, 7,* 341–353.

Brown, J. D., Novick, N. J., Lord, K. A., & Richards, J. M. (1992). When Gulliver travels: Social context, psychological closeness, and self-appraisals. *Journal of Personality and Social Psychology, 62,* 717–727.

Brown, R., & Kulik, J. (1977). Flashbulb memories. *Cognition, 5,* 73–99.

Brown, T. S., & Wallace, P. (1980). *Physiological psychology.* New York: Academic Press.

Brownell, K. D. (1991). Dieting and the search for the perfect body: Where psychology and culture collide. *Behavior Therapy, 22,* 1–12.

Brownmiller, S. (1975). *Against our will: Men, women and rape.* New York: Simon & Schuster.

Brozan, N. (1985, March 13). U.S. leads industrialized nations in teenage births and abortions. *New York Times,* p. P1.

Bruch, H. (1973). *Eating disorders: Obesity, anorexia nervosa, and the person within.* New York: Basic Books.

Bruner, J. S. (1983). *Child's talk.* New York: Norton.

Bruner, J. S. (1992). Another look at New Look I. *American Psychologist, 47,* 780–783.

Bruning, N. S., & Frew, D. R. (1987). Effects of exercise, relaxation and management skills training on physiological stress indicators: A field experiment. *Journal of Applied Psychology, 72,* 515–521.

Bryan, J., III. (1986). *Hodgepodge: A commonplace book.* New York: Ballantine.

Bryant, R. A., & McConkey, K. M. (1989). Hypnotic blindness: A behavioral and experimental analysis. *Journal of Abnormal Psychology, 98,* 71–77.

Buchanan, C. M., Eccles, J. S., & Becker, J. B. (1992). Are adolescents the victims of raging hormones? Evidence for activational effects of hormones on moods and behaviors at adolescence. *Psychological Bulletin, 111,* 62–107.

Buchsbaum, M. S., & Haier, R. J. (1987). Functional and anatomical brain imaging: Import on schizophrenia research. *Schizophrenia Bulletin, 1391,* 115–132.

Buck, L., & Axel, R. (1991). A novel multigene family may encode odorant receptors: A molecular basis for odor recognition. *Cell, 65,* 175–187.

Buck, R., & Ginsburg, B. (1991). Spontaneous communication and altruism: The communicative gene hypothesis. In M. S. Clark (Ed.), *Prosocial behavior.* Newbury Park, CA: Sage.

Bureau of the Census. (1992). *Statistical abstract of the U.S.* Washington, DC: U.S. Government Printing Office.

Burgess, A. W., & Holmstrom, L. L. (1974). Rape trauma syndrome. *American Journal of Psychiatry, 131,* 981–986.

Buri, J. R., Louiselle, P. A., Misukanis, T. M., & Mueller, R. A. (1988). Effects of parental authoritarianism and authoritativeness on self-esteem. *Personality and Social Psychology Bulletin, 14,* 271–282.

Burke, K. C., Burke, J. D., Rae, D. S., & Regier, D. A. (1991). Comparing age at onset of major depression and other psychiatric disorders by birth cohorts in five U.S. community populations. *Archives of General Psychiatry, 48,* 789–795.

Burns, M. O., & Seligman, M. E. P. (1989). Explanatory style across the life span: Evidence for stability over 52 years. *Journal of Personality and Social Psychology, 56,* 471–477.

Burnstein, E. (1983). Persuasion as argument processing. In M. Brandstatter, J. H. Davis, & G. Stocker-Kreichgauer (Eds.), *Group decision processes.* London: Academic Press.

Burrows, G. D., & Dennestein, L. (1988). *Handbook of hypnosis and psychosomatic medicine.* New York: Elsevier.

Burton, D. (1988). Do anxious swimmers swim slower? Reexamining the elusive anxiety-performance relationship. *Journal of Sport and Exercise Psychology, 10,* 45–61.

Buser, P., & Imbert, M. (1992). *Audition.* Cambridge, MA: MIT Press.

Buss, A. H., & Plomin, R. (1984). *Temperament: Early developing personality traits.* Hillsdale, NJ: Erlbaum.

Buss, D. M. (1991). Evolutionary personality theory. *Annual Review of Psychology, 42,* 459–491.

Butcher, J. N., & Dunn, L. (1989). Human responses and treatment needs in airline disasters. In R. Gist & B. Lubin (Eds.), *Psychosocial aspects of disaster.* New York: Wiley.

Butcher, J. N., & Hatcher, C. (1988). The neglected entity in air disaster planning: Psychological services. *American Psychologist, 43,* 724–729.

Byrne, D., & Clore, G. L. (1970). A reinforcement model of evaluative responses. *Personality: An International Journal, 1,* 103–128.

Byrne, D., Clore, G. L., & Smeaton, G. (1986). The attraction hypothesis: Do similar attitudes affect anything? *Journal of Personality and Social Psychology, 51,* 1167–1170.

Byrne, D., & Greendlinger, V. (1989). *Need for affiliation as a predictor of classroom friendships.* Unpublished manuscript, State University of New York at Albany.

Byrne, D., & Nelson, D. (1965). Attraction as a linear function of proportion of positive reinforcements. *Journal of Personality and Social Psychology, 1,* 659–663.

Cairns, H. (1952). Disturbances of consciousness in lesions of the mid-brain and diencephalon. *Brain, 75,* 107–114.

Calabrese, J. R., Kling, M. A., & Gold, P. W. (1987). Alterations in immunocompetence during stress, bereavement, and depression: Focus on neuroendocrine regulation. *American Journal of Psychiatry, 144,* 1123–1134.

Calhoun, J. B. (1962). Population density and social pathology. *Scientific American, 206*(2), 139–148.

Cameron, N. (1963). *Personality development and psychopathology.* Boston: Houghton Mifflin.

Camic, P. M., & Brown, F. D. (Eds.). (1989). *Assessing chronic pain: A multidisciplinary handbook.* New York: Springer-Verlag.

Campbell, D. T. (1969). Reforms as experiments. *American Psychologist, 24,* 409–429.

Campbell, R. E., & Cellini, J. V. (1981). A diagnostic taxonomy of adult career problems. *Journal of Vocational Behavior, 19,* 175–190.

Campbell, S. S., & Gillin, J. C. (1987). Sleep measures in depression: How sensitive? How specific? *Psychiatric Annals, 17,* 647–653.

Cannon, W. B., & Washburn, A. L. (1912). An explanation of hunger. *American Journal of Physiology, 29,* 441–454.

Carew, T. J., et al. (1990). The development of learning and memory in *Aplysia.* In J. L. McGaugh, N. M. Weinberger, & G. Lynch (Eds.), *Brain organization and memory: Cells, systems, and circuits.* New York: Oxford.

Carey, F. (1977). The child as a word learner. In M. Halle, J. Bresnan, & G. Miller (Eds.), *Linguistic theory and psychological reality.* Cambridge, MA: MIT Press.

Carey, G., & Gottesman, I. I. (1981). Twin and family studies of anxiety, phobic and obsession disorders. In D. F. Klein & J. Rabkin (Eds.), *Anxiety: New research and changing concepts.* New York: Raven.

Cargan, L., & Melko, M. (1982). *Singles: Myths and realities.* Beverly Hills, CA: Sage.

Carlat, D. J., & Camargo, C. A. (1991). Review of bulimia nervosa in males. *American Journal of Psychiatry, 148,* 831–843.

Carlson, J. G., & Hatfield, E. (1992). *Psychology of emotion.* Ft. Worth, TX: Harcourt Brace Jovanovich.

Carnegie Council on Adolescent Development. (1989, June). *Turning points: Preparing American youth for the 21st century.* New York: Carnegie.

Carpenter, W. T., Jr., & Heinrichs, D. W. (1983). Early intervention, time-limited, targeted pharmacotherapy of schizophrenia. *Schizophrenia Bulletin, 9,* 533–542.

Carruthers, M. (1981). Field studies: Emotion and beta-blockade. In M. J. Christie & P. G. Mellett (Eds.), *Foundations of psychosomatics.* Chichester, England: Wiley.

Carson, R. C., Butcher, J. N., & Coleman, J. C. (1988). *Abnormal psychology and modern life* (8th ed.). Glenview, IL: Scott, Foresman.

Carstensen, L. L. (1987). Age-related changes in social activity. In L. L. Carstensen & B. A. Edelstern (Eds.), *Handbook of clinical gerontology.* New York: Pergamon.

Cartwright, R. C. (1977). *Night life: Explorations in dreaming.* Englewood Cliffs, NJ: Prentice-Hall.

Carver, C. S. (1989). How should multifaceted constructs be tested? Issues illustrated by self-monitoring, attributional style, and hardiness. *Journal of Personality and Social Psychology, 56,* 577–585.

Carver, C. S., & Scheier, M. F. (1992). *Perspectives on personality* (2nd ed.). Boston: Allyn & Bacon.

Caspi, A. (1989). On the continuities and consequences of personality: A life-course perspective. In D. M. Buss & N. Cantor (Eds.), *Personality psychology: Recent trends and emerging directions.* New York: Springer-Verlag.

Caspi, A., & Benn, D. J. (1990). Personality continuity and change across the life course. In L. A. Pervin (Ed.), *Handbook of personality: Theory and research.* New York: Guilford.

Caspi, A., Elder, G. H., & Bem, D. J. (1988). Moving away from the world: Life-course patterns of shy children. *Developmental Psychology, 24,* 824–831.

Caspi, A., & Herbᵉner, E. S. (1990). Continuity and change: Assortative marriage and the consistency of personality in adulthood. *Journal of Personality and Social Psychology, 58,* 250–258.

Castellan, N. J., Jr. (Ed.). (1993). *Individual and group decision making.* Hillsdale, NJ: Erlbaum.

Cattell, R. B. (1965). *The scientific analysis of personality.* Chicago: Aldine.

Cattell, R. B. (1971). *Abilities: Their growth, structure, and action.* Boston: Houghton Mifflin.

Cattell, R. B. (1990). Advances in Cattellian personality theory. In L. A. Pervin (Ed.), *Handbook of personality: Theory and research.* New York: Guilford.

Ceci, S. J., Toglia, M. P., & Ross, D. F. (Eds.). (1987). *Children's testimony.* New York: Springer-Verlag.

Cernoch, J. M., & Porter, R. H. (1985). Recognition of maternal axillary odors by infants. *Child Development, 56,* 1593–1598.

Cervone, D. (1992). The role of self-referent cognitions in goal-setting, motivation, and performance. In M. Rabinowitz (Ed.), *Applied cognition.* New York: Ablex.

Cervone, D., & Williams, S. L. (1992). Social cognitive theory and personality. In G. V. Caprara & G. L. Van Heck (Eds.), *Modern personality psychology: Critical reviews and new directions.* New York: Wiley.

Chaiken, S. (1987). The heuristic model of persuasion. In M. P. Zanna, J. M. Olson, & C. P. Herman (Eds.), *Social influence: The Ontario symposium* (Vol. 5). Hillsdale, NJ: Erlbaum.

Chapman, L. J., & Chapman, J. P. (1969). Illusory correlations as an obstacle to the use of valid psychodiagnostic signs. *Journal of Abnormal Psychology, 74,* 271–280

Chase, W. G., & Simon, H. A. (1973). Perception in chess. *Cognitive Psychology, 4,* 55–81.

Cheek, J. M., & Watson, A. K. (1989). The definition of shyness: Psychological imperialism or construct validity? *Journal of Social Behavior and Personality, 4,* 85–95.

Chen, H-T. (1990). *Theory-driven evaluations.* Newbury Park, CA: Sage.

Cheng, P. W., & Holyoak, K. J. (1985). Pragmatic reasoning schemas. *Cognitive Psychology, 17,* 391–416.

Cherniss, C. (1980). *Staff burnout: Job stress in the human services.* Beverly Hills, CA: Sage.

Chess, S., & Thomas, A. (1982). Infant bonding: Mystique and reality. *American Journal of Orthopsychiatry, 52,* 213–222.

Chess, S., & Thomas, A. (1984). *Origins and evolution of behavior disorders.* New York: Brunner/Mazel.

Chi, M. T. H., Feltovich, P. J., & Glaser, R. (1981). Categorization and representation of physics problems by experts and novices. *Cognitive Science, 5,* 121–152.

Chi, M. T. H., Glaser, R., & Farr, M. J. (Eds.). (1988). *The nature of expertise.* Hillsdale, NJ: Erlbaum.

Chiesi, H. L., Spillich, G. J., & Voss, J. F. (1979). Acquisition of domain-related information in relation to high and low domain knowledge. *Journal of Verbal Learning and Verbal Behavior, 18,* 257–274.

Chiriboga, D. A. (1989). Mental health at the midpoint: Crisis, challenge, or relief? In S. Hunter & M. Sundel (Eds.), *Midlife myths: Issues, findings, and practice implications* (pp. 116–144). Newbury Park, CA: Sage.

Choca, J. P., Shanley, L. A., & Van Denburg, E. (1992). *Interpretive guide to the Millon Clinical Multiaxial Inventory.* Washington, DC: American Psychological Association.

Chomsky, N. (1957). *Syntactic structures.* The Hague: Mouton.

Chomsky, N. (1965). *Aspects of a theory of syntax.* Cambridge, MA: MIT Press.

Chomsky, N. (1987). Language in a psychological setting. *Sophia Linguistic Working Papers in Linguistics, 22,* Sophia University, Tokyo.

Christiansen, B. A., Smith, G. T., Roehling, P. V., & Goldman, M. S. (1989). Using alcohol expectancies to predict adolescent drinking behavior after one year. *Journal of Consulting and Chemical Psychology, 57,* 93–99.

Christiansen, K. O. (1977). A review of studies of criminality among twins. In S. A. Mednick & K. O. Christiansen (Eds.), *Biosocial basis of criminal behavior.* New York: Gardner.

Christman, R. J. (1970). *Sensory experience* (2nd ed.). New York: Harper & Row.

Chugari, H. T., & Phelps, M. E. (1986). Maturational changes in cerebral function in infants determined by 18FDC position emission tomography. *Science, 231,* 840–843.

Chwalisz, K., Diener, E., & Gallagher, D. (1988). Autonomic arousal feedback and emotional experience: Evidence from the spinal cord injured. *Journal of Personality and Social Psychology, 54,* 820–828.

Cialdini, R. B. (1988). *Influence: Science and practice* (2nd ed.). Glenview, IL: Scott, Foresman.

Cialdini, R. B., Borden, R. J., Thorne, A., Walker, M. R., Freeman, S., & Sloan, L. R. (1976). Basking in reflected glory: Three (football) field studies. *Journal of Personality and Social Psychology, 34,* 366–375.

Cialdini, R. B., Schaller, M., Hoolihan, D., Arps, K., Fultz, J., & Beaman, A. L. (1987). Empathy-based helping: Is it selflessly or selfishly motivated? *Journal of Personality and Social Psychology, 52,* 749–758.

Cialdini, R. B., Vincent, J. E., Lewis, S. K., Catalan, J., Wheeler, D., & Darby, B. L. (1975). Reciprocal concessions procedure for inducing compliance: The door-in-the-face technique. *Journal of Personality and Social Psychology, 31,* 206–215.

Cicirelli, V. G. (1982, August). *An attachment model of sibling helping behavior in old age.* Paper presented at the meetings of the American Psychological Association, Washington, DC.

Cioffi, D. (1991). Asymmetry of doubt in medical self-diagnosis: The ambiguity of "uncertain wellness." *Journal of Personality and Social Psychology, 61,* 969–980.

Clark, D. A., Beck, A. T., & Brown, G. (1989). Cognitive mediation in general psychiatric outpatients: A test of the content-specificity hypothesis. *Journal of Personality and Social Psychology, 56,* 958–964.

Clark, D. M. (1988). A cognitive model of panic attacks. In S. Rachman & J. D. Maser (Eds.), *Panic: Psychological perspectives.* Hillsdale, NJ: Erlbaum.

Clark, H. H. (1979). Responding to indirect speech acts. *Cognitive Psychology, 11,* 430–477.

Clark, H. H., & Clark, E. V. (1977). *The psychology of language.* New York: Harcourt Brace Jovanovich.

Clark, L. A., & Watson, D. (1991). Tripartite model of anxiety and depression: Psychometric evidence and taxonomic implications. *Journal of Abnormal Psychology, 100,* 316–336.

Clark, M. S., Ouellette, R., Powell, M. C., & Milberg, S. (1987). Recipient's mood, relationship type, and helping. *Journal of Personality and Social Psychology, 53,* 94–103.

Clarke, A. M., & Clarke, A. D. B. (1976). *Early experience: Myth and evidence.* New York: Free Press.

Clarke-Stewart, K. A. (1982). *Day care.* Cambridge, MA: Harvard University Press.

Clarke-Stewart, K. A. (1989). Infant day care: Maligned or malignant? *American Psychologist, 44,* 266–273.

Clarke-Stewart, K. A., & Hevey, C. M. (1981). Longitudinal relations in repeated observations of mother-child interaction from one to two and a half years. *Developmental Psychology, 17,* 127–145.

Clarkin, J. F., Marziali, E., & Munroe-Blum, H. (1992). *Borderline personality disorder.* New York: Guilford.

Clarkson-Smith, L., & Hartley, A. A. (1990). Structural equation models of relationships between exercise and cognitive abilities. *Psychology and Aging, 5,* 437–446.

Clary, E. G., & Snyder, M. A. (1991). A functional analysis of altruism and prosocial behavior: The case of volunteerism. In M. S. Clark (Ed.), *Prosocial behavior.* Newbury Park, CA: Sage.

Cloninger, C. R., & Gottesman, I. I. (1989). Genetic and environmental factors in antisocial behavior disorders. In S. Mednick, T. Moffitt, & S. Strack (Eds.), *The causes of crime: New biological approaches.* New York: Cambridge University Press.

Cobb, S., & Rose, R. M. (1973). Hypertension, peptic ulcer and diabetes and the traffic controllers. *Journal of the American Medical Association. 224,* 489–492.

Coffey, C. E., et al. (1991). Brain anatomic effects of electroconvulsive therapy: A prospective magnetic resonance imaging study. *Archives of General Psychiatry, 48,* 1013–1020.

Cohen, J. B., & Reed, D. (1985). The Type A behavior pattern and coronary heart disease among Japanese men in Hawaii. *Journal of Behavioral Medicine, 8,* 343–352.

Cohen, J. D., & Servan-Schreber, D. S. (1992). Context, cortex, and dopamine: A connectionist approach to behavior and biology in schizophrenia. *Psychological Review, 99,* 45–77.

Cohen, S. (1988). Psychosocial models of the role of social support in the etiology of physical disease. *Health Psychology, 7,* 269–297.

Cohen, S., & Edwards, J. R. (1989). Personality characteristics as moderators of the relationship between stress and disorder. In R. W. J. Neufeld (Ed.), *Advances in the investigation of psychological stress.* New York: Wiley.

Cohen, S., Evans, G. W., Stokols, D., & Krantz, D. S. (1986). *Behavior, health, and environmental stress.* New York: Plenum.

Cohen, S., et al. (1989). Debunking myths about self-quitting: Evidence from 10 prospective studies of persons who attempt to quit smoking by themselves. *American Psychologist, 44,* 1355–1365.

Cohen, S., & Williamson, G. M. (1991). Stress and infectious disease in humans. *Psychological Bulletin, 109,* 5–24.

Colbach, E. M. (1987). Hysteria again and again and again. *International Journal of Offender Therapy and Comparative Criminology, 31,* 41–48.

Colby, A., Kohlberg, L., Gibbs, J., & Lieberman, M. (1983). A longitudinal study of moral judgment. *Monographs of the Society for Research in Child Development, 48* (1–2, Serial No. 200).

Cole, M., & Cole, S. R. (1989). *The development of children.* New York: Scientific American Books.

Coleman, L. M., & Antonucci, T. C. (1983). Impact of work on women at midlife. *Developmental Psychology, 19,* 290–294.

Collins, A. M., & Loftus, E. F. (1975). A spreading activation theory of semantic processing. *Psychological Review, 82,* 407–428.

Coltheart, M. The right hemisphere and disorders of reading. In A. W. Young (Ed.), *The functions of the right hemisphere.* London: Academic Press.

Comer, R. J. (1992). *Abnormal psychology.* New York: Freeman.

Commons, M. L., Rachlin, H., & Nevin, J. A. (Eds.). (1984). *Quantitative analyses of behavior.* Vol. 5, *Reinforcement value: The effect of delay and intervening events.* Cambridge, MA: Ballinger.

Compas, B. E., Davis, G. E., Forsythe, C. J., & Wagner, B. (1987). Assessment of major and daily stressful events during adolescence: The Adolescent Perceived Events Scale. *Journal of Consulting and Clinical Psychology, 55,* 534–541.

Condon, J. W., & Crano, W. D. (1988). Inferred evaluation and the relationship between attitude similarity and interpersonal attraction. *Journal of Personality and Social Psychology, 54,* 789–797.

Cook, M., Mineka, S., Woklenstein, B., & Laitsch, K. (1985). Observational conditioning of snake fear in unrelated rhesus monkeys. *Journal of Abnormal Psychology, 94,* 591–610.

Cook, T. D., & Campbell, D. T. (1979). *Quasiexperimentation.* Chicago: Rand McNally.

Cooley, C. H. (1902). *Human nature and the social order.* New York: Schocken Books.

Cooper, J. R. (1986). *The biochemical basis of neuropharmacology* (5th ed.). New York: Oxford.

Coren, S., & Ward, L. (1989). *Sensation and perception.* New York: Harcourt Brace Jovanovich.

Corkin, S. (1984). Lasting consequences of bilateral medial temporal lobectomy: Clinical course and experimental findings. *Seminars in Neurology, 4,* 249–259.

Corless, I. B., & Pittman-Linderman, M. (Eds.). (1987). *AIDS: Principles, practices and politics.* New York: Hemisphere.

Cornell, E. H., & McDonnell, P. M. (1986). Infants' acuity at twenty feet. *Investigative Opthalmology*

and Visual Science, 17, 1417–1420.

Corso, J. F. (1977). Auditory perception and communication. In J. E. Birren & K. W. Schaie (Eds.), *Handbook of the psychology of aging.* New York: Van Nostrand.

Cosmides, L., & Tooby, J. (1987). From evolution to behavior: Evolutionary psychology as the missing link. In J. Dupre (Ed.), *The latest on the best.* Cambridge, MA: MIT Press.

Costantini, E., & Craik, K. H. (1980). Personality and politicians: California party leaders, 1960–1976. *Journal of Personality and Social Psychology, 38,* 641–661.

Cotman, C. W., Bridges, R. J., Taube, J. S., Clark, A. S., Geddes, J. W., & Managhan, D. T. (1989). The role of the NMDA receptor in central nervous system plasticity and pathology. *Journal of NIH Research, 1*(2), 65–74.

Cowen, E. L. (1985). Person-centered approaches in primary prevention in mental health: Situation-focused and competence enhancement. *American Journal of Community Psychology, 13,* 31–48.

Coyne, J. C., Burchill, S. A. L., & Stiles, W. B. (1991). An interactional perspective on depression. In C. R. Snyder & D. R. Forsyth (Eds.), *Handbook of social and clinical psychology: The health perspective.* New York: Pergamon.

Craik, F. I. M., & Lockhart, R. S. (1972). Levels of processing: A framework for memory research. *Journal of Verbal Learning and Verbal Behavior, 11,* 671–684.

Crain, W. C. (1985). *Theories of development: Concepts and applications.* Englewood Cliffs, NJ: Prentice-Hall.

Crandall, C. S. (1988). Social contagion of binge eating. *Journal of Personality and Social Psychology, 55,* 588–598.

Craske, M. G. (1991). Phobic fear and panic attacks: The same emotional states triggered by different cues? *Clinical Psychology Review, 11,* 599–620.

Craske, M. G., Brown, T. H., & Barlow, D. H. (1991). Behavioral treatment of panic: A two-year follow-up. *Behavior Therapy, 22,* 289–304.

Crawford, C. B., & Anderson, J. L. (1989). Sociobiology: An environmentalist discipline? *American Psychologist, 44,* 1449–1459.

Crawford, H. J., Wallace, B., Normura, K., & Slater, H. (1986). Eidetic-like imagery in hypnosis: Rare but there. *American Journal of Psychology, 99,* 527–546.

Creese, I., Burd, D. R., & Snyder, S. H. (1976). Dopamine receptor binding predicts clinical and pharmacological potencies of antischizophrenic drugs. *Science, 192,* 481–483.

Crick, F., & Mitchson, G. (1983). The function of dream sleep. *Nature, 304,* 111–114.

Crick, F., & Mitchson, G. (1986). REM sleep and neural nets. *Journal of Mind and Behavior, 7,* 229–250.

Crisp, D., Weinberg, H., & Podrouzek, K. W. (1991). Imaging techniques in the localization of epileptiform abnormalities. *International Journal of Neuroscience, 60,* 33–58.

Crits-Christoph, P., Cooper, A., & Luborsky, L. (1988). The accuracy of therapists' interpretations and the outcome of dynamic psychotherapy. *Journal of Consulting and Clinical Psychology, 56,* 490–495.

Crits-Christoph, P., & Mintz, J. (1991). Implications of

therapist effects for the design and analysis of comparative studies of psychotherapies. *Journal of Consulting and Clinical Psychology, 59,* 20–26.

Crocker, P. R. E. (1989). A follow-up of cognitive-affective stress management training. *Journal of Sport and Exercise Psychology, 11,* 236–242.

Cronbach, L. R. (1990). *Essentials of psychological testing* (5th ed.). New York: Harper & Row.

Cross, S., & Markus, H. (1991). Possible selves across the life span. *Human Development, 34,* 230–255.

Crovitz, H. F. (1971). The capacity of memory loci in artifical memory. *Psychonomic Science, 24,* 187–188.

Crow, T. J. (1985). The two-syndrome concept: Origins and current status. *Schizophrenia Bulletin, 11,* 471–485.

Crowe, L. C., & George, W. H. (1989). Alcohol and human sexuality: A review and integration. *Psychological Bulletin, 105,* 374–386.

Croyle, R. T., & Cooper, J. (1983). Dissonance arousal: Physiological evidence. *Journal of Personality and Social Psychology, 45,* 782–791.

Csapo, M. (1972). Peer models reverse the "one bad apple spoils the barrel" theory. *Teaching Exceptional Children, 4,* 20–24.

Csikszentmihalyi, M. (1990). *Flow: The psychology of optimal experience.* New York: Harper & Row.

Csikszentmihalyi, M., & Larson, R. (1984). *Being adolescent: Conflict and growth in the teenage years.* New York: Basic Books.

Cumming, E., & Henry, W. E. (1961). *Growing old.* New York: Basic Books.

Curtiss, S. (1977). *Genie: A psychological study of a modern day "wild child."* New York: Academic Press.

Cutler, W. B., Preti, G., Huggins, G. R., Ramon-Garcia, C., & Lawley, H. J. (1986). Human axillary secretions influence women's menstrual cycles: The role of donor extract from men. *Hormones and Behavior, 20,* 463–473.

Cutting, J. E. (1987). Perception and information. *Annual Review of Psychology, 38,* 61–90.

Cytowic, R. E. (1989). *Synesthesia: A union of the senses.* New York: Springer-Verlag.

Czeisler, C. A., Allan, J. S., Strogatz, S. H., Ronda, J. M., Sanchez, R., Rios, C. D., Freitag, W. O., Richardson, G. S., & Kronauer, R. E. (1986). Bright light resets the human circadian pacemaker independent of the timing of the sleep-wake cycle. *Science, 233,* 667–671.

Dallas, T. L., & Finn, R. S. (1989). Role of the anesthesiologist in the treatment of pain. In P. M. Camic & F. D. Brown (Eds.), *Assessing chronic pain: A multidisciplinary approach.* New York: Springer-Verlag.

Daneman, M., & Carpenter, P. A. (1980). Individual differences in working memory and reading. *Journal of Verbal Learning and Verbal Behavior, 19,* 450–466.

Dannemiller, J. L., & Stephens, B. R. (1988). A critical test of infant pattern preference models. *Child Development, 59,* 210–216.

Darley, J. M., & Gross, P. H. (1983). A hypothesis-confirming bias in labeling effects. *Journal of Personality and Social Psychology, 44,* 20–33.

Darley, J. M., & Latané, B. (1968). Bystander intervention in emergencies: Diffusion of responsibility.

Journal of Personality and Social Psychology, 8, 377–383.

Darling, C. A., & Davidson, J. K. (1986). Coitally active university students: Sexual behaviors, concerns and challenges. *Adolescence, 21,* 403–419.

Darling, C. A., Davidson, J. K., & Passarello, L. C. (1992). The mystique of first intercourse among college youth: The role of partners, contraceptive practices, and psychological reactions. *Journal of Youth and Adolescence, 21,* 97–117.

Darlington, R. B. (1986). Long-term effects of preschool programs. In U. Neisser (Ed.), *The school achievement of minority children.* Hillsdale, NJ: Erlbaum.

Darwin, C. J., Turvey, M. T., & Crowder, R. G. (1972). An auditory analogue of the Sperling partial report procedures. *Cognitive Psychology, 3,* 255–267.

Darwin, C. R. (1965). *The expression of emotions in man and animals.* Chicago: University of Chicago Press. (Original work published 1872)

Das, J. P., Kirby, J., & Jarman, R. F. (1979). *Simultaneous and successive cognitive processes.* New York: Academic Press.

Davey, G. (1990). *Ecological learning theory.* New York: Routledge.

Davidson, A. R., & Jaccard, J. J. (1979). Variables that moderate the attitude-behavior relation: Results of a longitudinal survey. *Journal of Personality and Social Psychology, 37,* 1364–1376.

Davidson, J. R. T., & Foa, E. B. (1992). *Posttraumatic stress disorder: DSM-IV and beyond.* Washington, DC: American Psychiatric Press.

Davidson, R. J. (1978). Specificity and patterning in biobehavioral systems: Implications for behavior change. *American Psychologist, 33,* 430–436.

Davidson, R. J. (1988). Cerebral asymmetry, affective style, and psychopathology. In M. Kinsbourne (Ed.), *Cerebral hemisphere function in depression.* Washington, DC: American Psychiatric Press.

Davidson, R. J. (1991). Biological approaches to the study of personality. In N. J. Derlega, B. A. Winstead, & W. H. Jones (Eds.), *Personality: Contemporary theory and research.* Chicago: Nelson-Hall.

Davidson, R. J., Ekman, P., Saron, C. D., Senulis, J. A., & Friesen, W. V. (1990). Approach-withdrawal and cerebral asymmetry: Emotional expression and brain physiology I. *Journal of Personality and Social Psychology, 58,* 330–341.

Davidson, R. J., & Fox, N. A. (1988). Cerebral asymmetry and emotion: Developmental and individual differences. In D. L. Molfese & S. J. Segalowitz (Eds.), *Brain lateralization in children: Developmental implications.* New York: Guilford.

Davidson, R. J., & Fox, N. A. (1989). Frontal brain asymmetry predicts infants' response to maternal separation. *Journal of Abnormal Psychology, 98,* 127–131.

Davidson, R. J., & Schwartz, G. E. (1976). Psychobiology of relaxation and related states: A multiprocess theory. In D. Mostofsky (Ed.), *Behavior modification and control of physiologic activity.* Englewood Cliffs, NJ: Prentice-Hall.

Davis, M. (1992). The role of the amygdala in fear and anxiety. *Annual Review of Neuroscience, 15,* 311–327.

Davison, G. C., & Darke, L. (1991). Managing pain. In D. Druckman & R. A. Bjork (Eds.), *In the mind's eye: Enhancing human performance.* Washington, DC: National Academy Press.

Davison, G. C., & Pirozzolo, F. J. (1991). Meditation. In D. Druckman & R. A. Bjork (Eds.), *In the mind's eye: Enhancing human performance.* Washington, DC: National Academy Press.

Davitz, J. R. (1970). A dictionary and grammar of emotion. In M. Arnold (Ed.), *Feelings and emotions.* New York: Academic Press.

Dawes, R. M., Faust, D., & Meehl, P. E. (1989). Clinical vs. actuarial judgment. *Science, 243,* 1668–1674.

Dawson, M. E., Schell, A. M., & Tweddle-Banis, H. (1986). Greater resistance to extinction of electrodermal responses conditioned to potentially phobic CSs: A noncognitive process? *Psychophysiology, 23,* 522–561.

Day, R., et. al. (1987). Stressful life events preceding the acute onset of schizophrenia: A cross-national study from the World Health Organization. *Culture, Medicine, & Psychiatry, 11,* 123–205.

DeBono, K. G., & Snyder, M. (1989). Understanding consumer decision-making processes: The role of form and function in product evaluation. *Journal of Applied Social Psychology, 19,* 416–424.

DeCasper, A. J., & Spence, M. J. (1986). Prenatal maternal speech influences newborns' perception of speech sounds. *Infant Behavior and Development, 9,* 133–150.

DeCharms, R., & Moeller, G. H. (1962). Values expressed in American children's readers: 1800 to 1950. *Journal of Abnormal and Social Psychology, 64,* 135–142.

Deci, E. L., & Ryan, R. M. (1985). *Intrinsic motivation and self-determination in human behavior.* New York: Plenum.

Delmonte, M. M. (1984). Physiological responses during meditation and rest. *Biofeedback and Self-Regulation, 9,* 181–200.

Dement, W. C. (1974). *Some must watch while some must sleep.* San Francisco: Freeman.

Demo, D. H., & Acock, A. C. (1988). The impact of divorce on children. *Journal of Marriage and the Family, 50,* 619–648.

Denny, M. R. (1991). Relaxation/relief: The effect of removing, postponing, or terminating aversive stimuli. In M. R. Denny (Ed.), *Fear, avoidance, and phobias: A fundamental analysis.* Hillsdale, NJ: Erlbaum.

DePaulo, B. M. (1992). Nonverbal behaviors and self-presentation. *Psychological Bulletin, 111,* 203–243.

Depue, R. A. (1992). *Neurobehavioral systems, personality, and psychopathology.* New York: Springer-Verlag.

Depue, R. A., & Iacono, W. G. (1989). Neurobehavioral aspects of affective disorders. *Annual Review of Psychology, 40,* 457–492.

Depue, R. A., & Monroe, S. M. (1986). Conceptualization and measurement of human disorder in life stress research: The problem of chronic disturbance. *Psychological Bulletin, 99,* 36–51.

Der-Karabetian, A., & Gebharp, N. (1986). Effect of physical fitness programs in the workplace. *Journal of Business Psychology, 1,* 51–57.

Derlega, V. J., Hendrick, S. S., Winstead, B. A., & Berg, J. H. (1991). *Psychotherapy as a personal relationship.* New York: Guilford.

Derlega, V. J., Winstead, B. A., & Jones, W. H. (Eds.). (1991). *Personality: Contemporary theory and research.* Chicago: Nelson-Hall.

De Rogatis, L. R. (1986). *Clinical psychopharmacology.* Menlo Park, CA: Addison-Wesley.

Des Jarlais, D. C., & Friedman, S. R. (1988). The psychology of preventing AIDS among intravenous drug users: A social learning conceptualization. *American Psychologist, 43,* 865–870.

DeValois, R. L., & DeValois, K. K. (1988). *Spatial vision.* New York: Oxford.

Dewsbury, D. A. (1991). Psychobiology. *American Psychologist, 46,* 198–205.

Dichter, M. A., & Ayala, G. F. (1987). Cellular mechanisms of epilepsy: A status report. *Science, 237,* 157–164.

DiClemente, R. J. (1992). *Adolescents and AIDS: A generation in jeopardy.* Newbury Park, CA: Sage.

Diener, E. (1980). Deindividuation: The absence of self-awareness and self-regulation in group members. In P. B. Paulus (Ed.), *The psychology of group influence.* Hillsdale, NJ: Erlbaum.

Dienstbier, R. A. (1989). Arousal and physiological toughness: Implications for mental and physical health. *Psychological Review, 96,* 84–100.

DiGiulio, R. C. (1989). *Beyond widowhood: From bereavement to emergence and hope.* New York: Free Press.

Digman, J. M. (1990). Personality structure: Emergence of the five-factor model. *Annual Review of Psychology, 41,* 417–440.

Dillbeck, M. D., & Orme-Johnson, D. W. (1987). Physiological differences between transcendental meditation and rest. *American Psychologist, 42,* 879–881.

Dion, K. K., Berscheid, E., & Walster, E. (1972). What is beautiful is good. *Journal of Personality and Social Psychology, 24,* 285–290.

Dishman, R. K. (1988). *Exercise adherence: Its impact on public health.* Champaign, IL: Human Kinetics.

Dixon, N. F. (1981). *Preconscious processing.* New York: Wiley.

Dobson, K. S. (1989). A meta-analysis of the efficacy of cognitive therapy for depression. *Journal of Consulting and Clinical Psychology, 57,* 414–419.

Dobson, P., & Williams, A. (1989). The validation of the selection of male British Army officers. *Journal of Occupational Psychology, 62,* 313–325.

Dollard, J., Doob, L., Miller, N., Mowrer, O. H., & Sears, R. R. (1939). *Frustration and aggression.* New Haven, CT: Yale University Press.

Donnerstien, E., Linz, D., & Penrod, S. (1987). *The question of pornography.* New York: Free Press.

Doob, A. N., & Kirshenbaum, H. (1973). Bias in police lineups: Partial remembering. *Journal of Police Science and Administration, 1,* 287–293.

Doppelt, J. E., & Wallace, W. L. (1955). Standardization of the Wechsler Adult Intelligence Scale for older persons. *Journal of Abnormal and Social Psychology, 51,* 312–330.

Dorfman, H., & Kuehl, K. (1989). *The mental game of baseball.* South Bend, IN: Diamond Publications.

Dorfman, H. A. (1990). Reflections on providing personal and performance enhancement consulting services in professional baseball. *The Sport Psychologist, 4,* 341–346.

Doris, J. (Ed.). (1991). *The suggestibility of children's recollections: Implications for eyewitness testi-*

mony. Washington, DC: American Psychological Association.

Dornbush, S. M., Ritter, P. L., Liederman, P. H., Roberts, D. F., & Fraleigh, M. J. (1987). The relation of parenting style to adolescent school performance. *Child Development, 58,* 1244–1257.

Dovidio, J. F. (1984). Helping behavior and altruism: An empirical and conceptual overview. In L. Berkowitz (Ed.), *Advances in experimental social psychology* (Vol. 17). New York: Academic Press.

Dovidio, J. F., Allen, J. L., & Schroeder, D. A. (1990). Specificity of empathy-induced helping: Evidence for altruistic motivation. *Journal of Personality and Social Psychology, 59,* 249–260.

Doyle, A. C. (1892). Silver Blaze. *Strand Magazine* (London).

Dryfoos, J. G. (1990). *Adolescents at risk: Prevalence and prevention.* New York: Oxford.

Dublin, J. (1976). Gestalt therapy, existential-Gestalt therapy, and/versus ''Perls-ism.'' In E. Smith (Ed.), *The growing edge of Gestalt therapy.* New York: Bruner/Mazel.

Duclos, S. E., Laird, J. D., Schneider, E., Sexten, M., Stern, L., & Van Lighten, O. (1989). Emotion-specific effects of facial expressions and postures on emotional experience. *Journal of Personality and Social Psychology, 57,* 100–108.

Duke, P. M., Carlsmith, J. M., Jennings, D., Martin, J. A., Dornbusch, S. M., Gross, R. T., & Siegel-Gorelick, B. (1982). Educational correlates of early and late sexual maturation in adolescence. *Journal of Pediatrics, 100,* 633–637.

Duncan, G. E., & Stumpf, W. E. (1991). Brain activity patterns: Assessment by high resolution autoradiographic imaging of radiolabeled 2-deoxyglucose and glucose uptake. *Progress in Neurobiology, 37,* 365–382.

Dunn, J., & Plomin, R. (1990). *Separate lives: Why siblings are so different.* New York: Basic Books.

Dush, D. M., Hirt, M. L., & Schroeder, H. E. (1989). Self-statement modification in the treatment of child behavior disorders: A meta-analysis. *Psychological Bulletin, 106,* 97–106.

Duvall, D., & Silverstein, R. M. (1986). *Chemical signals in vertebrates: Ecology, evolution, and comparative biology.* New York: Plenum.

Eagly, A. H., Ashmore, R. D., Makhijani, M. G., & Longo, L. C. (1991). What is beautiful is good, but . . . A meta-analytic review of research on the physical attractiveness stereotype. *Psychological Bulletin, 110,* 109–128.

Eagly, A. H., & Steffen, V. J. (1986). Gender and aggressive behavior: A meta-analytic review of the social psychology literature. *Psychological Bulletin, 100,* 309–330.

Ebbinghaus, H. (1964). *Memory: A contribution to experimental psychology* (H. A. Ruger & E. R. Busemius, Trans.). New York: Dover. (Original work published 1885)

Eccles, J. (1991). Gender-role socialization. In R. M. Baron, W. G. Graziano, & C. Stangor (Eds.), *Social psychology.* Ft. Worth, TX: Holt, Rinehart & Winston.

Edelstein, B. A. (1989). Generalization: Terminological, methodological, and conceptual issues. *Behavior Therapy, 20,* 311–324.

Edwards, A. E. (1962). A demonstration of the long-term retention of a conditioned galvanic skin response. *Psychosomatic Medicine, 24,* 459–463.

Edwards, K. (1990). The interplay of affect and cognition in attitude formation and change. *Journal of Personality and Social Psychology, 59,* 202–211.

Egeland, B., & Farber, E. A. (1984). Infant-mother attachment: Factors related to its development and changes over time. *Child Development, 55,* 753–771.

Eibl-Eibesfeldt, I. (1973). The expressive behavior of the deaf-and-blind-born. In M. von Cranach & I. Vine (Eds.), *Social communication and movement.* New York: Academic Press.

Eich, E., & Hyman, R. (1991). Subliminal self-help. In D. Druckman & R. A. Bjork (Eds.), *In the mind's eye: Enhancing human performance.* Washington, DC: National Academy Press.

Eiseley, L. (1946). *The immense journey.* New York: Random House.

Ekman, P., et al. (1976). Universal and cultural difference in the judgments of social expressions of emotions. *Journal of Personality and Social Psychology, 53,* 712–717.

Ekman, P., Davidson, R. J., & Friesen, W. V. (1990). The Duchenne smile: Emotional expression and brain physiology II. *Journal of Personality and Social Psychology, 58,* 342–353.

Ekman, P., & Friesen, W. V. (1987). *Facial action coding system.* Palo Alto, CA: Consulting Psychologists Press.

Ekman, P., Friesen, W. V., & O'Sullivan, M. (1988). Smiles when lying. *Journal of Personality and Social Psychology, 54,* 414–420.

Ekman, P., Levenson, R. W., & Friesen, W. V. (1983). Autonomic nervous system distinguishes among emotions. *Science, 221,* 1208–1210.

Ellis, A. (1962). *Reason and emotion in psychotherapy.* New York: Lyle Stuart.

Ellis, A., & Dryden, W. (1987). *The practice of rational-emotive psychotherapy.* New York: Springer-Verlag.

Ellis, A. W., & Young, A. W. (1988). *Human cognitive neuropsychology.* Hillsdale, NJ: Erlbaum.

Ellis, L., & Ames, M.A. (1987). Neurohormonal functioning and sexual orientation: A theory of homosexuality-heterosexuality. *Psychology Bulletin, 101,* 233–258.

Ellman, S. J., & Antrobus, J. S. (Eds.). (1991). *The mind in sleep: Psychology and psychophysiology* (2nd ed.). New York: Wiley.

Elmer-DeWitt, P. (1989, December 9). Fighting noise with antinoise. *Time,* p. 94.

Emmons, R. A. (1990). Motives and life goals. In S. Briggs, R. Hogan, & W. H. Jones (Eds.), *Handbook of personality psychology.* Orlando, FL: Academic Press.

Emmons, R. A., & King, L. A. (1988). Conflict among personal stirrings: Immediate and long-term implications for psychological and physical well-being. *Journal of Personality and Social Psychology, 54,* 1040–1048.

Epstein, J. A., & Harackiewicz, J. M. (1992). Winning is not enough: The effects of competition and achievement orientation on intrinsic interest. *Personality and Social Psychology Bulletin, 18,* 128–138.

Epstein, L. H., & Jennings, J. R. (1986). Smoking, stress, cardiovascular reactivity, and coronary heart disease. In K. A. Matthews et al. (Eds.), *Handbook of stress, reactivity, and cardiovascular disease.* New York: Wiley.

Epstein, S. (1983). Aggregation and beyond: Some basic issues on the production of behavior. *Journal of Personality, 51,* 360–392.

Epstein, S. (1990). Cognitive-experiential self theory. In L. A. Pervin (Ed.), *Handbook of personality: Theory and research.* New York: Guilford.

Epstein, S., & Katz, L. (1992). Coping ability, stress, productive load, and symptoms. *Journal of Personality and Social Psychology, 62,* 813–825.

Erdberg, P. (1990). Rorschach assessment. In G. Goldstern & M. Hersen (Eds.), *Handbook of psychological assessment.* New York: Pergamon.

Erdelyi, M. H. (1985). *Psychoanalysis: Freud's cognitive psychology.* New York: Freeman.

Erdelyi, M. H. (1988). Repression, reconstruction, and defense: History and integration of the psychoanalytic and experimental frameworks. In J. Singer (Ed.), *Repression: Defense mechanism and cognitive style.* Chicago: University of Chicago Press.

Erikson, E. H. (1950). *Childhood and society.* New York: Norton.

Erikson, E. H. (1963). *Childhood and society.* New York: Norton.

Erikson, E. H. (1968). *Identity, youth and crisis.* New York: Norton.

Erikson, E. H. (1980). *Identity and the life cycle.* New York: Norton. (Original work published 1959)

Erikson, E. H., Erikson, J. M., & Kivnick, H. Q. (1986). *Vital involvement in old age.* New York: Norton.

Eron, L. D. (1987). The development of aggressive behavior from the perspective of a developing behaviorism. *American Psychologist, 42,* 435–442.

Estes, T. H., & Vaughn, J. L. (1985). *Reading and learning in the content classroom: Diagrams and instructional strategies* (3rd ed.). Boston: Allyn & Bacon.

Estes, W. K. (1991). Cognitive architectures from the standpoint of an experimental psychologist. *Annual Review of Psychology, 42,* 1–28.

Ewart, C. K. (1991). Social action theory for a public health psychology. *American Psychologist, 46,* 931–946.

Ewin, D. M. (1984). Hypnosis in surgery and anesthesia. In W. C. Wester & A. H. Smith (Eds.), *Clinical hypnosis: A multidisciplinary approach.* Philadelphia: Lippincott.

Eysenck, H. J. (1967). *The biological basis of personality.* Springfield, IL: Charles C Thomas.

Eysenck, H. J. (1990). Biological dimensions of personality. In L. A. Pervin (Ed.), *Handbook of personality: Theory and research.* New York: Guilford.

Eysenck, H. J., & Grossarth-Marticek, R. (1991). Creative novation behavior therapy as a prophylactic treatment for cancer and coronary heart disease: 2. Effects of treatment. *Behavior Research and Therapy, 29,* 17–31.

Eysenck, H. J., & Kamin, L. J. (1981). *The intelligence controversy.* New York: Wiley.

Eysenck, M. W. (1989). Personality, stress arousal, and congitive processes in stress transactions. In R. W. J. Newfeld (Ed.), *Advances in the investigation of psychological stress.* New York: Wiley.

Fagley, N. S. (1987). Positional response bias in multiple-choice tests of learning: Its relation to test-wiseness and guessing strategy. *Journal of Educational Psychology, 79,* 95–97.

Fagot, B. I., Leinbach, M. D., & O'Boyle, C. (1992). Gender labeling, gender stereotyping, and parenting behaviors. *Developmental Psychology, 28,* 225–230.

Falbo, T., & Peplau, L. A. (1980). Power strategies in intimate relationships. *Journal of Personality and Social Psychology, 38,* 618–628.

Fanselow, M. S. (1991). Analgesia as a response to aversive Pavlovian conditional stimuli: Cognitive and emotional mediators. In M. R. Denny (Ed.), *Fear, avoidance, and phobias: A fundamental analysis.* Hillsdale, NJ: Erlbaum.

Fantz, R. L., & Nevis, S. (1967). Pattern preferences and perceptual-cognitive development in early infancy. *Merrill-Palmer Quarterly, 13,* 88–108.

Farberow, N. L. (1970). Ten years of suicide prevention/Past and future. *Bulletin of Suicidology, 6,* 5–11.

Farberow, N. L. (1974). Suicide. Morristown, NJ: General Learning Press.

Fava, M., Copeland, P. M., Schweiger, U., & Herzog, D. B. (1989). Neurochemical abnormalities of anorexia nervosa and bulimia nervosa. *American Journal of Psychiatry, 146,* 963–971.

Fazio, R. H., Zanna, M. P., & Cooper, J. (1977). Dissonance and self-perception: An integrative view of each theory's proper domain of application. *Journal of Experimental Social Psychology, 13,* 464–479.

Federation CECOS, Schwartz, D., & Mayaux, M. J. (1982). Female fecundity as a function of age. *New England Journal of Medicine, 306,* 404–406.

Feingold, A. (1988). Matching for attractiveness in romantic partners and same-sex friends: A meta-analysis and theoretical critique. *Psychological Bulletin, 104,* 226–235.

Feist, J., & Brannon, L. (1988). *Health psychology: An introduction to behavior and health.* Belmont, CA: Wadsworth.

Felten, D. L., Cohen, N., Ader, R., Felten, S. Y., Carlson, S. L., & Roszman, T. L. (1990). Central neural circuits involved in neural-immune interactions. In R. Ader, N. Cohen, & D. L. Felten (Eds.), *Psychoneuroimmunology II.* New York: Academic Press.

Feltz, D. L., Landers, D. M., & Becker, B. J. (1988). A revised meta-analysis of the mental practice literature on motor skill learning. In D. Druckman & J. Swets (Eds.), *Enhancing human performance: Issues and techniques.* Washington, DC: National Academy Press.

Fenton, W. S., & McGlaskan, T. H. (1991a). Natural history of schizophrenia subtypes: 1. Longitudinal study of paranoid, hebephonic, and undifferentiated schizophrenia. *Archives of General Psychiatry, 48,* 969–977.

Fenton, W. S., & McGlaskan, T. H. (1991b). Natural history of schizophrenia subtypes: 2. Positive and negative symptoms and long-term course. *Archives of General Psychiatry, 48,* 978–986.

Fernald, A., Taeschner, T., Dunn, J., Papousek, M., De Boysson-Bardies, B., & Fukui, I. (1989). A cross-cultural study of prosodic modification in mothers' and fathers' speech to preverbal infants. *Journal of Child Language, 16,* 477–501.

Ferrari, N. A. (1962). *Institutionalization and attitude change in an aged population.* Unpublished doctoral dissertation, Western Reserve University, Cleveland.

Ferster, C. B., & Skinner, B. F. (1957). *Schedules of reinforcement.* Englewood Cliffs, NJ: Prentice-Hall.

Fessler, R. G. (1989). Physiology, anatomy, and pharmacology of pain perception. In P. M. Camic & F. D. Brown (Eds.), *Assessing chronic pain: A multidisciplinary approach.* New York: Springer-Verlag.

Festinger, L. (1957). *A theory of cognitive dissonance.* Stanford, CA: Stanford University Press.

Festinger, L., & Carlsmith, J. M. (1959). Cognitive consequences of forced compliance. *Journal of Abnormal and Social Psychology, 58,* 203–210.

Festinger, L., Pepitone, A., & Newcomb, T. (1952). Some consequences of deindividuation in a group. *Journal of Abnormal and Social Psychology, 47,* 382–389.

Festinger, L., Riecken, H. W., & Schacter, S. (1956). *When prophesy fails.* Minneapolis: University of Minnesota Press.

Festinger, L., Schacter, S., & Back, K. (1950). *Social pressures in informal groups: A study of a housing community.* New York: Harper & Bros.

Fetterman, D. M. (1988). *Excellence and equality: A qualitatively different perspective on gifted and talented education.* Albany: State University of New York Press.

Feuer, D. (1987). Domino's Pizza: Training for fast times. *Training, 24,* 25–30.

Fichter, M. M., & Noegel, R. (1990). Concordance for bulimia nervosa in twins. *International Journal of Eating Disorders, 9,* 255–263.

Fiedler, F. E. (1978). Contingency model and the leadership process. In L. Berkowitz (Ed.), *Advances in experimental social psychology* (Vol. 11). New York: Academic Press.

Fiedler, F. E., & Garcia, J. E. (1987). *Leadership: Cognitive resources and performance.* New York: Wiley.

Field, T. M., Schanberg, S. M., Scafidi, F., Bauer, C. R., Vega-Lahr, N., Garcia, R., Nystrom, J., & Kuhn, C. M. (1986). Tactile/kinesthetic stimulation effects on preterm neonates. *Pediatrics, 77,* 654–658.

Field, T. M., Woodson, R., Cohen, D., Garcia, R., & Greenberg, R. (1983). Discrimination and imitation of facial expressions by term and preterm neonates. *Infant Behavior and Development, 6,* 485–490.

Fieve, R. R. (1976). *Moodswing: The third revolution in psychiatry.* New York: Bantam.

Fine, A. (1986). Transplantation in the central nervous system. *Scientific American, 255*(8), 52–58.

Fishbein, M., & Ajzen, I. (1974). Attitudes toward objects as predictors of single and multiple behavioral criteria. *Psychological Review, 81,* 59–74.

Fishbein, M., & Ajzen, I. (1980). Predicting and understanding consumer behavior: Attitude, behavior correspondence. In I. Ajzen & M. Fishbein (Eds.), *Understanding attitudes and predicting social behavior.* Englewood Cliffs, NJ: Prentice-Hall.

Fisher, W. A., & Barak, A. (1989). Sex education as a corrective: Immunizing against possible effects of pornography. In D. Zilmann & J. Bryant (Eds.), *Pornography: Research advances and policy decisions.* Hillsdale, NJ: Erlbaum.

Fiske, S. T., & Taylor, S. E. (1991). *Social cognition*

(2nd ed.). New York: McGraw-Hill.

Flavell, J. H. (1970). Developmental studies of mediated behavior. In H. W. Reese & L. P. Lipsett (Eds.), *Advances in child development and behavior* (Vol. 5). New York: Academic Press.

Flavell, J. H. (1982). On cognitive development. *Child Development, 53,* 1–10.

Flavell, J. H. (1985). *Cognitive development* (2nd ed.). Englewood Cliffs, NJ: Prentice-Hall.

Fleming, I., Baum, A., & Weiss, L. (1987). Social density and perceived control as mediators of crowding stress in high-density residential neighborhoods. *Journal of Personality and Social Psychology, 52,* 899–906.

Flynn, J. P. (1975). Experimental analysis of aggression and its neural basis. In J. P. Flynn (Ed.), *Advances in behavioral biology: The neurophysiology of aggression.* New York: Academic Press.

Flynn, J. R. (1987). Massive IQ gains in 14 nations: What IQ tests really measure. *Psychological Bulletin, 101,* 171–191.

Foa, E. B., & Kozak, M. J. (1986). Emotional processing of fear: Exposure to corrective information. *Psychological Bulletin, 99,* 20–35.

Fodor, J. (1983). *The modularity of mind.* Cambridge, MA: MIT/Bradford.

Folkman, S., & Lazarus, R. S. (1988). Coping as a mediator of emotion. *Journal of Personality and Social Psychology, 54,* 466–475.

Fontana, A. F., Kerns, R. D., Rosenberg, R. L., & Colonese, K. L. (1989). Support, stress and, recovery from coronary heart disease: A longitudinal causal model. *Health Psychology, 8,* 175–193.

Fordyce, W. E. (1988). Pain and suffering: A reappraisal. *American Psychologist, 43,* 276–283.

Fowles, D. (1983, May-June). The changing older population. *Aging,* pp. 6–9.

Fowles, D. C. (1992). Schizophrenia: Diathesis-stress revisited. *Annual Review of Psychology, 43,* 303–336.

Fox, N. A., & Davidson, R. J. (1991). Hemispheric specialization and attachment behaviors: Developmental processes and individual differences in separation process. In J. L. Gewirtz & W. M. Kurtines (Eds.), *Interactions with attachment.* Hillsdale, NJ: Erlbaum.

Fozard, J. L., Wolf, E., Bell, B., McFarland, R. A., & Stephen, P. (1977). Visual perception and communication. In J. E. Birren & K. W. Schaie (Eds.), *Handbook of psychology of aging* (pp. 497–534). New York: Van Nostrand.

Frances, A. J., & Widiger, T. (1986). The classification of personality disorders: An overview of problems and solutions. *Annual Review of Psychiatry, 5,* 240–257.

Frank, E., Anderson, C., & Rubinstein, D. (1978). Frequency of sexual dysfunction in "normal" couples. *New England Journal of Medicine, 299,* 111–115.

Frank, J. D. (1973). *Persuasion and healing.* Baltimore: Johns Hopkins Press.

Frankenhaeuser, M., Lundberg, U., & Chesney, M. (1991). *Women, work, and health: Stress and opportunities.* New York: Plenum.

Frankenhaeuser, M., Lundberg, U., & Forsman, L. (1980). Dissociation between sympathetic-adrenal and pituitary-adrenal response to an achievement situation characterized by high controllability: Comparison between Type A and Type B males and females. *Biological Psychology, 10,* 79–91.

Franklin, J. (1987). *Molecules of the mind: The brave new science of molecular psychology.* New York: Atheneum.

Franz, C. E., McClelland, D. C., & Weinberger, J. (1991). Childhood antecedents of conventional social accomplishment in midlife adults: A 36-year prospective study. *Journal of Personality and Social Psychology, 60,* 586–595.

Frazier, K. (Ed.). (1981). *Paranormal borderlands of science.* Buffalo, NY: Prometheus Books.

Frazier, K. (Ed.). (1986). *Science confronts the paranormal.* Buffalo, NY: Prometheus Books.

Fredrickson, B. L., & Carstensen, L. L. (1990). Choosing social partners: How old age and anticipated endings make people more selective. *Psychology and Aging, 5,* 335–347.

Freedman, J. L. (1988). Television violence and aggression: What the evidence shows. In S. Oskamp (Ed.), *Television as a social issue.* Newbury Park, CA: Sage.

Freud, S. (1935). *A general introduction to psychoanalysis.* New York: Washington Square Press.

Freud, S. (1953). *A general introduction to psychoanalysis.* New York: Perma-books.

Freud, S. (1953). The interpretation of dreams. In J. Strachey (Ed. and Trans.), *The standard edition of the complete psychological works of Sigmund Freud* (Vols. 4, 5). London: Hogarth Press. (Original work published 1900)

Freud, S. (1957). Mourning and melancholia. In J. Strachey (Ed. and Trans.), *The standard edition of the complete psychological works of Sigmund Freud* (Vol. 14). London: Hogarth Press. (Original work published 1917)

Freud, S. (1964). *New introductory lectures in psychoanalysis.* New York: Norton. (Original work published 1933)

Friedberg, J. (1975). Let's stop blasting the brain. *Psychology Today, 35,* 18–26.

Friedman, H. S. (Ed.). (1991). *Hostility, coping, and health.* Washington, DC: American Psychological Association.

Friedman, H. S., & Booth-Kewley, S. (1987). The "disease-prone personality": A meta-analytic view of the construct. *American Psychologist, 42,* 539–555.

Friedman, H. S., & DiMatteo, M. R. (1989). *Health psychology.* Englewood Cliffs, NJ: Prentice-Hall.

Friedman, W. J., Robinson, A. B., & Friedman, B. L. (1987). Sex differences in moral judgments? A test of Gilligan's theory. *Psychology of Women Quarterly, 11,* 37–46.

Frijda, N.H. (1986). *The emotions.* New York: Cambridge.

Frisby, J. P. (1980). *Seeing: Illusion, brain, and mind.* Oxford: Oxford.

Fuller, J. L. (1986). *Perspectives in behavior genetics.* Hillsdale, NJ: Erlbaum.

Furman, W., & Buhrmester, D. (1992). Age and sex differences in perceptions of networks of personal relationships. *Child Development, 63,* 103–115.

Furnham, A., & Taylor, L. (1990). Lay theories of homosexuality: Aetiology, behaviours, and "cures." *British Journal of Social Psychology, 29,* 135–147.

Furstenberg, F. F., Jr., Brooks-Gunn, J., & Morgan, S. T. (1987). *Adolescent mothers in later life.* New York: Cambridge.

Furumoto, L. (1979). Mary Whiton Calkins (1863–1930): Fourteenth president of the American Psychological Association. *Journal of the History of the Behavioral Sciences, 15,* 346–356.

Gainotti, G. (1972). Emotional behavior and hemispheric side of lesion. *Cortex, 8,* 41–55.

Gallagher, D. E., Breckenridge, J. N., Thompson, L. W., & Peterson, J. A. (1983). Effects of bereavement on indicators of mental health in elderly widows and widowers. *Journal of Gerontology, 38,* 565–571.

Gallup, G. G., Jr. (1979). Self-awareness in primates. *American Scientist, 67,* 417–421.

Gallup, G. G., Jr., & Suarez, S. D. (1986). Self-awareness and the emergence of mind in humans and other primates. In J. Suls & A. G. Greenwald (Eds.), *Psychological perspectives on the self* (Vol. 3). Hillsdale, NJ: Erlbaum.

Gallup, G. H., Jr., & Newport, F. (1991, Winter). Belief in paranormal phenomena among adult Americans. *Skeptical Inquirer,* pp. 137–146.

Gallup Organization. (1988). *American's youth 1977–1988.* Princeton, NJ: Author.

Galton, F. (1869). *Hereditary genius: An inquiry into its laws and consequences.* New York: Appleton.

Gangestad, S. W. (1989). The evolutionary history of genetic variation: An emerging issue in the behavioral genetic study of personality. In D. M. Buss & N. Cantor (Eds.), *Personality psychology: Recent trends and emerging directions.* New York: Springer-Verlag.

Garber, J., & Dodge, K. A. (Eds.). (1991). *The development of emotion regulation and dysregulation.* New York: Cambridge.

Gardner, B. T., & Gardner, R. A. (1975). Evidence for sentence constituents in the early utterances of child and chimpanzee. *Journal of Experimental Psychology: General, 104,* 244–267.

Gardner, H. (1983). *Frames of mind: The theory of multiple intelligences.* New York: Basic Books.

Garfield, C. A. (1979). A child dies. In C. A. Garfield (Ed.), *Stress and survival: The emotional realities of life-threatening illness.* St. Louis: Mosby.

Garfield, S. L. (1989). *The practice of brief psychotherapy.* New York: Pergamon.

Garfield, S. L., & Bergin, A. E. (1986). Introduction and historical overview. In S. L. Garfield & A. E. Bergin (Eds.), *Handbook of psychotherapy and behavior change* (2nd ed.). New York: Wiley.

Garfinkel, P. E. (1992). Evidence in support of attitudes to shape and weight as a diagnostic criterion of bulimia nervosa. *International Journal of Eating Disorders, 11,* 321–325.

Garfinkel, P. E., & Garner, D. M. (1982). *Anorexia nervosa: A multidimensional perspective.* New York: Brunner-Mazel.

Garland, D. J., & Barry, J. R. (1991). Cognitive advantage in sport: The nature of perceptual structures. *American Journal of Psychology, 104,* 211–228.

Garmezy, N. (1983). *Stress, coping, and development in children.* New York: McGraw-Hill.

Gatewood, R. D., & Field, H. S. (1990). *Human resource selection.* Orlando, FL: Dryden.

Gaugler, B. B., Rosenthal, D. B., Thornton, G. C., & Bentson, C. (1987). Meta-analysis of assessment center validity. *Journal of Applied Psychology, 72,* 493–511.

Gawin, F. H. (1991). Cocaine addiction: Psychology and neurophysiology. *Science, 257,* 1580–1586.

Gaylord-Ross, R. (1990). *Issues and research in special education.* New York: Teachers College Press.

Gazzaniga, M. S. (1967). The split brain in man. *Scientific American, 217*(8), 24–29.

Gazzaniga, M. S. (1985). *The social brain.* New York: Basic Books.

Gazzaniga, M. S., & Smylie, C. S. (1983). Facial recognition and brain asymmetries: Clues to underlying mechanisms. *Annals of Neurology, 13,* 536–540.

Gazzaniga, M. S., Steen, D., & Volpe, B. T. (1979). *Functional neuroscience.* New York: Harper & Row.

Geen, R. G., & Thomas, S. L. (1986). The immediate effects of media violence on behavior. *Journal of Social Issues, 42,* 7–28.

Gelman, R., & Baillargeon, R. (1983). A review of some Piagetian concepts. In J. H. Flavell & E. M. Markman (Eds.), *Handbook of child psychology: Cognitive development* (Vol. 3). New York: Wiley.

Gelman, R., & Gallistel, C. R. (1978). *The child's understanding of number.* Cambridge, MA: Harvard University Press.

George, C., & Main, M. (1979). Social interactions of young abused children: Approach, avoidance, and aggression. *Child Development, 50,* 306–318.

George, L. (1980). *Role transitions in later life.* Monterey, CA: Brooks/Cole.

George, W. H., Derman, K. H., & Nochajski, T. H. (1989). Alcohol expectancy set, self-report expectancies, and predispositional factors: Predicting interest in violence and erotica. *Journal of Studies on Alcohol, 50,* 541–551.

George, W. H., & Marlatt, G. A. (1986). The effects of alcohol and anger on interest in violence, erotica, and deviance. *Journal of Abnormal Psychology, 95,* 150–158.

Gerrard, M. (1987). Sex, guilt, and contraceptive use revisited: The 1980s. *Journal of Personality and Social Psychology, 52,* 975–980.

Gershon, E. S., Berrettini, W. H., & Golden, L. E. (1989). Mood disorders: Genetic aspects. In H. I. Kaplan & B. J. Sadock (Eds.), *Comprehensive textbook of psychiatry.* Baltimore: Williams & Wilkins.

Giambra, L. M. (1982). Daydreaming: A black-white comparison for 17–34-year-olds. *Journal of Personality and Social Psychology, 42,* 1146–1156.

Gibson, E. J. (1988). Exploratory behavior in the development of perceiving, acting and the acquiring of knowledge. *Annual Review of Psychology, 39,* 1–42.

Gibson, J. J. (1979). *The ecological approach to visual perception.* Boston: Houghton Mifflin.

Gilbert, D., & Jones, E. E. (1986). Perceiver-induced constraint: Interpretations of self-generated reality. *Journal of Personality and Social Psychology, 50,* 269–280.

Gilbert, D. T. (1989). Thinking lightly about others: Automatic components of the social inference process. In J. S. Uleman & J. A. Bargh (Eds.), *Unintended thought: Limits of awareness, intention, and control.* New York: Guilford.

Gilbert, L. A., Hollahan, C., & Manning, L. (1981). Coping and conflict between professional and maternal roles. *Family Relations, 30,* 419–426.

Gilligan, C. (1982). *In a different voice: Psychological*

theory and women's development. Cambridge, MA: Harvard University Press.

Gilligan, C., Murphy, J. M., & Tappan, M. B. (1990). Moral development beyond adolescence. In C. N. Alexander & E. J. Langer (Eds.). *Higher stages of human development: Perspectives on adult growth.* New York: Oxford.

Gilovich, T., Vallone, R., & Tversky, A. (1985). The hot hand in basketball: On the misperceptions of random sequences. *Cognitive Psychology, 17,* 295–314.

Giordano, J. A. (1988). Parents of the baby boomers: A new generation of young-old. *Family Relations, 37,* 411–414.

Glanzer, M., & Cunitz, A. R. (1966). Two storage mechanisms in free recall. *Journal of Verbal Learning and Verbal Behavior, 5,* 351–360.

Glaser, R., & Bassok, M. (1989). Learning theory and the study of instruction. *Annual Review of Psychology, 40,* 631–666.

Glaser, R., Rice, J., Sheridan, J., Fertel, R., Stout, J., Spreicher, C., Pinskey, D., Kotur, M., Post, A., Beck, M., & Kiecolt-Glaser, J. (1987). Stress-related immune suppression: Health implications. *Brain, Behavior, and Immunity, 1,* 17–26.

Glass, D. C., & Singer, J. E. (1972). *Urban stress.* New York: Academic Press.

Glasscote, R. (1978). What programs work and what programs do not work for chronic mental patients? In J. A. Talbott (Ed.), *The chronic mental patient: Problems, solutions, and recommendations for a public policy.* Washington, DC: American Psychiatric Association.

Glenberg, A. M., Sanocki, T., Epstein, W., & Morris, C. (1987). Enhancing calibration of comprehension. *Journal of Experimental Psychology: General, 116,* 119–136.

Glenn, N., & McLanahan, S. (1982). Children and marital happiness: A further specification of the relationship. *Journal of Marriage and the Family, 44,* 63–72.

Glick, P. C. (1989). Remarried families, stepfamilies, and stepchildren: A brief demographic profile. *Family Relations, 38,* 24–27.

Godden, D. R., & Baddeley, A. D. (1975). Context-dependent memory in two natural environments: On land and under water. *British Journal of Psychology, 66,* 325–332.

Goetzel, E. J., Turck, C. W., & Sreedharan, S. P. (1990). Production and recognition of neuropeptides by cells of the immune system. In R. Ader, N. Cohen, & D. L. Felten (Eds.), *Psychoneuroimmunology II.* New York: Academic Press.

Goffman, E. (1961). *Asylums: Essays on the social situation of mental patients and other inmates.* New York: Doubleday.

Goldberg, L. R., Grenier, J. R., Guion, R. M., Sechiest, L. B., & Wing, H. (1991). *Questionnaires used in the prediction of trustworthiness in preemployment selection decisions: An APA task force report.* Washington, DC: American Psychological Association.

Golding, J. M., Smith, R., & Kashner, M. (1991). Does somatization disorder occur in men? *Archives of General Psychiatry, 48,* 231–235.

Goldman-Rakic, P. S. (1992). Working memory and the mind. *Scientific American, 267*(3), 110–117.

Goldsmith, R. F. (1990). Utility analysis and its application to the study of cost-effectiveness of the as-

sessment center method. In K. R. Murphy & F. E. Saal (Eds.), *Psychology in organizations: Integrating science and practice.* Hillsdale, NJ: Erlbaum.

Goldstein, G., & Hersen, M. (Eds.). (1990). *Handbook of psychological assessment* (2nd ed). New York: Pergamon.

Goleman, D. (1988, June 14). In old age, Erikson expands his view of life. *New York Times,* pp. C1, C14.

Goodglass, H., & Butters, N. (1988). Psychobiology of cognitive processes. In R. C. Atkinson, R. J. Herrnstein, G. Lindzey, & R. D. Luce (Eds.), *Stevens' handbook of experimental psychology:* Vol. 2. *Learning and cognition* (2nd ed., pp. 863–952). New York: Wiley.

Goodman, W. (1982, August 9). Of mice, monkeys, and men. *Newsweek,* p. 61.

Goodwin, C. J. (1991). Misportraying Pavlov's apparatus. *American Journal of Psychology, 104,* 135–141.

Gorczynski, R., & Kennedy, M. (1987). Behavioral trait associated with conditioned immunity. *Brain, Behavior, and Immunity, 1,* 27–32.

Gorczynski, R., Macrae, S., & Kennedy, M. (1982). Conditioned immune response associated with allogenic skin grafts in mice. *Journal of Immunology, 129,* 704–709.

Gorman, J. M., & Kertzner, R. M. (Eds.). (1991). *Psychoimmunology update.* Washington, DC: American Psychiatric Press.

Gormezano, I., & Wasserman, E. A. (Eds.). (1992). *Learning and memory: The behavioral and biological substrates.* Hillsdale, NJ: Erlbaum.

Gottesman, I. I. (1991). *Schizophrenia genesis: The origins of madness.* New York: Freeman.

Gottman, J. M. (1986). The world of coordinated play: Same- and cross-sex friendship in young children. In J. M. Gottman & J. G. Parker (Eds.), *Conversations of friends: Speculations of affective development.* Cambridge, England: Cambridge.

Gottman, J. M., & Krokoff, L. J. (1989). Marital interaction and satisfaction: A longitudinal view. *Journal of Consulting and Clinical Psychology, 57,* 47–52.

Gottman, J. M., & Levinson, R. (1992). Marital processes predictive of later dissolution: Behavior, psychology and health. *Journal of Personality and Social Psychology, 63,* 221–233.

Gottschalk, L. A., et al. (1991). Anxiety levels in dreams: Relations to localized cerebral glucose metabolic rate. *Brain Research, 538,* 107–110.

Gould, D. (1987). Understanding attrition in children's sport. In D. Gould & M. R. Weiss (Eds.), *Advances in pediatric sport sciences:* Vol. 2. *Behavioral issues.* Champaign, IL: Human Kinetics.

Gould, R. L. (1972). The phases of adult life: A study in developmental psychology. *American Journal of Psychiatry, 129,* 521–531.

Gournay, K. (Ed.). (1989). *Agoraphobia: Current perspectives on theory and treatment.* New York: Routledge.

Graf, M. V., & Kastin, A. J. (1984). Delta sleep-inducing peptide: A review. *Neuroscience and Biobehavioral Reviews, 8,* 83–93.

Graham, N. V. (1989). *Visual pattern analyzers.* New York: Oxford.

Green, J., Bax, M., & Tsitsikas, H. (1989). Neonatal behavior and early temperament: A longitudinal study of the first six months of life. *American Journal*

of Orthopsychiatry, 59, 82–93.

Greenberg, L. S., & Safran, J. D. (1989). Emotion in psychotherapy. *American Psychologist, 44,* 19–29.

Greenberg, M. S., & Beck, A. T. (1989). Depression versus anxiety: A test of the content-specificity hypothesis. *Journal of Abnormal Psychology, 98,* 9–13.

Greene, R. L. (1992). *Human memory: Paradigms and paradoxes.* Hillsdale, NJ: Erlbaum.

Greenough, W., & Sirevaag, A. M. (1991). A neuroanatomical approach to substrates of behavioral plasticity. In H. N. Shair, G. A. Barr, & M. A. Hofer (Eds.), *Developmental psychology: New methods and changing concepts.* New York: Oxford.

Greenwald, A. G. (1990). What cognitive representations underlie social attitudes? *Bulletin of the Psychonomic Society, 28,* 254–260.

Greenwald, A. G. (1992). New look 3: Unconscious cognition reclaimed. *American Psychologist, 47,* 766–779.

Greenwald, A. G., Spangenberg, E. R., Pratkanis, A. R., & Eskenazi, J. (1991). Double-blind tests of subliminal self-help tapes. *Psychological Science, 2,* 119–122.

Greer, H. S., Morris, T., & Pettingale, K. W. (1979). Psychological response to breast cancer: Effect on outcome. *Lancet, 2,* 785–787.

Gregory, R. L. (1966). *Eye and brain.* New York: McGraw-Hill.

Gregory, W. L., & Burroughs, W. J. (1989). *Introduction to applied psychology.* Glenview, IL: Scott, Foresman.

Griffin, E., & Sparks, G. G. (1990). Friends forever: A longitudinal exploration of intimacy in same-sex friends and platonic pairs. *Journal of Social and Personal Relationships, 7,* 29–46.

Griggs, R. A., & Cox, J. R. (1982). The elusive thematic-materials effect in Wason's selection task. *British Journal of Psychology, 73,* 407–420.

Grilly, D. M. (1989). *Drugs and human behavior.* Boston: Allyn & Bacon.

Grossberg, J. M., & Grant, B. (1978). Clinical psychophysics: Applications of ratio scaling and signal detection methods to research on pain, fear, drugs, and medical decision making. *Psychological Bulletin, 85,* 1154–1176.

Grossberg, S., & Rudd, M. E. (1992). Cortical dynamics of visual motion perception: Short-range and long-range apparent motion. *Psychological Review, 99,* 78–121.

Guidubaldi, J., & Perry, J. D. (1984). Divorce, socioeconomic status, and children's cognitive-social competence at school entry. *American Journal of Orthopsychiatry, 54,* 459–468.

Guilford, J. P. (1959a). *Personality.* New York: McGraw-Hill.

Guilford, J. P. (1959b). Three faces of intellect. *American Psychologist, 14,* 469–479.

Guilford, J.P. (1967). *The nature of human intelligence.* New York: McGraw-Hill.

Guion, R. M., & Gibson, W. M. (1988). Personnel selection and placement. *Annual Review of Psychology, 39,* 349–374.

Gurman, A. S., Kniskern, D. P., & Pinsof, W. M. (1986). Research on the process and outcome of marital and family therapy. In S. L. Garfield & A. E. Bergin (Eds.), *Handbook of psychotherapy and behavior change* (2nd ed.). New York: Wiley.

Gustafson, S. B., & Magnusson, D. (1991). *Female life careers: A pattern approach.* Hillsdale, NJ: Erlbaum.

Haaga, D. A., & Davison, G. C. (1986). Cognitive change methods. In F. H. Kanfer & A. P. Goldstein (Eds.), *Helping people change: A textbook of methods* (3rd ed., pp. 236–282). New York: Pergamon.

Haaga, D. A., Dyck, M. J., & Ernst, D. (1991). Empirical status of cognitive theory of depression. *Psychological Bulletin, 110,* 215–236.

Haas, H., Fink, H., & Hartfelder, G. (1959). Das placeboproblem (translation). *Psychopharmacology Service Center Bulletin, 2,* 1–65.

Hackman, J. R. (1991). *Work design.* In R. M. Steers & L. W. Porter (Eds.), *Motivation and work behavior.* New York: McGraw-Hill.

Hackman, J. R., & Oldham, G. R. (1980). *Work redesign.* Reading, MA: Addison-Wesley.

Hadigan, C. M., & Walsh, B. T. (1991). Body shape concerns in bulimia nervosa. *International Journal of Eating Disorders, 10,* 323–331.

Hall, G. S. (1904). *Adolescence* (Vols. 1, 2). New York: Appleton-Century-Crofts.

Hall, H. (1983). Hypnosis and the immune system: A review with implications for cancer and the psychology of healing. *American Journal of Clinical Hypnosis, 25,* 92–103.

Hall, M. R. S., & O'Grady, M. (1990). Psychosocial interventions and immune function. In R. Ader, N. Cohen, & D. L. Felton (Eds.), *Psychoneuroimmunology II.* New York: Academic Press.

Halpern, D. (1986). *Sex differences in cognitive abilities.* Hillsdale, NJ: Erlbaum.

Hamilton, V. L., Blumenfeld, P. C., Akoh, H., & Miura, K. (1991). Group and gender in Japanese and American elementary classrooms. *Journal of Cross-Cultural Psychology, 22,* 317–346.

Hammen, C. (1991). *Depression runs in families: The social context of risk and resilience in children of depressed mothers.* New York: Springer-Verlag.

Hammen, C., Davila, J., Brown, G., Ellicott, A., & Gitlin, M. (1992). Psychiatric history and stress: Predictors of severity of unipolar depression. *Journal of Abnormal Psychology, 101,* 45–52.

Hammen, C., Elliott, A., Gitlin, M., & Jamison, K. R. (1989). Sociotropy/autonomy and vulnerability to specific life events in patients with unipolar depression and bipolar disorders. *Journal of Abnormal Psychology, 98,* 154–160.

Hammer, R. (1987). *The CBS murders.* New York: New American Library.

Hampson, E., & Kimura, D. (1992). Sex differences and hormonal influences on cognitive function in humans. In J. B. Becker, S. M. Breedlove, & D. Crews (Eds.), *Behavioral endocrinology.* Cambridge, MA: MIT Press.

Hansen, C. H., & Hansen, R. D. (1988). Finding the face in the crowd: An anger superiority effect. *Journal of Personality and Social Psychology, 54,* 917–924.

Hardiman, P. T., Dufresne, R., & Mestre, J. P. (1989). The relation between problem categorization and problem solving among experts and novices. *Memory and Cognition, 17,* 627–638.

Harlow, H. F. (1958). The nature of love. *American Psychologist, 13,* 673–685.

Harlow, H. F., & Suomi, S. J. (1970). The nature of love-simplified. *American Psychologist, 25,* 161–168.

Harper, R. M. (1983). Cardiorespiratory and state control in infants at risk for the sudden death syndrome. In M. H. Chase & E. D. Weitzman (Eds.), *Sleep disorders: Basic and clinical research.* New York: Spectrum.

Harrell, T. W., & Harrell, M. S. (1945). Army General Classification Test scores for civilian occupations. *Educational and Psychological Measurement, 5,* 229–239.

Harrington, D. M., Block, J. H., & Black, J. (1987). Testing aspects of Carl Rogers's theory of creative environments: Child-rearing antecedents of creative potential in young adolescents. *Journal of Personality and Social Psychology, 52,* 851–856.

Harris, J. E., & Morris, P. E. (1984). *Everyday memory, actions, and absent-mindedness.* London: Academic Press.

Harris, J. P. (1987). Contingent perceptual aftereffect. In R. L. Gregory (Ed.), *The Oxford companion to the mind.* Oxford: Oxford.

Harter, S. (1983). Developmental perspectives on the self-system. In E. M. Hetherington (Ed.), *Handbook of child psychology: Socialization, personality, and social development.* New York: Wiley.

Hartigan, J. A., & Wigdor, A. K. (Eds.). (1989). *Fairness in employment testing.* Washington, DC: National Academy Press.

Harvey, S. M. (1987). Female sexual behavior: Fluctuation during the menstrual cycle. *Journal of Psychosomatic Research, 31,* 101–110.

Hatfield, E. (1988). Passionate and companionate love. In R. J. Sternberg & M. L. Barnes (Eds.), *The psychology of love.* New Haven, CT: Yale University Press.

Hatfield, E., & Rapson, R. L. (1987). Passionate love/sexual desire: Can the same paradigm explain both? *Archives of Sexual Behavior, 16,* 259–278.

Havighurst, R. J. (1972). *Developmental tasks and education.* New York: McKay.

Havighurst, R. J. (1982). The world of work. In J. Wolman (Ed.), *Handbook of developmental psychology.* Englewood Cliffs, NJ: Prentice-Hall.

Hayashi, C. (1988). *National character of the Japanese.* Tokyo: Statistical Bureau, Japan.

Hayes, J. R. (1989). *The complete problem solver* (2nd ed.). Hillsdale, NJ: Erlbaum.

Haynes, M. E. (1987). *Personal time management.* Los Altos, CA: Crisp Publications.

Haynes, S. G., Feinleib, M., & Kannel, W. B. (1980). The relationship of psychosocial factors to coronary heart disease in the Framingham Study: I. Methods and risk factors. *American Journal of Epidemiology, 107,* 362–383.

Haynes, S. N. (1990). Behavioral assessment of adults. In G. Goldstein & M. Hersen (Eds.), *Handbook of psychological assessment.* Elmsford, NY: Pergamon.

Hayslip, B., & Panek, P. E. (1989). *Adult development and aging.* New York: Harper & Row.

Healy, A. F., Kosslyn, S. M., & Shiffrin, R. M. (Eds.). (1992). *From learning processes to cognitive processes: Essays in honor of William K. Estes* (Vol. 2). Hillsdale, NJ: Erlbaum.

Hearold, S. (1986). A synthesis of 1043 effects of television on social behavior. In G. Comstock (Ed.), *Public communications and behavior* (Vol. 1). New York: Academic Press.

Heatherton, T. F., Herman, C. P., & Polivy, J. (1991). Effects of physical threat and ego threat on eating behavior. *Journal of Personality and Social Psychology, 60,* 138–143.

Heckhausen, H. (1991). *Motivation and action* (2nd ed.). New York: Springer-Verlag.

Heckhausen, H., Schmidt, H., & Schneider, K. (1985). *Achievement motivation in perspective.* Orlando, FL: Academic Press.

Heider, E. R., & Olivier, D. C. (1972). The structure of the color space in naming and memory for two languages. *Cognitive Psychology, 3,* 337–354.

Heider, F. (1958). *The psychology of interpersonal relations.* New York: Wiley.

Heilbrun, K. S. (1980). Silverman's subliminal psychodynamic activation: A failure to replicate. *Journal of Abnormal Psychology, 89,* 560–566.

Heller, J., Groff, B., & Soloman, S. (1977). Toward an understanding of crowding: The role of physical interaction. *Journal of Personality and Social Psychology, 35,* 183–190.

Heller, K. (1990). Social and community interventions. *Annual Review of Psychology, 41,* 141–168.

Heller, M. A., & Schiff, W. (Eds.). (1991). *The psychology of touch.* Hillsdale, NJ: Erlbaum.

Hellriegel, D., Slocum, J. W., Jr., & Woodman, R. W. (1989). *Organizational behavior* (5th ed.). St. Paul, MN: West.

Hendrick, C. (Ed.). (1989). *Close relationships.* Newbury Park, CA: Sage.

Hendrick, C., & Hendrick, S. (1986). A theory and method of love. *Journal of Personality and Social Psychology, 50,* 392–402.

Hendrick, C., Hendrick, S., Foote, F. H., & Slapion-Foote, M. J. (1984). Do men and women love differently? *Journal of Social and Personal Relationships, 1,* 177–185.

Hendrick, S. S., Hendrick, C., & Adler, N. L. (1988). Romantic relationships: Love, satisfaction, and staying together. *Journal of Personality and Social Psychology, 54,* 980–988.

Henriques, J. B., & Davidson, R. J. (1990). Regional brain electrical asymmetries discriminate between previously depressed and healthy control subjects. *Journal of Abnormal Psychology, 99,* 22–31.

Herd, J. A. (1986). Neuroendocrine mechanisms in coronary heart disease. In K. A. Matthews et al. (Eds.), *Handbook of stress, reactivity, and cardiovascular disease.* New York: Wiley.

Herdt, G., & Lindenbaum, S. (Eds.). (1992). *Social analysis in the time of AIDS.* Newbury Park, CA: Sage.

Herman, C. P., Polivy, J., Lank, C. N., & Heatherton, T. H. (1987). Anxiety, hunger, and eating behavior. *Journal of Abnormal Psychology, 96,* 264–269.

Hertzog, C., & Schaie, K. W. (1986). Stability and change in adult intelligence: 1. Analysis of longitudinal covariance structures. *Psychology and Aging, 1,* 159–171.

Herzog, A. R., House, J. S., & Morgan, J. N. (1991). Relation of work and retirement to health and well-being in older age. *Psychology and Aging, 6,* 202–211.

Hetherington, E. M. (1987). Family relations six years after divorce. In K. Pasley & M. Ihinger-Tallman (Eds.), *Remarriage and stepparenting: Current research and theory.* New York: Guilford.

Hibler, N. S. (1984). Investigative aspects of forensic

hypnosis. In W. C. Webster & A. H. Smith (Eds.), *Clinical hypnosis: A multidisciplinary approach.* Philadelphia: Lippincott.

Higgins, E. T. (1987). Self-discrepancy: A theory relating self and affect. *Psychological Review, 94,* 319–340.

Hilgard, E. R. (1977). *Divided consciousness: Multiple controls in human thought and action.* New York: Wiley.

Hilgard, E. R. (1987). Research advances in hypnosis: Issues and methods. *International Journal of Clinical and Experimental Hypnosis, 35,* 248–264.

Hilgard, E. R., & Loftus, E. F. (1979). Effective interrogation of the eyewitness. *International Journal of Clinical and Experimental Hypnosis, 27,* 342–357.

Hill, C. A. (1987). Affiliation motivation: People who need people but in different ways. *Journal of Personality and Social Psychology, 52,* 1008–1018.

Hill, T., & Lewicki, P. (1991). The unconscious. In N. J. Derlega, B. A. Winstead, & W. H. Jones (Eds.), *Personality: Contemporary theory and research.* Chicago: Nelson-Hall.

Hite, S. (1988). *Women and love: A cultural revolution in progress.* New York: Knopf.

Hobfoll, S. E., Lomranz, J., Eyal, N., Bridges, A., & Tzemach, M. (1989). Pulse of a nation: Depressive mood reactions of Israelis to the Israel-Lebanon war. *Journal of Personality and Social Psychology, 56,* 1002–1012.

Hobson, J. A. (1989). *Sleep.* New York: Freeman.

Hodes, R. L. (1981). *A psychophysiological investigation of the classical conditioning model of fears and phobias.* Unpublished doctoral dissertation, University of Wisconsin, Madison.

Hofmann, A. (1980). *LSD, my problem child.* New York: McGraw-Hill.

Hogan, R., & Nicholson, R. A. (1988). The meaning of personality test scores. *American Psychologist, 43,* 621–626.

Hogarty, G. E., et al. (1986). Family psychoeducation, social skills training, and maintenance chemotherapy in the aftercare treatment of schizophrenia: One-year effects of a controlled study on relapse and expressed emotion. *Archives of General Psychiatry, 43,* 633–642.

Holahan, C. J., & Moos, R. H. (1990). Life stressors, resistance factors, and improved psychological functioning: An extension of the stress resistance paradigm. *Journal of Personality and Social Psychology, 58,* 909–917.

Holahan, C. K. (1988). Relation of life goals at age 70 to activity participation and health and psychological well-being among Terman's gifted men and women. *Psychology and Aging, 3,* 286–291.

Holden, C. (1989). Women (not) in math. *Science, 246,* 574.

Holden, C. (1991). Probing the complex genetics of alcoholism. *Science, 251,* 163–164.

Holland, J. L. (1985). *Making vocational choices: A theory of vocational personalities and work environments* (2nd ed.). Englewood Cliffs, NJ: Prentice-Hall.

Holland, J. L., & Gottfredson, G. D. (1981). Using a typology of persons and environments to explain careers: Some extensions and clarifications. In D. H. Montross & C. J. Shinkman (Eds.), *Career development in the 1980s: Theory and practice* (pp.

5–27). Springfield, IL: Charles C Thomas.

Holland, P. C. (1992). Event representation in Pavlovian conditioning: Image and action. In C. R. Gallistel (Ed.), *Animal cognition.* Cambridge, MA: MIT Press.

Hollister, L. E. (1986). Health aspects of cannabis. *Pharmacological Reviews, 38,* 1–20.

Hollon, S. D., Shelton, R. C., & Loosen, P. T. (1991). Cognitive therapy and pharmacotherapy for depression. *Journal of Consulting and Clinical Psychology, 59,* 88–99.

Holloway, M. (1991). Rx for addiction. *Scientific American, 264*(3), 95–103.

Holmes, D. S. (1984). Meditation and somatic arousal reduction: A review of the experimental evidence. *American Psychologist, 39,* 1–10.

Holmes, D. S., & McCaul, K. D. (1989). Laboratory research on defense mechanisms. In R. W. J. Neufeld (Ed.), *Advances in the investigation of psychological stress.* New York: Wiley.

Holmes, T. H., & Rahe, R. H. (1987). The Social Readjustment Rating Scale. *Journal of Psychosomatic Research, 11,* 213–218.

Honts, C. R. (1991). The emperor's new clothes: Application of polygraph tests in the American workplace. *Forensic Reports, 4,* 91–116.

Honts, C. R., & Perry, M. V. (1992). Polygraph admissibility: Changes and challenges. *Law and Human Behavior, 16,* 357–379.

Hooker, K., & Ventis, D. G. (1984). Work ethic, daily activities, and retirement satisfaction. *Journal of Gerontology, 39,* 478–484.

Hooker, W. D., & Hones, R. T. (1987). Increased susceptibility to memory intrusions and the Stroop interference effect during acute marijuana intoxication. *Psychophysiology, 91,* 20–24.

Hooley, J. M. (1985). Expressed emotion: A review of the critical literature. *Clinical Psychology Review, 5,* 119–139.

Hooper, J. (1986). *The three-pound universe.* New York: Macmillan.

Hooyman, N. R., & Kiyak, H. A. (1988). *Social gerontology: A multidisciplinary perspective.* Boston: Allyn & Bacon.

Horn, J. L. (1985). Remodeling old models of intelligence. In B. B. Wolman (Ed.), *Handbook of intelligence: Theory, measurement, and application* (pp. 267–300). New York: Wiley-Interscience.

Horne, J. (1988). *Why we sleep: The functions of sleep in humans and other mammals.* New York: Oxford.

Horowitz, I. A. (1991). Social psychology and the law. In R. M. Baron & W. G. Graziano (Eds.), *Social psychology.* Ft. Worth, TX: Holt, Rinehart & Winston.

Horowitz, M. (1988). *Psychodynamics and cognition.* Chicago: University of Chicago Press.

Houck, J. C., Kimball, C., Chang, C., Pedigo, N. W., & Yamamura, H. I. (1980). Placental B-endorphin-like peptides. *Science, 207,* 78–79.

House, J. S., Landis, K. R., & Umberson, D. (1988). Social relationships and health. *Science, 241,* 540–545.

Houston, B. K., Smith, M. A., & Cates, D. S. (1989). Hostility patterns and cardiovascular reactivity to stress. *Psychophysiology, 26,* 337–342.

Houston, J. P. (1992). *Fundamentals of learning and memory.* Ft. Worth, TX: Harcourt Brace Jovanovich.

Howard, K. I., Kopta, S. M., Krause, M. S., & Orlinsky, D. E. (1986). The dose-effect relationship in psychotherapy. *American Psychologist, 41,* 159–164.

Howe, G. R., et al. (1990). Dietary factors and risk of breast cancer: Combined analysis of 12 case-control studies. *Journal of the National Cancer Institute, 82,* 561–569.

Howes, C., & Olenick, M. (1986). Child care and family influences on toddlers' compliance. *Child Development, 57,* 202–216.

Hubel, D. H. (1982). Explorations of the primary visual cortex. *Nature, 299,* 515–524.

Hubel, D. H., & Wiesel, T. N. (1979). Brain mechanisms of vision. *Scientific American, 241*(9), 150–162.

Huebner, R. R., & Izard, C. E. (1988). Mothers' responses to infants' facial expressions of sadness, anger, and physical distress. *Motivation and Emotion, 12,* 185–196.

Hull, C. L. (1951). *Essentials of behavior.* New Haven, CT: Yale University Press.

Hull, J. G., & Bond, C. F. (1986). Social and behavioral consequence of alcohol consumption and expectancy: A meta-analysis. *Psychological Bulletin, 99,* 347–360.

Humphreys, M. S., & Tehan, G. A. (1992). A simultaneous examination of recency and cuing effects. In A. F. Healy, S. M. Kosslyn, & R. M. Shiffrin (Eds.), *From learning processes to cognitive processes: Essays in honor of William K. Estes* (Vol. 2). Hillsdale, NJ: Erlbaum.

Humphriss, N. (1989, November 20). Letters. *Time,* p. 12.

Hunt, E. (1978). Mechanics of verbal ability. *Psychological Review, 85,* 109–130.

Hunt, E. (1987). The next word on verbal ability. In P. Vernon (Ed.), *Speed of information processing and intelligence* (pp. 347–392). Norwood, NJ: Ablex.

Hunt, E. (1989). Cognitive science: Definition, status, and questions. *Annual Review of Psychology, 40,* 603–630.

Hunt, E., & Agnoli, F. (1991). The Whorfian hypothesis: A cognitive psychology perspective. *Psychological Review, 98,* 377–389.

Hunt, E., Lunneborg, C. E., & Lewis, J. (1975). What does it mean to be high verbal? *Cognitive Psychology, 7,* 194–227.

Hunt, M. (1987, August 30). Navigating the therapy maze. *New York Times Magazine,* pp. 28–49.

Hunter, F. T., & Youniss, J. (1982). Changes in functions of three relations during adolescence. *Developmental Psychology, 18,* 806–811.

Hunter, J. E., & Hunter, R. F. (1984). Validity and utility of alternative predictors of job performance. *Pychological Bulletin, 96,* 72–98.

Hunter, J. E., & Schmidt, F. L. (1982). Fitting people to jobs: The impact of personnel selection on national productivity. In M. D. Dunnette & E. A. Fleishman (Eds.), *Human performance and productivity:* Vol. 1. *Human capability assessment* (pp. 233–384). Hillsdale, NJ: Erlbaum.

Hunziker, U. A., & Barr, R. B. (1986). Increased carrying reduces infant crying: A randomized controlled trial. *Pediatrics, 77,* 641–648.

Huselid, M. A., & Day, N. E. (1991). Organizational commitment, job involvement, and turnover: A substantive and methodological analysis. *Journal of Ap-*

plied Psychology, 76, 380–391.

Huttenlocher, P. R. (1979). Synaptic density in human frontal cortex: Developmental changes and effects of aging. *Brain Research, 163,* 195–205.

Hyde, J. S. (1990). *Understanding human sexuality* (4th ed.). New York: McGraw-Hill.

Hyde, J. S., Fennema, E., & Lamon, S. J. (1990). Gender differences in mathematics performance: A meta-analysis. *Psychological Bulletin, 107,* 139–155.

Hygge, S., & Ohman, A. (1978). Modeling processes in the acquisition of fears: Vicarious electrodermal conditioning to fear-relevant stimuli. *Journal of Personality and Social Psychology, 36,* 271–279.

Hyman, S. E., & Nestler, E. (1992). *The molecular foundations of psychiatry.* Washington, DC: American Psychiatric Press.

Ikemi, Y., & Nakagawa, A. (1962). A psychosomatic study of contagious dermatitis. *Kyushu Journal of Medical Science, 13,* 335–350.

Ingelhart, R., & Rabier, J. R. (1986). Aspirations adapt to situations—but why are the Belgians so much happier than the French? A cross-cultural study of the quality of life. In F. M. Andrews (Ed.), *Research on the quality of life.* Ann Arbor: Institute for Social Research, University of Michigan.

Ingram, R. E. (Ed.). (1991). *Contemporary psychological approaches to depression: Theory, research, and treatment.* New York: Plenum.

Inhelder, B., & Piaget, J. (1958). *The growth of logical thinking from childhood to adolescence* (Anne Parsons & Stanley Milgram, Trans.). New York: Basic Books.

Inouye, S. (1989). *Biology of sleep substances.* Boca Raton, FL: CRC Press.

Inque, S., & Schneider-Helmert, D. (Eds.). (1988). *Sleep peptides: Basic and clinical approaches.* New York: Springer-Verlag.

Insel, P. M., & Roth, W. P. (1976). *Health in a changing society.* Palo Alto, CA: Mayfield.

Ironside, R., & Batchelor, I. R. C. (1945). The ocular manifestations of hysteria in relation to flying. *British Journal of Ophthalmology, 29,* 88–98.

Isaacson, R. L. (1964). Relation between *n* Achievement, test anxiety, and curricular choice. *Journal of Abnormal Psychology, 68,* 447–452.

Iversen, L. L. (1979). The chemistry of the brain. *Scientific American, 241*(9), 134–149.

Izard, C. E. (1977). *Human emotions.* New York: Plenum.

Izard, C. E. (1981). Differential emotions theory and the facial feedback hypothesis: Comments on Tourajean and Ellsworth's "The role of facial response in the experience of emotion." *Journal of Personality and Social Psychology, 40,* 350–354.

Izard, C. E. (1989). The structure and functions of emotions: Implications for cognition, motivation, and personality. In I. S. Cohen (Ed.), *The G. Stanley Hall lecture series* (Vol. 9). Washington, DC: American Psychological Association.

Izard, C. E. (1990). Facial expressions and the regulation of emotions. *Journal of Personality and Social Psychology, 58,* 487–498.

Izard, C. E., & Malatesta, C. Z. (1987). Perspectives on emotional development: 1. Differential emotions theory of early emotional development. In J. D. Osofsky (Ed.), *Handbook of infant development* (2nd ed.). New York: Wiley-Interscience.

Jacobs, K. M., & Donoghue, J. P. (1991). Reshaping the cortical motor map by unmasking latent intra-cortical connections. *Science, 251,* 944–946.

Jacobs, M. K., & Goodman, G. (1989). Psychology and self-help groups: Predictions on a partnership. *American Psychologist, 44,* 536–545.

Jacobson, E. (1938). *Progressive relaxation* (2nd ed.). Chicago: University of Chicago Press.

Jacobson, M. B., Antonelli, J., Winning, P. U., & Opeil, D. (1977). Women as authority figures: The use and nonuse of authority. *Sex Roles, 4,* 365–376.

James, W. (1902). *The varieties of religious experience: A study in human nature.* New York: Longmans, Green.

James, W. (1950). *Principles of psychology* (Vol. 2). New York: Dover. (Original work published 1890)

Jameson, D., & Hurvich, L. M. (1989). Essay concerning color constancy. *Annual Review of Psychology, 40,* 1–22.

Janis, I. L. (Ed.). (1982). *Counseling on personal decisions: Theory and research on short-term helping relationships.* New Haven, CT: Yale University Press.

Janis, I. L. (1983). *Groupthink: Psychological studies of policy decisions and fiascos* (2nd ed.). Boston: Houghton Mifflin.

Jarvik, L. F., & Winograd, C. H. (1988). *Treatments for the Alzheimer patient.* New York: Springer-Verlag.

Jemmott, J. B., et al. (1990). Motivational syndrome associated with natural killer cell activity. *Journal of Behavioural Medicine, 13,* 53–73.

Jenkins, J. G., & Dallenbach, K. M. (1924). Oblivescence during sleep and waking. *American Journal of Psychology, 35,* 605–612.

Jensen, A. R. (1980). *Bias in mental testing.* New York: Free Press.

Jepsen, C., & Chaiken, S. (1986, August). *The effects of anxiety on the systematic processing of persuasive communications.* Paper presented at the annual meeting of the American Psychological Association, Washington, DC.

Jernigan, T. L., Zisook, S., Heaton, R. K., Moranville, J. T., Hesselink, J. R., & Braff, D. L. (1991). Magnetic resonance imaging abnormalities in lenticular nuclei and cerebral cortex in schizophrenia. *Archives of General Psychiatry, 48,* 881–890.

John, O. P. (1989). Toward a taxonomy of personality descriptors. In N. Cantor & D. M. Buss (Eds.), *Personality psychology: Recent trends and emerging directions.* New York: Springer-Verlag.

Johnson, J. E., Lauver, D. R., & Nail, L. M. (1989). Process of coping with radiation therapy. *Journal of Consulting and Clinical Psychology, 57,* 358–364.

Johnson, J. S., & Newport, E. L. (1989). Critical period effects in second language learning: The influence of maturational state on the acquisition of English as a second language. *Cognitive Psychology, 21,* 60–99.

Johnson, K. (1987, June 3). Youth described Getz as "soft," witness recalls. *New York Times,* p. 16.

Johnson, V. S. (1985). *Electrophysiological changes induced by androstenol: A potential human pheromone.* Unpublished manuscript, New Mexico State University, Las Cruces.

Johnson-Laird, P. N. (1983). *Mental models.* Cambridge, MA: Harvard University Press.

Johnston, L. D., O'Malley, P. M., & Bachman, J. G. (1988). *Monitoring the Future project.* Ann Arbor: Institute for Social Research, University of Michigan.

Johnston, L. D., O'Malley, P. M., & Bachman, J. G. (1991). *Drug use among American high school seniors, college students, and adults, 1975–1990* (Vol. 1; Department of Health and Human Services Publication No. 91–1813). Washington, DC: U.S. Government Printing Office.

Joiner, T. E., Alfano, M. S., & Metalsky, G. I. (1992). When depression breeds contempt: Reassurance seeking, self-esteem, and rejection of depressed college students by their roommates. *Journal of Abnormal Psychology, 101,* 165–173.

Jorgensen, S. R. (1992). Adolescent pregnancy and parenting. In T. Gullotta, G. R. Adams, & R. Montemayor (Eds.), *Adolescent sexuality.* Newbury Park, CA: Sage.

Julien, R. M. (1991). *A primer of drug action* (6th ed.). New York: Freeman.

Just, M. A., & Carpenter, P. A. (1992). A capacity theory of comprehension: Individual differences in working memory. *Psychological Review, 99,* 122–149.

Kaas, J. H. (1987). The organization of neocortex in mammals: Implications for theories of brain function. *Annual Review of Psychology, 38,* 129–157.

Kagan, J. (1989). Temperamental contributions to social behavior. *American Psychologist, 44,* 668–674.

Kagan, J., Reznick, S., & Snidman, N. (1988). Biological bases of childhood shyness. *Science, 240,* 167–171.

Kagan, J., & Snidman, N. (1991). Infant predictors of inhibited and uninhibited profiles. *Psychological Science, 2,* 40–44.

Kagitcibasi, C., & Berry, J. W. (1989). Cross-cultural psychology: Current research and trends. *Annual Review of Psychology, 40,* 493–532.

Kahneman, D., & Tversky, A. (1979). Prospect theory: An analysis of decisions under risk. *Econometrica, 47,* 263–291.

Kail, R., & Pellegrino, J. W. (1985). *Human intelligence: Perspectives and prospects.* San Francisco: Freeman.

Kaiser, R. B. (1970). *R. F. K. must die: A history of the Robert Kennedy assassination and its aftermath.* New York: Dutton.

Kalick, S. M., & Hamilton, T. E., III. (1988). Closer look at a matching simulation: Reply to Aron. *Journal of Personality and Social Psychology, 54,* 447–451.

Kalish, R. A., & Reynolds, D. K. (1977). The role of age in death attitudes. *Death Education, 1,* 205–230.

Kandel, E. R., & Hawkins, R. D. (1992). The biological basis of learning and individuality. *Scientific American, 267*(3), 78–87.

Kandel, E. R., & Schwartz, J. H. (1982). Molecular biology of learning: Modulation of transmitter release. *Science, 218,* 433–443.

Kane, J. M. (Ed.). (1992). *Tardive dyskinesia: A task force report of the American Psychiatric Association.* Washington, DC: American Psychiatric Press.

Kanfer, F. H., & Gaelick, L. (1986). Self-management methods. In F. H. Kanfer & A. P. Goldstein (Eds.), *Helping people change: A textbook of methods* (3rd ed., pp. 283–345). New York: Pergamon.

Kanfer, F. H., & Goldstein, A. P. (Eds.). (1991). *Helping people change: A textbook of methods* (4th ed.). New York: Pergamon.

Kaplan, H. S. (1986, February). Quoted in W. Gallagher, The etiology of orgasm. *Discover*, pp. 51–59.

Kaplan, R. M. (1985). The controversy related to the use of psychologist tests. In B. B. Wolman (Ed.), *Handbook of intelligence: Theory, measurement, and applications.* New York: Wiley-Interscience.

Kaprio, J., Koskenvu, M., & Rita, H. (1987). Mortality after bereavement: A prospective study of 95,647 widowed persons. *American Journal of Public Health, 77,* 283–287.

Katz, J., & Melzack, R. (1990). Pain "memories" in phantom limbs: Review and clinical observations. *Pain, 43,* 319–336.

Katz, L., & Epstein, S. (1991). Constructive thinking and coping with laboratory-induced stress. *Journal of Personality and Social Psychology, 61,* 789–800.

Kaufman, A. S., Kamphaus, R. W., & Kaufman, N. L. (1985). New directions in intelligence testing: The Kaufman Assessment Battery for Children (K-ABC). In B. B. Wolman (Ed.), *Handbook of intelligence: Theory, measurement, and applications* (pp. 663–698). New York: Wiley-Interscience.

Kay, L. (1982). *Spatial perception through an acoustic sensor.* Christchurch, New Zealand: University of Canterbury Press.

Kaye, H. L. (1986). *The social meaning of modern biology: From social Darwinism to sociobiology.* New Haven, CT: Yale University Press.

Kazdin, A. E. (1982). The token economy: A year later. *Journal of Applied Behavior Analysis, 15,* 431–445.

Kazdin, A. E. (1986). Research designs and methodology. In S. L. Garfield & A. E. Bergin (Eds.), *Handbook of psychotherapy and behavior change* (2nd ed.). New York: Wiley.

Kazdin, A. E. (1989). Developmental psychopathology: Current research, issues, and directions. *American Psychologist, 44,* 180–187.

Kazdin, A. E., & Bass, D. (1989). Power to detect differences between alternative treatments in comparative psychotherapy research. *Journal of Consulting and Clinical Psychology, 57,* 138–147.

Keating, D. P. (1980). Thinking processes in adolescence. In J. Adelson (Ed.), *Handbook of adolescent psychology.* New York: Wiley.

Keating, J. P. (1987, August). *An overview of research on human response during disasters: Major fires, earthquakes, tornadoes, and airplane disasters since 1980.* Paper presented at the annual meeting of the American Psychological Association, New York.

Keefe, F. J., et al. (1990). Pain coping skills training in the management of osteoarthritic knee pain: Followup results. *Behavior Therapy, 21,* 435–447.

Keil, F. C. (1986). Conceptual development and category structure. In U. Neisser (Ed.), *Concepts and conceptual development: Ecological and intellectual factors in categorization.* Cambridge, England: Cambridge.

Keirstead, S. A., et al. (1989). Electrophysiologic responses in hamster superior colliculus evoked by regenerating retinal neurons. *Science, 246,* 255–256.

Keller, L. S., Butcher, J. N., & Slutske, W. S. (1990). Objective personality assessment. In G. Goldstein & M. Hersen (Eds.), *Handbook of psychological as-*

sessment (2nd ed.). New York: Pergamon.

Keller, S., & Serganian, P. (1984). Physical fitness and autonomic reactivity to psychosocial stress. *Journal of Psychosomatic Research, 28,* 279–287.

Kelley, H. H. (1973). The process of causal attribution. *American Psychologist, 28,* 107–128.

Kelley, H. H. (1979). *Personal relationships: Their structures and processes.* Hillsdale, NJ: Erlbaum.

Kelley, H. H. (1992). Common-sense psychology and scientific psychology. *Annual Review of Psychology, 43,* 1–23.

Kellner, R. (1992). *Psychosomatic syndromes and somatic symptoms.* Washington, DC: American Psychiatric Press.

Kelly, J. A., St. Lawrence, J. S., & Brasfield, T. L. (1991). Predictors of vulnerability to AIDS risk behavior relapse. *Journal of Consulting and Clinical Psychology, 59,* 163–166.

Kelly, J. A., St. Lawrence, J. S., Hood, H. V., & Brasfield, T. L. (1989). Behavioral intervention to reduce AIDS risk activities. *Journal of Consulting and Clinical Psychology, 57,* 60–67.

Kelly, T. A., & Strupp, H. H. (1992). Patient and therapist values in psychotherapy: Perceived changes, assimilation, similarity, and outcome. *Journal of Consulting and Clinical Psychology, 60,* 34–40.

Kenrick, D. T., & Funder, D. C. (1988). Profiting from controversy: Lessons from the person-situation debate. *American Psychologist, 43,* 23–34.

Kenrick, D. T., & Funder, D. C. (1991). The person-situation debate: Do personality traits really exist? In N. J. Derlega, B. A. Winstead, & W. H. Jones (Eds.), *Personality: Contemporary theory and research.* Chicago: Nelson-Hall.

Kerr, N. L., & Bruun, S. E. (1983). The dispensability of member effort and group motivation losses: Free-rider effects. *Journal of Personality and Social Psychology, 44,* 78–94.

Kessler, R. C., McLeod, J. D., & Wethington, E. (1985). The costs of sharing: A perspective on the relationship between stress and psychological distress. In I. G. Sarason & B. R. Sarason (Eds.), *Social support: Theory, research, and applications.* Washington, DC: Hemisphere.

Keverne, E. B. (1977). Pheromones and sexual behavior. In J. Money & M. Musaph (Eds.), *Handbook of sexology.* Amsterdam: Excerpta Medica.

Keyes, D. (1982). *The minds of Billy Milligan.* New York: Bantam.

Kiesler, C. A. (1982). Mental hospitals and alternative care: Noninstitutionalization as potential public policy for mental patients. *American Psychologist, 37,* 349–360.

Kiesler, C. A. (1992). U.S. mental health policy: Doomed to fail. *American Psychologist, 47,* 1077–1082.

Kihlstrom, J. F. (1987). The cognitive unconscious. *Science, 237,* 1445–1452.

Kihlstrom, J. F., Barnhardt, T. M., & Tataryn, D. J. (1992). The psychological unconscious: Found, lost, and regained. *American Psychologist, 47,* 788–791.

Kihlstrom, J. F., & Shor, R. E. (1978). Recall and recognition during posthypnotic amnesia. *International Journal of Clinical and Experimental Hypnosis, 26,* 330–349.

Kimble, D. P. (1992). *Biological psychology* (2nd ed). Ft. Worth, TX: Harcourt Brace Jovanovich.

Kimura, D. (1992). Sex differences in the brain. *Scientific American, 267*(9), 119–125.

Kinsey, A. C., Pomeroy, W. B., Martin, C. E., & Gebhard, P. H. (1953). *Sexual behavior in the human female.* Philadelphia: Saunders.

Kirmeyer, S. L., & Biggers, K. (1988). Environmental demand and demand engineering behavior: An observational analysis of the Type A pattern. *Journal of Personality and Social Psychology, 54,* 997–1005.

Klein, S. B., & Mowrer, R. R. (1989a). *Contemporary learning theories: Vol 1. Pavlovian conditioning and the status of tradition.* Hillsdale, NJ: Erlbaum.

Klein, S. B., & Mowrer, R. R. (1989b). *Contemporary learning theories: Vol 2. Instrumental conditioning theory and the impact of biological constraints on learning.* Hillsdale, NJ: Erlbaum.

Kleinmuntz, B. (1980). *Essentials of abnormal psychology* (2nd ed.). New York: Harper & Row.

Kluznik, J. C., Speed, N., VanDalkenburg, C., & Magraw, R. (1986). Forty-year follow-up of United States prisoners of war. *American Journal of Psychiatry, 143,* 1443–1446.

Knapp, P. H. (1988). Steps toward a lexicon: Discussion of unconsciously determined defensive strategies. In M. Horowitz (Ed.), *Psychodynamics and cognition.* Chicago: University of Chicago Press.

Koestler, A. (1964). *The act of creation.* New York: Macmillan.

Koestner, R., & McClelland, D. C. (1990). Perspectives on competence motivation. In L. A. Pervin (Ed.), *Handbook of personality theory and research.* New York: Guilford.

Kohlberg, L. (1963). The development of children's orientations toward a moral order: 1. Sequence in the development of moral thought. *Human Development, 6,* 11–33.

Kohlberg, L. (1978). Revisions in the theory and practice of moral development. *New Directions for Child Development, 2,* 83–88.

Kohlberg, L. (1984). *The psychology of moral development: Essays on moral development* (Vol. 2). New York: Harper & Row.

Kohlenberg, R. J., & Tsai, M. (1991). *Functional analytic psychotherapy.* New York: Plenum.

Kohn, P. M., Lafreniere, K., & Guervich, M. (1991). Hassles, health, and personality. *Journal of Personality and Social Psychology, 61,* 478–482.

Kolb, B. (1989). Brain development, plasticity, and behavior. *American Psychologist, 44,* 1203–1212.

Kolb, B., & Whishaw, I. Q. (1989). Plasticity in the neocortex: Mechanisms underlying recovery from early brain damage. *Progress in Neurobiology, 32,* 235–276.

Korb, M. P., Gorrell, J., & Van De Riet, V. (1989). *Gestalt therapy: Practice and theory* (2nd ed.). New York: Pergamon.

Kosambi, D. D. (1967). Living prehistory in India. *Scientific American, 216*(2), 105.

Kraft, C. L. (1978). A psychophysical contribution to air safety: Simulator studies of visual illusions in night visual approaches. In H. L. Pick, Jr., H. W. Leibowitz, J. E. Singer, A. Steinschneider, & H. W. Stevenson (Eds.), *Psychology: From research to practice.* New York: Plenum.

Krause, N., Jay, G., & Liang, J. (1991). Financial strain and psychological well-being among the American and Japanese elderly. *Psychology and Aging, 6,* 170–181.

Krauss, R. M., Geller, V., & Olson, C. (1976, September). *Modalities and cues in the detection of deception.* Paper presented at the annual meeting of the American Psychological Association, Washington, DC.

Krausz, M. (1982). Policies of organizational choice at different vocational life stages. *Vocational Guidance Quarterly, 31,* 60–68.

Kraut, R. E. (1982). Social presence, facial feedback, and emotion. *Journal of Personality and Social Psychology, 42,* 853–863.

Kroeber, A. L. (1948). *Anthropology.* New York: Harcourt Brace Jovanovich.

Krosnick, J. A., Betz, A. L., Jussim, L. J., & Lynn, A. R. (1992). Subliminal conditioning of attitudes. *Personality and Social Psychology Bulletin, 18,* 152–162.

Krueger, J. M. (1989, May-June). No simple slumber: Exploring the enigma of sleep. *The Sciences,* pp. 36–41.

Krystal, H. (1968). *Massive psychic trauma.* New York: International Universities Press.

Kübler-Ross, E. (1969). *On death and dying.* New York: Macmillan.

Kuiper, N. A., & Olinger, L. J. (1989). Stress and cognitive vulnerability for depression: A self-worth contingency model. In R. W. J. Neufeld (Ed.), *Advances in the investigation of psychological stress.* New York: Wiley.

Kukla, A. (1975). Preferences among impossibly difficult and trivially easy tasks: A revision of Atkinson's theory of choice. *Journal of Personality and Social Psychology, 32,* 338–345.

Kulik, J. A., & Mahler, H. I. M. (1989). Social support and recovery from surgery. *Health Psychology, 8,* 221–238.

Kurtz, P. (1986). Debunking, neutrality, and skepticism in science. In K. Frazier (Ed.), *Science confronts the paranormal.* Buffalo, NY: Prometheus Books.

Kurzweil, E. (1989). *The Freudians: A comparative perspective.* New Haven, CT: Yale University Press.

Kurzweil, S. R. (1988). Recognition of mother from multisensory interactions in early infancy. *Infant Behavior & Development, 11,* 235–243.

Kutchins, H., & Kirk, S. A. (1986). The reliability of DSM-III: A critical review. *Social Work Research and Abstracts, 16,* 3–12.

Kuykendall, D., & Keating, J. P. (1990). Altering thoughts and judgments through repeated association. *British Journal of Social Psychology, 29,* 79–86.

Kwong, K. K., Belliveau, J. W., et al. (1992). Dynamic magnetic resonance imaging of human brain activity during primary sensory stimulation. *Proceedings of the National Academy of Sciences, 89,* 5675–5679.

Lacey, J. I., & Lacey, B. C. (1970). Some autonomic–central nervous system interrelationships. In P. Black (Ed.), *Physiological correlates of emotion.* New York: Academic Press.

Lafferty, P., Beutler, L. E., & Crago, M. (1989). Differences between more and less effective psychotherapists: A study of select therapist variables. *Journal of Consulting and Clinical Psychology, 57,* 76–80.

Laing, R. D. (1967). *The politics of experience.* New York: Pantheon Books.

Laird, J. D. (1974). Self-attribution of emotion: The effects of expressive behavior on the quality of emotional experience. *Journal of Personality and Social Psychology, 29,* 475–486.

Laird, J. D. (1984). The real role of facial response in the experience of emotion: A reply to Touranglow and Ellsworth, and others. *Journal of Personality and Social Psychology, 47,* 909–917.

Lakein, A. (1973). *How to get control of your time and your life.* New York: Wyden.

Lamal, P. A. (Ed.). (1991). *Behavioral analysis of societies and cultural practices.* Bristol, PA: Hemisphere.

Lambert, M. J., Shapiro, D. A., & Bergin, A. E. (1986). The effectiveness of psychotherapy. In S. L. Garfield & A. E. Bergin (Eds.), *Handbook of psychotherapy and behavior change* (3rd ed.). New York: Wiley.

Lamke, L. K. (1982). The impact of sex-role orientation on self-esteem in early adolescence. *Child Development, 53,* 1530–1535.

Landers, D., & Pirozzolo, F. J. (1991). Optimizing performance under pressure. In D. Druckman & R. A. Bjork (Eds.), *In the mind's eye: Enhancing human performance.* Washington, DC: National Academy Press.

Landfield, P., Cadwallander, L. B., & Vinsant, S. (1988). Quantitative changes in hippocampal structure following long-term exposure to delta-9-tetrahydrocannabinol: Possible mediation by glucocorticoid systems. *Brain Research, 443,* 47–62.

Lang, A. R., Goeckner, D. J., Adesso, V. J., & Marlatt, G. A. (1975). Effects of alcohol on aggression in male social drinkers. *Journal of Abnormal Psychology, 84,* 508–518.

Langer, E. J. (1989). *Mindlessness.* Reading, MA: Addison-Wesley.

Langer, E. J., & Abelson, R. P. (1974). A patient by any other name . . . Clinicians' group difference in labelling bias. *Journal of Consulting and Clinical Psychology, 42,* 4–9.

Lanzetta, J. T., Cartwright-Smith, J. E., & Kleck, R. E. (1976). Effects of nonverbal dissimulation on emotional experience and autonomic arousal. *Journal of Personality and Social Psychology, 33,* 354–370.

LaPiere, R. T. (1934). Attitudes and actions. *Social Forces, 13,* 230–237.

Larsen, R. J., & Ketelaar, T. (1991). Personality and susceptibility to positive and negative emotional states. *Journal of Personality and Social Psychology, 61,* 132–140.

Larson, E. B., Kukull, W. A., & Katzman, R. L. (1992). Cognitive impairment: Dementia and Alzheimer's disease. *Annual Review of Public Health, 13,* 342–367.

Latané, B., Williams, K., & Harkins, S. (1979). Many hands make light the work: The causes and consequents of social loafing. *Journal of Personality and Social Psychology, 37,* 822–832.

Lau, R. R., & Russell, D. (1980). Attribution in the sports pages. *Journal of Personality and Social Psychology, 39,* 29–38.

Laughlin, H. P. (1967). *The neuroses.* Washington, DC: Butterworth.

Laurent, H. (1968). Research on the identification of management potential. In J. A. Myers (Ed.), *Predicting managerial success.* Ann Arbor, MI: Foundation for Research on Human Behavior.

LaVoie, J. C. (1976). Ego identity formation in middle adolescence. *Journal of Youth and Adolescence, 5,* 371–385.

Lazarus, R. S. (1991a). Progress on a cognitive-motivational-relational theory of emotion. *American Psychologist, 46,* 819–834.

Lazarus, R. S. (1991b). *Emotion and adaptation.* New York: Oxford.

Lazarus, R. S. (1991c). Cognition and motivation in emotion. *American Psychologist, 46,* 352–367.

Lazarus, R. S. (1992). Constructs of the mind in adaptation. In N. Stein, B. Leventhal, & T. Trabasso (Eds.), *Psychological and biological approaches to emotion.* Hillsdale, NJ: Erlbaum.

Le Doux, J. E. (1986). The neurobiology of emotion. In J. E. Le Doux & W. Hirst (Eds.), *Mind and brain: Dialogues in cognitive neuroscience.* Cambridge, England: Cambridge.

Le Doux, J. E. (1989). Cognitive-emotional interactions in the brain. *Cognition and Emotion, 3,* 267–289.

Le Doux, J. E. (1992). Systems and synapses of emotional memory. In L. R. Squire, N. M. Weinberger, G. Lynch, & J. L. McGaugh (Eds.), *Memory: Organization and locus of change.* New York: Oxford.

Lee, J. A. (1973). *Colors of love.* Toronto: New Press.

Lee, V. E., Brooks-Gunn, J., & Schnur, E. (1988). Does Head Start work? A 1-year follow-up comparison of disadvantaged children attending Head Start, no preschool, and other preschool programs. *Developmental Psychology, 24,* 210–222.

Leff, J., & Vaughan, C. (1985). *Expressed emotion in families.* New York: Guilford.

Lehman, D. R., Wortman, C. B., & Williams, A. F. (1987). Long-term effects of losing a spouse or child in a motor vehicle crash. *Journal of Personality and Social Psychology, 52,* 218–231.

Lehmann-Haupt, C. (1988, August 4). Books of the times: How an actor found success, and himself. *New York Times,* p. 2.

Leippe, M. R., Romanczyk, A., & Manion, A. P. (1991). Eyewitness memory for a touching experience: Accuracy differences between child and adult witnesses. *Journal of Applied Psychology, 76,* 367–379.

Leitenberg, H., Gross, J., Peterson, J., & Rosen, J. C. (1984). Analysis of an anxiety model and the process of change during exposure plus response prevention treatment of bulimia nervosa. *Behavior Therapy, 15,* 3–20.

Lenneberg, E. H. (1967). *Biological foundations of language.* New York: Wiley.

Lenzenweger, M. F., Dworkin, R. H., & Wethington, E. (1989). Models of positive and negative symptoms in schizophrenia: An empirical evaluation of latent structure. *Journal of Abnormal Psychology, 98,* 62–70.

Leonard, W. E. (1927). *The locomotive god.* New York: Appleton-Century-Crofts.

Lerner, M. J. (1980). *The belief in a just world: A fundamental delusion.* New York: Plenum.

Lerner, R. M. (1987). A life-span perspective for early adolescence. In R. M. Lerner & T. T. Foch (Eds.), *Biological-psychosocial interactions in early adolescence.* Hillsdale, NJ: Erlbaum.

Lerner, S. E., & Burns, R. S. (1978). PCP use among youth: History, epidemiology, and acute and chronic intoxication. In R. C. Petersen & R. C. Stillman (Eds.), *PCP phencyclidine abuse: An appraisal* (NIDA Research Monograph No. 21). Washington, DC: U.S. Department of Health, Education, and Welfare.

Lesgold, A. (1988). Problem solving. In R. J. Sternberg & E. E. Smith (Eds.), *The psychology of human thought*. Cambridge: Cambridge University Press.

Lethem, J., Slade, P. O., Troup, J. D. G., & Bentley, G. (1983). Outline of a fear-avoidance model of exaggerated pain perception: I. *Behavior Research and Therapy, 21,* 401–408.

LeVay, Simon. (1991). A difference in hypothalamic structure between heterosexual and homosexual men. *Science, 253,* 1034–1037.

Levenson, R. W., Carstensen, L. L., Friesen, W. V., & Ekman, P. (1991). Emotion, physiology and expression in old age. *Psychology and Aging, 6,* 28–35.

Levenson, R. W., Ekman, P., & Friesen, W. V. (1990). Voluntary facial action generates emotion-specific autonomic nervous system activity. *Psychophysiology, 27,* 363–384.

Leventhal, E. A., Leventhal, H., Shacham, S., & Easterling, D. V. (1989). Active coping reduces reports of pain from childbirth. *Journal of Consulting and Clinical Psychology, 57,* 365–371.

Leventhal, H., & Tomarken, A. J. (1986). Emotion: Today's problems. *Annual Review of Psychology, 37,* 565–610.

Levin, I. P., Schnittjer, S. K., & Thee, S. L. (1988). Information framing effects in social and personal decisions. *Journal of Experimental Social Psychology, 24,* 520–529.

Levin, J. D. (1989). *Alcoholism: A bio-psycho-social approach.* New York: Hemisphere.

Levine, J. D., Gordon, N., & Fields, H. (1978). The mechanism of placebo analgesia. *Lancet, 2,* 654–657.

Levine, M. W., & Shefner, J. M. (1991). *Fundamentals of sensation and perception* (2nd ed.). Pacific Grove, CA: Brooks/Cole.

Levinger, G. (1988). Can we picture "love"? In R. J. Sternberg & M. L. Barnes (Eds.), *The psychology of love.* New Haven, CT: Yale University Press.

Levinson, D. J. (1986). A conception of adult development. *American Psychologist, 41,* 3–13.

Levinson, D. J. (1990). A theory of life structure development in adulthood. In C. N. Alexander & E. J. Langer (Eds.), *Higher stages of human development: Perspectives on adult growth.* New York: Oxford.

Levinson, D. J., Darow, C. N., Klein, E. B., Levinson, M. H., & McKee, B. (1978). *The seasons of a man's life.* New York: Knopf.

Levinthal, C. F. (1990). *Introduction to physiological psychology* (3rd ed.) Englewood Cliffs: Prentice-Hall.

Levit, D. B. (1991). Gender differences in ego defenses in adolescence: Sex roles as one way to understand the differences. *Journal of Personality and Social Psychology, 61,* 992–999.

Levy, J. (1983). Language, cognition, and the right hemisphere: A response to Gazzaniga. *American Psychologist, 38,* 538–541.

Levy, S., Marrow, L., Bagley, C., & Lippman, M. (1989). Survival hazards analysis in first recurrent breast cancer patients: Seven-year follow-up. *Psy-*

chosomatic Medicine, 50, 520–528.

Lewin, K. (1935). *A dynamic theory of personality.* New York: McGraw-Hill.

Lewin, R. (1987). Brain grafts benefit Parkinson's patients. *Science, 236,* 149.

Lewinsohn, P. M., Hoberman, H., Teri, L., & Hantzinger, M. (1985). An integrative theory of depression. In S. Reiss & R. Bootzin (Eds.), *Theoretical issues in behavior therapy.* New York: Academic Press.

Lewinsohn, P. M., Mischel, W., Chaplain, W., & Barton, R. (1980). Social competence and depression: The role of illusory self-perceptions. *Journal of Abnormal Psychology, 89,* 203–212.

Lewinsohn, P. M., Zeiss, A. M., & Duncan, E. M. (1989). Probability of relapse after recovery from an episode of depression. *Journal of Abnormal Psychology, 98,* 107–116.

Lewis, M., & Brooks-Gunn, J. (1979). *Social cognition and the acquisition of self.* New York: Plenum.

Lewis, R., & Roberts, C. (1982). Postparental fathers in distress. In K. Soloman & N. Levy (Eds.), *Men in transition.* New York: Plenum.

Lewy, A. J., Sack, L., Miller, S., & Hoban, T. M. (1987). Antidepressant and circadian phase-shifting effects of light. *Science, 235,* 352–354.

Liberman, A. M., & Mattingly, I. G. (1989). A specialization for speech perception. *Science, 243,* 489–494.

Lickey, M. E., & Gordon, B. (1991). *Medicine and mental illness: The use of drugs in psychiatry.* New York: Freeman.

Liddy, G. G. (1980, October). Liddy. *Playboy,* pp. 37–46.

Lieberman, P. (1984). *The biology and evolution of language.* Cambridge, MA: Harvard University Press.

Liebert, R. M., Sprafkin, J. N., & Davidson, E. S. (1989). *The early window: Effects of television on children and youth* (3rd ed.). New York: Pergamon.

Liem, R., & Rayman, P. (1982). Health and social costs of unemployment. *American Psychologist, 37,* 1116–1123.

Lincoln, J. R. (1989). Employee work attitudes and management practice in the U.S. and Japan: Evidence from a large comparative survey. *California Management Review, 32,* 89–106.

Lindzey, G., Loehlin, J. C., & Spuhler, J. (1975). *Racial differences in intelligence.* San Francisco: Freeman.

Linn, R. L. (Ed.). (1989). Intelligence: Measurement, theory and public policy. *Proceedings of a symposium in honor of Lloyd G. Humphreys.* Urbana, IL: University of Illinois Press.

Linz, D. (1989). Exposure to sexually explicit materials and attitudes toward rape: A comparison of study results. *Journal of Sex Research, 26,* 50–84.

Linz, D., & Donnerstein, E. (1989). The effects of countertransformation on the acceptance of rape myths. In D. Zillmann & J. Bryant (Eds.), *Pornography: Research advances and policy considerations.* Hillsdale, NJ: Erlbaum.

Lion, J. R., Bach-Y-Rita, G., & Ervin, F. R. (1969). Enigmas of violence. *Science, 164,* 1465.

Lipkin, R. (1988). Making machines in mind's image. *Insight, 4*(7), 8–12.

Litman, G. K. (1986). Alcoholism survival: The prevention of relapse. In W. R. Miller & N. Heather

(Eds.), *Treating addictive behaviors: Processes of change.* New York: Plenum.

Litt, M. D. (1988). Self-efficacy and perceived control: Cognitive mediators of pain tolerance. *Journal of Personality and Social Psychology, 54,* 149–160.

Littlefield, C. H., & Rushton, J. P. (1989). Levels of explanation in sociobiology and psychology: A rejoinder to Archer. *Journal of Personality and Social Psychology, 56,* 625–628.

Livingstone, M. S. (1988). Art, illusion, and the visual system. *Scientific American, 258*(1), 38–45.

Locke, D. C. (1992). *Multicultural understanding: A comprehensive model.* Newbury Park, CA: Sage.

Locke, E. A. (1990). The nature and causes of job satisfaction. In M. Dunnette (Ed.), *Handbook of industrial and organizational psychology* (2nd ed.). Chicago: Rand McNally.

Locke, E. A., & Latham, G. P. (1990). *A theory of goal setting and task performance.* Englewood Cliffs, NJ: Prentice-Hall.

Locke, S., & Colligan, D. (1986). *The healer within.* New York: Dutton.

Loehlin, J. C. (1992). *Genes and environment in personality development.* Newbury Park, CA: Sage.

Loehlin, J. C., Willerman, L., & Horn, J. M. (1988). Genetics and human behavior. *Annual Review of Psychology, 39,* 101–134.

Loewenstein, R. J. (1991). Psychogenic amnesia and psychogenic fugue: A comprehensive review. In A. Tasman & S. M. Goldfinger (Eds.), *American Psychiatric Press review of psychiatry* (Vol. 10). Washington, DC: American Psychiatric Association.

Loftus, E. F. (1979). *Eyewitness testimony.* Cambridge, MA: Harvard University Press.

Loftus, E. F., & Ketcham, K. (1991). *Witness for the defense.* New York: St. Martin's.

Loftus, E. F., Miller, D. G., & Burns, H. J. (1978). Semantic integration of verbal information into a visual memory. *Journal of Experimental Psychology: Human Learning and Memory, 4,* 19–31.

Loftus, E. F., & Monahan, J. (1980). Trial by data: Psychological research as legal evidence. *American Psychologist, 35,* 270–283.

Loftus, E. F., & Zanni, G. (1975). Eyewitness testimony: The influence of the wording of a question. *Bulletin of the Psychonomic Society, 5,* 86–88.

Logue, A. W. (1991). *The psychology of eating and drinking* (2nd ed.). New York: Freeman.

Long, M. E. (1987). What is this thing called sleep? *National Geographic, 172,* 787–821.

Lorayne, H., & Lucas, J. (1974). *The memory book.* New York: Ballantine.

Lorenz, K. (1966). *On aggression.* New York: Harcourt Brace Jovanovich.

Losch, M. E., & Cacioppo, J. T. (1990). Cognitive dissonance may enhance sympathetic tonus, but attitudes are changed to reduce negative affect rather than arousal. *Journal of Experimental Social Psychology, 26,* 289–304.

Lovaas, O. I. (1977). *The autistic child.* New York: Irvington.

Love, A. J. (1991). *Internal evaluation: Building organizations from within.* Newbury Park, CA: Sage.

Low, B. S. (1989). Cross-cultural patterns in the training of children: An evolutionary perspective. *Journal of Comparative Psychology, 103,* 311–319.

Luchins, A. J. (1942). Mechanization in problem solving: The effect of Einstellung. *Psychological Monographs, 54*(6, Whole No. 248).

Lucker, W., Rosenfield, D., Sikes, J., & Aronson, E. (1977). Performance in the interdependent classroom: A field study. *American Educational Research Journal, 13,* 115–123.

Luria, A. R. (1966). *Human brain and psychological processes.* New York: Harper & Row.

Luria, A. R. (1968). *The mind of a mnemonist: A little book about a vast memory.* New York: Basic Books.

Lydic, R., & Biebuyck, J. F. (Eds.). (1989). *Clinical physiology of sleep.* New York: Oxford.

Lynch, G., & Baudry, M. (1984). The biochemistry of memory: A new and specific hypothesis. *Science, 224,* 1057–1063.

Lynn, R. (1982). IQ in Japan and the United States shows a growing disparity. *Nature, 297,* 222–223.

Lynn, S. J., & Rhue, J. W. (1986). The fantasy-prone person: Hypnosis, imagination, and creativity. *Journal of Personality and Social Psychology, 51,* 404–408.

Lytton, H., & Romney, D. M. (1991). Parents' differential socialization of boys and girls: A meta-analysis. *Psychological Bulletin, 109,* 267–296.

Maass, A., & Clark, R. D., III (1984). Hidden impact of minorities: Fifteen years of minority influence research. *Psychological Bulletin, 95,* 428–450.

Maccoby, E. E. (1988). Gender as a social category. *Developmental Psychology, 24,* 755–765.

Maccoby, E. E. (1990). Gender and relationships: A developmental account. *American Psychologist, 45,* 513–520.

Maccoby, E. E., & Martin, J. A. (1983). Socialization in the context of the family: Parent-child interaction. In E. M. Hetherington (Ed.), *Handbook of child psychology: Socialization, personality, and social development.* New York: Wiley.

MacCulloch, M. J., Snowden, P. R., Wood, P. J. W., & Mills, H. E. (1983). Sadistic fantasy, sadistic behaviour, and offending. *British Journal of Psychiatry, 143,* 20–29.

Mackie, D. M. (1986). Social identification effects in group polarization. *Journal of Personality and Social Psychology, 50,* 720–728.

Mackie, D. M., & Cooper, J. (1984). Attitude polarization: Effects of group membership. *Journal of Personality and Social Psychology, 46,* 575–585.

Maddox, J. E. (1991). Personal efficacy. In N. J. Derlega, B. A. Winstead, & W. H. Jones (Eds.), *Personality: Contemporary theory and research.* Chicago: Nelson-Hall.

Madraza, I., Drucker-Colin, R., Diaz, V., Martinez-Mata, J., Torres, C., & Becerril, J. J. (1987). Open microsurgical autograph of adrenal medulla to the right candate nucleus in two patients with intractible Parkinson's disease. *New England Journal of Medicine, 316,* 831–834.

Magnuson, S. (1986). "A serious deficiency": The Rogers Commission faults NASA's "flawed" decision-making process. *Time* (International Edition), pp. 40–42.

Magnusson, D., Stattin, H., & Allen, V. L. (1986). Differential maturation among girls and its relation to social adjustment: A longitudinal perspective. In P. B. Altes, D. L. Featherman, & R. M. Lerner (Eds.), *Lifespan development and behavior* (Vol. 7). Hillsdale, NJ: Erlbaum.

Mahoney, M. J. (1974). *Cognition and behavior modification.* Cambridge, MA: Ballinger.

Mahrer, A. R. (1988). Discovery-oriented psychotherapy research: Rationale, aims, and methods. *American Psychologist, 43,* 694–702.

Major, B., Carrington, P. I., & Carnevale, P. J. D. (1984). Physical attractiveness and self-esteem: Attributions for praise from an other-sex evaluator. *Personality and Social Psychology Bulletin, 10,* 43–50.

Makin, J. W., & Porter, R. H. (1989). Attractiveness of lactating females' breast odors to neonates. *Child Development, 60,* 803–810.

Mandell, A. (1978, September). The Sunday syndrome. *Proceedings of the National Amphetamine Conference.* San Francisco.

Mandler, G. (1988). Problems and directions in the study of consciousness. In M. Horowitz (Ed.), *Psychodynamics and cognition.* Chicago: University of Chicago Press.

Mandler, G., & Nakamura, Y. (1987). Aspects of consciousness. *Personality and Social Psychology Bulletin, 13,* 299–313.

Mann, L. (1981). The baiting crowd in episodes of threatened suicide. *Journal of Personality and Social Psychology, 41,* 703–709.

Manne, S. L., & Zautra, A. J. (1989). Spouse criticism and support: Their association with psychological adjustment among women with rheumatoid arthritis. *Journal of Personality and Social Psychology, 56,* 608–617.

Manning, M. M., & Wright, T. L. (1983). Self-efficacy expectancies, outcome expectancies, and the persistence of pain control in childbirth. *Journal of Personality and Social Psychology, 45,* 421–431.

Marcia, J. E. (1980). Identity in adolescence. In J. Adelson (Ed.), *Handbook of adolescent psychology.* New York: Wiley.

Margolin, D. I. (1992). *Cognitive neuropsychology in clinical practice.* New York: Oxford.

Markovits, H., & Nantel, G. (1989). The belief-bias effect in the production and evaluation of logical conclusions. *Memory and Cognition, 17,* 11–17.

Marks, I. M. (1977). Phobias and obsessions: Clinical phenomena in search of laboratory models. In J. Maser & M. E. P. Seligman (Eds.), *Psychopathology: Experimental models.* San Francisco: Freeman.

Marks, I. M. (1991). Self-administered behavioural treatment. *Behavioural Psychotherapy, 19,* 42–46.

Markus, H. R. (1977). Self-schemata and processing information about the self. *Journal of Personality and Social Psychology, 35,* 63–78.

Markus, H. R., & Kitayama, S. (1991). Culture and the self: Implications for cognition, emotion, and motivation. *Psychological Review, 98,* 224–253.

Markus, H. R., & Nurius, P. (1986). Possible selves. *American Psychologist, 41,* 954–969.

Markus, H. R., & Wurf, E. (1987). The dynamic self-concept: A social psychological perspective. *Annual Review of Psychology, 38,* 299–337.

Marlatt, G. A., Baer, J. S., Donovan, D. M., & Kivlahan, D. R. (1988). Addictive behaviors: Etiology and treatment. *Annual Review of Psychology, 39,* 223–252.

Marlatt, G. A., & Gordon, J. R. (1985). *Relapse prevention: Maintenance strategies in the treatment of addictive behaviors.* New York: Guilford.

Marshall, W. L. (1988). The use of sexually explicit stimuli by rapists, child molesters, and nonoffenders. *Journal of Sex Research, 25,* 267–288.

Martens, R. (1986). Youth sport in the U.S.A. In M. R. Weiss & D. Gould (Eds.), *Sport for children and youths.* Champaign, IL: Human Kinetics.

Martin, E. (1970). Toward an analysis of subjective phrase structure. *Psychological Bulletin, 74,* 153–166.

Martin, G., & Pear, J. (1992). *Behavior modification: What it is and how to do it.* Englewood Cliffs, NJ: Prentice-Hall.

Martin, J. B. (1987). Molecular genetics: Applications to the clinical neurosciences. *Science, 238,* 765–772.

Martin, J. E., & Dubbert, P. M. (1985). Adherence in exercise. In R. I. Terjung (Ed.), *Exercise and sport sciences review* (Vol. 13). New York: Macmillan.

Marttunen, M. J., Aro, H. M., Hillevi, M., Henrikkson, M. M., & Lonngvist, J. K. (1991). Mental disorders in adolescent suicide: DSM-III-R Axes I and II diagnoses in suicides among 13- to 19-year-olds in Finland. *Archives of General Psychiatry, 48,* 834–839.

Marvin, R. S. (1977). An ethological-cognitive model for the attenuation of mother-child attachment behavior. In T. Alloway, P. Pliner, & L. Krames (Eds.), *Advances in the study of communication and affect* (Vol. 3, pp. 25–68). New York: Plenum.

Marx, J. (1991). Mutation identified as possible cause of Alzheimer's disease. *Science, 251,* 866–867.

Marzuk, P. M., Tierney, H., Tarfidd, K., Gross, E. M., Morgan, E. B., Hsu, M. A., & Mann, J. G. (1988). Increased risk of suicide in persons with AIDS. *Journal of the American Medical Association, 259,* 1332–1333.

Mason, A., & Blankenship, V. (1987). Power and affiliation motivation, stress, and abuse in intimate relationships. *Journal of Personality and Social Psychology, 52,* 203–210.

Masters, J. C. (1991). Strategies and mechanisms for the personal and social control of emotion. In J. Garber & K. A. Dodge (Eds.), *The development of emotion regulation and dysregulation.* New York: Cambridge.

Masters, W. H., & Johnson, V. E. (1966). *Human sexual response.* London: Churchill.

Masters, W. H., & Johnson, V. E. (1970). *Human sexual inadequacy.* Boston: Little, Brown.

Masters, W. H., Johnson, V. E., & Kolodny, R. C. (1988). *Human Sexuality* (3rd ed.). Boston: Little, Brown.

Matson, J. L., & Gardner, W. I. (1991). Behavioral learning theory and current applications to severe behavior problems in persons with mental retardation. *Clinical Psychology Review, 11,* 175–183.

Matthews, K. A., & Haynes, S. G. (1986). Type A behavior pattern and coronary risk: Update and critical evaluations. *American Journal of Epidemiology, 123,* 923–960.

Mauro, R., Sato, K., & Tucker, J. (1992). The role of appraisal in human emotions: A cross-cultural study. *Journal of Personality and Social Psychology, 62,* 301–317.

Mavromatis, A. (1991). *Hypnogogia.* New York: Routledge.

May, J. R., & Sieb, G. E. (1987). Athletic injuries: Psychosocial factors in the onset, sequellae, rehabilitation, and prevention. In J. R. May & M. J. Asken (Eds.), *Sport psychology: The psychological health of the athlete*. New York: PMA Publishing Corporation.

May, R. (1961). The emergence of existential psychology. In R. May (Ed.), *Existential psychology*. New York: Random House.

Mayer, J. D., Salovey, P., Gomberg-Kaufman, S., & Blainey, K. (1991). A broader conception of mood experience. *Journal of Personality and Social Psychology, 60*, 100–111.

Mays, V. M., Albee, G. W., & Schneider, S. F. (1989). *The primary prevention of AIDS: Psychological approaches*. Newbury Park, CA: Sage.

McAdams, D. T. (1992). The five-factor model in personality: A critical appraisal. *Journal of Personality and Social Psychology, 60*, 329–361.

McCall, R. B. (1977). Childhood IQs as predictors of adult educational and occupational status. *Science, 1977, 197*, 482–483.

McCallum, W. C. (1986). *Cerebral psychophysiology: Studies in event related potentials*. New York: Elsevier.

McCann, T., & Sheehan, P. W. (1988). Hypnotically induced pseudomemories: Sampling their conditions among hypnotizable subjects. *Journal of Personality and Social Psychology, 54*, 339–346.

McCarthy, C. (1988, December 31). Koop versus booze. *Washington Post*, p. A19.

McCartney, K. (1984). Effects of quality day care environment on children's language development. *Developmental Psychology, 20*, 244–260.

McCaul, K. D., & Malott, J. J. (1984). Distraction and coping with pain. *Psychological Bulletin, 95*, 516–533.

McClearn, G. E., Plomen, R., Gora-Mazlak, G., & Crable, J. C. (1991). The gene search in behavioral science. *Psychological Science, 2*, 222–230.

McClelland, D. C. (1989). *Human motivation*. New York: Cambridge.

McClelland, D. C., Koestner, R., & Weinberger, J. (1989). How do self-attributed and implicit motives differ? *Psychology Review, 96*, 690–702.

McClintock, M. K. (1971). Menstrual synchrony and suppression. *Nature, 229*, 244–245.

McCloskey, M., & Zaragoza, M. (1985). Misleading post-event information and memory for events: Arguments and evidence against memory impairment hypotheses. *Journal of Experimental Psychology: General, 114*, 1–16.

McConnell, S. R. (1983). Retirement and employment. In D. S. Woodruff & J. E. Birren (Eds.), *Aging: Scientific perspectives and social issues* (2nd ed., pp. 333–350). Monterey, CA: Brooks/Cole.

McCoy, D. F., Roszman, T. L., Miller, J. S., Kelly, K. S., & Titus, M. J. (1986). Some parameters of conditioned immunosuppression: Species difference and CS-US delay. *Physiology and Behavior, 36*, 731–736.

McCrae, R. R., (1989). Why I advocate the five-factor model: Joint factor analyses of the NEO-PI with other instruments. In D. M. Buss & N. Cantor (Eds.), *Personality psychology: Recent trends and emerging directions*. New York: Springer-Verlag.

McCrae, R. R., & Costa, P. T. (1982). Self-concept and the stability of personality: Cross-sectional comparisons of self-reports and ratings. *Journal of Personality and Social Psychology, 43*, 1282–1292.

McCrae, R. R., & Costa, P. T. (1989). The structure of interpersonal traits: Wiggins' circumplex and the five-factor model. *Journal of Personality and Social Psychology, 56*, 586–595.

McCrae, R. R., & Costa, P. T. (1990). *Personality in adulthood*. New York: Guilford.

McCrystal, J. L. (1978). Videotaped trials: A primer. *Judicature, 61*, 279–298.

McCubbin, H., Couble, E., & Patterson, J. (1982). *Family stress, coping, and social support*. Springfield, IL: Charles C Thomas.

McGarrigle, J., & Donaldson, M. (1974–1975). Conservation accidents. *Cognition, 3*, 341–350.

McGaugh, J. L., Weinberger, N. M., & Lynch, G. (Eds.). (1990). *Brain organization and memory: Cells, systems, and circuits*. New York: Oxford.

McGlaskan, T. H., & Fenton, W. S. (1992). The positive-negative distinction in schizophrenia: Review of natural history validators. *Archives of General Psychiatry, 49*, 63–72.

McGrath, E., Keita, G. P., Strickland, B. R., & Russo, N. F. (1990). *Women and depression*. Washington, DC: American Psychological Association.

McGuire, T. W., Kiesler, S., & Siegel, J. (1987). Group and computer-mediated discussion effects in risk decision making. *Journal of Personality and Social Psychology, 52*, 917–930.

McGuire, W. J. (1985). Attitudes and attitude change. In G. Lindzey & E. Aronson (Eds.), *Handbook of social psychology* (3rd ed.). New York: Random House.

McNally, R. J. (1987). Preparedness and phobias: A review. *Psychological Bulletin, 101*, 283–303.

McWhirter, D. P., Sanders, S. A., & Remsch, J. M. (Eds.). (1990). *Homsexuality/heterosexuality: Concepts of sexual orientation*. New York: Oxford.

Meador, B., & Rogers, C. R. (1984). Person-centered therapy. In R. Corsini (Ed.), *Current psychotherapies* (3rd ed.). Itaska, IL: Peacock.

Mearns, J. (1991). Coping with a breakup: Negative mood regulation expectancies and depression following the end of a romantic relationship. *Journal of Personality and Social Psychology, 60*, 327–334.

Megargee, E. I. (1966). Undercontrolled and overcontrolled personality types in extreme anti-social aggression. *Psychological Monographs, 80* (11, Whole No. 611).

Meichenbaum, D. (1985). *Stress inoculation training*. New York: Pergamon.

Meier, R. P. (1991). Language acquisition by deaf children. *American Scientist, 79*, 61–70.

Meilman, P. W. (1979). Cross-sectional age changes in ego identity status during adolescence. *Developmental Psychology, 15*, 230–231.

Meltzoff, A. N. (1988). Imitation of televised models by infants. *Child Development, 59*, 1221–1229.

Meltzoff, A. N., & Moore, M. K. (1983). Newborn infants imitate adult facial gestures. *Child Development, 54*, 702–709.

Melzack, R. (1990). The tragedy of needless pain. *Scientific American, 262*(2), 27–33.

Melzack, R., & Wall, P. (1983). *The challenge of pain*. New York: Basic Books.

Menard, S. (1991). *Longitudinal research*. Newbury Park, CA: Sage.

Meredith, N. (1986). Testing the talking cure. *Science, 232*, 31–37.

Merikle, P. M. (1988). Subliminal auditory messages: An evaluation. *Psychology and Marketing, 5*, 342–351.

Merritt, J. O. (1979). None in a million: Results of mass screening for eidetic ability using objective tests published in newspapers and magazines. *Behavioral and Brain Sciences, 2*, 612.

Mershon, B., & Gorsuch, R. L. (1988). Number of factors in the personality sphere: Does increase in factors increase predictability of real-life criteria? *Journal of Personality and Social Psychology, 55*, 675–680.

Messenger, J. C. (1971). Sex and repression in an Irish folk community. In D. S. Marshall & R. C. Suggs (Eds.), *Human sexual behavior*. Englewood Cliffs, NJ: Prentice-Hall.

Metts, S., Cupach, W. R., & Bejlovec, R. A. (1989). ''I love you too much to ever start liking you'': Redefining romantic relationships. *Journal of Social and Personal Relationships, 6*, 259–274.

Meyer, B. (1980). The development of girls' sex-role attitudes. *Child Development, 51*, 508–514.

Meyer, C. B., & Taylor, S. E. (1986). Adjustment to rape. *Journal of Personality and Social Psychology, 50*, 1226–1234.

Meyer, D. E., & Schvaneveldt, R. W. (1971). Facilitation in recognizing pairs of words: Evidence of a dependence between retrieval operations. *Journal of Experimental Psychology, 90*, 227–234.

Meyer, R. G., & Osborne, Y. H. (1987). *Case studies in abnormal behavior* (2nd ed.). Boston: Allyn & Bacon.

Michaels, J. W., Blommel, J. M., Brocato, R. M., Linkous, R. A., & Rowe, J. S. (1982). Social facilitation and inhibition in a natural setting. *Replications in Social Psychology, 2*, 21–24.

Michelson, L. K., & Marchione, K. (1991). Behavioral, cognitive, and pharmacological treatments of panic disorder with agoraphobia: Critique and synthesis. *Journal of Consulting and Clinical Psychology, 59*, 100–114.

Middlebrooks, J. C., & Green, D. M. (1991). Sound localization by human listeners. *Annual Review of Psychology, 42*, 135–159.

Mikulincer, J. (1989). Cognitive interference and learned helplessness: The effects of off-task cognition on performance following unsolvable problems. *Journal of Personality and Social Psychology, 57*, 129–135.

Milgram, S. (1974). *Obedience to authority: An experimental view*. New York: Harper & Row.

Millar, M. G., & Millar, K. U. (1990). Attitude change as a function of attitude type and argument type. *Journal of Personality and Social Psychology, 59*, 217–227.

Miller, B. C., Card, J. J., Paikoff, R. L., & Peterson, J. L. (Eds.). (1992). *Preventing adolescent pregnancy: Model programs and evaluations*. Newbury Park, CA: Sage.

Miller, G. A. (1956). The magical number seven, plus or minus two: Some limits on our capacity for processing information. *Psychological Review, 63*, 81–97.

Miller, J. (1983). *States of mind*. New York: Pantheon.

Miller, J. B. (1976). *Toward a new psychology of woman*. Boston: Beacon Press.

Miller, K. F., & Stigler, J. (1987). Counting in Chinese: Cultural variation in a basic cognitive skill. *Cognitive Development, 9,* 279–305.

Miller, L. (1991). *Freud's brain: Neuropsychodynamic foundations of psychoanalysis.* New York: Guilford.

Miller, L. C. (1990). Intimacy and liking: Mutual influence and the role of unique relationships. *Journal of Personality and Social Psychology, 59,* 50–60.

Miller, M. E., & Bowers, K. S. (1986). Hypnotic analgesia and stress inoculation in the reduction of pain. *Journal of Abnormal Psychology, 95,* 6–14.

Miller, N. E. (1989). Biomedical foundations for biofeedback. *Advances, 6,* 30–36.

Miller, S., Rossbach, J., & Munson, R. (1981). Social density and affiliative tendency as determinants of dormitory residential outcomes. *Journal of Applied Social Psychology, 11,* 356–365.

Miller, S. D., Blackburn, T., Scholes, G., White, G. L., & Mamales, N. (1991). Optical differences in multiple personality disorder: A second look. *Journal of Nervous and Mental Disease, 179,* 132–135.

Miller, W. R., & Hester, R. K. (1986). The effectiveness of alcoholism treatment: What research reveals. In W. R. Miller & N. Heather (Eds.), *Treating addictive behaviors: Processes of change.* New York: Plenum.

Millman, J., Bishop, C. H., & Ebel, R. (1965). An analysis of testwiseness. *Educational and Psychological Measurement, 25,* 707–726.

Millon, T. (1991). Classification in psychopathology: Rationale, alternatives, and standards. *Journal of Abnormal Psychology, 100,* 245–261.

Millon, T., & Everly, G. S. (1985). *Personality and its disorders: A biosocial learning approach.* New York: Wiley.

Milner, B. R. (1966). Amnesia following operations on the temporal lobes. In C. W. M. Whitty & O. L. Zangwill (Eds.), *Amnesia.* London: Butterworth.

Milner, B. R. (1970). Memory and medial temporal regions of the brain. In K. H. Pribram & D. R. Broadbent (Eds.), *Biology of memory.* Orlando, FL: Academic Press.

Mineka, S. (1985). Animal models of anxiety-based disorders: Their usefulness and limitations. In A. H. Tuma & J. D. Maser (Eds.), *Anxiety and the anxiety disorders* (pp. 199–244). Hillsdale, NJ: Erlbaum.

Minuchin, S. (1974). *Families and family therapy.* Cambridge, MA: Harvard University Press.

Mirande, A. (1985). *The Chicano experience: An alternative perspective.* Notre Dame, IN: University of Notre Dame Press.

Mischel, W. (1984). Convergences and challenges in the search for consistency. *American Psychologist, 39,* 351–364.

Mischel, W. (1986). *Introduction to personality: A new look.* (4th ed.). New York: Holt, Rinehart & Winston.

Mischel, W. (1990). Personality disposition revisited and revised: A view after three decades. In L. A. Pervin (Ed.), *Handbook of personality: Theory and research.* New York: Guilford.

Misumi, J. (1985). *The behavioral science of leadership: An interdisciplinary Japanese research program.* Ann Arbor: University of Michigan Press.

Mitchell, J. E. (1987). Scope and significance of eating disorders. *Journal of Consulting and Clinical Psychology, 55,* 628–634.

Mitler, M. M., Carskadon, M. A., Czeisler, C. A., Dement, W. C., Dinges, D. F., & Graeber, R. C. (1988). Catastrophes, sleep, and public policy: Consensus report. *Sleep, 11*(1), 100–109.

Moffitt, T. E., Caspi, A., Belsky, J., & Silva, P. A. (1992). Childhood experience and the onset of menarche: A test of a sociobiological model. *Child Development, 63,* 47–58.

Mogg, K., Mathews, A., Bird, C., & Macgregor-Morris, R. (1990). Effects of stress and anxiety on the processing of threat stimuli. *Journal of Personality and Social Psychology, 59,* 1230–1237.

Monahan, J. (1980). *The clinical prediction of violent behavior.* Washington, DC: U.S. Government Printing Office.

Monahan, J. (1992). Mental disorders and violent behavior: Perceptions and evidence. *American Psychologist, 47,* 511–521.

Money, J. (1987). Sin, sickness, or status. *American Psychologist, 42,* 384–399.

Monk, T. H. (1989). Circadian rhythm. *Clinics in Geriatric Medicine, 5,* 331–346.

Monmaney, T. (1987, April). Are we led by the nose? *Discover,* pp. 48–56.

Monroe, S. M., & Peterman, A. M. (1988). Life stress and psychopathology. In L. H. Cohen (Ed.), *Life events and psychological functioning: Theoretical and methodological issues.* Newbury Park, CA: Sage.

Montepare, J. M., & Zebrowitz-McArthur, L. (1987). Perceptions of adults with childlike voices in two cultures. *Journal of Experimental Social Psychology, 23,* 331–349.

Montgomery, G. (1989, December). Molecules of memory. *Discover,* pp. 46–55.

Moody, R. L. (1946). Bodily changes during abreaction. *Lancet, 2,* 934–935.

Moore, J. W., & Desmond, J. E. (1992). A cerebellar neural network implementation of a temporally adaptive conditioned response. In I. Gormezano & E. A. Wasserman (Eds.), *Learning and memory: The behavioral and biological substrates.* Hillsdale, NJ: Erlbaum.

Moore-Ede, M. C., Sulzman, F. M., & Fuller, C. A. (1982). *The clocks that time us.* Cambridge, MA: Harvard University Press.

Morgan, W. P., Horstman, D. H., Cymerman, A., & Stokes, J. (1983). Facilitation of physical performance by means of a cognitive strategy. *Cognitive Therapy and Research, 7,* 251–264.

Morris, C., Bransford, J. D., & Franks, J. J. (1977). Levels of processing versus transfer appropriate processing. *Journal of Verbal Learning and Verbal Behavior, 16,* 519–533.

Morris, D., Collett, P., Marsh, P., & O'Shaughnessy, M. (1979). *Gestures.* New York: Stein & Day.

Morris, J. C. (1966). Propensity for risk-taking as a determinant of vocational choice. *Journal of Personality and Social Psychology, 3,* 328–335.

Morris, N. M., & Udry, J. R. (1978). Pheromonal influences on human sexual behavior: An experimental search. *Journal of Biosocial Science, 10,* 147–157.

Morris, R. J. (1991). Fear reduction methods. In F. G. Kanfer & A. P. Goldstein (Eds.), *Helping people change: A textbook of methods* (4th ed.). New York: Pergamon.

Morrison, A. R. (1983). A window on the sleeping brain. *Scientific American, 248*(4), 94–102.

Moscovici, S. (1985). Social influence and conformity. In G. Lindzey & E. Aronson (Eds.), *Handbook of social psychology* (3rd ed.). New York: Random House.

Moss, C. S. (1972). *Recovery with aphasia.* Urbana: University of Illinois Press.

Muir, C. S., & Sasco, A. J. (1990). Prospects for cancer control in the 1990s. *Annual Review of Public Health, 11,* 143–163.

Mullen, B. (1986). Atrocity as a function of lynch mob composition: A self-attention perspective. *Personality and Social Psychology Bulletin, 12,* 187–197.

Muller, G. A. (1981). *Language and speech.* New York: Freeman.

Muller, J. B. (1976). *Toward a new psychology of women.* Boston: Beacon Press.

Munsterberg, H. (1908). *On the witness stand: Essays on psychology and crime.* New York: McClure.

Murdock, B. B. (1962). The serial position effect of free recall. *Journal of Experimental Psychology, 64,* 482–488.

Murphy, E. A. (1982). Muddling, meddling, and modeling. In V. E. Anderson, W. A. Houser, J. K. Penry, & C. F. Sing (Eds.), *Genetic basis of the epilepsies.* New York: Raven Press.

Murphy, S. M. (1992, May). *Mental imagery training and sport performance.* Paper presented to the American College of Sports Medicine, Dallas, TX.

Murray, A. W., & Szostak, J. W. (1987). Artificial chromosomes. *Scientific American, 257*(5), 62–68.

Mussen, P., & Eisenberg-Berg, N. (1977). *Roots of caring, sharing, and helping.* San Francisco: Freeman.

Myers, D. G. (1990). *Social psychology* (3rd ed.). New York: McGraw-Hill.

Myers, D. G. (1992). *Well-being: Who is happy—and why.* New York: Morrow.

Nadler, A., & Ben-Slushan, D. (1989). Forty years later: Long-term consequences of massive traumatization as manifested by holocaust survivors from the city and the kibbutz. *Journal of Consulting and Clinical Psychology, 57,* 287–293.

Nakayama, K., & Tyler, C. W. (1981). Psychophysical isolation of movement sensitivity by removal of familiar position cues. *Vision Research, 21,* 427–433.

Natale, J. A. (1988, April). Are you open to suggestion? *Psychology Today,* pp. 28–30.

Nathan, P. E. (1984). John Johnson's love for life. In J. D. Matarazzo, S. Weiss, J. A. Herd, N. E. Miller, & S. M. Weiss (Eds.), *Behavioral health.* New York: Wiley.

Nathans, J., Thomas, D., & Hogness, D. S. (1986). Molecular genetics of human color vision: The genes encoding blue, green and red pigments. *Science, 232,* 193–202.

National Institute of Drug Abuse. (1989). *Report of drug use: 1988.* Washington, DC: Author.

National Institutes of Health. (1989). *Decade of the brain: Answers through scientific research.* Washington, DC: Author.

Neimark, E. D. (1982). Adolescent thought: Transition to formal operations. In B. B. Wolman (Ed.), *Handbook of developmental psychology.* Englewood Cliffs, NJ: Prentice-Hall.

Neimeyer, R. A., & Mitchell, K. A. (1988). Similarity

and attraction: A longitudinal study. *Journal of Social and Personal Relationships, 5,* 131–148.

Neisser, U. (1967). *Cognitive psychology.* New York: Appleton-Century-Crofts.

Neisser, U. (1981). John Dean's memory: A case study. *Cognition, 9,* 1–22.

Nelson-Gray, R. O. (1991). DSM-IV: Empirical guidelines from psychometrics. *Journal of Abnormal Psychology, 100,* 308–315.

Nemeth, C., Mayseless, O., Sherman, J., & Brown, Y. (1990). Exposure to dissent and recall of information. *Journal of Personality and Social Psychology, 58,* 429–437.

Nemiah, J. C. (1978). Psychoneurotic disorders. In A. M. Nicholi (Ed.), *Harvard guide to modern psychiatry.* Cambridge, MA: Harvard University Press.

Neufeld, R. W. J., & Paterson, R. J. (1989). Issues concerning control and its implementation. In R. W. J. Neufeld (Ed.), *Advances in the investigation of psychological stress.* New York: Wiley.

Neugarten, B. L., & Hall, E. (1980, April). Acting one's age: New roles for old. *Psychology Today,* pp. 66–80.

Neugarten, B. L., Wood, V., Kraines, R. J., & Loomis, B. (1968). Women's attitudes toward the menopause. In B. L. Neugarten (Ed.), *Middle age and aging: A reader in social psychology.* Chicago: University of Chicago Press.

Newcomb, M. D., & Harlow, L. L. (1986). Life events and substance use among adolescents: Mediating effects of perceived loss of control and meaninglessness in life. *Journal of Personality and Social Psychology, 51,* 564–577.

Newcomb, M. D., & McGee, L. (1991). Influence of sensation seeking on general deviance and specific problem behaviors from adolescence to young adulthood. *Journal of Personality and Social Psychology, 61,* 614–628.

Newcomb, T. M. (1963). Persistence and regression of changed attitudes: Long-range studies. *Journal of Social Issues, 19,* 3–14.

Newell, A., & Simon, H. A. (1972). *Human problem solving.* Englewood Cliffs, NJ: Prentice-Hall.

Newell, K. M. (1991). Motor skill acquisition. *Annual Review of Psychology, 42,* 213–238.

Newman, B. M., & Newman, P. R. (1991). *Development through life: A psychosocial approach* (5th ed.). Pacific Grove, CA: Brooks/Cole.

Nickerson, R. S., & Adams, M. J. (1979). Long term memory for a common object. *Cognitive Psychology, 11,* 287–307.

Nideffer, R. M. (1986). Concentration and attention control training. In J. M. Williams (Ed.), *Applied sport psychology: Personal growth to peak performance.* Menlo Park, CA: Mayfield.

Nideffer, R. M. (1989). Anxiety, attention, and performance in sports: Theoretical and practical considerations. In D. Hackfort & C. D. Spielberger (Eds.), *Anxiety in sports: An international perspective.* New York: Hemisphere.

Nigel, A. J. (1984). *Biofeedback and behavioral strategies in pain treatment.* New York: Medical and Scientific Books.

Nigg, J. T., Lohr, N. E., Westen, D., & Gold, L. J. (1992). Malevolent object representation in borderline personality disorder and major depression. *Journal of Abnormal Psychology, 101,* 61–67.

Noel, R. C. (1980). The effect of visuomotor behavior rehearsal on tennis performance. *Journal of Sport Psychology, 2,* 221–226.

Nolen-Hoeksema, S. (1988). Life span views on depression. In P. B. Baltes, D. L. Featherman, & R. M. Lerner (Eds.), *Life span development and behavior* (Vol. 9). Hillsdale, NJ: Erlbaum.

Nolen-Hoeksema, S., & Morrow, J. (1991). A prospective study of depression and post-traumatic stress symptoms following a natural disaster: The 1989 Loma Prieta earthquake. *Journal of Personality and Social Psychology, 61,* 115–121.

Norcross, J. C., & Prochaska, J. O. (1982). National survey of clinical psychologists: Affiliations and orientations. *Clinical Psychologist, 35,* 1–6.

Norem, J. K. (1989). Cognitive strategies as personality: Effectiveness, specificity, flexibility, and change. In D. M. Buss & N. Cantor (Eds.), *Personality psychology: Recent trends and emerging directions.* New York: Springer-Verlag.

Norris, F. H., & Murrell, S. A. (1990). Social support, life events, and stress as modifiers of adjustment to bereavement by older adults. *Psychology and Aging, 5,* 429–436.

North, T. C. (1989, September). *Effect of exercise and psychotherapeutic treatments on depression: A meta-analysis.* Paper presented at the meeting of the Association for the Advancement of Applied Sport Psychology, Seattle.

Norton, G. R., Harrison, B., Hauch, J., & Rhodes, L. (1985). Characteristics of people with infrequent panic attacks. *Abnormal Psychiatry, 94,* 216–221.

Nye, R. D. (1992). *Three psychologies: Perspectives from Freud, Skinner, and Rogers* (4th ed.). Pacific Grove, CA: Brooks/Cole.

Oatley, K., & Jenkins, J. M. (1992). Human emotions: Function and dysfunction. *Annual Review of Psychology, 43,* 55–85.

O'Bryant, S. L. (1988). Sibling support and older widows' well-being. *Journal of Marriage and the Family, 50,* 173–183.

Ogg, L. W. (1988). The clonal selection theory. *The Scientist.*

Ohman, A. (1986). Face the beast and fear the face: Animal and social fears as prototypes for evolutionary analyses of emotion. *Psychophysiology, 23,* 123–145.

Ohman, A., Dimberg, U., & Ost, L. G. (1985). Animal and social phobias: Biological constraints on learned fear responses. In S. Reiss & R. R. Bootzin (Eds.), *Theoretical issues in behavior therapy* (pp. 123–175). New York: Academic Press.

Oldenburg, D. (1990, April 3). Hidden messages. *Washington Post,* p. C5.

Oldridge, N. B. (1984). Adherence to adult exercise fitness programs. In J. D. Matarzzo, Sh. M. Weiss, J. A. Herd, N. E. Miller, & St. M. Weiss (Eds.), *Behavioral health: A handbook of health enhancement and disease prevention.* New York: Wiley.

O'Leary, A. (1990). Stress, emotion, and human immune function. *Psychological Bulletin, 108,* 363–382.

O'Leary, K. D., & Wilson, G. T. (1987). *Behavior therapy: Application and outcome.* Englewood Cliffs, NJ: Prentice-Hall.

Oller, D. K. (1978). The emergence of the sounds of speech in infancy. In G. H. Yeni-Komshian, J. F. Kavanaugh, & C. A. Ferguson (Eds.), *Child phonology: Perception and production.* New York: Academic Press.

Olson, J. M., & Zanna, M. P. (1991). Attitude change and attitude-behavior consistency. In R. M. Baron, W. G. Graziano, & C. Stangor (Eds.), *Social psychology.* Ft. Worth, TX: Holt, Rinehart & Winston.

Olweus, D. (1980). Familial and temperamental determinants of aggressive behavior in adolescent boys: A causal analysis. *Developmental Psychology, 16,* 644–666.

O'Neal, E. C. (1991). Violence and aggression. In R. M. Baron, W. G. Graziano, & C. Stangor (Eds.), *Social psychology.* Ft. Worth, TX: Holt, Rinehart & Winston.

O'Regan, B. (1984). Multiple personality—mirrors of a new model of mind? *Institute of Noetic Sciences Investigations, 1,* 1.

O'Reilly, C. A., III (1991). Organizational behavior: Where we've been, where we're going. *Annual Review of Psychology, 42,* 427–458.

Orlick, T. (1989). Reflections on sportpsych consulting with individual and team sport athletes at Summer and Winter Olympic games. *Sport Psychologist, 3,* 358–365.

Orlinsky, D. E., & Howard, K. I. (1986). Process and outcome in psychotherapy. In S. L. Garfield & A. E. Bergin (Eds.), *Handbook of psychology and behavior change* (3rd ed.). New York: Wiley.

Ormel, J., & Wohlforth, T. (1991). How neuroticism, long-term difficulties, and life situation change influence psychological distress. *Journal of Personality and Social Psychology, 60,* 744–755.

Orne, M. T. (1959). The nature of hypnosis: Artifact and essence. *Journal of Abnormal and Social Psychology, 58,* 277–299.

Ornstein, R. (1986). *Multimind: A new way of looking at human behavior.* Boston: Houghton Mifflin.

Orton, I. K., Beiman, I., LaPointe, K., & Lanksford, A. (1983). Induced states of anxiety and depression: Effects on self-reported affect and tonic psychophysiological response. *Cognitive Therapy and Research, 1,* 233–244.

Ortony, A. (1989). *The cognitive structure of emotions.* New York: Cambridge.

Osborn, A. F. (1963). *Applied imagination: Principles and procedures for creative problem-solving* (3rd ed.). New York: Scribners.

Ouchi, W. G. (1981). *Theory Z: How American business can meet the Japanese challenge.* Reading, MA: Addison-Wesley.

Ozer, D. J. (1989). Construct validity in personality assessment. In D. M. Buss & N. Cantor (Eds.), *Personality psychology: Recent trends and emerging directions.* New York: Springer-Verlag.

Ozer, E. M., & Bandura, A. (1990). Mechanisms governing empowerment effects: A self-efficacy analysis. *Journal of Personality and Social Psychology, 58,* 472–486.

Paffenbarger, R. J., Jr., Hyde, R. T., Wing, A. L., & Hsieh, C-C. (1986). Physical activity, all-cause mortality, and longevity of college alumni. *New England Journal of Medicine, 314,* 605–612.

Pagano, R. R., & Warrenburg, S. (1983). Meditation: In search of a unique effect. In R. J. Davidson, G. E. Schwartz, & D. Shapiro (Eds.), *Consciousness and self-regulation* (Vol. 3). New York: Plenum.

Paivio, A. (1969). Mental imagery in associative learning and memory. *Psychological Review, 76,* 241–263.

Paivio, A. (1986). *Mental representations: A dual coding approach.* New York: Oxford.

Palfai, T., & Jankiewicz, H. (1991). *Drugs and human behavior.* Dubuque, IA: William C. Brown.

Palmere, M., Benton, S. L., Glover, J. A., & Ronning, R. (1983). Elaboration and recall of main ideas in prose. *Journal of Educational Psychology, 75,* 898–907.

Panitz, D. R., McConchie, R. D., Sauber, S. R., & Fonseca, J. A. (1983). The role of machismo and the Hispanic family in the etiology and treatment of alcoholism in Hispanic American males. *American Journal of Family Therapy, 11,* 31–44.

Panksepp, J. (1986). The neurochemistry of behavior. *Annual Review of Psychology, 37,* 77–107.

Papanicolaou, A. C. (1989). *Emotion: A reconsideration of the somatic theory.* New York: Gordon & Breach.

Parker, L. E., & Lepper, M. R. (1992). Effects of fantasy contexts on children's learning and motivation: Making learning more fun. *Journal of Personality and Social Psychology, 62,* 625–633.

Parkes, C. M., & Weiss, R. S. (1983). *Recovery from bereavement.* New York: Basic Books.

Parloff, M. B., London, P., & Wolfe, B. (1976). Individual psychotherapy and behavior change. *Annual Review of Psychology, 37,* 321–350.

Paterson, R. J., & Neufeld, R. W. J. (1989). The stress response and parameters of stressful situations. In R. W. J. Neufeld (Ed.), *Advances in the investigation of psychological stress.* New York: Wiley.

Patterson, G. R. (1982). *Coercive family processes.* Eugene, OR: Castalia Press.

Patterson, G. R. (1986). Maternal rejection: Determinant or product for deviant child behavior. In W. W. Hartup & Z. Rubin (Eds.), *On relationships and development.* Hillsdale, NJ: Erlbaum.

Patterson, G. R., Littman, R. A., & Bricker, W. (1967). Assertive behavior in children: A step toward a theory of aggression. *Monographs of the Society for Research in Child Development, 32* (Whole No. 5).

Paul, G. L., & Lentz, R. J. (1977). *Psychosocial treatment of chronic mental patients: Milieu versus social learning programs.* Cambridge, MA: Harvard University Press.

Paulhus, D. (1989). Socially desirable responding: Some new solutions to old problems. In D. M. Buss & N. Cantor (Eds), *Personality psychology: Recent trends and emerging directions.* New York: Springer-Verlag.

Paulus, P. B. (1980). Crowding. In P. B. Paulus (Ed.), *Psychology of group influence.* Hillsdale, NJ: Erlbaum.

Paulus, P. B., & Garcia, J. E. (1991). The dynamics of groups and organizations. In R. M. Baron, W. G. Graziano, & C. Stangor (Eds.), *Social psychology.* Ft. Worth, TX: Holt, Rinehart & Winston.

Paunonen, S. V., Jackson, D. N., Trzebinski, J., & Forsterling, F. (1992). Personality structure across cultures: A multimethod evaluation. *Journal of Personality and Social Psychology, 62,* 447–456.

Pavlov, I. P. (1906). The scientific investigation of the psychical faculties or processes in the higher animals. *Science, 24,* 613–619.

Pavlov, I. P. (1928). *Lectures on conditioned reflexes* (Vol. 1; W. H. Gantt, Trans.). New York: International.

Pearce, J. M. (1987). A model for stimulus generalization in Pavlovian conditioning. *Psychological Review, 94,* 61–73.

Pearlin, L. I., & Schooler, C. (1978). The structure of coping. *Journal of Health and Social Behavior, 19,* 2–21.

Peck, R. C. (1968). Psychological developments in the second half of life. In B. L. Neugarten (Ed.), *Middle age and aging.* Chicago: University of Chicago Press.

Pederson, N. L., Plomin, R., McClearn, G. E., & Griberg, L. (1988). Neuroticism, extraversion, and related traits in adult twins reared apart and reared together. *Journal of Personality and Social Psychology, 55,* 950–957.

Pennebaker, J. W. (1990). *Opening up: The healing power of confiding in others.* New York: Morrow.

Pennebaker, J. W., Barger, S. D., & Tiebout, J. (1989). Disclosure of traumas and health among Holocaust survivors. *Psychosomatic Medicine, 51,* 577–589.

Pennington, N., & Hastie, R. (1990). Practical implications of psychological research on juror and jury decision making. *Personality and Social Psychology Bulletin, 16,* 90–105.

Perdue, C. W., Dovidio, J. F., Gurtman, M. B., & Tyler, R. B. (1990). Us and them: Social categorization and the process of intergroup bias. *Journal of Personality and Social Psychology, 59,* 475–486.

Perls, F. S. (1972). Gestalt therapy. In A. Bry (Ed.), *Inside psychotherapy.* New York: Basic Books.

Pert, C. B. (1986). The wisdom of the receptors: Neuropeptides, the emotions, and bodymind. *Advances, 3,* 8–16.

Peschel, E. R., & Peschel, R. E. (1987). Medical insights into the castrati in opera. *American Scientist, 75,* 578–583.

Peterson, A. C. (1987). The nature of biological-psychosocial interactions: The sample case of early adolescence. In R. M. Lerner & T. T. Foch (Eds.), *Biological-psychosocial interactions in early adolescence.* Hillsdale, NJ: Erlbaum.

Peterson, C., Seligman, M. E. P., & Vaillant, G. E. (1988). Pessimistic explanatory style as a risk factor for physical illness: A thirty-five-year longitudinal study. *Journal of Personality and Social Psychology, 55,* 23–32.

Peterson, K. C., Prout, M. F., & Schwarz, R. A. (1991). *Post-traumatic stress disorder: A clinician's guide.* New York: Plenum.

Peterson, L. R., & Peterson, M. J. (1959). Short term retention of individual verbal items. *Journal of Experimental Psychology, 58,* 193–198.

Pettinate, H. M. (Ed.). (1988). *Hypnosis and Memory.* New York: Guilford.

Petty, R. E., & Cacioppo, J. T. (1986). *Communication and persuasion: Central and peripheral routes to attitude change.* New York: Springer-Verlag.

Phares, E. J. (1992). *Clinical psychology: Concepts, methods, and profession.* Pacific Grove, CA: Brooks/Cole.

Phillips, D., McCartney, K., & Scarr, S. (1987). Child care quality and children's social development. *Developmental Psychology, 23,* 537–543.

Phillips, M. T., & Sechzer, J. A. (1989). *Animal research and ethical conflict.* New York: Springer-Verlag.

Piaget, J. (1926). *The language and thought of the child.* New York: Meridian.

Piaget, J., & Inhelder, B. (1956). *The child's conception of space.* London: Routledge.

Piccione, C., Hilgard, E. R., & Zimbardo, P. G. (1989). On the degree of measured hypnotizability over a 25-year period. *Journal of Personality and Social Psychology, 56,* 289–295.

Pichter, M. A., & Ayala, G. F. (1987). Cellular mechanisms of epilepsy: A status report. *Science, 237,* 157–164.

Pierce, G. R., Sarason, I. G., & Sarason, B. R. (1991). General and relationship-based perceptions of social support: Are two constructs better than one? *Journal of Personality and Social Psychology, 61,* 1028–1039.

Pilbeam, D. (1984). The descent of hominoids and hominids. *Scientific American, 250*(3), 84–97.

Pines, A., & Aronson, E. (1981). *Burnout: From tedium to personal growth.* New York: Free Press.

Pitz, G. F., & Sachs, N. J. (1984). Judgment and decision: Theory and application. *Annual Review of Psychology, 35,* 139–163.

Plomin, R. (1989). Environment and genes: Determinants of behavior. *American Psychologist, 44,* 105–111.

Plomin, R. (1990). *Nature and nurture: An introduction to behavior genetics.* Pacific Grove, CA: Brooks/Cole.

Plomin, R., De Fries, J. C., & McClearn, G. E. (1990). *Behavior genetics: A primer* (2nd ed.). New York: Freeman.

Plomin, R., & Rende, R. (1991). Human behavioral genetics. *Annual Review of Psychology, 42,* 161–190.

Plutchik, R. (Ed.). (1986). *Biological foundations of emotion.* Orlando, FL: Academic Press.

Poggio, G. F., & Fischer, B. (1977). Binocular interaction and depth sensitivity of striate and prestriate cortical neurons of behaving rhesus monkeys. *Journal of Neurophysiology, 40,* 1392–1405.

Polansky, N. A. (1991). *Integrated ego psychology.* Hawthorne, NY: Aldine de Gruyter.

Polivy, J., & Herman, C. P. (1992). Undieting: A program to help people stop dieting. *International Journal of Eating Disorders, 11,* 261–268.

Postman, L., & Phillips, L. W. (1965). Short-term temporal changes in free recall. *Quarterly Journal of Experimental Psychology, 17,* 132–138.

Poulos, C. X., & Cappell, H. (1991). Homeostatic theory of drug tolerance: A general model of physiological adaptation. *Psychological Review, 98,* 390–408.

Powell, M. C., & Fazio, R. M. (1984). Attitude accessibility as a function of repeated attitudinal expression. *Personality and Social Psychology Bulletin, 10,* 139–148.

Prentice-Dunn, S., & Rogers, R. W. (1982). Effects of public and private self-awareness on deindividuation and aggression. *Journal of Personality and Social Psychology, 43,* 503–513.

Prentice-Dunn, S., & Spivey, C. B. (1986). Extreme deindividuation in the laboratory: Its magnitude and subjective components. *Personality and Social Psychology Bulletin, 12,* 206–215.

Press, G. A., Amaral, D. G., & Squire, L. R. (1989). Hippocampus abnormalities in amnesic patients revealed by high-resolution magnetic resonance imagery. *Nature, 341,* 54–57.

Pressley, M., Snyder, B. L., Levin, J. R., Murray, H. G., & Ghatala, E. S. (1987). Perceived readiness for examination performance (PREP) produced by initial reading of text and text containing adjunct questions. *Reading Research Quarterly, 22,* 219–236.

Preti, G., Cutler, W. B., Garcia, G. R., Huggins, G. R., & Lawley, J. J. (1986). Human axillary secretions influence women's menstrual cycles: The role of donor extract from females. *Hormones and Behavior, 20,* 473–480.

Pritchard, R. M. (1961, June). Stabilized images on the retina. *Scientific American, 204*(12), 72–78.

Probst, L. R., Ostrom, R., Watkins, P., Dean, T., & Mashburn, D. (1992). Comparative efficacy of religious and non-religious cognitive-behavioral therapy for the treatment of clinical depression in religious individuals. *Journal of Consulting and Clinical Psychology, 60,* 94–103.

Ptacek, J. T., Smith, R. E., & Zanas, J. (1992). Gender, appraisal, and coping: A longitudinal analysis. *Journal of Personality, 60,* 747–770.

Pulkkinen, L. (1982). Self-control and continuity in childhood and delayed adolescence. In P. Baltes & O. Brim (Eds.), *Life span development and behavior* (Vol. 4). New York: Academic Press.

Putnam, F. W. (1984). The psychophysiologic investigation of multiple personality disorder: A review. *Psychiatric Clinics of North America, 7,* 31–39.

Putnam, F. W. (1989). *Diagnosis and treatment of multiple personality disorder.* New York: Guilford.

Pyszczynski, T., & Greenberg, J. (1987). Toward an integration of cognitive and motivational perspectives on social inference: A biased hypothesis-testing model. In L. Berkowitz (Ed.), *Advances in experimental social psychology* (Vol. 20). Orlando, FL: Academic Press.

Pyszczynski, T., Hamilton, J. C., Greenberg, J., & Becker, S. E. (1991). Self-awareness and psychological dysfunction. In C. R. Snyder & D. O. Forsyth (Eds.), *Handbook of social and clinical psychology: The health perspective.* New York: Pergamon.

Quinsey, V. L., Maguire, A., & Varney, G. W. (1983). Assertion and overcontrolled hostility among mentally disordered murderers. *Journal of Consulting and Clinical Psychology, 51,* 550–566.

Quintero, N. (1980). Coming of age the Apache way. *National Geographic, 157,* 262–271.

Rachlin, H. (1991). *Introduction to modern behaviorism* (3rd ed.). New York: Freeman.

Rachman, S. J. (1991). Neo-conditioning and the classical theory of fear acquisition. *Clinical Psychology Review, 11,* 155–173.

Rachman, S. J., & Hodgson, R. J. (1980). *Obsessions and compulsions.* Englewood Cliffs, NJ: Prentice-Hall.

Ragland, D. R., & Brand, R. J. (1988). Type A behavior and mortality from coronary heart disease. *New England Journal of Medicine, 318,* 65–69.

Ragozin, A. S., Basham, R. B., Crnic, K. A., Greenberg, M. T., & Robinson, M. M. (1982). Effects of maternal age on parenting role. *Developmental Psychology, 18,* 627–635.

Raichle, M. R. (1992). Modular organization of infor-

mation processing in the living brain: Studies with positive emission tomography. In L. R. Squire, N. M. Weinberger, G. Lynch, & J. L. McGaugh (Eds.), *Memory: Organization and locus of change.* New York: Oxford.

Raven, B. H., & Rubin, J. Z. (1983). *Social psychology* (2nd ed.). New York: Wiley.

Ray, O. S. (1983). *Drugs, society, and human behavior* (3rd ed.). St. Louis: Mosby.

Ray, O. S., & Ksir, C. (1987). *Drugs, society, and human behavior* (4th ed.). St. Louis: Mosby.

Reeve, J. (1992). *Understanding motivation and emotion.* Ft. Worth, TX: Harcourt Brace Jovanovich.

Reeves, B. F. (1970). *The first year of Sesame Street: The formative research.* New York: Children's Television Workshop.

Register, P. A., & Kihlstrom, J. F. (1987). Hypnotic effects on hyperamnesia. *International Journal of Clinical and Experimental Hypnosis, 35,* 155–170.

Reich, J. W., & Zautra, A. J. (1988). Direct and stress-moderating effects of positive life experiences. In L. H. Cohen (Ed.), *Life events and psychological functioning: Theoretical and methodological causes.* Newbury Park, CA: Sage.

Reisberg, D. (Ed.). (1992). *Auditory imagery.* Hillsdale, NJ: Erlbaum.

Reite, M., Nagel, K., & Ruddy, J. (1990). *Concise guide to evaluation and management of sleep disorders.* Washington, DC: American Psychiatric Press.

Remmers, J. E. (1983). Obstructive sleep apnea: Reflections on breathing and the sleeping brain. In M. H. Chase & E. D. Weitzman (Eds.), *Sleep disorders: Basic and clinical research.* New York: Spectrum.

Renner, M. T. (1987). *Enriched and impoverished environments: Effects on brain and behavior.* New York: Springer-Verlag.

Renwick, P. A., & Lawler, E. E. (1978, May). What do you really want from a job? *Psychology Today,* pp. 53–65.

Rescorla, R. A. (1988). Pavlovian conditioning: It's not what you think it is. *American Psychologist, 43,* 151–160.

Rescorla, R. A., & Solomon, R. L. (1967). Two-process learning theory: Relationships between Pavlovian conditioning and instrumental learning. *Psychological Review, 74,* 151–182.

Rest, J. R. (1983). Morality. In J. H. Flavell & E. M. Markman (Eds.), *Handbook of child psychology: Cognitive development* (Vol. 3). New York: Wiley.

Restak, R. R. (1988). *The mind.* New York: Educational Broadcasting Corporation.

Revenson, T. A., & Felton, B. J. (1989). Disability and coping as predictors of psychological adjustment to rheumatoid arthritis. *Journal of Consulting and Clinical Psychology, 57,* 344–348.

Reznick, J. S., Gibbons, J., Johnson, M. O., & McDonough, P. (1992). Behavioral inhibition in a normative sample. In J. S. Reznick (Ed.), *Perspectives in behavioral inhibition.* Chicago: University of Chicago Press.

Riccio, D. C., & Spear, N. E. (1991). Changes in memory for aversively motivated learning. In M. R. Denny (Ed.), *Fear, avoidance, and phobias: A fundamental analysis.* Hillsdale, NJ: Erlbaum.

Richards, F. A., & Commons, M. L. (1990). Postformal cognitive-developmental theory and research: Review of its current status. In C. N. Alexander & E.

J. Langer (Eds.), *Higher stages of human development: Perspectives on adult growth.* New York: Oxford.

Richardson, D. R. (1991). Interpersonal attraction and love. In R. M. Baron, W. G. Graziano, & C. Stangor (Eds.), *Social psychology.* Ft. Worth, TX: Holt, Rinehart & Winston.

Riegel, K. (1973). Dialectic operations: The final period of cognitive development. *Human Development, 16,* 346–370.

Riley, D. M., & Furedy, J. J. (1985). Psychological and physiological systems: Modes of operation and interaction. In S. R. Burchfield (Ed.), *Stress: Psychological and physiological interactions.* Washington, DC: Hemisphere Publishing Corporation.

Riley, D. M., Sobell, L. C., Leo, G. I., Sobell, M. B., & Klajner, F. (1987). Behavioral treatment of alcohol problems: A review and a comparison of behavioral and nonbehavioral studies. In W. M. Cox (Ed.), *Treatment and prevention of alcohol problems: A resource manual.* New York: Academic Press.

Rilling, M. (1992). An ecological approach to stimulus control and tracking. In W. K. Honig & J. G. Fetterman (Eds.), *Cognitive aspects of stimulus control.* Hillsdale, NJ: Erlbaum.

Rips, L. J. (1988). Deduction. In R. J. Sternberg & E. E. Smith (Eds.), *The psychology of human thought.* Cambridge, MA: Cambridge.

Roberts, P., & Newton, P. M. (1987). Levinsonian studies of women's adult development. *Psychology and Aging, 2,* 154–163.

Robins, L. N. (1966). *Deviant children grow up.* Baltimore: Williams & Wilkins.

Robins, L. N., & Regier, D. A. (Eds.). (1991). *Psychiatric disorders in America: The Epidemiological Catchment Area Study.* New York: Free Press.

Robinson, B. E., & Barret, R. L. (1986). *The developing father.* New York: Guilford.

Robinson, F. P. (1970). *Effective study* (4th ed.). New York: Harper & Row.

Rock, I. (1983). *The logic of perception.* Cambridge, MA: MIT Press.

Rodgers, J. E. (1982). The malleable memory of eyewitnesses. *Science Digest, 3,* 32–35.

Rodgers, R., & Hunter, J. E. (1991). Impact of management by objectives on organizational productivity. *Journal of Applied Psychology, 76,* 322–336.

Rodin, J. (1986). Aging and health: Effects of the sense of control. *Science, 233,* 1271–1276.

Rodin, J., Bartoshuk, L., Peterson, C., & Schank, D. (1990). Bulimia and taste: Possible interactions. *Journal of Abnormal Psychology, 99,* 32–39.

Rodin, J., & Langer, E. J. (1977). Long-term effects of a control-relevant intervention with the institutionalized aged. *Journal of Personality and Social Psychology, 35,* 879–902.

Rodin, J., & Salovey, P. (1989). Health psychology. *Annual Review of Psychology, 40,* 533–579.

Roediger, H. L., III. (1990). Implicit memory: Retention without remembering. *American Psychologist, 45,* 1043–1056.

Rogers, C. R. (1951). *Client-centered therapy.* Boston: Houghton Mifflin.

Rogers, C. R. (1959). A theory of therapy, personality, and interpersonal relationships, as developed in the client-centered framework. In S. Koch (Ed.), *Psychology: A study of a science* (Vol. 3). New York:

McGraw-Hill.

Rogers, C. R. (1970). *Carl Rogers on encounter groups.* New York: Harper & Row.

Rogers, C. R. (1980). *A way of being.* Boston: Houghton Mifflin.

Rogers, R. W. (1983). Cognitive and psychological processes in fear appeals and attitude change: A revised theory of protection motivation. In J. Cacioppo & R. Petty (Eds.), *Social psychophysiology: A sourcebook.* New York: Guilford.

Rogers, T. B., Kuyper, N. A., & Kirker, W. S. (1977). Self-reference and the encoding of personal information. *Journal of Personality and Social Psychology, 35,* 677–688.

Rollins, B. (1989). Marital quality at midlife. In S. Hunter & M. Sundel (Eds.), *Midlife myths: Issues, findings, and practice implications* (pp. 184–194). Newbury Park, CA: Sage.

Roosa, M. W. (1988). The effect of age in the transition to parenthood: Are delayed childbearers a unique group? *Family Relations, 37,* 322–327.

Root, M. P. P., Fallon, P., & Friedrich, W. N. (1986). *Bulimia: A systems approach to treatment.* New York: Norton.

Rosch, E. (1973). On the internal structure of perceptual and semantic categories. In T. E. Moore (Ed.), *Cognitive development and the acquisition of language.* New York: Academic Press.

Rosch, E. (1977). Human categorization. In N. Warren (Ed.), *Advances in cross-cultural psychology* (Vol. 1). London: Academic Press.

Rose, R. J. (1988). Genetic and environmental variance in content dimensions of the MMPI. *Journal of Personality and Social Psychology, 55,* 302–311.

Rose, S. (1973). *The conscious brain.* New York: Knopf.

Rosekind, M. R., Coates, T. J., & Thoresen, C. E. (1978). Telephone transmission of all-night polysomnographic data from subjects' homes. *Journal of Nervous and Mental Disease, 166,* 438–441.

Rosen, J. C., & Leitenberg, H. (1982). Bulimia nervosa: Treatment with exposure and response prevention. *Behavior Therapy, 13,* 117–124.

Rosenbaum, M. E. (1986). The repulsion hypothesis: On the nondevelopment of relationships. *Journal of Personality and Social Psychology, 51,* 1156–1166.

Rosenberg, M. (1985). Self-concept and psychological well-being in adolescence. In R. L. Leahy (Ed.), *The development of the self.* Orlando, FL: Academic Press.

Rosenhan, D. L., & Seligman, M. E. P. (1989). *Abnormal psychology* (2nd ed.). New York: Norton.

Rosenman, R. H., Brand, R. J., Jenkins, C. D., Friedman, M., Straus, R., & Wurm, M. (1975). Coronary heart disease in the Western Collaborative Group Study. *Journal of the American Medical Association, 233,* 872–877.

Rosenstein, D., & Oster, H. (1988). Differential facial responses to four basic tastes in newborns. *Child Development, 59,* 1555–1568.

Rosenthal, R. (1985). From unconscious experimenter bias to teacher expectancy effects. In J. B. Dusek, V. C. Hall, & W. J. Meyer (Eds.), *Teacher expectancies.* Hillsdale, NJ: Erlbaum.

Rosenthal, R., Archer, D., DiMatteo, M. R., Koivumaki, J. H., & Rogers, P. L. (1974). Body talk and tone of voice: The language without words. *Psy-*

chology Today, 2, 64–71.

Rosenthal, R., & Jacobson, L. (1968). *Pygmalion in the classroom: Teacher expectations and pupils' intellectual development.* New York: Holt, Rinehart & Winston.

Rosenthal, R., & Rubin, D. (1978). Interpersonal expectancy effects: The first 345 studies. *Behavioral and Brain Sciences, 3,* 377–415.

Rosenzweig, M. R. (1984). Experience, memory, and the brain. *American Psychologist, 39,* 365–376.

Roskies, E., Seraganian, P., Oseasohn, R., Smilga, S., Martin, N., & Hanley, J. A. (1989). Treatment of psychological stress responses in healthy Type A men. In R. W. J. Neufeld (Ed.), *Advances in the investigation of psychological stress.* New York: Wiley.

Ross, B. M. (1992). *Remembering the personal past: Descriptions of autobiographical memory.* New York: Oxford.

Ross, L. (1977). The intuitive psychologist and his shortcomings: Distortions in the attribution process. In L. Berkowitz (Ed.), *Advances in experimental social psychology* (Vol. 10). New York: Academic Press.

Ross, L., & Nisbett, R. E. (1991). *The person and the situation: Perspectives of social psychology.* New York: McGraw-Hill.

Roszman, T. L., & Carlson, S. L. (1990). Neurotransmitters and molecular signalling in the immune response. In R. Ader, N. Cohen, & D. L. Felten (Eds.), *Psychoneuroimmunology II.* New York: Academic Press.

Rothblum, E. D. (1990). Fear of failure: The psychodynamic, need achievement, fear of success, and procrastination models. In H. Lertenberg (Ed.), *Handbook of social and evaluation anxiety.* New York: Plenum.

Rother, L. (1987, January 4). Women gain degrees, but not tenure. *New York Times,* p. 9.

Rothstein, W. G. (1980). The significance of occupations in work careers: An empirical and theoretical review. *Journal of Vocational Behavior, 17,* 328–343.

Rowe, D. C. (1989). Personality theory and behavioral genetics: Contributions and causes. In D. M. Buss & N. Cantor (Eds.), *Personality psychology: Recent trends and emerging directions.* New York: Springer-Verlag.

Rowe, D. C. (1991). Heredity. In N. J. Derlega, B. A. Winstead, & W. H. Jones (Eds.), *Personality: Contemporary theory and research.* Chicago: Nelson-Hall.

Rubenstein, C. (1982, June). Wellness is all: A report on *Psychology Today's* survey of beliefs about health. *Psychology Today,* pp. 28–37.

Rubin, Z., Hill, C. T., Peplau, L. A., & Dunkel-Schetter, C. (1980). Self-disclosure in dating couples: Sex roles and the ethic of openness. *Journal of Marriage and the Family, 42,* 305–317.

Rubonis, A. V., & Bickman, L. (1991). Psychological impairment in the wake of disaster: The disaster-psychopathology relationship. *Psychological Bulletin, 109,* 384–399.

Rudman, D., Feller, A. G., Nagraj, H. S., Gergans, G. A., Lalitha, P. Y., Goldberg, A. F., Schlenker, R. A., Cohn, L., Rudman, I. W., & Mattson, D. E. (1990). Effects of human growth hormone in men over 60

years old. *New England Journal of Medicine, 323,* 1–6.

Ruhlen, M. (1976). *A guide to the languages of the world.* Stanford, CA: Language Universals Project, Stanford University.

Ruhm, C. J. (1989). Why older Americans stop working. *Gerontologist, 29,* 294–299.

Rumelhart, D. E., & McClelland, J. L. (Eds.). (1986). *Parallel distributed processing: Explorations in the microstructure of cognition* (Vol. 1). Cambridge, MA: MIT Press.

Rushton, J. P. (1989). Genetic similarity, human altruism, and group selection. *Behavioral and Brain Sciences, 12,* 503–559.

Russell, D. W., & Cutrona, C. E. (1991). Social support, stress, and depressive symptoms among the elderly: Test of a process model. *Psychology and Aging, 6,* 190–201.

Russell, J. A. (1991). In defense of a prototype approach to emotion concepts. *Journal of Personality and Social Psychology, 60,* 37–47.

Ryff, C. D. (1991). Possible selves in adulthood and old age: A tale of shifting horizons. *Psychology and Aging, 6,* 286–295.

Ryn, Z. (1990). The evolution of mental disturbances in the concentration camp syndrome (KZ-Syndrom). *Genetic, Social, and General Psychology Monographs, 116,* 21–36.

Sacks, O. (1985, 1986). *The man who mistook his wife for a hat and other clinical tales.* New York: Summit Books and Simon & Schuster.

Sagi, A., & Hoffman, M. L. (1976). Empathic distress in the newborn. *Developmental Psychology, 12,* 175–176.

Sagi, A., Van IJzendoorn, M. H., & Koren-Karie, N. (1991). Primary appraisal of the Strange Situation: A cross-cultural analysis of preseparation episodes. *Developmental Psychology, 27,* 587–596.

Saltz, B., et al. (1991). Prospective study of tardive dyskinesia incidence in the elderly. *Journal of the American Medical Association, 266,* 2402–2406.

Sandler, J. (1986). Aversion methods. In F. H. Kanfer & A. P. Goldstein (Eds.), *Helping people change: A textbook of methods* (3rd ed.). New York: Pergamon.

Sapolsky, R. M. (1992). Neuroendocrinology of the stress response. In J. B. Becker, S. M. Breedlove, & D. Crews (Eds.), *Behavioral endocrinology.* Cambridge, MA: MIT Press.

Sarason, I. G. (1984). Stress, anxiety, and cognitive interference: Reactions to tests. *Journal of Personality and Social Psychology, 46,* 929–938.

Sarason, I. G., & Sarason, B. R. (1990). Test anxiety. In H. Leitenberg (Ed.), *Handbook of social and evaluation anxiety.* New York: Plenum.

Sarason, I. G., & Sarason, B. R. (1993). *Abnormal psychology: The problem of maladaptive behavior* (7th ed.). Englewood Cliffs, NJ: Prentice-Hall.

Sarason, I. G., Sarason, B. R., Pierce, G. R., Shearin, E. N., & Sayers, M. H. (1991). A social learning approach to increasing blood donations. *Journal of Applied Social Psychology, 21,* 896–918.

Sarbin, T. R., & Coe, W. C. (1972). *Hypnosis: A social psychological analysis of influence communication.* New York: Holt, Rinehart & Winston.

Sarrel, P., & Sarrel, L. (1980). The Redbook report on sexual relationships. *Redbook, 155,* 73–80.

Satir, V. (1967). *Conjoint family therapy.* Palo Alto, CA: Science and Behavior Books.

Savage-Rumbaugh, E. S., Pate, J. L., Lawson, J., Smith, S. T., & Rosenbaum, S. (1983). Can a chimpanzee make a statement? *Journal of Experimental Psychology: General, 112,* 457–492.

Sawaguchi, T., & Goldman-Rakic, P. S. (1991). DI dopamine receptors in prefrontal cortex: Involvement in working memory. *Science, 251,* 947–949.

Sawrey, W. L., & Weiss, J. D. (1956). An experimental method of producing gastric ulcers. *Journal of Comparative and Physiological Psychology, 49,* 269.

Saxe, G. B. (1981). Body parts as numerals: A developmental analysis of numeration among the Oksapmin in Papua New Guinea. *Child Development, 52,* 306–316.

Scarr, S. (1992). Developmental theories for the 1990s: Development and individual differences. *Child Development, 63,* 1–19.

Scarr, S., & McCartney, K. (1983). How people make their own environments: A theory of genotype environmental effects. *Child Development, 54,* 424–435.

Scarr, S., & Weinberg, R. A. (1976). IQ test performance of black children adopted by white families. *American Psychologist, 31,* 726–739.

Schachter, S., & Latané, B. (1964). Crime, cognition, and the autonomic nervous system. In D. Levine (Ed.), *Nebraska Symposium on Maturation.* Lincoln: University of Nebraska Press.

Schachter, S., & Wheeler, L. (1962). Epinephrine, chlorpromazine, and amusement. *Journal of Abnormal and Social Psychology, 65,* 121–128.

Schacter, D. L. (1992). Understanding implicit memory: A cognitive neuroscience approach. *American Psychologist, 47,* 559–569.

Schacter, D. L., Cooper, L. A., & Delaney, S. (1990). Implicit memory for unfamiliar objects depends on access to structural descriptions. *Journal of Experimental Psychology: General, 119,* 5–24.

Schaie, K. W. (1983). Age changes in intelligence. In D. F. Woodruff & J. E. Birren (Eds.), *Aging: Scientific perspectives and social issues* (Vol. 2). New York: Van Nostrand.

Schaie, K. W. (1987, April). *Old dogs can learn new tricks: Intellectual decline and its remediation in later adulthood.* Paper presented at the Eastern Psychological Association, Philadelphia, PA.

Schaie, K. W., & Strother, C. R. (1968). A cross-sequential study of age changes in cognitive behavior. *Psychological Bulletin, 70,* 671–680.

Schaie, K. W., & Willis, S. L. (1986). *Adult development and aging* (2nd ed.). Boston: Little, Brown.

Schardein, J. L. (1985). *Chemically induced birth defects.* New York: Dekker.

Schatzberg, A. F., & Cole, J. O. (1991). *Manual of clinical psychopharmacology* (2nd ed.). Washington, DC: American Psychiatric Press.

Scheff, T. J. (1966). *Being mentally ill: A sociological theory.* Chicago: Aldine.

Scherer, K. R. (1984). On the nature and function of emotion: A component process approach. In K. Scherer & P. Ekman (Eds.), *Approaches to emotion.* Hillsdale, NJ: Erlbaum.

Scherer, K. R. (1988). *Facets of emotion: Recent research.* Hillsdale, NJ: Erlbaum.

Schlenker, B. R., & Weigold, M. F. (1992). Interpersonal processes involving impression regulation and management. *Annual Review of Psychology, 43,* 133–168.

Schlesier-Stropp, B. (1984). Bulimia: A review of the literature. *Psychological Bulletin, 95,* 247–257.

Schmidt, F. L., Ones, D. S., & Hunter, J. E. (1992). Personnel selection. *Annual Review of Psychology, 43,* 627–670.

Schmidt, G. (1975). Male-female differences in sexual arousal during and after exposure to sexually erotic stimuli. *Archives of Sexual Behavior, 4,* 353–364.

Schmidt, G. (1978). Letter to the editor on H. Geise and G. Schmidt, 1968. *Archives of Sexual Behavior, 7,* 73–74.

Schmidt, G., & Weiner, B. (1988). An attributional-affect-action theory of behavior: Replications of judgments of helping. *Personality and Social Psychology Bulletin, 14,* 610–621.

Schmidt, N., & Klimoski, R. J. (1991). *Research methods in human research management.* Cincinnati: Southwestern Books.

Schmitt, N., & Robertson, I. (1990). Personnel selection. *Annual Review of Psychology, 41,* 289–319.

Schneider, W., & Shiffrin, R. M. (1977). Controlled and automated human information processing: 1. Detection, search, and attention. *Psychological Review, 84,* 1–66.

Schneidman, E. S. (Ed.). (1976). *Suicidology: Contemporary developments.* New York: Grune & Stratton.

Schofield, J. W., & Sagar, H. A. (1979). Unplanned social learning in an interracial school. In R. Rist (Ed.), *Inside desegregated schools: Taking stock of a great American experiment.* New York: Academic Press.

Schoicket, S. L., Bertelson, A. D., & Locks, P. (1988). Is sleep hygiene a sufficient treatment for sleep maintenance insomnia? *Behavior Therapy, 19,* 183–190.

Schreber, S. L. (1991). Chemistry and biology of the immunophilins and their immunosuppressive ligands. *Science, 251,* 283–287.

Schroeder, C. S., & Gordon, B. N. (1991). *Assessment and treatment of childhood problems: A clinician's guide.* New York: Guilford.

Schroeder, D., & Costa, P. (1984). Influence of life event stress on physical illness: Substantive effects or methodological laws? *Journal of Personality and Social Psychology, 46,* 853–863.

Schuckit, M. A. (1987). Biological vulnerability to alcoholism. *Journal of Consulting and Clinical Psychology, 55,* 301–309.

Schulz, R., & Aderman, D. (1980). Clinical research and the stages of dying. In R. A. Kalish (Ed.), *Death, dying, and transcending.* Farmindale, NY: Baywood.

Schusterman, R. J., (1989). Please parse the sentence: Animal cognition in the Procrustean bed of animal linguistics. *Psychological Record, 39,* 3–18.

Schutte, N. S., Malouff, J. M., Post-Gorden, J. C., & Rodasts, A. L. (1988). Effect of playing video games on children's aggressive and other behavior. *Journal of Applied Social Psychology, 18,* 454–460.

Schwartz, B. (1986). *The battle for human nature: Science, morality, and modern life.* New York: Norton.

Schwartz, L. L., & Kaslow, F. W. (1981). The cult phenomenon: Historical, sociological, and familial factors contributing to their development and appeal. *Marriage and Family Review, 4,* 3–30.

Schwartz, R. (1984). Body weight regulation. *University of Washington Medicine, 10,* 16–20.

Schweder, R. A., & Sullivan, L. (1990). The semiotic subject of cultural psychology. In L. A. Pervin (Ed.), *Handbook of personality: Theory and research.* New York: Guilford.

Scott, R., & Angwin, M. J. (1986). *Time out for motherhood.* Los Angeles: Jeremy Tarcher.

Scoville, W. B., & Milner, B. (1957). Loss of recent memory after bilateral hippocampal lesions. *Journal of Neurology, Neurosurgery, and Psychiatry, 20,* 11–21.

Sears, A. E. (1989). The legal case for restricting pornography. In D. Zillman & J. Bryant (Eds.), *Pornography: Research advances and policy considerations.* Hillsdale, NJ: Erlbaum.

Sears, R. R. (1970). Relation of early socialization experiences to self-concepts and gender role in middle childhood. *Child Development, 41,* 267–289.

Sears, R. R. (1977). Sources of life satisfaction of the Terman gifted men. *American Psychologist, 32,* 119–128.

Sears, R. R., Maccoby, E. E., & Levin, H. (1957). *Patterns of child rearing.* Evanston, IL: Row, Peterson.

Seligman, M. E. P. (1991). *Learned optimism.* New York: Knopf.

Selkoe, D. J. (1991). The molecular pathology of Alzheimer's Disease. *Neuron, 6,* 487–498.

Selman, R. L. (1981). The child as a friendship philosopher. In S. R. Asher & J. M. Gottman (Eds.), *The development of children's friendships.* Cambridge, MA: Cambridge.

Selye, H. (1976). *The stress of life* (rev. ed.) New York: McGraw-Hill.

Senden, M. von (1960). *Space and sight: The perception of space and shape in the congenitally blind before and after operation* (P. Heath, Trans.). New York: Free Press.

Seta, J. J., Seta, C. E., & Wang, M. A. (1991). Feelings of negativity and stress: An averaging-summation analysis of impressions of negative life experiences. *Personality and Social Psychology Bulletin, 17,* 376–384.

Shaffer, D. R. (1989). *Developmental psychology: Childhood and adolescence.* Pacific Grove, CA: Brooks/Cole.

Shair, H. N., Barr, G. A., & Hofer, M. A. (Eds.). (1991). *Developmental psychobiology.* New York: Oxford.

Shallice, T., & Burgess, P. (1991). Higher-order cognitive impairments and frontal-lobe lesions in man. In H. S. Levin, H. M. Eisenberg, & A. L. Benton (Eds.), *Frontal lobe function and dysfunction.* New York: Oxford.

Shapiro, D. H., & Walsh, R. N. (Eds.). (1984). *Meditation: Classical and contemporary perspectives.* Hawthorne, NY: Aldine.

Shapley, R. (1990). Visual sensitivity and parallel retinocortical channels. *Annual Review of Psychology, 41,* 635–658.

Shaver, K. (1987). *Principles of social psychology* (3rd ed.). Hillsdale, NJ: Erlbaum.

Shaver, P., Hazan, C., & Bradshaw, D. (1988). Love as attachment: The integration of three behavioral systems. In R. J. Sternberg & M. L. Barnes (Eds.), *The psychology of love.* New Haven, CT: Yale University Press.

Shavit, Y. (1990). Stress-induced immune modulation

in animals: Opiates and endogenous opioid peptides. In R. Ader, N. Cohen, & D. L. Felten (Eds.), *Psychoneuroimmunology II.* New York: Academic Press.

Sheehan, P. W., & Statham, D. (1989). Hypnosis, the timing of its introduction, and acceptance of misleading information. *Journal of Abnormal Psychology, 98,* 170–176.

Shekelle, R. B., et al. (1985). The MRFIT behavior pattern study: II. Type A behavior and incidence of coronary heart disease. *American Journal of Epidemiology, 122,* 559–570.

Shepard, R. N. (1990). *Mind sights: Original visual illusions, ambiguities, and other anomalies, with a commentary on the play of mind in perception and art.* New York: Freeman.

Shepard, R. N., & Cooper, L. A. (1982). *Mental images and their transformations.* Cambridge, MA: MIT Press.

Sherif, M. (1935). A study of some social factors in perception. *Archives of Psychology* (No. 187).

Sherif, M., Harvey, O., White, B., Hood, W., & Sherif, C. (1961). *Intergroup conflict and cooperation: The Robbers Cave experiment.* Norman: University of Oklahoma Press.

Sherrington, C. S. (1950). The physical basis of mind. In P. Laslett (Ed.), *The physical basis of mind.* New York: Macmillan.

Sherrod, D. R., Hage, J. N., Halpern, P. L., & Moore, B. S. (1977). Effects of personal causation and perceived control on responses to an aversive environment: The more control, the better. *Journal of Experimental Social Psychology, 13,* 14–27.

Sherwood, L. (1991). *Fundamentals of physiology: A human perspective.* St. Paul, MN: West.

Shevrin, H. (1988). Unconscious conflict: A convergent psychodynamic and electrophysiological approach. In M. Horowitz (Ed.), *Psychodynamics and cognition.* Chicago: University of Chicago Press.

Shimizu, H., Ross, R. K., Bernstein, L., Pike, M. C., & Henderson, B. E. (1990). Serum estrogen levels in post-menopausal women: Comparison of American whites and Japanese in Japan. *British Journal of Cancer, 62,* 451–453.

Shinkman, C. J. (1981). Career development in the early college years. In D. H. Montross & C. J. Shinkman (Eds.), *Career development in the 1980s: Theory and practice.* Springfield, IL: Charles C Thomas.

Shoor, S. M., & Holman, H. R. (1984). Development of an instrument to explore psychological mediators in chronic arthritis. *Transactions of the Association of American Physicians, 97,* 325–331.

Shortcliffe, E. H. (1983). Medical consultation systems: Designing for doctors. In M. E. Sime & M. J. Coombs (Eds.), *Designing for human computer communication.* New York: Academic Press.

Shumaker, S. A., & Hill, D. R. (1991). Gender differences in social support and physical health. *Health Psychology, 10,* 102–111.

Siegel, R. K. (1977). Hallucinations. *Scientific American, 237*(10), 132–139.

Siegel, R. K. (1989). *Intoxication: Life in pursuit of artificial paradise.* New York: Dutton.

Siegel, R. K. (1990). *Intoxication.* New York: Pocket Books.

Siegel, S. (1984). Pavlovian conditioning and heroin overdose: Reports from overdose victims. *Bulletin of the Psychonomic Society, 22,* 428–430.

Siegler, R. S. (1986). *Children's thinking.* Englewood Cliffs, NJ: Prentice-Hall.

Sigelman, C. K., & Shaffer, D. R. (1991). *Life-span human development.* Pacific Grove, CA: Brooks/Cole.

Silverman, L. H. (1983). The subliminal psychodynamic activation method: Overview and comprehensive listing of studies. In J. Masling (Ed.), *Empirical studies of psychoanalytic theories* (Vol. 1). Hillsdale, NJ: Erlbaum.

Simon, H. A. (1990). Invariants of human behavior. *Annual Review of Psychology, 41,* 1–20.

Singer, J. L. (1975). *The inner world of daydreaming.* New York: Harper & Row.

Singer, J. L. (1988). Sampling ongoing consciousness and emotional experience: Implications for health. In M. J. Horowitz (Ed.), *Psychodynamics and cognition.* Chicago: University of Chicago Press.

Skinner, B. F. (1957). *Verbal behavior.* Englewood Cliffs, NJ: Prentice-Hall.

Skinner, B. F. (1977). *Upon further reflection.* Englewood Cliffs, NJ: Prentice-Hall.

Skinner, B. F. (1989). The origins of cognitive thought. *American Psychologist, 44,* 13–18.

Sklar, L. S., & Anisman, H. (1981). Stress and cancer. *Psychological Bulletin, 89,* 369–406.

Slade, P. D., Troup, J. D. G., Lethem, J., & Bentley, G. (1983). The fear-avoidance model of exaggerated pain perception: 2. Preliminary studies of coping strategies for pain. *Behaviour Research and Therapy, 21,* 409–416.

Slater, A. (1989). Visual memory and perception in early infancy. In A. Slater & G. Bremner (Eds.), *Infant development.* Hillsdale, NJ: Erlbaum.

Slavin, R. E. (1990). *Cooperative learning: Theory, research, and practice.* Englewood Cliffs, NJ: Prentice-Hall.

Smith, A. N., & Spence, C. M. (1981). National day care study: Optimizing the day care environment. *American Journal of Orthopsychiatry, 50,* 718–721.

Smith, C. A. (1989). Dimensions of appraisal and physiologic response in emotion. *Journal of Personality and Social Psychology, 56,* 339–353.

Smith, C. A. (1991). The self, appraisal, and coping. In C. R. Snyder & D. R. Forsythe (Eds.), *Handbook of social and clinical psychology: The health perspective.* New York: Pergamon.

Smith, C. A., & Ellsworth, P. C. (1985). Patterns of cognitive approach in emotion. *Journal of Personality and Social Psychology, 48,* 813–838.

Smith, C. A., & Ellsworth, P. C. (1987). Patterns of appraisal and emotion related to taking an exam. *Journal of Personality and Social Psychology, 52,* 475–488.

Smith, D. (1982). Trends in counseling and psychotherapy. *American Psychologist, 37,* 802–809.

Smith, E. R., & Zarate, M. A. (1992). Exemplar-based model of social judgment. *Psychological Review, 99,* 3–21.

Smith, M. E. (1926). An investigation of the development of the sentence and the extent of vocabulary in young children. *University of Iowa Studies in Child Welfare, 3* (No. 5).

Smith, M. L., & Glass, G. V. (1977). Meta-analyses of psychotherapy outcome studies. *American Psychologist, 32,* 752–760.

Smith, N. J., Smith, R. E., & Smoll, F. L. (1983). *Kidsports: A survival guide for parents.* Reading, MA: Addison-Wesley.

Smith, P., & Pederson, D. R. (1988). Maternal sensitivity and patterns of infant-mother attachment. *Child Development, 59,* 1097–1101.

Smith, R. E. (1989). Effects of coping skills training on generalized self-efficacy and locus of control. *Journal of Personality and Social Psychology, 56,* 228–233.

Smith, R. E. (1992). *Psychological skills in professional baseball.* Houston: Houston Astros Baseball Club.

Smith, R. E., & Johnson, J. (1990). An organizational empowerment approach to consultation in professional baseball. *The Sport Psychologist, 4,* 347–357.

Smith, R. E., & Nye, F. L. (1989). A comparison of induced effect and covert rehearsal in the acquisition of stress management coping skills. *Journal of Counseling Psychology, 36,* 17–23.

Smith, R. E., & Rohsenow, D. J. (1987). Cognitive-affective stress management training: A treatment and resource manual. *Social and Behavioral Sciences Documents, 17*(2), Document No. 2829.

Smith, R. E., & Smoll, F. L. (1990). Sport performance anxiety. In H. Leitenberg (Ed.), *Handbook of social and evaluation anxiety.* New York: Plenum.

Smith, R. E., Smoll, F. L., & Ptacek, J. T. (1989). Conjunctive moderator variables in vulnerability and resiliency research: Life stress, social support and coping skills, and adolescent sport injuries. *Journal of Personality and Social Psychology, 58,* 360–370.

Smith, R. E., Smoll, F. L., & Schutz, R. W. (1990). Measurement and correlates of sport-specific cognitive and somatic trait anxiety: The Sport Anxiety Scale. *Anxiety Research, 2,* 263–280.

Smith, R. E., Vanderbilt, K., & Callen, M. B. (1973). Social comparison and bystander intervention in emergencies. *Journal of Applied Social Psychology, 3,* 186–196.

Smith, S. M., & Rothkopf, E. Z. (1984). Contextual enrichment and distribution of practice in the classroom. *Cognition and Instruction, 1,* 341–358.

Smoll, F. L., Smith, R. E., Barnett, M. P., & Everett, J. J. (1993). Enhancement of children's self-esteem through social support training for youth sport coaches. *Journal of Applied Psychology.*

Snarey, J. (1987a). A question of morality. *Psychological Bulletin, 97,* 202–232.

Snarey, J. (1987b). Promoting moral maturity among adolescents: An ethnographic study of the Israeli kibbutz. *Comparative Education Review, 31,* 241–259.

Snow, M. E., Jacklin, C. N., & Maccoby, E. E. (1983). Sex-of-child differences in father-child interaction at one year of age. *Child Development, 54,* 227–232.

Snyder, D. K., Wills, R. M., & Grady-Fletcher, A. (1991). Long-term effectiveness of behavioral versus insight-oriented marital therapy: A 4-year follow-up study. *Journal of Consulting and Clinical Psychology, 59,* 138–141.

Snyder, M. (1987). *Public appearances, private realities: The psychology of self-monitoring.* New York: Freeman.

Snyder, M., Berscheid, E., & Glick, P. (1985). Focusing on the exterior and the interior: Two investigations of the initiation of personal relationships. *Journal of Personality and Social Psychology, 48,* 1427–1439.

Snyder, M., & Gangestad, S. (1986). On the nature of self-monitoring: Matters of assessment, matters of validity. *Journal of Personality and Social Psychology, 51,* 125–139.

Snyder, M., & Swann, W. B., Jr. (1976). When actions reflect attitudes: The politics of impression management. *Journal of Personality and Social Psychology, 34,* 1034–1042.

Snyder, S. H. (1986). *Drugs and the brain.* New York: Scientific American Library.

Sobel, N. R., & Pridgen, D. (1981). *Eyewitness identification: Legal and practical problems.* New York: Clark Boardman.

Sokolov, E. N. (1992). Local plasticity in neuronal learning. In L. R. Squire, N. M. Weinberger, G. Lynch, & J. L. McGaugh (Eds.), *Memory: Organization and locus of change.* New York: Oxford.

Solomon, Z., Mikulincer, M., & Avitzur, E. (1988). Coping, locus of control, social support, and combat-related posttraumatic stress disorder: A prospective study. *Journal of Personality and Social Psychology, 55,* 279–285.

Sorenson, S. B., & Rutler, C. M. (1991). Transgenerational patterns of suicide attempt. *Journal of Consulting and Clinical Psychology, 59,* 861–866.

Spady, D. (1987). Effects of mothers' smoking on their infants' body composition as determined by total body potassium. *Pediatric Research, 20,* 716–719.

Spanos, N. P. (1991). Hypnosis, hypnotizability, and hypnotherapy. In C. R. Snyder & D. R. Forsythe (Eds.), *Handbook of social and clinical psychology: The health perspective.* New York: Pergamon.

Spanos, N. P., & Chaves, J. F. (Eds.). (1988). *Hypnosis: The cognitive-behavioral perspective.* Buffalo, NY: Prometheus Books.

Spanos, N. P., & Katsanis, J. (1989). Effects of institutional set on attributions of nonvolition during hypnotic and nonhypnotic analgesia. *Journal of Personality and Social Psychology, 56,* 182–188.

Spanos, N. P., Lush, N., & Gwynn, M. I. (1989). Cognitive skill training enhancement of hypnotizability: Generalization effects and trance logic responding. *Journal of Personality and Social Psychology, 56,* 795–804.

Spearman, C. (1923). *The nature of "intelligence" and the principles of cognition.* London: Macmillan.

Spector, P. E., & Jex, S. M. (1991). Relations of job characteristics from multiple data sources with employee affect, absence, turnover intentions, and health. *Journal of Applied Psychology, 76,* 46–53.

Speisman, J., Lazarus, R. S., Mordkoff, A., & Davison, L. (1964). Experimental reduction of stress based on ego-defense theory. *Journal of Abnormal and Social Psychology, 68,* 367–380.

Speisman, J. C. (1959). Depth of interpretation and verbal resistance in psychotherapy. *Journal of Consulting Psychology, 23,* 93–99.

Sperling, G. (1960). The information available in brief visual presentations. *Psychological Monographs, 74* (11, Whole No. 498).

Sperling, G. (1984). A unified theory of attention and signal detection. In R. Parasuraman & D. R. Davies (Eds.), *Varieties of attention.* New York: Academic Press.

Sperry, R. W. (1970). Perception in the absence of neocortical commissures. In Association for Research in Nervous and Mental Disease, *Perception and its*

disorders. New York: Williams & Wilkins.

Spiegel, D., Bloom. J. R., Kraemer, H. C., & Gottlieb, E. (1989). Effect of psychosocial treatment on survival of patients with metastatic breast cancer. *Lancet, 2,* 888–891.

Spielberger, C. D., & DeNike, L. D. (1966). Descriptive behaviorism versus cognitive theory in verbal operant conditioning. *Psychological Review, 73,* 306–326.

Spitzer, R. L., Skodol, A. E., Gibbon, M., & Williams, J. B. W. (1983). *Psychopathology: A casebook.* New York: McGraw-Hill.

Sprafkin, J. N., Liebert, R. M., & Poulos, R. W. (1975). Effects of a prosocial televised example on children's helping. *Journal of Experimental Child Psychology, 20,* 119–126.

Spring, B., Chiodo, J., & Bowen, D. J. (1987). Carbohydrates, tryptophan, and behavior: A methodological review. *Psychological Bulletin, 102,* 234–256.

Springer, S., & Deutsch, G. (1989). *Left brain, right brain* (3rd ed.) New York: Freeman.

Squire, L. R. (1987). *Memory and brain.* Oxford: Oxford.

Squire, L. R. (1992). Memory and the hippocampus: A synthesis from findings with rats, monkeys, and humans. *Psychological Review, 99,* 195–231.

Squire, L. R., & Zola-Morgan, S. (1991). The medial temporal lobe memory system. *Science, 253,* 1380–1386.

Sroufe, L. A., Cooper, R. G., & De Hart, G. B. (1992). *Child development: Its nature and course.* New York: McGraw-Hill.

Stall. R., & Biernacki, P. (1986). Spontaneous remission from the problematic use of substances: An inductive model derived from a comparative analysis of the alcohol, opiate. tobacco, and food/obesity literatures. *International Journal of the Addictions, 21,* 1–23.

Stampfl, T. G. (1991). Analysis of aversive events in human psychopathology: Fear and avoidance. In M. R. Denny (Ed.), *Fear, avoidance, and phobias: A fundamental analysis.* Hillsdale, NJ: Erlbaum.

Staples, R. (1981). The myth of the black matriarchy. *Black Scholar, 12,* 26–34.

Steele, C. M. (1988). The psychology of self-affirmation: Sustaining the integrity of the self. In L. Berkowitz (Ed.), *Advances in experimental social psychology* (Vol. 21). New York: Academic Press.

Steele, C. M., & Josephs, R. A. (1990). Alcohol myopia: Its prized and dangerous effects. *American Psychologist, 45,* 921–933.

Steele, C. M., Southwick, L. L., & Critchlow, B. (1981). Dissonance and alcohol: Drinking your troubles away. *Journal of Personality and Social Psychology, 41,* 831–846.

Steers, R. M., & Porter, L. W. (Eds.). (1991). *Motivation and work behavior* (5th ed.). New York: McGraw-Hill.

Stein, A. H., & Friedrich, L. K. (1972). Television content and young children's behavior. In J. P. Murray, E. A. Rubinstein, & G. A. Comstock (Eds.), *Television and social behavior:* Vol. 2. *Television and social learning.* Washington, DC: U.S. Government Printing Office.

Stein, M., Miller, A. H., & Trestman, R. L. (1990). Depression and the immune system. In R. Ader, N.

Cohen, & D. L. Felten (Eds.), *Psychoneuroimmunology II.* New York: Academic Press.

Steinberg, L. (1987, September). Bound to bicker. *Psychology Today,* pp. 36–39.

Steinberg, L. D., & Silverberg, S. (1986). The vicissitudes of autonomy in early adolescence. *Child Development, 57,* 841–851.

Stephan, W. G. (1990). School desegregation: Short-term and long-term effects. In H. Knopke (Ed.), *Opening doors: An appraisal of race relations in America.* Tuscaloosa: University of Alabama Press.

Stephan, W. G. (1991). Intergroup relations and prejudice. In R. M. Baron, W. G. Graziano, & C. Stangor (Eds.), *Social psychology.* Ft. Worth, TX: Holt, Rinehart & Winston.

Stern, R. (1987). *Theories of the unconscious and theories of the self.* Hillsdale, NJ: Analytic Press.

Sternbach, R. (Ed.). (1987). *The psychology of pain.* New York: Raven Press.

Sternberg, R. J. (1985a). Cognitive approaches to intelligence. In B. B. Wolman (Ed.), *Handbook of intelligence: Theory, measurement, and applications* (pp. 59–118). New York: Wiley-Interscience.

Sternberg, R. J. (1985b). *Beyond IQ: A triarchic theory of human intelligence.* London: Cambridge.

Sternberg, R. J. (1986). A triangular theory of love. *Psychological Review, 93,* 119–135.

Sternberg, R. J. (1988a). Triangulating love. In R. J. Sternberg & M. L. Barnes (Eds.), *The psychology of love.* New Haven, CT: Yale University Press.

Sternberg, R. J. (1988b). *The triarchic mind: A new theory of human intelligence.* New York: Viking Press.

Sternberg, R. J., & Powell, J. S. (1983). Comprehending verbal comprehension. *American Psychologist, 38,* 878–893.

Stitzer, R. L., Skodal, A. E., Gibbon, M., & Williams, J. B. W. (1983). *Psychopathology: A casebook.* New York: McGraw-Hill.

Stock, W. A., Okun, M. A., Haring, M. J., & Witter, R. A. (1983). Age and subjective well-being: A meta-analysis. In R. J. Light (Ed.), *Evaluation studies: Review annual* (Vol. 8). Beverly Hills, CA: Sage.

Stokols, D. (1976). The experience of crowding in primary and secondary environments. *Environment and Behavior, 8,* 49–86.

Stokols, D. (1978). A typology of crowding experiences. In A. Baum & Y. Epstein (Eds.), *Human response to crowding.* Hillsdale, NJ: Erlbaum.

Stokols, D. (1992). Establishing and maintaining healthy environments: Toward a social ecology of health promotion. *American Psychologist, 47,* 6–22.

Stokols, D., & Baron, R. M. (1991). The environmental context of behavior. In R. M. Baron, W. G. Graziano, & C. Stangor (Eds.), *Social psychology.* Ft. Worth, TX: Holt, Rinehart & Winston.

Stone, M. H. (1986). Borderline personality disorder. In R. Michels & J. O. Cavenar (Eds.), *Psychiatry* (Vol 1). New York: Basic Books.

Storms, M. D. (1981). Theories of sexual orientation. *Journal of Personality and Social Psychology, 38,* 783–792.

Strack, F., Martin, L. L., & Stepper, S. (1988). Inhibiting and facilitating conditions of facial expressions: A non-obtrusive test of the facial feedback hypothesis. *Journal of Personality and Social Psychology,*

54, 768–777.

Strauman, T. J. (1992). Self-guide, autobiographical memory, and anxiety and dysphoria: Toward a cognitive model of vulnerability to emotional distress. *Journal of Abnormal Psychology, 101,* 87–95.

Straus, M. A., Gelles, R. J., & Steinmetz, S. K. (1980). *Behind closed doors: Violence in the American family.* Garden City, NY: Doubleday (Anchor).

Streissguth, A. P., Clarren, S. K., & Jones, K. L. (1985). Natural history of the fetal alcohol syndrome: A 10-year follow-up of eleven patients. *Lancet, 2,* 85–91.

Strentz, H. (1984, December 25). The road to imbecility. *Cleveland Plain Dealer,* p. B23.

Strentz, T., & Auerbach, S. M. (1988). Adjustment to the stress of simulated captivity: Effects of emotion-focused versus problem-focused preparation on hostages differing in locus of control. *Journal of Personality and Social Psychology, 55,* 652–660.

Stricker, G. (1992). The relation of research to clinical practice. *American Psychologist, 47,* 543–549.

Strober, M., & Humphrey, L. L. (1987). Familial contributions to the etiology and course of anorexia nervosa and bulimia. *Journal of Consulting and Clinical Psychology, 55,* 654–659.

Stroebe, M. S., & Stroebe, W. (1983). Who suffers more? Sex differences in health risks of the widowed. *Psychological Bulletin, 93,* 279–301.

Stromeyer, C. F., & Psotka, J. (1970). The detailed texture of eidetic images. *Nature, 225,* 346–349.

Strube, M. J. (1989). Evidence for the *type* in Type A behavior: A taxometric analysis. *Journal of Personality and Social Psychology, 56,* 972–987.

Strupp, H. H. (1989). Psychotherapy: Can the practitioner learn from the researcher? *American Psychologist, 44,* 717–724.

Stryer, L. (1987). The molecules of visual excitation. *Scientific American, 257*(1), 42–50.

Stunkard, A. J. (1982). Obesity. In A. S. Bellak, M. Hersen, & A. E. Kazdin (Eds.), *International handbook of behavior modification and therapy.* New York: Plenum.

Sue, D. W., & Sue, D. (1990). *Counseling the culturally different: Theory and practice.* New York: Wiley.

Sue, D., Sue, D. W., & Sue, S. (1990). *Understanding abnormal behavior* (3rd ed.). Boston: Houghton Mifflin.

Sue, S., Smith, R. E., & Caldwell, C. (1973). Effects of inadmissible evidence on the decisions of simulated jurors: A moral dilemma. *Journal of Applied Social Psychology, 3,* 345–353.

Suggs, R. (1962). *The hidden worlds of Polynesia.* New York: Harcourt Brace Jovanovich.

Suls, J., & Marco, C. (1991). The self. In R. M. Baron, W. G. Graziano, & C. Stangor (Eds.), *Social psychology.* Ft. Worth, TX: Holt, Rinehart & Winston.

Suls, J., & Wan, C. K. (1989). Effects of sensory and procedural information on coping with stressful medical procedures and pain: A meta-analysis. *Journal of Consulting and Clinical Psychology, 57,* 372–379.

Super, D. E. (1981). A developmental theory: Implementing a self-concept. In D. H. Montross & C. J. Shinkman (Eds.), *Career development in the 1980s: Theory and practice.* Springfield, IL: Charles C Thomas.

Sur, M., Garraghty, P. E., & Roe, A. W. (1988). Experimentally induced visual perceptions into auditory thalamus and cortex. *Science, 242,* 1437–1440.

Swan, G. E., Dame, A., & Carmelli, D. (1991). Involuntary retirement, Type A behavior, and current functioning in elderly men: 27-year followup of the Western Collaborative Group Study. *Psychology and Aging, 6,* 384–391.

Swann, W. B., Jr., Hixon, J. G., & De La Ronde, C. (1992). Embracing the ''bitter truth'': Negative self-concepts and marital commitment. *Psychological Science, 3,* 118–121.

Swann, W. B., Jr., Stein-Seroussi, A., & Giesler, R. B. (1992). Why people self-verify. *Journal of Personality and Social Psychology, 62,* 392–401.

Swets, J. A. (1992). The science of choosing the right decision threshold in high-stakes diagnostics. *American Psychologist, 47,* 522–532.

Szasz, T. (1974). *The myth of mental illness* (rev. ed.). New York: Harper & Row.

Szasz, T. (1987). *Insanity: The idea and its consequences.* New York: Wiley.

Tajfel, H., & Turner, J. C. (1986). The social identity theory of intergroup behavior. In S. Worchel & W. G. Austin (Eds.), *The psychology of intergroup relations* (2nd ed.). Chicago: Nelson-Hall.

Talbot, J. D., Marrett, S., Evans, A. C., Meyer, E., Bushnell, M. C., & Duncan, G. H. (1991). Multiple representations of pain in human cerebral cortex. *Science, 251,* 1355–1358.

Tanner, J. M. (1970). Physical growth. In P. H. Mussen (Ed.), *Carmichael's manual of child psychology* (3rd ed., Vol. 1). New York: Wiley.

Tanner, J. M. (1978). *Fetus into man: Physical growth from conception to maturity.* Cambridge, MA: Harvard University Press.

Tapp, J. (1976). Psychology and the law: An overture. *Annual Review of Psychology, 27,* 358–404.

Task Force on DSM IV. (1991). *DSM IV options book: Work in progress* (9/1/91). Washington, DC: American Psychiatric Association.

Taube, C. A., & Barrett, S. A. (Eds.). (1985). *NIMH: Mental health U.S. 1985.* Washington, DC: U.S. Government Printing Office.

Taylor, F. W. (1911). *The principles of scientific management.* New York: Harper & Bros.

Taylor, S. E. (1991). *Health psychology* (2nd ed.). New York: McGraw-Hill.

Taylor, S. E., & Brown, J. D. (1988). Illusion and well-being: A social psychological perspective on mental health. *Psychological Bulletin, 103,* 193–210.

Teasdale, J. D., & Fogarty, F. J. (1979). Differential effects of induced mood on retrieval of pleasant and unpleasant events from episodic memory. *Journal of Abnormal Psychology, 88,* 248–257.

Teicher, M. H., Glod, C., & Cole, J. O. (1990). Emergence of intense suicidal preoccupation during fluoxetive treatment. *American Journal of Psychiatry, 147,* 207–210.

Telch, M. J., Lucas, J. A., & Nelson, P. (1989). Nonclinical panic in college students: An investigation of prevalence and symptomatology. *Journal of Abnormal Psychology, 98,* 300–306.

Tellegen, A., Lykken, D. T., Bouchard, T. J., Wilcox, K. J., Segal, N. L., & Rich, S. (1988). Personality similarity in twins reared apart and together. *Journal of Personality and Social Psychology, 54,* 1031–1039.

Tennant, C., Goulston, K. J., & Dent, O. F. (1986). The psychological effects of being a prisoner of war: Forty years after release. *American Journal of Psychiatry, 143,* 618–621.

Terrace, H. M., Petitto, L. A., Sanders, R. J., & Bever, T. G. (1979). Can an ape create a sentence? *Science, 206,* 891–902.

Tesser, A. (1988). Toward a self-evaluation maintenance model of social behavior. In L. Berkowitz (Ed.), *Advances in experimental social psychology* (Vol 21). Orlando, FL: Academic Press.

Tesser, A., & Shaffer, D. (1990). Attitudes and attitude change. *Annual Review of Psychology, 41,* 479–523.

Teyber, E. (1992). *Interpersonal process in psychotherapy: A guide for clinical training.* Pacific Grove, CA: Brooks/Cole.

Thatch, W. T., Goodkin, H. P., & Keating, J. G. (1992). The cerebellum and the adaptive coordination of movement. *Annual Review of Neuroscience, 15,* 161–182.

Thayer, R. E. (1987). Energy, tiredness, and tension effects of a sugar snack versus moderate exercise. *Journal of Personality and Social Psychology, 52,* 119–125.

Thibaut, J. W., & Kelley, H. H. (1959). *The social psychology of groups.* New York: Wiley.

Thomas, A., & Chess, S. (1977). *Temperament and development.* New York: Brunner/Mazel.

Thomas, A., & Chess, S. (1980). *The dynamics of psychological development.* New York: Brunner/Mazel.

Thomas, A., & Chess, S. (1986). The New York Longitudinal Study: From infancy to early adult life. In R. Plomin & J. Dunn (Eds.), *The study of temperament: Changes, continuities, and challenges.* New York: Brunner/Mazel.

Thomas, G. V., & Blackman, D. (1991). Are animal experiments on the way out? *Psychologist, 14,* 208–212.

Thomas, L. (1974). *The lives of a cell.* New York: Viking Press.

Thompson, J. G. (1988). *The psychobiology of emotions.* New York: Plenum.

Thompson, R. F. (1985). *The brain: An introduction to neuroscience.* New York: Freeman.

Thompson, R. F., & Gluck, M. A. (1992). Basic substrates of associative learning and memory. In R. G. Lister & H. J. Weingartner (Eds.), *Perspectives on cognitive neuroscience.* New York: Oxford.

Thompson, R. F., & Steinmetz, J. E. (1992). The essential memory trace circuit for a basic form of associative learning. In I. Gormezano & E. A. Wasserman (Eds.), *Learning and memory: The behavioral and biological substrates.* Hillsdale, NJ: Erlbaum.

Thoresen, C. E., & Patillo, J. R. (1988). Exploring the Type A behavior pattern in children and adolescents. In B. K. Houston & C. R. Snyder (Eds.), *Type A behavior pattern: Current trends and future directions.* New York: Wiley.

Thorndike, R. L., Hagen, E. P., & Sattler, J. M. (1986). *The Stanford-Binet Intelligence Scale: Guide for administering and scoring* (4th ed.). Chicago: Riverside.

Thorpy, M. (1990). *Handbook of sleep disorders.* New York: Dekker, Marcel.

Thyer, B. A., Baum, M., & Reid, L. D. (1988). Exposure techniques in the reduction of fear: A comparative review of the procedure in animals and humans. *Advances in Behavior Research and Therapy, 10,* 105–127.

Thyer, B. A., Parrish, R. T., Curtis, G. C., Neese, R. M., & Cameron, O. G. (1985). Ages of onset of *DSM-III* anxiety disorders. *Comprehensive Psychiatry, 26,* 113–122.

Timiras, P. S. (1972). *Developmental psychology and aging.* New York: Macmillan.

Tims, F. M., & Leukefeld, C. G. (Eds.). (1986). *Relapse and recovery in drug abuse* (NIDA Research Monograph 72). Rockville, MD: NIDA.

Tobin, J. J., & Friedman, J. (1983). Spirits, shamans, and nightmare death: Survivor stress in a Hmong refugee. *American Journal of Orthopsychiatry, 53,* 439–448.

Toch, H. (1992). *Violent men: An inquiry into the psychology of violence* (rev. ed.). Washington, DC: American Psychological Association.

Tolman, E. C., & Honzik, C. H. (1930). Introduction and removal of reward and maze performance in rats. *University of California Publications in Psychology, 4,* 257–275.

Tomarken, A. J., Davidson, R. J., & Henriques, J. B. (1990). Resting frontal brain asymmetry predicts affective responses to films. *Journal of Personality and Social Psychology, 59,* 791–801.

Tomarken, A. J., Davidson, R. J., Wheeler, R. E., & Doss, R. C. (1992). Individual differences in anterior brain symmetry and fundamental dimensions of emotion. *Journal of Personality and Social Psychology, 62,* 676–687.

Tomkins, S. S. (1991). *Affect, imagery, consciousness: 3. Anger and fear.* New York: Springer-Verlag.

Tooby, J., & Cosmides, L. (1989). Evolutionary psychology and the generation of culture: 1. Theoretical considerations. *Ethology and Sociobiology, 10,* 29–49.

Triandis, H. C. (1989). Cross-cultural studies of individualism and collectivism. In J. J. Berman (Ed.), *Nebraska Symposium on Motivation 1989* (Vol. 37). Lincoln: University of Nebraska Press.

Tricker, R., & Cook, D. L. (1990). *Athletes at risk: Drugs and sport.* Dubuque, IA: William C. Brown.

Triplett, N. (1898). The dynamogenic factors in pacemaking and competition. *American Journal of Psychology, 9,* 507–533.

Troll, L. E. (1982). *Continuations: Adult development and aging.* Monterey, CA: Brooks/Cole.

Troll, L. E. (1985). *Early and middle adulthood* (2nd ed.). Monterey, CA: Brooks/Cole.

Trope, Y., Cohen, O., & Maoz, Y. (1988). Perceptual and inferential effects of situational inducements on dispositional attribution. *Journal of Personality and Social Psychology, 55,* 165–177.

Tulving, E. (1983). *Elements of episodic memory.* Oxford: Oxford.

Tulving, E., & Pearlstone, Z. (1966). Availability versus accessibility of information in memory for words. *Journal of Verbal Learning and Verbal Behavior, 5,* 381–391.

Tulving, E., & Schacter, D. L. (1990). Timing and human memory systems. *Science, 247,* 301–306.

Tulving, E., & Tholmson, D. M. (1973). Encoding specificity and retrieval processes in episodic memory. *Journal of Experimental Psychology, 80,*

352–373.

Turk, D. C., Meichenbaum, D., & Genest, M. (1983). *Pain and behavioral medicine: A cognitive-behavioral perspective.* New York: Guilford.

Turner, A. M., & Greenough, W. T. (1985). Differential rearing effects on rat visual cortex synapses: 1. Synaptic and neural density and synapses per neuron. *Brain Research, 329,* 195–203.

Tversky, A., & Kahneman, D. (1980). Causal schemas in judgments under uncertainty. In M. Fishbein (Ed.), *Progress in social psychology.* Hillsdale, NJ: Erlbaum.

Tversky, A., & Kahneman, D. (1982). Judgments of and by representativeness. In D. Kahneman, P. Slovic, & A. Tversky (Eds.), *Judgment under uncertainty: Heuristics and biases.* Cambridge, England: Cambridge.

Tversky, B., & Tuchin, M. (1989). A reconciliation of the evidence on eyewitness testimony: Comments on McCloskey and Zaragoza. *Journal of Experimental Psychology: General, 118,* 86–91.

Tye, M. (1991). *The imagery debate.* Cambridge, MA: MIT Press.

Tyler, F. B., Brome, D. R., & Williams, J. E. (1991). *Ethnic validity, ecology, and psychotherapy: A psychosocial competence model.* New York: Plenum.

Underwood, B. J. (1970). A breakdown of the total-time law in free-recall learning. *Journal of Verbal Learning and Verbal Behavior, 9,* 573–580.

Ursin, H. (1978). Activation, coping, and psychosomatics. In H. Ursin, E. Baade, & S. Levine (Eds.), *Psychology of stress: A study of coping men.* New York: Academic Press.

Ursin, H., Baade, E., & Levine, S. (1978). *Psychology of stress: A study of coping men.* New York: Academic Press.

U.S. Public Health Service. (1979). *Healthy people: The Surgeon General's report on health promotion and disease prevention.* Washington, DC: U.S. Government Printing Office.

Uttal, W. R. (1973). *The psychobiology of sensory coding.* New York: Harper & Row.

Vaillant, G. E. (1977). *Adaptation to life.* Boston: Little, Brown.

Valenti, A., & Downing, L. (1975). Differential effects of jury size on verdicts following deliberation as a function of the apparent guilt of the defendant. *Journal of Personality and Social Psychology, 32,* 655–663.

Valle, R. S., & Halling, S. (Eds.). (1989). *Existential-phenomenological perspectives in psychology: Exploring the breadth of human experience.* New York: Plenum.

Vallis, T. M., Howes, J. L., & Miller, P. C. (Eds.). (1991). *The challenge of cognitive therapy.* New York: Plenum.

Vandell, D. L., & Corasaniti, M. A. (1988). The relation between third graders' after-school care and social, academic, and emotional functioning. *Child Development, 59,* 868–875.

Vandell, D. L., Henderson, V. K., & Wilson, K. S. (1988). A longitudinal study of children with daycare experiences of varying quality. *Child Development, 59,* 1286–1292.

Vandell, D. L., & Ramanan, J. (1991). Children of the National Longitudinal Survey of Youth: Choices in after-school care and child development. *Develop-*

mental Psychology, 27, 637–643.

Van den Hout, M., & Merckelbach, H. (1991). Classical conditioning: Still going strong. *Behavioral Psychotherapy, 19,* 59–79.

van der Heijden, A. H. C. (1991). *Selective attention in vision.* New York: Routledge.

Van Deuzen-Smith, E. (1988). *Existential counseling in practice.* Newbury Park, CA: Sage.

van Doornen, L. J. P., & de Geus, E. J. C. (1989). Aerobic fitness and the cardiovascular response to stress. *Psychophysiology, 26,* 17–28.

Vanek, J. (1980). Household work, wage work, and sexual equality. In S. F. Berk (Ed.), *Women and household labor.* Beverly Hills, CA: Sage.

Van Houdenhove, B. (1986). Prevalence and psychodynamic interpretation of premorbid hyperactivity in patients with chronic pain. *Psychotherapy and Psychosomatics, 45,* 195–200.

Van IJzendoorn, M. H., & Kroonenberg, P. M. (1988). Cross-cultural patterns of attachment: A meta-analysis of the Strange Situation. *Child Development, 59,* 147–156.

Verbrugge, L. M. (1979). Marital status and health. *Journal of Marriage and the Family, 41,* 267–285.

Verrillo, R. T., & Verrillo, V. (1985). Sensory and perceptual performance. In N. Charness (Ed.), *Aging and human performance* (pp. 1–46). New York: Wiley.

Vischi, T. R., Jones, K. R., Shank, E. L., & Lima, L. H. (1980). *The alcohol, drug abuse, and mental health national data book.* Rockville, MD: Alcohol, Drug Abuse, and Mental Health Administration.

Vitaliano, P. P., Katon, W., Maiuro, R. D., & Russo, J. (1989). Coping in chest pain patients with and without psychiatric disorders. *Journal of Consulting and Clinical Psychology, 57,* 338–343.

Vitiello, M. V., Carlin, A. S., Becker, J., Barris, B. P., & Dutton, J. (1989). The effect of subliminal Oedipal and competitive stimulation on dart throwing: Another miss. *Journal of Abnormal Psychology, 98,* 54–56.

Von der Heydt, R., Adorjani, C., Hanney, P., & Baumgartner, G. (1978). Disparity, sensitivity, and receptive field incongruity of units in the cat striate cortex. *Experimental Brain Research, 31,* 523–545.

Vurpillot, E. (1968). The development of scanning strategies and their relation to visual differentiations. *Journal of Experimental Child Psychology, 6,* 632–650.

Wachs, T. D. (1992). *The nature of nurture.* Newbury Park, CA: Sage.

Wade, C., & Cirese, S. (1992). *Human sexuality* (2nd ed.). Chicago: Harcourt Brace Jovanovich.

Wade, N. J., & Swanston, M. (1991). *Visual perception: An introduction.* New York: Routledge.

Wagner, E. H., La Croix, A. Z., Buckner, D. M., & Larson, E. B. (1992). Effects of physical activity on health status in older adults: 1. Observational studies. *Annual Review of Public Health, 13,* 368–392.

Walen, S. (1980). Cognitive factors in sexual behavior. *Journal of Sex and Marital Therapy, 6,* 87–101.

Walk, R. D. (1981). *Perceptual development.* Monterey, CA: Brooks/Cole.

Walker, L. J. (1987, April). *Moral orientations: A comparison of two models.* Paper presented at the biennial meetings of the Society for Research in Child Development, Baltimore.

Walker, T. G., & Main, E. C. (1973). Choice-shifts in political decision making: Federal judges and civil liberties cases. *Journal of Applied Social Psychology, 2,* 39–48.

Wall, P. D., & Melzack, R. (Eds.). (1989). *Textbook of pain* (2nd ed.). London: Churchill Livingstone.

Wallbott, H., & Scherer, K. (1988). How universal and specific is emotional experience? Evidence from 27 countries and five continents. In K. Scherer (Ed.), *Facets of emotion: Recent research.* Hillsdale, NJ: Erlbaum.

Wallerstein, J. S. (1984). Children of divorce: Preliminary report of a ten-year follow-up of young children. *American Journal of Orthopsychiatry, 54,* 444–458.

Wallerstein, J. S. (1989). *Second chances.* New York: Tickner & Fields.

Wallerstein, J. S., & Kelly, J. B. (1980). *Surviving the break-up: How children actually cope with divorce.* New York: Basic Books.

Warga, C. (1987, September). Pain's gatekeeper. *Psychology Today,* pp. 50–59.

Wason, P. C., & Johnson-Laird, P. N. (1972). *Psychology of reasoning: Structure and content.* London: Batsford.

Wasserman, E. A. (1989). Pavlovian conditioning: Is temporal contiguity irrelevant? *American Psychologist, 44,* 1550–1551.

Waters, E., Vaughn, B. E., & Egeland, B. R. (1980). Individual differences in mother-attachment relationships at age one. *Child Development, 51,* 208–216.

Watson, D. (1989). Strangers' ratings of the five robust personality factors: Evidence of a surprising convergence with self-report. *Journal of Personality and Social Psychology, 57,* 120–128.

Watson, D., & Clark, L. A. (1992). Affects separable and inseparable: On the hierarchical arrangement of the negative affects. *Journal of Personality and Social Psychology, 62,* 489–505.

Watson, D., & Pennebaker, J. W. (1989). Health complaints, stress, and distress: Exploring the central role of negative affectivity. *Psychological Review, 96,* 234–254.

Watson, D. L., & Tharp, R. G. (1989). *Self-directed behavior: Self-modification for personal adjustment* (4th ed.). Pacific Grove, CA: Brooks/Cole.

Watson, J. B. (1924). *Behaviorism.* New York: People's Institute.

Weaver, C. (1980). Job satisfaction in the United States in the 1970s. *Journal of Applied Psychology, 65,* 364–367.

Webb, E. J., Campbell, D. T., Schwartz, R. D., & Sechrest, L. (1966). *Unobtrusive measures: Nonreactive research in the social sciences.* Chicago: Rand McNally.

Webb, W. B. (1974). Sleep as an adaptive response. *Perceptual and Motor Skills, 38,* 1023–1027.

Weg, R. B. (1983). Changing physiology of aging: Normal and pathological. In D. S. Woodruff & J. E. Birren (Eds.), *Aging: Scientific perspectives and social issues* (2nd ed.; pp. 242–284). Monterey, CA: Brooks/Cole.

Weinberger, M., Hiner, S. L., & Tierney, W. M. (1987). In support of hassles as a measure of stress in predicting health outcomes. *Journal of Behavioral Medicine, 10,* 19–31.

Weiner, B. (1992). *Human motivation: Metaphors, theories, and research.* Newbury Park, CA: Sage.

Weiner, R. D., & Coffey, C. E. (1988). Indications for the use of electroconvulsive therapy. In A. J. Francis & R. E. Hales (Eds.), *Review of Psychiatry* (Vol. 7). Washington, DC: American Psychatric Press.

Weinstein, C. S. (1991). The classroom as a social context for learning. *Annual Review of Psychology, 42,* 493–525.

Weiss, J. M., Glazer, H. I., & Pohoresky, L. A. (1976). Coping behavior and neurochemical change in rats: An alternative explanation for the original ''learned helplessness'' experiments. In G. Serban & A. King (Eds.), *Animal models in human psychobiology.* New York: Plenum.

Weissman, M. M., Geshon, E. S., Kidd, K. K., Prusoff, B. A., Leckman, J. F., Dibble, E., Hamovit, J., Thompson, W. D., Pauls, D. L., & Guroff, J. J. (1984). Psychiatric disorders in the relatives of probands with affective disorders. *Archives of General Psychiatry, 41,* 13–21.

Weitzman, E. D., Czeisler, C. A., Zimmerman, J. C., Moore-Ede, M. C., & Ronda, J. M. (1983). Biological rhythms in man: Internal organization of the physiology during non-restrained (free-running) conditions and applied to delayed sleep phase syndrome. In M. H. Chase & E. D. Weitzman (Eds.), *Sleep disorders: Basic and clinical research.* New York: Spectrum.

Wells, G. L. (1984). The psychology of lineup identifications. *Journal of Applied Social Psychology, 14,* 89–103.

Wells, G. L. (1988). *Eyewitness identification: A system handbook.* Toronto: Carswell Legal Publications.

Wells, G. L., & Luus, C. A. E. (1990). Police lineups as experiments: Social methodology as a framework for properly conducted lineups. *Personality and Social Psychology Bulletin, 16,* 106–117.

Wells, R. A., & Gianetti, V. J. (Eds.). (1990). *Handbook of the brief psychotherapies.* New York: Plenum.

Wender, P. H., Kety, S. S., Rosenthal, D., Schulsinger, F., Ortmann, J., & Lunde, I. (1986). Psychiatric disorders in the biological and adoptive families of adopted individuals with affective disorders. *Archives of General Psychiatry, 43,* 923–929.

Wenzlaff, R. M., Wegner, D. M., & Roper, D. W. (1988). Depression and mental control: The resurgence of unwanted negative thoughts. *Journal of Personality and Social Psychology, 55,* 882–892.

Werker, J. F., & Tees, R. C. (1992). The organization and reorganization of human speech perception. *Annual Review of Neuroscience, 15,* 86–101.

Werner, E. E. (1989a). Children of the Garden Island. *Scientific American, 260* (4), 106–111.

Werner, E. E. (1989b). High risk children in young adulthood: A longitudinal study from birth to 32 years. *American Journal of Orthopsychiatry, 59,* 72–81.

Werner, E. E., & Smith, R. S. (1982). *Vulnerable but invincible: A longitudinal study of resilient children.* New York: McGraw-Hill.

West, S. G., Whitney, G., & Schnedler, R. (1975). Helping a motorist in distress: The effects of sex, race, and neighborhood. *Journal of Personality and Social Psychology, 31,* 691–698.

Westen, D. (1990). Psychoanalytic approaches to personality. In L. A. Pervin (Ed.), *Handbook of personality: Theory and research.* New York: Guilford.

Westoff, C. F. (1980). Women's reaction to pregnancy. *Family Planning Perspective, 12,* 135–139.

Wexler, K., & Culicover, P. W. (1980). *Formal principles of language acquisition.* Cambridge, MA: MIT Press.

Wexley, K. N., & Yukl, G. A. (1977). *Organizational behavior and personnel psychology.* Homewood, IL: Irwin.

Whalen, R. E., & Simon, N. G. (1984). Biological motivation. *Annual Review of Psychology, 35,* 257–276.

Whisman, M. A., Miller, I. W., Norman, W. H., & Keitner, G. I. (1991). Cognitive therapy with depressed inpatients: Specific effects on dysfunctional cognitions. *Journal of Consulting and Clinical Psychology, 59,* 282–288.

Whitbourne, S. K. (1985). *The aging body: Physiological changes and psychological consequences.* New York: Springer-Verlag.

White, G. L., & Kight, T. D. (1984). Misattribution of arousal and attraction: Effects of salience of explanations for arousal. *Journal of Experimental Social Psychology, 20,* 55–64.

White, L., Tursky, B., & Schwartz, G. E. (Eds.). (1985). *Placebo: Theory, research and mechanism.* New York: Guilford.

White, M. (1987). *The Japanese educational challenge: A commitment to children.* New York: Free Press.

White, N. M., & Milner, P. M. (1992). The psychobiology of reinforcers. *Annual Review of Psychology, 43,* 443–472.

White, R. K. (1968). *Nobody wanted war.* Garden City, NY: Doubleday.

Whitley, B. E., Jr. (1990). The relationship of heterosexuals' attributions for the causes of behavior to attitudes toward lesbians and gay men. *Personality and Social Psychology Bulletin, 16,* 369–377.

Whitmont, E. C., & Perera, S. B. (1990). *Dreams: A portal to the source.* New York: Routledge.

Whorf, B. L. (1966). Science and linguistics. In J. D. Carroll (Ed.), *Language, thought, and reality: Selected writings of Benjamin Lee Whorf.* Cambridge, MA: MIT Press.

Wicker, A. W. (1969). Attitudes versus actions: The relationship between verbal and overt behavioral responses to attitude objects. *Journal of Social Issues, 25,* 41–78.

Widom, C. S. (1983). A methodology for studying noninstitutionalized psychopaths. In R. D. Hare & D. A. Schaling (Eds.), *Psychopathic behavior: Approaches to research.* Chichester, England: Wiley.

Wiedenfeld, S. A., O'Leary, A., Bandura, A., Brown, S., Levine, S., & Raska, K. (1990). Impact of perceived self-efficacy in coping with stressors on components of the immune system. *Journal of Personality and Social Psychology, 59,* 1082–1094.

Wiens, A. N., & Menustik, C. E. (1983). Treatment outcome and patient characteristics in an aversion therapy program for alcoholism. *American Psychologist, 38,* 1089–1096.

Wigdor, A. K., & Garner, W. R. (1982). *Ability testing: Uses, consequences, and controversies.* Washington, DC: National Academy Press.

Wiggins, J. S., & Pincus, A. L. (1992). Personality: Structure and assessment. *Annual Review of Psychology, 43*, 473–504.

Wilcoxon, H. C., Dragoin, W. B., & Kral, P. A. (1971). Illness-induced aversions in rat and quail: Relative salience of visual and gustatory cues. *Science, 171*, 826–828.

Wilkie, J. R. (1981). The trend toward delayed parenthood. *Journal of Marriage and the Family, 43*, 583–591.

Williams, C. N., Solomon, S. D., & Bartone, P. (1988). Primary prevention in aircraft disasters: Integrating research and practice. *American Psychologist, 43*, 730–739.

Williams, J. E., Bennett, S. M., & Best, D. L. (1975). Awareness and expression of sex stereotypes in young children. *Developmental Psychology, 11*, 635–642.

Williams, J. M. (1992). *Applied sport psychology: Peak performance to personal growth* (2nd ed.). Menlo Park, CA: Mayfield Press.

Williams, K. D., Nida, S. A., Baca, L. D., & Latané, B. (1989). Social loafing and swimming: Effects of identifiability on individual and relayed performance of intercollegiate swimmers. *Basic and Applied Social Psychology, 10*, 73–82.

Williams, R. L., Moore, C. A., & Karacan, I. (Eds.). (1988). *Sleep disorders: Diagnosis and treatment* (2nd ed.). New York: Wiley.

Williams, R. M. (1970). *American society: A sociological interpretation.* New York: Knopf.

Williams, S. L., Kinney, P. J., & Falbo, J. (1989). Generalization of therapeutic changes in agoraphobia: The role of perceived self-efficacy. *Journal of Consulting and Clinical Psychology, 57*, 436–442.

Willis, S. L. (1989). Adult intelligence. In S. Hunter & M. Sundel (Eds.), *Midlife myths: Issues, findings, and practice implications* (pp. 97–111). Newbury Park, CA: Sage.

Wills, T. A. (1991). Social comparison processes in coping and health. In C. R. Snyder & D. R. Forsyth (Eds.), *Handbook of social and clinical psychology: The health perspective.* New York: Pergamon.

Wilson, G. T., & Walsh, B. T. (1991). Eating disorders in the DSM-IV. *Journal of Abnormal Psychology, 100*, 362–365.

Wilson, S. C., & Barber, T. X. (1983). The fantasy-prone personality: Implications for understanding imagery, hypnosis, and parapsychological phenomena. In A. A. Sheikh (Ed.), *Imagery: Current theory, research and applications.* New York: Wiley.

Wincze, J. P., & Carey, M. P. (1991). *Sexual dysfunction: A guide for assessment and treatment.* New York: Guilford.

Windle, M., Barnes, G. M., & Welte, J. (1989). Causal models of adolescent substance abuse: An examination of gender differences using distribution-free estimators. *Journal of Personality and Social Psychology, 56*, 132–142.

Wingfield, A., & Byrnes, D. L. (1981). *The psychology of human memory.* New York: Academic Press.

Winson, J. (1990). The meaning of dreams. *Scientific American, 260* (11), 86–96.

Winter, D. G. (1988). The power motive in women and men. *Journal of Personality and Social Psychology, 54*, 510–519.

WISC III: Wechsler Intelligence Scale for Children—

Third Edition. (1991). San Antonio, TX: Psychological Corporation.

Wise, R. A., & Rompre, P.-P. (1989). Brain dopamine and reward. *Annual Review of Psychology, 40*, 191–226.

Wissler, R. L., & Saks, M. J. (1985). On inefficacy of limiting instructions: When jurors use prior conviction evidence to decide on guilt. *Law and Human Behavior, 9*, 37–48.

Wolberg, L. R. (1967). *The technique of psychotherapy* (2nd ed.). New York: Grune & Stratton.

Wolf, E. M., & Crowther, J. H. (1992). An evaluation of behavioral and cognitive-behavioral group interventions for the treatment of bulimia nervosa in women. *International Journal of Eating Disorders, 11*, 3–16.

Wolfe, L. (1980). The sexual profile of that Cosmopolitan girl. *Cosmopolitan, 189*, 254–257, 263–265.

Wolff, P. H. (1969). The natural history of crying and other vocalizations in early infancy. In B. M. Foss (Ed.), *Determinants of infant behavior* (Vol. 4). London: Methuen.

Wolman, B. B. (Ed.). (1985). *Handbook of intelligence: Theory, measurement, and applications.* New York: Wiley-Interscience.

Wolpe, J. (1958). *Psychotherapy by reciprocal inhibition.* Stanford, CA: Stanford University Press.

Wong, D. F., et al. (1986). Positron emission tomography reveals elevated D_2 dopamine receptors in drug-naive schizophrenics. *Science, 234*, 1558–1563.

Wong, M. M., & Csikszentmihalyi, M. (1991). Affiliation motivation and daily experience: Some issues on gender differences. *Journal of Personality and Social Psychology, 60*, 154–164.

Woody, C. D. (1986). Understanding the cellular basis of memory and learning. *Annual Review of Psychology, 37*, 433–493.

Woolfolk, A. (1990). *Educational Psychology* (4th ed.). Englewood Cliffs, NJ: Prentice-Hall.

Worth, L. T., Allison, S. T., & Messick, D. M. (1987). Impact of a group decision on perception of one's own and others' attitudes. *Journal of Personality and Social Psychology, 53*, 673–682.

Wortman, C. B., & Silver, R. C. (1989). The myths of coping with loss. *Journal of Consulting and Clinical Psychology, 57*, 349–357.

Wright, A. A. (1992). The study of animal cognitive processes. In W. K. Honig & J. G. Fetterman (Eds.), *Cognitive aspects of stimulus control.* Hillsdale, NJ: Erlbaum.

Wright, B. A. (1991). Labeling: The need for greater person-environment individuation. In C. R. Snyder & D. R. Forsyth (Eds.), *Handbook of social and clinical psychology: The health perspective.* New York: Pergamon.

Wylie, R. C. (1989). *Measures of self-concept.* Lincoln: University of Nebraska Press.

Yablonsky, L. (1962). *The violent gang.* New York: Macmillan.

Yang, K. S. (1986). Chinese personality and its change. In M. H. Bond (Ed.), *The psychology of the Chinese people.* New York: Oxford.

Yankelovich, D. (1981). *New rules: Searching for self-fulfillment in a world turned upside-down.* New York: Random House.

Yerkes, R. M., & Dodson, J. D. (1908). The relation of strength of stimulus to rapidity of habit-formation.

Journal of Comparative Neurological Psychology, 18, 459–482.

Yin, T. C. T., & Kuwada, S. (1984). Neuronal mechanisms of binaural interaction. In G. M. Edelman, W. M. Cowan, & W. E. Gall (Eds.), *Dynamic aspects of neocortical function.* New York: Wiley.

Yinon, Y., & Dovrat, N. (1987). The reciprocity-arousing potential of the requestor's occupation and helping behavior. *Journal of Applied Social Psychology, 17*, 429–435.

Young, T. Y., Lawson, G. W., & Gacono, C. B. (1987). Clinical aspects of phencyclidine (PCP). *International Journal of the Addictions, 22*, 1–15.

Young, V. (1970). Family and childhood in a southern Negro community. *American Anthropologist, 72*, 269–288.

Zaccaro, S. J., Foti, R. J., & Kerney, D. A. (1991). Self-monitoring and trait-based variance in leadership: An investigation of leader flexibility across multiple group situations. *Journal of Applied Psychology, 76*, 308–315.

Zahn-Waxler, C., Radke-Yarrow, M., & King, R. A. (1979). Child rearing and children's prosocial initiations towards victims of distress. *Child Development, 50*, 319–330.

Zahn-Waxler, C., Radke-Yarrow, M., Wagner, E., & Chapman, M. (1992). Development of concern for others. *Developmental Psychology, 28*, 126–136.

Zajonc, R. B. (1965). Social facilitation. *Science, 149*, 269–274.

Zajonc, R. B. (1980a). Compresence. In P. Paulus (Ed.), *The psychology of group influence.* Hillsdale, NJ: Erlbaum.

Zajonc, R. B. (1980b). Feeling and thinking: Preferences need no inferences. *American Psychologist, 35*, 151–175.

Zajonc, R. B. (1984). On the primacy of affect. *American Psychologist, 39*, 117–123.

Zajonc, R. B. (1985). Emotion and facial efference: A theory reclaimed. *Science, 228*, 15–21.

Zajonc, R. B., Murphy, S. T., & Inglehart, M. (1989). Feeling and facial efference: Implications of a vascular theory of emotion. *Psychological Review, 96*, 395–416.

Zanna, M. P., & Cooper, J. (1974). Dissonance and the pill: An attribution approach to studying the arousal properties of dissonance. *Journal of Personality and Social Psychology, 29*, 703–709.

Zatzick, D. F., & Dinsdale, J. E. (1990). Cultural variations in response to painful stimuli. *Psychosomatic Medicine, 52*, 544–557.

Zautra, A. J., Okun, M. A., Robinson, S. E., Lee, D., Roth, S. H., & Emmanual, J. (1989). Life stress and lymphocyte alterations among patients with rheumatoid arthritis. *Health Psychology, 8*, 1–14.

Zelnick, M., Kantner, J. F., & Ford, K. (1981). *Sex and pregnancy in adolescence.* Beverly Hills, CA: Sage.

Zilbergeld, B., & Evans, M. (1980, May). The inadequacy of Masters and Johnson. *Psychology Today*, pp. 29–43.

Zillmann, D. (1979). *Hostility and aggression.* New York: Halsted Press.

Zillmann, D. (1984). *Connections between sex and aggression.* Hillsdale, NJ: Erlbaum.

Zillmann, D. (1989). Pornography, research, and public policy. In D. Zillman & J. Bryant (Eds.), *Pornography: Research advances and policy consider-*

ations. Hillsdale, NJ: Erlbaum.

Zillmann, D., & Bryant, J. (Eds.). (1989). *Pornography: Research advances and policy considerations.* Hillsdale, NJ: Erlbaum.

Zimbardo, P. G. (1972). Pathology of imprisonment. *Society, 9*(6), 4–8.

Zimbardo, P. G., Haney, C., Banks, W. C., & Jaffe, D. (1973, April 8). The mind is a formidable jailer: A Pirandellian prison. *New York Times Magazine,* pp. 12–16.

Zimbardo, P. G., & Leippe, M. R. (1991). *The psychology of attitude change and social influence.*

New York: McGraw-Hill.

Zinbarg, R. E., Barlow, D. H., Brown, T. A., & Hertz, R. M. (1992). Cognitive-behavioral approaches to the nature and treatment of anxiety disorders. *Annual Review of Psychology, 43,* 235–268.

Zirkel, S. (1992). Developing independence in a life transition: Investing the self in the concerns of the day. *Journal of Personality and Social Psychology, 62,* 506–521.

Zivian, M. T., & Darjes, M. T. (1983). Free recall by in-school and out-of-school adults: Performance and metamemory. *Developmental Psychology, 19,*

513–520.

Zuckerman, M. (1975). Belief in a just world and altruistic behavior. *Journal of Personality and Social Psychology, 31,* 972–976.

Zuckerman, M. (1991). *Psychobiology of personality.* New York: Cambridge.

Zuckerman, M., Gioioso, C., & Tellini, S. (1988). Control orientation, self-monitoring, and preference for image versus quality approach to advertising. *Journal of Research in Personality, 22,* 89–100.

Name Index

Subject Index

Page numbers in italics refer to figures, and those followed by "t" refer to tables.

Hidden observer, 246
Higher order conditioning, 269
Hindbrain, 71–73
Hippocampus, *72,* 74, 77, 308
    damage to, and memory, 307
Hispanic Americans, intelligence and, 359–360
HIV virus. *See* Human immunodeficiency virus
    (HIV)
Hmong sudden death syndrome case study, 37–38
Homelessness, mental illness and, 564–565
Homeostasis, 372
·Homosexuality:
    AIDS transmission and, 658
    genetics and, 387
    percentages of, 385
    theories on cause of, 386–387
Homozygous genes, 101
Hormones, 86–87
    emotions and, 406
    gender differences of intelligence and, 360
    puberty and, 137
    stress and, 470
Hospice organizations, 165
Hospitalization syndrome, 563
Hostile aggression, 624
Human growth hormone (HGH), delaying aging
    process and, 153
Human immunodeficiency virus (HIV), 88, *89*
Humanistic perspective, 18–19
    on anxiety disorders, 508–509
    assessment techniques used, 461t
    on depression, 21, 516
    history of, 18
    intrapsychic, 18
    on motivation, 371–372
    on psychoactive drugs, 257
    on treatment of psychological disorders, *536,*
        539–542
    on personality, 446–449
    on psychological disorders, 498–499
    self-actualization, 18
    summary of, 19t
Humanistic psychotherapies, *536,* 539–542
    client-centered therapy, 540–541
    Gestalt therapy, 541–542
Human Sexual Inadequacy (Masters/Johnson),
    553
Human Sexual Response (Masters/Johnson), 382
Humors, 435
Hunger:
    chemical control, 374
    as motivation, 372–375
    neural control and, 372–373
    regulation of eating, 372–375
    set point theory, 374, 375
Hypercolumns, 182, *183*
Hyperopia, 177
Hypersomnia, 239
Hypnosis, 242–246, 537
    crime eyewitnesses and, 244
    dissociation and, 246
    hidden observer, 246
    history of, 242–243
    imagination and, 246
    increased pain tolerance and, 244–245
    memory and, 243–244
    physiological effects of, 244

    role theory of, 246
    scientific study of, 243
    theories of, 245–246
Hypnotic susceptibility scales, 243
Hypothalamus, 86
    aggression and, 625
    immune system and, 89–90
    motivation and emotion, 73–74
    regulation of eating and, 373–374
    sexual hormones and, 381
Hypothesis, 30–31
    inductive reasoning and, 338–339
Hysteria, 11–12

I

Iconic storage, 303
Id, 442
Ideal self, 131
Identical twins. *See also* Twin studies
    behavioral traits and, 10
Identification, 120
Identity achievement, 142–143
    foreclosure, 142
    moratorium and, 142
Identity crises, in Erikson's psychosocial theory,
    121–122
Idiot savants, 354
Illness, stress and, 475–476
Illusions:
    false perceptual hypotheses, 208–210
    perceptual constancies as basis for, 210–211
    Ponzo illusion, 210, *211*
Imagery, problem solving and, 342–343
Imaginal coding, 312–314
    eidetic imagery, 313–314
    use of schemas in, 313
Imaginal thought, 331
Imagination, hypnosis and, 246
Imitation:
    neonate's ability of, 104–105
    during sensorimotor stage, 111
    television and, 111
Immune system, 87–92
    cells and functions of, 88
    classical conditioning and, 267–268
    depression and, 90
    disorders of, 88–89
    emotional restraint and stress, 90
    enhancement of, 92
    nervous system and, 89–90
    positive emotions and, 90–91
    stress and, 90, 475–476, 481
Implicit memory, 301
Implicit personality theories, 608–609
    central traits, 608–609
    peripheral traits, 609
Impulse control disorders, 502t
Incubation, 344
Independent variables, 43–44
    manipulating one, 44–46
    manipulating two, 46–47
India, pain and hook-hanging ritual, 219, *220*
Indiscriminate attachment, 124, *125*
Individualism, 17
Individual psychology (Adler), 444
Inductive reasoning, 336–339

    definition of, 332
    heuristics and decision making, 340–342
    problem solving and, 336–339
Indulgent parents, 130
Industrial psychology, 6t
Industry, in Erikson's psychosocial theory, 121
Infants:
    attachment and, 124–127
    emotional expression of, 408
    insecurely attached, 125–126
    securely attached, 125, 126
    self-awareness and, 131
    sex typing and, 130
    temperament, 122
Information-processing theory, of cognitive
    development and, 114–115
Information-processing theory, of memory,
    301–302
    encoding, 301
    retrieval, 301
    storage, 301
Informed consent, 53–54
Initiation ceremonies, 136
Initiative, in Erikson's psychosocial theory, 121
Insanity, 503
Insanity plea, 503
Insecurely attached infants:
    anxious-avoidant, 125–126
    anxious-resistant, 125, 126
Insight, 14
    in psychoanalysis, 537
Insomnia, 239
    delayed sleep phase syndrome, 239
Instinctive drift, 292
Institutional treatment, 562–563
Instrumental aggression, 624
Instrumental behaviors, 411–413
    emotional arousal and performance, 411–412
    role of task difficulty, 412–413
Integrated coping response, 490
Integration, principle of, 106
Integrity, in psychosocial theory, 146
Intellectualization, as defense mechanism, 444t
Intelligence, 346–363
    changes in adulthood, 157–159
    cognitively disabled, 361–362
    crystallized vs. fluid intelligence, 353
    definition of, 347
    gender differences in cognitive skills, 360–361
    genetics and environment, 356–358
    measured in longitudinal studies, 156
    measured in cross-sectional studies, 156–157
    measuring, 347–351
    nature of, 351–356
    physical exercise in elderly and, 158
    psychometric approach, 352–354
    racial differences in, 359–360
    theory of multiple intelligence, 354
    triarchic theory of intelligence, 355–356
Intelligence quotient (IQ), 348
    standardization of, 348
Intelligence tests:
    achievement tests vs. aptitude tests, 350–351
    Binet's method of, 347–349
    group intelligence tests, 349–350
    as mental age scales, 348
    predictive validity of, 351

behavior correlates of, 393
  gender, 393–394
Power of suggestion, 244
Preconscious, 232
Preconscious mind, 442
Preconventional level, of moral reasoning, 140, 141t
Preferential looking procedure, 103, *104*
Pregnancy:
  drug use during, 102
  older women and, 162
Prejudice, 610–611
  definition of, 610
  realistic conflict theory and, 610
  social identity theory, 610
Premature ejaculation, 554
Premises, in deductive reasoning, 332
Prenatal development, 101–103
  maternal drug use and, 102
  maternal illness during, 102
  stages of, 102
Preoperational stage, of cognitive development:
  conservation, 112, *113*
  egocentrism, 100t, 112–113
  object classification, 110t, 112
  object representation, 110t, 112
Preparedness:
  fear and, 292–293
  in learning, 292
Preventive mental health, 564–565
Primacy effect, 306
Primary appraisal, 469
Primary mental abilities, 352–353
Primary prevention, 565
Primary reinforcers, 270
Primary sex characteristics, 137
Priming, 312
Prioritizing, 23
Prison-simulation study, 570
Proactive interference, 324–325
Problem finding, in adult cognitive development, 156
Problem-focused coping strategies, 477–478
  controllability and coping efficacy, 478–479
Problem solving:
  algorithms and, 339–340
  guidelines for creative, 343–345
  heuristics, 340–342
  imagery, 342–343
  inductive reasoning and, 337–339
Problem-solving schemas:
  role of, in expertise, 335–336
  as substitute for deductive reasoning, 334–335
Procedural memory, 301, 308
Professional specialization in Piaget cognitive development theory, 156
Program evaluation, 635–640
  definition of, 635
  designing evaluation research, 636–638
  evaluation of cooperative learning programs, 639–640
  formative evaluation, 637
  multiracial programs, 638–639
  outcome evaluation, 637–638
Progressive muscle relaxation, 489, 490–491
Projection, as defense mechanism, 444t
Projective hypothesis, 459
Projective tests, 459–460

Propositional thought, 331
Propositions, 331–332
Prosocial behavior, 617–623
  altruism and empathy, 621–622
  behavioral perspective, 620
  bystander intervention, 618–619
  increasing likelihood and effectiveness of, 622–623
  just world hypothesis, 620–621
  negative state relied model, 622
  sociobiological perspective, 620–621
  victim characteristics, 619–620
Protective factors, 479–487
Prototypes, 331–332
Proximity,
  in Gestalt perception theory, 205, *206*
  interpersonal attraction, 611–612
Proximodistal principle, 106
Psychoactive drugs, compensatory response, 268
Psychiatric social workers, 536
Psychiatrists, 536
Psychoactive drugs, 249–257
  addiction, 249
  classical conditioning and tolerance/drug overdoses, 268
  definition of, 249
  dependence, 249
  depressants, 249–251
  effects of major, 254t
  hallucinogens, 253–255
  marijuana, 255
  mechanisms of drug action, 249–251
  multiple determinants of drug effects, 257
  narcotics, 252
  neurotransmitters and, 66
  overcoming addiction, 255–257
  stimulant, 251–253
  tolerance, 249
Psychoanalysis, 10–12, 537–539
  aggression drives, 12
  free association, 11–12, 537
  hysteria, 11–12
  insight, 537
  interpretation, 539
  interpretation of dreams, 537
  repression, 12
  resistance, 537–538
  sexual drives, 12
  transference, 538–539
Psychoanalytic theory:
  on anger, 516
  on antisocial personality disorders, 531
  anxiety and, 508
  assessment techniques used, 461t
  defense mechanisms, 508
  on depression, 516
  on dissociative disorders, 511
  evaluation of, 445–446
  Freud's theory, 441–443
  neoanalytic theories, 443–445
  on schizophrenia, 515
Psychobiology:
  aggression hypothesis, 629–630
  memory and, 307–310
  treatments for sexual dysfunction, 553–554
Psychodynamic perspective, 10–12. *See also* Psychoanalysis
  on aggression, 628–629

on antisocial personality disorder, 531
on anxiety, 508
definition of, 10–12
on depression, 21, 516
on dissociative disorders, 511
on dreaming, 238
on emotion-eliciting stimuli, 402
on forgetting, 325
on hypnosis, 246
on learning, 269–270
on motivation, 370–371
on psychoactive drugs, 257
on treatment of psychological disorders, *536, 537*
on personality, 441–446
on psychological disorders, 498
on schizophrenia, 515
summary of, 19t
on unconscious influences on emotion, 422–424
Psychodynamic psychotherapies, *536, 537*–539
  brief psychodynamic therapies, 539
  psychoanalysis, 537–539
Psychogenic amnesia, 510
Psychogenic fugue, 510
Psychological disorders, 495–531. *See also* Psychotherapies
  anxiety disorders, 504–510
  asylums, 497–498
  conversion disorders, 511–512
  critical issues in diagnostic labeling, 501, 503–504
  definition of abnormal behavior, 499–500
  demonological perspective, 497
  depressive disorders, 513–521
  diagnosis of abnormal behavior, 500–504
  dissociative disorders, 510–511
  early biological and psychological views, 497
  early medical approaches, 498
  historical perspective, 496–499
  personality disorders, 526–531
  psychophysiological disorders, 511–513
  schizophrenic disorders, 521–526
Psychological perspectives:
  causal interaction and, 19–21
  comparison of, 19
  integration of, 19–20
  on psychological disorders, 498–499
Psychologists:
  as expert witnesses, 650–651
  major speciality areas, 5, 6t
  work settings of, 5, 6t
Psychology: *See also* Behavioral perspective; Biological perspective; Cognitive perspective; Humanistic perspective; Psychodynamic perspective
  definition of, 4
  major speciality areas within, 5, 6t
  perspectives in, 5–19
  scope of, 4–5
Psychometrics, 352–354
  cognitive process theories, 355–356
  crystallized vs. fluid intelligence, 353
  definition of, 352
  g factor, 352
  primary mental abilities, 352–353
  theory of multiple intelligence, 354
Psychomotor retardation, 513

Psychoneuroimmunology, 87
Psychopharmacology, 557
Psychophysics, 172
Psychophysiological disorders, 476, 511–513
Psychoses, 498
Psychosexual development, stages of, 120–121
Psychosocial development, stages of, 146–147
Psychosocial theory (Erikson), 121–122, 146–147
   identity crises and, 121
   stages of, 121–122
   successful resolution of stages and wisdom of
     aged, 146–147
Psychosomatic disorders, classical conditioning
   and, 266–267
Psychotherapies:
   behavioral perspective on, *536,* 546–550
   biological perspective on, *536,* 557–560
   cognitive perspective on, *536,* 542–545
   deinstitutional movement, 563–564
   evaluating, 554–557
   factors affecting the outcome of, 556–557
   guidelines for seeking psychological treatment,
     565–566
   humanistic perspective on, *536,* 539–542
   institutional treatment, 562–563
   meta-analysis of, 555–556
   preventative mental health, 564–565
   psychodynamic, *536,* 537–539
   therapist/client relationship, 535–536
Psychotherapy by Reciprocal Inhibition (Wolpe),
   547
Psychotomimetic drugs, 253–255
Puberty, 137
Punishment, 279–281
   aversive, 279–280
   definition of, 279
   vs. extinction, 279
   internal self-evaluation as, 287–288
   negative aspects of, 280
   response cost, 279, 280–281
   therapeutic use of, 549–550
Pupil, 176

Q

Quantitative psychology, 6t

R

Race, intelligence and, 359–360
Radical behaviorists, 15–16
Rape trauma syndrome, 473
Rational–emotive therapy (Ellis), 543–544, 545t
Rationalization, as defense mechanism, 444t
Rational–theoretical approach, 457–458
Ratio schedules, 274
Reaction formation, as defense mechanism, 444t
Reaction range, 357–358
   genetic–environmental influences, 357–358
Reactivity, 49
Realistic conflict theory, 610
Reality principle, 442
Reason and Emotion in Psychotherapy (Ellis),
   543
Reasoned action, theory of, 579
Reasoning:
   deductive, 332–336
   inductive, and problem solving, 337–339

Recall, 299
   mood-congruent, 318
   primacy effect, 306
   recency effect, 306
Recency effect, 306
Receptor site, 64
Recessive genes, 101
Reciprocal causal relations, 21
Reciprocal determinism, 451–452
Recognition, 299
Recognition-by-components theory, 208
Reconstructive memory, 318–320
   schemas and, 318
Reference groups, 571
Reflected appraisals, 603
Reflecting, in client-centered therapy, 540
Reflexes:
   present at birth, 104, 105t
   rate of, and meditation, 242
   sensorimotor stage and, 110–111
Refractory period, 63, 383–384
Regression, 515
Rehearsal, memory and, 114–115
Reinforcement:
   conditioning, 270
   definition of, 270
   internal self-evaluation as, 287–288
   negative, 277–279
   positive, 270
   primary, 270
   secondary, 270
   self-administered positive, 284
Reinforcement, schedules of, 274–277
   continuous reinforcement, 274
   effect of, on learning and extinction, 276–277
   fixed-interval (FI), 276
   fixed-ratio (FR), 274–275
   intermittent, 274
   interval, 274
   ratio, 274
   variable-interval (VI), 276
Relapse prevention, 257
Relationships, close. *See* Close relationships
Relaxation, systematic desensitization and, 547
Relaxation response:
   cognitive, 242
   somatic, 242
Relearning, 299–300
Reliability, types of, for personality measures,
   455
Reminiscence, 324
REM rebound effect, 238
REM sleep, 236
   as erasing process, 239
   memory and, 238–239
Representative heuristic, 340–341
Representative sample, 36
Repression, 12, 325
   as defense mechanism, 443, 444t
Research. *See also* Scientific research
   applied, 5
   basic, 5
   goals of, 5
Residual rules, 500
Resistance, 537–538, 566
Response cost, 279, 280–281
Resting potential, 62, *63*

Reticular formation:
   attention and, 73
   as brain's gatekeeper, 72–73
   effect of alcohol on, 250
   LSD and, 253
   sleep and wakefulness, 73
Retina, 176
Retirement, 160
Retrieval, in memory, 301, 315–320
   context-dependent memory, 317
   distinctiveness, 316
   encoding specificity principle, 317
   levels of processing and, 316
   mood-congruent recall 318
   reconstructive process and, 318–320
   state-dependent, 318
   transfer-appropriate processing, 317
Retrieval cues, 315–316
Retroactive interference, 324–325
Retrograde amnesia, 325
Reuptake, 64
Revolving door phenomenon, 563–564
Rewards, intrinsic/extrinsic motivation and, 369
Rheumatoid arthritis, 89
Right hemisphere, of brain:
   child abuse and language development, 96
   damage to, 78
   depression and, 515–516
   emotions and, 78–79, 405
   left-handed people and, 78
   mental, artistic, spatial abilities and, 78
   panic attacks and, 507–508
   patterns and, 80
   split-brain research and, 79–80
Rods, 177–178
   regeneration rates of, and dark adaptation,
     179–180
   wavelength and brightness sensitivity, 179
Role confusion, during adolescence, 142–143
Role theory of hypnosis, 246
Rooting reflex, 105t
Rorschach inkblots, 459–460

S

Sampling, 36–37
   representative, 36
Scatter plots, 42, *43*
Schemas, 311–312, 313
   in Piagetian theory, 109
   reconstructive memory and, 318
Schizophrenic disorders, 66, 502t, 521–526
   acute vs. chronic, 522
   biological causal factors, 523–525
   categorization of, 522–523
   characteristics of, 522
   cognitive causal factors, 526
   dopamine hypothesis, 524
   drug therapy, 558
   environmental causal factors, 515–516
   genetic factors, 524–525
   intrapsychic causal factors, 515
   major subtypes of, 523t
   negative symptoms, 523
   positive symptoms, 523
   token economy in therapy, 548
   ventricles and, 523–524

Acknowledgments

Fig. 1.1 (left) © OneWorld Photographic, 1992; (top right) © Alan Tannenbaum, Sygma; (bottom right) © Frank Siteman 1992. Fig. 1.2 © Bob Daemmrich Photography. Fig. 1.3 © Dave Black Photography. Fig. 1.7 © Jim Amos, Photo Researchers, Inc. Fig. 1.8 © M. W. Tweedie, Photo Researchers, Inc. Fig. 1.10 © Nebbia, Woodfin Camp and Associates. Fig. 1.12 © P. Forden, Sygma. Fig. 1.13 Mary Evans Picture Library. Fig. 1.14 Art Resource. Fig. 1.15 Archivist of the History of American Psychology, University of Akron. Fig. 1.16 *Water* by Acrimboldo, Kunsthistorisches Museum, Vienna. Fig. 1.17 Yerkes Regional Primate Research Center, Emory University. Fig. 1.18 © Anderson, Monkmeyer Press. Fig. 1.19 Archives of the History of American Psychology, University of Akron. Fig. 1.20 © Falk, Monkmeyer Press. Fig. 1.21 © Charles Painter, Stanford University News Service. Fig. 1.22 © Duomo, Steven E. Sutton 1985. p. 24 © Ida Wyman, Monkmeyer Press. p. 25 © Richard Hutchings, Photo Edit. Fig. 2.1 Bibb Latane/John M. Darley, "The Unresponsive Bystander; Why Doesn't He Help?," © 1970, p. 98. Adapted by permission of Prentice Hall. Fig. 2.3 UPI/Bettmann. Fig. 2.5 (top left) © Richard Pasley, Stock Boston, Inc.; (bottom left) © David Young-Wolff, Photo Edit; (right) Photo courtesy of Sensormedics Corp. Fig. 2.7 UPI/Bettmann. Fig. 2.8 From *West's American Government,* © 1992 West Publishing Co. Fig. 2.10 From the film *Obedience,* by Stanley Milgram, The Pennsylvania State University, Audio Visual Services. Fig. 2.14 (top) © Mark Richards, Photo Edit; (bottom) © Bill Aron, Photo Edit. p. 51 © Mark Richards, Photo Edit. Fig. 2.19 (top) © Lawrence Migdale 1990, Photo Researchers, Inc.; (bottom) © Will and Deni McIntyre, Photo Researchers, Inc. Fig. 2.20 Courtesy of Foundation for Biomedical Research. Fig. 2.21 © Michel Tcherevkoff, The Image Bank. Fig. 3.3 (left) © Cabisco,Visuals Unlimited; (right) © John D. Cunningham, Visuals Unlimited. Fig. 3.6 Chiras, D., *Human Biology: Health, Homeostatis, and the Environment,* © 1991 West Publishing Co. Fig. 3.9 (left) © Grant Leduc, Monkmeyer Press; (right) © John D. Cunningham, Visuals Unlimited. Fig. 3.10 © Grant Leduc, Monkmeyer Press. Fig. 3.11 NIH/Science Source, Photo Researchers, Inc. Fig. 3.12 CNRI/Science Photo Library, Photo Researchers, Inc. Fig. 3.14 Chiras, D., *Human Biology: Health, Homeostatis, and the Environment,* © 1991 West Publishing Co. Fig. 3.17 Sherwood L., *Human Physiology: From Cells to Systems,* © 1989 West Publishing Co. Fig. 3.20 Gazzaniga, M. S., & Smylie, C. S., 1983. "Facial recognition and brain asymmetries: Clues to underlying mechanisms." *Annals of Neurology,* 13, 536–540. Fig. 3.21 From *Decade of the Brain,* National Institutes of Health. Courtesy of Dr. Joo Ho Sung, University of Minnesota Hospital. Fig. 3.22 From "Experimental Treatment for Parkinsons Disease," *Discover Magazine,* Courtesy of Dr. Lewis Calvert, University of Texas. Fig. 3.23 From *Decade of the Brain,* January 1989, National Institutes of Health. Courtesy of P. Hunter Peckham Ph.D, Case Western Reserve University. Fig. 3.26 © Boehringer Ingelheim GmbH. Photo by Lennart Nilsson. Fig. 3.28 Sherwood L., *Human Physiology: From Cells to Systems,* © 1989 West Publishing Co. Fig. 4.1 From *Genie, A Psychological Study of a Modern Day "Wild Child,"* 1977 by Susan Curtis. Reprinted by permission of Academic Press. Fig. 4.2 © Merritt Vincent, Photo Edit. Table 4.2 From *The Development of Children,* by Michael Cole and Sheila Cole. © 1989 by Michael Cole, Sheila R. Cole, and Judith Boies. Reprinted by permission of W. H. Freeman and Company. Fig. 4.3 Saxe, G. B., *Body Parts as Numerals,* 1981. Fig. 4.5 © C. Edelmann/La Villette, Photo Researchers, Inc. Fig. 4.8 (top left) © Petit-Format/Nestle, Photo Researchers, Inc.; (top right) © Petit-Format/Guigoz, Photo Researchers, Inc.; (bottom left) © Petit-Format/Nestle, Photo Researchers, Inc.; (bottom right) © J. Stevenson, Photo Researchers, Inc. Fig. 4.9 Courtesy of the University of Washington, School of Medicine. Fig. 4.11 © Enrico Ferorelli/DOT. Fig. 4.12 Courtesy of A. N. Meltzoff and M. K. Moore, *Science,* 1977. Fig. 4.13 Dworetsky, J. P., *Introduction to Child Development, 4/e,* © 1990 West Publishing Co. Fig. 4.15 From Conel, J. L., *The Postnatal Development of the Human Cerebral Cortex, Vols. I–VI.* © Harvard University Press. Fig. 4.16 Courtesy of Dr. Mark R. Rosenzweig, University of California, Berkeley. Fig. 4.17 © Bill Anderson, Monkmeyer Press. Fig. 4.18 © Doug Goodman, Monkmeyer Press. Fig. 4.19 Courtesy of Marie Hanak. Fig. 4.20 © Tony Freeman, Photo Edit. Fig. 4.22 Vurpillot, E., "The Development of Scanning Strategies and Their Relations to Visual Differentation." *Journal of Experimental Psychology, 6/e,* 1968, p. 632–650. Fig. 4.24 © Robert Brenner 1991, Photo Edit. Fig. 4.25 © Lawrence Migdale, Stock Boston, Inc. Fig. 4.26 © David Young-Wolff, Photo Edit. Fig. 4.27 © Arlene Collins, Monkmeyer Press. Fig. 4.28 Harry F. Harlow, University of Wisconsin Primate Laboratory. Fig. 4.30 © Wyrleen Ferguson, Photo Edit. Fig. 4.31 Harry F. Harlow, University of Wisconsin Primate Laboratory. Fig. 4.32 © G. Goodwin, Monkmeyer Press. Fig. 4.34 (left) © Frank Siteman, Stock Boston, Inc.; (right) © Sybil Shackman, Monkmeyer Press. Fig. 5.1 Bill E. Hess. Fig. 5.3 © Rick Kopstein, Monkmeyer Press. Fig. 5.4 © Tony Freeman, Photo Edit. Fig. 5.5 © Mimi Forsyth, Monkmeyer Press. Fig. 5.7 © Michael Newman, Photo Edit. Fig. 5.9 Hunter, F. T., & Youniss, J., 1982, "Changes in functions of three relations during adolescence," *Developmental Psychology,* 18, 806–811. Fig. 5.10 Figure from *Being Adolescent* by M. Csikszentmihalyi and R. Larson, © 1984 by Basic Books, Inc. Reprinted by permission of Basic Books, a division of HarperCollins Publishers, Inc. Fig. 5.12 © Robert Brenner, Photo Edit. Fig. 5.13 From *The Seasons of a Man's Life* by Daniel J. Levinson et al., © 1978 by Daniel J. Levinson. Reprinted by permission of Alfred A. Knopf, Inc. Fig. 5.14 Cross, S., & Markus, H., 1991. "Possible selves across the life span." *Human Development,* 34, 230–255. Reprinted by permission of S. Karger AG, Basel. Fig. 5.15 Ryff, C.D., 1991, "Possible selves in adulthood and old age: A tale of shifting horizons." *Psychology and Aging,* 6, 286–295. Fig. 5.18 Focus on Sports, Inc. Fig. 5.19 © Frank Siteman, Monkmeyer Press. Fig. 5.21 Levenson, R. W., Carstensen, L. L., Friesen, W. V., & Ekman, P., 1991. "Emotion, pnysiology and expression in old age," *Psychology and Aging,* 6, 28–35. Fig. 5.22 © Christopher Fitzgerald, Picture Group. Fig. 5.23 Doppelt, J. E., & Wallace, W. L., 1955. "Standardization of the Wechsler Adult Intelligence Scale for older persons." *Journal of Abnormal and Social Psychology,* 51, 312–330. Fig. 5.24 Schaie, K. W., & Strother, C. R., 1968. "A cross-sequential study of age changes in cognitive behavior." *Psychological Bulletin,* 70, 671–680. Fig. 5.25 (left) © Ellis Herwig, Stock Boston, Inc.; (right) UPI/Bettmann. Fig. 5.26 © Peter Byron, Monkmeyer Press. Fig. 5.27 © Robert Brenner, Photo Edit. Fig. 5.28 © Myrleen Ferguson, Photo Edit. Fig. 5.29 © Cary Wolinsky, Stock Boston, Inc. Fig. 5.30 © Bob Daemmrich, Stock Boston, Inc. Fig. 5.31 UPI/Bettmann. Fig. 5.32 © Spencer Grant, Stock Boston, Inc. Fig. 6.2 © Steve Goldberg, Monkmeyer Press. Table 6.3 Figure from *Sensory Experience, 2/e,* by R. J. Christman. © 1979 by Harper & Row Publishers, Inc. Reprinted by permission of HarperCollins Publishers. Fig. 6.5 © Hank Morgan, Photo Researchers, Inc. Fig. 6.6 © Dr. Mazziotta, Photo Researchers, Inc. Fig. 6.7 Chiras, D., *Human Biology: Health, Homeostatis, and the Environment,* © 1991 West Publishing Co. Fig. 6.8 Chiras, D., *Human Biology: Health, Homeostatis, and the Environment,* © 1991 West Publishing Co. Fig. 6.10 © Omikron, Photo Researchers, Inc. Fig. 6.11 Chiras, D., *Human Biology: Health, Homeostatis, and the Environment,* © 1991 West Publishing Co. Fig. 6.13 © Rhoda Sidney, Monkmeyer Press. Fig. 6.15 © Paul Conklin, Monkmeyer Press. Fig. 6.20 © Fritz Goro, *Life Magazine* 1971. Fig. 6.25 Sherwood L., *Human Physiology: From Cells to Systems,* © 1989 West Publishing Co. **Fig. 6.26** Culver Pictures. **Fig. 6.27** © Rick Gemmell Photography. **Fig. 6.29** Chiras, D., *Human Biology: Health, Homeostatis, and the Environment,* © 1991 West Publishing Co. **Fig. 6.30** © Al Rubi, Stock Boston, Inc. **Fig. 6.31** © Vic Bider, Photo Edit. **Fig. 6.32** Greenwald, A. G., Spangenberg, E. R., Pratkanis, A. R., & Eskenazi, J., 1991. "Double-blind tests of subliminal self-help tapes." *Psychological Science,* 2, 119–122. **Fig. 7.1** Sygma. **Fig. 7.2** © Bill Nation, Sygma. **Fig. 7.4** © Dan Helms, Duomo. **Fig. 7.5** *Pintos* by Bev Doolittle, © The Greenwich Workshop, Inc. **Fig. 7.8** From *Seeing: Illusion, Brain and Mind,* by Frisbee, 1980. Reprinted with permission of Roxby Press Ltd. **Fig. 7.9** Reprinted by permission of *International Herald Tribune.* **Fig. 7.11** © David Young-Wolff, Photo Edit. **Fig. 7.12** © Dawson Jones, Stock Boston, Inc. **Fig. 7.14** © Rogers, Monkmeyer Press. **Fig. 7.15** © David Young-Wolff, Photo Edit. **Fig. 7.16** (top) © C. Vergara, Photo Researchers, Inc. **Fig. 7.18** *Uncomposed in Space 1929,* by Paul Klee, © 1992 Artists Rights Society, New York, Bild-Kunst, Bonn. **Fig. 7.20** © Art Hupy Photography, La Conner, Wa. **Fig. 7.21** *Drawing Hands* by M. C. Escher, collection of Haags Gemeentemuseum-The Hague. **Fig. 7.22** *The School of Athens* by Sanzio, Photo Researchers, Inc. **Fig. 7.25** © Duomo 1991. **Fig. 7.28** © J. P. Laffont, Sygma. **Fig. 7.29** Sygma. **Fig. 7.31** Bandura, A., O'Leary A., Taylor, C. B., Gauthier, J., & Gossard, D., 1987. "Perceived self-efficacy and pain control: Opioid and nonopioid mechanisms." *Journal of Personality and Social Psychology,* 53, 563–571. **Fig. 7.32** Blakemore, C., Cooper, G. G., 1970. "Development of the grain depends on visual environment." *Nature.* Reprinted by permission of Macmillan Magazines Ltd. **Fig. 8.2** Illustration by Iselin, Alan D., "Hallucinations" by Ronald K. Siegel, *Scientific American,* October, 1977, p. 136. **Fig. 8.3** © Duomo, Adam J. Stoltman 1989. **Fig. 8.4** © Jack Fields 1981, Photo Researchers, Inc. **Fig. 8.5** © Louis Psihoyos 1988, Matrix International, Inc. **Fig. 8.7** Photo courtesy of Sensormedics Inc. **Fig. 8.11** © Louis Psihoyos 1990, Matrix International, Inc. **Fig. 8.12** Monkmeyer Press. **Fig. 8.13** UPI/Bettmann. **Fig. 8.14** UPI/Bettmann. **Fig. 8.15** Wide World Photos. **Fig. 8.16** UPI/Bettmann. **Fig. 8.17** (left) Courtesy of Ernest R. Hilgard Ph. D., Stanford University. **Fig. 8.18** Putnam, F. W., 1984. "The psychophysiologic investigation of multiple personality disorder: A review." *Psychiatric Clinics of North America,* 7, 31–39. **Fig. 8.20** Magnum Photo Library. **Fig. 8.21** © Claudia Andujar, Photo Researchers, Inc. **Fig. 9.1** Culver Pictures, Inc. **Fig. 9.6** © Jim Pickerell 1991, Stock Boston, Inc. **Fig. 9.7** © Rubin Klass Photography. **Fig. 9.8** © Sybil Shelton, Monkmeyer Press. **Fig. 9.10** Yerkes Regional Primate Research Center of Emory University. **Fig. 9.11** Photo courtesy of Monte Costa, Sea Life Park, Hawaii. **Fig. 9.13** © Brad Bower, Picture Group. **Fig. 9.15** © Jim Teeny, Teeny Nymph Co. **Fig. 9.19** © Myrleen Ferguson, Photo Edit. **Fig. 9.21** © David Young-Wolff, Photo Edit. **Fig. 9.22** © Duomo, David Madison. **Fig. 9.26** Spielberger, C. D., & DeNike, L. D., 1966. "Descriptive behaviorism versus cognitive theory in verbal operant conditioning." *Psychological Review,* 73, 306–326. **Fig. 9.28** Bandura, A., 1965. "Influence of models' reinforcement contingencies on the acquisition of imitated responses." *Journal of Personality and Social Psychology,* 1, 589–595. **Fig. 9.29** © Rick Kop-

stein, Monkmeyer Press. **Fig. 9.31** © Edlan, IBM. **Fig. 9.32** © Pat and Tom Leeson, Photo Researchers, Inc. **Fig. 9.33** © Mimi Forsyth, Monkmeyer Press. **Fig. 10.1** UPI/Bettmann. **Table 10.2** Bartlett, F. C., 1932. *Remembering: A Study in Experimental and Social Psychology.* Cambridge University Press, New York. **Fig. 10.7** © Duomo, David Madison. **Fig. 10.9** © J. P. Laffont, Sygma. **Fig. 10.10** Peterson, L. R. & Peterson, M. J., 1959. "Short term retention of individual verbal items." *Journal of Experimental Psychology,* 58, 193–198. **Fig. 10.11** Drawing by Ed Fisher, © 1983. **Fig. 10.14** Squire, L. R., & Zola-Morgan, S., 1991. "The medial temporal lobe memory system." *Science,* 253, 1380–1386. **Fig. 10.15** © John Karapelou 1989, Discover Magazine. **Fig. 10.16** © Joseph Nettis, Stock Boston, Inc. **Fig. 10.17** Bower, G. H., Clark, M. C., Lesgold, M. A., & Winzenz, D., 1969. "Hierarchical retrieval schemes in recall of categorized word lists." *Journal of Verbal Learning and Verbal Behavior,* 8, 323–343. **Fig. 10.19** Collins, A. M., & Loftus, E. F., 1975. "A spreading activation theory of semantic processing." *Psychological Review,* 82, 407–428. **Fig. 10.21** Merritt, J. O., 1979. "None in a million: Results of mass screening for eidetic ability using objective tests published in newspapers and magazines." *Behavioral and Brain Sciences,* 2, 612. **Fig. 10.22** © Richard Hutchings, Photo Edit. **Fig. 10.24** © A. Tannenbaum, Sygma. **Fig. 10.25** © Laboute, Photo Researchers, Inc. **Fig. 10.26** (left) UPI/Bettmann; (right) UPI/Bettmann. **Fig. 10.31** Nickerson, R. S., & Adams, M. J., 1979. "Long term memory for a common object." *Cognitive Psychology,* 11, 287–307. **Fig. 10.33** Jenkins, J. G., & Dallenbach, K. M., 1924. "Oblivescence during sleep and waking." *American Journal of Psychology,* 35, 605–612. **Fig. 11.1** © James Cachero, Sygma. **Fig. 11.2** © John D. Cunningham, Visuals Unlimited. **Fig. 11.7** (left) © Julie Houck, Stock Boston, Inc.; (top right) © Mark Richards, Photo Edit; (bottom right) © Bob Daemmrich, Stock Boston, Inc. **Fig. 11.14** Shepard, R. N. & Cooper, L. A., 1982. *Mental Images and Their Transformations.* MIT Press, Cambridge, Ma. **Fig. 11.19** Stock Boston, Inc. **Fig. 11.24** (left) © Melloul/Rancinan, Sygma; (right) © Ira Wyman, Sygma. **Fig. 11.27** © Paul Conklin, Photo Edit. **Fig. 11.29** Kimura, D., 1992. "Sex Differences in the brain." *Scientific American,* 267 (3), 119–195. **Fig. 11.30** © Richard Hutchings, Photo Edit. **Fig. 12.1** Focus on Sports. **Table 12.1** Markus, H., & Nurius, P., 1986. "Possible selves." *American Psychologist,* 41, 954–969. **Fig. 12.2** (top) © W. K. Almond, Stock Boston, Inc.; (center) © Myrleen Ferguson, Photo Edit; (bottom) © J. Patrick Forden, Sygma. **Table 12.3** Sarason, I. G., 1984. "Stress, anxiety, and cognitive interference; Reactions to tests." *Journal of Personality and Social Psychology,* 46, 929–938. **Fig. 12.8** Courtesy of Neal E. Miller, Professor Emeritus, Yale University. **Fig. 12.10** Bray, G. A., 1978. "Definitions, measurements, and classification of the syndromes of obesity." *International Journal of Obesity,* 2, 99–112. **Fig. 12.12** © Johnny Horne, Picture Group. **Fig. 12.13** Harry F. Harlow, University of Wisconsin Primate Laboratory. **Fig. 12.14** (left) © Myrleen Ferguson, Photo Edit; (right) © Tim Lynch, Stock Boston, Inc. **Fig. 12.15** © Dellenback, The Kinsey Institute. **Fig. 12.17** UPI/Bettmann Newsphotos. **Fig. 12.18** Masters and Johnson Institute. **Fig. 12.20** (left) © Amanda Merullo, Stock Boston, Inc.; (right) © Fa-

bricius-Taylor, Stock Boston, Inc. **Fig. 12.21** Courtesy Capilano State Park, North Vancouver, B.C. **Fig. 12.24** Irvington Publishers, N.Y. **Fig. 12.25** DeCharms, R., & Moeller, G. H., 1962. "Values expressed in American children's readers: 1800 to 1950." *Journal of Abnormal and Social Psychology,* 64, 135–142. **Fig. 12.26** © Charles Gupto, Stock Boston, Inc. **Fig. 12.27** Drawing by Lorenz; © 1975. **Fig. 12.28** © Michal Heron, Monkmeyer Press. **Fig. 13.1** (left) © Duomo 1991; (right) © David Austen, Stock Boston, Inc. **Fig. 13.2** © Tony Freeman, Photo Edit. **Fig. 13.4** © T. Matsumoto, Sygma. **Fig. 13.7** Davidson, R. J., & Fox, N. A., 1988. "Cerebral asymmetry and emotion: Developmental and individual differences," D. L. Molfese & S. J. Segalowitz (Eds.), *Brain Lateralization in Children: Developmental Implications.* Guildord Press, New York. **Fig. 13.8** UPI/Bettmann. **Fig. 13.9** (bottom) © W. B. Spunbarg, Photo Edit. **Fig. 13.10** © Paul Ekman, 1975. **Fig. 13.11** © Paul Ekman, 1988. **Fig. 13.12** © Duomo 1990. **p. 71** Photos courtesy of Dr. John Belliveau, Department of Radiology, Harvard Medical School. **Fig. 13.17** © Tony Freeman, Photo Edit. **Fig. 13.19** Speisman, J., Lazarus, R. S., Mordkoff, A., & Davidson, L., 1964. "Experimental reduction of stress based on ego-defense theory." *Journal of Abnormal and Social Psychology,* 68, 367–380. **Fig. 13.25** Archive Photos. **Fig. 14.1** © Michael Newman, Photo Edit. **Table 14.2** Tellegen, A., Lykken, D. T., Bouchard, T. J., Segal, N. L., & Rich, S., 1988. "Personality similarity in twins raised apart and together." *Journal of Personality and Social Psychology,* 54, 1031–1039. **Fig. 14.9** From *The Scientific Analysis of Personality* by R. B. Catell, 1965. Reprinted by permission of IPAT. **Fig. 14.7** Courtesy of Dr. David Buss, Department of Psychology, University of Michigan. **Fig. 14.8** © Trapper, Sygma. **Fig. 14.9** (left) © Owen Franken, Stock Boston, Inc.; (right) © Tony Freeman, Photo Edit. **Fig. 14.11** © Mark Gerson. **Fig. 14.12** Eysenck, H. J., 1967. *Biological Basis of Personality.* **Fig. 14.13** © Louie Psihoyos 1990, Matrix International. Inc. **Fig. 14.15** (left) UPI/Bettmann; (right) UPI/Bettmann. **Fig. 14.16** Courtesy of The Carl Rogers Memorial Library. **Fig. 14.19** The Ohio State University Archives, Photographic Collection. **Fig. 14.20** © Tony Freeman, Photo Edit. **Fig. 14.23** Bandura, A., & Cervone, D., 1983. "Self-evaluative and self-efficacy mechanisms governing the motivational effects of goal systems." *Journal of Personality and Social Psychology,* 45, 1017–1028. **Fig. 14.26** © Bob Daemmrich, Stock Boston, Inc. **Fig. 14.27** © Mimi Forsyth, Monkmeyer Press. **Fig. 14.28** Minnesota Multiphasic Personality Inventory-2. © Regents University of Minnesota, 1942, 1943 (renewed 1970), 1989. This profile from 1989. **Fig. 14.29** © Lew Merrim, Monkmeyer Press. **Fig. 15.2** (top left) © Doug Menuez, Stock Boston, Inc.; (top right) © Tony Freeman 1990, Photo Edit; (bottom) © Robert Brenner, Photo Edit. **Fig. 15.3** UPI/Bettmann. **Table 15.3** Meichenbaum, P., *Stress Innoculation Training.* Simon & Schuster International. **Fig. 15.6** UPI/Bettmann. **Fig. 15.7** Burton, D., 1988. "Do anxious swimmers swim slower? Reexamining the elusive anxiety-performance relationship." *Journal of Sport and Exercise Psychology,* 10, 45–61. © 1988 by Human Kinetics Publishers, Inc. Reprinted by permission. **Fig. 15.8** Sygma. **Fig. 15.11** Archive Photos. **Fig. 15.15** © Jeff Persons, Stock Boston, Inc. **Fig. 15.16** Baron, R. S., Cutrona, C. E.,

Hicklin, D., Russell, D. W., & Lubaroff, D. M., 1990. "Social support and immune function among spouses of cancer patients." *Journal of Personality and Social Psychology,* 59, 344–352. **Fig. 15.17** Ozer, E. M., & Bandura, A. 1990. "Mechanisms governing empowerment effects: A self-efficacy analysis." *Journal of Personality and Social Psychology,* 58, 472–486. **Fig. 15.18** Wiedenfeld, S. A., O'Leary, A., Bandura, A., Brown, S., Levine, S., & Raska, K., 1990. "Impact of perceived self-efficacy in coping with stressors on components of the immune system." *Journal of Personality and Social Psychology,* 59, 1082–1094. **Fig. 15.19** Charles S. Carver and Michael F. Scheier, *Perspectives on Personality, 2/e.* © 1992 by Allyn and Bacon. Reprinted with permission. **Fig. 16.2** © Paul Conklin, Monkmeyer Press. **Fig. 16.3** Courtesy Department Library Services, American Museum of Natural History. **Fig. 16.4** Goya, *Witches' Sabbath.* Lazaro Galdiano Museum, Madrid. © Scala, Art Resource. **Fig. 16.5** From Coon, D., *Introduction to Psychology 6/e,* © 1992 West Publishing Co. **Fig. 16.6** *Pinel,* © Rapho, Photo Researchers, Inc. **Fig. 16.8** (left) © Roddey E. Mims, Sygma; (right) Sygma. **Fig. 16.9** © Geo. Goodwin, Monkmeyer Press. **Fig. 16.10** © Gwendolen Cates, Outline. **Fig. 16.12** Monkmeyer Press. **Fig. 16.13** S. Fishman/D. Sheehan, © *Psychology Today Magazine* 1985, Sussex Publishers, Inc. **Fig. 16.15** AP/Wide World Photos. **Fig. 16.16** Moody, R. L., 1946. "Bodily changes during abreaction." *The Lancett,* 2, 934–935. **Fig. 16.17** © Stacy Pick 1990, Stock Boston, Inc. **Fig. 16.18** © J. Gerald Smith, Monkmeyer Press. **Fig. 16.21** © Alan Oddie, Photo Edit. **p. 520** © Rhoda Sidney, Photo Edit. **p. 521** D. Kleinmuntz, 1980. *Essentials of Abnormal Psychology.* University of Illinois, Chicago. **Fig. 16.24** William Blake, *Unizen.* Courtesy of the National Library of Congress. **Fig. 16.25** Courtesy of the National Institute of Mental Health. **Fig. 16.26** Courtesy of the National Institute of Mental Health. **Fig. 16.27** Monkmeyer Press. **Fig. 16.28** Sygma. **Fig. 16.30** © Kochaniec, Sygma. **Fig. 17.4** © Ann Chwatsky, The Picture Cube. **p. 538** Wolberg, L. R., 1967. *The Technique of Psychotherapy.* Grune & Stratton, New York. **Fig. 17.5** Howard, K. I., Kopta, S. M., Krause, M. S., & Orlinsky, D. E., 1986. "The dose-effect relationship in psychotherapy." *American Psychologist,* 41, 159–164. **Fig. 17.6** Courtesy of Center for Studies of the Person, La Jolla, Ca. **Fig. 17.7** © Paul Herbert, Eslalen Institute, Big Sur, Ca. **Fig. 17.9** Courtesy of the Institute for Rational-Emotive Therapy. **Fig. 17.10** Courtesy of University of Pennsylvania, Psy-

chiatry Department. **Fig. 17.13** Ayllon, T., & Azrin, N. H., 1968. *The Token Economy: A Motivational System for Therapy and Rehabilitation.* Appleton-Century-Crofts, New York. **Fig. 17.14** Bandura, A., Blanchard, E. B., & Ritter, B., 1969. "The relative efficacy of desensitization and modeling approaches for inducing behavioral, affective and attitudinal changes." *Journal of Personality and Social Psychology,* 13, 173–199. **Fig. 17.15** Monkmeyer Press. **Fig. 17.20** © Michael Newman, Photo Edit. **Fig. 17.21** © Will and Deni McIntyre, Photo Researchers, Inc. **Fig. 17.24** © Lawrence Migdale 1987, Stock Boston, Inc. **Fig. 17.25** © Rhoda Sidney, Monkmeyer Press. **Fig. 17.26** © Bob Rashid, Monkmeyer Press. **Fig. 18.1** Courtesy of Stanford University, Department of Psychology. **Table 18.1** Stokols, D., 1976. "The experience of crowding in primary and secondary environments." *Environment and Behavior,* 8, 49–86. **Fig. 18.2** © Owen Franken, Stock Boston, Inc. **Fig. 18.3** (left) © Giansanti, Sygma; (right) UPI/Bettmann. **Fig. 18.4** C. G. Scofield, courtesy of Bennington College. **Fig. 18.6** © Bob Daemmrich, Stock Boston, Inc. **Fig. 18.7** © William Vandivert, *Scientific American Magazine.* **Fig. 18.8** Drawing by Handelsman; © 1972. **Fig. 18.9** © Sygma. **Fig. 18.10** © Tannenbaum, Sygma. **Fig. 18.11** The Bettmann Archive. **Fig. 18.16** © Freda Leinwand, Monkmeyer Press. **Fig. 18.19** © Mitchell Layton, Duomo. **Fig. 18.23** Drawing by Dana Fradon; © 1980. **Fig. 18.24** Drawing by H. Martin; © 1979. **Fig. 18.26** Bettmann. **Fig. 18.27** (left) © Paul Conklin, Photo Edit; (right) © Rhoda Sidney, Photo Edit. **Fig. 18.28** © Rubin Klass Photography. **Fig. 18.31** © David Young-Wolff, Photo Edit. **Fig. 18.32** © Michael Newman, Photo Edit. **Table 19.1** Snyder, M., & Gangestad, S., 1986. "On the nature of self-monitoring; Matters of assessment, matters of validity." *Journal of Personality and Social Psychology,* 51, 125–139. **Fig. 19.2** Asch, S. E., 1946. "Forming impressions of personality." *Journal of Abnormal and Social Psychology,* 41, 258–290. **Fig. 19.3** Drawing by Dana Fradon; © 1971. **Table 19.3** Hill, C. A., 1987, "Affiliation motivation: People who need people but in different ways." *Journal of Personality and Social Psychology,* 52, 1008–1018. **Table 19.4** Hendrick, C., & Hendrick, S., 1986. "A theory and method of love." *Journal of Personality and Social Psychology,* 50, 392–402. **Fig. 19.5** Sygma. **Table 19.5** From *The Psychology of Love,* "Love as Attachment: The Integration of Three Behavioral Systems," by Shaver, Hazen and Bradshaw, 1988. Reprinted with permission of Yale Uni-

versity Press. **Fig. 19.9** Perdue, C. W., Dovidio, J. F., Gurtman, M. B., & Tyler, R. B., 1990. "Us and them: Social categorization and the process of intergroup bias." *Journal of Personality and Social Psychology,* 59, 475–486. **Fig. 19.10** © Cramer Gilmore, Picture Group. **Fig. 19.11** © Elizabeth Zuckerman, Photo Edit. **Fig. 19.12** © R. Maiman, Sygma. **Fig. 19.13** Archive Photos. **Fig. 19.14** Byrne, D., & Nelson, D., 1965. "Attraction as a linear function of proportion of positive reinforcements." *Journal of Personality and Social Psychology,* 1, 659–663. **Fig. 19.16** Brehm, S. S., & Kassin, S. M. *Social Psychology, 2/e.* © Houghton Mifflin Co., used with permission. **Fig. 19.17** Sternberg, R. J., 1986. "A triangular theory of love." *Psychological Review,* 93, 119–135. **Fig. 19.18** © Robert Brenner, Photo Edit. **Fig. 19.21** © Joe McDonald, Visuals Unlimited. **Fig. 19.23** Courtesy of Irwin G. and Barbara R. Sarason. **Fig. 19.24** © Tom McHugh 1974, Photo Researchers, Inc. **Fig. 19.27** *The Fifth Horseman,* by Pat Oliphant, © 1984. Used by permission of Universal Press Sindicate. **Fig. 20.1** (left) © Myrleen Ferguson, Photo Edit; (right) © Bob Daemmrich, Stock Boston, Inc.; (bottom) © Richard Pasley, Stock Boston, Inc. **Table 20.1** Wells, G. L., & Luus, C. A. E., 1990. "Police lineups as experiments: Social methodology as a framework for properly conducted lineups." *Personality and Social Psychology Bulletin,* 16, 106–117. Reprinted by permission of Sage Publications, Inc. **Fig. 20.4** CTW/John A. Barrett; © 1992 Children's Television Workshop. **Fig. 20.5** © Paul Conklin, Monkmeyer Press. **Fig. 20.6** © Charles Gupton, Stock Boston, Inc. **Fig. 20.9** © Bob Daemmrich, Stock Boston, Inc. **Fig. 20.14** © Jim Pickerell 1992, Stock Boston, Inc. **Fig. 20.16** © Lawrence Migdale, Stock Boston, Inc. **Fig. 20.17** Smith, R. E. & Smoll, F. L., 1990. "Self-esteem and children's reactions to youth sport coaching behaviors: A field study of self-enhancement processes." *Developmental Psychology,* 26, 987–993. **Fig. 20.19** © Harvey Gruyaert, Magnum. **Fig. 20.22** Brown, J. D., 1991. "Staying fit and staying well: Physical fitness as a moderator of life stress." *Journal of Personality and Social Psychology,* 60, 555–561. **Fig. 20.23** Kelly, J. A., St. Lawrence, J. S., & Brasfield, T. L., 1989. "Predictors of vulnerability to AIDS risk behavior relapse." *Journal of Consulting and Clinical Psychology,* 57, 163–166. **Fig. 20.24** © Kevin Larkin, Sygma. **Fig. 20.25** © Mark Richardson/DOT. **Fig. 20.27** © Tony Freeman, Photo Edit. **B.1** *Psychological Abstracts,* June, 1992, p. 2399, Abstract Number 19861.